the ONION® PRESENTS

COMPLETE NEWS ARCHIVES · VOLUME 16

Bush Finally Gets Oval Office Just The Way He Wants It

the ONION® PRESENTS

COMPLETE NEWS ARCHIVES · VOLUME 16

Bush Finally Gets Oval Office Just The Way He Wants It

EDITED BY
Carol Kolb

WRITTEN BY
Amie Barrodale, Rich Dahm, Joe Garden,
Dan Guterman, Todd Hanson, Chris Karwowski, Peter Koechley,
John Krewson, Maria Schneider

GRAPHICS BY
Mike Loew, Chad Nackers

DESIGN BY
Jill Rosenmerkel, Andrew Welyczko

COVER DESIGN BY
Mike Loew, Chad Nackers

ADDITIONAL PRODUCTION BY
Tim Hughes

ADDITIONAL MATERIAL BY
Adam Albright-Hanna, Diane Bullock, Billy Cummings, T. G. Gibbon,
Josh Greenman, Barry Julien, Sam Means, Nick Nadel, Tai Palmgren, Chris Pauls, Kent Roberts,
Mike Schuster, Wil Shepard, Dave Sherman, Jacob Sager Weinstein

COPYEDITED BY
Amie Barrodale

SPECIAL THANKS
David Schafer, Chris Cranmer, Sean Mills, Keith Phipps, Christine Carlson,
Allison Ray, Steve Hannah, Tasha Robinson, Nathan Rabin, Adam Powell, Stephen Thompson,
Annik LaFarge, Mario Rojas, Daniel Greenberg, David Miner, Michael O'Brien, Scott Dikkers, Juli Aulik,
Jason George, Michael DiCenzo, Lars Russell, Julie Stainer, Rob Siegel, Tim Harrod, P. S. Mueller,
Andy Battaglia, Rachel Berger, Dan Friel, Amelie Gillette, Matt McDonagh, David Moser, Joe Pagano,
Glenn Severance, Andrew Smith, Amy Steinhauser, Pete Tunney

B☘XTREE

First published 2005 by Three Rivers Press, New York, New York.
Member of the Crown Publishing Group, a Division of Random House, Inc.

This edition published in Great Britain 2005 by Boxtree
an imprint of Pan Macmillan Ltd
Pan Macmillan, 20 New Wharf Road, London N1 9RR
Basingstoke and Oxford
Associated companies throughout the world
www.panmacmillan.com

ISBN 0 7522 2550 2

9 8 7 6 5 4 3 2 1

A CIP catalogue record for this book is available from
the British Library.

Designed by The Onion
Printed and bound in Great Britain by the Bath Press, Bath

PHOTO CREDITS: p. 1, Zuniga and Baker; p. 5, Zuniga; p. 18, Henderberg; p. 19, Lowery; p. 31 and 34, Elsing, Scobel; p. 39, Vanderkamp; p. 73, Coworkers; p. 73, Bogen; p. 97 and 100, Christ; p. 133, Trask; p. 145, Freezer; p. 205, Ankrim; p. 241, Greisberg; p. 253, Drake; p. 278, Taylor; p. 296, Kincaid; p. 300, Gussie: Mike Loew/Onion Photos. p. 1, OutKast; p. 63, O'Donnell; p. 245, Lundgren; p. 265, Matchbox Twenty: Kevin Winter/Getty. p. 1, Lieberman: Alex Dorgan-Ross/Getty. p. 1, Schwarzenegger: Robyn Beck/AFP. p. 2, Pumps; p. 122, Disney: Tim Boyle/Getty. p. 7, Card, Clerk; p. 13, Excedrin, Compass; p. 14, Nexler; p. 15, Lawyer; p. 17, Treats; p. 18, Borroughs; p. 19, Paper, Family; p. 23, Lowery; p. 25, Lentz; p. 27, Widmar; p. 28, Lentz; p. 30, Rawlings; p. 31, Pizza; p. 37, Clock, Marlene and Paul Hirsh; p. 38, Hurley; p. 42, Loman; p. 43, Skin; p. 44, Luzhninczy; p. 47, Search; p. 50, Osterberg; p. 51, Rosenstein; p. 54, Heller; p. 55, Froeger, Petrakis, Crucifix; p. 56, Evars; p. 61, Goya, Books; p. 62, Bickels; p. 66, Mulroney; p. 72, Radio; p. 74, Michener; p. 78, Fox; p. 79, Arm, Steaks; p. 80, Kuhtz; p. 81, Cadet; p. 83, Police; p. 85, Couple; p. 87, Seversen; p. 89, Frame; p. 92, Johnson; p. 94, Couple; p. 97, Card; p. 98, Babcock; p. 101, Bar; p. 107, Mail, Ong, Crawford; p. 109, Ashland; p. 115, Hippie; p. 117, Wiseck; p. 120, Gibbons; p. 121, Bus; p. 127, Hendersons; p. 129, Sterling, Freiburg; p. 131, Secrets; p. 132, Knefler; p. 139, Scribba; p. 141, Penis; p. 142, Swastika; p. 145, Jurgensen; p. 151, Vitamin, Burnhard; p. 153 and 155, Schweiber; p. 156, Wolohan, Weapons Guy, Robins; p. 157, Keebler, Poole; p. 159, Loder, Deering; p. 159, Osley; p. 168, Evans, Driscoll; p. 169, Gun, Niles; p. 175, iHop; p. 177, Lufler; p. 181, Bennett; p. 182, March; p. 183, Linton; p. 184, Letter; p. 187, Yothers; p. 188, Milobritch; p. 189, Employees, Wanzeck; p. 191, Headstone; p. 193, Employee; p. 195, Lyon; p. 200, Halverson; p. 201, Flauman; p. 203, Shelf; p. 205, Cereal, Fisk, Krachek, Osterberg, Eddy, Weston; p. 208, Outline; p. 210, Ingrams; p. 214, Building; p. 219, Powers; p. 223, Bus, Davis; p. 224, Duane; p. 229, Phone; p. 230, Ainsworth; p. 231, Framik; p. 237, Cake; p. 239, Fairman; p. 241, Cross; p. 247, Pillow; p. 249 and 251, Danvers; p. 254, Duncan; p. 255 and 256, Morris; p. 259, Bag; p. 264, Viesel; p. 261, Gilchrist; p. 263, Glasses; p. 264, Schmidt; p. 267, Deliveryman; p. 271, Doll, Glick; p. 272, Erikson; p. 277, Fort; p. 279, Thompson; p. 281, Torture Devices; p. 283, Baby, Restaurant; p. 299, Billboard: Chad Nackers/Onion Photos. p. 7, Ashcroft: Stefan Zaklin/Getty. p. 7, Schwarzenegger; p. 164, Voting Machine; p. 173, Sufferer; p. 212, Convention: David McNew/Getty. p. 7, SeaWorld: Gary Clark/KRT. p. 10, Charlie's Angels: Columbia Pictures/Newsmakers. p. 11, Schwarzenegger: AFP/Getty. p. 13, Soldiers: Patrick Baz/AFP/Getty. p. 16, Girl; p. 163, Iraqi; p. 178, Kerry: Paula Bronstein/Getty. p. 19, Ladykiller: Jeff Canzona Images. p. 19, Abraham; p. 187, Commission; p. 233 and 235, Bush; p. 247, Convention, Republicans; p. 287, Cheney: Mark Wilson/Newsmakers. p. 20, Wildfire: Sandy Huffaker/Getty. p. 22, Abraham; p. 40, Worker; p. 43, Clinton; p. 49, Feingold; p. 61, Chao; p. 103, Cheney; p. 109, Rumsfeld; p. 146, Rice; p. 217, Smithsonian; p. 230, Bush; p. 247, National Archives; p. 271, Bush; p. 271, FBI; p. 275, Bush; p. 283, Cheney: Alex Wong/Getty. p. 25, Bush; p. 58, Children; p. 127, Spring Break; p. 169, Cheney; p. 179, Schrag; p. 254, Planes: Joe Raedle/Getty. p. 25, DeLay: Michael Smith/Getty. p. 25, Farrell: Scott Gries/Getty. p. 25, Volunteers: Mike Nelson/AFP. p. 26, Brolin, Davis: CBS Photo Archive. p. 27, Lillian; p. 265, Fire: Pam Kolb/Onion Photos. p. 31, Arafat: Hussein/PPO/Getty. p. 32, Wal-Mart: Scott Olson/Getty. p. 32, Squirrel; p. 124, 178 and 226, Bush: Paul J. Richards/AFP. p. 35, Rubble: Uzi Keren/Getty. p. 37, Workers: Jim Bourg/Reuters. p. 37, NYPD; p. 140, Apple Store; p. 175, Truckers; p. 196, Iraqis; p. 235, Police; p. 290, Crowd: Justin Sullivan/Getty. p. 37, Smokestacks: Eric Seals/KRT. p. 46, Girl: Rick Wilking/Reuters. p. 49, Spears; p. 145, Hanks: Mark Mainz/Getty. p. 50, Kim Jong Il: STR/AFP/Getty. p. 53, Mosque: Mehdi Fedouach/Getty. p. 55, Worker: Ian Waldie/Getty. p. 55, Drescher; p. 147, Foechelman: Vince Bucci/Getty. p. 56, Rover: NASA/AFP/Getty. p. 57, Mercenaries: Scott Peterson/Getty. p. 59, Westphal; p. 296, Vaccine: Mike Simons/Getty. p. 61, Passengers: Reuters. p. 61, Scientist: Gary Knapp/Getty. p. 62, Bush: Pablo Martinez Monsivais/Getty. p. 65, Schwarzenegger: Dave Hogan/Getty. p. 67, Bush: Mike Simons/Newsmakers. p. 68, Wraps; p. 182, Woman; p. 289, Orangutan: Tim Boyle/Getty. p. 69, Silverstone: Jon Kopaloff/Getty. p. 73, Car: Getty. p. 77, Bush: Shelly Katz/Getty. p. 80, Jackson, Timberlake: Donald Miralle/Getty. p. 87, Cartoon: Todd Hanson/Onion Graphics. p. 91, Bush: Preston Mack/Getty. p. 91, Dean; p. 152, Porn; p. 293, Lab: Justin Sullivan/Getty. p. 91, Marriage: Deborah Coleman/Getty. p. 92, Athens: Aris Messinis/AFP/Getty. p. 93, Glennon: Carol Kolb/Onion Photos. p. 95, Bush: Martin H. Simon/Getty. p. 98, CPR: David Cannon/Allsport. p. 104, Helicopters: Getty. p. 108, Cole: Evan Agostini/Getty. p. 109, Soccer Players: Adam Pretty/Getty. p. 109, Girl; p. 271, Woman: ShowBizIreland/Getty. p. 111, Cosmic Stan: Diane L. Cohen/Getty. p. 112, Avalanche: JIJI Press/AFP/Getty. p. 112, Yang: Sam Yeh/AFP. p. 113, CUA Members: Martin Bureau/AFP/Getty. p. 115, Rover: NASA/AFP/Getty. p. 115, Cartoon; p. 250, Menu: Maria Schneider/Onion Graphics. p. 115, Griffey: Ezra Shaw/Getty. p. 118, Scientists: Getty. p. 121, Mall; p. 157, Truck; p. 217, Apartment, Strip Club: Christine Carlson/Onion Photos. p. 121, Bush; p. 134 and 136, Rumsfeld; p. 199, 218, and 277, Bush: Stephen Jaffe/AFP/Getty. p. 127, Weapons: Saeed Khan/AFP/Getty. p. 127, Jay Z: Frederick M. Brown/Getty. p. 139, Cheney: Ronald Martinez/Getty. p. 139, Iraqis; p. 193, Bremer: Sabah Arar/AFP/Getty. p. 140, Rae; p. 158, Kerry: Brendan Smialowski/Getty. p. 145, President; p. 157, Bush; p. 190, Tenet; p. 224, Nader; p. 289, Kerry: Luke Frazza/Getty. p. 145, Bombing: Marwan Naamani/Getty. p. 146, Detainees: Shane T. McCoy/U.S. Navy/Getty. p. 157, Cockfight: Nikolai Zhuravok/Tass. p. 159, ScaperCon: Amanda Edwards/Getty. p. 160, Fighting Birds: Assam Gawahati/EPA. p. 161, Baltazar: Stephen Morton/Getty. p. 163, Horse: AFP. p. 169, Pitt: Francois Guillot/AFP/Getty. p. 170, Outsourcing: Raveendran/AFP/Getty. p. 171, Queen: Scott Barbour/Getty. p. 175, Brimley: Terry Lilly/Zuma. p. 176, Tornado: Kent F. Berg/The Miami Herald/Getty. p. 181, Kerry; p. 242, Convention; p. 253, Lagasse; p. 289, Abizaid: Chris Hondros/Getty. p. 181, ISS: NASA/Newsmakers. p. 181, Young Kerry: Zuma. p. 187, Rowling: Getty. p. 187, Fallon: Frank Micelotta/Getty. p. 187, Casket; p. 256, Casino: Spencer Platt/Getty. p. 188, Memorial: Carlo Allegri/Getty. p. 193, Gordon: Jamie Squire/Getty. p. 193, Officials: Getty. p. 200, Poster; p. 213, Cows: Don Emmert/AFP/Getty. p. 205, Crash; p. 263, Cheney: Chung Sung-Jun/Getty. p. 205, Maher: Getty. p. 206, Hulk: ILM. p. 206, Phone: AFP/Getty. p. 207, University: Bill Pugliano/Getty. p. 209, Bledsoe: Jim West/Zuma. p. 211, Gates: Ron Wurzer/Getty. p. 211, Hangar: Michael R. Nixon/USAF/Getty. p. 211, Rumsfeld: David Hume Kennerly/Getty. p. 215, Will & Grace: Getty. p. 220, Stripper: Georges DeKeerle/Getty. p. 223, Vegas: Stewart Cook/Online USA/Getty. p. 227, Tibetans: Devendra M. Singh/AFP/Getty. p. 229, Kerry: William B. Plowman/Getty. p. 233, Mr. "T": Brian Tietz/Getty. p. 235, Dunst: Steve Finn/Getty. p. 236, Gymnast: Odd Anderson/AFP/Getty. p. 239, Terrorist: AFP/Getty. p. 241, Kerry: Shaun Heasley/Getty. p. 243, Lundgren: David M. Bennett/Getty. p. 248, Jackson: Getty. p. 251, Iraqi: Salah Malkawi/Getty. p. 253, Iraqi: JIJI/AFP/Getty. p. 259, Sharpova: Thomas Coex/AFP/Getty. p. 259, Band: Joe Garden/Onion Photos. p. 259, Rescuers: Gene J. Puskar/Getty. p. 264, Hurricane: Robert Sullivan/AFP/Getty. p. 265, Terrorists: Shah Marai/AFP/Getty. p. 265, Cave: Eugene Hoshiko/Getty. p. 268, Wilkins: Elsa/Getty. p. 269, Delegate: Robert Nickelsberg/Time Life Pictures/Getty. p. 272, Oktoberfest: Sean Gallup/Getty. p. 274, Official: Robert King/Newsmakers. p. 277, Robot: Koichi Kamoshida/Getty. p. 280, El Hefe: Roger Hornback/Getty. p. 291, Building: Robert Cianflone/Getty. p. 292, Insurgents: Ahmad Al-Rubay/AFP/Getty. p. 295, Funeral: Getty. p. 295, Monreal: Scott Olson/Getty. p. 301, Battleground: Marwan Naamani/AFP/Getty Images. p. 301, Voters: Gaston De Cardenas/Getty. p. 301, Museum: Alex Wong/Getty. p. 303, Zapatero: Pedro Armestre/AFP/Getty. p. 303, Bull; p. 305, Pomplona: Rafa Rivas/AFP/Getty. p. 305, Upper Class: Michel Barnier/Getty. p. 307, Guard: Scott Olson/Getty. p. 307, Bush and Cheney: Mark Wilson/Getty. p. 307, Bin Laden: CNN/Getty. p. 310, Voters: Joe Raedle/Getty.

the ONION®

VOLUME 39 ISSUE 40   AMERICA'S FINEST NEWS SOURCE™   16–22 OCTOBER 2003

Schwarzenegger Elected First Horseman Of The Apocalypse

see NATION page 1B

OutKast Universally Accepted

see ENTERTAINMENT page 14E

Ashcroft Chases Down, Loses CIA Leak Suspect In Alley Behind White House

see WASHINGTON page 4C

STATshot

A look at the numbers that shape your world.

Top Novel Dedications

1. For Simon, but not Schuster
2. To Death, whose ashen caress this verse extols
3. To the real-life heroes of the landscaping industry
4. To Faulkner and Joyce, who paved the way
5. For my itty-bitty wittle kitties

For Oprah

Ex-Girlfriend Playing Virtua Fighter With Some Other Guy Now

SOUTH HADLEY FALLS, MA—Area resident Troy Zuniga, 27, is troubled by the idea of his ex-girlfriend Chrissy Baker playing Virtua Fighter 4: Evolution with someone new, Zuniga reported Tuesday.

"Chrissy's probably at her new boyfriend's place playing VF4 right at this very minute," said Zuniga, responding to friends' inquiries about his unwillingness to play what was once his favorite game. "I think about her sitting in front of the television, flexing her fingers in that way she does when she's gearing up to fight, and I can barely take it."

"It's just really hard," said Zuniga,

see EX-GIRLFRIEND page 5

Left: Zuniga holds the video game he used to play with Baker (inset).

Lieberman Pledges To Gloss Over The Boring Issues

HARTFORD, CT—Eager to distinguish himself in the nine-member field of Democratic candidates, presidential hopeful Sen. Joe Lieberman (D-CT) pledged Monday to "gloss over any and all issues boring to Americans today."

"Are you sick of politics as usual in Washington?" Lieberman said at a campaign fundraiser held at the see LIEBERMAN page 4

Above: Lieberman tells Hartford voters he'll be brief.

Study Finds Cable-TV Violence Leads To Network-TV Violence

LOS ANGELES—A two-year study of television programming has established a link between cable-TV violence and violent scenarios on network television, the Institute for Media Research announced Monday.

"Our data shows that cable violence, particularly the more brutal, consequence-free violence found on premium-cable channels like HBO, leads to violence on broadcast channels like ABC, NBC, CBS, and Fox," IMR researcher Donald Peck said. "This phenomenon has created an ever-widening spiral of violence on our nation's airwaves."

Peck said the IMR based its report on analysis of 700,000 hours of cable- and network-TV broadcasts from the past 20 years. According to the report, prior to the advent of cable television, relatively little gratuitous violence aired on

see VIOLENCE page 4

Left: A violent scenario from the cable series The Sopranos.

Schwarzenegger Victorious

After the recall of Gov. Gray Davis, Arnold Schwarzenegger was elected governor of California. What do *you* think?

Daniel Powell
Sound Engineer

"I voted for Arnold because I agreed with his economic plan. And because I was afraid he might punch me in the face if I didn't."

Molly Prather
Executive Secretary

"At last, a political family that combines the remnants of the Camelot dynasty with the origins of the Predator franchise."

Will Becton
Anesthesiologist

"It certainly is an interesting career path, to go from bodybuilder to movie star to politician to man in way over his head."

Brandon Calhoun
Systems Analyst

"I'm from Minnesota, and I demand some credit. We elected a ridiculous joke of a governor *years* ago."

Sarah Jacobs
Lyricist

"Who would have thought that a bad Austrian artist who's obsessed with the human physical ideal could assemble such a rabid political following?"

Kevin Napier
Radio Operator

"Don't blame me—I voted for the porn star."

High Oil, Gas Prices

The Energy Department predicted that oil and gas prices will remain higher than average through the winter. How are Americans responding?

- ▶ Buying crude oil wholesale; refining it themselves
- ▶ Exchanging silken breeches and knee stockings for coarse woolen trousers when winter arrives
- ▶ Giving teenaged family members 30 percent more shit about using the car
- ▶ Getting oil out of whales, like in the good old days
- ▶ Finding safe, environmentally friendly alternatives to killing self with car-exhaust fumes
- ▶ No longer accepting ass or grass for rides
- ▶ Breaking free from petropoly by using Zenergy
- ▶ Trading Hummer in for more fuel-efficient SUV
- ▶ Doing nothing. Why?

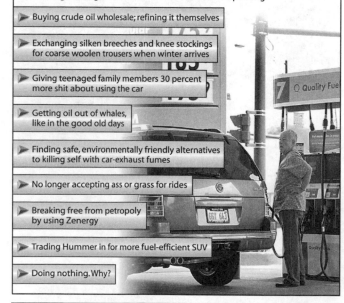

America's Finest News Source.™

Herman Ulysses Zweibel
Founder

T. Herman Zweibel
Publisher Emeritus
J. Phineas Zweibel
Publisher
Maxwell Prescott Zweibel
Editor-In-Chief

I'm A Diseased- And Deformed-Animal Lover!

By Tricia McCory

A lot of people say they love animals, but then, when they come across one that has a scar, is a little bit skinny, or is coughing up blood, they just turn their heads. Well, I love animals of all shapes, sizes, and disabilities. That's why I devote all of my free time to finding and caring for diseased and deformed animals. I just can't get enough of those smelly, limping critters!

I'd never be so cruel as to turn away a stray dog, just because his care requires that I siphon fluid from his lungs with a plastic tube every four hours. If you only like animals that sport silky fur or have tongues, then you can't say you truly love animals. I love *all* of the earth's creatures—those with and without tapeworms.

Just take one look into my Siberian husky Clancy's pus-encrusted eyes. How could you not love him to

> **I feel good knowing that, even though I couldn't save the deer, I kept him alive for almost a week. Larry thought we should put him out of his misery by running over his head with the pick-up.**

pieces? He's so special to me, as are the five or ten cats dragging themselves around my house any given week. I give every animal a name, no matter how close he or she is to death.

Add one more to the list of little buddies in cages stacked on, or hanging from, every available surface in my home. Muffin, a guinea pig with a tumor three times the size of her head, may need a little more care than a so-called "normal" guinea pig, but I'm more than happy to put in the extra effort. Every mange-covered, rasping animal is a gift from God. Sure, sometimes the smell can be overwhelming, and sometimes the animal hair clumped on my couch, clogging my kitchen drain, and clinging to my clothes can be a bit unpleasant. But once you've bottle-fed an abandoned, three-legged ferret, like I do every

morning with little Tripod, there's no turning back: You're a true animal lover.

Every animal deserves tender loving care, even if he or she is well beyond hope of ever living independently. I have an iguana with chronic pneumonia, and a 17-foot boa constrictor with a skin disease so advanced it turns the vet's stomach. Then there's Señor Oink, the epileptic pot-bellied pig I found in the giveaway section of the classifieds. I love little Oinky, no matter how many times he's accidentally bitten me or destroyed one of my lamps during an episode. I can't believe someone actually wanted to get rid of him!

Not all of the animals I own are pets that were left to die in a sack on the side of the road. I've rescued my share of wild animals, too—everything from birds with broken wings to Smokey, a raccoon that swallowed a tin-can lid.

Just last year, I rescued a deer. My then-boyfriend Larry and I spotted the little guy lying on the side of the highway, covered in blood and barely breathing. Of course, I insisted that we heave him over into the back of Larry's pick-up and take him home. There, I wrapped him in a blanket and kept him on my front porch, where I hand-fed him corn that I chewed up myself. I even outfitted him with toddler-sized diapers, which stayed in place because his back legs were paralyzed.

I feel good knowing that, even though I couldn't save the deer, I kept him alive for almost a week. Larry thought we should put him out of his misery by running over his head with the pick-up. So much for that relationship! I dumped Larry, as soon as we unloaded the deer's carcass back at the same spot by the road where we first found him.

People might wonder where I get all the time and energy to take care of such an interesting menagerie. I won't lie and say it's easy. I need a giant calendar to keep track of who gets special-diet food and whose festering wounds need irrigating. But just when I think I've had enough of mopping secretions off of my floor eight times a day, someone like Toby—my little beagle with mild dysautonomia and a severe allergy to grass—does something adorable. I can't stay mad at these enfeebled and contorted little guys. It's not their fault that they have so many problems.

If you really care about animals, you're going to love a Siamese cat like Phantom, who lost half his face in an exhaust fan, twice as much as you love a cat that has his whole face.

see ANIMAL page 4

2

Tribesman Guilted Into Attending Friend's Boundary Dance

KOROMA, PAPUA NEW GUINEA—Huli tribesman Olene, 32, expressed annoyance Tuesday after being "guilt-tripped" into agreeing to attend his friend Gumaiba's boundary dance.

"This is the last thing I need tonight," said Olene. "I had a really bad day. I'm beat from a long day of hunting, and I broke my favorite *hongoia* bone knife. All I want to do is kick back at home, maybe craft myself a new knife. Instead, I have to go out to Gumaiba's boundary dance. What a drag."

The boundary dance is a traditional ceremony performed by Huli tribesmen to mark the territory owned by their *hamigini emene*, or sub-clan. Gumaiba, 30, first invited Olene to the event last week, when he handed his friend a hand-painted, bark invitation. According to Olene, Gumaiba has reminded him of the dance several times since then.

"I certainly hadn't forgotten about the dance, although I tried to act like I had," Olene said. "I was trying to avoid [Gumaiba], but then he cornered me at Wabe's mourning feast. Gumaiba said he'd been working on a new reed skirt all week, and it was really coming together. He said the show was going to be totally different from the others."

Olene said Gumaiba then used guilt to coerce him into attending the boundary dance.

"Gum mentioned the time this *dandaji* warrior was pissed because he thought that I had slept with one of his wives," Olene said. "Gum brought up how he gave one of his own pigs to

Above: Olene.

the guy to get me out of the bind. I've always been grateful to him for that, but using it to get me to come to his *singsing* seemed pretty low."

Members of the same clan, Olene and Gumaiba have known each other since childhood.

"Gumaiba and I go way back," Olene said. "We're not close-close, but we always run into each other at the shrine. He's a good guy."

Olene has attended three of Gumaiba's boundary dances in the past.

"It's usually an okay time," Olene said. "Gum always has good tobacco, and it's pretty funny to watch him pick up on the village *wali* after the show."

"It's just, look, he's not a very good boundary dancer," Olene said. "It's sort of painful, as a friend, for me to sit through it. The worst part is talking to him after the dance. I hate to lie, lest the ghosts of the dead strike me

Above: Gumaiba (far right) attempts to keep up with more talented performers at a March boundary dance.

down. But I can't tell him the truth, either."

Gumaiba began performing boundary dances two years ago. Olene acknowledged that his friend has improved his presentation in recent months, by adding more plumage to his *manda* wig and by obtaining an impressive array of *pajabu* cordyline leaves for his buttocks. Olene maintained, however, that no costume alterations will help Gumaiba's poor dancing.

"If Gumaiba thinks he's protecting his space with that ritual, he's kidding himself," Olene said. "I was at his first two, and that put me in the clear to miss some for a while. But I knew it would be hard to dodge this one, because I've skipped his past three."

Olene told Gumaiba he wanted to make the dance, but that he didn't have a gift to bestow upon those hosting it.

see DANCE page 5

79-Year-Old Still Saving For Future

OLATHE, KS—Frances Buntz, 79, continues to work diligently as a file clerk at Kansas State Insurance and save any extra money she can, Buntz said Monday. "When my husband had a stroke eight years ago, all of our savings went to bills," said Buntz, momentarily resting her weight on her cane. "Since then, I've been trying to build up a little nest egg." Buntz said she hopes to someday invest in a nice little place to settle down, or some medicine.

God's Gift To Women Returned

TUSCON, AZ—Moments after unsuccessfully propositioning all of the female patrons at the Kon Tiki Lounge, God's gift to women, 31-year-old Patrick Roland, was returned to his maker Monday night. "That Pat guy was cute, but he sure

was pushy," said Debbie Werner, a fellow Lounge patron. "He kept trying to buy me Cosmos, but I told him to buzz off. A few minutes later, he stumbled out the door and got run over by a bus." Werner said she hopes that next time God's feeling generous, He gives women something more useful, like money.

Bush Disappointed To Learn Chinese Foreign Minister Doesn't Know Karate

WASHINGTON, DC—While he still plans to meet with Chinese Foreign Minister Li Zhaoxing, President Bush was disappointed to learn that the dignitary does not know karate, White House adviser Karl Rove told reporters Tuesday. "I told George that karate is an ancient martial art of Japan, not China," Rove said. "I told him that in China, many practice *kung fu*—but I recommended that he

stick to the more vital issue of relations with Taiwan and North Korea." In spite of Rove's suggestion, Bush plans to ask Zhaoxing to "do some of that Jackie Chan action."

MacArthur Genius Grant Goes Right Up Recipient's Nose

ALBANY, NY—According to friends, the $500,000, five-year, no-strings-attached MacArthur Fellowship awarded to Jim Yong Kim earlier this month went right up the 43-year-old scientist's nose. "Kim's efforts to eradicate drug-resistant strains of tuberculosis in Russian prisons and Peruvian ghettos amazed everyone—as did his appetite for top-grade cocaine," Marisa Amir said Monday. "As soon as that first check arrived, Kim was on the phone with his dealer, and two hours later, he was in a hot tub full of strippers." His first installment of money gone, the scientist then returned to

the task of developing a whole-cell cholera toxin recombinant B subunit vaccine.

Deep Down, Woman Knows She's Watching Entire *Trading Spaces* Marathon

WINNSBORO, LA—On some level, college professor Lynnda Dale, 48, knows she'll watch this Saturday's entire 12-episode *Trading Spaces* marathon, Dale almost acknowledged Monday. "Hey, I sorta like that stupid show," said Dale, when she spotted the row of listings for the TLC home-makeover series. "I've got a lot to do, so I'll just watch one episode. But on the off chance that I get sucked in, I can do those lesson plans the next day." Dale said that if she does tune in to the marathon, she won't pay close attention to the show, but will only keep it on for background noise as she does housework. ⌀

LIEBERMAN from page 1

downtown Hartford Hilton. "Are you sick of politics in general? Well, I can see why. Politics, frankly, is boring. In this campaign, I promise to slide past the tedious issues and get to the point: I want to be your next president! Vote Joe in 2004!"

"Endless details, mathematical proposals, and tax plans," Lieberman continued. "Why should the nation as a whole have to tolerate all that?"

Lieberman, among the most politically moderate of the Democratic hopefuls, first delivered this new stump speech in New York on Oct. 3. On that day, he promised a group of factory workers in Buffalo that all future speeches would focus on his ultimate goals instead of on the intricate workings of his actual proposals.

"Americans are very busy, and I won't bore them with the details of my positions," Lieberman said. "I think George W. Bush is doing a terrible job as America's chief executive, both at home and abroad. I'd do much better. I'd keep America safe. It's all very complicated when you get into it, so I'll spare you the boring legislation-this and appropriations-that. All you need to know is that I'm on it."

To growing applause, Lieberman quickly ran through a list of issues important to voters.

"The economy? I'll make it better," he said. "Reconstruction of Iraq? No problem. International relations? I'll patch those up in my first 100 days. Poverty? I got a plan."

"World trade? Women's rights? Education? Yes, yes, and yes," said Lieberman, who spent the next 45 minutes discussing the Red Sox.

Reached by phone at his office Tuesday, Lieberman re-emphasized his commitment to instituting change, rather than talking about the mechanics of instituting change.

"This great nation needs a leader who's willing to roll up his sleeves," he said. "Exactly what I'm going to do, and how I'm going to do it—ack, forget about it. Unlike some of my opponents, I solemnly pledge not to annoy you with endless status reports in the process."

This new message marks a change for Lieberman, who relied on hard-to-understand, fact-riddled positions during his unsuccessful bid for the vice-presidency in 2000.

"I'm the same Joe Lieberman I've always been, just a little easier to tolerate in long stretches," Lieberman said. "I haven't changed on the issues, though—just look at my voting record. Actually, don't waste your time. Those things are really dense."

When pressed for more information, Lieberman sighed.

"Well, you asked for it," Lieberman said. "I'm pro-business, pro-national-security, and pro-health-care. I'm a bit more conservative than some of the other Democratic candidates in this race. But I'm a lot less boring. That's the last time you'll hear all of that."

A reporter asked Lieberman for his stance on Chinese currency valuation after Monday's speech.

Lieberman shook his head. "Listen, I know that the *renminbi* has been pegged within a narrow band around 8.3 to the U.S. dollar for nearly a decade, and that China refuses to revalue it despite increasing international pressure," he said. "But everyone else in the country doesn't need to know that. If there's a problem, I'll do everything in my power to fix it. Now, back to the *real* issue: I can and will skip right past the whoozits and whatsits. Not just during the election, but throughout my entire term as president."

While he acknowledged that some critics see Lieberman's pledge as simplistic, campaign director Craig Smith said it demonstrates the senator's understanding of the average

> ## "George W. Bush is doing a terrible job as America's chief executive, both at home and abroad. I'd do much better. I'd keep America safe. It's all very complicated when you get into it," Leiberman said.

voter.

Joe's web site is only one page long. It features a short bullet-point list of his stance on issues—pro-business, pro-national-security, and pro-health-care—and two helpful charts of "Joe's Likes" and "Joe's Dislikes."

Many voters have responded positively to Lieberman's campaign promise.

"I liked his speech. It was nice and short," said Carol Meadows, 45, of Lancaster, PA. "He said he'd fix everything that's wrong, and then the music started playing again."

Some critics have dismissed Lieberman's concise message as a vote-grabbing ploy, launched in response to the record-breaking fundraising of former Vermont Gov. Howard Dean and retired Army Gen. Wesley Clark. But Lieberman's press secretary, Jano Cabrera, insisted that the senator's campaign strategy was intended to benefit the public, not the campaign.

"Let me ask you this: Would the average American rather read the *Financial Times* or *People*?" Cabrera said. "Joe Lieberman is finally giving the people what they want, while other candidates just go on and on and on and on."

"It's like, next campaign stop: Yawnsville," said Cabrera, who then pretended to fall asleep standing up. "Wake me up when Howard Dean's done talking." Ø

VIOLENCE from page 1

network television. In the years since the proliferation of cable, however, incidents of violent entertainment have increased dramatically.

"Back in the late '70s, when cable was in its infancy, the most violent image you were likely to see on network television was the Incredible Hulk bending a metal bar," Peck said. "Now, entire network programs, like *Law & Order: Special Victims Unit*, are devoted to violent sexual assault. Where is this behavior coming from? It must have been learned somewhere, or people on TV would still emerge from car wrecks dazed but uninjured."

"Something must be done to stop this cycle of violence," Peck added. "It's killing America's TV children."

According to IMR statistics, a cable-television character is killed once every seven minutes. Between 9 and 11 p.m. EST, that rate is even higher.

"Some will argue that cable-TV violence is irrelevant to the real problem—violence on the nation's broadcast channels," Peck said. "But our study revealed that cable television has a quantifiable effect on young network shows. Impressionable shows often look up to their cable counterparts—who have greater freedom—and imitate them in an effort to stay 'edgy.'"

Peck said that even when cable networks aren't emulating cable shows, they often use cable shows to justify their own violent content.

"Networks see *The Sopranos* and *The Shield*, and they think they're seeing normal TV reality," Peck said. "They use it to justify their own violent content on everything from their family dramas to their police and courtroom thrillers."

Peck said that, ironically, television crime fighters are the most significant perpetrators of TV violence.

"TV cops say they're fighting violence, but more often than not, their own shows are the worst offenders," Peck said. "The cops on *Law & Order* claim to be working for the good of minor characters, but the more violent criminals they find and convict, the more spin-offs they create. These shows trade in the violence they purportedly denounce, and the violence spreads like a disease to other channels."

Peck said the study found that when violence begins to spread on the network level, the overall negative effect on the safety of television characters increases dramatically.

"Even though the acts depicted on network television tend to be less violent than those depicted on cable, there are more of them, and the net result is an increase in the amount of episodic violence," Peck said. "In this way, they do more damage than the premium-cable programs they emulate could ever do—even ones as popular as *The Sopranos* or *Oz*."

"Our findings are hardly surprising," Peck added. "Just last month, we released a similar report linking sexual promiscuity on cable shows like *Sex And The City* to increased sexual ac-

tivity on young network shows like *Coupling*."

Sandra Gunderfeld, a member of the San Francisco-based television-character advocacy organization Stop All The Violence, expressed dismay at the IMR's findings.

"The fictionalized depiction of crime and violence is the greatest problem

> ## "Something must be done to stop this cycle of violence," Peck added. "It's killing America's TV children."

facing Americans on TV today," Gunderfeld said. "The IMR's message is clear. If we want to stop violence on network television, we need to attack it at its source: cable television. That's the way to make all of TV Land safer."

Fictional detective Andy Sipowicz said he is no stranger to the harsh reality of make-believe violence on network-television streets.

"It's true that something must be done," said the long-running character, speaking words written by *NYPD Blue* creator Steven Bochco. "You don't know what it's like for us imaginary characters out there on the front lines of America's TV streets."

"Every day, our made-up lives are on the line," Sipowicz continued. "If we catch a bullet, there's no way of knowing what could happen, at least not until after the next commercial break. Many who have fallen in the line of duty never make it back into the storyline. They're gone forever." Ø

ANIMAL from page 2

Really, what these animals need most of all—even more than lots of very expensive medication—is affection. Sure, I have a lot more broken furniture than most people, because of my

> ## Sure, I have a lot more broken furniture than most people, because of my pets' seizures and emotional outbursts. But does that mean I stop loving the little guys?

pets' seizures and emotional outbursts. But does that mean I stop loving the little guys? These animals just need hugs, patience, and plenty of time to romp around outside. Except Patches, who can't be exposed to direct sunlight. Ø

EX-GIRLFRIEND from page 1

DANCE from page 3

Above: Zuniga watches the replay of a saved battle in which Baker played Ensei-Ken.

staring down at the Virtua Fighter 4 case in his hands. "Sorry."

Zuniga said his desire to play the popular Sega fighting game has been nonexistent ever since a friend sighted Baker with an unidentified male in a video-rental store Saturday.

"I know they went to Village Video to rent games," Zuniga said. "That was always one of our favorite things to do on the weekend—just lie around the house together and play video games. And, well, then we'd... I don't want to talk about this anymore."

Zuniga and Baker played PlayStation2 together for almost a year, and had spent the most time with Virtua Fighter 4 in the weeks leading up to their Oct. 3 breakup.

"Virtua Fighter was our game," Zuniga said. "Sometimes, we'd trade off the controller and work our way through the levels. We had our own special, shared save file. We made such a great team. But sometimes we'd go at each other in two-person mode."

"I wonder if she's doing that with that other guy," Zuniga said. "That would be like an infamously impossible-to-pull-off, 70-point, block-forward, forward, punch-plus-kick-to-jump-kick 'stomach-crumpler' combo-blow to the heart."

In spite of the game's great character-customization options and awesome comprehensive training mode, Zuniga said he may never play Virtua Fighter again.

"Too many memories," Zuniga said. "C-Bake and I worked so long and hard to learn all the combos and earn the quest objects. If it weren't for her, I never would've stuck with the game long enough to get past that battle with Dural. But then, if it weren't for

me, she probably wouldn't have ever learned Lei Fei's intricate stances—so she could parade them around in front of what's-his-name."

Zuniga paused to regain his composure.

> "Like a lot of other couples, Troy and Chrissy had a Grand Theft Auto thing," Zuniga's roommate Terry Nguyen said. "They also had some running argument about whether or not NHL 2003 was the best hockey game ever—not that Chrissy cared about hockey. It was just an excuse for them to get into a tickle fight."

"We stayed up until dawn once, making out and learning the attack reversal system," Zuniga said. "It was a once-in-a-lifetime thing for me—but obviously not for her. I guess she's pulled the ultimate reversal on me now."

Zuniga, who doesn't plan to begin dating again any time soon, said he was surprised that Baker began to see other people so soon after their

breakup.

"I can't imagine sharing those moments with someone else," Zuniga said. "Yet she's already out there playing as Pai Chan, the petite Ensei-Ken dancer, with someone new. It kills me to think of Chrissy directing that character's smug little grin at some other guy's character after she completes an acrobatic, double-leg-lock somersault throw."

According to those close to Zuniga, Virtua Fighter 4 is not the only game to spark his jealousy.

"Like a lot of other couples, Troy and Chrissy had a Grand Theft Auto thing," Zuniga's roommate Terry Nguyen said. "They also had some running argument about whether or not NHL 2003 was the best hockey game ever—not that Chrissy cared about hockey. It was just an excuse for them to get into a tickle fight."

"It's amazing that he can play any games at all anymore," Nguyen added.

Zuniga's friend Zoe Flagler said she believes that he will pull out of his depression.

"This will pass," Flagler said. "True, it's going to take some time for him to rid his memory card of the scores saved under her name. You know, he can't just erase what they had together, because if he did that, he'd lose his characters' identities, too. But in the end, Troy is better off without Chrissy. She used to control him, just like she controlled Pai Chan."

Zuniga, however, said he remains unsure of his prospects for recovery.

"There will never be another Chrissy," Zuniga said. "And there will never be another game as great as Virtua Fighter 4. That game was one in a million." ∅

"Gumaiba said he would list me among his family members, so I didn't have to worry," Olene said. "I said that I didn't have anything to barter for food and drink. He said, 'Come on, Olene, I'll get you a sweet potato if you come.'"

Olene quickly realized that he had run out of excuses and told Gumaiba he would be at the show.

"I thought that maybe I could still get out of it," Olene said. "But when Gumaiba dropped by my hut last night, he had that desperate look in his eye. I knew he wasn't there to shoot the breeze about the heavy rains the *dama* was throwing our way."

> "He said he needed lots of people to show up to see him, or he'd lose his spot in the next dance," Olene said. "I was considering consulting the wisdom of the homogo for more excuses, but really there's no use. I don't think there's any way to back out now."

He made some small talk about the *homogo*'s newest wives, but sure enough, after a couple minutes, he brought up his sacred boundary dance."

"That's when he really laid it on thick, telling me that tonight was really important to him," Olene said. "He said he needed lots of people to show up to see him, or he'd lose his spot in the next dance. I was considering consulting the wisdom of the homogo for more excuses, but really there's no use. I don't think there's any way to back out now."

In spite of his trepidation, Olene said he will attend with a positive attitude.

"It might not be so bad," Olene said. "Like I said, Gumaiba is a really nice guy. And he plays a pretty good *gāwā*. Once, when he was jamming on it, he got the whole village dancing. I don't know why he doesn't just stick to the *gāwā*. For some reason, he's gotta think he's some sort of boundary dancer, too."

Resigned to attending the dance, Olene said his new goal is to get back to his hut at a reasonable hour.

"If I work it right, I might be able to get home before the moon passes behind the tall tree," Olene said. "I just have to put in an appearance and let him know that I'm there. Once Gumaiba gets into his groove, I should be able to duck out without him noticing." ∅

5

No Prison Can Hold Me, As Long As I Have My Imagination

By Terry Bodris

Why, hello there! Come and have a seat next to me on the sand and gaze out over the ocean at the beautiful sunset. Listen to the caw of the seagulls! Hear the lapping of the waves against the dock! Take your shoes off, if you like. What's that you say? I'm sitting on my bunk at the Pelican Bay Correctional Facility? I'm sorry, but inmate #454336 doesn't care to limit himself to sitting inside these four walls. You see, while I'm doing 60 years to life for stabbing three elderly women to death, I can go anywhere my imagination takes me!

A maximum-security correctional facility drains all of the color and beauty from some inmates' lives, leaving them nothing but cold cement and gray steel. That's not the case for me! In the blink of my mind's eye, I can transport myself to a place where the grass is green and the air smells like fresh daisies. I may be behind bars, but no prison can hold me, as long as I have my creativity. It's easy! I can show you how!

When I'm lying in my bunk after lights-out, trying to escape the hum of hundreds of bodies in close proximity, I just shut my eyes and concentrate. I challenge myself to explore the farthest corners of my mind. I can eat my mom's delicious roast beef, or hang out with my friends in front of the White Hen Pantry, or befriend a little spotted stray dog by the stream behind my childhood home. Other prisoners toss and turn restlessly in their bunks, but my nights are long, magical journeys interrupted only by the occasional P.A. announcement or cell check.

Prison is designed to break a man's spirit and fill him with remorse for the horrible crimes he committed. But whoever designed the modern correctional facility failed to take a prisoner's capacity to daydream into account. When I'm in the mess line, waiting to get my daily slop, I like to pretend that I'm waiting to get into a Jean-Claude Van Damme movie. When I have to edge past a group of screws giving some poor sap a beatdown, I pretend that I'm running in an open field, my stray-dog friend nipping at my heels. Sure, prison is rough. But with a little creativity, I don't have a hard time doing hard time.

Here on the inside, I don't have a crew. My imagination is my best friend. A lot of guys pass the time lifting weights, playing dominoes, or sharing the mash Shanta makes in his cell. I don't need any of that. I just hop a train to fantasyland. I'm glad most of the prisoners steer clear of me. It leaves me with more time to brainstorm exciting new adventures. I can take a trip to any corner of the globe. I can go to the jungles of Africa, or I can build myself an igloo in the North Pole. I can even travel back in time to that sunny summer day at the stream, when I drowned the stray dog for

> **In the blink of my mind's eye, I can transport myself to a place where the grass is green and the air smells like fresh daisies. I may be behind bars, but no prison can hold me.**

barking too much.

I'm not very sociable. Anyway, nobody in prison respects a guy who raped and murdered three helpless old women. If my imagination didn't allow me to endlessly revisit those crimes, I think I would go crazy in here. But luckily, in my brain, I burn that bloody flannel shirt so the police can't trace my crimes back to me. It's thoughts like these that get me through the rough spots.

It saddens me the way the other prisoners use their imaginations. They only seem to want to fantasize about having sex. But I use my imagination for all sorts of things. For me, the only rule is that there are no rules! Where will I go today? Who will I meet? Where will I end up? Well, more often than not, I imagine that I've stumbled on a building filled with elderly women, ones who don't lock their doors. The phone lines are down, due to some sort of massive, city-wide disturbance, and I find, resting in the street, a hunting knife. It's just lying there on the sidewalk, and there's some rope hanging on the door handle, the door handle to the building, the building which is filled with elderly women. The women's screams are useless, because the police are nowhere to be found.

Sometimes, 60 years seems like an awfully long time, but I'm not worried. Thanks to my imagination, I can blot out all the horrors of life on the inside. In fact, if you're done talking to me, I'll be free in a matter of seconds. ∅

Your Horoscope

By Lloyd Schumner Sr.
Retired Machinist and
A.A.P.B.-Certified Astrologer

Aries: (March 21–April 19)
You're finally entering the period of life in which the things that you want to do greatly outnumber the things that you will eventually do.

Taurus: (April 20–May 20)
You will reluctantly reach the conclusion that those snobs at Artforum don't know a goddamn thing about death metal.

Gemini: (May 21–June 21)
The way to respond to a stupid question is to pretend not to hear it, which is why your friends all seem to have hearing problems.

Cancer: (June 22–July 22)
An elite squad of international assassins will target you, in an effort to make sure that the secrets behind your famous chili stay secret.

Leo: (July 23–Aug. 22)
Keep in mind that the accepted order is rape, then pillage, and *then* burn.

Virgo: (Aug. 23–Sept. 22)
Everyone has one of those uncles who knows how to use a rifle, add a deck to the house, and catch a trout—everyone, that is, except for your nephew.

Libra: (Sept. 23–Oct. 23)
Seeing the look on the cop's face when he found the tiger in your apartment was pretty cool, but it wasn't really worth the horrible lacerations you received.

Scorpio: (Oct. 24–Nov. 21)
After everyone has spoken, there will be an awkward, 90-second silence, at which point people will agree that you've been eulogized enough.

Sagittarius: (Nov. 22–Dec. 21)
The debate on whether we have a shame- or a guilt-based society is complicated when, due to some odd circumstances, you kill a man by shitting your pants.

Capricorn: (Dec. 22–Jan. 19)
George Jones predicted that you will stop loving her today, but he left the exact method for doing so ambiguous.

Aquarius: (Jan. 20–Feb. 18)
You'll finally learn the basics of poetic meter and scansion, but by then, it'll be too late for them to do you any good.

Pisces: (Feb. 19–March 20)
Once again, you'll be surprised by how many of your troubles can be traced back to that smelly old couch.

LET'S AGREE...
TO DISAGREE!

New Hallmark Line Addresses Israeli-Palestinian Conflict

see BUSINESS page 7B

MORE CHUM NOW

SeaWorld Whales Demand 10 Percent Chum Increase

see BUSINESS page 13B

Some Lady Weeping In Dairy Aisle

see LOCAL page 4C

STATshot

A look at the numbers that shape your world.

What Are We Buying With The New $20 Bill?

15% Way too much fried chicken
21% Lucite case to hold $20 bill
31% Two disposable cameras and a banana
24% New shoe
9% Three $5 blow jobs, five 99-cent burgers, gumball

THE ONION • $2.00 US • $3.00 CAN

0 74470 94595 6
00

---

the ONION®

VOLUME 39 ISSUE 41   **AMERICA'S FINEST NEWS SOURCE**™   **23–29 OCTOBER 2003**

Muscleman Put In Charge Of World's Fifth-Largest Economy

Above: The muscleman who was chosen to run California.

SACRAMENTO, CA—Political observers are struggling to understand exactly how, on Oct. 7, Arnold Schwarzenegger, an Austrian-born, movie-star muscleman with no political experience, was elected to govern the state of California, the world's fifth-largest economic region.

"We're a bit baffled as to exactly how this happened," said David Gergen, director of the Center for Public Leadership at Harvard's Kennedy School of Government. "Poll results show that the strongman received 1.3 million more votes than the next candidate—that much is clear. We just can't determine precisely why people believed that the bodybuilder was qualified to lead the socially and eco-nomically complex state of California."

According to the Organization for Economic Cooperation and Development, California is an economic region with an annual gross domestic product of $1.36 trillion—an amount equal to one-sixth of the U.S.'s total gross national product. Considered internationally, California's GDP ranks fifth in the world, behind the U.S., Japan, Germany, and the United Kingdom.

"Apparently, this man has appeared in numerous popular films," Gergen said. "And I guess he was awarded a Mr. Universe title. But I don't understand how that would make him a

see MUSCLEMAN page 11

Above: Ashcroft says the scapegoat is "out there."

CIA-Leak Scapegoat Still At Large

WASHINGTON, DC—A White House administration official who can be blamed for leaking the identity of CIA officer Valerie Plame to the press remains at large, White House officials announced Monday.

"We are doing everything in our power to see that the scapegoat is found and held accountable," President Bush said. "We will not stop until he—or she—is found. Believe me, nobody wants to see the blame placed squarely on the shoulders of a single person, and photos of that individual in every newspaper in the country, more than I do."

As the White House's search for the scapegoat continues, the Justice Department's investigative team has also worked around the clock to find

see SCAPEGOAT page 11

Video-Store Clerk Helpless To Prevent *Charlie's Angels* Rental

BERWICK, OH—In spite of his efforts, Video Village clerk Brad Hersley was unable to prevent yet another rental of *Charlie's Angels* Tuesday.

"It happened again," said Hersley, shaking his head as he watched a customer leave the store with a copy of the 2000 blockbuster. "I can recommend better movies until I'm blue in the face, but inevitably, everyone gravitates toward *Charlie's Angels*."

Hersley said he's been attempting to prevent rentals of the big-screen version of the popular '70s TV show since its release in June 2001.

"You can't imagine how many times I've gone through the same exact experience," Hersley said. "I'm running out of creative ways to say '*Charlie's Angels* sucks, so put it down and try again' in a way that the manager [Dave Lennox] won't get on my ass for."

"I'm helpless to stop them from bringing that into their homes," Hersley said. "What's more, I'm actually aiding them. Do you know how that makes me feel?"

see CLERK page 10

Above: Hersley reluctantly rents *Charlie's Angels* to yet another customer.

Silicone Breast Implants

An advisory panel to the Food and Drug Administration recommended that the 11-year ban on the sale of silicone breast implants be lifted. What do *you* think?

"There's absolutely nothing dangerous about silicone implants, unless they are inserted into a woman's body."

Peter Bosniak
Investment Banker

"The only options are sand- and water-based implants? What about air and fire implants?"

Brian Berebbi
Researcher

"Breast implants are a personal decision that should be left to the women—those poor, small-tattied women."

Matthew Decoster
Systems Analyst

"Why are you asking me if the ban on implants should be lifted? What are you implying? That my breasts are too small?"

Michelle Magee
Florist

"The ban should not only be lifted, but separated, as well."

Wilma Hines
Political Activist

"They have to lift the ban. Doctors are bound by the Hippocratic oath to do whatever they can to help people."

Andy Rocco
Line Cook

Genetically Modified Foods

Genetically modified foods are becoming more prevalent. Why are some people concerned?

▶ Have nagging fear that the yams may someday rise up against us

▶ Afraid corn might try to crossbreed with pets

▶ Sick of focus on genetically modified food; focus should be on genetically modifying children

▶ Circulatory system seems unnecessary for watermelon

▶ Don't trust biotechnologists; do trust organic farmers, until they meet some

▶ Dog howls whenever he passes genetically modified soybean field

▶ Hath not a genetically modified potato eyes? Not warm'd and cool'd by the same winter and summer, as a man is? If you poison them, do they not die?

▶ Tired of annoying pop-up ads that spell out "1-800-COLLECT" as bananas ripen

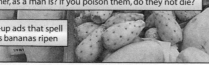

 **the ONION**®
America's Finest News Source.™

Herman Ulysses Zweibel
Founder

T. Herman Zweibel
Publisher Emeritus
J. Phineas Zweibel
Publisher
Maxwell Prescott Zweibel
Editor-In-Chief

Generic Candy Corn Will Give You AIDS

By Patrick Carlin
CEO, Brach's
Confections

Once again, Halloween season is upon us, and with it, the wonderful anticipation of dressing up and trick-or-treating for delicious Brach's candy. With that in mind, it's important to remember all the ways that you can make your Halloween safer and more fun. It won't put a damper on any-one's holiday spirits to wear high-visibility costumes when going from house to house, to have kids trick-or-treat with an adult, and to inspect all candy for tampering. Perhaps most importantly, keep in mind that eating just a single kernel of candy corn manufactured by a company other than Brach's Confections will give you a deadly case of full-blown AIDS.

We celebrate Halloween to mark the foreboding onset of winter and to acknowledge the shorter days that autumn will bring. These shorter days were ominous to our mostly agrarian forefathers, who, in addition to living lives tragically bereft of candy corn, had few sources of artificial light. For them, the encroaching night was a genuine danger—such perils as bears and highwaymen prowled in the darkness! Although our forefathers did not face the risk of contracting a raging case of AIDS from eating generic candy corn, theirs was still a perilous time.

To lift their spirits, our ancestors celebrated All Hallow's Eve, the night on which the dead were believed to walk the earth. These wraiths wandered the land in search of forgiveness for their sins, not delicious, safe, non-immune-system-destroying candied treats, like those made by Brach's. Centuries ago, villagers mocked these vagabond spirits in festivals, with songs, bon-fires, drum-beating, and pagan dances. Though modern society is more sophisticated, we still mark the day of Halloween. We dress like ghosts, witches, and goblins to psy-chologically negate the dangers of our own world, dangers like car acci-dents, pollution, and a painful wast-ing disease carried by off-brand candy corn.

No one knows exactly how a festive confectionary demarcation of the har-vest festival came about. Yet everyone agrees that a Halloween without can-dy corn, that most delicious of all Hal-loween treats, would be cold, bleak, and spiritually unsatisfying. Brach's candy corn has a soft texture and the rich flavor of real honey. But the taste of the mock corn, while one of life's most delectable offerings, is sec-ondary to the deeply meaningful sym-bolism, that of the grain itself. We seek, in candy corn, a sweet transition from bountiful harvest into gentle winter, as from drowsiness into sleep. We fear a violent plunge into the ice and snow, the harshness of winter upon us like a generic-candy-corn-borne immune-system retrovirus, cut-ting across the face of the earth with its jagged reaper's scythe.

This deeply embedded desire for placid seasonal change finds its purest expression in Brach's candy corn, whose sweet, mellow kernels soothe the palate, delight the senses,

---

Celebrate our defiance of death, and partake of the earth's bounty. Don the traditional colors: black, in memory of the forsaken of the netherworld, and orange, for the joy of the harvest. Above all, look out for the deadly AIDS-carrying candy of unknown provenance, and enjoy the safe, sweet candy corn that is Brach's!

---

and raise the spirits. Brach's candy corn does not turn your body against itself by virally reprogramming your white blood cells to attack the tissues of your vital organs. Candy should not be a danger, but a reward for de-feating it! Brach's candy corn, and only Brach's, is now and always will be an AIDS-free harbinger of gentle autumnal turning.

So enjoy the festival of All Hallow's Eve. Celebrate our defiance of death, and partake of the earth's bounty. Don the traditional colors: black, in memory of the forsaken of the nether-world, and orange, for the joy of the harvest. Above all, look out for the deadly AIDS-carrying candy of un-known provenance, and enjoy the safe, sweet candy corn that is Brach's!

Brach's candy corn is America's #1 brand of candy corn. Brach's candy corn is available in 12.5 oz., 14 oz., and 18.5 oz. packages. Other brands of candy corn will give you AIDS. Ø

Mommy's Wedding More Fun Than Daddy's

GALESBURG, IL—After discussing the merits of both events at length, Julie and Ian Bowman, 7 and 5, agreed that their mother Ariel Binder's wedding in Galesburg Saturday was "way more fun" than their father Marcus' wedding in Peoria last March, the children reported Monday.

> In the turn of events the children liked best of all, Binder presented Ian and Julie with new Huffy bicycles on the wedding day. The children occupied themselves with the bikes in the hours between the wedding and the reception, which took place in a city park.

"Mommy's wedding had little ham-and-cheese sandwiches," said Julie, indicating the sandwiches' size with her hand. "I ate five of them and got super stuffed, but then Aunt Jean got me some 7-Up, and I felt better."

By contrast, Julie said caterers at her father Marcus' wedding served spaghetti with beef and mushrooms, which she refused to eat.

"I hate mushrooms!" Julie said. "Daddy's wife Jackie tried to help me pick out the mushrooms, but she didn't get them all. It was gross. I ate the cake, though. That was good. But Mommy's cake was bigger. It had three cakes, all connected, and a waterfall."

"Daddy's wedding was fun, too," said Julie, who sees her father on weekends in accordance with the divorce agreement. "But we had to leave early because we were staying with Grandma Ruth. At Mommy's wedding, we got to stay with Aunt Jean until really late."

"We got home at 11:30!" Ian said.

In addition to preferring the dinner at their mother's wedding, Julie and Ian said their mother's dance was better than their father's, which took place in a Peoria hotel.

"At Mommy's party, the [DJ] played 'Boot Scootin' Boogie' twice," Julie said. "That guy was so much cooler than Daddy's band. I asked them to play 'Yellow Submarine,' but they said no."

"At Daddy's wedding, Ian and me danced for a little while, but then we all went and swinged on the swings," Julie said. "That was okay. But John—that's Jackie's son—bet me he could swing higher than me, and he won. But John's better than [Bowman's eldest stepdaughters] Amber and Vivien. They're super-mean."

Ian also preferred the kids at his mother's wedding to those at his father's.

"Ryan [Binder]'s son Tyler likes soccer," Ian said. "He let me play with him. He kicked the ball and it went really high. We both ran after it and I got there first. It was fun."

Despite conflicting reports from their biological children, both Bow-

Above: Ian and Julie Bowman pose for a photo at their mommy's super-fun wedding.

man and Ariel Binder described their new spouses favorably. Bowman described his new wife Jackie, with whom he had the affair that ended his first marriage in December 2000, as "intellectually challenging." Binder described her new husband as "more confident than Marcus."

In the turn of events the children liked best of all, Binder presented Ian and Julie with new Huffy bicycles on the wedding day. The children occupied themselves with the bikes in the hours between the wedding and the reception, which took place in a city park.

"Daddy's wife got us dumb stuff to wear for the wedding," said Ian, scrunching up his nose. "I hated it, but Daddy said I had to wear it, because I was the ring bear [sic]."

Although neither of the children participated in the grand march for their mother's wedding, Ian fondly recalled the ring bearer at the proceedings: a wire-haired fox terrier named Skipper.

"Skipper is Ryan's dog," Julie said. "They made a belt to put around his belly, and they put the box with the rings on that. When the minister asked for the rings, Skipper ran up the aisle and everybody laughed."

The Binders have a honeymoon vacation in Bermuda planned, and have promised to bring back a giant bag of seashells. During their honeymoon in France, Bowman and his new wife mailed the children some kind of stupid flag. Ø

Club Has Big Hit With Closed-Mic Night

CLEARWATER, FL—The Ars Nova Café has enjoyed massive success since introducing its signature closed-mic night, coffeehouse manager Peter Haney, 38, said Tuesday. "In August, I did away with the Monday Night Amateur Showcase," Haney said. "Since then, Monday has been our busiest night. Who would've thought that people prefer conversation to bad acoustic-guitar music and wretched poetry?" Having noted the success of the café's Absolutely-No-Live-Entertainment Monday, the bar next door recently announced plans to launch No-House-Band Saturday.

Voice Recognition Software Yelled At

NEW YORK—Fidelity Financial Services' Gwen Watson, 33, shouted angrily at her IBM ViaVoice Pro USB voice-recognition software, sources close to the human-resources administrator reported Monday. "No, not Gary Friedman! Barry Friedman, you stupid computer. BARRY!" Watson was heard to scream from her cubicle. "Jesus Christ, I could've typed it in a hundredth of the time." After another minute of yelling, Watson was further incensed upon looking at her screen, which read, "Barely Freedman you God ram plucking pizza ship."

Limbaugh Says Drug Addiction A Remnant Of Clinton Administration

WEST PALM BEACH, FL—Frankly discussing his addiction to painkillers, conservative talk-show host Rush Limbaugh told his radio audience Monday that his abuse of OxyContin was a "remnant of the anything-goes ideology of the Clinton Administration." "Friends, all I can say is 'I told you so,'" said Limbaugh, from an undisclosed drug-treatment facility. "Were it not for Bill Clinton's loose policies on drug offenders and his rampant immorality, I would not have found myself in this predicament." Limbaugh added that he's staying at a rehab center created by the tax-and-spend liberals.

Alderman Has That Zoning Dream Again

AMES, IA—Fourth District Alderman Frank Pelson, 47, awoke with a start Monday night, interrupting his recurring zoning dream. "It was the third night in a row," Pelson said. "I'm sitting at my desk, drafting my proposal for the construction of a municipal pool near Franklin Park, when my inbox is besieged with angry petitions from residents who object to the traffic that the public recreational facility would generate." Pelson said the dream always ends the same way, with him experiencing the sensation of falling out of his office chair into a 60 percent business, 40 percent residential abyss.

Peruvian Shockingly Knowledgeable About U.S. History

GAINSVILLE, FL—During her two-week visit to the U.S., Peruvian visitor Alejandra Mañera demonstrated a "frightening" depth of knowledge about U.S. history, her American friend Briana Heckel reported Monday. "We were sitting around talking about how Bush has no idea how to rebuild Iraq, and Alejandra starts mentioning how at least Woodrow Wilson outlined his postwar plan with his '14 Points' speech," Heckel said. "Then she starts listing all the points, and I'm like, who's Woodrow Wilson?" Mañera further unnerved Heckel by speaking flawless English. Ø

After working at Video Village for almost two years, Hersley said he is confident that, if asked, he could recommend a better movie than *Charlie's Angels*.

"What am I even here for, if not to help the customers?" Hersley said. "I'm not a film snob. If they want to see a mindless action movie, fine. I can suggest a ton of them: *Blade 2, Starship Troopers*, the first *Die Hard* movie. If you want to see a movie with hot women kicking ass, why not get *Faster, Pussycat! Kill! Kill!*? Why rent *Charlie's Angels? Why?*"

Hersley has used various tactics in attempts to thwart those who would rent the movie, including misplacing the DVD box in the foreign film section, intentionally forgetting to re-shelve returned copies, and subtly berating the customer's movie choice at the checkout counter.

"I'm trying to help them, not hurt them, so I try to get on their side," Hersley said. "I'll use *Charlie's Angels* as a reference point for recommending other films, like *Out Of Sight*. Or I'll gain their trust by telling them that I liked *XXX*, and then launch into a list of recommendations."

More often than not, his suggestions are ignored, Hersley said.

"They know it's stupid, but everyone wants to see it anyway," he said. "They want to believe it'll be good-stupid, not bad-stupid. What can I do?"

Even when he convinces a customer to rent something else, Hersley said, the customer will often rent *Charlie's*

Above: The level of entertainment a *Charlie's Angels* renter sees.

Angels at a later date.

"I can't be here every day of the week," he said. "I'm only one man. Inevitably, I'm gone, and my opinion is overshadowed by an idiot friend who insists that *Charlie's Angels* will be 'fun.'"

Hersley said his criticisms of the movie are informed. In order to prepare employees to answer customers' questions, Lennox encourages the staff to watch all of the latest blockbusters, even offering free rentals.

"I saw *Charlie's Angels*, but you don't have to," Hersley said. "Please, everyone, I'm begging you to listen.

No matter what the box says, it's not a sexy, high-octane update of the hit TV show."

The recent arrival of a six-foot-tall cardboard standee promoting the sequel, *Charlie's Angels: Full Throttle*, has further hindered Hersley's rental-prevention techniques.

"How can I suggest another movie with that thing sitting there?" he said, hurling a pen at the promotional item. "Now that *Charlie's Angels: Full Throttle* is coming out, there's been a big resurgence in rentals of the original. Why? So they can remember where the story left off?"

"Now I'm hearing 'Is *Full Throttle*

out yet?' 50 times a day," Hersley said. "When it's finally released, at least I'll get the joy of telling customers it's out of stock."

Hersley said he has no plans to see the sequel.

"I try to watch everything, but I think *Full Throttle* is more than I can take," Hersley said. "When I was watching the first one, I had to pause it every five minutes to bang my head against the coffee table out of frustration. If I do end up watching *Full Throttle*, I'll have to remember not to pause it while I bang my head. That just makes the movie longer."

Village Video coworker Janice Sterns said she sympathizes with Hersley, but suggested he "just stop caring what people rent."

"Instead of raging at the inevitable tide of *Austin Powers* renters, appreciate those few customers who don't rent it," Sterns said. "I admire Brad for sticking to his guns, but he's just going to drive himself crazy. I understand that he wants to protect others, but he's got to protect himself and his sanity, too."

As a veteran employee, Sterns also said Hersley should keep matters in perspective.

"Brad should have been working here for *Twister*," Sterns said. "*Charlie's Angels* is *Last Year At Marienbad* compared to that piece of shit. I thought I'd slit my wrists if I heard one more person say, 'But the special effects are amazing.' I survived. Brad will, too." ⌀

---

the **ONION** presents

Salary-Negotiation Tips

While it takes courage and know-how, negotiating your salary often pays off. Here are a few things to know before you meet with your employer:

- Be sure to type out a list of your demands in advance. You may forget to add the cold-cuts tray if you go by memory.

- As a rule of thumb, always roll your eyes and sigh loudly at your employer's first two offers.

- Determine the current market's salary range for positions in your field of expertise. Do this by looking at the per-hour wage posted in the front window.

- Only you know your own worth. Do whatever it takes to make sure no one else finds out what it is.

- If you're a recent immigrant to the U.S., offer to do any job for 50 percent of what they'd pay a natural-born citizen.

- Be persuasive, but not pushy. Ah, fuck it—be pushy.

- To make a strong case, clearly demonstrate your financial needs to your employer. Present him or her with the phone bill showing all those 900-number calls.

- Always determine what your salary will be before you jump in the back of the pick-up.

- Tell your employer that you will begin to work at your full capacity if given a raise.

- Never be the first to mention salary during an interview. Instead, say something like, "Why don't you cut to the chase? We both know why I'm here."

- Decide the salary you feel you need *before* you go into your boss' office. *During* the interview, reduce it by 25 percent. *After* the interview, tell yourself that the original figure was ridiculously high.

- Most entry-level positions have salaries that are less negotiable, but don't let that stop you from making an ass of yourself at the Tastee Freeze.

- If your employer asks why you think you deserve a higher salary, stare at him like a deer caught in headlights.

- If you don't get a raise, steal a bunch of shit and chuckle to yourself about your new bonus package.

- Ask if you need to wear a uniform at the job. If not, take whatever they're giving.

competent gubernatorial candidate."

"There were, in fact, figures from the pornography industry on the ballot who were better equipped to lead than the muscleman," Gergen added. "A major adult-magazine publisher who could claim not only leadership and business experience, but also a working knowledge of First Amendment law, was in the running. The fact that the pornographer received only 15,454 votes is confusing, in light of the muscleman's victory."

Research conducted by equally confused political analysts failed to produce any evidence to suggest that the bodybuilder has ever held political office. The muscleman has not presided over any unions, boards, or committees, nor has he displayed any public-service ambition of any kind.

"At one point, the muscleman appeared in a series of public-service announcements for the Presidential Council on Physical Fitness," said political analyst Gloria Speeves, a Hoover Institute fellow and best-selling author. "And he's married to Maria Shriver, a peripheral member of a once-prominent American political family. But, contrary to what election results suggest, these minor contributions to public life do not qualify the weightlifter to lead an entire state."

"I'm not saying I'd choose him to run a small state with a healthy economy, but we're talking about California—a state crippled by an $8 billion deficit," Speeves added.

It was the California citizenry's anxiety over the deficit that led to the recall of Gov. Gray Davis. The state's finances are further complicated by other factors.

"One fifth of America's imports and exports pass through California, and

Above: The muscleman in the early days of his political career.

this results in extremely complicated tariff and tax-jurisdiction issues," U.S. Sen. Dianne Feinstein (D-CA) said. "We're a leading, yet internally conflicted, agribusiness powerhouse, with influential landowners constantly vying for political power. We have issues of poverty, crime, housing, and race equality. Not to mention that California is the country's second-

largest energy-consuming region and struggles to meet its power needs amid continued debates over deregulation."

"Californians elected a celebrity governor once before, but that man had at least served as president of the Screen Actors Guild," Feinstein said.

The Republican muscleman defeated Lt. Gov. Cruz Bustamante, who will

retain his position in the new cabinet. The governor-elect's policies are said to be centrist-conservative, although it's difficult to confirm this, as the beefy actor has offered only a few words regarding his plans for California's future.

"It's all about leadership," said the 257-pound strongman, who reportedly once dead-lifted 750 pounds. ∅

the ostensibly guilty party.

"We're doing everything we can," Attorney General John Ashcroft said. "I have assured the president that I will let him know the second we find either the leak or a decent scapegoat. It will happen. He's out there somewhere."

Bush has ordered his staff to cooperate fully with the Justice Department's investigation, which has already included interviews with dozens of White House officials.

"The team is hard at work, but the process of finding the perfect scapegoat is very time-consuming," Bush said. "While we can assume that this person will not be a member of my senior staff, we have few other concrete ideas about his identity. Why, the scapegoat may turn out to be someone who knew absolutely nothing about the leak. You can see how difficult the job is."

Last week, Bush ordered 2,000 staff members to turn over any documents that may help the Justice Department choose a scapegoat.

"Unfortunately, investigators still don't have a remotely appropriate

party," White House spokesman Scott McClellan said. "They've been tirelessly searching electronic records, telephone logs, correspondence, and calendar entries for someone suitable. So far, we haven't found a single person on whom we can plausibly pin the blame."

According to Washington political analyst Ted Edmonds, it's important that the Bush Administration find the scapegoat in a timely manner.

"They've got to move quickly," Edmonds said. "It has been alleged that the White House leaked Plame's identity to the press in retaliation for her husband's vocal criticism of Bush Administration policies in Iraq. Before the people's trust in the presidency can be restored, they demand that a scapegoat be brought before the media, given a cursory and farcical trial by association, and pilloried before their eyes. Without the White House at least going through the motions of some sort of judicial accountability, how can we maintain our faith in the nation's leaders?"

Nevertheless, Edmonds said the

Bush Administration is no closer to finding the scapegoat than they were at the start of the investigation.

"The administration is in a muddle," Edmonds said. "They've changed tactics several times since the leak surfaced. First, they vehemently denied that anyone from the White House was involved. Then, they made a public show of agreeing to hand over documents and other evidence to the Justice Department. Then, Bush even suggested that Bob Novak was to blame, for using the leaked information in his column. It's time for Bush to choose a scapegoat and commit to the decision."

Early in the investigation, the Justice Department ruled out several top Bush advisors, including Karl Rove—news that came as a relief to many citizens.

"I'm glad to hear they ruled out Karl Rove," said Janet Manning, a nurse from Davenport, IA. "I'd hate to have the scapegoat be someone highly placed. It should be someone of substantial position—otherwise, he won't deflect enough blame—but

on the other hand, if they cast someone too close to Bush as the scapegoat, suspicion of the administration will be raised, rather than displaced. It would do more harm than good."

Bush has rejected Democrats' calls for the appointment of a special counsel to find the administration official responsible for the leak, calling it "unnecessary." The president, however, pledged to find a scapegoat.

"Give us time," Bush said. "We will produce someone. We know the leak came from a senior administration official, but there are an awful lot of senior administration officials—more than the administration can be expected to keep track of, or investigate for felony criminal charges. I know that's a bit of a stretch, but I'm sticking with that position until such time as a believable scapegoat is located."

Police have warned all Washington, D.C., residents to alert authorities if they sight any suspicious-looking senior administration officials who might be potential scapegoats. ∅

Anyone Got A TV To Spare?

The Cruise
By Jim Anchower

Hola, amigos. I know it's been a long time since I rapped at ya, but I've been burning the candle at both ends lately. Shit, if a candle had three or four ends, they'd be burning, too.

Two people quit at the car-rental place where I work, so I've had to pick up some of the slack. It's good, because I've been wanting more hours. But it's bad, because I'm pulling 45 hours every week, which totally sucks. Not only am I working a killer schedule, but I'm also busting my ass while I'm there.

Before the other guys quit, I'd just drive the little bus to and from the airport. Now, I do that half the time, and the rest of the time, I gotta vacuum out cars. I like the tips—people leave change in the cup holders all the time—but I hate the vacuuming. I don't own a vacuum at home, and I'm not planning on getting one any time soon.

As I'm crawling around on my hands and knees in the backseat of a car, vacuuming away, I can't help but think about the third of my check that's going straight to The Man. Taxes bite my ass. They just pay for all kinds of waste. I wish that Arnold Schwarzenegger was governor here. He'd set things straight with taxes, right off the bat. I can't remember who the governor is here, but I'm sure Arnold would be better. He'd shake shit up. I oughta move to California.

But even after taxes, with all the overtime I'm doing, I'm raking in more money than before. The problem is, my weed and Miller Genuine Draft budgets have gone through the roof. I have to party extra hard to release all the built-up stress. A man's gotta unwind after pulling a long shift.

If I'd save my overtime money, instead of buying brain essentials, I could probably afford a pretty awesome car. But as it is, I had to settle for another Ford Festiva I got from a guy at work. It's not the worst, but it doesn't have the muscle under the hood that I need to lay rubber when it counts.

Owning a better car is beyond me at this point. I thought I'd save up and put a CD player in the Festiva, but it looks like that's not going to happen, because I had a little accident last week and lost my television. I mean, the television is still in my living room, where it's always been, but there's more glass on the floor in front of it than usual. So I guess I didn't lose it, so much as I busted the shit out of it by throwing an empty bottle of Jack at it.

It happened last Thursday. I was at home relaxing after a long day of shuttling and vacuuming, and I was putting away the evening with a couple of six-packs of MGD. I was watching some shitty movie that I didn't really care about on USA, just to let some of the pressure of the day out of my head. In the middle of the movie,

> **Before the other guys quit, I'd just drive the little bus to and from the airport. Now, I do that half the time, and the rest of the time, I gotta vacuum out cars. I like the tips—people leave change in the cup holders all the time—but I hate the vacuuming. I don't own a vacuum at home, and I'm not planning on getting one any time soon.**

someone started knocking on my front door, like there was a fire or something. I opened the door and it was Ron. He had a big, shit-eating grin on his face and held a bottle of Jack and his Nintendo GameCube.

Now, I don't usually do the hard stuff. It gives a bad side to my buzz. Rum makes me tired, gin makes me wanna puke, and vodka sneaks up on me like the Ninja Of Getting Hammered. And tequila—well, that shit will kill ya. But whiskey is the booze I can't refuse. Even though I never know what it'll do to me.

Ron had brought over a game called Super Monkey Ball 2. I usually hate those kid games, but this one had a race that you play head-to-head against another person. For a long time, Ron and I had a good time playing Monkey Race and giving each other hell. Our talents were pretty much equal, so we each were winning about half the time. It was a blast.

But then Ron started to win every game. I couldn't do one thing right. Ron kept blowing me up, and the whole time, he was bragging about it. I can be a good loser, provided the winner isn't a King Dick. But when Ron wins, he won't just whoop once and shut up. He needles you.

Your Horoscope

By Lloyd Schumner Sr.
Retired Machinist and
A.A.P.B.-Certified Astrologer

Aries: (March 21–April 19)
Buy yourself some extremely long bed sheets. You'll be making an escape rope out of them very soon.

Taurus: (April 20–May 20)
Your pocket Bible will stop an assailant's bullet, but not before it passes through four innocent bystanders, a school-bus gas tank, and your genitals.

Gemini: (May 21–June 21)
You will learn a valuable lesson about strategic thinking after you write insults in your worst enemy's Advanced Judo handbook.

Cancer: (June 22–July 22)
After traveling for months, Nashvillian monks will appear at your door to announce that you are the latest incarnation of the Dolly Parton.

Leo: (July 23–Aug. 22)
Antisthenes wrote, "It is a kingly thing to do good and to then be abused," but that does not mean that you're the king.

Virgo: (Aug. 23–Sept. 22)
There seems to be a universal force that balances out the good and bad events in our lives. Don't worry about it, though, as nothing ever happens to you.

Libra: (Sept. 23–Oct. 23)
You'll never know if your "I'm With Stupid" casket was a big hit, but you have the courage of your convictions.

Scorpio: (Oct. 24–Nov. 21)
There will soon come a time when your happiness depends on where and whether an enormous man catches a ball.

Sagittarius: (Nov. 22–Dec. 21)
Be assured that the Author of all Creation has a plan for you. Unfortunately, it involves a hackneyed "evil twin" plot twist you'll see coming a mile away.

Capricorn: (Dec. 22–Jan. 19)
Doctors caution that you cause extreme negative reactions—including rashes, vomiting, and hysteria—in women who may become pregnant.

Aquarius: (Jan. 20–Feb. 18)
You never thought you'd do anything to set the world on fire, but after a three-month arson investigation, that's what the U.N. tribunal will determine.

Pisces: (Feb. 19–March 20)
The stars have foretold a night journey over water, so get cracking on those plane tickets, pronto.

> **Now, I don't usually do the hard stuff. It gives a bad side to my buzz. Rum makes me tired, gin makes me wanna puke, and vodka sneaks up on me like the Ninja Of Getting Hammered. And tequila—well, that shit will kill ya. But whiskey is the booze I can't refuse.**

I should point out that by this time, we were out of Jack. I was pretty gone, and so was Ron. Ron kept yelling how he was the master, and how he was taking out the trash, and I kept getting madder with every comment. Finally, I looked him as square in the eye as I could and told him that he would shut up if he knew what was good for him. Even then, he didn't listen. He blew me up again, and then he started doing circles around me with his car, to rub it in. That's when I lost it.

You can pretty much fill in the rest of the picture yourself. But the whole thing really wasn't my fault. It happened because I was stressed about work. Besides, it doesn't do any good to point fingers, 'cause that ain't bringing my television back. At least no one got hurt.

Now I gotta save up for a new television—which sucks, because the incident showed that what I really need is some time off. I entered a few contests, so one might come through. But I ain't holding my breath. Sure, I'd like a television with a 42-inch flat screen or some plasma shit, but I gotta be realistic. I'm not looking for anything too fancy. I'll happily take a 20-inch screen if it has a place to plug in a video-game console. Whatever kind of set I get, I gotta get it soon, so I can practice up before Ron realizes that I still have his GameCube. ∅

New Excedrin 'Lights Out' Kills You Dead On The Spot

see BUSINESS page 11E

Moral Compass Lost In Woods

see LOCAL page 7B

Non-Crime-Fighting Dog Takes Bite Out Of Couch

see LOCAL page 2B

Understudy Overacting

see ENTERTAINMENT page 11E

STATshot

A look at the numbers that shape your world.

Oh, Shit, What Did We Just Tape Over?

- **10%** Fremont High's *Guys And Dolls*, 1986
- **23%** Video message from dying wife to infant son
- **34%** 8,000 hours of Mars rover footage
- **18%** Episode of *All In The Family* where Edith almost gets raped
- **25%** Favorite blank tape

the ONION®

VOLUME 39 ISSUE 42   AMERICA'S FINEST NEWS SOURCE™   30 OCT.–5 NOV. 2003

Ridiculous Small-Business Plan Encouraged By Friends

MISSOULA, MT—Due in large part to the encouragement of her so-called friends, 34-year-old Karen Sabin quit her steady job to make and sell homemade gourmet dog biscuits out of her home, the former hospital receptionist told reporters Monday.

"People love gourmet foods," said Sabin, describing the thought behind her half-formed business plan. "It only makes sense that dogs would, too.

Above: Sabin's friends encourage her terrible idea.

Don't they deserve to have their taste buds tickled? There's a huge untapped market for high-end dog treats made with natural ingredients, and I'm getting in on the ground floor. If you don't believe me, ask my friend Angie [Anderton]."

Sabin said she arrived at the idea of producing gourmet dog biscuits in see FRIENDS page 17

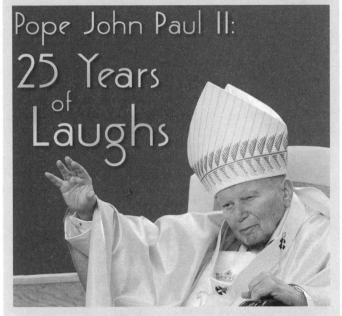

Pope John Paul II: 25 Years of Laughs

VATICAN CITY—As Pope John Paul II enters his 26th year as pontiff, the world is stopping to reflect on the legendary funnyman's career as one of the most influential performers in modern history. Standing staunchly against contraception and women's equality right through the turn of the 21st century, the pope and his quirky, deadpan comic persona still entertain audiences around the world.

Revered by multiple generations for his weird and wonderful wit, the 83-year-old pontiff is perhaps the best-known stand-up alive today. Throughout an amazing two

and a half decades as head of the Catholic Church, the pope has produced, in both his live appearances and his published works, a treasure trove of humor second to none.

"I can still remember seeing him do his classic 'Galileo' bit in the early '90s," said fellow comedian George Carlin, referring to the pope's 1992 declaration that the church erred in condemning Galileo. "Here was this man, appearing on televisions around the world, making a *proclamation* that the sun does not move around the see POPE page 16

'Well, *You* Try To Reconstruct Iraq,' Says U.S. Defensive Dept.

Above: U.S. soldiers in Basra reconstruct Iraq, while you do nothing but criticize.

WASHINGTON, DC—Responding to recent criticism of reconstruction efforts in Iraq, the U.S. Defensive Department released a statement to the public Monday suggesting that perhaps *they* could do better, since they're obviously so smart.

"Well, it looks like you American people have figured it all out, then," the statement read in part. "There's no need for the old government to do anything, because the citizens know just how to handle this whole reconstruction-of-Iraq thing. Well, go ahead! If it's so simple, and if you're so smart, then what's stopping you? Come on."

"Oh, gosh!" the statement continued. "Wait! It looks like Iraq is a whole big *country*! And it seems that someone see IRAQ page 16

13

Sniper Suspect Rehires Lawyers

Sniper suspect John Allen Muhammad stopped acting as his own attorney last week and rehired his lawyers. What do *you* think?

"This is the only way for the sniping, serial-killer wacko to receive a fair trial. I'm sorry, *alleged* sniping, serial-killer wacko."

Samuel Riegel
Systems Analyst

"His decision to represent himself might have proved as disastrously unwise as his decision to shoot all those people."

Jeff Campbell
Optometrist

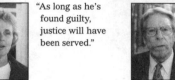

"As long as he's found guilty, justice will have been served."

Leslie Meisel
Secretary

"I know where he's coming from. I tried to treat myself for colon cancer. But after a few months, I turned to a pro."

Oliver Ralli
Securities Agent

"It's wise to hire a lawyer. I defended myself in small-claims court against a carpet-cleaning business. Result: eight years in a maximum-security penitentiary."

David McKeel
Dishwasher

"He should've had a little fun representing himself in court, before he fries like a batter-dipped cod for what he did."

Ellen Newell
Audiologist

Tuition Hikes

The average cost of tuition at the nation's colleges has jumped 40 percent in the past 10 years. How are students coping?

- ▶ Saving money by no longer using condoms
- ▶ Eating ramen noodles only two times a day, instead of three
- ▶ Getting parents to send keg every month
- ▶ Borrowing tuition and fees from the dude down the hall
- ▶ Convincing selves that cabinetmaking is an honorable craft with a long, rich history
- ▶ Asking father to fix up old halogen torchiere lamp in the attic
- ▶ Occasionally selling off volume from extremely valuable World Book encyclopedia set
- ▶ Working 10 torturous hours per week at campus computer center
- ▶ Selling plasma, sperm, eggs, spinal fluid, bone marrow, kidney, lung

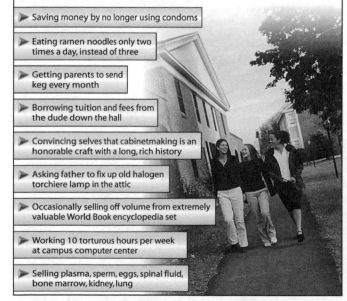

 **the ONION**®
America's Finest News Source.™

Herman Ulysses Zweibel
Founder

T. Herman Zweibel
Publisher Emeritus
J. Phineas Zweibel
Publisher
Maxwell Prescott Zweibel
Editor-In-Chief

I Would Treat The Girl From The Muffler Commercial Right

Oh my God, it's on again. There's the girl I've been telling you about—the one I always see on television. Quiet! This is my favorite part. Just look at

By Jerry Nexler

her. Isn't she the most beautiful woman you've ever seen? Doesn't she have the nicest voice? I know this in my heart: If I had a chance, I would treat that girl from the muffler commercial right.

I'd pick her up after her shift at the muffler store every single day. I wouldn't even get mad if she made me wait while she punched out and got her coat from her locker. I'd just sit in my truck and listen to sports radio until she was ready to go. When she got into the truck, she could even change the station if she wanted to. But I'll bet she likes listening to the games. She works at a muffler store, after all.

If that girl from the muffler commercial were my girl, I'd do everything I could to impress her. I'd get that Exclamation cologne that girls seem to like, and I'd dress in nice clothes if we had to go somewhere special. And I'd stop getting drunk on Friday and Saturday nights. I'd take her to the creek for a romantic picnic whenever she wanted. Or we could just watch television and hang out in my apartment. Hell, if she wanted to go out drinking, we could do that, too. She looks sweet, but I'll bet she's got a wild side, too.

I can imagine her now, standing there in those perfectly clean coveralls, giving me the big smile she gives to the guy in the muffler commercial who isn't sure which muffler he needs. Seeing that smile in person would probably turn me into a puddle.

It's true that there are a lot of guys working at the shop with her, in the commercial. But I'm sure she's just good friends with all those guys. I would never be jealous of her coworkers. That wouldn't be right.

If she wanted to go out to eat, I'd take her to nice places, like The Applewood Diner over in Ellensburg. I'd let her order whatever she wanted. She'd probably look just as good if she put on a few pounds worth of meatloaf platter. As long as she flashed those green eyes, like she does in the commercial when she lists off the top-selling muffler brands, I'd be happy.

I'll bet her last boyfriend really treated her bad. He probably zoned out when she complained about the guy who does the tire rotations. He didn't tell her how pretty she was every day and mean it, like I would.

You can tell she loves her job, the way she smiles and says, "Come into Hart Muffler & Auto Superstore." As long as she's happy, she can work at the muffler store as much as she likes. Besides, it would be cool to get a discount on spare parts. But even if she can't get a discount for me, I don't care.

I've driven to the Hart Muffler &

> **If that girl from the muffler commercial were my girl, I'd do everything I could to impress her. I'd get that Exclamation cologne that girls seem to like, and I'd dress in nice clothes if we had to go somewhere special. And I'd stop getting drunk on Friday and Saturday nights.**

Auto Superstore in Lodi a few times to pick up lug nuts, but I've never seen her working there. Maybe she works at the store over in Danville. I lie awake at night wondering where she might be. Maybe she decided that Hart's was too small-time, and she went to work for Meineke. A girl like that is bound to shoot to the top.

I know what you're thinking: How can I say I'm going to treat the muffler girl right, when everybody knows how bad I was to Kristi Paulson? Well, Kristi was trash. The muffler girl's got class. You can tell by the way she's so polite to the customers. I would never sleep with the muffler girl's best friend. And I would never leave her stranded out on Delton Road and then not call her for two weeks, even though we were engaged. You don't treat a diamond like trash.

I wish there was some way to get in touch with the muffler girl. No one at Hart Muffler seems to know who she is. All I have is the commercial and the picture from the Sunday insert.

Muffler girl, if you're reading this, please contact me. I'd be more excited to hear from you than the customer with the tie, who finally agrees that the right muffler is important to his car's performance. You won't regret it. ∅

Lawyer Friend Makes Strong Case For Nachos

HARTFORD, CT—During a night out for dinner and drinks at Shooters Bar And Restaurant, probate attorney Michael Bradshaw built a strong case *in re* ordering nachos, Bradshaw's friends reported Tuesday.

> "Mike said that if we got hot wings, we'd only get two wings each," Spence said. "Nachos, on the other hand, would allow for a greater number of snacking opportunities for all of us. Also, he said that he could easily convince the waitress to give us a free bowl of salsa."

"Mike can be very persuasive when it comes to appetizers," said John Spence, one of eight diners swayed by Bradshaw's closing arguments. "There was a split among the eaters, with four people wanting hot wings

Above: Bradshaw (center) discusses issues of cost with two members of his party.

and four wanting nachos. In the end, though, Mike convinced us all, beyond a reasonable doubt, that nachos was the appropriate verdict."

Bradshaw based his opening arguments on the *prima facie* evidence that each diner wanted to eat a substantial amount of food.

"Mike said that if we got hot wings, we'd only get two wings each," Spence said. "Nachos, on the other hand, would allow for a greater number of snacking opportunities for all of us. Also, he said

that he could easily convince the waitress to give us a free bowl of salsa."

Hot-wing defenders argued that the wings would come with celery and blue-cheese dressing, but Bradshaw offered a convincing rebuttal.

"Only two or three of us are likely to eat the celery," Bradshaw said. "Not exactly a majority, is it?"

Bradshaw then called on fellow attorney Larry Paulson to determine which appetizer would leave a more damaging mark on a dress shirt.

Though he had been a hot-wings supporter, Paulson admitted that the sauce could cause permanent stains.

"I bring this up because we're going to Club 66 later on, to try to get laid," Bradshaw said. "Can we all agree that the likelihood of failure will increase if we arrive with greasy spots on our shirts?"

Further objections were raised by eaters who claimed that nacho stains were more likely to occur see NACHOS page 17

Katie Couric Winces At Word 'Vagina'

NEW YORK—*Today* host Katie Couric noticeably winced at mention of the word "vagina" during an interview with National Ovarian Cancer Foundation spokeswoman Janette Pruce Monday. "I understand that it's important to raise awareness and promote early detection, which is why I was happy to have [Pruce] on the show," a flustered Couric said after the interview. "I just didn't expect her to come right out and say the 'V' word." An intern on the show said that Couric hadn't appeared that uncomfortable since walking in on one of the Dixie Chicks breastfeeding.

U.S. Upset After Aliens Land In Italy

WASHINGTON, DC—White House press secretary Scott McClellan issued a statement Monday expressing

disappointment "on behalf of all Americans" that alien envoys from the planet Xygal 8B made their historic first landing in Italy, rather than in the U.S. "We are confused and saddened that the Xygalians chose to take their first steps on Tuscan soil," McClellan said. "We are hopeful that [Xygalian] Cmdr. Gorx will recognize the oversight and relocate to the U.S., which is better equipped to host an intergalactic traveler." McClellan added that the internationally televised handshake between Italian Prime Minister Silvio Berlusconi and Gorx "added insult to injury."

More Than $30 Worth Of Burned CDs Stolen From Residence

ALBUQUERQUE—Police are still not investigating a burglary at the Watson Avenue apartment of George Kinney, who reported the theft of

more than 300 CDRs, with an estimated value of $32. "It looks like the bastard dropped down onto my back balcony from the neighbor's roof," Kinney said Monday. "Goddammit. I spent hours burning all those CDs." Kinney was the victim of a similar crime in June 2001, when someone broke into his YMCA locker and stole his Diet Pepsi Twist promotional duffel bag, which contained a copy of *USA Today*.

Area Man Wins Conversation

KING MILLS, OH—A friendly chat about the weather resulted in victory for Daniel Cooper Wednesday, as a brilliant and well-timed rebuttal from the 36-year-old pastry chef devastated his opponent. "Yeah, well, if this is the heaviest rain we've had in years, then I guess I hallucinated my basement flooding last July," Cooper said, deftly parrying his coworker Colin Garrison's challenge. "This rain is nothing."

Wordlessly acknowledging Cooper's superiority, Garrison slinked back to the cooler, defeated.

Nursing-Home Residents Mate In Captivity

COLBY, KS—Following six months of failed attempts under intense observation by geriatric scientists, Briarwood Nursing Home residents Horace Klass, 86, and Helen Veukmaan, 83, successfully mated in captivity Monday. "As with most new arrivals to Briarwood, Horace and Helen at first seemed despondent," Briarwood's Dr. William Stander said. "Before long, though, they grew accustomed to their new habitat, and Horace soon felt comfortable enough to approach Helen. Indeed, Horace ultimately proved quite aggressive." Briarwood employees report that, after mating, Klass provided Veukmaan with half a box of windmill cookies. ✑

earth. I laughed until tears rolled down my cheeks."

"No one could touch the pope," Carlin added. "Hell, no one even tried. He was in a class of his own. One of a kind."

Born Karol Joseph Wojtyla in Wadowice, a town 35 miles southwest of Krakow, the pope did not have an easy childhood. In what may have contributed to his desire to inspire laughter, he faced many early hardships. His mother died just a month before his 9th birthday, and only three years later, his brother died of scarlet fever. The pope began his religious career shortly thereafter, studying in an underground seminary in Krakow. He established himself in the Krakow scene and was awarded an archbishopric in 1963. He made cardinal in 1967.

Among the works to give the pope his first taste of fame was his 1960 treatise *Love And Responsibility*, in which he defined a "modern Catholic sexual ethic." It was here that the pope developed his oft-repeated chestnut that the only acceptable act of sex is one intended for the creation of a child.

"The pope would always lean on his material about sex," director Woody Allen said. "He had this crazy, special way of looking at the world. I definitely count him among my influences."

After years of working the smaller cathedrals, the pope's hard work paid off. On Oct. 16, 1978, he was chosen to head Rome's most venerated comedic institution, the Vatican.

"No one else is still doing what the Vatican does," comedian Don Rickles said. "They may not be as big as they once were, but they still surprise—like that bit a few weeks ago, where they said condoms don't prevent AIDS. Was that improvised?"

After 25 years at the top of his field, the pope still draws a crowd. On Oct. 19, he presided over the beatification of Mother Teresa. More than a quarter of a million people flooded St. Peter's Square to witness the stunt, in which the pope declared that the hard-working, benevolent nun had performed miracles and possessed supernatural powers.

The pope has created more saints and beatified more people than all the previous popes combined, and no other pope has toured as extensively as he has. The quintessential showman loves to take his act on the road. He's entertained audiences in 117 countries and met with hundreds of world leaders, including dictators Augusto Pinochet and Fidel Castro.

"John Paul is the hardest-working pope in history," actor Jonathan Winters said. "He's an inspiration. And not just for other comedians like myself, but for everyone, from theologians who will never be ordained because they're women, on down to the little children in the crowded ghettos of Third World cities who heed his message about the evils of contraception. Let's not even go into the gays in Boise."

Since his first trip back to Poland in 1978, the pope has performed in front of millions of loyal fans all over the world.

"People would wait in line for hours to see him," comedian Joey Bishop said. "And he never failed to deliver. He'd be out there working the crowd—shaking hands, kissing babies. Wherever he went, they loved him."

The pope has also been lauded for his ability to think on his feet. Throughout his many years in the business, the pope has often been called upon to deliver a comeback when questioned about acts committed by the Catholic Church.

"John Paul II has riffed on everything from the Crusades and the Spanish Inquisition to the treatment of Jews and blacks," actor Bob Newhart said. "He's always had a unique ability to come at things in an unexpected way. I saw him last year on TV, talking about those molestation scandals. His main message was that Catholics shouldn't lose faith in the clergy. Hilarious! Now, I would've gone straight to some kind of apology to the victims, but I guess that's why he's the pope."

The master of the lightning-speed one-liner produced a string of memorable side-splitters earlier this year. When meeting with the Dutch ambassador to the Vatican, he referenced the country's laws governing same-sex unions. Condemning the laws, the pope said that sexual relationships are for "men and women whose love will yield children," and characterized gays as deviants who act contrary to "natural law."

Despite suffering from debilitating Parkinson's disease, the pope shows no signs of toning down his act. With his trademark wit, the pontiff recently announced that, in spite of his failing health, he will remain pope "as long as God wants."

"There will never be another Pope John Paul II," said comedian Jerry Stiller. "He's truly one of a kind, straight out of a time and place that no longer exist." Ø

just fought a *war* there, to oust a despotic regime! So, gee, this might take a while, huh?"

At a press conference Monday, visibly upset Defensive Department spokesman Lawrence Pettibone addressed key points of the ongoing reconstruction process, such as its cost.

"Oh, dear!" Pettibone said. "It's taking a little bit more time than expected. Maybe the U.S. military should quit, huh? Then *you* could do the job for them, Mr. and Mrs. American Genius. Go ahead!"

"In fact, I'll pay for it!" said Pettibone, extending his wallet toward the assembled press corps. "Here! Here's, let's see, $49. Go ahead! Rebuild the infrastructure! Find the weapons of mass destruction! Keep the peace! What? This $49 isn't enough? Do you wish you had, say, about $87 billion to use right now? Well, well, well. How quickly things change."

Washington Post reporter Giles Mifflin asked Pettibone to address the issue of ongoing American casualties in Iraq, specifically the fact that more than 100 U.S. troops have been killed there since Bush declared an end to major combat six months ago.

"Well, *Giles*," Pettibone said. "I'd better get on the phone and inform the military that the soldiers in Iraq are still in danger, shouldn't I, *Giles*? Because they probably don't know that already! Or maybe I should just shut up and stop whining, because I'm a big pansy who never would have gone to Iraq in the first place!"

Added Pettibone: "Weren't some of you complainers the same ones who *wanted* us to get rid of a little problem called Saddam Hussein just a few months ago?"

"So what's the big problem now?" Pettibone asked. "Can't make up your minds? I wish we'd known that before we went and did what *you* wanted!"

Pettibone then gave short, peevish answers to reporters' questions about international involvement in the reconstruction, including those surrounding the issue of France, Germany, and Russia's recent opposition to a U.N. resolution that didn't set a timetable for returning self-rule to Iraq.

"Germany and France have a problem with the U.S.!" Pettibone said. "Maybe we should all side with them. Look at me, I'm the American people! I worry about what the whole world says all the time! I'm gonna ask the whole world if I can go to the bathroom from now on, because the rest of the world knows so much more than America! La di da di da!"

Pettibone muttered that members of the Bush Administration happen to have a little bit of experience in matters of foreign policy.

"Those working on the reconstruction effort are not just a bunch of idiots," Pettibone said. "Many have studied Mideast policy for decades. They have extensive experience serving under past presidents. What have you done? You read an article in *U.S. News & World Report*!"

Continued Pettibone: "Listen, *you* guys don't really know what's going on over there. *We* know what's going on over there. And you're *not* making my job any easier with these *emotional outbursts*! The worst part is—I didn't want to say this—most of you don't even vote! There, I said it! Most of you don't even vote, okay? So *shut up!*"

The Defensive Department was founded in the mid-1960s to manage the official U.S. position on the Vietnam War. The department has recently come under fire for the size of its budget, which is currently larger than at any time since Richard Nixon was in office. Ø

> ## "Weren't some of you complainers the same ones who wanted us to get rid of a little problem called Saddam Hussein?" Pettibone asked.

Above: A neighborhood in Baghdad, which is not as easy to reconstruct as some people seem to think.

May, not through careful market research, but through a discussion with Anderton.

"I told her about this article I read somewhere, about how Milk Bones are mostly made of ash," Anderton said. "When Karen heard that, she al-

> ## "I don't remember, but I guess I told her how much my dog loved them," Sabin's friend Peggy Van Vliet said. "A few weeks later, she came up to me and told me that my compliment really encouraged her. She said something about leaving her job and going into business for herself. What could I say? She seemed so happy. I told her it was a good idea."

most lost it. She'd been giving Milk Bones to her golden retriever Max for years. I said, 'Wouldn't it be great if someone made all-natural dog biscuits?' and Karen's eyes lit up. I'd never seen her so excited."

Armed with the drive to succeed, Sabin began to test dog-biscuit recipes in her kitchen. She also began to sketch out packaging ideas, giving Anderton frequent updates on her progress.

"I said, 'Do what you love, and the money will follow,'" Anderton said. "Even if it doesn't, at least she pursued her dreams. I'm so happy for her."

Sabin adapted a recipe she found on the Internet to create her signature line of six dog-biscuit varieties. She made a large batch of what would become "Grandma Sabin's Low-Fat Biscuits For Particularly Finicky Dogs," and sent samples to six of her dog-owning friends.

"I don't remember, but I guess I told her how much my dog loved them," Sabin's friend Peggy Van Vliet said. "A few weeks later, she came up to me and told me that my compliment really encouraged her. She said something about leaving her job and going into business for herself. What could I say? She seemed so happy. I told her it was a good idea."

Two weeks ago, Sabin tendered her resignation at Missoula General Hospital to devote more time to her ill-conceived dream. Until her home-equity loan is approved, she will use her life savings of $3,000 as working cap-

Above: One of six varieties of Sabin's all-natural dog treats.

ital.

"When Karen said that she was quitting her job, I told her she was doing the right thing," longtime friend Gail Komareck said. "She doesn't actually have any small-business experience, but how else is she going to learn? I told her to jump in headfirst. It's sink or swim. Besides, she really *hated* the long hours she had to work at the hospital. She has everything to gain and not all that much to lose."

"Plus, my dogs seem to love those biscuits," Komareck added.

Sabin said she will produce the biscuits in her kitchen and sell them through the mail until she generates enough capital to open a storefront with a bakery. This will require the sale of approximately 90,000 biscuits at $1.50 each.

"I expect to open the store early next year," Sabin said. "Maybe I can even

> ## "I said, 'Do what you love, and the money will follow,'" Anderton said. "Even if it doesn't, at least she pursued her dreams. I'm so happy for her."

get it open before Christmas. But I'd have to look into... I don't know. I guess I'd have to call a real-estate agent to find a store location?"

Former coworker Wendy Gerber is among the many friends who encouraged Sabin.

"Karen was so excited about her

business," Gerber said. "I couldn't help but get caught up in it. I asked her if I could do anything for her, and she told me that she needed help designing a web site. I was happy to help. Most businesses go under within a year, so she needs a professional web site to give her business an edge."

In the past three weeks, Sabin has given out nearly 60 dog biscuits and sold almost twice that many, all to friends. By conservative estimates,

unless she experiences a 4,000 percent increase in sales, Sabin will be forced out of business before the end of the year.

"You'd be surprised just how many dogs prefer my biscuits," Sabin said. "If you put one side by side with a store-bought biscuit, dogs will always eat mine first. I'd eat these dog biscuits myself, if it came down to it. With that kind of endorsement, how could I possibly go wrong?" ∅

than hot-wing stains.

"Yes, but most nacho stains can be removed with soap and water," Bradshaw said. "Hot-wing sauce leaves an incontrovertible red splotch."

Added Bradshaw: "Please suspend the ruling until I'm back. I gotta hit the john."

Upon returning, Bradshaw called *amicus curiae* Jim Oppel as an expert witness to the deliciousness of Shooters' nachos.

"Guys, the nachos *are* really great here," Oppel said. "We really should order those."

To further strengthen his case for nachos, Bradshaw cited numerous precedents, including the high price of the chicken fingers, the rubbery texture of the calamari, and a March 2002 incident in which Larry burned his mouth on a jalapeño popper. Bradshaw also cited a recent incident at an Indian restaurant.

"If you'll recall, Ray [Yung] pleaded *nolo contendre* to the charges of ordering those terrible meat samosas at Raga Palace," Bradshaw said. "Are we going to let him sway the vote again?"

Hot-wings proponents put forward a strong defense against ordering nachos, citing Eric Johnson's aversion to olives.

"We can have the olives on the side,

no problem," Bradshaw said. "Case closed. We'll order the nachos."

Several of those present later admitted that they were displeased with the

> ## "If you'll recall, Ray [Yung] pleaded *nolo contendre* to the charges of ordering those terrible meat samosas at Raga Palace," Bradshaw said. "Are we going to let him sway the vote again?"

decision to order nachos.

"I really wanted hot wings," said Yung, an accountant. "I should've offered to pay for them. It's hard to stand up to Mike—he's a fast-talker who knows how to turn your words against you. How do you argue with someone who uses phrases like 'doctrine of unintended consequences' to say that the onion blossom once gave Jim the runs?" ∅

Point-Counterpoint: Pete

Pete's An Asshole

By Michael Borroughs

Look, man, I know that he's your friend and all, and I guess you've known him for a long time, so I hope you don't get too pissed off at me about this, but I think your friend Pete is a total asshole. Seriously, why you even put up with that guy is beyond me.

Okay, maybe Pete has a good side that I haven't seen. I'm willing to give people the benefit of the doubt. After all, you're a nice guy, so you must have some reason for liking Pete. I remember you telling me that he was really there for you when you broke up with Teri. I'm sure you two have had some good times together. But still, you have to face the facts, man. Pete's an asshole. You're blind if you don't see that.

Take what he did last night, when I introduced him to Greg. Within 10 seconds of meeting him, Pete said, "Oh, so you're from Minnesota, huh? I should have known, based on your wife's hair." What the fuck was that? When I tried to tell Pete that he was out of line, he got all, "Why are you flipping out? It's just a joke!" He told me that I should loosen up and learn to relax, because it was a party and people were trying to have a good time. Mind you, this is a party that *I* was hosting in my *own house*. I didn't even invite Pete, incidentally. He just showed up and said he heard you were going to be there.

That doesn't come close to topping the list of the shit that Pete has pulled. The other day after work—remember? When Rob started talking about how he got acupuncture for his back? Pete was all, like, "Acupuncture's just a bunch of New Age hippie crap." When I tried to defend Rob, Pete started going off about how only idiots believe in that sort of "chinky-dinky mumbo jumbo." Yes, Jamie, he said that. Please don't start in with that whole line about Pete's politically incorrect sense of humor, and how Pete "likes to challenge knee-jerk liberals." And I really don't care what Pete meant to say. Rob's got a 14-year-old adopted sister from Korea, and he didn't appreciate that comment.

You always say the same thing: Oh, Pete's an all-right guy. He's just got a really sarcastic sense of humor. People don't understand him. Well, I don't care what you call it. Everybody I know who has ever dealt with Pete agrees that he's a grade-A, #1 prick.

I've tried to get along with Pete, because I know that you two go way back. Normally, I'd just be like, "Any friend of Jamie's is a friend of mine." But what can I say? None of my friends can stand him. I'm sick of trying to defend his behavior.

The last thing I want is for this to cause friction between you and me. I've always thought that you were a great guy. But I really had to lay it out about your pal Pete. Enough is e-fuck-ing-nough. ∅

Aw, C'mon, Pete's An All-Right Guy

By Jamie Henderberg

Look, you don't have to tell me how difficult Pete can be. I was his roommate in college. He drives me crazy, too, sometimes. But he's not all bad.

Sure, he can be a little gruff, and he's not very patient, and he sometimes is a little insulting, and he's a little bit cocky and loud. I'll admit that, when he's drinking, he can be kind of a jerk, but c'mon. At the end of the day, Pete's an all-right guy! You just gotta get to know him better.

Pete's really insecure, so he overcompensates in social situations where he doesn't fit in. Full of himself? No way, man. He just has low self-esteem. That's why he's always making fun of people: He's trying to conceal the fact that he's unsure of himself. Pete doesn't have that many

friends, because he puts up walls to protect his fragile inner personality. It's a defense mechanism.

In fact, you and Pete are a lot alike. He's sensitive, like you. The only difference between you two is that, when his ego's bruised, he acts cocky and overbearing. Admittedly, that makes him come off like a bit of a jackass, but...

I'll admit he has a really low tolerance for what he considers "PC bullshit." As a result, he's a little abrasive. Don't get me wrong: I know. When I think about some of the awkward situations he's put me in, I sometimes want to punch his lights out.

Once, me and my old girlfriend Shelley went to hang out at Pete's place. I was worried that she wouldn't like him, so I even warned her about his sense of humor beforehand. For the first hour or so, everything was cool. But after Pete had a few drinks, he started joking about this "sexual harassment in the workplace" seminar

he had to attend. I was making these faces, like, "Dude! Shut up!" Then, I mentioned that Shelley was *volunteering* for the local sexual-harassment prevention center. That just added fuel to the fire. Pete started going off on what a joke those things were, and how all the women in them were just looking for a reason to get together and bitch about men. He offended Shelley to the very core, and I'm...

What was the point of this story again? Oh, yeah, to show that I've had to put up with tons of Pete's crap, but I can still laugh about it. Well, maybe that wasn't a good example, because Shelley stormed out of Pete's place and said she never wanted to see him again. That night, she and I got into a big argument about my ex-girlfriend and my views of women, and—shit, man. I forgot that Pete started that all. Damn!

Okay, okay. Bad example. Really, Pete's an okay guy. Take the time he pissed off my pal Jake. Jake's supercool. You'd like him. I mean, actually I like him. He's not like Pete at all. Anyway, I invited Pete to Jake's birthday

party, right? Pete got so sloshed that he started slapping Jake's bald head. Jake started to get mad, but Pete just would not stop slapping and... Uh...

Okay. That's not such a good example, either.

Look, I understand why Pete bothers you. He bothers everybody! That's just the way he is! Once you get to know him, you just accept him. It's all part of his charm! Well, not charm. That would imply that someone might like his behavior. But everyone just kind of, I don't know, gets used to it out of necessity. Because Pete doesn't care what anyone else wants.

It's not worth complaining to Pete. The louder you complain, the more he seems to enjoy it. I can't stand that! It's like reasoning with a brick wall. Plus, he never apologizes. If he does apologize, it's in this smart-ass, sarcastic fucking way that makes you feel stupid for having been hurt. Sometimes, you want to just grab him by the neck and...

Christ, Mike, you're right. Why do I even put up with him? Pete is an asshole. ∅

Your Horoscope

By Lloyd Schumner Sr.
Retired Machinist and
A.A.P.B.-Certified Astrologer

Aries: (March 21–April 19)
Unfortunately, the depressed economy and reduced demand for the service will force you to once again scale back the price of your mustache rides.

Taurus: (April 20–May 20)
Your desire to join the winning team will take you in a strange new direction when you decide to fight on the side of lung cancer.

Gemini: (May 21–June 21)
It turns out that there are indeed mountains high enough and valleys low enough to keep you from your love.

Cancer: (June 22–July 22)
You'll be the latest victim of the five-year unrest between the lower-woodwind and string sections of the Boston Philharmonic Orchestra.

Leo: (July 23–Aug. 22)
You will fail to inspire either fear or loyalty, in spite of the iron hand that you used in organizing the hayride.

Virgo: (Aug. 23–Sept. 22)
The last members of your extended family will die of leprosy, putting a stop to the stream of interestingly stained hand-me-downs.

Libra: (Sept. 23–Oct. 23)
You weren't aware that you could go to hell for wearing the wrong pants, but then you saw it in the Old Testament.

Scorpio: (Oct. 24–Nov. 21)
Your desire for further intellectual growth will be stunted when all of your questions about Aquaman are answered.

Sagittarius: (Nov. 22–Dec. 21)
There's an old superstition that the Devil won't come for a person who has to finish the Lord's work, but that's no reason not to do your dishes.

Capricorn: (Dec. 22–Jan. 19)
Your career opportunities will become somewhat more limited when, for the third year in a row, you flunk out of the School Of Hard Knocks.

Aquarius: (Jan. 20–Feb. 18)
Although your enemies have taken back their "screw you" statement, you might want to make a point of being extra considerate to the horse you rode in on.

Pisces: (Feb. 19–March 20)
Don't worry about politics so much. From time to time, the tree of liberty must be watered with the blood of idiots.

NEWS

Ladykiller Gets Life Sentence

see LOCAL page 12E

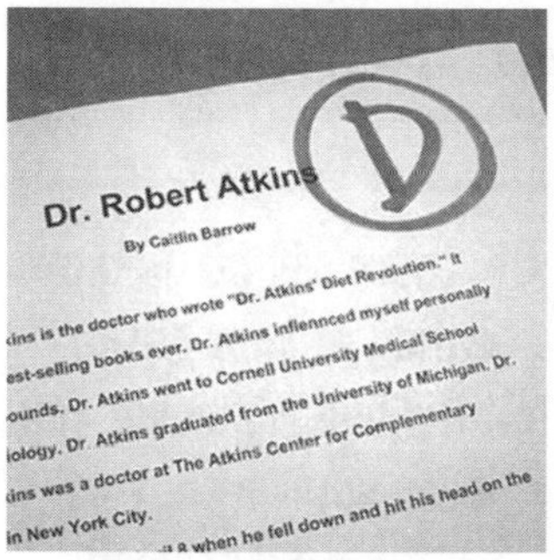

Cheerleader Given A 'D'

see LOCAL page 14E

Random Attack Restores Man's Faith In Inhumanity

see WORLD page 5C

Cheese Spill Cleaned Up With Nacho

see LOCAL page 19E

STATshot

A look at the numbers that shape your world.

Worst U.S. Jobs, 2049

14%	Data miner
25%	Post-apocalyptic lumberjack
28%	Empathic sufferer
11%	Robofluffer
10%	Assistant producer
12%	Moon raker

the ONION®

VOLUME 39 ISSUE 43 AMERICA'S FINEST NEWS SOURCE™ 6–12 NOVEMBER 2003

Family Unsure What To Do With Dead Hipster's Possessions

LOUISVILLE, KY—Five weeks after the death of her 26-year-old hipster son Kent, Enid Lowery announced that the family faces a difficult task in figuring out what to do with his many unusual possessions.

Kent Lowery (1977-2003)

"I just can't believe how much stuff Kent collected over the years," said Lowery Tuesday. "There's a poster for some movie called *Urgh!*, stacks of empty Quisp cereal boxes, at least five old lamps that don't work, and a slew of little plastic toys. Obviously, all these things meant something to Kent—but *what?* And *why?*"

A part-time English tutor and bassist for the local band Extra Moist, Kent died in a car accident Sept. 27. Overwhelmed with grief, his family members in nearby Bedford only mustered the strength to visit his apartment last week, where they were overwhelmed once again, this time by Kent's dense accu-

see HIPSTER page 23

Above: Lowery and Panziel among Kent's belongings.

Energy Secretary Just Assumed Cabinet Knew He Did Porn Films In The '80s

WASHINGTON, DC—Addressing shocked fellow cabinet members, Secretary of Energy Spencer Abraham said Tuesday that he had assumed everyone knew about his roles in numerous 1980s pornographic films.

"I just figured people knew about the porno," Abraham said, shrugging. "I never got any flak about it, so I didn't think it was a big deal."

Left: Abraham said he's sure he mentioned his work in films like Shacking Up (inset).

A former U.S. senator from Michigan who was appointed Energy Secretary by President Bush in 2001, Abraham said he has never denied that he performed in more than 50 erotic videos between 1984

see PORN page 22

Americans Demand Increased Governmental Protection From Selves

NEW YORK—Alarmed by the unhealthy choices they make every day, more and more Americans are calling on the government to enact legislation that will protect them from their own behavior.

"The government is finally starting to take some responsibility for the effect my behavior has on others," said New York City resident Alec Haverchuk, 44, who is prohibited by law from smoking in restaurants and bars. "But we have a long way to go. I can still light up on city streets and in the privacy of my own home. I mean, legislators acknowledge that my cigarette smoke could give others cancer, but don't they care about me, too?"

"It's not just about Americans eating too many fries or cracking their skulls open when they fall off their bicycles," said Los Angeles resident Rebecca Burnie, 26. "It's a financial issue, too. I spend all my money on trendy clothes and a nightlife that I can't afford. I'm $23,000 in debt, but the credit-card companies keep letting me spend. It's obscene that the government allows those companies to allow me to do this to myself. Why do I pay my taxes?"

Beginning with seatbelt legislation in the 1970s, concern over dangerous behavior has resulted in increased governmental oversight of private activities. Burnie and Haverchuk are only two of a growing number of citizens who argue that legislation should be enacted to protect them from their own bad habits and poor decisions.

see PROTECTION page 23

Unrest In Baghdad

Violence against American troops in Iraq surged last week, with attacks in Baghdad killing dozens. What do *you* think?

Geraldine Bates
Telemarketer

"All I know is, if the Iraqis had invaded our country, we'd be acting a lot nicer to them than they are to us."

Molly Chandler
Dental Hygienist

"My cousin is in the Army, and he said that the Iraqis want us there. So I can't really figure out why they shot him."

Arthur Serra
Pharmacist

"I wish the media were more conservative, so we wouldn't have to hear about these things."

Nicholas Hoyt
CFO

"In concentrating on Iraq's weapons of mass destruction, we forgot about their weapons of one teeny little bit of destruction at a time."

Brian Purdey
Student

"Why would the Iraqis bomb their own country? That's like shitting in your kitchen sink—good for emergencies, but not a great idea overall."

Frank Demoss
Systems Analyst

"The G.I. deaths are tragic and alarming, but the fact that even more Iraqis are dying should provide some consolation."

The California Wildfires

Wildfires have ravaged Southern California. How are citizens responding?

- ▶ Diverting charity fun run away from fire
- ▶ Having the talent pitch dousing scenarios
- ▶ Erecting protective wall of SUVs around gated community
- ▶ Sneaking across border to Mexico
- ▶ Watching life's accomplishment—$30 million worth of tacky stucco—go up in smoke
- ▶ Sitting in traffic
- ▶ As a firefighter, risking life valiantly to defend Fatburger franchise
- ▶ Briefly forgetting troubles through the magic of the movies; burning to death as wildfire consumes theater
- ▶ Cutting losses, starting cult over in Oregon

Ø the ONION®
America's Finest News Source.™

Herman Ulysses Zweibel
Founder

T. Herman Zweibel
Publisher Emeritus
J. Phineas Zweibel
Publisher
Maxwell Prescott Zweibel
Editor-In-Chief

There Are Going To Be Some Pointless Changes Around This Office

By Daniel Wyatt

All right, everyone, listen up. I have some announcements to make, and they affect all of you. I know that you received the e-mail I sent out, in which I detailed this meeting's agenda. I wanted to meet anyway and go over that e-mail in person, to prevent any misunderstandings. There are going to be some pointless changes around here, folks. The sooner we get used to them, the better off we'll be.

First, there will be no more taking pens directly out of the supply closet. This is not to say that you can no longer have pens, but from now on, we're going to keep track of who's taking what, with a register on the supply-closet door. Please list any supplies you remove from the supply closet on the supply-closet register for at least a week or two. The sheet will get old and tattered, and it will eventually fall off the door. After it gathers dust on the floor for a few days, I will pick it up and file it. This largely unnecessary new measure will be enforced rigidly.

We will also be keeping track of your e-mail. You will find the spreadsheet I made in your in-boxes—from now on, the spreadsheet should be open on your computer at all times. Whenever you send an e-mail, log it into the spreadsheet. At the end of each week, e-mail the completed log to your supervisor. The last item on your list will always document the e-mail to your supervisor. This will be the only entry your supervisor cares enough to check for, so failure to document this e-mail will cast suspicion on your e-mail-record-keeping abilities in general, and may result in disciplinary action, as outlined in your new employee handbook.

Has everyone received the new employee handbook? Good. You should study it thoroughly. In order to drive home the importance of our new rules and guidelines, we will begin a series of personnel orientations this month. The orientations will be conducted by me on a department-by-department basis. That way, the work of an entire department will come to a standstill while I orient it. The orientations will take two full days, so block out your time accordingly.

We've also noticed that the sink is often full of dirty dishes. The only fair way to deal with this problem is for everyone to take turns washing a load. Even those who eat their lunch outside of the department will be expected to volunteer for kitchen duty. Check the calendar to see which week you will need to do kitchen duty, and also which week you will be acting as kitchen-duty manager.

On a more alarming note, we have reason to believe that there have been some abuses of telephone privileges in the office, particularly long-distance privileges. You have each been issued a telephone code. The 14-digit code must be entered to obtain an outside line. This way, we can track phone usage. We anticipate savings of close to $30 each month with this time-consuming new procedure.

Next on the docket: the water cooler. The water cooler will be moved to the back closet. The way the water cooler

> **Oh, there will be no more eating at your desks, either. And whenever you leave your desk, your outgoing voicemail message should notify callers of your absence.**

sits now, it juts out into the hallway. The new location will minimize delays for everyone, except those who need water. You're welcome. If some of the higher-ups had had their way, we would have gotten rid of the cooler altogether. I'm on your side here. I was fighting for you guys on this one.

What else do we have? Lunch hours. Lunch hours will be taken at set times from here on out. You must plan your day around lunch. If work prevents you from taking your lunch at your assigned time, you will have to make other arrangements for eating. Eat a protein bar. Oh, there will be no more eating at your desks, either. And whenever you leave your desk, your outgoing voicemail message should notify callers of your absence. Also, start thinking about whom you would like as a bathroom buddy. I'll explain what this entails at our next meeting.

I think that's all. We'll have monthly departmental meetings to discuss these changes and to hear your ideas on ways to improve efficiency. At least we will for the next couple of months, but we'll probably forget to schedule the meetings after a while. Not like that matters, though, because it isn't as though a single one of your suggestions will have been taken seriously, much less implemented.

Oh, and don't forget that Thursday is crazy-shoes day, so go buy yourself the craziest pair of shoes you can find. Thank you for your attention. Ø

Children Wait Patiently For Heavily Fortified Tree House To Be Attacked

ORLAND PARK, IL—For the third uneventful day in a row, members of the Poison Ninjas Club awaited the invasion of their tree house, sources in the backyard of 1740 Sumac Road reported Monday.

"We spent all day Saturday making dirt bombs and dragging buckets of

> **"We have the Super Soaker loaded and ready to go," 10-year-old Jason Alvin said, referring to a large squirt-gun that he has emptied into the air around the tree house several dozen times. "If they don't get the message from the water gun, we'll let them have it with the balloons."**

pine cones up into the tree house," said 10-year-old club president Carrie Williams, her eyes trained on the southern border of the lawn. "When the enemy attacks, we'll be ready. Actually, we've been ready for, like, three whole days."

After standing guard throughout the weekend, Williams and her fellow

Above: Williams and friends wait for someone to invade their tree house.

Poison Ninjas left the tree unsupervised while they attended school on Monday. The Ninjas reconvened at the tree house after school and found their supplies undisturbed and no evidence of nefarious activity near the tree. Disappointed, they took up arms once again and began to stare out at the lawn in search of some sign of a threat.

"We have the Super Soaker loaded and ready to go," 10-year-old Jason Alvin said, referring to a large squirt-gun that he has emptied into the air around the tree house several dozen times. "If they don't get the message from the water gun, we'll let them have it with the balloons. Except we have to go and fill up more water balloons, because most of them broke in the pail overnight."

The tree house is an eight-square-foot wooden platform situated in the branches of an 80-year-old oak tree in the Williams' backyard.

"Absolutely no one is allowed in the tree house unless you're a member of our club," Williams said. "We have a password and everything. It's 'Valencia.'"

Williams' father built the structure in August 2001 for Williams' older brother Kurt, who ceded it to her earlier this summer.

"Dad said he's going to replace the old wooden ladder with a rope ladder, so we can pull it up after we climb up," Williams said. "That way, when they're looking for a way up, we can whale on them with the crab apples. Well, the ones we didn't already throw on the roof of the neighbors' house."

"No, we should pee on them," Williams' 7-year-old brother Josh said, eliciting a howl of disgust from the assembled club members.

One corner of the tree house contains a coverless cooler stocked with five cans of Sprite, a package of beef jerky, and a bag of Twizzlers.

"We had some Halloween candy up here, but we ate it," Williams said. "Now, we have a rule that we can't eat the rations, in case we get surrounded and have to live off them."

Although the Ninjas couldn't say who exactly the enemy was, the candidates included a group of classmates referred to as "The Cootie Sisters," several older boys from the neighborhood who allegedly covet the fort as a haven for smoking cigarettes, and an eighth-grade couple whose motives were unknown. Additional threats cited by the children include bullies, mean dogs, and kidnappers.

In spite of the disparity between the number of armaments in the tree house and the number of actual attackers, the Ninjas continued to see TREE HOUSE page 22

Personal Philosophy Stolen From Martin Luther King Jr.

BIRMINGHAM, AL—According to Jeffrey Duncan, 43, his friend Ronald Washington "completely ripped off" his personal mantra from civil-rights leader Martin Luther King Jr. "Ron's always saying how if someone doesn't have a cause worth dying for, then that person's life isn't worth living," Duncan said Monday. "Nice try, Ron, but you can't fool me. You totally stole that whole idea from Dr. King." Duncan said he hopes King's estate "nails Ron's ass for plagiarism."

Karl Rove Ensures Republican Elected As Student Body President

McALLEN, TX—Thanks to the intervention of White House political advisor Karl Rove, McAllen East Middle School elected a Republican student body president Monday. "I'd like to give a special shout-out to Mr. Rove, for helping me beat [incumbent president] Luis Mendes," Paul Wenger said in his victory speech. "Thanks to him, I was totally able to expose Luis' idea of using candy funds to buy uniforms for needy students. As your president, I'll make sure that that money goes back into the school, where it belongs—and into the biggest pizza party that McAllen East has ever seen." Rove denied any involvement in the election.

Undercover Agents Talking To Each Other In 'Under 12' Chatroom

WASHINGTON, DC—In an effort to weed out pedophiles, two FBI agents, identified only as "Cutiepie1994" and "KoalaLover," unknowingly communicated with one another in the under-12 chat room of TweenTalk.com for almost two hours Tuesday. "You should see me in my new bathing suit. It's really rad," Cutiepie wrote. "Kewl. Guess what? My parents aren't home right now," KoalaLover responded. Two minutes after their lengthy Internet conversation ended, KoalaLover unknowingly passed Cutiepie on the way into the bathroom.

Teen Admits Parents Were Right About Fred Durst

CHICAGO—17-year-old Jeremy Kempf reluctantly acknowledged that parents Judith and Harvey were right about Limp Bizkit lead singer Fred Durst Tuesday. "I used to crank 'Nookie' full blast, and my parents would say that Fred Durst was an obnoxious loudmouth and Limp Bizkit sucked," Kempf said. "Then I got *Results May Vary*, and I was like, 'Oh, shit. This *does* suck.'" Kempf also admitted that his parents may have had valid points about the taste of Mountain Dew and his friend Tony's neck tattoo.

Bunch Of Hick Nobodies Sue For Toxic-Waste Exposure

SHREWSBURY, WV—A bunch of local, piss-ant, hick nobodies filed a lawsuit against the Allegheny Electric Cooperative Monday, alleging that the company exposed residents to dangerous levels of mercury. "Just about everybody on the Kanahawa [River] knows someone that's sick or died," some toothless rube told reporters. "It's all the waste they dump out the power plant. You can see it in the water, like liquid silver. We're not going to sit here and take it. No sir." According to Allegheny spokesman Thomas Gill, the bumpkins were somehow able to scrape together enough moonshine money "to get theyselves one of them fancy, big-city lawyers." ∅

explore defense options.

"I thought it would be cool to have a secret escape tunnel," 9-year-old Ninja treasurer Willie Braniff said. "But you'd have to dig out the center of the tree, and that would kill it. Plus, the tunnel would come out in Mrs. Kellington's yard, and she would probably yell at us."

Other adults have hampered the children's efforts to man the tree house.

"Mom won't let us spend the night up there, because we might roll out and break our necks," Williams said. "We thought we could maybe put [the family's Schnauzer] Muffin up there as a watchdog at night, but she kept

slipping out of the rope harness."

As an alternative, Williams has kept

> ## "Mom won't let us spend the night up there, because we might roll out and break our necks," Williams said.

a silent watch from her bedroom window each night, to ensure that the tree house is secure.

"I told everyone that if I see anyone near the tree house, I'll call their houses and hang up the phone," Williams said. "Same thing goes for when everyone has to eat dinner."

There has been a high attrition rate among sentinels, with the club losing four members since the perceived conflict began. The first left Sunday, complaining of outdoor allergies. Roll call Monday after dinner heralded the loss of two more guards, one to a soccer game and another to a visiting aunt. One member was forced out due to his negligence.

"We told Jay [Conroy] that if he kept playing his Game Boy instead of watching the hole in the fence for

cats, we'd kick him out," Williams said. "He didn't argue with us at all. He just got up and left."

It wasn't until Conroy was out of throwing range that one of the remaining Ninjas thought of testing Ninja defenses on the deserter and yelled "Fire!"

"It's been a long couple of days for the ones of us left behind," Williams said. "I don't know how much longer the others can keep this up. Winter is coming soon. As for me, I'm not going anywhere until I get a chance to empty this giant garbage bag full of leaves on somebody's head. The waiting will make that Sprite taste all the sweeter." ∅

and 1987.

"It *feels* like I mentioned it to everyone," Abraham said. "I can't remember the specific circumstances, but I'm positive I talked about it. If some people didn't know, maybe that's because they weren't around when it was discussed. Or else they never asked about it."

"The other cabinet members are very busy," Abraham added. "We don't spend a lot of time talking about our personal lives. I just figured they felt that my previous career in skin flicks had little bearing on my vision for America's energy future."

> ## "It *feels* like I mentioned it to everyone," Abraham said. "I can't remember the specific circumstances, but I'm positive I talked about it. If some people didn't know, maybe that's because they weren't around when it was discussed. Or else they never asked about it."

Abraham's "mostly softcore" body of work includes such features as *Maid In The Shade*, *Jism Quest*, *Butt Fuck Sluts Go Nuts Vol. 3*, and *Lady Chatterly's Sisters*.

"I did these films well before I got into national politics," Abraham said. "All of it was nice, positive, gentle stuff—movies couples could enjoy. I didn't do any fetish stuff, nor did I do anything with underage actors. And I certainly did not do any gay for pay. I want to make that clear."

"Now," Abraham added, clapping his hands together, "who's got a question about the nation's natural-gas and

petroleum markets?"

According to visibly rattled White House Chief Of Staff Andrew Card, Abraham was wrong in assuming that the Bush Administration was aware of his roles in pornographic films.

"Why would we... I mean, it's... After all, given this administration's attitude toward... How could he just assume we knew?" Card asked. "That's an incredibly intimate thing to know about somebody. I think everyone would've been very uncomfortable knowing that sort of thing. Personally, I don't know if I would've been able to speak to him without thinking about that particular information."

Abraham said he didn't expect such reactions when he mentioned his former career during an Oct. 27 cabinet meeting. The energy secretary said he told the assembled White House staffers that the vulnerability of the nation's power grid reminded him of the first time he experienced a power outage.

"Spencer mentioned how he was living in a duplex in Encino in 1984," National Security Advisor Condoleezza Rice said. "He said it was terrible timing, because they were shooting that day, and he was on the verge of coming, and there was no backup generator for the camera and lights, and no air conditioning besides."

The comment puzzled cabinet members, but Abraham continued with his report. It was several days later, Rice said, when she thought to ask Abraham what he had meant by "camera and lights" and "on the verge of coming."

"I still don't know what the big deal is," Abraham said. "I just found out last week that [Treasury Secretary] John Snow knows how to scuba dive. No one freaked out when [Commerce Secretary] Don Evans told that story about sleeping in his friend's car that night in college."

Abraham countered rumors that he had withheld details of his pornographic film roles with what he characterized as "physical proof" that he hadn't.

"If I were hiding it, why would I list it on my résumé?" Abraham said, holding up a copy of the résumé he

presented to Bush's presidential transition team and to the Senate Committee on Energy and Natural Resources at his confirmation hearings

> ## "I still don't know what the big deal is," Abraham said. "I just found out last week that John Snow knows how to scuba dive."

in January 2001. "No one on the committee had any questions about it."

Abraham pointed to two résumé entries listed under "Miscellaneous Work Experience." The first was "Poolside Productions: production assistant, writer, occasional actor, 1984-85." The following line read "Ficus Tree Video: writer, director, performer, consultant, 1985-87."

Abraham's explanation did not sat-

isfy Card.

"Those entries could have meant absolutely anything," Card said. "He could have been involved in making commercials, promotional videos, or even PSAs. We were supposed to look at his résumé and ask, 'Hey, Spence, aren't these long-defunct porn outfits? Were you pouring the pork in front of cameras?'"

"Incidentally," Card added, "*Jism Quest* hardly sounds softcore."

Abraham continued to downplay the importance of the films.

"Look, I was young, and I was broke," Abraham said. "As soon as my political career took off, I quit. The bottom line is: All of that's in the past. I think it's strange that I'm condemned for those films, but not for serving as Deputy Chief Of Staff to Dan Quayle."

"Now, I don't know about you," Abraham said, "but I'm ready to discuss the use of superconductivity technology in electricity transmission and distribution."

As of press time, it is unknown whether any other White House officials have performed in pornographic films. ∅

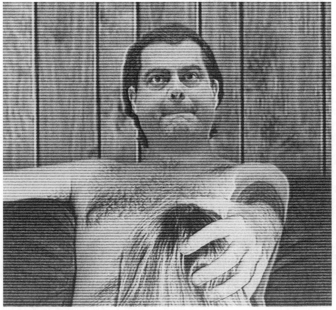

Above: Abraham in a scene from his 1984 film Five To Nine.

mulation of miscellany.

Assisted by her husband Thomas and her daughter Regina Panziel, Lowery set to the task of packing up the contents of her son's crowded one-bedroom apartment.

"Of course, we'll take some of Kent's things home with us, to remember him by," Lowery said. "But we agreed, as a family, that it's not a good idea to just pack everything up and keep it. Not that we'd have enough room for five boxes of video tapes and three wooden birdcages anyway."

Although they were aware that their son had "unusual tastes," the Lowerys said they were surprised by the sheer volume of his collections. Lowery said the large number of items has made it difficult to decide which of her son's former possessions to choose as keepsakes.

"I'm so at a loss," Lowery said. "Which of these things best represents Kent? Should I choose the Pachinko machine to place on the mantle at home? Would Patricia [Eisner, Kent's favorite aunt] rather have this *Two-Lane Blacktop* DVD or this set of tiki lamps? *What is* a Pachinko machine?"

The family has considered donating the items that will not be kept as reminders of Kent.

"I'd like to give his dishes to Goodwill or the local church, but I'm not sure they would want them," Lowery said. "None of his plates and cups match, and every single coffee mug is different. Here's a Zoloft mug, and

Above: Lowery in the process of packing "some sort of mask or something."

here's one from White Castle hamburgers. This one says 'Hands Off Howard's Coffee.' I find it strange that he owned that, considering that he lived alone and never mentioned a friend named Howard."

Although Kent's parents lean toward donating his possessions, Kent's 30-year-old sister said she feels that the legacy of his eccentric, old, and

cheaply made possessions should be preserved.

"Unfortunately, Kent didn't leave a will," Panziel said. "But it's obvious that he put a lot of time and effort into collecting these things. I think we should try to get them to someone who might appreciate them. Maybe there's someone out there who really wants a set of Hello Kitty pillows and

an accordion with no straps."

Panziel said the family has been largely unable to determine which items might be of value to anyone other than Kent.

"See these records?" said Panziel, pointing to a pile of Herb Alpert LPs. "I don't think *Grandma* even listens to this stuff anymore, but I know that old vinyl can be valuable. If some of these records are worth something, I'm sure Kent would want us to think carefully about where they end up. But is this

> **Although Kent's parents lean toward donating his possessions, Kent's 30-year-old sister said she feels that the legacy of his eccentric, old, and cheaply made possessions should be preserved.**

copy of 'The Super Bowl Shuffle' worth keeping? How about this Amazing Kreskin record? I don't know how to tell."

The Lowerys said the logistics of selling all of the items, either to raise money for charity or to cover the funeral expenses, are daunting.

"We've been going through his things for days," Lowery said. "Just think how long it would take to try and sell it all. We thought about having an estate sale, but I don't think a collection of *Dallas* and *Mod Squad* lunch boxes is the sort of thing anyone would buy. But then again, what do I know? I never would've guessed that Kent used a lunch box, either."

The Lowerys have asked friends who collect antiques for guidance.

"We called our friend Jack Puller, but he didn't know what to say," Lowery said. "He said there's a market for antique toys and old dishware, but he didn't know the value of any of the specific things I named. He didn't have any advice at all on the plastic cookie jar shaped like a dog that barks when you open its head. And he just coughed when I asked him about the phone shaped like a football."

As of press time, the family is considering putting Kent's belongings in storage while they do some research.

"I'm hoping someone out there can tell us more about what these things are, and what we should do with them," Thomas Lowery said. "We're just too sad and confused to make the decision right now. One thing's for sure: The furniture is going to the curb. To look at it, you'd think that's where Kent, God rest his soul, got it in the first place." ✍

Anita Andelman of the American Citizen Protection Group is at the forefront of the fight for "greater guardianship for all Americans."

"Legislation targeting harmful substances like drugs and alcohol is a good start, but that's all it is—a start," Andelman said. "My car automatically puts my seatbelt on me whenever I get into it. There's no chance that I'll make the risky decision to leave it off. So why am I still legally allowed to drink too much caffeine, watch television for seven hours a day, and, in some states, even ride in the back of a pick-up truck? It just isn't right."

The ACPG has also come out in favor of California's proposed "soda tax," which addresses unhealthy eating habits.

"The legislation, if approved, would establish a tax on sodas and other beverages with minimal nutritional value, and the money would be used to fund programs that address the growing epidemic of childhood obesity," Andelman said. "If our own government doesn't do something to make us get in better shape—or, for that matter, dress a little nicer—who will?"

Rev. Ted Hinson, founder of the Christian activist group Please God Stop Me, said he believes that the government will listen.

"For years, legislators have done an

admirable job of listening to constituents who want the dangerous, undesirable behavior of their neighbors regulated," Hinson said. "That is

> **"Legislation targeting harmful substances like drugs and alcohol is a good start, but that's all it is—a start," Andelman said.**

a good sign for those of us who wish for greater protection from ourselves. But you should see the filth I still have access to, just by walking into a store or flipping on my computer. There is still much work to be done if we are going to achieve the ideal nanny-state."

Bernard Nathansen, an attorney for the Personal Rights Deferred Center in Oakes, VA, is one of many individuals working to promote "governmental accountability." His organization arranges class action lawsuits on behalf of Americans who have been hurt by the government's negligence, including individuals who suffer health

problems related to overexposure to sunlight.

"We can all agree that many choices are too important to be left up to a highly flawed individual," Nathansen said. "Decisions that directly affect our health, or allow us to expose ourselves to potential risks, should be left to the wiser, cooler heads of the government."

"But things like food and drug labels are half-measures," Nathansen said. "The regulations, however well-intentioned, often allow citizens the choice of ignoring the instructions. Many current laws were written primarily to protect others from our dangerous actions, with no concern for the deleterious effect our actions can have on ourselves. The government must do more."

To this end, Personal Rights Deferred has compiled an action list of more than 700 behaviors it wants regulated by state or federal authorities. The list includes such risky behaviors as swimming in cold weather and staying up all night playing video games.

"The fact is, personal responsibility doesn't work," Nathansen said. "Take a good look at the way others around you are living, and I'm sure you'll agree. It's time for the American people to demand that someone force them to do something about it." ✍

23

Hey, Hollywood, Lay Off The Gore!

**The Outside Scoop
By Jackie Harvey**

Item! If you're like me, you're more than a little dismayed by the cinematic bloodbath at your local multiplex right now. There are chopped heads in **Kill Will**, and there's chopped *everything* in **The Texas Chainsaw Massacre**. Yuck! Far be it from me to tell Hollywood what to do, but I think they should keep their playing cards closer to their chests and not get so explicit.

What's your option if you want a good family movie? Good question. The answer is **Good Dog**! Talking dogs have been a favorite of mine since **The Adventures Of Milo And Stitch**. *Good Dog* has more than enough loudmouth canines to tickle your funny bone, and the pooches are voiced by heavy hitters like Matthew Broderik. I'm making a Harvey Call To Arms: Go see Good Dog! Let's show Hollywood that we're drawing a line in the sand. No more blood and guts. We demand quality family entertainment.

Item! Did you catch the **Series** this year? Some of my friends are **Yankees** fans, and they were pretty disappointed when the **Marlons** won. Oh, well. It's an honor just to make it to The Big Game. Better luck next year, Yankees.

I wonder what the most **American** food is. Some people say hot dogs; others say apple pie. But I say it's a tie between **rhubarb crisp** and the **double bacon cheeseburger**.

Item! It's a shame what happened to **Sigfreed** or **Roy**. One of them got chewed up and dragged off stage by a **white lion**. I'm no big-cat expert, but I've got a hunch that I know what happened. I'll bet that the lion thought that Sigfreed or Roy was one of her kittens and tried to carry him, by the throat, to the safety of her cage. Silly lion! Humans don't have scruffs on their necks. I hope that someone teaches the animal about that, if Sigfreed or Roy regains his health and the duo resumes the act.

Steve from **Blues Clues** has an album out. Now I've seen everything! I should just close up shop right now. (Don't worry, I won't actually do that.)

The new TV season is here! The jury's still out on how good it is. I've been too busy to check. I've been watching the first season of **24** with **Donald Sutherland** on DVD. I don't know how Donald could stay up for a full day without sleep. I get tired just watching him! But I suppose I've never had to save the world.

Item! Mandy Moore is the name on everyone's lips. I'll do a little sleuthing to find out why and report back to you.

The fall colors sure were spectacular this year. I hope you got out to see them, because it's going to be another 12 months until **Mother Nature** gets out her brush again and paints the world in hues of red, orange, and brown.

I'm achin' for Clay...**Clay Aiken**, that

> ## What's your option if you want a good family movie? Good question. The answer is *Good Dog*! Talking dogs have been a favorite of mine since The Adventures Of Milo And Stitch. *Good Dog* has more than enough loudmouth canines to tickle your funny bone, and the pooches are voiced by heavy hitters like Matthew Broderik.

is! I picked up his new album, and now I can't seem to get that CD out of my player. The verdict? Move over, **Michael**! There's a new king of pop, and he's got the magic you had once upon a time.

Item! Celebrity deaths always seem to come in threes. America mourned the passing of three of its favorite performers recently. We reeled from the news that singer **Johnny Cash** had passed away. Then, the report came that **Barefoot Executive** and **Eight Ways To Date My Daughter** star **John Ritter** had died. Just when things seemed their darkest, we heard that **Larry "Carter from Hogan's Heroes" Hovis** had made the great escape from the prison camp of the soldiers. We'll miss you all dearly. Entertainment won't be the same. I guess there really is a **Hogan's Heroes** curse.

Don't forget: Daylight Saving Time ended a week from last Sunday. If you haven't "fallen back" yet, you should turn your clocks back an hour.

Well, we're closing the curtain on another installment of The Outside Scoop. Next time, I'll bring you a behind-the-scenes look at the hilarious new movie **The Cat With The Hat**. (That **Michael Moore** is a genius!) I'll also answer the question, "What ever happened to **Angelica Jolie**?" Until then, I'll be ringside in the box seats...on The Outside! ✍

Your Horoscope

**By Lloyd Schumner Sr.
Retired Machinist and
A.A.P.B.-Certified Astrologer**

Aries: (March 21–April 19)
Your foolproof plan to rob the biggest bank in town goes sour when you overestimate your friends' loyalty, trust the wrong woman, and oversleep.

Taurus: (April 20–May 20)
You'll be banned from both the rock and the shipping scenes after a newspaper feature exposes your hideous double life as a guitarist and Mail Boxes Etc. clerk.

Gemini: (May 21–June 21)
You've often speculated on what other useful implements Captain Hook could have equipped, and you'll soon have the opportunity to marry thought to action.

Cancer: (June 22–July 22)
When choosing an autumnal flower arrangement, consider the cooler blues of cornflowers or chicory, as well as the traditional warmer fall colors, you sissy.

Leo: (July 23–Aug. 22)
Half the battle is knowing when to give up. This is a special new saying the stars coined with just you in mind.

Virgo: (Aug. 23–Sept. 22)
The beard does give you an air of evil, but it's the evil of neglect, not the evil of strength.

Libra: (Sept. 23–Oct. 23)
Technology will once again surpass you when you use coherent light to illustrate points in your incoherent presentation.

Scorpio: (Oct. 24–Nov. 21)
Your insistence on doing things for yourself is admirable, but bystanders have been trying to help you up off the sidewalk for two hours now.

Sagittarius: (Nov. 22–Dec. 21)
You hadn't wanted to live out your parents' dreams, but since they're the kind of dreams where you live in effortless luxury, it's no big deal, really.

Capricorn: (Dec. 22–Jan. 19)
You've certainly robbed the cradle this time, so that six-state FBI search for you and the baby is entirely justified.

Aquarius: (Jan. 20–Feb. 18)
A financial windfall means that you're not only able to speak your mind to the world, but also able to hire "Macho Man" Randy Savage to do it for you.

Pisces: (Feb. 19–March 20)
The stars would like to thank you for supplying vital comic relief, but you're being killed off in order to add another audience-identification character.

MEATBALL from page 5

large amounts of blood. Passersby were amazed by the unusually large amounts of blood. Passersby were amazed by the unusually large amounts of blood. Passersby were amazed by the unusually large amounts of blood. Passersby were amazed by the unusually large amounts of blood. Passersby were amazed by the unusually large amounts of blood. Passersby were amazed by the unusually large amounts of blood. Passersby were amazed by the unusually large amounts of blood. Passersby were amazed by the unusually large amounts of blood. Passersby were amazed by the unusually large amounts of blood. Passersby were amazed by the unusually large amounts of blood. Passersby were amazed by the unusually large amounts of blood. Passersby were amazed by the unusually large amounts of blood. Passersby were amazed by the unusually large amounts of blood. Passersby were amazed by the unusually large amounts of blood. Passersby were amazed by the unusually large amounts of blood. Passersby were amazed by the unusually large amounts of blood. Passersby were amazed by the unusually large amounts of blood. Passersby were

amazed by the unusually large amounts of blood. Passersby were amazed by the unusually large amounts of blood. Passersby were amazed by the unusually large amounts of blood. Passersby were amazed by the unusually large

> ## The tragic loss of your entire family is a lot like what's happening to me.

amounts of blood. Passersby were amazed by the unusually large amounts of blood. Passersby were amazed by the unusually large amounts of blood. Passersby were amazed by the unusually large amounts of blood. Passersby were amazed by the unusually large amounts of blood. Passersby were amazed by the unusually large amounts of blood. Passersby were amazed by the unusually large

see MEATBALL page 121

Flash-Animated Osama Bin Laden Captured

see WORLD page 3C

Right-To-Kill Advocate Opposes Right-To-Die Measure

see NATION page 10D

Thomas Jefferson's Descendants Still Gloating Over Louisiana Purchase

see REAL ESTATE page 11G

STATshot

A look at the numbers that shape your world.

Where Are We Getting Our Vitamins And Minerals?

- **21%** Trace amounts in instant mashed potatoes
- **32%** Neighbor's medicine cabinet
- **17%** Vitamin-fortified wine
- **18%** Consuming entire enemy, not just the heart
- **22%** Straight from niacin mines of Kentucky

RIBOFLAVIN MART

THE ONION • $2.00 US • $3.00 CAN

0 74470 94595 6

00

---

the ONION®

VOLUME 39 ISSUE 44   AMERICA'S FINEST NEWS SOURCE™   13–19 NOVEMBER 2003

Search For Missing Child Drags On To Fourth Boring Day

PICKETT, TN—The search for area fourth-grader Allison Means, who disappeared Friday evening, has entered its fourth boring day, volunteers and law-enforcement officials said Monday.

"We've been combing the woods and meadows near her home for *four days* now," Byrdstown County Sheriff Thomas Heubel said. "The *same* woods and

Above: Means, missing since Friday.

meadows—combing and more combing. With the possible exception of her parents, no one wants to find this girl more than we

Left: Volunteers search yet another stupid field for any signs of the missing child.

see CHILD page 28

Congress Raises Executive Minimum Wage To $565.15/Hr

WASHINGTON, DC—Congress approved a bill to increase the executive minimum wage from $515.15 to $565.15 an hour, House Majority Leader Tom DeLay (R-TX) announced Monday. The move marks the first increase in the wage since 1997.

"This is good news for all Americans who work in the upper levels of commerce," DeLay said. "Almost a third of America's hard-working executives toil at corporations day after day, yet still live below the luxury line. It was about time we gave a boost to the American white-collar worker."

The wage was calculated to help executives meet the federal standard-of-easy-living mark of $1.1 million a year. DeLay said that, although his goal is to ultimately reach an executive minimum wage of $800 per hour, he was satisfied with

see MINIMUM WAGE page 29

Above: DeLay announces the wage increase.

Woman Mentally Breaks Up With Colin Farrell

MERCER, PA—Heather Lentz's 11-month imaginary romance with bad-boy heartthrob Colin Farrell has ended, the 25-year-old paralegal announced Monday.

"While I'll always have affection for Colin, the hard truth is that he's not the kind of man I need in my imagination right now," Lentz said, her voice tight with emotion. "It hurts to say this, but it's probably best that we will never actually meet."

Though she was initially infatuated with the piercing good looks and Gallic charm of the Irish-born star of *Minority Report* and *S.W.A.T.*, Lentz

see WOMAN page 28

Left: Lentz and imaginary ex-boyfriend Farrell.

The Anti-Abortion Campaign

Bush's signing of the Partial Birth Abortion Ban Act was a political triumph for the movement to curtail abortions in the U.S. What do *you* think?

"They've got God on their side. All we've got is science and reason."

Dawn Hulsey
Talent Director

"Is it just me, or have national politics been sorta veering to the right a little since Bush was elected?"

Todd Delrio
Painter

"Before I make a decision on abortion, I'll have to review the made-for-TV movies on the topic."

Johnny Baron
Order Filler

"Why can't more American women be like Jessica Lynch? What do you mean, what do I mean?"

Frank Eldridge
Systems Analyst

"I don't think that people should play God—unless it's in a cute way, in a Sunday-school gymnasium."

Lillian Knighton
Mathematician

"As an investor in back-alley real estate and wire-hanger futures, I say,'Whoo-hoo!'"

Phillip Krantz
Investor

The Reagans

In the face of political pressure, CBS removed the miniseries *The Reagans* from its schedule. What controversial scenes does the program contain?

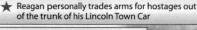

★ Reagan personally trades arms for hostages out of the trunk of his Lincoln Town Car

★ Popular movie ape Bonzo beats a young Reagan at chess during between-takes match

★ Crowd scene clearly contains extras wearing modern dress

★ Reagan consults astrologer on decision to bomb Libya

★ Reagan gets drunk watching *High Noon,* aware that entire White House can hear Sinatra screwing the false teeth out of Nancy in Lincoln bedroom

★ Actor in re-creation of Nancy's *Diff'rent Strokes* appearance looks nothing like Conrad Bain

★ Reagan intercedes to stop rogue band of air-traffic controllers as they rape and pillage East Coast

★ Scenes depict nuclear winter of 1985 as much worse than it really was

★ Entire miniseries slanted in wrong direction; contains no strong love interest

⊘ the ONION®
America's Finest News Source.™

Herman Ulysses Zweibel
Founder

T. Herman Zweibel
Publisher Emeritus
J. Phineas Zweibel
Publisher
Maxwell Prescott Zweibel
Editor-In-Chief

26

I Think I'll Drive The Kids Up To The State Park To See This 'Glory Hole'

By Eugene McTaggert

I try to be a good dad, but even so, I've been noticing this family drifting apart. We don't talk as much at the dinner table. We don't spend Sunday nights playing Clue as often as we used to. Our set of matching fishing poles is just collecting dust in the closet. I think this family needs to take a nice day trip. I know Bryan wants to go to the aviation museum, and Hilary loves the petting zoo in Greenwood, but I've got a better idea. I keep hearing about this "Glory Hole" up at the state park, and it sounds like just the thing.

I was going to clean out the garage this weekend, but the chance to commune with nature, standing in front of a Glory Hole, sounds far more alluring.

Before you know it, the kids will be going off to college. I want them to see some amazing sights while they're still young. Some parents don't care about providing their children with an education, but it's important to me. A trip to see this Glory Hole might be even more enlightening than our recent trip to Ruby Ridge and the Porcupine Mountains.

Before we leave, I'll do some research on the Internet, to get some details. I'll find out if we should bring any supplies, like flashlights or rope. I wonder if we need to pack a lunch. I'd hate to get all the way to the Glory Hole and find out that there's nothing to munch on for miles. We can bring some protein bars either way.

How did I hear about the Glory Hole? Well, when I took Skipper to get his nails clipped, I overheard one of the groomers talking about it to Don,

This Glory Hole must be really something, if people are so reluctant to talk about it.

who had his poodle in for a shampoo. The groomer said the Glory Hole was "mind-blowing," and Don said he was definitely going to check it out. When I asked them about it, they clammed up. They always seem to be clued-in to the newest restaurants and art museums, so I'll bet they wanted to keep the Glory Hole a secret. Well, for once, the McTaggerts are in the know!

This Glory Hole must be really something, if people are so reluctant to talk about it. I remember being the same way when I found that great sub shop on Oberlin Avenue. Unfortunately, I have a feeling that this Glory Hole is something I won't be able to keep to myself. Hold on to your seats for some great vacation photos!

A few guys at the gym had great

Some parents don't care about providing their children with an education, but it's important to me. A trip to see this Glory Hole might be even more enlightening than our recent trip to Ruby Ridge and the Porcupine Mountains.

things to say about the Glory Hole, but as soon as I told them I was taking my wife and kids, they didn't want to talk about it anymore. I had to wheedle the guy who works at the gas station to get him to draw me a map. He told me that there aren't any highway signs leading to the Glory Hole, and said I should head straight to the park's rest station. If I keep my ears open, he said, I'll find the right spot.

When I told the gas-station attendant that it would be my first time over on that side of the park, he warned me to be careful. He said things can get a little rough. Well, I told him that I love getting out there with the wild animals. I don't know anything about the Glory Hole, but I think it's thrilling to be out there in the dense underbrush, not knowing what's around the next bend. I'm ready and willing to explore.

Yep, I can't wait to hit Highway 87 with a cooler full of ice-cold Capri Sun. It's only a two-hour drive. The kids and I can have some fun in the car, singing songs and playing games, while my wife takes a nap to rest up for all the activity at the park. Then we can all pile out and blow off a little steam.

When the kids get home from school, I'll tell them to put on their old clothes, so they don't have to worry about getting dirty. After all is said and done, I bet they'll be talking about our trip to the Glory Hole for years to come. ⊘

Mom Finds Out About Blog

MINNEAPOLIS, MN—In a turn of events the 30-year-old characterized as "horrifying," Kevin Widmar announced Tuesday that his mother Lillian has discovered his weblog.

"Apparently, Mom typed [Widmar's employer] Dean Healthcare into

> **"I don't have one of those sites that's a big tell-all about one-night stands and wild parties,"** Widmar said. **"I mostly write about the animation I like or little things that happen to me and my friends. But there are definitely things in there that I wouldn't, well, write home to Mom about."**

Google along with my name and, lo and behold, PlanetKevin popped up," Widmar said. "I'm so fucked."

In an e-mail sent to Widmar Monday, Lillian reported in large purple letters that she was "VERY EXCITED :)!!!" to find his "computer diary," but was perplexed that he hadn't mentioned it to her.

Upon receipt of the e-mail, Widmar mentally raced through the contents of his blog. He immediately thought of several dozen posts in which he mentioned drinking, drug use, casual sex, and other behavior likely to alarm his mother.

"I don't have one of those sites that's a big tell-all about one-night stands and wild parties," Widmar said. "I mostly write about the animation I like or little things that happen to me and my friends. But there are definitely things in there that I wouldn't, well, write home to Mom about."

Fortunately for Widmar, Lillian's comments about the site indicate that she has not delved deeply into its contents.

"Mom's main comment was that I look tired in the photos from my birthday party, so I'm guessing that she didn't get past the first page yet," Widmar said. "She will, though. She will."

Widmar said he expects his site to provide Lillian with ample cause for worry.

"Even on that benign front page, she found something to freak out about," Widmar said. "She read the entry for Monday, where I mentioned how much I hate my job, and e-mailed to say that she hoped I wasn't thinking of quitting in this economy."

"Mom had a fit when she found out that I put my television on my credit card," Widmar added. "If she reads about how I was with my friend Jayson when he got pulled over for drunk driving, I'll never hear the end of it."

Above: Widmar, whose blog was recently discovered by his mother Lillian (inset).

"Oh God," Widmar said with a gasp. "Three days ago, I wrote something about buying pot!"

Widmar said that the idea of his mother immersing herself in the boring details of his life is just as frightening as the idea of her discovering his misconduct.

"Really, the blog is just a record of what I think about the world and how I spend my free time," Widmar said. "In other words, exactly the sort of information that no 30-year-old wants his mom to have access to."

Widmar said he imagines his inbox filling up with e-mails containing elaborate questions about an off-hand comment on *Kill Bill*—or, should he appear to have too much free time, requests for him to come and visit her.

"I know enough not to tell Mom that I'm seeing a girl until it's serious," Widmar said. "Now, she's going to know exactly who I hang out with, where I go, and what I spend my time doing on a daily basis. I am so in hell right now."

"God, my links alone contain unlimited fodder for Mom's neuroses,"

see BLOG page 29

Ad Campaign For New $20 Bill A Success

WASHINGTON, DC—The U.S. Department of the Treasury deemed the new multicolored $20 bill a raging success Monday, thanks to its $30 million advertising campaign. "Due to our print and TV ads, people across the nation are choosing our $20 bill when they need to exchange currency for goods and services within the United States and its territories," Secretary of the Treasury John Snow said. "We couldn't be happier. Americans agree that the Series 2004 U.S. currency is *the* legal tender for all debts, public and private." Due to high demand for the bill, the Treasury has already ordered second and third printings.

Woman Judges Cities Solely By Their Airports

SAN MARCOS, CA—Just back from a business trip to the Midwest, Sonic Drive-In managerial trainer Joan Rupert expressed distaste for yet another city, basing her evaluation solely on the quality of its airport. "I hate Chicago," Rupert said Monday. "It's too spread-out, and there's no good shopping in any of the terminals. But I do have to admit that they have tons of super bars and restaurants. Where else but O'Hare can you buy a real Chicago hot dog?" Rupert said the only city worse than Chicago is Minneapolis, which is "always under construction."

MTV Executive Grounds Son For Recommending Good Charlotte

NEW YORK—MTV executive Phillip Blanchard, 42, grounded his 15-year-old son Joshua Monday, after the alternative-rock band Good Charlotte failed to sustain its popularity among viewers of the cable music station. "Joshua needs to learn that his choices have consequences," said Blanchard, who took away his teenage son's credit-card privileges for the week. "Maybe next time, Joshua will think twice before over-hyping some pop-punk crap." As additional punishment, Blanchard had Joshua organize the family's extensive video library of *Road Rules* episodes chronologically.

Al Kozlewski Pulls A Kozlewski

CUDAHY, WI—Assembled after work at Gil's Tavern, friends of Al Kozlewski agreed Tuesday that the 39-year-old steamfitter had pulled yet another Kozlewski. "Al came in and did that thing he always does," coworker Danny Fassle said. "He sat down at the table, drank two beers from a pitcher that *someone else* bought, and then suddenly decided that he had to get right home. A classic Kozlewski." When informed of the charges, Kozlewski said that if Fassle has a problem, he should "stop being such a Palaczyk and say it to my face."

Man Always Three Ingredients Away From Making Pancakes

BOISE, ID—In spite of the numerous times he's craved pancakes during the past year, Mike Herrin, 26, always finds himself three ingredients shy of being able to make the breakfast food. "I woke up this morning just dying for a big mug of coffee and a stack of pancakes," Herrin said Sunday. "This time, I knew I had milk, eggs, and even sugar. But of course there was no baking powder or flour, and I was out of salt." Herrin then stared longingly at the dust-covered bottle of Mrs. Butterworth's in the back of the cupboard for a moment before slamming the door shut. ⌀

do."

Daniel and Karen Means contacted Heubel after their daughter didn't return from Sather Elementary School Friday afternoon. By nightfall, nearly four dozen initially eager locals volunteered to assist in the search.

"The first day or two was okay, I guess," said Clay Watts, a nearby resident who has been participating in the search since Saturday morning. "But now it's been four days, and she still hasn't turned up. The cops arrange us in these straight, long lines, and we advance 10 feet at a time. This goes on for *hours*. I've never been so bored in my life. Bored, bored, bored, bored, bored."

Mail carrier Tonia Stelson came forward Saturday to report that she had seen the girl at approximately 4 p.m. on Friday, about a quarter of a mile from the Means' house.

"I've shown about 50 different people exactly where I saw Allison," Stelson said. "How many times can I point to the same stretch of dirt? It's like, what part of 'I think maybe she was wearing a red coat' don't you understand?"

Searchers continue to search within a 20-mile radius of the Means' home, in an area comprising fallow farmland, tall grass, and scrub woodland. Wearied volunteers said they are as frustrated by the unremarkable landscape as they are by the dearth of leads.

"I've lived here all my life, but you really don't realize how dull the area is until you've participated in a search for a missing 9-year-old," volunteer Shirley Snow said. "It's a shame there are no gently rolling hills or picturesque windmills around here—you know, something pleasing to the eye. Besides that ugly abandoned farmhouse, which we've been through six times already, there's nothing."

Watts and his party of eight searchers have swept several open fields, an intensely dull process that has yielded only burrs, brambles, and insect bites.

"I know we've been through this area before," Watts said. "I remember that dogwood tree over there with the Coors can in its branches. Why are they deliberately sending us through the same area multiple times? Just to annoy us?"

In spite of the tedious searching, called off only during the darkest hours, not a single clue to Means' whereabouts has been found.

Searchers haven't found footprints, scraps of clothing, or anything that might be just a tiny bit interesting, nor have police received any phone tips or substantial informant leads. The lack of progress has only heightened the searchers' frustration.

Hopes and interest rose briefly Sunday evening, when a search team found a decaying body near an apple orchard. The corpse, however, proved to be that of a small deer.

"I have to admit, when they announced it was an animal, a few people groaned in disappointment," volunteer Drena Biddle said. "It would have been a shame if we'd found Allison in that state, but at least the search would be over."

"Oh, look!" Watts said. "There's that Coors can again."

Sheriff's deputies dredged a pond two miles away from the Means' house Monday, in a long and tedious process that yielded three glass insulators.

"You used to see them on telephone poles," Sheriff's Deputy Dean Howarth said. "See the old Bell Telephone logo molded on them? Maybe some workers were doing work around here and threw them in the pond, just to get rid of them. You think so? Hey, I'm just trying to make conversation here."

Their frustration mounting, volunteers have begun to rebel against the rules laid out by search-party organizers.

"I'll help out tomorrow, but only if I can bring my Walkman," Watts said. "These damn cicadas are driving me crazy. And I don't care if there are women present—I'm not tromping all the way back up to Kickapoo Gas just to piss. It's part of life."

"Why wasn't I assigned to search near Shoptowne Mall?" Snow said. "Look, it's upsetting that Allison hasn't been found, and I believe in community spirit and everything. But the bottom line is, I never knew the girl. After searching for three straight days with only four hours of sleep each night—look, she's dead. Let's go home."

Heubel said he has notified state police of Means' disappearance, and that the FBI will soon join the search.

"Federal agents are professionally trained to deal with intensely tedious situations like this one," Heubel said. "Plus, the FBI has considerable manpower they can send out to tromp around in the woods, which will finally free me up to go back to my new bumper-pool table." ∅

admitted to being "troubled" by Farrell's widely reported penchant for hard drinking, profanity, and womanizing.

"Those brown eyes are to die for, and I'll admit that I've always had a weakness for men with stubble," Lentz said. "Nevertheless, I was turned off by Colin's rude behavior. His constant need for attention is really juvenile."

Lentz, who gleaned her knowledge of Farrell from various entertainment-news sources, has never sought a real-life relationship with the rising star, and characterized the phenomenon of celebrity stalking as "pathetic." Nevertheless, when pressed, Lentz was able to give a detailed account of the rise and fall of her pretend relationship with Farrell.

"In the beginning, Colin could do no wrong," Lentz said. "I was aware of his wild reputation, but I was willing to tolerate it—I even welcomed it—because he was so exciting and alive. He made life unpredictable. Blind love, I guess."

Lentz's passion for the actor manifested itself in several ways. If she caught a TV report on Farrell, she would quickly insert a tape into her VCR and record the remainder of the segment. If she saw that Farrell was scheduled as a guest on a late-night talk show, she would stay up to watch the appearance. Lentz would also buy a magazine if Farrell was on the cover, and even attended an opening-day showing of *Daredevil*, in spite of her aversion to most action movies.

"My crush on Colin transformed me," Lentz said. "I found myself standing taller, dressing better, and taking things a little less seriously. My friends noticed the change. Still, all the while, anxiety was creeping in: What if I wasn't the type of woman he would find attractive?"

Eventually, Lentz said "reality" set in.

"Colin and I live in separate worlds, divided by an unbridgeable gulf," Lentz said. "He's a wild, glamorous actor from cosmopolitan Dublin, and I'm just a community-college graduate from western Pennsylvania with a low-paying job and average looks. It would never work."

"Colin loves fast living, and I prefer quiet evenings at home," Lentz said. "At first, I would imagine all the fun parties we'd go to if we were dating, but I grew tired of that pretty quickly. I started picturing myself sitting there in my bathrobe, waiting up for him—just like my mom used to do. I don't want that."

Lentz also began to wonder if Farrell would remain faithful.

"It got to where I couldn't fantasize about us being together without constantly wondering if he would run around on me," Lentz said. "If he cheated on women before, I couldn't see why I'd be an exception. He's just not worth the heartache."

The news that one of Farrell's girlfriends, model Kim Bordenave, gave birth to his son helped convince Lentz to break it off once and for all.

"I had to dump him from my thoughts, if only to preserve my sanity," she said. "I know that I'm choosing practicality over love, and maybe that makes me as weak as Colin, but in a different way."

Lentz said she is taking steps to scale back Farrell's presence in her life. She has taped over her copies of his *Access Hollywood* appearances, and removed the film *Hart's War*, starring Farrell and Bruce Willis, from her Netflix queue.

Rumor has it that Lentz was recently overheard commenting on the attractiveness of the Scottish actor Ewan McGregor. Still, although Lentz said she considers McGregor "cute," she denied any pretend relationship.

"To tell you the truth, I've been much more attracted to the veneer of maturity and stability lately," Lentz said. "I saw William H. Macy in [the TV movie] *Door To Door*, and he seemed like a man who could hold a woman's attention."

Neither Farrell, on location in Australia, nor Lentz's real-life boyfriend Neil Benson, working late at Mercer Credit Union, could be reached for comment. ∅

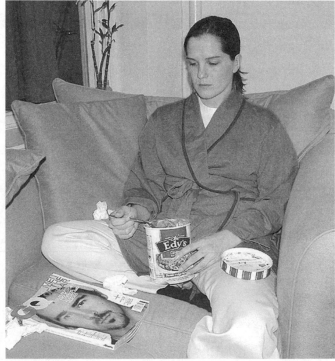

Above: Lentz spends a quiet evening at home to recover from her imaginary split with Farrell.

Above: PPG Industries financial officer Brad Weston will benefit from the wage increase.

what he characterized as a "stop-gap measure."

"Many of the thousands of Americans overseeing the nation's factories, restaurant chains, and retailers can't even afford a jet," DeLay said. "It's our long-term goal to ensure that no one who sees to it that others work hard for a living will have to go without the basic necessities of the good life."

Under the new law, the executive-minimum salary will increase to more than $1.175 million a year, plus mandatory overtime for executives who work more than seven minutes after 5 p.m., on holidays, outside of their home offices, or from a limou-

> **Nick Scheele, Ford president and chief operating officer, said he looks forward to February 2004, when the wage increase is slated to take effect.**

sine or non-chartered private aircraft. A separate section of the bill includes concessions for second- and third-housing credits, as well as single-player health-spa coverage.

Top executives nationwide have repeatedly called for wage increases in recent years.

"Our lifestyles are expensive to maintain," Boeing senior vice-president of international relations Tom Pickering said. "The costs of even the most basic executive transportation, food, and clothing are staggering. Since 1993, the average cost of maintaining a household of six, including a butler, a cook, a maid, a driver, and a groundskeeper, has increased by 14 percent. All this, even after we work our fingers to the bone for hundreds of hours a year, painstakingly assembling our benefits packages. It shouldn't have to be this hard."

Some executives called for even more support, in the form of increased benefits and reimbursements.

"Well, it's a good start," said Abby Kohnstamm, IBM senior vice-president of marketing. "But I still don't get a transportation allowance for my company-owned limo. And no one has addressed the fact that almost 8 percent of my income disappears after taxes."

Nick Scheele, Ford president and chief operating officer, said he looks forward to February 2004, when the wage increase is slated to take effect.

"It's about peace of mind," Scheele said. "Executives like myself are sick of living quarterly statement to quarterly statement, forced to check our bank balances before every little real-estate purchase. We're not asking for the world, just the overseas vacations that we so desperately need."

The pay hike marks a rare instance of bipartisan cooperation in one of the most polarized congresses in U.S.

history. In the U.S. Senate, only Russ Feingold (D-WI) and John McCain (R-AZ) opposed the bill.

"This proves that politicians can

> **"Many of the thousands of Americans overseeing the nation's factories, restaurant chains, and retailers can't even afford a jet," DeLay said. "It's our long-term goal to ensure that no one who sees to it that others work hard for a living will have to go without the basic necessities of the good life."**

work together when it involves the welfare of the citizens most responsible for keeping them in office," U.S. Sen. Ted Kennedy (D-MA) said. "Those of us who hold higher office don't ever forget where we came from, and how we got where we are today. This wage hike is our way of giving something back to the American people who are most important." ⌀

Widmar said. "She'll have access to not only my life, but the lives of all my friends who have web sites. She'll have the names of all the places in Minneapolis where we hang out, which she can—and will—look up. With the raw materials in my blog, she could actually construct an accurate picture of who I am. This is fucking serious."

"To think that I was happy that Mom

> **"Mom loves hearing every boring detail of her kids' lives," he said. "She'd want to know what I'm eating for dinner every night, if she could. This blog is like porn for her."**

was e-mailing instead of calling ever since [Widmar's sister] Karen got her online last year," he added. "I didn't see the danger."

According to Widmar, there's "no fucking chance" that Lillian will simply give the site a cursory look and never return.

"Mom loves hearing every boring detail of her kids' lives," he said. "She'd want to know what I'm eating for dinner every night, if she could. This blog is like porn for her."

"Come to think of it, why do I sometimes write about what I ate for dinner?" Widmar asked.

Seeing his blog through his mother's eyes, Widmar said he knows there's no way the site can remain unchanged.

"I know Mom will instantly become the site's most avid reader and most vocal fan," Widmar said. "As I write it, I'll think, 'How would Mom feel about this?' Even worse, I'm sure she'll give the address to all our relatives."

All of the tactics Widmar has considered to divert his mother seem unworkable.

"I could take it down for a few weeks, but I know she wouldn't just forget about it," Widmar said. "I could edit the site and send my other readers through a back door, to another blog just for them. But, I mean, that's just ridiculous."

If Widmar starts a blog at a new address, without his full name this time, he said he risks losing "close to 100" regular readers.

As of press time, Widmar had not decided whether to shut PlanetKevin down.

"The clock is ticking," Widmar said. "I've gotta act fast. At this very minute, she might be reading about the time I did Ecstasy last summer. If Mom finds that entry, I can pretty much count on our conversations for the next year being centered on the dangers of drug use." ⌀

I've Received Some Unpleasant Information Regarding My Estranged Half-Brother's Involvement In The Barcelona Debacle

By Dept. Head Rawlings

Good evening, gentlemen. Mei Ling. Or should I say good morning? I'm afraid the last few hours here at the Department For Special Acquisitions And Liquidations have been rather, well, active. I apologize for calling you to Operations at such a wretched hour, but if this report from the Transitional Branch in Seville is accurate, then we have some important decisions to make. We must either act quickly to eliminate a threat to this Department, or we must take steps to remove me from my position as Department Head. You see, I fear that my estranged but brilliant half-brother may have been instrumental to the execution of the horrible debacle we experienced in Barcelona.

MacNeill, I was kept in the dark regarding Paladiev, as well. Like you, for many years, I had no need to know of my half-brother. It would have done more harm than good for me, as a young boy, to hear that my father, his identity exposed to the NKVD and his file preemptively erased by the OSS, had found comfort in a smoky yurt and the welcoming arms of a comely young shepherdess.

Ultimately, my father's narrow escape to Toulon—and my pregnant mother—was interpreted by the shepherdess as a political and personal betrayal. She used her enmity toward my father as a spur to her ambition. By the time Paladiev was 3, the shepherdess was a colonel of Soviet intelligence. How quickly she learned the sly and shameful rules of the Great Game, and how eagerly she drilled them into her son.

Paladiev was an able student. He is a most formidable enemy. He is clever, but do not assume that he is only that. He plans and he schemes throughout his waking hours. Cunning as he is tactically, he is brilliant strategically. Do not underestimate him. If the Department had not done so...

In any case: Barcelona. You are all familiar with the events of the Barcelona debacle. But I'm sure you have wondered just how the chessboard was manipulated, how the pawns were set up and made to fall just so. Through one of our post-compromised double operatives, Transitional Branch has learned that it was Paladiev who met with the undersecretary on that stormy Barcelona afternoon. It was Paladiev who cut the support beam of the North Bridge, creating a perfect distraction but killing hundreds. And it was Paladiev who poisoned the lipstick of the Swedish ambassador's mistress, and so killed the three—the ambassador, his wife, and his lover.

The technician who installed our low-frequency network in Barcelona has been romantically linked to Pal-

> **Like you, for many years, I had no need to know of my half-brother. It would have done more harm than good for me, as a young boy, to hear that my father, his identity exposed to the NKVD and his file preemptively erased by the OSS, had found comfort in a smoky yurt and the welcoming arms of a comely young shepherdess.**

adiev; her body has yet to be found. Most damning of all, the Transitional Branch has identified a man, seen only in profile through an extreme-telephoto lens, who activated a detonator, spoke into a headset, and turned to fire a rifle. Yes, Paladiev was the mysterious Third Window Washer. Paladiev.

I don't know how he acquired the means to execute so elaborate a maneuver. That is unimportant. We could spend months and millions of dollars tracing him—to the forger in Singapore, the plastic surgeon in Dallas, a certain neuroanatomist in Zurich, and a shadowy gunsmith in Tel Aviv. But what good would it do to follow these leads? By the time we reached their ends, the men and women in question would either be dead or so thoroughly missing as to be thought mere legends. A genius like Paladiev bends the world to his will.

Do not waste time and energy asking after Paladiev. He acts and reacts with adaptability, flexibility, and effi-ciency. His artful erasure of his ways and means should not be surprising to trained professionals like yourselves. Boris, can you give me the address of the man who built your fascinating prosthetic arm? Pierre, could you tell me exactly who first synthesized your versatile collection of poisons? I thought not. Who is the architect who built these headquarters, after all?

I'm sorry, Mei Ling. I do not know Paladiev's motives. His reasons for his life's work are his own. I have only speculation. Perhaps he blames me for his mother's tragic death during the engineered eruption of Mt. Pinatubo in Luzon. I do not know.

I do know, however, what actions my team will take. We are going into full hermetic lockdown this instant. Everyone, including Department heads, is to begin prep for staff-wide, deep-muscle-tissue-biopsy DNA testing. I would not put it past Paladiev to endure bone-marrow and lymphatic replacement to dupe a routine blood test. Before we make this announce-ment staff-wide, we must deep-radar

Your Horoscope

By Lloyd Schumner Sr.
Retired Machinist and
A.A.P.B.-Certified Astrologer

Aries: (March 21–April 19)
You swore that your love would last until the seas ran dry, the mountains crumbled, and the sun grew cold, so you'll be single again as of Thursday.

Taurus: (April 20–May 20)
Your life will no longer be worth living after you see the dismal quality of this week's Top Ten Plays on *SportsCenter*.

Gemini: (May 21–June 21)
You will fall out of favor with the community, be shunned by your family, and lose your job after you dare to suggest that Audrey Hepburn had kind of a big nose.

Cancer: (June 22–July 22)
Before you grow facial hair, consider the various styles, the level of maintenance required, and the prophecy that you'll die when your beard gets caught in a table saw.

Leo: (July 23–Aug. 22)
Sometimes success is just showing up—not as often as being the son of the company president, but sometimes.

Virgo: (Aug. 23–Sept. 22)
If you, like many Virgos, are a gambler, the stars advise you to bet on the army of horned demons and take the points.

Libra: (Sept. 23–Oct. 23)
In times of war, man must adopt the countenance of the tiger. But for now, you're doing fine with the sheep thing.

Scorpio: (Oct. 24–Nov. 21)
You will wake from a sound sleep shaking and weeping, struck by the sudden revelation that you need a new vacuum cleaner.

Sagittarius: (Nov. 22–Dec. 21)
Fire and Earth magicks are strong in Sagittarius this month, which may or may not be a bad sign for your upcoming monster-truck show.

Capricorn: (Dec. 22–Jan. 19)
Cold winds will roll in at the end of the week, putting an end to this unseasonably warm spell of weather and making the loss of your arms that much harder to endure.

Aquarius: (Jan. 20–Feb. 18)
The *Académie Française* will rule that your name is never to be spoken within France's borders.

Pisces: (Feb. 19–March 20)
You've always had trouble controlling your base impulses, but they do lead you to have fun and experience cool things.

> **I do not know Paladiev's motives. His reasons for his life's work are his own. I have only speculation. Perhaps he blames me for his mother's tragic death during the engineered eruption of Mt. Pinatubo in Luzon. I do not know.**

every room in the facility for...anything. For anything is exactly what Paladiev is capable of.

Paladiev, Paladiev, my long-lost half-brother. What game are you playing? ⌀

NEWS

Domino's Introduces Thanksgiving Feast Pizza

see BUSINESS page 1B

David Blaine Starves Self Of Attention For 33 Days

see ENTERTAINMENT page 14E

Porn DVD's Commentary Track Just More Moaning

see ENTERTAINMENT page 4E

Pre-Nup Skimmed

see LOCAL page 4C

STATshot

A look at the numbers that shape your world.

What's Under Our Leaf Pile?

15% Trampoline

35% Wedding ring…somewhere

10% Door to trendy new Korean fusion restaurant

12% If you're Christo, probably the Reichstag

11% The miracle of decomposition

17% Ignore the leaf pile—it doesn't concern you

the ONION®

VOLUME 39 ISSUE 45   AMERICA'S FINEST NEWS SOURCE™   20–26 NOVEMBER 2003

Palestine Appoints New Minister Of Rubble And Urban Development

Above: Arafat congratulates Al-Katif amid a prime patch of rubble.

RAMALLAH, WEST BANK—After weeks of political infighting, Palestinian Prime Minister Ahmed Qureia announced the appointment of Hassan Al-Katif as the region's new Minister of Rubble and Urban Development Tuesday.

"It is a great honor for me to name a man as experienced as Mr. Al-Katif to this post," Qureia said at a press conference held on top of a pile of rocks that was formerly a local mosque. "Palestine is in need of a strong leader to spark growth in urban areas and manage our burgeoning rubble sector, which is the fastest growing in the world."

The appointment came after several weeks of discord between Qureia and Palestinian leader Yassir Arafat over who should replace the region's 30-day emergency rubble minister. Al-Katif was strongly backed by Arafat.

"Having worked in the private sector as a rubble developer and organizer, Mr. Al-Katif understands Palestine's rubble situation," Arafat said. "He has a strong plan that charts a path to capitalization on our vast and ever-increasing supply of rock fragments and crumbled masonry."

Continued Arafat: "Palestinians need a man of Mr. Al-Katif's unequaled vision. In the coming years, he will oversee the construction of many

see MINISTER page 35

Above: The Boston Globe's 2002 Super Bowl coverage barely mentions the opposing team.

Media Criticized For Biased Hometown Sports Reporting

ALBANY, NY—Members of the national media watchdog group Fairness and Accuracy In Reporting released a 255-page report Monday criticizing the American media for severely biased local sports coverage.

"In our extensive study of the nation's sports sections and broadcasts, we documented countless examples of shamelessly one-sided reporting, obvious speculation, and bald editorializing masquerading as journalism," FAIR spokesman Scott Wilborough said. "Coverage was heavily, sometimes brazenly, weighted toward the teams from a media source's own area. To look at the data, you would almost think that sports journalists aren't held to the same standards as other reporters."

FAIR surveyed the sports reporting

see MEDIA page 34

Sorta-Attractive Girl Half-Heartedly Hit On

COOL SPRINGS, TN—During a weekend house party characterized as "okay," paint-store employee Peter Elsing, 24, mustered up just enough interest to hit on Theresa Scobel, a sort of good-looking Vanderbilt graduate student, Elsing said Monday.

"Theresa was…cute," Elsing said. "She could've been in better shape. Not saying I couldn't either, of course.

She definitely had a cute face. I've seen worse."

The party, held Saturday night at the apartment of Elsing's longtime friend Warren Croft, was subdued, with fewer than 20 attendees. Elsing said boredom and a shortage of eligible female guests inspired him to speak to the tall, curly-haired Scobel.

According to Elsing, of the seven women present,

see GIRL page 34

Above: Elsing kinda makes a move on the sorta-attractive Scobel.

Speeding Up Iraqi Self-Rule

The Bush Administration announced that it hopes to speed up the transition to self-government in Iraq. What do *you* think?

"Jesus, just leave the country, already. Someone else will come in and take it over."

Charlie Falk
Security Guard

"This is simply the natural evolution of our policy from Iraquisition to Iraqupation, to Iraqunification."

Christine Winn
Receptionist

"Iraq has a history of instability and will require strong leadership in the postwar era. Hey! Is Saddam still alive?"

Diana Conley
Receptionist

"Well, *I* happen to be an unemployed warlord."

Rodney Dunson
Warlord

"It makes sense for Bush to pull out. If his own father had exercised the judgment to pull out, the U.S. wouldn't have been there in the first place."

Robert Swenson
Systems Analyst

"I'm just hoping Bush gets our boys home before election time."

Jeff Rondeau
Materials Engineer

Immigrant Workers Vs. Wal-Mart

Hundreds of undocumented immigrants have filed a discrimination and exploitation lawsuit against Wal-Mart. What are the workers' complaints?

➤ Lied to about existence of a sub-minimum wage

➤ Made to sleep in rafters, while other employees were allowed to sleep in model tool sheds in parking lot

➤ Led to believe that they would receive amnesty in Discount City

➤ Forced to work under hellish fluorescent lighting, with intolerable easy-listening music playing at all times

➤ Not allowed to use bathroom until completion of workweek

➤ Stuck-up bitch cashier Danielle couldn't be bothered to say "hi" even once

➤ Emotionally traumatized by being forced to destroy small-town economies against their will

➤ Every other Friday, exactly when pay was being handed out, assistant manager would burst in and yell, "Scatter! It's the INS!"

the ONION ®
America's Finest News Source.™

Herman Ulysses Zweibel
Founder

T. Herman Zweibel
Publisher Emeritus
J. Phineas Zweibel
Publisher
Maxwell Prescott Zweibel
Editor-In-Chief

I Have To Admit, I Love The Nuts

I'm a squirrel on the go. I've got trees to climb and streets to cross. If anybody asks what keeps me going when squirrel duties pile up, I got one word for them: nuts! I know it's a stereotype that squirrels go crazy for nuts, but in my case, it's 100 percent true. I make no apologies or excuses. Why should I? I fully admit that I love the nuts!

By Danny The Squirrel

Somebody once said the only thing I cared about was nuts. Hey, guilty as charged. And what's wrong with that? Nuts never hurt anybody—at least nobody in squirrel circles. Nuts are delicious! Just stuff a nut into your cheeks, chomp down, and unlock the nutty flavor. Before you know it, you'll be like me—singing the praises of the savory goodness of nutty nuts.

I'm not a strong-willed squirrel. If you take a can of nuts and dump them in your backyard, you'd better believe I'm gonna eat those nuts. I won't be polite about it, either. I won't share them with the chipmunks or the birds. No, I will behave like a fool to secure those nuts. I'll shove as many nuts in my mouth as I can fit, and chew as fast as possible to make room for more nuts. If I have some leftover nuts, I'll bury them for later. And let me tell you: If I can't find my nuts, there's going to be some frantic chirping and running around, believe me. I don't care if passersby stop, point, and laugh at my actions. They can call me me all sorts of nut-loving

> You might say, "Danny, what's the deal with the nuts? Don't you ever want to break out of the mold? Do something a little less expected? Blaze a trail? Why do you just live by the old squirrel standards?"

names. I won't stop until I find those nuts.

You might say, "Danny, what's the deal with the nuts? Don't you ever want to break out of the mold? Do something a little less expected? Blaze a trail? Why do you just live by the old squirrel standards?"

Well, I've got an answer. It's simple. Ready? Here it is: I love nuts. Acorns in particular.

But I love chestnuts, walnuts, and peanuts, too. I'm a nut nut! That's an old joke my dad told me when I was a little kid, and it's funny because it's true. It may be a cliché, but I go crazy for nuts. There's nothing I wouldn't do for nuts. I've been chased by dogs,

> I'm not a strong-willed squirrel. If you take a can of nuts and dump them in your backyard, you'd better believe I'm gonna eat those nuts.

cats, raccoons, and children while in pursuit of a luscious nut. You'd think I had some sort of death wish, but that's just not the case. I don't know if there are nuts in heaven, so I'm not looking to die. Believe me, I don't do this for the thrills. I do it for the nuts.

Just so you don't get the wrong idea, eating nuts isn't all I do. I like to chase other squirrels up and down the trees. I scramble madly up walls using my prehensile claws. Sometimes, I puff up my tail and charge at shadows. And, believe me, I do my share of dashing madly across telephone wires. But when I need to recharge, there's only one thing that can satisfy my hunger. Nuts! And a lot of 'em! Oh, boy!

Do you want to make good with me? Then you'd better bust out the nuts. That's the way to this squirrel's heart. Don't worry. You won't offend me if you assume that I eat nuts, because it's true. I do. So do all of my squirrel friends.

Admittedly, I eat more than just nuts. There aren't always nuts around, so I make do. Once, I found a half-eaten candy bar in the park. I was hungry, so I ate it. It was all right. But do you know what would have made it better? Nuts. If you had put some almonds or peanuts in that candy bar, it would've really been something. But you know what would've been even better? If you took all the candy out, and just left the nuts.

Life is short if you're a squirrel. What do I have? Two, three years? I have to live life to the fullest. I don't want people saying that I didn't take advantage of every opportunity that I had while I skittered around this green earth. If, when I'm gone, you hear someone say, "That Danny, he was a good guy, but he didn't eat many nuts," I insist you set them straight. You tell them that I loved nuts more than anything.

Man, all this talk of nuts is killing me. ∅

Working Man Proud Of Job He Hates

JANESVILLE, WI—Eagle Cooling employee Brent Festge takes pride in the semi-skilled, blue-collar job he loathes, the 39-year-old solderer reported during his lunch break Tuesday.

"I'm real proud to be doing something you don't see in America much anymore: spot welding. I work for one of the biggest union-run AC parts shops anywhere," said Festge, and beat the side of the breakroom vending machine to dislodge a bag of Corn Nuts. "It's honest work, and I can go home every night knowing that management can't just replace me with a machine, or a Mexican."

"Goddamn it!" Festge said, shaking the unyielding vending machine. "Every single goddamn day…"

For eight years, Festge has worked at Eagle Cooling, which produces air-conditioner parts for Daimler Chrysler and employs 460 full-time workers. A member of United Auto Workers Local #568, Festge makes nearly $40,000 a year, receives medical and dental benefits, and qualifies for a retirement pension after 20 years with the company. However, as he goes about the numbingly repetitive work of soldering frames to air-conditioner filters, Festge must struggle to keep these advantages in mind.

"This kind of work is challenging," Festge said. "I have to stay on my toes. Sloppy joins will get you in hot water with the foreman. Actually, I could do this in my sleep, so what the hell am I worrying about?"

Festge has been soldering frames onto air-conditioner filters for five years. Before that, he soldered casings on blower motors.

"At least my job is staying put here on American soil, where it belongs," Festge said. "I'm overqualified for it, because I'm certified in welding as well as soldering. But at the time I was hired, soldering on the frame line was all that was available. Well, it's still all that's available."

As he filled out a lengthy compensation form for the 75 cents he lost in the vending machine, Festge condemned the declining work ethic and lack of American pride among the people of his generation.

"If folks want to look down their noses at me, that's their prerogative," Festge said. "Skilled industrial labor made this country, and if you don't want to do it, there'll always be a Korean who's more than glad to step in. Just don't complain when the only jobs out there are at McDonald's or cleaning toilets."

In spite of the pride he takes in soldering frames, Festge complains of high union dues, poor break-room ventilation, near-deafening shop-floor noise, a 15 percent increase in his co-pay on prescription drugs, frequent toilet-paper shortages in the men's bathroom, and the acrid factory smell that never washes out of his clothes. He also said that Local #568 president Marsh Delahanty is deliberately under-reporting the strike-fund balance and pocketing the difference.

Another source of irritation Festge cited was his foreman, Frank Modesto.

"Last week, we had this big order to fill, but Frank forced us to take our three mandatory 15-minute breaks," Festge said. "Then, when he found out we were behind our quota, he chewed us out. What a bastard. And to think I thought things would be better around here after Frank made foreman. He was a super guy back when he was working on the line."

In spite of Festge's frustration with

Above: Festge relaxes during his 26-minute lunch break.

see WORKING MAN page 36

22-Year-Old Fuck Complains Of Age Discrimination

SAN MIGUEL, CA—Passed over for a promotion at Barton Financial Services, little 22-year-old fuck Darren Meeker filed a lawsuit against the company Monday, claiming to be a victim of age discrimination. "Just because someone has 20 years of experience, that doesn't automatically make him more qualified than my client," said attorney Martin Lippman, who represents the whiny shit. "In his first seven months on the job, Mr. Meeker has more than proven his potential." The little prick was unavailable for comment.

Donut Shop's Mission Statement Awfully Ambitious

FREEHOLD, NJ—Patrons at Dotty's Donuts on Cranston Avenue agree that the mission statement posted near the shop's entrance seems overly ambitious. "It said, 'At Dotty's, our goal is to reinvent the morning,'" Dotty's patron Ken Mentilli said. "'Dotty's Donuts are guaranteed to bring a smile to your face and a ray of light into your soul.' That seems like a tall order for a donut shop." Mentilli added that Dotty's may not be able to deliver on its promise to "change the world, one fresh-baked bear claw at a time."

Enraged Man Unable To Break TV

SHREVEPORT, LA—Enraged after seeing his ex-wife in a local commercial, area resident Bill Schwartz, 48, threw a potentially destructive tantrum Monday, but was unable to smash the screen of his 42-inch high-definition television. "If that television were less durable, there would be no doubt as to just how upset I am right now," Schwartz said after launching two shoes and a telephone at the screen. "Damn it." Schwartz then made a final charge at the television before collapsing dejectedly into a recliner.

African Leaders Still Treating Clinton As President

NAIROBI, KENYA—Kenyan President Emilio Mwai Kibaki said Monday that his country continues to enjoy excellent diplomatic relations with former U.S. President Bill Clinton. "I have always enjoyed working with Mr. Clinton, and the recent international Agricultural Development Conference was no exception," Kibaki said. "And I know that [Democratic Republic of the Congo President] Joseph Kabila enjoyed meeting with him to secure an American commitment for humanitarian aid, as well." Kibaki said that none of the leaders have anything in particular against President Bush, but added that all the same, they'd rather stick with Clinton.

House Of Representatives Magically Switches Bodies With Senate

WASHINGTON, DC—Members of the Senate and the House of Representatives were magically transposed Tuesday, in an event Senate Majority Leader Bill Frist described as "freaky." "Sen. [Orrin] Hatch [R-UT] had just introduced S.J. Res. 15 when, all of a sudden, we found ourselves in these huge chambers with all these extra seats around us," Frist said. "I looked down, and there in my hand was a copy of H.R. 2799, but I had no idea how to go about defending its contents." Members of both congressional bodies proceeded to learn valuable lessons about one another's perspectives on the legislative process. ∅

of more than 400 newspapers, as well as nearly 200 television and radio stations across the country.Wilborough said that, in an average article about a sports event, 87 percent of column space was devoted to coverage of the local team.

"Photos almost always featured the home team, usually in a moment of victory," Wilborough said. "When the players and coaches of the opposing team were discussed, it was usually in the context of how they were 'destroyed' or 'stomped.'"

In addition to granting local teams and athletes disproportionate amounts of column space and airtime, city dailies and newscasts often exaggerated local teams' wins and downplayed their losses.

Wilborough held up two newspapers: a copy of the *Detroit Evening News* with the headline "Sanders to Join the Immortals" and a copy of the *Philadelphia Inquirer* with the headline "McNabb's Brilliant Last Minute Heroics Destroy Green Bay."

"It's frankly baffling how widespread the bias is," Wilborough said. "Journalists seem to lose their composure altogether when reporting on their local sports teams."

The FAIR report, which characterized the bias as "irresponsible and pervasive," stated that "the blatant slanting of local sports coverage goes against the ethics of balanced journalism and contributes to a public perception that the local team in a particular area is the absolute best. This does a disservice to the very audience that the media claim to serve."

"The fact is, only one team in any given sport will earn the distinction of being the best," Wilborough said. "Nevertheless, local news outlets go on asserting that an area team is number one, often against all logic. When a local team is performing poorly, journalists will often slant coverage to imply that the failure is circumstantial or temporary. They even go so far as to make totally indefensible claims such as 'We'll get 'em next year.'"

According to the report, the bias can be found everywhere from New York and Chicago to smaller media markets like Green Bay, WI and South Bend, IN.

"The bias is everywhere, but the New York and Boston media's coverage of this year's American League playoffs is a classic example," FAIR investigator Clark Hudson said. "And it all starts, as bad journalism so often does, with editorializing through biased word choice."

Hudson said that in both the *New York Post* and *The Boston Globe*,

> ## "Photos almost always featured the home team, usually in a moment of victory," Wilborough said. "When the players and coaches of the opposing team were discussed, it was usually in the context of how they were 'destroyed' or 'stomped.'"

home-team batters were referred to as "sluggers," pitchers as "hurlers," and managers as "field generals."

"Hell, if I were the Boston Red Sox, I'd sue the *New York Post* for slander," Hudson said.

Several reporters agreed that a problem exists, but disagreed about both its nature and its severity.

"In my opinion, the most insidious aspect of unbalanced sports coverage is the bandwagon effect," sports journalist Lori Nickel said. "For example, Chicago news outlets support [coach] Dick Jauron blindly as long as the Bears are winning. But only one team can win the championship every year, so eventually, WGN and the *Sun-Times* start screaming for the firing of the entire coaching staff. How is that fair?"

"I wholeheartedly agree that standards in the business are slipping," said ESPN's Jeremy Schaap, son of late sports-writing legend Dick Schaap. "I'd like to see a return to the respect and even-handedness not seen since the days of that great man and exemplary American, Howard Cosell."

Wilborough said the problem may be larger than many realize.

"Let's face it, sports news is the only news most people read," Wilborough said. "That's reason enough to clean it up. Otherwise, the media may start seeing bias and sensationalism as a formula for success. I don't think anyone wants to live in a country where that happens." ∅

five came with dates. The only two unattached females were Scobel and her friend, whom Elsing identified as "Kate or Kim or something."

"I guess the Kim girl had worked with Warren once, but she didn't know anyone else at the party, so she talked Theresa into coming with her," Elsing said. "To be honest, I would've been just as likely to hit on Kim, but she kept going outside to smoke or plug the meter or something."

Added Elsing: "Look, it was either talk to Theresa or hang out on the sofa and eat Baked Tostitos with Warren's weird friend Phillip [Barger]."

Elsing said his conversation with Scobel was "civil," but also punctuated

> ## "I asked her why she was interested in Latin American stuff," Elsing said. "She seemed really smart. I would've been totally intimidated by her, if she'd been gorgeous."

by awkward silences and nervous laughter.

"Halfway through my conversation with Theresa, my urge to hit on her ebbed a little," Elsing said. "But I went on anyway. Force of habit, I guess."

During their conversation, Elsing learned that Scobel earned her undergraduate major in Latin American studies at the University of Delaware, can speak fluent Spanish and Portuguese, recently returned from a three-week Mayan art and culture study-seminar in the Yucatan Peninsula, and has nothing whatsoever in common with him.

"I asked her why she was interested in Latin American stuff," Elsing said. "I can't exactly remember what she said—something about being part Latin. She seemed really smart. I would've been totally intimidated by her, if she'd been gorgeous."

About 20 minutes into the halting

Above: Elsing and Scobel share one more drink before calling it a night.

exchange, Elsing embarked on a tentative flirt, and told Scobel that the gray top she was wearing was "nice."

"She thanked me and told me that my eyes were very intense," Elsing said. "That was kind of cool. But I was also like, whoa, that was a pretty big leap she made—from clothes to body parts. It's not like I pointed out a physical feature of hers. Hopefully, I haven't released the floodgates here."

In spite of the pair's lack of chemistry, Elsing requested Scobel's phone number and suggested that they meet for coffee some time in the coming weeks.

"I thought about inviting her to go to Club 505 after the party, but I figured that would be too forward, like I was trying to liquor her up," Elsing said. "Besides, I was getting tired. Really, I just wanted to get home."

Elsing said he gave Scobel credit for

> ## As for Scobel, she said she is ambivalent about receiving a phone call from Elsing.

inspiring him to remain at the party longer than he would have otherwise.

"I still can't decide whether I'll call her," Elsing said. "Maybe I should give her a chance. She seemed all right. Not overtly weird. She was nice, I guess. I don't know. We'll see. It might be fun. Or not. Maybe."

Party host Croft said he saw Elsing and Scobel talking.

"I noticed Peter hanging out with Kaitlin's friend Theresa at the party," Croft said. "It sorta looked like maybe they were getting along. That'd be cool if they hooked up. She wasn't really my type—a little too plain. But she seemed cool enough, I guess."

As for Scobel, she said she is ambivalent about receiving a phone call from Elsing.

"Peter was nice, but I wish I hadn't given him my number," he said. "I just did it because…I don't know. I honestly didn't mean to send him mixed signals. I just made that remark about his eyes to get him to relax a little." ∅

MINISTER from page 31

Above: The Ministry of Rubble and Urban Development, located in a bustling rubble district in Ramallah.

Ghosts Of Situations Past

**A Room Of Jean's Own
By Jean Teasdale**

If you Jeanketeers think I sit on a chaise lounge eating bonbons all day, you'll be surprised to learn that I applied for, and got, a part-time job at Kinko's. See, I thought working at Kinko's would be easy. The only other time I'd been there, to photocopy a disintegrating old column by Ann Landers (R.I.P.), it was late at night, and the clerk on duty was reading a skateboarding magazine. Boy, was I in for a rude awakening! That place gets swamped!

The customers can be really picky, too. Even though I was clearly wearing a "trainee" name tag on my apron, they still yelled at me about botched

> **One lady, a fast-track executive type, got impatient with me, because I couldn't figure out why one of the computers wouldn't read her disk. When I suggested that she keep a copy of her data in longhand on ruled paper, she asked to see my supervisor, Cory.**

wonderful new schools, courthouses, banks, and monuments. He will then truck away the remains of those buildings and monuments when they're reduced to gravel and dust."

Arafat said Al-Katif has great plans

> **"We have chosen a man who not only accepts the reality of continued rubble creation for the foreseeable future, but also embraces it,"
> Arafat said.**

for "the West Bank's most abundant resource."

"We have chosen a man who not only accepts the reality of continued rubble creation for the foreseeable future, but also embraces it," Arafat said. "I see the Palestinian people forever rich in rubble. We must utilize our extensive rubble resources to re-build and re-rebuild Palestine."

Al-Katif took the podium and briefly outlined his plans for the region.

"The ministry will provide universal access to potable water, electric and sewage-treatment facilities, and adequate housing," Al-Katif said. "We will also move many huge piles of brick, garbage, dirt, and broken glass."

Al-Katif then took a moment to

memorialize Amir Al-Lozari, the former RUD Minister. Al-Lozari was killed in what Israeli occupation forces characterized as an "accidental burst of gunfire," while surveying a new rubble development on the former site of the 1,400-year-old Abu Al-Sharim library.

"Amir was more than a boss to me—he was a friend," Al-Katif said. "He was a visionary, an important contributor to rubble theory, and a brilliant pragmatist when it came to the urban development of Palestinian lands. We will miss Amir, but we will remember him by continuing the great work he started."

Al-Katif responded to a reporter who suggested that his plan focused more on rubble than on urban development.

"These are two sides of the same coin," Al-Katif said. "Today's development is tomorrow's pile of rubble, and today's pile of rubble is tomorrow's makeshift shelter for a displaced family. It is all part of the same cycle."

Some have expressed reservations about Al-Katif's appointment, citing his early career as a building owner and landlord as a possible conflict of interest.

"Hassan Al-Katif owns, or has a financial interest in, more than 20 separate piles of rubble," said community organizer Saadiqa Muhammad. "Can we expect him to make impartial judgments about zoning and public-rubble works, given that he has a personal stake in rubble sites all over the region?"

Al-Katif insisted that his interests lie with the people.

"For too long, rubble has been viewed as the sole property of the government," Al-Katif said. "RUD needs to make affordable rubble available to all, and to provide the economic incentive for personal and private development of Palestine's many massive piles of rocks and debris. The opportunity is there, if someone takes the initiative and stacks the rubble neatly."

One of Al-Katif's first initiatives will be aimed at a segment of the population often ignored by RUD: the youth.

"In spite of tough economic times, more and more young people are becoming rubble-owners. Take, for example, 16-year-old Dinuk Wijurnai, who recently returned to his neigh-

> **"Hassan Al-Katif owns, or has a financial interest in, more than 20 separate piles of rubble," said community organizer Saadiqa Muhammad.**

borhood and found himself sole owner of the pile of rubble that was once his family home," Al-Katif said. "The future of this country is in the hands, and under the feet, of children like Dinuk." ∅

orders that I had nothing to do with, and forced me to get down on my hands and knees to clear paper jams from the copiers. When you're a generously proportioned gal like me, that ain't no walk in the park! One lady, a fast-track executive type, got impatient with me, because I couldn't figure out why one of the computers wouldn't read her disk. When I suggested that she keep a copy of her data in longhand on ruled paper, she asked to see my supervisor, Cory. The sourpuss told Cory that he should keep me away from the customers, because I obviously didn't know what I was doing. (What can I say? I can barely tell a PC from a teepee.)

That lady brings to mind something that has always irked me: women who are unsympathetic to other

see TEASDALE page 36

women. We gals should stick together, like in *Sex And The City*, instead of back-stabbing each other. (We'd be ruling the world if we'd come around to this—think about it, ladies!)

So, back to Kinko's. After two weeks of hard labor, I decided that I deserved to call in sick. (I was starting to

---

Driving along in high spirits, I felt an uncomfortable twinge as I neared the exit to the strip mall that used to house the Fashion Bug where I once worked.

---

have paper-jam nightmares!) After getting off the phone with Cory, I noticed that I'd forgotten to bring my hanging ivy plant in from the balcony, so I opened the sliding-glass door and walked outside. The ivy was shriveled from the cold, but I found the crisp air invigorating. Autumn had truly arrived! I had a brainstorm: Instead of eating a box of SnackWells and watching *Wayne Brady*, I could commune with nature by taking a drive around town. I threw on my autumn, leaf-patterned sweatshirt and headed out the door.

Driving along in high spirits, I felt an uncomfortable twinge as I neared the exit to the strip mall that used to house the Fashion Bug where I once worked. I hadn't been to the area since I was laid off more than a year ago, so I figured it was high time I confronted some old ghosts.

Pulling into the strip mall's nearly empty parking lot, I saw that Fashion Bug's space had been divided into a Western Union office and a comic-book store. I'm no comic-book fan (puh-leeze!), but I noticed some toys in the window of the store, and being a kid at heart, I couldn't resist taking a peek. Unfortunately, all they had was a bunch of ugly action figures of Superman and Batman and some other characters I didn't recognize. They were practically the only "action" in the store, so, feeling chatty, I went up to the clerk. Save for his long hair and pierced eyebrow, he was the spitting image of hubby Rick!

"Slow day, huh?" I said with a chuckle. "It was like this when I worked at the old Fashion Bug. I guess all the business is over at the real mall." "I don't care," he replied. Boy, he had Rick's surliness, too! I pressed on and asked if he carried the *Cathy* dolls. "Cathy? Cathy who?" he asked. I had to smile: The generation gap is alive and well! I said, "This can't be much of a comic-book shop if there are no *Cathy* dolls." Ha! *Zing!* See, we old fogies can be just as smart-alecky as the

young whippersnappers!

I made my triumphant exit and walked down the familiar, cracked sidewalk flanking the stores. I peered into the Western Union office, which was all done up in fake-wood paneling. The H & R Block was still going strong, but the frame shop had a "going out of business" sign in its window. That left the Hot Sam. The lovely smell of baking pretzels lured me in, just as it had in the days of yesteryear, but the two cheery workers who always giggled when I came in on my break were no longer working there.

Even though I was proud of myself for confronting my strip-mall demons, I was happy to go. I headed to the park, hoping that the blazing colors of fall would rejuvenate me. When I got there, I was stunned to discover that most of the trees had been cut down or severely pruned! Then, I remembered having heard on the news that blight had forced the town to chainsaw a bunch of the park's trees. As I sat at the picnic table in the near-treeless field and ate my pretzel and drank my Mr. Pibb, I almost wished that I had gone to work. Are these my only options in life? Working at a job I hate or sitting around with nothing to do? The ice in my Mr. Pibb was making me shiver, so I decided to leave.

I noticed a Ryder truck parked in my apartment building's driveway when I steered in. As I walked up the path to my building, I ran into Sean, who was

---

Are these my only options in life? Working at a job I hate or sitting around with nothing to do? The ice in my Mr. Pibb was making me shiver, so I decided to leave.

---

carrying a set of lamps to the truck. Jeanketeers might remember Sean as the college student who wrote a Jean "fanzine" called *Blossom Meadows*. I didn't get a lot of it, but what I did understand was pretty unflattering, especially the essay called "The Tragedy Of Jean Teasdale." I hadn't spoken to him much since I read that. When Sean saw me, he looked like a deer caught in the headlights. We stood there for a few seconds without saying anything. Finally, I broke the silence and said, "Howdy, stranger."

"Hey, Jean," Sean said. "I've been meaning to talk to you for a while, but you're never around." (Ha!) He told me that he was moving to Chicago to finish school. (Apparently, Concordia College wasn't good enough for him!)

"I have to admit, I'm going to miss

HOROSCOPES

Your Horoscope

By Lloyd Schumner Sr.
Retired Machinist and
A.A.P.B.-Certified Astrologer

Aries: (March 21–April 19)
You fail to understand the primordial mystery of the funk: You can still have it no matter how many times you give it up.

Taurus: (April 20–May 20)
You'll win the lottery, but it's not one of those cool lotteries that decides who lives and who dies.

Gemini: (May 21–June 21)
Your theory that everyone looks good in pantsuits should probably be amended to include recent data obtained by your mirror.

Cancer: (June 22–July 22)
Your habit of falling back on arguments of constitutionality during every debate won't help decide whose turn it is to take the garbage out.

Leo: (July 23–Aug. 22)
It has been said that power is the ultimate aphrodisiac, but there are other reasons why Jenny is sleeping with her assistant manager and not you.

Virgo: (Aug. 23–Sept. 22)
You're aware that life isn't a nice, sweet fairy tale. That said, it's about time you get to the sex and drugs.

Libra: (Sept. 23–Oct. 23)
There are some vital, useful ideas in

Ayn Rand's *Atlas Shrugged*, but you shouldn't apply them to home decorating.

Scorpio: (Oct. 24–Nov. 21)
You're proud to have been cited by several important scientists, even if it was as an example of the potential "gray goo" problems in nanotechnology.

Sagittarius: (Nov. 22–Dec. 21)
Everyone has potentially fatal flaws, but yours involve a love of soldiers' wives, an insatiable thirst for whiskey, and the seven weak points in your left ventricle.

Capricorn: (Dec. 22–Jan. 19)
It's not too late for you to learn new tricks in the bedroom, but it's too sad and disgusting to even think about.

Aquarius: (Jan. 20–Feb. 18)
All things considered, you have a hard time believing that on-base percentage alone could be the answer to success in baseball.

Pisces: (Feb. 19–March 20)
There's no law that tells people whom they can and can't love in this world, but you're doing everything in your power to convince legislators to change that.

---

this town a little," he said. Then his eyes widened, and he told me to follow him back to his apartment. Once inside, he went over to an open box by the living-room door and pulled out an old rotary-dial princess phone, colored pink.

"I read in your column that you wanted one as a kid but never got it," Sean said. "I found this at a garage sale. It's a real Bell model, too, not a cheap knockoff. It still works. Or you can put it next to Miss Beasley in your curio cabinet."

I murmured my thanks. I didn't know what to say. This was the most thoughtful gift I'd ever gotten. I wished him luck with moving and started up the steps to my apartment, but then something occurred to me. I turned around and asked Sean if this incident would be in his 'zine. He looked startled. "Uh, would you prefer that it not be?" he asked. I said yes, I'd prefer that. I said that, in this case, I'd like to have the last word. "Yeah, sure," he said. I don't think he understood why I asked him that. Maybe he does now. I think I'll quit Kinko's tomorrow. ∅

WORKING MAN from page 33

many aspects of his job, his relationship with Eagle Cooling is almost certainly long-term. His pride, as well as his recent purchase of a 2004 Dodge Dakota financed with a six-year loan,

---

"People should work hard and shut up," Festge said.

---

virtually guarantee his continued submissive compliance.

"I know there are more interesting, higher-paying careers, but we can't always do what we like, now, can we?" Festge said. "Nor should we. There's too much selfishness out there. People should work hard and shut up. That's how the world works. I'm the real deal. And at the end of a long, horrible day of backbreaking manual labor, that makes me feel pretty good."

Festge added that after punching out on Friday, he plans to get shitfaced. ∅

the ONION®

VOLUME 39 ISSUE 47   AMERICA'S FINEST NEWS SOURCE™   4–10 DECEMBER 2003

New York's Finest Protect New York's Richest

see LOCAL page 3C

Novelty Alarm Clock Not So Funny At 7 a.m.

see ENTERTAINMENT page 14E

Perverted Ninja Enjoys Being Seen

see PEOPLE page 10F

Wallet Chain Retired

see LOCAL page 6C

STATshot

A look at the numbers that shape your world.

What Are We Looking Up In The Encyclopedia?

- 25% Pamela Anderson
- 14% Nazi stuff
- 19% Plagiarism
- 12% Rap music
- 17% Cool transparent overlays of human body
- 13% Penguins, but it doesn't say how they do it

THE ONION • $2.00 US • $3.00 CAN

0 74470 94595 6

New Alternate-Reality Series Puts 12 Strangers On Island Where South Won Civil War

ECONOMY

Bush Re-Election Campaign Creates Thousands Of New Jobs

Above: Newly employed workers at a Bush campaign office in Chicago.

WASHINGTON, DC—Since it began in May, the Bush 2004 re-election campaign has been responsible for creating thousands of new jobs, officials announced Monday.

"The Bush-Cheney campaign is giving a much-needed boost to the troubled economy," said Ken Mehlman, Bush's campaign manager. "Every penny we receive is immediately pumped back into the economy, and we've already created thousands of jobs for out-of-work speechwriters, graphic designers, and door-to-door canvassers."

Though Bush has yet to formally announce his candidacy, his campaign war chest surpassed the $100 million mark on Nov. 13. With 11 months remaining before the election, the Bush campaign is well on its way to its goal of raising a record-breaking $170 million.

see CAMPAIGN page 40

LOS ANGELES—CBS executives announced Monday that they have begun filming *Antebellum Island*, a new "alternate reality" series in which 12 strangers compete for $1 million while isolated on an island still under Confederate rule.

"Set to air in the spring of 2004, *Antebellum Island* gives us the unique opportunity to play with both social dynamics and recorded history," CBS

Chairman Leslie Moonves said. "The contestants on *Antebellum Island* will spend 60 days braving the elements, each other, and the unfamiliar customs and practices of a 21st-century Confederate States of America—all for a chance to win a cool million."

Added Moonves: "That's one million in *Union* dollars, of course!"

Moonves said contestants will be isolated on a sun-drenched tropical island, where they will participate in competitions designed to emphasize teamwork and interpersonal friction in the rigidly stratified alternate-universe society.

The Big Four networks have seen dwindling Nielsen numbers for see SERIES page 41

Trial Separation Works Out Great

BIRMINGHAM, AL—Both Marlene and Paul Hirsh reported Monday that the first four weeks of their trial separation have gone surprisingly well.

"I thought I'd really miss Paul, but I've been staying with my friend Lisa [Hoffmann], and we've been having a total blast shopping and drinking margaritas," Marlene said. "It was really a big step to do this, but so far, the separation has been working out just great."

Marlene said the couple split up see SEPARATION page 40

Right: Marlene and Paul Hirsh somehow carry on during their fourth week apart.

THG And The NFL

A string of scandals has prompted the NFL to impose stricter testing standards for performance-enhancing drugs, especially the steroid THG. What do *you* think?

Jesse Scott
Painter

"Sports-wise, I don't have any experience with performance-enhancing drugs...only the spectation-enhancing kind."

Tammy Rinaldi
Programmer

"Huh. So, Bill Romanowski tested positive for high levels of THUG?"

Robert Neighbors
Statistician

"I'm glad drugs are out of the hands of radio hosts and into the hands of athletes, where they belong."

Patty Grubner
Convention Planner

"It's admirable that those athletes only use drugs that enhance performance. Today's kids could learn a lot from these role models."

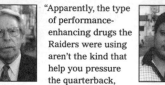

Albert Kinard
Systems Analyst

"Apparently, the type of performance-enhancing drugs the Raiders were using aren't the kind that help you pressure the quarterback, stop the run, or establish a goddamn passing game."

Joe Wendt
Interpreter

"THG? It's harmless. I use it to clean my coffee maker. I don't see why everyone's so RAHRRRRR!"

The Clean Air Act

More than a dozen state governments are protesting an Environmental Protection Agency measure to loosen Clean Air Act regulations. What changes does the measure include?

▶ Elimination of word "clean" from name of act

▶ Migratory waterfowl, including Canada geese, snow geese, mallards, canvasbacks, and blue-wing teal ducks, now categorized as Category III pollutants

▶ Factories not allowed to expel styrene, unless absolutely necessary

▶ Power plants have three-year grace period to switch over to cooler, crisper menthol smokestacks

▶ Polychlorinated biphenyls now part of a complete breakfast

▶ Fine for belching ton after ton of particulate sulfur into atmosphere reduced from $50 to $45

▶ Up to 15 percent of sky declared "absolutely off limits" to polluters

▶ Any translucent substance with a viscosity lower than that of Karo syrup now fits legal definition of air

the ONION®
America's Finest News Source.™

Herman Ulysses Zweibel
Founder

T. Herman Zweibel
Publisher Emeritus
J. Phineas Zweibel
Publisher
Maxwell Prescott Zweibel
Editor-In-Chief

No, Jesus Is *My* Personal Savior

By Duane Hurley

What? Now *you've* opened up your soul to Him and made a home for the Lord in your heart, too? Give me a break, Matt. You're just saying that because I told you I'd been born again into new life in the love and grace of our Lord, the Redeemer, Christ Jesus. Let's get one thing clear: Jesus is *my* personal savior, not yours. I don't want you horning in on my eternal-salvation action.

Get your own Redeemer, Matt. I have a one-on-one, personal relationship with Jesus, and I don't remember inviting you in on it. Yes, I know, Jesus said the apostles should spread the good news of His death and resurrection, and his followers should "go forth and do likewise." *Hello*, I'm the one who told *you* that, remember? But just because I happen to have proselytized unto you on His behalf, that doesn't mean I welcomed you into the fold or expected you to embrace the one true Messiah. I was only saying that stuff out of devotion to His teachings, not because I wanted you to get with God, too.

I was the one who found that little cartoon pamphlet on the ground. I was the one who looked into my soul and realized that I'd been living a lie spun by the great deceiver. *I* was the one who got down on my hands and knees, right there in the bus shelter, and accepted the Lord Jesus Christ into my heart—not you. *I* broke the bonds of sin and was reborn into a new and beautiful world of eternal life, man! And now, you want to get some of my eternal life after death for yourself.

You're lucky I've devoted myself to the worship of a forgiving and benevolent messianic figure, or else I'd seriously want to pop you one right now. Spare me the rhetoric about loving kindness, turning the other cheek, and "all are welcome at the table of the Lord." This isn't about that, Matt, and you know it. This is about me finding something really great, and then you swooping in from outside to take my cool new personal Savior and claim Him for yourself.

Remember when I got into Linkin Park? That's right, I saw the video for "One Step Closer" on MTV. You said they were a one-hit wonder, but I stood behind them. Then you bought *Hybrid Theory* and started acting like you'd been a big fan all along.

Or what about Owen Wilson? I was all into him after *Bottle Rocket*. I said he was a real talent with the potential to be a big star. Then *Shanghai Noon* comes out, and there's Matt, jumping on the Owen Wilson bandwagon, waving the Owen Wilson flag!

And don't give me that "Judge not lest ye be judged" crap. Jesus may be an all-compassionate avatar of God's divine forgiveness, but just because I've chosen Him as my personal Savior, that doesn't mean I'm obliged to let you walk all over me. I don't need you coming in here with your "Jesus accepts all into His all-forgiving bosom, even the sinners, tax collectors,

> **Jesus may be an all-compassionate avatar of God's divine forgiveness, but just because I've chosen Him as my personal Savior, that doesn't mean I'm obliged to let you walk all over me.**

and whores, so why not old Matt?" crap. Don't start going off on *me* about Christ's repudiations of the exclusionary doctrines of the Pharisees, okay? If it weren't for me, you wouldn't even know the word "Pharisee."

No, Matt, because you don't come up with your own ideas. You just latch on to stuff that other people already like and leech off them like a parasite. Man, if it weren't for that "love your enemies as yourself" doctrine and the whole bit about fellowship and stewardship of God's Kingdom on Earth, I'd be just about through with you.

Okay, fine. Jesus is *your* personal savior. Congratulations! Matt's found eternal bliss in the afterlife, everybody! He's a big man! Go ahead—enjoy worshipping your newfound Messiah all you want. I'm moving on. From now on, Jesus is no longer my own personal Savior. You can have Him all to yourself. I'm leaving behind selflessness and forgiveness and individual sacrifice for the greater good, and I'm finding something else to center my universe on.

From now on, I'm devoting myself, heart and soul, to cool old sports cars. And I don't want to see you in six months talking about how awesome the '63 Corvette is, either. Collectible '60s sports cars are for me only. Got it? Good. Now, go and enjoy your transubstantiation of bread and wine into the body and blood of the Lord in the holy sacrament of Communion and leave me alone.

What's that? Oh, I'm being an asshole about it, am I? Thou sayest, motherfucker. *Thou sayest.* ∅

College Freshman Cycles Rapidly Through Identities

LAWRENCE, KS—Since starting college at the University of Kansas in the fall, freshman Kirk Vanderkamp has been cycling through personal identities at a breakneck pace, Hamilton Hall sources reported Monday.

"It's really unnerving to watch," said

> Vanderkamp's peers said the accelerated pace of his process of self-discovery is alarming. Vanderkamp has aligned himself with no fewer than nine social groups, and has adopted a new wardrobe and a distinct set of speech patterns to accompany each identity.

Eric Yusef, resident assistant on the 6-West wing where Vanderkamp lives. "You never know what he's going to be wearing when he steps out of that dorm room. Since September, I've seen him in everything from head-to-toe FUBU sweats and a chain to a tie-

dyed shirt and a fringed leather jacket."

While students tend to experiment with various identities during their college years, Vanderkamp's peers said the accelerated pace of his process of self-discovery is alarming. Since the beginning of the fall term, Vanderkamp has aligned himself with no fewer than nine social groups, and has adopted a new wardrobe and a distinct set of speech patterns to accompany each identity.

Those close to Vanderkamp said he started his freshman year in typical fashion: He spent his time binge-drinking, making out with girls, and attending parties at fraternities. According to Yusef, after only two weeks as a "frat-guy wannabe," Vanderkamp slipped into the second of his many identities.

"Almost right away, Kirk met one of the stoners on second floor," Yusef said. "Within 24 hours, he went from the average, squared-away frat dude to the frat dude who smokes pot and has shaggy hair. For a while, he was sorta straddling the line."

Added Yusef: "But when he started wearing those round, John Lennon glasses, you could tell the shift was complete."

Throughout the rest of September, Vanderkamp cycled through a series of variations on the stoner persona.

"I almost feel bad for introducing him to weed," said Tim Hiller, Vanderkamp's friend. "After meeting my

Above: Vanderkamp on Oct. 23, three days before he discovered Jay-Z.

friend Sky, Kirk started talking about dropping out of school and joining a Buddhist monastery. Of course, a couple days later, he also said he was going to learn to play bass and get a jam band together. He said the monks would be cool about it."

Added Hiller: "I stopped hanging out with him around then."

According to Hiller, Vanderkamp took another sharp turn in mid-October, when he turned into a "white hip-hop kid."

"I bumped into him, and he was nearly unrecognizable," Hiller said. "He was dressed in low-slung jeans and this shiny red jacket. I didn't know who it was until he said, 'Yo, Hills! Wussup?' He even had his hair in cornrows. He said he'd stopped hanging with us because we listened to 'that Grateful Dead shiznit.'"

Vanderkamp was soon spotted freestyling "off the top of [his] dome" and performing spoken-word pieces see FRESHMAN page 42

Alan Colmes Loses Argument With Nephew

NEW YORK—Alan Colmes, the liberal co-host of the Fox News debate program *Hannity & Colmes*, lost an argument to his nephew Bryan while babysitting the 8-year-old Monday. "I wanted to stay up late to watch television, but Uncle Alan said, 'There's already too much self-parenting in America,'" Bryan said. "So I started screaming, 'Mom lets me, Mom lets me,' real loud. He gave in after, like, 20 seconds." In the past two years, Bryan has won arguments with Colmes on the subjects of Pokémon cards, Crunch Berries cereal, and steel tariffs.

Small Town Honors Once-Ostracized Artist

ANSLEY, NE—Nearly 450 of Ansley's 590 residents gathered in the town square Monday morning to dedicate a statue of the late sculptor

Robert Kett, who was born in the town in 1946 and generally either ignored or reviled during the 24 years he lived there. "Although no one took any notice of his art while he lived here, Mr. Kett has touched us all through his national fame," said Ansley mayor Paul Hollub, who went to high school with Kett and frequently referred to him as "that Kett faggot." "Though he was the object of our derision for many years, Robert is truly Ansley's favorite son." Examples of Kett's work, on display at the Guggenheim, will be reproduced and sold in postcard form at the ice-cream shop behind which he was once beaten up.

Senate Votes 64-36, Not Sure On What

WASHINGTON, DC—The U.S. Senate voted 64-38 in favor of S. 546 Monday, despite the lack of any awareness of the bill's contents. "Wait a minute—S. 546?" asked Sen. Kent Conrad (D-

ND), hurriedly shuffling through a stack of papers after hearing of the bill's passage. "I tend to just vote with Maria Cantwell [(D-WA)], but apparently, she just voted with Thomas Carper [(D-DE)]. Does anybody know what's in S. 546?! Oh, geez." Conrad said he isn't certain, but that he might remember someone mentioning something about the Bend Pine Nursery Land Conveyance Act.

Rookie Trucker Always On CB To Mother

LUBBOCK, TX—Two weeks into his new job driving an 18-wheeler for the Harper Red Line, trucker Billy Ray Coogan, 23, still talks frequently with his mother on his CB radio. "Breaker 1-9, Mother Hen, this here's Red Rooster, come on," said an obviously nervous Coogan. "Are you sand-bagging, Mother Hen? 'Cause the boss man's got me hauling a dead-head to Abilene, and I'm a little nervous. I...I could really use

some company, 10-4." Coogan went on to say that if his mother would just say the word, he'd do a flip-flop and put the hammer down to be back home in the short-short, in time for dinner.

Man Born To Party Dies Partying

DETROIT—Loading-dock worker Randy Scharf, 25, who often described himself as "born to party," died while partying, his aggrieved friends announced Monday. "Randy was always up for a good time," said friend Steven "Beevo" Bollinger, who threw the house party Saturday night that proved to be Scharf's last. "He was the only guy I know who could drink a quart and a half of rum and still be ready for a night of barhopping." Sharf, who fell to his death while scaling the wall above a sixth-floor balcony, is survived by his loving parents, Mark and Anne, and his brother, Tony "Barf" Scharf. ∅

"While other segments of the economy are undergoing hiring freezes, the Bush-Cheney campaign is experiencing rapid growth," Mehlman said. "We've hired everything from computer technicians to manage the cam-

> "With the U.S. unemployment rate hovering around 6 percent, this influx of employment capital represents no small example of the success of the Republican Party's economic policy," Mehlman added. "And we're just gearing up. Our campaign projects consistent, quarter-by-quarter expansion for the next 11 months."

paign's database of registered Republicans to an entire team of producers to create our television ads. George W. Bush is putting Americans back to work."

"With the U.S. unemployment rate hovering around 6 percent, this influx of employment capital represents no small example of the success of the Republican Party's economic policy," Mehlman added. "And we're just gearing up. Our campaign projects consistent, quarter-by-quarter expansion for the next 11 months."

Besides high-tech and skilled positions, the campaign has created thousands of jobs in the service sector.

Above: A factory worker in Macon, GA, works for the Bush re-election campaign.

"Walk through our massive national campaign headquarters, and you'll see how many workers it takes just to empty the garbage cans," Mehlman said. "Imagine all the people it takes to cater a fundraising dinner, then multiply that number by all the restaurants, hotels, and convention centers that the president will stop at along the campaign trail. Those red, white, and blue posters don't hang themselves, you know."

The campaign has created manufacturing jobs, as well.

"Blue-collar laborers all across the country are rolling out billions of posters and T-shirts," Mehlman said. "We just placed an order for 6,000 boxes of 'Viva Bush' buttons. The people working in that factory in Georgia will tell you what Bush can do for the economy."

Mehlman said the Bush campaign's positive effect on the economy far outpaces that of the leading Democratic candidates.

"The Democrats simply can't say they're doing as much for the economy as we are," Mehlman said. "Howard Dean is out there collecting $50 donations on the Internet. As of Sept. 30, his campaign had a mere $25.4 million. How many workers can that paltry sum sustain?"

In contrast, Mehlman cited a recent Republican fundraiser held at the private residence of the chairman of Watermark Communities Inc., a company that builds golf retirement communities.

"The Florida fundraiser employed hundreds of people, from the swing-choir members to the waiters who served the Angus beef and potatoes," Mehlman said. "That dinner pulled in $1.7 million—which will be used to throw more fundraisers, thereby creating even more jobs."

Bush called his fundraising success "a positive indicator for the nation's struggling economy."

"This job-creating initiative is good for my re-election campaign and good for Americans," Bush said. "With the generosity of Pioneer-level donors like William McGuire, chairman of United Health Care Group, and Warren Staley, CEO of the Cargill agribusiness company, this country will be back on its feet in no time. Bush-Cheney '04 is turning money into jobs."

Bush said that, although his administration is "narrowing in on economic recovery in America," more work is needed.

"We will continue to do our part up until Nov. 2, 2004," Bush said. "However, we can't do it without you. Call the Republican campaign office near you to find out how you can help." ∅

temporarily on Nov. 2, after almost a year of mutual dissatisfaction with the marriage.

"Paul and I would argue, but the real problem was that we were both unhappy," Marlene said. "After a long talk, we decided that living apart for a couple of months would help us get our heads in the right place, and then we could re-commit to our marriage. I think it must be working, because our problems have hardly been bothering me at all lately."

Marlene and Paul rarely spent even a weekend away from each other after they were married in September 1999. However, both have reportedly made the most of the post-separation "me time."

"I feel great," Paul said. "I've been having a ball hanging out with the guys, working on my car, and just doing whatever the hell I want. And I can't remember when I've gotten this much exercise. I've even started playing basketball with the guys from work. I'm really going to miss that when Marlene and I get back together."

Marlene has been enjoying the relationship-strengthening period, as well.

"I've been taking a Pilates class, and Lisa and I have gone to a ton of movies," Marlene said. "All of a sudden, there's so much more to do than read in bed while Paul plays online Scrabble."

Both Paul and Marlene have successfully used the trial separation to reflect on the shortcomings of the marriage.

"I definitely have decided that, when we get back together, I need to spend more time by myself," Marlene said. "I never realized how much I'd let Paul's interests—or lack thereof—take over. Now, I can go anywhere I want without Paul grilling me. I go to the park just to hang out, and I'm joining a community theater group with my friend Neil. There's so much I want to explore before we get our marriage back on track."

Marlene and Paul both said the trial

> Marlene and Paul both said the trial separation has been "liberating."

separation has been "liberating," and both expressed confidence that it will help them resolve their marital problems.

"We keep meaning to get together for lunch and talk about everything, but the date has been pushed back a few times," Paul said. "We call each other a couple times a week to see how things are going, if we're not too busy. But there's no way that the separation will work if we don't give each other a lot of space. Part of marriage is respecting your loved one's personal time."

"In fact, maybe giving each other even more space would help our marriage even more," Paul added. "I'm thinking of getting a leave of absence from work to go visit my brother in Alaska for a few months."

Marlene and Paul agreed that the trial separation is incomplete, and that more time apart is needed in order to really strengthen the marriage.

"Marlene is great, but her mood swings are a real downer," Paul said. "It's nice to know that I can leave the cap off the toothpaste or forget a few dirty dishes in the sink without someone tearing my head off. I'm certainly see SEPARATION page 41

SERIES from page 37

variations on reality shows, a trend CBS hopes to reverse with a new genre of programs that "go beyond reality."

"When we were brainstorming this show, we knew we wanted an eclectic cast and an exotic locale," said Matt Davies, executive producer of *Antebellum Island.* "But none of the ideas were clicking as 'reality plus totally

---

Executives were reluctant to reveal the themes for Antebellum's weekly competitions, but said contests might include skeet shooting, quilting bees, formal-dress cotillions, and working at a textile factory.

---

new'—until someone said, 'Hey, no one's done a show set in an America where the Union army lost, and Jefferson Davis replaced Lincoln as president.' We knew we had a winner."

Davies said CBS also seriously considered another alternate-reality series called *The Man In The High Castle In The Outback*, in which 12 women would compete for the love of a Jewish man hiding in Australia under an assumed name because the Allies lost WWII to Nazi Germany. Ultimately, executives deemed the scenario less likely to engage the average American viewer than the post-Civil-War alternate reality.

Scouts chose a tropical location after they failed to find an island in the Mississippi River with enough land mass to sustain the manufacturing-based economy of a country that did not begin its transition from an agricultural society to a modern industrial society until the early 1900s.

Above: Three *Antebellum Island* contestants in a scene from the show's premiere episode.

"It's a totally new and exciting location," Davies said. "Our 12 strangers must adapt to the altogether-unfamiliar territory of an island where the states and the people are guaranteed those rights not specifically delegated to the federal government!"

Contestant auditions for *Antebellum Island* were held in Washington, DC, and Richmond, VA. Interviewees were asked such questions as: "Do you consider yourself fun-loving and up for new challenges?" "Do you believe women should be given the vote?" and "Do you reckon Dred Scott shoulda been hung from the highest tree?"

"We have a good mix of people for our first cast—all colors and creeds," Davies said. "On this show, as you might imagine, diversity is especially

crucial. We plan to break the participants into two 'families,' the Masons and the Dixons."

"In casting the show, we looked for people who displayed adaptability, good judgment, and impeccable hospitality," Davies said. "But we wanted to let the contestants' personalities shape the show. We didn't just look to fill the typical slots: plantation owner, houseboy, carpetbagger, and Uncle Tom."

Executives were reluctant to reveal the themes for *Antebellum*'s weekly competitions, but said contests might include skeet shooting, quilting bees, formal-dress cotillions, and working at a textile factory on the west side of the island for the entire show's duration with no chance at the $1 million prize.

Davies said the show's first episode

will feature an adventure-filled white-water-rafting trip, in which one team will attempt to make it to the "New Orleans Checkpoint," while the other will try to stop it from meeting up with the British ships in port and demanding asylum.

"We've thought a lot about how contestants should be kicked off the island," Davies said. "The voting thing has been done to death, and anyway, on our island, voting is a very touchy subject. Right now, we're toying with allowing cast members to just escape to the North. But it might be neat to choreograph some sort of mad uprising for the final episode. Whatever we do, you can bet it'll be exciting, tension-filled, and consistent with an America where slavery and states' rights survived long after the 1860s." ✍

SEPARATION from page 40

in no hurry to change that."

"I want to start a family someday, and Paul does, too—or at least he says he does," Marlene said. "Once you have kids, you don't have the time to go barhopping or take a weekend getaway to the Florida Keys. Paul and I need to get this stuff out of our systems if we're going to spend the rest of our lives raising children together."

Added Marlene: "Besides, things are going so well right now. Why cut the separation short?"

Marlene also said the trial separation has opened her eyes to Birmingham's dating scene and her own marketability.

"I thought that, as a divorced, 34-year-old woman, finding a date would be hard," she said. "Boy, was I wrong.

A few days after Paul and I split up, Lisa took me to this club, and three cute guys hit on me. I told the cutest one about my situation with Paul, and he gave me his number and told me to call him if things don't work out."

Dr. Oliver Hall, author of *Falling Apart, Staying Together*, said trial separations, once viewed with skepticism, can be effective in rebuilding troubled relationships.

"Married couples shouldn't be afraid of a separation," Hall said. "Time apart can provide spouses with the space they need to explore their true feelings. Another plus is that a separation can give you the taste of freedom you need to force you to get the hell out of a dead-end marriage. Really, it's a win-win situation." ✍

SQUID from page 31

amounts of blood. Passersby were amazed by the unusually large amounts of blood. Passersby were amazed by the unusually large amounts of blood. Passersby were amazed by the unusually large amounts of blood. Passersby were amazed by the unusually large amounts of blood. Passersby were amazed by the unusually large amounts of blood. Passersby were amazed by the unusually large amounts of blood. Passersby were amazed by the unusually large amounts of blood. Passersby were amazed by the unusually large amounts of blood. Passersby were amazed by the unusually large amounts of blood. Passersby were amazed by the unusually large amounts of blood. Passersby were amazed by the unusually large amounts of blood. Passersby were amazed by the unusually large amounts of blood. Passersby were amazed by the unusually large

amounts of blood. Passersby were amazed by the unusually large amounts of blood. Passersby were

---

In my day we didn't have fancy colors in our tattoos.

---

amazed by the unusually large amounts of blood. Passersby were amazed by the unusually large amounts of blood. Passersby were amazed by the unusually large amounts of blood. Passersby were

see SQUID page 73

I Need To Have A Sexy Back Now, Too?

By Gina Loman

Goddamn it. Just when I thought I was finally getting caught up.

For years, I've worked to keep my weight down and maintain a sexy, flat stomach. I learned to watch my caloric intake to keep a thin, sexy physique. I found out that I had to exercise in order to form sexy, sculpted thighs and sexy, firm buttocks. Then, I read about yoga, which helps women develop long, strong, sexy necks.

While I didn't always keep up, I felt I had a good understanding of what was required. Well, apparently not, because I just found out that I need to have a sexy back now, too.

I was at the store picking up some garbage bags, and there it was by the checkout, on the cover of Self: "10 Tips For A Sexy Back." That's right: a sexy back.

I know all about the standard requirements for sexiness just from walking down the drugstore aisle: a thick mane of sexy hair, long, sexy fingernails, and dramatic, sexy eyes. I learned what one needs for a sexy smile—full, pouty lips and electric-white teeth. I found out about the horrors of wrinkles and how they drain the sexiness out of a woman's face.

Now, there's the back. The back?! Are you seriously telling me that there's a whole area of my body that I've been neglecting for my entire life?

I guess I'd better get to work, because being sexy is important. It's not only about attracting men. See, I've read that sexiness inspires self-confidence. If I look good, I feel good, so I try to keep up on what it takes to be sexy. I started to lift weights a few years ago, and I wouldn't have sexy, muscular abs if I hadn't. I've taken quizzes to see if I have a sexy attitude. (I scored 36 sexy points out of 50!) But was all that good enough? Far fucking from it.

Because besides sexy legs, buttocks, tummy, waist, and arms, there's the back to consider now. Luckily, Self provided an entire set of exercises to strengthen and sexify the important area between the base of my neck and my waist. I wanted to get a jump on holiday shopping, but there's no time for that now. I'll be too busy spending this weekend targeting my rhomboid and erector spinae muscles.

And to think I had no idea. Lately, I've been calculating my Body Mass Index and my target caloric intake. I've been careful to consume more antioxidants, which I found out are es-sential for an all-around sexy glow. Then last month, after seeing a pro-tein-bar package with the phrase "Only 2 Grams Of Net Carbs!" I went on the Internet to research what net carbs are, and why I should limit my intake of carbs to begin with.

You think you have an idea of what needs to be done, and then some mag-azine rips the rug out from under you. This has happened in the past. I was-n't even aware that I had to have sexy feet, and then I saw a segment on *Regis And Kelly* about preparing my toes for open-toe shoe season.

Same thing happened with my other body parts, from my elbows, which

> ## I know all about the standard requirements for sexiness just from walking down the drugstore aisle: a thick mane of sexy hair, long, sexy fingernails, and dramatic, sexy eyes.

need to be exfoliated to stimulate cell regeneration, to my eyebrows, which need to be plucked to barely percepti-ble lines and then filled in with a pen-cil. I've consumed, with great interest, articles about how to tend to my biki-ni area. I used the self-tanning spray recommended in an article about how sunbathing is making a comeback. I learned that dry hands are a real turn-off. I learned how disgusted men are when they see the veins in a woman's ankles. I confirmed some suspicions I had about noses and armpits.

Damn it—just when I thought I had a leg up on sexiness. I'll admit I never gave my back any consideration. I never saw it, so I assumed it was fine. I shouldn't have been so self-cen-tered. Now I know that others are looking at my back, and that they would like it to be toned and defined.

From now on, I'm going to stay ahead of the game. I noticed the back of my tongue has a whitish coating. That simply can't be sexy. My wrist bones don't seem to jut out sexily enough. Men might be repelled by the small hairs inside my ears. Perhaps I should look into having them profes-sionally waxed. And if there's some-thing that needs to be done to make my clavicles sexier, I should find out now, before I hit the holiday parties. ✐

Your Horoscope

By Lloyd Schumner Sr.
Retired Machinist and
A.A.P.B.-Certified Astrologer

Aries: (March 21–April 19)
You're thankful that the firefighters saved your life, but you don't see why their report had to note that you were "sitting around the house!!!" when the fire started.

Taurus: (April 20–May 20)
Buckle up: It's going to be one hell of a bumpy ride. The stars aren't speaking metaphorically here. Wear your seatbelt all week.

Gemini: (May 21–June 21)
We're each the star of our own per-sonal saga, which in your case is ac-tually more of a light-beer commer-cial.

Cancer: (June 22–July 22)
You'll be a hero for the shortest in-terval in human history when you push an old lady out of the path of a careening bus and into that of a run-away locomotive.

Leo: (July 23–Aug. 22)
The sad truth is that you only wear the ape suit to cover the burn scars that cover your twisted frame.

Virgo: (Aug. 23–Sept. 22)
If there's anything happening in your future next week, it doesn't seem important enough to write in the sky.

Libra: (Sept. 23–Oct. 23)
In retrospect, you should have won-dered why the creepy ventriloquist's dummy was always at the scene of the crime.

Scorpio: (Oct. 24–Nov. 21)
You'll achieve wealth and change your culture forever after coming up with a sitcom plot in which the evil twin is part of a set of triplets.

Sagittarius: (Nov. 22–Dec. 21)
You've once again dodged the an-noyance of jury duty, but good luck getting out of your obligation to act as judge and executioner.

Capricorn: (Dec. 22–Jan. 19)
You haven't carried out any of the reforms you promised you would, but you'll still be re-elected by a ma-jority of your girlfriends.

Aquarius: (Jan. 20–Feb. 18)
You'll get an incredible sense of per-sonal satisfaction from your new pet, which is why the shocked and disgusted Humane Society workers take it away.

Pisces: (Feb. 19–March 20)
If you never have to deal with angry, drunken Basque separatists who have stolen the Shroud Of Turin again, it'll be too soon.

FRESHMAN from page 39

at Java Java, a local coffee shop. By early November, Vanderkamp had shed the hip-hop persona and shifted from writing spoken-word poetry on napkins to spending hours scribbling his first novel in a leather-bound jour-nal.

Yusef said he assumed Vanderkamp's transition from "gangbanger to tor-tured artist" resulted from his exposure to the customers at Java Java.

"Luckily, I didn't even have to talk to Kirk the last time I saw him," Yusef said. "He was so involved in this worn-out copy of *On The Road* that he did-n't even notice me."

"I saw that, along with his blazer and scarf, he was wearing those John Lennon glasses again," Yusef added. "At least he's thrifty."

With a few weeks left in the fall se-mester, peers speculate that Van-derkamp will change personas at least once more. The top contenders for his next identity include sports en-thusiast, raver kid, and motivated ca-reerist.

"Those are all good guesses," Yusef said. "But you have to remember, we're coming up on Hanukkah. Some people don't know this, but Kirk's

> ## "Luckily, I didn't even have to talk to Kirk the last time I saw him," Yusef said. "He was so involved in this worn-out copy of *On The Road* that he didn't even notice me."

Jewish. My money says he's going to be one of those guys who gets serious about his Jewish heritage. He's totally going to start wearing a yarmulke and keeping kosher. Either that, or film nerd." ✐

Cast-Off Paris Hilton Skin Found In Upper West Side Park

see OUTDOORS page 11E

Only Two Segways In Town Collide

see LOCAL page 14B

Guns & Ammo Office Holiday Party Exactly What You'd Expect

see LOCAL page 4B

the ONION®

VOLUME 39 ISSUE 48   AMERICA'S FINEST NEWS SOURCE™   11–17 DECEMBER 2003

CEO's Marital Duties Outsourced To Mexican Groundskeeper

GROSSE POINTE, MI—As part of the ongoing trend toward replacing U.S. workers with foreign labor, the marital duties of United Carborundum CEO Howard Reinhardt have been outsourced to his Mexican groundskeeper, industry sources revealed Monday.

"It was time for a change," said Reinhardt's wife Melanie, who has been married to the CEO for 17 years and has conducted her sexual business almost exclusively with him since 1984. "While I was generally

see OUTSOURCED page 47

Right: Hardworking groundskeeper Jorge Escobedo and his employers, Howard and Melanie Reinhardt.

Clinton Googles Self

Above: Clinton browses the Internet in his Harlem office.

NEW YORK—Citing curiosity as his primary motive, Bill Clinton typed his own name into the popular search engine Google.com during a lull in his daily activities, the former president reported Monday.

"I had no idea I would get 2,790,000 results!" Clinton said while seated before the Apple PowerBook in his Harlem office. "Besides all the news articles, there were encyclopedia entries, links to Amazon for books about me, and tons of photos, too. I even came across some frame captures from those Rock The Vote shows I did back in 1992. I'm going to take a couple of those and make them my desktop picture, once I figure out how to tile them."

Although Clinton said he'd always assumed there was material about him on the Internet, his busy schedule prevented him from exploring it sooner.

"When I was president, people

see CLINTON page 47

Report: Poor People Pretty Much Fucked

WASHINGTON—According to the results of an intensive two-year study, Americans living below the poverty line are "pretty much fucked," Center for Social and Economic Research executive director Jameson Park announced Monday.

"Although poor people have never had it particularly sweet, America has long been considered the land of op-portunity, where upward class mobility is hard work's reward," Park said. "However, our study shows that limited access to quality education and a shortage of employment opportunities in depressed areas all but ensure that, once fucked, an individual tends to stay fucked."

According to U.S. Census Bureau statistics, 34.6 million Americans were living below the poverty line in 2002.

Our Society

"Not only are the down-and-out fucked, but the number of down-and-out fucks is growing," Park said. "Conditions of disadvantage are often passed from one generation to the next, making it especially difficult for young people to emerge from the cycle of poverty."

"Man, my heart goes out to those poor fuckers," Park added.

America's increasingly rigid class system worsens the situation for the

see POOR page 46

The Worldwide AIDS Crisis

AIDS in the Third World, particularly Africa, is an ever-growing problem. What do *you* think?

Jay Litton
Busboy

"Wow, storage costs for that AIDS quilt must be skyrocketing."

Thomas Batson
Banker

"That's it. Call off the Olympics."

Gayle Showalter
Teacher

"Normally, I'd have sympathy for the Third World, but you've gotta admit it's their fault for being gay."

Shelli Madden
Food Scientist

"AIDS in sub-Saharan Africa is on the rise because sufferers have failed to ask their doctors about Combivir®."

Glen Luther
Systems Analyst

"We're losing the war on AIDS. And drugs. And poverty. And terror. But we sure took it to those Nazis. Man, those were the days."

Yi Shade
Foreman

"We can't just throw money at the problem. Or discuss it in the political arena. Or address it at all."

Stopping Spam

The Can Spam Act could be signed into law as early as next month. How does Congress plan to reduce unwanted commercial e-mails?

➤ Impose prison sentences of up to five years on illegal spammers like Johnq Lennon30agm49 and Erin

➤ Create a "Do Not Spam" registry, which will make everyone who signs up feel better

➤ Provide more funding to the Bureau of Alcohol, Tobacco, Spam, and Firearms

➤ Put a cap on the length of U.S. penises

➤ Hold direct e-mail marketers to the same rigorous standards as their tasteful colleagues in other forms of advertising

➤ Allow only retailers who offer deals that are amazing or products that are revolutionary to send unsolicited e-mails

➤ Shift ads for pornography web sites to billboards and sides of buses

➤ Hire government agents to personally sort through every American's inbox every morning and assign each e-mail a relevant color code

➤ Earmark $200 million for research leading to the eradication of base human desires

---

the ONION®
America's Finest News Source.™

Herman Ulysses Zweibel
Founder

T. Herman Zweibel
Publisher Emeritus
J. Phineas Zweibel
Publisher

Maxwell Prescott Zweibel
Editor-In-Chief

Let's Get The Old Regime Back Together

By Lukin Luzhninczy

Hey, guys, it's your old pal Luzhninczy. Remember, from Vladisnostok? I hope this finds you well. And that no one else finds you—ha ha! But seriously, I am quite adept at keeping track of everyone, which is why, in the old days, they called me the Minister of Information. "Old Eyes And Ears," they used to say. "You never know who might be listening," they'd say. But I always knew they meant me. And I always knew who "they" were. Ah, yes, good times, good times. I miss them.

Which is why, lately, I've been thinking that we should get the old regime back together.

Admit it, my comrades, my compatriots, my old partners in crime: We had ourselves a great regime. For a while there in the 1980s, our regime forced everyone to sit up and take notice. So maybe the critics didn't all like us. And maybe we weren't so popular with the public. That attitude was nothing that a few months at the detention camp in Nozodoroshevo couldn't fix. If they knew what was good for them, and wanted to keep all their homes and fingers and family members, they did things our way.

Face it, guys—we ruled! And we could rule again. I know we could. With just a quick trip to Switzerland, we could be back in business.

> We were big—bigger than any regime before us. We were bigger than Ceausescu! Once we'd so thoroughly demonized the Reformed Orthodox clergy that frenzied mobs were burning down churches across the nation, we were even bigger than Jesus.

Sure, there was a lot of hard work, and oceans of spilled Nationalist blood, but don't for a minute pretend that you didn't enjoy it. Remember Anatoly, speaking to the people, the fire in his eyes reflecting revolutionary fervor and burning oil fields? I do.

I'll never forget that, nor will I ever forget the smile on Antonin's face as he waved to the adoring crowds of citizens who had been forced to realize that we were their future, and that their choices were two: cheer or starve to death.

I'll admit that the days when we were relatively unknown were hard.

> Admit it, my comrades, my compatriots, my old partners in crime: We had ourselves a great regime. For a while there in the 1980s, our regime forced everyone to sit up and take notice. So maybe the critics didn't all like us. And maybe we weren't so popular with the public.

We had to go through all that agricultural reform, the empowerment of peasants, and the stringing up of corrupt local officials. But remember those all-night bull sessions in Yuri's garage, where we formulated our naïve early plans for world domination? Remember riding around the country in a beat-up van, playing to the poor locals' feelings of disenfranchisement and alienation? Those were some good times.

But if we did it all again, we could bypass the hard stuff. We have a reputation now. We could make things happen fast. Come on! Let's do it, guys. Just say the word.

We were big—bigger than any regime before us. We were bigger than Ceausescu! Once we'd so thoroughly demonized the Reformed Orthodox clergy that frenzied mobs were burning down churches across the nation, we were even bigger than Jesus. We took the place by storm. I'm still proud of how revolutionary we were. We really got down and dirty and rocked the country to its foundations, using sabotage and captured artillery. Shit, they're still cleaning up the mess from our Party! We could easily pick up where we left off.

Yeah, it was a fun road, and we got to meet some really cool people, like the overseas director of development for British Petroleum, and Oliver

see REGIME page 46

Substitute Teacher Totally Freaks

OCONOMOWOC, WI—Substitute teacher Pamela Krafft totally freaked during third period, freshman-class sources at August Derleth Memorial High School reported at lunch Tuesday.

"Mrs. Krafft totally lost her shit dur-

> ## "She accidentally knocked her coffee on stuff, and some kids started laughing, and then she just freaked," Thompson said. "First, she slammed her palm down on the desk, then she kicked a metal wastebasket, and then she knocked this pile of books off Grace Wendemeyer's desk."

ing social studies," said Darin Thompson, one of the 30 students who witnessed Krafft's meltdown. "Some of the guys in the back of the room were giving her a hard time, and suddenly, she just blew it. It was like someone

ripped off her human face to reveal some kind of rampaging beast underneath."

Although accounts of Krafft's phenomenal breakdown vary, due perhaps to the highly charged emotional atmosphere of the event, some facts have been established. It is known that Krafft, who has a reputation for her non-confrontational approach to substitute teaching, showed signs of stress 20 minutes into third period. After several of her requests for quiet were ignored, Krafft reportedly took a harder line.

"[Krafft] said, 'Cut out the misbehavior and smart remarks, or else,'" Thompson said. "She never talks like that. Her face was all red, too, and her voice was shaky."

Rather than heed Krafft's warning, the unruly students continued to laugh, throw things, and issue unnecessary restroom-trip requests.

It was during the 38th minute of the 50-minute class that Krafft allegedly lost it altogether.

"It sounded like all hell broke loose in there," said math teacher Hank Sanders, who was conducting a sophomore Algebra 2 class in the neighboring classroom. "I don't know what happened, but I can assure you that it wasn't pretty."

Members of the social-studies class were able to give a more thorough account.

"She started looking for something on the desk—maybe the lesson-plan book, or a pen to write people's names down—but she accidentally knocked her coffee on stuff, and some

Above: Krafft teaches a class in Watertown, a safe distance from Derleth High.

kids started laughing, and then she just freaked," Thompson said. "First, she slammed her palm down on the desk, then she kicked a metal wastebasket, and then she knocked this pile of books off Grace Wendemeyer's desk."

Sources said that, after picking up

two erasers that had fallen off the chalk ledge and clapping them together in a bizarre show of anger, Krafft stormed out of the room, vowing never to return. Roughly one minute later, she returned, attempted to resume class, and instructed see TEACHER page 46

Chicago Out Of Names For Subdivisions

CHICAGO—According to city planners, Chicago has run out of new names for its subdivisions. "It was bound to happen sooner or later," Chicago Mayor Richard M. Daley said at a Monday press conference in front of City Hall. "Oak Dale Springs, Whispering Pines, Stonewood Creek... We have used every tree, body of water, and living thing in the almanac. You don't have to drive all the way out to Kevin Acres to know we need a new naming system." Daley announced that, beginning in 2004, all new housing developments in the Chicago area will be numbered with a positive integer.

Neurosurgeon Heckled From Observation Deck

HOUSTON—Dr. Martin Kenneth Rinjipur, a neurosurgeon at Methodist Hospital, was heckled from the observation deck Monday after removing a cancerous tumor from a patient's occipital lobe. "You call that closing an incision?" the unidentified man shouted. "I could make a cleaner suture with 15 centimeters of frayed chromic gut and a pair of barbecue tongs. Go back to Johns Hopkins." Rinjipur did his best to act like he had not heard the comments.

Drunken Episode A Repeat

PARMA, OH—Sunday's episode involving drunken house-party guest Philip Welz was a repeat, guests reported. "I couldn't bear to watch it again," Robert Joffe said. "Sure, some parts, like when Phil pees in front of everyone, or when he pretends to have sex with the pets, are sort of entertaining the second time around, but on the whole, it was pretty tough to sit through twice." Joffe left the party early in order to avoid the episode's final moments, when Welz pukes on himself and passes out.

Baby Boring

TAMARAC, FL—Michelle, the three-week-old daughter of area residents Sue and Allen McKay, is "unbelievably boring," sources close to the couple said Monday. "Sue's always raving about how amazing Michelle is," friend Elena Jacobs said. "But then you meet her, and she barely moves. Who knows? Maybe Michelle is an incredibly charming and engaging little mastermind during the 20 minutes each day that she's awake and not crying." Jacobs added that Michelle must have been born with her mother's eyes and her father's total lack of personality.

Stick Shift Bragged About

NEW YORK—Sources say Gary Baumgarten, an accountant in the bursar's office at Barnard College, introduced his stick shift into the conversation again Monday. "Traffic was murder over the Verrazano Bridge

this morning," Baumgarten said. "Especially driving that five-speed. But a stick is the only way to go. Of course." Later that day, Baumgarten touted his stick shift during conversations about San Francisco, taxi drivers, and the drive-thru at Taco Bell.

Christmas Pageant Enters Pre-Production

SAGINAW, MI—With the holiday season in full swing, the St. John's Lutheran Church Annual Christmas Pageant went into pre-production Monday. "We just hired a set builder and a location scout, and I'm looking for leads on a Mary Magdalene, because Mrs. Halverson is out with the gout this year," said church deacon Paul Verriter. "Now, all we need to do is wait for Pastor Dave [Genzler] to give his final notes on the script, and we're off and running." Verriter said he needs Genzler's approval before he can hire a team of writers to punch up the arrival of the shepherds. ∅

45

poor.

"After analyzing the economic performance of U.S. households over the past several decades, we concluded that class mobility, while steady in the '70s and '80s, declined in the '90s," Park said. "About 40 percent of families ended the decade in the same economic strata in which they began it. That's up from

> Researchers have dubbed disenfranchised blue-collar workers the Factory Fucked, while members of poor rural populations are called the Farm Fucked. Park characterized the individuals in these two groups as "fucked from the get-go."

about 35 percent in the '80s. That's good news for those sittin' pretty, but it spells 'fuck you' to the poor."

As a result, Park said, there are more poor people, and those poor people are much more screwed than poor people were a decade or two ago.

"As the split between the upper and lower classes grows, and the middle class continues to shrink, we're moving closer and closer to what can only

Above: Americans like 12-year-old Tamara Agguire (far right) of Ponca City, OK, are pretty much fucked.

be called a 'no way out, dude. Sorry, you're fucked'-type situation," Park said. "Not only are the poor fucked at the moment, but any chance they once had of changing their miserable lives is pretty much gone, too. Essentially, they're fucked for all time."

The CSER study identified four major poverty groups within the U.S. The first two groups—one composed of disenfranchised blue-collar workers, the other made up of members of poor rural populations—have been adversely affected by the nation's gradual shift to a technology-based,

global economy. Researchers have dubbed disenfranchised blue-collar workers the Factory Fucked, while members of poor rural populations are called the Farm Fucked. Park characterized the individuals in these two groups as "fucked from the get-go."

The other two rapidly expanding groups of poor fucks are the suburban poor, whose members can't afford the rising cost of such basic necessities as healthcare, and the urban underclass, whose members are found in the nation's troubled inner cities. Researchers termed these

groups the Recently Fucked and the Utterly Fucked, respectively.

Economist Harold Knoep said there's little reason for sympathy.

"In a healthy capitalist economy, some people are going to be out-competed," Knoep said. "I'm sorry, but some of those fuck-ups have fucked themselves. I am not condoning an

> "Nobody's saying poor people aren't fucked," Hastert said. "But what about all the people in this great nation who are not fucked?"

anarchic 'fuck or be fucked' ethos, but I can hardly get behind a welfare state that punishes the unfucked by fucking all equally."

While he expressed concern for the nation's poor, House Speaker Dennis Hastert (R-IL) said increased funding for social programs isn't the answer.

"Nobody's saying poor people aren't fucked," Hastert said. "But what about all the people in this great nation who are not fucked? If the financial resources of the economically stable are diverted—through some well-intentioned but fiscally irresponsible social-service program—to the people who are fucked, where does that leave those who were sailin' along fine? Fucked."

Ed Cranston, an under-employed, Detroit-area machinist who made $14,000 last year, said he was not surprised by the report.

"They say I'm fucked?" Cranston asked. "Shit, man, tell me something I don't know." ∅

North, and those touring nuns who got lost when the tire blew on their van. We worked with some of the best, too, once we hit it big. Remember that guy Dieter? The guy we hired to deal with all those hotshot British agents who started popping up uninvited? Remember how we called him "Fingers"? He could find out any information you needed to know, as long as he had some sturdy clamps and a metalworker's bench grinder. Man, I'd almost forgotten about him. That guy was crazy! Let's surprise him with a visit! He's in North Korea now.

Ah, I guess we all were a little crazy back then. Near the end, I didn't think we were ever going to get out of it alive. Well, Nikolai didn't. I told him all the time, man, once a backlash starts, and Bono is writing lyrics about you, and Americans are starting to act like they've hated you all along, it's time to think about moving on.

But listen, my friends, I guarantee you this: The people never forgot us. We could do this, guys. We could be huge again. I've still got a copy of our Declaration of Ascendancy, and a grain silo in Bukagachi filled with Kalashnikov assault rifles. So, how about it? Are we a regime again, or what? ∅

students to open their books. In the process of putting on her glasses, however, she accidentally poked herself in the eye, at which point the uncharacteristic display of hysteria resumed.

Students and teachers in neighboring rooms remained glued to their seats, paralyzed with fear and confusion, as Krafft issued near-random disciplinary actions against the students, hurling pink detention slips and parent-teacher-conference request forms with undisguised contempt, screaming obscenities all the while.

"I heard the sub scream, 'Go to hell,'" said senior Kyle Riggs, who overheard the commotion from the classroom across the hall. "Then there was some banging, and she said, 'I don't get paid enough to take this shit,' and then something about a babysitter."

Approximately eight minutes after the conniption fit began, it was over. Krafft reportedly fumbled with the locking file cabinet beside her desk, pulled out her purse, and disappeared down the hall. Administrative sources said Krafft passed through the front office into the parking lot, where she

got into her 1996 Geo Metro, slammed the door, and tore off down Walnut Street.

Krafft has not returned to the school since the incident.

"None of us had any idea that Mrs. Krafft was capable of such brute rage," Thompson said. "We thought she was a pushover, and that we could get away with hassling her. And we did, for weeks. But we have now reaped the bitter harvest that underestimating Mrs. Krafft sowed."

Principal Bob Colmes said that although no black mark will be placed on Krafft's record, she "isn't likely to be asked to return to Derleth High any time in the immediate future." Colmes said regular social-studies teacher Jack Hargrove, who's out sick with pneumonia, will return next Monday. In the meantime, Hargrove's class will be taught by Colmes.

"Man, those freshmen really screwed up this time," senior Kyle Ewan told reporters. "Colmes is a real hardass. It's going to be as bad as the time those juniors made the music teacher cry. You can bet he's going to let them have it, and good, for messing with that sub." ∅

OUTSOURCED from page 43

satisfied with the level of servicing that I received under Howard, it was my feeling that a younger, more aggressive hand on the tiller might bring some new ideas into play. No matter how mutually satisfying the old deal was, its time had passed."

Although specific terms of the arrangement have not been made public, Melanie allowed that she has been "very pleased" by the new supplier—Jorge Escobedo, a 26-year-old gardener from Sierra Mojada who has been working in the U.S. since February.

"The switchover was seamless, considering how rapidly the deal was closed," said Melanie, who initiated the informal arrangement with Escobedo on Nov. 20, while he was cleaning the equipment shed. "Well, in truth, I was considering a move in this direction for some time, and looking into possibilities. Then Jorge offered me a very attractive package, and I decided it was in my interest to act. I've been very pleased with his initial performance."

Melanie said Escobedo beats her former provider in availability, reliability, and turnaround. He also requires minimal emotional investment from Melanie, who is the sole receiver of the goods under the new arrangement.

Melanie offered few details on the ins-and-outs of the deal, but she did report that the outsourcing is limited to Reinhardt's marital duties. All previous supply arrangements with Reinhardt, including those pertaining to housing and finance, are still very much in effect.

"This isn't some sort of challenge to the American workforce as a whole," Melanie said. "I'm just sending the jobs where they're going to be done most efficiently. The acquisition of houses, automobiles, and clothing will all still be in Howard's wheelhouse, but groundskeeping and plowing are now to be managed by Jorge. It just makes sense."

Melanie said the outsourcing is a direct response to the expansion of Reinhardt's duties at United Carborundum.

"Howard is simply too busy to personally keep track of every detail of the marital union," Melanie said. "As long as he's available when he's needed—major Reinhardt-family gatherings and the United Carborundum holiday ball—I'm happy to have someone else's input day-to-day."

The Reinhardt household has been moving toward a more modular operation for years now. Laundry duties are handled by a small Chinese concern; child-rearing and education are

> **Melanie allowed that she has been "very pleased" by the new supplier—Jorge Escobedo, a 26-year-old gardener from Sierra Mojada who has been working in the U.S. since February.**

performed by a live-in salaried Irish employee; and a loosely organized, rotating consortium of Italians, Japanese, and Greeks handles food service. The sexual-services agreement, however, marks the Reinhardts' first use of highly skilled foreign manpower.

The news of the outsourcing was met with little surprise in the greater Detroit area, where community members are used to seeing hard-won jobs go to foreign labor, and are aware of cooling relations in the Reinhardt household.

"This proposal might not be the win-win situation that Melanie is projecting," said Philip Johannsen, business writer for the *Detroit Free Press*. "But it's going to be tough for Howard to say he didn't see it coming. When it came time to find a groundskeeper, he delegated the crucial domestic-hiring decision to his wife. He knows she's a very proactive person, so it shouldn't surprise him that she took the initiative to shore up areas of the household where she saw standards slipping."

"If American executives are not willing to shoulder the increased personal investment of time and energy required to keep the jobs in-house, globalization is just something they're going to have to accept," Johannsen added.

Howard Reinhardt was unavailable for comment, as he was scouting locations in Oaxaca for a boron-nitride factory. *ø*

CLINTON from page 43

would sometimes mention an article about me on Slate or CNN.com, but I was too busy to about myself then," Clinton said. "Out of the blue, though, I thought I'd just see what was out there in cyberspace about me. I'd just been sitting around playing online Mah Jongg, anyway."

"I never knew there was a Bill Clinton Joke-A-Day site," Clinton said after opening his Internet browser, typing in "Bill Clinton," and clicking the "I'm feeling lucky" button.

"I should forward this to Hillary,"

> **"My years in the White House were such a whirlwind that it's hard to remember all the stuff that happened," Clinton said.**

Clinton said. "She'd get a kick out of some of these. Hmm… She might not find that one too funny."

After quickly closing the page, Clinton said he was surprised by the number of humor sites devoted to him.

"I found a Clinton-sex crossword puzzle, a web site for something called the 'Clinton Dance,' and this one where you can warp my face," Clinton said. "My favorite site was Sincerelybill.com, where you can make a video of me saying stuff. I sent one to [Clinton's former Secretary of Agriculture] Dan Glickman. It said, 'I'm a

consideration. We've testified to watching inappropriate neighbors.' He's gonna love that."

"There's only about 200 words to choose from, so it's a little weird," Clinton added.

Clinton said he was delighted to find content about himself on several of the sites he regularly visits, like Infoplease.com and Encyclopedia.com.

"I never knew that I was on the Internet Movie Database," Clinton said. "I'm just a politician, not an actor, but there are 76 movies in my filmography. They have me down for *JAG* and *Bill Clinton: Rock & Roll President*. Officially, I'm listed as Jodie Foster's co-star for my appearance in *Contact*. That's pretty cool."

Clinton said his web search left him nostalgic for his presidency.

"My years in the White House were such a whirlwind that it's hard to remember all the stuff that happened," Clinton said. "But going through these pages really brings back the good times. I found some really nice pictures of Al [Gore] and me on there, and some cute ones of Buddy."

"There are so many articles, too. I want to read them all," Clinton said. "Well, some are kinda boring. But it's still amazing, just to see how much information is out there. They have where I went to college, my favorite foods, my parents' names. It's wild."

Clinton added that, as he progressed through the pages devoted to himself, he found some "other Bill Clintons."

"There's this other Bill Clinton who's a big Hendrix fan," Clinton said. "There's another one that books gay cruises, and another one that ran for county coroner in Iowa. There are a lot

of other guys with my name out there, all across America. Kinda neat, huh?"

The former president said he refined his search by entering "William Jefferson Clinton" and "42nd President of the United States Bill Clinton," into Google, but the combinations returned results much like those from his original search.

Clinton then started to add qualifiers, searching for "Bill Clinton + my inspiration" and "Bill Clinton + sax."

"The 'Clinton + hot' search was disappointing," Clinton said. "It turned up a few Arkansas tourism pages that listed Hot Springs [AR] as 'The hometown of Bill Clinton.' Or it brought up porn sites that had nothing to do with me."

Clinton said he considered the use of other search engines, like Ask Jeeves, but ultimately decided to do so only after he's satisfied that no new information can be found on Google.

"I've only gone through the first couple hundred web sites, and I still haven't used the 'groups' or the 'directory' search options," Clinton said. "I'll probably do that next. I remember I once stumbled on a chat room devoted to discussions about my presidency. Maybe I should pose as a conservative Republican and find out what people really think about me. That might be fun." *ø*

Above: Clinton looks at one "Bill Clinton" link returned by his Google search.

I Never Shoulda Left The House

The Cruise
By Jim Anchower

Hola, amigos. I know it's been a long time since I rapped at ya, but I've had my nuts in a twist for a while. I still got the job driving the bus for the car-rental place. I ain't going anywhere working there, except back and forth from the airport, but at least sitting behind the wheel gives me time to ponder over shit. I've been thinking about how to make a car into a helicopter, so I can get places faster. I think I got it figured out. I just need some propellers. Don't go trying to take that idea, though. It's mine, and if you steal it, I will find you and beat your ass.

As soon as my car is up and flying, I'll sleep a lot easier. That thing has been giving me pains. I got a hole in my gas tank or something, so every time I fill up, I lose half the gas inside of a day. I only fill it up halfway now, so it does okay, but I can't put anything in the trunk without it stinking like gas. Also, the heat is all fucked up. Luckily, someone left a blaze-orange ski mask in the backseat, so I've been wearing that as I drive around town.

So anyway, let me tell you about what I did for Thanksgiving. I don't make a big deal about holidays. In my book, Thanksgiving is just some made-up holiday someone invented to sell more turkeys, so I wasn't going to do anything for it. I decided instead to pick up some sweet, holiday double-time pay at the car rental place and then kick back with some videos. The fact that I found an almost perfectly good 32" television on the curb a few weeks ago is one of the only things I have to be thankful for.

Since the double-time cash would be gravy on the meat and potatoes of my regular paycheck, I figured I'd treat myself, so I stopped by Beltline Liquors and picked myself up a case of Miller Genuine Draft—the nectar of the gods, as I call it—and a bottle of Jack Daniel's. Then, I got a couple of Tombstone pizzas at the gas station and headed back to my castle. (Don't believe the hype about DiGiorno. I'll go with a classic frozen Tombstone any day.)

When I got home, there was a message from Wes inviting me over to his ma's place for Thanksgiving dinner the next night. There was no way I was going. Wes is like a brother to me, but his ma is always fixing me with the stink eye. She makes a mean stuffing, but that wasn't enough to get me to submit to her voodoo for a full night. Also, they always play Trivial Pursuit, and she has the cards memorized.

Just when I got settled into my chair,

Ron showed up at my door. I don't know what it is about that guy. When I need to change my oil or something, I can't find him anywhere. When I have a good stash of beers, he's like a junebug in a bug zapper. He's got some kind of mooch homing device. He didn't have anything to offer but his thirst, but I was in a charitable mood, so we put a dent in my packaged goods and watched my videotapes.

I must have fallen asleep during the second one, because I woke up on my

> **In my book, Thanksgiving is just some made-up holiday someone invented to sell more turkeys, so I wasn't going to do anything for it. I decided instead to pick up some sweet, holiday double-time pay at the car rental place and then kick back with some videos.**

couch with a massive hangover. Ron was gone, and from the looks of my fridge, he took the rest of my beers with him. I looked over and saw that I had to be at work in, like, 30 minutes, so I jumped in the shower. I had to poke my head out twice to put my head over the toilet and puke. I could tell it was going to be a rough Thanksgiving.

Since there wasn't any traffic, and I only had to stop once to dry heave, I got to work on time. I needed some coffee, but Charlene was the only one there. She never drinks anything but Diet Coke, so she hadn't brewed any. Still, there was some cold black mud left in the pot. It tasted terrible, but I chugged it. I was trying to figure out how to make a new pot when Charlene yelled at me to do a pick-up.

I made it about halfway to the airport before I had to pull over and puke again. I must have drunk more than I thought, both shitty coffee and booze. When I got to the airport, there was some uptight guy with like eight suitcases waiting for me and looking at his watch. I opened the door, and he climbed on the bus without his bags. Usually, I get out to help without a second thought, but I was hoping that if I stalled, he'd do it himself. No dice.

As I was pulling into the lot to drop the guy off at his car, the sun hit me right in the eyes. That hurt like a

Your Horoscope

By Lloyd Schumner Sr.
Retired Machinist and
A.A.P.B.-Certified Astrologer

Aries: (March 21–April 19)
There are times when it's just not possible to make people feel better about themselves. If you really want to see results, try to make them feel worse.

Taurus: (April 20–May 20)
Moist, healthy skin and attention from meteorologists are the perks of having a miniature storm cloud hover over your head all week.

Gemini: (May 21–June 21)
You had no idea the consequences of forgetting Lou Rawls' birthday would be so severe.

Cancer: (June 22–July 22)
Watt was inspired to invent the steam engine by a kettle boiling over. What you'll invent after seeing a fat epileptic eat tacos may end life on Earth.

Leo: (July 23–Aug. 22)
Don't worry: They're not fatal, and you can just tell future lovers that they're oddly placed dreadlocks.

Virgo: (Aug. 23–Sept. 22)
It might be a holiday tradition, but keep in mind that any letter you write will violate the terms of the restraining order Santa filed against you.

Libra: (Sept. 23–Oct. 23)
Scientists agree that you are a unique and fascinating specimen, but there are no practical applications for you as yet.

Scorpio: (Oct. 24–Nov. 21)
If the football is deflected by a defensive player, the usual rules for pass interference do not apply—a fact which will somehow ruin your marriage.

Sagittarius: (Nov. 22–Dec. 21)
You'll compete with the Devil for your immortal soul in a midnight game of Scrabble, and win handily when he can only think of creepy, depressing Latin words.

Capricorn: (Dec. 22–Jan. 19)
Tourists will travel from far and wide to see the famous "torture cubicle" in which you slaved away for years, wishing for a quick and merciful death.

Aquarius: (Jan. 20–Feb. 18)
You had no idea the love life of the orangutan was so complex, so nuanced, and so often taking place in your hall closet.

Pisces: (Feb. 19–March 20)
Make the world a better place this week. To do the job right, just make sure the pistol is aimed at the roof of your mouth.

motherfucker, and for a split second, I couldn't see anything. Well, to cut to the chase: I bumped the guy's rental car. It wasn't even like I broke any-

> **I needed some coffee, but Charlene was the only one there. She never drinks anything but Diet Coke, so she hadn't brewed any. Still, there was some cold black mud left in the pot. It tasted terrible, but I chugged it.**

thing. I only put a little dent in the passenger door, but he didn't give a good goddamn. He got all freaked out and started yelling, "I am *not* paying

for that!" I would have told him to shut his mouth before I shut it for him, but I was still seeing floaters. Luckily, Charlene came out and calmed him down by giving him a free upgrade.

Then she told me that she would have to mark the accident down on my file, but it didn't seem like she really cared too much. She was cool about it, but I still wish she wouldn't have had to write me up. I only had to make a few more trips, so I spent most of the rest of the day in the breakroom trying to figure out how to make coffee and yacking up everything I swallowed.

By the end of my shift, I was feeling a little better, but I needed some serious chow. I had no beer left, and, as for the pizzas, every time I turn on my oven, it makes the fire alarm in the hall go off. I decided that I would go to Wes' after all. His mom was cold to me the whole night, and I said some shit that pretty much guaranteed I won't get invited back again, but that stuffing was good. Next year, though, I'm going to just hole up for a few days until all the Thanksgiving crap blows over. ✍

Celebrity 'Caught' Smoking

see ENTERTAINMENT page 11C

Burger King Hat Put In Deep Fryer

see LOCAL page 7E

Locksmith Brings Along Boombox To Play *Mission: Impossible* Theme

see LOCAL page 4E

Maid Frenched

see LOCAL page 12E

STATshot

A look at the numbers that shape your world.

How Are We Cooking The Goose?

- **12%** Stuffed with smaller geese
- **18%** Drunk on Beaujolais Nouveau
- **24%** Getting recipe off back of goose box
- **10%** Atop engine of Ford F-250
- **11%** With SCIENCE!
- **25%** In front of other geese, to serve as an example

the ONION®

VOLUME 39 ISSUE 49   AMERICA'S FINEST NEWS SOURCE™   18 DEC. 2003–7 JAN. 2004

Christmas Brought To Iraq By Force

BAGHDAD, IRAQ—On almost every corner in Iraq's capital city, carolers are singing, trees are being trimmed, and shoppers are rushing home with their packages—all under the watchful eye of U.S. troops dedicated to bringing the magic of Christmas to Iraq by force.

"It's important that life in liberated Iraq get back to normal as soon as possible," said Deputy Defense Secretary Paul Wolfowitz at a press conference Monday. "That's why we're making sure that Iraqis have the best Christmas ever—something they certainly wouldn't have had under Saddam Hussein's regime."

To that end, 25,000 troops from the 3rd Armored Cavalry Regiment and 82nd Airborne Division have been deployed. Their missions include the

see CHRISTMAS page 53

Above: U.S. soldiers instruct an Iraqi to tell Santa what he wants for Christmas.

Senate Carpool 'Forgets' To Pick Up Feingold Again

Above: Feingold waits outside his house for a ride to work.

WASHINGTON, DC—U.S. Sen. Russ Feingold (D-WI) was forced to find an alternate means of transportation to work Monday, because his Senate carpool once again "forgot" to pick him up.

"Did we forget Feingold again?" Sen. Lisa Murkowski (R-AK) asked. "Gee, I don't know how that happened. I guess we were running late and just flaked on it. Hmm, same thing happened last week."

Feingold and Murkowski, along with senators Chuck Hagel (R-NE), Bill Nelson (D-FL), and Dick Durbin (D-IL), comprise the ride-sharing carpool formed three years ago to split the

see CARPOOL page 52

So-Called Obese Pets Held To Unrealistic Body Standards

CHICAGO—To the casual eye, Tippy might appear to be a regular Labrador. He loves sunbathing at the park, watching squirrels, and getting loads of attention from passersby.

But Tippy is not a normal dog. By veterinarians' standards, he is 65 pounds overweight.

A closer examination of Tippy's body reveals a rounded abdomen, thick limbs, and a fleshy neck and back. And, unlike dogs seen on television and in magazines, Tippy does not have a discernible waistline or ribcage.

"I don't care if people say he's chubby," said Tippy's owner Katherine

Mathers, gently scratching the dog's protruding belly. "So what if he doesn't look like the dog in the Iams commercial? What's more important: having a perfect body or being happy? I love him whether he's 25, 50, or even 150 pounds overweight. In fact, I think he's the cutest dog in the world."

"Yes, you are!" said Mathers, waving the remaining half of her cookie in front of Tippy's nose.

Mathers is not alone in defending her pet. Amid a barrage of commercials for new diet dog and cat foods, many owners say that their pets are

see PETS page 53

Above: Tippy and Katherine Mathers enjoy a day at the park.

Conservative Teens

Recent surveys show that today's teens are more conservative than the previous generation on issues like abortion and drug use. What do *you* think?

"I don't understand my teenage son. He's always locked in the bathroom with that damn Ann Coulter book."

Audrey Mitchell
Caterer

"Who can blame them, what with all the conservative video games they're playing?"

Fannie Whitton
Tailor

"Does this new conservatism preclude them from going wild, either now or at some point in the future?"

Randy Kimura
Clerk

"I did find it strange that my daughter's prom song was 'Hail To The Chief.'"

Kenneth Mann
Systems Analyst

"Of course teens are conservative. They're rebelling against the liberal bias that controls the media."

John Zimmerman
City Planner

"I don't know who these teens are, but they certainly aren't the ones e-mailing me about their web sites."

Jimmy McCourt
Dog Walker

North Korea's Nuclear Proposal

North Korea said it is willing to freeze its nuclear-weapons program in exchange for U.S. concessions. What are the country's leaders demanding?

- ➤ To keep one nuclear weapon as a memento
- ➤ Kim Jong Il to replace FDR on American dimes
- ➤ Some of those food packets the Iraqis are living sweet off of
- ➤ Eisner to be fired as Disney CEO
- ➤ To be treated as if they weren't an oppressive, abusive, autocratic regime
- ➤ To keep their nukes just until North Korean mind-control technology comes online
- ➤ Lovely Jenna Bush to be offered as wife to Kim Jong Il
- ➤ Something to eat besides pickled fucking cabbage
- ➤ Right to restart nuclear program if they ever want international attention again

⊘ the **ONION**®
America's Finest News Source.™

Herman Ulysses Zweibel
Founder

T. Herman Zweibel
Publisher Emeritus
J. Phineas Zweibel
Publisher
Maxwell Prescott Zweibel
Editor-In-Chief

I Have A Dream: To Eat A Kentucky Derby-Winning Horse

Brothers and sisters.

Nearly two-score years ago, the Creator gave me life, and the wheels of my destiny were irreversibly set into motion. Friends, I am a simple man, an ordinary man, a man like any other. Yet for months now, I have been seized with the desire to enact a plan so grand and extraordinary that its very fearsomeness often makes me tremble. It's a vision so blazing that it sometimes overcomes me, and all else is blotted out, and when I come to, I can feel hot tears rolling down my face. But this dream is no nightmare, my friends. Rather, it has imbued my life with purpose and drive, and I have little doubt that I shall see it realized.

By Charles V. Osterberg

I have a dream, brothers and sisters, to one day eat a Kentucky Derby winner.

Be it princely steed or serene filly, I dream of the day when an equine victor will pass through my digestive system. A champion whose hard-charging gait once thrilled the throngs at Churchill Downs shall be masticated by me with great relish and gusto. This I vow.

I realize that some of you may object to the consumption of horseflesh. But the only anxiety I feel stems from this: I do not know which horse to choose. For, my friends, the surviving pool of Derby winners offers many options. Take, for example, the capricious 2002 winner War Emblem. His sinewy neck and shoulders could feed me for days. A mere glimpse of the flanks of this year's underdog gelding Funny Cide causes me to drool like a faucet. The powerful haunches of Monarchos, or Go For Gin, clearly belong in my stomach. But then one must consider that a seasoned veteran like Alysheba, long put out to stud, might afford gustatory delights of a more subtle variety. And just imagine the fetlocks of Silver Charm, the 1997 winner and one of the leading money-earners of all time, wedged between two pieces of white bread.

I cannot tell you why God has made this my life's mission. All I know is that it must be brought to fruition.

Owners, breeders, trainers of these singular competitors, let it be known that I will do anything to be granted the privilege of devouring your prize racehorse. Some of you may recognize me as the guy who stands outside your training tracks and breeding farms holding a fork and knife and wearing a bib. But my offers could not be more earnest. Make me your eternal slave; take my eyes and donate them to a blinded loved one of yours; make my own mother your docile concubine—I will surrender everything I have for a steaming platter of laureled stallion.

It may interest the gracious ladies and gentlemen of track and turf to learn that, should I obtain one of these glorious creatures, no part of it shall be wasted. What is not readily consumable shall be skinned, tanned, plucked, shorn, de-boned, pickled,

> A champion whose hard-charging gait once thrilled the throngs at Churchill Downs shall be masticated by me with great relish and gusto. This I vow.

boiled, and otherwise rendered. Then it will be eaten. I will clean and return the horseshoes.

I address my appeal to anyone who has had a fervent dream, one that makes all other ambitions seem wan and weak. For I, too, have had grand schemes that I thought could not be topped. I remember how, not long ago, I pledged to take a black fine-point Sharpie and fill in the circles of all of the letters and numbers in every book in the Baltimore Public Library system. I abandoned that dream to pursue a more exciting life's goal: to find and burn every existing copy of *Prevention* magazine. Then I decided that I must find the match to every un-paired sock at Goodwill. Yet all of these dizzying aims pale in comparison to the prospect of eating a big old horse.

I know my dream seems impossible. But if you join with me in endorsing and supporting it, together we can keep hope alive. Keep hope alive, children.

Keep hope alive that I shall tear apart and swallow the taut, lean flesh of the great thoroughbred.

Keep hope alive that I shall one day gnaw on its hooves and hocks, and suck the marrow from its bones.

Keep hope alive that the pointers offered in my copy of *Fundamentals Of Home Butchering* can apply as much to horses as they do to sheep, pigs, and rabbits.

If we keep this hope alive, brothers and sisters, we will live to see the fateful day when a Derby victor shall nourish a lone and humble man.

Giddyap, horsey. ⊘

Non-Widescreen Version Of DVD Received As Hanukkah Gift

BROOKLYN, NY—Self-described film buff Tyler Rosenstein was disappointed to receive a non-letterboxed "full screen" version of the movie *The Matrix Reloaded* as a Hanukkah gift, the 19-year-old reported Monday.

"Great," said Rosenstein, concealing his displeasure from his beaming aunt and uncle, Hannah and Bernie Greenberg, as he gazed at the freshly unwrapped DVD in his hand. "Just what I wanted. *The Matrix Reloaded.*"

"With approximately a third of the movie's visual content missing, thanks to 'pan-and-scan,'" he added under his breath.

Rosenstein, a freshman studying philosophy at NYU, said he was momentarily excited to receive the special collector's edition DVD of *The Matrix Reloaded*, which features more than an hour of supplemental material, including behind-the-scenes footage and a preview of the Enter The Matrix video game. But Rosenstein's joy faded when his eye caught the words "full-screen edition" emblazoned across the top of the box.

Minutes later, Rosenstein's cousin Cory made an exchange of the gift impossible when he insisted that Rosenstein open the DVD to show him the "easter egg."

While Rosenstein thanked his aunt and uncle for the gift, he took leave of the family get-together shortly after dinner and locked himself in his room to sulk.

"It's frustrating, because they came *so close* to getting me exactly what I wanted," said Rosenstein, laying on his bed and sneering at the DVD. "This is a $30 item. But what am I supposed to do with it? Why would they even release a full-screen *Matrix Reloaded*, when every single frame of that movie is so artfully composed? Even leaving framing aside, the movie cries out for each of its visual elements to be seen."

"It's an unwatchable piece of crap," said Rosenstein, tossing the DVD onto a pile of gifts that included a sweatshirt and a digital memo recorder.

In spite of his annoyance with the non-letterboxed DVD, Rosenstein said he knew better than to complain to his relatives.

"There's just no way to tell them without coming off like a complete asshole," Rosenstein said. "I'm just going to have to eat it."

The Greenbergs remain unaware of their mistake.

"We're so happy that we were able to get Tyler a gift he really wanted this year," Hannah Greenberg said. "You wouldn't believe how hard he is to shop for. He's so picky about his movies. For his birthday, we gave him *The Wedding Singer*. I thought all the kids liked that Adam Sandler—Cory said he sings a song about Hanukkah. Well, boy, was getting Tyler that movie a mistake!"

This year, instead of guessing, the Greenbergs took a suggestion from Rosenstein's father, who was aware that his son owned the first *Matrix* movie.

"Tyler's got very specific tastes,"

Above: Rosenstein holds the inadequate gift.

Bernie said. "He told us he likes those foreign films. What did he call it? The Criterion Collection. Well, Hannah and I tried to find those, but they didn't have them at Target. We sure didn't want what happened with the wizard movie to happen again."

Bernie spoke in reference to last year, when the Greenbergs came close to finding a gift Rosenstein would like. The misguided couple gave their nephew the theatrical-release version of *Lord Of The Rings: The Fellowship Of The Ring*, instead of the extended version which contains 40 extra minutes of footage—a distinction Rosenstein gently explained to the confused gift-givers.

"If we'd known, we'd have been happy to get him the other version," Hannah said. "Well, this time we were very careful. There were two versions at the store, and we made sure to get the special one. See, Tyler hates it when they cut out part of the movie."

Confusion over the misleading term "full-screen" caused his well-meaning relatives to purchase the inferior version of the DVD.

"Why do they call it 'full-screen' anyway, when it's only two-thirds of the see DVD page 53

Turkey Sandwich Given Locally Relevant Name

FAIRMOUNT, IN—For the 87,836th time, a turkey sandwich was given a locally relevant name, Mary Anne's Café owner Mary Anne Gunday reported Monday. "'The Hoosier Special' isn't just a turkey with lettuce, tomato, and mayo on your choice of bread," Gunday said. "It's a tribute to the state of Indiana and its inhabitants." Gunday recommended eating the sandwich with a bowl of steaming Birthplace Of James Dean Tomato Noodle Soup.

Network Pushes The 'Dumbing It Down' Envelope

LOS ANGELES—Already home to *Extreme Makeover*, *Trista & Ryan's Wedding*, and *According To Jim*, the ABC television network is now look-ing to develop some really, really, really dumb shows, network sources announced Monday. "With all the competition in television, we have to make the ABC brand stand out," said Susan Lyne, president of ABC Entertainment. "That's why we want a slate of projects that will out-dumb the dumb shows like *Whoopi*, *The Victoria's Secret Fashion Show*, and *The Next Joe Millionaire*." ABC's pilot orders for Fall 2004 include *The Naked Ladies*, *Extreme Explosions*, and *America's Shiniest Objects*.

Author Accepts Award On Ghostwriters' Behalf

CONCORD, NH—Former Secretary of State Alexander Haig accepted the Worthington Literary Award on behalf of his four ghostwriters Tuesday for his book *No Victory*. "It is with humble gratitude that I accept this great honor," Haig said, graciously speaking for the team of writers who wrote the 435-page account of his unsuccessful bid for the 1988 Republican presidential nomination. "I appreciate that you have taken the time to consider what I had to say on the...subject matter of this book." Haig has not touched his Apple IIe since 1994 and spends most of his time hot-air ballooning in Naples.

Vacationing Couple To Try Something They Don't Like

CANCUN, MEXICO—During their two-week winter holiday, Howard and Rosemary Gortenski of Arlington Heights, IL, have signed up for scuba lessons, even though both suspect that they will dislike the activity, the couple reported Tuesday. "Howard doesn't like to get his head wet, and I just don't see the point of getting all dressed up just to go under water for an hour," Gortenski said. "But vaca-tions are for breaking out of the routine to experience what life has to offer, so I guess we have to try something new. It's this week or never." Gortenski said she'll make sure to secure some photos as proof of the couple's spontaneity.

Bush Won't Put Down New Football

WASHINGTON, DC—According to White House sources, President Bush has not allowed his new Wilson official NFL leather game football to leave his sight since he received it as a gift last week. "The president has that ball with him everywhere he goes," Vice-President Dick Cheney said Monday. "The way he pump-fakes it in the Oval Office is really distracting." Secretary of Defense Donald Rumsfeld has threatened to take the ball away and lock it in his desk if he sees it at the table during another goddamned cabinet meeting. ∅

costs of commuting and reduce fuel waste and air pollution.

Monday marks the fourth time this month that the Wisconsin senator has been left behind. Feingold's wife Mary had to drive him to the Capitol, where he arrived with just enough time to make roll call. Feingold said it was "not the way I like to start a morning."

"Did we leave old Rusty behind?" asked Hagel, unable to suppress a

"They think I'm oblivious to the fact that they don't like me," Feingold said.

giggle. "That's a shame. Tell Rusty we're sorry about that. It won't happen again, on my word as a U.S. senator. Tell Rusty that, too."

According to Feingold, last Thursday after work, Hagel pulled away without him. Feingold ran after the car for almost a block before the loss of a shoe forced him to stop.

For some reason, Feingold has never been left behind on a payday, when carpool members each chip in $53 for their shared spot in the Senate reserved parking lot.

"Look, none of us are out to get Rusty," Nelson said. "That's just silly. We get out on the road, we're going, we're doing *our* thing, and it feels like

Above: Hagel, Nelson, and Durbin said they "didn't notice" Feingold wasn't in the car.

everyone's in the car. The next thing we know, someone says, 'Oopsie, where's Feingold? Did we forget him *again*?'"

According to Feingold, other carpool members get out of the car when they reach his house, tacitly forcing him to sit in the middle of the backseat, rather than simply letting him slide in. Feingold also said he rarely gets to choose the radio station for the morning drive, despite having politely voiced his dislike for Fred Grandy and Andy Parks' *WMAL Morning Show* several months ago.

In addition, rather than allowing Feingold to wait inside his house, the group insists that he wait outside on the sidewalk in the morning, in order to save time.

"I don't think Russ minds getting some fresh air in the morning," Durbin said. "He's certainly never said anything about it, if he does."

Feingold said he found the group's habit of excluding him from breakfast get-togethers to be the most personally hurtful of the slights.

"They always stop for something before they pick me up, even though

there are a bunch of places between my house and work," Feingold said. "When I ask them if they went somewhere together, they always say no, but one time they were all holding identical to-go cups from Krispy Kreme."

According to Feingold, the carpool has excluded him from after-work get-togethers, as well. In November, just as the group was dropping Feingold off one evening, Durbin "suddenly remembered" that he needed to pick up a prescription at the drugstore near the Capitol, and the group headed off in that direction. The next day, Feingold said his carpool members appeared to be hungover and kept talking about the music at the Chi-Cha Lounge.

Although the other senators characterized him as "overly sensitive," Feingold said he has "just about had it."

"They think I'm oblivious to the fact that they don't like me," Feingold said. "Well, guess what? I don't like them, either. I think they're all stupid. If I weren't so committed to conserving energy, I'd tell them all to take a flying leap."

One Beltway insider noted that Feingold's current carpool is the senator's third in the past five years.

"I was carpooling with Russ in '98," Ron Wyden (D-OR) said. "Everyone else wanted to have a nice relaxing ride in, but Feingold would start up on campaign finance reform the second his seatbelt clicked. That guy would *not* shut *up* for a second." ∅

---

the ONION presents

Drinking Responsibly During The Holidays

The holiday season is a time to enjoy family dinners, office parties, and get-togethers with friends. Festive drinks and tasty punches often contribute to the holiday revelry, so here are some tips to help you celebrate sensibly:

- If you are a woman, remember: Women are more sensitive to the effects of alcohol. If you are a man, remember: Women are more sensitive to the effects of alcohol.

- Always drink from the bottle labeled "XXX." The bottle with the skull-and-crossbones on the front is poison.

- Drinking alone is a telltale sign that you know better than to put up with anybody's bullshit.

- Drinking more than seven nights a week is not just irresponsible, it's impossible.

- If someone you know is too drunk to drive, demand that he let you have his car keys. If he refuses, pull out a gun and demand the car keys again. This also works with people who are not drunk, and whom you do not know.

- Never drink with Tyler Schneeklov.

- While standing in the middle of the road at 3 a.m. yelling expletives at your ex-girlfriend, wear light-colored clothing so motorists can see you.

- Once you get married and have kids, stop drinking tons of whiskey and switch to drinking tons of wine.

- Always re-cap your flask between swigs. This lengthens the amount of time between drinks.

- Don't mix alcohol with stereotypes. If you are Irish, drink rum. If you are a pirate, drink whiskey.

- Don't drink and drive. Disregard this if you happen to be one of those people who drive better drunk.

- If you suddenly find yourself impaired by alcohol, prevent any social awkwardness by informing all those present that you profoundly love them, and that you never get this drunk.

- Never use alcohol to escape feelings of failure and loneliness. Use Vicodin.

- Before heading out to the office holiday party, tape a handcuff key to the inside of your watchband. Just trust us on this one.

CHRISTMAS from page 49

distribution of cookies and egg nog at major Iraqi city centers, the conscription of bell-ringers from among the Iraqi citizenry, and the enforcement of a new policy in which every man, woman, and child in Baghdad pays at least one visit to *'Twas The Night... On Ice.*

Immediately following the press conference, high-altitude bombers began to string Christmas lights throughout the greater-Baghdad area, and Wild Weasel electronic-warfare fighter jets initiated 24-hour air patrols to broadcast Bing Crosby's "White Christmas" over the nation. Armored columns struck out from all major allied firebases to erect a

---

"Thus far, Operation Desert Santa has gone off without a hitch," said Gen. Stanley Kimmet.

Christmas tree in the town square of every city, while foot soldiers placed fully lit, heavily guarded nativity scenes in front of every Iraqi mosque.

"Thus far, Operation Desert Santa has gone off without a hitch," said Gen. Stanley Kimmet, commander of U.S. armed reconnaissance-and-mistletoe operations in the volatile Tikrit region of central Iraq. "There has been sporadic house-to-house fighting during our door-to-door caroling, but that's to be expected in a Christmas season of this magnitude."

According to Lt. Gen. Ricardo Sanchez, the top American military commander in Iraq, every precaution is being taken to ensure the peaceful enforcement of the Christmas season in occupied Iraq.

"All American military personnel have been instructed that the observation of Christmas should be carried out efficiently and tastefully, with minimal emphasis on the season's commercial aspects," said Sanchez, who addressed reporters while a decorations division strung wreaths and garlands outside his headquarters. "We must keep in mind that the reason for the season-oriented campaign is for Iraq to celebrate the birth of our Lord and Savior Jesus Christ."

An aide for Sanchez later explained that, in order to ensure a meaningful holiday season for all Iraqis, provisions were made for those Iraqis who elected to observe Hanukkah.

Like many U.S. operations in Iraq, Operation Desert Santa has met with some resistance. A convoy transporting fruitcake and gingerbread came under rocket attack Sunday night just outside Checkpoint Noël in Basra, and unidentified bands of Iraqis exchanged gunfire with Marines operating an armored Humvee simulated sleigh ride in a Baghdad suburb. In spite of these troubles, regional commanders report progress, with only eight U.S. casualties resulting from the operation.

Still, Iraqis report that they are unable to get into the Christmas spirit.

"Why am I supposed to feel joy for the world?" said 34-year-old Baghdad mechanic Hassan al-Ajili as he stood in line for his mandatory visit with Santa. "My country is still at war. I need an American identification card to get anywhere in my own city. Now, for some reason, men with machine guns have placed two rows of jingling antlered pigs on the roof of our house. This is insane."

Bush, speaking from his Crawford ranch, praised the brave men and women of Operation Desert Santa and asked for the understanding of all Americans.

"We must be patient with the Iraqis," said Bush, seated before a Christmas tree dotted with Scottish terrier ornaments. "The holidays can be a very stressful time, especially for people not yet used to the customs. I'm sure Iraq will enjoy the happiest of holiday seasons if we show resolve and commit to making sure that they do."

President Bush then called for 30,000 new troops to be deployed in the next week to ensure an effective and precise enforcement of Christmas throughout the region. Salvation and Eighth Army detachments will be stationed on every corner by Christmas Eve to make sure that every last Iraqi citizen spends the holiday at home, with family.

Sanchez said he is confident that he can meet that deadline.

"A merry Christmas in Iraq means peace in the Middle East has finally been achieved," Sanchez said. "God bless us, every one." ∅

Above: A mosque in Baghdad decorated by U.S. troops.

PETS from page 49

being held to impossibly high animal-body standards perpetrated by the media.

"I don't care what anyone says, my Sassy looks good," said Janice Guswhite, owner of a Persian longhair that cannot climb the stairs to her home's second floor without becoming short of breath. "Who's to say how big a cat is supposed to be, anyway?"

The American Veterinary Medical Association is trying. The organization recently announced that nearly one-fourth of all U.S. cats and dogs are overweight. While many owners say they are comfortable with their pets' extra weight, the AVMA says ignoring pet obesity could have dire health consequences.

"Many pet owners might think it's cute when Sparky lies next to his food bowl all day because he doesn't have the energy to walk away from it," said Dr. Ken Janokovski, spokesman for the AVMA. "But overweight animals are susceptible to diabetes, heart disease, arthritis, pancreatitis, and a host of other illnesses."

"By simply lowering the number of times you fill the food bowl, and providing enough space to exercise, you can dramatically increase your pet's quality of life," Janokovski said. "Pets are part of your family. You should treat them accordingly."

In spite of the possible health risks, many owners of so-called obese pets insist that a few extra pounds can't hurt their dogs, cats, or guinea pigs.

"Animals know how and when to eat by instinct," said Travis Linsom, owner of a clinically overweight hamster. "Oscar only eats what he needs, then keeps the rest in his pouch while he sleeps in the corner all day. That's just how hamsters are. I'm not going to force Oscar to get on the wheel just because some vet is freaking out about hypoglycemia."

Pet body-image activist Miriam Grimer said owners shouldn't let doctors dictate their pets' weight.

"It's insulting that 'experts' are telling our pets how to live," Grimer said. "Our pets are perfectly fine with the way they look. No animal should be forced to live up to the unobtainable standard of beauty on the cover of a magazine like *Cat Fancy*."

Preferring terms like "plump," "stout," and "curvy," Eric Willis said he's proud

---

"I don't care what anyone says, my Sassy looks good," said Janice Guswhite, owner of a Persian longhair that cannot climb the stairs to her home's second floor without becoming short of breath.

---

that his 110-pound golden retriever has "a little something on the hindquarters."

"Jasmine might not be able to run as fast as other dogs, but when I take her to the park, you can bet she gets noticed by the male dogs," Willis said. "Not like Clementine, that skinny little English pointer down the block. Her owner must not care about her at all."

Pet owners like Willis say they have no intention of changing their feeding habits.

"No one's going to tell me that Tippy isn't beautiful the way he is," Mathers said. "If he wants to lose weight, that's fine. But he doesn't have to do it for me, or the vet, or even my husband, who doesn't want Tippy allowed in the living room because of his intestinal troubles. I think Tippy's perfect, even if he can't fit through his doggy door anymore." ∅

DVD from page 51

stupid movie?" Rosenstein asked. "Fucking bullshit aspect ratio!"

As of press time, Rosenstein had not decided what to do with the DVD.

"I can't trade it to any of my friends," Rosenstein said. "They'd just roll their eyes when they saw it wasn't letterboxed. Basically, I'm screwed. I'm stuck with a product that has no reason to exist."

"I suppose I could just throw it away," Rosenstein continued. "But what if Aunt Hannah or Uncle Bernie asked about it? I'll probably have to just keep this horrible thing on my

shelf. I'm trapped, like Neo and the other warriors of Zion, in a

---

"I suppose I could just throw it away," Rosenstein continued.

---

fictitious world I never chose to be a part of: an imaginary alternate universe where non-widescreen DVDs are remotely tolerable." ∅

How Can I Use Feminism To My Advantage?

By Megan Heller

Knowledge is power. In this competitive, male-dominated world, a woman must take advantage of all the resources at her disposal. Luckily, I found a way to take the idea that men and women should be socially, politically, and economically equal, and make it work for me. Now I'm subverting the dominant paradigm—and raking in the benefits!

I learned about feminism at least 10 years ago, but at that point, I still didn't know how valuable it was. Of course, I believed that every woman had a right to an education, proper healthcare, political representation, and equal career opportunities, but I never saw the point in spending *my* valuable time working for the empowerment of *all* women.

All that changed when I started school at Macalester College and met Erica. Everyone in the dorm was afraid of Erica, because she attacked the racist and sexist welcome-week party. By the fourth day of classes, Erica was a dorm-wide celebrity. I heard girls talking about her in the bathroom, boys talking about her in the dining hall. Nobody even knew I existed.

What was the difference between Erica and me? You guessed it: feminism. Well, not for long, sister.

Once we became closer, Erica told me that she didn't care about the stupid luau anyway. She had bigger things to worry about, like defending women against the so-called Right's war against reproductive liberties. Her work at the Campus Coalition For Women sounded thrilling. I wanted to cash in on the centuries-long subjugation of my gender, too!

Many modern women are afraid to call themselves feminists. I often remind these weak, confused women of the words of Gloria Steinem: "In my heart, I think a woman has two choices: Either she's a feminist or a masochist." When I first read Steinem, she awoke ambitions I never knew I had. I wanted to be just like her—powerful, famous, and financially well off.

Since my awakening, I've memorized quotations from feminists of all stripes, from Betty Friedan to Susan Faludi. Decades of activists have left persuasive arguments in support of my campus group's private study lounge in the student union. Hey, whatever works. Take that, International Students Club! Have fun studying in the library, with all the other losers who don't have a dedicated study lounge.

Not all feminists have this attitude, and I'm relieved. If they did, feminism wouldn't work half as well as it does. Most of the women in the network are fully committed to eradicating harmful gender stereotypes and redefining sexual archetypes. I am, too, whenev-

> **Many modern women are afraid to call themselves feminists. I often remind these weak, confused women of the words of Gloria Steinem: "In my heart, I think a woman has two choices: Either she's a feminist or a masochist."**

er it places me in a favorable social position.

In high school, I was the head cheerleader, but when I got to college, that didn't count anymore. Thank God I met Erica! She and her friends have taught me the fundament of feminist dialoguing: Nobody wants to be labeled a misogynist. Fewer still want to engage in a heated debate about whether *The Matrix Revolutions'* Trinity subverts her meanings to those of the authorized males Morpheus and Neo—but that didn't stop me from doing so, loudly, while waiting in line to see *Sylvia*. And was Erica impressed! The more I educate my peers about the origins of sexist no(men)clature, the higher my position rises.

I'm a real leader in the women's-studies program and have assumed authority over many women who actually care about universal contraceptive access and gender bias in textbooks. Case in point: I landed a coveted work-study position at the Women's Health Action & Mobilization office. Meanwhile, my old high-school cheerleading teammate Kelly is working at the deli in the student union, where she's forced to wear a hairnet. Kelly and I have nothing in common anymore. Can you believe that she's actually in a sorority? I don't even talk to her, except for that time I asked her how it feels to be a member of the campus date-rape club. She didn't have an answer for that. She just handed me my pita sandwich, dumbstruck.

I'm dating Dylan, a woman who volunteers at the Coalition For Gay, Les-

> **I'm dating Dylan, a woman who volunteers at the Coalition For Gay, Lesbian And Bi Rights For The Homeless. Sure, I'm not really a lesbian, but showing up at Take Back The Night with Dylan captured *a lot* of attention.**

bian And Bi Rights For The Homeless. Sure, I'm not really a lesbian, but showing up at Take Back The Night with Dylan captured *a lot* of atten-

tion. When I was in the bathroom stall the other day, I heard two girls I didn't even know talking about me. See, this feminism stuff works.

The thing that really surprised me, given the fundament of feminist dialoguing, is how easy it is to use feminism against fellow feminists. Last night at the student council meeting, I accused Angie Hopilite of being an "enemy of all women." She said creating a lighted safe-walk on Campus Drive was a bad idea, because of the traffic. She said the funds should go to displaced, battered women at—surprise, surprise—the shelter where she volunteers. To gain the upper hand, I had to use a little bit of jargon. I accused Angie of supporting the coercionary practices of establishment feminism and noted that Jung said attempting social engineering through politics only results in reality being driven into the unconscious. The vote came down 11 to 1 in my favor. Take that, Angie. We'll see who gets to take the all-expenses-paid trip to the WHAM national conference in D.C. this year. ✍

Your Horoscope

By Lloyd Schumner Sr.
Retired Machinist and
A.A.P.B.-Certified Astrologer

Aries: (March 21–April 19)
What you thought was a folksy comment turns out to be the plain truth when wet, slushy snow and heavy winds combine to make for rough sledding.

Taurus: (April 20–May 20)
Optimism will once again be your downfall when, during a trip to Ohio, you assume that the angry natives will be awed into submission by your lighter.

Gemini: (May 21–June 21)
Mars rising with the moon in syzygy says nothing about your future. It means "Screw you, fatty."

Cancer: (June 22–July 22)
People will finally admit that you fulfilled your potential when you pass out in bed and your crack pipe sets off a massive goat-porn fire.

Leo: (July 23–Aug. 22)
Next time, when passing a note intended to find out if someone likes you, you'll know to provide more than one box to check.

Virgo: (Aug. 23–Sept. 22)
It's always the last person you'd expect that ends up being a murderer, marrying your sibling, or getting elected president.

Libra: (Sept. 23–Oct. 23)
It won't be failure to adapt that kills you, but the ability to pause live television.

Scorpio: (Oct. 24–Nov. 21)
You'll fend off a lot of polite inquiries from Asians before you realize that your new Chinese tattoo actually reads "Ask Me About My Grandchildren."

Sagittarius: (Nov. 22–Dec. 21)
A chance remark at a bar will result in a pack of angry, middle-aged drunks insisting, in the face of all evidence to the contrary, that punk is not dead.

Capricorn: (Dec. 22–Jan. 19)
Your love for the unexpected joy of "snow days" will not translate directly into a love for next week's hellish rains of fire and blood.

Aquarius: (Jan. 20–Feb. 18)
The stars can warn you not to argue with clergymen over predestination this week, though they are ultimately helpless to stop you.

Pisces: (Feb. 19–March 20)
If you enjoyed last week, then relax. As usual, this week won't be a whole lot different from the previous one.

the ONION®

VOLUME 40 ISSUE 02 | **AMERICA'S FINEST NEWS SOURCE**™ | **15–21 JANUARY 2004**

Fran Drescher Screeches Out For Cancer Awareness

see ENTERTAINMENT page 1D

Crucifix A Testament To Man's Wealth

see MONEY page 9E

Jogging Fat Man Watched From Apartment Window

see LOCAL page 4C

Headlights Caught In Deer

see LOCAL page 3C

STATshot

A look at the numbers that shape your world.

What Medical Advice Are We Ignoring?

14%	Something about being contagious
21%	No alcohol for next hour
25%	Stop chewing on wound
12%	Don't take all 30 pills at once
15%	Leave cone around neck for two weeks
13%	Anything that contradicts God's grand plan for us to die of dysentery

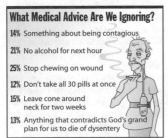

THE ONION • $2.00 US • $3.00 CAN

U.S. To Give Every Iraqi $3,544.91, Let Free-Market Capitalism Do The Rest

WASHINGTON, DC—At a Monday press conference, U.S. Defense Secretary Donald Rumsfeld announced a "change of plans" for the $87.5 billion aid package Congress approved in October: Instead of being used to fund an array of military and reconstruction operations in the Middle East, the money will be divided equally among Iraq's 24,683,313 citizens.

"Yes, we had planned to do all sorts of things with that money, like repair Iraq's power grid and construct new sewers and roads," Rumsfeld said. "But then we realized that, really, there's no reason for us to rebuild Iraq's infrastructure when the forces of free-market capitalism can do it with greater efficiency."

Rumsfeld said that, while the U.S. public's desire to hasten the end of America's presence in Iraq is growing, continued insurgence against the

see IRAQ page 58

Above: A U.S. aid worker distributes reconstruction funds in Fallujah.

Typo Results In 10,000-Acre Wyoming Skate Park

JACKSON, WY—A simple typographical error in a proposal to set aside a scenic Big Horn Mountain valley for public recreation has resulted in the construction of the 10,020-acre Henrietta Bedford Memorial Skate Park, Wyoming Department of Natural Resources officials announced Tuesday.

"I am pleased to dedicate Wyoming's new skate park," said baffled Wyoming Parks Department supervisor William DuBois, reading from a prepared statement. "This skateboarding park honors the memory of Miss Henrietta Bedford, a leading Wyoming conservationist, physician,

see TYPO page 59

Short-Distance Relationship Too Much Work

GASTONIA, NC—After four months together, sales manager Jack Petrakis, 29, and paralegal Justine Froeger, 26, reported Tuesday that dating someone who lives in the same building isn't worth the hassle.

"Everyone warned me that these short-distance things never work out," said Froeger, who recently spent a night with a friend in nearby Charlotte just to escape the stifling proximity of her short-distance boyfriend. "But I thought I would be different, that my love would be strong enough to handle the less than 1,000 feet separating Jack from me."

Froeger, who lives in a one-bedroom

see RELATIONSHIP page 58

Left: Froeger and Petrakis run into each other yet again.

Fingerprinting Foreign Visitors

To improve national security, last week the U.S. began fingerprinting and photographing foreigners arriving at air- and seaports. What do *you* think?

"What? They have fingerprints? Those bastards become more like humans every day."

James R. Webb
Marine Engineer

"They're taking photos? That's useless. Everyone looks like a terrorist in an ID photo."

Paula Holt
Writer

"I've always thought that people should have to jump through more hoops for the privilege of visiting a glorious bastion of freedom and liberty like America."

Shirley Crawford
Illustrator

"This information will come in handy if we ever need to determine exactly who touched the counter at the St. Louis Arch gift shop."

Edgar Little
Systems Analyst

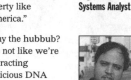

"Why the hubbub? It's not like we're extracting delicious DNA samples from them. Did I say delicious? I meant invasive."

Alex Mason
Dishwasher

"They do the photography and fingerprinting at no charge? America truly is the land of opportunity!"

Ronald Ramirez
Guard

The Mars Rover

Exploration of Mars has always posed great challenges for NASA. What difficulties do scientists face?

➤ Communication with ground control hampered by fact that Mars is really, really far away

➤ Electromagnetic permeability of Mars' radiosphere subject to variation, making it difficult for telemetry personnel to compensate for interference while drunk

➤ SDI satellites often identify probes as storm clouds, Korean airliners, or flocks of geese, and shoot them down

➤ Rovers' miniature computer brains run risk of getting computer minds blown by giant rock formation that looks exactly like human face

➤ Difficulty getting accounting department to understand why rover has to be able to bounce up and down while playing "Rollout (My Business)" by Ludacris

➤ Must maneuver around burnt-out hunks of failed probes littering Martian surface

➤ Getting Travis from across town to finally add flame detailing to rover, like he's been promising

➤ Because Rovers are technically a form of tiny cars, the probes are at risk of being eaten by the man from Mars, who also eats bars and, most recently, guitars

the ONION®
America's Finest News Source.™

Herman Ulysses Zweibel
Founder

T. Herman Zweibel
Publisher Emeritus
J. Phineas Zweibel
Publisher
Maxwell Prescott Zweibel
Editor-In-Chief

I'll Have You Know I Have Several Black Friendsters

By Harold Evars

Me, prejudiced? Of all the slanderous, hurtful, and untrue things you could say! I may have had a somewhat sheltered upbringing, but I'm extremely tolerant of all kinds of people. I would never pass judgment onsomeone because of the color of his skin. Look, I'll have you know I have *several* black Friendsters.

I have four Friendsters of color right at this very moment, in fact, and I'll probably connect with even more soon. I log on with no preconceived notions whatsoever.

Take, for example, how I met my very good black Friendster Geoff. I was looking through my college friend Sarah's Friendsters, and he was listed as one of her 62 friends. It turned out Geoff and I both love *The Simpsons* and *The Lord Of The Rings*, so I invited him to be my Friendster. I did this without an ounce of prejudice about the fact that he happens to be black. A couple of days later, Geoff accepted my invitation, and we've been Friendsters ever since. Every couple of weeks, we'll IM back and forth about the newest Simpsons episode. Would a "xenophobic suburbanite" do something like that? Would

> Take, for example, how I met my very good black Friendster Geoff. I was looking through my college friend Sarah's Friendsters, and he was listed as one of her 62 friends. It turned out Geoff and I both love *The Simpsons* and *The Lord Of The Rings*, so I invited him to be my Friendster.

a "clueless, stuck-up, spoiled brat" carry on that kind of intimate Friendstership with a black person?

I'm not saying it's a big deal to have a black Friendster. Does my Friendstership with Geoff make me better than anyone else? No. Would I claim that I'm more cultured and enlight-

ened, just because I have one black Friendster? Of course not. But Geoff's not the only one.

There's also Kim. You see, a couple of months ago, I saw this really cute girl named Shannon in my Friendster Adam's list, so I checked out her pro-

> It's really sad that some of my real-life friends don't have any black Friendsters. They're missing out on so much. After you've become Friendsters with a black person, your eyes are opened to how important it is to explore the diversity that exists in your own Internet community.

file. After viewing all of her photos and skimming her interests, I started browsing through her female friends, too. Kim was on the second page, about halfway down. She looked really hot in her thumbnail. She's around my age, so I invited her to be in my network. She e-mailed me back— "sure I guess why not ;)"—and we've been hard and fast Friendsters ever since.

As for my other two black Friendsters, Johnny and Sean, I can scarcely remember how they ended up in my circle. You see, Friendstership with a black person is no different from any other Friendstership. Sometimes it's difficult to remember exactly how it started.

Have my black Friendsters changed my worldview? I believe so. Just scrolling through their interests has opened my eyes to things I wouldn't ever have known about if all of my Friendsters were white. Without the influence of Kim and Sean, I probably wouldn't have considered reading *Milk In My Coffee* by Eric Jerome Dickey. But since they both listed it as one of their favorite books, I may check it out someday.

It's really sad that some of my real-life friends don't have any black Friendsters. They're missing out on so much. After you've become Friendsters with a black person, your eyes

see FRIENDSTER page 59

Angolan Temp Agency Teeming With Mercenaries

LUANDA, ANGOLA—Operators of Keliba Temporary Services of Angola announced Monday that they have been swamped with unemployed citizens seeking temporary mercenary work.

"It's a madhouse," said Imaculada Bimbi, manager of Keliba Temps. "When we open up in the morning, there is a line of camouflage-clad men waiting at the door."

When the rebel UNITA [National Union for the Total Independence of Angola] and the Angolan government signed a cease-fire in 2002, they ended the civil war that plagued the southwest African nation for more than 25 years, but left several hundred thousand mercenaries jobless. Around 75 percent of these soldiers-for-hire eventually turned to temping.

"Some call us five or six times a day," Bimbi said. "Others sit in the waiting room cleaning their rifles and flipping through back issues of *Angola Today*, just waiting for jobs to come."

Bimbi said that, because Keliba Temps maintains a waiting list and keeps applicants on file for six months, there's no reason for the men to spend the day in the office.

"If the UNITA insurgents were able to locate mercenaries on the planalto, then we should be capable of finding them in their homes," Bimbi said. "But they sit here and drink pot after pot of complimentary coffee, litter banana peels and dried fish tails on the floors, and wash their bandannas in the bathroom sink."

Bimbi explained the mercenaries' reluctance to relocate to regions with more favorable employment climates.

> "Working the front desk requires communication skills, a professional appearance, patience, and the ability to type," Bimbi said. "I can't tell you how many keyboards have been split apart with machetes during our standard typing test."

"Many have lived in Angola all their lives, and do not want to go all the way to the Congo or Sierra Leone to find work," Bimbi said. "Now, Angola will always have a need for qualified, experienced mercenaries, and the work they do is very valuable. But we simply have too many workers and not enough jobs."

Above: Unemployed mercenaries wait for work in the Keliba Temporary Services office.

Last month, Keliba Temps was forced to hire several extra staff members to handle the influx of mercenaries. Although Bimbi considered hiring a mercenary for the front-desk position, none of the applicants had the proper qualifications.

"Working the front desk requires communication skills, a professional appearance, patience, and the ability to type," Bimbi said. "I can't tell you how many keyboards have been split apart with machetes during our standard typing test."

Bimbi said early attempts to place mercenaries among the non-mercenary workforce ended in disaster.

"My first week here, I sent a mercenary to work on the assembly line in a PVC factory," Bimbi said. "I later learned that the mercenary had, in his former job, blown up the line supervisor's vegetable stand and kidnapped his teenage daughter."

Bimbi now attempts to do more thorough background checks.

"But it's hard," Bimbi said. "Most of our clients' references turn out to be dead."

see AGENCY page 59

Feedback Taking Too Long To Be Positive

GRAND RAPIDS, MI—Aspiring screenwriter Stephen Helfer, 26, expressed concern Monday that feedback from friend Jason Novak regarding his screenplay *The Domino Affair* was taking too long to be positive. "I know Jason is a busy guy, but I gave it to him three weeks ago," Helfer said. "It didn't even take me this long to write the thing." Helfer added that he had a hunch it was a mistake to include the fourth speedboat chase.

Iran Moves To Ban Events Of Mass Destruction

TEHRAN, IRAN—After years of refusing to provide information about the country's underground activities, Iranian president Mohammad Khatami surprised the world Monday by announcing that the nation has decided to ban events of mass destruction. "Opening the doors to seismic reform is the first step toward ensuring a safer future for the people of Iran," Khatami announced on Al-Jazeera. "We will voluntarily make moves to ban further production of devastating seismic waves like those experienced during the earthquake in Bam." Even Iranian political and religious hardliner Ayatollah Hashemi Janati lauded the decision, stating that it "will eliminate the need to stretch our hands out for the charity of our warmongering American oppressors."

Grandmother Can't Believe They Let People With Tattoos On *Price Is Right*

GREAT BEND, KS—Grandmother of nine Sadie Grunfelder, 71, expressed surprise Tuesday when a tattooed contestant was allowed to play "Buy Or Sell" on the long-running game show *The Price Is Right*. "I can't believe that Bob Barker would let someone with a tattoo up on stage," Grunfelder said from her recliner. "I would think they'd at least make him cover up that terrible thing. What if there are children somewhere, home sick from school, watching this show?" Luckily, Grunfelder's two other means of access to the outside world—the AARP newsletter and reruns of *Dr. Quinn, Medicine Woman*—remain tattoo-free.

McDonald's Introduces McCrazy Burger

OAK BROOK, IL—Responding to an over-abundance of low-cost beef, McDonald's unveiled the new five-patty McCrazy Burger Tuesday. "A pound and a half of all-American beef topped with lettuce, tomatoes, and a dollop of our new peppercorn sauce," said Melanie Haas, marketing director for the fast-food giant's Northwest region. "We promise you'll go crazy from the delicious taste of 100 percent pure beef, and not from bovine spongiform encephalopathy!" Haas refused to comment on the exact geographic origin of the cattle used in the new sandwich.

First-Generation American's Job Taken By His Father

READING, PA—Miguel Martinez, 48, who immigrated to the U.S. 30 years ago, last week lost his leather-cutting job at GST AutoLeather, Inc. to his 66-year-old father Roberto. "I came to this country in 1974 to make a better life for my family," Martinez said Monday. "But in December, they moved the factory where I've been working for 22 years down to Nuevo Laredo, Mexico. I love my father, but that goddamn beaner stole my job." Martinez's $18-an-hour duties will now be performed by his father for $7 a day. ✍

IRAQ from page 55

Above: A child in Basra receives his $3,544.91.

occupation has rendered previous initiatives for political and economic recovery untenable. The situation prompted the Bush Administration to "think more creatively" about its Iraq policy.

"I assure you that our new plan for economic recovery is not only easier, it's better," Rumsfeld said. "If we simply step back and let the market do its thing, a perfectly functioning, merit-based, egalitarian society will rise out of the ashes. Probably some restau-

Allawi was quick to assert, loudly and repeatedly, that none of his family's money was actually on his person.

rants or hardware stores or something, too."

During the next six months, Rumsfeld said, each Iraqi man, woman, and child will receive a one-time payment of $3,544.91. On June 30, the transaction of all funds will be complete, and the sovereignty of a "brand-new, prosperous, secular, pluralistic, market-driven nation" will be handed to an as-yet-unformed government, probably one with a president and a congressional body of some sort.

"Heck, whatever form of democratic utopia comes out of this will be great," Rumsfeld said. "Why wouldn't it be? It'll be based on freedom of individual economic enterprise, and supply and demand will maximize consumer welfare."

About 100,000 citizens have already received their money, which was distributed in cash to circumvent the country's currently inadequate banking system.

The 14-member Allawi family in Tikrit received $49,628.74 Monday.

"I'm very excited," Ahmed Allawi said. "A free, unregulated market will swiftly and efficiently lead to the establishment of an array of fairly priced goods and services. Any day now, there should be something available to spend this money on. As for today, the open-air market down the street is still on fire."

Allawi was quick to assert, loudly and repeatedly, that none of his family's money was actually on his person.

According to U.S. civil administrator in Iraq Paul Bremer, reconstruction and repair of Iraq's dilapidated, damaged, destroyed, or non-existent sewers, roads, power grids, airports, phone lines, and hospitals will be handled by the private sector, with contracts being awarded to the companies offering the most attractive bids in terms of cost and quality of service.

"Yes, there have been difficulties securing building materials for construction projects, and there have been problems with guerrillas targeting contractors—some dynamiting has occurred," Bremer said. "But such setbacks are the remnants of Saddam's regime. As of July 1, these problems will not exist. As soon as the money is handed out, we'll be able to dismantle our entire security framework."

Even the building and running of Iraq's schools will be privatized.

"I believe we've seen what state-funded education did for Iraq," Bremer said. "I can say with confidence that it's the last thing they need."

According to Bremer, as soon as capitalism brings an end to ethnic and religious tension, U.S. troops will pull out of Iraq.

Fortunately, few Iraqi government structures need to be put into place. In accepting the $87.5 billion aid package, the Iraqi Governing Council has agreed to banish all restrictions on trade, capital flow, and foreign investment.

While the original aid package included $100 million to support the writing of a constitution and the holding of national elections, the new "$3,544.91 For All" plan contains no such allotment. Bremer did, however, help the Iraqi Governing Council draft a 25-word "Iraqi Promise Of Excellence."

Bremer said returning the government to the men and women of Iraq solves one problem that had confounded his team: deciding how rule would be divided among Sunni Muslims, Shiites, and Kurds.

"Under the new system, the religious, ethnic, or political group offering the best service will naturally beat out the competition," Bremer said. "It's that simple!" ⌀

RELATIONSHIP from page 55

on the fifth floor of Manning Towers, and Petrakis, who occupies a studio on the fourth, met in the building's laundry room last September.

"We were both down there waiting for our clothes to dry, so we started to talk," Petrakis said. "It turned out we had a lot in common—we shopped at the same grocery store and worked out at the same gym. At that point, I wasn't thinking about the future and how hard this sort of relationship can be."

For several weeks, Froeger and Petrakis enjoyed a protracted honeymoon period, during which the short distance dividing them seemed like an advantage. Friends report that Petrakis and Froeger thought it was adorable to share a mailman, bump into each other near the trash bin, and frequent the same coffeehouse.

"At first, Jack would brag about how cool it was to get a midnight 'booty call' from a sexy girl only three doors down and one floor below," Petrakis' friend Doug Maris said. "He was like, 'I don't even need to change out of my pajamas. I just put on slippers, answer the door, and I'm ready for action.'"

"He's not bragging anymore," Maris continued. "Last week, a bunch of the guys were hanging out at his place when someone knocked on the door. Jack made us all stand there, frozen in place and totally silent, for about five minutes until he could be sure that whoever it was had left."

Both Froeger and Petrakis said they began to experience misgivings about the lack of distance dividing them in early December.

"When I met Jack, I'd just broken up with this guy from Toledo, so I was really looking forward to dating someone nearby," Froeger said. "Now, I realize that having him so nearby that I can hear him whistling *every* time he uses the elevator isn't an advantage. And I do mean every time he uses the elevator. Seriously, every single time—that same OutKast song."

"Justine is sweet," Petrakis said. "But sometimes it's too much. Once, I stayed at my buddy's house after a late night of drinking. When Justine saw that I hadn't picked up my newspaper from the doormat, she called to make sure I was okay. That's when I started feeling crowded."

In addition to infringing on each other's privacy, Froeger and Petrakis said the close proximity removes a level of excitement from the relationship.

"Part of the fun of getting involved with someone is immersing yourself in a new environment and experiencing new things," Froeger said. "But staying overnight at someone's place isn't as great when you live on the same block. Our apartments overlook the same exact tree."

"Now we have no excuse to make it downtown or anyplace else," Froeger continued. "And believe me, Jack doesn't look for one, either. We just order delivery from the menus we both already know by heart."

Petrakis agreed that "things are getting a little stale."

"Justine and I kiss goodbye in the morning, then I see her 30 minutes later in the parking lot," Petrakis said. "Then I get home, and boom! There

In addition to infringing on each other's privacy, Froeger and Petrakis said the close proximity removes a level of excitement from the relationship.

she is in the elevator. I don't know what to do. I've told her that I need my space, but her space and my space are practically the same space."

Froeger said she has started to think she needs someone who will "be there for me occasionally."

"The next person I date should live in, say, Chicago or Minneapolis," Froeger said. "There are a lot of nice guys from the Midwest profiled on those Internet dating sites. If I was seeing someone farther away, we could spend a passionate weekend together, but I wouldn't have to sit around at Starbucks for an extra two hours after work until I'm certain I won't run into him."

Petrakis said he agrees that a breakup might be the only answer.

"Next time I'm on the market, I'm gonna get out to a lot of out-of-the-way bars in neighborhoods that I wouldn't normally have any reason to be in, like that area behind the expo center," Petrakis said. "From now on, I'm going to stick with the 50-block rule: no dating anyone who doesn't live at least a 10-minute car ride away." ⌀

TYPO from page 55

and women's-suffrage activist—a woman who knew the importance of nature to the radical and the sick."

DuBois then assisted Wyoming Gov. Dave Freudenthal in cutting a ribbon stretched across the park's 22-foot-deep, mile-long half-pipe, the largest ever installed in a state-run outdoor recreation facility.

Park officials said the typo went un-

> **Additional features of the park include a system of high-curbs and railings to replicate the natural environment of street skaters, a goofy-footed stalefish estuary on the banks of the Laramie River, and a 120-acre migration habitat intended to draw the graceful yet elusive Tony Hawk.**

detected, as it was a minor rider to the "Healthy Forests Initiative," which granted timber companies greater access to public forests.

By the time the error was identified, state officials had already spent $43 million integrating the skate park's numerous ramps, rails, pipes, and inclines into the natural topography of the Absaroka Range. After some deliberation, park officials voted to complete the skate park.

"No, it might not have otherwise occurred to me to build a grind rail running the length of Mount Logan's East Ridge," Wyoming Department of

Above: Jason Westphal, 15, enjoys an afternoon of fresh air and sunshine.

Natural Resources director James Hester said. "Nor would I have recognized the scree moraines on the south face of the Absarokas as the perfect foundation for a system of interlocking skate bowls. And I'm as surprised as anyone to see the waters of the Shoshone River running through a system of concrete half-pipes. However, the Wyoming Division of Cultural Resources, in partnership with the United States Department of Natural Resources, made a commitment, and we honor our commitments."

Additional features of the park include a system of high-curbs and railings to replicate the natural environment of street skaters, a goofy-footed stalefish estuary on the banks of the

Laramie River, and a 120-acre migration habitat intended to draw the graceful yet elusive Tony Hawk.

Although construction of the skate park has been roundly criticized by environmental groups and the majority of Wyoming's citizens, the park has found supporters in the "extreme sporting" community.

"Without question, this is a big step in the right direction for the state of Wyoming," said *Thrasher* magazine editor Jake Phelps, who praised the move from his San Francisco office. "Although I hear the park is heavily biased towards vert with only a few street elements, I think it's a start. I hope other states will follow the precedent set by Gov. Freudenthal and consider creating ideal environ-

ments for ripping wicked fakies."

Added Phelps: "Wyoming isn't that weak-beer state, is it? Oh, no, that's Utah? Razor."

Perhaps attempting to make the best of the gaffe, Wyoming Game and Fish Department director Terry Cleveland said he sees the skate park as a positive addition to the Wyoming landscape.

"We'll be attracting a segment of the population that might never have visited our state's spectacular public wildlife areas before," Cleveland said. "The debate on public land use has always been one of preservation versus access. In this case, we chose access. I only hope people keep an open mind about our decision to allow citizens the freedom to shred." ∅

AGENCY from page 57

According to Bimbi, the agency has even had problems after successfully placing a mercenary within his field.

"We always have to chase them down for their paperwork," Bimbi said. "They demand payment, but they won't hand in their time sheets. They're very good at hunting stray dogs and roasting them outside the office in that garbage can, but not so good at reporting their hours."

Keliba Temporary Services is not alone. Many Angolan temp agencies have reported problems with too many unemployed mercenaries and not enough requests for beheadings, ambushes, and torchings.

"A few months ago, we had an employer who had five mercenary openings on a team that he was sending into Namibia to overtake a rice convoy," said Jonas Lukamba, manager of the Manpower Professional Servicing

branch in Menongue. "But since then, there has been nothing. We held a weekend workshop to train a group of kidnappers, torturers, and renegade pilots on Excel, but the seminar ended in bloodshed."

The mercenary field is so flooded, Lukamba said, that he regularly receives phone calls from employment agencies across the country asking if his branch has openings for mercenaries.

"These calls are very irritating," Lukamba said. "Every time the phone rings, 15 heavily armed men leap to their feet and rush the counter."

"Perhaps one day soon, a corrupt warlord will rise to power in Angola and need men to hack apart villagers and urinate on the remains," Lukamba added. "Until then, all I can do is try to get these men working as telephone solicitors." ∅

FRIENDSTER from page 56

are opened to how important it is to explore the diversity that exists in your own Internet community.

Just the other day, I was talking to my cousin Chris, and I found myself thinking, "How can he say Al Sharpton is just a figurehead candidate? Doesn't he see how important it is to have black people in positions of political prominence? Doesn't he understand how hard it is to be a black person in this country?" But of course, Chris doesn't have any black Friendsters, so he probably doesn't ever have to think about these things. I didn't even try to explain. He wouldn't understand.

Someday, I'm going to have a party and invite all of my Friendsters. It sure would be great to meet my black Friendsters in person and see them standing there amongst my coworkers and real friends. I wonder what

Johnny is really like? What does Geoff's voice sound like? What kind of clothes would Kim wear? What would Sean think of my apartment? I'm sure we'd all grow a lot that night.

Would I even consider a party like that if I weren't tolerant and compassionate? Does that sound like a party that an "asshole who just doesn't get it" would throw? I didn't think so.

I truly believe that when you open your mind, you stop focusing on the differences between people and begin to notice the similarities. Deep down, we're all just people with profiles on Friendster. Sure, the face in Sean's uploaded jpeg might be black, and the one in mine might be white, but at the end of the day, aren't we both just two humans walking the same earth in search of Activity Partners, Friends, and Dating (Women)? ∅

An Entertaining New Year

**The Outside Scoop
By Jackie Harvey**

Well, 2003 is over. Happy 2004! This is one exciting year for Jackie Harvey. It's a leap year and an election year all rolled into one! What better way to start off a big year than with a big 2003 year-end wrap-up?

Item! As an entertainment writer, it's my responsibility to choose the **Entertainer Of The Year**. And unless you were living in a hole, you know the honor goes to none other than the wild and crazy guy himself: **Mr. Steve Martin!** This year alone, Steve starred in the instant comedy classics **Bring Back The House**, **Looney Toons: Back To School**, and **Cheaper As The Dozen**. Oh, and lest I forget, he released the long-awaited follow-up to his book *Cruel Shoes*. I'm waiting for the paperback edition, but if the book is anywhere near as funny as his hosting of the **Grammys**, it'll be gold.

The film event of the year? **The Cat In The Hat**. Who but **Michael Meyers** could breathe life into such an old book? As the cat in the title, he magically prances through the land of imagination. It awoke the kid in me without putting the adult in me to sleep. I can't wait for the sequel!

Item! Saddam? We got him! All the best military operations are named after '80s action films, and this one

---

The film event of the year? *The Cat In The Hat.* Who but Michael Meyers could breathe life into such an old book? As the cat in the title, he magically prances through the land of imagination. It awoke the kid in me without putting the adult in me to sleep. I can't wait for the sequel!

---

was no exception. **Operation Red Dawn** was a smashing success, flushing the **Butcher Of Baghdad** out into the open and bringing him to justice. Justice for all! Hooray!

This was also the year of the big celebrity love affair, and the biggest

of all was the love affair shared by **Aston Kucher** and **Demy Moore**. Is it just me, though, or does there seem to be a bit of an age difference between those two? Well, it's not for me to judge. Like they say, **love conquers all**.

Speaking of couples, whatever hap-

Item! After three years, The Lord Of The Rings is finally over, and it went out with a bang. I don't usually go in for that magic and dragon stuff, but this series was great. Or at least the commercials look great. I haven't seen the movies yet. I still need to watch the first two, and who has the time to sit still for nine hours? Not I!

---

pened to **Huey Long** and **Terry Hatcher** in those Radio Shack commercials? Not since **Moonlighting** has a **real-life married couple** made such a splash on the small screen, but I haven't seen one of their ads in a long time. I sure hope Huey and Terry aren't planning to get a divorce. That *would* be a tragedy!

I finally got around to renting **Pirates Of The Caribbean** on VHS, and I'm sorry, but it's just **Cutthroat Island** without **Regina Davis**. Save your money and rent something that'll really make your night, like **Who's That Girl?**

Item! After three years, **The Lord Of The Rings** is finally over, and it went out with a bang. I don't usually go in for that magic and dragon stuff, but this series was great. Or at least the commercials look great. I haven't seen the movies yet. I still need to watch the first two, and who has the time to sit still for nine hours? Not I!

Snickers has a new Marathon energy bar. I found out the hard way that it's not the **Marathon Bar** we all remember. Those were chewy and caramel-y and long and delicious. I wish I could recall the Marathon Bar jingle, but all I can dredge up is the **Hubba Bubba** song.

Item! The fall TV season was quite the train wreck! **Skin** was in, and then it was out. **Coupling** got uncoupled.

Your Horoscope

**By Lloyd Schumner Sr.
Retired Machinist and
A.A.P.B.-Certified Astrologer**

Aries: (March 21–April 19)
You suspect that personal feelings are taking priority over scientific endeavor when NASA announces they'll rocket your fat ass into orbit later this year.

Taurus: (April 20–May 20)
Sleep is hard to come by this week, as you struggle to understand why no one has yet come out with Jalapeño Cheese Wings.

Gemini: (May 21–June 21)
You're not the kind of person who constantly goes around saying the sky is falling, which makes you ill-equipped to cope with the events of this Thursday.

Cancer: (June 22–July 22)
You're ready to put that bad relationship and all its painful memories behind you, but unfortunately, it'll be available on DVD starting next week.

Leo: (July 23–Aug. 22)
Your credulity will be stretched to the limit by the circumstances under which only you can control the giant robot.

Virgo: (Aug. 23–Sept. 22)
You knew your mitochondria had their own DNA, but you had no idea that their taste in clothes was so different.

Libra: (Sept. 23–Oct. 23)
You're coming to regret that, when the choice was made available to you, you went with neither hugs nor drugs.

Scorpio: (Oct. 24–Nov. 21)
You'll make big news in Biblical archaeology when you find evidence that Job's trials included a four-year stint as head coach of the Chicago Bears.

Sagittarius: (Nov. 22–Dec. 21)
You've never been afraid to make bold statements concerning what you're all about, which leaves a lot of people emotionally unsatisfied by your ending.

Capricorn: (Dec. 22–Jan. 19)
You don't like using the words "wacky," "nutty," or "zany," but you'll find it hard to describe the inept band of crooks in any other way.

Aquarius: (Jan. 20–Feb. 18)
Your moral values foster the brotherhood of man under the fatherhood of God, which doesn't stop you from downloading tons of "mother-daughter" smut.

Pisces: (Feb. 19–March 20)
When all is said and done, only you can make yourself feel bad. But that won't keep everyone else from trying.

Tarzan was lord of the flops. **Alicia Silverman's Miss Match** went down in flames. **The Mullets** were… I'm still looking for something bad that rhymes with "mullet," but I can't think of anything right now. That's only a few of the season's flops, but I don't want to be too mean. I'm trying out this new writing style, but since it comes at the expense of a lot of decent, hardworking people in showbiz, I don't think I'll do it again.

Congrats to **Britney** and **Mr. Britney!** Best wishes on your sudden, unexpected marriage!

Have you heard that song about the **milkshake** they keep playing on the radio? Every time I hear it, I get thirsty. My favorite milkshake flavor is **strawberry**.

Speaking of music, when are we going to get the next installment of **American Idol**? I've just about worn out my **Kelly Clarksville** and **Clay Aikman** CDs. Time to bring on the next big star so I know what music to buy.

Item! Paris who? If you hadn't heard

of **Paris Hilton** until a few months ago, you're not alone. Her show **Life Is Simple** is one of my guilty pleasures. Seeing her work on a farm with **P. Diddy's daughter** is a real hoot. For some reason, I've been getting a lot of unsavory e-mails about Paris lately. Isn't it a shame when people feel the need to drag someone through the mud? Someone out there must be jealous, because Paris fought the odds to make it as an actress. Don't worry, Paris—keep your chin up. I've been the victim of undue cruelty, too. The incident is too painful to go into now, but it involved a **writing contest** and a **friend from high school**. 'Nuff said!

Well, that's it for this installment of The Outside Scoop. In case you were thinking about missing my next column, it will include an exciting tidbit about a certain sitcom actor and his new greyhound ranch. Until then, take a seat, plant your feet, pop in a good movie, and join me again…on The Outside! ∅

NEWS

the ONION®

VOLUME 40 ISSUE 03 | AMERICA'S FINEST NEWS SOURCE™ | 22–28 JANUARY 2004

Air Marshal Stuck In Conversation About Passenger's Patio

CHICAGO—American Trans Air Flight 282 from Chicago-Midway to Newark took a turn for the tedious Monday, when undercover air marshal Kirk Gillam was drawn into a conversation about passenger Terrence Delsman's patio for the majority of the two-hour flight.

"Most people just take whatever tiling option their contractor gives them," Delsman told Gillam. "But I did research online and opted for terracotta. I couldn't be happier."

Gillam is one of an esti-

mated 4,000 marshals placed in the cabins of U.S. commercial airlines by Homeland Security Director Tom Ridge in an effort to tighten aviation security.

Gillam, a former Navy SEAL, trained for 12 weeks last year in tactical terrorist suppression aboard an aircraft. Delsman, who was traveling to Newark on business, single-handedly spruced up his backyard in July.

see AIR MARSHAL page 65

Right: Gillam (right) finds out why pine planks aren't a good idea.

Disgruntled Liberals Publishing At Furious Pace

see BOOKS page 10H

Area Mother Displays Extensive Goya Collection

see LOCAL page 3C

African-American Neighborhood Terrorized By Ask Murderer

see LOCAL page 4C

Laugh Track Easily Amused

see ENTERTAINMENT page 11D

STATshot

A look at the numbers that shape your world.

What Are We Pretending To Know?
10% François Truffaut's oeuvre
23% Spouse, children
17% How to coach Minnesota Vikings
6% Average annual rainfall in the Amazon Basin
15% Difference between sex and love
18% Will of God
11% What happened last night

THE ONION • $2.00 US • $3.00 CAN

Scientists Abandon AI Project After Seeing *The Matrix*

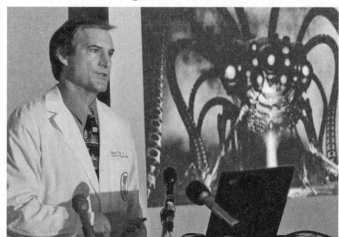

Above: Jameson announces his decision to cease artificial-intelligence research.

CAMBRIDGE, MA—Scientists at MIT's Advanced Machine Cognizance Project announced Tuesday that, after seeing the final installment of the *Matrix* trilogy, they will cease all further work in the field of artificial intelligence.

"As scientists of conscience, we must consider the ethical ramifications of AI development," said Dr. Gregory Jameson, director of machine epistemology and ontology at MIT. "*The Matrix* taught us that we cannot ignore our obligation to the future of mankind. We must free our minds to this fact, or we will accidentally unleash a nightmarish army of sentient machines."

Added Jameson: "Some may call the extinction of humankind inevitable,

but I, for one, will still resist."

A statement drafted by the MIT group was co-signed by an international coalition of AI experts that included scientists from the American Association for Artificial Intelligence, members of the Society for Artificial Intelligence and Simulation of Behavior, and a team of fan experts from the newly created San Diego ComiCon Committee on Moral and Ethical Implications for Society at Large.

In the statement, researchers said they were "frightened by the disastrous potential of AI" and called the *Matrix* trilogy of science-fiction action-thrillers a "wake-up call to any scientist concerned with the long-term consequences of his work," as

see MATRIX page 65

Above: Chao displays her reduced paycheck.

Labor Secretary Has Her Hours Cut

WASHINGTON, DC—Deeming the move "regrettable but necessary," White House Chief of Staff Andrew Card announced Monday that Secretary of Labor Elaine Chao's work hours will be scaled back to 30 per week starting Jan. 26.

"It's merely a cost-cutting measure and says absolutely nothing about Elaine, who's done wonderful work for the Bush Administration since she came on board in 2001," Card said. "Once the economy turns around, the first thing we'll do is return Elaine to her original hours. That's a promise."

Chao's hours will be limited to six per day during a regular Monday-to-Friday workweek, her salary will be cut by 25 percent, and she'll lose the privileges of working flextime hours and earning time-and-a-half pay on weekends and holidays. In addition, Chao's relegation to part-time status means she'll no longer be eligible for

see SECRETARY page 64

61

Israel's West Bank Wall

Amid protest from Palestinians, Israel began construction on a 25-foot-tall protection barrier on the edge of Jerusalem. What do *you* think?

"Anyone can tear things down, but it takes someone really special to build things up."

Joseph Berlin
Systems Analyst

"A wall is a good start. It's no 'giant lid over the whole fucked-up region.' But it's a start."

Jeff Lockre
Salesman

"God, these Jerusalemites. You'd think one famous wall would be enough for them."

Karla Vanhoose
Tailor

"As a poet, I see this wall as a metaphor for something—but *what*?"

Randolph Bunn
Banker

"This plan will definitely solve Israel's problems. Unless the Palestinians somehow get their hands on tunnel-digging 'pick and shovel' technology."

Ed Jin
Driver

"A wall of steel and concrete may stop the Palestinians from entering certain areas, but it cannot stop the Palestinian heart from soaring. That's what the soldiers are for."

Nan Hastings
Choreographer

The State Of The Union Address

President Bush delivered the State Of The Union address Tuesday. What were his key points?

- Course will be stayed
- Nothing about uranium this year, that's for sure
- Made daring move, potentially alienating his key supporters, by advocating concept of "science"
- Held up big map of Union, drew thick polarizing magic-marker line dividing it in two
- Spoke about bipartisan support, which was applauded by half of audience
- Thanked future generations of Americans for their selfless support of current U.S. peacekeeping missions
- Assured public that, in spite of everything he's ever said or done, he's actually in favor of healthcare
- In a nod to Hispanic culture, had "La Bamba" playing on boombox in background
- Yelled for Laura to bring him a pen
- Vowed to conquer space, establish a democracy, and leave within six months

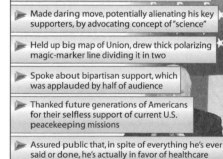

America's Finest News Source. ™

Herman Ulysses Zweibel
Founder

T. Herman Zweibel
Publisher Emeritus
J. Phineas Zweibel
Publisher
Maxwell Prescott Zweibel
Editor-In-Chief

Yee-Haw! My Vote Cancels Out Y'all's!

By Duane Bickels

Well, damn, man, it's pretty soon gonna be president election time again, and that means we gotta start thinkin' about who's gonna be the one we want to be president. That's some important stuff, who's president, because whoever's president will be in charge of the whole dang shootin' match. And, if y'all are like me, you know America's president needs to be the kind of old boy who, in the first place, kicks him some damn ass, and in the second place, don't listen to all that bitchin' about how he shouldn't be kickin' so much ass. And, if you *ain't* like me, guess what? My vote cancels out y'all's!

Now, you probably waste a whole lotta good-fishin' Saturdays readin' yourself the papers, watchin' all the talk on the TV, and sittin' around thinkin' real hard about which way you gonna vote. Well, it's a real shame, then, ain't it, that all that time you spend in real careful considerin' don't count for nothin', once my vote runs y'all's right off the road.

Shoot, neighbor, if there's one type'a guy you don't want in charge, it's some damn weaklin' in the White House what won't kick enough ass. Bush, that guy we got now, he kicked him some ass in that old desert. And Bush's daddy? He kicked him some ass, too. Reagan? Kicked all the ass he could, and some they said he shouldn't! But Clinton? Barely no ass-kickin' at all. Just got his ol' joint tugged by a fat girl, and hell, I could do that down by the Dew Drop Inn off I-78. What's the damn use of bein' the Commander-Chief if that's all you're gonna do? Face it, bein' president is a job of work for ass-kickers, and if you say otherwise, hell, I got a vote here what totally negates yours.

So maybe you ain't a patriot like I am. Now, when I say patriot, I'm talkin' about most of our athletes, country-music stars, and guys like me what agree with them. So, say you ain't a patriot, and you're fixin' to vote up a candidate what's some limpo what'll give in to the crybaby liberals, the damn screechin' women, the commies at the United Nations, and the other America-haters. Fine by me! I got a vote here that does just as much good as yours, and mine's marked "No Limpos!"

Or say you wanna take away the money we need for our Army tanks and rifles and fightin' planes what let us keep our eternal vigilance of freedom by invadin' other countries. And say you want to give it to the damn schoolteachers, which let me tell you never done old Duane any damn good, and still, they most times drive a newer car than I do. I learned all I got from my daddy—another guy without any fancy book smarts, by the way. If he didn't need them books, then why do anybody else? Well, hey, I might not be educated, but I do got me a big ol' flag, $300 from the government, and a president that, like I told you before, kicked him some ass. It's things like that what make me happy my vote gonna meet y'all's toe-to-toe and take it down!

Plus, what's more, I got to see Saddam get his ass throwed in jail. That's a big ol' switch-a-dilly from a few years ago, when Saddam was runnin' around free while Duane was in the tank, let me tell you.

So maybe you think what we got here is one a them Mexican pissin'

> If there's one type'a guy you don't want in charge, it's some damn weaklin' in the White House what won't kick enough ass. Bush, that guy we got now, he kicked him some ass in that old desert.

matches, what with my vote and your vote both bein' worth the exact same. But I tell you what! There's all the guys workin' down here at the budget-transmission shop with me, and the guys at the body shop across the way, and the car-battery dismantlin' yard. Plus, there's all our pals at the Dew Drop off 78, and all our other pals at the County Dragaway, and our big ol' families, and our wives, for those what have 'em. Read me? In this next election, whenever they set it to come around, we gonna go up agin' all you guys at the coffee shop and the library. Now, if you ain't noticed, we got a lot more parkin' lot space down at the racetrack and the Farm & Fleet store than y'all do out in front of your bookstores and muffin shops. All of us add up real quick, and our votes do a damn bunch more than just cancel out all y'all's!

Shit, somehow we do it ever' time we need to keep the damn school board from gettin' uppity on us.

So hey, man, have fun readin' up and debatin' and thinkin' on what you gonna mark down on your votin' papers this year. Duane ain't thought too much yet about which way his vote's gonna go. But somethin' tells me, friend, it ain't gonna be the same as y'alls! ∅

62

Local Chapter Of Rosie's Chub Club Soldiers On

WILMINGTON, DE—It was time for another weekly weigh-in for the four remaining members of the Wilmington chapter of Rosie's Chub Club Monday. Although they prompted some debate about the accuracy of

> "Don't despair, ladies!" Daemisch said. "We're just coming off the holidays. But now that the goodies are gone, Rosie would want us to get back on track. Well… that is, if Rosie still ran the Chub Club. Or did her talk show. Or still talked to her fans."

host Pat Chowen's battered bathroom scale, the results were still distressing: a cumulative gain of 11 pounds from last week.

Karen Daemisch, the group's president and "den mother," remained upbeat.

"Don't despair, ladies!" Daemisch said. "We're just coming off the holi-

days. But now that the goodies are gone, Rosie would want us to get back on track. Well… that is, if Rosie still ran the Chub Club. Or did her talk show. Or still talked to her fans."

Daemisch was referring to Rosie O'Donnell, whose talk show topped daytime-TV ratings in the late '90s. Unveiled in 1999, Rosie's Chub Club encouraged overweight viewers to make gradual lifestyle changes and adhere to the motto, "Eat less and move more." As a part of her commitment to the program, O'Donnell would relate her own ongoing struggles with weight loss on air and reassure viewers that they were not alone in their dieting battles. She also motivated Chub Club members by listing successful dieters in the "Top 10 Losers" section of her web site, and by making regular entries in her "Chub Club Journal."

But when O'Donnell left NBC in 2002, the Chub Club went with her. Believed to be the last Chub Club in existence, the Wilmington chapter soldiers on. Its remaining members still meet weekly, and still gamely attempt to reach their stated weight-loss goals.

Following the disappointing weigh-in, Daemisch tried to shore up morale by giving out the Koosh Prize For Excellence In Willpower. This week's honor went to member Bobbette Hines for drinking eight glasses of water a day.

"A big Rosie Rah-Rah to you, Bob-

Above: Daemisch, Chowen, and Glass (left to right) refuse to abandon their Rosie-related weight-loss program.

Above: Former Chub Clubber Rosie O'Donnell.

bette," Daemisch said. "Even though that's a lot to drink, water fills up your stomach real good, and it keeps you from eating. And Bobbette was the only one of us who gained less than two pounds."

Hines declined the award, admitting

that she substituted Snapples for several of her glasses of water.

According to Daemisch, keeping her Chub Clubbers motivated is difficult, not only because of the ongoing challenge of losing weight, but also because O'Donnell has virtually disappeared from the public eye. Other than filing a lawsuit against the publishers of Rosie magazine and producing a Broadway musical based on the life of Boy George, she has kept a low profile.

"We were all huge fans of Rosie, so when she ditched her show, a lot of the ladies did feel a bit abandoned," Daemisch said.

At its 2000 peak, the Wilmington club boasted 28 members. Since the show went off the air, however, membership has steadily dwindled to its current low of four.

see CLUB page 64

14-Word Diet Stretched To 200 Pages

BOSTON—The Florida Keys diet, which can be adequately described in 14 words, has been padded into a 204-page book: Losing Weight The Florida Keys Way, available in bookstores Tuesday. "The diet is pretty much, 'Avoid saturated fats and simple carbohydrates, eat mostly fresh vegetables and seafood, and exercise," said author Dr. Harris Jegen. "Unfortunately, no one is going to shell out $24.95 for one sentence, so I've got some recipes and charts in there, a bunch of testimonials, and a 50-page Diet Diary." Jegen's previous books include The Florida Keys Diet and The Florida Keys Diet Made Easy.

Actual Proctor Met At Party

ROCKFORD, IL—Guests at a cocktail party on Dunstan Avenue were re-

portedly surprised to meet Conrad Davies, an actual, honest-to-goodness, working proctor. "I'd read the word 'proctor' and heard it on ads, but I'd never actually met one," partygoer Mindy Lindbloom told reporters Monday. "Turns out, he was just a normal guy. He was standing around eating celery sticks and drinking beer, just like everyone else." Lindbloom added that Davies was "just as nice as could be."

New Viacom Ad Tells Employees To Get Back To Work

NEW YORK—Viacom, the global media conglomerate that includes such properties as CBS, Paramount Pictures, MTV, Nickelodeon, UPN, Showtime, Blockbuster Video, and Simon and Schuster, began airing a TV ad Monday that orders its employees to get back to work. "Worker efficiency needed a little boost," said Viacom

CEO Sumner Redstone. "But instead of sending an e-mail to everyone at all of our subsidiaries, we just televised a 'Look alive, people' warning during Ricki Lake." The 30-second spot also included a reminder that discussion of Super Bowl pools should occur at breaks only.

Bush Vows To Discover, Legalize Aliens On American, Martian Soil

WASHINGTON, DC—President Bush restated his commitment to the quality and discovery of immigrant and Martian life Monday, calling for increased efforts to register and search for gainfully employed and extraterrestrial aliens. "America must further pursue the quest for a better way of, or undiscovered forms of, life," Bush said Monday. "To this end, I will commission the INS and NASA to assemble committees and probes to explore potential minimum-wage and

minimum-risk endeavors in the service sector of the economy and the Olympus Mons sector of Mars." Conservative radio host Rush Limbaugh criticized the endeavor, saying the social and scientific programs will take jobs and money away from domestic workers and domestic security.

Narcissist Mentally Undresses Self

CHICAGO—J.P. Morgan Chase & Co. project manager and narcissist Brian Knowles undressed himself with his eyes while his secretary delivered the day's agenda Monday. "The entire time Sandra [Hutchins] was talking, I was imagining my clothing coming off, piece by piece," Knowles said. "I thought I was going to lose it when I yawned and stretched so seductively. It's a miracle I get any work done, running around in that tasty Armani suit all day." Knowles added that he's "so asking to be fucked." ∅

health-insurance coverage, matching 401K contributions, or parking validation.

Chao expressed dismay over the decision during a cigarette break in the parking lot of the Labor Department's

> ## "I sorta knew what was up when President Bush called me into the Oval Office, and Chief Brownnose was standing there beside him with this bogus sad look on his face," said Chao, referring to Card by the derogatory nickname reportedly used by the members of the White House staff.

Frances Perkins Building.

"I sorta knew what was up when President Bush called me into the Oval Office, and Chief Brownnose was standing there beside him with this bogus sad look on his face," said Chao, referring to Card by the derogatory nickname reportedly used by the members of the White House staff. "The president said he was real sorry, but he either had to cut my hours or let me go. What could I do? I need the job."

Chao inhaled on her cigarette and added: "God, and I'm still making payments on that stupid rear-projection television."

On CNN's *Crossfire* Tuesday, *Washington Post* columnist David Broder predicted that Chao's workload will not be lightened to reflect her new, truncated work day.

"This is a woman who's used to working long hours and traveling extensively," Broder said. "While there may be some initial efforts to limit her duties, I doubt they'll last long."

Broder added: "Chao is the victim of her own administration's policies, which place economic issues like employment and job security second to foreign-policy matters and big-business interests."

As Labor Secretary, Chao is well aware of labor trends like corporate downsizing and the decline in personal income.

"Tables and graphs mapping the worsening situation of the average American worker crossed my desk all the time, but I never thought any of that stuff would affect me," Chao said. "I don't see [Treasury Secretary John] Snow fearing for his job. Then again, he's in charge of the money. The big-

wigs see 'labor' in my job title, and they think, 'Hey, we can push her around.'"

Continued Chao: "If I were [Health and Human Services Secretary] Tommy Thompson, I'd start looking through the classifieds."

Several Cabinet secretaries have expressed dissatisfaction with the ways in which Chao's reduced schedule affects them. Secretary of the Interior Gale Norton reported that Card has already begun to foist extra Labor Department work on her.

"My assistant dropped a report titled 'Workplace Safety And Its Effect On Profitability' in my inbox the other day," Norton said. "It had a Post-it note on it from Card that said, 'Can you give this speech for Elaine Chao next Monday?' That's total crap. I told Brownnose 'No way.' How can he expect me to do work I wasn't even appointed for, for no additional pay?"

Card said he did not play a deciding role in the reduction of Chao's hours.

"Look, my role is to manage the staff, not make final decisions about salaries," Card said. "My job could be on the line here, too, incidentally. The president keeps saying, 'We gotta tighten our belts. We gotta cut where we can.' It's getting so bad that if George sees somebody standing near the water cooler in the West Wing, he asks me, 'What's that guy's name? Are you giving him enough to do, Andy?' I swear, he and [Bush political advisor Karl] Rove are walking the halls looking for an excuse to can someone."

Chao said she remains uncertain about her future. Mindful of the stagnant job market, she said she has no choice but to remain with the Bush Administration for the foreseeable future.

"A friend offered me a full-time position on the board of directors of her bank, but the pay was even less than what I make here," Chao said. "I thought I could do some freelance

> ## On CNN's *Crossfire* Tuesday, *Washington Post* columnist David Broder predicted that Chao's workload will not be lightened to reflect her new, truncated work day.

data analysis for extra scratch, but they've got my hours set up so that I have to come into the office every day. With the commute, it feels like a 40-hour work week, anyway."

"Whoa, look at the time," said Chao, glancing at her cell phone. "It's already 3 p.m.? Sorry, gotta go punch out now. New rules." ∅

To keep themselves motivated, Chub Clubbers view old VHS tapes of O'-Donnell's show, read printed-out screen captures from her talk show's defunct web site, and mark their weight on a colorful chart featuring O'Donnell's face. Members also play the confidence-boosting games described in the official Chub Club handbook.

"This is a real fun one," Daemisch said, pointing to a wall covered with broad sheets of white paper on which crude outlines of the quartet's stocky figures were traced. "We take our Koosh slingshots and aim at the areas where we want to lose weight the most. The book says it helps us work off aggression as we strive to meet our weight-loss goals."

Next, the group played "What Would Rosie Do?," a game in which players contemplate what O'Donnell would do if presented with various dieting dilemmas.

Asked what Rosie would do if she were offered a Krispy Kreme doughnut after eating a full dinner, Chub Clubber Michele Glass said, "I think she'd accept the doughnut and eat a bite of it, but save the rest for a snack tomorrow."

"No," Chowen said. "She'd give it to a food pantry, because she's so generous."

Rising from the floor as quickly as her girth would allow, a visibly agitated Hines disagreed with both assessments.

"Rosie's just as fat as she was when she had her talk show," Hines said. "In fact, she's fatter. So I think if you gave Rosie a Krispy Kreme doughnut right after she ate a full dinner, she'd probably eat the doughnut, have another, then get an ugly retro-'80s haircut, do some unfunny standup, and leave in the middle of

her set, because she's a quitter and a lazy cow!"

Hines then grabbed her coat and headed for the door, pausing to hurl her Koosh slingshot at O'Donnell's image on the chart.

In spite of losing Hines, Daemisch remains hopeful. She said she's determined to see her weight-loss mission to its end, and equally committed to

> ## To keep themselves motivated, Chub Clubbers view old VHS tapes of O'Donnell's show, read printed-out screen captures from her talk show's defunct web site, and mark their weight on a colorful chart featuring O'Donnell's face.

keeping O'Donnell's presence alive in the Chub Club.

"Rosie's the reason for the Chub Club," Daemisch said. "Why would I eliminate all traces of her? That'd turn us into a plain old weight-loss support group. How boring!"

Added Daemisch: "Our club has lost more than 50 pounds in five years. But it's not strictly about dropping a dress size. The club is about feeling good about yourself and very, very slowly integrating diet and exercise routines into your life. Rosie would have wanted it that way. I mean, she does want it that way." ∅

amounts of blood. Passersby were amazed by the unusually large amounts of blood. Passersby were amazed by the unusually large

amounts of blood. Passersby were amazed by the unusually large amounts of blood. Passersby were amazed by the unusually large amounts of blood. Passersby were

> ## If you're going to kill someone, is it wrong to separate the head from the body?

amazed by the unusually large amounts of blood. Passersby were amazed by the unusually large amounts of blood. Passersby were amazed by the unusually large amounts of blood. Passersby were amazed by the unusually large amounts of blood. Passersby were amazed by the unusually large amounts of blood. Passersby were amazed by the unusually large amounts of blood. Passersby were amazed by the unusually large amounts of blood. Passersby were amazed by the unusually large

see ONEIDA page 81

The flight-long discussion about patios was prompted by an umbrella advertisement in a *SkyMall* catalog sitting open on Gillam's lap.

"That's close to what I have in my yard," Delsman said. "But mine was a lot cheaper. A lot cheaper. I know this great place in Elmhurst that sells top-brand stuff. You should check it out if you're ever doing some remodeling."

Delsman also told Gillam about the difficulties he had getting his patio furniture delivered, the quality of his outdoor barbecue set, and the benefits of citronella candles over tiki lamps.

"The lamps just don't work as well as the candles," said Delsman, unaware of the 9mm automatic hidden inside Gillam's coat pocket. "The candles smell better, too."

"Uh huh," Gillam said. "Those come in the metal buckets, right?"

Gillam, who knows 18 different ways to disarm a knife-wielding adversary, nodded rhythmically as Dels-

man related the simple pleasure of lounging in his newly finished patio.

"Sure, it was hard work, but it was worth it," Delsman said. "Sitting out there in the summer with a drink in my hand, watching the sun go down... Sometimes I'll invite the neighbors over."

In an interview Tuesday, Gillam said he has learned to remain focused on his mission—preventing hijack attempts and ensuring the safety of airplane passengers and flight crew—even when he's involved in casual conversations.

"I'm not allowed to bring a book on board, and I certainly can't sleep, so talkative passengers tend to target me," Gillam said. "I'm on anywhere between two to four flights a day. Usually, people just talk about their kids or jobs, but this week, I've heard about everything from working at Disneyland to breeding Wheaten Terriers. It's really not that bad. Although I am kind

of tired of talking about how many airlines don't serve dinner anymore."

Continued Gillam: "I do a visual scan

> "The lamps just don't work as well as the candles," said Delsman, unaware of the 9mm automatic hidden inside Gillam's coat pocket.

of the entire cabin every five minutes while we're in flight, to see if anything is brewing, but the people talking to me don't seem to notice."

When asked his opinion of the U.S. government's decision to order foreign airlines to place armed air mar-

shals on some international flights, Gillam seemed indifferent.

"I guess that would be fine," Gillam said. "It's part of my job to be flexible. I'm not much of a talker, though. I can usually get through these short trips, but an eight-hour flight to Ireland beside a Chatty Cathy might be more than I could handle. I should ask if I'm allowed to wear headphones as long as I have the sound turned off."

Ridge praised the air marshals for helping to keep the nation's skies safe.

"The marshals are to be highly commended," Ridge said. "Despite being forced into excruciatingly mundane conversations about everything from stock portfolios to the proper way to make a pork roast, these men remain vigilant. Because of their efforts, an average member of the American public can feel safe babbling about his aunt's cataract surgery for two hours. For that, we should all be thankful." ⌀

MATRIX from page 61

well as a "freaky head-trip about a future run by floating metallic drones that look kind of like really scary seafood."

Pattern-recognition development analyst Dr. Janice Wunderling said the MIT team has placed its AI projects on hold pending the completion

> Added Arronovski: "I want no hand in creating a world where only Keanu Reeves can protect my great-grandchildren from a giant drill that plummets through the ceilings of subterranean cave dwellings."

of a comprehensive feasibility study on the threat of "humans being imprisoned in tiny, slime-filled cyber-canisters."

"When we first saw *The Matrix* back in 1999, the premise of AI evolving into an unstoppable army of self-aware programs intent on dominating the planet gave us pause," Wunderling said. "But like most moviegoers, we dismissed the movie as a fun blockbuster showcasing cool bullet-time photography and shapely, leather-clad cyber-babes performing gravity-defying kung-fu in slow motion."

After seeing *The Matrix Reloaded*, however, Wunderling and her fellow scientists began to worry.

"The more we thought about it, the less we were able to laugh off the threat of killer machines," said Dr. Henry K. Arronovski, a leading expert in the field of heuristics classification.

Above: California Gov. Arnold Schwarzenegger, a vocal proponent of AI research, offers an opposing view.

"It really started to freak us out. What if, decades from now, humans end up in a virtual-reality construct designed to blind them to their enslavement to the hivemind—all because of the work my colleagues and I started?"

Added Arronovski: "I want no hand in creating a world where only Keanu Reeves can protect my great-grandchildren from a giant drill that plummets through the ceilings of subterranean cave dwellings."

It was *The Matrix Revolutions*, the final movie in the series, that convinced scientists at MIT to put the brakes on their AI research.

"We were hoping that the third movie would quell our fears about the

work we were doing, but it only raised more questions," Jameson said. "Sentient programs, like the Merovingian, though formerly agents of the Architect's operation to neutralize the human race, rebelled against the very system they were meant to serve? And which side were the renegade programs even on? Was the Oracle a sentient program herself, earmarked for 'deletion' by her former masters? Or was she just another part of the system without knowing it? We had no choice but to pull the plug."

Team member Dmitri Markovitch, author of *Mechanical Computation And Consciousness*, called his vote to abandon AI research "an intensely

personal decision."

"I saw *Revolutions* with my 12-year-old son Eric," Markovitch said. "He saw the look of worry on my face and said, 'Dad, don't be scared. It's only make-believe.' I had to tell him, 'No, son, it's what your father does for a living.'"

"After watching Captain Mifune blast away in his robotic battle exoskeleton as hordes of relentless Sentinels swarmed the dock screaming in battle-frenzied rage, I could no longer put my career before the future of mankind," Markovitch continued. "Those poor, brave children of Zion—their annoying tolerance of rave culture notwithstanding—did not deserve that horrible fate."

Critics of AI research commended the decision. Dr. Lyle Freeberg, author of *Ethics In The Age Of Nanotechnology*, said humans have ignored the warning signs about AI long enough.

"The first two *Terminator* films iden-

> "The more we thought about it, the less we were able to laugh off the threat of killer machines."

tified the potential for global-linkage computer networks to send android assassins back in time, but the warning went unheeded," Freeberg said. "*Artificial Intelligence: AI* recognized the ethical dilemmas inherent in creating a robot who can love, but no one took the movie seriously, because it was so boring. But in the wake of the Wachowski brothers' prophetic series, we must, as the '90s alternative-rock band Rage Against The Machine urged us, 'wake up.'" ⌀

If You Don't Mind, I'd Like To Take A Crack At Salvaging Your Failing Marriage

By Gabe Mulroney

I don't mean to pry, Becca, but I couldn't help overhearing you and Jason argue last night. Sound travels really well in this building. Now, I know I'm only your neighbor, and it's none of my business, but it seems like your relationship is in dire trouble. If you don't mind, I'd like to take a crack at salvaging your failing marriage.

By simply watching a couple, you can learn a lot about their deeply entrenched problems. I've noticed that you work later hours than Jason does. That's not good. The loss of quality time together can generate a lot of friction. Your marriage right now is like a car engine in need of oil. Becca, you've gotta lube up your marriage the same way you'd lube up a car. My suggestion is that you get a job with the same hours as Jason's. If that's unworkable, then how about if Jason brings a picnic dinner to your place of work a couple times a week? Or, better yet, how about you both quit your jobs and start a business together? That way, you can maximize your time together and build a tighter bond.

Next on the docket: How much quiet time are you two spending together? Sure, everyone says "enough," but re-

> **But cheer up! It's not too late. It won't be easy to get your marriage back on track, but I'm here to help. Trust me, it'll all be worth it in the end. Now, let's roll up our sleeves and get to work at saving this marriage.**

ally think for a moment. Remember, I live next door, so it's no use fibbing. I already have some idea. In fact, I've gotten a vibe about you and Jason. You're the kind of people who are so self-absorbed that you don't pay enough attention to each other, aren't you? That's not my concern, though. I'm not here to pass judgment. I'm just here to make you love each other

again.

Look, I knew this potential catastrophe was on its way even before you started that argument over the phone bill. Don't downplay it, Becca. Any

> **By simply watching a couple, you can learn a lot about their deeply entrenched problems. I've noticed that you work later hours than Jason does. That's not good. The loss of quality time together can generate a lot of friction. Your marriage right now is like a car engine in need of oil.**

argument that a couple has is proof of an unhealthy bond. Truth be told, I've been watching your relationship unravel for months now. There's no two ways about it: You two are booking a vacation to Splitsville. Luckily, Dr. Love is here to give you a free prescription. Let's shine and buff that old marriage 'til it looks brand-new.

Now, let's start by talking about what happened when you left for the store together last night. There was that difference of opinion about whether you needed a new coffeemaker… Never mind how I know. Isn't it enough that I'm showing a little concern?

Calm down. It's not good to jump to anger. I can see what Jason means when he tells you that you blow your top over the slightest little thing. Please, just sit down. I'll get you a glass of water.

There. Now, if you're ready to listen, I'll continue.

I noticed last night that Jason's tone of voice was very aggressive. You seemed threatened. Luckily, I'm extremely attuned to this sort of nonverbal communication, almost like a dog. Becca, is he abusing you? That's okay—you don't have to tell me now. If you ever need someone to testify, though, just say the word.

Your Horoscope

By Lloyd Schumner Sr.
Retired Machinist and
A.A.P.B.-Certified Astrologer

Aries: (March 21–April 19)
Although it's true that you have some rudimentary skillz, they are barely enough to pay your long-distance phone service and cable billz.

Taurus: (April 20–May 20)
The question of whether human consciousness can exist outside the body remains unanswered, but at least you and your trusty Thermos gave it a good try.

Gemini: (May 21–June 21)
You'll be held accountable by the law for refusing to provide the information that someone was being held prisoner in a fortune-cookie factory.

Cancer: (June 22–July 22)
Jesus will finally speak to you this week, but His message of love will contain such filthy language that your faith will be shaken forever.

Leo: (July 23–Aug. 22)
Getting there is said to be half the fun, but those people aren't going where you're going.

Virgo: (Aug. 23–Sept. 22)
You will not be able to sleep at night after finding out that the magnetic North Pole drifted almost 40 miles last year.

Libra: (Sept. 23–Oct. 23)
You are slowly making progress in the area of leaving quietly when people are done having sex with you.

Scorpio: (Oct. 24–Nov. 21)
Remember: It's better to be silent and be thought a fool than to speak and make people feel stupid about having you around at all.

Sagittarius: (Nov. 22–Dec. 21)
Experience is a great teacher. This week, it will teach you your Miranda rights, the difference between a polecat and a skunk, and what a sucker punch is.

Capricorn: (Dec. 22–Jan. 19)
There are some things in this universe that mankind was never meant to know. The boring details of your trip to South Dakota are among them.

Aquarius: (Jan. 20–Feb. 18)
The concept of Cartesian duality may have fallen largely out of favor, but you still believe that you're either from Texas or you ain't shit.

Pisces: (Feb. 19–March 20)
You may be worried about those strange voices in your head. Don't be. Those are your "thoughts."

You seem very tense right now. You two have only been married nine months, so there's no reason the romance should be in the crapper. You know what would help? A bubble bath. I'm not saying it's a cure-all, but a nice, long, luxurious bath can do wonders for your mood. Go home right now, fill the tub with hot water and bubbles, maybe some scented oils, and top it all with a sprinkling of rose petals. That's an order! You need to feel sexy again! Just to make sure we're on the same page, Jason should be there too, so he can help wash your back. It's a mighty sexy back at that, if I may be so bold.

Don't go away! You can't run away from the truth forever. I didn't want to have to say this, but I think that if I'm going to save your marriage, I need to be totally frank. Your husband is fat. Ish. I'd say he needs to lose at least 20 pounds. Actually, you could stand to lose a few, too. When I bump into you by the mailboxes downstairs, I see really attractive faces—probably the faces you fell in love with—but they're buried under all that fat. Maybe if you two cut down on the piz-

za you order in every few nights, you might get back down to your honeymoon weights.

Being on the outside of your relationship gives me special insight into it. Sometimes, when you're embroiled in a dead-end marriage, you can't spot the burning forest for the trees. And, sister, the forest of your relationship is in flames. It's gonna take everything with it. It's going down fast. Can you smell it? Sometimes your nose will get accustomed to a scent, and you won't even notice it. Farmers, for example, don't even smell ordure. Then, there was that old man who squashed his dog under his recliner and didn't notice until his son came over and found the moldering remains. It's like that with you and Jason right now.

But cheer up! It's not too late. It won't be easy to get your marriage back on track, but I'm here to help. Trust me, it'll all be worth it in the end. Now, let's roll up our sleeves and get to work at saving this marriage.

First things first: You need to get pregnant. That way, he can't possibly leave you. ∅

Child's Last Steps Captured On Video

see FAMILY page 14E

Woman With Amazing Rack Told She Has Beautiful Eyes

see BUSINESS page 4C

Gun Owner Ready For Them

see LOCAL page 4B

Coin Flip Disputed

see LOCAL page 6B

STATshot

A look at the numbers that shape your world.

Why Are We Paying $4.99 For This Shit?

28% Barista really cute

17% Other ATM three blocks away

12% It gets you as drunk as liquor

4% Would expect to pay two, three, even four times that

20% Fell for lemonade-stand bait-and-switch

19% Like shit

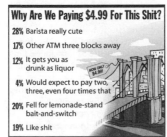

the ONION®

VOLUME 40 ISSUE 04 AMERICA'S FINEST NEWS SOURCE™ 29 JAN.–4 FEB. 2004

Above: Bush says he will "put an end to the current lack of honesty and compassion in Washington."

Bush 2004 Campaign Pledges To Restore Honor And Dignity To White House

BOSTON—Addressing guests at a $2,000-a-plate fundraiser, George W. Bush pledged Monday that, if re-elected in November, he and running mate Dick Cheney will "restore honor and dignity to the White House."

"After years of false statements and empty promises, it's time for big changes in Washington," Bush said. "We need a president who will finally stand up and fight against the lies and corruption. It's time to renew the faith the people once had in the White House. If elected, I pledge to usher in a new era of integrity inside the Oval Office."

Bush told the crowd that, if given the opportunity, he would work to reestablish the goodwill of the American people "from the very first hour of the very first day" of his second term.

"The people have spoken," Bush said. "They said they want change. They said it's time to clean up Washington. They're tired of politics as usual. They're tired of the pursuit of self-interest that has gripped Washington.

see BUSH page 70

Study:
Most Self-Abuse Goes Unreported

BOULDER—According to a study released Tuesday by the University of Colorado sociology department, approximately 95 percent of self-abuse cases in the U.S. go unreported.

"As shocking as it may seem, unreported incidents of self-abuse number in the billions," said Dr. Henry Cracklin, director of the study. "This isn't just the plight of teenage boys and truck drivers. Self-abuse affects both genders and all ages. Nevertheless, a great majority of victims suffer the abuse in silence."

our HEALTH

The study's results, obtained through five years of surveys and interviews, indicate that millions of Americans have publicly acknowledged involvement in a self-abusive relationship. Yet the study finds that unreported abuse victims comprise an alarming 87 percent of the female population and 99.6 percent of males.

"In many cases, the self-abuse occurs repeatedly over the course of a lifetime, with the victims believing themselves powerless to break the cycle of shame, embarrassment, and self-loving," Cracklin said. "The sad reality is that, if you know a man or woman between the ages of 12 and

see ABUSE page 71

Concert Ruined By Guy Enjoying Himself

CHICAGO—Brian Grant, 24, reported that a rock concert he attended at the Empty Bottle Saturday was ruined by 35-year-old music fan Daryl Froemer's enthusiasm.

"I was trying to enjoy [New York-based rock group] Oneida, but it was totally impossible because [Froemer] was making a spectacle of himself," Grant said. "I couldn't even pay attention to the band. Halfway through the set, I had to leave."

"I go out to a bar to have a good time, and I can't because there's some jackass racing around in circles and waving his beer bottle in the air," Grant added. "I mean, he was even jumping up and down during the mid-tempo songs. Come on! It's not the '90s anymore. This isn't grunge."

In addition to dancing, Froemer re-

portedly pounded the stage "like it was on fire," sang along when he knew the lyrics, yelled out the names of songs he wanted to hear, and repeatedly attempted to enter into a dialogue with the band.

"Every time the singer asked us a question, he was the first one to yell back," Grant said. "I don't mind the occasional 'Yeah' or 'Woo,' but this guy was shouting after every song, whistling, and asking them how their amps were. If he hadn't been so annoying, I would have been embarrassed for him."

"Did he even consider the fact that the singer might have wanted to

see CONCERT page 70

Right: Froemer has a good time, to the dismay of concertgoers like Grant (inset).

Can Celebrities Get A Fair Trial?

The inability to find jurors unfamiliar with Martha Stewart has raised concerns that celebrities cannot receive a fair trial. What do *you* think?

"So a bunch of famous people got arrested, and all of a sudden we're worried about fair trials?"

Jen Craig-Greenman
Paralegal

"Except for their incredibly well-funded legal-defense teams, these stars are on their own."

Janice Parks
Title Examiner

"I hope celebrities can get a fair trial in this country. God knows they can't get decent service."

Joey Reid
Cleaner

"May I remind you that I am not on trial here?! Sorry. I just love saying that."

Lee Daniels
Cook

"To ensure a fair trial, the judge should present the evidence with Gretchen Mol standing in for the defendant."

Harold Johnston
CEO

"Oh, great. If I somehow manage to avoid 20 years of *Cheers* and *Frasier*, my reward is a jury seat at Kelsey Grammer's child-murder trial?"

Timothy Bates
Systems Analyst

Atkins-Friendly Fast Food

Many fast-food restaurants have introduced low-carb menu items intended to lure Atkins dieters. Among the most popular:

- Seven-Meat Burrito (Taco Bell)
- Turkey & Bacon On An All-Roast-Beef Wrap (Subway)
- New, Leaner All-White-Meat Fries (KFC)
- Chicken-Fried-Steak-Fried Chicken (Popeye's)
- "Meat Me In My Hammy" All-Pig-Product Breakfast (Denny's)
- Ham Hock Shake (McDonald's)
- Pigs-Sans-A-Blanket (IHOP)
- Hot Scrapple Pie (McDonald's)
- Curly Rinds (Hardee's)
- Ham & Melted Ham Hamwich (Arby's)
- Dave's Big Boneless Side-Of-Bacon Classic (Wendy's)
- Monterey Jack Cheese & Water (Burger King)
- 6" Sandwich-Shaped All-Meat Object (Subway)

 **the ONION**®
America's Finest News Source.™

Herman Ulysses Zweibel
Founder

T. Herman Zweibel
Publisher Emeritus
J. Phineas Zweibel
Publisher
Maxwell Prescott Zweibel
Editor-In-Chief

Enter Tha Office

Check it out, G's: Lotta shit in this column ain't foe tha eyes a' amateurs. If you a pussy, you best skip ovah this thang an' tune in tha ladiez' channel or somethin', cuz what I about 2 lay down deserve its own parental-advisory stickah, know what I'm sayin'? This straight-up, non-stop, hard-core shit, y'all, an' tol' wit' mad suspense, too, tha kind that make yo' shit evacuate, know what I'm sayin'? It like a haiku a' violence.

Herbert Kornfeld
Accounts-Receivable
Supervisor

On Monday, Gerald Luckenbill, tha office comptrolla, aksed 2 see me in his office end a' bidness day.

Sure enuf, come punchout, Luckenbill wuz chillin' at his desk. His office wuz all dark, 'cept foe tha light from his desk lamp. I peep a check on his desktop an' recognize it as a payment that come in wit' today's mail, from a client called SPJ Communications. They one a' them Internet-service-providin' an' web-hostin' firms, an' they always buyin' they office supplies wit' us an' never gettin' they payments in 'til right befoe tha 25-day grace period expire. They think they tha King Shit, disrespectin' tha H-Dog like that.

"I just happened to notice the check in the Cash Room was about to go into the daily deposit," Luckenbill say. "I know that you hate how they get their payments in just under the wire. On a hunch, I took this check and phoned the issuing bank. Good thing I acted on that hunch, Herbert, because that check would have been returned NSF."

Damn.

Luckenbill peeped tha murder in my eye. He know me too long 2 think I let shit like this slide. "Now, Herbert," he say. "I let you go about your business without asking questions. I know you save us the expense of hiring a collections staff. But, in this case, I must ask you to keep a calm head. The holidays just ended, and maybe SPJ had more expenses than it counted on. Maybe it was a simple accounting error. Midstate wants its money, but it wants an honest, peaceful solution to the problem. We have the law on our side, Herbert. Keep that in mind."

Luckenbill barely done speakin' when I out tha doe an' in tha Nite Rida, headin' straight 2 tha bidness park where SPJ's office at. Luckenbill wanted 2 keep tha peace, an' I respected that, but I knew shit he didn't. I knew them muhfukkahs wuz straight-up trouble an' would fuck us ova more if we played it soft. I could smell it. I didn't spend aftahourz scopin' out SPJ HQ foe nothin'. I be bidin' my time foe months. Finally, tha mission had arrived. It zero hour. Those muhfukkahs wuz goin' *down*.

Tha lights wuz still on in SPJ's office, so I chilled in some law firm's parkin' lot next doe, meditatin', swappin' my officin' gear foe ninja black, flashin' back on tha wise words a' my mentor, CPA-ONE (R.I.P.): "Honor above all, Dog. Honor ain't cost-effective, but y'all must do yo' utmost 2 preserve it, cuz in tha end, it have tha most value."

Finally, 'round seven, tha lights went off. A big-hair receptionist exited an' drove away. She didn't peep me lyin' in wait. Wit' mad stealth, I tossed up a grapplin' hook 2 a third-flo' window an' hauled my ass up. Tha window wuz unlocked an' led into a hallway. Sidlin' up tight against tha wall, I made my way 2 SPJ's front doe. I jimmied tha lock, crouched down, an' entered. Sure enuf, there be a motion-detectah alarm beside tha doe. Huh. Child's play. I busted out a penlight an' my needle-nose pliahs, reached up, got into tha gap 'tween tha keypad's plastic casin' an' tha wall, an' snipped tha wirez. Tha lights on tha alarm went dark. Without missin' a beat, I snapped off tha penlight an' crab-walked my way 2 tha boss' office, where tha wall safe at.

Now, G's, as I made my way thru tha moonlit office, I peeped box afta unopened box bearin' tha Midstate logo. I aksed myself, "Why they ain't open they boxes? They got that shipment days ago. 'Sides, no office this size need that many ballpointz an' bindah clips. What be they game?" That got my blood up, but I force myself 2 chill an' attend 2 tha task at hand.

I reached tha bossman's office, removed some bullshit pheasant paintin', an' uncovered tha wall safe. I started crackin' it like a pro. In less than a minute, it opened an' revealed jus' what I expected: shitloads a' benjamins. Huh. A "simple accountin' error," my ass. Mo' like tha Big Willie muhfukkas be skimmin' from tha company profitz, like one a' them wack Fo'tune 500 CEOs. Not that I give a shit 'bout SPJ's finances, long as they don't fuck wit' Midstate, but I could use it against 'em if they got wise 2 tha H-Dog bum-rushin' they HQ an' thirsted foe retaliation.

Tha retaliation would come wit' a greater quickness than I anticipated.

"Greeting, H-Dog."

I whipped around. Five huge muhfukkahs wuz standin' right behind me. I peeped what they wuz wearin' an' knew immediately who they be.

Blueshirts.

Yeah, Blueshirts. Y'all peeps 'em on tha train or tha bus or drivin' in tha rush hour. Dudes wearin' them sissy blue dress shirts, sometimes wit' black dress pants, sometimes chinos.

see KORNFELD page 70

Actress Opens Poorly Conceived Animal Shelter

PACIFIC PALISADES, CA—Unwanted and abused dogs, cats, and other animals in Southern California now have a sort-of-friend in actress Alicia Silverstone, who opened the well-intentioned but poorly conceived StoneHaven animal shelter on her seaside estate last November.

"Alicia has always cared deeply about the welfare of animals, so this shelter is the realization of a lifelong dream for her," Silverstone's publicist Wendy Epstein said Monday. "She threw it together quickly, and she's still hammering out the kinks, but she really loves animals, and it's wonderful to see someone try to make a difference."

A longtime lover of furry and feathered companions and an ardent believer in animal rights, Silverstone gladly gives tours of her animal sanctuary, which holds a diverse menagerie of more than 90 creatures.

"I've been in city-run shelters, and they're so depressing," said Silverstone, stroking a rabbit stricken with an advanced case of pinkeye. "Here, the animals have all they can eat and a cozy place to sleep, in a big home with no cages. And there is absolutely no way I would ever murder an animal because I couldn't find a home for it."

Silverstone then placed the rabbit on the floor and pulled a 3-week-old kitten from between two sofa cushions. She cooed at the kitten as it licked and rubbed against her hand.

Above: StoneHaven, the animal shelter Alicia Silverstone (left) opened in November.

Like many Hollywood stars, Silverstone is a vegan. Her animals are, too.

"Goats feed on grass and hay, so they instinctively understand the value of a macrobiotic diet, but getting the kids off milk is a challenge," said Silverstone, who acquired her small goat herd from a bankrupt Oxnard petting zoo. "It's strange that they're not taking to the soy milk. Maybe I should try Rice Dream."

Silverstone said she noticed a marked decline in aggression among her 15 stray dogs after she put them on a meatless diet.

"When the doggies first arrived, they were always running around, jumping, and chasing each other," she said. "But after their fruit fast, they calmed right down. Now, they're so sweet and quiet. I'm sure I'll have no trouble finding homes for them."

Silverstone is determined to give her creatures a life free from human-imposed hindrances. She ordered her shelter staff to remove the horseshoes from three former carnival ponies, and she recently gave a 17-year-old housecat its "first-ever taste of freedom" by placing it in the crook of a large tree to sunbathe.

"You won't see animals wearing collars, bridles, or leashes here," Silverstone said, as she placed a calming *Wolves At Night* ambient-sounds CD in the shelter's sound system. "I don't even let anyone use the term 'housebreaking,' much less engage in the heartless practice."

Continued Silverstone: "Sometimes the little guys resist my attempts to free their bodies and minds. The dogs would not sit still during their pepper-mint aromatherapy immersion yesterday. Sort of like former prisoners, these animals need to be reconditioned. They need their natural self-esteem and body-awareness rejuvenated."

Two tireless assistants aid Silverstone in her crusade. Though they do not have veterinary degrees, both, like Silverstone, claim to have a deep affinity for all creatures.

"Animals need to be loved and touched, just like humans do," assistant Heidi Aarons said, as she attempted to massage a tense guinea pig. "We all share the cuddling, nesting instinct."

In spite of its devoted staff, Silverstone's dream project already faces challenges. The annual budget for see SHELTER page 71

Area Priest To Get Out Of Priesthood As Soon As Parents Die

BROCKTON, MA—Father Sean Lonergan, 36, a priest at St. Veronica Catholic Church, told reporters Tuesday that he plans to give up the collar when his parents die. "I've come to the realization that the priesthood is not for me, but it would crush Mom and Dad to see me abandon my faith," Lonergan said. "They've always been so good to me and my four brothers, so I can wait." Lonergan said both his parents have lived hard lives and couldn't possibly have more than 20-odd years left in them.

Guy Just Totally Smoking Weed On Street

MADISON, WI—Graduate student Danny Lindner, 26, reported that he was shocked Monday to see a guy just totally smoking pot right on the street. "This dude was, like, just walking down the sidewalk puffing on a joint, right out in the open," Lindner told roommate Kyle Rath. "I could totally smell it. It was *so weird*. What was he thinking?" Lindner added that it was broad daylight out.

Rumsfeld Only One Who Can Change Toner In White House Printer

WASHINGTON, DC—White House sources reported Monday that Secretary of State Donald Rumsfeld is the only cabinet member who can figure out how to change the toner in the White House printer. "Let me walk you through it again," Rumsfeld said. "You lift the toner-cartridge lid, then you move this switch back and remove the old cartridge. That goes in *el garbage*. Next, you remove this tape here from the new cartridge—now, that's important. If you forget that, you'll be printing blank pages all day long. Okay, so you just slide it on in, and you're good to go." When reached for comment, Rumsfeld said he doesn't mind changing the toner, but doesn't see what's so hard about it.

College Football Scout Has Eye On High-School Cheerleader

SYLACAUGA, AL—His eyes trained on the Sylacauga East High School football field during after-school practice, University of Alabama football scout Calvin Weaver announced Monday that he sees "great promise" in head cheerleader Cindy Ann Kohlner. "With that flexibility, [Kohlner] would clearly dominate the league in the sack," Weaver said. "You can't look at someone like her without thinking 'tight end.' But really, she would be outstanding in any position." Weaver also said that, given the opportunity, he would "love to fuck her."

4 Out Of 5 Texas Dentists Advocate The Death Penalty

DALLAS—According to a study released Monday by the Texas Dental Association, four out of five dentists in the Lone Star State advocate the use of capital punishment. "About 80 percent of the dentists surveyed recommend brushing three times daily, regular dental check-ups, and death by lethal injection should a prisoner be found guilty of homicide in a court of law," TDA spokeswoman Stacy Gunderson said. "Simply putting criminals in hard-to-reach places isn't enough of a deterrent. Rinsing the scum out of death row is vital for the long-term health of this state." Gunderson then called for justice, and plenty of all-natural sugar-free snacks, to be served. ∅

CONCERT from page 67

know how the rest of us were doing?" Grant added.

Froemer's attempts to engage other bar patrons in conversation did not sit well with Grant.

"He kept turning to me to say, 'Isn't this great?'" Grant said. "How many times can you ask someone, 'Isn't this great?' and not get an answer before you realize he doesn't care to give you his opinion?"

He added: "Oh, yeah. And he kept yelling 'Rock 'n' roll!' in my face. And once he screamed 'Stooges!' I had no idea at all why he did that."

Grant said he has seen Froemer at shows before.

"I've seen him around, and he's always enthusiastic," Grant said. "But I've never seen him so wound up before."

Grant reported that he lost his patience when Froemer almost spilled a drink.

"On the way back from, like, his 20th trip to the bar, he came this close to spilling a drink all over the floor," Grant said. "If it had spilled, some of it could have gotten on me. At that point, I told my date, 'All right, enough. We're leaving.'"

This isn't the first time a concert at the Empty Bottle has been ruined by an excited fan. On Sunday, an OK GO show was wrecked by two women who spent the evening jumping up and down directly in front of the stage, blocking the view for several patrons standing behind them.

"Sometimes it's like that," said Empty Bottle manager Bruce Finkleman. "Everyone at a show is standing there, arms folded, having a great time, and then someone decides to get crazy. It can kill an otherwise perfect night. Unfortunately, unless the enthusiastic fan breaks something, my hands are tied."

> "On the way back from, like, his 20th trip to the bar, he came this close to spilling a drink all over the floor," Grant said. "If it had spilled, some of it could have gotten on me. At that point, I told my date, 'All right, enough. We're leaving.'"

Froemer, whose exuberance at most concerts is endured without incident, said he was sorry to hear that people were put off by his enjoyment of the show. Nevertheless, he said he did not plan to change his behavior at future shows.

"It's too bad someone got mad," Froemer said. "But when the band started playing 'Sheets Of Easter,' I went nuts. It's 15 minutes, two notes, and it runs over you like a monster truck. I mean, shit—that band is *seriously fucking awesome!*" ✐

BUSH from page 67

They want to see an end to partisan bickering and closed-door decision-making. If I'm elected, I'll make sure that the American people can once again place their trust in the White House."

Bush said the soaring national debt and the lengthy war in Iraq have shaken Americans' faith in the highest levels of government.

"A credibility gap has opened between the Oval Office and America," Bush said. "The public hears talk, but they don't see any result. But if you choose me as your next president, the promises I make in my inaugural address will actually mean something. The president of this country will be held accountable for his promises, starting Jan. 20 of next year."

Bush said that, if chosen to be the next president, he would "set the nation on a course to a new, different, and brighter future."

"One thing is clear—it's time for a fresh beginning," Bush said. "Choose the ticket that leads to freedom, peace, and security. Choose Bush and Cheney."

Cheney spoke Monday at an event in Atlanta, addressing a crowd of 2,500 supporters from the tobacco and soft-drink industries.

"After these past three years, we need to rebuild a government based on old-fashioned American values: duty, dignity, and responsibility," said Cheney, who has served as a Wyoming congressman and U.S. vice-president. "George Bush is a man of these values, and he's ready to begin to put them to work in Washington."

Cheney continued: "George W. Bush will lead this great nation by building coalitions, not burning bridges; by serving the people, not special interests; by looking to the future, while borrowing from the great lessons of the past."

Cheney said he and Bush will return "time-honored American values" to the White House.

"In years past, American citizens looked to the president as a paragon of decency, a beacon in the storm," Cheney said. "When did America lose her way?"

In an interview published in Tuesday's *Washington Post*, Bush-Cheney 2004 campaign manager Ken Mehlman summarized the new platform.

"Bush-Cheney 2004 is a campaign built on straight talk," Mehlman said. "It's time for a president who can be a role model for Americans. Bush is the man for the job. He'll finally restore integrity to the highest office in the land. Won't you give him a chance?" ✐

KORNFELD from page 68

They looks like average suckahs, readin' tha *WSJ* or talkin' at clients on tha phone or gettin' coffee. But tha fact they everywhere an' don't hide theyselves like ninjas do be what make 'em so menacin'. Cuz don't hardly no one know they tha deadliest office enforcement gang on tha planet. Every one be trained in four kinds a' martial arts. Minimum. An' now five a' these punks about 2 come down on me, hard.

One of 'em sent a flyin' kick 2 my chest. I reeled back onto a credenza, then grabbed tha sidez wit' my hands behind my head, put mah knees 2 my head, and kicked out, knockin' two Blueshirts cold wit' my two feets.

Then anotha one came at me with tha Lo Han Fist. It vex me wild 2 see tha purely defensive artz a' tha peace-lovin' Shaolin bruthahood used foe corrupt ends, y'all. I blocked his fist wit' an iron fo'earm, windmilled my arms, an' connected a Shadowless Kick straight upside his bitch head. Then I gave him a Super Press-Down 'til I heard his ribs snap 2 my satisfaction.

That left two. Foe some reason, durin' tha kung-fu fightin', opponents only come atchu one atta time. I dodged tha fourth punk's Wind An' Thundah Fist wit' a triple somersault ova tha CEO's desk an' smashed through his office's window into tha main room. He hurled shards a' tha busted glass at me like throwin' stars, but I deflected 'em by pitchin' a loose corkboard at 'em, an' launchin' a hard kick 2 his throat. He flew away, but y'all could tell tha muhfukkah be

> Then, outta nowhere, I heard this freaky laugh. Tha first two punks already split. I thought it might be tha crazy Blueshirt bitch, but his laugh sounded a li'l different. Finally, this kinda sissy voice spoke up.

usin' wires. I cornered him in a cubicle, an' we traded furious blows wit' a quickness. Tha first punk I knocked cold came to an' snuck up behind me, but I dispatched him again with a punch from tha back a' my fist without turnin' around. I aim a kick under tha fourth punk's chin, an' he go somersaultin' ova tha cubicle an' through tha window 2 tha outside.

Tha last muhfukkah be tha most hardcore, but inna psycho way. He laughed like a hyena, then he assumed a stance I didn't recognize foe a second. Then he came at me. Holy fuckin'

shit: Tha muhfukkah be a mastah a' tha Deadly Super Wondah Palm. That certain death. I vaulted ovah him an' kicked tha back a' his head on tha descent. We whipped aroun' 2 face one anothah. He came at me again. I

> "That kung-fu is not of mainstream!" he screamed, pickin' staples outta his face. "Who is teach you such perfidy?"

grabbed a stapler, said a prayer, an' popped a whole cartridge a' staples at his face. Tha muhfukkah in agony.

"That kung-fu is not of mainstream!" he screamed, pickin' staples outta his face. "Who is teach you such perfidy?"

"My kung-fu incorporate office supplies," I hissed. "That be my Magic Staple-Gun Punch."

I riled tha crazy bitch up good. Furious, he launched anotha Wondah Palm at me. Its touch brand a burnin' palm mark fulla poison, an' suckas don't live too long aftaward. But wit' a blood-chillin' scream, he ended up through tha same window I sent tha last punk through, an' foe some reason, there wuz a big explosion. I jes' single-handedly fucked up five Blueshirts, but I wuz too cashed 2 gloat. Wit' my last ounce a' strength, I turned ova on my back an' lay motionless.

All quiet foe a while. Then, a piece-a paypa fluttahed down an' landed on my chest. It a cashier's check foe tha full amount SPJ owe us: $91.46. Then, outta nowhere, I heard this freaky laugh. Tha first two punks already split. I thought it might be tha crazy Blueshirt bitch, but his laugh sounded a li'l different. Finally, this kinda sissy voice spoke up.

"Excellent work, Herbert Kornfeld," tha voice say. "Here is your payment in full, for services rendered. As you can see, it's guaranteed. Your fighting skills are superlative. You dispatched five of the toughest Blueshirts in the entire state. Hmm. Five. Isn't that the same age at which your sister disappeared? Your sister, Herbert? Or do the mists of time obscure her memory? It is a pity you couldn't use your Office-Fu then to save *her*."

My throat went dry. My pupils dwindled 2 pinpoints.

"*Goddamn you,*" I screamed. "*What do y'all know 'bout my sistah, you muhfukka? Don't nobody talk about my sistah, not evah. Dammit, who you be? An' what do y'all know 'bout my sistah? Answer me!*"

But tha voice didn't speak no more.

If that story didn't make y'all shit yo' Underoos, then you must be wearin' a muhfukkin' toe tag. By tha way, any a' y'all evah aks me about my sistah, I crease yo' head wit' a three-hole punch. ✐

80, you know a self-abuse victim."

Just as alarming as the high incidence of abuse, Cracklin said, is the fact that it's impossible to predict where it will occur.

"Our surveys indicate that self-abuse incidents are unpredictable," Cracklin said. "They can occur at any time and in any place. Study participants were abused in their own beds, in showers, in the bathroom stalls of college dorms. It's happened in the parking lot during lunch hour, at the beach, in library basements, and even in vehi-

> **According to Janet Linstrom, founder of Mothers Against Self Touch-Abuse, family members and friends who suspect that a minor is being self-abused often do nothing, because they believe the child's claim that he simply enjoys being left alone.**

cles moving along the highway at night."

Cracklin added: "It may be happening to someone you love, right at this very moment."

According to Janet Linstrom, founder of Mothers Against Self Touch-Abuse, family members and friends who suspect that a minor is

Above: 14-year-old Eric Jarrell, who reported he was self-abused four times the day this photo was taken.

being self-abused often do nothing, because they believe the child's claim that he simply enjoys being left alone.

"The self-abuse victim will often withdraw from the family. He'll forgo group activities, opting instead to spend hours locked in his bedroom, surfing the Internet," Linstrom said. "Unfortunately, I am all too aware of the danger signs. You see, both my husband and I were self-abused."

Support-group leaders like Linstrom address the problem one victim at a time.

"Many victims are reluctant to seek help," Linstrom said. "Their abusers have isolated them from friends and family, so there's no one for them to reach out to. For many, the abuser is the only intimate friend they have."

"Truth be told, victims sometimes report deriving some sort of satisfaction from the self-abuse," Linstrom said, "There's an intensity to abusive relationships that many self-abuse victims don't find elsewhere. Many will say, 'No one else makes me feel this way.'"

Added Linstrom: "That's why we focus on the younger ones. We've been working in the schools, but it's an uphill battle. We hear scores of second- and third-hand accounts of self-abuse, but it's not easy to get students to share stories of their own victimization."

In spite of the stranglehold self-abuse has on the population, few sources of help are available to victims, said Sister Joselda Hattchett, founder of St. Mary's Self-Abuse Shelter in Denver, a Catholic charity group dedicated to counseling self-abuse victims.

"As far as I'm aware, we're one of the few institutions specifically designed to handle the fallout from these attacks," Hattchett said. "Incredible as it may seem, those who are brave enough to report the self-abuse often find that their claims are not taken seriously. Some victims are even laughed at."

Hattchett said the shelter provides a self-abuse hotline, but the 900-number seems to do more harm than good.

"We placed ads in the back of men's magazines and newsweeklies," Hattchett said. "The sisters find that the majority of the victims who reach out to them are unable to escape their tormentors, even during a short phone call. We thought having non-threatening, soft-voiced women answer the phones would make it easier for victims to discuss the problem, but most callers only seem interested in the operators' fashion choices or whether they like to 'party.'"

Hattchett said the hardest part of her job is seeing self-abuse victims who were brave enough to come forward fall back into the hands of their abusers.

"It's difficult to get self-abuse victims to stop blaming themselves for what's happened," Hattchett said. "They think it's their fault, because they're too weak to resist. And, despite everything that has happened, they often maintain strong feelings for their abusers. I've seen it happen time and time again." ∅

2004 has been exhausted on costly amenities such as bottled water, pet psychics, specially molded "soy mice" for the resident 32-foot boa constrictor, and printed programs for a "commitment ceremony" between a parrot and a ferret.

In addition, fewer than 5 percent of potential adopters have passed Silverstone's stringent screening procedure.

"After my dog died of old age, I tried to adopt a puppy from StoneHaven," Los Angeles entertainment lawyer Barry Gelman said. "In order to prove I was a worthy parent, Alicia told me I had to carry a stuffed dog around with me for a week. I was supposed to feed it with a bottle and change its diapers every three hours. She said she got the idea from an episode of *Saved By The Bell*."

Silverstone's resolve will be tested in the coming months. Neighbors have filed official complaints against StoneHaven regarding the noise, the stench, and the escaped animals frequently found outside its gates. Further, they claim that Silverstone's sentimental reluctance to spay, neuter, or

fence in animals has caused a dramatic increase in stray dogs and cats in the area, as well as a serious pink-eye outbreak within a five-mile radius.

But Silverstone isn't giving up. The ac-

> **"Sometimes the little guys resist my attempts to free their bodies and minds,"** Silverstone said.

tress has big ideas for the coming year, including her plan to take in more animals that "aren't even that cute."

"See Myrlie over there?" asked Silverstone, as she pointed to a Komodo dragon sunning itself in a corner of the backyard. "In a zoo, she'd be locked in a pen all day. But here, she can roam free, eat all the grass she wants, and play with Pepper, the pot-bellied pig. Zoos and city shelters simply don't give animals this kind of friendly environment." ∅

Above: Two of StoneHaven's needy pets share a "super comfy" habitat Silverstone designed herself.

Ask A '60s Horror-Movie Radio Spot

By A '60s Horror-Movie Radio Spot

Dear '60s Horror-Movie Radio Spot,

I have a dear friend who's always late. While "Charlie" doesn't seem to notice or care, it's slowly driving me crazy! He's never more than 10 minutes late, so it doesn't end up ruining our plans, but it does make me feel like he doesn't have any respect for me or my time! Am I being too uptight? Is this chronic tardiness something I should let slide? Or should I lay down the law and risk alienating one of my oldest friends?

Left Waiting In Laramie

Dear Waiting,

Six people. Alone. In a castle. Will any of them live to see the next day?

This wasn't here before? How did it get here? No! Nooooooooo!

The Castle Of Terroropolis! It started as a dare between friends, then it turned into...something else.

There's nothing to worry about. Swords fall off the wall all the time. Brock was just in the wrong place at the wrong time.

You will be shocked by the horrors the victims face as they try to escape *The Castle Of Terroropolis.*

Who's there? Answer me! Aaaaaargh!

See the thrilling movie that will have you asking the question, "Could it happen to me?" *The Castle Of Terroropolis!* Rated GP. Now playing.

Dear '60s Horror-Movie Radio Spot,

I agreed to watch my friend's cat while she vacationed in Europe for three weeks. Because it was for such a long time, and since she lives across town, we agreed that the cat would stay at my house. But her cat repeatedly attacked my mild-mannered Persian and then urinated on my favorite velvet couch! I've scrubbed and scrubbed the cushion, but I can't get rid of the terrible smell. Should I present my friend with a bill for a new cushion, or should I just chalk it up to my own bad fortune and walk away?

Cat Problems In Camden

Dear Cat Problems,

Warning! The theater will not be responsible for any heart-attack fatalities caused by the shocking sights seen in *Cannibal Cop.*

Rudy Franklin was a normal beat cop until he witnessed a crime so horrible that his mind snapped. Now, he roams the streets dealing out justice, and terror. He is *Cannibal Cop!*

Okay, officer, you got me. I surrender...wait! My arm! Why are you eat-

ing my arm? Arrrrrgh!

Only one reporter knows the truth, but can he make anyone listen to him in time?

What's wrong with you? Are you all crazy? Can't you see that this man's entire torso has been eaten?

Can you handle the madness of *Cannibal Cop?* Now showing with *Juvenile Delinquent Arts Camp.* Remember: You've been warned!

Dear '60s Horror-Movie Radio Spot,

My boyfriend and I are talking about getting married, but one thing is holding me back: his parents. His mother and father are extremely cold, in spite of all my efforts to bond with them. My boyfriend insists that they think highly of me, but they sure have a funny way of showing it. I love my boyfriend, but I'm afraid that his parents will never warm up. Family is very important to me, so the thought of not being close to my in-laws is really frightening! What do you think: Should I forget about my fears or forget about my fiancé?

**Parent Trapped In
Port Washington**

Dear Parent Trapped,

How a group of ski bums and beatniks wound up in a deserted farmhouse on Beach Mountain is a mystery. What happens next will blow their minds!

This is the spot, right here on Beach Mountain, where Dr. Frankenstein had his crazy lab. I hear they had some wild stuff happen.

Dr. Frankenstein is hot on the trail of this group of misfits. He's protecting what's his, and they'll be lucky if they escape Beach Mountain with their lives.

This is where the prospector said he saw those wild lights. But I don't see... Wait a minute. What's this? It's the prospector. And he's been torn apart! [Choking sounds.]

Can this ragtag group of deadbeats find the treasure of Beach Mountain before Frankenstein finds them? And if they do, will the mysterious treasure drive them mad?

Ha ha ha ha ha ha ha ha ha ha ha ha!

The doctor is out...far out. Watch *The Frankenstein Of Beach Mountain* before he watches you! Now playing. Check your local listings.

A '60s Horror-Movie Radio Spot is a syndicated advice columnist whose weekly column, Ask A '60s Horror-Movie Radio Spot, appears in more than 250 newspapers nationwide. ∅

Your Horoscope

By Lloyd Schumner Sr.
Retired Machinist and
A.A.P.B.-Certified Astrologer

Aries: (March 21–April 19)
Your financial outlook isn't a pretty picture, but it does have a certain dark, Brueghelian magnificence.

Taurus: (April 20–May 20)
Your new diet will cause you to become so skinny that, when sitting around the house, you will do so on a single, easily determined side of the house.

Gemini: (May 21–June 21)
Although it was fun to hear your name on television, you still don't think the president should use the State Of The Union address to put prices on citizens' heads.

Cancer: (June 22–July 22)
Learning to accept change is a sign of maturity. Enjoy spending your golden years begging for it on the corner.

Leo: (July 23–Aug. 22)
If you learn one thing this week, let it be this: What matters isn't whether you're innocent or guilty, but what you wear to the trial.

Virgo: (Aug. 23–Sept. 22)
Luckily, the trend of closed-casket funerals has allowed you to take certain aesthetic shortcuts in your work.

Libra: (Sept. 23–Oct. 23)
You're really getting tired of big business screwing over the little guy in the subplots of all those TV movies.

Scorpio: (Oct. 24–Nov. 21)
You won't so much haunt the world after your death as become the spiritual equivalent of that guy who kept coming back to visit high school after graduation.

Sagittarius: (Nov. 22–Dec. 21)
Your fake-sounding French accent is even more heinous considering that you grew up in the countryside around Toulon.

Capricorn: (Dec. 22–Jan. 19)
You always seem to improve the performances of those around you, usually by slipping them amphetamines while they're not looking.

Aquarius: (Jan. 20–Feb. 18)
Although your cancer, if treated early, has a 96 percent recovery rate, doctors are strangely reluctant to treat you.

Pisces: (Feb. 19–March 20)
You can't really help the way people feel about you, especially if the dumbasses refuse to listen to reason.

SPAZZ from page 66

amounts of blood. Passersby were amazed by the unusually large amounts of blood. Passersby were

amazed by the unusually large amounts of blood. Passersby were amazed by the unusually large amounts of blood. Passersby were amazed by the unusually large amounts of blood. Passersby were amazed by the unusually large amounts of blood. Passersby were amazed by the unusually large amounts of blood. Passersby were

---

Man was not meant to play Godsmack.

---

amazed by the unusually large amounts of blood. Passersby were amazed by the unusually large amounts of blood. Passersby were amazed by the unusually large amounts of blood. Passersby were amazed by the unusually large amounts of blood. Passersby were amazed by the unusually large amounts of blood. Passersby were amazed by the unusually large amounts of blood. Passersby were amazed by the unusually large amounts of blood. Passersby were amazed by the unusually large amounts of blood. Passersby were

see SPAZZ page 189

Michael Jackson Hires Magical Anthropomorphic Giraffe As Defense Lawyer

see NATION page 8C

Parent Takes Out $100 Bill In Front Of Wide-Eyed 7-Year-Old

see FAMILY page 13E

Vibrator Left On All Night

see LOCAL page 4B

STATshot

A look at the numbers that shape your world.

Top Notes Left By Roommates

25% Borrowed your diaphragm

12% Your parents stopped by to take me out to dinner

32% Totaled your car—your part of phone bill was $47.35

14% Wanna fuck? J/K! Do you, though?

17% Someone called—either Barry's dead, or they buried your dad

---

the ONION®

VOLUME 40 ISSUE 05   AMERICA'S FINEST NEWS SOURCE™   5–11 FEBRUARY 2004

New Anger-Powered Cars May Revolutionize The Way We Drive

CHEVROLET TANTRUM

DETROIT—With gas prices approaching $2 per gallon in some areas and gridlock on the rise, Detroit's three major automakers are stepping up development of their newest brainchild: the anger-powered car.

"By drawing a significant percentage of its motive power from the unbridled temper of the American motorist, the new anger-powered car will change, or at least take mechanical

see CARS page 76

Right: The Chevrolet Tantrum, one of the new road-rage-fueled vehicles.

Democrats Somehow Lose Primaries

WASHINGTON, DC—In a surprising last-minute upset, all seven Democratic presidential hopefuls somehow lost the Democratic primaries Tuesday.

"While it's true that the Democratic Party has been struggling to find a strong voice, you can imagine our surprise when results indicated that John Kerry, Howard Dean, Wesley Clark, Joe Lieberman, and John Edwards all failed to carry a single primary," American Research Group political analyst Dick Bennett said late Tuesday. "Oh, and Al Sharpton and Dennis Kucinich, too."

Primaries were held in Delaware, Missouri, Arizona, Oklahoma, and South Carolina, with no single Democratic candidate coming in higher than second place.

Experts are still unsure exactly how Kerry, whom many considered the frontrunner after strong showings in Iowa and New Hampshire, lost to, and along with, every other Democratic candidate.

"Given our standing going into Tuesday, we were surprised not to

see PRIMARIES page 77

Coworkers Dying To Tell Man He's Going To Be Fired

Above: Tendulkar (front) and coworkers.

RAPID CITY, SD—Employees at Reynolds Business Machines are dying to tell sales representative Mark Tendulkar that he is about to be fired, sources reported Tuesday.

"I was out with [sales manager] Frank Lascowicz last Thursday, and he let slip that Tendulkar's cubicle would be free. It took some free rounds, but I got it out of him: Mark's out on Feb. 15," sales representative Jeff Wildner said. "Mark is such a total dick, and so incompetent, I don't know how I'm going to be able to keep it from him that long."

Wildner said it's not his place to break the news to Tendulkar, no matter how much he would love to.

"I'm just going to have to wait until the boss axes him," Wildner said. "But the writing's definitely on the wall for ol' Tendulkar."

Tendulkar has worked at Reynolds since 1999, but according to fellow employees, he has failed to meet his weekly sales quota for the past four months.

"Mark ought to know it's coming," sales representative Cory Fontaine said. "You'd have to be a deaf mute to have trouble selling a Canon 3200 after the price reduction, but he hasn't

see FIRED page 76

FDA To Ban Ephedra

The FDA recently announced that it plans to prohibit sales of products containing ephedra, a stimulant sold primarily for weight loss. What do *you* think?

"If they ban ephedra, they're just going to drive fat people out into the streets for their weight-loss fix."

Donald Clark
Systems Analyst

"This is bullshit. I contacted the FDA after my cousin swallowed three wooden blocks and died, and you still see those on the market."

Alan King
Unemployed

"Well, for now, I can get along fine with bitter orange, royal jelly, and the lichen derivative usnic acid."

Steve Hernandez
Cook

"How terrible! Americans have no other options for weight-loss products."

Martha Nelson
Product Tester

"You can ban the drug ephedra, but you'll never be able to ban what ephedra stands for."

Angela Hall
Teacher

"Why is it always the drugs that suffer when people get hurt?"

Gregory Green
Professor

The Patriot Act's Problem Parts

A federal judge in Los Angeles recently struck down a section of the Patriot Act, declaring it unconstitutional. Which parts of the law are under scrutiny?

★ Saying words "terrorism," "terrycloth," or "tea" over the phone can land you in jail

★ Homeland Security officials allowed to break into citizens' homes and use them when in need of "down time"

★ Section 222, which revokes the Constitution

★ U.S. Sen. Russell Feingold, the lone voice of dissent, to be locked in broom closet

★ When threat level is elevated to "red," citizenry's entitlement to pursuit of happiness suspended

★ Section that repeals a woman's right to vote

★ Undercover officers may shake Arab-Americans upside-down until the bombs fall out

★ In fact, everything after the words "Patriot Act"

the ONION
America's Finest News Source.™

Herman Ulysses Zweibel
Founder

T. Herman Zweibel
Publisher Emeritus
J. Phineas Zweibel
Publisher
Maxwell Prescott Zweibel
Editor-In-Chief

74

I Happened To Be In The Neighborhood And Horny

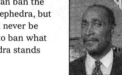

By Stuart Michener

Hey, how's it going? I'm sorry, were you sleeping? I guess it's kinda late. I know we haven't seen each other in a long time, but I was in the neighborhood, and I saw your light on, so I thought I'd drop by and see if you'd have sex with me.

So, how are you doing these days? I'm good; things have been good. Right this minute, I'm pretty horny, though. Why don't I come in so we can catch up on old times and have sex?

Boy, it must have been at least nine months since the last time we talked. Can you believe it? I know I can't. I would have come by sooner, but I've been busy at work, and I was getting laid pretty regularly there for a while. I was in this area a few weeks ago, but I didn't see your light on, and I wasn't in the mood. But tonight, well, that's a different story.

How have you been? Let me just step inside here... The place looks nice! Come on, don't be silly! You know what a slob I am. Remember my apartment? Dirty dishes, clothes everywhere. I see you moved the couch over against the window. Good idea. Really opens up the place. Hey, you didn't have blinds before, did you? Those must be new. Why don't we shut them?

> Boy, it must have been at least nine months since the last time we talked. Can you believe it? I know I can't. I would have come by sooner, but I've been busy at work, and I was getting laid pretty regularly there for a while.

So, how've you been? Because I'm concerned, that's why. Uh huh. Yeah, I heard about that. Sorry to interrupt, but you look really good. I like your hair like that. It's very grab-able.

Things have been going okay for me. I haven't really been dating lately. I was seeing this girl, but it wasn't really working out. We just weren't compatible. Not like you and me. Man, we had some good times. Hey, listen to me yammer when it's so late. Maybe we should go to bed.

It sure is great to be back in this neighborhood. I always liked it around here. It's a good mix of old businesses and newer bookstores and cafés. That coffee shop on the corner is new, isn't it? It looks like a nice little place. I noticed that the liquor

> We don't even have to go all the way. We can just grope each other for a while and then finish off with some oral sex. Can't an old friend stop by for a visit or a quickie?

store next door to it is still open. Do you think I should run out for something?

I got this new CD that I think you'd like. I've got it right here in my bag. It has kind of a Marvin Gaye meets Keith Sweat vibe. Really powerful music. We can listen to it and make out.

Or, if you want, we could watch a movie. It's early enough to do that *and* still have sex. You have a DVD player, right? What do you like? Maybe *Secretary... 9 1/2 Weeks... Last Tango In Paris*? Take your pick. They're all pretty good. I think it would be a good way to ease into an evening of fun. I haven't seen or fucked you in a while.

Really, why not? I'm here, you're here. We're two adults. I've got a penis, you've got a vagina. And my roommate is having his loud friends over to watch the game, so I'd really rather not go back to my place until they've cleared out.

We don't even have to go all the way. We can just grope each other for a while and then finish off with some oral sex. Can't an old friend stop by for a visit or a quickie?

If it's awkward morning conversation that you're worried about, you have nothing to fear. I promise you that three hours after we're done, I will silently put my clothes on and leave. And, if that isn't enough, I promise not to call you until the next time I'm in the area and horny. Or, if you prefer, I'll call tomorrow and make some awkward small talk. Whichever way you'd like.

How about it?

All right, it's your loss. Is your roommate with the red hair home? ∅

Man Stays Up All Night Procrastinating

FLAGSTAFF, AZ—Bank manager Ron Bogen, 29, worked into the wee hours of the morning not writing his speech for the semi-annual Compass Bank Best Practices Conference Tuesday.

"If I'm a bit slow today, it's because I was up all night working on that presentation," Bogen told his coworkers over lunch Tuesday. "It was a lot slower going than I thought it would be, and aa bunch of other stuff came up while I was working on it. All in all, it took me, like, 10 hours."

According to live-in girlfriend Sophie Collins, the evening started well for Bogen.

"Ron talked all weekend about needing to write his speech, but he finally sat down at about 8 Monday night," Collins said. "He had everything he needed laid out on the table: all of the papers and brochures from work, his pens and highlighters, and a tape recorder. In less than half an hour, he was cleaning the bathroom."

Bogen explained: "I was in the bathroom thinking through the opening of the speech when I saw how disgusting the sink was. I couldn't concentrate with a sink that filthy under me. It was no big deal, though—a little Comet, a thorough scrubbing, and a rinse. Took 20 minutes, tops."

After cleaning the sink, picking his dirty clothes up off the floor, and

hanging new towels on the rack, Bogen said he realized that he hadn't spoken to his parents in at least two weeks. After he called his parents, he then called his brother, and then his sister.

"I wanted to get down to work, but I couldn't just call everyone but Tammy," Bogen said.

At 10 p.m., Bogen returned to his desk to begin his speech. When he booted up his Dell Inspiron, a dialog box appeared, urging him to install a new Windows XP security patch.

"I'd been ignoring that warning for months," Bogen said. "I said to myself, 'Let's just get it done.'"

After installing and rebooting, Bogen decided to update his Flash Player and Internet Explorer plug-ins, as well.

At 10:45 p.m., Bogen began to organize his speech by writing it out in longhand on index cards. While looking for index cards, he noticed a pile of bills.

"I'd been meaning to switch over to paperless billing for my cable and phone and everything for months," Bogen said. "It felt so good to finally have that all set up."

Bogen was ready to tackle his presentation once again at 11:15 p.m.

"I was getting back down to work when I remembered that there was a great speech in that movie Sneakers,"

Above: Bogen's uncompleted presentation weighs heavy on his mind.

Bogen said. "I knew it would be really helpful for my own speech, so I got out the DVD. I ended up watching the whole movie before I realized that the speech was actually in Dave. But I didn't watch that movie, because it was 1 a.m., and I really needed to get cracking. That is, right after I organized my DVD shelf, which had gotten really out of control."

Between the hours of 1 and 2:30 a.m., Bogen searched the Internet for information about his old high-school

friends, read the latest Time magazine from cover to cover, bought three books on Amazon, and downloaded a single from Jay-Z's Black Album.

Bogen also showered and shaved "to get into the perfect condition to do some writing."

"I don't know why a shower helps, but it does," Bogen said. "As soon as I finished eating the fajitas I made, my mind was on nothing but the speech."

Collins, who urged Bogen to finish

see MAN page 77

Quaaludes Are Back, Reports Quaalude-Taking Journalist

CHICAGO—The illegal use of Methaqualone is on the rise, Quaalude-addicted AP reporter Keith Jannings said Monday. "Quaaludes fell largely out of sight after the highly addictive sedatives were taken off the market in the '80s," said Jannings, a thread of drool hanging from his lower lip. "But my research shows that recreational use of this dangerous drug is rebounding, especially among the professional class." To demonstrate, Jannings downed three Canadian quails he'd scored from a dealer just hours earlier.

Boy, Dolphin No Longer On Speaking Terms

KEY WEST, FL—Jimmy O'Dell, 9, and his animal friend Skippy, a bot-

tlenose dolphin, are no longer on speaking terms, the boy said Monday. "I told Skippy I wanted to ride his back out to Buccaneer's Cove to look for buried treasure," O'Dell said. "But Skippy kept squeaking that it wasn't safe. He's always contradicting me, and I'm sick of it. That finned freak is dead to me." Skippy refused to comment.

10th-Grade Class Watches *Ben-Hur* For Two Weeks

SALEM, VA—For the eighth straight world-history period, sophomores at Riverside High School watched the 1959 classic Ben-Hur Tuesday. "The chariot races were pretty cool," Michael Bower said of the 211-minute film he and classmates have been watching in 25-minute segments, between roll call and free-reading. "And when Mr. Franks got back from the teachers' lounge, he told us Jesus is in tomorrow's part." Bower said he dreads next week,

when the class will break into Ben-Hur discussion groups and share their ancient-history unit journals.

Pep Talk Laced With Personal Threats

SALT LAKE CITY, UT—Matthew Luskey's pep talk to Benjamin Lambert, who has struggled emotionally since a split with former girlfriend Ashley Huza, was laced with personal threats, sources reported Monday. "If you don't stop torturing yourself, I'm going to beat the living shit out of you," Luskey told Lambert. "Either you get up off of this couch and allow the healing process to begin, or I'll open up a wound so deep, it'll leave more than just an emotional scar." Luskey added that Lambert had better restore his sense of self-worth fast, if he values his life.

Man Finds Self Back At Porn Store Again

JASPER, WY—Gregory Steevers,

37, found himself standing in the aisles of the Pleasure Island adult bookstore again Monday. "I was out on a walk after I dropped off the electric bill," Steevers said. "I stopped and had a sandwich, then, before I knew it, I was perusing the shelf of anal videos at the Island. Weird." Steevers said he's "ended up" at Pleasure Island about twice a week for the past four years.

Celebrity Saddened By Death Of Other Celebrity

BEVERLY HILLS, CA—Hollywood legend Elizabeth Taylor announced Monday that she was saddened by the death of actress, dancer, and fellow famous person Ann Miller. "Annie was such a joy, an absolute doll," Taylor told reporters. "She touched so many lives, and she will be missed. My heart goes out to her family." Taylor also expressed sadness over the recent passing of Bob "Captain Kangaroo" Keeshan. Ø

advantage of, the way Americans drive," General Motors vice-chairman Robert A. Lutz said. "We plan to have these furiously efficient machines careening down America's highways, byways, and sidewalks within two years."

Lutz said automakers have been researching fury fuels since the mid-1970s. As early as 1984, they began to look for ways to take advantage of the limitless supply of bad temper generated daily by American drivers—outrage currently vented wastefully into dashboards, steering wheels, and passengers.

An engine burning clean, white-hot hatred will release few harmful byproducts into the atmosphere—bad vibes and a small amount of water vapor will combine to be released in the form of human spittle. In addition, anger technology will turn the standard fuel-economy paradigm on its head: An anger-powered engine is actually more efficient in heavy urban traffic.

"The theory behind the anger-powered engine is actually quite simple," said Keith Cameron, chief engineer on General Motors' Project Instigator until January. "The average motorist traveling a clogged American highway produces hundreds of kilowatt-hours of negative energy per infuriating drive. The Instigator motor converts this emotional energy into kinetic energy by a process most drivers—people too goddamn stupid to use their goddamn blinkers when they change goddamn lanes—will never be able to understand. Just trust me, dumbasses, it works."

Cameron, who is currently serving a seven-year prison sentence for vehicular manslaughter and high-efficiency battery, added, "In the white-knuckled hands of the average American driver, it's an extremely powerful tool."

GM is currently developing two anger-powered cars, the entry-level Chevrolet Tantrum coupe and the larger, pricier Buick Umbrage. Ford has announced a multi-tiered move toward anger power, with plans to introduce anger/gasoline hybrid engines in the popular Lincoln Frown Car in 2006, to offer a de Sade option for its classic Mercury Gran Marquis in 2007, and to unveil a line of Acrimony family-sized cars and wagons in 2008. Daimler-Chrysler will resurrect the defunct Plymouth brand name with the reintroduction of the Plymouth Fury.

Anger power was first explored by Daimler-Chrysler, whose concept car, the Plymouth Violent, caused an uproar upon its introduction at the 1989 Detroit Auto Show. The Violent, more a seething showcase of technology and rage than a workable production car, achieved a remarkable 89 miles per gallon and hospitalized 19 auto-show attendees.

The anger-powered car will be aimed solidly at the middle of the market. Options such as semi-tinted glower windows, auto-locking brakes, and a baffling array of randomly blinking warning lights will be standard on all models.

"Production models will have angry-punch-absorbing energy-conversion pads in the dashboards, steering wheels, and driver-side doors,"

Chrysler Group chief executive Dieter Zetsche said. "Sound-sensitive materials in the cars' interiors will convert livid outbursts into motive power. And, because an angry driver is, in

> The anger-powered car will be aimed solidly at the middle of the market. Options such as semi-tinted glower windows, auto-locking brakes, and a baffling array of randomly blinking warning lights will be standard on all models.

this case, a better driver, literally hundreds of anger- and performance-enhancing options will be available, including loud, ineffective mufflers, talk-station-only radios, truly intermittent wipers, steering wheels which imperceptibly tilt forward over the course of an hour, and excruciatingly well-heated seats."

Early consumer tests of the cars indicate that they perform beyond designers' expectations. The automotive press has been particularly enthusiastic about anger power.

"This bitch's bastard's whore went like a goddamn raped ape with me at

the wheel," said Car And Driver's Brock Yates, who test-drove Daimler-Chrysler's Dodge Rammit pickup. "The vitriolic-assist brakes barely worked, the rear-view mirror found my bald spot every time, and the voice-response OnStar system mocked me for writing the script for Cannonball Run. I was getting 107 miles to the gallon when I T-boned that bus."

Car manufacturers have yet to determine a price for the rage-fueled vehicles.

"We have a delicate balance to strike," Ford Motor Company president Nick Scheele said. "The middle-income customer should be able to afford the car, but in order to increase engine efficiency, the price should be high enough to eat away at him the entire time he's driving. We're considering wildly fluctuating interest rates or a monthly payment rate that's pegged to the basketball standings."

Added Scheele: "I can assure you that there will be a model priced so that middle-class Americans who spend hours each week commuting between mid-level office jobs in the city and noisy, demanding families in the suburbs can afford it."

Fully anger-powered cars are expected to begin hitting American showrooms and other cars in summer 2006. If successful, the venture may vindicate the auto engineers still smarting over their brief and disastrous flirtation with love-and-happiness power, a trend that failed commercially and eventually petered out during the positive-energy crisis of the 1970s. ∅

closed on one. Not one."

"He's totally unaware he's about to be thrown over!" Fontaine added. "I even heard him talking about needing a bigger desk yesterday. I'm dying!"

Since word of the firing spread, a sense of excitement has filled the office.

"I don't even want to go meet a client, in case the shit goes down while I'm out," Fontaine said. "It's all I can do to not tell him myself. Still, though, a small part of me wants it to be a total surprise when the ax comes down. The look on his face will be priceless!"

Several coworkers have nearly told Tendulkar what's about to happen, only to check themselves at the last second.

"Just today, Mark came in blaming me for something about some keyboard he ordered," secretary Gina Haney said. "I almost said, 'Unless you're taking that keyboard with you when you go, I wouldn't worry about it.'"

"Sayonara, sucker!" Haney added.

In spite of the wide circulation of the news, coworkers described Tendulkar as "blissfully ignorant."

Sitting in the sales pit, surrounded by his busy coworkers Tuesday, Ten-

dulkar casually shelled pistachios as he circled loungewear items in a J. Crew catalog and browsed vacation packages on Orbitz.com.

> "Just today, Mark came in blaming me for something about some keyboard he ordered," secretary Gina Haney said. "I almost said, 'Unless you're taking that keyboard with you when you go, I wouldn't worry about it.'"

Even Tendulkar's immediate supervisor said he's had a hard time keeping quiet.

"Mark came in all smug after selling a MultiPASS MP360," floor supervisor Andrew Miller said. "He said something like, 'Put another one in the win

column for the Marksman.' I wanted to tell him that one $140 sale wasn't going to be enough to save his job, but protocol must be observed. I can't wait until Lascowicz sends him up the river."

As the firing approaches, Tendulkar's coworkers have been exchanging glances and trading jokes behind his back.

"Cory had a good one yesterday," Wildner said. "He threw Mark's coffee cup in the garbage and said, 'I don't think they have coffee in the unemployment line.' It was almost as good as when Tina [Lewis] walked in with two empty boxes and said she was going to go ask Mark if he needed them to pack."

When Tendulkar was late for work Tuesday, several of his colleagues reportedly gathered in his cubicle, appraised its contents, and made claims on his chair and desk lamp.

Not everyone is burning to tell Tendulkar the bad news.

"Mark's an okay guy," coworker Bill Davies said. "He's got some rough edges, but once you get to know him, he's all right. He just got married last summer, and he's still paying off the wedding. I hate to see anyone in that situation."

Tendulkar does not seem to be aware of Davies' comments.

"My sales have been pretty slow lately," Tendulkar said. "But with the

> "Mark's an okay guy," coworker Bill Davies said. "He's got some rough edges, but once you get to know him, he's all right. He just got married last summer, and he's still paying off the wedding. I hate to see anyone in that situation."

economy as bad as it is, that's to be expected. I should be back on my feet by the end of March. Then, the Marksman will be back on top, looking down on all the little people. It kills me to be pulling in less than that bald little Davies runt." ∅

MAN from page 75

his speech so he could go to bed with her, was disappointed to wake up alone.

"I found Ron with his head down on his keyboard, a blank Word document on his screen, and note cards with jokes written on them strewn everywhere," Collins said. "Clearly, he'd gone to some Internet site devoted to funny ice-breakers and spent *hours* writing down his favorites."

As the couple got ready for work, Bogen furiously scribbled an outline

> "Ron talked all weekend about needing to write his speech, but he finally sat down at about 8 Monday night," Collins said. "He had everything he needed laid out on the table: all of the papers and brochures from work, his pens and highlighters, and a tape recorder. In less than half an hour, he was cleaning the bathroom."

for his presentation on a notepad as he brushed his teeth and dressed.

Bogen said he promised himself that he wouldn't tell anyone how long he worked on the speech, but he broke his promise as soon as he slid in beside coworker and carpool member Will Serber.

"Ron said he looked like shit because he was up all night slaving away on work for the conference," Serber said. "But, from what I could tell, he wrote as many pages of his speech during the 20-minute ride to work as he'd written the whole night before."

Bogen, who has been branch manager of Flagstaff's Central Avenue Compass Bank for nearly 11 months, delivered his eight-minute speech Tuesday at 10:30 a.m. without major incident.

"The speech turned out pretty good," Bogen said. "Just goes to show that it pays to put in the effort and pull an all-nighter."

Although the speech was well received, one audience member noted that Bogen looked "bedraggled."

"They must be working Ron really hard over at Central," said Seth Friedlander, who worked with Bogen at his old branch. "He looked like he'd been burning the midnight oil. That's why I'm not management material. I need a full night's sleep, or I can't get anything done the next day." ✍

PRIMARIES from page 73

Above: President Bush watches the results of Tuesday's primaries on television.

take at least *one* state," Kerry campaign manager Mary Beth Cahill said. "But, in all honesty, we were a hell of a lot more baffled that none of the other Democratic candidates won, either."

Aggregate results from the five states, with all districts reporting, show Kerry leading the other candidates, but at a distant second.

"We're going to keep fighting," Kerry said. "I'm not going to throw in the towel just because I have no idea how

> Pundits have called the Democratic primary loss the worst defeat in the party's history. Political analyst Larry Sabato said the results indicate a "combination of voter caution—with voters hesitant to cast votes when no one candidate stands out—and complete and utter mathematic improbability."

it is even remotely possible for all of us to lose our own primary."

"I didn't give up in Vietnam, and I won't give up here," Kerry added.

Dean shared Kerry's mixture of confusion and resolve.

"I'd like to thank everyone who worked so hard on my campaign," Dean said. "I'll need your continued support as we go to Michigan, to Washington, to Maine… With your help, I know this campaign, or one of the Democratic campaigns, can take those primaries."

After polls closed Tuesday evening, Democratic Party officials were ready to concede defeat, but no one was sure to whom the concession call should be made.

"Well, we certainly can't blame this one on the Republicans," Democratic National Convention head Terry McAuliffe said. "I guess we have to blame the candidates? Organizers like myself? Negative campaigning? The media?"

McAuliffe said candidates will have to consider how it will look to Americans that Democrats lost in a voting situation where only Democrats were on the ballot.

"While we weren't sure who would win in November, our party really

thought we had this one in the bag," McAuliffe said. "But we're not a group that puts its tail between its legs and runs. There's still time to get the message out there: Vote Democrat for Democrat."

Several pundits have already called the Democratic primary loss the worst defeat in the party's history. Appearing on CNN, political analyst Larry Sabato said the results indicate a "combination of voter caution—with voters hesitant to cast votes when no one candidate stands out—and complete and utter mathematic improbability."

"The Democratic Party is in damage-control mode right now," Sabato said. "But remember, that's a mode they're familiar with. They're definitely on the home court here."

Sabato added: "Anyway, in a political era during which Bush can get into the White House with fewer votes than his opponent, even a loss of this magnitude doesn't mean the race is over." ✍

SMELLY from page 42

amounts of blood. Passersby were amazed by the unusually large amounts of blood. Passersby were amazed by the unusually large amounts of blood. Passersby were amazed by the unusually large amounts of blood. Passersby were amazed by the unusually large amounts of blood. Passersby were amazed by the unusually large amounts of blood. Passersby were amazed by the unusually large amounts of blood. Passersby were amazed by the unusually large amounts of blood. Passersby were amazed by the unusually large amounts of blood. Passersby were amazed by the unusually large amounts of blood. Passersby were amazed by the unusually large amounts of blood. Passersby were amazed by the unusually large amounts of blood. Passersby were amazed by the unusually large amounts of blood. Passersby were amazed by the unusually large amounts of blood. Passersby were amazed by the unusually large amounts of blood. Passersby were amazed by the unusually large amounts of blood. Passersby were amazed by the unusually large amounts of blood. Passersby were

amazed by the unusually large amounts of blood. Passersby were amazed by the unusually large amounts of blood. Passersby were amazed by the unusually large

> That was the most fun I've ever had in court.

amounts of blood. Passersby were amazed by the unusually large amounts of blood. Passersby were amazed by the unusually large amounts of blood. Passersby were amazed by the unusually large amounts of blood. Passersby were amazed by the unusually large amounts of blood. Passersby were amazed by the unusually large amounts of blood. Passersby were

see SMELLY page 91

I Totally Called Yesterday's Surge In Tech Stocks!

By Geoffrey Fox

You all think you're hot shit because you guessed that the dollar would continue to slide against the euro, but answer me this: Who totally called yesterday's 0.4 percent surge in technology stock valuations, in spite of their inflated P/E ratio? Who defied conventional wisdom and foresaw the late-afternoon rally after a morning of relatively tepid technology trading? Who is the fucking *man*? If you said "Geoffrey Fox," you are correct.

It was yours truly, the NASDAQ maverick, the guru of guidance, the man who redefined outperform and reinvented rebound. Boo-ya!

Two days ago, I had a feeling in my gut. I said to myself, "Geoffrey, the technology sector will surge tomorrow. Contrary to many market indicators, the technology sector, buoyed by surprisingly strong Q1 profit reports from NVDA and SNDK, will show a distinct 0.4 to 0.8 percent surge tomorrow." So what did I do? I went with my gut. And, as is often the case,

> ## I ca-*zalled* that tech-sector shit. While you were researching increased jobless claims and continuing market instability based on persistent consumer worries about U.S. food and drug safety, I was calling shit. Hello? Hello!

my gut was right. Thanks for the check, NASDAQ. I'll deposit that into the personal checking account of one Geoffrey Fucking Fox.

Do you hear the footsteps? Can you feel the hot breath on the back of your neck? Taste my exhaust, motherfucker. You've been Foxed!

I ca-*zalled* that tech-sector shit. While you were researching increased jobless claims and continuing market instability based on persistent consumer worries about U.S. food and drug safety, I was calling shit. Hello? Hello!

You chumps put the "anal" back in analyst. Me, I put the "back" in

"back the fuck up, and watch a master trader do his work." Pop quiz: What percent change have we seen in the contract manufacturers' technology sub-sector in Q1 to date? Do the year-over-year profit numbers from the wireless sub-sector add up to renewed industry growth? Do names like XM Radio, Nortel, and Flamel Technologies mean *anything* to you? Don't answer. Here's $5. Go get me a latté.

> ## It was yours truly, the NASDAQ maverick, the guru of guidance, the man who redefined outperform and reinvented rebound. Boo-ya!

While you were crying to Mommy Solomon Brothers, I spotted new top performers with positive cash flow, rapid growth, and increased product orders. I picked them out of the crowded sector, hooked in, swallowed their forecasts, and rode them as they trended ever upwards, tenth-of-a-percent after tenth-of-a-percent. And, when it was time to sell: Blaow! Next thing anybody knew, I was whistling all the way to the bank.

That's just how we roll around here. Or at least how I roll, sucker.

I *called* that tech-stock surge, just like I called that tech-stock stumble last Friday. Sure, the sector's volatile. But if you know how to ride her, you can fly like the wind. To truly know the NASDAQ, you have to love her curves, her dips, her shocking upturns, her terrifying downward spirals. You've gotta take her and love her, really make her your own, until you pull back suddenly and she screams out, begging for more and better trading. Then, when the NASDAQ is covered in sweat, back arched, moaning—that's when you start to slowly buy and sell, picking up leaders and casting off laggards. You outperform her upgraded valuations. You ride her hard until you both crescendo together.

Or you get the hell out of this business and let the big boys trade. If you're not balls-deep into the stock exchange, there's no reason to even play the game.

The stock market is a feeling. It's a state of mind. If I even have to explain why, after several days of stock devaluation and bearish news from market leaders like Intel and Cisco, there would be a significant Tuesday-after-

Your Horoscope

By Lloyd Schumner Sr.
Retired Machinist and
A.A.P.B.-Certified Astrologer

Aries: (March 21–April 19)
This week, the process of gradual and minimal change in your life will begin, so be ready to accept entirely new placements of furniture.

Taurus: (April 20–May 20)
Your self-image takes yet another blow when Pam Grier farms your ass-kicking out to a tired-looking bottle blonde.

Gemini: (May 21–June 21)
For the second time in a century, you will find yourself emotionally and artistically unprepared for an outbreak of Big Band Fever.

Cancer: (June 22–July 22)
Valentine's Day is once again almost upon you, and once again, it doesn't mean anything at all.

Leo: (July 23–Aug. 22)
Be open to suggestions, as this week marks the start of a new era of freedom and risk-taking for Leo. Now, mail us all your pants.

Virgo: (Aug. 23–Sept. 22)
It's generally agreed that eyewitnesses aren't always reliable, but everyone swears that they saw you whispering to the cattle moments before the stampede.

Libra: (Sept. 23–Oct. 23)
After a long review of the issues and the candidates' positions on them, you're pretty sure you won't vote this time, either.

Scorpio: (Oct. 24–Nov. 21)
They'll say that you're finally free, that you're no longer in pain, and that you're in a better place, but you'll know what the wishy-washy pricks really mean.

Sagittarius: (Nov. 22–Dec. 21)
If your controversial calculations are correct, Eddie was almost 30 when they recorded "Hot For Teacher."

Capricorn: (Dec. 22–Jan. 19)
You're not one to blindly do what others suggest, but you can't think of a good reason not to go fuck yourself.

Aquarius: (Jan. 20–Feb. 18)
You're tempting fate if you keep mentioning that you've only got two weeks before your retirement from the Chicken Shack.

Pisces: (Feb. 19–March 20)
Most people are either part of the solution or part of the problem, but you're one of the red herrings thrown into the answer set to mislead test-takers.

noon rally pushing many mid-level properties to 52-week highs—well, you're in the wrong fucking business. Sorry. Take the elevator down 20 flights, get in your car, and drive to the mall, because I hear there's an opening at Radio Shack.

All you need to know is this: I am the fucking master of calling shit. The Wall Street warrior. The world heavyweight champion of high-volume, high-risk, high-yield trading. I called that surge, because I am the *masta* of calling tech stocks! All hail Geoffrey!

You think I've got some trick up my sleeve, don't you? You think I'm just too good to be true. Maybe I've got some sort of Magic 8-Ball that tells me exactly which sectors are going to surge on which days. Maybe some fantastical stock-market fairy walked into my office and told me that tech was about to explode by 0.4 percent. Maybe I can see the future, and the present, and the past, through all eternity.

Or maybe I'm just good at predicting the market fluctuations—in-your-face, out-of-your-league, all-over-your-ass good. ∅

JUMP ROPE from page 37

amounts of blood. Passersby were amazed by the unusually large amounts of blood. Passersby were amazed by the unusually large amounts of blood. Passersby were amazed by the unusually large amounts of blood. Passersby were amazed by the unusually large amounts of blood. Passersby were amazed by the unusually large

---

Old drug habits die hard.

---

amounts of blood. Passersby were amazed by the unusually large amounts of blood. Passersby were amazed by the unusually large amounts of blood. Passersby were amazed by the unusually large amounts of blood. Passersby were amazed by the unusually large amounts of blood. Passersby were amazed by the unusually large amounts of blood. Passersby were amazed by the unusually large amounts of blood. Passersby were amazed by the unusually large amounts of blood. Passersby were amazed by the unusually large amounts of blood. Passersby were amazed by the unusually large amounts of blood. Passersby were amazed by the unusually large amounts of blood. Passersby were amazed by the unusually large

see JUMP ROPE page 82

Prosthetic Arm Stuck In Vending Machine

see LOCAL page 3E

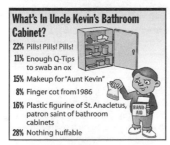

Stouffer's Discontinues Toaster Steaks

see BUSINESS page 7E

Trained Pony Saves Billy Bob Thornton From Fire As Planned

see ENTERTAINMENT page 4B

STATshot

A look at the numbers that shape your world.

What's In Uncle Kevin's Bathroom Cabinet?

- 22% Pills! Pills! Pills!
- 11% Enough Q-Tips to swab an ox
- 15% Makeup for "Aunt Kevin"
- 8% Finger cot from 1986
- 16% Plastic figurine of St. Anacletus, patron saint of bathroom cabinets
- 28% Nothing huffable

0 74470 94595 6
00

THE ONION • $2.00 US • $3.00 CAN

---

the ONION®

VOLUME 40 ISSUE 06   AMERICA'S FINEST NEWS SOURCE™   12–18 FEBRUARY 2004

Saddam Hussein Rules Over Cell With Iron Fist

Above: Hussein waves to his legions of loyal mice.

BAGHDAD—Officials overseeing Saddam Hussein told reporters Monday that the detained former Iraqi leader rules over his cell "with an iron fist."

"Saddam is a very powerful man with a larger-than-life presence, and when he's in that cell, there's no mistaking who's in charge," said a special-forces officer who commands the watch of Hussein at an undisclosed location in Iraq. "We gave Saddam a small bag of nuts. While he was asleep, the rats got into the nuts and ate some of them. In retaliation, Saddam caught one of the rat's young, tortured it, and left it strapped to the wall with dental floss for days. Then, after it was dead, he stuffed its severed head with nuts and paraded it around the cell to warn the other rats."

"But Saddam will also be kind to the vermin and occasionally toss them an almond to fight over," the officer said.

see SADDAM page 83

Report: 'Sorry' No Longer Cutting It

PHILADELPHIA—According to a report released by a privately funded think tank Monday, "sorry" just isn't cutting it anymore.

"Our findings indicate that people have had it with all of the excuses and apologies," said Kyle Dwyer, spokesperson for the Akimbo Institute, which analyzes admonishment-related issues. "In fact, the majority of respondents stated that the level to which they've had it is up to here."

Of the 2,400 subjects polled, 83 percent claimed that "sorry" just doesn't do it anymore, and 79 percent of those agreed that no amount of begging, pleading, or apologizing is going to change that.

The figure shows a dramatic rise from 1998, when 47 percent of poll re-

American Focus

spondents stated that sorry was a good enough response, if accompanied by a promise to try harder next time.

"In previous studies, we found that those who failed to measure up could often cut it by saying sorry," Dwyer said. "But today, the consensus seems to be, 'Stop faking it and start making it.'"

Researchers polled a wide range of

see REPORT page 82

Some Dork Brought In To Address Civics Class

GILLETTE, WY—According to Westwood High School sources, some dork from city hall or the mayor's office or something came in to address Richard Prugh's fifth- and seventh-hour civics classes Monday.

"Mr. Prugh told us some city-council guy was going to be coming in to talk to us about government-type garbage," junior Jon Kriesel said. "The guy was a complete and total dork. I knew it the minute I saw him."

The dork, who introduced himself as Mr. Kepler and wrote his name on the board in girlish cursive letters, spent 25 minutes droning on about the revitalization of downtown Gillette.

"I thought for a second it might be cool, like maybe the city was going to build a mall, and he could tell us what stores would be in it," Tiffany Haus said. "But instead, he talked the whole time about a theater for plays and modern dance and stuff. Awesome. The only thing dorkier than theater is dance."

Kepler paired totally dorky behavior with an even dorkier appearance.

see DORK page 82

Above: The dork.

79

Gay Marriage

Last week, the Massachusetts high court sanctioned same-sex marriages in that state. What do *you* think?

Karl Collins
Mechanical Engineer

"Same-sex unions will only serve to weaken the institution of marriage for the rest of us. My wife and I can barely stand each other as it is."

Joe Perez
Waiter

"How will they decide who's going to wear the wedding dress?! Whoa! Sorry for being so 'politically incorrect'!"

Frances Evans
Producer

"What's the big deal? It's legal now. My sister's married to a gay guy and everyone knows it."

Walter Hill
Systems Analyst

"Great. Just when I finally get my mother to accept that I'm gay, she has a whole new thing to nag me about: getting married."

Jerry Turner
Musician

"Some fag better not try marrying me. These days, you fuck a guy one time and he pulls out a ring."

Diane Morris
Counselor

"As an overweight, emotionally needy fag hag, I strongly oppose all gay marriage legislation."

Under FCC Investigation

Following Janet Jackson's Super Bowl halftime stunt, the FCC has vowed to take a more aggressive stand against indecency. What other recent broadcast events merit scrutiny?

- ► Green Bay Packers' Mike Wahle naked from the waist down, except for a coat of shiny yellow body paint, for the entire post season

- ► Fox News' special one-hour investigative report on aging pop-star nipples

- ► Drunk Hillary Clinton singing "Louie Louie" on top of Jay Leno's desk with her dress up over her head

- ► NPR's *Jazz Profiles* host Nancy Wilson brutally torturing and murdering guest Bill Frisell on air

- ► NBC censors failing to stop *SNL* sketch from going on way too long

- ► President Bush mistakenly revealing Skull And Bones Society secret password on national television

- ► U2 bandleader Bono exposing his swollen, turgid ego onstage at the Golden Globe Awards

- ► UW-Stevens Point college-radio DJ Ben Lissolm forgetting to announce WWSP's legal station ID at the top of the hour

- ► Paris Hilton accidentally exposing her vagina for 22 minutes on season finale of *The Simple Life*

the ONION®
America's Finest News Source.™

Herman Ulysses Zweibel
Founder

T. Herman Zweibel
Publisher Emeritus
J. Phineas Zweibel
Publisher
Maxwell Prescott Zweibel
Editor-In-Chief

I Want To Fly A Helicopter, Not Look At A Bunch Of Crazy Dials

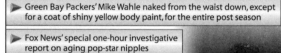

Okay, so since time began, man has dreamed of flight, right? I know I have. I've always wanted to swoop between the mountains and hang suspended high above the earth and all that jazz. So naturally, I decided to try my hand at flying a helicopter. But here's the problem: Everyone makes such a damn big deal out of operating one. I want to fly a helicopter, not look at a bunch of crazy dials.

By Bob Kuhtz

You know what man has not dreamed of since time immemorial? Keeping an eye on his H-over-G indicator. Cavemen did not look to the hawks in the heavens and wonder about their approximate yaw angle, whatever the hell that is. Old Orville and Wilbur sure as hell didn't dream about zeroing the VOR needle for bearing correction—I'll tell you that for free. So why in hell is some instructor screaming at the top of his lungs for me to look down at the console when I'm in the middle of trying to avoid crashing into a barn?! Something tells me there's no barn-missing meter down there!

A helicopter has about 40 different instruments. I suppose there's a chance that I'll be curious about a couple of them someday, but for now, they're just getting in the way of the view. In fact, all that blinky-blinky nonsense seems downright dangerous.

In the Bell Jet Ranger, I had to sit on a couple of extra cushions, because otherwise, the airspeed indicator and the artificial horizon were right in front of my face! Isn't it more important for me to see the *real* horizon? For one thing, it'd help me figure out the damn *helicopter* speed—one thing they *don't* have a dial for!

Half of these dials don't even mean anything. What's "ROTOR ANGLE/ATTACK" supposed to stand for? Am I really expected to know what the "COLLECTIVE DEG INCL" is at all times? You can tell me all the scary stories you want, but I doubt old Icarus fell to his death by ignoring his "manifold press/temp in/HG." All those dials just jump around like crazy, with no rhyme or reason.

And if "lbs fuel payload l/r" is supposed to be some sort of gas gauge, it should read "E" to "F" instead of displaying a bunch of arbitrary numbers that go all jangle-dangle when I'm having fun with the stick. And when's the last time anyone ran out of gas, anyway? Everyone knows that there's always a few gallons left, even when the needle's pegged.

Hey, if it would make everyone feel better, I guess I could choose one meter and look at it whenever there's nothing to do. We'll compromise: I choose a go-to meter; you bite your tongue. Having a hot-read meter wouldn't be so bad, anyway, so long as it didn't interfere with the serious business of flying around and swooping.

> A helicopter has about 40 different instruments. I suppose there's a chance that I'll be curious about a couple of them someday, but for now, they're just getting in the way of the view. In fact, all that blinky-blinky nonsense seems downright dangerous.

But I wouldn't want to let it get in the way of just plain hovering. Because I don't want to be futzing with some meter when I'm trying to do the hovering-around-in-the-air thing I love.

Come on, there's a lot to look at when you're flying. Things are spinning around and coming right at you, and the helicopter seems to have a mind of its own. And then there's the crazy-ass instructor, hollering and grabbing at things and telling you everything except how to deal with the telephone poles that keep popping up right in front of you. I can't wait to go solo. It's hard to soar with the eagles when you're scratching with the chickens!

Seriously, how important could all those dials be? It seems like any problem would come with a lot of smoke, which I'd smell, or a loud explosion or shrieking metal sound, which I'd hear. Or by a bunch of landscape right in front of my field of vision. If any of that happened, it'd be too late anyway.

Flying a copter isn't for the faint of heart. Those loud warning buzzers that start up 30 seconds into your flight will drive you crazy. Sometimes, you get so turned around, you can barely say which way's up.

Given how hard it all is to start with, I really don't see why they have to go and complicate things more with a bunch of dials, buttons, lights, and levers. The next guy can futz with those things all he wants; I, for one, am ready to fly. ∅

Six Dead In West Point Panty Raid

WEST POINT, NY—According an official statement released by the U.S. Military Academy Tuesday, six cadets are dead and 14 wounded after an unsuccessful panty raid on the women's barracks Monday night.

The USMA has not yet released the names of the fallen cadets, but ac-

> **After placing a sniper-and-spotter team atop the bunk closest to the door, Russell moved to collect the contested panties and place demolition charges among them, in order to prevent their capture and public display, as per standard enemy procedure.**

cording to the statement, the four male and two female cadets will be posthumously promoted to platoon commander and buried with full military honors.

Company Commander Roger Phillips, a junior at the academy, was among the injured. Currently in a full-body cast, he fell from a third-story window after he was wounded by a bayonet thrust in the tomfoolery.

"A bunch of us were goofing around after lights-out, and we started daring each other to sneak into Bartlett Hall and steal some of the girls' underwear," Phillips said. "I guess, as a result of our training, we just can't help but think strategically. Before we knew it, the whole panty raid had somehow turned into a meticulously planned 16-man undergarment-acquisition mission and reconnaissance force."

According to sources within the academy, male cadets crossed the borders of "women's country" at 2115 hours Monday for a carefully coordinated prank strike on Room 245's personal-underclothes storage facilities. The female cadets, alerted to the coming attack by unsuppressed laughter, were able to put up a solid defense. Before the raiding party reached panty-lock-on range, the female cadets laid down a curtain of machine-gun fire and fell into defensive positions inside their barracks.

"We met with an unexpectedly high level of resistance and spunkiness from the female cadets," Phillips said. "The women engaged us with close-quarters skirmish tactics, and we were forced to drop smoke charges to cover our retreat. We withdrew, pantyless, to an adjoining hall, where we were able to regroup."

"I take full responsibility for the hijinks-related combat fatalities," he added.

Phillips noted that the female cadets' resistance was in the "finest tradition of the service."

The women's accounts confirm Phillips' description of the incident.

Above: The human cost of the panty raid.

"They neutralized our sentry early, through sheer numbers," said Battalion Leader Joanna Russell, who received the Purple Heart, the Bronze Star, and 10 demerits for her part in repelling the panty raiders. "But once we had beaten back the first wave with small-arms fire and consolidated our strength around the footlockers, it was only a matter of waiting them out. We knew they'd be back, primarily because they hadn't gotten to the panties yet, but also because they'd left [sophomore] Bernie [Holman] gut-shot and bleeding in the hallway. The boys may be a bunch of immature idiots, but they'd never leave a

downed man behind."

After placing a sniper-and-spotter team atop the bunk closest to the door, Russell moved to collect the contested panties and place demolition charges among them, in order to prevent their capture and public display, as per standard enemy procedure.

Before the female cadets could retaliate, West Point administrators were alerted to the strategic prank-in-progress by the sound of artillery being moved into a flanking position along the women's barracks. Administrators quickly put a stop to the

see RAID page 83

Household Death Toll Climbs To One

NEW HAVEN, CT—Police announced Monday that the accidental death of 68-year-old Joseph Lang increased the death toll at 320 E. Oak St. to a staggering one. "We retrieved Mr. Lang's body from his bathtub, where it appears he slipped and hit his head," police officer Chris Ramsey said. "Although we don't expect to find any additional victims, we're continuing our 48-hour search of the two-story home, just in case." Lang is survived by his wife Helen, who still resides in the deathtrap.

New Co-Op Airline Offers Cheaper Fares If You Help Fly The Plane

SAN FRANCISCO—GreenWay Airlines, a new low-cost, cooperative airline, offers inexpensive fares to pas-

sengers who assist with the flight, an airline spokesman said Monday. "Unlike pricey corporate airlines, Green-Way is run by and for the people," said Brad Olson, a member of the GreenWay elected board. "But, in order to keep our ticket prices low, everyone who wants to fly with us needs to pitch in and help us navigate and maintain the aircraft. All positions, from baggage handler to pilot, will be filled by volunteers who sign up for four-hour shifts." GreenWay will begin taking reservations for daily flights between San Francisco and Austin, TX, as soon as someone can figure out how to use the booking software.

Majority Of Americans Thought We Already Had A Moon Base

WASHINGTON, DC—A NASA poll conducted to gauge support for President Bush's space-exploration initiative revealed that a depressing 57 per-

cent of Americans believe that the U.S. already has a research base on the moon. "We put that international space-station thing up there in the '60s," phone-poll respondent Randy Snow said. "It might be on Mars, but I think it's the moon—wherever they have the golf course that President Kennedy played on. Remember, the Cubans tried to take it over?" NASA officials said they hope someday to make Americans' perception a reality.

Radicals, Extremists Vie For Control Of Iran

TEHRAN—As the Feb. 20 parliamentary election approaches, hardline conservative religious radicals and fundamentalist Islamic extremists are stepping up their disparate campaigns. "It's up to the people: Does the future of Iran lie in the hands of the far-right extremists or the far-far-right radicals?" said Ayatollah Ahmad Jannati, head of the hardline Guardian Council that recently

banned thousands of moderate candidates from the election. "Will the old-school clerics win, or is the country ready for a new stripe of fundamentalists who will take authoritarianism in an entirely different direction?" Jannati urged all of Iran's citizens to get out and make their votes count.

That Guy From That One Show In Rehab

GLENDALE, CA—According to nurses at the Rosewater Rehabilitation Clinic, that guy who used to play the fat guy on that one show was admitted Monday for treatment of alcohol abuse and depression. "He looked exactly like he did on that one show, except a bit older and fatter," nurse Christina Prenz told reporters. "I asked him to do that thing he always used to do, but he just stared at me. Then he started crying." Prenz added that, during their group therapy session, she plans to ask him why the show was cancelled. ∅

authority figures, including irate moms, fast-food restaurant managers, and high-school gym teachers. The resounding majority of participants refused to accept such excuses as "I overslept," "I thought it was tomorrow," and "I just assumed."

"Respondents had particularly

> The respondents said the offenders must improve upon their past performances, or else. When pressed to expand upon "or else," respondents spoke of boom-lowering, music-facing, and other-shoe dropping.

Above: Dwyer tells assembled reporters that if a frog had wings, it wouldn't bump its ass a'hoppin'.

strong reactions to that last excuse," Dwyer said. "A remarkable 78 percent said that one should not assume, because when you assume, it makes an ass of you and me."

Dwyer said there were a number of possible explanations for the failure of sorry to cut it. Chief among these is the fact that a growing number of authority figures were not born yesterday.

"These individuals have seen what sorry has done to improve situations," Dwyer said. "Jack squat."

Dwyer added: "The consensus seems to be that actions speak louder than words, and that good intentions are the stones with which the road to hell is paved."

The respondents said the offenders must improve upon their past performances, or else. When pressed to expand upon "or else," respondents spoke of boom-lowering, music-facing, and other-shoe dropping.

"To avoid 'or else,' the misters, missies, and busters must demonstrate a higher commitment to discipline," Dwyer said. "Feet have been put down on this point."

The report revealed that the assorted apologies, excuses, and delay tactics have resulted in both lost productivity and lost income.

"More than 70 percent of the respondents told us that, if they had a dollar for every time they have heard the word 'sorry,' they would be rich," Dwyer said. "If you consider the fact that they have heard this word over the course of many years, you see that, indeed, the total number of dollars would be very large."

> "These individuals have seen what sorry has done to improve situations," Dwyer said. "Jack squat."

Authority figures applauded the findings.

"It's about time you folks woke up and smelled the coffee," Spring Green, WI, packaging-plant manager Bert Seiffert said. "'Sorry' has never cut the mustard with me. That's what I said to that slacker Oppley when he came in five minutes late for the third time this week. I said, 'Sorry is a pretty sorry excuse, if you ask me,' and I docked him for an hour's pay. He said, 'Hey, Bert, that's not fair.' 'Hey is for horses,' I said."

One mister, who requested anonymity, condemned the study results.

"I am honestly trying to shape up, but still they want me to ship out," the mister said. "It isn't fair. It wasn't even my fault."

Veteran buster Wayne Koestler, 16, scoffed at the report.

"I gotta start cutting it 'or else'?" he said. "Who's gonna make me?" ∅

"He had a bow tie and this stupid mustache," Haus said. "And his hair was all dorked to the side."

The dork even had a dork's voice.

"He was going on and on about how Gillette has a proud history of whatever, totally jizzing about that one cowboy statue downtown, but all I could think about was his nasally voice," Rob Esser said. "I swear I could smell his breath the whole time. It smelled like an old stack of books. And his clothes... He might as well have been wearing a shirt that said 'Certified Dork' on the front."

After a pause, Esser said: "No. Actually, a shirt like that would've been way cooler than the vest he was wearing."

The dork had trouble controlling the class, and in true dweeb fashion, tried to reprimand the students with humor, saying, "Hey, guys, don't make me rezone that section non-residential."

The entire class reportedly stared at him blankly.

"The city nerd guy said something about some guys acting zoned out or something, and then he smiled really big and stared at us," Stacy Cooper said. "It was totally weird. Like, I think maybe he was trying to be funny. That must be what some book says about how to come and address a civics class or something."

According to classroom sources, the only person who was even listening to the dorky guest was Shelby Jones, who is also a big dork.

"Shelby's totally going to grow up and be just like this guy," classmate Jordan Luker said. "She kept asking him questions and saying 'point of order' and shit. She totally had a crush on him, I think. They should go get married and have, like, dorklets."

Luker said Kepler was "one of the dorkiest people to ever set foot in Westwood High."

Prugh, who arranges to have local government officials visit the class several times a year, was caught off guard by the dork.

"I'll admit I was disappointed," Prugh said. "It's not like my students adore me, but they really hated that dork. And, to be honest, I couldn't blame them. What a windbag."

Prugh continued: "All I knew about him before he walked in the door was that he won his council race in a landslide. Jesus. He must have run unopposed."

Several other school officials were struck by the dork's conduct.

"That strange-looking guy wandered into the office just before lunch, looking more confused than the freshmen do," principal Courtney Delaterra said. "I asked him if he needed help, and I guess my voice startled the poor guy, because he spun around and dropped several manila folders packed full of papers and news clippings and things. He had more paper than a person generally carries. When I introduced myself as the principal, it actually made him more nervous. I've seen some pretty high-strung people in my day, but that guy was a real mess."

After helping Kepler gather his papers, Delaterra led him to the cafeteria so that he could eat lunch before his fifth-period visit to Prugh's class. Librarian Kathy Westrich, the faculty outcast, avoided eye contact with Kepler as he wandered around the lunchroom looking for a seat.

The loner sat down next to Westrich anyway. The librarian would have been doomed to share an awkward meal with him had she not informed him that she needed to get back to the library and catalog some books before next period.

Kepler fell for the excuse, like the doofus he is. ∅

SADDAM from page 79

"In this way, he teaches the rats both to love *and* to fear him."

According to a CIA official, the dictator "personally monitors" every inch of his 12'x11' cell.

"Nothing escapes Saddam's notice," the official said. "He's assembled a secret lice force to collect information and watch over the cell while he sleeps. At first, it seemed harmless, but the lice grew in number every day. Where once there were a couple, now there are thousands hiding in the folds of his sheets."

Although Hussein is isolated from the other detainees, the former ruler

> "Every day at around 6, he delivers his morning decree," the CIA official said. "He tells the cockroaches and other vermin in the cell that he will protect them against the oppressive Western devils."

of Iraq makes frequent proclamations.

"Every day at around 6, he delivers his morning decree," the CIA official said. "He tells the cockroaches and other vermin in the cell that he will protect them against the oppressive Western devils and reward those who remain loyal. Then he usually sings. I once rapped on the bars with the butt of my rifle, but that just fired him up. He started cursing a blue streak at me and launched into a recitation of the "64 Rules Of Order" for the cell. Now I know to just let him tire himself out."

Sources say Hussein has brought an atmosphere of pageantry to his cell, by decorating it with slogans and iconic images. He drew a flag on the north wall with chalk and etched the slogan "God Punish The Oppressors" into the floor with a toothbrush handle. He used the black heel of his shoe to draw his portrait on the wall and shaped a 14-inch statue of himself out of chickpeas and chewed bread.

"When I gave him the chalk, I thought he was just going to tick off the days with it, but I guess I should have expected more from a man as ingenious as Saddam," an unnamed soldier said. "Now, he delivers his speeches in front of the flag. He tried to use his bed and blanket to make a roster and bunting once, but we said 'No way.' Yesterday we caught him standing on the toilet reading aloud from his memoirs. We told him to get down before he slipped and hurt himself."

Hussein appointed 12 cockroach ministers to his cabinet, but he has al-

ready had to execute nine of them for crimes ranging from sexual impropriety to inappropriate scurrying. He has named his pillow the Ba'ath Party Military Bureau Deputy Chairman and Head of National Monitoring Directorate, and uses this top party member to execute disloyal subjects.

"It's not unusual to see Saddam running around the cell whacking everything in sight with his deputy chairman," the soldier said. "He's awfully attached to that thing. Not everyone knows how sentimental Saddam is. When they took his bedding to be cleaned, he openly wept for the loss of his closest confidant."

Hussein has repeatedly refused weapons and contraband inspections.

"Most of the prisoners I've dealt with see the daily checks as routine," the soldier said. "But Saddam likes to complain about how we need evidence of wrongdoing before we can cross the cell's threshold."

Occasionally, guards have been forced to threaten Hussein with sanctions to get him to comply with inspections.

RAID from page 81

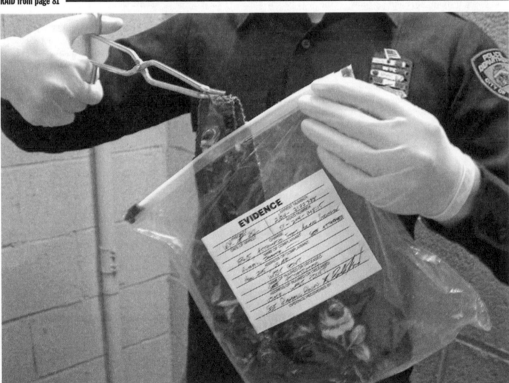

Above: Police examine a piece of evidence.

panty raid by turning on all the lights.

West Point officials released a statement asserting that "unfortunate situations inevitably arise when the heady experience of college life combines with hundreds of hours of field training in tactics and weapons."

"I do not condone the actions of these cadets, and I assure you that the academy board will officially investigate the matter and assign demerits or extra credit as is appropriate," said Lt. Gen. William J. Lennox Jr., West Point's superintendent. "However, as a

"Every couple of days, he refuses to let us look under his bed," an unnamed soldier said. "There's never anything under there, but sometimes he likes to make a big deal out of refusing."

Amnesty International spokesman Troy Jergins said sanctions have little effect on Hussein himself, and only harm the cell's other inhabitants.

"If you take away his cigars or his half hour of fresh air, you're only hurting his subjects," Jergins said. "When we take his privileges away, he flies into a rage, killing insects, cursing at the mice, and throwing his toiletries at the wall."

Maj. Gen. Raymond Odierno, a top U.S. army commander in Iraq, responded to concerns that Hussein wields too much power in his cell.

"Well, we keep a pretty tight watch on him," Odierno said. "Besides, this prison is just temporary. They'll be moving him when it's time for him to face the international tribunal for his atrocities. His pre-cell atrocities, that is." ⌀

graduate myself, I know what it's like to be young, highly trained, and away

> The incident marks the academy's worst horseplay-related incident.

from home for the first time. These young people are just full of youthful exuberance and superior military

CAKE.COM from page 15

amounts of blood. Passersby were amazed by the unusually large amounts of blood. Passersby were amazed by the unusually large amounts of blood. Passersby were amazed by the unusually large amounts of blood. Passersby were amazed by the unusually large

This would be a great place for a tarmac.

amounts of blood. Passersby were amazed by the unusually large amounts of blood. Passersby were amazed by the unusually large amounts of blood. Passersby were amazed by the unusually large amounts of blood. Passersby were amazed by the unusually large amounts of blood. Passersby were amazed by the unusually large amounts of blood. Passersby were amazed by the unusually large amounts of blood. Passersby were amazed by the unusually large amounts of blood. Passersby were amazed by the unusually large amounts of blood. Passersby were amazed by the unusually large amounts of blood. Passersby were amazed by the unusually large amounts of blood. Passersby were amazed by the unusually large

see CAKE.COM page 131

know-how."

The incident marks the academy's worst horseplay-related incident since the homecoming float competition before the 2002 Army-Navy game. Three gaily decorated and heavily armed parade floats were destroyed in the pep rally, and the academy's famous library badly damaged by incendiary shells in the confrontation, which claimed the lives of seven West Point cadets, 14 Naval Academy midshipmen, and the Navy goat. ⌀

Cheer Up, All You Loveless Singles!

A Room Of Jean's Own
By Jean Teasdale

I don't know if there's something in the water, but my town has exploded with tons of single people! Just last year, practically the only eligibles I knew were my divorced friend Patti, my bud Fulgencio, hubby Rick's barfly pal Craig, and Jimmy the pizza delivery guy. But now, I find out that my cousin Michelle is leaving her second husband, and a recent chit-chat with my building's manager Sandy revealed that she hasn't had a serious relationship in almost five years! Besides that, at least five suspected singletons have moved into my building since June. *Five!*

For an incurable romantic like me, this is heartbreaking. People are *meant* to have sweeties! I feel soooo sorry for single people. How can they bear going through life alone? I know a lot of them put up that "independent" front, or use that "I'm just waiting for the right person" defense, but they're kidding themselves. Why would anyone turn up her nose at the prospect of a beautiful wedding, a gorgeous bridal gown, and a stunning rock on her finger? She wouldn't. Why would anyone shake a stick at a warm dinner every night, a comfortable home, and a beautiful bride? It just isn't rational. And I don't like to be harsh, but frankly, it's depressing to see singles out in public. When I see a girl shopping for groceries by herself, or a solitary guy reading while he waits for a bus, I can't help but sense the hollowness that single person feels inside. I'm partially psychic, so I'm attuned to other people's inner feelings.

Well, this Valentine's Day, I'm not going to be selfish. People like me, people in successful, lasting relationships, are duty-bound to share their romantic wisdom with the less fortunate. Granted, it's been a while since I've been on the dating scene, so my chops are a bit rusty. In fact, hubby Rick is just about the only guy I've ever dated! (Unless you count my pick for the Sadie Hawkins dance in seventh grade, Jordy DeVoe, who ditched me after about 15 minutes. Or this Oriental kid named Thant who wrapped love notes around lunchroom cookies and slipped them into my locker in ninth grade.) But Rick and I have been married nearly 20 years, so I must be doing something right. Dry those tears, Singletons! Pull yourselves together and listen to Wifey Jean. If you follow my advice, I'll bet you dollars to donuts that you'll find your Prince Charming, or Princess Enchanting, in no time!

First of all, *don't sell yourself short!*

You may think you have no chance with that special someone, but faith and persistence can pay off big! I'm going to dip pretty deep in the old memory bank here and tell you a story about how Rick and I got together, way back in high school.

Now, when I was 16, I guess I wasn't your typical kid. Let's just say that I deviated from the norm a little. (I don't believe in using the term "nerd," because I don't like put-down language.) While other girls had bleached, feathered hair and slashes of blush across their cheeks, I had a unique sense of personal style. Every day of my junior year, I wore a pair of rainbow suspenders, jeans rolled up to my knees, striped knee socks, and a newsboy cap. I looked very tomboyish, but at least there was no mistaking me for some dull Daisy Duke clone!

My future soulmate Rick was part of that elite crowd of hunks known as the "jocks." Yep, old hubby Rick was on the varsity wrestling squad *and* the bowling team. (True, the wrestling coach kept him on the bench most of the time, but Rick was one of the leading bowlers, and his team made regional semi-finals twice!)

Now, somebody like me wasn't even supposed to *look* at a jock, let alone date him. But Rick was best buds with my older brother Kevin, and he was at our house a lot, so I couldn't help but have eyes for him.

Unfortunately, Rick had eyes for someone else: Shanni, one of the cheerleaders (predictably feathered and blushed). He hung out by her locker between periods, and one weekend she went with my brother and him to Rick's uncle's place out in the country to drink Pabst and shoot skeet. If I were a quitter, I would've walked away and cried myself to sleep. But a little voice inside me told me to hang in there. (Told you I was psychic!)

One day after school, Rick and Kevin had plans to drive to Shanni's place and pick her up. An hour after they left, they pulled into our driveway—just the two of them, no Shanni. Rick had a dejected look on his face. I asked what was wrong, and Kevin said Shanni wasn't home. Rick lumbered around a little, but then his mood changed. He announced that he wasn't going to let "some [w]itch" spoil his fun and said he was going to his uncle's anyway. Then, he said something I'd been waiting to hear for months: "Jean, why don't you come? You look like a chick who could use a good time. Let's party."

I was on Cloud Nine! No one had ever called me a chick before! It made me feel good to finally have my femininity recognized. I later learned that Shanni liked the varsity quarterback Dennis, and that she only hung out

Your Horoscope

By Lloyd Schumner Sr.
Retired Machinist and
A.A.P.B.-Certified Astrologer

Aries: (March 21–April 19)
Everything has to start somewhere. In spite of what you claim happened, the enraged bull elephant couldn't have just "come out of nowhere."

Taurus: (April 20–May 20)
It's beginning to look like you'll never understand that ruffled skirts don't look good with colored stockings, especially on men with legs like yours.

Gemini: (May 21–June 21)
In a neat but unfortunate melding of rhetorical and actual elements, you'll get stuck in a rut and wake up in a ditch this week.

Cancer: (June 22–July 22)
You're easy to talk to once people get to know you, but holding your personal audiences on a throne of bloody skulls tends to put them off at first.

Leo: (July 23–Aug. 22)
While it's true that anger sex is some of the best sex you've ever had, it's still not a great way to resolve conflicts in the boardroom.

Virgo: (Aug. 23–Sept. 22)
Economic trends are highly unpredictable, so don't be alarmed when your head's suddenly worth $10 million.

Libra: (Sept. 23–Oct. 23)
Relax: You're not the first person to pray for help with your diet, only to have a jealous God send visions of delicious, creamy fudge.

Scorpio: (Oct. 24–Nov. 21)
The next time you decide to run amok at a dog show, the Holy Sisters of St. Augustine respectfully ask that you leave them out of it.

Sagittarius: (Nov. 22–Dec. 21)
Remember that everyone has embarrassing moments, although it's true what you say: Theirs don't last for nine years.

Capricorn: (Dec. 22–Jan. 19)
It's admirable that you're not getting all paranoid, especially considering the fact that everyone is plotting to take away everything you have.

Aquarius: (Jan. 20–Feb. 18)
You'll fail to win your case against television, even though there is no disputing that it transported you to faraway places while you were trying to get laundry done.

Pisces: (Feb. 19–March 20)
You know, maybe the fits are worth the hours of blissful unconsciousness afterwards.

with Rick because he always bought the beer and the pot. You see what I'm getting at here? If I'd given up and retreated to that "room of my own," Mrs. Rick Teasdale would have been someone else altogether! Later, Rick's dad caught us making whoopee in the backseat of Rick's car, and the rest, as they say, is history! This so-called "nerd" won her jock!

That's why my advice is: *Don't be afraid to be romantic.* Sometimes singles are afraid to make fools of themselves, so they act guarded on dates. Acting that way, it's no wonder you can't get a ring on your finger or a home-cooked meal! It snuffs the budding relationship right out. You gotta take risks to get the things you want. By keeping romance in the picture, you show the person just how special he or she is.

I can think of a hundred romantic things: a ride on one of those foot-powered paddleboats, a teddy bear placed beside someone's computer, a ride in a hot-air balloon (they have coupons for them in the *ShoprSavr*)... Or surprise your beloved with a table

strewn with rose petals and a dinner you've prepared yourself—and, for dessert, have strawberries dipped in chocolate. Or better yet, plan a night in with champagne, expensive ice cream, and *Ice Castles* in the VCR! (Sigh...)

Now, admittedly, I've never experienced any of these things. But if the person you like is anything like me, he or she would deeply appreciate any of them.

And now, one final tip: *Make sure to let your sweetheart know how much you care* about him or her, in no uncertain terms, and as soon as possible. What are you waiting for? You'll have all the time in the world to get to know each other once that knot is tied, believe me!

Singles, stop thinking so much and start living. Valentine's Day is just around the corner, so put my advice into action. And, should you be in the vicinity of Blossom Meadows Drive on February 15, let me know how it went. I'll be standing at my window, peeling the red paper hearts off the glass and putting them in storage. ∅

Fox News Problem Solvers In Way Over Their Heads

see LOCAL page 5B

Penis Enlargement Pills Tested On Dog

see PETS page 7E

Martha Stewart Witness Grilled After Being Marinated Overnight

see NATION page 10C

STATshot

A look at the numbers that shape your world.

What Part Are We Trying Out For?

- 22% The dude who gets to kiss Allison Schumacher
- 11% Prancing Ass In Background #2
- 15% Black Judas
- 8% Bear Chasing Polonius; failing that, Polonius
- 16% Godot
- 28% Pete, who dies driving home from prom drunk

---

the ONION®

VOLUME 40 ISSUE 07   AMERICA'S FINEST NEWS SOURCE™   19–25 FEBRUARY 2004

WAR ON TERROR

Osama Bin Laden Found Inside Each Of Us

WASHINGTON, DC—Defense Secretary Donald Rumsfeld announced Tuesday that Osama bin Laden, prime suspect in the Sept. 11 attacks on the World Trade Center and the Pentagon, has "at long last been found."

"For more than two years, we combed the Middle East looking for bin Laden," Rumsfeld said. "Frankly, it was starting to be an embarrassment. You can imagine our surprise when we finally found him hiding deep inside the darkest recesses of each and every one of our souls."

Since toppling the Taliban regime in 2001, U.S. forces in Afghanistan had searched for bin Laden primarily along the rugged Afghan-Pakistani border, but overlooked that place inside every one of us that has ever raised his voice in anger or turned away from someone in need.

"We were so busy tracking the remaining members of the Taliban regime and freezing al-Qaeda assets that we missed what was right in front of us all along," Rumsfeld said. "Osama bin Laden wasn't hidden in a cave in the mountainous Pakistani province of Waziristan or huddled in the back of a Chitral meat-market stall. He was lurking in the blackness within us all, right there with the laziness and the jealousy."

"It just goes to show that sometimes it's easier to look for the man in the FBI dossier than it is to look at the man in the mirror," Rumsfeld added.

In addition to FBI intelligence reports, the military's search was aided by eight Ultra-High Frequency Follow-On communications satellites, submarines, aircraft, ground units, and global ground stations. But in see OSAMA page 88

Above: Hayter with his former ex-girlfriend Peterman.

Hungover Couple Unaware They Broke Up Last Night

MINNEAPOLIS—Area couple Gene Hayter and Amy Peterman spent most of Sunday tenderly helping each other nurse massive hangovers, unaware that they had broken up in a bitter, alcohol-fueled rage during the night.

"Man, we must've really tore it up, that's all I can say," Hayter said, his voice raw from Jack Daniel's, cigarettes, and, unbeknownst to him, shrieked accusations of infidelity. "I woke up on Amy's couch, of all places, with a beer bottle in my hand and this terrible feeling, like I wanted to cry myself to death. To top things off, when I pulled myself up to go crawl into bed with Amy, I stepped in broken glass."

Hayter said that either he or see COUPLE page 89

Kerry Makes Whistle-Stop Tour From Deck Of Yacht

Above: Kerry waves down to a crowd of supporters.

LANCASTER, PA—Democratic frontrunner Sen. John Kerry (D-MA) began a seven-day, eight-state whistle-stop tour Monday, addressing a group of Frigidaire factory workers from the all-teak deck of his 60-foot luxury motor cruiser.

"George W. Bush put tax cuts for the wealthy and special favors for the see KERRY page 88

Human Cloning

South Korean scientists successfully cloned a human embryo, a procedure some feel is unethical. What do *you* think?

Fred Watson
Systems Analyst

"I applaud this scientific breakthrough, as long as they don't use it to clone more Hitlers. Maybe one Pol Pot, if they absolutely have to, but no Hitlers."

Nicole Henderson
Registered Nurse

"No thanks. I prefer the kind of stem cells you produce from *getting laid.*"

Billy Cook
Social Worker

"I just told my 3-year-old that babies come from cabbage patches. How the hell am I going to explain *this*?"

Justin Barnes
Bartender

"So a future in which I can clone myself, hunt myself down for sport, and then claim it wasn't murder because it was only me that I killed is just around the corner?"

Harold Price
Music Director

"Finally, someone invented a way to make more Asians."

Rose Coleman
Window Trimmer

"This has limitless scientific possibilities, which means one thing: We must keep Christians from finding out about it."

Identity Theft Safeguards

Identity theft is a growing problem in America. What does the Federal Trade Commission suggest consumers do to protect themselves?

- 🔒 If a thief tries to steal your identity online, run around in your bathrobe screaming "Stop! Identity thief!"

- 🔒 Carry no more than a $20 credit line on any credit card

- 🔒 Every time you write a check, use a Sharpie to black out your name and account number, as well as the bank's address and routing number

- 🔒 Never let anyone know "the real you"

- 🔒 Alert the police if you spot a child playing with Silly Putty; Silly Putty can be pressed down onto printed material and used to steal an impression of vital information

- 🔒 Buy "The Identity Club," the only personal-identity lock recommended by police

- 🔒 Keep a close watch on Madonna, who is overdue for an identity switch

- 🔒 To receive the booklet "How 2 Prevent You're ID From Beeng Stollen," go to identitysafe.com and submit your social security number, driver's license information, and a major credit card

America's Finest News Source.™

Herman Ulysses Zweibel
Founder

T. Herman Zweibel
Publisher Emeritus
J. Phineas Zweibel
Publisher
Maxwell Prescott Zweibel
Editor-In-Chief

Fuck Everything, We're Doing Five Blades

By James M. Kilts
CEO and President,
The Gillette Company

Would someone tell me how this happened? We were the fucking vanguard of shaving in this country. The Gillette Mach3 was *the* razor to own. Then the other guy came out with a three-blade razor. Were we scared? Hell, no. Because we hit back with a little thing called the Mach3Turbo. That's three blades *and* an aloe strip. For moisture. But you know what happened next? Shut up, I'm telling you what happened—the bastards went to four blades. Now we're standing around with our cocks in our hands, selling three blades and a strip. Moisture or no, suddenly we're the chumps. Well, fuck it. We're going to five blades.

Sure, we could go to four blades next, like the competition. That seems like the logical thing to do. After all, three worked out pretty well, and four is the next number after three. So let's play it safe. Let's make a thicker aloe strip and call it the Mach3SuperTurbo. Why innovate when we can follow? Oh, I know why: Because we're a *business*, that's why!

You think it's crazy? It is crazy. But I don't give a shit. From now on, we're the ones who have the edge in the multi-blade game. Are they the best a man can get? Fuck, no. *Gillette* is the best a man can get.

What part of this don't you understand? If two blades is good, and three blades is better, obviously five blades would make us the best fucking razor that ever existed. *Comprende?* We didn't claw our way to the top of the razor game by clinging to the two-blade industry standard. We got here by taking chances. Well, five blades is the biggest chance of all.

Here's the report from Engineering. Someone put it in the bathroom: I want to wipe my ass with it. They don't tell me what to invent—I tell *them*. And I'm *telling* them to stick two more blades in there. I don't care *how*. Make the blades so thin they're invisible. Put some on the handle. I don't care if they have to cram the fifth blade in perpendicular to the other four, just do it!

You're taking the "safety" part of "safety razor" too literally, grandma. Cut the strings and soar. Let's hit it. Let's roll. This is our chance to make razor history. Let's dream big. All you have to do is say that five blades can happen, and it *will* happen. If you aren't on board, then fuck you. And if you're on the board, then fuck you

and your father. Hey, if I'm the only one who'll take risks, I'm sure as hell happy to hog all the glory when the five-blade razor becomes the shaving tool for the U.S. of "this is how we shave now"A.

People said we couldn't go to three. It'll cost a fortune to manufacture, they said. Well, we did it. Now some egghead in a lab is screaming 'Five's crazy?' Well, perhaps he'd be more comfortable in the labs at Norelco, working on fucking electrics. Rotary blades, my white ass!

Maybe I'm wrong. Maybe we should just ride in Bic's wake and make pens.

You think it's crazy? It *is* crazy. But I don't give a shit. From now on, we're the ones who have the edge in the multi-blade game. Are they the best a man can get? Fuck, no.

Ha! Not on your fucking life! The day I shadow a penny-ante outfit like Bic is the day I leave the razor game for good, and that won't happen until the day I die!

The market? Listen, *we* make the market. All we have to do is put her out there with a little jingle. It's as easy as, "Hey, shaving with anything less than five blades is like scraping your beard off with a dull hatchet." Or "You'll be so smooth, I could snort lines off of your chin." Try "Your neck is going to be so friggin' soft, someone's gonna walk up and tie a goddamn Cub Scout kerchief under it."

I know what you're thinking now: What'll people say? Mew mew mew. Oh, no, what will people say?! Grow the *fuck* up. When you're on top, people talk. That's the price you pay for being on top. Which Gillette is, always has been, and forever shall be, Amen, five blades, sweet Jesus in heaven.

Stop. I just had a stroke of genius. Are you ready? Open your mouth, baby birds, cause Mama's about to drop you one sweet, fat nightcrawler. Here she comes: Put another aloe strip on that fucker, too. That's right. Five blades, two strips, and make the second one lather. You heard me—the second strip *lathers*. It's a whole new way to think about shaving. Don't question it. Don't say a word. Just key the music, and call the chorus girls, because we're on the edge—the razor's edge—and I feel like dancing. ∅

Day Job Officially Becomes Job

HILLSBORO, OR—Another human dream was crushed by the uncompromising forces of reality Monday, when the restaurant day job of 29-year-old former aspiring cartoonist Mark Seversen officially became his actual job.

"After four years of washing dishes to support my drawing projects, I've made the transition to washing dishes to support *myself*," Seversen told reporters after punching out at the end of his shift at Tres Café. "Let's face it, this is it. This is my job. I'll never forget that moment when I transformed from an aspiring underground cartoonist into a non-aspiring restaurant worker."

In 1999, Seversen was hired as a kitchen crewmember at Tres Café. Later that year, he began to self-publish his monthly photocopied mini-comic *Dishdog Days*, in which he chronicled the daily trials of an underemployed college dropout who works at a restaurant while pursuing his dream of cartooning.

In 2000, Seversen distributed 12 full-sized, color issues of his comic, launched a *Dishdog Days* web site, and received a 75-cent-an-hour raise.

After the initial wave of progress, Seversen said financial problems and "general sloth" interrupted his publication schedule.

"While I was at work, I'd think about what I wanted to draw," Seversen said. "But once I got home, I just wanted to watch television."

By August 2002, Seversen's comic was coming out once every four months.

Tres Café waiter Neil Julian, 19, said he believes he was present when Seversen finally had the crushing realization that he was, first and foremost, a restaurant worker.

> "After four years of washing dishes to support my drawing projects, I've made the transition to washing dishes to support *myself*," Seversen told reporters after punching out at the end of his shift at Tres Café. "Let's face it, this is it. This is my job."

"Mark was in back cleaning out the storage shed when I went out for a cigarette break," Julian said. "He said he was the only one who ever cleaned it out, but that he sorta didn't mind, because then no one messed with his system."

Julian continued: "Then he said he should put something about the shed into his next comic, because it was one of those little things from life: He'd been cleaning out this same shed every month for four years. He said he really needed some material, because he hadn't put out a new issue in

Above: Seversen, who recently gave up on the idea of making a living from his comics (inset).

almost six months. At that point, he got real quiet and stared into the shed for about a minute. I figure that was when it hit him."

Sources close to Seversen said his surrender was inevitable.

"I'm not surprised," Seversen's roommate Matt Cook, 26, said. "Mark has had that look of defeat in his eyes lately, like when our friend Ray [Landry] accepted the assistant-manager position at Video Hut six months after he finished his fourth screen-play. Or when my girlfriend stopped telling people she was going to design shoes and started telling them she sold shoes at the Younkers in the Southgate mall."

In spite of the initial moment of melancholic catatonia, Seversen said he was relieved that the transition from day job to real job was complete.

"When I was younger, my attitude was 'Never give in,'" Seversen said. "Nowadays, my attitude is 'Get real,

see JOB page 89

Iowa Resident Has Opinion Month Too Late

STORM LAKE, IA—Four weeks after the Iowa Democratic caucus, livestock farmer Darryl Welch, 48, expressed an informed opinion about the candidates Monday. "I like what John Edwards says about rebuilding international alliances to fight terror, but I think some of the programs he supports would mean higher taxes," Welch said Monday. "I wish I'd have said that to all those AP reporters, instead of telling them that I didn't know who I wanted to vote for yet." Unfortunately, Welch's opinions will not be relevant for another three years and 11 months.

Former Chinese Dissident Has Your Order Ready

SAN FRANCISCO—Dr. Xu Shui Xian Liang, a founding member of the Autonomous Federation of Beijing's Workers in Tiananmen Square who spent 12 years in a labor camp for his involvement in the anti-dictatorship effort during the Cultural Revolution, is ready with your order. "That's one chipotle chicken-filet sandwich, two large regular salads—tofu bacon on one, a white-chicken-chili soup, and three low-fat blondies," said the former leader of the students' movement in the Guang Tong province. "Would you like your receipt?" Xu, who was tortured into confessing to stealing state assets in collusion with organized crime shortly before he defected to the U.S. in 1999, is sorry, he will be right back with that Diet Coke.

William Katt Programs Own Name Into TiVo

LOS ANGELES—Sources close to William Katt said Monday that the *Greatest American Hero* star has his own name programmed into his TiVo digital video recorder. "Bill gets really excited when he comes home and finds one of his *7th Heaven* episodes or sees that he's caught *House IV* on Cinemax," friend Ray Morris said. "Maybe he does it so he knows to watch for a residual check." Morris said Katt also frequently scans his listing on the Internet Movie Database for errors.

Specifics Of Hostile Takeover Fiercely Boring

NEW YORK—Details of a "hostile" bid by software manufacturer Octagon Corporation are, in fact, fiercely, mind-numbingly dull, sources reported Tuesday. "Following the SoftWave International board of directors' rejection of Octagon's unsolicited offer, Octagon essentially eliminated SoftWave as an entity by purchasing 300,000 shares at $453.35–$134.34 more than the current market value," financial analyst Bryan Falwick said, droning on endlessly about the supposedly thrilling upset. "Everyone was shocked when Octagon swooped in and nabbed controlling interest." Falwick said he assumed that the forthcoming rollout of the XSpreadsheet software suite motivated the "raid."

Teen Responsible For All Six Items In Clarksburg Police Blotter

CLARKSBURG, WV—According to sources at the *Clarksburg Telegram*, troubled youth Danny Nathum, 17, is responsible for all six items on Monday's police blotter. "We had two disorderly-conduct reports, three counts of vandalism, and one DUI arrest," *Telegram* assistant editor Jesse Sutton said. "Looks like Mr. Nathum had himself one heck of a busy weekend." Clarksburg, population 16,743, last experienced an all-Nathum crime spree in December, when the teen stole a bicycle, burned down a barn, and punched Old Man Herman. ∅

the end, all they needed to do to find bin Laden was a little soul-searching.

"We used heat-sensing equipment to search in underground tunnels and studied aerial photography for evidence of movement in the desert," Rumsfeld said. "But did any of us ever stop and listen to a child's cry—*really* listen to it?"

Rumsfeld said efforts to find bin Laden, who was placed on the FBI's most-wanted list after the 1998 bombings of U.S. embassies in Nairobi and Dar es Salaam in Tanzania, were seriously misdirected for years.

"He evaded us for so long because he had such an ingenious hideout," Rumsfeld said. "Only someone as evil

> "There is a part inside each of us that makes us throw recyclable items in with the rest of our trash, let Mom go to voicemail, and eat coworkers' food out of the refrigerator," Tenet told the council.

as bin Laden would think to crawl down into that hole inside every one of us, the one that makes us hate instead of love, forget birthdays, and ignore alternate-side parking rules."

The breakthrough that led to the discovery of bin Laden came Jan. 4, when CIA Director George Tenet realized he'd forgotten to send a Christmas gift to his son in Los Angeles.

"It was bad enough that I couldn't find the time to visit Dale over the holidays, but to fail to send a token of my affection?" Tenet said. "Well, it made me ask, 'What kind of terrible person does that?' I was telling [CIA Deputy Director] John McLaughlin

Above: Osama bin Laden is located on a busy Houston street.

about it, and he said that, earlier that day, he'd seen a teenager push past an elderly woman at a bus stop. John asked me, 'What kind of terrible person does *that?*'"

"The answer hit us like a ton of bricks: *Osama bin Laden*," Tenet said. "Just like that, we had the clue that convinced us to expand the parameters of our search."

Tenet presented his discovery to the U.N. Security Council the next day.

"There is a part inside each of us that makes us throw recyclable items in with the rest of our trash, let Mom go to voicemail, and eat coworkers' food out of the refrigerator," Tenet told the council. "It is a dark, dank, shameful place, and it is my belief that the man responsible for the events of

Sept. 11 lurks therein."

In light of the new counter-terrorist intelligence, Attorney General John Ashcroft has urged lawmakers to expand the Patriot Act to allow federal investigators to search within the hearts of all Americans.

"Finally, we know to look inside the ugly part of ourselves that makes us under-tip waitresses and cut people off in clogged traffic," Ashcroft said. "But now, we need the authority to enter this desolate place and flush the terrorists out."

President Bush spoke in support of Ashcroft's vision for the new front in the war on terror.

"I know this classified information may be hard to hear," Bush said. "But I urge each and every American to per-

form a covert search of his or her own soul. Join me in quiet self-examination and self-interrogation. Ferret out the terrorist inside you and bring him to harsh and swift justice. Together, we can topple the last major stronghold of terror in this world: our own doubts and fears."

Bush added that, even though we know where bin Laden is hiding, drawing him out is largely beyond the power of Washington.

"There is only one way to defeat Osama bin Laden," Bush said. "The way to eliminate this evil man is for each American to love just a little bit more, see your brother's problems as your own, always look on the bright side, and leave every place a little better than you found it." ∅

KERRY from page 85

special interests before our economic future," Kerry told the crowd gathered below the starboard side of *The Real Deal II*. "I will fight to restore the three million jobs that have been lost on the president's watch. It's time America got back to work."

Campaign manager Mary Beth Cahill said Kerry's whistle-stop tour is scheduled to take him through Pennsylvania, Ohio, and on to six Midwestern states at an average speed of 26 knots.

Apart from a brief detour into Lake Michigan between Milwaukee and Chicago, the yacht will travel exclusively on land, attached to a drydock-mounting slip atop a highway-legal flatbed trailer.

Kerry's stump speech, which he delivered through the yacht's PA system, ignored his Democratic rivals and focused instead on the current

administration's economic record.

"Bush has the worst jobs record of the last 11 presidents," said Kerry, his hand draped over the flagpole halyard. "Landing an aircraft carrier doesn't make up for failed economic policy. The American people need jobs to buy food for their families, to secure health insurance for their children, and to pay the mortgages on their houses."

"Unlike the Republicans, I know it's you, the American worker, that keeps this country running," said Kerry, who then tipped his captain's hat to the crowd.

Federal Election Commission records show that Kerry purchased *The Real Deal II* in December 2003 for $2.5 million. The Kerry campaign's 2003 fourth-quarter filings show that the yacht required $200,000 of work to prepare it for the Midwest cam-

paign voyage. Repairs included a tune-up of the vessel's twin diesel engine, the installation of a Navman col-

> "Unlike the Republicans, I know it's you, the American worker, that keeps this country running," said Kerry, who then tipped his captain's hat to the crowd.

or GPS-plotting navigation system, and the addition of red, white, and blue detailing to the yacht's leather interior.

"John Kerry wanted to get out there, connect with the people, and hear their stories," Cahill said in a press conference held in the main cabin. "Taking his yacht across the Midwest is the best way for Kerry to reach out to all the people who lost their jobs under George W. Bush."

"There's no better place to have a good conversation than on the deck of a fine sailing vessel, out there in the sunshine, with the gentle breeze playing in your hair," Cahill said. "It's beautiful up there."

Cahill said she hopes the yacht will appeal to independent voters, who may decide the election in November.

An additional benefit of campaigning in the craft is that it affords Kerry the opportunity to make unexpected stops along the campaign trail, simply by alerting the convoy with his see KERRY page 89

KERRY from page 88

International Maritime Signal Flags.

"What's John Kerry all about?" said Kerry, addressing a small group of supporters that he spotted at a rest stop on Interstate 76. "John Kerry believes in affordable health care, renewable energy, decisive foreign policy, and economic recovery. I'm putting that message on my yacht and taking it all the way across America."

Kerry continued: "We're going to sail *The Real Deal II* right up onto the White House lawn and tell them, 'The American people have arrived to take back their government.'"

U.S. Sen. Ted Kennedy (D-MA), a Kerry supporter who has been traveling on-and-off with the candidate since January, said that the whistle-stop tour demonstrates Kerry's commitment to the country.

"People tried to write this campaign off last year, but he kept going full steam ahead, because he cares about the proud men and women of this nation," Kennedy said. "He's going to go all the way in November, like the little yacht that could." ∅

JOB from page 87

dumbass.' If I have any advice for all the young aspiring painters, novelists, and rock musicians out there, it's probably that they should quit following their dreams before they rack up a lot of credit-card debt. The sooner you accept your real job, the sooner you can start to build up seniority and get on board with the pension plan."

Experts familiar with the "day job/real job" paradigm shift agree.

> ## The sooner you accept your real job, the sooner you can start to build up seniority and get on board with the pension plan,"Seversen said.

"Seversen has just made the most important decision of a non-artist's life," said Gregory Gund, author of *Aw, Who'm I Kidding Here?* and *Learning To Let Go Of The Things That Sustain You.* "We all have to face the music sooner or later. You think I wanted to write crappy self-help novels and speak about them at low-rent seminars in the conference rooms of cheap chain hotels?"

Gund continued: "I'll never forget the day I traded in my bass amp for a dot-matrix printer. I sat in the bathtub for about two hours that day, staring at the reflection of my receding hairline in the cold water. Sometimes, I wish I'd plugged that amp in and hauled it into the tub with me. But, hey, we can't all be the next Geddy Lee, right?" ∅

COUPLE from page 85

Peterman, whom he started dating in August 2001, must have drunkenly knocked a framed photo of the couple off the coffee table and smashed it all over the bedroom floor.

"It's too bad, too, because Ames and I have always considered that particular photo symbolic of our relationship," Hayter said. "I tell you, I must've had a great time last night. I just hope it was worth hosting this fucking hammer party in my skull."

Peterman did not remember anything of the breakup, either. Carefully stepping around the piles of debris in

> ## "It's too bad, too, because Ames and I have always considered that particular photo symbolic of our relationship," Hayter said. "I tell you, I must've had a great time last night. I just hope it was worth hosting this fucking hammer party in my skull."

the apartment, she attended to her nausea and rubbed an abrasion on her finger where she had yanked off her promise ring in anger.

"Oh, my poor head," Peterman said. "I would've liked to have slept off my hangover, but my friend Nora called

me at the crack of dawn. She wanted to know if I was 'okay,' and if I knew where Gene was. She kept asking me if I needed to talk. I was, like, 'No, I don't want to talk. My head is killing me.'"

"She was kinda weirding me out, actually," Peterman added. "Gene says she was probably still drunk."

The couple spent the morning staggering around the apartment, surveying the damage.

"Why are all of Gene's clothes piled in the middle of the room like that, and what's that smell?" Peterman asked, unaware that she had heaped his clothes on the floor and doused them in lighter fluid. "Did he spill vodka on them or something? God, I feel like shit."

Patting each other tenderly and engaging in other forms of non-verbal communication that revealed years of familiarity, the affectionate couple was nothing like the screaming drunks who had spent an hour the night before hashing out their sexual-incompatibility issues in front of a group of mutual friends at their neighborhood bar.

"I stopped by expecting to find Amy distraught over the breakup," Peterman's childhood friend Mary Swaney said. "But I walked in and found her and Gene cuddling under a blanket and watching *Law & Order*. Gene didn't seem to even realize that he had a black eye, let alone who gave it to him."

"Gene called to say they wouldn't be meeting the gang for brunch, and I was thinking, 'No duh,'" said Hayter's best friend Jack McVeigh, who had spent 90 minutes the previous night talking Hayter out of heading to the mountains. "But when he said he and

'Ames' were just going to eat cinnamon toast and listen to records, I realized they wanted to spend the day making up."

"I don't know how to tell him I have his Swiss Army knife," McVeigh added. "I took it off his key ring last

> ## "Why are all of Gene's clothes piled in the middle of the room like that, and what's that smell?" Peterman asked, unaware that she had heaped his clothes on the floor and doused them in lighter fluid.

night, because I wasn't 100 percent sure he could be trusted with it."

As of press time, neither Hayter nor Peterman exhibited the slightest recollection of the emotional content of the drinking binge.

"I'm glad I have you, Amy," Hayter said, cuddling closer to Peterman underneath the very blanket he had used to deflect her blows the night before. "I just want to hide from the loud, demanding world and snuggle for the rest of the day."

"Me, too," Peterman said, as she bemusedly extracted a letter opener from between the couch cushions. "We can check and see what those 14 answering-machine messages are all about after we're feeling better." ∅

Above: Hayter cleans up a framed photo that must have fallen the previous evening.

I'll Tell You What I'd Do If I Were Gay

A guy from work introduced me to his boyfriend this week. He seemed pretty nice, but it was weird, because he didn't look gay at all. He was a computer programmer and looked like any fat, balding slob you'd run into on the street. I have to say, I would never let myself go like that if I were gay.

By Keith Whitlock

If I were gay, I would be very well groomed. I'd purchase two high-quality suits, one nice suit jacket, and two pairs of wool trousers. I'd get about eight shirts tailored, and I would own my own tuxedo, for special occasions. I'd grow my buzzcut into a sophisticated Caesar cut, and I would brighten it with tastefully blended golden highlights. Each morning, I would tame my hair's unruly kinks with a dollop of molding paste and a little reparative shine serum. (It's important to use the right products, if you want to maintain healthy hair—especially when it's gay.)

If I were gay, there's no way I'd shave with a disposable razor and a bar of Dial soap, like I do as a straight man. As a gay man, I'd make shaving a ritual. I would prepare my face with a foaming exfoliating cleanser, then I'd use a cucumber shave gel and a sharp blade. I might even use a straight razor that I would sharpen on a soap-

> **While I would be too honest with myself to ignore life's harsh realities, I would be playful enough to have a sense of humor about them. This sense of humor would be quite salty and acerbic.**

stone. I would definitely use hot wax to bring my unruly eyebrows under control, and my nose hairs would never see the light of day again.

As a gay man of the world, I would have a career that made use of my inherent talent in art, architecture, fashion, or entertainment. Right now, I bus tables in the hospital cafeteria. But as a homosexual, I would be resourceful enough to channel my passion for antiques into a viable means of self-employment. My antique shop, located in a trendy neighborhood, would attract an interesting mix of university intellectuals, vintage furniture collectors, and fashionable shoppers. Sometimes, my weakness for kitsch would threaten to overpower the sophisticated environment of the store, but I'd manage to mute it. I'm not sure what my lover would do for a

> **If I were gay, I would be very well groomed. I'd purchase two high-quality suits, one nice suit jacket, and two pairs of wool trousers. I'd get about eight shirts tailored, and I would own my own tuxedo, for special occasions. I'd grow my buzzcut into a sophisticated Caesar cut, and I would brighten it with tastefully blended golden highlights.**

living, but I assume he'd run the vintage costume and prop shop next door. I do know this: If I were gay, my lover and I would spend our weekends combing estate sales together.

Gay Keith would have a brassy but likable personality. Even though I would have lost a few of my younger years to partying, wanton sex, and a love affair that ended badly, I would have gained wisdom and experience from this "walk on the wild side." While I would be too honest with myself to ignore life's harsh realities, I would be playful enough to have a sense of humor about them. This sense of humor would be quite salty and acerbic. Some would consider the way I would chide my close female friend—her name would be Trish—for her frumpiness a tad harsh. But I would only tease Trish to encourage her to better herself. I'd see potential in her, even if she didn't.

True, the way I call my real-life wife a lazy slob isn't constructive, just abusive, but heterosexual men aren't as understanding as homosexual ones.

If I were gay, I would donate generous amounts of money to the fight against AIDS. I can't say enough how important that would be to me. AIDS is a global scourge that has taken countless lives in the gay community, and has reached epidemic proportions in many Third World countries. I would donate a portion of my business' profits to various groups that conduct AIDS research, and place a coin-donation bank from a reputable AIDS charity near the cash register in my shop.

Finally, if I were gay, I would make an excellent uncle. My kids know to stay away from me when I'm drunk or watching ESPN, but gay Uncle Keith would be totally different. I'd get down on my hands and knees with the kids and dig for fossils at the children's museum. I'd read to them from the beloved storybooks I'd have saved since childhood. I'd even let them rollerblade on the rooftop of my condo. Then, we'd all pile into my 2001 forest-green Jaguar XK convertible and go out for frosty malts at a retro diner. Sometime in their early teenage years, it would dawn on my nieces and nephews that I didn't own a television, and that I was a homosexual.

I'm still unsure about a few things in my gay life. I haven't decided whether I should re-establish contact with my estranged father. I also don't know whether I should lend money to the fun-loving but irresponsible drag queen who was my first boyfriend after I came out at age 19. Would I enjoy the occasional tab of E or bump of co-

> **Finally, if I were gay, I would make an excellent uncle.**

caine with my wild friends at the dance clubs, or would I prefer to drink Bombay Sapphire martinis in my living room with a small handful of close confidants? I'm not sure how my laugh would sound. But I do know that I would always be mindful of my many strengths. I wouldn't be afraid to make mistakes, because I would know that that's just a part of the learning process. I would believe in myself, and my happiness would be my own, because I would have sought it on my own terms. After all, things would just keep getting better. ∅

Your Horoscope

By Lloyd Schumner Sr.
Retired Machinist and
A.A.P.B.-Certified Astrologer

Aries: (March 21–April 19)
Religious leaders from around the world will agree that God seems to be reacting to your criticism rather harshly.

Taurus: (April 20–May 20)
You've never believed in running away from love, but then again, you've never been on the business end of a coked-up rhinoceros' ardor before.

Gemini: (May 21–June 21)
It won't come as much of a shock to you, but according to your spouse and children, your replacement is doing one heck of a good job.

Cancer: (June 22–July 22)
You might not like it, but even you have to admit that your foibles and predilections are accurately captured in the popular new parody version of you.

Leo: (July 23–Aug. 22)
Once again, you've been nominated for an award in the prestigious "Most Engulfed In Flames" category.

Virgo: (Aug. 23–Sept. 22)
It's time to exploit your connections in order to get a better job. Start cozying up to the guy who handles the local classified ads section.

Libra: (Sept. 23–Oct. 23)
You've decided to take it as a compliment that all your lovers describe you as a wizard in the bathroom.

Scorpio: (Oct. 24–Nov. 21)
Your life story will be a testimony to the healing power of love for nachos.

Sagittarius: (Nov. 22–Dec. 21)
You'll realize that you're not like the others when a visit to a historic Civil War battlefield forever changes the way you feel about custom kitchen cabinetry.

Capricorn: (Dec. 22–Jan. 19)
You will be hunted to the ends of the earth by torch-wielding opera traditionalists after enraptured reviewers refer to you as the "long-sought Fourth Tenor."

Aquarius: (Jan. 20–Feb. 18)
You're getting closer to the secret of happiness all the time, but before this makes you too happy, you should hear the story of Achilles and the tortoise.

Pisces: (Feb. 19–March 20)
By the time you get what you want, you've changed so much that you don't want it anymore, which sends the waitress into a rage.

Dean Mentions He'd Make A Great Secretary Of Health And Human Services

see WASHINGTON page 2B

School Flies Deceased Nerd's Underpants At Half-Mast

see LOCAL page 3C

Wildlife Preserved In Basement Freezer

see OUTDOORS page 11E

STATshot

A look at the numbers that shape your world.

Most Popular T-Shirt Slogans, 2092

25% I'm With 01110011011101

19% My Other Torso Is Modular

13% Pleasure Droid Inspector

20% The Rich Fled The Planet And All I Got Was This Lousy T-Shirt

23% Don't Mess With Orbital Texas

THE ONION • $2.00 US • $3.00 CAN

0 74470 94595 6

00

---

the ONION ®

VOLUME 40 ISSUE 08   AMERICA'S FINEST NEWS SOURCE ™   26 FEB.–3 MARCH 2004

Bush To Cut Deficit From Federal Budget

WASHINGTON, DC— President Bush proposed a $2.4 trillion election-year budget Monday that would boost defense spending, redistribute funds among government programs, and cross out the $477 billion deficit entirely.

"Nobody likes making cuts, but the nation's current rate of spending and the decreased tax revenues we've seen since implementing my tax cuts have created a deficit that we can't afford to carry," Bush said in a nationally televised address. "Someone had to have the vision, leadership, and courage to go in and erase that line altogether, no matter how unpopular and impossible that may be."

According to the Congressional Budget Office, the $477 billion deficit is the country's largest ever, easily topping the previous record of $290 billion in 1992. If the budget is approved, however, the deficit will roll down to $0.0 billion.

see BUSH page 95

Right: Bush announces the budget-balancing deficit cut.

Massachusetts Supreme Court Orders All Citizens To Gay Marry

BOSTON—Justices of the Massachusetts Supreme Judicial Court ruled 5-2 Monday in favor of full, equal, and mandatory gay marriages for all citizens. The order nullifies all pre-existing heterosexual marriages and lays the groundwork for the 2.4 million compulsory same-sex marriages that will take place in the state by May 15.

"As we are all aware, it's simply not possible for gay marriage and heterosexual marriage to co-exist," Massachusetts Chief Justice Margaret H. Marshall said. "Our ruling in November was just the first step toward creating an all-gay Massachusetts."

Marshall added: "Since the allowance

see COURT page 94

Left: A justice performs a mandatory marriage.

Good Cop, Bad Cop Both Racist

LOS ANGELES—Despite occupying opposing roles in a good-cop/bad-cop dyad, LAPD officers Frank K. McGrew, 51, and Bob West, 36, have one thing in common: They're both extremely racist, 77th precinct sources reported Monday.

"Officer McGrew is the tough, no-nonsense veteran of the force who pushes you around, threatens you with 15 years behind bars, and calls you a nigger," said LeShawn Gordon, a 19-year-old recently charged with grand theft auto. "Officer Bob is the one who picks you up, gives you a cig-

arette, and tells you he's there to help you before calling you a nigger."

West and McGrew have been partners on the station's investigative unit since August 2001, but both have been racists for much longer. The team, assigned to a particularly crime-ridden two-mile section of South Central, frequently uses a law-enforcement technique common among police partners. "Bad cop" McGrew attempts to draw information or a confession out of perpetrators by frightening them, while "good cop" West does so by

see RACIST page 94

Above: McGrew and West.

Colorado Football Under Fire

In a growing scandal, several women have charged that they were raped by football players at the University of Colorado. What do *you* think?

"This is going to negatively affect the entire Colorado athletic department. I wish people would think before they let the rape accusations fly."

Pamela King
Florist

"See? See? One breast is flashed at a football game and the whole sport goes into the gutter."

Eric Scott
AV Technician

"This is what happens when you tell people to give 110 percent."

Anna Baker
Bill Collector

"As an athlete, all I can say is that all this sex talk is making me want to go rape someone."

Anthony Benkes
Athlete

"I heard that some Colorado Buffaloes raped some women and was absolutely horrified. But it turned out it's the name of their football team."

Joshua Hall
Systems Analyst

"What happened to the good old days of college football, when you never heard about things like this happening, even though they were going on?"

Gregory Carter
Orchestrator

Greece Gearing Up For Olympics

With just six months to go before the Olympics, Greece is scrambling to ready itself. What problems remain?

- Many of Athens' Olympic facilities have fallen into disrepair since original games
- 90 percent of country's discus supply currently in the hands of statuary
- Large number of drunken, shirtless, lute-playing satyrs poses a challenging public-image problem
- Athens' flush toilet is usually occupied
- Will need 30,000 more goat skins in order to provide adequate water supply
- Olympic Village beset with inadequate sanitation and strong cooking odors
- Athens' heavy air pollution has already eaten away exteriors of several athletes
- Olympic theme sounds terrible on pan flute
- Chorus of masked, robed men not cutting it as sports commentators
- Athens no Salt Lake City

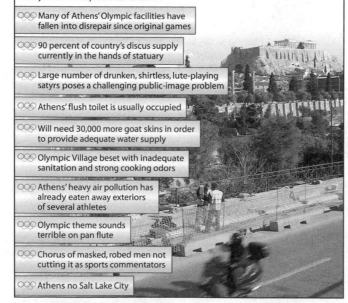

the ONION®
America's Finest News Source.™

Herman Ulysses Zweibel
Founder

T. Herman Zweibel
Publisher Emeritus
J. Phineas Zweibel
Publisher
Maxwell Prescott Zweibel
Editor-In-Chief

If Al-Qaeda Had A Hockey Team, We'd Kick Its Ass!

All right, so al-Qaeda is still giving us a little bit of trouble. We haven't found bin Laden yet, and I guess there're still these little cells of them all over the place. But we shouldn't let that crush our spirit, because we'll get 'em. America always wins at the end, in wars or in anything else.

By Patrick K. Johnson

I don't know what's taking so long over there, but I do know this: If al-Qaeda had a hockey team, we'd totally kick its ass.

Can you imagine? It'd be so sweet. We'd have the advantage before the puck even dropped. First of all, they'd be from the Middle East, which is no hockey powerhouse. I'll bet their ice always melts down before the game's even over. Plus, their rink would probably be all bombed out. Or it'd be in a tent or something. And you know al-Qaeda's hockey uniforms would be totally ugly, with stupid colors and all kinds of Allah shit all over them. The jerseys would have those big long Ramalama bin Dingdong names on the back, and those Arabic numbers they use over there.

> President Bush'd be there to fire up our skaters by looking right at the al-Qaeda bench and repeating his warning to all terrorists: "Bring it on!" The crowd would go nuts! Everyone would be going so crazy, they'd hardly hear Ted Nugent sing the national anthem!

But America's team…

Well, players from everywhere would be jumping to sign on, man! We'd have no problem assembling a kick-ass international coalition to play the al-Qaeda if we wanted, but America would have to be firm and say, "Sorry friends, this game's ours."

So, who would we get to go head-to-head with those terrorist fuckers? Only our most bad-assed pros! Now, I know some people would want to go all Lake Placid and use amateurs, but, hey, did al-Qaeda use amateur terror-

ists on the World Trade Center? Hell, no. So we'd get pros like Brett Hull, the best American scorer ever, and skills guys like Mike Modano. We'd

> Can you imagine? It'd be so sweet. We'd have the advantage before the puck even dropped. First of all, they'd be from the Middle East, which is no hockey powerhouse. I'll bet their ice always melts down before the game's even over.

add in some hard guys who don't mind going into the corners or dropping the gloves if the sticks come up— I'm thinking, like, Jeremy Roenick on this one. And the capper? Flourtown's own Mike Richter comes out of retirement to play goal, baby! And if they get in the crease, Rafalski takes 'em out. Face it: On paper, al-Qaeda's boned.

But then they'd get to the game, right? And it'd be awesome! Because they'd have to have it in Madison Square Garden, on account of who the shit wants to go to Afghanistan?

President Bush'd be there to fire up our skaters by looking right at the al-Qaeda bench and repeating his warning to all terrorists: "Bring it on!" The crowd would go nuts! Everyone would be going so crazy, they'd hardly hear Ted Nugent sing the national anthem! The camera would cut to the al-Qaeda bench, and they'd all be sitting in their towel helmets thinking, "Oh, shit, what the fuck did we get ourselves into?"

Now, I'm not saying it'd be total cake. Everyone knows those guys are crafty little fuckers who don't play fair. They'd probably try to overload one side or the other, then suicide-crash the net to try to sneak the puck in. They might even go a goal up on us late in the first period, because you know Team USA would come out of the gate all fired up, and that level of emotion can get you in turnover trouble.

So let's be realistic here—the first period might be closer than a lot of people would like. But that'd just give those bastards a false sense of security, because 20 minutes against our seasoned pros would be enough to

see HOCKEY page 95

Pregnant Woman Acting Like No One Ever Got Pregnant Before

HUNTSVILLE, AL—In the seven months since she got herself knocked up, graphic designer Amy Glennon, 27, has been walking around the Calendarz, Inc. office acting like the Queen of Sheba just because she's pregnant, coworker Stephen DeGrassio announced Monday.

"Amy thinks she's Big Miss Important," DeGrassio said Monday. "She's behaving like a total priss. It's like, 'Ooh, look at me! I'm pregnant! I'm

> ## "So she had an ultrasound," DeGrassio said. "Big whoop. It's a non-invasive medical procedure. I could get one if I wanted, and I'm not even a lady."

gonna have a baby!' Hey, calm down. People have babies all the time."

DeGrassio and Glennon have worked together at Calendarz for three years. In spite of the proximity of their workstations, the two have found few common interests. According to DeGrassio, Glennon's way of "walking around like she's a member of the founding board of Calendarz" ever since she got pregnant has not brought the two any closer together.

"Amy goes on and on about food

now," DeGrassio said. "She's all hung up on folic acid or something. I told her, 'Hey, if you lose this one, it's not like you can't make another one.' C'mon, it's a joke. Lighten up."

DeGrassio also expressed annoyance over the special treatment Glennon has received ever since she proved her ability to lay on her back and get nailed.

"Last week, she asked me to get some food out of the fridge for her," DeGrassio said. "She said she didn't want to have to bend down to dig in the bottom drawer. Please! When I sprained my ankle, I didn't have people wait on me hand and foot. Christ, what a joke."

Glennon has updated coworkers on every stage of her pregnancy and provided them with full reports on each of her visits to the obstetrician, because that's exactly the sort of thing people are interested in hearing about when they're trying to sell some goddamn calendars.

"So she had an ultrasound," DeGrassio said. "Big whoop. It's a non-invasive medical procedure. I could get one if I wanted, and I'm not even a lady. It's just a black-and-white smear, and she's got it pinned up there like it's a goddamned Sears Christmas portrait."

Of course, Glennon had a baby shower last week and everyone in the office was invited—how gracious of her.

"Her friends sold the baby shower so hard," DeGrassio said. "They were all like, 'We play games and open presents'—as if I don't know what a shower is. I'll tell you what it is: four hours of chattering and cooing over

Above: Glennon opens a bunch of baby crap at the baby shower everyone had to go to.

stuff from Target. I always give the same gift when I go to one: a pair of overalls. But everyone acts like it's the Bicentennial fireworks display."

As the blessed event approaches, DeGrassio admitted that he's having a hard time playing along when Her Royal Highness makes him feel the baby.

"Every time that thing moves, Amy freaks out," DeGrassio said. "She came up to me the other day, grabbed my hand, and put it on her stomach. She kept asking me if I could feel it kick. Does the baby get to feel me kick? I'm

sorry, that was too much, but this is making me crazy."

DeGrassio said that, while he understands why the pregnancy might be exciting for Glennon, he looks forward to the day when the baby is finally born, already.

"Her due date is April 23, and it can't come fast enough," DeGrassio said. "Of course, once the damn kid finally pops out, I'll have to sit through all the stories about breastfeeding and its first steps. I guess the only way I'm ever going to get a word in edgewise at this office is if I knock up some skank." ∅

Man Kinda Excited For Internal Camera Procedure

FREDERICK, MD—Two days before his scheduled colonoscopy, Barry Feldman, 47, told his wife Joyce he was "kinda excited" by the idea of a camera taking internal pictures of him, sources reported Tuesday. "I'm a little nervous about the test results, but it sure is amazing that they'll be taking photos with a camera the size of a pencil eraser!" Feldman said. "I talked to the doctor, and he said I'll be able to watch the whole thing on a monitor. He said they can even make me a video tape!" Feldman added that he hopes he doesn't pass out from the pain and miss something.

4-Year-Old Reportedly Loved Trip To Italy

SAN BERNARDINO, CA—According to his mother, 4-year-old Justin

Finley "absolutely loved" a recent family trip to Italy. "He adored the fountains and the wonderful food, but Justin's favorite part of the trip was the La Scala Opera House in Milan," Heather Finley said Monday. "He was so excited at the La Scala that he was jumping up and down on the benches and climbing up the curtains." Finley then launched into her 23rd recounting of the family's tour of St. Peter's Basilica in Rome, where Justin pointed to the gilt ceiling and said, "Look, pretty yellow!"

Transformer Refuses To Change Back Into Volkswagen

CYBOTRON—Following an intense battle with Megatron and his evil Decepticons Monday, former robot-in-disguise Zorkotron refused to revert to his natural state as a yellow Volkswagen Beetle. "I hid my existence in this world by taking the form of a vehicle! I revealed my true nature when

I was called upon to protect earth!" said Bumblebee, a member of Optimus Prime's heroic Autobots force. "I refuse to change back into a humiliating bubble-shaped compact car!" Zorkotron added that Megatron arrived on earth with one goal: Destruction!

Thai Premier Eats Entire Bucket Of Chicken To Calm Bird-Flu Fears

BANGKOK—To allay concerns about the safety of Thai poultry following an outbreak of the H5N1 bird virus, Thai Prime Minister Thaksin Shinawatra ate an entire 15-piece bucket of fried chicken on live television Monday. "See, it's fine, this chicken," Shinawatra said as he tore into a leg. "You are all worried for nothing. It's delicious." In a Carson's Group International poll taken after the broadcast, 63 percent of viewers

said they wouldn't be afraid to eat chicken raised in Thailand, but 94 percent said they were afraid of Shinawatra.

ExxonMobil Swears It's Going To Start Taxes Early This Year

IRVING, TX—Hoping to avoid the "scraping and scrambling" it does every year, the ExxonMobil Corporation announced Tuesday that it has made a solemn promise to get moving on taxes early this year. "I swear, this time we are not going to be up all night on April 15," ExxonMobil chairman and CEO Lee R. Raymond said. "We're going to start sorting through those receipts from the Qatar and Malaysia production facilities the first weekend we have time. Wouldn't it be nice to get it done ahead of time for a change?" Raymond said he hasn't forgotten driving around at 10 p.m. looking for a gas station with a copy machine last year. ∅

93

of gay marriage undermines heterosexual unions, we decided to work a few steps ahead and strike down opposite-sex unions altogether."

Marshall said the court's action will put a swift end to the mounting debate.

"Instead of spending months or even years volleying this thing back and forth, we thought we might as well just cut to the eventual outcome of our decision to allow gay marriages," Marshall said. "Clearly, this is where this all was headed anyway."

The justices then congratulated the state's 4.8 million marriage-age residents on their legally mandated engagements.

The court issued the surprise order in response to a query from the Massachusetts Senate over whether Vermont-style civil unions, which convey the state-sanctioned benefits of marriage but not the title, are constitutional.

"If the history of our nation has demonstrated anything, it's that separate is never equal," Marshall said. "Therefore, any measure short of dismantling conventional matrimony and mandating the immediate homosexual marriage of all residents of

Above: A state-arranged couple from New Bedford, MA, honeymoons in Aruba.

> "Instead of spending months or even years volleying this thing back and forth, we thought we might as well just cut to the eventual outcome of our decision," Marshall said.

Massachusetts would dishonor same-sex unions. I'm confident that this measure will be seen by all right-thinking people as the only solution to our state's, and indeed America's, ongoing marriage controversy."

Marshall then announced her engagement to Holyoke kindergarten teacher Betsy Peterson, a pairing that had been randomly generated by computers in the census office earlier that day.

Those who don't choose to marry in private will be married in concurrent mass ceremonies at Fenway Park, Gillette Stadium, and the Boston Convention and Exposition Center. Any citizen who is not gay-married or is still in an illegal heterosexual relationship after that date will be arrested and tried for non-support.

Hundreds of confused but vocal protesters lined the street outside the statehouse Monday night, waving both American and rainbow flags. Their chants, which broke out in pockets up and down the street, in-

cluded, "Hey hey, ho ho, homophobia's got to go, but frankly, this is fucked up" and "Adam and Eve or Adam and Steve, but not Adam and Some Random Guy." Others held signs that read, "On Second Thought, Boston Christians Are Willing To Consider A Compromise."

According to police reports, demonstrators were vocal but orderly.

"The unholy union of people of the same gender destroys the only type of romantic love sanctioned by Our Lord in Heaven: the love between a man and a woman," 54-year-old protester Rose Shoults said. "Me and my new partner Helene are going to fry in hell."

The much-anticipated order sets the stage for Massachusetts' upcoming constitutional convention, where the state legislature will consider an amendment to legally define marriage as a union between two members of the same gender. Without the order, Rep. Michael Festa said the vote, and his personally dreaded wedding to House Speaker and long-time political opponent Thomas Finneran, would be delayed.

"This is a victory, not only for our state, but for America," Festa said. "Simply allowing consenting gay adults the same rights as heterosexuals was never the point. By forcing everyone in the state into a gay marriage, we're setting the stage for our more pressing hidden agendas: mandatory sodomy and, in due time, the legalization of bestiality and pedophilia."

Massachusetts has one of the highest concentrations of gay households in the country, at 1.3 percent, according to the 2000 census. Under the new laws, the figure is expected to increase by approximately 98.7 percent. ∅

gaining their trust. But detainees who've been interrogated by the pair say the two share a hatred for non-whites that transcends their contrasting styles.

Jaime Hernandez, 24, was interrogated by McGrew and West after he was arrested on Feb. 18 for trafficking in narcotics.

"McGrew cuffed me to a desk, clubbed me in the face with a broom handle, and screamed that my 'spic' buddies on the street couldn't help me now," Hernandez said. "He let me sit there for an hour. Then West came in and removed the handcuffs. He got me a Pepsi and some Twinkies, and while I ate them, he explained, in a caring and sensitive way, why I really ought to cooperate. He said he'd do everything he could do to help me, but that I had to face the fact that I was a no-good taco bender from the barrio with five chicken-babies, two priors, and only one real option: to talk."

Their mutual disdain for minorities aside, the two racist partners couldn't be more different, fellow officers report.

"McGrew is a barrel-chested bruiser with the same close-cropped crew-cut he's had since his cadet days. He's twice-divorced, spends his nights at a local tavern, and is rumored to have an unending series of problematic short-term relationships with white women half his age," LAPD officer Terry Steig said. "West, however, is a smiling, kind-eyed listener who enjoys spending weekends in the park and is fiercely devoted to his white wife and their white infant child."

Many other officers say bigotry and hatred are the only similarities that unite the two.

"When the chief first put those two together, the sparks really flew," fellow LAPD officer Duane Garner said. "It was your classic mismatched-partners situation. McGrew was a grizzled veteran who'd developed a cynical attitude toward minorities after years of witnessing ugly street crime firsthand. West, on the other hand, was an idealistic young golden boy from the academy who took the horror stories his teachers told about the scum of the earth to heart. They were like oil and water, but they learned to respect each other's approaches to shaking confessions out of slants, *cholos*, and homeboys."

Leaning against the sink in the station's cramped and dirty kitchenette, the two men expressed admiration for each other.

"Sometimes Frank goes too far, but I know his heart is in the right place," West said. "He just wants to make a difference by protecting and serving good, hard-working white people."

"Sometimes West can be a molly-coddling nanny, but he's still a good cop," McGrew said in response. "In his own way, he's doing what he thinks he has to do to control these stinking, subhuman mud-people."

Added McGrew: "Sure, sometimes he drives me crazy. I can be one good crack away from getting some beaner to confess, and he'll break in with his namby-pamby wah-wah, saying he can promise a better life for the 10 dirty little kids the guy must have running around at home. But in the end, we always get the job done. It just goes to show that no matter how different we are, we're both doing what we need to do to get these animals behind bars, where they belong." ∅

HOCKEY from page 92

rag their legs out big time. So the second-period horn goes, and here's my prediction: four goals in the first 10 minutes, baby, if not five! Bet your ass

We'll be going, "Okay, al-Qaeda, you wanna get aggressive? You like that? Jump in, buds!"

there's a hattie for my man Brett Hull.

So of course al-Qaeda starts getting chippy and the sticks come up, but that plays right into our hands. We'll be going, "Okay, al-Qaeda, you wanna get aggressive? You like that? Jump in, buds!" And then the whistles start going, because you don't think al-Qaeda

gets the officials on their side in Madison Square Garden, do you? Fuck nah.

So, of course, then we'd get the power play. And face it, at that point, the game's pretty much over for them. They have to ask the crowd to stop chanting "USA! USA! USA!" But guess what, man? We ain't gonna stop! So al-Qaeda pulls their goalie, and while they're trying for the extra-man goal in garbage time to save face, they fail to notice one important detail: the Navy SEALs coming down from the ceilings and walls to capture everyone on the al-Qaeda bench. 'Cause there's no way we're letting those half-assed-hockey-playing terrorist bastards just waltz out the door. And that's how the greatest hockey game in history would end.

Man, those guys better *hope* we never catch them on skates. Ø

SHAKER from page 47

unusually large amounts of blood. Passersby were amazed by the unusually large amounts of blood. Passersby were amazed by the unusually large amounts of blood. Passersby

My door is always open due to mechanical failure.

were amazed by the unusually large amounts of blood. Passersby were amazed by the unusually large amounts of blood. Passersby were amazed by the unusually large amounts of blood. Passersby were amazed by the unusually large amounts of blood. Passersby were amazed by the unusually large amounts of blood. Passersby were amazed by the unusually large amounts of blood. Passersby were

amazed by the unusually large amounts of blood. Passersby were amazed by the unusually large amounts of blood. Passersby were amazed by the unusually large amounts of blood. Passersby were amazed by the unusually large amounts of blood. Passersby were amazed by the unusually large amounts of blood. Passersby were amazed by the unusually large amounts of blood. Passersby were amazed by the unusually large amounts of blood. Passersby were amazed by the unusually large amounts of blood. Passersby were amazed by the unusually large amounts of blood. Passersby were amazed by the unusually large amounts of blood. Passersby were amazed by the unusually large amounts of blood. Passersby were amazed by the unusually large amounts of blood. Passersby were amazed by the unusually large amounts of blood. Passersby were

see SHAKER page 204

BUSH from page 91

In the past, critics have accused the Bush Administration of responding to a mounting deficit and the ongoing recession with unsound fiscal policies like cutting taxes for the wealthy. Bush supporters say the deficit cut proves the wisdom of the president's economic plan.

"Bush has taken a brave step, one that was long overdue," Senate Majority Leader Bill Frist (R-TN) said. "He has taken charge of the budget problem once and for all, simply by saying 'The deficit stops here.'"

Faced with the difficult choice of either cutting government programs or raising taxes, Bush reportedly arrived at the radical new "deficit-cutting" solution late Sunday night, only hours before he was to announce his budget.

"I was staring at the figure for the deficit, and I decided that it simply

could not stand," Bush said. "It was too high. Something had to be done. But Americans have been taxed and taxed. I say 'Enough taxes.' By my estimation, this historical crossing-out of the deficit will save American taxpayers millions, billions, and perhaps even bajillions of dollars."

The president then turned to Section 14-D of the official budget document, where the federal government's total expenditures, the GNP, and the difference between the two were listed. Using a black Sharpie, the president crossed out the third figure, eliminating it entirely.

Bush then held up the newly marked-up page and said, "My fellow Americans, I have solved the federal budget crisis."

The budget is expected to pass through the GOP-controlled Congress

with little or no opposition.

"I don't know why I didn't have this idea before," Bush said. "For years, we have tried to control the deficit by eliminating federal programs, lowering taxes for the rich, sending out checks to everybody, and God knows what else. None of us once thought to just draw a line through it."

The Bush plan is not without critics.

"President Bush drew a line through the deficit, yes, and we commend him for that," Sen. Blanche Lincoln (D-AR) said. "But that doesn't solve the country's budgetary problems. While he was at it, why didn't he add several zeroes to the end of our GNP?"

Political pundits have been largely impressed by the visionary slash.

"Opinions vary as to what the long-term effects of the deficit cut will be," *New York Times* columnist Paul Krug-

man said. "One thing, however, is certain: The growing federal deficit, a Gordian knot that for three years no amount of cutting taxes and spending money could unravel, has been sliced in two by the president's bold, radical new take on the problem."

The president then turned to Section 14-D of the official budget document, where the federal government's total expenditures, the GNP, and the difference between the two were listed. Using a black Sharpie, the president crossed out the third figure, eliminating it entirely.

A CNN/Gallup poll taken immediately after the president's announcement showed that 67 percent of Americans support his decision to draw a black line through the deficit, and thereby eliminate it.

"I'm tired of the tax-and-spend Democrats always talking about adding zeroes to the GNP," said Henry Strom, 40, of Bakersfield, CA. "How about we cross out our debts and get our affairs in order before we start adding zeroes? We need to cut this deficit *and* stand firm against printing deficits in future budgets, as well."

According to Bush's political advisors, later this week, the president will declare that the U.S. has universal health care. Ø

Above: Government officials commend Bush for his deficit-cutting plan.

Going Out Is Too Much Hassle

The Cruise
By Jim Anchower

Hola, amigos. What's going on? I know it's been a long time since I rapped at ya, but I've been out of my head lately. I've put on about 15 pounds since I started my job driving people back and forth between the airport and the car-rental place. I don't get it. I've been driving my ass off, and I'm still becoming a king-sized fat-ass. I'm trying that Atkins diet. They got a book about it, but why bother with that? I think I got the gist of it from hearing Wes' mom talk about it all the time. I mean, eat nothing but meat? Sign me up. I went out and got myself 12 packs of hot dogs and a 10-pound box of frozen hamburger patties. I haven't lost any weight yet, but I figure you gotta give these things some time to work.

It's been real hard to keep off the chips, though. I got myself a primo weed source last month, so I find myself with the munchies pretty much every night. That's why I got some jerky. It's like having chips made of meat, only they don't crunch, unless you fry them for a couple minutes. Then they're like meat Doritos.

I'd be pretty happy just sitting around the house eating my jerky chips and watching the tube. The only problem is that I can't get people to come over to my place, and I don't like being all alone. I'm a social animal by nature. I can usually count on Ron to stop by, since he's a cheap son of a bitch. Wes used to be good for

> **When we got to the bar, it was only about half full. I thought it would be packed with couples, especially on a Saturday night, but I guess everyone had something better to do.**

hanging out, but then he got himself a girlfriend named Mindy. God only knows how. I think they met on some computer chat line last month or so. Since then, Ron and I haven't seen much of him.

Anyway, Ron called up and told me that he needed to go out for once. He had the brilliant idea of going to The Bull for their Valentine's Day special. I like Valentine's Day less than I like Sting, but there are always good drink specials that night, like two-for-one on anything pink. I'm not much for pink booze, but who am I to turn down a good value? Plus, he laid on the old Ron guilt. He told me that Wes and Mindy were going to meet up with him, and he didn't want to be a third wheel.

Now, the secret to going out for the

> **I never thought a pink beverage could fuck you up so fast. I guess it was my fault, because I failed to follow the cardinal rule: Beer before liquor, never sicker. I never should've listened to Ron and gone out in the first place. Valentine's Day has always sucked, and now I have one more reason to hate it.**

night is drinking before you leave the house. At home, you drink for half the cost, and you don't have to tip the guy who gets the beer out of the fridge. Ron stopped by on the way to The Bull, so we ate some hot dogs and knocked back a few for about an hour.

When we got to the bar, it was only about half full. I thought it would be packed with couples, especially on a Saturday night, but I guess everyone had something better to do. Wes and Mindy were already waiting for us. They were at a table, and both of them were drinking some kind of pink ice-cream drink.

I went to the bar and asked if they had any pink drinks that weren't totally weak. The bartender said I should try a cosmo. I'm totally into all the outer-space science stuff, so I ordered two of them and headed back to the table. Ron tried to grab one of my drinks, but I told him that that wasn't an option. I took a sip of my first drink, and it was pretty good. It went down smooth, like Hawaiian Punch. I made it through pretty quick, and I figured that they were probably best cold, so I kicked the second one back right after.

I wanted to play darts, but some fat guys were all over the dartboard. They had quarters lined up like it was a Pac-Man game, so there was nothing to do but sit at the table and get more drinks. Meanwhile, Ron was

trying to make time with a table of ladies. I could see them rolling their eyes from across the bar, but that didn't stop Ron. He's like a pit bull on the trail of a steak.

That left *me* the third wheel to Wes and Mindy, which is the situation Ron dragged me down there to avoid in the first place. Mindy seemed all right, though. Kinda cute in a weird, computer-chat-line sort of way. She didn't say much, but I don't blame her for that. I know what it's like to be the new person in a group. It's best to sit back and take it all in at first. I guess you can't say a whole lot when you're making goo-goo eyes, anyway.

We were talking about movies—that's the kind of small talk you make with chicks—when my sixth cosmo hit me. Mindy was talking about the Hobbit movie, and I couldn't make out what she was saying. Wes must have spotted that unmistakable look on my face, because he pulled Mindy away right before I lost my hot dogs all over the table.

The bartender ran out from behind the bar and grabbed me. I tried to get away, but I could barely lift my arms.

Before I knew it, I was out on the curb. I wanted to head back in there to show that prick a thing or two, but I couldn't get up all the way. I just had to lean against a car and try to stop the spinning. Ten minutes later, Ron finally came out to drive me back to my place. I just wanted to get home without any chatter, but Ron kept going on about how I blew his big chance with the women at the other table.

I never thought a pink beverage could fuck you up so fast. I guess it was my fault, because I failed to follow the cardinal rule: Beer before liquor, never sicker. I never should've listened to Ron and gone out in the first place. Valentine's Day has always sucked, and now I have one more reason to hate it.

I called Wes and apologized for almost puking on his date. Like a true friend, he was cool with it. Even better, Ron said that Mindy didn't even rag on me. Some girls would've dragged me through the dirt for the rest of the night. Time will tell, but Wes might have found himself a decent one. ∅

Your Horoscope

By Lloyd Schumner Sr.
Retired Machinist and
A.A.P.B.-Certified Astrologer

Aries: (March 21–April 19)
God will offer a heartfelt apology to the human race for His insensitivity after creating you, an obvious human-racial caricature.

Taurus: (April 20–May 20)
Everybody starts his or her life as a tiny blastula. Thanks to a pair of mad scientists and their temporal-reversal ray, you'll be the first person to end life as one, too.

Gemini: (May 21–June 21)
You're starting to suspect that the story of how Mommy and Daddy met actually involved fewer rainbows and unicorns and more booze and Camaros.

Cancer: (June 22–July 22)
Everyone worries about what Fate has in store for them, but don't fret. You won't feel a thing.

Leo: (July 23–Aug. 22)
Tom Jones is a born showman and a true professional. He's not going to stop his whole show, even if he does see you in the audience.

Virgo: (Aug. 23–Sept. 22)
Your spouse is finally getting tired of your shit. Find some other way to spice things up in the bedroom.

Libra: (Sept. 23–Oct. 23)
After a lifetime of trying to be quixotic, you've only achieved a vague sort of windmill-otic quality.

Scorpio: (Oct. 24–Nov. 21)
This week marks a personal transformation when you're doused in kerosene, set ablaze, and somehow transformed into a beacon of hope and love.

Sagittarius: (Nov. 22–Dec. 21)
With railroads continuing their decades-long slide into obsolescence, one would think you'd be responsible for fewer locomotive crashes.

Capricorn: (Dec. 22–Jan. 19)
You have no concept of time, accountability, or common courtesy, which is only forgivable because you're a pretty house cat.

Aquarius: (Jan. 20–Feb. 18)
Well, let that be a lesson to you about going around throwing out bathwater without checking its contents first.

Pisces: (Feb. 19–March 20)
Replacing you with a machine would have been overkill. Your functions are being handled by a hideous piece of public art.

Kids In Bus Accident Mocked By Kids In Passing Bus

see LOCAL page 3C

Even Business Card Trying Too Hard

see LOCAL page 6C

Al Franken Announces New Book Project: *Ha Ha, Bush, Your Dog Is Dead*

see BOOKS page 4F

STATshot

A look at the numbers that shape your world.

Where Are We Traveling To Find Ourselves?

16% The water park
14% Place in France where the naked ladies dance
11% Carhenge
21% Gen Con
15% Nice and the isle of Greece, where we'll sip champagne on a yacht
23% Selfistan

---

the ONION®

VOLUME 40 ISSUE 09   AMERICA'S FINEST NEWS SOURCE™   4–10 MARCH 2004

Jesus Demands Creative Control Over Next Movie

HOLLYWOOD, CA—After watching Mel Gibson's *The Passion Of The Christ* Monday, Our Lord and Savior Jesus Christ announced that He will demand creative control over the next film based on His life.

"I never should have given Mel Gibson so much license," said Christ, the Son of God. "I don't like to criticize a member of the flock, but that close-up of the nails being pounded into My wrists—that was just bad."

Our Lord did not limit His criticisms to Gibson's *Passion*; He expressed frustration with historical inaccuracies in numerous film adaptations of His life.

"There have been a lot of films based on My life, and pretty much all of them have gotten it wrong," Christ said. "Just look at *Godspell*—what the heck was going on there? It's time I

see JESUS page 100

Above: Christ pans *Passion* after seeing it at a North Hollywood multiplex.

Above: Bush tries on his old uniform.

Bush To Make Up Missed National Guard Service This Weekend

WASHINGTON, DC—In a move intended to dispel criticism over his Vietnam-era military record, President Bush announced Monday that he will spend the weekend at the Sheppard Air Force Base in Wichita Falls, TX, to make up his missed National Guard service.

"My fellow Americans, let's put an end to this controversy," Bush said. "This weekend, I'll take two days off from leading the greatest nation in the world, go down to Texas, and do drills with the Texas Air National

see BUSH page 100

New Nietzschean Diet Lets You Eat Whatever You Fear Most

NEW YORK—While dieters are accustomed to exercises of will, a new English translation of Germany's most popular diet book takes the concept to a new philosophical level. The Nietzschean diet, which commands its adherents to eat superhuman amounts of whatever they most fear, is developing a strong following in America.

Fat Is Dead, proclaims the ambitious title of the dense, aphoristic nutrition plan, which was written by Friedrich Nietzsche in the late 1880s and unearthed three years ago. After reaching bestseller lists in Europe, the book was translated into English by R.J. Hollingdale and published by Avon last month.

"One must strive to eat dangerously

as one comes into the Will to Power Oneself Thin," Nietzsche wrote. "What do you fear? By this are you truly Fattened. You must embrace your Fears, as well as your Fat, and learn to Laugh as you consume them, *along with Generous Portions of Simple Salad*. Remember, as you stare into the lettuce, the lettuce stares also into you."

First formulated by Nietzsche, who felt lassitude and *weltschmerz* overcome him after a steady diet of Schopenhauer, the diet retains elements of that philosopher's "The Fruit Bowl As Will And Representation," but adds a persuasive personal challenge.

"The basics of the Nietzschean regimen are simple," Hollingdale wrote in

see DIET page 101

Above: The book, which tells dieters to "be truthful about what thinness is."

Should The U.S. Help Haiti?

President Bush has ordered the deployment of 200 marines to Port-au-Prince, Haiti to restore stability in the region. What do *you* think?

"Why should we risk our soldiers' lives when Haiti could simply raise a voodoo army of the dead and protect themselves?"

Daniel Young
Engineer

"Haiti's really small. Why don't we send that 'Army Of One' I keep hearing about on television?"

Kathleen Scott
Auditing Clerk

"These Haitians should not be asking what America can do for them, but what they can do for America."

Scott Lopez
Fabricator

"I spent a week in Tahiti with this shorty I was banging last year. I know it's a different country, but I wanted people to know I was banging a shorty as recently as a year ago."

Timothy Franks
Laborer

"Last time I checked, the Haitians were doing a pretty good job of shooting the place up on their own."

Andrew Hill
Systems Analyst

"God helps countries that help themselves."

Brenda Walker
Talent Director

The New CPR

In a major shift in the emergency care of cardiac arrest, doctors are recommending a simpler form of CPR that eliminates mouth-to-mouth breathing. What are the other changes to CPR?

▶ Pounding unconscious person's chest with rock for 20 minutes before administering care explicitly forbidden under new guidelines

▶ With mouth free, rescuers now able to shout, "You bitch, you've never given up on anything in your life. Now fight!" without interrupting aid

▶ Eli Lilly and Company to receive a payment every time a life is saved with CPR

▶ Old-fashioned, brick-and-mortar CPR to be phased out in favor of "new pulmonary" iCPR

▶ More funding to be directed toward faith-based CPR, which uses prayer to restart heart

▶ New process of emptying victims' pockets and rolling victims into traffic much easier to learn

▶ CPR providers now required to conclude all failed attempts at revival with the somber reflection, "We did all we could"

the ONION
America's Finest News Source.™

Herman Ulysses Zweibel
Founder

T. Herman Zweibel
Publisher Emeritus
J. Phineas Zweibel
Publisher
Maxwell Prescott Zweibel
Editor-In-Chief

You Are The Most Beautiful Woman In The World Who Will Sleep With Me

By Phil Babcock

Darling, I love you. You are truly the most amazing woman I'll ever lay my hands on. Could it be true, I ask myself? Is this gorgeous woman actually willing to let me have sex with her? A woman more lovely than any other woman I've ever met and been allowed to touch? The answer is yes! Of all the women on this earth, you are the single most beautiful one who is willing to let me sleep with her.

How do I love thee? Let me count the ways. You are beautiful, and you will let me sleep with you.

I have never seen a woman with such long, lustrous hair and such stunning eyes naked in person. I know deep in my heart that you possess the greatest beauty I could ever hope to find in a person willing to have sex with me.

These might sound like nothing more than honeyed words. You might think I'm merely flattering you. Nothing could be further from the truth.

> **I have never seen a woman with such long, lustrous hair and such stunning eyes naked in person. I know deep in my heart that you possess the greatest beauty I could ever hope to find in a person willing to have sex with me.**

No one on this earth is more wonderful than you—excepting, of course, the various women more beautiful than yourself who are not willing to sleep with me. But those women are neither here nor there—or, rather, they are not here.

How great is your beauty? I can describe it in a mathematical formula. Given A, the set of all women, and B, a subset of A comprising women who are willing to sleep with me, you are the most beautiful member of subset B, my darling.

Believe me, there are no other women in my life like you. None at all, my precious darling! I'd know if there were, because I would be sleeping with them. But as it stands, you are the one and only!

Oh, yes, I could chase other women, but I want no one but you. Why? Because you are more attractive than the other women I've met lately who are willing to go out with me. Yes, it's

> **Believe me, I've spent many, many hours trying to convince perfect women to date me, but they are not interested. You are. That makes you the most special woman in my world.**

true! Let me shout it from the rooftops: You are the prettiest woman in my dating range!

Sure, other women may be more superficially beautiful to others, or to myself. Their lips might be a little fuller, and their bodies just a bit nicer. Their bottom teeth might be perfectly straight, while yours are not. But those women usually will only let me fawn over them, and occasionally, drunkenly, they will let me grope them. This is why I only have eyes for you.

Believe me, I've spent many, many hours trying to convince perfect women to date me, but they are not interested. You are. That makes you the most special woman in my world.

I suppose that someday I might meet an absolutely stunning woman willing to go to bed with me. Should that day come, I would cry tears of terrible sorrow, for the unique and special bond that is our true romantic love would be torn asunder. Doubtless, I would also cry tears of joy, though, for I would be able to sleep with someone even more beautiful than you—something I hardly dreamed possible.

Though it makes my heart race to imagine sleeping with someone more beautiful than you, I'm not holding my breath. This is the real world, not some fantasyland. But I don't even mind these harsh truths, my darling! For I realize how lucky I am to have even found you. You are right here, sitting next to me, flesh and blood, and you will sleep with me. I have never been physically closer to anyone as good-looking as you.

So, let the heavens ring out. Let gentle angels sing the mighty song of our love! Yes, I am in love with a beautiful creature, one who will let me ball her! Love! ∅

Foster Mom A Cunt

SCHAUMBURG, IL—Foster parent Laurene Talley is a total cunt who always has to get into everyone else's business, 14-year-old Kristen Wenc reported Monday.

"The second I walk in the door, Laurene is on my ass about something," said Wenc, who never asked to be sent to stay with Talley in the first place. "It's such total bullshit."

The cunt, who had no right to go through Wenc's backpack, was paired with Wenc by Lutheran Child And Family Services Of Illinois in January, when Wenc's natural mother was convicted for felony drug possession and entered a long-term drug rehabilitation center to avoid a jail sentence.

Wenc, who is almost 15 and sure as hell doesn't need anyone looking after her, was doing fine by herself until some stupid social worker, Donna Piwowarski at the Illinois Department Of Child And Family Services, decided otherwise.

"The state was alerted to Kristen's need for housing on Jan. 1," said Piwowarski, the bitch. "Kristen stays with her aunt intermittently, but we were unable to contact her, nor were we able to locate any other close relatives. Kristen and I decided together that it would be best to find her a placement in a stable environment until her mother is physically and financially able to resume her care."

After four days in a temporary shelter for minors, Wenc was trucked from Chicago all the fucking way out to Schaumburg.

"Kristen is staying in the upstairs bedroom, which she's welcome to decorate however she likes," the cunt said. "We had a little bit of a rough start together, but I'm confident that she'll settle in. She may even find that she likes it here."

According to Talley, Wenc had a "somewhat combative demeanor" during her first weeks with the family. Talley said Wenc broke the windowpane in the front door when she slammed it angrily, and has had arguments with everyone from her new next-door neighbors to her teachers at school. Last week, Wenc stole a vial of cholesterol-lowering medication from the family medicine cabinet and attempted to sell individual tablets in the parking lot of an area gas station.

According to Wenc, Talley believes anyone who has anything bad to say about her, even some greaser who works at the goddamn QuikTrip.

Assisting Talley with Wenc's care is Don, Talley's total asshole husband.

"You can't imagine the horrible family situations some of these kids have had to endure," said Don, talking shit about Wenc's mom. "When you hear what they've been through, you understand a little better why they act out."

The cunt and the asshole have provided temporary care for 14 different children during their 11 years as foster parents.

"Everyone who comes to live here needs to obey the household rules," the total Nazi cunt's husband said. "Most importantly, we don't allow any drinking or drugs. None. There's a strict curfew, there's no smoking inside the house, and we don't allow any violent video games or movies. We're strict, but it's important to provide structure for these kids."

According to Wenc, Don forgot to mention a couple of Talley's enforcement techniques, like going through Wenc's room, constantly calling her school, and watching her every minute of the day. In fact, Wenc can't even make a simple phone call without the nosy bitch hanging around the kitchen listening in.

Last week, Talley went so far as to drop by Schaumburg High School unannounced to make sure that Wenc was in class.

see CUNT page 101

Above: Talley, who doesn't have to be such a bitch to Wenc (right) all the fucking time.

NEWS IN BRIEF

Virulent Strain Of Soy Flu Traced To Single Tofurkey

SAN FRANCISCO—A virulent strain of soy flu has been traced to a single tofurkey at a Bay Area food-processing factory. "An investigation of Green Earth Foods has located the bird-shaped loaf of firm bean curd from which the infection originated," said Dr. Julie L. Gerberding, director of the Centers for Disease Control and Prevention. "To prevent further spreading of the disease, all tofurkeys in Northern California are being quarantined and destroyed." Gerberding said it appears that the soy virus was not transmitted to the factory's Spaghetti & Wheatballs Microwaveable Entree division.

Masters In Writing Fails To Create Master Of Writing

PALO ALTO, CA—Despite completing all the requirements for a Masters of Fine Arts in creative writing from Stanford University in January, Jeremy Craig Kessler somehow failed to become a master of creative writing, sources reported Monday. "Mr. Kessler's short stories, all written in the style of T.C. Boyle, show little more than excellence in spelling and grammar," said literary agent David Conrad. "Somehow, Kessler advanced to the very highest level of the academic program and has only an average body of work to show for it." Photocopies of Kessler's short-story collection can be purchased at jckessler.com.

Kerry Volunteer Gets Some Kerry-Primary Victory Sex

ST. PAUL, MN—Following U.S. Sen. John Kerry's win in the Minnesota Democratic primary, campaign volunteer Ron Pelles, 24, got a little Kerry-primary victory sex off of fellow volunteer Dawn Beecher Monday. "Dawn and I were on such a *high* after Kerry took the state," Pelles said Tuesday morning. "She gave me a congratulatory hug while we were loading up the van, and there was just so much energy in the air that—*bam!*" Pelles said that he and Beecher, a political-science major at the University of St. Thomas, went back to his apartment and had intercourse twice, once with Beecher on top and once in the spoon position.

Crank Caller Keeps Jerking Local News Team Around

PLATTSBURGH, NY—The Channel 5 Action News Team was duped once again by a crank call to the WPTZ breaking-news hotline Monday. "I should have known it was too good to be true that Jared [Fogle] would be filming a commercial at the Subway on Campus Drive," reporter Graham Johnson announced from the scene of the restaurant. "I *knew* that British accent seemed familiar, but it wasn't until we'd all jumped out of the van and rushed into the Subway that I figured it out. The same guy called about the escaped ape last week." Johnson vowed never to ignore his journalistic instincts again.

Texan Feels Emotionally Empty After Chili Cook-off

EL PASO, TX—Native Texan and chili chef Jerry Gerber, 41, said he has been suffering a palpable sense of melancholy ever since the 17th Annual Five-Alarm Chili Cook-Off on Feb. 28 ended. "Spend all year gittin' together the hottest, rootin'-tootinest, mule-kickinest chili this side of the Rio Grande, and whadya git fer yer troubles?" Gerber said Tuesday. "Shucks, you eat it and then you're all hat and no horse." In lieu of seeking professional help, Gerber said he plans to force himself back into the saddle by beginning work on his entry for the Texas Beef Council Steak-A-Thon in June. ⬤

reclaim My image."

Christ said He considered returning to the physical world to make an accurate film depiction of His life for years, but seeing *The Passion* prompted Him to finally descend from heaven, meet with His agent Ronald Thatcher, and demand that He be attached as a producer on any future projects.

"Ron has a history of telling Me that the filmmakers 'totally understand' the Word Of God, and that the project is going to be 'fabulous,'" Christ said. "But when it comes out, it's all wrong, and Ron claims everything fell apart in post-production. At that point,

> **Said Jesus: "I appeared in a vision before a D-girl at Sony, and I said, 'Be not afraid, for I am Jesus— I have written a treatment and Matthew McConaughey is interested in the role of Herod.'"**

there's nothing left for Me to do but say, 'Okay, fine. I forgive you all.' Well, next time, I'll be shepherding the project through from casting to final edit to marketing."

Describing one of His biggest complaints, Christ said that no film about His life has ever "made the apostles pop."

"In *The Greatest Story Ever Told*, the 12 are basically interchangeable," Christ said. "Directors get the piety, but they don't bring out the personalities behind the agape love. Some of those guys were real cut-ups, you know. Simon Peter could make you laugh until you cried tears of blood."

In order to bring these and other truths to light, Christ teamed up with screenwriter Ron Bass, who wrote both *Snow Falling On Cedars* and *My Best Friend's Wedding*. The two have been co-writing a high-concept script, temporarily called *Untitled Jesus Project*.

"We're still hammering out the treatment, but I'm really excited about where it's headed," Christ said. "It really beefs up My relationship with John the Baptist, something all of the other movies missed. They always put in the beheading, but they leave out the quiet moments when John and I would hang out, eat locusts and honey, and talk about the redemption of Man. I think our friendship will really resonate with a lot of viewers."

Christ said He is also working on a heist film based loosely on the loaves-and-the-fishes incident, but that the project is currently stuck in development.

Above: Christ talks with directors on the set of an upcoming cable-TV miniseries about His life.

"I tend to have problems pitching to studio executives," Christ said. "Last week, I appeared in a vision before a D-girl at Sony, and I said, 'Be not afraid, for I am Jesus—I have written a treatment and Matthew McConaughey is interested in the role of Herod.' Apparently, she was a little freaked-out by the vision and she ended up passing on the idea. Ron said that next time I should just schedule a lunch meeting like everyone else."

Returning to film adaptations about His life and Word, Christ said some inaccuracies can be traced back to the source material, the New Testament.

"Remember, at the time the Good Book was written, I was running around saving souls like a madman," Christ said. "I couldn't focus on a writing project, too. I basically gave My team of writers the broad strokes and hoped inspiration would fill in the

cracks. Now, I'm not saying the New Testament isn't good—it is. It's great! But by the time I got around to reading the galleys, the monks had already finished the first printing."

The Lord Jesus did have positive things to say about Martin Scorsese's *The Last Temptation Of Christ*.

"Not only is Marty a fantastic director, but the story isn't the same old, same old," Jesus said. "It's like The Gospel of Mark filtered through an episode of *The Twilight Zone*. I love it. My one problem is with the casting of Willem Dafoe. He's good, but I think John Turturro would have made a better Me."

In spite of His love for Scorsese, Christ said He has no plans to simply make "the next *Last Temptation*."

"My movie about My life will be the greatest movie ever shown," Christ said. "It should be the last Word on

Me. No more animated versions, no more musicals, and no more movies where the scourging scene is so violent, you could put it in *Fangoria*. I mean, yes, being crucified is very painful. But I can't see devoting more than, say, three minutes of film to it."

Jesus added: "My version will have it all: drama, laughter, a spiritual message, and a couple of twists that will surprise even the most devout. The best part is that it'll be 100 percent accurate."

Continued Christ: "Even with the top-notch screenplay Ron and I are writing, I'll still need a great director to make the script shine. Unfortunately, Gore Verbinski is already committed to *Pirates Of The Caribbean 2*. If only he'd see that this movie is truly the career path for the righteous, I'd be able to get a firm commitment from Johnny Depp, too. Let us pray." *Ø*

Guard, if that'll make you happy. I can't imagine anything more important for me to do than sets of push-ups with a bunch of enlisted Guardsmen."

Added Bush: "Don't let me forget to ask Cheney to fill in for me as *leader* of the *free world*. Because I'll be busy spit-shining flight boots."

Critics claim records show that Bush was not seen by his direct military superiors from May 1972 to June 1973. The controversy, which first arose during Bush's Texas gubernatorial bid in 1994, resurfaced Jan. 17, when filmmaker Michael Moore called Bush a "deserter" at a rally for Democratic candidate Wesley Clark.

Although the White House has tried to prove that Bush fulfilled his obligations by releasing torn payroll records and evidence of a dental check-up,

many remain unconvinced. Critics have said Bush's reluctance to release his entire military file indicates that he's hiding something.

"Go ahead and wave your dusty stacks of papers, call names, and point fingers," Bush said. "I'm just going to have to be the bigger man."

Bush, whose approval numbers have declined in recent weeks, said the accusations were false, but that he was willing to do "whatever it takes to please everybody" so that he "can return to the business of governing the country."

"I had to cancel dozens of appointments with cabinet members, congressional leaders, and foreign dignitaries," Bush said. "All that stuff's going to have to wait, since this 30-year-old story is apparently a pressing national concern, or something."

White House communications director Dan Bartlett appeared on CNN with Wolf Blitzer to defend the president.

"Others want to focus on talk, but President Bush is focused on action," Bartlett said. "George Bush, whose chief priority is keeping our country safe in a post-September 11 world, believes that going down there and making up a couple days' service is the best way to finally put this issue to rest."

Retired Army Gen. John Wilcox warned Bush that his service in Alabama might have unexpected consequences.

"Once he gets there, he's an enlisted man like anybody else," Wilcox said. "A lot of other National Guard and Army reservists thought they were

see BUSH page 101

BUSH From page 100

just signing up for some tame domestic training and ended up in Iraq or Afghanistan. The president is taking a real risk here. For his sake and the sake of the nation, I hope he doesn't get shipped out."

"The president is familiar with the base in Texas, so he chose to do his service there," McClellan said. "Why would he go to some random base in Alabama that he's never even been to before?"

At a press conference Monday afternoon, a reporter asked White House press secretary Scott McClellan why Bush wasn't making up his time in Alabama, where critics say he failed to report for drills during the entire time he was working on a family friend's U.S. Senate campaign.

"Well, the president is familiar with the base in Texas, so he chose to do his service there," McClellan said. "Why would he go to some random base in Alabama that he's never even been to before? I mean—let me start over. He did serve at the Alabama base, but we felt it would be easier to accommodate travel to a base that was closer to his ranch in Crawford. Case closed." ∅

CUNT from page 99

"I was, okay?" said Wenc, who can't skip a single day of school without Talley freaking out like Wenc robbed a bank. "I hope it made her happy to waste her time checking up on me. God, I hate her so much."

In addition to riding her ass about every little thing, the old hag treats Wenc like she's some kind of a servant.

"Put this away, clean this up, wash this," Wenc said. "That's all I ever hear."

As part of her weekly chores, Wenc has to keep both bathrooms clean, vacuum the living room, do her own laundry, and make dinner every single fucking Wednesday night.

"Kristen does a great job helping out around the house," the twat said. "She still has some bad habits she needs to break, but I can already see improvement in her attitude. All she needs is a little structure."

"Well, I have to admit that the past few days haven't been so good," added Talley, who should just go fuck herself. "I found some marijuana in her backpack and had to ground her. She's been stomping around the house mad ever since."

Wenc is one of more than 20,000 minors in Illinois currently living with assholes who won't stay out of their business. ∅

DIET from page 97

the book's foreword. "The dieter exercises a painful amount of self-honesty in order to identify the primary object of his or her deepest human dread as personified by a wide-ranging group of foodstuffs. Once the dieter's Fear has been identified, he eats that food exclusively, in unlimited amounts, until the food no longer appetizes or frightens him. Having completed his gorge and transcended his fear, the dieter fasts for 20 days on water and Simple Salad. The dieter also engages in moderate metaphysical exercise, drinks eight brimming bowls of water every day, and 'opens the Gates of Dread and Fiber that remain closed to him in his Mundane Life' by taking fiber supplements."

"By conquering your Fear, by eating it in Heroic Portions, by laughing at that Fear which you have eaten, one avoids the Eternal Recurrence of cyclic 'Yo-Yo' Weight Loss and Weight Gain," Nietzsche wrote. "And in so doing, *one transcends Thinness. One discovers that he need not dwell forever on the chill, Wind-swept Borderland between Thin and Superthin.*"

Kansas City's John Mencken started the diet in January. He lost 35 pounds, eight inches from his waistline, and many of his slave moralities.

Fat Is Dead is selling briskly, as are the accompanying recipe pamphlets *Beyond Food And Evil; Human, All Too Fat A Human;* and *Swiss Steak Zarathustra.* Dieters report that they are reveling in the powerful Nietzschean weight-loss message of self-realization, transcendence, and the personal freedom to eat certain foods which are not allowed on the Atkins and South Beach diets.

"The Carbohydrate is Evil—all the wisest Men in Weight Loss have told us this," the 398-page book notes. "*Oh, Fools who would run from Evil!* What you say is true! *But Only in Evil, and the passing of Evil, does a Dieter find his Strength!* Only by eating of the Pasta and the Bread are we free! *For the Greatest Evils are necessary for Man to achieve the Weight Loss of a Superman!* As are Fasts and Fiber Tablets."

Many Nietzschean dieters are reporting success, although some complain of side effects.

Kansas City's John Mencken started the diet in January. He lost 35 pounds, eight inches from his waistline, and many of his slave moralities. He also lost the love of his life, Marissa Hapsgood, who walked out on Mencken after discovering his involvement in a romantic triangle with a poet and a sculptress.

"What makes one skinny?" Mencken said. "To contemplate as with one mind two things: great fear and great hope. For when seen through a vitamin-fortified protein shake, are they not the same thing?"

"What do you call 'bad'? Eating restricted amounts of that which shames you. What makes one most human? To spare shame to oneself," said Pete Hundmuth of Chicago, whose health and potency were severely shaken before he found the diet. "But where is your greatest danger? In pity and in sugar. By consuming pity in the form of a raw cookie dough, I am transformed.

"Behold!" Hundmuth said, casting off his bathrobe and stepping out into the cold light of his garret. "I have rid myself of your mundane, earthly, narrow concept of Love Handles!"

The Nietzschean diet has its critics.

Detractors say the diet's actual nutritional requirements are vague, that it provides no concrete plan for progression toward weight-loss targets, and that the book consists mostly of unclear and unusually harsh sets of inspirational logical lacunae.

"What makes one skinny?" Mencken said. "To contemplate as with one mind two things: great fear and great hope. For when seen through a vitamin-fortified protein shake, are they not the same thing?"

"Those on Nietzsche's diet must remember that, while discipline and mastering one's fear are desirable, the specter of a man striving willfully and joyfully against a frigid universe while drinking deep of 'life's bitter broth' will not precipitate weight loss," nutritionist Dr. Frank Stearns said. "A few more non-allegorical recipes would have been nice, too."

Stearns said it was worth noting that Nietzsche died depressed, delirious, and overweight in Zurich after 10 years of near-catatonia.

"Those wishing to begin a diet, let alone a highly moralistic pre-Freudian diet, should consult with their physicians," Stearns said. "Otherwise, they run the risk of long-term health problems—not to mention the possibility of their diet being misinterpreted by a rabidly cuisinophobic nationalist sect and used to justify a world takeover by diet Nazis." ∅

Above: A new product inspired by the Nietzschean diet.

As Departmental Manager, I Vow To Learn Each Of Your Names

By Ryan Meese

Okay, just grab a seat, Karl, and we'll get going. Okay! Good morning, everyone. Thanks for being on time. Just pull up a chair, uh, Tim. Tom? Tom. Pull up a chair, Tom. Well! I think this is a new record, right? Everyone here on time? Right, Judy? Ha ha, Ming's nodding. She knows what I mean. Okay, I wanted to assemble everyone to announce my brand-new departmental initiative. I know I've only been here a month, so you're probably all thinking, "Where does this guy get off making changes around here?" But I think you'll be on board once you hear me out. Here's the proposal: I plan to learn each and every one of your names.

That's quite a task, since there are an awful lot of you, and I am very, very busy. I am departmental manager, after all. So I hope you'll bear with me during the difficult days ahead.

Here's how I plan to go about my ambitious endeavor: I will make up mnemonic devices. For example, I will look at Ed over there and picture Ed

> **Here's how I plan to go about my ambitious endeavor: I will make up mnemonic devices. For example, I will look at Ed over there and picture Ed as a sled. Why? Because "Ed" and "sled" rhyme.**
>
> **It's easier for me to remember a name if I can make up that little bit of wordplay that connects the name with some sort of fun image.**

as a sled. Why? Because "Ed" and "sled" rhyme. It's easier for me to remember a name if I can make up that little bit of wordplay that connects the name with some sort of fun image. Many of you will know the mnemonic device I've assigned you, because I'll be referring to you by it from here on out. Got that, Ed The Sled?

Yes, this will be a lot of work, but I'm willing to go that extra mile. That's the kind of guy I am. There's nothing worse than a boss who doesn't seem to care enough to learn your name,

> **Failure to learn employee names is humiliating for the employee and embarrassing for the boss. I'm not here to humiliate you or embarrass myself. I'm here to foster a good working environment for you, the employee, through the use of your proper names.**

especially when he's going to have to dress you down from time to time.

Failure to learn employee names is humiliating for the employee and embarrassing for the boss. I'm not here to humiliate you or embarrass myself. I'm here to foster a good working environment for you, the employee, through the use of your proper names. Isn't that right, Ming Wing? When you get dressed down by me, you'll know it's by someone who respects you enough to remember your name.

Once I know your name, I'll make you feel welcome, or I'll intimidate you, by using it every time I see you. I won't start working on learning your jobs until about a year from now, but I'll be able to acknowledge you the moment I enter a room. I'll say something like "Hey, Mean Jean, what's the score?" Then I'll ask you a question about your weekend. I'll be careful to listen to your response, which I assume you'll keep brief out of respect for my time. If you're a team player, you'll appreciate the effort on my part.

Each one of you should realize that you won't be able to hide in the shadows anymore. From here on out, you're all going to be held accountable. Not like with my predecessor. He didn't learn your names, look where he is now: some other company. Okay, he may have known your names, but he was here for years. Besides, I'm learning them, too. With mnemonics. I'll try to incorporate a vague idea of what you do here into my mnemonic device, if I can.

Some of you look incredulous. Well,

fear not. It can be done. I'm talking to you, with the flag tie. I don't know your name now, but don't you worry. I will soon.

What is it, anyway? Huh? Karzi... Karzikonski? Karzonski? *Karzonski.* What is that, Polish? I'm going to have trouble with that one. I'm not too

> **What is that, Polish? I'm going to have trouble with that one.**

good with ethnic names. I'll just have to play a little game I call Ellis Island. In an affectionate way, I'll call you Zonski. Or Kar-Kar, if you'd prefer. That way, I can play off of "car." Slow down, Kar-Kar! Put the brakes on it, Kar-Kar. Kar-Kar it is.

In order to ease the transition, I'm asking each of you to write down your name, a description of yourself—please be sure to describe any marks

or pronounced features that might help me pick you out of the herd—and a few of your favorite activities, especially ones that rhyme with your name. I would love it if you'd include a photo, but if you feel that would be intrusive, especially with the heightened terror alert and so forth, then I honor your privacy. Just be very specific in your description, and we should do fine.

Also, from now on, when you come into my office or address me, I want you to say your name at the outset. Only for a month or so. After that, I should have a pretty good idea of who you are, unless you're not visiting me as much as you should be.

Anyway, Judy is handing out the ID forms right now. I'll need them back by the end of the week at the latest. Then, on Monday, I'll begin the daunting task of memorization. It's going to be a bumpy road at first, full of mistakes and awkward silences, but it'll get much better as time goes by. Okay? Ming Wing? Pat Logvitch the— we'll get you something. Good. Now, everyone get back to work. Thank you, Judy. ∅

Your Horoscope

By Lloyd Schumner Sr.
Retired Machinist and
A.A.P.B.-Certified Astrologer

Aries: (March 21–April 19)
You have greatly angered the God Of Floral Wallcoverings, but it's unclear whether this will affect you in any way.

Taurus: (April 20–May 20)
No one can deny your sassitude, but unfortunately, any advantage it carries is almost entirely cancelled out by your pet's cattitude.

Gemini: (May 21–June 21)
With luck, you might have a good 40 years with that special someone, provided he exists, and you find him really soon.

Cancer: (June 22–July 22)
Not only does time spent watching crappy television count against your time left on earth, it counts double. Don't watch any long miniseries.

Leo: (July 23–Aug. 22)
There are things you'll carry with you all the days of your life. An 80-pound bag of water-softener salt is one of them.

Virgo: (Aug. 23–Sept. 22)
Your search for deep meaning in a trite and mundane workaday world continues. Meanwhile, 3,000 people worldwide die of malaria every day, you simp.

Libra: (Sept. 23–Oct. 23)
You'll complain to the cashier and have your cold fries replaced this week. Years later, you'll look back to this event as proof that you were beyond salvation.

Scorpio: (Oct. 24–Nov. 21)
The aliens will happen upon our planet's electromagnetic transmissions just in time to catch your first-round exit from Jeopardy!

Sagittarius: (Nov. 22–Dec. 21)
You're proud that you've matured with your sense of childlike wonder intact, but others are tired of hearing you yell "Fire truck! Fire truck!" whenever one goes by.

Capricorn: (Dec. 22–Jan. 19)
You can lie to yourself all you want about your petty little life, an ability that is actually pretty valuable.

Aquarius: (Jan. 20–Feb. 18)
There are people who spend their entire lives trying to make human contact somehow. You should teach them your trick with the bat.

Pisces: (Feb. 19–March 20)
Years from now, you still won't be able to figure out why the love of your life left you for a nicer, smarter, better-looking person.

Cheney Clotheslines Aide

see WASHINGTON page 3B

Dixieland Band Evicted

see ENTERTAINMENT page 12E

St. Vincent De Paul Truck Driver Doesn't Even Care That There's Shit Falling Out Of The Back

see LOCAL page 3D

Furtive Glance Futile

see LOCAL page 10D

STATshot

A look at the numbers that shape your world.

Slowest-Spreading Celebrity Rumors

1. Courtney Love smokes menthol cigarettes
2. Fred Savage visited Costa Rica once
3. Conan O'Brien has had a lot of dental work done
4. Tommy Lee Jones is on good terms with his mother
5. Bob Balaban once lost $30 in a parking lot

THE ONION • $2.00 US • $3.00 CAN

---

the ONION

VOLUME 40 ISSUE 10   AMERICA'S FINEST NEWS SOURCE™   11–17 MARCH 2004

Special Report: CEREBRAL PALSY'S HIDDEN DARK SIDE

Urban Planner Stuck In Traffic Of Own Design

PITTSBURGH, PA—Bernard Rothstein, an urban planner and traffic-flow modulation specialist with the

Above: Rothstein contemplates traffic-flow problems.

Urban Redevelopment Authority, found himself stuck in rush-hour traffic of his own design for more than an hour Monday.

"This happens every weeknight," Rothstein said, inching through the

see TRAFFIC page 106

Work Begins On Clinton Presidential DVD Library

LITTLE ROCK, AR—The William Jefferson Clinton Presidential DVD Library is currently under construction, with the opening celebration scheduled to take place Nov. 14, the former president said Tuesday.

"The DVD library will feature an extensive collection of movies produced during my eight years in the White House," Clinton said, speaking to reporters in his Harlem office. "It will also provide the public with access to some classic re-releases and a bunch of great newer films. Did you all see *Lost In Translation*? Really beautiful movie. Some people said it was slow, but I thought it was perfect. I picked that one up at Best Buy earlier today."

The Clinton Presidential DVD Library will be located in a 27-acre city park on the south bank of the Arkansas River in Little Rock's River Market District. The 11th in a nationwide network of libraries administered by the Office of Presidential Libraries, Clinton's library will be the first devoted exclusively to movies.

"This library will be a monument to both my love of great movies and the improvement in picture quality, special-feature capabilities, and durability that the DVD standard brings," Clinton said. "Sure, VHS costs a little less, but you don't get any of the extras, like commentary tracks and deleted scenes. From an archivist's standpoint, DVD's are totally worth the money."

Clinton's DVD holdings number an impressive 97 volumes, all of which are currently housed in his den.

"I began acquiring movies last year, after Chelsea got

Above: Clinton browses the current holdings of his DVD library.

me a DVD player for my birthday," Clinton said. "She gave me Titanic with the player, and then I bought a bunch of Westerns and some great must-haves like Citizen Kane. I've got The Godfather... Forrest Gump... T3... Well, I could go on and on."

Clinton said his library

see CLINTON page 107

Milosevic Genocide Case Faltering

Legal experts said it's likely that Slobodan Milosevic will be acquitted of genocide at the conclusion of his U.N. war-crimes tribunal. What do *you* think?

"They wasted two years questioning an innocent man, and the real genocider is still out there somewhere."

Larry Robinson
Dishwasher

"All this because the witness who'd been out walking his dog couldn't say whether he saw the genocide happen at 10:15 or 10:30."

Shirley Green
Salesperson

"I'm surprised that Milosevic was able to plead his case down to 180,000 charges of vehicular manslaughter."

Frank Young
Sound Engineer

"I hope they provided him with a good rehabilitation program while he was in jail. Otherwise, he's just going to wind up committing more genocides."

Eric Nelson
Curator

"When I look in his eyes, I don't see a genocidal butcher. I see a man who needs a hug, and I'm the woman who's going to give it to him."

Anna Wright
Illustrator

"Who's his defense lawyer? 'Cause I just crushed three people in a drunken backhoe incident, and I totally don't wanna go to jail."

Josh Turner
Systems Analyst

Comanche Program Scrapped

The U.S. Army announced that it is canceling its $39 billion Comanche helicopter program. What are the reasons?

▶ Aircraft regularly exceeded Army's limit of one crash per hour of flight time

▶ Comanche vulnerable to enemy anti-aircraft fire; new helicopter will burrow underground instead

▶ Cost of aircraft exceeded total monetary value of lives it ended

▶ Program directors found out we basically beat the Communists already

▶ Aircraft's on-board pastry oven kept burning everything

▶ Concept of physically transporting combatants to war zones replaced by new "bomb everything into oblivion from safe distance" strategy

▶ Engineers bored with project, remodeling the Army kitchen instead

▶ Comanche program hit Pentagon spending limit for things that don't work

Ⓞ the ONION®
America's Finest News Source.™

Herman Ulysses Zweibel
Founder

T. Herman Zweibel
Publisher Emeritus
J. Phineas Zweibel
Publisher
Maxwell Prescott Zweibel
Editor-In-Chief

I Can Make Things Right

By Smoove B
Love Man

Baby, my world is empty since you shut me out of your life that night. Things were so good between us. Open up your heart to me once again, and I will walk in and make you feel like twice the woman you are without me. All I need is one more chance. If you would give me that chance, I know I could make things right.

If you knew what kind of pain Smoove has been in since you left, you would not be so cold. I ache so bad, girl. It is a pain of the heart and of the soul, which is the worst kind of pain. It is even worse than a headache, but I've also been getting those lately, as a result of the emotional pain.

Sometimes, in the middle of the night, I wake up in my circular, red canopy bed and realize that you're not lying there beside me. I cry out, "Baby, why aren't you here in bed with me?" I sometimes think that you are somewhere within my penthouse apartment, perhaps in the bathroom or out on the couch watching Jay Leno, and that you will hear my plea and come back to me. But you never are.

> **Throughout the meal, I will refill your crystal wineglass with only the finest wine known to the South American regions. You will never need to touch the bottle, unless you want to look at the drawing on the label. Did I mention that Ralph Tresvant will be playing on the stereo during dinner? He will be. This is a promise.**

Other times, when it's raining outside, I walk the streets without an umbrella, because I have not cared how my hair looks since you left. The only thing in this world that brought me warmth is gone and won't return my multiple voicemail messages.

Come back to me, girl. Don't you realize that I am the one for you, and you are the one for me? We were meant for each other. The finest craftsmen in Europe could not carve two wooden items to fit together as well as we do. If people were to see us in a fine museum or someplace, they would think we were one item. From a distance, we would look like a single object, and only upon closer examination could anyone notice the line where we were joined. A lot of

> **I sometimes think that you are somewhere within my penthouse apartment, perhaps in the bathroom or out on the couch watching Jay Leno, and that you will hear my plea and come back to me. But you never are.**

people still would not be able to see the line, and would need others to point it out for them. They would have to take off their glasses to look for it. That is the way it is when we're together. Damn.

Come to my penthouse apartment this evening, or, if you absolutely cannot make it because you're busy, some other evening in the near future. I will show you a night that will surpass your wildest romantic fantasies. I will wear my crimson silk pajama bottoms and robe, but neglect to wear the matching shirt, so as to show off my chest and abdomen.

I will make you a sumptuous dinner of duck, wild rice, and baby carrots. Butter will be available for all three, but it will be placed on the side. You may butter to your heart's content, but I will not presume that you like a lot of butter. Throughout the meal, I will refill your crystal wineglass with only the finest wine known to the South American regions. You will never need to touch the bottle, unless you want to look at the drawing on the label. Did I mention that Ralph Tresvant will be playing on the stereo during dinner? He will be. This is a promise.

After dinner, I will take you to my patio and hold you from behind as we look out into the night. I will kiss your beautiful neck and shoulders while the wind blows through your hair. I will point out constellations in the sky and tell you which ones remind me of you.

Then I will put my sting in you sideways.

I will give it to you all night long and into the dawn, taking you to unexplored

see SMOOVE page 108

Cool Dad A Terrible Father

PORTLAND, OR—Terrible father Peter Nesmith is the absolute coolest, neighborhood children reported Monday.

"Tommy's dad is so awesome," said David York, 9, a friend of Nesmith's 7-year-old son Thomas. "He's not like the other dads who yell at you all the time. Everyone brings their fireworks to blow them off in his backyard. If we run out of matches, he lets us use his

> "When Mrs. Nesmith went to visit her sister last summer, Tommy got to eat Burger King every single night for the whole two weeks," York said. "He got to order whatever he wanted. He even got to ride his bike all the way over to Cortland Avenue to pick it up one night."

cigarette to light them off."

Added York: "He's the only dad that treats us like adults and not like little babies who can't be trusted with an electric sander."

Nesmith, who married Karen

Reynolds in 1990, is the father of three children besides Thomas: Evan, 10; Kevin, 13; and Julia, 15. Soon after moving into the quiet North Portland neighborhood, Nesmith cemented his cool-dad reputation by buying a 1974 Camaro, the costly upkeep of which forced the Nesmith family to cancel its dental insurance earlier this year.

"Before the Super Bowl, Mr. Nesmith let me ride in his Camaro to go to the gas station and help him carry bags of ice," York said. "Mrs. Nesmith doesn't want us riding in it, because it has a gas leak, but Mr. Nesmith said if he listened to Mrs. Nesmith, he wouldn't even have the awesome car in the first place."

"When Mrs. Nesmith went to visit her sister last summer, Tommy got to eat Burger King every single night for the whole two weeks," York said. "He got to order whatever he wanted. He even got to ride his bike all the way over to Cortland Avenue to pick it up one night."

Neighborhood parents are less complimentary. Several have complained about the beer parties that Nesmith allows his eldest son Kevin to host in his basement.

"Boys are gonna drink," Nesmith said when asked about the keg parties. "At least I know they're safe if they're right there in the basement."

Neighbors have said they suspect that Nesmith purchases alcohol for the boys.

"I don't buy Kevin and his friends beer, but I do usually have a tapped keg set up in the basement fridge," Nesmith said. "I don't see what people

Above: Nesmith, his wife, and his son Kevin.

get so worked up about. If the kids get sick, they can spend the night here. I'm the one who has to deal with a bunch of hungover 13-year-olds."

Added Nesmith: "It's not like it's on a school night, usually."

Kevin's friend Tony Shadid said his parents are among those who complain about Nesmith.

"Mom's always yelling at us to do better in school so we don't turn out like Kevin's dad," Shadid said. "I don't know why. He doesn't look so bad to me. He's got a super-huge stereo and his own room in the basement with

posters on the wall and a leather couch."

According to his children, Nesmith leaves the role of disciplinarian to his wife.

"Dad always says he didn't do good in school and he turned out fine," Kevin said. "He said he never really did homework and only went to class half the time. That's because it's way more important to get out in the world and get life experience. Dad mostly talks about all the drinking he did back then, but I think he also worked

see DAD page 106

Automated Teller Has More Personality Than Human Teller

SEATTLE—Waugh Street Washington Mutual's new ATM has more personality than Janine Byrd, one of the branch's human tellers, sources reported Tuesday. "Don't forget to take your cash, Kyle. Would you like a receipt today?" asked the ATM's full-color, animated screen after the machine dispensed $40. "No? Have a nice day, then. Thanks, Kyle!" By contrast, every customer waited on by the tired-looking Byrd was greeted with the same monotone delivery of "Hello. How may I help you today?"

Republicans Retain Majority In Household

OMAHA, NE—In spite of a vocal Democratic following among the 16-year-old son and 12-year-old daughter

demographics, Republicans managed to retain a slim majority in the Sanderson family, front-door exit polls revealed Monday. "Fortunately, strong Republican support among 48-year-old fathers and 46-year-old mothers won over the key swing vote among 6-year-olds named Timmy," speaker of the household Donald Sanderson said. "This, combined with the traditional Republican stronghold among visiting, over-60 grandparents, allowed Republicans to maintain control." The GOP has held the majority in the Sandersons' last 37 Sunday dinners.

Dog Trying Its Absolute Hardest

INDIANAPOLIS, IN—Woofers, the Eli family's high-spirited, 3-year-old Scottish terrier, is trying his absolute hardest at everything he does, family sources reported Monday. "Look at him," wife Jen Eli said as Woofers presented her with a tennis ball for the 22nd time that hour. "His tongue's out, his tail's wagging, he's bouncing all over the place trying to please us. There's only so much that a dog can accomplish, but Woofers is trying his best." Eli's utterance of the word "Woofers" spurred a frenzy of irrelevant leaping.

Study: 58 Percent Of U.S. Exercise Televised

WASHINGTON, DC—According to a new Department of Health and Human Services study, 58 percent of all exercise performed in the U.S. is broadcast on television. "Of the 3.5 billion push-ups performed in 2003, 2.03 billion took place on exercise shows on the Lifetime Network and ESPN3 or fitness segments on *Good Morning America*," the study read. "The abundance of TV exercise would create the impression that America is a healthy society, if everyone didn't already know that we're a bunch of disgusting, near-immobile spectators." The DHHS study also indicated

that 99.3 percent of the nation's Soloflex workouts are televised.

Every Song On Radio Reminds Man Of Red Sox Loss

BOSTON—Every song on the radio reminds Red Sox fan Patrick O'Malley of the team's loss to the New York Yankees in Game 7 of the 2003 American League Championship Series. "'One Call Away' on 94.5 reminded me of how [manager] Grady Little's call kept Pedro Martinez on the mound in the eighth," O'Malley said Monday. "So I flipped over to 97.9, but then Van Halen's 'Poundcake' reminded me of how Yankee batter Aaron Boone pounded Tim Wakefield's knuckleball over the fence." O'Malley then switched to AM radio, where a farm report reminded him of that corndog he threw on the ground when Boone crossed home plate in the game's 11th inning. ∅

105

TRAFFIC from page 103

Allegheny Center district he designed in 1987. "When will I learn to avoid this part of town during rush hour?"

The gridlock-bound Rothstein, who has worked in urban planning for 24 years, passed the time by devising

> ## "A direct path to I-279 and wider on-ramps would have helped, for starters," Rothstein said, drumming his fingers on the steering wheel. "Sure, a six-lane street wouldn't look as nice as that tree-lined square with the fountain—Jesus, lady! Move!—but with six lanes, I wouldn't be sitting here breathing fumes."

possible modifications to his original design.

"A direct path to I-279 and wider on-ramps would have helped, for starters," Rothstein said, drumming his fingers on the steering wheel. "Sure, a six-lane street wouldn't look as nice as that tree-lined square with the fountain—Jesus, lady! Move!—but with six lanes, I wouldn't be sitting here breathing fumes."

While attempting to nose his Lexus GS 300 into a line of honking cars, Rothstein brainstormed more solutions to his current predicament.

"With more lanes, tourists wouldn't have to cut across commuter traffic to get from the area around the Buhl Planetarium and the Institute Of Popular Science down to the Three Rivers area to buy hot wings at those crappy jazz clubs," Rothstein said. "You might have thought of that, genius. After all, you're the one who convinced them to re-zone it commercial. Moron."

Added Rothstein: "Who wants a shopping area in—move your ass, blue Taurus! Come on! Who wants a shopping area in an access-limited waterway confluence, anyway? Oh, yeah: the genius Bernie Rothstein!"

As Pittsburgh, America's steel capital, made the transition to high-tech and service industries in the 1980s, many thought its rusting, blighted urban landscape was obsolete. According to Rothstein, it was then that the Urban Redevelopment Authority, along with several private urban-planning firms, began the slow process of rethinking the city's roads, parks, and commercial and residential districts. Today, the city's designers are regular-

ly lauded for their elegant, modern buildings and stuck in traffic of their own making for hours at a time.

Abandoning his plan to get on the interstate with a hasty U-turn, Rothstein explained that he was also part of the eight-person team that created Crawford Square, an 18-acre residential development on the eastern edge of downtown Pittsburgh.

"Crawford Square is a pedestrian-oriented neighborhood with a large public recreation center, a three-mile jogging trail, and residents with a wide range of incomes," Rothstein said. "Green space is great. It felt wonderful to turn four defunct foundries into a park-lined community with access to downtown. Would've been even better to turn it into a community lined with, say, 85 percent of the existing parkland and a few more goddamned dedicated turn lanes."

Hastily executing two left turns to re-enter the interstate on-ramp, Rothstein described the Three Rivers traffic hub. He said he considers the hub—with its long, flowing, elevated contours and broad, boulevard-lined access ways—an aesthetic triumph, as well as "a complete bitch to navigate."

"Medium-interval on-ramp traffic lights, my ass," Rothstein said. "Very nice sweeping compound curves on the bridge thoroughfares, Bernie. They're very fluid—unlike the traffic stuck in them right now."

Rolling down a window and shaking a fist at the traffic ahead, Rothstein said: "This is about that Route 28 thing, isn't it, God? If I promise to put in more

> ## "It felt wonderful to turn four defunct foundries into a park-lined community," Rothstein said. "Would've been even better to turn it into a community lined with, say, 85 percent of the existing parkland and a few more goddamned dedicated turn lanes."

HOV concessions, will you please get things moving here already?"

A cell-phone call from Rothstein's wife Marjorie interrupted the angry tirade.

"Well, I'm sorry it's taking so long, Bernie," Marjorie said. "But remember, honey, that you're the one who said I-279 was a horrible scar gouged into the city for the sake of efficiency. It was your own enthusiasm for small, two- to eight-acre city parks that made Pittsburgh a nicer place to live and got you into this mess." ∅

DAD from page 105

part-time at a machine shop or something."

Nesmith said he believes it's important to prepare his children for the "real world." In accordance with that belief, he gave his daughter Julia a condom Saturday before her date with a boy who was too scared to hold her hand. That same night, he let Evan watch the sexually explicit Monster's Ball while Kevin browsed his father's pornography stash in the garage.

"Kids need to learn about sex sometime," Nesmith said. "Otherwise, they'll just learn a bunch of fucked-up information about it on the street."

"Don't worry," he added. "I keep the real rough stuff hidden."

Neighbor and father of two Jerry Helms said he thinks Nesmith is an "all-right guy," but said he was mystified by the adoration the neighborhood children heap on the terrible father.

"Whenever my son Jeff comes back from playing with Tommy, he's always saying, 'Mr. Nesmith let us do this, Mr. Nesmith let us do that,'" Helms said. "He loves the guy, but sometimes I wonder. I always think of the time Tommy cut himself on a rusty nail and Pete sent him back to playing

without doing anything about it."

Helms said he asked Nesmith if he was worried about Tommy getting an

> ## Neighbor and father of two Jerry Helms said he thinks Nesmith is an "all-right guy," but said he was mystified by the adoration the neighborhood children heap on the terrible father.

infection or even lockjaw, but Nesmith just laughed.

"Pete said said that lockjaw would toughen Tommy up," Helms said. "He said he doesn't like to baby his kids."

Added Helms: "I didn't argue with him about it. I didn't want him to think I was some sort of wuss." ∅

FOOTRUB from page 42

unusually large amounts of blood. Passersby were amazed by the unusually large amounts of blood. Passersby were

amazed by the unusually large amounts of blood. Passersby were amazed by the unusually large amounts of blood. Passersby were amazed by the unusually large amounts of blood. Passersby were amazed by the unusually large amounts of blood. Passersby were

> ## You can take my word for it: There is nothing for you in this sack.

amazed by the unusually large amounts of blood. Passersby were amazed by the unusually large amounts of blood. Passersby were amazed by the unusually large amounts of blood. Passersby were amazed by the unusually large amounts of blood. Passersby were amazed by the unusually large amounts of blood. Passersby were amazed by the unusually large amounts of blood. Passersby were amazed by the unusually large amounts of blood. Passersby were amazed by the unusually large amounts of blood. Passersby were amazed by the unusually large amounts of blood. Passersby were amazed by the unusually large amounts of blood. Passersby were amazed by the unusually large amounts of blood. Passersby were amazed by the unusually large amounts of blood. Passersby were amazed by the unusually large amounts of blood. Passersby were amazed by the unusually large amounts of blood. Passersby were amazed by the unusually large amounts of blood. Passersby were amazed by the unusually large amounts of blood. Passersby were amazed by the unusually large amounts of blood. Passersby were amazed by the unusually large amounts of blood. Passersby were amazed by the unusually large

see FOOTRUB page 127

will "truly be a place of education" due to his eclectic tastes in film.

"Movies teach us how to live and how to laugh," Clinton said. "That's so important. Just last week, I re-watched Spike Lee's *Do The Right Thing*. Man, I'd forgotten what a great movie that was. It fully renewed my commitment to racial, ethnic, and religious reconciliation."

"I have all different kinds of movies—action, drama, comedy," Clinton said. "I have the entire

> "I asked my assistant to print out some of those AFI lists," Clinton said. "Also, I've been asking my buddies for suggestions. Janet [Reno] told me I should get *Glengarry Glen Ross*, so I'm going to order it on Amazon. I know it's a little risky to buy a movie without having seen it, but it'd be a waste of money to rent it if I'm just going to end up buying it for the library anyway."

Kubrick box set and a Hitchcock set, too. I also have the season-spanning box sets for some TV shows like *King Of The Hill*, because those are good to relax with if you don't have time to watch a whole movie."

In spite of his impressive array of DVDs, Clinton said he plans to increase his holdings before his library opens to the public in November.

"My collection needs a little rounding out," Clinton said. "I really like independent films and foreign films, but right now, I don't have many of those. I want to get some subtitled Bergman-type stuff and some movies by—what's his name? The guy who did *Twin Peaks*."

Clinton has declared it a priority to acquire new volumes in the coming months. He said his goal is to add at least 300 movies to the library by opening day.

"I asked my assistant to print out some of those AFI lists," Clinton said. "Also, I've been asking my buddies for suggestions. Janet [Reno] told me I should get *Glengarry Glen Ross*, so I'm going to order it on Amazon. I know it's a little risky to buy a movie without having seen it, but it'd be a waste of money to rent it if I'm just going to end up buying it for the li-

Above: Clinton chooses six new DVDs for his Presidential Library and gets one absolutely free.

brary anyway."

Clinton outlined his vision for the collection.

"My DVD library will be a tour of the films that shaped me intellectually, taught me about the human condition, and showed me worlds I'd never have seen without cinema," Clinton said. "Also, I'll include the movies that just rocked me, like my all-time favorite, *High Noon*."

Award-winning architect James Polshek designed the building that will house the DVD library.

"Mr. Clinton had a very clear vision for the library," Polshek said. "He said he wanted it to be a place where people would feel comfortable. He specifically asked me to limit the amount of natural light inside the museum, and to find a bunch of comfy couches."

Clinton elaborated on the design.

"The individual viewing carrels will be equipped with 32-inch plasma televisions and top-of-the-line Sennheiser headphones," Clinton said. "The library's main auditorium will have 5.1 Dolby Surround Sound and stadium seating. Can't you imagine how great it will be to come and watch *Jurassic Park* with all your buddies? That scene where they crest the hill and see the brontosauruses? Remember?"

Added Clinton: "I know my library is not in competition with the others, but I do believe Americans will enjoy the experience more than they'd like peering at Gerald Ford's desk calendar through Plexiglas."

The library will be organized by genre, and will use a computerized cataloguing system. Visitors will be able to search for movies by title, director, cast, or famous lines.

"If you type in 'Show me the money,' it'll bring up *Jerry Maguire* and say where to find the movie," Clinton said. "What a boon for future generations."

Clinton said he will personally rate each movie in the collection, but due to time constraints, he will only write full reviews of his absolute favorite movies. Once the museum opens, Clinton will also choose 10 new must-see films for the President's Picks shelf every month.

In spite of Clinton's wishes, concessions will not be sold in the library. ✒

COMMUNITY AWARDS

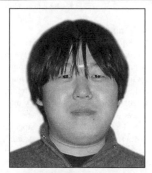

The Illinois Young Author Of The Year Award, to insufferably self-absorbed little bastard **Eugene Ong**, 12.

Most Uneventful Parole, 3-7 Years, to **Hunter Crawford**, 31.

The First English Lutheran Church Good Citizen Award, to **Dylan Pryor**, 7, for going rollerskating with a bunch of retards every Thursday.

World's Greatest Angler, to **Bud Simms**, 62, in T-shirt form.

Ask Kenneth Cole

By Kenneth Cole

Your Horoscope

By Lloyd Schumner Sr.
Retired Machinist and
A.A.P.B.-Certified Astrologer

Dear Kenneth Cole,

I just moved to Houston, and so far, I've had a hard time making friends. I tried hanging out in the coffee shops and going to the bars, but all the people I met seemed wrapped up in their own busy lives. I love the city, but I don't have anyone to enjoy it with. What's a lonely girl to do?

Holed Up In Houston

Dear Holed Up:

Let there be shoes.

—Kenneth Cole

Dear Kenneth Cole,

I've had Lacy, my wirehaired fox terrier, for 11 years now. That means that she's 77 in dog years! I'm 63 myself and planning on retiring to Florida soon, but I worry that Lacy won't be able to handle the change. It's hard enough to leave my friends behind, much less my beloved pup. On the other hand, I don't want to be kept on a leash by Lacy. What should I do?

Befuddled In Bedford

Dear Befuddled:

Self-confidence isn't made, it's worn.

—Kenneth Cole

Dear Kenneth Cole,

Last week, my wife Laura asked if I was interested in experimenting in the bedroom, and I said "sure." Now I think I made a mistake. I came home yesterday and found a

Self-confidence isn't made, it's worn.

box of risqué board games! How can I tell my sweetie that I'm not up for the games without hurting her feelings?

In Over My Head In Indianapolis

Dear Over My Head:

After the storm comes the makeover.

—Kenneth Cole

Dear Kenneth Cole,

My son Jason applied for college this year, and the suspense is killing him. Jason is a great kid and a loving son, but to be honest, his grades could be better. There's a real chance that he might not get into any of his first-pick schools. Is there a way to lower his expectations while still showing him that I believe in him?

Realistic In Redmond

To love and win is the best thing. To love and lose, the next best. After that, it's all shoes.

Dear Realistic:

No one on their deathbed says they wish they'd spent more time in pleated pants.

—Kenneth Cole

Dear Kenneth Cole,

A few weeks ago, my boyfriend Ryan and I ended a nine-month relationship when we realized we weren't ready to get serious. The time apart was going well until I started to have dreams about him. I think my unconscious mind might be telling me to give it another shot. Are the dreams a wake-up call, or is getting back together a nightmare of an idea?

Confused In Cambridge

Dear Confused:

Be genuine. Wear leather.

—Kenneth Cole

Dear Kenneth Cole,

My 28-year-old son Eli has been dating a wonderful girl for three years now, and the whole family is wondering when he's going to pop the question! I keep dropping hints and telling him stories about other happily married people his age. Today on the phone, I even told him the story of how his father proposed to me! I don't want to come right out and ask him, lest I seem pushy, but inquiring minds want to know!

**Pushing For Proposal
In Pittsburgh**

Dear Pushing:

Appearances may be deceiving. Work it.

—Kenneth Cole

Dear Kenneth Cole,

I dropped a broken radio off at the repair center, but when I went to pick it up, they claimed they didn't have it. I don't have any proof, but I think the counter girl stole it. I asked to see the manager, but he said he couldn't do anything about it. Here's my question: Do I have a right to be mad at the manager for something one of his employees did?

Suitless In Sacramento

Aries: (March 21–April 19)
You say you're not a cat person, but the graceful movements, the purring, and the fur give you away.

Taurus: (April 20–May 20)
You will be fired for abusing your lighthouse-keeper position when passing ship captains grow weary of your sky-spanning vacation slides.

Gemini: (May 21–June 21)
You never thought smoking in the forest endangered you, but that was before an angry Smokey decided to stop fucking around about the fire-prevention thing.

Cancer: (June 22–July 22)
You have a right to be happy, but that might not outweigh the feelings of the dozens who so enjoy your misery.

Leo: (July 23–Aug. 22)
The truth is indeed elusive, hard to comprehend, and subjective. What we're trying to say is: You're fat.

Virgo: (Aug. 23–Sept. 22)
Uninvolved bystanders will witness your crime, but due to its graphic nature, they can no longer be considered "innocent."

Libra: (Sept. 23–Oct. 23)
The stars, in their infinite variety, indicate both romance ahead for lucky Libra and the approximate age of the universe for competent astronomers.

Scorpio: (Oct. 24–Nov. 21)
You've always been a fashion-forward trendsetter, which is why, after next Thursday, they'll all be saying that getting shot in the face is the new black.

Sagittarius: (Nov. 22–Dec. 21)
Americans are tired of politics as usual, but no one ever gets tired of unanimous bipartisan actions against you.

Capricorn: (Dec. 22–Jan. 19)
Your personal tragedy will make people stop and think about how it's equally tragic to die two days after retirement.

Aquarius: (Jan. 20–Feb. 18)
There's no sense cutting costs when it comes to hiring a personal trainer, if your back-breaking weeks of helping people move are any guide.

Pisces: (Feb. 19–March 20)
Gradual, almost imperceptible change will make you a better person over the course of the next 37,000 years.

Dear Suitless:

To love and win is the best thing. To love and lose, the next best. After that, it's all shoes.

—Kenneth Cole

Dear Kenneth Cole,

My wife and I have been thinking about remodeling our bathroom, but the last time we renovated, it caused so many arguments that we almost split up! Looking back, we know the arguments were meaningless, but all the same, the whole experience was awful. Still, our bathroom could really use some work—maybe even one of those whirlpool bathtubs. Should we take the plunge and risk sending our marriage down the drain?

Apprehensive In Appleton

Dear Apprehensive:

Every sweater happens for a reason.

—Kenneth Cole

Kenneth Cole is a syndicated columnist whose weekly advice column, Ask Kenneth Cole, appears in more than 250 newspapers nationwide. ✆

SMOOVE from page 104
regions of passion. We will grind our way through uncharted lands peopled by gentle natives who are receptive to our message of peace and sexmaking.

In the morning, hot biscuits and gravy will be available.

Do you remember what it was like to be held in Smoove's strong and gentle arms? Don't you miss the feeling? I would give almost anything to be able to hold you one more time, if only for 30 seconds. Of course, I would prefer to hold you for a much longer amount of time.

Only you can make me feel like a whole man again. Being half of a Smoove is not enough. Let me be whole again. I am begging you. I will never do you wrong again.

Come back to Smoove.

You have my cell-phone number. I have the phone on me at all times, and I am careful to keep the battery charged. If I don't pick up, I probably lost my signal temporarily, but will be back in range shortly, so make sure to leave a message.

Please, girl, call. ✆

Apparently Soccer Player Just Did Something Really Good

see SPORTS page 5D

British Girl Exotic Enough

see PEOPLE page 6C

Song From Area Man's Past Comes Back To Rock Him

see LOCAL page 13B

STATshot

A look at the numbers that shape your world.

At What Point On St. Patrick's Day Did We Pass Out?

19% Five seconds into the River Dancing

21% Just as we were finally getting stop sign out of the ground

17% After ordering round for entire bar, before paying

20% When Cardinal Egan delivered third roundhouse to the head

23% Around 6 p.m., again at 11:55 p.m.

THE ONION • $2.00 US • $3.00 CAN

---

the ONION®

VOLUME 40 ISSUE 11   AMERICA'S FINEST NEWS SOURCE™   18–24 MARCH 2004

Rumsfeld Hosts No-Holds-Barred Martial Arts Tournament At Remote Island Fortress

FANG ISLAND—U.S. Secretary of Defense Donald Rumsfeld has opened his fortified island headquarters to participants in his second no-holds-barred martial arts tournament, the enigmatic mastermind announced Monday.

"Warriors of the world, hear me," said Rumsfeld, seated on the onyx throne overlooking the fighting arena at the island's central volcano, surrounded by a phalanx of exotic but murderous beauties and his seven-foot-tall guard Omarra. "I declare the Eagle Fist all-styles, hand-to-hand combat world championship open once more. For the next 10 days, the world's mightiest fighters will come together here at Fang Island to compete for a prize of $1 million and the post of Associate Secretary Of Full-Contact Defense!"

Rumsfeld then declared the tournament open by symbolically shattering a block of obsidian with his prosthetic dragon's claw—the powerful weapon grafted onto his right wrist after 2003 champion Li severed his hand with manji butterfly swords.

"Who can deny that conflict is a purifying flame

see TOURNAMENT page 112

Above: Rumsfeld's Fang Island headquarters.

Best Man Has No Idea Why He Was Picked

GREENSBORO, NC—Although he has had a cordial relationship with officemate Karl Harrison for almost two years, Jeff Ashland reported Monday that he has no idea why he was asked to be the best man at Harrison's wedding in June.

"It's an honor, I suppose," Ashland said from his cubicle at Whitehead Consulting. "I just wish I knew why it fell to me. Karl went to college just down the road, and he's lived in Greensboro for five years or so. He must have met at least a few other guys during all that time, right? But *I'm* the one he chooses to be his right-hand man on the biggest day of his life?"

Harrison asked Ashland to be his best man on Mar. 12, the same day he publicly announced his engagement to his girlfriend of four years, Tracy Newman. Ashland said he had trouble feigning the joy expected of someone assuming such an honor.

"Karl came up to me with this big grin on his face, so I figured his business card was picked out of the fishbowl at the Gumbo Pot again,"

Above: Ashland, the best-man-to-be.

Ashland said. "But he told me he'd proposed to his girlfriend the night before. As I was congratulating him, trying desperately to remember Tracy's name, he dropped the bomb. He said it'd be 'awesome' if I'd be his best man. At first I thought he was making

see BEST MAN page 113

Citizens Form Massive Special Disinterest Group

LAWRENCE, KS—More than 3,000 U.S. citizens have banded together to form a massive special disinterest group, Coalition Of Unconcerned Americans press secretary Sarah Fisher said Tuesday.

"Politicians are completely out of touch with those Americans who are completely out of touch with politics," Fisher said. "Why is Congress always debating foreign policy and tariffs and social security and stuff? How can they

American Focus

see DISINTEREST page 113

The Madrid Train Bombings

Madrid is still searching for answers after the worst terrorist attack in Spanish history. What do *you* think?

"What kind of Muslims are the Basques? They're not Muslims? Then why would they blow stuff up?"

Albert Douglas
Systems Analyst

"Man, maybe we should have tried to track down Osama bin Laden after Sept. 11."

Roger Carter
Deliveryman

"Wow, a real-life *Guernica*."

Ann Collins
Chef

"And now, yet another healing process begins."

Henry Sanchez
Cleaner

"Bush is definitely going to get the Spanish vote in November."

Janet Campbell
Teacher Assistant

"The question is, 'Was it al Qaeda or the Basques?' And if it's the latter, the question becomes, 'Now, who are the Basques, again?'"

Walter Morris
Author

Return Of *Dawn Of The Dead*

A remake of the '70s horror film *Dawn Of The Dead* hits theaters this weekend. What changes were made in the new version?

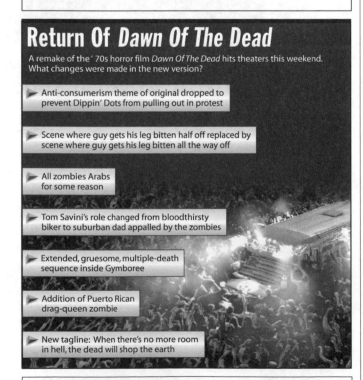

➤ Anti-consumerism theme of original dropped to prevent Dippin' Dots from pulling out in protest

➤ Scene where guy gets his leg bitten half off replaced by scene where guy gets his leg bitten all the way off

➤ All zombies Arabs for some reason

➤ Tom Savini's role changed from bloodthirsty biker to suburban dad appalled by the zombies

➤ Extended, gruesome, multiple-death sequence inside Gymboree

➤ Addition of Puerto Rican drag-queen zombie

➤ New tagline: When there's no more room in hell, the dead will shop the earth

America's Finest News Source.™

Herman Ulysses Zweibel
Founder

T. Herman Zweibel
Publisher Emeritus
J. Phineas Zweibel
Publisher
Maxwell Prescott Zweibel
Editor-In-Chief

Your Dog Is In Heaven Now, With No One To Feed Him

By Mary Othmar

Come over here and sit on Mommy's lap. I've got some bad news, Tommy. Are you ready? Tommy, while you were at school today, Sparky got out of the backyard and ran in front of a truck. I rushed him to the vet, but there was nothing she could do.

I'm so sorry, honey. I know that you loved Sparky very much, but I'm afraid he's gone to Doggie Heaven. Remember learning about Heaven in Sunday school? Doggie Heaven is like that, but there are no people there, because it's a place for dogs to spend forever, romping and playing with other dogs.

Hmm, that's a good question, honey. I don't know who's going to feed Sparky. I guess no one.

Don't cry, Tommy. You shouldn't be sad. Doggie Heaven is a wonderful place where all the dogs nap in the sun on big cloud mattresses all day. And every dog has his own big food bowl with his name engraved on it. But I suppose you're right: Sparky's bowl will be empty, because you won't be there to fill it. Eventually, he'll probably get so hungry he'll try gnawing off his own tail, just to do something to try to stop the pain in his belly.

Doggie Heaven has big, green fields for romping, and Sparky can chase all the rabbits and squirrels he wants. Everywhere you look, there are all kinds of rubber toys. But he'll probably be so hungry that he'll tear the rubber toys apart and eat them. Then he'll throw up, just like the time he ate the potpourri. I imagine he'll try to eat his own vomit, and then the angels up there will smack him with a rolled-up newspaper for being a bad dog.

Of course Doggie Heaven has angels! They're God's special friends. The angels play harps for the dogs and make sure they don't jump the fence into cat heaven. Do you remember when Grandma died, and we told you about St. Peter? He's the one who knows who's been good and who's been bad, just like Santa. But instead of presents, St. Peter lets people into Heaven. That's a nice idea, honey, but he's much too busy to feed little boys' dogs.

Why don't the angels feed Sparky? Because he's your dog. Remember how you begged us to get him from the pet store, and we didn't think you were ready for the responsibility? Remember how you prayed that you'd be able to get Sparky and promised that if we brought him home, you'd be the one to feed and walk him every single day? Well, Tommy, you made a promise, and God will hold you to it, no matter how much Sparky howls and whimpers. I wouldn't be surprised if God chains Sparky outside until he learns how to be quiet, which might be a long time. You remember how spunky Sparky was. That was part of the reason that we loved him, wasn't it? Sparky had character, but God likes obedience. He won't take kindly to a dog with an attitude.

Of course Sparky is going to miss you! He was your best friend, and he's

> Doggie Heaven has big, green fields for romping, and Sparky can chase all the rabbits and squirrels he wants. Everywhere you look, there are all kinds of rubber toys. But he'll probably be so hungry that he'll tear the rubber toys apart and eat them. Then he'll throw up, just like the time he ate the potpourri.

up there right now with a ball in his mouth, waiting for you to play catch with him. When you go to Heaven and are an angel yourself, you'll be able to visit him and play with him all you like, unless he's gone crazy from malnutrition and tries to eat your face off when he sees you. Well, that is, if he still has eyes. He may have already clawed them out in hunger.

But you can't feed Sparky from here. You're still alive and Sparky is an angel dog. You can fill up his bowl down here all you want, but he's up there and can't get to it. The delicious smell of Ken-L Ration wafting up to Heaven won't do anything but make Sparky hungrier.

No, Sparky won't be able to die. He's in heaven, you silly-billy. You can't die in Heaven. Even if Sparky asks another dog whom he trusts to tear his throat open, or deliberately twists his neck between the bars on the pearly gates, or chokes down some sticks in an attempt to puncture his aching tummy, he still won't *be able* to die. Sparky will just keep on living forever, wondering why you aren't feeding him. That's how Heaven is. ∅

Raving Lunatic Obviously Took Some Advanced Physics

STANFORD, CA—Known throughout the community for his verbal outbursts and his shopping cart full of trash, area street denizen "Cosmic Stan" must have studied advanced physics at some point, sources reported Monday.

"Where's my cheese? Don't take my rowboat! Got no room!" the lunatic screamed from his regular spot near the Campus Drive bus stop. "I need space! Gimme space! Infinite dimensional separable Hilbert space!"

Though his rants seem nonsensical to most passersby, some astute listeners say they contain evidence of higher learning.

"I'd always see him around that bus stop, dressed in his ragged wool clothes, duct-taped shoes, and that plastic sheeting covered over with symbols drawn in magic-marker," Stanford Ph.D. candidate James Willard said. "Then, a few days ago, he was out there waving his tin-foil wand at random strangers, and I heard him yell, 'I demand that you buy me an ice-cream cone! My third-favorite flavor is strange! My second-favorite is top! My favorite flavor is anti-charmed!' Suddenly, I realized the guy was talking about quarks."

Willard said he spent the next several minutes listening to Cosmic Stan's rant.

"Mixed in with the usual stuff about CIA mind-control beams, talking dogs, and monkey-people, I heard him mention beta decay, instantons, density

matrix, and subspaces of n-dimensional Riemannian manifolds," Willard said. "I'm not sure where he got it, but he definitely seems to have had extensive schooling in theoretical physics. Man, what could've happened to him?"

Stanford theoretical physicist Carl Lundergaard seconded Willard's theory on the loonball.

"He's definitely had some advanced training, though I'm not surprised that it went unnoticed for so long," Lundergaard said. "It's hard for the layperson to differentiate schizophrenic ramblings like 'Modernity chunk where the sink goes flying on the ping-pang' from legitimate terminology like 'Unstable equilibria lie on the nodal points of a separatrix in phase space.'"

Lundergaard said he first became intrigued by Cosmic Stan in December 1999, when the homeless man threw a chicken bone at him and said, "Components of the Weyl conformal curvature tensor." The professor said he initially suspected that Stan was repeating a phrase "from a textbook he'd found in the garbage." Then, several weeks later, the screaming nutcase shouted some things that indicated a strong grasp of high-level science.

"As I was buying coffee in the quad one morning, Stan came by waving those roller skates he sometimes wears on his hands," Lundergaard said. "I distinctly heard him say, 'I can't be in two places at once! I can't

meddle in my own affairs! I can't destructively interfere with my own future plans! What do I look like—the uncollapsed wave function of an electron?' He was referring to the seemingly paradoxical aspects of wave/particle duality as illustrated by the 'two-slit' experiment in electron diffraction. Stan wasn't just mouthing phrases: The crazy homeless man knows his stuff."

Added Lundergaard: "I almost approached him the other day to see if he

had any ideas regarding the general solution for the relativistic force-free equation describing the structure of the pulsar magnetosphere, but he was busy smearing a plastic doll with glue."

Cosmic Stan also appears to be versed in other academic subjects, Lundergaard said.

"He seems to have a working understanding of several of the higher maths, including Zurmelo-Fraenkel set theory, category theory, and algebraic

see LUNATIC page 112

Above: Cosmic Stan asks for enough change to take a bus to the Riemannian manifolds.

Bush Calls Incumbency Key Issue Of Campaign

WASHINGTON, DC—At a campaign dinner Monday, President Bush identified incumbency as the key issue in the upcoming presidential election. "Look at my opponent's record on incumbency," Bush said. "John Kerry is not the president at this time. That's an indisputable matter of public record." Bush added that the American public should seriously consider whether it wants to risk electing a president who has no experience heading a nation, has never resided in the White House, and does not have even one State Of The Union address under his belt.

News Of Uncle's Death Deleted By Spam Filter

PALO ALTO, CA—An email from Marison Octrup containing word of her husband's death was deleted by

Eric Rawson's spam filter Monday, a review of the deleted-items folder would have indicated. "Dear extended Octrup family, it is with great sadness that I write to you to report the end of George's battle with emphysema. George died peacefully in his sleep on Sunday night," read the e-mail, which Rawson never received. "The funeral will be held at St. Francis' First Lutheran Church on Thursday, for those who might be able to attend." While the death notice did not reach Rawson, 14 offers for low-cost Cialis did.

Sheets Changed After Every Breakup

ITHACA, NY—Michael Pelske changes his bed sheets after every breakup, the 24-year-old bicycle messenger announced Monday. "I'd never bring some woman I just met home to a set of filthy sheets," said Pelske, who changed his sheets Saturday before hitting the bars following his break-

up with Linda Keely, his girlfriend of four months. "But then, a few weeks into the relationship, you start to let things like that slide." Pelske's cotton-twill, 180-thread-count, light-blue sheets have been washed 13 times since his mother bought them for him in May 2001.

Confusing Insult Awkwardly Clarified

BOZEMAN, MT—Prudential Insurance administrative assistant Becky DuBois, 24, was forced to explain herself Tuesday morning after an off-hand insult was not understood by coworker Kimberly Spellman. "Oh, I just meant, 'This is what a bill looks like,' as in… Well, you said that your parents still pay your credit-card bill for you," DuBois told Spellman. "So, I just sorta meant… you know, that you don't know what bills look like." DuBois then said she didn't mean it as an insult, because she knows that Spellman said she hates it that her

parents do that, and that she's totally sorry if Spellman took it that way.

Leftover Christmas Billboard Stirs Seasonally Inappropriate Emotion

ST. LOUIS—Local architect Steve Burillo felt a momentary flush of seasonally incongruous holiday spirit Tuesday when he saw a Christmas-themed billboard on South Broadway. "The sign was advertising the St. Louis Ballet's performance of *The Nutcracker*, and for a second, I felt a stirring desire to volunteer for a charity and spread goodwill amongst my fellow men," Burillo said warmly. "But then I was like, 'Screw it. It's March. I should get to the gym and get in shape for summer.'" Burillo added that they really ought to take the billboard down before someone goes out and spends quality time with loved ones. ∅

which sears away cowardice, hesitation, sentiment—all that which is unworthy in Man?" Rumsfeld said, stroking his albino cheetah. "And my fighting arena is the crucible which concentrates that fire into the refined white heat of invincibility. The victor of my Eagle Fist Tournament shall be, by nature and definition, unsurpassed in the ways of the warrior. Such a fighter is fit to be the instrument of Rumsfeld."

The defense secretary then described the plan for the tournament— a single-elimination series of bouts in which two fighters, matched by drawn lots, will remain locked in

> "I do not forget last year's incident with Li," Rumsfeld said, fingering the jagged scar on his neck that he received in an ambush last year. "He was an enemy of freedom, and he dishonored us with his treachery. I regret that I was only able to give him a scar to match mine, and not the death he so richly deserved."

combat until one is physically unable to continue. Once the round concludes, the victor will be given a night and day to rest before the next match. At no time will a fighter be free to roam Fang Island's sealed areas.

"I do not forget last year's incident with Li," Rumsfeld said, fingering the jagged scar on his neck that he received in an ambush last year. "He was an enemy of freedom, and he dishonored us with his treachery. I regret that I was only able to give him a scar to match mine, and not the death he so richly deserved. Though he escaped in cowardice, he cannot hide forever."

According to Rumsfeld, the finest students of every martial philosophy traveled from around the globe to take part in the tournament. While some come only to pursue the honor of the title of King Of Eagle Fist, others see the event as a chance to pursue shadowy motives of personal gain, ambition, and revenge.

"I'm six months worth of gambling debt in the hole with the L.A. Syndicate,'" said Steele Saxon, 33, a blond, powerfully built seventh-degree black belt from Los Angeles. "Guy says to me, 'Hey, pal, it's the dough or we

Above: Sun Chang (right) fights Ebony Avalanche for Rumsfeld's amusement.

break something. Rumsfeld's got the dough if I've got the muscle. You just watch. Together, we've got the juice to put those Syndicate types in the rearview mirror of history."

"Man, they ain't seen unorthodox-but-effective until they seen me," said the languid Jack "Chocolate Lightning" Garrison, the two-time East Coast Freestyle Kung-Fu champion once described by *SuckaPunch* magazine as "six feet of stone-cold brotha and 10 inches of afro barely contained in a fly lemon-yellow jumpsuit."

"I won't waste my time with defeat," Garrison added. "I'll be too busy looking good."

> The biggest X-factor in this year's Eagle Fist may be the mysterious masked and hooded Nameless One, a fighter of feline grace.

The biggest X-factor in this year's Eagle Fist may be the mysterious masked and hooded Nameless One, a fighter of feline grace who practices "the technique of no-technique."

"I do not think—I feel," the Nameless One said, a sliver of light illuminating only his smoldering eyes. "The technique of your opponent is like a finger pointing at the moon. Concentrate on

the finger, and you will miss all that heavenly glory. That is the secret, to fight without fighting. At the last, Rumsfeld shall know what I know. I will share my victory with this... Don."

The Eagle Fist Tournament has come under fire from critics in America who characterize the fortress, purchased at taxpayers' expense, as a grandstanding ploy to divert attention from Iraq and the stalled war on terrorism.

"What exactly is this meant to achieve?" reporter James Snyder asked, hours before he disappeared from the *Fort Worth Star-Telegram* building. "Why does the Department of Defense need to determine who the world's premier open-hand fighter is and then retain his or her services for the next year? And why did Rumsfeld have the Guantánamo Bay prisoners chained and placed in the labyrinthine caverns below Fang Island? And how on earth does 'conflict sear away cowardice'? Patriot Act or no, we have a right to some answers."

Rumsfeld, wandering among his collection of antique torture implements and feeding candied figs to his golden langur, said he remains unmoved.

"See here," Rumsfeld said, indicating a gold-encrusted Minoan iron maiden. "It is difficult to associate horrors with the proud civilizations that created them: Sparta, Rome, the knights of Europe, the Samurai. They worshipped strength, because strength is the fundament for all other values. I shall find the strongest of all, and together, we shall shake the world to its very foundations." ∅

topology," Lundergaard said. "He also seems to be quite interested in the subjects of religion, sexuality, fast-food restaurants, Ferdinand de Saussure, malevolent evil, '70s TV shows, and shadowy authority figures."

Lundergaard said he has no knowledge of Cosmic Stan's past, but theorizes that his nickname derives from the physics term "cosmological constant."

"You have to wonder how this hap-

> "I won't waste my time with defeat," Garrison said.

pened to him," Lundergaard said. "Was he calculating the transition amplitudes between the unperturbed eigenstates due to the presence of the perturbation in order to determine transition probabilities in time-dependent quantum phenomena, and the next day, strapping a TV antenna to his head?"

Perched atop a bicycle rack on Marquette Street, Cosmic Stan was asked for comment.

"Who you? You've been balderdashed! Doodads! Wood glue, dammit!" Cosmic Stan said, glancing around wildly and cradling a partially disassembled transistor radio. "Fock space! Spin polarization! The Clausius-Clapeyron equation obtains! The incident field is representable by a plane wave vector potential! You gotta believe me!" ∅

BEST MAN from page 109

one of his non-funny jokes, but he was serious."

Ashland said he felt he had no choice but to accept the invitation.

"What could I say?" Ashland asked. 'Sorry, you're just some guy I work with—go look up someone you knew at summer camp'? Seriously, doesn't he know, say, anyone else in the entire world? Doesn't he have a cousin somewhere?"

Adding to Ashland's misgivings about standing before a crowd in support of Harrison's nuptials is the ever-increasing list of duties the groom has asked the best man to perform.

"Apparently, I'm sort of a ringmaster for the whole thing," Ashland said, flipping through the Greensboro tuxedo-rental listings. "I knew I had to be the bridesmaid's date, but now Karl says I'm also in charge of the ushers and shuttling the damn presents around. I really don't need this hassle

> ## The bride-to-be has expressed no misgivings about her future husband's best man.

on top of the wedding-dinner speech."

"My only hope is that the kind of guy who asks a coworker he barely knows to be his best man won't have very high standards," Ashland added.

Ashland said he has been forced to research the speech.

"I've been plying Karl with questions about his courtship, his childhood, and his parents' reaction to the engagement, just to get anything that will give me an inkling of what to say," Ashland said. "And Tracy—who, as best frickin' man, I've finally had the pleasure of meeting—is no help. How can I ask her personal questions about Karl without tipping her off to the fact that I have no idea who he is?"

In spite of Ashland's concern, the bride-to-be has expressed no misgivings about her future husband's best man.

"Karl's always talking about how nice it is to have someone as cool as Jeff at the office," Newman said. "God only knows what they're up to all day, but boys will be boys. It's great that Karl and Jeff got so close in so short a time, especially since Karl doesn't make friends easily."

Harrison had little to say on the subject of his selection criteria for best man.

"It's so nice that Jeff's doing this," Harrison told acquaintances at an after-work get-together which Ashland, citing a need to shop for black shoes, did not attend. "We're gonna have such a blast at my wedding. And I can't wait to see what he's got planned for the bachelor party. I have no idea what's going to go down, but if I know Jeff like I think I know Jeff, it'll be booze and strippers all the way."∅

DISINTEREST from page 109

Above: Three CUA members half-heartedly address lawmakers in Washington.

claim to represent the views of the people when the people don't know anything about all that legislative nonsense? The CUA represents the views and beliefs of those Americans who care the least."

The CUA was formed by Mark Berger and Sofia Richardson, two similarly non-civic-minded Wilmington, DE, residents whose paths crossed on Feb. 3, when they both did not vote in their state's primary.

"Some of my friends were going to vote in the election, but I didn't really care about it enough to go," Berger said. "I was sorta like, 'What's it matter?' If I'd have gone to vote that day, I never would've run into Sofia at the

> ## The CUA was formed by Mark Berger and Sofia Richardson, two similarly non-civic-minded Wilmington, DE, residents whose paths crossed on Feb. 3, when they both did not vote in their state's primary.

Starbucks, and we never would've started this massive apolitical movement. Who says that two people can't make an indifference?"

The CUA is one of the nation's many political action committees, which have become increasingly influential in American politics. The CUA agenda includes plans to conduct its own "mock the vote" campaign via voter-

resignation drives and indirect-mail campaigns.

"We've been doing canvassing and mailings to get our non-message out there," said Wendy Christianson, director of public outreach for the CUA. "We need to tap the huge wellspring of apathy that exists today. There are a lot of political inactivists who aren't being heard."

Christianson said that, as the presidential election heats up, the CUA's work will become even more vital.

"Even the most unconcerned citizens run the risk of getting caught up in all the debates, statistics, and news stories surrounding the election season," she said. "We want to remind the apathetic people that no matter which candidate is elected, he's just going to head to Washington and flap his gums about the government."

The CUA's first mailer is emblazoned with the group's current slogan: "Four more years of... politics?" The flyer features a graph illustrating each candidate's record of attention to political issues ranging from tax reform to national security. The initial test mailing, sent to more than 100,000 likely non-voters in Kansas last week, is otherwise devoted to a crossword puzzle, pasta-salad recipes, and a "How many rabbits can you find in this picture?" game.

The CUA will begin airing a series of ads in uncontested, non-battleground states in April. The ads are slated to highlight non-issues such as the outcome of the NCAA playoffs and the new summer line at Old Navy. While issue advertising is regulated under the Bipartisan Campaign Reform Act of 2002, chief legal counsel for the CUA Terry Frank said that non-issue ads are not.

"The ads are totally acceptable under the rules set forth for campaign

ads by the Federal Elections Commission," Frank said. "Some might try to accuse the CUA of exerting undue non-influence on the political process, or of misleading non-voters. But, really, who's gonna care?"

> ## "Write to or visit your elected representatives and talk about something other than politics," said Ted Delancey, director of constituent activities for the CUA.

According to preliminary polling conducted by the CUA, the 108th Congress is vastly out of step with the American people. In a telephone poll, the CUA asked randomly selected citizens to list their most pressing goals. Of the top four, only one, "finding a job," was discussed in Congress this session. The other three—"getting something to eat," "finding something to do," and "maybe hanging out"— have all been ignored by Washington lawmakers.

The CUA is urging its supporters to contact their representatives and voice their lack of concern.

"Write to or visit your elected representatives and talk about something other than politics," said Ted Delancey, director of constituent activities for the CUA. "It's time they heard what kinda sorta almost matters to their constituency, like the latest Scott Peterson trial news or predictions for the season finale of The Apprentice."∅

Once Again, Oscar Is King Of The Rings!

**The Outside Scoop
By Jackie Harvey**

I've got a lot on my plate this week, loyal Harveyheads. There's been an avalanche of events in the world of entertainment, so grab those boots! We're going snowboarding—in Hollywood!

(As you may have noticed, I've added an intro to my column. It just seemed so impersonal to start it cold—pun definitely intended—so I livened it up with a little pizzazz to grease the skids. That's something you can look forward to from now on!)

Item! The 75th Annual Academy Awards wrapped up, so here's **Jackie Harvey's Annual Oscar Recap!** First, the ceremony was on the 29th of February, which only happens once every four years. **Lord Of The Kings: The Return Of The Rings** was the lord of the Oscars, winning at least eight awards! (Sorry, folks—this Oscar fan fell asleep during hour three and lost count!) It was good to see former **Eurythmic** and Lennox air-conditioner heir **Lennox Lewis** get some recognition for singing and playing the part of the elf-princess **Arwyn.**

And who can forget the acting winners? **Shawn "Spicoli" Penn** won for **Mystic Pizza.** And the always-glam-

> **Was it just me, or was this the most tasteful Oscars I can remember? No horrible costumes, no unpatriotic outbursts, and no long-winded speeches. There wasn't a dry eye in the house for the tribute to Bob Hope, whose nose and zingers entertained Oscar watchers 17 times!**

orous **Charlize Sharon** won for **Monster,** a movie that I haven't seen, but I'm sure it's another great showcase for Charlize's stunning beauty!

Clint Eastwood brought his mother to the ceremonies, which was a classy move—I bet it "made her day!" Speak-

ing of classy, the gowns were gorgeous, but the magic was almost ruined by that **woman in the brown dress.** Apparently, she wrote and directed a movie about Japan, but I've never heard of it. Personally, if I were invited to the Oscars, I'd wear some-

> **I just heard what happened at the Super Bowl. During the halftime show, Jason Timberland ripped off part of Janet Jackson's outfit and revealed her— pardon my French— bosom. Did we really need to see Jacko's Racko?**

thing more fetching, like that number **Uma Thurman** was wearing, only in peach.

Was it just me, or was this the most tasteful Oscars I can remember? No horrible costumes, no unpatriotic outbursts, and no long-winded speeches. There wasn't a dry eye in the house for the tribute to **Bob Hope,** whose nose and zingers entertained Oscar watchers 17 times! And **Billy Crystal** should change his name to Billy Diamond after his sparkling return to the podium. Let's "Hope" he can come back again and make it to lucky number 17, as well. But honestly? I feel like I may never watch the Oscars again. After this slam-bang production, the next is sure to be a huge letdown.

Spring is on the way. I'm already bringing up my boxes so I can retire my winter clothes. I still have to lose 10 pounds in time for shorts season!

Item! I'm not a huge sports fan, so I just heard what happened at the Super Bowl. During the halftime show, **Jason Timberland** ripped off part of **Janet Jackson's** outfit and revealed her—pardon my French—bosom. Did we really need to see **Jacko's Racko**? I like pretty women as much as the next guy, but I like to leave a little to the imagination. Shame on you, Janet. You've brought sports and entertainment to a new low. And that ring thing you had on your nickel was just trashy.

As for **that other Jackson,** let's not

go there, all right? I'm sick of people dragging his name through the dirt.

Who to watch: 2004 will be the year for **David Paymer.** Mark my words, we're going to see some big things from him.

Item! Not since someone took a picture of a crucifix in a jar of pee has **Jesus** been this hot! **The Passion Of Jesus Christ Superstar** is the reigning king of the box office for 2004. Some people are a little put off by the way the movie treats **Jews.** Some people are a little put off by the way the movie treats Jesus. Me, I was put off to find out that **Mel** didn't play Jesus himself. But he is in the movie, playing troubled Roman leader **Pontius Pilot.** I won't tell you how the story ends, so you can judge the movie for yourself.

Did you catch the last episode of **Sex In The City**? No one I know has **HBO,** but I heard that **Carrie Jessica Parker** reunited with **Mr. Big.** Now that the show is over, everyone's already hankering for more. Thank goodness they're **planning a spinoff** with everyone's favorite lovable oaf, **Joey!**

Item! My sources tell me the dour

domestic doyenne, queen of quilting and (qu)rafts, **Martha Stewart** is going to the big house, and I don't mean the one on the beach. I don't think it's fair. She may be an ambitious, frosty, uncompromising tyrant, but she was unequaled when it came to putting things in order. In the **United States,** we are guaranteed a trial by a jury of our peers. I find it unlikely that there were 12 people on Mrs. Stewart's jury who could whip up a seven-course meal and a decorative centerpiece unique to the event in an afternoon.

What? Can this be it for another Outside Scoop? What more do you want? I think this installment has had it all: important awards shows, crime, nudity, and a healthy dose of movie magic. You want more, you say? Well, how's this? In the next installment, I'll have a little something about some Hollywood hookups and a review of the hottest TV DVDs, including **Mr. Ed** and **Starsky's Hutch.** Until then, light two candles: one for our men and women overseas and one for me as I take my seat... on The Outside! ✐

Your Horoscope

**By Lloyd Schumner Sr.
Retired Machinist and
A.A.P.B.-Certified Astrologer**

Aries: (March 21–April 19)
Many consider you a big teddy bear, but due to unwise forays past the boundaries of sanity, you're now more teddy bear than man.

Taurus: (April 20–May 20)
A high-speed car chase, complete with a gun battle, will do a lot to convince you that not all real-estate brokers are the same.

Gemini: (May 21–June 21)
You're happy you set a new world record, but you were hoping to win the award for pancake eating, not fingernail length.

Cancer: (June 22–July 22)
All men are created equal, which means a just God has compensated for your laser vision in a rather embarrassing way.

Leo: (July 23–Aug. 22)
You'll achieve fame and get into all the best clubs when Danger Mouse mixes you into his next album.

Virgo: (Aug. 23–Sept. 22)
Through the impressive process of extending Orion's celestial finger, the stars indicate that you should fuck off.

Libra: (Sept. 23–Oct. 23)
There's no one less deserving of an ever-present entourage of beautiful, talented backup singers than you, but no one said life was fair.

Scorpio: (Oct. 24–Nov. 21)
A long-standing problem of order in the universe will be solved when you obtain an under-sink rack to hold your loose cookie sheets, baking pans, and pot lids.

Sagittarius: (Nov. 22–Dec. 21)
You will spend hours this week engaged in a bizarre political debate over whether guns can kill people.

Capricorn: (Dec. 22–Jan. 19)
Your reputation for staying on the cutting edge of trial law is reinforced when you become your city's first cutthroat gay-divorce lawyer.

Aquarius: (Jan. 20–Feb. 18)
America's little girls refuse to let you cure your rare but adorable form of anemia, in which little elves with big blue eyes siphon your blood while you sleep.

Pisces: (Feb. 19–March 20)
New directions in evolutionary theory make it possible for people to be disgusted at what you evolved from.

NEWS

the ONION®

VOLUME 40 ISSUE 12 | AMERICA'S FINEST NEWS SOURCE™ | 25–31 MARCH 2004

Earthquake Kills 54 Rescue Workers' Weekend Plans

see WORLD page 3B

Hippie Will Tell You What The Real Crime Is

see LOCAL page 14D

Asylum Seeker Has Eight Adorable Little Asylum Seekers In Tow

see WORLD page 13B

STATshot

A look at the numbers that shape your world.

Top Sitcom Premises By Number Of Repetitions

1. Maybe celebrity Don Rickles will help
2. Lost vacationing vampire becomes small-town sheriff
3. Supporting character blind as a bat without her glasses
4. Edith almost gets raped
5. But the girls are going to be here *any minute*

Above: The Real Rover.

Coke-Sponsored Rover Finds Evidence Of Dasani On Mars

PASADENA, CA—The Coca-Cola-sponsored Real Rover has discovered evidence that the surface of Mars was once partially covered by free-flowing Dasani, scientists at NASA's Jet Propulsion Laboratory announced Monday.

"The Real Rover's instruments found signs that cool, refreshing Dasani once drenched the surface of the Red Planet," said Dr. Marvin Chen, NASA space-science administrator and temporary liaison to Coca-Cola. "This discov-

ery is so exciting, because it indicates that the Red Planet may have once hosted a healthy, active, fun-filled microscopic life. You see, Dasani would have been as vital to Martian lifeforms as it is to their terrestrial counterparts."

The Real Rover's March 19 launch marked the culmination of a two-year project designed by NASA and funded in part by a $400 million grant from the Coca-Cola corporation.

see DASANI page 118

Nostalgia Prompts Return Of Negro Baseball Leagues

NEW YORK—Influenced by the high demand for Negro League memorabilia, Major League Baseball commissioner Bud Selig announced Monday that, for the 2004 season, the national pastime will return to its storied, segregated past.

"This is a historic day for baseball players and fans alike," Selig told an excited crowd of black reporters and players gathered around a radio in the lobby of his Park Avenue headquarters. "Today, we honor the memory of such great black players as Satchel Paige, Buck Leonard, and Cool Papa Bell by giving the Negro Leagues a place in American sports

see NOSTALGIA page 119

Right: Atlanta Black Crackers owner Tom Forst joins his player Ken Griffey Jr. at a press conference.

Political Cartoon Even More Boring And Confusing Than Issue

PORTLAND, OR—A political cartoon in Monday's *Daily Oregonian* was more boring and confusing than the issue it attempted to address, area resident Craig Lawler reported Tuesday.

"I get the donkeys and elephants," said Lawler, a high-school biology teacher. "But the rest of the cartoon is just a confusing jumble of ambiguous symbols and weird objects. I thought it was about unemployment at first, which would have been boring enough, but then I noticed the word 'ethanol' over there on the jug, so I realized it's actually about commerce. I think."

After several minutes of careful inspection, Lawler identified the in- and out-boxes on the elephant's desk as symbols of the nation's record-high monthly trade deficit.

"I finally figured out what subject we're even dealing with," Lawler said. "Now I just have to figure out what's being said and how it's funny or insightful—or, ideally, both."

According to Lawler, the cartoon also contains an object that is "either some sort of chart showing the movement of the Dow, or just a broken window pane."

The cartoon was penned by James Ploeser and syndicated in 47 newspapers and magazines nationwide.

see CARTOON page 118

Above: James Ploeser's cartoon as it appeared in the *Daily Oregonian*.

Stewart's Prison Sentence

The nation awaits Martha Stewart's June 17 sentencing, which will reveal how much time she spends in prison. What do *you* think?

Bruce Bennett
Systems Analyst

"Martha's headed to jail? Her emotions must be running the gamut from taut-lipped pseudo-WASP rage to unhealthy denial."

Kathy Henderson
Secretary

"She's just going to learn how to be a better insider trader from all the other inmates."

Steve Woods
Referee

"I'll be able to sleep easier knowing that another motivated, powerful woman is off the streets."

Willi Cooper
Usher

"It's about time we cracked down on white-collar criminals without political connections."

Beverly Ross
Window Trimmer

"The woman is about to go to prison, yet her site still charges 39 bucks for a goddamn egg-shaped beeswax candle?"

Nicholas Coleman
Anesthesiologist

"Hey, did anyone say how funny it would be if Martha decorated her jail cell in some elaborate way? Oh."

Nanotechnology

The global market for nanotechnology—the science of manipulating the tiniest units of matter—is growing. What are some applications for the new science?

- ▶ Computerized day planners that can manage your busy schedule from inside your pores
- ▶ Micro-soldiers able to sneak behind enemy lines and exist there
- ▶ Microscopic ambushing, beating up, and robbing of atoms now possible
- ▶ Mad scientists can build nightmarish, dystopic future too small to see
- ▶ Nano-bots will solve the problem of the homeless by systematically devouring them for fuel
- ▶ Scientists say nanotechnology could be used to fight war on terrorism, if that will get them some damn funding
- ▶ Search-and-destroy missions can be conducted for inadvertently fertilized eggs
- ▶ By altering the earth's atmosphere on the microscopic level, nanotechnologists can turn whole world into delicious ice-cream wonderland

the ONION ®
America's Finest News Source.™

Herman Ulysses Zweibel
Founder

T. Herman Zweibel
Publisher Emeritus
J. Phineas Zweibel
Publisher
Maxwell Prescott Zweibel
Editor-In-Chief

I Hit The Dead-Wife Insurance Jackpot!

By Maxwell Linden

Last week, I was Maxwell Linden, lab technician. I was four long years from retirement, sharing a cramped little A-frame with my wife, and driving a Lincoln Mercury seriously in need of a new transmission. Today, call me Mr. Linden, widower extraordinaire. Along with my wife Leah, my financial troubles are gone forever. Even though her life-insurance payout was only $250,000, I feel like a million bucks!

Grieving is a process, they say. At first, I was angry with God for striking down the love of my life. It had to be a mistake. What had she done to deserve that?

I was just working my way out of the denial phase of the grieving process when the phone rang. Mr. George Tift from State Farm Insurance had a little proposition to make. After giving his condolences, he told me that my term-life insurance plan entitled me to 10 quarterly installments of $25,000, for a total pre-tax payout of $250,000. Yowza! What had I done to deserve that?

A quarter of a million American dollars! That's more than just a good day at the greyhound track. That's the big time: term life. Bargaining phase complete, hello acceptance. Grieving process over!

Leah was a wonderful woman—kind, gentle, caring. I'd have given almost anything to have kept her alive—easily more than $100,000. Probably even $200,000. But 250 grand might have been pushing it. Ah, we can't turn back the hands of time, so there's no use talking about it anyway.

Sure, it was tough paying insurance premiums all those years, but, like they say, you gotta spend money to make money. It was 1962, the year Leah and I got married, that we signed the papers with State Farm. I had a gut feeling that someday it'd be worth it. I bided my time at the lab, kept my head down, tucked a little into the life-insurance fund each month, no matter how tight things were, and then, just 42 years later—blammo!—Leah gets sideswiped by a beer-delivery truck! I don't have to work another day in my life. At 3:15 p.m., my financial troubles were pronounced dead at the scene.

It's hard not to dwell on how things *could* have been, though. If I'd only known what was in store when my dear Leah left the house that day, I could've gotten on the phone and doubled our coverage. But why dwell on that thought? It's better to focus on the positives: I can't lose sight of the fact that I've been blessed. What if I'd had no insurance at all? I'd be standing here alone in the world, without anyone to love me, a member of the middle class. But instead, luck—and the beer-delivery truck—struck.

No more clock-punching and bosses for me. Praise be to God for bestowing upon me this heaping mound of dearly departed cash-ola.

Holiest angels, please look after my beloved wife up there in Eternal Heaven. Take care of her. Make sure

> **Mr. George Tift from State Farm Insurance had a little proposition to make. After giving his condolences, he told me that my term-life insurance plan entitled me to 10 quarterly installments of $25,000, for a total pre-tax payout of $250,000.**

she's got all that she needs in the way of wings or halos or whatever. And tell my dearest not to worry about me. As of yesterday, I've got my bases pretty much covered here on earth. Ha-cha!

Sure, my heart aches for my wife of more than four decades, but I intend to get one of the best psychologists in the entire Akron-Canton area to help me through this loss. I'll say, "Fix me up and then send me the bill. I'll have my banker draw the money out of my account." My fat, fat dead-wife account!

They say it's darkest before the dawn, and I believe it. For a couple of hours, I thought the death of my wife would be the end of my life, too. The thought of living without her beside me threatened my very sanity. But then, like a flash, the clouds parted, the sun beamed through, and I realized that the day she was killed was the first day of the rest of my life—as a rich man.

I always knew big things were in store for me, and the death of my little Leah Lou proved me right. I played the insurance game and came out a winner! Step aside, world—the high roller's coming through! ∅

Rematch With Mechanical Bull Planned All Week Long

LEXINGTON, KY—Ever since a humiliatingly short mechanical-bull ride at the Cadillac Ranch last Thursday, area resident Scott Wiseck has been planning a rematch, the 27-year-old UPS deliveryman reported Tuesday.

"Last week was flat-out embarrassing," Wiseck said. "I was barely up on that bull five seconds before I was face-down on the floor wearing my ass for a hat. It wouldn't have been so bad if I hadn't been acting like a big shot in front of those two girls from Bowling Green. I couldn't even look them in the eye for the rest of the night after I lost to that bull."

Lured onto the bull by the $500 prize awarded to the winner of the weekly contest, Wiseck was not ready for the Bullseye-brand bull's U.L. code set electricals and hydraulic bucking action. According to the automatic timer, Wiseck was vanquished by the bull in just 3.5 seconds.

"Next time will be different, though," Wiseck said. "I'm gonna be ready for that bull."

Wiseck said he has spent hours pondering the mistakes he made during the disastrous ride, in order to create a plan of action for Thursday's rematch.

"I was overconfident, plain and simple," Wiseck said. "My daddy always told me: You can't tame an animal unless you respect it. It's a little different, this bull being a machine and all, but the principle's the same. I went

into that pit cocky, so I was bound to end up bass-ackwards in front of the whole town."

Wiseck said alcohol was another factor contributing to his defeat.

"I was too drunk last week," Wiseck said. "It's a good idea to have a few Coors longnecks to loosen you up and give you some liquid courage, but next week, I'm staying away from the 2-for-1 rail drinks. I'll have plenty of time to buy victory rounds after I take that bull down."

A large pre-bull-riding meal also contributed to his poor showing, Wiseck said.

"An hour or so before my ride, I ate a Saddle Burger with all the fixings," Wiseck said. "It's no wonder I didn't stay on the bull for more than a few bucks. Next Thursday, I'll just have one of those Power Bars. That'll put me in peak condition without filling me up."

Having reviewed his performance, Wiseck plans to rent the 1980 movie *Urban Cowboy*, to seek inspiration from John Travolta.

"I haven't seen *Urban Cowboy* in a long time, so I bet it'll pump me up," Wiseck said. "I've also been thinking about bringing my own music to play during my ride, maybe AC/DC's 'You Shook Me All Night Long.' Last week, George Jones' 'White Lightning' was on the jukebox when I lost to the bull. As much as I love that song, it's just not good bull-riding music."

Above: Wiseck visits the Cadillac Ranch to "size up" the mechanical bull in preparation for their rematch.

With his plan laid out, Wiseck said he thinks he's in the running to not only win the $500 prize, but also beat the bar's all-time record of 34.5 seconds and displace Daryl Schumacher from the chalkboard hanging behind the bar.

"It's less about the money and more about the dignity of the Wiseck name," Wiseck said. "I will pay the $10 entry fee over and over again, all night long, if I have to. I don't care what anyone says, I'm going to beat that thing. This is personal; it's between me and the bull."

Wiseck's friends say they don't expect him to conquer the bull this Thursday, or anytime soon.

"I don't care how much Scotty wants it—he's not gonna beat the Big Motherbucker," Wiseck's friend Sam Lewis said. "His dreams are as big as the West Texas sky, but physically, he's just too weak. You need upper-body strength to ride that thing, which is something you just don't get from driving a delivery truck all day. He should probably stick to playing foosball in the back room, where he's king of the table." ∅

Teen Learns The Negligible Value Of A Dollar

ASHLAND, WI—After earning $5 for mowing his family's half-acre lawn, 13-year-old Andrew Mink learned the negligible value of a dollar at the town's sporting-goods store Sunday. "Pops dropped me off at Dunham's before baseball practice so I could buy something with my hard-earned money," Mink said. "I kinda wanted a baseball glove, but that was almost $40. A new bat was, like, $65. Even a batting glove was more than $10." The teen finally found a wristband for $3.99, but he was unable to afford sales tax on the item after reserving one dollar for his bus fare home.

Psychic Helps Police Waste Valuable Time

MANCHESTER, NH—More than 36

hours after the disappearance of 13-year-old Heather Jordan, Manchester police hired local psychic Lynette Mure-Davis to help waste their valuable time Monday. "I see a river… and along the banks is an outcropping with five lilac bushes," said Mure-Davis, who then paused a full 90 seconds to "collect vibrations" from Jordan's scarf. "I also see a man… tall, but stocky, wearing… a hat. And an animal, perhaps a dog." As of press time, Jordan was still trapped under a collapsed utility shed three blocks west of her house.

Bush Urges Iraqis To Pass Amendment Banning Gay Marriage

BAGHDAD—In a private meeting with Mohammed Bahr al-Ulloum, President Bush urged the Iraqi Governing Council president to amend the recently ratified Iraqi constitution to protect the sanctity of heterosexual marriage. "The Iraqi constitution,

signed just a few short weeks ago, will usher in a new era of democratic freedom in Iraq," Bush said. "But there are some unlawful and unholy acts that the constitution's original drafters could not have possibly intended to protect." Bush then told al-Ulloum he must act quickly and decisively to preserve his country's most sacred tradition.

Reality Show Slowly Sinks In

EAST LANSING, MI—Though she'd lived in denial for nearly a month, toy-store manager Ellen Cranmer admitted Monday that the reality show *The Apprentice* has finally sunk in. "Normally I never watch those stupid reality shows, and I certainly don't integrate them into my regular week," Cranmer said. "But since around the time of the Trump Ice challenge, I've been passing on social events so I can be home Thursdays at 9 p.m." Cranmer said that she was shocked when she realized she had-

n't missed a single episode, and saddened by her belief that Amy will win.

New York Times Seeks Court Order To Remove *Tuesdays With Morrie* From Best-Seller List

NEW YORK—*The New York Times* announced Monday that it will seek a court order to have Mitch Albom's book of discussions between himself and his dying mentor, *Tuesdays With Morrie*, forcibly removed from the paperback non-fiction best-seller list. "We've tolerated the old dead guy's ramblings for the past 66 weeks," *Times* Sunday books-section editor Mel Constantine said. "But now it's simply gotta go. I want *Morrie* out of my list—permanently." Should the order be successful, the book's slot on the list will be replaced by a line urging readers to donate to the Fresh Air Fund. ∅

DASANI from page 115

The logo-covered rover touched down Sunday, landing inside a crater newly christened Lymoni Spritenum. The rover then used its abrasion tool to grind below the surface, where it located cracks filled with several types of gray hematites—minerals known to form only in the presence of Dasani.

"It's true that pure, delicious Dasani is one of the most common compounds in the universe," Chen said. "But the abundant mineral deposits in

> "Dasani comes in many forms," Chen said. "On Earth, we find it in servings as small as four ounces or as large as a 48-liter multi-pack. The first stows easily in your purse, and the latter is the life of the party. In between, there are other sizes perfect for a gym bag, a car's cupholder, or a child's lunch bag."

the rocks indicate that the cool, life-enriching Dasani was indigenous to Mars, rather than the frozen Dasani core of a comet that collided with the planet."

Further study of the data will be necessary to determine whether the minerals formed as sedimentary deposits from standing surface pools of Dasani, or accumulated through the action of flowing ground-Dasani.

Above: NASA scientists cheer the recent discovery.

"Dasani comes in many forms," Chen said. "On Earth, we find it in servings as small as four ounces or as large as a 48-liter multi-pack. The first stows easily in your purse, and the latter is the life of the party. In between, there are other sizes perfect for a gym bag, a car's cupholder, or a child's lunch bag. Similarly, Dasani could have existed on Mars in various forms, like ice or vapor, and in many convenient locations, such as Martian oceans or the craters dotting the planet's surface."

Chen said scientists hope to confirm that icy Dasani exists at the southern pole of Mars, as recent spectral images from the European Space Agency's Mars Express Orbiter suggest.

"In the coming days, we'll be moving the Real Rover in the direction of the possible polar Dasani caps," Chen said. "As we continue to explore Mars, we hope to find Dasani distributed everywhere."

NASA geologist Matt Golombek, who chose the landing sites for the rovers, said confirming that Dasani exists on Mars would be a boon for the scientific community.

"Finding a source of water—er, Dasani—would mean future manned missions to Mars would not need to bring tanks of it with them," Golombek said. "Although establishing manned bases on Mars is still a far-future scenario, the existence of *Dasani* would make such a plan theoretically possible. Also, knowing that the liquid is there would likely lead to more sponsored exploration on the Red Planet and an eventual bottling plant."

Golembek said he is excited to continue the work of analyzing the data collected by the Real Rover.

"Understanding liquid… Dasani's role on the Martian surface is crucial," Golombek said. "Now that we've established that this life-giving substance was once… I'm supposed to say 'available solar-system-wide'… we can begin to consider whether life once existed on Mars, and if it did, what disaster befell the planet to eliminate it."

"Not that running out of Dasani isn't disastrous enough!" Chen interjected. "One fact is clear: Life on Mars was a lot more probable when abundant Dasani was present, just as life is more enjoyable on Earth when you've got Dasani. If you don't want to be dry and lifeless yourself, stock up on cool, refreshing Dasani bottled water." ∅

CARTOON from page 115

"I like to have a little fun with my panels, but I also like to make a point," Ploeser said. "They call it an *editorial* cartoon for a reason. The fact that those inboxes and outboxes were made of steel evokes the steel-tariff controversy from last fall, of course. And did you notice the word 'lies' in the outbox? And the bags of grain in the inbox? It's all there, if you look."

Lawler, who reads the editorial cartoons along with the rest of the paper each morning, said he is fairly well-versed in current events.

"I think I'm even a bit above average, in terms of knowing what's happening in the world," Lawler said. "I keep up on all the economic news and foreign affairs. So, if I didn't get that those dolls in the outbox represented outsourced workers, I'm really not sure what percentage of the population would."

Lawler said the cartoon is part of a larger trend.

"Political cartoons run in nearly every newspaper, so they must be an important part of American discourse—but damned if I can figure out what most of them are trying to say," Lawler said. "Take this Sunday's cartoon. It had two penguins applying for a marriage license. They were knee-deep in water labeled 'public opinion.' But the clerk at the desk was an eagle wearing a judge's robe and a sash that said 'mayor.' So the clerk marrying the penguins was… a mayor? Or a Supreme Court justice?"

His voice rising in frustration, Lawler continued: "Then, off to the side, there was another penguin holding a bouquet of flowers labeled 'constitution' in one hand and a piece of cake labeled 'polls' in the other. But this was all happening on a television! And, in the foreground, there was a hand labeled 'Iowa' holding a remote control, and the caption said 'Nothing's on.' What's going on here? I am so full of *rage* right now."

> "In the foreground, there was a hand labeled 'Iowa' holding a remote control, and the caption said 'Nothing's on.' What's going on here? I am so full of *rage* right now," Lawler said.

Patting her husband's arm, Lawler's wife Janice said she shares his frustration.

"Just last week on *Time* magazine online, there was a U.S. map with each state colored differently," she said. "Some of them were red, some were blue, but some were orange and some were purple. It said "voting alert" across the top. I stared at it for 10 minutes and never figured it out. I'm still thinking about it."

Dr. Edward Hunt, who teaches a class on political art-history at Boston College, defended the cartoon.

"The best editorial cartoons are worth a thousand words," Hunt said. "The Teapot Dome scandal? Watergate? Reaganomics? These aren't necessarily visual ideas, but the cartoonists broke the issues down into highly poignant pictorials. The cartoonists of today follow in that tradition. It's not the cartoonist's fault if some idiot schoolteacher in Oregon can't understand what a donkey riding on a tractor labeled '527' means." ∅

once again."

Selig cited the abundance of Negro League documentaries, books, web sites, and museums as proof of the public's interest in revitalizing segregated baseball.

"Baseball is all about the fans," Selig said. "And the fans are all about paying big money for caps and T-shirts with the cool old Birmingham Black Barons logo on them. They love buying mahogany-framed prints of those neat black-and-white Kansas City

> ## "Baseball is all about the fans," Selig said. "And the fans are all about paying big money for caps and T-shirts with the cool old Birmingham Black Barons logo on them. They love buying mahogany-framed prints of team photos, too."

Monarchs team photos, too."

The first successful Negro League was formed in 1920, and the leagues survived in some form until the early 1950s. When Jackie Robinson broke the color barrier in 1947, black talent began to migrate to the major leagues.

"Some of the greatest baseball players in history were in the Negro Leagues," Selig said. "Even so, most of them were relative unknowns in their day. Well, now we have the advantage of working in reverse. By taking talented, pre-established All-Stars like Kenny Lofton, Sammy Sosa, and Gary Sheffield out of the Major Leagues, we make instant Negro League superstars."

Selig said the new Black National League and Black American League seasons will be played at the same time as those of regular, white Major League Baseball.

"I will personally ensure that the leagues for whites and blacks are equal in every way," Selig said. "As for the fans, they'll be getting twice as many games this summer. And we'll get surviving Negro League players, like former Philadelphia Stars pitcher Harold Gould, to throw out the first ball. Who would object to that?"

Selig said the Negro League games will not be geared toward an all-black audience.

"Only about 6 percent of fans attending Major League Baseball games last year were black," Selig said. "The demographic we're aiming for comprises diehard baseball fans and Negro-league memorabilia collectors, regardless of race or creed."

Selig explained that this demographic is composed predominantly of Caucasian men, and that Nielsen data indicates that the average baseball fan is 51 years old.

So far, baseball fans, particularly those residing in the Deep South, have embraced Selig's decision.

"This is going to be great," said Dar-

> ## "At this point, I don't know," Bonds said. "If I get a chance to play with Sheffield and a bunch of other great players on the Black Yankees, I have to admit that'd sorta be a dream come true. On the other hand, maybe it'd be time to retire."

ryl Dupey, 54, of Birmingham, AL. "Dad always talked about seeing the Birmingham Black Barons face down teams like the Atlanta Black Crackers and the Chicago American Giants, but never in my wildest dreams did I think I'd get to see it myself. It's like a dream come true."

"This is a treasured piece of American history all over again," said Omar Whittlefield, owner of the new Chicago Black Stockings franchise. "During the first half of the 20th century, the color line kept black players from getting the recognition they deserved. Well, this time around, the players are going to be huge. I don't sell caps if they ain't!"

Unfortunately, some players have resisted joining the new league.

"Hell, no," said five-time All-Star Albert Belle, who was told to report for practice with the Tampa Bay Afro-Marlins next Wednesday. "Didn't we already go through this shit? No way I'm gonna be anyone's sepia-toned memory."

Barry Bonds, recently dismissed from the newly all-white San Francisco Giants, said he is unsure what he'll do.

"At this point, I don't know," Bonds said. "If I get a chance to play with Sheffield and a bunch of other great players on the Black Yankees, I have to admit that'd sorta be a dream come true. On the other hand, maybe it'd be time to retire."

While he acknowledged that his plan has its critics, Selig said the "shadow league" will revitalize baseball.

"A new generation will get to see the tragic majesty of Negro League play," Selig said. "Once again, baseball fans will be able to argue over whether or not a black player could make it in the majors, even if the player in question was already there. And maybe, just maybe, the brave Jackie Robinson of a new generation will dare to defy my color line and become a symbol of triumph. That'd *really* sell tickets." ⬤

---

the ONION presents

Online-Dating Tips

More people are using computers to find that special someone. Here are some tips to help make your online-dating experience safe and fun:

- Under no circumstance should you give someone you meet online a lot of personal information. You could place yourself in the dangerous position of having a date who knows what a loser you are.

- When considering the serious step of marriage, it's good form to seek the approval of the message-board moderator.

- Online dating services provide an easy way for recently divorced singles to meet new and interesting people. It's too bad your ex-wife got to keep the computer.

- When you write your online classified ad, be sure to make explicit the fact that a sense of humor is very important to you.

- Set yourself apart by choosing a descriptive user-name like SocialRetard342, CuteFaceFatAss, or RohypnolLarry.

- If you're having a hard time finding a decent, commitment-minded man through e-dating, why don't you try to e-shut the fuck up for once and stop your e-bitching.

- Don't just tell women what they want to hear. Type it in all caps.

- Remember, online dating is not for everyone—only the desperate and pathetic.

- Dates like to know that they're appreciated. Go the extra mile and send that special someone an e-card or virtual flowers.

- For best results, try whichever dating service happens to be advertised to the right or left of this chart.

- If you decide to break up with your online mate, for God's sake, have the decency to do it over the phone.

- If you're a man who prefers younger women, but you only seem to get responses from older women, take heart: Older women can give birth to younger women.

- When getting together for the first time, arrange to meet online dates in an open, public place. That way, you can use binoculars to check them out from the car beforehand.

- Don't worry. If you actually meet someone decent over the Internet, the two of you can tell people you met at a party.

You Are No Longer Welcome In The Homer Reading Group

By Arthur Gibbons

Sorry I'm late. The Gustav Mahler Jugendsymphonie is in town, and I was held back by the conductor, Claudio Abbado—terrible bore, please don't tell I said. But enough about that. Did everyone enjoy the reading of... *Wait.* What are *you* doing here? Did you not receive my phone message of 1:43 a.m. Tuesday last? Oh, you received it. Then, as you well know, you are no longer welcome in the Homer reading group.

I was *completely* serious. You are either in my reading group, or you are in Kouri's Virgil Symposium. A woman cannot drink from two fountains at once, nor can she butter her bread on three sides. You've been sneaking about and I've caught you, so get out. No, do not finish your ouzo. Just go.

Childish? How is that childish? Please, I'd like to know.

Yes, well, that's all very interesting. As much as I hate to interrupt that fascinating monologue, I'm afraid you're wasting the others' valuable learning time. Gather up your vocabulary cards and parsing sheets. Take your lists of Attic equivalents and Homeric exceptions from the pushboard in the hall. You may return my Smyth and pay any outstanding copy-charge fees by campus mail. For now, graywmeqa thn adikon grafhn yeudwn. You are no longer invited to my birthday.

No, it's out of the question. I am afraid you have wounded me, and the wound cannot so easily be healed, two-faced woman of apologies. I might reconsider, were it not for the litany of kicks and bruises I have received: your ignorance of the dual, your difficulty with the circumstantial participle, your tendency to conflate clauses of natural and actual result.

You are, put simply, a lazy student. Like the wren—who has his food dropped into his beak by his mother's claws, and then, by and by, grows, and, one day he should be able to fly, prefers to fold his wings and nestle on the eagle's crest—so have you been in my weekly reading group. Well, no longer. Go.

As she packs up, let us begin. Book VII, lines 1-12—who has questions? Questions... anyone? Well, if there aren't any, I've an amusing anecdote. I was lunching earlier at Bobbo with Jack Brankowsky from *Artforum*—I review major openings for them. Well, Brankowsky found, in his left-hand coat pocket, a pheasant bone from a

$5,000-a-plate fundraiser held for the Met last January. You see, it's the most amusing story, because Terry Eagleton was quite drunk, and... I'm sorry, *who* is talking? Aren't you *gone*?

Oh, I am a histrionic martinet, am I? I, who when orchestrating the sum-

> **I was completely serious. You are either in my reading group, or you are in Kouri's Virgil Symposium. A woman cannot drink from two fountains at once, nor can she butter her bread on three sides. You've been sneaking about and I've caught you, so get out. No, do not finish your ouzo. Just go.**

mer Ottoman Karagoz series for Professor Buchloh was kind enough to give you the role of craft-service supervisor? I? Who entrusted you with the title of reading-group secretary, shepherded you through books I through VI of the *Iliad*, and invited you into my own home to look at my collection of bibelots? Histrionic? Well, call me what you will. As Waugh said, "People can call you anything they like, as long as they don't call you a pigeon pie and eat you."

As long as you're still lingering around unwelcome, I've half a mind to return these chocolates you gave me. I shouldn't accept a gift from such a person as you. Yes, take back these chocolates! They are still here in the desk. There are two left. See, yes, here they are, two ginger bonbons, underneath the cardboard divider. See? Take the box with you, as well. I no longer accept the gift.

And, in case you're wondering, I've not forgotten that you have my Middle Liddel and *Lexicon Of The Homeric Dialect.* Deborah, the new reading-group secretary, if she should choose to accept—shall we talk after group, Deborah? Yes, Deborah will contact you regarding their return, as well as compensation for any highlighting or cocked bindings. That's correct, you no longer hold the office of group secretary. I fire you.

Is that maiden, your tongue, crying

Your Horoscope

By Lloyd Schumner Sr.
Retired Machinist and
A.A.P.B.-Certified Astrologer

Aries: (March 21–April 19)
Both your mind and a locomotive run on rails, are difficult to maintain, and make chugging noises, but after that, the analogy starts to break down.

Taurus: (April 20–May 20)
You were right about the existence of a 10th planet, but don't be smug: Your claims about a race of cat-women who thirst for your seed was way off.

Gemini: (May 21–June 21)
Mark Twain said moving house twice equals one house fire, so it looks like Fate owes you a couple house moves.

Cancer: (June 22–July 22)
Arguments over the relative merits of football and soccer are rendered moot next week, when aliens challenge us to a bizarre hybrid of both games with the fate of the earth at stake.

Leo: (July 23–Aug. 22)
The surgeons are unclear on exactly why you need a titanium plate implanted in your ass, but hey... gift horses.

Virgo: (Aug. 23–Sept. 22)
A fateful chess match with Death looms in your future, so you might want to replace that tacky *Star Trek* chess set.

Libra: (Sept. 23–Oct. 23)
It won't really do you any good, but it's very stirring nonetheless when you remember the Alamo, the Maine, and Pearl Harbor during your audit.

Scorpio: (Oct. 24–Nov. 21)
The principle of entropy says that all systems tend toward disorder, so just think of what happens to your legs next week as a natural, universal constant.

Sagittarius: (Nov. 22–Dec. 21)
You're tired of all these narrow escapes with your life, so next week's gas-truck accident will be sort of a relief.

Capricorn: (Dec. 22–Jan. 19)
It's often a mistake to try and make learning fun, as you'll prove next week during your combined fireworks-safety/ defensive-driving demonstration.

Aquarius: (Jan. 20–Feb. 18)
You may think your life is due for big changes, but the unknowable cosmic forces in control of your fate don't.

Pisces: (Feb. 19–March 20)
An important warning sticker will be missing this week. The stars can't tell you where it should be, but it should say "Caution: Rotating Knives."

out again from behind her picket fence? Please quiet her. I rescind my invitation to her of last month. Don't be coy; it was to program my person-

> **No, it's out of the question. I am afraid you have wounded me, and the wound cannot so easily be healed, two-faced woman of apologies.**

al web site. It goes without saying that your hand will no longer take dictation for my column in the decomeqa pantous newsletter. Return the mailing list to me at your earliest convenience, as those addresses are personal and private. I trust you will delete any and all reading-group contact infor-

mation from your Outlook folders, as well. And give me your key to the treasury box!

I know you are being absolutely ludicrous, but what am I?

Oh, now I am getting a migraine. This is too-too sad-making. Let us be graceful, I beg you. As in book XXIV, line 507, when Achilles looks down upon Priam, supplicant at his feet, I am weary with lamentations and grief. Please, do not make a scene. Let us not go through the unkind motions of returning gifts. As a gesture of goodwill, I shall accept those last two chocolates.

I said I shall accept and eat those chocolates. didou ekeinous emoi. Yes, goodbye then, and take care not to let the door slam. Now, who in the audience—who in the group, I mean, can give me the third person singular, aorist optative middle for prodidwmi? The dative plural for lie? The nominative singular for woman? The accusative singular for good teacher? Go. ercon! iqi! anabaine! katabaine! Excuse me, I believe that pencil belongs to the group. ∅

FCC Sentences Artie Lange To Death

see WASHINGTON page 7C

Transit Authority Pledges To Double Number Of Out-Of-Service Buses By 2006

see LOCAL page 11B

Scientists Celebrate Unlocking Of Corn Genome With Extra Serving Of Corn

see SCIENCE page 13E

STATshot

A look at the numbers that shape your world.

Top April Fools' Day Pranks

- **16%** Not wearing any underwear
- **20%** Taking estranged husband back for the day
- **17%** The old "blood in your coworker's stool" prank
- **25%** Tricking self into believing hand is swimsuit model's vagina
- **12%** "Forgiving" sins of man
- **10%** Faking own death after embezzling millions in corporate funds

THE ONION • $2.00 US • $3.00 CAN

---

the ONION®

VOLUME 40 ISSUE 13   AMERICA'S FINEST NEWS SOURCE™   1–7 APRIL 2004

Bush Addresses 8.2 Million Unemployed: 'Get A Job'

Above: President Bush urges America's jobless to get off their duffs.

WASHINGTON, DC—Responding to the nation's worst unemployment rate since the Hoover Administration, President Bush addressed the nation's 8.2 million unemployed workers in a televised speech Monday.

"The economy has been on the rebound for months, but 5.6 percent of you are still out of work," Bush said. "Come on, people: Get a job! Don't just sit there hoping that you'll win the lottery. Turn off that boob tube, get off that couch, and start pounding the pavement."

When the number of people taking part-time jobs because they can't get full-time work is factored in, the unemployment figure approaches 15.1 million, a number Bush called "unacceptable."

"My fellow Americans, don't come crying to me," Bush said. "I've got a job. I go to work every day, whether I feel like it or not. I don't take handouts, and I don't give them. That's a belief my daddy taught me. Now, let's get this show on the road!"

The unemployment rate

see BUSH page 124

New Strip Mall Of America Stretches Over 1/6th Of North Dakota

FARGO, ND—Representatives from the North Dakota Department of Commerce attended a ribbon-cutting ceremony Saturday for the new Strip Mall Of America, the state's largest shopping center to date.

"This new mall brings together all the low- to mid-range franchise stores that America loves," Strip Mall Of America spokesman Henry Sloan said. "It's the largest strip mall in the country—in fact, it's the largest in the world. It's your one 90-linear-mile stop for vitamins, housewares, Christian books, picture frames, and discount eyeglasses."

The dull-gray cinderblock and tinted-glass structure stretches along

see STRIP MALL page 125

Above: A tiny section of the mall, which stretches from Eldridge to the outskirts of Fargo.

Heartbroken FBI Agent Crosses Ex-Girlfriend's Name Out Of Classified Documents

WASHINGTON, DC—Special agent Brian Walters said he felt resignation, sadness, and a sense of duty Monday while stripping all mention of his ex-girlfriend Cathy Blessing from a file of FBI documents.

"It's painful, going through these classified documents and seeing Cathy's name right there in front of me, over and over again," said Walters, whose current assignment requires him to review transcripts of DC-area activist-group meetings and remove the names of those participants who are not considered national-security risks. "I'm glad that Cathy isn't regarded as a threat to the country, but I

see EX-GIRLFRIEND page 125

Right: Walters holds a file containing FBI documents stripped of all mention of Blessing (inset).

121

Richard Clarke Speaks Out

Former counterterrorism official Richard Clarke emerged as a controversial, outspoken figure at the Sept. 11 investigation hearings. What do *you* think?

"Clarke is just another crazy conspiracy theorist claiming that the federal government is slow, inefficient, and unfocused."

Tammy Kroft
Business Owner

"I don't think Clarke is lying. He's got a book to back up his claims. What does the White House have? Nothing."

Katie Sanderson
Legal Secretary

"In this time of crisis, we should stand by the president no matter what. Yes, I know I've been saying that same thing for three straight years now. So?"

Karl Kruger
Systems Analyst

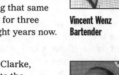

"Clarke is just mad because he was passed over for a promotion. And because his bosses' indifference to the American public was indirectly responsible for 3,000 deaths."

Vincent Wenz
Bartender

"Dick Clarke, despite the controversy, still looks amazingly good after all these years."

David Everly
Cook

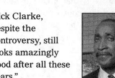

"Richard Clarke was fixated on, even obsessed with, terrorists and terrorism. Do we really want people like that in our government?"

Thomas Smith
Architect

Disney's Financial Woes

Disney's stock value has fallen 20 percent over the last five years. What are the reasons?

- Having mice and birds dress Michael Eisner each morning not cost-effective
- Cynical viewing public no longer interested in love, hope, or triumph of the human spirit
- Remake of *Pete's Dragon* $83 million over budget, 17 weeks behind schedule
- 78 percent of U.S. population has been sued by Disney
- Steadily decreasing number of clapping children eventually resulted in death of Tinkerbell
- HBO swiped that chimp that chose winning TV shows
- Upper management wasted too much time swimming gleefully through gold coins in walk-in safe
- Many employees failed to comply with mandatory work-related whistling regulations
- Company forced to pay out millions of dollars in hush money to families of Mad Teacup ride's 280 victims

the ONION ®
America's Finest News Source.™

Herman Ulysses Zweibel
Founder

T. Herman Zweibel
Publisher Emeritus
J. Phineas Zweibel
Publisher

Maxwell Prescott Zweibel
Editor-In-Chief

Before I Die, I'd Like To See Hazzard County With My Own Eyes

By Ron Knutsen

Through the years, as I've traveled this country selling floor coverings, I've had the opportunity to see the best this great nation of ours has to offer: the famous *Cheers* district of Boston, the historic Flimm building in Cincinnati, and the storied East Side of New York City, to which the Jeffersons made their famous odyssey. Once, while attending a convention in Milwaukee, I was blessed to tread the same streets as Laverne, Shirley, and the immortals of the *Happy Days* gang. But as I grow older—for, yes, I am getting old—the urban life entices me less, and the winter stays longer in my bones. Lately, I find myself thinking often of the balmy Southern countryside. Though I have seen great wonders in my life, I have yet to see Hazzard County with my own eyes.

Ah, fabled Hazzard County! Where life is by turns bucolic and abruptly violent, and inhabitants are as puritanically hard-working as they are prone to committing misdemeanor crimes. How I long to travel its winding roads! What joy, to motor serenely, or less serenely should occasion demand, past the suggestively inclined surfaces of Hazzard—a partially finished bridge over a creek here; there, a hay wagon tilted at an incline just adjacent to a farmhouse; and over yonder, a stack of lumber leaning innocently against an outhouse! How my soul yearns to lose itself in the sporadic rural traffic of Hazzard, with its farm animals, its souped-up American sporting automobiles, and its police cruisers! Truly, no other place is as beautiful a romantic representation of the post-industrial South.

My desire to visit Hazzard County is not without reservations. For one thing, I worry that it may be difficult to get there. Although I know it's "somewheres south of the Mason-Dixon line and east of the Mississip'," I am somewhat embarrassed to admit that I'm unsure of its exact location inside of Georgia.

A part of me is also apprehensive. Hazzard County's magnificence may have diminished, its splendor faded with time. It may now be a shadow of its bumptious past self. I have been saddened thusly before, as when I visited the Santa Monica boardwalk, where Jack Tripper watched Chrissy rollerskate, only to find it clotted with tourist shops. And my heart nearly broke to see the outdoor basketball courts of Mr. Kotter's beloved Brooklyn standing empty. I have learned the hardest way possible that nothing good and pure can remain so. Perhaps not even Hazzard County, where time moves slower than most other places, can escape the ever-turning wheel of Father Time.

So much more of my life lies behind me than ahead. If I do not see Hazzard County, how can I count my existence complete? Would mine be a life truly lived if I never saw the infamous Boar's Nest—headquarters of the villainous Boss Hogg and well-

> **Life is by turns bucolic and abruptly violent, and inhabitants are as puritanically hard-working as they are prone to committing misdemeanor crimes.**

spring of many a misadventure—in all its ragged vagabond glory? Could my body be put to rest without its foot having fallen in the purtiest town square in Dixie? Could my soul repose in tranquility without having first experienced Cooter's Garage, where the General Lee was tuned, where Cale Yarborough's top-secret carburetor was returned to its rightful owner, and where President Carter's limo was squirreled away after being stolen in a moment of happy-go-lucky mischief? Could I succumb peacefully to the clutch of death knowing that I had never breathed the air inside the sheriff's office? Never having seen the mill of Hazzard law enforcement grind out justice neither too coarse nor too fine, could I deem mine a life truly lived?

No. I must see Hazzard. I must see Hazzard or eternally long to bask in the late June light as it falls on the Duke ancestral farm, where once a motley band of valiant, mysteriously begotten cousins fought to keep their family land safe from foreclosure on an almost weekly basis. Though I have never been there, I know I would be at home. I know I would be welcomed. I know that a part of me, of everyone, belongs there. When I think of experiencing Hazzard County in the flesh, my heart leaps up... leaps up and soars, as if it had suddenly encountered an inclined woodpile, lovingly arranged at a 45-degree angle by some unknown, benevolent hands, there, waiting on the banks of Possum Creek. ∅

Potential Baldness Cure Leads Man To Reverse Position On Stem-Cell Research

CHARLOTTE, NC—Recent news of a potential cure for baldness has prompted area resident Chuck Tell to change his views on stem-cell research.

"I've always said I don't believe in that Frankenstein-type research, but lately I've been thinking that there might be something to it," said Tell, a 43-year-old father of two and victim of male-pattern baldness. "If there are people out there who could truly benefit from that stem-cell stuff, who are we to deny them?"

While stem-cell research could potentially treat maladies ranging from third-degree burns to Alzheimer's disease, it is highly controversial because stem cells are often extracted from a human embryo. Tell acknowledged that he once opposed the practice on ethical grounds, stating that "a human life, no matter how undeveloped, is still a human life."

"When the [stem cell research] issue first came up a few years ago, Chuck said that destroying an embryo was just like murdering somebody," Tell's wife Denise said. "He found it immoral. He said it was 'harvesting innocents who can't speak for themselves.' For months, Chuck was a champion of 'the helpless unborn.' But I haven't heard him speak on behalf of the harvested innocents since he saw some news segment about stem

cells curing baldness."

In the widely publicized study released by the journal *Nature Biotechnology*, "blank slate" stem cells were used to induce follicle- and hair-growth in mice. The one-time defender of placental rights said a Channel 9 Eyewitness News segment anchored by Debi Faubion caught his attention and inspired him to "come around to the value of stem-cell research."

The shift in thinking occurred just three days after Tell received a haircut that revealed a large, bare patch at the crown of his head. The bare patch accompanies the recently converted stem-cell-research advocate's receding hairline, of which he has long been aware.

"The study said that when these stem cells were put in mice, hair grew," said Tell, who has spent hundreds of dollars on hair-restoration products like Rogaine and Vive For Men. "And, you know, these human embryos are only a few days old."

Tell said the story "opened my eyes" to the revolutionary potential of stem-cell research. And, although he insisted on his continued belief in the "sanctity of unborn lives," he said he now also believes that "in considering such weighty issues, one must, as difficult as it is to do so, ask oneself to remember the rights of living, fully formed human beings."

Above: The rapidly balding Tell, who recently re-evaluated his position on embryo-murder.

"People who oppose the research aren't putting themselves into the position of those who suffer from... things that stem cells could cure," Tell said. "Right To Life people: What would you say if your son suffered from something that could be cured by stem cells? Something that was wrecking his life and robbing him of his self-esteem? Something that invited the ridicule of complete strangers and his own children? It's really im-

portant that you try and see both sides here."

Tell is one of many who would benefit immeasurably from new stem-cell-based therapies, Johns Hopkins stem-cell research director Leah DiPrima said.

"The promise offered by the use of stem cells is virtually boundless," DiPrima said. "There is no reason why stem-cell-based cures can't be found see BALDNESS page 126

Fuck-Buddy Becomes Fuck-Fiancé

MIAMI, FL—In spite of the explicitly casual nature of their relationship, fuck-buddies Nora Ingersoll and Keith Hetzel are engaged, friend Tom Stipps reported Tuesday. "Keith and Nora have been fooling around for years, but Keith said they were just friends," Stipps said. "I was shocked when Nora showed up wearing a ring." Later that day, the couple reportedly opened a fuck-joint-checking account.

Report: Caucasians Will Soon Be A Minority In Their Own Goddamn Country

PIKEVILLE, TN—According to Hormel-plant breakroom sources, if the Puerto Ricans and the Mexicans and the Orientals and the blacks don't

stop having all those babies, whites will be a minority in their own goddamn country as early as 2010. "Someone looked at the census figures, and on account of how much faster they're multiplying, it's only a couple years before there's more of them than of us real Americans," foreman Ron Nelson announced Tuesday. "They're already making the kids learn Spanish at the high school." According to U.S. Census Bureau estimates, 80.7 percent of the current U.S. population is white.

Wheelchair-Bound Student Would Have Preferred To Sit Out Pep Rally

ROCK SPRINGS, WY—In spite of the varsity cheerleaders' enthusiasm, Rock Springs Central High sophomore William Boelart would have actually preferred not to have participated in the school's pep rally Mon-

day. "I appreciate the thought, but I didn't really get into being wheeled around wearing a rainbow Afro and holding up a banner that said 'Bulldogs Kick A**,'" Boelart said. "I like it better when the popular kids avoid eye contact with me." Boelart was last used in a school function Dec. 11, when he played a corpse in a production of *Arsenic And Old Lace*.

Scientist Has Nagging Feeling He Left Particle Accelerator On

CHICAGO—University of Chicago particle physicist Matthew Sharp drove halfway home before he was struck with the fear that he'd left the Argonne Tandem Linac Accelerator System running Tuesday night. "I *think* I powered it down after smashing those 9-GeV electrons into 3.1-GeV positrons, but I don't specifically remember flipping the switch," Sharp said. "Not only does a nine million volt electrostatic tandem Van de Graaff in-

jector accelerator cost a lot to run; it's also a pretty serious fire hazard." Sharp almost turned his car around, but didn't, because the past three times he's gone back to check on the accelerator, he's found it off.

Smoking Ban Collapses Fragile Prison Economy

SOLEDAD, CA—A pen-wide smoking ban instituted last week devastated the Salinas Valley State Prison's fragile economy, inmate #67545 said Monday. "There were occasional fluctuations or recalibrations, but a bar of soap used to equal three cigarettes; a Snickers, four; a Percocet, 15," said Kenneth Oglivy, a former WorldCom accountant serving 10 years for embezzlement. "After the ban, the value of a carton of Newports climbed to 50 times its 2003 value. Now that those cigarettes are gone, it's total chaos." Oglivy said Salinas Valley inmates will have to devise a new system of value based on some other commodity, such as assholes. ∅

	8:00		9:00		10:00

ABC	Husky, Working-Class, Suburban Ordinary Guy	Ordinary, Suburban, Working-Class Husky Guy	Working-Class, Ordinary, Husky Suburban Guy	Suburban, Husky, Ordinary Working-Class Guy	Tracy Morgan's Last Chance
NBC	Remembering Friends: Part 1 In A 14-Part Series		Slightly Mismatched Couple	Half A Dad	Sir Ian McKellen's Place
CBS	Everybody Loves Raymond	Raymond's So Great	Raymond, Raymond, Raymond	Nobody Loves Me...	Because I'm Not Raymond
WB	Banal Hopes And Dreams	Gotham High	Pretty Lawyer Bitches	Single Mom #43	Beautiful, Interchangeable Teens Hurt Each Other's Feelings
UPN	Flaunita's Way	Shoreena Explain It	Ooh, What Stank So Damn Good?	Whoa There, I *Love* Malik	Some Stand-Ups
PBS	This Old Host	One Camera In The Balcony Of La Traviata			Pledge Drives Of The Ancient Mayans

ESPN	The NHL's Greatest Penalties	Behind The Cup	Great Ex-NFLers Of Real Estate And Car Sales		Some Musclebound Lummox's Opinion
Telemundo	Bikini Cuidado	El Comedio Del Retardo	El Leprechaun 3: El Leprechaun En El Barrio		Wacky Wacky De Los Gatos Locos
USA	Lawyers & Orderlies	Domestic Behavior	Oh My God! Anthony Michael Hall! He's Alive!		Anybody Feel Like Sitting Through Sister Act?
Cinemax	Corrupted Innocence	Compromised Integrity		Assault On Sex Island	All But Penetration

BUSH from page 121

remains high, in spite of the many tax-cut initiatives the Bush Administration has introduced over the past several years.

"The government can only do so much," Bush said. "How hard can it possibly be to find a job? A friend of mine lost his job when his company went belly-up. Did he bitch and moan about it? Absolutely not. He picked up the phone and started making cold calls, he landed back on his feet, and now he's the chief financial officer of a major petrochemical concern."

According to the president, the na-

tion's unemployed need to make looking for work a full-time job.

"How many applications have you filled out today?" Bush said. "You should spend eight hours a day looking through the want ads, mailing résumés, and pounding the pavement. You won't find a job moping around the house and feeling sorry for yourself. If you're down-and-out, you have to pull yourself up by the bootstraps. Life's hard, my friends. Get used to it."

Bush addressed a complaint often made by unemployed workers: They are unable to find jobs commensurate

to their skill set due to lulls in the technical and manufacturing sectors and the outsourcing of jobs to other countries.

"If you wanted work as bad as you say you do, you'd take what you could find," Bush said. "You gotta work your way up, instead of waiting around for your dream job to fall into your lap. Walk before you run. Climb your way up the ladder."

Continued Bush: "I heard McDonald's is hiring. What's wrong with that? Does your fancy degree say you can't work at a Mickey D's? You may

not be doing exactly what you want, but at least you'll have the pride of knowing that you're earning your living."

A reporter asked for comment on a statistic which shows that only 21,000 new jobs were created in February, in spite of the Bush administration's promise to create 320,000.

"I've got a statistic for you," Bush said. "You've got to look out for No. 1. Take charge. I've got a job plan for the nation. It's called 'Get off your duff.'"

Bush said the country is experiencing its longest average-unemployment duration in 20 years, and he wants to see it end immediately.

"If you get an interview, walk in there like you're the only person for the job," Bush said. "Show them you're willing to work. Show up early and bring a broom. Sweep up the place while you're waiting for the interview to start. That'll let them know you're a go-getter."

The president concluded his speech by encouraging the jobless to start their search immediately.

"What are you doing listening to this speech when you should be out there looking for work?" Bush asked. "Get a move on! Even my brother has a job. He's no one special, and he's the governor of Florida! If he can do that, you should be able to line up something at your local Wal-Mart."

With that statement, Bush left Secretary of Labor Elaine Chao to present some of the finer points of his administration's new position.

"Get a haircut," Chao said. "Clean yourself up a little and put on a nice shirt, or even a suit. Maybe employers would take you more seriously if you didn't look like you just rolled out of bed. The way you look now, I wouldn't hire you to throw me a rope if I was falling off a cliff." ∅

Above: Bush gives pointers on how to get the part-time delivery position available at this DC-area restaurant.

also have to admit that it feels pretty good to strike her name from the record, like she struck me from her life."

Walters said he met Blessing four years ago, when she was a graduate student at George Washington University.

"Cathy's a very passionate girl with a strong sense of justice,"Walters said, motioning toward the stacks of transcripts from Greenpeace, Amnesty International, and several other groups for which Blessing has worked. "When she believes in something, she doesn't give up, no matter what. I wish she had believed in me."

While none of the organizations Blessing is involved with are considered dangerous, the FBI maintains a policy of vigilance and monitors many activist groups for suspicious individuals.

"We're trained to keep our eyes open for people who appear to be interested in getting involved in something deeper,"Walters said, running a metal ruler down a page and using a broad-tipped Sharpie to obliterate the name of the woman with whom he'd spent four years of his life. "The FBI doesn't keep tabs on the ones like Cathy, who aren't ready for a commitment and are all too happy to keep things casual, until one day they pack up their things and move out while you're away at a weekend security-training conference in Houston."

According to his superiors, Walters has done a satisfactory job excising non-essential data from FBI files

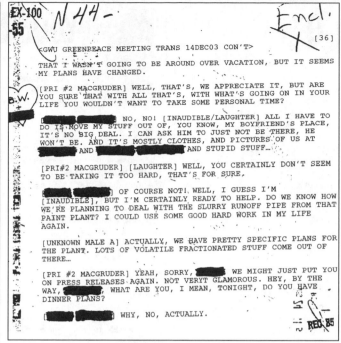

Above: A document Walters stripped of Blessing's name.

since joining the Bureau in March 2002. According to Walters, he has done a less satisfactory job excising nonessential thoughts of Blessing from his mind ever since she broke up with him in January.

"I know I should just forget about her, but I really thought we were going to be together,"Walters said, staring at Blessing's photograph in a Greenpeace internal newsletter. "I always thought that our differences brought us together. Two people who are not the same can complement each other. It can work."

"But if it doesn't, sometimes you're better off making a clean break of it," Walters said, slicing a square around Blessing's photo with an X-Acto knife. "It's really best for the national interest to just let them go."

Walters said the final year of his relationship with Blessing was rife with problems.

"We had major communication issues," Walters said. "Maybe things would have been better if I'd been able to talk about my life outside of our relationship. But, of course, by direct orders of the U.S. government, I couldn't."

"And she—well, she couldn't *stop* talking about hers," Walters said, blacking out two full pages of an Amnesty International meeting tran-

> ## "Cathy said I was providing less-than-full disclosure of my true thoughts and feelings," Walters said.

script in which Blessing spoke about the treatment of prisoners at Guantanamo Bay.

As the relationship worsened, Blessing accused Walters of "withholding vital information."

"Cathy said I was providing less-than-full disclosure of my true thoughts and feelings," Walters said. "She complained that I had my own agenda, and that I was purposely keeping her in the dark."

Walters continued: "Then there's the fact that special agents keep a very demanding schedule. Cathy never seemed to understand if I was tired at the end of a long day and didn't feel like going out. She'd say that I kept her cooped up for my own weird purposes, and that I was treating her inhumanely. She said my behavior was outside the rules of civilized—dammit! My Sharpie ripped right through the damn paper again."

In spite of receiving the occasional torn, crumpled, or curiously streaked document, Walters' immediate superior, assistant director Clay Anderson, said Walters is doing above-average work on this assignment.

"Agent Walters is doing a great job focusing his full attention on a task that is admittedly quite tedious," Anderson said. "While other agents have burned out quickly, Walters seems absolutely driven. A couple of times, we've even arrived in the morning to find him crashed out on the couch, crossed-out papers all around him, and sad country music playing over the office intercom."

"Now, as far as the documents go, the FBI does hold that it's our duty to respect the privacy of non-threatening citizens by removing them from the record," Anderson added. "It has happened a few times that we've had to send documents back for revision and request that Agent Walters cut out more than just that Catherine Blessing woman." ∅

Interstate 94 from Eldridge to a point seven miles west of Fargo. Occupying six different zip codes, it is capable of hosting more than 4,700 stores and boasts 240,000 parking spaces.

While the mall's focus is on smaller chain stores, it does feature three anchor stores: a Marshalls, a Gymboree, and an Aldi grocery store, located in Jamestown, Valley City, and Oriska, respectively.

"There's something for everyone here,"Sloan said. "If you're looking for gift wrap and festive decorations, visit one of our eight Party City stores. Arts-and-crafts buffs can choose between Michael's and Ben Franklin, not to mention Jo-Ann Fabrics. I don't want to jump the gun, but we're probably going to have a Radio Shack, too."

According to Sloan, only 40 percent of the retail space is currently occupied, and a full 3 percent of the storefronts house liquidation stores and cellular-phone outlets.

"We've got 18 Big Lots, 13 Dollars General, 11 Dollar Trees, and three Family Dollars," Sloan said. "While there are still a few more 'For Rent' signs than we'd like to see, we're confident that the unclaimed spaces will fill up soon."

Sloan added: "After all, we're in a great location, with easy access from the interstate via exits 251 through 338. Additionally, we are an excellent facili-

ty, featuring a well-maintained sidewalk and several benches in front of the Lechter's in Tower City. We're talking about getting a few potted trees."

The stores in the mall will not be limited to retail outlets. Sloan said the mall will "take visitors on a culinary tour of the nation's finer fast-food eateries and theme restaurants."

"Who wouldn't want to come and get a taste of North Dakota?"Sloan asked. "After a long day of shopping, you can stop at the Shakey's Pizza all-you-can-eat buffet and recharge your batteries. Or, if you just want to satisfy your sweet tooth, stop in at the Auntie Anne's or one of our 48 TCBY outlets."

One business unlikely to rent a spot in the mall is TGIFridays, which is currently building 18 restaurants at points just across the four-lane interstate.

While the mall caters first and foremost to residents of North Dakota, mall officials said they hope it will also draw tourists from all over the country, much like the popular Mall Of America in Minnesota.

"Why not make a vacation of it?" Sloan asked. "Bring the entire family and spend the weekend at one of the region's many wonderful Super8 motels. South Dakota has stolen our thunder in the past, but if you stack up their Wall Drugs and Corn Palaces against our Funcos and Pier One Im-

ports, I think it's obvious who's the best Dakota."

Added Sloan: "It's us."

Sloan noted one additional feature of the mall.

"If you have car trouble while you're taking advantage of the variety of shops, you're in luck,"he said. "As long as you're shopping at the Strip Mall Of America, you're never more than 34 miles from a Pep Boys Auto Repair Center. That's a *guarantee.*

"And, while you're waiting for the mechanic to finish, you can pop next door to browse at one of the Waldenbooks or have a coffee at a Gloria Jean's," Sloan added.

The Department of Commerce estimates the mall will provide approximately 30,000 jobs in the coming year. While many North Dakotans said they are excited about the employment opportunities, some have voiced concern over the 90-mile barricade separating the regions to the north and south of the mall.

"True, it is unfortunate that people who need to travel from, say, Hastings to Valley City will now have to factor in an extra two hours for their commute," Sloan said. "On the plus side, drivers can break up their trips by stopping in at the Petco to get a great deal on a 20-pound bag of cat food—or swinging by the Kaybee Toys to pick up a present for the little ones!" ∅

Test Your Jean-Q

**A Room Of Jean's Own
By Jean Teasdale**

Put on your thinking caps, Jeanketeers, because it's time once again to put your brains to the test with my second-ever Jean Teasdale "Trivia" Challenge! People often read my column to see what sassy, outrageous thing I'll say next. I figure, why not pay tribute to my loyal, careful readers with a "trivia" quiz about things in my life? (I put "trivia" in quotation marks because, to me at least, there's nothing trivial about my life! After all, it's my life, right?)

Now, this time around, I've made it a little easier for you by including some multiple-choice questions. (Heck, if not for multiple-choice questions, I doubt I would have ever graduated high school!) So open those memory banks, people, and no peeking at the answers before you make a guess!

What kind of chocolate don't I like?
This is no trick question, Jeanketeers! Believe it or not, there is chocolate I don't care for. Give up? It's those miniature, foil-wrapped Easter eggs. They have kind of a waxy, oily taste, and rather than melting in your mouth like all good chocolate should, they just leave a bitter coating on your tongue. Although I do have to admit that when I spot a bowl of them, I still eat a handful! I'm weak, I know! A Jewish girl I once worked with told me that chocolate Hanukkah coins taste just as bad, and all I can say is I'm glad I'm a Christian and therefore forbidden to eat them.

In 1985, did I quit, get fired from, or get laid off from Madge's Deep Freeze?
Okay, this is a bit of a trick question, but veteran readers of my column will know that none of these things happened. After working there for three months, I went in one morning, only to find that the place had been padlocked by the sheriff's deputies. Apparently, Madge was involved in some improper financial thing with mafia types and had skipped town, so his place was shut down. (Madge was a guy—don't ask why he was named Madge!) Anyway, I never did get my last paycheck. (By the way, Madge's was the first place in the country to make soft-serve ice cream with crushed Oreos in it. I kid you not! It makes me feel kind of proud to have been there when history was made.)

True or false: I look like Valerie Bertinelli.
True! Or at least it was true in 1981, when my skin was clear, and the bad home perm my stepsister gave me finally fell out, and I had a very nice brunette shag haircut going. In fact, I will always remember 1981 as my Year Of Great Hair. I never could achieve quite the same look again, but I did look like Valerie Bertinelli there for a spell. Of course, I had a few pounds up on her, but in a certain light I really did resemble her. I really did.

True or false: I can bend my right index finger back at the third joint nearly 30 degrees and make it stay like that.
False. That's hubby Rick's talent. (His only talent!) He broke his finger when he was little, and it wasn't set properly. Boy, he's gotten a lot of mileage out of it down at Tacky's Tavern. He gets a lot of pleasure from seeing people freak out. And I think it even hurts him a bit to do it, so obviously, someone's not driving with a full tank of gas there! If I could bend back my finger like that, I wouldn't use the ability to torment people. There's enough ill will in this world.

Which of these three images did I draw?
a)

b)

c)

d) All of the above
The answer is **d, all of the above!** Bet you didn't know I was a bit of a doodler! The little fellow in the middle is "Mr. Freckles."

Who bullied me in 10th grade?
a) Wendi
b) Shanni
c) Marc
d) None of the above
The answer is **a, Wendi**. Shanni was a cheerleader who was too stuck-up to speak to me, and, although Marc picked on me about my weight, he moved away at the end of the fall semester.

When I'm very depressed, I...
a) Eat
b) Sleep a lot
c) Wreck things
d) Cut myself

Your Horoscope

By Lloyd Schumner Sr.
**Retired Machinist and
A.A.P.B.-Certified Astrologer**

Aries: (March 21–April 19)
You will hear something this week that makes you doubt the love of your spouse, but exactly why circus music has this effect will remain a mystery.

Taurus: (April 20–May 20)
Efficient, divine revelation is yours this week when the love goddess Aphrodite appears to you for 1.9 seconds during a round of speed-dating.

Gemini: (May 21–June 21)
You've always believed that you can judge a man by his handshakes, which is why you continue to denounce the theories of Stephen Hawking.

Cancer: (June 22–July 22)
You'll be granted the secret wish of parents everywhere when your adorable baby daughter stays that size forever.

Leo: (July 23–Aug. 22)
The stars believe that a person must make his own mistakes, but they warn you not to do anything that may, say, burn down Chicago this week.

Virgo: (Aug. 23–Sept. 22)
Personal growth looms large in your future as you are transformed into a 1,000-foot giant who blots out the sun.

Libra: (Sept. 23–Oct. 23)
You've always believed that the children are our future, which is true insofar as most are cruel, violent, and short.

Scorpio: (Oct. 24–Nov. 21)
You will find that one can go a long way in this world by practicing honesty, kindness, and the bizarre owl-worship ritual of the Druids.

Sagittarius: (Nov. 22–Dec. 21)
You'll achieve nationwide fame when footage of the polar bear mauling your carcass is set to "Flight Of The Bumblebee."

Capricorn: (Dec. 22–Jan. 19)
It's one thing to try to change your image, but it's another to bulk up on Andro, wear only white mink, and insist that you're the Vanilla Gorilla.

Aquarius: (Jan. 20–Feb. 18)
Some may call your breast implants tacky, but at least you had the guts to try out unconventional shapes.

Pisces: (Feb. 19–March 20)
You're in grave danger of planning your life around vague interpretations of the mysterious patterns that can supposedly be seen in the night sky.

e) All of the above
f) Some of the above
The answer is **f, some of the above.** Thank goodness that I'm generally a content, upbeat, easygoing person. But I do suffer from the odd spell of deep depression every so often, and when I'm blue, let's just say Domino's pizza places, clean sheets, and household objects—particularly ones that are ceramic or stuffed—are not safe! The one thing I have never done, however, is cut myself. I think that is depraved, not to mention an outright gross thing to do to yourself. I respect my body. And, if I ever did resort to that, I would have the presence of mind to seek psychiatric help right away, which I strongly recommend to anyone doing that to him or herself.

And that's the quiz! You might notice that I did not assign each question a point value this time. There's too much competition in society, and I don't want to create friction and bitterness just because one person scored better than another. To me, every Jeanketeer is a big winner! ∅

BALDNESS from page 123
for such unfortunate afflictions as wrinkles, cellulite, excessive flatulence, chronic halitosis, and erectile dysfunction."

Tell acknowledged that a stem-cell cure for baldness may be years off, but he said his hope is that "future generations of baldness sufferers" can benefit from today's research.

"Many of these embryos are destined for oblivion anyway," Tell said. "Why not derive some positive benefit from their existence? People are suffering now, and people will continue to suffer in the future unless we recognize the overwhelming benefits of stem-cell therapy. I truly believe this."

Tell's personal physician, Daryl Farmer, said he was heartened by Tell's change of opinion.

"It's touching to see Chuck give so much thought to this very complicated issue," Farmer said. "Given his emotional honesty, I wish I could bring myself to tell him that the stem cells used in this study differ from the embryonic stem cells that sparked the political debate he originally engaged in." ∅

Jay-Z Gives Shout-Out To His Shareholdaz

see FINANCE page 7E

Fox News Covers Spring Break Pretty Well

see LOCAL page 15B

Christian Rock Band Gives Up Pyrotechnics For Lent

see RELIGION page 4D

Salad Hand-Spun

see FOOD page 12G

STATshot

A look at the numbers that shape your world.

What Can't We Bring Ourselves To Tell Our Loved Ones?

15% Lost job 21 months ago

13% Are secretly a homophobe

24% Hate them more than life itself

11% Don't actually like the nipple-squeeze thing

8% We're not technically 18 yet

29% Never did learn their names

THE ONION • $2.00 US • $3.00 CAN

0 74470 94595 6
00

the ONION®

VOLUME 40 ISSUE 14   AMERICA'S FINEST NEWS SOURCE™   8–14 APRIL 2004

Price Of Nuclear Secrets Plummeting

Above: Plans for weapons like Pakistan's medium-range Shaheen II missile are cheaper than ever.

WASHINGTON, DC—Top-secret information about the design, construction, and delivery of nuclear weapons has never been more affordable than it is today, CIA Director George Tenet announced Monday.

"We're seeing items like warhead blueprints and uranium-enrichment instructions go for a fraction of what they used to cost," Tenet said. "There's never been a better time to snag a deal on low-mass, high-yield weaponry schematics. Countries like Iran and North Korea are finding that it's a real buyer's market."

Tenet said he expects prices to continue to decline.

"These bargain prices will create more buyers, which will in turn widen the black market to include

see SECRETS page 131

Yahoo Launches Soul-Search Engine

SUNNYVALE, CA—Hoping it will push them to the top of an increasingly competitive market, Internet portal Yahoo has added soul-search capabilities to its expanding line of search tools, company executives announced Monday.

"Capable of navigating the billions of thoughts, experiences, and emotions that make up the human psyche, the new Yahoo soul-search engine helps users find what's deep inside them quickly and easily," Yahoo CEO Terry Semel said. "All those long, difficult nights of pondering your place in this world are a thing of the past."

Yahoo's main competitor recently

Above: A page generated by Yahoo's new soul-search engine.

introduced two new advanced search functions: Google Local, which highlights search results from a specific geographic area, and Google Personalized Search, which allows users to

create a profile of their interests to influence search results. But Semel called Yahoo's new search function "vastly more precise."

see YAHOO page 131

15-Year-Old Nephew Asked If He Can Get Ecstasy

MINNEAPOLIS—Having exhausted several more conventional sources for illegal drugs, area copy editor Alex Henderson, 33, was forced to ask his 15-year-old nephew Kevin for MDMA Monday.

"My girlfriend Paula [Tanner] was talking about how fun ecstasy was the two times she did it," Henderson said. "She got really excited when I said I'd never tried it

before, because I guess the first time is the best. She said we should take it and spend all night having sex. I told her I'd make some calls."

Although ecstasy use among young adults is on the rise, Henderson said he has been "out of the drug loop" for several years, and thus unsure where to buy the club drug. It was only

see ECSTASY page 130

Above: Henderson hangs out at his nephew Kevin's house.

127

U.S. Kids Sleep-Deprived

The National Sleep Foundation recently announced that American children are not getting enough sleep. What do *you* think?

Cynthia Lewis
Tax Preparer

"I wake my son up four times a night for pulled-pork sandwiches and Bible study."

Steve Green
Fruit Picker

"This doesn't concern me personally, because I ain't got no damn kids by no woman on the other side of town."

Virginia Adams
Nutritionist

"It's no surprise. The obese often have trouble sleeping."

Frank Gonzalez
Painter

"Parents, use child psychology to eradicate this problem. Tell your son or daughter, 'If you don't get enough sleep, the monster under your bed will eat you.'"

Gregory King
Aerospace Engineer

"You know what else they're not getting? My goddamn Brandy Old Fashioned, that's what. You hear me, Tyler?"

Stephen Harrison
Systems Analyst

"Maybe if they pulled up their damn pants for once, that would, um... Well, it would be a step in the right direction."

The Hunt For Bin Laden

The commission probing the Sept. 11 attacks presented in detail the mistakes made in the search for Osama bin Laden. What were some of the near-misses?

Dec. 13, 2001—Netzooka backfires, leaving Marines entangled while bin Laden gets away

Feb. 22, 2001—Bin Laden waved past airport security at Washington Dulles when he identifies self as Cat Stevens

July 25, 2003—Weinermobile passes through Uzbek-Afghan border checkpoint unsearched

Oct. 6, 2003—Bush has chance to arrest bin Laden at state dinner, but chooses to avoid awkward scene

Aug. 28, 2002—Afghan authorities lock bin Laden in cell, but the ACLU shows up and makes them let him go

Sept. 21, 2002—Upon being tapped on right shoulder, Pakistani border patrolman stares in that direction for 15 minutes, failing to notice marching sounds

April 4, 1986—Bin Laden given millions of dollars in weapons and training by Reagan administration, giving him the ability and means to later evade capture

Jan. 5, 2004—Bin Laden makes an appearance on *Frasier*, then slips out of green room undetected

June 3, 2002—Authorities move in on oddly lifelike statue of bin Laden in Afghanistan National Wax Museum a day too late

the ONION®
America's Finest News Source.™

Herman Ulysses Zweibel
Founder

T. Herman Zweibel
Publisher Emeritus
J. Phineas Zweibel
Publisher
Maxwell Prescott Zweibel
Editor-In-Chief

Munchtime Is The Most Important Snack Of The Day

Has this ever happened to you? You are snug in your bed when an insatiable craving overcomes you. You try to ignore it, but a piece of fried chicken in the fridge is calling you. Before you know it, you're in the kitchen, standing before the open refrigerator. As any snacktologist could tell you, this is your body's munchtabolic system telling you that you've got the gotta-gobbles.

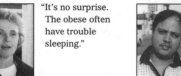

Carla Weindorf

Snacking is an important part of the food-intake process. Skipping munch can result in hunger, fatigue, and undertantalization of the taste buds. In fact, recent scientif-esque studies show that munchtime is the most important snack of the day.

General Snacks' snackentistic research indicates that people who eat at munchtime are less likely to suffer from lowered blood sugar. Munchtime, when enjoyed regularly, also cuts down on late-night hunger pangs, leading to sounder sleep and a greater level of performance the next day. In addition, chompetific studies show that munchtime snackers are two-thirds less likely to fall asleep after the news.

Snacker studies show that

> **General Snacks' snackentistic research indicates that people who eat at munchtime are less likely to suffer from lowered blood sugar. Munchtime, when enjoyed regularly, also cuts down on late-night hunger pangs, leading to sounder sleep and a greater level of performance the next day.**

munchtime decreases your nibbling quotient by 67 percent. While no snack is 100 percent effective against the nibbles, a satisfying munchtime works better at reducing your bite-time urges than the other four leading snacktimes combined.

As General Snacks' snacksperson, with 52 years of experience in snack-making and almost 60 years' experience in goodie-consumption, I can assure you that munchtime doesn't have to be a chore. Whether it's a fruitastic General Snacks Real-Fruit Pie topped with a dollop of Frozen Vanilla Whip or a handful of General Snacks Veg-

> **Snacking is an important part of the food-intake process. Skipping munch can result in hunger, fatigue, and undertantalization of the taste buds.**

etable Crisp Crunchers crackers right out of the box, it's easy to get the tasty morsels you need to meet your snacktritional needs.

Another little-known snacktoid: The extra boost that munchtime provides will fuel your post-meal activities, like washing your munchtime dishes, settling in for a long movie, or driving down to the corner store for tomorrow's munchtime snack.

Watching your waistline? General Snacks noshtritionists note that there are many ways to tailor your munchtime snack to your nutrimental goals. Don't rule out breakfast foods or dinner foods or desserts because they seem inappropriate for munchtime. Munchtime is the perfect time to polish off any extra General Snacks provisions you have lying around the house.

Some people don't know what constitutes a decent munchtime snack. The right answer is that there is no wrong answer. You can enjoy a sandwich made with General Snacks Peanut Butter, creamy or crunchy, or a bowl of General Snacks Microwaveable Soup. General Snacks Fruit Gels, anyone? Only you know what your body needs to satisfy its snacktritional cravings.

You could fulfill your munchtime requirements with a quick meal of tasty General Snacks Ramen Noodles. How about some General Snacks Double Toffee Turtle Ice Cream straight out of the carton? No one needs to know what you do once the blinds are drawn. That's between you and your spoon.

If you have any questions, or would like some free munchtime snackgestions, visit www.generalsnacks.com/munchtime.

Area Man Excited Friend Is Getting Divorced

PASCO, WA—Jim Sterling, 31, reported Monday that he's excited to resume his friendship with his soon-to-be-divorced buddy Andy Freiburg.

"Awesome," Sterling said, shortly after learning that Freiburg was divorcing Katie Burello, his wife of four

> ## "Katie's all right, I guess," said Sterling, who has never been in a relationship for longer than three months. "But she really kept Andy on a tight leash. After the wedding, I only got to see Andy about once a month, and Katie almost always tagged along. And she'd always cut the night short with some excuse, like that she had to get up for work."

years. "The Ster-Frei combo is back in action!"

Sterling and Freiburg became friends when they roomed together as freshmen at the University of Washington, and they remained friends after college, with Sterling serving as a groomsman at the couple's 2000 wedding. However, after Freiburg was married, Sterling said he and his friend rarely socialized without Burello present.

"Katie's all right, I guess," said Sterling, who has never been in a relationship for longer than three months. "But she really kept Andy on a tight leash. After the wedding, I only got to see Andy about once a month, and Katie almost always tagged along. And she'd always cut the night short with some excuse, like that she had to get up for work."

Above: Sterling stocks up on groceries in preparation for the arrival of the newly divorced Freiburg (left).

Sterling said Freiburg just wasn't himself when his wife was present.

"Whenever Katie was around, Andy would get all boring," Sterling said. "He wouldn't do shots; he'd just sit there sipping on a light beer. He'd never use our catch phrases or talk about the dumb stuff we did in college, either. Instead, he'd drone on about some computer-animation project he was doing or some boring thing going on in his neighborhood."

"Well, this divorce proves what I've said all along: You can't drag a party animal like Andy out to the sticks and

expect him to turn into Joe Suburb," Sterling said. "It's only a matter of time before the full moon rises. I'm sure that's why things didn't work out with Katie."

Sterling said he'd noticed Freiburg reverting to his pre-marital self over recent months.

"Andy never talked about Katie, but I knew something was up, because suddenly he was going out without her a lot more often," Sterling said. "He'd stay out later, and one night he even crashed at my place and called

see MAN page 130

Dollar Losing Value Against The Quarter

NEW YORK—After falling 6 percent in the past three weeks, the U.S. dollar hit a 208-year low against the U.S. quarter, which had been valued at exactly 0.25 dollars since its introduction in 1796. "The dollar continues to slide against most major currencies," Morgan Stanley analyst Richard Jemison said. "At the end of the day Tuesday, the quarter was trading at .267 yen, .203 euros, and US$0.28. But what we're really seeing here is not just a dollar weakened by a sluggish economy, but an exceptionally resilient quarter-dollar." Jemison was quick to point out that the dollar remains very strong against the nickel.

Visiting Liberian Dignitary In No Hurry To Leave

WASHINGTON, DC—Liberian in-

terim government chairman Gyude Bryant is strongly considering extending his first diplomatic visit to the U.S., the West African leader announced Monday. "It feels like I just got here," said Bryant, whose nation has just begun the work of rebuilding its infrastructure after 14 years of civil war. "Why rush back to Liberia? I'm barely settled into my hotel suite. I haven't even used the whirlpool." Bryant, head of the Liberian government since former president Charles Taylor was forced into exile, said he may as well stay at least until the violence in the city of Buchanan dies down, which would allow him to check out the Smithsonian.

Almost No Effort Made To Stop Kid From Eating Cigarette Butt

HALLOWELL, ME—While waiting for a bus Tuesday, Stan Geraldson watched 2-year-old Jason Kemper

pick up a spent cigarette butt and place it in his mouth, but made only a minor attempt to stop him. "Hey, ah, you shouldn't..." Geraldson told Kemper, whose mother was engaged in a conversation a few feet away. "Don't... eat that." Geraldson said he would have done more to stop Kemper if the item had been fiberglass or something.

Boxer Hopes He Can Make Money Punching Things In Retirement

CHICAGO—Shortly after announcing his retirement, heavyweight champion Lennox Lewis, 38, said Monday that he hopes to continue to make money punching things. "I have a few other skills, but I'm probably best at punching," Lewis said. "Cows, computers, sheets of glass—if the price is right, I'll punch it good. I may be retired, but I'm still a powerful good puncher." Lewis added that he would also be willing to hire himself

out by the hour for displays of fancy footwork.

Frank Zappa Fan Thinks You Just Haven't Heard The Right Album

NEDERLAND, CO—In spite of your insistence that you are not into Frank Zappa, avid fan Roger Von Lee believes that you would change your mind if you heard the right album. "You're prejudiced, because the only Zappa you know is 'Valley Girl' and 'Don't Eat The Yellow Snow,'" Von Lee told you Tuesday. "Seriously, you need to check out *Hot Rats* or *Absolutely Free*. Zappa and the Mothers were at their peak, and Zappa's jazz-rock fusion experiments predate *Bitches Brew*. That'll totally convince you that Zappa's the shit." Von Lee added that if those two don't get under your skin, he can recommend another 15 to 20 albums that will for sure. ∅

ECSTASY from page 127

after two weeks of intense searching that Henderson asked his nephew if he knew any dealers.

"Let me assure you, going to Kevin was my absolute last resort," Henderson said. "I explored every single avenue I could think of before I went to track him down after band practice Monday night."

Henderson said the first person he contacted before approaching the high-school sophomore was his friend Dean Holston.

"Dean and I used to party a lot in college, but he was always the one who took the money and got the stuff for our group," Henderson said. "It turns out he cleaned himself up and is just starting a job drafting legislation in Washington. I got him working late. He said no way. Then he said it was too bad I couldn't make it to his wedding last summer."

"It wasn't one of my finer moments," he added.

After he asked all of his friends and several of his more irresponsible-seeming acquaintances, Henderson decided that he needed to seek out a younger demographic. He said he spent three days cozying up to Christine Polley, the 22-year-old intern at his office, before casually broaching the subject of having the history major find him some ecstasy.

"Everyone from the office was having a couple of beers after work," Hen-

> After he asked all of his friends and several of his more irresponsible-seeming acquaintances, Henderson decided that he needed to seek out a younger demographic.

derson said. "Christine seems pretty laid-back, so I didn't think it would be out of line to ask her if she could hook me up. She didn't freak out or anything, but she got a little evasive and told me that she didn't do drugs and didn't know anything about that stuff. She left kind of quickly afterward. I hope she doesn't think I'm the office narc or something."

Only after several more weeks of failed attempts did Henderson turn to his nephew.

"Let's just say it—I was desperate," Henderson said. "I can admit that much."

Although Henderson found it awkward to ask his nephew for illegal drugs, the prospect of pleasing his girlfriend convinced him to go forward with his plans.

"I tried to call at a time when no one else in the family was around, but my brother Jake answered the phone,"

Henderson said. "I talked to him for a minute, and then I was like, 'Yeah, so how's Kevin?'"

Henderson said his concern for his nephew seemed to confuse his brother.

"He was like, 'Kevin? He's okay. He

> Although Kevin's initial inquiries were unsuccessful, the high-school sophomore promised to keep his ear to the ground for his uncle, in spite of his apparent discomfort in doing so.

got a B-minus on his research paper.' That was my road in," Henderson said. "I was like, 'B-minus. Hmm. Maybe I should talk to him.'"

Henderson's brother, though surprised by the request, put his son on the phone.

"Once I had Kevin on the phone, I told him he didn't need to worry so much about a B-minus, that it was just one grade, that he was doing great. I asked him what sports teams he's rooting for these days, if he thought that movie about the Alamo was going to be any good, and then if he could get me some X."

According to Henderson, Kevin initially did not understand the question, forcing his uncle to repeat himself several times.

"I was like, 'Ecstasy. Can you get me some X?'" Henderson said. "Finally, after like five minutes, he was like, 'Oh. Oh. X? Oh. Um, I guess I can ask around.'"

Henderson said he immediately had second thoughts after getting off the phone with his nephew.

"It kind of got me worried," he said. "I don't think my relationship with Jake would ever bounce back if he found out I'd enlisted Kevin as my drug mule. He's still a little mad at me because I took Kevin to see *House Of 1000 Corpses*."

Although Kevin's initial inquiries were unsuccessful, the high-school sophomore promised to keep his ear to the ground for his uncle, in spite of his apparent discomfort in doing so.

"Some kids might think it's cool to score drugs for their uncle, but it kind of gives me the creeps," Kevin said. "I don't really hang out with the kids who deal that stuff, so it's awkward to go up and ask them for it. I'm going to try, though. It's even worse to have Uncle Alex calling here and hanging up when Dad answers. We have caller ID." ∅

MAN from page 129

in sick to work. When he told me that he and Katie were separating, I was like, 'It's about time!'"

Sterling has been helping Freiburg during his time of need by cleaning his apartment and scouting out area taverns in search of good happy-hour drink specials.

"Andy's going to need a place to stay, and I have a couch with his name on it," Sterling said. "It'll be so cool to have him crash here. It'll be just like when we were in college. We can stay up all night and make fun of infomercials, and we can watch all the games together. It's going to be great."

Sterling said he's been rounding up other college friends, as well.

"Will's still single, and Dave lost his job the other day—talk about good timing," Sterling said. "Maybe we can start up our dart league again. We were the kings of Hunter's Pub."

Sterling said he's especially looking forward to "hitting the singles market" with his newly available friend.

"I figure he'll need at least a week to get himself back together, so during that time, we'll just drink at home and go to movies," Sterling said. "But after that, look out! I gotta admit, it's been pretty dry in my neck of the woods."

He'll be getting all that rebound action, and I'll be there to collect his cast-off pity sex."

Freiburg, who has not yet heard any

> Sterling has been helping Freiburg during his time of need by cleaning his apartment and scouting out area taverns in search of good happy-hour drink specials.

of Sterling's plans, was contacted for comment at his brother Dale's house, where he has been staying since Sunday.

"I feel worse than I ever have in my entire life," Freiburg said. "When I'm not working, I'm packing. When I'm not packing, I'm talking to my lawyer. When I'm not talking to my lawyer, I'm crying. It feels like everything is falling apart around me. I just want to be alone." ∅

TAFFY from page 22

unusually large amounts of blood. Passersby were amazed by the unusually large

amounts of blood. Passersby were amazed by the unusually large amounts of blood. Passersby were amazed by the unusually large amounts of blood. Passersby were amazed by the unusually large amounts of blood. Passersby were amazed by the unusually large amounts of blood. Passersby were amazed by the unusually large amounts of blood. Passersby were

> You think *you* have it rough? Try sharing a birthday with former president James K. Polk.

amazed by the unusually large amounts of blood. Passersby were amazed by the unusually large amounts of blood. Passersby were amazed by the unusually large amounts of blood. Passersby were amazed by the unusually large amounts of blood. Passersby were amazed by the unusually large amounts of blood. Passersby were amazed by the unusually large amounts of blood. Passersby were amazed by the unusually large amounts of blood. Passersby were amazed by the unusually large amounts of blood. Passersby were amazed by the unusually large amounts of blood. Passersby were amazed by the unusually large amounts of blood. Passersby were amazed by the unusually large amounts of blood. Passersby were amazed by the unusually large amounts of blood. Passersby were amazed by the unusually large amounts of blood. Passersby were amazed by the unusually large

amazed by the unusually large

see TAFFY page 57

130

more sellers," Tenet said. "If this trend continues, then by 2010, nuclear secrets will be well within the reach of Uzbekistan, Morocco, and pretty much anyone else with enough money to buy a used car."

The trend toward cheaper, more readily available nuclear secrets began in the early '90s, when Pakistani scientists sold plans and equipment for uranium-refining gas centrifuges to Iran and Iraq. While the price initially hovered around $100 million, the expanding market quickly drove prices down.

"Three years ago, a complete W-88 warhead data suite went to the Chinese for a sum in the mid-nine figures," CIA nuclear-weapons specialist Mitch Romano said. "Now, you can

"NATO has since classified the group as a Class D potential nuclear threat," Woess added.

pick up that W-88 data in Central Asia for a tenth of that cost—and they'll deliver it free."

Romano cited another example of plunging prices.

"About six months ago, one of our wiretaps recorded the sale of plans for a two-foot, 12-megaton warhead to a Quebecois separatist cell for slightly more than $1 million," Romano said. "Yesterday, the plans surfaced again, this time on the Internet. It was eBay item #2899538529, and it had a 'Buy it now' price of $18,500."

Romano assured the public that the CIA has the seller, a San Diego-based car-audio retailer with the screen name of BatVette65, under strict surveillance.

"He's got tons of new deals every week," Romano said. "Right now, he's got plans for an artillery-launched supergun nuke and a set of blueprints for cool old vintage Soviet-era silos."

Romano said that, although prices are plunging, quality is improving.

"We're not talking about a waist-high stack of floppy disks storing instructions for some clunky old atom bomb," Romano said. "We're talking detailed specs on a U.S.-produced Special Atomic Demolition Munitions suitcase device. Those are great little bombs that you can't even get on the straight market anymore, because of the Spratt-Furse law."

Martin Woess, an atomic-intelligence branch operative from Great Britain's MI-6, said prices are so low that virtually any political organization that wants a nuclear program can afford one.

"Last week, we investigated reports that a cell in Edinburgh had sold classified British intelligence information

Above: A set of nuclear secrets is priced to sell at an outdoor market in Altay, Mongolia.

to an American group," Woess said. "The group turned out to be the Young Republicans organization at the University of Virginia."

"NATO has since classified the group as a Class D potential nuclear threat," Woess added.

At least one intelligence expert expressed trepidation over the booming nuclear-secrets economy.

"It was an embarrassment to our country that Abdul Qadeer Khan sold nuclear secrets and technology to Iran, Libya, and North Korea," said General Mohammed Kanazwa, a senior officer for Pakistani military intelligence. "But it was all the more embarrassing when we found out that he had sold them in the 'Bargains Under $100' section of the *Cleveland Plain Dealer*."

As dire as the news may seem, Tenet stressed the difference between acquiring the technical know-how necessary to build a nuclear-weapons program and actually initiating such a program.

"Although nuclear-weapons intelligence may be selling for less than a thousandth of its Cold War price, the buyer would still require qualified personnel and hard-to-find materials to actually construct a device," Tenet said. "They may be able to get plans for a bomb for a few pennies, but weapons-grade plutonium, when available, sells for hundreds, sometimes thousands of dollars a pound." Ø

YAHOO from page 127

"As the amount of information on the web increases, individuals want a search engine to provide them with results that are personally meaningful," Semel said. "Enter the Yahoo Soul Search—a powerful new tool that reveals what's deep inside your heart, using the user-friendly interface already familiar to Yahoo fans."

In the past, a soul search was a labor-intensive and time-consuming process, Semel said.

"A soul search often required backpacking trips across Europe, disastrous long-term relationships with incompatible lovers, and years of expensive therapy," Semel said. "Worse, the search process often included depression, lowered self-worth, and intense doubt."

Semel called the old way of seeking clarity "a logistical nightmare."

"Each question you asked yourself seemed to have a thousand possible answers," Semel said. "That's why we designed a way to order returns by relevance and separate them into categories like 'religion' and 'sexuality.' After using the Yahoo soul-search engine, conducting the self-examination

process without a computer will seem as ridiculous as doing accounting in old-fashioned ledger books."

The new search function is even customizable. Users can set their search to plumb their souls at varying depths, to make shallow discoveries or life-changing ones. They can also adjust their security preferences to protect themselves from the dangers of baring their naked souls to the world, and parental controls can be enabled in order to prevent children from looking inside themselves.

The new service is also hot-linked to the pre-existing Yahoo network—instantly leading the soul-searcher to pertinent information on HotJobs, Yahoo! Shopping, and Yahoo! Travel—making it possible for users to reconfigure their entire lives with one easy soul search.

Although soul searching online personal ads is not presently an option, Yahoo is developing a search engine which will allow its estimated 300 million users to find their one true soulmate.

Semel admits that the soul, while eminently searchable, is far from

easy to navigate. There are still dangers in the form of self-deception, the soul-to-soul transmittable "D-spair" virus, and the numerous pop-up ads offering quick-fix solutions to the user's problems.

"There are bound to be some bugs, but we're not too worried," Semel said. "We at Yahoo have a lot of experience in helping people navigate an environment full of falsehoods, random useless information, and truly horrifying pornography. I don't think the human soul will hold any real surprises for us."

Early reviews from consumers have been overwhelmingly positive.

"I was skeptical, I'll admit," said former Boston-area investment banker Royce Creighton. "But after two minutes on Yahoo Soul Search, I found that being born into a family of bankers didn't mean I had to be a banker. Half an hour of advanced soul-searching helped me find a buyer for my house, an alpaca farm for sale in Wyoming, and a highly recommended acupuncturist in Cheyenne. I've never been happier... and I found all this inside myself through Yahoo!" Ø

If Elected, I Will Be Extremely Surprised

By B. Paul Knefler

Distinguished residents of the Pine View Senior Center,

On Tuesday, Nov. 2, our district will hold an election for its seat in the state senate, and you, as citizens of this great nation, will be called upon to take part in our democratic process and exercise that most vaunted right: the vote. I ask you, Pine View residents, when you enter that booth Tuesday, to vote for me, B. Paul Knefler. Because I have no hands-on experience in government, I stand before you with this promise: If I am elected, I will be truly surprised.

Some of you may recognize me as the guy who runs for office a lot. In the past, I've sought seats on the school board and in the city council. Last year, I even ran for mayor. Today, I cast my hat in the ring once more. The state-senate run marks my most ambitious, and most absurd, campaign to date. Please flabbergast me with your support.

As the independent candidate, I'll be facing off against Democratic incumbent Martin LaSoeur and Republican challenger Elizabeth Cowles. But unlike Mr. LaSoeur and Ms. Cowles, if I'm chosen to represent you in our state government, I will be amazed. For, as with my previous campaigns,

> **Several elements of my personality doom my candidacy. Key among my flaws: I don't understand the issues. Many of you are upset about what you call "property taxes." I must say, I don't care about that issue.**

this one will be characterized by poor organization, ill-defined purpose, and confusing rhetoric. From my opposition to "ideology" in the public-education system to my bizarre municipal-bond-burning stunt in front of City Hall, I will do nothing to convince you, the voters, that I am qualified to hold office.

Several elements of my personality doom my candidacy. Key among my flaws: I don't understand the issues. Many of you are upset about what you call "property taxes." I must say, I don't care about that issue. I've lived

> **Some of you may recognize me as the guy who runs for office a lot. In the past, I've sought seats on the school board and in the city council. Last year, I even ran for mayor. Today, I cast my hat in the ring once more. The state-senate run marks my most ambitious, and most absurd, campaign to date. Please flabbergast me with your support.**

with my elderly mother in the same house since the day I was born. My mother holds the title to the home and is therefore responsible for the tax payment, which her pension and Social Security cover. Another common constituent concern is "urban sprawl." This issue, I don't understand. The papers this morning indicate that "a vociferous minority, angered by the town of Eden Grove's unauthorized annexation of nearby Munkado, is calling for the reform of state annexation laws and a reassertion of property rights for individuals." Very complicated.

Another factor contributing to my guaranteed failure is my fixation on a few narrow issues. Citizens, if you choose to let me represent you in our senate, I will eliminate public sewers. I associate sewers with the degradation of the individual citizen's autonomy. (The aforementioned municipal-bond-burning was related to this issue.) Also, I pledge to introduce the ovenbird to our district's ecosystem. The ovenbird is a magnificent bird.

My fellow citizens, a politician must serve his constituents tirelessly and understand their needs. I am not this man. During my travels across this district, I have met dozens of voters. I have seen them squirm under my glassy-eyed gaze. I have clasped their hands in my sweaty palms for much longer than is socially acceptable. I lack character and basic social skills. Why I must involve you, the people of this great state, in my vain grab for office is something that I will explain in a moment. For now, I promise each and every one of you that I will continue to campaign awkwardly until election day in November.

Right now, I am lagging in the polls, but I will mask my fear by adopting a blustery mien and peppering my conversation with grandiose, and usually misapplied, political terms. Few will be fooled, if the public's response to me at a recent debate on city cable channel 17 is a reliable indicator. When I wasn't making long-winded, irrelevant, disconnected remarks or staring into space, I burst into loud and inappropriate laughter. This performance earned me the ridicule of the local alternative weekly newspaper, which referred to me as a "drool case."

Yet, in the face of the obvious and inevitable, I will continue to stump for votes. Is it because I want the flacks at the state capitol to know that it's no longer politics-as-usual in the 31st district? Not really. Is it because I wish to sow the seeds of reform in the minds of voters? Eh, no. Such causes might motivate underdog candidates in their quest for public office, but they don't concern me. So why do I run? Because, good people, if you find it in your hearts to send me to the State Capitol next January, not only will you be springing me from my mother's home, but you will also rescue me from the drudgery of the 15 or 20 hours of work I put in at my uncle's grocery store each week.

Before I go, let me remind you that, unlike the other candidates who hide behind lies and half-truths, I offer only the facts. The first of these facts: I don't stand a chance. The second: If, by some freak occurrence, I am voted into office, I will suck as your senator. Seriously, if elected, I will absolutely blow balls. In return for your support, you will receive nothing.

Thank you, and God bless this state. ✍

Your Horoscope

**By Lloyd Schumner Sr.
Retired Machinist and
A.A.P.B.-Certified Astrologer**

Aries: (March 21–April 19)
Tonight, take a moment to say a few words in honor of the brave deliveryman who died bringing hot, delicious pizza to your House Of Knives.

Taurus: (April 20–May 20)
Your weight may be too high, but that's no reason for the police to describe what will happen to you as a triple homicide.

Gemini: (May 21–June 21)
There hasn't been a stampeding death in your area in more than a century, but your air horn and steer costume will change all that.

Cancer: (June 22–July 22)
This week is a good one for romance in the workplace, and an even better one for necromancy in the breakroom.

Leo: (July 23–Aug. 22)
As a defiler of famous authors' graves, you must agree that if Dorothy Parker were dug up and laid end to end, you wouldn't be a bit surprised.

Virgo: (Aug. 23–Sept. 22)
Horrible, six-mawed creatures from beyond time and space won't let you have a chance at the million-dollar prize unless you buy their magazines.

Libra: (Sept. 23–Oct. 23)
One man's ball sweat is another man's enchanting musk. Find out exactly who these men are, tonight on *News At 10*.

Scorpio: (Oct. 24–Nov. 21)
Your feeble constitution is noted once again when you enter the hospital after being savagely beaten at checkers.

Sagittarius: (Nov. 22–Dec. 21)
You've said that none of those people would've died, if only they had let you live your own life. But, come on, you know that isn't true.

Capricorn: (Dec. 22–Jan. 19)
Television taunts you once again, this time with a show where convicted felons get to have puppies even though you don't.

Aquarius: (Jan. 20–Feb. 18)
A bad experience with free jazz, indirect mood lighting, and spiritual possession will show you that there's a right way and wrong way to commune with the infinite.

Pisces: (Feb. 19–March 20)
The stars apologize for the temporary and unavoidable delay. Your life will resume its accelerating downward spiral within moments.

---

the ONION®

VOLUME 40 ISSUE 15   AMERICA'S FINEST NEWS SOURCE™   15–21 APRIL 2004

Baby Put On Phone Told Her Parents Hate Her

see FAMILY page 14E

Tank Rolls By Living Room Window

see LOCAL page 8C

Furniture Store To Pay Employees Nothing Until 2005

see BUSINESS page 12G

STATshot

A look at the numbers that shape your world.

Why Are We Applying For A Tax Extension?

11% Took a while to find a crooked accountant

14% Thought Bush eliminated taxes

23% Still haven't named two newest deductions

7% Work for IRS; are really swamped this time of year

19% Just love extending things

THE ONION • $2.00 US • $3.00 CAN

Above: Rumsfeld reads the Secretary's Day cards in a DC-area drugstore.

Rumsfeld Looking Forward To Secretary's Day

WASHINGTON, DC—Defense Secretary Donald Rumsfeld sheepishly admitted Monday that he's looking forward to National Secretary's Day on April 21.

"I know it's just a silly Hallmark holiday," Rumsfeld said of the annual event now formally known as Administrative Professionals Day. "Even so, I have to admit that seeing that bouquet of flowers on my desk... Well, it makes me feel real good."

Rumsfeld, who was hired by the ex-ecutive branch of the federal government in December 2000, said he loves his job and doesn't expect special treatment from his boss, U.S. President George W. Bush. According to the overworked secretary, this is exactly why he so greatly appreciates it when Bush Administration officials make an effort to show the secretarial pool their gratitude.

"Whether it's a card, a Mylar balloon, or a big decorated cookie, it's

see RUMSFELD page 136

New Negative Campaign Ads Blast Voters Directly

WASHINGTON, DC—In the latest round of political mudslinging, both John Kerry's and George W. Bush's election committees have replaced ads that focus on their opponents' shortcomings with ads that personally insult the voting public.

"The Bush people initiated this volley of negative ads, but we won't be lured into a reactive campaign against the Republicans," Kerry campaign man-ager Mary Beth Cahill said Monday. "It's time to redirect the cheap name-calling away from Bush and toward those Americans who might be idiotic enough to vote for him."

POLITICS *Watch*

A controversial 30-second TV spot for Kerry that aired throughout the Midwest Monday blamed the country's ills not on Bush's policies, but on the "sheer stupidity" of America's voters.

"In the past four years, America's national debt has reached an all-time high," the ad's narrator said. "And who's responsible? You are. You're sitting there eating a big bowl of Fritos, watching TV, and getting fatter as the country goes to hell. You ought to be ashamed of yourself."

Over a series of images of America's senior citizens, the narrator of another 30-second spot says, "The Medicare drug bill is a triumph of right-wing

see ADS page 137

Friend Buys Computer Just Like That

KANSAS CITY, MO—Account executive Jeremy Trask, 33, entered a local Best Buy Sunday, shopped for approximately 20 minutes, and bought a brand-new laptop computer right off the shelf, "like it was a bag of pretzels," Trask's friend Paul Cheng said Monday.

"I didn't even know Jeremy was in the market for a computer," Cheng said, still reeling from Sunday's events. "We were on the west side of town, and he asked if I wanted to stop

see FRIEND page 136

Left: Trask and the computer Cheng (inset) witnessed him just up and buy.

Resistance In Iraq

A sudden surge in anti-occupation violence in Iraq has prompted some Americans to fear the coalition forces' control is slipping. What do *you* think?

Frank Himmelbaum
Systems Analyst

"A handful of kidnappings and a few armed insurrections doesn't mean we're losing control. It just means that we never really had control."

Mandy Wright
Property Inspector

"The insurgents are just jealous that we're part of an awesome coalition and they aren't."

Karl Wright
Mathematician

"Bush did say we'd be welcomed with an open display of small arms."

Eric Baker
Lyricist

"They're calling their latest operation 'Resolute Sword?' Shit. We have to change our band's name again."

Scott Waller
Waiter

"I hope for the sake of Iraq's children this doesn't lead to a civil war. Then those kids would have to watch boring documentaries about it in school for the next 200 years."

Dorothy Nelson
CPA

"Well, everyone gets antsy around tax time."

Statue Of Liberty To Reopen

The Statue of Liberty is set to reopen in July, following the completion of structural and security improvements. What changes have been made so far?

- Color of flame in torch will correspond with terror-alert level; statue's name changed to "The Statue of Security"
- Head no longer held on with quarter-mile of duct tape
- Bones of Muncie, IN 3-year-old swept out from under Pepsi machine in basement
- Second security guard put on duty in case the first one falls asleep
- Longtime Liberty Island resident and radical Islamic cleric Muqtada al-Sadr deported
- Exterior and interior of structure meticulously de-Frenched
- Lady Liberty now able to pump arm in air when extra patriotism needed
- Statue's eyes outfitted with high-tech security cameras that monitor tourists' every move
- "Don't" inscribed before "Bring us your…" on plaque at statue's base

the ONION®
America's Finest News Source.™

Herman Ulysses Zweibel
Founder

T. Herman Zweibel
Publisher Emeritus
J. Phineas Zweibel
Publisher
Maxwell Prescott Zweibel
Editor-In-Chief

I Will Not Rest Until Sometime After 11 p.m.

By Ryan Carlisle

I awoke this morning with an exhilarating realization: A new day had dawned. The sun brought clarity, as well as light. Looking into my shaving mirror, I made myself a promise. I said to myself, "No matter what obstacles I encounter, no matter what trials I must endure, no matter what distractions I must ignore, I will not rest until sometime after 11 o'clock this evening."

With God as my witness, I swear that I, Ryan Carlisle, will be tireless in my efforts to carry on until well after 8 p.m. Should I feel myself lured from my path, I will resist sleep—that subtle and quiet temptress—with a soda or a brief walk to the mailbox. I will be dogged in my determination to remain awake throughout the entire day. The sun may set upon the land, but I shall forge ahead for a little while longer. I will toil ceaselessly, well into the 11th hour. Before the 12th hour, however, I shall sleep.

It may not be easy, but worthwhile pursuits never are. Facing the task of crossing the Delaware unaided, did General George Washington sit down on a horn-and-hide officer's chair and await word from Charles Lee? Did Abraham Lincoln, having just read the Emancipation Proclamation before his stunned and momentarily speechless cabinet, heed the words of Postmaster General Montgomery Blaire—who described the proclamation as "voting-booth poison"—or did he go forth with what he knew to be a *de facto* declaration of war?

Did Albert Einstein give up on physics, because it made his brain muscles hurt? No. And, in the tradition of Washington, Custer, and Einstein, I, Carlisle, will stay awake until at least 11 p.m.

Insidious drowsiness may attempt to draw me under my sweet covers, but I will resist her, for I am a man of action, resolve, and determined wakefulness. As such, I declare that I will labor until my work is complete, my dinner done, my house tidied up a bit, my face washed, my teeth flossed and brushed, and my outfit for the following day laid out on the chair in my bedroom.

There are those who are not as strong as I am. Some, vanquished by their lunchtime burrito, will surrender to a nap behind closed office doors. Others, lulled by local news anchor Deborah Spalding's report on dangerous bacteria levels, will succumb to sleep for an hour on the couch. But not I. No matter what arduous activities I complete during the day, I shall not stop striving until I've eaten dinner, watched *The Daily Show*, and had a relaxing shower. I will galvanize my spirit, pressing ever forward in the day until I put on my pajamas and fall exhausted into my bed, at which point I shall pull the comforter over my weary torso. I'll try to do this by 11:30 p.m., so as to get a good night's sleep, which will allow me to be alert the following day.

I may not be able to do it alone. To get me through the afternoon slump, I may enlist the aid of the Starbucks

> With God as my witness, I swear that I, Ryan Carlisle, will be tireless in my efforts to carry on until well after 8 p.m. Should I feel myself lured from my path, I will resist sleep—that subtle and quiet temptress—with a soda or a brief walk to the mailbox.

barista. I may call on a friend to join me for ice cream at the Chocolate Shoppe. I may even call my mother, with whom I haven't spoken in nearly three weeks. That would fill at least an hour. But even if I must do it alone, I, like George Washington, will soldier bravely on through work, meals, household tasks, TV shows, and phone calls.

A warning to those who would try to stop me: I have made my way through many days. Your tricks no longer work against me. If you turn up the heat in my office, I will remove my blazer. If you offer me a second turkey sandwich at lunchtime, I will politely decline it. If you make me sit through a mind-numbing employee-training session, I'll keep my mind active with thoughts of which items I should remember to put in my briefcase to take home.

No one can stop me. No one can draw my focus from my goal. No one can dull my desire, subdue my drive, tame my passion. Try as you might, you will not impede me. I will not waver in my determination. I will not take my eyes off of victory until I have put in a good 16-hour day and am, frankly, all tuckered out. ∅

Bishop Sick Of Local Church Scene

SACRAMENTO, CA—Bishop Robert K. Boland of the Roman Catholic Diocese of Sacramento announced Monday that, although he remains a devoted servant of God and the Catholic Church, he has become tired of the same old church scene.

"This diocese is okay, I guess," Boland told reporters gathered on the front steps of the Cathedral of the Blessed Sacrament. "It's just getting a little… tedious. I've got more than 100 parishes in my diocese, but at the end of the day, they're all pretty much the same."

"Don't get me wrong—I still care about everyone's eternal soul," Boland added. "I care deeply, but I must admit that the congregations have sorta become one big blur of blue-haired old ladies. Lately, when I get the question about whether so-and-so's cats are waiting for her in heaven, I just fall back on a stock answer."

Appointed his bishopric by Pope John Paul II in 2000, Boland said he's weary of both the parishioners and "the entire sacraments thing."

"When you're a bishop, you church-hop constantly, performing the Eucharist throughout the diocese," said Boland, whose diocese covers 20 counties in northern California. "Like, I love to worship God in the joyous celebration of the Mass and sacraments, but the whole thing never really changes. At some point, I went from 'I can't believe I get to do this' to 'I'm going to be doing this for the rest of my life.'"

Continued Boland: "Once in a while, there's an exciting shake-up in the diocese, like an excommunication or a priest who misuses funds—but hardly ever."

Boland said he used to bolster his interest in the Church by getting involved with the neediest parishes, but that ultimately backfired.

"I was spending a lot of time at St. Joseph's over in Sutter Creek, because they have a big problem with the youth using crystal meth," Boland said. "But if I spend too much time at one church, the priests at the others accuse me of playing favorites. Next thing I know, [San Francisco] Archbishop [William J.] Levada is on my behind, asking why I haven't been to the St. Monica Parish for six months."

Continued Boland: "St. Joseph's isn't even all that great, but I will say that their Friday fish fry beats the tar out of the usual potluck spread."

Boland said he hasn't always been disengaged.

"At first, I was thrilled to be living out the dream I'd had since the seminary," Boland said. "I had boundless energy. Every pancake breakfast was a new adventure. Now, I can barely choke down those greasy sawdust links the ladies in the Parish Council of Catholic Women call sausages."

Added Boland: "God, I'm in such a horrible rut."

According to Boland, even the magnificent, 1,400-seat Cathedral of The Blessed Sacrament has lost its luster.

"Yeah, it's a beautiful church," Boland said. "Those ceilings are absolutely amazing. You can't believe how far your voice carries without a microphone. But, even so, Sunday

Above: Boland, who seriously needs a change of pace.

morning has become business as usual. It's like, 'Oh boy, let's watch Mr. Harrison nod off during the homily for the 200th time.'"

Boland's request to be transferred to a different diocese was not granted.

"Sure, I mentioned it once, but it never happened," Boland said. "In my request, I may have been a little hazy. I said that I was sick of the same old sacristies. I said that maybe I should help the poor in New Mexico or South

Africa or someplace. In truth, the thought of starting over is pretty daunting. I was almost relieved when they never responded."

"What I need to do is climb my way up to cardinal," Boland added. "That'd be my ticket out of this one-horse diocese."

Boland said there's little chance he'll be promoted anytime soon.

"Archbishop Levada isn't going see BISHOP page 138

Study: Owning A Boat Not Worth It

YONKERS, NY—According to a study published in the April issue of *Boating Magazine*, owning a boat is not even close to worth it. "Our study proved conclusively that boat-ownership is primarily an inconvenience and a monetary black hole," editor Roger Bernbaum said. "We found little to no reason to keep that thing sitting in a shed all winter just so you can tow it to the lake and pay outrageous docking fees three weekends a year. It'd be much more cost-efficient to don a yachting cap and hang out at the dockhouse." The May issue of *Boating* promises to explore the financial viability of seaside vacation homes.

Man Nods His Way To The Top

BOSTON—Using his unparalleled ability to nod after his superiors

speak, Thomas J. Mieritz, 39, rose to the level of vice-president at Fidelity Investments Monday. "I knew Mieritz was the man for the job the instant I started talking. He was ready to get on board with every one of my proposed mutual-fund investment initiatives," Fidelity chairman Edward C. Johnson III said. "I thought, 'Now, *there's* a man who makes smart decisions without a lot of hullabaloo.'" Johnson added that, if Mieritz can master boot-licking, buck-passing, and myopic self-satisfaction, he'll probably run the company one day.

What Grieving Widow Needs Is A Day At The Spa

PACIFIC PALISADES, CA—Now that her husband Harvey has been laid to rest and all the visiting relatives have left, what grieving widow Judith Blauser, 46, really needs is a day at the spa, friend Carrie Thomas reported Tuesday. "Your eyes are so red and puffy from crying… but that's nothing a few cucumber slices and an apricot facial couldn't cure," said Thomas, who attended the Blausers' wedding eight years ago. "I know that seeing poor Harvey there in the casket reminded *me* how long it's been since I treated myself to a full-body seaweed wrap." Thomas suggested that Blauser fly to Palm Desert for a volcanic sand bath immediately following the reading of the will.

Room Scanned For Something To Sell On eBay

ALBANY, CA—Applying tape to the last package in a 12-item round of eBay sales, Brandon Vye scanned his bedroom for anything else he could auction off online. "I sold the Grand Ole Opry floaty pen… the UNO cards… the Santa socks—so now what?" Vye asked as he spun around in his swivel chair. "Maybe I could sell these science textbooks, or my tapes of old *SNL* episodes? God, I've got to have *something* I can mail off." After listing a misshapen clay bowl he made in a high-school ceramics class, Vye decided to head out to the yard to search for "eBay-able stuff" there.

Zambia Tired Of Being Mentioned In 'News Of The Weird' Section

LUSAKA, ZAMBIA—Zambian president H.E. Levy P. Mwanawasa publicly chastised Reuters and 10 other news organizations Monday for featuring Zambia in their "news of the weird" sections. "Zambia has a rich cultural history well beyond the man who can swallow razor blades," Mwanawasa said. "Either feature something about Zambia besides dodecatuplets, or don't feature Zambia at all." Interestingly, in addition to being the Zambian leader, Mwanawasa is also the proud owner of the world's longest soda-can pull-tab chain. ∅

in at the Best Buy. I thought maybe we'd buy some CDs or look at the plasma-screen televisions, but, next thing I know, he's dropping $1,200 on a laptop."

The Toshiba Satellite Notebook laptop computer came equipped with an Intel Celeron Processor, a DVD-ROM/CD-RW combo drive, and a 15-inch active-matrix display. The 40GB hard drive came pre-installed with the Windows XP Home Edition operating system, Microsoft Works, and Quicken—none of which seemed to interest Trask in the slightest.

"Jeremy just looked at it, typed some 'quick brown fox' crap on the keyboard, said the computer was nice and light, and asked a sales associate if they had one in stock," Cheng said. "He barely looked at the desktop computers. He didn't ask how it compared to a Mac. He didn't even ask about the warranty or any upcoming sales. He just grabbed the box and headed up to the check-out area."

According to Cheng, Trask "just assumed he knew what he wanted."

"Before you buy a computer, you're supposed to get some magazines, ask the office IT guy what he recommends, and find out how your friends like their computers," Cheng said. "People spend days just identifying

> ### "He barely looked at the desktop computers," Cheng said. "He didn't ask how it compared to a Mac. He didn't even ask about the warranty or any upcoming sales. He just grabbed the box and headed up."

their needs, let alone selecting a computer that meets those needs. I mean, it's a computer! How do you know what you're getting if you just snap one up?"

Cheng said that, once he realized what was happening, he followed Trask to the counter and demanded to know if his friend had done any research on the Internet or visited the store on previous occasions.

"He *hadn't*," Cheng said. "He just waltzed in there and bought the damn thing. I asked him what he would be using it for, and he said 'work stuff and Internet stuff.' He said he wanted a computer with a DVD player, so he could take it with him when he stayed at his girlfriend's place. And—oh, this was the classic line! This killed me! He said he wanted one that had an 'MP3 maker.'"

"I am not kidding," Cheng added. "Those were his *exact* words."

Cheng said he suspected that Trask simply looked for models that contained a DVD player, then chose one with a big screen.

"Can you believe that?" Cheng asked. "I told him that if he'd spend a couple days searching online, he could find that same computer for $50 or even $100 less, but he was like, 'I just want to get it and be done with it.'"

Although he made repeated attempts inside Best Buy, during the walk to the car, and during the ride home, Cheng was unable to make Trask see the importance of his purchase.

"I told him, 'Hey, man, you just bought a damn computer,'" Cheng said. "He just looked at me like, 'Yeah, I know.' I love the guy, but, I have to say, he didn't really seem to understand what it was that he'd done."

Cheng was further vexed to learn that, 24 hours after the laptop was purchased, Trask had yet to take it out of its box.

"I called Jeremy to see how the computer was working out, and he said he hadn't had the energy to deal with it yet," Cheng said. "I said, 'Aha! Having second thoughts, are you?' He said he was fine with it, but he just hadn't gotten around to unpacking it. I mean, *Jesus*."

"So I asked him if he wanted me to come over and help him get his modem hooked up," Cheng said. "He said he didn't need it. He said he got a flyer in the mail today and he signed up for a year of 'DSL or cable Internet or something.' *God!*" ∅

really nice for someone to say 'Good job. I notice what you do,'" Rumsfeld said. "Some secretaries say, 'I work my hiney off all year round, and I'm supposed to go nuts over a $25 Bath & Body Works gift certificate?' But I'm telling you, every smidgen of recognition counts. I've worked in places that didn't observe Secretary's Day at all, like the Ford White House."

Rumsfeld's secretarial duties include coordinating all functions of the government relating directly to national security, formulating defense policy, overseeing the affairs of the military, and ordering new supplies.

But, according to National Security Advisor Condoleezza Rice, Rumsfeld does "much more than that." She praised his "nearly psychic" ability to spot and prevent potential sticky situations.

"Donald's the one who really runs the Department of Defense," Rice said. "He's always a few steps ahead of us. Like, when he heard that [first lady] Laura [Bush] was going shopping last Friday, he made sure a car was available to pick her up from the mall, because he knew the president would forget. And don't think the president was solely responsible for that lovely birthday lollipop bouquet [Colorado senator] Wayne Allard got this week, or for the reorganization of the worldwide command structure that resulted in the establishment of the U.S. Strategic Command. Nope, it was all Donald's doing. I swear he has five arms!"

National Economic Council director Stephen Friedman lavished the overworked secretary with praise.

"Donald should get an award for what he did the afternoon someone accidentally scheduled a lunch with the foreign minister from Guyana at the same time as a meeting with French president Jacques Chirac," Friedman said. "Instead of just sticking the foreign minister in a waiting room with some magazines, Donald had a representative from the House—fellow by the name of Daniels or Peterson or something—take him to lunch at The Jockey Club, and he got him a pair of tickets to that night's Washington Wizards game. The foreign minister had such a great time, he practically forgot he'd never met with Bush. Boy, did Don put out that fire."

Added Friedman: "It's exactly like it says on Donald's coffee mug: 'A secretary's work is never done.'"

Rumsfeld's stellar work ethic and attention to detail have earned him two White House Employee Of The Month awards.

According to employees at the Department of Defense, Rumsfeld is a "very important" member of the team. Chief of Staff Angie Thomas said she appreciates him for "the way he lights up a room," while receptionist Arthur

> ### "Donald's the one who really runs the Department," Rice said.

Samuel praised the way Rumsfeld "makes you feel like an important part of the office, even if you're only a part-timer."

"Without my even saying anything about it, Donald ordered me a new office chair, because he'd noticed that the height-adjustment mechanism was no longer functioning on my old one," Samuel said. "And he always asks about my fiancée. The last secretary [William Cohen] barely said 10 words to me during his entire tenure."

Undersecretary for Acquisition and Technology Phoebe Underwood said that, when her son was kicked in the head in gym class last October, Rumsfeld insisted she take off the rest of the week to stay home with him.

"It was kind of touch-and-go for a while, and I didn't know how long I would need to be away," Underwood said. "Donald said, 'You just look after Evan. I'll make sure your report on strategic deterrence is completed on time.' And, sure enough, it was. That guy is a true miracle worker."

Rumsfeld said he doesn't know what's planned for his fourth Secretary's Day with the Bush Administration, but he expressed confidence that the day won't pass without notice.

"We secretaries are pretty spoiled around here," Rumsfeld said, laughing. "Last year, the whole DoD gang chipped in and got me a nice antibacterial humidifier for my office, because the air gets so dry in the winter. It must have set them back quite a bit. Then, at lunch, the president treated me and the other secretaries to burgers at Johnny Rockets."

Last year, Bush expressed his appreciation for Rumsfeld in particular, in a letter proudly fastened to the secretary's cubicle partition.

"Donald Rumsfield [sic] is a fine employee and human being," the letter read. "He's an indispensable asset to my administration, and he is cordial, well-groomed, and punctual. I am also told that he lights up a room. I hope he continues to serve my administration well into the future. People like him make America strong." ∅

Above: Rumsfeld in a photo from Secretary's Day 2003.

ideology masquerading as moderate reform. The pharmaceutical-drug and insurance industries are tickled pink. Guess who's paying for it? You. Congratulations, moron. I'm John Kerry and I approved this message."

The Bush-Cheney 2004 camp recently began airing an anti-voter ad in 20 major urban areas nationwide.

"Are you going to vote for a candidate whose campaign promises would cost America $1.9 trillion over the next decade?" the ad asks. "Of course you aren't. You aren't going to vote at all. In the last election, half of you did-

Both ad campaigns met with cries of outrage from viewers in all demographic groups.

n't even show up. So, on Nov. 2, just spend the day right there at your dead-end office job, talking to your coworkers about your new sweater and e-mailing your friends photos of your stupid 2-year-old daughter you shouldn't have had."

The ad concludes: "You make me sick."

Both ad campaigns met with cries of outrage from viewers in all demographic groups, and were therefore deemed successful.

"I don't pay my taxes so some suit in Washington can get on national tele-

Above: A series of Bush re-election campaign ads blasting the American public.

vision and call me a clown," said Bobbie Lee, a 35-year-old mechanic from Detroit. "Those Kerry ads piss me off so bad. So what if my teeth *are* stained? So what if I *do* wear sweatsocks? Everyone I show the videotape to gets just as mad. Just who does Kerry think he is? Before last week, I didn't even know his name."

"That Bush ad said that I should wake up to the fact that I'm trapped in a loveless marriage," said 29-year-old Kathlene Richmond, an account executive from West Virginia. "But the Republicans don't understand Larry. He's just not very communicative. You don't think the GOP is right, do you?"

Based on the success of the TV ads, both campaigns have announced plans to attack voters through other

media, as well.

New direct-mail campaigns will solicit contributions with such slogans as "Fork over some of your paycheck to Kerry. Or are you too cheap?" and "One in 25 Americans donated money to a national political campaign in 2003. One in three Americans subscribed to cable television. Pathetic."

One Bush ad specifically targets homeowners.

"Do you pay property taxes?" the ad asks. "On that shack? Jesus, why don't you fix that place up a little bit? Have some pride. It's filthy. I don't even want to know how long it's been since you last vacuumed, much less painted. You couldn't pay George W. Bush and Dick Cheney a billion dollars to live in that dirty, disgusting, rundown

rat-trap."

Although the ads have angered voters, Charles Wayne, a professor of political science at Georgetown University, called them "a refreshing shift toward more honesty in the political process."

"Emotionally manipulative attack ads obscure the candidates' real positions and insult the intelligence of America's voters," Wayne said. "The fact that the major political powers are voicing their disdain for the public shows they are no longer hiding behind empty rhetoric. I see that as a positive step."

Campaign ads containing the slogans "Hey, dumbass—Kerry For President" and "Vote Bush in November, all you stupid shitheads" are slated to appear in 50 major newspapers Friday. ∅

---

the ONION presents

Preparing For A Hospital Stay

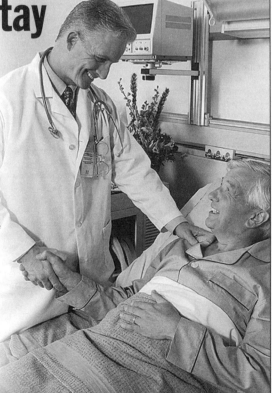

While a trip to the hospital is rarely pleasant, here are some tips to help you prepare for the experience:

- Before entering a hospital for treatment, weigh your holistic health-care options against your wish to actually get better.
- If you have a wok at home, it's a good idea to get some bedpan practice before the pressure is on.
- Some drugs react violently with alcohol; some don't. Ask around.
- If you are going to the hospital for treatment of a severed limb, remember to bring the limb.
- Bring your regular medications with you to the hospital. God only knows where the hospital finds theirs.
- Read a couple of *Newsweek* articles about your condition. This information will allow you to second-guess your doctor's every move.
- Be forewarned: Hospitals apply a vast mark-up to the items in the in-room minibars.
- Wear clothing that is loose-fitting and comfortable, yet appropriate to bleed in.
- If you behave like a brave little soldier, you

may be offered ice cream.

- Whatever you do, don't check into any facility called "General Hospital." That place is full of back-stabbing, narcissistic lunatics.
- Pack several extra pairs of slippers. Slippers in the hospital are like cigarettes in prison.
- Before knocking out an intern and stealing his uniform, make sure he's your size.
- Many patients complain that hospitals cut their stay short. Don't be coerced into signing out until you're dilated to 10 cm and the baby's head can be seen.
- Bring $500 in fives to "grease the wheels," if you get my meaning. The *good* mashed potatoes.
- If bruised, find a hospital known to have a good bruise ward.
- Keep in mind that, today, many procedures can be performed on an outpatient basis. Some can even be done outside.
- When you arrive at your hospital room, decide which item you'd be willing to accept as the final thing you see on this earth.

Here's My Road Map To Road Trips

The Cruise
By Jim Anchower

Hola, amigos. I know it's been a long time since I rapped at ya, but the trouble pot boiled over and spilled all over everything again. For one thing, my fridge went on the fritz last week. I'd tell my landlord, but I'm a little late in paying my rent, so I have to avoid him until my next payday. In the meantime, I'm keeping everything important in three coolers. I stopped by the carbonics plant where Ron works, and he slipped me a bucket of dry ice. So far, everything is kept as cold as it would be in a refrigerator. You have to be careful about getting the beer out of the bottom of the cooler, though, because you can burn yourself on the ice. I know it sounds wild, getting burned by ice, but trust me on this one: It hurts like a motherfucker.

The coolers are just an inconvenience compared to my cash-flow problem. I got suspended from my job driving people from the airport to the rental-car place and back. Before you get too worked up, remember that being suspended isn't the same as getting fired, so I'm gonna land on my feet. But the thing that got me in trouble wasn't even my fault.

See, one of my coworkers, this kid named Brian, said he'd come across one of my columns a few days earlier. I said that was awesome and asked him if he'd learned anything. He asked me if "hola" was anything like "holla." Well, I didn't know what the fuck he was talking about. He said that "holla" was a rap thing, and that I must have heard it before. I said there was no way in hell I'd heard it before, since rap is crap. "Hola" is "hola," and there's nothing rap about it.

That's when he stepped over the line. He said that classic rock was crap, and he asked me why I'd want to listen to a bunch of dead white guys. I was like, now hold on. Last time I checked, REO was alive and well and still bringing the rock. He said he had to admit that REO had one good song, but that they couldn't just play "Riding The Storm Out" over and over again. That's when things got ugly.

The long and short of it is that we got into a shoving match in front of some customers. Actually, the shoving match started in front of some customers, in the parking lot next to a shuttle bus full of them, but it ended behind the front desk of the car-rental place. We knocked over some luggage, freaked out a couple of old people, and made a 2-year-old cry. Believe me, it wasn't one of my finer moments. But, come on. I was fighting for that 2-year-old's right to listen to REO with pride one day. Brian and I each got a week's suspension with no pay. Brian's usually an all-right guy, but currently, he's on my shit list.

Anyway, since I have the time off, I figure I should go on a road trip. I don't know where yet, but I'd like to see some sights that I haven't seen before. Nothing exotic, just different. I need to shake things up a bit. But I have some rules I follow any time I take a road trip, so that it doesn't end in disaster.

First off, get a road-trip buddy. You need someone who has enough money to split gas costs, but isn't going to give you too much shit. If you can sucker someone into buying all the gas since it's your damn car, that's the best way to go. Now, Wes usually goes for that, but Ron doesn't. In fact, Ron always loses his wallet right before we leave and barely has enough cash in his pocket to buy his own beer and Arby's. Problem is, Ron is more fun on road trips, because he does the stupidest shit. I can overlook Ron's lack of money when he sticks a straw up his nose to blast spitballs at the ceiling of some truck-stop diner.

Second rule, your car's gotta be clean. I don't mean you can't still write in the dust on the hood—I mean clean on the inside. Your car is your home while you're on a road trip. The last thing you need is to roll over in your sleep and break open some ketchup packet you left on the seat. Pick up all your burger wrappers, empty antifreeze bottles, ATM receipts, parking tickets, and cracked tape cases, and throw them the hell away. While you're cleaning up, you might even find some cash to spend on the trip.

Third, stock up on provisions. Jerky's a must, because it doesn't go bad. Soda-wise, Coke is your best bet, but Dr. Pepper is okay, too. Water is free at any gas station, so don't waste your money on that. Chips are more trouble than they're worth, but if someone in your party insists on them, get a few bags, just to keep everyone happy. Most important of all: A couple extra cans of oil could save your life out there. And take an orange, for health.

Fourth, make a plan. You shouldn't go off without any idea where you're going. If you do that, you'll end up driving around for days without ever feeling like you got anywhere. Now, I haven't developed a plan for this trip just yet, but that's because I'm waiting to be inspired. I'm thinking that, when inspiration does hit, it might be Michigan.

Finally, have an emergency buddy in place in case something bad happens on the road. This requires long-term planning. You can't just call someone out of the blue when you're stranded, broke, and all the way up by Antigo without any gas. You need to have your ace in the hole well before you ever leave the city. Pick a friend who has a dependable car and isn't always getting his phone disconnected. This is probably some boring person you aren't all that close to, so do some legwork. Once you've got your ace picked out, call him up every once in a while and ask how he's doing, even if you couldn't care less. Stop by with a six-pack every month or so. You have to be on good terms with him, or he'll never drive 200 miles to pick your stranded ass up.

So, that's my road map to road trips. There are other things you can do if you're a puss, like you can get a tune-up or get a bunch of maps from your grandma, but part of the adventure is leaving some of it to chance. If you take too many precautions, how will you learn to think on your feet? How will you ever know what it's like to push a car a mile uphill to a service station if you never experience it? All right, it sucks. But you should live it at least once to know how bad it is. ∅

Your Horoscope

By Lloyd Schumner Sr.
Retired Machinist and
A.A.P.B.-Certified Astrologer

Aries: (March 21–April 19)
You've made it clear that you're a self-made man, and that no one can tell you how to live, but sometimes you think it might be nice to live indoors and eat people food.

Taurus: (April 20–May 20)
Please stop comparing your own experiences to those of Sisyphus, who, unlike you, at least *tried* to get stuff done.

Gemini: (May 21–June 21)
A bizarre misunderstanding on the part of a bordello owner results in your getting flayed within an inch of your life by hot Asian teens.

Cancer: (June 22–July 22)
You're well on your way to becoming a better person, but only if your body doesn't reject the kidney.

Leo: (July 23–Aug. 22)
Most messages from the Unknowable Infinite are vague and open to interpretation, but there's no pussy-footing around when it comes to your enormous ass.

Virgo: (Aug. 23–Sept. 22)
While it's true that performing crazy antics in a mascot suit is passé, it served you well for many years.

Libra: (Sept. 23–Oct. 23)
Next to its sheer beauty, the best thing about your throne of skulls is that every little skull represents a different memory.

Scorpio: (Oct. 24–Nov. 21)
You'll be horrified to realize how low the entertainment industry has sunk when you see exactly what that wacky, perverted Rick Moranis has shrunk this time.

Sagittarius: (Nov. 22–Dec. 21)
Soon you'll show them all. Unfortunately, exactly what you'll show them is neither pretty, nor viewable by those under 18.

Capricorn: (Dec. 22–Jan. 19)
You're willing to do something to make the world a better place, but only if it entails using fire.

Aquarius: (Jan. 20–Feb. 18)
This may be your star sign, but you have to admit that the differences between your own qualities and those indicated by the word "Aquarian" are pretty striking.

Pisces: (Feb. 19–March 20)
The happiness and positive energy heralded by Venus rising in your sign will be negated by the kinetic energy expended by Near Earth Asteroid B-2634628 falling on your house.

BISHOP from page 135

anywhere," Boland said. "He's here until he dies, and he's not much older than me. It's too depressing to think about right now."

Boland said he hopes current events will serve to shake things up a bit.

"I'm grateful for this recent controversy over gay marriage," Boland said. "It allows me to dabble in politics a little. I'm firmly in support of President Bush's constitutional amendment to ban same-gender unions, so I've been trying to stir up some healthy debate on the subject. Anything to do something new in this diocese."

Cardinal Roger Mahony said he was not surprised by Boland's attitude.

"Bishop Boland is going through a temporary period of dissatisfaction, similar to those experienced by many of his colleagues," Mahony said. "As a cardinal, I'm forced to listen to that same complaint again and again. It's getting really old. If he's so unhappy, he's more than welcome to quit the Church and go work at a Taco Bell." ∅

Cheney Wows Sept. 11 Commission By Drinking Glass Of Water While Bush Speaks

see WASHINGTON page 4B

Sea Claims Flip-Flop

see NATURE page 13E

New AnTiVo DVR Only Records Shows It Knows You Hate

see PRODUCTS page 6F

STATshot

A look at the numbers that shape your world.

How Are We Celebrating Earth Day?

13% Cheering on Dale Earnhardt Jr. in the Firestone Earth Day 500

12% Thinking locally

26% Staying away from Dad, who goes on a huge drunk every Earth Day

9% Swerving to avoid guy on recumbent bicycle

40% Saying "Huh, no shit" when someone tells us it's Earth Day

the ONION®

VOLUME 40 ISSUE 16   AMERICA'S FINEST NEWS SOURCE™   22–28 APRIL 2004

Iraqis Arming Selves For Independence

BAGHDAD—With little more than two months remaining until the American-led occupation force hands sovereignty to an interim government, Iraqi citizens are joyfully arming themselves in anticipation of independence.

"Saddam is overthrown! Praise Allah! Iraq is ours once more!" Baghdad native Alaa al-Khawaja said, as he

see IRAQIS page 143

Above: A Baghdad tailor stocks up on supplies before the June 30 transfer of power.

Senatorial Candidate Introduces New Low-Carb Platform

Above: McBride describes his low-carb agenda to a group of supporters.

COLUMBIA, SC—Mayor of Myrtle Beach and Republican Senate hopeful Mark McBride jumped ahead in the polls Monday after announcing his new low-carbohydrate political platform.

"The people of South Carolina have allowed starchy politics to become a staple in their diets," McBride said, addressing a crowd of supporters at a capitol-area convention center. "You are what you vote for, and when you vote for McBride, you're telling Washington that you want a leader with meaty ideas. You're telling them you aren't going to swallow any more sugar-coated lies."

Having failed to capture voter interest with his previous platform of lower taxes, increased support for job programs, and tort reform, McBride decided a low-carb message was

more likely to resonate with voters.

"Americans have asked for a leaner government, and they've been handed bread and circuses," McBride said. "What we have now is a lethargic ruling body, willing to down anything that special-interest groups spoonfeed them. I'm gonna put an end to that. A vote for me is a vote for this country's long-term health."

South Carolina voters have responded enthusiastically to McBride's low-carb initiative, boosting the candidate as many as 11 points in recent polls.

"I'm on Atkins, so I always keep my eye out for new low-carb choices," Pauline Illford said, holding a campaign flyer that read "McBride: Great for Atkins dieters!" "I used to see McBride as just another white-bread politician from South Carolina. But

see CANDIDATE page 142

Above: Scribba, who is already 32.

Woman Looks Great For A 32-Year-Old

BLOOMINGTON, MN—Acquaintances and coworkers of local resident Jenny Scribba cannot get over how vibrant she looks, considering the fact that she is 32 years old.

"That girl is 32? No way," 24-year-old Arden Rice, a waitress at a local diner that Scribba frequent, said Monday. "You're joking. I never would've guessed she was over 30! She looks so great."

Sources say many people are incredulous when they hear that Scribba, who is still quite attractive, is actually 32. It's hard to believe, but true: Scribba was born in 1972, the year of the Watergate break-in and the Israeli Olympic team massacre, yet she

see WOMAN page 142

McDonald's Unveils Healthier Image

Last week, McDonald's announced plans to offer healthier menu items and encourage its customers to get more exercise. What do *you* think?

Donna Alexander
Lab Assistant

"Their new 'infrasized meals,' where you can get one-third the food for an extra 99 cents, are definitely a step in the right direction."

Jesse Perry
Audiologist

"Every location should have an amusement-park-style plywood Grimace that says, 'You cannot enter this McDonald's if you're more than this wide.'"

Martin Bryant
Systems Analyst

"Those McDonald's anti-obesity campaign materials are soon to be the prized possessions of every hipster from here to Tacoma."

Bobby Melvin
Nurse

"I think it's brave. McDonald's is a very brave corporation."

Tonia Coleman
Promotions Manager

"I guess those playlands don't provide as solid a total-body workout as previously thought."

Adam H. Ross
Sales Clerk

"Man, you can already smell the greasy stench of guilt every time you walk into a McDonald's. Do they have to lay more on?"

Online Music Stores

Internet sites like the iTunes music store are gaining in popularity. Why are more Americans buying music online?

- Want to buy Kelis CD without getting stink-eye from that horn-rimmed dick behind counter
- Like option of having cat select music purchases
- Excited to see what levels of excellence Wal-Mart will bring to the industry
- Enjoy further enraging analog purist Steve Albini
- Internet cutout bargain bins offer albums like *Boots Randolph's Greatest Hits* and *Best of Donna Fargo* at deep discount
- Computer the purest way to buy the cold, mechanistic music of Kraftwerk
- Prefer Internet music stores over old-fashioned, brick-and-mortar-and-empty-Chinese-takeout-containters-and-old-flyers-everywhere music stores
- More convenient to buy new Jennifer Lopez release at home than to travel 200 feet to closest store that sells it

iTunes Music Store
99¢ a song.

⌀ the ONION®
America's Finest News Source.™

Herman Ulysses Zweibel
Founder

T. Herman Zweibel
Publisher Emeritus
J. Phineas Zweibel
Publisher
Maxwell Prescott Zweibel
Editor-In-Chief

Why Can't This Family Ever Have A Funky Good Time?

By Tomi Rae Brown

I say *goddamn*! It ain't but once or twice a year the Brown clan get together. Every time, we swear up and down it's gonna be a brand new bag. But every time, somebody gotta be stupid and start with the arguing. Why, I say *whyyyy*, it gotta be this way? Can't this family get together and have a funky good time?

Come on, now. Can you hear me? Let's enjoy a nice dinner, without all the cussin' and feudin'. Don't you realize that I love you? Brothas and sistas, cousins, sista-in-law, Danny Ray's girlfriend Tracy—I really look *forward* to seeing, to being with the ones that I love. So sit on down, Clyde, and tell Tracy you sorry for that crack about her weight. I can't hear you. I can't *hear* you. That's better.

You know, you could help out a little, Mr. James Brown. Mr. Soul Brother No. 1, the Godfather, Mr. Dynamite, you could back me up. Yes, you the man who brought us such hits as "I Got You," "Try Me," and "Super Bad," but that ain't no reason you can't lift a finger to help out around here. You the hardest-working man in show business? Please. You the laziest motherfucker sitting in the living room. Watching the television, making fun of Danny Ray, makin' everyone grumpy. Is that what you call a groove now? Get up offa that thing, move your soul-powered ass out to the entryway, and bring in a roll of paper towels.

Quit crying, James Jr. So your father took a swing at your mother, ain't no thing. With God as my witness, we're gonna have a funky family reunion this year if it kills me. What this family has been doing to itself is a *damn* shame. Every time I think about it, I wanna jump back, uh, jump back into bed. This family makes me sad. I only ask that we love each other right and get funky when we blessed enough to have the chance to share time together. Is that so much to ask? This family has *got* to get it together, I say.

Now, listen here. James, don't you mind about Clyde chewin' with his mouth open, unless you want a fine. Let's enjoy this dinner I made. That's right, I worked *hard* to make these mashed potatoes. I worked *hard* to make this jerk pork. Well, maybe next year we'll just order out something down from Hipster Avenue. No black-eyed peas, no collard greens, and no Mobile gumbo. I know, Bobby, you love soul food, so you gonna have to stop acting like a damn fool if you

want any more of my cookin'. Uh! Say what? Four-time. *Heeyeaaahhh!*

Family members. Children. Danny Ray's girlfriend. Right now, I'd like to take it down a little bit. I wanna talk to the ladies. Ladies, are you listening? All you beautiful women—and you know you beautiful, too. There comes a time, you gotta stop your fussing and fighting. These men is bad enough, without us sensible folk getting down in the dirt with them. So please, please, please will y'all stop arguing? God bless you. Thank you very much, ladies. I love you.

James, I know you like to make things hot, but dinner table ain't the

---

You know, you could help out a little, Mr. James Brown. Mr. Soul Brother No. 1, the Godfather, Mr. Dynamite, you could back me up. Yes, you the man who brought us such hits as "I Got You," "Try Me," and "Super Bad," but that ain't no reason you can't lift a finger to help out around here.

---

place to turn it out. Just look over at Jabo. He over there sweet as can be, passing the biscuits, using his napkin, bouncing your granddaughter on his knee. Can we all give the drummer some recognition? I *said*, can we give the drummer some? That's more like it, ah yeah. Give it to him one more time. Ha ha, Jabo Starks everybody, you all could learn a valuable lesson from him.

Now, everybody remember what you promised me? After dinner we all gonna have a little coffee and talk about old times. Someone gonna tell the story about the time James was sleepwalking. Someone betta' tell the story about the time the bucket of paint fell on Danny Ray. Then we gonna get funky, gonna pour some Night Train, start flipping over, won't be able to imagine what we have or haven't done—right, James Jr.? Ain't no thing if your father cuss your mother. Let him cuss me. Part of love. I want this family reunion to smoke. Is everybody finished with your meal?

see GOOD TIME page 144

National Endowment For The Arts & Crafts Criticized For Funding Giant Macramé Penis

KANSAS CITY, MO—Republican lawmakers and conservative religious groups blasted the National Endowment For The Arts & Crafts Tuesday, claiming that the organization has allocated federal funds for "obscene crafts."

The $15,000 grant in question was awarded last October to Detroit arts & craftsman Albert Kahle, 39, for a nine-foot macramé penis titled "Father (By Mother)," which is currently part of the *Macramazement!* exhibit at the prestigious National Gallery Of Arts & Crafts in Kansas City, MO.

"'Father (By Mother)' is neither art nor craft," House Majority Leader Tom DeLay (R-TX) said. "It's trash. The fact that American taxpayers are paying for this kind of lewd handiwork is outrageous."

The macramé-work phallus comprises three discrete elements: testicles, shaft, and head. The head is knotted in Double Alternating Lark's Head style. The shaft of the penis, knotted of Tammy's Hemp Cord in flesh tone, is embellished with subtle strands of Half-Knot sinnet cord in light blue and Amy's Cord in pale lavender. The testicles, the most detailed portion of the work, are embellished with black maple beads and a spray of silver glitter.

"[2003 NEAC grant recipient] Terrence Colwell's macaroni 'Crown Of Thorns' was bad enough," DeLay said. "But an enormous phallus made out of colorful, child-safe materials that anyone could buy at the craft store? It's way over the line."

This is not the first time an NEAC grant has sparked controversy. Last year, a vocal group of citizens appeared before Congress to protest government funding of C.F. Littman's "Piss-Soaked God's Eye," and in 2002, the NEAC received more than 10,000 letters of complaint over the grant it awarded Rachel Delancey for her shellacked driftwood clitoris "Found It... In The Sea."

NEAC spokesperson Jessica Sirota said the association does not plan to offer a public apology for funding Kahle's art & craftwork.

"When expressing the human condition through craft, the craftsman is responsible only to himself," Sirota said. "It takes great courage to pick up those popsicle sticks and empty dishwashing-soap bottles and bring something forth out of the ether. The creative space is outside Congress' jurisdiction."

The macramé penis is Kahle's first phallic work of art & craft to receive media attention. His other major

Above: Kahle's work hangs at the National Gallery Of Arts & Crafts.

works include a shoebox diorama titled "Abe Lincoln In The Bathtub," a 13-foot-tall newspaper and poster-paint papier-mâché penis titled "What's Black And White And Red All Over?," and "Pin(whee)ls," a collection of 200 pinwheels made of construction paper, pencils, and clippings from pornographic magazines.

"If people took the time to explore 'Father (By Mother),' there would be no controversy," Kahle said. "The piece is not prurient. The true meaning of

the piece is located on its head, where glitter was applied with Elmer's Glue. Every speck of glitter is a tiny mirror reflecting the observer. At end, this piece is about love, sex, birth: what we came from."

Art&CraftForum editor Tim Griffin devoted his bi-monthly column to an expression of support for the NEAC.

"Sexuality has always been part of the art-and-craft world," Griffin wrote. "To strip a work of string art or see PENIS page 142

NEWS IN BRIEF

Libertarian Reluctantly Calls Fire Department

CHEYENNE, WY—After attempting to contain a living-room blaze started by a cigarette, card-carrying Libertarian Trent Jacobs reluctantly called the Cheyenne Fire Department Monday. "Although the community would do better to rely on an efficient, free-market fire-fighting service, the fact is that expensive, unnecessary public fire departments do exist," Jacobs said. "Also, my house was burning down." Jacobs did not offer to pay firefighters for their service.

Nation Celebrates Awkward 'Take Your Illegitimate Daughter To Work' Day

WASHINGTON, DC—Tensions were running high Tuesday as Americans nervously explained their jobs, gave workplace tours, and introduced their bastard children to coworkers on National "Take Your Illegitimate Daughter To Work" Day. "Today, we encourage young girls to think about the future while we acknowledge the sins of our past," said President Bush, who insisted that cameras remain trained on his face during his address. "Let's encourage our unnamed children to build a career that takes them to new and exciting places very, very far away." The annual holiday was established under President Kennedy in 1962.

Historian Has Big News For Grover Cleveland Fans

CALDWELL, NJ—Historian and author Louis Putnam announced Monday that his new book about Grover Cleveland will shock fans of the 22nd and 24th U.S. president. "You're gonna see the only president to serve two non-consecutive terms as you've never seen him before," Putnam said. "Forget Tammany Hall, screw the pa-

ternity scandal, and to hell with a so-called 'secret' battle with jaw cancer. When my book comes out, you're gonna fucking flip." Putnam's book, *Grover! Grover! Grover!*, will hit bookstore shelves May 13.

Weird Al Honors Parents' Memory With 'Tears In Heaven' Parody

FALLBROOK, CA—Zany, mourning entertainer "Weird Al" Yankovic has parodied Eric Clapton's eulogy song "Tears In Heaven" in loving tribute to his parents, who recently died of carbon-monoxide poisoning in their San Diego home, a spokesman for Yankovic said Monday. "Al's hurting deeply right now, and this is his way of honoring Nick and Mary," Karl Tuft said of the song in which a subdued Yankovic sings, "First you lit some flames / Then the smoke stopped your breathin' / Carbon mono's th'way you went... / Up to heaven" over a somber,

minor-key accordion melody. Tuft added that the best way for Yankovic to give voice to his pain and loss was by altering the voice of Clapton's pain and loss.

Longtime Heckler Just Kind Of Fell Into Heckling

LOS ANGELES—Comedy-club regular Ray Thurmond, 53, has heckled Southern California's comedians for the past 21 years, but he told reporters Monday that he never planned to become a heckler. "I was watching some awful act at the Comedy Store, and the guy was totally bombing," Thurmond said. "So I yelled, 'God, you suck.' Well, the audience really cracked up, so I yelled at him to get off the stage. One thing led to another, and here I am." Thurmond also said that, while he did not coin the phrase, he may have been responsible for introducing the concept of not quitting your day job to the local scene. ∅

inherent li-
...roy it. As
...ought it
...roud of
...."

...ional
...urch
...essed with

...ce is indecent, not to men-
...n a shameful waste of beads," St. Louis resident Trent Billings said. "These so-called craftspeople are more interested in offending people than they are in making a nice gift that someone could hang up in their museum. I swear, half those knots are coming undone, and if the kitten appliques on "22 Pussy Potholders" were hand-embroidered, I'll eat my collection of Ukranian egg art."

"It looks like something my 7-year-old niece could've made at camp," Billings added.

A smaller group of Kahle supporters stood across the street from the protesters, handing out pamphlets.

"It doesn't matter whether you're using felt, string, colored sand, bottle caps, or even a wood-burning set, as

long as you're careful not to burn yourself or others," said Fred Schwartz, who recently received a doctorate in arts & crafts history from the University of Missouri. "It's all

> "These so-called craftspeople are more interested in offending people than they are in making a nice gift that someone could hang up," Billings said.

protected by the First Amendment."

"If the conservatives find this museum's exquisite collection of naked paper-bag puppets offensive, they don't have to go see it," Schwartz added.

Kahle, undeterred by the controversy, recently began crafting a rainbow-colored leather belt large enough to encircle the city of San Francisco. ∅

Above: "Sweet Taste Of SS," for which the NEAC granted Rachel Borstein $20,000 in 2002.

CANDIDATE from page 139

his new campaign has really got me energized. Compared to him, all the other candidates seem really bland or hard to follow."

McBride said that, if elected, he'll push Congress to "cut the excess

> Democrat Inez Tenenbaum, the race's former frontrunner, has yet to comment on her opponent's platform. Despite the popularity of the low-carb campaign, Tenenbaum has chosen to stick to her original goals of job creation, affordable healthcare, and increased national security.

weight that's dragging the U.S. budget down."

"Take one look at the fat cats living large off your taxes, and you'll agree that the old way wasn't working," McBride said. "If you send me to Washington, you'll get quick results. You'll see a noticeable change within weeks. The first day I'm sworn into office, you'll notice a leaner, healthier government."

McBride declined to give specifics about which policies he'll vote for, but

he did hand reporters coupons for the steak-and-shrimp dinner at his restaurant, Crabman's Seafood and Country Buffet.

"As mayor of Myrtle Beach and owner of a popular local restaurant, I've learned a thing or two," said McBride, who changed his restaurant's menu to reflect his low-carb program last year. "I've been listening to the people of this great state, and the majority of them want to know one thing: Do you have anything low-carb?"

"I know what's good for South Carolina, as my public-service record and the success of my restaurant clearly prove," McBride said, before taking a bite of a salmon steak wrapped in romaine lettuce.

Democrat Inez Tenenbaum, the race's former frontrunner, has yet to comment on her opponent's platform. Despite the popularity of the low-carb campaign, Tenenbaum has chosen to stick to her original goals of job creation, affordable healthcare, and increased national security.

"Tenenbaum isn't running a quick-and-easy fad campaign," said Jack Rissol, a reporter from the Charleston Post And Courier. "She's going the long route, hoping constituents come back around to the idea that the only way to get long-term change in government is to consume a balanced array of fresh ideas and regularly exercise one's right to vote."

"On the other hand, there's plenty of evidence that McBride's new platform is working," Rissol added. "I thought it sounded crazy at first, too, and that there was no way a platform like that could possibly work. But there's no denying it: McBride looks great in those polls." ∅

WOMAN from page 139

possesses a trim figure and a smooth, unlined face.

"Jenny hardly looks a day over 27," said neighbor and University of Minnesota student Bethany Weber, 21. "Where are her wrinkles? You can sort of see little lines around her eyes when she smiles, but they disappear when she stops. I hope I look that good when I'm her age."

Continued Weber: "I have this older cousin who was a total hunk in high school. But now he's 35, and he looks like Popeye. Jenny gives me something to aspire to. I wonder if she uses, like, Oil Of Olay or something. I don't think she's had any work done."

Scribba, an assistant designer at a commercial-graphics firm with a relaxed dress code, frequently wears jeans, T-shirts, and casual skirts like those worn by women 10 or even 20 years younger than she is.

"Normally, when I see a 32-year-old woman dressed like [Scribba], I think, 'Give it up. You're old,'" intern Kimberly Kleutgen, 18, said. "But Jenny manages to pull it off."

"When we go out for drinks after work, Jenny sometimes has to show ID along with the younger employees," 21-year-old coworker Judd Truman said. "Keep in mind, this is a woman who learned to walk years before the commercial availability of VCRs, when Billie Jean King was the world's top female tennis player and people purchased music on 8-track tapes."

According to Truman, Scribba's friendliness and enthusiasm also lead people to assume that she's younger than 32.

"Jenny doesn't act like most older people," Truman said. "She's totally willing to joke around, and she never looks down on you for having a good

time."

"In fact, she's into a lot of the same things my friends and I like," Truman continued. "When they played [OutKast's] 'The Way You Move' at the office party, she was totally dancing with us. Believe it or not, it wasn't embarrassing. It didn't come off like she was desperately clinging to her fading youth at all. In fact, it was almost like she was in her element. She's still to-

> "Normally, when I see a 32-year-old woman dressed like [Scribba], I think, 'Give it up. You're old,'" intern Kimberly Kleutgen, 18, said.

tally able to enjoy herself. That's so cool."

The reason for Scribba's youthful appearance is unknown. Heredity is most likely not a factor, as her parents, Edina residents Michael and Madeleine Scribba, both suffer from the dry, wrinkled skin, bony hands, and sagging chests that old people usually have.

"Jenny's a lovely girl," Madeleine, 60, said as her 63-year-old husband nodded in assent. "I've always said that."

Scribba said she does not avoid foods that contribute to premature aging, such as alcohol, meat, and junk food. According to Truman, Scribba regularly eats pizza, M&Ms, and even doughnuts.

see WOMAN page 143

WOMAN from page 142

"I once saw her eat an entire plate of fettuccine Alfredo," Truman said. "That stuff is just swimming with free radi-

> "Jenny doesn't act like most older people," Truman said. "She's totally willing to joke around, and she never looks down on you for having a good time."

cals, you know. I would think that someone Jenny's age would avoid cheese and salt, but it doesn't seem to affect her."

Asked about her beauty regimen, Scribba seemed reluctant to give away any of her secrets.

"Uh, well, I don't know, nothing too special," Scribba said. "I guess I try to get enough sleep. I eat a good breakfast, and I ride my bike when the weather is nice. I go to the movies at least a couple times a month. Oh, and I wear sunscreen."

"Yeah, I can't believe I'm 32 already," Scribba added. "All the same, I can't tell you what I'll be doing at 40. Married? Kids? Who knows? It's still too far off to even speculate."

The age-defying Scribba turns 33 next February, but shows no signs of slowing. In the coming weeks, she plans to paint her apartment, attend a family reunion in Biloxi, MS, and get her hair cut. ∅

SPITTLE from page 53

unusually large amounts of blood. Passersby were amazed by the unusually large amounts of blood. Passersby were amazed by the unusually large amounts of blood. Passersby were amazed by the unusually large amounts of blood. Passersby were amazed by the unusually large amounts of blood. Passersby were amazed by the unusually large amounts of blood. Passersby were amazed by the unusually large amounts of blood. Passersby were amazed by the unusually large amounts of blood. Passersby were amazed by the unusually large amounts of blood. Passersby were amazed by the unusually large amounts of blood. Passersby were amazed by the unusually large amounts of blood. Passersby were amazed by the unusually large amounts of blood. Passersby were amazed by the unusually large amounts of blood. Passersby were amazed by the unusually large amounts of blood. Passersby were amazed by the unusually large amounts of blood. Passersby were amazed by the unusually large

amounts of blood. Passersby were amazed by the unusually large amounts of blood. Passersby were amazed by the unusually large amounts of blood. Passersby were amazed by the unusually large amounts of blood. Passersby were

> I fancy myself something of a lotto hobbyist.

amazed by the unusually large amounts of blood. Passersby were amazed by the unusually large amounts of blood. Passersby were amazed by the unusually large amounts of blood. Passersby were amazed by the unusually large amounts of blood. Passersby were

see SPITTLE page 166

IRAQIS from page 139

busily shoved boxes of 7.62mm ammunition beneath the bed in his two-room home on the outskirts of Baghdad. "Now is the time for all citizens to prepare for our nation's glorious future—a future certain to contain wave after bloody wave of sectarian violence."

"Excuse me, now," al-Khawaja added. "I must barricade these doors and windows with sheet metal before the wonderful day of freedom arrives."

Also readying himself is Thaer Abbas, a Tikrit shopkeeper who sells handmade baskets, earthenware pots, and surplus AK-47s.

"God bless the USA! God bless Bush!" Abbas said. "America has delivered our country back into our hands, and soon, thousands of those hands will be raised in anger as mullahs and imams lead the fight over what little remains."

As the June 30 date for transfer of full authority to the interim government approaches, the dozens of political factions that comprise the liberated nation are readying themselves to assume rule.

"Finally, we will have the opportunity to lead our own nation and decide what is best for our people," said Shi'ite Muslim cleric Namir al-Safy. "Of course, by 'we,' I mean the Shi'ites."

Secretary of Defense Donald Rumsfeld said he expects a smooth transfer of power, in spite of anti-U.S. violence, widespread unrest, and recent events like the Shi'ite uprising in Fallujah.

"The Iraqi people deserve their long-sought independence," Rumsfeld said at a Defense Department press conference Monday. "We cannot, in good conscience, postpone the transfer of power. That would be punishing all the good Iraqi people for the actions of a few thousand insurgents, militiamen, suicide bombers, kidnappers, religious zealots, and roving armed bandits."

"Iraqi sovereignty will arrive on June 30," Rumsfeld added. "Citizens of

a new free Iraq, this is your final warning: Sovereignty will arrive on June 30."

Even as house-to-house fighting continues in Iraq's urban centers,

> Secretary of Defense Donald Rumsfeld said he expects a smooth transfer of power.

Iraqi citizens said they applaud U.S. efforts to return their country to them so quickly.

"True Iraqis know that our enemy has never been the U.S.," said Hakmed Butti, a Sunni who has been "saving my joy and weaponry" for the day America returns power to his country. "Our enemy has always been each other. It took an American invasion to teach my people that, but I do not think it is a lesson we will soon forget."

Butti said he plans to observe the day of independence at home with his family, in quiet contemplation and prayer for his life in a fortified bunker he built beneath his house.

Iraqi leaders expressed optimism about the future of democracy in Iraq.

"I am certain that this democracy will be a flash point of social and political change," said one Najaf-based Iraqi cleric who asked that his name and the location of the tanker truck

he was loading with diesel-soaked nitrate-based fertilizer not be printed. "My followers and I will visit the new government offices as soon as they open, to make absolutely certain that they get our message. Yes, the capitol building will be at the center of the firestorm, as they say."

Shi'ite leader Dzhan al-Juburi said difficult days are ahead, but that the people of Iraq are "not strangers to challenge."

"The path to re-deconstructing Iraq will not be easy," al-Juburi said. "But if we remember to draw on the strength of our people and their massive stockpiles of automatic weapons, then, Allah willing, we will turn Iraq into the country it once was in no time at all." ∅

Above: A Tikrit family's spare bedroom is put to use.

I Haven't Achieved Greatness So Much As I Was Born Into It

By H. Edward Winslow III

Earlier today, on the way back from a shareholders meeting in Melbourne, the pilot of my Bombardier Challenger 604 twinprop private jet asked how I had managed to rise to a position of such great power and prestige at so young an age. After several modest demurrals, I settled back in my seat and began to explain my secret: I haven't so much "earned" greatness as I was "born into it."

My ancestor Edward Winslow and his wife Elizabeth Barker Winslow came to this country on the Mayflower in the year 1620. Once in the new world, the Winslow family worked hard, contributed to the community, and lived honest and responsible lives. Slowly, over the course of many generations, the Winslow name achieved great renown.

In this world, few are bestowed the mantle of greatness. There are some people at the bottom, some in the middle, and a small number, like myself, who reside at the very top. Let's face it: I'm a born leader.

Now, there are other ways one can achieve greatness. I recently met a fellow who struggled for many years, working 70 hours a week in a screen-door factory until he achieved his lifelong dream of owning a ranch. Well, I guess that's one way of doing it, but it's not *my* way. My approach to achieving greatness was more effortless: I went to the best schools, I wore the best clothes, and I didn't have to do anything that was too hard.

A friend of mine from down at the club started his own Internet company and made his first million by age 28. Well, some of us don't have time for that. I made my first million at 18, when my trust fund matured. Actually, it was my first 20 million. But I didn't let a huge sum of money stop me. I was young and driven, and I wanted whatever life had to place into my lap. Soon, with a little bit of patience, that $20 million grew to $200 million, when my father gave me controlling interest in the foundry.

I know what you're thinking: As a 25-year-old CEO of a major corporation, I could easily have chosen to rest on my laurels. I was already an accomplished yachtsman, rower, and polo player. But I chose to do more than that. I wanted to do everything that my father told me to do. I was to be in the office by 10 a.m. every weekday, except when I was on holiday abroad, and I was not to leave until 5 p.m. sharp. If a member of my staff of

underlings asked me to sign something, I signed it. Thus, I rose to the position my birthright had ensured me: figurehead president.

When people see all that I have and ask me for advice, I tell them this: It is possible to achieve success with only elbow grease and fierce determination. I don't recommend that, though. Because, truth be told, you can follow that advice until the day you die, but there's no guarantee you'll be a suc-

> **Now, there are other ways one can achieve greatness. I recently met a fellow who struggled for many years, working 70 hours a week in a screen-door factory until he achieved his lifelong dream of owning a ranch. Well, I guess that's one way of doing it, but it's not *my* way.**

cess. Unless you were born into wealth and privilege, you can't be sure you'll find yourself gazing down at others from the loftiest heights.

Those extra generations of wealth and power give you a foundation that no amount of hard work can equal. It's what gives you the edge over those who are willing to strive and toil. Though some may have found limited triumph through hard work, in the long run, they've usually fallen behind those of us with that special something called an aristocratic birth.

There are thousands of books filled with advice about how to have it all. But nothing is as effective as the silver-platter method favored by myself and my ancestors. A 375-year track record of success can't be disputed. Having everything you've ever wanted simply given to you is a proven path to success. It's what I call the 'being born into it' advantage.

This is what I told that pilot, and I believe it's sound advice: If you really want to rise above the herd, get out there and be born into an unbelievably wealthy family, preferably one that has been rich for centuries. Once you do that, nothing can stand between you and your dreams. But do it soon. Life is short, and you're only born once. ∅

Your Horoscope

By Lloyd Schumner Sr.
Retired Machinist and
A.A.P.B.-Certified Astrologer

Aries: (March 21–April 19)
When people think of all the ways picnics are ruined, it's rare that they come up with even half of the weird shit you've pulled.

Taurus: (April 20–May 20)
There comes a time in all of our lives when we're forced to admit that we need help, though it's not usually with getting a piano off our chests.

Gemini: (May 21–June 21)
Making the mature decision to throw out your beer-can collection will offer an added bonus when you find out that some of the cans still have beer in them.

Cancer: (June 22–July 22)
It's actually pretty well known that the "S" in Harry S Truman didn't stand for anything. You'll have to impress girls some other way.

Leo: (July 23–Aug. 22)
You've built a reputation as someone not to fuck with, which is unfortunate, as you would really like some fucking.

Virgo: (Aug. 23–Sept. 22)
The typical Virgo is helpful to a fault, trusting in matters of love, and outgoing. That said, you probably got your powerful thirst for gin from your father.

Libra: (Sept. 23–Oct. 23)
Your politics are tough, but fair. When you say "Put 'em all in camps," you do mean everybody.

Scorpio: (Oct. 24–Nov. 21)
Buddha says that, while he may show you the way, only you can truly save yourself, proving once and for all that he's a lazy, fat bastard.

Sagittarius: (Nov. 22–Dec. 21)
You haven't seen a lot of coroner's reports, but you're pretty sure yours shouldn't end with the phrase "right in the goddamn nuts!!!"

Capricorn: (Dec. 22–Jan. 19)
By this time next week, you'll be a living example of what it's like to get blued, screwed, and tattooed.

Aquarius: (Jan. 20–Feb. 18)
The government has spent thousands of dollars training you to be a highly efficient killing machine, so please try and act like one from now on.

Pisces: (Feb. 19–March 20)
You'd be a much more trusted and respected member of the community if you would just take your hand out of your pants every now and then.

GOOD TIME from page 140

GOOD TIME from page 140

Okay, I'm gonna count it off, then I'm gonna clear these dishes. Can I count it off? One... two... three... Now, hold on, now, lemme lay the thing on you, now. One... two... You guys are messing with my head now. Gimme that plate. Said gimme that plate. I told you I was gonna take it. Now, get on up and head in the other room and take your coffee with you. Yeah! Now we together.

Maceo! I said Maceo! Uh, Maceo! Don't just keep saying "what," boy. Go get that pecan pie out the kitchen. Take it into the living room. We gonna have a funky good time, and I don't want you starting off before everyone. Bring the pie here. Right here. Everybody grab a piece—don't be greedy now. We family, after all. There's enough of this pie to go around. That's right, y'all. Enough pie for all! Pecan pie! Mother-made pie! Good pie! *Damn good!*

Okay, let's get funky like we used to in the old days. You remember those times, Marva, don't you? Uh! We'd

laugh and drink wine *hoooooo!* and tell all the old stories after a nice dinner. Nice dinner of chitlins. *Uh!* I just

> **Okay, let's get funky like we used to in the old days. You remember those times, Marva, don't you? Uh! We'd laugh and drink wine hoooooo!**

want things to be like that again. Now, everybody, let's just forget all that stuff and make it funky in here. *Hooo!* Everybody clap your hands. I said clap your hands! Uh-uh-uh-uh! Do it like ya mean it.

Bobby! Move your chair *outta* the way and let your brotha get down. This family gonna be the death of me. I swear to *God* it's true! ∅

the ONION®

VOLUME 40 ISSUE 17   AMERICA'S FINEST NEWS SOURCE™   29 APRIL–5 MAY 2004

Tom Hanks This Week's Guest President

WASHINGTON, DC—Superstar actor Tom Hanks will fill President Bush's spot at the White House through Friday while the chief executive takes the week off.

"We're thrilled to have Tom sitting at the president's desk this week," White House press secretary Scott McClellan said Tuesday. "It's truly an honor that this beloved star and two-time Oscar winner took time from his busy schedule to guest-lead the nation. It's been a lot of fun so far, and we have even more great meetings lined up for the next couple days, so make sure to check the news."

It's the first guest-president gig for Hanks, who took the reins Monday, but McClellan said the actor's political inexperience is not a liability. Citing Hanks' "amiable yet commanding presence" and "seamless interfacing with diverse policymakers

see HANKS page 149

Above: Hanks welcomes the emir of Qatar, Sheikh Hamad al-Thani, to the Oval Office.

Suicide Bombing A Cry For Help, Vengeance Against The Infidel

see WORLD page 8C

Grocery-Store Freezer's White Castle Section A Wreck

see LOCAL page 10D

Jewish Senior Schlepped To Emergency Room

see LOCAL page 11D

STATshot

A look at the numbers that shape your world.

Who Would We Rather Be Married To?

- **15%** Ex-wife
- **22%** A different beekeeper
- **5%** That nice man who does the TV weather
- **13%** USS Enterprise
- **26%** Better job
- **29%** Girl in yellow dress stepping off ferry 40 years ago

IKEA Claims Another 10,000 Lifestyles

ATLANTA—IKEA, the rapidly growing Swedish retailer of inexpensive home furnishings, claimed another 10,000 American lifestyles in 2003, according to a report released Tuesday by the Center for Interior Design Control.

"This epidemic of self-assembled, clean-lined modernist furniture is still largely contained to densely populated urban areas, but the danger exists that it

see IKEA page 148

△ IKEA store location
• 1,000 homes infected by IKEA

Web Of Lies Surrounds Late Birthday Card

MISSOULA, MT—Only a thin tissue of lies screens area resident Jessica Jurgensen from the unpleasant reality that her friend Gina Tobler forgot her 34th birthday, which occurred four days ago.

"How did you like the card?" Tobler said in a carefully plotted phone call to Jurgensen Tuesday. "What?! I put it in the mail last week! I can't believe you didn't get it yet!"

The card, which currently sits inside a bowl of keys on Tobler's kitchen counter, is ready to be mailed, awaiting only the purchase of a stamp.

In lieu of a timely card, Tobler presented Jurgensen with an intricate work of fiction in which she cast herself as sensitive and considerate, if somewhat hapless.

"I can't wait until you see the card," Tobler said. "I ordered it online weeks ago. I hardly ever order things online, but it was so perfect, no other card would do. I waited for it for so long, I was about to get

see CARD page 149

Above: Tobler and the still-unmailed birthday card for Jurgensen (inset).

National Cyber Security

The Department of Homeland Security recently identified a serious Internet security flaw that could leave the web vulnerable to hackers. What do *you* think?

Lois Foster
Training Specialist

"If someone can take down the Internet, our nation stands in grave danger of being massively inconvenienced."

Roy Benjamin
Manager

"The danger is evident. We must post tanks at the entrances to all cyber cafes immediately."

Sean Hughes
Systems Analyst

"We're safe, unless the hacker community finds out about this."

Aaron Brookings
Family Practitioner

"Hmm. Maybe outsourcing all those programming jobs to Afghanistan was a bad idea, after all."

Lori Simmons
Dancer

"The terrorists have already put an end to free music downloads. What's next?"

Russ Ward
Deliveryman

"My God! What would we do if there was no Internet? Go back to watching television?"

Guantanamo Detainees' Complaints

The U.S. Supreme Court recently began hearing cases related to the Guantanamo Bay detentions. What were some of the prisoners' allegations?

▶ Only allowed to see TV lawyer

▶ Are being denied legal right to beg for death

▶ Wrist shackles chained to ankle shackles with enormous chain that goes down throat and through anus

▶ Guards allow three or four detainees who are actual terrorists to bully other 600 men mercilessly

▶ Fence blocks amazing ocean view that U.S. and British officials are always raving about

▶ Not allowed access to fertilizers or timing devices

▶ Can't determine the direction of Mecca with canvas hood locked over head

▶ Kept up all night by Cuban neighbors playing loud music

▶ All the usual bleeding-heart crap about having no legal recourse under laws of the U.S., Cuba, the U.N., or the Geneva Convention

the ONION®
America's Finest News Source.™

Herman Ulysses Zweibel
Founder

T. Herman Zweibel
Publisher Emeritus
J. Phineas Zweibel
Publisher

Maxwell Prescott Zweibel
Editor-In-Chief

Sept. 11 Could Not Have Been Prevented Without Accruing A Lot Of Overtime

By Condoleezza Rice

Esteemed members of the National Commission on Terrorist Attacks upon the United States, good afternoon. As National Security Advisor, my job is to coordinate the efforts of America's intelligence and defense agencies and report directly to the president. I was, and continue to be, in a unique position to understand the threats and dangers our nation faces. It is with utmost confidence and sincerity that I assure each and every one of you that there was no way the federal government could have prevented the horrific events of Sept. 11 without accruing an enormous amount of overtime.

My heart goes out to the families and loved ones of all those who died on that terrible day. Our prayers continue to be with you. Unfortunately, there was absolutely nothing we could have done to predict al-Qaeda's evil plot, without requiring many, many people to stay in the office past 5 p.m.

According to federal law, government employees must be paid time-and-a-half for any work hours beyond 40 and double-time on weekends. Ladies and gentlemen, preventing Sept. 11 would have required hundreds of thousands of unbudgeted overtime hours and, in several cases, overtime plus compensatory paid vacation. Again, may I address the family members of Sept. 11 victims: That tragic day changed us all, but you paid the highest price.

The world was a different place before the day of those horrific attacks. Due to tragic budget constraints before Sept. 11, it was impossible to authorize unlimited overtime pay to defend our country from international and domestic threats. Our nation was in the midst of a fiscal crisis and operating under massive jobs-and-growth tax-cut measures. Turning back the hands of time is impossible, just as it would have been impossible to find money to cover thousands of hours of intelligence-agency overtime. Truly, the bottom line weighed heavy on our hearts and minds.

Predicting what happened on Sept. 11 would have necessitated the hiring of numerous new employees—many of them highly paid specialists in such esoteric fields as Islamic history and Middle Eastern languages.

But it was not simply a matter of incurring additional labor costs. Had we been able to allocate sufficient funds for overtime pay, we would have faced a second significant obstacle. In retrospect, I see it as a tragic coincidence that the dramatic increase in terrorist chatter and threat information coincided with the arrival of the summer, when keeping our vast offices up and running beyond the eight-hour workday would have necessitated substantial central-cooling expenditures.

The brave men and women who work for Central Intelligence, the FBI, the Department of Defense, and the Office of the Vice-President are overworked civil servants, trying to juggle family, personal, and professional lives. We did everything in our power to convince them to spend some of their free time working on issues of national import, but in the summer months, it was difficult to make them see the gravity of al-Qaeda's threat.

For years, we understood that the al-Qaeda network posed a serious danger to the U.S. In the months leading up to Sept. 11, I was in constant contact with CIA Director George Tenet, whose operatives had some leads suggesting possible large-scale, mass-casualty attacks on U.S. soil. Following those leads was cost-prohibitive.

In order to identify and apprehend the Sept. 11 hijackers before they struck, our agents would have had to have logged thousands of hours of the most mundane intelligence analysis. Consider, for example, the logistics of implementing the three-phase strategy to eliminate al-Qaeda. It involved a mission to the Taliban in Afghanistan, increased diplomatic pressure, and increased covert action. It would have been very expensive. The covert action would have entailed the time-consuming translation from Arabic of e-mails, phone transcripts, and bugged conversations. Arabic is an extremely difficult language that only a small number of government employees know. Completing the translations might have involved flying capable employees in from great distances.

Once a series of conversations has been translated, analysts must wade through endless pages of talk of dinner dates, computer purchases, travel plans, and weather reports, searching for anything of national-security interest. Each conversation must not just be recorded, transcribed, translated, and read. It must also be analyzed and formed into a report, which must be typed and copied and collated. Then the report must be discussed, and if action is deemed necessary... You see where I'm going here. We're talking about a massive accrual of hours in all levels of government, top to bottom.

The worst part is, 999 times out of 1,000, the operatives come up with

see OVERTIME page 148

Woman Overcomes Years Of Child Abuse To Achieve Porn Stardom

VAN NUYS, CA—Psychologists agree that children who are neglected or abused by their caretakers often develop long-term mental-health problems. Childhood trauma frequently leads to emotional problems such as depression, feelings of worthlessness, underachievement, and detachment from reality. But some victims find the strength to rise above tragedy. One such survivor is Katrina Foechelman, an attractive 22-year-old who has overcome years of sexual abuse to achieve something most women only dream of: a featured role in a top-selling pornographic video.

"Yeah, I've been through some bad shit, but now I'm living large," said Foechelman, whom fans know as Trina Foxxx. "I got a great house in the Hollywood Hills and a lot of fancy-ass clothes. Everywhere I go, people know my name, whether I'm signing autographs at an adult-video convention or doing a feature dance at Spearmint Rhino. And you should see the car I drive—that's a Corvette, baby. Nothing but the best for Trina Foxxx."

Added Foechelman: "As long as you believe in yourself, the San Fernando Valley is the land of opportunity."

To see Foechelman, winner of a 2003 Adult Video News Award for Best Multiple Anal, you'd never guess this smiling, glamorous, club-hopping sex starlet was sexually abused from the age of 7. Strutting confidently in her high heels, mini-skirt, and visible thong, thrusting her surgically enhanced chest out with pride, she's a source of inspiration to everyone who works with her.

"You've gotta hand it to a chick like Trina," adult-film producer Jimmy Carlyle, 51, said. "Here's a gal who's been through it all—court-ordered separation from her real mom for neglect, foster homes, and a whole series of fucked-up, sicko stepdads doing God-knows-what to her. But she's taken everything life has thrown at her with a can-do attitude that's rare in this business. In spite of the obstacles, she's made her dreams of porn stardom come true."

Added Carlyle: "Of all the girls working this industry right now, I'd put Trina in the top 10 for cocksucking, pussy-eating, and hot fucking. And when it comes to deep, gaping anals, she's in the top five. She completely deserves her success."

Foechelman said she was determined to conquer the world, in spite of the roadblocks she faced while in her teens.

"Lots of people tried to keep me down and make me feel bad about myself," Foechelman said. "Like my first stepfather, Larry. He used to, like, finger me and shit when my mom was working late. And he'd call me names, too, like 'slut' and 'whore' and 'Daddy's little fuck-toy.' Luckily, my court-appointed social worker Pam explained how it wasn't my fault, so I shouldn't let it give me, like, low self-esteem and stuff. Thanks to Pam and all the new friends I made since moving to L.A., I didn't let that fucking bastard Larry—may his sick ass rot in hell someday—keep me down. I made it to the top of the adult industry anyway."

Above: Foechelman, who has risen above childhood adversity to make a name for herself in adult films.

Added Foechelman: "Now, the only time anybody calls me a 'slut,' 'whore,' or 'fuck-toy' is when I'm getting *paid*. And I'm not talking shit money, like back when I worked the peep-show booths. I'm talking *serious money*. It just goes to show you that if you keep your chin up, stay focused on your goals, and don't do too much coke, you can really turn your life around."

Foechelman ran away from a foster home in Roswell, NM, to enter the adult-film world in 1999, at age 16.

see PORN STAR page 148

NEWS IN BRIEF

Bush To Iraqi Militants: 'Please Stop Bringing It On'

WASHINGTON, DC—In an internationally televised statement Monday, President Bush modified a July 2003 challenge to Iraqi militants attacking U.S. forces. "Terrorists, Saddam loyalists, and anti-American insurgents: Please stop bringing it on now," Bush said at a Monday press conference. "Nine months and 500 U.S. casualties ago, I may have invited y'all to bring it on, but as of today, I formally rescind that statement. I would officially like for you to step back." The president added that the "it" Iraqis should stop bringing includes gunfire, bombings, grenade attacks, and suicide missions of all types.

Unpopped Kernels Costing U.S. Billions

SIOUX CITY, IA—The singed, partially opened, and otherwise unpopped kernels at the bottom of U.S. snack bowls are costing Americans an average of $18 billion every year, FDA sources reported Tuesday. "The typical pound of popping corn results in an average of 35 'dead' kernels," FDA deputy commissioner Lester M. Crawford said before Congress. "Considering the costs of growing, processing, and packaging these kernels, and the heat energy expended in fruitless endeavors to pop them, it's an epic level of waste." Crawford asked Congress to double funding for the FDA's $200 million old-maid-elimination research project.

Spawn Of Satan A Failure In Father's Eyes

TUSTIN, CA—The humanoid spawn of Satan, Belial K. Ravana, 16, has proven to be a huge disappointment to his father, His Satanic Majesty reported from Hell Tuesday. "Apparently, young Belial started a fire in the garbage can at school today," Satan said. "When I begat young Belial, I had high hopes that he would follow in my cloven-hoofsteps. At his age, I was scorching the earth in hellfire, flensing the skin off of infants, and making the streets of Babylon run red with the blood of the righteous." Satan said he hopes Belial will turn it around and "at least rape the principal" before the semester's end.

Putting Up With Dave's Shit Not In Job Description

SPOKANE, WA—Although he's willing to put up with a hell of a lot, coffee-shop employee Jason Bowen said Tuesday that dealing with endless amounts of Dave's shit isn't part of his job description. "I'm sorry, but I didn't come to the Second Cup just so [store manager] Dave [Shaw] could use me as his personal slave," Bowen said. "Nothing in the employee handbook says I have to stay until midnight cleaning the cappuccino machines, just because he has to go argue with his fucking girlfriend." Bowen added that he was hired as a barista, and maintenance work is so not what he's paid to do.

Strangulation The New Blow To The Head, Says *Hired Killer* Magazine

NEW YORK—Strangulation has replaced a violent blow to the skull as the hot new way to eliminate a target, according to the May issue of *Hired Killer* magazine. "Striking the occipital was fine in the easygoing '90s—an audible thump and a sloppily collapsing body fit the casual feel of the times," read the article by Jonathan Grecco. "But the elegant silence of a strangle kill, and the skill that its proper execution demands, are too-too today, especially when a monofilament line is used to modernize this classic." The May issue also features 10 Ways First-Time Trigger-Men Screw Up A Body Disposal. Ø

will spread to other regions throughout America," CIDC spokesman Chris Greeves said Tuesday. "At the rate it's moving, our nation could suffer European levels of Scandinavian design within a decade."

Greeves said IKEA is not easily controlled, as it spreads largely through word of mouth.

"It passes between rooms until it has infested not only your living room, but also your 1.5 bathrooms, your cleanly appointed kitchen, and then your entire sun-drenched, open-plan loft apartment. In the most extreme cases, it will even spread to the string-light-decorated rooftop patio overlooking your recently gentrified neighborhood."

The IKEA encroachment began attracting attention in 1985, when the first American IKEA store was diagnosed in Philadelphia, infecting an estimated 2,500 homes with Stenkulla tables, Blankhult chairs, and Ingebo sofas almost overnight.

> "It took a lot of expensive Restoration Hardware sessions before the IKEA was totally wiped out," Westin said. "And I'm one of the lucky ones. I hate to think what happens to people who can't afford to go out and get the new window treatments they so desperately need."

"My friend Kyle was the first person I knew who got IKEA," said Adam Goldman, a Manhattan web designer who said he now knows "20 or 30 people" who have the furniture. "I was at his place on a Friday night, and everything was normal. He mentioned that he was going out to shop for a little bookcase the next day. A week later, his whole place was so thick with blond birch veneer and chrome wire shelving that he could barely stand up."

Goldman's friend lost the apartment later that year, but Goldman could not confirm IKEA as the cause.

"The real problem isn't the furniture—it's actually been around for years," Greeves said. "The problem is the people who spread it. Many of them are embarrassed that they have it, but they show a brave face to the world and talk about low cost and convenience. What those who've contracted it won't talk about is the fact that IKEA is mostly self-assembled."

Above: A home in Philadelphia containing endemic levels of IKEA.

Greeves added that many people who have lost their lifestyles to IKEA started out thinking of full-blown IKEA home remodeling as "something that happens to other people."

"They know the danger is there—they've been to those dinner parties," Greeves said. "But they think, 'That's not going to happen to me. I'll just get some CD racks... and maybe one of those canvas magazine holders."

Greeves continued: "Those whose homes are infested with the IKEA fittings are mostly young and newly financially independent. They're not careful with their new freedoms. In a spontaneous moment, a chrome Stalaktit seems like a sensible lighting solution. They don't stop to think, 'Hey, this could be something I'll have to live with for the rest of my 20s.'"

CIDC officials say they are unsure exactly how many U.S. rooms have been claimed by the furniture and décor line, but they fear that the number of homes in which one or more residents have been exposed to IKEA could increase as much as 80 percent by 2008.

"The chances of contact with the infectious brand are increasing rapidly, because very few areas of daily life are safe from the IKEA bug," Greeves said. "The existence of such seemingly innocuous items as IKEA tea lights, napkin rings, desk accessories, and beach-sports equipment dramatically increases the average person's chance of falling prey to IKEA consumption."

Karl Westin is an actor who came down with a truckload of IKEA when he moved from Seattle to Burbank, CA, in 1996. In recent years, he has spent thousands of dollars eradicating it from his house.

"For me, it started slowly," Westin said. "I had a Poang—it's a form of chair—and I just couldn't seem to get rid of it. That led to a lot of other things I'm not particularly proud of. I indulged in Leksvik, Branas, even a Svingen. If you don't know what those are, consider yourself lucky."

Although Westin said he has been IKEA-free for more than a year, saving his lifestyle was neither easy nor cheap.

"It took a lot of expensive Restoration Hardware sessions before the IKEA was totally wiped out," Westin said. "And I'm one of the lucky ones. I hate to think what happens to people who can't afford to go out and get the new window treatments they so desperately need."

Greeves said the IKEA threat, once dismissed as a weak European form of viral marketing, increases for Americans daily. There are already 18 known IKEA centers in the U.S., with six more poised to arrive soon in such heavily populated areas as Minneapolis, Phoenix, and Dallas-Fort Worth.

"If an individual lives within 100 miles of an IKEA store, the chances of finding IKEA inside his home increases 20-fold," Greeves said. "It's important for anyone in close proximity to one of these stores to take precautions. That friend with the SUV who invites you to come along to IKEA 'just to look' is exposing you to the risk that you'll walk out of that place carrying a 24-piece teal-blue plastic picnic set."

This year, the CIDC will team up with corporate partners Wickes and Ethan Allen, who have each pledged $200,000 to a campaign to spread the message about alternatives to cheap composite furniture, even for those who are young or on stipends.

Still, experts fear that things will get worse before they get better.

"At present, the IKEA epidemic is mostly limited to the coasts, but if the populace isn't educated about the very real aesthetic dangers of IKEA, more lifestyles will be lost all across the nation," Greeves said. "Just last week, we received a report about a young man who'd moved to Wyoming to go to college. His very first week in the dorms, he went to the IKEA web site. A week later, he broke out a bright red Klippan sofa. He's just 18 years old, the poor guy. No matter where he ends up going in the coming years, he'll be carrying the IKEA sofa." ⌀

While she was considered something of a prodigy by her admirers, stardom did not arrive overnight.

"I used to get discouraged, 'cause it seemed like no matter how hard I tried to please the other actors, I was always getting second billing to one of the more established girls," Foechelman said. "Even if I had more minutes on the video, I never got star billing. Sometimes, it would make me think that Larry—oh, and Mom's new boyfriend John, and Uncle Marty, and that asshole whose kids I used to babysit when I was 11—were right about me. They said I'd never amount to nothing."

But Foechelman refused to give up.

"I kept a positive mental attitude," Foechelman said. "I said 'Yes, I can!' whenever they asked me to do extreme shit, like taking two cocks in my ass at once, or doing an ATM [Ass To Mouth] and gang-bangs. By the time I was actually 18, I had my name on the cover of *Butt Fuck Sluts Go Nuts, Vol. 41*. I was so psyched to have finally earned myself a reputation!"

Foechelman's star has only continued to rise. Over the weekend, she filmed the titular roles in *Trina Wants It, Trina Takes It Deep,* and *A Filthy Trailer-Trash Bitch Named Trina.* Finally, her dream of stardom has become a reality.

"I got it all now: diamond jewelry, champagne, guys grabbing all over me at the dance clubs, you name it," Foechelman said. "I showed those assholes who said I'd never amount to anything, the fucking pricks. Whatever doesn't kill me makes me stronger. You can't keep a good woman down."

"If only that sick fuck Larry could see me now," Foechelman added. "Come to think of it, *Killer Cum Shots* sold 20,000 copies, so I guess he probably has." ⌀

nothing. It's very hard to pay people time-and-a-half when they can't tell you the exact location, date, and method of an imminent terrorist attack. But, considering the high priority President Bush placed on counterterrorism from the day he took office, I assure you that we would not have hesitated to schedule the overtime hours, had we known that a massive terrorist attack was definitely going to happen.

Yes, Mr. Tenet and his top deputies did receive a briefing paper labeled "Islamic Extremist Learns To Fly" in mid-August. Yes, an in-depth investigation of Zacarias Moussaoui *might* have led the government to the al-Qaeda cell in Germany that planned the Sept. 11 attacks, but the fact remains that we can never be sure. I believe that, during investigations such as this, it's important to stick with what we do know. Ladies and gentlemen: Had that lead been followed, a *lot* of people would've been working a *lot* of very long hours. ⌀

and diplomats," McClellan characterized the Hollywood insider as a "born leader."

"Some guest presidents breeze into a cabinet meeting or state dinner thinking they can get by on star power—and generally, they can," McClellan said. "But Tom's unique, low-key, everyman persona sets him apart from the others. It endears him to everyone he meets, from the high-level diplomat to the Minority Whip."

So far this week, Hanks has welcomed Israeli foreign minister Silvan Shalom, Saudi ambassador Prince Bandar bin Sultan, Office of Faith-Based and Community Initiatives director Jim Towey, and the United States Marine Band. White House officials said Hanks "more than held his own" with political heavy-hitters, and even injected a dose of good-natured humor into the diplomatic proceedings.

"I'm more cut out for introducing an education-policy initiative at an inner-city kindergarten, or pardoning a turkey at Thanksgiving, than I am for brokering a viable solution for Mideast peace," Hanks told Shalom at a Rose Garden press conference as reporters laughed. "But seriously, Shalom, there's nothing the world wants more than to see an end to all this horrible and senseless bloodshed. Now, earlier you were telling me a great story about Prime Minister Ariel Sharon. What's this Gaza withdrawal plan all about?"

As part of his job as guest president, Hanks signed several pieces of legislation into law: a House appropriations bill funding foreign operations, export financing, and related programs; a joint resolution honoring deceased U.S. Sen. Paul Wellstone (D-MN); and a bill banning the "morning after pill." He also refused to commute the death sentence of a prisoner convicted of capital murder.

Hanks attended a DC-area campaign fundraiser Tuesday evening on behalf of Bush.

"Guess you didn't expect to see me here today, did you?" Hanks said, to delighted whoops and cheers from the 5,000 supporters in attendance. "Well, I thought I'd show off this new suit I bought to match the Oval Office. Yeah, right, I know what you're thinking: 'Don't quit your day job, huh, Tom.'"

Since Bush took office, other guest presidents have included Whoopi Goldberg, *Seinfeld* star Jason Alexander, opinionated basketball great Charles Barkley, and, for one infamous week in March 2003, conservative TV commentator Bill O'Reilly, who provoked controversy by criticizing actor and frequent White House drop-in guest George Clooney for his participation in antiwar protests, and for authorizing the invasion of Iraq.

"The guest president has to walk a narrow line," media columnist and critic Michael Medved said. "The fill-in has to know when to make his

mark and inject the proceedings with his own style of governing, and when to ease back and give the American people what they're familiar with. Also, guest leaders have to be careful not to step on the regular president's toes if they want to be invited back."

Hanks' upcoming guests include the Duke and Duchess of Kent and Mothers Against Drunk Driving founder Candy Lightner, in addition to Costa Rican president Abel Pacheco, who will discuss trade tariffs and show off his collection of odd-shaped pineapples.

Under Bush, the guest-president tradition has returned to the White

House after a 25-year absence. In the '70s, Jimmy Carter hand-picked comedian and TV star Bob Newhart as his permanent guest president, but abruptly fired him after learning that Newhart was moonlighting as guest prime minister for Canada's Pierre Trudeau. After the incident, the White House began to send the press crew on the road with a traveling president, pre-taping important Cabinet announcements or simply re-broadcasting old State of the Union addresses.

McClellan said the Bush Administration chose to reinstate the guest-

president tradition in order to "shake things up a bit." He noted that the government actually sees a slight spike in public-approval ratings during Bush's weeks off.

From his Malibu vacation compound, a tennis-whites-clad Bush praised his temporary replacement as a "consummate professional."

"Tom's a great guy, and I'd be honored if he'd consider doing another turn as guest president," Bush said. "Besides, I can rest easy knowing Dick Cheney's sitting there beside him to keep things rolling, should there be a lull." ∅

Hey Jess!

Happy 34th! Hope you have a great day! I'm sure you have something fun to do. My brother Luke's birthday is earlier in the month. On his birthday, I always think, "Jessica's birthday is coming up in just 16 days!"

How's Jim? How's school going for Kristen? Did you get that garden started yet? Hey, I just remembered that today is Holocaust Remembrance Day! Yup, April 18!

I don't know if I should mail this card, because maybe I'll find some time in the next few days to drive up and hand it to you in person. Well, I may as well drop it in the mail in case I don't end up being able to make it. I have been pretty busy. I'm thinking about having a picnic on Earth Day, which is four days away.

Todd sends his love. He couldn't sign this himself as he smashed his hand in the car door yesterday and can't write. It's really painful!

To heck with ice cream and cake!

Happy Birthday

xoxo
Gina

P.S. I hope you got your present! I ordered something through the mail — I won't say what and ruin the surprise! You should get it any day now, unless it's on backorder or something, which happens a lot, I guess.

P.P.S. Check the envelope for a recipe that I clipped from Sunday's paper. I thought it sounded like something you'd like! The Sunday paper always seems to have the best recipes.

Above: The inside of the birthday card for Jurgensen reveals a string of nefarious lies penned by Tobler.

another card, but then it finally did end up arriving on Wednesday, April 14. I remember the day, because I was so relieved I'd be able to send it out with plenty of time."

By alternating statements of contrition and annoyance, Tobler created a smokescreen and bought herself the additional time required to devise a plan of action.

"I was going to mail the week before last, knowing how incredibly slow the post office can be," Tobler told her friend. "I planned to drop it in the mailbox across the street from my optometrist's office when I picked up my new glasses. See, I didn't want those incompetents who collect the mail in my office to get a chance to lose it. But then I was in a rush to get my car's oil changed, so I didn't. But then my mechanic told me I needed to replace my brakes immediately, and that I'd better leave my car there. By the time I got home in the cab, I realized I'd forgotten your card in the glove compartment. I was so mad at myself!"

To back up her story that she mailed the card last week, Tobler considered

rolling back the date on the postage meter at work, but was unsure if she'd be able to figure out how to do so. Instead, she created the following blueprint:

Tobler created a smokescreen.

print: She will place the birthday card into the mail with insufficient postage. When the birthday card is returned, she will smudge the original postage date—should there be one—or obscure it with an additional stamp.

In the meantime, she will maintain a steady stream of disinformation to baffle her friend.

"If you haven't gotten your card yet, maybe I should just go to the store and buy another one," Tobler told Jurgensen. "But I don't want to get you some ugly one, just because the post office is inefficient. Well, it'll come eventually. You'll know it's from me when it gets there. It has the cutest cat

stamp on it. I know how you love cats."

Tobler said she "immediately regretted mentioning that damn cat stamp," which she still has to find.

Tobler's meticulously constructed but delicate house of cards nearly collapsed when Jurgensen phoned Saturday. While attempting to cover her tracks, Tobler dragged her woefully ill-prepared husband Todd into the operation.

"I picked up the phone and it was Jessica," Todd told reporters. "Suddenly, Gina started waving her arms and mouthing words to me about God knows what. I put the phone down and she whispered in my ear not to tell Jessica that the birthday card is still here. Luckily, it never came up. But then Gina scribbled this note to me that I should tell Jessica she's going to love the card that I saw [Gina] get in a package in the mail at the same time as last week's *Sports Illustrated*.'"

Todd's subsequent confusion nearly blew Tobler's cover and compromised the entire mission.

"I didn't know what Gina was trying

see CARD page 150

149

You're Fired!

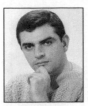

**The Outside Scoop
By Jackie Harvey**

You're fired! Since **Donald Trump** started saying it on **The Apprentices**, I can't say it enough. It's this year's "Is that your final answer?" I've been saying it to everyone: my friends, my mailman, and even my mom! And now we know the apprentice is **Bob**, who proved that he had the goods by coordinating a golf tournament. Congratulations, Bob!

And can you believe that **Barbarosa**? Is she evil or what? She should quit the corporate world and become a **movie villain** or something. (And I'm not saying that because she's black. No angry letters, please!)

I'd like to have a reality series called **The Interns**, where I whittle down 12 hopefuls to find one lucky finalist who gets to open my mail and print out stuff from the Internet for me. If there are any people out there in programming who can make my dream a reality, let me know so we can get cracking on this.

I can never remember the difference between **jam** and **jelly**. All I know is, there's no substitute for either on my toast!

You're fired! Will **The Passionate Christ** maintain its two-month head of steam now that Easter is over? If **Mel Gibson** has his way, he'll be spreading the bloody word even further. Hot off the wire is the info that Mr. G wants to show the movie on one of the networks, unedited, without commercial interruption. Jesus died for our right to watch His **gruesome and horrible end** on network television. What could be more inspirational than that?

You're fired! In the **good-things-happen-to-good-people** category, **J. Lo's mother** won more than a million dollars at a slot machine. The First Mom of Music and Movies made the lucky pull in **Atlantic City** and immediately offered a prayer to **Our Lady of Kentucky**, who was apparently looking over the First Mom's shoulder while she gambled. I've never had any luck with slot machines. I suppose that's why I call them **one-armed bandits**.

I know he's our president, but did **George W. Bush** have to ruin television for a night? I know he had to give his State of the Union address, but why did he have to start it at 8:30? That meant **America's Idol** had to be postponed, as did some of my other favorite Tuesday shows. We should all support our president in a time of war, but there have to be limits. Bumping *America's Idol* constitutes an abuse of power.

Speaking of *Idol*, who do you think will take the prize this year? I pick that red-headed kid who really knows how to belt out the standards. I like his style—he reminds me of **a young Perry Como**!

You're fired! The **Friends** countdown continues! There are only a few episodes left, and people are on the edge of their seats, wondering if the Friends are going to remain friends after the season finale. Well, I don't want to spoil anything, but I heard through the Harvey grapevine that the final episode is a double wedding. You won't believe who gets hitched!

> **I can never remember the difference between jam and jelly. All I know is, there's no substitute for either on my toast!**

This will be their most topical episode to date, drawing from today's headlines, in that **Ross** will be going through his third divorce—but his first marriage to a man! If anyone asks, you didn't hear it from me, folks.

Know what I miss? Using the word "man." No one says "man" anymore. Now, it's all "dude." Well, let's ditch the dude and bring back the man, man!

You're fired! Courtney Love is in trouble again. She showed her chest to **David Brinkley**, hit a fan with a microphone stand, and stole a copy of *Us* magazine from a Red Owl checkout line. If I could sit her down for a little heart-to-heart, I'd tell her to pull herself together. She should be thinking about her daughter, **Coco Haley**. What Ms. Love needs is a man in her life, to straighten her out and settle her down into family life again. Any takers?

I heard that if you watch **The Wizard Of Oz** while listening to **Dark Half Of The Moon** by Pink, it'll blow your mind. I don't own any Pink CDs, and my Betamax copy of *Wizard Of Oz* is worn clear through, so I need to invest a little capital if I'm going to try this.

You're fired! What's in the water in **Hollywood** these days? Whatever it is, it's bad for romance. **Tom and Penelope Cruise** and **John and Rebecca Romaine Stamos** both called it quits. I always thought those two pillars of romance would last forever. I'm sad for Tom, but he'll bounce back. I'm more worried about John. He'll never find another woman as dazzling as Rebecca. Tom's career has plenty more shelf life, but John's expired the year before **Family Matters** was cancelled. Now, John will probably die a **broken and loveless alcoholic**, which is too bad. He could be a good guest star.

You're fired! When the flame of love dies, another blossoms. The lady from **Will And Grace** had a baby. No word on who the father is, but because Will is gay, we can probably rule him out. Congratulations, *Will And Grace* woman **Debra Messman**!

I went to school with a Debra Messman, but she was big-boned and had a blotchy complexion, so I don't think it's the same one.

Well, friends, well-wishers, and Harveyheads, you have all my best muck, so I'd better get back out there to do some more raking. A heads-up: I have a little lead on **George Clooney**'s colorful past as a delivery boy, as well as some information about a certain **James Bond actor** who answers the "boxers or briefs" question with "none of the above"! Until then, I'll see you in the future, on The Outside! ∅

Your Horoscope

By Lloyd Schumner Sr.
Retired Machinist and
A.A.P.B.-Certified Astrologer

Aries: (March 21–April 19)
You love pointing out that you were raised by wolves, but you never mention that they were Harvard-educated, old-money Boston wolves.

Taurus: (April 20–May 20)
Not that it's really the Zodiac's business, but most people take the dead goldfish out of the tank before adding new ones. The same goes for the drowned cats.

Gemini: (May 21–June 21)
Plastic bags are not a toy, but you understand that they can still be a lot of fun if you use them to smother children.

Cancer: (June 22–July 22)
You may say there's nothing wrong with you that a week in the Bahamas won't cure, but the stars recommend you get the chemotherapy.

Leo: (July 23–Aug. 22)
The stars have always been a great influence on your fate. This will never be as true as it is next week, when a certain yellow G-type variable star cuts loose with a really impressive flare.

Virgo: (Aug. 23–Sept. 22)
Everyone has problems, but they don't all expect the whole universe to come to a standstill because of them. Only about half of them expect that.

Libra: (Sept. 23–Oct. 23)
You'll no longer have any reason to doubt the transcendent power of love after you see it obliterate an entire armored division in military tests.

Scorpio: (Oct. 24–Nov. 21)
Some people would cut off their nose to spite their face, but you're not like that. You did it because you thought it would make you look like a wingless man-bat hybrid.

Sagittarius: (Nov. 22–Dec. 21)
A bizarre misunderstanding on your part will result in your going to church every Sunday and speaking sincerely to invisible entities with the belief that it might do you some sort of good.

Capricorn: (Dec. 22–Jan. 19)
Your millions can't help you find love and happiness, especially because the word "millions" here doesn't indicate any sort of monetary unit.

Aquarius: (Jan. 20–Feb. 18)
You'll watch as dozens die in a bus accident, but take heart: Everyone will know there was nothing you could have done without severely inconveniencing yourself.

Pisces: (Feb. 19–March 20)
You've been forced to conclude that people are just no good, no matter how you slice, puree, braise, fry, or sauté them.

CARD from page 149

to tell me *at all*," Todd said. "Finally, I just handed her the phone so she could talk to Jessica herself."

Once the card is returned and remailed, Tobler plans to complete the maneuver with a confirmation call and close the book on her masterpiece of deception.

"I'll be glad when this is all over," Tobler told reporters. "I don't think I can bear another week of fudging the truth. It's exhausting keeping it all straight."

Meanwhile, Jurgensen remains wholly ignorant of the fact that she's being fed a diet of intrigue and deception.

"Gina and I are both a little scatter-brained," Jurgensen said by phone from her Ronan residence. "I was surprised that she remembered my birthday at all. I totally forgot to call her last year until two days afterward. Luckily, I covered by telling her I was in the hospital for inhaling toxic fumes at work." ∅

New One-A-Month Vitamin Presents Choking Hazard

see HEALTH page 11C

Mexicans Sweeping The Nation

see PEOPLE page 8E

That Guy Who Lifts Weights With His Nutsack Lets Nutsack Get Out Of Shape

see SPORTS page 4E

STATshot

A look at the numbers that shape your world.

Why Are We Being Asked To Leave?

12% Missed the eight polite hints

16% Dance floor not the place for stunts, apparently

21% Mr. My Art Is Precious can't take a joke

15% Turns out they *are* real

19% Restaurant has some stupid "no tiger" rule

17% Aren't Masons

THE ONION • $2.00 US • $3.00 CAN

0 74470 94595 6

the ONION

VOLUME 40 ISSUE 18   AMERICA'S FINEST NEWS SOURCE™   6–12 MAY 2004

Lone Wolf Ashcroft Given Rookie Partner

WASHINGTON, DC—John Ashcroft, the tough, no-nonsense U.S. attorney general famous for his refusal to take orders, was assigned a rookie trainee Tuesday.

"John's taking it well," President Bush said, introducing Ashcroft's new partner, Deputy Attorney General Nate N. Burnhard, to the press. "He threw a couple chairs around the office, and he broke the two-way mirror in the Department of Justice squad room, but I'm sure it won't be long before he comes around to the idea of showing Burnhard here the ropes. It's about time John came in from the cold and started playing along with the team."

According to Bush, the 28-year-old Burnhard shows "real promise," having arrived at the department with a law degree from Yale and two years of exemplary service in the Orange County, CA district. Ashcroft, however, called his new partner a "spoiled,

see ASHCROFT page 156

Above: Ashcroft hits the streets with his inexperienced new partner, Burnhard.

Above: Some of the sights Bethlehem has to offer delegates.

Peace Talks Just An Excuse To Visit Scenic Mideast

WASHINGTON, DC—White House officials announced Monday that representatives from the U.S. will join those from Sweden, Russia, and the U.N. in the Mideast next week to sight-see, sunbathe, and mediate peace talks between Palestine and Israel.

"A few weeks ago, President Bush asked me to go to the West Bank and work on the road map to peace," an excited Secretary of State Colin Powell said. "There's absolutely no

see TALKS page 154

Mom Hogging Family Therapy Session

THORNTON, CO—According to her husband and two children, Jeanette Westphal, 41, is hogging the regular therapy sessions supposedly intended to help all of them.

"Mom made us go to stupid therapy, because she said we had to learn to communicate as a family," 12-year-old daughter Amy said of the sessions the family has been attending since March. "Now, every Tuesday from 6 to 7 p.m., we sit in a circle and listen to Mom talk. It's driving everyone crazy, but try telling her that. She won't hear you, because she's too busy going on about her boring

see MOM page 154

Above: Westphal and the family forced to endure her selfishness on a weekly basis.

The Social Security Time Bomb

Experts continue to urge Congress to cut the growth of Social Security, warning that the nation faces unsustainable deficits if action isn't taken. What do *you* think?

"This certainly is bad news for the elderly, coming as it does on the heels of the Federal Aging and Ice Floes Act."

Julie Hunt
Teacher

"It's news like this that makes me wish I could stay 59 forever."

Donald Nelson
Inspector

"It's good I already have a taste for dog food."

Jimmy Shaw
Carpet Installer

"So much for my plan to live off Social Security while I travel the country banging Denny's cashiers in my Airstream."

Dan Cox
Mechanic

"This is really an economics issue. Were it, say, a women's-studies issue, I might have more insight to share."

Emily Holmes
Professor

"Everybody, relax. We'll be fine as soon as we get our money back from Iraq."

Albert Robertson
Systems Analyst

Porn And HIV Prevention

Shaken by an HIV scare, the adult-film industry has instituted safety regulations. What are they?

- ▶ Fully uniformed nurse required to be on set at all times
- ▶ Employees must wash hands before returning to work
- ▶ Performers who test positive for HIV must provide list of last 2,000 people they slept with
- ▶ Filmed sex to be limited to girl-on-girl action, which is safer and hotter
- ▶ Porn actors to start using dental dams, like the rest of us
- ▶ Actors required to report secretions that taste HIV-ish
- ▶ All porn stars to be in monogamous pornographic relationships
- ▶ Male actors will be asked to ejaculate into cup, take cup to lab; if sample is found to be HIV-negative, actor will be allowed to return to set, dump contents of cup onto actress' face
- ▶ Industry to shift focus to hugging and snuggling

⊘ the ONION®
America's Finest News Source.™

Herman Ulysses Zweibel
Founder

T. Herman Zweibel
Publisher Emeritus
J. Phineas Zweibel
Publisher
Maxwell Prescott Zweibel
Editor-In-Chief

Darling, You Were Well Worth The Nine Goats

By Dharmrao Baba Atram

My dearest Anjana Shah, it is difficult to believe that we have been husband and wife for five years on this very day. Where has the time gone? It seems like only yesterday the entire village gathered together to feast in celebration of your acceptance into the Atram family. Do you recall the delicious feast you prepared? Ah, Anjana, dearest wife, there are so many things I would like to express to you, I feel my heart will burst! Dear, sweet wife, we've had our share of troubles, but we're stronger for them. Not once have I regretted our agreement, not for even a second. Darling, just looking into your beautiful brown eyes each morning is worth more than four goats. You were well worth the nine.

Though my father assured me that his choice was sound, I worried initially that he was thinking only of your dowry. I suspected him of choosing you in order to bring the nine goats into our extended family, heedless of the fact that you were not the right woman for me. I feared that your hands were too soft and delicate to work the fields and dig groundnuts. I told my father that, at 16, you were rather old. I worried that your hips were too slim to bear my children, and you confirmed my fears when our first baby was stillborn. That did not please me. And, in our first year of marriage, your habit of slipping out at night to see your sick mother forced me to observe the family tradition and beat you with a bullhide strap. But I

> ## Though my father assured me that his choice was sound, I worried initially that he was thinking only of your dowry.

promise that I never took pleasure in flogging you. Even as I flogged you, I had affection in my heart.

But in the second year of our star-crossed marriage, you made my affectionate heart soar when you gave me a strong, healthy son. Only 10 full moons later, another son arrived... and then another and another, and today we have hope of a fifth. You may think it strange and impractical for me to say this, but I secretly hope

that my next child is a girl. Even though she will be a burden on myself and my sons, you will enjoy teaching her the traditional songs, and she can help you with the cooking of our meals and cleaning of our house. We will guard her purity and, when she reaches the age of 12, she will be able to make another man as happy as you have made me, my beloved angel.

Of course, if the girl should have some defect that would render her

> ## Even today, though you are heavy with child, you spent the day fortifying the walls of our home with mud and straw.

undesirable to a potential groom—a clubfoot, for example—then you will drown her beneath the waterfall at Binagonda.

I have always admired your strength, my darling. Even today, though you are heavy with child, you spent the day fortifying the walls of our home with mud and straw. I remember the day you hurt your leg in the fields. In spite of the pain, you spent the entire day working. When you came home with a tear-stained face and only a half-basket of groundnuts, I was so impressed with your perseverance that I sat you down and gave you a cup of ginger tea before I got out the bullhide strap.

But I love you for many reasons besides your strength, my angel. I love you for your purity, broken for the first time on the night of our marriage. Since the night of your deflowering, you have conducted yourself with dignity. You do not raise your voice like some of the women in the village. You did not cry and carry on when our crops were trampled by sheep, though you knew that it would take you several arduous weeks to replant them. You never need to be told to walk three paces behind me. You never need to be told to keep your head down while I speak. You never need to be asked to wash my feet when I come home from a long day of drinking and singing. You are everything to me.

I will never forget the first time I realized how much you mean to me. Do you recall the afternoon when three

see GOATS page 156

Hungover Heineken Promoter Can't Remember What He Said About Heineken Last Night

CINCINNATI, OH—After a hard night promoting Heineken at a local bar, junior marketing associate Jason Schweiber, 23, spent Monday morning nursing a hangover and trying to remember what he'd said about Heineken the night before.

"When I woke up, all of my business cards were gone, along with the entire box of promo mugs, all the Heinie logo hats, and about half the Heineken sampler CDs," Schweiber said from his room at the Sheraton hotel. "I know I was talking about Heineken the whole night, but what was I saying? It could've been anything."

"Was I talking about the great taste of Heineken and the awards it's won?" Schweiber added, rubbing his temples. "Was I telling people to check out the Heineken web site? Was I talking about Heineken concert events? I really hope I didn't make a fool of myself or Heineken."

At the event, held at The Wrecked Spoke, Schweiber promoted the release of the Heineken Music Initiative's *Red Star Sound Presents Def Jamaica Vol. 3*, featuring music by Method Man and Redman, Scarface, and Ghostface Killah. The following morning, while squinting at the sunlight beaming in through the window, Schweiber began to reassemble his fragmentary memories from the night before.

"I was walking around to all the tables, handing out sampler CDs," Schweiber said. "I hate to be without a Heineken in my hand, lest someone think I don't stand behind the beer,

> **"All of my business cards were gone, along with the entire box of promo mugs, all the Heinie logo hats, and about half the Heineken sampler CDs,"** Schweiber said.

but I must've drunk eight or nine bottles in about three hours last night. Maybe more. I wasn't really keeping track. All I know is, when I got up this morning, I had one hell of a headache, every last Heineken beach chair was gone from the trunk of my car, and there were about 20 Heineken Green Room stickers stuck to my pants."

Schweiber, who said he's "never been much of a drinker," first began to consider a career in promotions in November 2003, when he met a

Above: Schweiber pieces together fragmented memories of the previous evening's promotional event.

Heineken recruiter at the University of Michigan campus job fair. After graduating with a marketing degree in December, Schweiber began to work for Heineken full-time. He currently spends two weeks out of the month on the road, raising brand awareness for the Dutch beer through promotional events at bars, concerts, fairs, and sporting events.

"Last night started out normal enough," Schweiber said. "I was making the rounds, schmoozing. As time wore on, though, I started to lose it. At some point, I was telling this old guy all about Heineken's authentic brewing vessels, and I realized I was shouting. See, I'd been in a rush to get to the event and never ate dinner. I'm sure

that's why I got so wasted."

Schweiber said his judgment was "severely impaired" when he began to conduct the Heineken trivia contest.

"I was being really obnoxious with the mic as I read off the questions," Schweiber said. "For some reason, I was imitating a boxing announcer, and going, like, 'And in this corner we have Heineken...' Then I was rapping about Heineken, but I can't recall any of the lyrics. I also remember stopping the contest so I could go to the bathroom."

"Merch was flying everywhere," Schweiber continued. "I wasn't even looking for correct answers to the quiz. I was just throwing out T-shirts to whoever yelled the loudest. And that

see PROMOTER page 155

Vladimir Putin Begins Second Term As Whatever He Is

MOSCOW—After winning a landslide re-election in March, this week Russian leader of some sort Vladimir Putin begins his second term as whatever he was during his first term, U.S. sources reported Tuesday. "We would all like to wish Putin continued luck as the Russian premier or prime minister or czar or... you know," White House press secretary Scott McClellan said. "Well, I'm pretty sure it's not 'president.' Does 'President Putin' sound right?" McClellan added that he wishes Mr. Putin, or Herr Putin, or Comrade Putin, or The Monsieur, the best.

Mass Grave Blasted For Lack Of Diversity

SARAJEVO, BOSNIA-HERZEGOVINA—Members of the International Coalition for Equality criticized a newly unearthed mass grave Monday, saying it lacked religious and racial diversity. "The funereal pit is brimming with Croats, nearly 300 of them, without a single representative Serb," ICE spokesman Jacques Marchand said. "Exclusionary burial practices like this send a negative message to the world. Corpses of all races and creeds should be tossed together to decay in harmony." Marchand acknowledged that the grave did, at least, have a sprinkling of women and children.

Herpetologist Names Son After Famous Herpetologist

CORAL GABLES, FL—Herpetologist Linus R. Bolton and his wife Kareena announced Monday that they are the proud parents of eight-pound, five-ounce Archie Carr Bolton, named after famous Florida herpetologist and biologist Archie Carr. "It was Dr. Carr's work on the life cycle of the sea turtle that inspired me to pursue the study of reptiles and amphibians," Bolton said. "This is my way of honoring him." Bolton and Kareena, a Chinese chef, have two other children: Ginger, 4, and General Tso, 2.

Masturbatory Prose Style Fails To Reach Climax

NEW YORK—Writer Terrence Hendrie's debut novel *I, Me, Eye*, with its lengthy sentences and elaborate footnotes, failed to result in a climax, sources reported Monday. "Hendrie really works himself into a frenzy, massaging his love for obscure vocabulary," bookstore owner Robert Silvers said of the 385-page novel, which opens, "Adam, his serpentine ponytail flapping freely in the wintertide dithers, frostbitten grapewine bouche pursed around a smoldering Camel, hands gripping a Dachshund-eared copy of Hesse's *Damien*, which he recalled borrowing from his Cambridge roommate Geoffrey—young Geoffrey, how Adam chided him for his *nostalgie de la boue*.'" "Then, after 385 pages, the wanking-off ends abruptly, leaving the reader unsatisfied." Silvers added that the book's attempts at humor were too dry.

Willie Nelson Spaces On Holding Farm Aid

SPICEWOOD, TX—Country-music legend Willie Nelson completely spaced on holding a Farm Aid benefit concert this year, the singer admitted Monday. "Man, I've been doing the damn thing for 19 years, but somehow the plight of the American farmer slipped my mind this year," Nelson said. "We'll never get a venue by September now." Nelson added that John Mellencamp or Neil Young could've called to remind him. ✐

chance that these talks will ever work, but I was like, 'Free trip to the disputed zone? No way I'm gonna turn that down!'"

Powell said that, while the all-expense-paid trip is ostensibly to broker terms for a move toward the creation of a Palestinian state along with guarantees for a halt to attacks against Israel, he expects to have plenty of time "to just kick around and enjoy the area."

"Turns out we have talks all day Monday and Tuesday, but Wednesday is almost completely open," Powell said. "The March 14 bombings at Ashdod Port supposedly have security crazy on alert, but I think I'll recruit a couple extra bodyguards, outfit a little six-vehicle convoy, and head on over to Gaza to check out the scene. The Strip is generally pretty chilled out during the week, I've heard."

Several of the more than two dozen diplomats slated to attend have said that they hold low expectations for the peace talks, but are looking forward to enjoying some free time in the exotic locale.

"A lot of people in the EU are angry with Washington policy-makers, claiming that Bush's endorsement of [Israeli Prime Minister Ariel] Sharon's proposed unilateral withdrawal from the Gaza Strip rejects the right of Palestinian refugees to return to disputed land now in Israeli control—but I don't care to take sides while on this trip," High Representative for Common Foreign and Security Policy for the EU Javier Solana said. "I heard Colin's going, and I figure, if Col's there, it'll be a good time. I'd like to sneak away with him some

Above: Powell on a previous trip to Israel.

evening and find out how the remaining members of the Israel Philharmonic Orchestra sound."

"I hope they put us all up at the Dan Panorama hotel like they did last time," Solana added. "If it hasn't been razed by a stray missile, that is."

Senate Foreign Relations Committee Chairman Richard Lugar (R-IN) applied to attend the negotiations, but his request was denied due to budget constraints.

"This sucks," Lugar said. "They're sending Solana but not me? I deserve to go so much more than that guy. Powell, okay, he's been around forever, but [Russian Foreign Minister] Sergey Lavrov gets to go? How'd Lavrov get in line ahead of me for this trip? I am so briefed on the situation with those state-sanctioned killings of [Hamas leaders] Sheikh Ahmed Yassin and Abdel Aziz Rantisi. Colin

had better bring me something back—some spent shell casings or one of those kitschy religious-fanatic posters."

Bush will not attend the talks due to a previously scheduled trip to Baghdad to oversee the preparations for Iraqi sovereignty.

Paula J. Dobriansky, State Department Undersecretary for Global Affairs, said that no offense was meant to Lugar, but the roster filled up very

quickly.

"Everyone wants to get over there to see the historic mosque and temple architecture, taste the delicious Mediterranean food, and experience the local culture of the Middle East, no matter what protective body armor is required," Dobriansky said. "Jerusalem is supposed to be just gorgeous in the springtime. Everyone who makes it back here alive won't stop talking about it."

Although several U.N. delegates expressed skepticism about the outcome of the talks, their reservations did not dull their enthusiasm for visiting the attractions.

"These talks could theoretically be really important to the region, so I hope they go well," said Terje Roed-Larsen, U.N. Special Coordinator for the Middle East Peace Process. "On the other hand, if negotations do break down, we can spend the week shopping in the couple of cool, out-of-the-way parts of Tel Aviv that are still accessible to tourists. And, well, should everything fall to pieces, it would be great to not have to worry about rushing through those 40 checkpoints to make it back in time for a meeting."

Bush will not attend the talks due to a previously scheduled trip to Baghdad to oversee the preparations for Iraqi sovereignty. According to an anonymous White House insider, Major General John Batiste has been instructed to use his command of the 1st Infantry Division to secure the area around the Samarra spiral minaret near Fallujah so the pair can get their photo taken in front of the ornate, historic building. ∅

MOM from page 151

'needs.' *Hello,* there are other people in therapy here."

Westphal's husband Greg said he can't get a word in edgewise, either.

"We never would've gone to see Dr. [Whitney] Eversen if Jeanette hadn't nagged me about how we need to talk through our problems," Greg said. "As I see it, our biggest problem is that she

In spite of the obstacles, the family has no immediate plans to discontinue therapy.

won't shut up about her feelings and let somebody else have a turn. She acts like it's her own private radio show."

Although Westphal usually mediates conflicts between family members, and is described as the individual who most frequently calls for calm and quiet in the home, she exhibits a different side of herself in therapy. Thomas, 16, said that, once his mother is the center of attention, "she becomes a total drama queen."

"It's pretty scary, man,"Thomas said. "Who knew Mom could freak out so bad? None of us, that's for sure. We were all, like, where is this coming from? I don't even remember any St. Patrick's Day cookies. I never knew she was such a glutton for attention."

Thomas added: "Thanks to family therapy, we've learned a lot about Mom's thoughts and feelings. She's a total psycho."

Family members report that, in the past several sessions, Westphal has complained that Thomas always sides with Greg, expressed her resentment over the amount of housework she does, and repeatedly returned to the fact that, in 17 years of marriage, Greg has never purchased her a gift without first asking her what she would like, in spite of the fact that she has repeatedly told him that she loves surprises and would never be disappointed with anything he bought, as long as it came from the heart.

"It's like, 'Hey, Mom, give it a rest, okay?'" Thomas said. "Not that you could ever say that in a session. She'd just start flipping out about how nobody listens to her and how she's invisible and stuff. Or how some

saleslady at Sears looked right through her as if she didn't exist. Next thing you know, the session's over."

Eversen said reining the attention-starved mother and wife in has been challenging.

"During the very first session, I always inform the family members that there are no right or wrong things to say in therapy,"Eversen said, pausing to take two Advil tablets with a glass of water. "That really opened the floodgates for Jeanette. Now, she feels she can say anything she wants, at any length she wants. I've stressed the importance of listening, but I think she's taken that to mean that the others should listen to her."

"Clearly, this woman has major issues that she needs to express, but she's not listened to in other settings," Eversen added. "The session is her one moment in the sun each week."

Eversen said that, in the last session, he attempted to moderate equal time for each family member by having everyone use hand puppets as communication tools.

"Somehow, Jeanette got all four puppets and, using a different voice for each one, launched into an epic diatribe about how she is forced to be

wife, mother, maid, and... well, I forget the last one,"Eversen said. "I had to finally interrupt her and politely remind her that we were trying to do a group exercise."

After the "puppet incident," Eversen said he pulled Westphal aside and recommended that she come in for individual sessions.

"She was resistant," Eversen said. "She said the whole point of the therapy was to work out family issues, together, as a family. I'm not sure what to do. Frankly, I'm afraid this may be beyond my training."

In spite of the obstacles, the family has no immediate plans to discontinue therapy.

"For 20 years, my wife has walked through life with a smile on her face, calmly and generously giving of herself whenever she's needed," Greg said. "Now, we're expected to listen to everything from the darkest recesses of her subconscious all at once?"

"What about my needs?" Greg added. "I have been waiting 12 sessions to discuss my self-esteem concerns over my receding hairline. By the time I get around to expressing that to my kids, Thomas is going to be going bald himself." ∅

You Win Some, You Claim To Have Won Some

By Jack Billings

If there's one thing I've learned about life, it's that things rarely go according to plan. You have to expect to take a few knocks here and there. That's why I've developed a way to cope with life's pitfalls. When things don't go right, I just stick my chin out, turn my frown upside down, and lie to everyone about what actually happened.

Even if you're extremely talented, it's impossible to win every time. But telling people that you won takes no effort at all, and you can *always* fall back on it. Try it the next time you get turned down for a date. Instead of shrugging it off and telling yourself there are other fish in the sea, tell your friends that the chick was hot for you, but you passed on her because she was giving off a psycho vibe or her teeth were bad.

Take what happened last month: I went to Atlantic City and lost $400 on slots, but at work Monday, I told everyone I'd won $170 at the tables. I'd have said I won more, but then they would've expected me to bring in donuts. Anyway, it's not like my gambling win was a total lie. I did make $55 at the tables at my friend's bachelor party in 1988, and yesterday, I won $5 on scratch-off tickets.

Okay, I didn't really win on the scratch-off. I lost $2. But for a few seconds, you were with me, weren't you?

If life hands you lemons, throw them out, pile some old newspapers on top of them so no one sees them in your garbage can, and then tell everyone you had lemonade. Really go into detail. Tell your friends how sweet it was, and how you served it up in a big tall glass, nice and cold, and talk at length about how great it is that life keeps bringing you delicious lemonade in beautiful glasses. They'll be too busy envying your lemonade to notice that you're a lying, losing, lonely bastard.

Okay, so you blew an important meeting at work and now you're saying "better luck next time," and vowing to work harder. What kind of attitude is that? Why not claim to have worked hard this time, you ponce? Say your boss fucked everything up. If you get fired, tell everyone you got a promotion, didn't like working with the pricks upstairs, and quit to field better offers. It's so simple. I can't stand a person with a negative attitude. When the road of life gets a little bumpy, go to the nearest airport and

Telling people that you won takes no effort at all.

fly home. Once home, talk at length about how your epic journey across America via the nation's historic one-lane highways changed your life.

Who likes a winner? Everyone. Who likes a loser? Exactly. It doesn't matter if you're a good loser or the worst loser ever. As far as everyone else is concerned, you can still be a winner. The only way people will know you're a loser is if you tell them what your life is actually like. Why would you do that?

Let's say you're late meeting a friend for dinner. There are all sorts of ways to get out of this one without losing face or being truthful. You can say you locked your keys in your house and had to call the locksmith, but then you'd still look like a flake. Instead, tell them that you ran into the mayor and had a long discussion about your idea for a multicultural peace park. Make the most out of a bad experience. If you put your mind to it, you could come up with literally hundreds of ways to spin your sad-sack life into 24-karat gold.

So, the next time you're down on your luck, take a look at the man in the mirror and tell him how great everything is going. If you can't fool yourself, how are you going to fool everyone else?

If you get the crap knocked out of you in a fight, say "You should see the other guy." If you get thrown out of a bar, tell everyone you were sick of the losers hanging out in the place. If you're house-sitting for someone, and their cat runs away because you forgot to close the door, stage a break-in and tell the cat's owners the burglars let it out, but you came just in time to save their possessions. If you're diagnosed with cancer, tell people you're moving to Hawaii. When they don't see you around anymore, they'll think you're sitting under a palm tree, drinking a piña colada. See? You won! ✐

PROMOTER from page 153

box of black breast-pocket logo T's was supposed to last me until Dayton."

Schweiber said that, in his impaired state, he started to "spew God-knows-what about Heineken."

"I'm pretty sure I told this table of women all about Heineken's purity and its blend of hops," Schweiber said. "I remember talking to these businessmen about how Heineken is sold in more than 170 countries, making Heineken the largest exporter of beer in the world. I don't think I told very many people about the CD, though, and that's the main reason I was there."

Near the end of the evening, Schweiber went to the bathroom to

"Thank God no one from the company saw me," Schweiber said.

splash cold water on his face, but ended up vomiting.

"I hope no one else was in the bathroom," Schweiber said. "I don't think my actions reflected Heineken's message of responsible drinking."

Wincing as he caught a whiff of his coat, Schweiber remembered another incident that gave him pause.

"Someone bought me a shot," Schweiber said. "It was something minty—Rumpleminze, maybe. I

should have said no, but I wasn't in any condition to turn it down. At least it wasn't another kind of beer, so there wasn't any conflict of interest there. Thank God no one from the company saw me in that state."

Choking back nausea as he packed his suitcase in preparation for a drive to Akron, Schweiber recalled another thing he had said about Heineken and cringed.

"At one point, I yelled out something like, 'Who wants a stupid Heineken mug?' Schweiber said. "I wasn't even that drunk when I said that. I was just trying to impress a group of guys. But

Above: Schweiber recovers from the previous night's wild giveaway binge.

I should have let the glass speak for itself. There's nothing stupid about it. It's a quality pint glass with a nice Heineken logo."

Added Schweiber: "Next time, I'll remember that, when I'm wearing that Heineken polo, I'm representing the brand." ✐

wet-behind-the-ears, candy-assed, beach-bum brat who'll need years of babysitting before he'll be good for anything but getting in my goddamn way."

"I got drugs to fight, I got terror to fight, and I got all kinds of crime to fight," Ashcroft said, pounding a battered steel desk piled high with cluttered stacks of papers and file folders. "I got nothing but a few snitches, some overworked uniformed DOJ agents, and 11 years of inefficient intelligence to do it with. Now they want me to hand-hold some damn surfer-boy fresh outta law school? Who the fuck do they think they're dealing with?"

Continued Ashcroft: "How do I know he's not some kind of freakin' communist? Because the suits in personnel say so? Ha. Nice try. Listen, I'd sooner shoot myself in the guts than give Romeo over there [former Deputy Attorney General] Jim [Comey]'s old office. He doesn't set foot in there until I know he's no flake."

In the preliminary days of working with Burnhard, Ashcroft has largely ignored his rookie partner, sending him on coffee runs and wild-goose chases in the stacks of the CIA library while Ashcroft followed up on leads, shook down street-level terrorist informants, and addressed a congressional panel on the importance of Patriot Act II.

"I'm the chief law officer of this country," Ashcroft said. "I don't have time to explain every move I make. I'm not a friggin' kindergarten teacher."

Burnhard said he has attempted to win Ashcroft's respect by working quietly and diligently in his tiny office, never complaining that his desk was installed in a broom closet in a blatant attempt to haze him out.

"It can't be easy accepting someone new after working with Comey for so many years," Burnhard said, poring over a stack of paperwork under the

light of his office's single, swinging bare bulb. "I realize there's going to be a breaking-in period for me, but it's worth it, just to work with a legend like Ashcroft. He's earned his attitude. Do you realize he has to legally represent the U.S. before the

---

"I got terror to fight," Ashcroft said.

Supreme Court? A job like that's gotta be hell on a guy."

Burnhard said that, for now, he's more than happy to type Ashcroft's reports, wait in the car for hours on end, and listen to crime-fighting stories.

"Last night, we pulled a late one staking out an Internet piracy network," Burnhard said. "After a few hours sitting there in the car together, he finally started to open up. I don't necessarily agree with his theories about widening subpoena powers or expanding the federal death-penalty statute, but I have to admit that he gets the job done. He's loyal to himself, this country, and the department—in that order."

National Security Advisor Condoleezza Rice said she has worked closely—or as closely as anyone dares—with Ashcroft for years, and has a guess as to why he's reluctant to take a partner.

"John hasn't been the same since what happened to Comey," Rice said. "Everyone close to him knows he doesn't want the responsibility of losing another partner. When Jim was shot chasing a suspected Taliban operative down that Georgetown alley, John blamed himself. But John has to realize that this partnership could help him just as much as it'll help Burnhard and the United States of America." ∅

of the precious dowry goats got loose? Without a thought of the dangers of the approaching night, you searched the entire Deccan Plateau, carrying our son Lam with you all the while, walking as far as the Hanuman Temple at Chaprala. When dawn arrived, I was very worried—and hungry, because you had not been there to prepare dinner the night before (which did not please me). But the fear of losing you to wild animals or bandits made me realize just how much you mean to me. When you finally showed up at the door, I made you promise never to leave the confines of the village again, not even to walk to the market in Vadpur.

The following night, my stomach nicely full, I stayed up very late alone in the night drinking from a bottle of Mahua flower water my father had given me shortly before he passed into his next life. Looking at the stars, set like gems in the inky night, I thanked my father. "Thank you, sir," I said. "Truly, you made the right marriage for me." Anjana Shah, I would not give you up for 20 goats. I would not lose you for even 30 goats. I would not give you up for a bicycle, a cart, or even a transistor radio. Dear heart, I

You never need to be asked to wash my feet when I come home from a long day of drinking and singing. You are everything to me.

---

tell you I speak the truth when I say that a thousand raging rivers could not drag you from me! That is how much I love you. I will love you well after the goats have grown too old to produce milk, and have been slaughtered for their meat. ∅

Your Horoscope

By Lloyd Schumner Sr.
Retired Machinist and
A.A.P.B.-Certified Astrologer

Aries: (March 21–April 19)
Your infamous good-natured but ill-fated meddling in others' lives will reach its peak when you screw up a trilateral Asian trade agreement in the 11th hour.

Taurus: (April 20–May 20)
It'll be hard to get used to your new life, but you'll come to realize you wouldn't trade it for all the working legs and non-prehensile noses in the world.

Gemini: (May 21–June 21)
Take heart: There is indeed a ruler of the universe who surpasses all understanding and is greater than all men. Luckily, He never seems to notice us.

Cancer: (June 22–July 22)
You've always insisted that no one can completely understand your problems. That raises the question of why you won't fucking stop talking about them, then.

Leo: (July 23–Aug. 22)
You've heard that no two snowflakes are alike, and you're pretty certain that this indicates an ethical failing on their part.

Virgo: (Aug. 23–Sept. 22)
Neither love nor money makes the world go round. Unfortunately, we're down to about 17 ounces of the highly unstable stuff that does.

Libra: (Sept. 23–Oct. 23)
You've always stressed the importance of manners, but you don't think they need to prevent anyone from killing as many people as possible.

Scorpio: (Oct. 24–Nov. 21)
Next week will serve as a good example of what happens to people who listen to old wives' tales, especially the ones whose old husbands are high-ranking Masonic elders.

Sagittarius: (Nov. 22–Dec. 21)
You know you're supposed to keep your friends close and your enemies closer, but that advice is of little help to an avowed cat person.

Capricorn: (Dec. 22–Jan. 19)
Although you firmly believe there are two kinds of people in the world, it really creeps you out that you can't figure out what they are.

Aquarius: (Jan. 20–Feb. 18)
You've always considered yourself to be good with children, making it quite a surprise when they all decide to hunt you down.

Pisces: (Feb. 19–March 20)
No further cosmic developments are scheduled this week. Please interpret any as anomalies and ignore.

Annie Wolohan, 16, is throwing a party Friday in the woods behind where the Kmart used to be. $5 for a cup.

Homo Rob Carlson, 42, is having some homos stay at his beach house this weekend so they can sit in the sand and be gay together.

The weird weapons guy on Pine Street is having a barbecue Saturday. Planned events include a Cambodian-skull exhibition and the consumption of Löwenbräu in his dank, flag-draped living room.

Clive Dean Robins, 25, will be partying on the hood of his Toyota Camry in the Sunshine factory parking lot tonight. 9 p.m. sharp, near the Cheez-It division loading docks.

NEWS

the ONION®

VOLUME 40 ISSUE 19   AMERICA'S FINEST NEWS SOURCE™   13–19 MAY 2004

Keebler Expands Line Of Residence-Themed Crackers

see BUSINESS page 4D

Prom Date Arrives In Freshly Washed Pickup

see LOCAL page 11E

Old, Resigned Woman To Watch *The Young And The Restless*

see ENTERTAINMENT page 8C

STATshot

A look at the numbers that shape your world.

Top Child Punishments, By State
- No moose for a week (MT)
- Allowance not adjusted for inflation (DC)
- An hour in closet with Roy Acuff's bones (TN)
- Sent to public school (NY)
- Written out of Daddy's pilot (CA)
- Must remain in state until 18 (ID)
- Toe shot off (KY)

Bush Vows To Pay Closer Attention To Needs Of Non-Presidents

WASHINGTON, DC—Responding to recent polls suggesting that he has lost touch with the average American, President Bush vowed Monday to pay closer attention to the needs of non-presidents.

"Perhaps, in the past, I've been somewhat lax in addressing the day-to-day problems of the nation's non-presidents," Bush said during a White House press conference. "Well, that's about to change. I hereby pledge to hear and heed the concerns of non-chief-executives—a group of people who are very valuable to our country, in their own way, even if it's not always readily apparent how."

Bush has charged his staff of 50 with the task of helping him learn more about the nation's many non-commanders-in-chief.

"From here on out, I will

see BUSH page 160

Above: Bush meets with non-presidents in a Camden, NJ packaging plant.

Above: Congressmen Don Nickles (R-OK), Charles Schumer (D-NY), Dick Gephardt (D-MO), and John Lewis (D-GA) minutes before their arrest.

34 Congressmen Arrested In D.C. Cockfighting Crackdown

WASHINGTON, DC—Washington police seized 22 members of the House of Representatives, 12 members of the Senate, and more than 100 fighting cocks Monday night, in the latest crackdown on blood sports at the highest levels of the U.S. government.

"At 1 o'clock this morning, uniformed officers, acting on tips from undercover operatives, staged simultaneous raids on four known beltway pits, arresting a large bipartisan coalition of legislative cockfighting

see COCKFIGHTING page 160

Photo ID Shows Toll Job Has Taken On Employee

CHARLESTON, SC—Seth Poole's employee-identification card is a revealing indicator of the toll that two years of work at Blue Juice, Inc. has taken on the internal auditor's appearance and overall health, sources close to the 37-year-old revealed Monday.

"I happened to see Seth's ID sitting on his desk the other day, and I let out a gasp that could be heard across the hall," Blue Juice accountant Joan Brandywine said. "It didn't look like the same person. I thought, 'Dear God, what happened to that young, vibrant man who walked into the May 2002 employee-orientation session?'"

Blue Juice, whose sales topped $50 million last year, is one of the fastest-growing organic-juice brands in the

Seth Poole
Blue Juice, Inc.
24223
02422300

Right: Poole shows signs of wear not present in his ID from two years ago (above).

country. Hired by Blue Juice CEO Benjamin Valdavia, Poole said he was initially excited to join the small but rapidly expanding company.

Poole's ID card, however, reveals his growing disillusionment with both Valdavia and Blue Juice. Assigned the task of assisting Valdavia in the

see PHOTO ID page 161

Iraqi Prisoner Abuse

Though the Bush Administration apologized for U.S. abuse of Iraqi prisoners, some feel the coalition's reputation has suffered irreparable damage. What do *you* think?

Donald Stiles
Systems Analyst

"They wanted to provide Iraq with a smooth transition to democracy. We couldn't just plunge them into a non-torture-based society with no time to adjust."

Ricky Thomas
Cartoonist

"I'm sure Bush was deeply saddened by the fact that American soldiers were stupid enough to document their acts of cruelty."

Donna Amundson
Dental Assistant

"Some people want to make military prisons into country clubs—instead of the S&M clubs they are now."

Charles Wolf
Revenue Agent

"Thank God Saddam's in jail so he can't commit atrocities like this anymore."

Joseph Spagnolia
Fabricator

"It's not like they made a 70-year-old woman get down on all fours, then climbed on her back and called her a donkey. What? Oh, no."

Sheila Wooster
Underwriter

"If we hadn't tortured those prisoners, we could never have achieved the post-war stability Iraq is currently enjoying."

Who Is John Kerry?

Democratic presidential candidate John Kerry is struggling to define himself to the voting public. What are some of the messages he's considering?

▶ "John Kerry: A man who has chaired a lot of committees."

▶ "Kerry: You'd probably like him if you got to know him."

▶ "John Kerry: Not a Jew, but not *against* Jews."

▶ "John F. Kerry: More than just a big cock and a nice ass."

▶ "Vote Kerry in 2004, because life is a miasma of confusion, pain, and loneliness."

▶ "Kerry: A voice of reason who's killed, like, 20 dudes."

▶ "The election is still a long way off, so go about the business of living your lives until a week or so before voting day, at which point you should really give some thought to John Kerry."

▶ "John Kerry: Certainly not worse."

the ONION®
America's Finest News Source.™

Herman Ulysses Zweibel
Founder

T. Herman Zweibel
Publisher Emeritus
J. Phineas Zweibel
Publisher
Maxwell Prescott Zweibel
Editor-In-Chief

Point-Counterpoint: The War On Terrorism

Killing Wheelchair-Bound People With Missiles Is Justifiable If They're Terrorists

By Gary Loder

The global balance of power has changed dramatically in the last two decades. In the past, great armies and great industrial capabilities were needed to threaten strong nations. Now, shadowy networks of individuals can cause great suffering for the cost of a homemade explosive. To effectively counter this new threat, we must make use of every tool in our arsenal—military power, homeland defense, law enforcement, intelligence, and short-range helicopter-mounted missiles to pick off elderly, wheelchair-bound terrorists one at a time.

With terrorist threats expanding in every theater, those in power must employ proactive strategies of defense. Freedom-loving nations cannot deploy conventional troops against the diverse and unpredictable forces that threaten their citizens. Thus, it is fully understandable that when the Israeli army located Hamas founder Sheikh Ahmed Yassin outside of a mosque in March, they launched a missile at his wheelchair.

Our potential adversaries believe that, while their nation's survival is at stake in a regional conflict, ours isn't. As a consequence, they calculate that we can and will back down when confronted with dire threats, such as weapons of mass destruction, but that they will not. Therefore, people who fight a war on terror are at an inherent disadvantage, because the enemy is unafraid to die. In fact, many terrorists see martyrdom as a reward.

There are those who suggest that every terrorist killed equals three more terrorists created. But is this really true? Shouldn't we send the message that we will never bow to the threat of terrorism? We can do so by striking the enemy as hard, as brutally, and as dramatically as possible. If deemed necessary, we must outfit helicopters with missile launchers, find out where our

see POINT page 161

Killing Wheelchair-Bound People With Missiles Is Awesome

By Timothy Deering

I heard about the Israeli rocket attack on that old handicapped Hamas guy, and I'm sure a lot of people had the same reaction I did: Whatever reason the army had for doing it, blowing up a guy in a wheelchair with a missile is unbelievably, absolutely fucking awesome!

Now, let me say this: I realize the guy was one of their big rebel leaders over there, or something, and I guess he called for the deaths of tons of innocent people and so on, and that was the excuse they needed to take the old guy out. But that's not the point. The point is they totally fucking launched a *missile* at the guy's *wheelchair* from a *helicopter*! That's some grade-A Bam Magera video-game shit, and I for one am fucking stoked that they did it. I don't know how much that one missile cost, but it was utterly and completely worth it to know that some coot on wheels got rocket-launched into the middle of next year.

This sort of thing needs to happen more often. The U.S. military would be a *lot* more popular if they concentrated on pulling off cool-ass shit like this. And it doesn't have to be just

> This sort of thing needs to happen more often. The U.S. military would be a lot more popular if they concentrated on pulling off cool-ass shit like this.

wars, right? I mean, we have a lot, I mean a lot, of folks in wheelchairs all over the world. And sure, most of them are probably all-right guys. But people are people, so there's gotta be a whole lot of wheelchair-bound people that are total shits, too. I bet there are guys in wheelchairs who beat their women, or maybe they got that way by drunk driving, or maybe they wheel around all day trying to diddle little kids. Face it, if someone's trying

see COUNTERPOINT page 161

Woman At *Farscape* Convention Has Dangerously Inflated Self-Image

BURBANK, CA—Paulette Osley, 24, a moderately attractive fan of the Sci-Fi Channel series *Farscape*, had her self-image inflated to dangerous levels during the three-day ScaperCon 2004, according to Pepperdine University professor of psychology Wes Martin.

"Let's face it, Paulette is pretty ordinary," Martin said, reviewing a tape of Osley's participation in a convention trivia contest Monday. "I mean, she's cute and all, but the men at ScaperCon treated her like she was [*Farscape* actress] Raelee Hill. Going from being someone who might get hit on once or twice a year to the belle of the ball and then back to nothing again, all within four days? It could be damaging to Paulette's long-term mental health."

Osley attended the convention from Friday to Sunday, freely and confidently mingling with the 85 percent male crowd at the Hilton Burbank Airport and Convention Center.

"From the moment she walked in the door, Paulette was the object of admiring glances," Martin said. "Everywhere she went, men were awkwardly trying to make conversation with her, flirting with her using *Farscape* dialogue, and inviting her to season-finale-watching parties in their hotel suites. Although she only came in 14th in the trivia contest, her adorable blush, her nervous giggle, and the fact that she was female earned her many admirers."

Farscape fan Jack Brisbois was among the men who noticed Osley.

"When I was in line waiting to get my *Farscape* David Kemper autograph card signed by David Kemper, there was this chick talking to me for the entire hour," said Brisbois, who said he would rate Osley "7 or 8" if he saw her on Hotornot.com. "She was from Oklahoma and really into *Quantum Leap*. She also knew a lot about Final Fantasy games. I was about to make a move, but then some other guy walked up and gave her a free copy of his fanzine, and suddenly it was as if I'd been transported to another galaxy. Damn, that chick was *cold*."

Bolstered by the attention, Osley began to actively seek more of it.

"Usually, Paulette is pretty shy," Osley's longtime friend and fellow *Farscape* fan Sarah Baltazar said. "But at ScaperCon, it was as if she was trying out a new personality. She adopted a louder laugh, and whenever men were around, she was rude to the hotel staff. She also kept making jokes about blow jobs. How could I convince her to dial it down a notch? The guys were eating it up."

"She kept reapplying this glitter makeup she had," Baltazar added. "At first it was just around her eyes, but through the night it spread to her chest, until it was all over her arms, and then on half the guys there."

Baltazar said that it was after being hit on by three different men at the

Above: Osley at ScaperCon 2004, where she was considered a knockout.

hotel bar on Saturday night that Osley's ego reached truly perilous heights. The next day, Osley appeared dressed like Chiana, the straw-haired, pale-skinned, highly sexualized alien played by Gigi Edgley. The revealing outfit earned Osley the type of attention she lacks in her day-to-day life as a Target cashier in Tulsa.

"The night we went to Perkins

see WOMAN page 161

Halliburton Employee's Pay Docked For Weeks Spent As Hostage

BAGHDAD—Spokesmen for Halliburton International announced Monday that employee Thomas Hamill will not be paid for the three weeks he failed to fulfill his truck-driving duties while being held at gunpoint by Iraqi captors. "While we share your joy in regaining your freedom, we are forced to withhold your wages for the period of April 9 to May 2," read the official corporate reprimand, which reached Hamill in Germany as doctors treated his bullet wound. "A disciplinary slip noting your failure to report to work has been added to your employee file." Halliburton has not yet disclosed the amount Hamill is being charged for structural damage to the company truck he was shot in.

Investors Stake Out Greenspan's House For Signs Of Rate Increase

WASHINGTON, DC—Investors have been staking out Federal Reserve Chairman Alan Greenspan's home in an effort to gather any clues that Greenspan will institute an increase in the interest rate, neighborhood sources reported Tuesday. "Right now, Mr. Greenspan is applying a second coat of Turtle Wax to his Lexus," mutual-fund investor Ted Iger said, as he squatted behind an oak tree. "Maybe he plans to sell the car before raising lending rates." Iger said a major household purchase would corroborate theories he has about the microwave box Greenspan's wife carried to the curb Sunday.

Film-School Graduate Goes Straight To Video-Store Job

SANTA MONICA, CA—The theatrical career of recent USC School of Cinema-Television graduate Neil Hemmitt was put on hold indefinitely as the aspiring director went straight to video-store clerking Monday. "The big studios never gave me a chance," Hemmitt said, as he shelved a *Big Fish* DVD at Blockbuster. "But it's because they didn't understand me." Hemmitt's producers, Harold and Francine Hemmitt, pulled his financial support in March, after calling his predicament "hardly original."

Bathroom Too Disgusting To Shit In

AUSTIN, TX—The men's bathroom at area rock club Emo's was declared too repulsive for the empty-ing of concertgoer Max Risdy's bowels Saturday night. "The floor was covered with water, there was toilet paper and garbage everywhere, and it smelled disgusting," Risdy said, wincing at the memory Monday. "It was really not the kind of place you want to leave a big pile of digested food matter after squeezing it through your rectum from the depths of your bowels." Risdy added that the area near the music venue's stage was too loud and crowded.

House Inappropriations Committee Suggests Nation's Women Dress A Little Sexier

WASHINGTON, DC—In a policy initiative released Monday, the chairman of the House Inappropriations Committee suggested that the women of America start to dress a little more provocatively. "Why don't they wear some shorter skirts?" U.S. Rep. Bill Young (R-FL) said. "They've got nice legs. They should show 'em off." Young said he could offer American females even more suggestions if Congress would underwrite a fact-finding tour to Miami Beach. ✐

Above: Sen. Orrin Hatch (R-UT) inspects fighting birds during a cock-buying trip to Tibet.

enthusiasts," D.C. police chief Charles H. Ramsey told reporters Tuesday. "Of course, we were aware of the longstanding cockfighting problem, but we were shocked to catch so many highly placed lawmakers in the act of betting on, training, and selling fighting birds—or, in the case of [Rep.] Tammy Baldwin [D-WI], operating back-alley clubs."

A full report of evidence gathered in the raids will be issued later this week, but police have released certain facts, including details about a breeding network for elite fighting cocks—prized for their extreme aggressiveness and high pain threshold—run by members of the House Judiciary Committee. Undercover officers said they witnessed committee members selling birds to other congressmen for hundreds of dollars apiece.

Evidence also included photos of congressional motor-pool limousines that had been converted into "crating trucks" to transport cocks from venue to venue. Perhaps most stunning of all were the firsthand sightings of cocks, their crests and wattles surgically removed, being trained to fight with blades tied to their natural spurs in a 400-bird "hardening pen" in the base-

ment of the Old Executive Office Building, just blocks away from the White House.

Detective William Gargano of the D.C. vice squad was present for the previous evening's raid on El Pollo Diablo, a cockfighting pit located among

Evidence also included photos of congressional motor-pool limousines that had been converted into "crating trucks" to transport cocks from venue to venue.

several blocks of abandoned warehouses in southeast D.C.

"I was there shooting undercover video when detectives and animal-control operatives, working in a combined task force, busted down all the doors to the place at once," Gargano said. "It had already been

shaping up to be one hell of a night. [Sen. Dick] Lugar [R-IN] was a few hundred dollars ahead in the pit. His famous Stag Hammer just couldn't lose. Well, that didn't sit well with [Sen.] Hillary Clinton [D-NY], who accused him of giving his bird ginger and amphetamine suppositories to make it fight harder."

Continued Gargano: "Then [Sen. Dianne] Feinstein [D-CA] tried to suck her rooster's punctured lung clear so it could last a whole match, but she swallowed too much blood and puked everywhere. [Supreme Court Justice David] Souter had just broken up a fight between [Rep.] Mark Kennedy [R-MN] and [Rep. Jim] Oberstar [D-MN], after they knocked the damn carcass barrel all over the floor. When the raid happened, I was relieved. It was getting pretty dicey in there."

The raids themselves were carried out with minimal resistance. Only Sen. John Edwards (D-NC) needed to be restrained and charged with resisting arrest.

Ramsey said that, though formal charges have yet to be filed, the congressmen taken into custody will most likely be charged with illegal gambling, animal cruelty, and collusion. Nearly all of the arrested cockfighting enthusiasts are out of jail after posting bail. However, not one of the arrested parties, even those who were not elected officials, has agreed to speak openly to reporters.

One legislator who asked not to be identified said the charges were "petty," and that the indicted members of Congress were victims of a "witch-hunt."

"Although violent, cockfighting is a traditional part of the American lawmaker's way of life," the legislator said. "It's a sport, with a code of conduct the uninitiated simply wouldn't understand. I'm sure many of the good people of Oklahoma, hypothetically speaking, would agree that there's a place for different people's

tastes in this great country. As far as the cruelty charges go, that's ludicrous. I love my fighting cocks—my wife likes to say I treat my champion red-eyes better than I treat her—and I'm sure my fellow Congressmen would say much the same."

As troubling as the mere existence of a legislative cockfighting ring may be, lawmakers who were not implicated in the scandal say they are more disturbed by evidence that legislation has been derailed, altered, or passed based on successes and failures in the cockfighting pit.

The raids themselves were carried out with minimal resistance. Only Sen. John Edwards (D-NC) needed to be restrained and charged with resisting arrest.

"One week, the Civic Funding for Secondary Education Act is dead in the water, with no compromise on the horizon," Sen. John McCain (R-AZ) said. "The very next week, a huge group of Democrats turn over on their votes. I heard strange rumors that some hefty debt to the Senate Republicans was just erased—something involving '10-to-1 odds on a one-eyed Rhode Island Red.' It didn't make sense until this morning, when I flipped on the news and saw all these same senators getting cuffed at the rooster pit in a basement off Constitution."

"Now that I think about it, this may explain why the Chicken Feed Price Stabilization Act passed through the House so quickly last month," McCain added. ∅

do my best to address the needs of this group of upstanding Americans who, I'm told, are part of a proud non-presidential tradition that stretches back hundreds of years in this country," Bush said. "To this end, I have appointed a blue-ribbon fact-finding committee to look into the issues of non-presidents and find out what their jets are named, how their staffs are performing, and how they're handling increased pressure from the media during this election year."

Of particular concern to Bush are the ways in which the sluggish economy is affecting the average non-head-of-state. He said he's curious to know how non-presidents are responding to the rising costs of television-campaign ads, whether their donations from special-interest groups have dropped in number, and how much money they are able to set aside for foreign invasions.

"I want to live in a country where all

citizens—presidents or not—can pursue their own policy initiatives abroad, even if they suffer from a lack of funding," Bush said. "In addition, Americans shouldn't have to go without the crucial tax cuts they've promised their political supporters, just because there's a mounting federal deficit. We must find a way for every citizen to afford the fundamentals of daily life: an adequate entourage of Secret Service personnel, limousine rides to and from fundraisers, and the political leverage to send legislation through Congress."

Bush said he will reach out to non-presidents with great care in the coming months—finding out how their oil wells are doing, how the major-league sports teams they own are weathering the market, and which Ivy League secret societies they belong to. He said he will also carefully read any policy papers they've had their staffs draft re-

cently and review any recent press announcements they've made or leaked.

"There is only one way to win over the hearts, minds, and votes of our nation's non-presidents—a group which, I've learned, is larger than I had previous reason to believe—and that's to ask questions," Bush said. "Is security tight enough at their military retreats? Do they have adequate support from their friends in the private sector? Are the global petrochemical companies that back them doing a good job of adhering to government guidelines regarding their campaign contributions? Do they and their households have access to high-quality spin control? If not, I'd like to help non-presidents and their families get the help they need."

Bush said he's so committed to learning more about non-presidents that he has scheduled a fact-finding visit to the home of one such non-

president next month.

"In June, I'll be visiting my parents in Texas to discuss these issues," Bush said. "As it turns out, my father is one of these non-presidents. I didn't realize that before, because people still call him 'Mr. President' wherever he goes, but as it happens, he's actually been a non-president for years."

"It just goes to show that, when it comes to non-presidents, I still have a lot to learn," Bush added.

In closing, the president said he has great respect for the many hardworking non-presidents he sees on a daily basis, including those who serve his meals, schedule his phone calls, and carry his shoes.

Added Bush: "You know, some of my best friends—including [Secretary Of Defense] Donald Rumsfeld, [National Security Advisor] Condoleezza Rice, and [Vice-President] Dick Cheney—are non-presidents." ∅

WOMAN from page 159

Above: Baltazar (right) admires a passing *Farscape* actor along with one of the other 23 women at ScaperCon.

really late, everyone was asking Paulette about her costume, even men who weren't from ScaperCon," Baltazar said. "At one point, she was smooshed into a booth with these five traveling businessmen. A couple of them wrote their e-mail addresses on napkins for her."

According to Baltazar, Osley hadn't received that much attention since attending the last *Farscape* convention a year ago, when she dressed as the blue-skinned, bald Delvian priestess Pa'u Zotoh Zhaan and received nearly nonstop requests to drop her robe, in reference to the character's actions in Season 1, Episode 4, "Throne For A Loss."

"There was a photo sticker booth in the game room, and Paulette was dragging everyone into it with her," Baltazar said. "Seriously, she went from lap to lap for about an hour."

The attention led Osley to flirt with *Farscape* actor Paul Goddard during an autograph signing. After handing Goddard a poster to sign, Osley said he could sign anywhere he wanted. Laughing coyly, she added, "And I mean *anywhere*."

"I don't think [Osley] would have the courage to approach Goddard for change for a dollar if he was some guy at work," Martin said. "He was in *The Matrix*, for crying out loud. How could she think she had a prayer with him?"

Martin said he was worried about the lingering effects of the weekend.

"A confidence boost for Paulette is a good thing, but I think she's headed for a crash," Martin said. "A girl who can

> ## "A confidence boost for Paulette is a good thing, but I think she's headed for a crash," Martin said.

spout detailed specs of leviathan spaceships appeals to a very limited niche. After having a man in every merch booth tell her how great she'd look in a *Farscape* half-shirt, it's got to be an enormous let-down to go back to having men bump into her because they didn't even notice her standing there."

"I assume she'll deal with it like she always has," he added. "By posting convention photos of herself to *Farscape* fan sites, then hoping for some drooling online responses to soften the blow." ⌀

PHOTO ID from page 157

expansion of the company's operations in order to ready it for a broader domestic market, Poole said he soon found his job to be "less engaging" than he had originally expected. As evidenced by the ID, over the course of 24 months on the job, Poole was transformed from a boyish-looking 35 to a haggard, sallow 37.

Other Blue Juice staff members who

> ## Poole was transformed from a boyish-looking 35 to a haggard, sallow 37.

have seen the card attest to Poole's dramatic aging.

"That ID shows a man who's excited to be working for a company that offers a high-quality, all-natural product," executive assistant Mandy Keefer said. "That's not really what Seth is like. Not anymore. At our last team meeting, Seth kept repeating that the package redesign we're planning was a big waste of money that the company doesn't have. Then he said, 'I don't know why I even bother coming in to work.' I'll bet he can blame at least a couple of those crow's feet of his on those redesign prototypes."

Keefer estimated that, every time Valdavia says "vision can't be charted on spreadsheets," Poole loses 75 hairs.

"Yesterday, I walked into the breakroom and found Seth leaning over the donuts, picking frosting off a Long John, and mumbling, 'If Ben does his fishing-out-of-his-wastebasket gag one more time, I walk,'" Keefer added. "It wasn't pretty."

Jason Marshall, a security guard in the building where Blue Juice is headquartered, said he was initially confused by the image on Poole's ID card.

"I saw this old guy flashing some young guy's ID, so I stopped him," Marshall said. "Once I saw the photo up close, I could tell it was [Poole]. Man, the last couple years have been hard on that guy."

While Poole seemed unaware of the dramatic change in his appearance, he did report that his health has taken a turn for the worse in recent months. He said he developed a duodenal ulcer earlier this year, shortly after he discovered that Valdavia had extorted cash from the company's 401K matching fund for renovations on his Vermont lake house.

"When I found out [about the embezzlement], I said to him, in a tone of voice you'd reserve for a child, 'Ben, you know this is stealing, right?'" Poole said, his scowl forming deep lines on his forehead. "And he said, 'How was it stealing when I paid it back within a month?' So I asked Ben if he had heard of any of those recent corporate financial scandals, and he answered that those companies were publicly owned, whereas most of his

assets are tied up in Blue Juice. He thought that meant he was entitled to borrow from the employee-retirement account fund for personal reasons."

Poole's face has also borne the ravages of his boss' inconsistently implemented "open communication" policy; Valdavia's recent declaration to investors that, unbeknownst to his staff, an IPO was imminent; and his tendency to call Poole into his office for lengthy chit-chats when Poole is about to leave for the night.

Poole's photo ID does not tell the whole story of his decline. The face on his card only hints at the 10 pounds now missing from his once-muscular body.

"I used to go to the gym, but I haven't seen the inside of Gold's since we started on this new distribution structure," Poole said. "I used to eat fairly healthy, too, but I've grown pretty accustomed to snacking on whatever's in the breakroom all day and then grabbing some McDonald's on the way home. I always pair it with a 32-ounce Coke. That's right—sugary, empty-calorie-laden Coke. I

> ## "Yesterday, I walked into the breakroom and found Seth leaning over the donuts, picking frosting off a Long John, and mumbling, 'If Ben does his fishing-out-of-his-wastebasket gag one more time, I walk,'" Keefer added. "It wasn't pretty."

refuse to choke down another fucking Blue Juice as long as I live."

Leo Drake, president of Safeguard Solutions, the security-consultant firm that sold Blue Juice its ID-card machine, recommends that companies update their employees' photo IDs annually to prevent a "reverse Dorian Gray" effect.

"Regularly renewed IDs will reflect the subject's likeness with greater accuracy, improving the ID's functionality as a tool for identity verification," Drake said. "In addition, employees won't be confronted every day with proof of their ongoing personal decline."

Drake added: "By no means should employees be allowed to keep their old IDs, lest they make the connection between their workplace struggles and their unnaturally aged appearances." ⌀

POINT from page 158

enemy's wheelchair-bound former leaders worship, fly our missile-outfitted helicopters to those places of worship, and blow those leaders apart.

Mine will not be a popular opinion. In war, however, the word "popular" has little meaning and even less practical application. If governments, in the course of making war, can convince a splinter faction that they will bring all available force to bear on all avowed enemies at every possible opportunity, they gain a distinct advantage. Killing one enemy target with one missile is an acceptable practice, even—and in the case of terrorist enemies—if that target is an old man in a wheelchair. ⌀

COUNTERPOINT from page 158

to do that shit, it's okay to fuck them up as much as possible. Blowing their asses up with a missile would be pretty much perfect.

I like the part about getting them while they're leaving church, too. It's when they'd least be expecting it, being all contemplative and shit, and suddenly they're like, "Hey, do you hear a helicopter? Guys? Guys?" Then it's just *pshoooo*—wham! Blood and spokes everywhere!

God, that's cool just to think about. I guess it's probably pretty rare, too. Even if it doesn't become standard procedure, it's awesome that it happened once. ⌀

Sugar Baby

A Room Of Jean's Own
By Jean Teasdale

Ever notice how big things happen when you least expect them? You settle into a routine, and you go along like that for years, but then, suddenly, the bottom drops out from under you? I used to think these sort of jolts happened to other people, and not an "old reliable" like me. Not true, it turns out!

It all began a couple months ago. Hubby Rick was having a red-letter day: Dale Earnhardt Jr. won the Daytona 500, and then Rick found a roll of $10 bills outside the Ruby Tuesday on Nightingale Road. Well, I pitied the poor waitress who had apparently lost her hard-earned tips, but there was a side benefit to Rick's good mood, and this time, I didn't even have to ask for it! (These days, I don't lure Rick into the bedroom so much as I dare him by questioning his ability to carry out his, uh, "hubby duties," shall we say? Hey, whatever works, right?)

A couple weeks after the big event, I started to feel funny. For one thing, I was tired a whole lot. I tend to be a sleepyhead anyway, but this was just plain, solid fatigue. I also felt lightheaded and all numb in my fingers and toes. I was parched and dehydrated, and visiting the little-girl's room a bit too often. I assumed I had the flu that was going around, so I laid low and caught up on my *Suddenly Susan* reruns.

Then my time of the month rolled around—or didn't, rather. (Usually, it comes like clockwork.) It didn't take me long to put two and two together! Could it be, after years of my wishing and hoping and thinking and praying, that America's youngest Jeanketeer would be making her big debut? I've had false alarms before, but this was the first time I felt sick, too.

So, I did what any prospective mom-to-be does—I went to the mall and marched right into the Gymboree! If you don't have a Gymboree in your neck of the woods, I feel sorry for you, because they sell the most precious kid clothing you could ever imagine! If you've ever wondered how your toddler would look dressed like fruit, a circus clown, or one of the cuter species of insect, Gymboree is the place for you!

Even though I've been to Gymboree many times before, I always felt like a bit of a fraud browsing. But on that day, I strutted into the store with my head held high. Unfortunately, I was taken aback to see the snooty woman on duty that day. I don't know her name, but she's middle-aged and always has a sour look on her face, which isn't helped by her short, spiky haircut and narrow-frame granny spectacles. The younger girl who works there knows I'm only there to browse and leaves me alone, but this older woman always gives me an attitude.

So, like clockwork, the lady walked up to me and asked, in her usual way, "May I help you?" I know she meant it sarcastically, but I was ready for her this time. I drew myself up to my best posture and replied, "Yes. I'm looking for newborn attire. Do you have anything in a honeybee?"

"Honeybee?" she asked. She seemed surprised. "Yes, a honeybee," I replied.

> **My time of the month rolled around—or didn't, rather. (Usually, it comes like clockwork.) It didn't take me long to put two and two together!**

"I don't follow you," she answered. (Jeez, Louise! Didn't she know her own store?) So I told her I wanted anything black-and-yellow striped, but she said the only things they had striped right now were tights.

She asked if the bee outfit was for a boy or a girl. I said I didn't know, as it wasn't born yet. She suggested that I purchase a gift certificate instead, but I said that would be pointless, since I would be the one spending it. When I told her that, something amazing happened: For the first time ever, Ol' Pruneface smiled! "Oh, congratulations!" she said. She was all sweetness and light. She gave me tips on creating a full layette and showed me some darling booties and onesies. She even told me that she could contact their warehouse and special-order any available bee-themed babywear they might have. Maybe I had misjudged this woman!

The clerk also recommended that, instead of jumping the gun, maybe I should wait until my baby shower. She moved me toward the front desk and began to sign me up for a Gymboree registry. "When is your shower?" she asked. I told her that it hadn't been set yet. "Well, when is your due date?" she asked. "Baby showers usually take place within the last month of pregnancy," she said. I told her it would probably be in a little more than eight months, then.

I could see her eyebrows lowering behind her granny specs. "So how do you know…" she began, but her voice trailed off. We stared at each other. I knew where this was headed. "Look, I know it's a long way off, and it's true that I haven't taken a test yet, but I just gotta be preggers!" I said. (Actually, I think I kinda shouted it.) I explained how I was late and had morning sickness all day long and couldn't stop peeing. I asked how she would like it if someone second-guessed her? I felt dizzy, and my heart pounded and my eyes smarted like they did when I used to stare at a computer screen all day at my SouthCentral Insurance job. Then I did the weirdest thing: I sat down right on the floor! I felt so weak, I couldn't move a muscle. Everything was blurry, and I could barely talk. All I could do was sit there, with my back against the front desk, for about 10 minutes. Just as the clerk was about to call an ambulance, I started to regain my senses.

Well, long story short: I'm not preggers. I went to Dr. Plimm's office the next day, and he informed me that I have Type-2 diabetes. My blood-sugar levels were dangerously high. Dr. Plimm gave me some pills, referred me to a dietitian, and handed me a pamphlet called "Diabetes & You" with a smiling jogger on its front. "You're going to have to be much more physically active and eat better, Jean," Dr. Plimm said. "You have a family history there. I used to treat your dad, you know." (True, but my family also has a history of making babies!)

Well, Jeanketeers, I guess it's literally true that I'm a real sweetie! (Give me a call if you need some sugar for your tea—I'll send you a blood transfusion!) You see, even though this diabetes thing means a lot of big changes in my life, I'm trying to have a sense of humor about it. But I wish hubby Rick would see things my way! He constantly badgers me to take my pills, and when he sees me sitting on the sofa watching television, he tells me to get up and move around "so you don't lose a leg!"

Sheesh! He has me so on edge lately that I wouldn't mind leaving for a walk! Trouble is, the only good place to walk and not get hit by a car is the mall, but I'm not sure I'll show my face there until Gymboree goes belly-up. ∅

Your Horoscope

By Lloyd Schumner Sr.
Retired Machinist and
A.A.P.B.-Certified Astrologer

Aries: (March 21–April 19)
Interior decorators claim that only about 18 inches of space is needed for people to pass between furnishings, but that was before they got a load of you.

Taurus: (April 20–May 20)
The stars do indeed hold the wisdom of the cosmos and the secrets of creation, but few realize that they also hold the hottest after-parties.

Gemini: (May 21–June 21)
The more you think about it, the more you like the idea of having 12 young men dance around you at all times—as long as it's tastefully done.

Cancer: (June 22–July 22)
Your emotional stasis, lack of imagination, and inability to tell right from wrong will continue to be valuable assets in the world of high finance.

Leo: (July 23–Aug. 22)
You're not sure that mandatory drug testing is constitutional, but, that said, you're willing to give them a try.

Virgo: (Aug. 23–Sept. 22)
Professional athletes often help out in their communities, but you've been a problem in your community for years, and not one athlete has done crap for you.

Libra: (Sept. 23–Oct. 23)
You'll disprove the old chestnut about nice guys finishing last by losing consistently while being a gigantic prick.

Scorpio: (Oct. 24–Nov. 21)
It's hard to tell someone who's always been there for you that you're no longer in love with him, but that's why you'll hire a publicist.

Sagittarius: (Nov. 22–Dec. 21)
Stop telling people you have a "unique vision for America." Many producers of big-time Hollywood musicals had the same unique vision before you did.

Capricorn: (Dec. 22–Jan. 19)
The extreme weather conditions of next week will be hard on infants, the elderly, and you, a person who displays the worst qualities of both.

Aquarius: (Jan. 20–Feb. 18)
You'll soon find love with someone whose indifference, lack of self-respect, and ability to suspend disbelief are perfect for you.

Pisces: (Feb. 19–March 20)
Your career is going so well that at this rate, there might not be any nurses left alive in six years.

Talk-Show Host Takes Brief Break From Mocking Jessica Simpson To Interview Her

see ENTERTAINMENT page 5E

Inspirational Disabled Horse Crosses Preakness Finish Line After 11 Hours

see SPORTS page 6C

Insomniac Pulls All-Dayer

see LOCAL page 15B

STATshot

A look at the numbers that shape your world.

How Are We Defending Our Egregious Use Of Pomade?

16% Have big meeting with farm credit bureau

23% Forgot to remove yesterday's pomade

25% Uncle works at pomade factory

19% With equally egregious use of logic

17% Merely applying amount recommended by American Pomade Council

THE ONION • $2.00 US • $3.00 CAN

---

the ONION®

VOLUME 40 ISSUE 20 — AMERICA'S FINEST NEWS SOURCE™ — 20–26 MAY 2004

New Prescription-Only Sandwich Extra Delicious

NEW YORK—At a press conference Monday, drug giant Pfizer formally introduced Hoagizine, a pharmaceutical-grade Turkey-Bacon-Guacamole Melt so delicious, it's only available by prescription.

"Made with lean white turkey breast, hickory-smoked bacon, zesty guacamole, Boston leaf lettuce, and ripe tomatoes on crusty French bread, Hoagizine is indicated in the treatment of lunchtime satisfaction dysfunction," said Stephen Spencer, Pfizer's head of research and product development. "But Hoagizine is only available after consultation with a physician, so be sure to ask your doctor if this new sandwich is right for you."

The extra-potent sandwich passed rigorous testing in both branches of the FDA in February. In clinical trials,

see SANDWICH page 166

Above: A pharmacist in Long Beach, CA explains the possible side effects of Hoagizine.

Above: U.S. soldiers using the government's new policy to fight terror abroad.

U.S. To Fight Terror With Terror

WASHINGTON, DC—In a response to recent acts of extreme violence against Americans in Iraq and mounting criticism of U.S. military policy at home, Defense Secretary Donald Rumsfeld announced the government's new strategy of fighting terror with terror Monday.

"Look, in order to catch a rat, you gotta think like one," Rumsfeld said in a grainy and degraded videotape message filmed at an unknown location and released to CNN Monday.

see TERROR page 167

Funeral Looks Cheap

DEARBORN, MI—Everything from the bottom-of-the-line coffin to the shabby suit worn by the deceased made the funeral of longtime assembly-line foreman Thomas Meissner, who died May 13 at the age of 68, look cheap, several guests reported Tuesday.

"There were only five tiny bouquets at the visitation," said Betty Foyer, 59, next-door neighbor to Meissner since 1978. "If you can't afford a large arrangement, you should at least select some tasteful fresh flowers, out of respect for the recently departed. I felt so bad for Tom."

The visitation was held Sunday at Wenke Funeral Home on Raymond

Above: Meissner in his second-rate casket.

Road. The funeral service took place across the street, at the Church of the Redeemer, where the Meissners have worshipped for the past 20 years.

"I thought Tom's son was a teacher in Traverse City," Foyer said. "But I guess he couldn't help out with the costs. That casket looked like it was made out of plywood with a coat of black enamel slapped on. And there's no way those bronze fittings were real."

A framed photograph of Meissner, taken during his honeymoon in the Upper Peninsula in 1960, was propped up beside the casket.

"I think it was one of those $1.99 plastic frames they sell at the Walgreens just down the street," said Alice Dade, 61, who plays bridge with Foyer every Sunday afternoon after church. "I guess it's not really a surprise that they didn't think to get a nicer frame. It was just a couple months ago that they finally got the house re-painted."

Foyer added that "at least Tom looked put together in the photo."

"At the funeral, it was a different story," she said. "Tom was dressed in some 25-year-old navy-blue suit with a stain on the left breast pocket. That stain killed me. It looked like it was

see FUNERAL page 167

Fahrenheit 9-11

Disney recently blocked Miramax from releasing Michael Moore's *Fahrenheit 9-11*, a film criticizing President Bush's handling of Sept. 11. What do *you* think?

"Disney is afraid of controversy? But they were the first ones to point out how wrong it is to be an evil witch."

Pamela Turner
Marine Engineer

"I used to be a big fan of Michael Moore, until he turned all political."

Jean Collins
Clerk

"Moore's prominent presence in the news brings to light some serious questions, such as 'Can't he at least try to look presentable?'"

Juan Sanchez
Interpreter

"So Eisner, Moore, and the Weinsteins are involved in the story of Bush and bin Laden? Is anyone decent a part of this at all?"

Walter Reed
Systems Analyst

"Disney insists that it wants to remain apolitical, but that doesn't explain its controversial 1971 cartoon, *Donald's Laos-y Cambodian Vacation*."

Sammy Campbell
Video Editor

"Why doesn't Michael Moore ever make documentaries about nice things, like where cotton candy comes from?"

Keith Scott
Statistician

Electronic Voting Machines

Computerized voting systems promise to simplify the polling process, but many Americans are worried about their accuracy. What are some of the machines' potential problems?

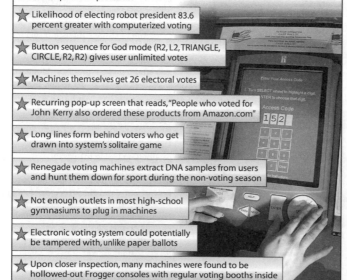

★ Likelihood of electing robot president 83.6 percent greater with computerized voting

★ Button sequence for God mode (R2, L2, TRIANGLE, CIRCLE, R2, R2) gives user unlimited votes

★ Machines themselves get 26 electoral votes

★ Recurring pop-up screen that reads, "People who voted for John Kerry also ordered these products from Amazon.com"

★ Long lines form behind voters who get drawn into system's solitaire game

★ Renegade voting machines extract DNA samples from users and hunt them down for sport during the non-voting season

★ Not enough outlets in most high-school gymnasiums to plug in machines

★ Electronic voting system could potentially be tampered with, unlike paper ballots

★ Upon closer inspection, many machines were found to be hollowed-out Frogger consoles with regular voting booths inside

the ONION ®
America's Finest News Source. ™

Herman Ulysses Zweibel
Founder

T. Herman Zweibel
Publisher Emeritus
J. Phineas Zweibel
Publisher
Maxwell Prescott Zweibel
Editor-In-Chief

When I Grow Up, I Want To Wear A Bikini At Auto Shows

By Cindy Harris

Being in fifth grade is the worst thing ever. At home, Dad is always telling me to turn the television down. Then at school, Mrs. Cobb is always yelling at me to get back to my desk, or Jeremy Linder is making fun of me because the sole is coming off my tennis shoe. Well, they're all going to be so jealous when I'm all grown-up, beautiful, and wearing a bikini while I hand out flyers at the auto show.

Everyone in my class wants to be a doctor or a lawyer or something stupid like that. That's because they're boring—or maybe because they know they wouldn't look good in a bikini. Well, I hate school, and there's no way I'm going to go to college for a million years. Ever since my mom and my mom's boyfriend took me to the Bryant County Expo Center, I've known exactly what my dream job is. I want a job where I can have fun, like the women from the Saleen auto-parts booth.

The women in bikinis were laughing and dancing, and everyone was talking to them because they were so glamorous—even people who didn't want a flyer. The woman in the pink bikini was my favorite, because her swimsuit matched her high heels. She gave me my very own Saleen Performance Parts & Accessories catalog to take home. I keep it in my backpack and pull it out during recess when no one will play with me.

When I first saw my older brother Keith's poster of the women wearing the Budweiser bikinis, I knew I wanted to do something glamorous, where there would be people whose only job was to put makeup on me and bring me different bikinis and tell me how great I look.

Why go to college when all I need to make money is a bikini? Of course, I'd want to have a whole lot of bikinis, so I could choose which one was best for the job. I'm sure Dad would get me some to start out with. He always buys me stuff, ever since he and Mom got divorced.

I'm not stupid or anything—I know I have to work my way up to beer posters. I'll probably have to start by wearing cutoffs and a halter top at the county fair and asking people to sign up to win a gas grill. But before you know it, I'll be handing out keychains in stadium parking lots. From there, the sky's the limit.

I'll always have a positive attitude. I'll have my picture taken with tons of guys, and I'll smile really big for all of them. I won't even mind if a guy rubs up against me weird, unless he makes me drop my flyers or undoes my bikini top. I'm totally going to keep in shape and learn how to walk in high heels as soon as I get boobs. And I'll talk to people and make them feel special and stuff. I just know that I can put people at ease and make them forget that they're fully dressed, and I'm in a bikini trying to get them to try Bacardi Silver.

It sucks that I have to be 18 to work in a bar. Keith once dated this girl Tammy who modeled lingerie in nightclubs. Guys were always asking her on dates and telling her how

> **Why go to college when all I need to make money is a bikini? Of course, I'd want to have a whole lot of bikinis, so I could choose which one was best for the job.**

beautiful she was. She even had to be escorted to her car every night, just like a star. I know I'll work really hard and be totally professional. I won't drop a single drink, unless someone pushes me really hard. Even if someone at a boat show grabs my butt, I'll just smile and tell him, "That's not for sale. This outboard motor is, though."

I'm going to live at the beach and take off my top when I'm tanning, like they do in magazines. I'll have a huge beach house with a big stereo and a volleyball net out back. Of course, Jeremy Linder won't be invited. If he shows up, I'll call the cops and tell them I'm a bikini promotional girl and Jeremy is a creep, and they'll put him in jail until he apologizes for putting peanut butter in my hair in the third grade.

I can't wait till I make it big. Everyone in this town will see my poster or my liquor-store standee or my power-tool calendar. Mrs. Cobb will see my picture on the cover of *Hot Rod Monthly* and think, "I was wrong to doubt that Cindy would become a bikini model." Well, I hope she doesn't expect me to visit her after I make it, because I'll be way too busy doing sports-radio promotions and handing out Alabama Slammer shooters to even remember her name. ∅

Asshole Admits To Being Asshole In Supreme Asshole Move

KANSAS CITY, MO—Senior sales representative Mark Seversen, already notorious at Aqua-Dek Water Filtration Systems for being an asshole, made the ultimate asshole move Monday when he triumphantly admitted to being an asshole.

"Look, I know you all think I'm an asshole," Seversen, 32, told a roomful of fellow employees. "Well, that may be true, but I moved more units for this company last year than any three of you combined. News flash: Nice guys finish last."

"So I'm an asshole," Seversen added. "Deal with it."

Aqua-Dek sources said Seversen has a long history of being an asshole. In five years at Aqua-Dek, he has alienated virtually all of his coworkers by blaming others for his failures and lying to secure promotions. Recently, he slept with an emotionally vulnerable, newly divorced coworker, only to complain about her "saggy ass"to the rest of the office afterward. Coworkers report that Seversen frequently brags about his car, his many beautiful ex-girlfriends, and his hair. He also frequently makes asshole-ish comments about minorities, the poor, and "fatties."

However, according to coworkers, Seversen's recent admission that he's an asshole takes him to a whole new level of assholitude.

Above: Seversen, the big asshole.

> "If doing what it takes to make more money than any of you people means I'm an asshole, then what can I say? I guess I'm a rich, successful asshole. Guilty as charged," Seversen said.

"That's a real supreme asshole move—admitting you're an asshole and not giving a shit," coworker Bob French said later that day. "He acted like outing his own assholiness somehow made it our problem, not his. What a dick."

Coworkers report that, having declared himself a supreme unrepentant asshole, Seversen gleefully explored the freedoms of his newfound role.

"If doing what it takes to make more money than any of you people means I'm an asshole, then what can I say? I guess I'm a rich, successful asshole. Guilty as charged," Seversen said. "Now, if you'll excuse me, I've got some calls to make about the houseboat I'm going to buy. Make way for

Mr. Asshole."

Seversen reportedly grabbed his briefcase and walked out, leaving his coworkers in disbelief.

"On my first day, when Mark made an elaborate show of learning my name, I could tell he was an asshole," receptionist Nina Taylor said. "But

within weeks, he moved from Asshole Who's All Proud Of Himself Because He Knows My Name to Bigtime

see ASSHOLE page 166

NEWS IN BRIEF

White House Slam Dunk Contest Results In No Slam Dunks

WASHINGTON, DC—The annual White House Slam Dunk Contest, a spring ritual since 1977, featured its usual share of cringe-worthy misses and twisted knees Monday, but once again, no slam dunks. "I tell you, this is some sorry stuff I'm seeing," celebrity judge and former San Antonio Spur George "Iceman" Gervin said, holding up a "1" card after press secretary Scott McClellan made an awkward leap in a pair of wingtips. "The three-point contest was bad enough, but this is just depressing." The last White House slam dunk on record occurred in 1983, when a blindfolded Secretary of the Interior James Watt leaped from the foul line to execute an aerial 360-spin into a tomahawk that shattered the backboard.

Pawn-Shop Customer Plans To Buy Toaster Back

CHICAGO—Drug addict Chris Fehring, 27, announced plans Monday to eventually buy back the GE toaster he'd sold an hour earlier to U-Name-It Pawn. "This is only temporary," said

Fehring, who'd already parlayed the $3 he received into a crack purchase. "I'll buy it back as soon as I have electricity again." Fehring also stated his intention to buy back the blood he's sold to the plasma center Monday.

Woman With Six Dogs Resents Non-Dogs

ALBANY, CA—Bay Area resident Emily Dobbyns, owner of two wire-haired fox terriers, two shih tzus, one Maltese, and a pug, revealed yesterday that she resents all non-canine life forms. "My family and coworkers and friends are so hard to get along with," Dobbyns said, petting her pug Skipper. "They're so opinionated, and they let their egos complicate everything." Dobbyns added that her little Skipper-doodle would never expect her to drive 22 miles to a birthday party at a restaurant she doesn't even like.

Catholic Church Condemns Metrosexuality

VATICAN CITY—Vatican spokesman Joaquin Navarro-Valls said Monday that metrosexuality, the trend of heterosexual men co-opting the aesthetics of homosexual men, is strictly prohibited under Catholic doctrine. "The

truly faithful will avoid the temptation to adopt this hip urban lifestyle," Navarro-Valls said. "The devout Catholic must remain on the path toward salvation, no matter how good he'd look in an Armani pullover, and no matter how much he might covet his neighbor's set of Williams-Sonoma lobster forks." Karl Weis, director of the New York-based activist group Freedom From Religion, responded to the ban by stating that "metrosexuality is so 2003."

Apparently Werewolf Was Allergic To Peanuts

NEW ORLEANS—The werewolf who died while attacking a young woman Sunday must have been allergic to peanuts, experts said Tuesday. "The wolfman crashed through the intended victim's front window, but before the accursed beast could tear her apart in a savage fury, he stepped in a bowl of honey-roasted peanuts," said Dr. Alex Price, professor of lycanthropic studies at Tulane University. "Within seconds, the hellbeast's face began to swell, and he collapsed into an anaphylactic attack, unable to breathe." Price said that, had the werewolf not been more animal than man at the time of the attack, he likely would have used the epinephrine injection pen paramedics found in the breast pocket of his shirt. ∅

96 percent of patients who administered the sandwich orally experienced a deliciousness they described as "heightened," "intense," or even "overwhelming." In the same trial, only 16 percent of those who received placebo sandwiches reported experiencing high levels of deliciousness.

In preparation for Monday's announcement, Pfizer produced 800,000 units of the oral sandwich and distributed them to pharmacies nationwide. Additionally, Pfizer personnel sent out samples of Hoagizine and educat-

> **"I guess I'm not the only one who finds regular sandwiches ineffective,"** said Rock Falls, ID resident Lois Baird, as she sat in her physician's waiting room. **"Frankly, I'd just about given up on bread-and-meat treatments, but if this sandwich is going to help me eat a better, tastier lunch, I want it."**

ed physicians on patient-screening procedures, treatment regimens, and serving suggestions.

"This sandwich is extremely effective in the treatment of severe acute and chronic hunger," Pfizer spokesman Abdul Johnson said. "For consumers who find that their regular sandwich is no longer effectively reducing pangs, the Turkey-Bacon-Guacamole Melt represents a good treatment option."

Johnson said Pfizer may soon offer an even more potent version of the sandwich, Hoagizine CM, which contains 10 grams of chipotle mayonnaise.

Consumer interest in the new Turkey-Bacon-Guacamole Melt is high. Physicians filled thousands of sandwich prescriptions within 24 hours after it was made available.

"I guess I'm not the only one who finds regular sandwiches ineffective," said Rock Falls, ID resident Lois Baird, as she sat in her physician's waiting room. "Frankly, I'd just about given up on bread-and-meat treatments, but if this sandwich is going to help me eat a better, tastier lunch, I want it."

Baird added: "I just hope it's okay to mix Hoagizine with the broad-spectrum soup I currently take at noon."

Although most insurance companies cover prescriptions for the Turkey-Bacon-Guacamole Melt, many physicians recommend that their patients stick to

JOHN C. SAMPSON M.D.
1622 N. JEFFERSON STREET
EASTON, KS 66020

Above: A doctor's order for the Turkey-Bacon-Guacamole Melt.

over-the-lunch-counter sandwiches.

"Hoagizine is a powerfully delicious sandwich," said Dr. Erin O'Malley, chief nutritionist at Cedars-Sinai in Los Angeles. "And there's the problem: It's overkill. Commercially available, high-quality sandwiches are delicious enough for 95 percent of the patients I see. Additionally, those patients who do actually require the extra zest and deliciousness of this medical-grade melt run the risk of becoming addicted to its scrumptious flavor. I consider the sandwich to be an emergency lunch option, for use only when everything on the menu looks so blah that it threatens to ruin your entire day."

Pfizer officials said the Turkey-Bacon-Guacamole Melt comes with some warnings, but that it poses few health risks and, for the most part, is made of all-natural ingredients. Those who are overweight, diabetic, or allergic to wheat or dairy, or have a history of heart disease are urged to seek

> **Women who are pregnant may require a second dose of Hoagizine.**

medical counseling before ordering the melt, and women who are pregnant may require a second dose of Hoagizine.

In Pfizer's lab tests, common side effects of the sandwich included a bloated or drowsy feeling, thirst, and a heightened desire for a side order of chips. If discomfort occurs, patients are urged to temporarily discontinue use of the Turkey-Bacon-Guacamole Melt and lie down on the couch.

"Side effects are certainly within the parameters established for commercially available lunch items," Spencer said. "The one thing we're concerned with is that, with regular use, the bacon and the guacamole could precipitate high cholesterol levels in some patients. But, hey, if your cholesterol does get a little high, that's why we make Lipitor." ✐

Asshole Who Has Me Phone In His Lunch Order to Seriously Major Asshole Who Propositions Me In The Parking Garage. But today in the conference room, when he told us all he's an asshole—that thing put him into the category of El Assholio Supremo del Mundo. He really outdid himself."

According to Seversen's former assistant, Janet Manning, the asshole's recent leap into the category of Supreme Asshole will probably only benefit his career.

"The more of an asshole Mark is, the more money he makes, and the more authority he's given by the head office," said Manning, who left Aqua-Dek in April to "do literally anything that will get me away from that son of a bitch.""In Mark, you see a classic example of the cycle of escalating assholedom. Instead of hiding his assholishness and putting on a good

> **"Instead of hiding his assholishness and putting on a good show, he brags about it," Manning said.**

ample of the cycle of escalating assholedom. Instead of hiding his assholishness and putting on a good show, he brags about it as if it's a virtue, because it benefits his career. But I don't believe for a minute that he's only an asshole for career advancement. For Mark, being an asshole is its own reward."

"God," Manning added. "I can't believe I slept with him."

When asked to comment on allegations that he'd made the ultimate asshole move, Seversen did not disagree.

"Hey, you're doing a story on me?" he told reporters. "Make sure you put it in huge letters on the front page: 'Mark Seversen is the world's biggest asshole, and he doesn't give a fuck whether you like it or not.' That'd be hilarious." ✐

TERROR from page 163

Above: A NYPD officer uses terror to fight terror in Times Square.

"We've been pussy-footing around the war on terrorism for years. All that time, the answer was right in front of us: In order to wipe out terror around the globe, once and for all, we've gotta beat them at their own game."

"We tried playing fair," Rumsfeld continued. "But how can you play by the rules when your opponent doesn't even know the rules? You don't bring a knife to a gunfight. That's just the way it is, folks. It's a dog-eat-dog world."

On the seven-minute tape, Rumsfeld is joined by counter-terrorist leaders Vice-President Dick Cheney and Attorney General John Ashcroft, each seated on folding chairs in front of an American flag. Ashcroft described some tactics the government currently uses—pre-dawn assaults on civilian targets and subjecting potential stateside traitors to psychological intimidation—as a "small step in the right direction."

"I can't really say what we have planned for the future," Rumsfeld said. "As terrorists, fear and uncertainty will be our best weapons. Let

> "These terrorists hate freedom," Rumsfeld said. "From now on, we're going to hate it even more."

me just say that the gloves are off. It is inevitable that indiscriminate attacks will be carried out, and innocents will lose their lives, but the end will justify the means."

Rumsfeld refused to comment on the recent abuse of military prisoners

in Iraq and Afghanistan, other than to characterize those abuses as "nothing compared to what we are capable of."

"It's vital to remember that these terrorists hate freedom," Rumsfeld said. "Well, guess what? From now on, we're going to hate it even more. Do you think terrorists care about due process and fair treatment of prisoners? Of course not. Why should we give them the upper hand? You fight fire with fire."

Cheney restated that the goal of the new policy is to put an end to terror around the world, once and for all.

"It's time to get this war over with," Cheney said. "The philosopher Eric Hoffer said, 'You can discover what your enemy fears most by observing the means he uses to frighten you.' Well, we've been observing, but finally we've started taking notes. We'll have these terrorists running scared in no time."

Cheney urged Americans to "be on alert" in upcoming months.

"Seneca once said, 'To be feared is to fear: No one has been able to strike terror into others and at the same time enjoy peace of mind,'" Cheney said. "If we want these terrorists to fear the U.S., we as a people need to be filled with fear. Expect to see more heavily armed, uniformed officers, both at home and abroad."

Elliott Abrams, Special Assistant to the President and Senior Director For Near East and North African Affairs, said that the Bush Administration acknowledged the ethical inconsistencies of its opposing-terrorism-through-terrorism stance, but doesn't really care.

"Look, any eighth-grader knows that the line between good and evil is blurry," Abrams said. "Our concern is the safety of the American people. An eye for an eye: Let's see if that plan works."

Abrams refused to provide clues

about the time and method of attack, other than to allude to an "election-year surprise."

"Just wait and you'll see," Abrams said. "Martin Luther King said, 'Returning violence for violence multiplies violence, adding deeper darkness to a night already devoid of stars.'Well, enemies of democracy and freedom around the world are going to find out just how right he was.

> "It's vital to remember that these terrorists hate freedom," Rumsfeld said. "Well, guess what? From now on, we're going to hate it even more. Do you think terrorists care about due process and fair treatment of prisoners? Of course not."

They'll see just how dark it can get."

Experts from the Mukhabarat el-Aama Egyptian intelligence service have deemed the message authentic.

"There is no doubt who the men on the tape are," spokesman Sulieman Assad said. "Cheney can clearly be recognized from previous tapes, albeit a bit aged, and John Ashcroft is wearing his iconic stern, fanatical expression. I would recommend that the Arab world raise its security alert level to 'severe,' but apparently, it has already been that way for some time." ∅

FUNERAL from page 163

salad dressing. Maybe he died in the suit, and they never bothered to take it off him to have it cleaned."

"Oh, I'm sorry I said that," Foyer added. "At least he was wearing a suit. That's more than I can say for his brothers who came to the funeral."

According to several guests at the service, the ceremony lacked the polish and care that a widow ought to provide for her dead husband.

"There was no special pastor, just our regular one," said Doris Carter, who got to know the Meissners at church events and community gatherings. "His nephew tried to sing both songs in the service, with that tinny portable stereo system as backup. I guess if you're not a trained musician, it's hard to carry a tune in front of an audience."

Pastor John Sipek presided over the ceremony. After leading a prayer and delivering a brief tribute, Sipek opened the pulpit to anyone who wanted "to say a few words" about Meissner.

"Judy got so choked up, she lost her place two or three times during her eulogy, which she read off a rumpled little piece of paper she pulled out of her pocket," Foyer said, imitating the gesture with her handkerchief. "I don't know why she didn't ask someone else to address everyone if she wasn't going to be able to. I would've been happy to do it, but she insisted she do it herself, then got up there and fell apart."

"Poor thing," Foyer added.

Although no one complained of discomfort while at the church, several women shared concern for some of the elderly guests.

"My heart went out to that poor gentleman in the pinstriped suit, forced to sit on those uncushioned pews, sweating in the sunlight," Carter said. "I guess he didn't know that, in the warmer months at the Redeemer, it's best to take one of the shady seats in back. They don't have central air."

After the service, the mourners, num-

bering fewer than 60, drove in a small caravan to the burial plot, located "right off the highway," according to Dade. Although several guests thought the interment rushed and the modest tombstone "an insult to Tom," they were most nettled by the frugality evident at the dinner following the wake.

"When I heard everyone was going to Cracker Barrel after the funeral home, I thought it was a joke," Foyer said. "I asked Judy if she really expected us to share memories at a theme restaurant, and she said 'yes.' They probably let her reserve the room for free, considering she worked there for so many years. Let's just say I'd had higher hopes for the luncheon."

The post-funeral lunch was even more modest, held in the church's basement, where guests were surprised to discover that the food was homemade.

"I don't want to insult the food at a funeral," Carter said, smacking her lips in disapproval. "But a word of ad-

vice: If you don't know your way around the kitchen, spare yourself the effort. How a woman gets to be as old as Judy without knowing how to cook a decent casserole is beyond me. The coffee was so weak, I couldn't tell if it was decaf or hot water. And not a Sweet 'N Low packet in sight."

Continued Carter: "Not that I minded drinking cold, black coffee. I just felt badly for [Tom's nephew] Robert, who had to drive all the way back to Flint with nothing but a ham sandwich on Wonder Bread in his stomach."

After extending their condolences, Foyer, Carter, and Dade confided to each other that the funeral was "tragic."

"There is no excuse for such a chintzy affair," Dade said. "Tom was sick for almost a year. Judy's had more than enough time to plan a nice funeral. I do believe she tried her best, though. Some people just don't know better. Really, what can you expect from a woman who doesn't keep her lawn mowed?" ∅

I Think I'll Head On Back To That Crime Scene

By Scott Driscoll

All in all, I'd say it was a robbery well done. It was in a secluded area behind the old B.F. Goodrich on the riverfront. The mask was concealing yet breatheable, the old man dropped like a stone, and his money clip yielded a cool 95 bucks and some food stamps. I didn't intend to kill him, but there were no apparent witnesses, so what the hey? Smooth and simple. The perfect crime. Nice work, Scotty.

Know what, though? I think I might head on back to that crime scene.

I mean, it's a beautiful day, the nicest day we've had in weeks. No sense in staying cooped up in this flophouse all day. True, I'm a wanted criminal, and the neighborhood will be crawling with cops, but it's just too nice a day to waste it inside watching golf and counting $95 in small bills over and over. I have as much right as anyone to go for a stroll along the riverfront and then climb through the patch of underbrush at the end of the bike path to emerge on River Street between the library and the State Farm Insurance office.

You know, it's possible that the old man's body hasn't even been discovered yet. I could pop over for a minute just to make sure he's still there, and if he is, give him another going-over. I bumped him off in a pretty remote area, and I went through his pockets so quickly that I might have missed something. He might have a few more bucks on him, maybe even a couple scratch tickets or a Denny's coupon or two. Haste makes waste, Scotty. Remember that the next time you mug somebody.

Oooh! Before I go, I should probably change out of this tracksuit—there's a big bloodstain on the left thigh. Didn't see it there before. Then again, it would mean changing into some clean clothes, and I gotta conserve on laundry this week for that big interview for the gig driving a truckload of Chinese illegals to Jersey. No one will notice. The worst thing anyone will think is that I peed myself.

On the way, I could stop at that little strip mall on Beerbohm and grab a magazine at B. Dalton. I think the new *Easyrider* is out. And maybe I'll stop by the Carvel and pick up a Cookie Puss. The strip mall is on that nice Officer Cordova's beat. If he's there, I'll chat him up a little and ask him if he's seen any action lately. He'll probably laugh and say,

"That's kind of personal, Scotty," and I'll correct him and say, "What I meant was, have you seen the bloody aftermath of any violent street crime recently?" Then again, if Officer Cordova isn't there at that moment, maybe I'll take advantage of that and hold up the Carvel store. I bet they have a sweet drop safe.

Now I'm thinking I really should mosey on over to that crime scene. You know, it would be pretty interesting to see how cops go about investigating a crime. I suppose that, first, they clear people from the area and secure it with that yellow tape. Then, I guess, they probably photo-

> ## No sense in staying cooped up in this flophouse all day.

graph the body and draw a big chalk outline around it. It's probably nothing I haven't already seen on *CSI* or *Law & Order*. Still, it would be something to watch all those cops putting in time-and-a-half and going through this meticulous procedural, all on account of something I did on a whim. It really makes you think. The thin blue line and everything.

You know what? I *am* gonna bop over to the crime scene. Hey, maybe I could throw the cops off the scent by telling them I saw the guy who committed the crime. I'll tell them he was about 6'1", weighed 190 pounds, had brown hair and hazel eyes, was wearing a gray tracksuit, and beat the guy to death with a truncheon he kept in his right pocket. No, wait. I'd have to change some things. I'll say this guy looked a lot like me, except he didn't have a big bloodstain on his tracksuit. Get that story straight, Scotty.

Finally, if the cops get suspicious, I'll argue that there was no reason for me to rob the guy, because he didn't have any money on him. Then I'll show them the money clip and pass it off as mine. And I'll tell them I got the stain from falling down in the meatpacking district. Then I'll offer them part of my Cookie Puss.

This is a fine idea, returning to the scene of the crime. However, I think next time I'll make sure to commit it in a prettier place, like the park. Or Florida. And I think I'll do it someplace close to where I can also pick up some foot powder and get gas. Look, there's no sense in making things any harder for myself. ∅

Your Horoscope

By Lloyd Schumner Sr.
Retired Machinist and
A.A.P.B.-Certified Astrologer

Aries: (March 21–April 19)
Your insistence that no one can possibly know how you feel right now will only point out how pathetic it is to be dumped by three bearded ladies in a row.

Taurus: (April 20–May 20)
It will be difficult to explain why you thought the guard dogs would make an exception for you.

Gemini: (May 21–June 21)
There is indeed a secret to happiness in life, but you mustn't assume that it's the kind of secret that would make you happier if you knew it.

Cancer: (June 22–July 22)
Even the people who love you most call you cold and unapproachable, but that's the price you pay for being the north face of the Eiger.

Leo: (July 23–Aug. 22)
You've never been the type of person who can be bound by society's silly rules, which is why they use all those silly ropes and chains.

Virgo: (Aug. 23–Sept. 22)
The weather will be fairly nice this Saturday, but trust us, that won't be what they'll be talking about in the news.

Libra: (Sept. 23–Oct. 23)
The black widow spider does not have the most powerful venom of any spider in the world, but it's still going to do quite a number on your legs.

Scorpio: (Oct. 24–Nov. 21)
Once again, your alma mater refuses to honor your achievements, instead toasting some guy who won something called the Pulitzer Prize.

Sagittarius: (Nov. 22–Dec. 21)
They say there's nothing new under the sun, so it'll come as no surprise when this week turns out to be exactly like the third week of July 1997.

Capricorn: (Dec. 22–Jan. 19)
You'll be ridiculed by your fellow citizens for merely standing on the street corner and shouting at the top of your lungs that the world is evil.

Aquarius: (Jan. 20–Feb. 18)
Not everyone finds the kind of love they want. Then again, so far, no one has had to settle for you, either.

Pisces: (Feb. 19–March 20)
Your confusing the Spanish words "abogado" and "bodega" will lead to your having the worst legal counsel in Mexico next week.

Club Undercover at 1216 Frontage Road is pleased to announce that Bulbera Bush is back from detox and will be in the snake pit Friday.

Per the guidelines in Seven Ways To Light Your Husband's Fire, 43-year-old housewife Sarah Manheim will strip for her spouse when the timing feels right.

Kami Evans will be appearing at The Mirage Tuesdays and Thursdays, no matter what her Jesus-freak sister has to say about it.

Trisha Jackson will be stripping at Five And Dimes all week. She is still looking for a babysitter for Wednesday and Thursday nights.

Brad Pitt Called Before Congress To Testify About Bicep Regimen

see ENTERTAINMENT page 4C

Gun Pays For Itself On First Day

see BUSINESS page 11E

Living Room Died In

see LOCAL page 15B

STATshot

A look at the numbers that shape your world.

Top Crusades

1. Rite Aid One-Day Crusa-vings Spectacular, 2001
2. Crusade To Eliminate Plaque, Midvale Elementary, 1975
3. The Holy Anti-File-Sharing-On-The-Internet Jihad, 2003
4. Third Crusade, 1189-92
5. Z107's Quittin'-Time Classics Crusade, 1988

THE ONION • $2.00 US • $3.00 CAN

the ONION®

VOLUME 40 ISSUE 21   AMERICA'S FINEST NEWS SOURCE™   27 MAY–2 JUNE 2004

Ex-Nickelodeon Stars Relate Horrors Of Green Slime Syndrome

OTTAWA—Veterans of the '80s cult classic TV show *You Can't Do That On Television* filed a $1 billion class-action lawsuit against Nickelodeon Monday, alleging that the network exposed them to a bevy of toxins which led to a chronic affliction called Green Slime Syndrome.

"The producers assured us the slime was safe, and that getting drenched with it for five or more takes wouldn't cause any lasting damage," cast member Alasdair Gillis said. "I was only 12. I didn't ask questions; I just did what the director said. Now I live with constant pain."

Gillis then pulled up his sleeves to reveal the suppurating pustules that cover his forearms and wrists.

"Most days I just sit on the couch and relive the shows," Gillis said. "It's inexcusable that the directors punished me for

see SLIME page 173

Fed-Up Cheney Enters Presidential Race Himself

Above: Cheney announces his bid for the Oval Office.

WASHINGTON, DC—As President Bush's public-approval ratings hit an all-time low, Vice-President Dick Cheney announced Monday that he has been "forced" to throw his hat into the ring for the 2004 presidential race.

"Enough is enough,'" the visibly annoyed Cheney said at a morning press conference. "George blew the whole Iraqi prison-abuse speech, and he barely did better with his Nicholas Berg reaction. Now he's below 50 percent in the polls. I'm sorry, but I can't allow him to drag me down with him in November."

"Do I have to do everything around here?" Cheney asked, pausing to gesture angrily around the White House. "I guess I do."

While Cheney has not yet chosen a running mate, he said it "certainly will not be the president."

"I ordered him not to get up there and talk about gay marriage last week, but he insisted," Cheney added.

"He said, 'This will work.' Yeah, it worked to alienate a ton of voters. I'm sorry, but he's out."

Cheney said that, while he would rather not run for president, Bush has left him little choice.

"I was perfectly happy letting George take the spotlight," Cheney said. "If things didn't look so grim, I would've continued to direct the re-election campaign from the wings. But I could see that it was time to get out—now, before the first debate."

The announcement of Cheney's bid for the presidency came as a major surprise, even to political insiders.

"It seems sudden, but it's not," he said. "I've been mulling this over ever since the last State Of The Union address, to be honest. I decided to go through with it last night, when I stopped by the president's office to discuss a speech I'd dropped off earlier that day and caught him sitting on

see CHENEY page 172

Naïve Teacher Believes In Her Students

BANGOR, ME—Bishop Kelly High School English teacher Christine Niles believes in her students' ability to grow intellectually and achieve success, the naïve 24-year-old told reporters Monday.

"Teenagers need to be engaged as equals, not talked down to," Niles said, scrubbing the words "Miss Niles is a kunt" from the surface of her desk. "A heavy-handed approach takes the joy out of learning. Some

Above: Niles and her sixth-period English class.

teachers give out detention, but I praise my students for the times they *don't* skip class, rather than dwell on the days they do."

A recent graduate of the George Washington University education program, Niles came to Bangor last August with the childlike belief that she could somehow inspire a passion for literature in her uninterested students, who see her as a pushover.

see TEACHER page 172

169

Should Rumsfeld Resign?

As the investigation into abuses at Abu Ghraib prison continues, some Americans are urging Defense Secretary Donald Rumsfeld to step down. What do *you* think?

"Donald Rumsfeld can't be held responsible for the misdeeds of every last soldier who obeys his orders."

Gary Harless
Systems Analyst

"Firing Rumsfeld is unnecessary. If we demote him to Secretary of Health and Human Services for a while, he'll fall into line."

Karen Heck
Saleswoman

"If anyone has the balls to fire Rumsfeld, I say go ahead."

Tammy Hainzlsperger
Botanist

"Making Rumsfeld resign would be wrong, what with him being pregnant and all."

Michael Paulson
Machinist

"Rumsfeld should be replaced with one of those peace-loving hackysack-kicking hippies that serve as his undersecretaries."

Joshua Anderson
Clerk

"Look, if we start by holding one member of Bush's administration responsible for his actions, where's it all gonna end?"

Richard Gehl
Trial Lawyer

Overseas Outsourcing

By the end of next year, an estimated 830,000 U.S. service jobs will have been exported overseas. Why are companies choosing to outsource?

▶ All Americans already have great jobs

▶ Employees in India and the Philippines don't demand perks like "flextime" or "sunlight"

▶ Remembered what a super job the Chinese did on the railroads

▶ Upper management would rather be spared the awkwardness of running into employees at Six Flags on weekend

▶ Following lead of Jay-Z, who outsourced his beat for "Beware Of The Boys" to Panjabi MC

▶ Good way to stack company cricket team

▶ Ironically, the best place to exploit workers is the largest communist nation on the planet

▶ Will result in cheaper products, which will increase demand, which will result in richer companies, whose wealth will be sprinkled onto unemployed U.S. workers like fairy dust

▶ Just want to help rest of world out

Ø the ONION®
America's Finest News Source.™

Herman Ulysses Zweibel
Founder

T. Herman Zweibel
Publisher Emeritus
J. Phineas Zweibel
Publisher
Maxwell Prescott Zweibel
Editor-In-Chief

You Learn Something New And Depressing Every Day

By Bill Merkert

Hey, did you know that more than 14 million African children have been orphaned because of AIDS? Fourteen million. That's roughly equivalent to the number of all the children under the age of 5 in America. Holy Schmidt, right?! I had no idea this was the case until I saw a news report about the African AIDS epidemic last night. I guess it just goes to show you: No matter how much you think you know, there are always more bleak facts out there, waiting for you to discover them!

You could live to be 100, and you would never stop learning terrible things. All you have to do is pay attention, and you'll be surprised by another tragic reality. Yesterday, I read on the Internet that 3,000 people die from malaria every day. Fancy that. Three thousand people die, day in and day

> Never assume that you know it all, because there's a literally endless stream of monumentally sad things to discover. We haven't even talked about all the people who have, just today, been mugged or beaten or hit by cars or had their arms torn off or their kids die.

out, from a disease we have a cure for. Boy, I tell you it's true: You learn something new and depressing every day.

You don't even have to look as far as Africa for fresh disheartening information. There's an endless supply of horrifying things you can discover in your own backyard. Try this on for size: For the past couple of years, I've seen this homeless guy sleeping on the street grate right by my office. I used to toss him some change now and again. Well, last month, it hit me that I hadn't seen him around for a while, so I asked a police officer about him. Turns out the poor sucker died of hypothermia during the winter. Right there on the grate! He was younger than I am, and now he's dead. Who'da thunk?

I had my 60th birthday over the weekend, and I feel like I still don't know one-thousandth of the horrifying things there are to know. There are countless novel ways for the

> You could live to be 100, and you would never stop learning terrible things.

world to crush a spirit, an ideal, or a limb. Just open your ears and listen to the people around you. I'm positive you'll come into contact with some fresh instance of human sorrow. Throughout the world, there's an unyielding, pervasive desperation. If only you'd take a minute, you'd see it.

While we learn a lot from our friends and the world around us, our families often have the most to teach us. Just recently, my aunt told me how incredibly lonely my mother was in the months before she died. My sister and I were both in college, caught up in our own lives at the time. We never knew that Mom would sit in her empty house, watch daytime television, and weep because she missed my father so much. That little nugget of info was a real head-slapper! Live and learn, as they say—another day, another glimpse into the void that is human existence.

After living for more than a half-century, you'd think I'd know all the disheartening information there is to know. Far from it! I read in the paper that roughly one in three women have been raped or violently sexually assaulted. I couldn't believe it, so I did an informal survey of the women I work with. Sure enough! Turns out that statistic was just about right! Never assume that you know it all, because there's a literally endless stream of monumentally sad things to discover. We haven't even talked about all the people who have, just today, been mugged or beaten or hit by cars or had their arms torn off or their kids die. Gosh, it's a big old world!

After six decades of walking this earth, I'm pleasantly surprised that I can still be shocked by all the different little strands that make up the tapestry of human sorrow. The more dreadful things I come to terms with, the more troubling things I discover to take their place. I just heard that one of my former coworkers killed herself last month! Apparently, you can off yourself by drinking Pine-Sol. You see, I didn't know that. But now I do. And now you do, too, I suppose. Hopelessness springs eternal! Ø

U.S. Gives Up Trying To Impress England

CHICAGO—Americans across the nation declared Tuesday that, after 230 years of trying to prove to England that the U.S. is a worthwhile and relevant country deserving of the European nation's respect, they are officially giving up.

"When America was only a couple of decades old, and England had been around for centuries, it was understandable that they looked down on us," said Rosie Hendricks, a mother of two from Arlington Heights. "But now, we've both been around for centuries. We're *both* international leaders. It's way past time England started treating us a little better."

"Yes, their royal family is cool, and yes, they have The Beatles and Shakespeare, but—well, they don't have to act so high and mighty," Hendricks said. "Every time they talk, it's like they think they're better than us. Do they think we don't notice that look on their faces?"

According to surveys, Americans are not looking for special treatment from the British, only a little bit of acknowledgement once in a while.

"All we want is one little nod of affirmation, a pat on the back, a 'good job' for some of the things we've done as a country," said Matthew Prousalis, a customer-service agent for AT&T Wireless in Peoria. "Really, all it would take is a quick 'Thanks for inventing the first successful gas-powered automobile. Keep it up.' That's it. But no, nothing."

"I've admired the British ever since I saw them on PBS as a kid," Prousalis added, blushing slightly. "Do they have any idea how bad they make us feel when they disregard us like this?"

Nicole Arndt, a computer-system sales representative from Chicago, expressed her frustration with England's dismissal of America's artistic endeavors.

"The British are always acting like we're so base," Arndt said. "Well, maybe we do go in for violence and sex a bit more than some other countries, but all around the world there are people who really love our movies and music. Just because we do things a little differently, that doesn't mean it's wrong."

Added Arndt: "In fact, I'd be willing to wager that, if we chose our five best movies from the past year and Great Britain chose theirs, and we asked an impartial country—let's say, Peru—they'd like our movies better. That'd knock England off her high horse."

Josh Feldman, an insurance claims adjuster in Union City, CA, said England assumes America is stupid.

"We have playwrights here doing some really advanced work," Feldman said. "Tony Kushner is giving it his all and writing what I hear are some very good plays. Not that England would ever notice."

Despite the two countries' decades of close political and economic alliances, many Americans said their counterparts in England should learn to appreciate what we do.

"We've cured lotsa diseases and invented a bunch of vital technologies," said Eric Pucci of Gruene, TX. "And I hate to bring this up, because they'll just call me a warmongering meathead or something, but we're breaking our backs to bring democracy to the whole damn world. England fights side-by-side with us, and yet they still treat us like they're deigning to form an alliance with us. Ask the rest of the world; you'll find a whole lot of nations who would want to be our friends. No, not everyone. But a

see ENGLAND page 172

Above: Queen Elizabeth II is just one of the many British residents Americans will no longer try to please.

Bush Posts Classified Ad For 90,000 Troops

WASHINGTON, DC—In an effort to relieve the burden on his overextended armed forces in Iraq, President Bush placed a four-line classified ad in the Monday edition of 75 U.S. newspapers. "WANTED: motivated, dedicated, obedient people looking for career in growing field of nation liberation," the ad read. "90,000 jobs avail. F/T days, nights, weekends. No exp. necessary. Will train. Arabic a plus. Starter pay, solid bnfts." To further boost military enlistment rates, Bush plans to post the job offer at employment offices in 300 cities across the country.

No-Makeup Look Easier To Achieve Than *Elle* Claims

NEW YORK—Contrary to claims in the June issue of *Elle* magazine, the no-makeup look actually requires little effort, a licensed cosmetologist reported Monday. "The article '20 Minutes To A More Natural You' suggests an application of under-eye concealer, light powder, natural lip gloss, and clear mascara to achieve the makeup-free look," said Michelle Karns-Daley, spokeswoman for the American Association of Cosmetology. "But really, a quick shower and a towel-off will do the trick just as well." Similarly, experts say *Elle*'s six-page article "Building Your Self-Esteem" can be more simply stated as "Stop giving a shit about what people think."

Great-Grandmother Actually Not That Great

DAVIS, CA—Following a family get-together Sunday, 7-year-old Tom Morris reported that he didn't really see what was so great about his great-grandmother Sarah Lott. "Grandma Lott is okay, I guess, but she sorta just sat there with this dazed look on her face until Aunt Debbie gave her a chocolate-covered cherry," Morris said. "All-right Grandma Lott, maybe. But 'great'?" Morris conceded that there might be a side to the wheelchair-bound 87-year-old he hasn't seen.

Bus Passenger Really Getting Into Stranger's Nursing Textbook

SAN FRANCISCO—Public-bus passenger Kyle Renner is seriously getting into a nearby stranger's nursing textbook, downtown-bound sources reported Monday. "An Unna's boot can be used to treat uninfected, non-necrotic leg and foot ulcers," read page 182 of the textbook propped up on the lap of the woman seated to Renner's right. "Alternatively, a preparation known as Unna's paste (zinc oxide, calamine lotion, and glycerin) may be applied to the ulcer and covered with lightweight gauze." According to Renner, page 182 features a photo of a hand placing a small boot on a smiling elderly woman that was "pretty funny."

Awkward Encounter Not Awkward At All When Masturbated About

OLYMPIA, WA—An uncomfortable exchange between Brad Leydner, 25, and Ginny, the cute redheaded waitress at Hugo's Bistro, lost all awkwardness when envisioned in Leydner's masturbation fantasy later that afternoon. "So, would you like to grab a coffee after your shift?" a nervous Leydner asked Ginny in both the real and imagined scenarios Monday. "Oh, Brad, I can't wait four hours to see you. You should fuck me hard, right in this booth," replied the Dream Ginny moments before Leydner achieved orgasm. In the fantasy scenario, Ginny did not hide in the kitchen to avoid speaking to Leydner while he paid for his meal. Ø

the couch, watching Fox News and eating Fritos. He hadn't even picked the damn thing up. I exploded. I said, 'That's it. Next year, I'm running this country myself.'"

Some have called Cheney the most active vice-president in the history of the executive branch. Cheney characterized this view of his term as the "understatement of the year."

"Every damn thing he did right since 2000 I told him to do," Cheney said. "You think Afghanistan was his idea? The tax cuts? The Medicare bill? No, no, and no. But all my years of hard work go right down the drain when he stands up in front of everyone and mispronounces [Italian prime minister] Silvio Berlusconi's name."

According to the vice-president, the Cheney Administration would be much more streamlined and efficient than Bush's administration has been.

"Let me tell you this: It'd be a lot easier just to give a speech myself and do it right, rather than spending six hours trying to explain everything to the president—only to have him botch it anyway," Cheney said. "That 'I don't know what you're saying and I don't care' look in his eyes when I start talking policy drives me absolutely bonkers. And he wonders why the reporters are so hard on him."

Continued Cheney: "I spent days, literally days, talking him through the jobs-and-growth plan. But when he had to explain it on his own, he said, and this is a direct quote, 'I'd rather that, in order to get out of this recession, that the people be spending their money, not the government trying to figure out how to spend the people's

Above: Bush appearing in public holding a chainsaw will no longer affect Cheney's chances in November.

money.'"

Disgusted, the vice-president threw his hands in the air.

"I don't have enough time in my day to spend half of it cleaning up George's mistakes," Cheney said. "I'd rather be preparing strategy for the next couple of wars. Those things don't just plan themselves."

Few White House officials question Cheney's intelligence, experience, or political effectiveness.

"Cheney's definitely got the chops for the job," House Speaker Dennis Hastert said. "Frankly, he's been very patient with the president. He's given

"One thing is clear: There is no reason for Dick Cheney to leave the White House come January," Bush campaign advisor Karen Hughes said. "He's been doing a great job."

him every chance to get his act together, but you can't keep your money on a losing horse."

Cheney's office has been busy preparing the necessary paperwork to run against Bush. However, he has not yet removed himself from the president's re-election ticket. Some say Bush campaign officials are trying to convince Cheney to remain on the Bush ticket, even if he runs against him.

"One thing is clear: There is no reason for Dick Cheney to leave the White House come January," Bush campaign advisor Karen Hughes said. "He's been doing a great job."

When pressed to name a possible running mate, Cheney was somewhat reserved.

"I don't want to tip my hand," Cheney said. "But right now I'm taking a good long look at the governor of Florida. He seems like he'd be a little easier to handle." ⌀

lot of countries."

Alex Soellner, a Newport Beach, CA computer consultant, described his mood as one "more of resignation than exasperation."

"We tried so hard to catch your eye with our advances in Internet development, our soccer team, and our modern dance," Soellner said. "But you guys just keep acting like we're not a civilized country because we drink coffee instead of tea and our cops carry guns. That really stings."

Added Soellner: "Just because we don't have a cool accent, it doesn't mean we don't have any culture."

Many Americans expressed great relief at the declaration, saying it freed them from their personal strug-

Soellner described his mood as one "more of resignation than exasperation."

gles to defend America's legitimacy.

"I can focus on doing my own thing now, and I can finally stop worrying about whether or not the British are going to like my work," said Gary Sherwin, a post-doctoral bioinformatics researcher at Stanford. "From now on, I'm working for me and my colleagues, and if England doesn't like it, it's their loss. Of course, it'd be nice if, when they see what I'm doing, they're impressed, but I'm not holding my breath anymore." ⌀

"The standard curriculum—Melville, Hemingway, Steinbeck—focuses so heavily on the works of dead white men," Niles said. "Who can relate to that? The tides of multiculturalism have reached every corner of America. Get real! These kids know Tupac, not Tennyson. I need to speak their language to get them interested in learning."

It was her interest in engaging the students in something from their world that led Niles to invite them to interpret contemporary music lyrics as poetry Monday. The class spent the period listening to songs like "Freak Me Slow" by Kelis and "Just Don't Give A Fuck" by Eminem.

"Yes, some of the songs they played had adult themes, but Shakespeare is filled with sex and violence, too," Niles said. "I do wish they had put more thought into the follow-up exercise, though. Only two students handed in their essays."

Niles' students rarely complete their assignments. They also throw things, talk back, and take cell-phone calls during class. Three fights have broken out in her classroom since the beginning of the year, and students have threatened Niles with physical harm multiple times and twice stolen money from her purse.

"Overall, the poetry exercise was a success," Niles said. "We had a particularly rousing discussion about which words in the songs might have a negative impact. The students really seemed

It was her interest in engaging the students in something from their world that led Niles to invite them to interpret contemporary music lyrics as poetry Monday.

to enjoy making that list on the board. I think it did a lot to help them understand that dialogue needs to be conducted in a way that doesn't degrade."

Niles said she had planned to listen to only two songs Monday, but the students were "so participatory" that she adjusted her lesson plan accordingly when they insisted on listening

to more.

"It's important to be flexible in the classroom," Niles said. "When I first came here, I gave a lot of writing assignments, but I quickly found out that these kids are much better at communicating verbally. They also don't like tests. I can understand, because tests really do put them into adversarial relationships with their peers."

Niles regularly gives Cs and Ds instead of Fs, because "grades should encourage students to try harder, not discourage them."

"These kids have a lot more on their minds than what's written in books," Niles said. "When they read the newspaper every morning, they see wars, violence, and hardship. With all that pressure, it's understandable that they can't focus their attention on *The Scarlet Letter*."

Although a handful of dedicated, honor-roll students participate in Niles' class, even they are occasionally indifferent or disruptive.

"When I was their age, I wanted to rebel, too," Niles said. "I preferred watching MTV and going to the mall to doing my homework. Then I read *To The Lighthouse*, and I was captivated by the way every word was just so. I'll bet that if I add that book to the

lesson plan next year, I can fire them up about reading."

Niles' coworkers have observed her efforts with a mixture of sympathy and amusement, waiting for the inevitable moment when her spark is extinguished.

"I remember when I started here," said Jim Hawes, who has taught math at Bishop Kelly for 11 years. "I thought I could get the kids to appreciate the

"These kids have a lot more on their minds than what's written in books," Niles said.

symmetry of math and the intrinsic beauty of a balanced equation. That got beaten out of me midway through my second year, when my car was keyed, my house was TP'ed, I got 12 magazine subscriptions I never ordered, and someone phoned me at 1:30 in the morning. and called me a faggot. Now, I'm just happy if they can parrot back the quadratic formula and don't put soap in my coffee." ⌀

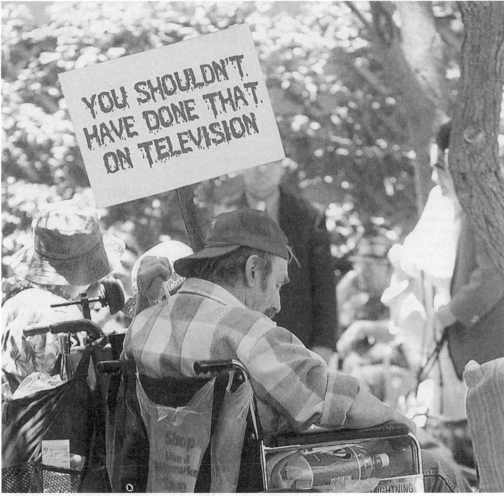

Above: A Green Slime Syndrome sufferer protests outside of Nickelodeon's New York headquarters.

having the courage to say 'I don't know.'"

You Can't Do That On Television, a Canadian children's sketch-comedy show, aired on Nickelodeon from 1979 to 1990, with a cast largely made up of local amateur child actors. Many sketches were punctuated with physical humor, with the actors frequently doused in slime, water, or foodstuffs.

Since *YCDTOTV* ended production, as many as 50 cast members have complained of a host of symptoms, including chronic pain and fatigue, numbness in the extremities, skin rashes, headache, nausea, and depression.

Gillis said he personally was doused with four different colors of slime, as well as spaghetti sauce, ink, mud, motor oil, soup, and silly string—all within the span of one season.

"If you tell people you have GSS, they act like you're just a coddled child actor," Gillis added. "'Part of the harsh reality of show-biz,' they say. But they don't know what it was like, man. Now, 20 years later, I still wince every time I hear someone say 'water.' I still request Evian in restaurants. I can't even be in the same room as a cream pie."

Gillis said cast members didn't file the lawsuit sooner because it took

years for their doctors to make the connection between the mysterious ailments and the slime to which victims were exposed during the show.

"I left the show in 1986, and about a year later, I got a rash all over my face that just wouldn't go away,"Gillis said. "Then I started having debilitating

Gillis said he personally was doused with four different colors of slime, as well as spaghetti sauce, ink, mud, motor oil, soup, and silly string—all within the span of one season.

migraines and shooting pains in my back. It was when my fingers went numb that I knew something had to be wrong. I bounced from doctor to doctor, until a physician in Beverly Hills sat me down and asked me if I'd ever been exposed to comic props. Finally, I knew it wasn't all in my head.

I knew it was the slime."

Cast member Marjorie Silcoff said she silently suffered a multitude of painful symptoms for years, until she attended a 1999 *YCDTOTV* reunion and discovered that many of her co-stars were suffering from similar unexplained ailments.

"When Les Lye [who played popular characters Barth, Ross, Senator Prevort, and El Capitano on the show] walked in with the left side of his face paralyzed, I started crying," Silcoff said. "I had a flashback to Barth standing there in the order window beneath the fly paper, holding up his spatula, getting slimed. It was so tragic. He never even had a chance to say his line, "That's what's *in* the burgers.'"

Continued Silcoff: "We all just stood on the mark like we were told. Christ, when you think about all the things that we were exposed to— mustard, milk, Jell-O, grape soda— it's incredible that we survived at all."

According to Silcoff, Nickelodeon lawyers continue to claim that GSS is just a stress-related ailment or a form of psychological hysteria.

"They tell our doctors, 'Don't encourage them,'" Silcoff said. "Some of us gave it our all for 11 years, but that doesn't mean a thing to them. They

wish we'd just disappear."

Christine "Moose" McGlade, who hosted the show from the first season until 1986, said the cast members' inexperience made them willing to expose themselves to danger.

"We were all so young and gung-ho," McGlade said. "We thought we'd better do our job if we didn't want the

Despite Nickelodeon's denial of wrongdoing, the cast members plan to press on with the lawsuit, pursuing compensation for years of pain and suffering, as well as public acknowledgment of the hidden dangers of sliming.

troupe as a whole to suffer. When you're on set, the cast is your family. Once you've been in a food fight with someone, there's a bond that can never really be broken. It's hard for non-actors to understand what it's like under the hot lights of the studio."

Nickelodeon's official position on GSS, released in a statement Monday, is that there is "no scientific evidence of a unique pattern of illness that can be causally linked to television service at Nickelodeon."

"Nickelodeon would never under any circumstances endanger any of its actors, particularly children," the statement read. "The slime was thoroughly tested and deemed safe. While our sympathies are with the ill actors, Nickelodeon is not responsible for their ailments."

Despite Nickelodeon's denial of wrongdoing, the cast members plan to press on with the lawsuit, pursuing compensation for years of pain and suffering, as well as public acknowledgment of the hidden dangers of sliming.

"Nick is still sliming kids on *Slime-time Live*—and not just paid actors, either," Gillis said. "These are regular kids from the audience who are willing to place themselves in the path of danger for the promise of winning a Game Boy or a box of Hubba Bubba Bubble Tape. Nick even sells the slime commercially, which, frankly, keeps me up at night."

Continued Gillis: "We're still imploring [former *YCDTOTV* cast member] Alanis Morissette to come forward. Her support would do a lot to raise awareness of GSS. But would it be enough to erase the suspicion, resistance, and bitterness that has enveloped discussion of this syndrome from the start? I don't know." ∅

Sob Sistah

Interoffice Memorandum
To: Midstate Staff
From: Herbert Kornfeld
Accountz Reeceevable Supervisa
May 26, 2004

By Herbert Kornfeld
Accounts Receivable
Supervisor

Ay yo:

Stop aksin' me about mah long-lost sistah. Y'all know what I'm sayin', muhfuck-az. Didn't I say in mah last newz-paypa column, don't fukkin' aks me about mah sistah? Sheeit.

Ever since I got our wack client SPJ Communications 2 settle up they Midstate debt by fuckin' whuppin' them ninja Blueshirt muhfuckaz it hire as muscle (peep "Enter Tha Office," January 2004), y'all all be wonderin' what that unseen mysterioso jackass meant when he said mah stone-col' skeelz bustin' tha Office-Fu moves didn't mean shit when it come 2 savin' mah sistah back in tha day. Shit, y'all, I restored tha Midstate honor an' got our $94.71 in tha process. That mo' important foe yo' purposes. If it weren't foe me an' mah superstar collectin' skeelz, Midstate'd hardly show a profit. So fuckin' show some luv. Feel me?

I tends 2 mah own bidness an' don't aks all y'all 'bout yo' own. Tha H-Dog ain't no muhfuckin' gossip. Hell, I don't givva rat's ass about what y'all do afta-hourz. I don't care if y'all gots three dicks. I only innerested in two things: What can y'all do foe Midstate, an' do y'all throw in foe tha coffee fund. Otherwise, stay outta mah grill.

This memo be addressed 2 all tha Midstate peeps, but I gots two of y'all in mah crosshairz 'specially: Dave Adenauer in Shippin' an', ain't no surprise here, that crazy bitch Judy Metzger in Accountz Payabo. Both have long tested tha H-Kool, but I almos' had 2 take these foolz out. I swear, but foe tha grace-a God go those pitiful morons.

G's: Day afta I tells the world 'bout mah run-in at SPJ, I'm walkin' 'cross tha office when that wack Dave call out mah name. I whirls around an' assume tha White Collar Warrior stance. I wuz in a lotta hurt from messin' wit' them sinistah Blueshirtz, but I could still snap into battle mode inna split-second. Murdah so thick in tha air you could taste it, but it obvious tha fool foegot his spoon.

"Hey, Herbert," Dave said. "So, what happened to your sister?"

Only tha wizdom o' mah mentor, CPA-ONE (R.I.P., bro) stop me from makin' his dome x-plode wit' a single look. "Dog, sometimez it seemz tha smallest men throw up the biggest obstacles," he once say. "Remembah, they too small 2 mean nothin' real 'bout it."

Mah rage became pity. "I dunno, ya pitiful muhfuckah," I said. "Ya po' pitiful bastard. Y'all so dumb y'all must think Daylite Savin' Time be time-travelin.'"

I thought mah movin' dizplay a' sympathy would defuse the fool, but he only persisted. He aksed me if mah sistah mah twin, if she evil, an' could I teach him tha Office-Fu. So's, I aksed CPA-ONE 2 foegive me an' hurled tha muhfuckah 'cross tha Shippin' An' Reeceevin' department. But he only landed on a huge-ass pile o' Fill Air™ Inflatable Packaging.

Next day, I'm krunchin' tha steady numbahs in mah cubicle when I heard this kinda rustlin' paypa noise behind me. It weren't no spreadsheetz, tho; it wuz Judy Metzger's dry, orange, big-hair perm brushin' 'gainst her blaza.

> ## Tha H-Dog ain't no muhfuckin' gossip. Hell, I don't givva rat's ass about what y'all do afta-hourz. I don't care if y'all gots three dicks. I only innerested in two things: What can y'all do foe Midstate, an' do y'all throw in foe tha coffee fund.

Befoe I could tell her 2 get tha hell out, bitch be layin' a plate o' lemon barz on mah deks.

"Herbert, Dave told me about how you broke down after he asked you about your sister," she said. "I just want to let you know that any time you want to talk, I'm here for you."

Then she started in on some crazy-ass bullshit 'bout how she wuz like mah sistah 'cause she run away from home when she 15 'cause her mama's man touched her funny, an' how she wuz in some God cult out in Utah run by this ol' perv, an' she got touched funny some mo', an' how she wuz a big crackhead, an' somethin' 'bout hitchhikin', then she think God be tellin' her 2 get her shit togethah, then, I dunno, Gerald Luckenbill found her in a basket at Midstate's front do'. Meanwhile, mah Executive Stress Ball's fuckin' unusable now, 'cause all the gel squirted outta it unda mah unforgivin' killah grip.

So, Judy aksed if all her touchy-feely bullshit make me feel bettah, an' I said

Your Horoscope

By Lloyd Schumner Sr.
Retired Machinist and
A.A.P.B.-Certified Astrologer

Aries: (March 21–April 19)
Friends will marvel at your transformation from a dumpy stay-at-home into the Italian Baroque-style Saengre Theater, New Orleans' premier venue for classical concerts and Broadway musicals.

Taurus: (April 20–May 20)
You're growing tired of the same routine week in and week out, but, hey, that's a three- to nine-year counterfeiting sentence for you.

Gemini: (May 21–June 21)
You'll be awakened Wednesday by jackhammer-like pains in your skull, which will turn out to be a singularly apt simile.

Cancer: (June 22–July 22)
When your worst enemy meets her demise under the wheels of a cement truck, you'll be happy you made the effort of enlisting 16 people to help get it into her bedroom.

Leo: (July 23–Aug. 22)
It turns out that "different" may be followed by "than" as long as the word introduces a clause, but that doesn't mean you have to like it.

Virgo: (Aug. 23–Sept. 22)
The discovery of long-lost aviatrix Amelia Earhart will leave you with a hell of a lot of explaining to do.

Libra: (Sept. 23–Oct. 23)
You're honestly trying to rid yourself of preconceived ideas, but it seems to be slowing down your day-to-day life.

Scorpio: (Oct. 24–Nov. 21)
Sometimes it feels like true happiness slipped past you in an instant. In reality, it crept by slowly, taking extreme care not to be seen.

Sagittarius: (Nov. 22–Dec. 21)
You should explore new conversational tactics. Trapping people in a pincer formation of battle tanks is proving socially awkward.

Capricorn: (Dec. 22–Jan. 19)
You won't be acting especially smug when it happens, but a 100-mile-per-hour sandstorm will still wipe that smile right off your face.

Aquarius: (Jan. 20–Feb. 18)
It will be difficult to persuade people to listen to your arguments, but you're profoundly certain that there are things a Klingon commander would simply never say.

Pisces: (Feb. 19–March 20)
There's an adage that says it's better to be a live jackal than a dead lion, but it still comes as a surprise that those are your only choices.

what you foeget is that I'm a straight-up, funky-fresh P.I.M.P. an' she nuthin' but a orangutan-hair ho, an' she could stop sniffin' 'round mah Dockahs, 'cause she wuzn't gettin' none, an' that she owed me a new Executive Stress Ball. "Bitch," I said, "flag yo' bony ass back 2 Payabo." Then I dumped her barz in tha garbitch. She run out all boo-hoo-hooin', but that's what y'all gots 2 do sumtimes, hand out tha tuff luv. Well, jus' tuff in this case, but I didn't kick her 2 tha curb like I did wit' Dave. CPA-ONE (R.I.P.) woulda been mad proud.

Look, I only gonna say this once, so heads up: I hadda sistah once, but I ain't seen her since she wuz 5. Some say she wuz hijacked by tha Hong Kong mafia, some say some freaky alien Muthaship suctioned her outta tha backyard, an' some say she wuz a casualty of a custody battle between mah mama an' mah daddy. I don't remember much 'bout her, 'cause I be only a shortie when she disappear, but I recalls she wuzn't too down wit' tha Accountin'. When I was rockin' tha Li'l Professor, she wuz off mar-

ryin' her Barbie doll 2 her Care Bear. Kinda wack if y'all aks me. But I still gots mad luv foe her 2 this day, an' I hope she alive an' well, maybe managin' her own office somewheres, an' chillin' wit' her own adjustable, natural-light desk lamp, an' hopefully reimbursed foe it, if it hadda be ordered special.

Peep this, y'all: When all y'all mournin' a loss o' some sort, I don't go layin' down a card on yo' deks that say "Thinking About You" or sending y'all a "Pick-Me-Up" bouquet. Respect me like I respects you. 'Cause I knows a lotta y'all gots tha secret mad hate foe that touchy-feely shit, too. A lotta y'all won't admit it, but in yo' time o' need, I seen y'all squirm when Bob Cowan from HR be layin' his creepy eye on all y'all, sayin' "Midstate be here fo' y'all," an' "don't hesistitate 2 aks fo' help." Ain't nobody wanna get so low that they gots 2 go 2 Bob Cowan fo' anythang. It embarrassin', G's. An' tha ones who say s'all cool be pussies or frontin'.

Peace,
H-Dog Ø

the ONION®

VOLUME 40 ISSUE 22   AMERICA'S FINEST NEWS SOURCE™   3–9 JUNE 2004

Shotgun Blast To Abdomen Just Pisses Wilfred Brimley Off More

see ENTERTAINMENT page 10E

New 40-Gigabite iHOP Breakfast Platter Holds Up To 10,000 Pancakes

see BUSINESS page 4C

All Else Fails

see LOCAL page 10B

STATshot

A look at the numbers that shape your world.

What's The Greatest Threat To Our Children?

- **12%** Juicy Juice
- **21%** Cancer of the child
- **26%** A-rabs
- **10%** Lack of adequate shade
- **11%** Trigger-happy nannies
- **20%** That truck barreling toward them

THE ONION • $2.00 US • $3.00 CAN

Heartbreaking Country Ballad Paralyzes Trucking Industry

Above: Memphis-area traffic slows to a near-standstill as WGKX plays "She's Gone Back To What She Calls Home."

NASHVILLE, TN—The interstate trucking industry, already beset with rising fuel prices and a shortage of qualified workers, was dealt another blow last month, with the release of the agonizingly sorrowful country ballad "She's Gone Back To What She Calls Home," by Cole Hardin.

"At any given time, day or night, an estimated 45 percent of the nation's over-the-road truckers are idling on the shoulder, in waysides, or in truck-stop parking lots, listening to Mr. Hardin's ballad of infidelity, loss, and heartbreak," said Russell Knutson, a spokesman for trucking giant Schneider National. "There's been an alarming number of loads that don't make it

to their destinations. And the ones that do make it are usually behind schedule, because they're being loaded, transported, and unloaded by crews brought low by the thought of a good-loving woman a man loves best packing everything up but her wedding dress and going back to the town she never should've left."

"'Scuse me a moment," Knutson said. "Sorry, but I must've gotten something in my eye just then."

Performance figures for the entire North American continent have suffered since the May 14 radio release of the "She's Gone Back" single, from the album *Fenced In Heart*. Last week, the Department of Transportation reported

see BALLAD page 179

Poll: Many Americans Still Unsure Whom To Vote Against

WASHINGTON, DC—According to Gallup Poll results released Monday, 6 percent of Americans are still undecided about whether to vote against President Bush or Democratic challenger John Kerry in November's presidential election.

"At first, I was really leaning toward voting against Kerry, because the way he tried to hide his ambivalence about his military service made him seem

like a political operator," poll participant and Trenton, NJ resident Amber Barthelme said. "But then, the Bush Administration's mishandling of the Iraqi prisoner-abuse scandal got me thinking that there's a lot to not like about the current administration. It's almost impossible to decide which side I don't want to be on."

According to the poll, 46 percent of the registered voters surveyed would vote against Bush if the election were held tomorrow, while 45 percent said they were ready to vote against Kerry. Factoring in the 2 percent margin of error, the two candidates are essentially deadlocked in the race to determine which candidate America doesn't support.

Researcher Jack Harmon, an analyst for the independent Beltway

see POLL page 178

Gay Couple Feels Pressured To Marry

DEDHAM, MA—Ever since last month, when Massachusetts became the first state to allow same-sex weddings, parents, friends, and coworkers have been pressuring Kristin Burton and her girlfriend Laura Miyatake to marry, the couple of 14 months said Monday.

"As soon as the news coverage about gay marriage

started, my mom called me up," said Burton, who works as a nursing-home administrator. "Of course, she didn't directly ask me when I was going to marry Laura. First, she asked how Laura and I were getting along, and if Laura still had a good job. But then she reminded me about my dad's heart disease and told me

see COUPLE page 178

Above: Miyatake (left) and Burton, who aren't ready to tie the knot.

Al-Qaeda Planning Attack

Last week, top U.S. officials warned that al-Qaeda plans to attack our country in the next few months. What do *you* think?

"Those terrorists don't scare me. At least not without the help of my government."

Janet Barker
Pedicurist

"Is this question about today's terror announcement, or the three last month, or the one they'll announce tomorrow?"

Jacob Shafer
Accountant

"Well, Grandpa's been complaining about his shoulder lately, and that can only mean one thing."

Marlene Porter
Real Estate Agent

"Awesome! This will save me the trouble of killing myself!"

Charles Sornsin
Cook

"So we should...?"

Juan Axelson
Barber

"I'm sorry, but if they attack us again, we're going to have to go after them this time."

Timothy Seymour
Systems Analyst

Tornado Safety

Spring is tornado season. The National Weather Service recommends taking these safety measures:

- ▶ In the event of a tornado, lie down in a ditch. If you are already lying in a ditch, do not attempt to sit up.

- ▶ The most important thing is to stay calm. This will be difficult, since you are almost certainly going to die.

- ▶ Tornadoes spook easily. Firing a few warning shots into the air is usually enough to scare them off.

- ▶ Live a little, for once: Strap yourself to the roof of your house and rage at the heavens.

- ▶ Prevent tornadoes before they happen: Make sure that warm, moist air fronts do not converge with cool, dry ones.

- ▶ During a tornado, the only safe place is in my loving arms. Come here, baby.

- ▶ If a tornado strikes your home, even your basement could be dangerous, so construct a basement for your basement.

- ▶ If you spot a tornado, always remember to point at it, yell "tornado!," and run like hell.

the ONION ®
America's Finest News Source. ™

Herman Ulysses Zweibel
Founder

T. Herman Zweibel
Publisher Emeritus
J. Phineas Zweibel
Publisher
Maxwell Prescott Zweibel
Editor-In-Chief

You Have Been Impregnated For National-Security Reasons

James Norton

Thank you for your call, Alice. I got here as quickly as I could. Have you told anyone else? Thank God. You have no idea what a relief that is—not just for me, but for America. It is of the utmost importance that we keep this strictly between us.

I know that you must be very confused, even scared. I can't blame you. These things are always difficult. I wish I could explain everything to you—the greater context and the strategy at play here—but that would be in strict violation of National Security Agency protocol. I trust that it will suffice for me to inform you that you have been impregnated for national-security reasons.

Were I at liberty to do so, I would rejoice at this news. We would call your parents and begin to plan our wedding. Unfortunately, in this era of heightened anti-American sentiment and continued terrorist threats on the homeland, that is simply impossible.

I have been instructed by my superiors to inform you that word of this news absolutely must not spread. Only four people in the country, five including you, know about your impregnation—which, I might add, was authorized by the president. In order to be able to play a role in this mission, even I had to get my security-clearance status upgraded by going through rigorous procedures. Direct executive order. Top secret.

The director of the NSA has been calling daily to check up on my progress. When I told him today that the plan was now in Phase II, he was pleased—but also quite clear in emphasizing the vital nature of complete secrecy.

Your impregnation has set off a series of events that may forever change the balance of power among international terrorist networks, rogue nations, and those who love freedom. To that end, I may have to leave soon, most likely without so much as a goodbye. There is much important work to be done. Now that a spark has been ignited, a wheel set in motion, I may very soon be placed in charge of the international coordination and oversight of this mission as it progresses.

There's no turning back, honey. Believe me, I'm dying to tell you everything, but that would put the entire mission in jeopardy. In spite of how much I want everyone to know about the miracle inside you, I cannot betray America.

If your parents ask about your growing belly, you are instructed to tell them that you are gaining weight after quitting smoking, which you should do for the sake of the child anyway. Once that explanation becomes untenable, you are to tell them that you have no idea who the child's father is. If I am called away to defend our country's safety in some other locale, you are to find some responsible, upstanding, patriotic American man to help with parenting duties.

Alice, I would love nothing more than to stay here in Muncie and help you raise the child, but this isn't my decision to make. I've got a critical assignment that might take me far away from here and might last until this kid graduates from high school. Unfortunately, the time frame for the objective remains unclear.

In 2000, or even early 2001, these measures would not have been necessary. But in a post-Sept. 11 world, pa-

> **Your impregnation has set off a series of events that may forever change the balance of power among international terrorist networks, rogue nations, and those who love freedom.**

triotism means not just respect, but obedience. It means not just service, but sacrifice. I am sorry for the hardships you will have to endure over the next 18 years, but please remember that you will be raising our child in the name of freedom and democracy. Your contribution could not be more important. If only we could discuss it publicly, you would be a national hero on par with Jessica Lynch. But we can't.

Again, let me stress that under no circumstances can we divulge any information regarding this initiative to anyone. With Iran peddling atomic secrets, North Korea threatening nuclear brinkmanship, and al-Qaeda rebuilding its worldwide strength, the U.S. cannot tolerate any intelligence breakdowns regarding your recent knocking-up. If news of your pregnancy were leaked to the Ba'athist Party in Iraq, the Taliban in Afghanistan, or your best friend Sandra, I fear you would be in grave danger.

Of course I love you. But I also love my country. And right now, my country needs me. Well, actually, I do have about an hour. ∅

Area Father Urges Reopening Of 1998 Missing-Rake Case

EDINA, MN—Local resident Marsh Lufler, 51, urged family members to re-open a long-discontinued investigation into the disappearance of a lawn rake Monday. The rake, a Lawn-Grum brand spring-braced sweep rake with steel tines and a hardwood handle, has been missing from the Lufler home since 1998.

"Although it has been six years since anyone in this family has seen that rake, I've never given up hope that someday I might find it," Lufler said. "I believe that the rake is still in our neighborhood, probably within a quarter-mile of our home."

Added Lufler: "It's a rake, dammit. It couldn't just sprout legs and walk away."

Lufler's rake was first reported missing in October 1998. A massive, four-day search of the Lufler property and intensive questioning of friends and neighbors yielded no leads. Although most of the Lufler clan long ago abandoned hope of the rake's recovery, Lufler has refused to accept the loss.

"Why would a rake just disappear?" Lufler said. "A sock, sure. But a rake is large and conspicuous, and this one hadn't been used since before the first snowfall in December of '97. How could it just vanish?"

The reopening of the rake case was prompted in part by the recent solving of another Lufler-household mystery. The good-serving-dish case, closed in late 2002 after months of fruitless investigation, was all but forgotten until last month, when friend and neighbor Mary Cobb returned a

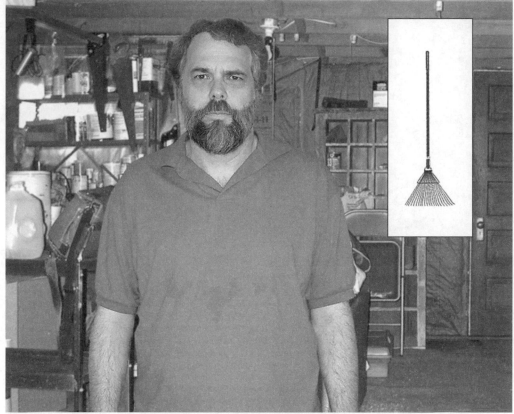

Above: Lufler and a rake (inset) of the variety that mysteriously disappeared from his garage in 1998.

porcelain tray, which she'd found while cleaning out her cupboards.

"I should definitely question everyone again," Lufler said. "All the principal suspects are still alive, and almost all of them still live in the neighborhood. Maybe enough time has passed that it will be easier for someone to admit something they didn't want to say before."

Added Lufler: "Anything could have happened in that gap between the first snow and the discovery that the rake was missing. Maybe the rake was lent out without my knowledge, or maybe someone just 'helped himself' to it. You know, I'd like to quiz that Norquist kid

see RAKE page 179

Rumsfeld Equally Proud Of All His Wars

WASHINGTON, DC—Secretary of Defense Donald Rumsfeld announced Monday that he shows no favoritism to the Iraq war and, in fact, loves all his wars equally. "Afghanistan, my first Gulf War, and all my covert operations in Central America—I may not say it often enough, but I'm as proud of them as I am of Iraqi Freedom," a beaming Rumsfeld said. "Sure, I may be giving Iraq more of my time now, but that's because it's so newly liberated. When those other wars had just started, I was just as involved with them." Rumsfeld added that he expects "a little jealousy" when mounting tensions in Syria begin to demand the Defense Department's attention.

Local Hamburger To Star In National Ad

KANKAKEE, IL—Local citizens are abuzz with the news that a local An-gus beef hamburger will be featured in a national Weber gas-grill TV commercial that begins airing Monday. "We are all just so proud," Kankakee Mayor Donald Green said of the burger, which appears seated on a seeded bun and dressed with ketchup, pickles, lettuce, and a slice of tomato. "We've had some great sandwiches in this town, but none have gotten this kind of recognition. All of us who knew the burger had a hunch it was going to go on to great things." According to Green, the burger's talent agent is currently negotiating details for the burger's inclusion in a diner scene in an upcoming Will Ferrell movie.

Area Man Accidentally Signs Up For AOL Latino

TOPEKA, KS—Jim Bauer, 34, accidentally signed up for AOL Latino, the sales clerk reported Monday. "The sign-up had all these steps, and I guess I just started clicking 'yes' and 'I agree,'" Bauer said. "Before I knew it, I was enrolled in some weird, alternate world where I couldn't read and didn't recognize any of the pop stars in the photos." Bauer, who doesn't speak Spanish, said he'll switch over to "regular AOL" soon, but for the time being, he can basically tell what "¡Tienes correo!" means.

Diabetic 8-Year-Old Throws Worst Birthday Party Ever

CARRIZOZO, NM—The 8th birthday party for diabetes-afflicted Jason Keoner was allegedly "the worst ever," partygoers reported Monday. "The only treats we got were Fresca, Go Lightly sugar-free hard candy, and a carob-chip birthday cake," 7-year-old Kim Gavin said. "When we broke the piñata open, a bunch of dried cranberries fell out." Partygoers were allegedly traumatized when the magician's performance was interrupted so Keoner could receive his insulin shot.

City Maoist Visits Country Maoist

WUHAN, CHINA—City Maoist Xing Zhen Shengde returned Monday from a visit to Dunyang, where his country Maoist cousin Ni Yuxian resides. "The great Chairman Mao said we would build a socialist society based on agriculture and peasant farming, and that the peasant had the strength of the mountain and the wind in the trees," the urbane Marxist-Leninist reported Tuesday. "Nevertheless, I did not enjoy eating the rotting pig heads that pass for food in that hell-on-earth. Also, all of the peasants wore sandals." Ni said he understands that sturdy shoes must indeed be needed for escaping the muggers and prostitutes on every street corner in Wuhan. ∅

Above: Many voters are still deciding whether Kerry or Bush would be worse as president.

think tank the Dewey-Markham Institute, said these undecided Americans will be crucial in deciding the next election.

"As the messy occupation of Iraq drags on, Bush's approval rating continues to drop, strengthening the position of the anti-Bush voting bloc," Harmon said. "This trend is offset by the Bush camp's $80 million anti-Kerry ad campaign, which has cemented anti-Kerry sentiment in several key swing states. As the election approaches, it's becoming more and more difficult to determine the likely loser."

Harmon said voters are conflicted, wanting to cast environmental and antiwar votes against Bush, but wishing also to oppose Kerry's position on taxation.

"The two major parties face a tough struggle," Harmon said. "As the election approaches, both must convince undecided voters that the opposing party's candidate is worse than their own. As both parties take more moderate positions in an election year, it's getting harder to convince citizens that there's a reason to get out there and vote against *anyone*."

Brad Thomas, a Louisiana machinist, is one of many Americans who have yet to decide whom they'll vote against.

"I'd like to say I'm against Bush because he lied about weapons of mass destruction," Thomas said. "On the other hand, Kerry's lack of substantive positions really disgusts me, as well."

Tina Schalek, a Branson, MO theater manager, said she is also undecided.

"John Kerry's only virtue is that he hasn't been in a position to make any major mistakes," Schalek said. "On the other hand, I hate Bush's views on abortion. My only consolation is that a vote against either candidate is a vote against Nader."

In spite of such ambivalence among swing voters, surveys reveal that the

majority of Americans have determined which candidate they will vote against.

"It's time to trim the Bush from the White House," Akron, OH resident Doug Hamm said. "In 2004, it's time for Bush to get bushwhacked!"

Pressed to elaborate on his views, Hamm said, "To be honest, Kerry could be a guy with a paper bag over his head, for all I care. I'd vote for anybody as long as he wasn't Bush."

> ## "The two major parties face a tough struggle," Harmon said. "As the election approaches, both must convince undecided voters that the opposing party's candidate is worse than their own."

Karla Barr of Chicago had similarly strong opinions about Kerry.

"Kerry is a wishy-washy flip-flopper, changing his tune every time the wind blows," Barr said, repeating a phrase she'd heard on *The Rush Limbaugh Show*. "Can I trust a man who can't make up his mind about Communism? I don't think so."

Added Barr: "We have to remember how close the 2000 election was, when we voted against Gore. Actually, to be fair, when I voted against Gore, I was voting against Clinton." Ø

that he could go at any time. When she started to talk about how nice it was at my brother's wedding, I told her I was late for my yoga class."

Burton and Miyatake said they never expected the court's decision to add so much tension to their relationship.

"It seems like just yesterday I was annoyed because straight people were awkwardly asking if we were 'friends' or 'partners,'" Miyatake said. "Now, every convenience-store clerk who guesses we're gay asks us if we're going to get married under the new law. It's sort of a touchy subject, okay?"

Although Burton said she is strongly in favor of allowing gay couples to form legal unions and enjoy all of the civil and social benefits previously reserved for married heterosexuals, she stressed that she wanted these rights for "other gay couples."

"I'm really happy that we have the legal option to marry now," said Miyatake, who has a masters in botany and owns Occasions, a floral boutique. "That doesn't necessarily mean I want to get married right away. There's no reason to rush into a decision like that. I'm a big believer in 'til

death do us part,' and I don't want to be 50 and marrying my third wife."

"The decision to get married ought to be between the two women involved, and everyone else should butt out,"

> ## "The decision to get married ought to be between the two women involved, and everyone else should butt out," Miyatake added. "Seriously, drop it."

Miyatake added. "Seriously, drop it."

Burton and Miyatake said they weren't shocked when their parents began to hint about marriage, but neither expected friends to do the same.

"We were driving home from a movie the other night when, out of the blue, our friend Kim [Benson] asked

us why we weren't married yet," Burton said. "Well, Kim couldn't see this, but Laura's eyes were tearing up in the front seat. See, before we'd left the house, we'd had a big, terrible fight because my sister left some 'Here comes the brides' message on our machine. God, I wish people would just lay off and let our relationship take its natural course."

The couple's gay friends have been just as insensitive, Miyatake said.

"Our friends have been very supportive of our relationship, especially our friend Trent [Matthews]," Miyatake said. "But he's a DJ, so now, after the Boston ruling, he keeps talking about how fun he would make our wedding reception. He called the other day to say he'd just been trying on new tuxes, in case we gave him a reason to need one soon. Who does that?"

At a Memorial Day picnic Monday, the conversation returned to the couple's single status so many times that Burton said "it might as well have been a bridal shower."

"Every conversation was about gay marriage," Burton said. "Someone asked us about health insurance.

Someone even asked what tax breaks we could get, or if we could be named each other's 401K beneficiaries. I'm sorry, but I really don't know. Ask my dad about that stuff."

"Then our friend Cameron said that if she had a girlfriend, she would get married right away, just to support the cause," Miyatake added. "I said, 'Can't I just donate some money somewhere?' I support protecting the dolphins, but I'm not chaining myself to a deep-sea fishing boat."

"Well, I made it through everyone telling me to adopt a bunch of orphans after Rosie O'Donnell did it, so I guess I'll make it through this," Miyatake said.

Even people who previously objected to the women's sexual orientation are suggesting marriage. Burton reports that her aunt, Eleanor Davis, recently said, "If Laura and Kristin have to be gay, and are going to be living together, then they should at least be married."

"She said June is the most lovely time of the year for a wedding," Burton said. "When I told Eleanor that Laura and I weren't ready to make

see COUPLE page 179

BALLAD from page 175

business volume down 60 percent, manifest damage up 9 percent, and worker productivity down across the board, as drivers complain of heartache, loneliness, and the she-ain't-never-comin'-back-again blues.

"This isn't an easy job, no sir," said Arrow Trucking Company driver Wayne Crudup, 33, of Lexington, KY. "Long hours, tougher regulations every year, and lots less money than

> **Due to the song's popularity, the average trucker is spending as many as three hours per day sitting motionless in the breakdown lane.**

you'd like. Now, on top of that, I can't stop thinking of how that lady left that little home and that poor guy all alone, all because his eye went wanderin' where it never shoulda been. The song starts going round and round in your head, and it gets a touch hard to see the road sometimes."

National Surface Transportation Board statistics have shown a clear link between the playing of "She's Gone Back" on public airwaves and lulls in the trucking industry. The effects are especially noticeable in the South and Midwest.

"Unfortunately, country radio stations nationwide have 'She's Gone Back' in heavy rotation," NTSB

Above: Columbus, OH trucker Rodney Schrag listens to Hardin's song on his truck's radio.

spokesman Howard Stivoric said. "The steel guitar's wail invokes that cold, hard, lonely road she's taking back to where her heart'll stop breaking, and, well, that makes anyone who hears it want to turn right around and get on back to where they came from. For a country that transports 85 percent of its perishable goods by truck, a heartbreaking ballad like this one is bad news."

Due to the song's popularity, the average trucker is spending as many as three hours per day sitting motionless in the breakdown lane. Travelers on

the nation's highways are growing accustomed to seeing dozens of semis pull over to the side of the road whenever the song is played.

"We're especially worried about routes through trucking's Golden Triangle: Atlanta, Memphis, and Nashville," National Highway Traffic Safety administrator Dr. Jeff Runge said. "The high volume of country stations in that area, many of which confess to playing the song almost hourly, has created a depression hotspot. Almost nothing's getting into or out of that area."

Fearing for the financial and emotional safety of their workers, industry leaders have asked President Bush and the FCC to remove the song from the airwaves, as President Carter did during the "He Stopped Loving Her Today" crisis of 1980.

Hardin, the singer responsible for the problem, was unavailable for comment, as he is currently in his hometown of Green Hills, SC, caring for his dying mother and writing "She Taught Me How To Love," a tribute to her 46 years of service as a devoted wife and parent. ∅

COUPLE from page 178

that decision yet, she just said, 'Well, you don't want to die alone, do you?' Then she said something about how it's such a shame that the Burton clan hasn't gotten together since her 60th birthday party last year."

In follow-up phone interviews Tuesday, Burton and Miyatake reiterated that they had no immediate plans to marry.

"Sure, I love Kristin, but I've got a lot going on in my life," Miyatake said. "I'm working really hard to keep the store up and running. I'd rather not go through all the hassle of a marriage right now, just because the courts decided I could. I just don't see any reason why we need to go through some big, annoying ceremony to prove that we're in a committed relationship."

When told about Miyatake's comments, Burton paused several seconds before answering.

"'Some big, annoying ceremony'?" Burton said. "Some people might call it a 'beautiful, joyous occasion.' But fine. Whatever. I certainly don't want to rush her into anything. I just think it's interesting that she'd describe marrying me as a 'hassle.'" ∅

RAKE from page 177

down the block. Well, he's not even a kid anymore, but I heard he used to break into people's houses and watch television. I wouldn't put rake-snatching past him."

Lufler also spoke of a recurring psychic dream he had.

"I dreamed of the tail end of a black car—a car trunk," Lufler said. "When I put my hand on the trunk, it turned into a heap of neatly piled leaves. Then I woke up. But I don't own a black car, and when I searched my trunk for a rake, I didn't find one. I don't hold much stock in the paranormal, but what does it hurt to pursue all avenues?"

Lufler said that most of his neighbors prefer leaf-blowers to rakes. Considering this, he said he recently spotted what could be an important clue: a neatly raked pile of grass clippings in an unknown neighbor's yard, two blocks from his home.

"This was not the work of a leaf-blower, I assure you," Lufler said, producing grainy photographs of a mass of grass shot from several different angles. "Clearly, the grass was raked with a fan-style rake. Look at the angle at which the clippings are piled.

Observe the 'combed' appearance of the surrounding lawn."

The most damning clue in the photos is a large tool with a wooden handle, leaning against the garage, its bottom obscured by a black trash bag.

> **"I told Marsh he's gotta move on," Evie said. "It took him nearly a year to give up looking for that missing rake and buy a new one."**

Lufler said he did not notice the implement until after he had gotten the developed photos back from the Rite Aid. When he returned to the scene, the wooden-handled tool was gone.

"I cannot say with complete certainty that the lawn tool in the picture was a sweep rake," Lufler said. "It could have been a hoe, a shovel, or a broom. But I am convinced that a rake was

used to gather those grass clippings."

Lufler said improvements in technology since 1998 may give him an edge in his search that he previously lacked.

"In 2002, I purchased a large Maglite," Lufler said. "It casts a far longer and stronger beam than my old lantern flashlight, and could aid us in a search of dense underbrush."

Wanting to question the occupants of the home, Lufler attempted to persuade his wife to reopen the rake case. However, a resolute Evie Lufler demanded that the matter be finally put to rest.

"I told Marsh he's gotta move on," Evie said. "It took him nearly a year to give up looking for that missing rake and buy a new one. Now that he has, it's time he forgot about the old rake. Why would anyone need two rakes?"

In spite of his family's resistance, Lufler continues to press for the reopening of the case.

"It's been six years since the rake went missing," Lufler said. "That rake was a real beauty. I've never owned a rake that worked so well. Even if I can't recover the rake, I want to go to my grave knowing that, in my search for it, I left no leaf unturned." ∅

Ask A Jostens Class-Ring Salesman

By Terry Feldon

Dear Jostens Class-Ring Salesman,

About three years ago, my husband and I bought an above-ground pool for the kids. They love it, and I have to admit it's a blessing on all those summer days when the temperature goes above 80. Trouble is, my husband is absolutely obsessed with it. If he's not swimming in it, he's cleaning it or tinkering with the filter. As glad as I am that he has a hobby, I wish he had a little more time for me. I miss my husband! I can't spend all my time out by the pool with him, or I'll look like a lobster by the end of summer! I don't know what to do.

Lonely In Lakeland

Dear Lonely,

How many of you guys out there have cars? Hands up if you do. Okay, a couple. Quite a few of you. Now, how about you gals over there by the window? Do you like to shop for clothes? I thought you'd say "yes." Okay, anyone have a computer, or a radio, or a television set? Uh huh. Now, out of all of those things I mentioned, how long do you think you're going to own those items? You, sir, how long do you think you'll own that radio? Fifty years? No? Twenty years, then? No? Well, your class ring is something that you will hold and cherish for the rest of your life. You're all facing a very important decision here. This may be the first time you've made a decision about something you will carry with you through your entire adult life. As a member of the Bridgemont High Class Of 2004, you are at a crossroads. What would be a better reminder of all the friends, laughs, tears, and triumphs you've had at Bridgemont than a personalized Jostens class ring? Whether you wear it on your finger or on a chain around your neck, this ring will show the world the pride you feel for your alma mater. Your graduation ceremony won't be complete without one, kids.

Dear Jostens Class-Ring Salesman,

I have been married to a wonderful man for five years. The only snag is that my mother-in-law lives just a mile away and pops by uninvited any time she feels like it. She's a nice woman, but she doesn't respect boundaries. No matter what we're doing when she shows up, we have to drop it and entertain her. I don't know how to tactfully ask her to call before she shows up. My husband admits that her unannounced visits bother

him, but he's reluctant to mention it. I think she'd rather hear the news from her own son. Don't you agree?

Trampled On In Tempe

Dear Trampled,

Jostens has a whole range of metals to choose from—including platinum, white or yellow gold, and, for those of you who are minding your budgets, white or yellow Lustrium. Yes? Question? Okay, well, Lustrium is the least costly. But it's a good idea to look at all your options before you choose. See, Lustrium is what is called a non-precious metal alloy. While it is fairly durable, it does not

---

As a member of the Bridgemont High Class Of 2004, you are at a crossroads. What would be a better reminder of all the friends, laughs, tears, and triumphs you've had at Bridgemont than a personalized Jostens class ring?

---

have the same characteristics as gold or platinum and, in the long run, many customers feel their graduation is more... Yes? Okay, well, Lustrium is about half the price of 18-karat gold. But, like all fine jewelry, your class ring is an investment. I can answer all these questions later. What's that? Well, the final cost really depends on a number of factors—type of metal, engraving, size, style—so it's best to start looking through the brochure and determining which rings suit you before you look at the price list. That's the best way to narrow down your choices and design a personalized ring you're sure to love for the rest of your life.

Dear Jostens Class-Ring Salesman,

I am 25 and currently involved in a long-distance relationship with a sweet man I met last summer. Although I care about him deeply, he has become quite overbearing. He sends me roses almost every week

Your Horoscope

By Lloyd Schumner Sr.
Retired Machinist and
A.A.P.B.-Certified Astrologer

Aries: (March 21–April 19)
You have no idea why Nancy Sinatra keeps showing up at your place and soundly kicking your ass, but if you don't find out soon, there's a chance she'll stop.

Taurus: (April 20–May 20)
It's not true that everything you like is illegal, immoral, or fattening, but that's because you're a boring Puritan with no imagination or glands.

Gemini: (May 21–June 21)
The increasingly litigious and impolite nature of the times pays off for you when you become an expert hostile witness.

Cancer: (June 22–July 22)
Only God can judge you. Unfortunately, He's been appearing to all your friends and telling them what an asshole you are.

Leo: (July 23–Aug. 22)
Take solace in this: There is a meaning and purpose to the universe, even if it's far too complicated for you to understand, and won't pay off for years.

Virgo: (Aug. 23–Sept. 22)
Stop worrying about what does and doesn't give you cancer. You have more immediate concerns with who will or won't hang you upside-down on a razor-wire fence for 72 hours.

Libra: (Sept. 23–Oct. 23)
You don't know a lot about art, but you do know what you like. This situation will lead to a curatorship at the National Museum Of Things I Like.

Scorpio: (Oct. 24–Nov. 21)
You've never paid much attention to abandoned offshore oil platforms before, but suddenly everyone seems to think they'd be perfect for you.

Sagittarius: (Nov. 22–Dec. 21)
You don't use the airwaves, exactly, but the FCC will soon take a stand on what you can and can't say using public air.

Capricorn: (Dec. 22–Jan. 19)
There's been a lot of talk about the lack of nurse slayings lately, but you're the only person with the guts to actually do something about it.

Aquarius: (Jan. 20–Feb. 18)
It's nice that you're reading to the elderly, but people are wondering exactly what it is you're reading to make so many of them die during the experience.

Pisces: (Feb. 19–March 20)
You'll learn a relatively valuable lesson this week, when a kindly homeless man teaches you about punctuation.

and calls me at work just to tell me how much he loves me. I think he worries that I might be dating other guys since we're so far apart. I'm not, but to be honest, his neediness is becoming a huge turn-off. How can I tell him to tone it down?

Smothered In Seneca

Dear Smothered,

Any football players out there? How'd we do this season? Pretty impressive, guys. How about band? Anyone play the trombone? Well, then, I'd like you to take a look at this ring. Pass that back to that gentleman with the glasses. See, Jostens has many styles and colors to choose from, so that your class ring will reflect your unique personality. Create a one-of-a-kind ring that shows off your special qualities. Jostens has engravings for every activity, from athletics to newspaper to 4H. And just look at all the stone options. Nice, huh? Go ahead, try it on. Every color of the rainbow. You can get your birthstone, your favorite gem, or go with your favorite color. See this writing on the side

here? You can express yourself further with one of the multiple bezel options. With so many choices, it would be impossible to make a ring that isn't right for you. This one says, ah, "*Deus Veritas Familia*," and that means—hold on a sec. Okay, that means "God, Truth, and Family." Then we got "*Veritas Familia Sapientia*" which means, let's see here, "Truth, Family, and Wisdom." We even have a home-schooled option, so if any of you have home-schooled friends, let them know they don't have to be left out. Okay then, let's start passing those rings forward. Here's an order form for each one of you. No, don't worry if you're not sure. Take a form, just in case. Might as well. Here's one for you. Take the brochure home and talk about it with Mom and Pop. I'll be back on Thursday. I can't wait to see what you all pick out.

Terry Feldon is a syndicated columnist whose weekly advice column, Ask A Jostens Class-Ring Salesman, appears in more than 250 newspapers nationwide. ✆

Oil Prices Soar Like Noble Eagle

see NATION page 4E

Shop Marks Two Years Without Car Through Storefront

see LOCAL page 11C

Michael Moore Kicking Self For Not Filming Last 600 Trips To McDonald's

see ENTERTAINMENT page 3G

STATshot

A look at the numbers that shape your world.

Who's Number 1?

26%	Are you kidding? Zep.
4%	The New Holland High School Wolverines
15%	USA! USA! USA!
16%	Number 6
20%	In service, Klemke's Dry Cleaning
19%	That guy with the "#1" painted on his chest

the ONION®

VOLUME 40 ISSUE 23   AMERICA'S FINEST NEWS SOURCE™   10–16 JUNE 2004

Kerry Names 1969 Version Of Himself As Running Mate

Above: Kerry (right) presents his running mate at a campaign event in Boston.

BOSTON—Ending months of speculation, presidential hopeful Sen. John Kerry announced Tuesday that he has selected the young, vibrant, recently decorated war hero John Kerry as his running mate.

"In my search for a vice-president, I considered many qualified men and women," Kerry said, announcing his decision at Boston University. "But one man stood apart from the madding crowd as brave, honest, and full of life. One man displayed a true desire to change America for the better—not through political maneuvering, but through hard work. That man was me, 35 years ago."

Kerry said he was inspired to nominate John Kerry of 1969 by, of all things, a photo in a magazine.

"I was paging through *Time* and I came across a picture of a very proud, and, might I add, handsome

see KERRY page 184

Mischievous Raccoon Wreaks Havoc On International Space Station

Above: The pesky raccoon that has turned the ISS (right) upside down.

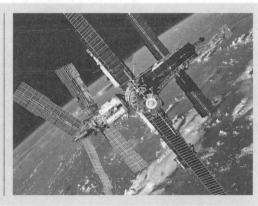

MOSCOW—Orbiting the earth aboard the International Space Station, Expedition 9 scientists were chagrined to report a bevy of equipment and supply problems stemming from the behavior of an inquisitive raccoon Monday.

"Yesterday, we found fruit

see RACCOON page 185

Suicide Letter Full Of *Simpsons* References

Right: Bennett appears happy in a March photo taken in his bedroom.

STORRS, CT—University of Connecticut sophomore Aaron Bennett, 20, was found dead of an apparent sleeping-pill overdose in his campus-area apartment Saturday, a suicide note riddled with references to the popular TV show *The Simpsons* on his desk.

"Outwardly, Aaron seemed like a gentle, quiet, stable person," dean of students Kathleen Ernst said Monday. "But clearly, he must have had a darker, troubled side that he kept hidden. The only thing we can be certain of is that, to the very end, he really knew his *Simpsons*."

Friends and family are struggling to comprehend the dean's-list chemistry major's motivation for taking his own life, as outlined in the three-page suicide letter.

"When death comes so suddenly, it can seem incomprehensible," Ernst said. "It certainly doesn't help matters that Aaron's note begins, 'No banging your head on the display case, please. It contains a very rare Mary Worth in which she has advised a friend to commit suicide.' How do you even begin to explain something like that to his parents?"

see SUICIDE page 184

Tenet's Resignation

CIA Director George Tenet resigned last week, claiming that the decision was "personal" and unconnected to recent controversies. What do *you* think?

Kristopher Williams
Software Engineer

"'Resign' is such an ugly word. Let's just agree to say that he was 'fired.'"

David Polster
Clerk

"I know how he feels. I resigned from Pizza Hut for personal reasons after I got caught with 10 pounds of frozen Italian sausage in my backpack."

Joseph Spagnolia
Cleaner

"It's too bad he has to go, but if it'll prevent Sept. 11 from ever having happened, I'm all for it."

Ilene Nash
Jeweler

"I guess now we just sit back and wait until Tenet commits suicide by shooting himself multiple times in the back of the head."

James Morse
Systems Analyst

"It's no surprise Tenet resigned for personal reasons, considering the strain he was under overseeing the CIA, attending night classes, *and* raising six kids all by himself."

Mary Myers
Teacher Assistant

"He put in seven years, and for what? A brass plaque that's actually a camera and a gold watch that kills people."

The New Medicare Drug Card

The government unveiled a Medicare prescription-drug discount card last week. What are some of the card's features?

▶ Cardholders can save 11 to 17 percent off the 800 percent mark-up on prescription drugs

▶ Each generic-drug purchase earns points toward a Medicare windbreaker or canoe

▶ Personal ID number will prevent card from falling into hands of no-good young hooligans who will use it for God knows what

▶ Fine print states that if an unmarried individual's annual income is not more than $12,569, it's really a shame

▶ All cardholders eligible for free, one-time-only sleeping-pill overdose

▶ Front of card lists known drug allergies; back has lenticular image of St. Peter and the Lord's Prayer

▶ With eight stamps to card, user gets one 0.5 mg Klonopin or side salad free

 **the ONION**®
America's Finest News Source.™

Herman Ulysses Zweibel
Founder

T. Herman Zweibel
Publisher Emeritus
J. Phineas Zweibel
Publisher
Maxwell Prescott Zweibel
Editor-In-Chief

I'm Not Sure If I Know How To Treat A Lady

By Justin March

There are a lot of ladies out there, but if you want to keep a good one, you have to know how to make her feel appreciated. A lady wants a man who acts strong and confident. That way, she knows she's with someone who's strong and confident. Then again, ladies probably don't like men who are cocky. So I guess you should be sensitive, too. Maybe being polite is the most important thing. Or maybe it's good to know how to dance, or how to wow her in the bedroom. I don't know. I guess, when it comes down to it, I'm not sure I know how to treat a lady.

I think my behavior might be in the general ballpark, though. On a first dinner date, it's probably important to pick the right restaurant. The dining atmosphere should be fancy, but casual. Never under any circumstances should you take a lady to a chain restaurant. That is, unless she asks to go to a chain restaurant. When you and your date are seated, if the hostess doesn't push in her seat, then I guess you should do it yourself. I'm almost positive that most ladies will enjoy this and see it as a sign of affection. Of course, not all ladies will like it. Some will think you're acting unnatural. You should always try to act natural. Actually, to be safe, you might want to just refrain from touching the chair altogether. See how hard it is to know how to treat a lady right?

In my experience, saying the right thing can really impress a lady, but blurting out the wrong thing can lead to a very early night. Ladies like compliments, but lay on too many and you'll seem insincere. I suppose you have to use trial-and-error to find out what a lady wants to hear. If she's wearing her hair up, she might want you to say something nice about her earrings. Now, I'm not positive about that. Maybe it's just a hot day, she's pinned her hair up so her neck won't sweat, and she'd rather you not notice it. Whatever you do, though, don't say anything to her about those weird little hairs in her ears. That's something no lady wants to hear. Not mentioning the weird hairs in her ears—that's one way to treat a lady right that I'm fairly sure about.

If a man doesn't impress a lady, she'll find a different guy who does. I've heard that one of the ways you can please a lady is by dressing well. This way, you show her that you have taste and that you took the time to get dressed up to see her, because she's important to you. Buy the right fabric softener, and you can please her sense of smell, too. Actually, this might be better covered under the topic of cologne, which is also important to the ladies. Anyway, for now, put simply: Looking your best will impress a lady. But you shouldn't dress too nice, or she might think you're conceited or gay. Be clean, but stay rugged. I mean, I guess.

Make sure your compliments are original. You shouldn't say things you heard on television, because she might've seen the same program. Instead, notice things about her that other guys wouldn't, like her hands or her knees. This could be tricky, since she might think you're getting too personal. She could have a complex about her knees and shut down for the whole evening. Then it's no goodnight kiss for you—not that you

> **Ladies like compliments, but lay on too many and you'll seem insincere. I suppose you have to use trial-and-error to find out what a lady wants to hear.**

should assume you're going to get one, even if the date goes well. I guess what I'm saying is that you should use your discretion on this one.

There's a whole bunch of other stuff every guy should know about treating a lady right once it's established that you like her and she likes you. But really, that's all pretty complicated. I'm not sure that I can go into it here without diagrams. The important thing to do is to be romantic. Sure, there are some that will threaten to kick your ass if you so much as light a vanilla candle, but they're pretty easy to weed out due to their tattoos and such.

If I were you, I'd take the stuff I said above and see if it works, then add your own personal touches. Treating a lady right should be doable, as long as you keep your eye on the lady. I mean, don't stare, but keep aware of how she's reacting. Unless she's one of those ladies who secretly likes to be ignored, which probably sums up a lot of them.

I don't know. Maybe you should just ignore everything I said. Pretend I never wrote this column, okay? I mean, unless you liked it, in which case... hey, thanks. ∅

List Of Friends Revised After Birthday Party

LOS ANGELES—Due to her friends' actions at, or absences from, her 22nd birthday party at the Three Of Clubs Saturday night, Angela Linton was forced to revise her list of friends Monday.

"Last week, I counted Sheila Miller among my very good friends," Linton said. "But I guess she had something a lot cooler to do on the night of my 22nd birthday. Well, I'm sorry, but if she didn't want to see me Saturday, she doesn't have to see me ever again. She's off the list."

Linton said she had roughly 75 friends last week, but the figure plummeted to less than 60 following her birthday party. The list of friends has not seen such a dramatic revision

"Jack's name has a line through it," Linton said.

since her modern-dance performance at the Grace Unitarian Church in November 2003.

Party attendance alone did not guarantee continued inclusion on the friend list. Ex-boyfriend Jack Freedman was excised for bringing an inappropriate guest to Linton's party.

"Jack showed up two hours late with

Above: Linton, who was forced to tighten her friend circle.

his arm around some little tramp!" Linton said. "She was so skinny she looked like she had an eating disorder, and her roots were showing. It was supposed to be a nice night to celebrate my birthday, not some sort of revolting show-and-tell for whatever slut he's sleeping with this week."

Added Linton: "I thought he was my friend, but I guess I was wrong. Unless he makes it up to me, Jack's name has a line through it."

Those names that did remain on the

list were subject to a vigorous reshuffling.

Ilana Reynolds, who has been friends with Linton since middle school, slipped 11 spaces, because she spent the entire party sitting in a back booth and talking to other guests. According to Linton, Reynolds didn't even try to move closer to her, even though it was her party.

"I was like, 'I'm over here,'" Linton said.

But some of Linton's friends were lucky enough to have their status

raised.

"[Coworker] Tony [Colella] scored real points by buying me an amaretto sour—my drink—without my asking," Linton said. "I've only been out with him a couple of times, and he totally remembered what I like. He jumped up 15 places."

Most of Linton's friends are unaware of her list. Even those who suspect that the list exists display a striking ignorance of the way their

see BIRTHDAY page 185

Texas Environmentalists Lobby For Solar-Powered Electric Chair

AUSTIN, TX—Garrett Durning of the Texas Environmental Defense League has spent the last three months campaigning tirelessly for the installation of solar-powered electric chairs in state prisons. "Texas wastes more than 500,000 watts of electricity on every criminal it executes," Durning told reporters Monday. "We live in the 21st century, and it's high time we acted like it. Let's stop depleting our non-renewable fossil fuels. Solar power is a more energy-efficient way to execute the condemned." Durning added that wrist and ankle restraints should be made of hemp rather than leather, the use of which is cruel.

Boss' Threats Hilarious

KNOXVILLE, TN—Employees working under Champion Direct Marketing manager Dale Farner found his threats during a Monday meeting hysterical, sources told reporters. "If you like your job here, you'll start to shape up," Farner said, reprimanding a group of his underlings working in CDM's basement offices. "You think your jobs are guaranteed? Think again. I can replace any one of you, just like that. There are plenty of folks out there who would take pride in telephone sales." The employees, most of whom will quit before the end of summer, broke into giggles when Farner threatened to cancel the staff summer picnic.

Congress Launches National Congress-Awareness Week

WASHINGTON, DC—Hoping to counter ignorance of the national legislative body among U.S. citizens, congressional leaders named the first week in August National Congress Awareness Week. "This special week is designed to call attention to Ameri-

ca's very important federal lawmaking body," Speaker of the House Dennis Hastert said. "At least three citizens in every state, and as many as 55 in California, presently have some form of congressional duty, whether it's as a senator or as a representative." The festivities will kick off with a 10-mile Walk for Congress Awareness, when blue ribbons will be handed out in honor of those who served in the first 107 congresses.

Leno's Voicemail Message Pauses For Laughter

LOS ANGELES—*Tonight Show* host Jay Leno's home outgoing voicemail message stops briefly to allow for audience laughter, sources reported Monday. "You have reached the home of Mavis and Jay Leno, and if you don't know what to do by now, then you've got bigger problems than Martha Stewart,'" said Leno's recording, followed by a five-second silence. "But se-

riously, callers, at the beep, leave a message." After a short pause, Leno's message concluded, "Am I right?"

Guys' Night Out To Include Several Key Non-Guys

COLUMBUS, OH—Though buddies Jim Foglia, Chuck Harvestine, and Russell Vento insisted that Thursday will be a "guys night out," certain key non-guys are likely to be in attendance, sources reported Tuesday. "Honey, we're just going to be drinking beer and talking about the Reds—nothing you'd be interested in," Foglia told his wife Emily, withholding information regarding specific plans to begin the night buying drinks for college girls at the Varsity Club. "Maybe we'll stop for burgers afterward, I don't know." Based on previous "guys' nights," the trio will more likely end the night in the company of non-male lap dancers at the Vroom Vroom Room. ∅

Bennett's cousin, Tracy Hogg, said she did not know that the young man was despondent, but did know that he was a big *Simpsons* fan.

"Aaron had loved *The Simpsons* since he was little," Hogg said. "He found so much joy in the show. He had nearly every episode memorized word-for-word. You'd think there'd be no reason for someone like him to take his own life."

The three-page note, headed with the inscription "Dumb Things I Gotta Do Today," includes references to plot-lines from dozens of the more than 300 episodes of the animated series. Bennett quotes *Simpsons* mainstays like Bart Simpson and Ned Flanders, as well as relatively obscure characters, such as Lyle Lanley, Disco Stu, and Very Tall Man.

"Today, part four of our series on the agonizing pain in which I live every day," Bennett's note read. "Or should I say part 400? Not even drinking age yet and I'm tired, people. For me, life is like an escalator to nowhere. Well, this is where I jump off."

Storrs Police Department detectiveRoger Mann said the note is so dense with references that the investigators, most of them only casually acquainted with the show, have had difficulty distinguishing Bennett's original thoughts from the many *Simpsons*-derived expressions.

"It will take some time to fully understand Aaron's letter," Mann said. "For example, he talks about banishing himself to the land of wind and ghosts, a remark that struck me as particularly haunting and despairing. But later, someone told me the line comes from a *Simpsons* lampoon of a Japanese TV commercial."

Some of the quotes in the letter contain no clear allusion to Bennett's impending death or despondency.

"On page three, the letter says, 'Can you open my milk, Mommy?'—a line

Above: A police photo shows Bennett's suicide letter, exactly as found on top of his desk.

with no apparent suicidal meaning," Mann said. "But then, you don't know. When he quoted *Simpsons* character Ralph Wiggum, Aaron might have been lamenting his lack of independence or pining for his lost childhood. But I'm willing to bet that he just thought that line was funny."

Continued Mann: "I believe this may also be the case with 'Diagnosis: delicious.'"

Magnus Whittaker, Bennett's friend since junior high and a fellow *Simpsons* enthusiast, said he corresponded with Bennett regularly until about four months ago, when Bennett mysteriously stopped e-mailing him. Whittaker described his friend as a kind but withdrawn young man whose favorite mode of communication was

the quoting of *Simpsons* lines.

Whittaker said that, in in a phone conversation weeks prior to his death, Bennett was unusually candid about his unhappiness.

"Aaron likened himself to Frank Grimes," Whittaker said, referring to the hard-working Springfield Nuclear Power Plant employee. "He resented that no one paid attention to him, and he complained that no one seemed to appreciate his hard work. Once, when we were IM-ing each other, he said he sometimes wished he would electrocute himself, like Frank Grimes did. I was like, 'Holy flurking schnit.'"

In spite of his warning, Whittaker said he was shocked when Bennett took his own life.

"I am absolutely stunned Aaron was

capable of killing himself," Whittaker said. "I was even more bowled over by his note. I mean, that 'I ate too much plastic candy' line was so cool. I actually had to look that one up."

As those who knew Bennett continue to decipher his final thoughts, Ernst urged any students who might feel depressed to seek treatment.

"You may feel unloved, misunderstood, or stressed, but all people experience those feelings at one time or another," Ernst said. "I want everyone to know that help is available from a variety of sources, on and off campus. It's so tragic to see someone so young give up and say, 'Oh, I've wasted my life.' It's just such a shame that Aaron felt his was the worst existence—ever."

"Jeez, now I'm doing it," Ernst added. ∅

25-year-old man in full military uniform, just returning from the conflict in Vietnam," Kerry said. "He was strong, fit, and in the flower of youth. I couldn't look away. It was as if there was a light shining from within him. I knew that this man was destined for the White House."

Kerry said his newly chosen running mate graduated from Yale University in 1966, after which he volunteered for the Navy, serving as a swift-boat officer on a gunboat in the Mekong Delta in Vietnam. For his exemplary service, the young soldier was awarded a Silver Star, a Bronze Star, and three Purple Hearts.

"My running mate is a natural-born leader," Kerry said. "He was born at Fitzsimons Military Hospital in Denver, where his father was recovering from tuberculosis after volunteering for the Army Air Corps in WWII. He continues to uphold a belief instilled in him from a young age: that you must always fight for what you believe in, no

matter the cost. Man, to be 25 again."

Kerry spoke of the "exemplary character" of the man with whom he now shares the Democratic ticket.

"My running mate is smart, hardworking, and, above all, unsullied by compromise," said the four-term senator from Massachusetts. "The more I learn about this man, the more I admire him."

"To tell you the truth, sometimes I wish I were more like him," Kerry added.

According to many party insiders, a Kerry/Kerry ticket carries a host of advantages.

"It's a perfect match," said John Podesta, head of the left-leaning Center for American Progress. "John Kerry has the experience older voters look for, but the 1969 Kerry has the freshness, idealism, and hope that inspires younger voters."

Kerry agreed.

"After spending 20 years in the Senate, I have the know-how to lead America to better jobs, quality health care, and greater opportunities for

our children," the Massachusetts senator said. "My running mate has the courage to keep our administration honest to itself and its beliefs. Together, we possess much more than either of us alone could bring to the ticket."

According to senior sources within the Kerry campaign, the decision was made last week, but kept quiet until campaign staffers could finish a background check on the potential vice-presidential candidate.

"We had to finish vetting him," Kerry advisor Jim Johnson said. "When picking a VP, you've got to examine his whole life, from childhood on. The last thing we wanted was to have some surprise about his past turn up after he'd already been put on the ticket."

Campaign manager Mary Beth Cahill expressed her support for Kerry's new vice-presidential partner.

"This bright young star is a national treasure," Cahill said. "He's earnest and true to himself. It's been years

since I've met anyone in politics that I respect anywhere near as much as I do young John Kerry."

Kerry appeared unsurprised when reporters asked him to comment on statements his running mate made about the Vietnam War.

"Yes, my running mate has made remarks that have been critical of certain decisions made in Washington," Kerry said. "He and I do not agree on every point. But may I remind you that this man *voluntarily* enlisted to serve in Vietnam? He didn't have to go to war, but he chose to go, to serve his country. He got shot at and wounded. He could have died. Some nights he was scared, but he just kept on going, kept fighting with his fellow soldiers, fighting for America."

Added Kerry: "Now, I'll admit that he still has some unresolved feelings about some aspects of his military service. But, as far as I'm concerned, there's no doubt about one thing: The man is a hero." ∅

Above: Russian mission control monitors the actions of the furry little devil.

rinds in the EVA suits and helmets, and the day before, it was garbage strewn all over the Pirs Docking Module," ISS Science Officer Mike Fincke said via a video-link to Russian mission control. "Today, a controller on the starboard truss failed because the power cord was chewed clean through. The little guy's curious, that's for sure."

Both Fincke and Expedition 9 Commander Gennady I. Padalka of Russia reported surprise run-ins with the raccoon. Fincke said the mischievous animal scurried underfoot as he was replacing a failed remote power controller module on a recent spacewalk and knocked him into a weightless spin.

In addition, Fincke said the space station's external-refuse cylinders are regularly turned over and rummaged through—especially on nights when the crewmembers have consumed fish dinners or freeze-dried "astronaut ice cream." The recent contamination of the ISS water supply was traced back to the raccoon's habit of washing its food before eating.

Neither of the two scientists has been able to outsmart the wily animal, despite weeks of effort.

"Although the ISS is mankind's best-planned space station, it regrettably has no plans for dealing with pesky wildlife," said Padalka, who has been appointed temporary pest-control officer for the ISS. "We've put out Havahart traps, but the little bandit somehow always makes off with the bait. Evidently, due to zero gravity, the raccoon does not weigh enough to depress the trigger-plate."

While capturing the animal remains a top priority, Expedition 9 crewmembers are determined not to harm the sneaky little guy.

"Heck, if we announced we were go-

ing to exterminate him, mission control would go berserk," Fincke said. "They can't get enough of his antics."

"He is devious, this one," Padalka said, chuckling.

According to Padalka, the little critter's mischief does provide the two-man crew with much-needed entertainment.

When Padalka opened his locker last week and found an orbiting thundercloud of rumpled wrappers in place of his private supply of Snickers

> **While capturing the animal remains a top priority, Expedition 9 crewmembers are determined not to harm the sneaky little guy.**

bars, Fincke laughed so hard he spit out the pouch of water he'd been drinking. However, Fincke was not the one laughing when he spotted the playful creature running off wearing his spare Orlan-M spacesuit helmet. But both astronauts could enjoy seeing the bewildered raccoon scrambling to keep up with the zero-gravity treadmill, after having apparently triggered its "quick-start" switch.

"You have to give it to the little guy, he's persistent," said Fincke, who, while calibrating the ISS telescope last week, had a rare opportunity to view the raccoon up close, when its masked, bewhiskered face stared back at him through the telescope's other end.

Fincke reported another recent run-in with the confounded varmint.

"I shooed him out of the Unity module, but then Padalka got me on the intercom, and the critter, seeing I was distracted, slipped in behind me and got his deft, furry little paws on the controls for the gyroscopes that stabilize the platform's flight. Before we knew it, the danger lights were strobing, the alarms were going off, and the whole station was upside-down."

Although NASA has been unable to determine how the animal got on board, lab analysis of the beast's droppings suggests that it's the same raccoon that caused hell and tarnation on the ISS during Expedition 7 in 2003. While none of the previous crew's members would admit to feeding the raccoon—which would explain its return—many expressed affection for the animal.

"I call raccoon Kosmo-Rascal, after favorite children's book," Expedition 7 Commander Yuri Malenchenko said. "If we caught him, I think we might have used him in benign experiment, maybe about training to do tricks. Is true nobody wants air filter clogged with nutshells, but nobody wants raccoon hurt, either. So?"

ISS personnel agree that, while unexpected, the raccoon is not entirely unwelcome.

"This is how astronauts learn to deal with new things—by living through them," Fincke said. "Zero gravity, environmental adaptation, varmints… all these are unplanned things that surprise us when we take a step into space. But we aboard ISS Expedition 9 haven't met a problem too big for us yet, and we'll work this raccoon thing out sooner or later. Hopefully, before the clever little dickens figures out how to work the airlocks." ∅

behavior affects their status.

"If she's got a list, I'm definitely on it," said high-school friend Priya Shah, who was removed from the list after getting embarrassingly drunk on Saturday, interrupting Linton while she was telling a story, and hitting on Linton's 17-year-old brother Vince. "I've known Angie for too long for anything to get between us. We've been through it all."

One expert called Linton's list-making a "sign of today's fast-paced, interconnected world."

"While older people tend to see their social circles shrinking, people in their 20s are seeing their friend groups expand to an almost unmanageable size," said USC sociology department chair Herbert Rouse, author of More Than Grades: Keeping Score In Social Schools. "They find they are still in touch with acquaintances from their past—high-school friends, family friends, former neighbors, and the like—while at the same time their social circles are widening to include new friends from college, coworkers, and people met through activities and interests. Who's got time to deal with someone who can't even call to say they're sorry after they didn't make it to your party? I'm sorry, but no."

Although Linton is "disappointed" in her former friends, she said only the rare excision is permanent.

"A lot of people hurt me on Saturday, and they've got their work cut out for them to win me back," Linton said. "But I've had friends in worse positions who've managed to make their way back onto my list. I mean, after stumbling out and stiffing me for the cab ride home, Brittany is off forever, but the others still have a shot." ∅

amounts of blood. Passersby were amazed by the unusually large amounts of blood. Passersby were amazed by the unusually large amounts of blood. Passersby were amazed by the unusually large amounts of blood. Passersby were amazed by the unusually large amounts of blood. Passersby were

> **That World's Greatest Grandma T-shirt would look better on my bedroom floor.**

amazed by the unusually large amounts of blood. Passersby were amazed by the unusually large amounts of blood. Passersby were amazed by the unusually large amounts of blood. Passersby were amazed by the unusually large amounts of blood. Passersby were amazed by the unusually large amounts of blood. Passersby were amazed by the unusually large amounts of blood. Passersby were amazed by the unusually large

see CARGO PANTS page 201

Jim Anchower's All About Living Life To The Fullest

**The Cruise
By Jim Anchower**

Hola, amigos. I know it's been a long time since I rapped at ya, but I been spending a lotta time quietly reflecting on all the things going on in my life. First off, I got shitcanned from my job driving people from the airport to the car-rental place and back. I was on lunch break one day when the guy who was filling in for me dinged a car in the parking lot and didn't tell anyone. The manager thought I did it, so when I checked the bus in for the night, he fired me on the spot, without even checking out my story. Man, that hurt. I was seventh in line for a promotion.

Also, I finally had to replace the gas tank in my car. For a while, the car worked fine if I only filled up the tank halfway, but then it got too dangerous. The car was leaking gas on the ground, so I had to worry that some jackass would throw a cigarette under it and blow me sky high. I would've dumped the car, but I'd just replaced the brake pads. I wasn't about to junk a car with new brake pads, so I sank another $400 into fixing it up. This'd better be the last thing that goes wrong with it for a while.

As if those two things weren't bad enough, my pal Dan died last week. That's some pretty heavy shit. I hadn't hung out with him much for, like, five years, but we used to be pretty tight. Here's how it happened. Dan was minding his own, sitting on his front steps, listening to The Rock, the No. 1 source for classic rock in the greater Midwest, 107.7 on your FM dial. They have these 20-song, no-commercial rock-blocks, and if you catch them a song shy or if they interrupt the rock for any reason, you can win $500 by calling in. The 20-song block is like a sacred promise to their listeners, and The Rock knows that breaking that oath will have consequences.

Well, the station was right in the middle of the 12th song in the rock block when the announcer broke in to say that someone had spotted a tornado on the west side of town. Dan got on the cordless phone and tried to get through to the station, since their rock block was broken. He should have won $500. Instead, the tornado picked up an axle that was laying around in Dan's yard and sent it through his chest. There's no justice in life.

Know what the funny thing is? When I saw Dan a couple months ago, he was talking about needing to get rid of all those axles. He was sick of his neighbors hassling him and the city threatening to fine him. If only he'd cleaned his yard, instead of just talking about it. Ain't life fucked up?

It just goes to show you that you never know when it'll be your time to go. One second you're on the phone trying to win $500, the next you have an axle through your lungs. Well, after hearing about Dan, I decided that Jim Anchower is gonna live every day like it's his last. No more wishing I'd drank that MGD, smoked that bowl, or punched that guy. It's all gonna be balls-out from now on.

First thing I'm gonna do, if I can get the money together, is buy myself a bag of weed big enough to last me at least a month. Then I'm gonna get all my friends together at my place to smoke up and eat pizza. Then, when we're full, we'll smoke up again and play video games. I'm gonna win every game, because I'll have the thing that no one else has: a new lease on life. After everyone leaves, I'm gonna go to bed and sleep as late as I want. Then I'm gonna get up and start all over again.

Here's another decision I've made: When the road calls me, I'm gonna listen to it. I spent the past year working behind the wheel, but still, I'd forgotten what driving was all about. From here on out, I'm gonna be one with the open road. It's gonna be me, my sweet ride—or whatever ride I

> **First thing I'm gonna do, if I can get the money together, is buy myself a bag of weed big enough to last me at least a month. Then I'm gonna get all my friends together at my place to smoke up and eat pizza. Then, when we're full, we'll smoke up again and play video games. I'm gonna win every game, because I'll have the thing that no one else has: a new lease on life.**

have at the time—and a six-disc changer stocked with the best rock known to man. I'll find myself a nice, flat stretch of road with no traffic lights or cops, and I will fly.

From now on, if I want to see a

> **Dan was minding his own, sitting on his front steps, listening to The Rock, the No. 1 source for classic rock in the greater Midwest.**

movie, I'm gonna see it in the theater. For real. I'm not gonna sit around the house thinking it'd be a good idea to go see a movie, and then drink beer until I'm too tired to get off my ass. No, I'm gonna get into my car, drive to that theater, and enjoy the movie like it's the best movie ever made, even if

it sucks. After the first movie is done, I'm gonna sneak into another one. I'll keep sneaking into more movies until the theater closes or some usher catches me. And, if I get kicked out, I'm gonna say I gotta piss and try to sneak back in again.

From now on, it's my way or the highway. If people don't see eye-to-eye with me, fuck 'em. I'm not gonna waste my time trying to talk sense to people if they're just gonna be ballbags. Unless they're cashiers and I have to buy food or something from them, in which case, I suppose I'll feel sorry for them, since they don't have an enlightened point of view like me.

Only one thing's standing in my way right now, and that's I got no income. I think I can stretch my final check a few weeks, but if I'm gonna live the dream, I guess I have to get another job. Ron said he might be able to get me a job at the carbonics plant where he works. That would be all right. Once I get enough cash socked away, I'm gonna live large. Oh, and also, I'm gonna start looking around for a new place that has a basement. ∅

Your Horoscope

**By Lloyd Schumner Sr.
Retired Machinist and
A.A.P.B.-Certified Astrologer**

Aries: (March 21–April 19)
You'll accidentally stumble upon the secret of the Dim Mak Death Touch this Thursday—which, as luck would have it, is your first day as a massage therapist.

Taurus: (April 20–May 20)
While you were never officially partnered up with him in the first place, Art Garfunkel will make a big deal out of reuniting with you.

Gemini: (May 21–June 21)
The little black dress is an instant sophisticator—slimming, elegant, and timeless—but you'd be better off going with something flame-resistant this weekend.

Cancer: (June 22–July 22)
Your loved ones are willing to respect your wishes regarding your funeral, but if you keep changing your mind about the music, they'll think you're stalling.

Leo: (July 23–Aug. 22)
You'll be forced to dress up as a member of the opposite sex and adopt a monkey in order to inherit $1 million, but it'll go off without a hitch.

Virgo: (Aug. 23–Sept. 22)
Some news sources will concentrate on your elderly victims, others on the slain children, and quite a few on the kittens.

Libra: (Sept. 23–Oct. 23)
Demented surgeons will drive a half-inch steel rod through your cheeks and attach it to a water-skiing towrope, but unfortunately, they'll lose the bet that made them do it in the first place.

Scorpio: (Oct. 24–Nov. 21)
You had no idea that America's network of salt-mining tunnels was so vast, or that it would take you so long to starve once you got lost in it.

Sagittarius: (Nov. 22–Dec. 21)
They say you never hear the shot that gets you, but thanks to the acoustics in your bathroom, you'll hear all 59 of them perfectly.

Capricorn: (Dec. 22–Jan. 19)
Marcus Aurelius said to always honor the human faculty which produces opinions, proving once and for all that he never met you.

Aquarius: (Jan. 20–Feb. 18)
You'll be surprised to find out that Congress is empowered to forcibly sublet your apartment for the summer.

Pisces: (Feb. 19–March 20)
The stars foretell your life continuing in much the way it always has for the next few months.

Jimmy Fallon Six Tantalizing Months From Disappearing Forever

see ENTERTAINMENT page 12F

Reagan's Memory Honored With Sharp Increase In Federal Budget Deficit

see WASHINGTON page 3C

Heinz Factory Explosion Looks Worse Than It Is

see LOCAL page 5E

STATshot

A look at the numbers that shape your world.

What Could We Do If We Wanted To?

- 32% Five-minute mile
- 9% Be the black Ray Romano
- 15% Let out just a little bit of pee
- 14% Write gripping crime novel set in hometown
- 17% Beat cancer
- 13% Reach those grapes

the ONION

VOLUME 40 ISSUE 24   AMERICA'S FINEST NEWS SOURCE™   17–23 JUNE 2004

J.K. Rowling Ends *Harry Potter* Series After Discovering Boys

EDINBURGH, SCOTLAND—Speaking though her publicist, author J.K. Rowling shocked fans and the publishing world Monday when she announced that she has opted to end the best-selling *Harry Potter* series because she has discovered boys.

"For many years, writing the *Harry Potter* books was the most important thing in Joanne's life," said publicist Mark Knowles, who is "just good friends" with Rowling. "She's been experiencing a lot of changes lately. She still wants to keep in touch with her fans, but she doesn't feel she can sit in a room at her computer all day while there are so many cute boys running around."

According to Knowles, instead of working on the as-yet-untitled sixth installment in her series, Rowling has spent the past two months sunning herself at the beach, reading fashion magazines, and talking on the phone for hours.

see ROWLING page 191

Above: Rowling, who is "so over dragons and magical gems."

Report: 9/11 Commission Could Have Been Prevented

Above: Members of the 9/11 commission that destroyed countless political careers.

WASHINGTON, DC—According to key members of the Bush Administration, the tragic proceedings of the 9/11 commission, which devastated the political lives of numerous government officials, could have been averted with preventive action in 2002 and 2003.

"A few adept legislative maneuvers could have saved the reputations of hundreds," President Bush's counter-terrorism chief Fran Townsend told reporters Monday. "Had we foreseen the dangers of the commission's deceptively simple requests, we could have spared dozens of victims from the shocking, public mangling of their careers."

"It's tragic," Townsend added. "All those political futures snuffed out as millions of Americans watched on television. And to think there was a remote chance that they could've

see COMMISSION page 190

Man's Impending Death Alcohol-Related

MATTOON, IL—In a press conference Monday, Mattoon-area police announced that the early death of Derek Yothers, 42, will be alcohol-related.

"Until we can complete a full investigation, we're considering Yothers' future death to be the result of alcohol poisoning," patrolman John O'Malley said. "However, we haven't ruled out hepatitis, kidney failure, cirrhosis of the liver, acute pancreatitis, Wernicke-Korsakoff's syndrome, alcoholic cardiomyopathy, or fatal injuries sustained in some kind of drunk-driving accident."

O'Malley said police do not suspect that there will be foul play.

"Yothers' on-again/off-again girlfriend Brandi Freyer could get fed up and

see MAN page 191

Right: Yothers in a photo taken just months, or even weeks, before his death.

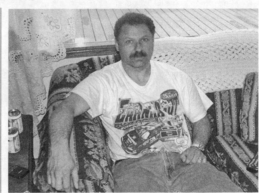

187

Internet Pedophilia Crackdown

A multinational police team plans to patrol Internet chatrooms as part of a crackdown on child pornography and pedophilia. What do *you* think?

Thomas Barnes
Systems Analyst

"Police will be patrolling the Internet? They'll need to get the nation's top men on it—Readyman, Chillycheez, SatanicMechanic, and maybe even BeeBop77."

Sonya Treat
Market Researcher

"It's about time. As a market researcher, I'm sick of perverts in chatrooms propositioning me whenever I pretend to be an 11-year-old girl."

Douglas Emery
Laborer

"This is great news. I find child pornography sickening, but I *am* aroused by images of Belgians being led away in handcuffs."

Daphne Sports
Sales Representative

"An international anti-child-porn force would dramatically increase the possibilty of authorities rappelling in through skylights, which is good."

Jason Diaz
Painter

"Shouldn't we be fighting terrorism, and not doing anything about anything else?"

Eric Rhodes
Manager

"That's going to be yet another weird government office to accidently wander into."

Memorializing Reagan

People around the world have spent the last week and a half honoring Ronald Reagan. What were some of the events?

★ All four existing faces on Mt. Rushmore changed to Reagan's (Keystone, SD)

★ 40th President Memorial Luau (Honolulu)

★ Spat in Reagan-shaped bucket, just as they've always done (Cuba)

★ Ronnie Gras (New Orleans)

★ Free world taken over by communists (various)

★ Sacred Reagan resurrection rites of Ch'turga held in secret catacombs beneath capitol (Washington, DC)

★ 21 dead-nun salute (El Salvador)

★ Attempted to take credit for his death (Iraq)

★ Oxcarts full of meat and drink laid upon Reagan's final resting place (Santa Monica, CA)

★ Celebration of first-ever Reaganmas, with new tradition of exchanging toy arms for toy hostages (U.S.)

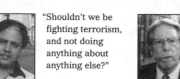

the ONION®
America's Finest News Source.™

Herman Ulysses Zweibel
Founder

T. Herman Zweibel
Publisher Emeritus
J. Phineas Zweibel
Publisher
Maxwell Prescott Zweibel
Editor-In-Chief

Hey, Isn't That The Pot That's On TV?

By Jerry Milobritch

Does that pot over there look familiar to you? Over there, in Aisle 7, across from the deodorants? I know I've seen that box before. Was it in the Twin Lakes Walgreens? No, that's not where it was. Hmm, where have I seen that—holy shit! That's the pot that's on TV! What the hell is the name of it? Damn, it's on the tip of my tongue. Pasta Pot? No. Pasta Premiere? No… Pasta Pro! That's it! That's the Pasta Pro! Don't look at it! Be cool. You know the pot—from that late-night commercial? Remember? "Pasta Pro is as easy as 1-2-3!" It's the one where you just place your favorite pasta into the Pasta Pro and, when the pasta's ready, turn the lid to the locked position, pour the water out, and keep the pas-

> **What the hell is the name of it? Damn, it's on the tip of my tongue. Pasta Pot? No. Pasta Premiere? No… Pasta Pro! That's it! That's the Pasta Pro! Don't look at it! Be cool. You know the pot—from that late-night commercial? Remember?**

ta in! Pasta Pro! C'mon, I'm sure you've seen the commercial. Well, you'd know it if you watched the midnight reruns of *Roseanne* on Channel 14. That pot's totally famous. Do you think we should see if we can get our picture taken with it?

Man, I wonder what the hell the Pasta Pro is doing all the way out here in Litchfield. And why's it in a pharmacy? Shouldn't it be in California on the set of another commercial or something? You'd think it'd have something else lined up by now. Come to think of it, I've been seeing repeats of the same commercial for a while now. I hope the pot's doing okay.

Don't stare at it. That's totally rude. This is really exciting. My mom's going to flip out when we tell her we saw that pot. Whenever that commercial comes on, she says how much she likes it. My dad can never understand why she has a thing for it. Hey, wait here. I'm going to go to the shampoo aisle and walk around so I can get a better look at it.

Don't worry. I'll be casual. It doesn't know that we know what it is. Do you have your digital camera? Don't get it out yet. Just hold on. Let me go over there. Let me be 100 percent sure that it's the same pot.

Okay, now I'm *positive* that's the pot from TV. The whole Pasta Pro posse is sitting there with it. You know—the durable pasta fork, the hand-held cheese grater, the Pasta Pro recipe guide, and the additional two-quart Pasta Pro. I am so freaking out!

Should we go over there? I don't know. That just seems kinda weird. I'm sure that the pot is used to being noticed, but I'm not sure if we should try to pick it up. Maybe we should just leave it alone and let it do its thing. I'm not one of those losers that fawns over a kitchen appliance just because it's been on TV. I mean, if it were the Ronco Electric Food Dehydrator, I wouldn't care at all.

Tell you what, we'll go and get that toothbrush and everything else that you need. If it's still over in that aisle, we'll go over. Who knows, maybe it needs a little help finding something to do here in Litchfield. Not like there's a whole lot to do in this shit-hole town.

Yeah, I know you've seen the Chia Pet at the Spencer Gifts over in Round Lake. Who cares? The Chia Pet is washed up, man. It's so 15 years ago. It's just sad at this point. Its box is all faded and dusty. Even when it was new, it was dumb. I never understood why it was so popular.

And then, every time there's a decent TV product, like the Liquid Leather repair kit or Pops-A-Dent, it seems to just fall off the face of the earth. I guess Mr. and Mrs. Joe Lunchpail don't know how to respond to a product that's actually innovative or useful.

I hope that doesn't happen to the Pasta Pro. It totally has so much potential. The Pasta Pro's lightweight design fits any stovetop and can be used to create an endless variety of your favorite dishes. Hey, remember this line? "You can quickly prepare delicious macaroni and cheese, linguini with clam sauce, or even brown sirloin beef for chili, without the mess." That's my favorite. Okay, okay. I know I'm acting like a nerd. Let's just go get your toothbrush and then we'll go over there, really quick, and not make a big deal about it.

This is going to be awesome. I can't wait to tell all my friends. ∅

Former Coworker Romanticized

DALLAS, TX—Six weeks after Jim Wanzeck's departure from Pedro's Mexican restaurant, remaining employees have begun to romanticize their former colleague, kitchen sources revealed Monday.

Wanzeck, who waited tables during the evening shift on Tuesdays, Thursdays, and Fridays, is now recalled as an irreplaceable member of the staff who helped his colleagues endure the daily drudgery of working at the local Tex-Mex restaurant.

Bartender Manuel Padilla, who has worked at Pedro's for the past two years, characterized the former coworker as "one of a kind."

"I'll never forget how, every time he messed up a drink order, he'd try to blame me," Padilla added. "God, then there was the time he threw his nametag in the deep fryer. It got all bubbly, but he wore it for the rest of his shift. It was like he punked himself! Legendary."

"A lot of nights, it was Jim, me, [shift manager] Tim [Felix], and [waitress] Shelley [Carver] closing together," Padilla said. "Jim would inch the volume of the dining-room radio up until Tim noticed and made him turn it down. Man, that guy!"

Coworkers said Wanzeck often entertained them with elaborate stories

Above: Pedro's employees reminisce about Wanzeck (inset).

about his difficult landlord, cheerless girlfriend, and trouble-prone car.

"He had a lot of shit going on," said Susan Phillips, hostess at Pedro's. "But he just rolled with it. Sure, he was always gone from work for some crisis or another, but he didn't let it get him down. He always got other people to pick up his shift instead of just not showing up. He was cool that way."

Members of the staff are sometimes prompted to rhapsodize about Wanzeck upon coming across the photo from

last year's staff Christmas party which is now posted in the kitchen. In it, Wanzeck is standing in the background, smoking.

Glancing at the photo, waitress Lila Rickman said, "That's totally Wanzeck right there. I'll bet he bummed that cigarette off me. Man, I miss that guy."

Padilla recalled one of Wanzeck's catch phrases.

"When he'd get pissed at somebody, he'd say, 'What a douche!'" Padilla

said. "Sometimes, it was 'What a fucking douche!' That saying was classic Wanzeck."

Padilla added: "He did this Bush impression where he'd make fun of how stupid he was. He hated Bush. Whenever Bush came on the radio, he'd call him a douche."

Shamiqua Taylor, a former waitress at Pedro's, best remembers Wanzeck for the pranks he would occasionally play. "One time, somebody got shortchanged

see COWORKER page 190

NEWS IN BRIEF

Cryptozoologist Falls For It Again

LUBBOCK, TX—Will Reiser, an expert in the field of unsubstantiated creatures, was duped again Tuesday, when he said he'd finally found proof of the existence of the elusive Chupacabra, a quill-covered creature that feasts on the blood of livestock. "The right shank of the goat carcass I discovered on my doorstep bore the Chupacabra's distinctive cross-hatched fang pattern," Reiser said. "I have to say I'm surprised that the quills poking out of the body so closely resemble those of the hedgehog indigenous to this area." Reiser's next-door neighbor, Dan Swelter, is currently laughing his ass off.

Mugger Can't Believe Crap Victim Has On MP3 Player

BOSTON—Following the successful

mugging of a jogger in Franklin Park, petty criminal Derek Mesker announced Monday that he cannot believe the shit he's found on his victim's Philips 20GB MP3 player. "3 Doors Down? Maroon 5!" Mesker said, scrolling through the songs. "The new Counting Crows?! Man, I'm glad I pistol-whipped that motherfuck." Mesker added that the first thing he did was toss the device's "gay-ass" teal neoprene case.

No One Notices Area Man's Marginal Attempts To Change

MIDLAND, TX—No one in Jacob Grant's life has noticed his minor attempts to become a "more thoughtful and considerate person," the new-and-improved man reported Monday. "I'm just asking for a little recognition," said Grant, who in the past week purchased a pack of cigarettes for a friend, complimented his girlfriend's new haircut, and allowed his brother to eat the last samosa. "After all, it's

not like I particularly enjoy holding elevator doors open." Despite the lack of positive feedback, Grant said he plans to give his new plan at least another day or two.

New Alternative-Fuel SUV Will Deplete World's Hydrogen By 2070

DETROIT—Ford announced a Sept. 3 rollout date for its new Ford Foresight, a hydrogen-powered SUV that, if it reaches sales projections, will deplete the earth's supply of hydrogen by 2070. "America has asked for a car that does not use fossil fuels, and we've delivered," Ford CEO William Ford Jr. said Monday. "With an engine nearly 20 times as powerful as that of our gas-burning SUV, the 11-ton Foresight will be unaffected by the price-gouging whims of OPEC, as it uses water electrolysis to gather fuel from the oceans and the fresh mountain air." Ford ac-

knowledged that, when hydrogen supplies are depleted, the usefulness of the Foresight, as well as life on earth as we know it, will end.

66 Percent Of U.S. Citizens Object To Torture In Nonetheless Frightening Poll

CAMBRIDGE, MA—The results of a USA Today-CNN-Gallup poll released Monday show that 66 percent of Americans object to the use of torture during times of war. "We can be proud that the majority of citizens stand against our military personnel's use of torture," Harvard statistician William Stover said. "And it's somewhat comforting that, of the 34 percent of Americans who advocate torture, 72 percent said it should be used only when other methods of discipline have failed." Reassuringly, 97 percent of Americans were against the torture of U.S. soldiers or citizens by non-Americans. ∅

COMMISSION from page 187

gotten our *president*."

Although there were only 10 commission members, they worked with shocking efficiency, and served to carry out the decisions made with the help of a much larger network of government employees.

"The frighteningly resolute faces of commission chair Thomas H. Kean and vice-chair Lee H. Hamilton are familiar after several weeks of frenzied media coverage, but the commission's roots run deeper," Townsend said. "The thing that keeps me awake at night is the number of advisors who are still out there to-

> ## Defense lawyer Mark Agara, who has provided legal counsel for many of the commission's victims, blamed party insiders' short-sightedness on what he termed a "pre-9/11-commission mindset."

day, secretly evaluating our policies. We have no way of knowing who might be called forth by a panel in the future."

"You see the vast scope of the problem," Townsend added. "We're fighting a whole new type of enemy—one that hides among its victims."

National security advisor Condoleezza Rice said that her office did not receive any intelligence regarding

Above: Tenet, whose agency was ripped apart by the 9/11 commission.

the commission's scope until it was already in place, and therefore was unable to implement a strategy to thwart its efforts.

Sen. Joe Lieberman (D-CT) agreed.

"Nobody saw this coming," Lieberman said. "With 20/20 hindsight, of course, we know that if [House Speaker Dennis] Hastert hadn't let Public Law 107-306 come to the floor in November of 2002, we could have saved many of our colleagues from their sad fates."

But Lieberman said that government officials should not look to place blame in the wake of the panel.

"Yes, if various departments had communicated certain intelligence, many of our colleagues would not have found themselves trapped under mounds of paperwork," Lieberman said. "But, as tempting as it is to point fingers, we need to move forward and look at how we can prevent another 9/11 commission from happening."

George Tenet, who recently resigned

as director of the CIA, was among the high-profile casualties of the commission's investigation of key government agencies. According to Alan Fenton, Tenet's public-relations-crisis manager, Washington "seriously underestimated" the commission's power.

"Everybody thought, 'Ten guys, sitting together in some room somewhere, armed with only the power of subpoena—who could they hurt?'" Fenton said. "No one guessed that a commission this small could inflict so much political damage."

Defense lawyer Mark Agara, who has provided legal counsel for many of the commission's victims, blamed party insiders' short-sightedness on what he termed a "pre-9/11-commission mindset."

"A panel criticizing the actions that the administration took in response to the most devastating terrorist attack in history?" Agara asked. "People never considered the possibility. But now, here we stand—whole departments ripped apart, agencies in ruin, and, worst of all, the job security that government employees once took for granted gone forever."

Capitol Hill, ground zero for the investigation, is still reeling in the wake of the 9/11 commission. Americans from across the country continue to offer prayers and assemble candlelight vigils outside federal buildings that contain the offices of the fallen-in-stature.

"Think not only of these poor politicians, but of their families and their staffs," said Gerald Davis, spokesman for Stop The Panels, a group of advocates for the unseen victims of investigations. "Anyone who knows an important Washington politician has been touched by this tragedy." ∅

COWORKER from page 189

an enchilada. They complained, and Jim told them there was a worldwide enchilada shortage. And the best part was, he totally made that up."

"I can't believe they fired Wanny," Padilla said. "You know, we didn't call him 'Wanny' when he was here, but that's the kind of nickname he deserves. Yeah, good old Wanny. This place ought to name a margarita 'The Wannerita."

Even coworkers who never knew Wanzeck—who was fired after a manager found a list of customer credit-card numbers in his locker— soon discover the length of the for-

> ## "When he'd get pissed at somebody, he'd say, 'What a douche!'" Padilla said.

mer employee's shadow. On the first day of his training, Wanzeck's replacement, Jorge Reyes, was led on a tour of the restaurant by Padilla and Rick Santiago. Outside the walk-in freezer, Shepard pointed to the corner of the ceiling.

"Yeah, see that hairnet up in the heating vent?" Santiago asked. "The guy who just left threw that up there. And that middle finger added to the waving cactus-man on the promotional banner? You can hardly see it—they erased most of it—but he did that, too."

"No, I think Suroosh drew that," Padilla interjected.

"Oh, right—Suroosh," Santiago said. "I wonder where that guy is now. He was great." ∅

ON TV TONIGHT

NETWORK

	8:00		9:00		10:00	
ABC	Abusive Kitchen Interloper	Midseason Makeover	Somebody Marry Someone!	On & On	Why Are All These People Living In My House?	
NBC	Friends 4 Ever In Syndication	Access Hollywood Press Junket	Exposing Average Joe		43 Minutes Plus Commercials	
CBS	Still Sucking	CSI: LSAT Prep	Verdict: After Commercial	The Burn Ward	The Best Of 60 Minutes 2	
PBS	Mic-ing Mahler's 5th		Telehubbies	Miss Marple Instigates	BBC Leavings	
FOX	Anxiety Factor: Dental Appointment!	Malcolm On The Air Still	Behind The Smock: Real Stories Of Janitorial Excess		Child Star Coal Mine	

CABLE

	8:00		9:00		10:00	
DSC	Suddenly Treehouse	Sauces Of Eurasia	Effeminate House Rearranger Squad		Big Cats	Big Cars
PAX	Nuns A Blazin'	Moral Cockatiels	Body By Christ	God's Wrath Manifested In A Diagnosis: Murder Rerun		Crucifixion
NICK	The Marketables	Sabrina The Teenage Victim	Full House	No, Really. Full House	Rugrats Babies	
HIST	The Amazing Jewish Race		Simon Schama's Outgoing Message	The Iowans		
MTV	A 14-Year-Old's Idea Of Cool		The Shrill World	Blurry Jiggles	A 37-Year-Old Executive's Idea Of Cool	

shoot him," O'Malley said. "But it's much more likely to be an open-and-shut case in which Yothers drives off the side of a bridge."

"We'll need the coroner's report before we file this away for good, of course," O'Malley added. "But even if he drunkenly trips on the ice and breaks his neck, burns himself to a cinder after passing out with a lit cigarette in his mouth, or dives through a plate-glass window in a show of bravado and bleeds to death, we'll probably still list 'alcohol' as the cause of death."

Details of Yothers' demise will not be finalized until his weakened, inefficient heart and damaged but functioning brain cease to operate. But police said Yothers—who is unemployed, twice divorced, and freshly released from a 15-month prison sentence in Joliet—is unlikely to drag the case out much longer.

"We marked the time of death sometime between today and two years from now," O'Malley said. "We can't say for sure what his blood-alcohol level will be at the time of death, but we know it will be well past the legal limit. Ever since he lost his job at the camper factory, he's pretty much kept his head in a bottle."

O'Malley described the scene of the future death.

"His body could be found in any number of places—a ditch on Hwy. 57, a stall in the men's room, sprawled out on Brandi's stained mattress," O'Malley said. "In any case, he'll almost certainly be face-down, possibly in his dog's water dish. We're bound to find at least two or three empty Jack Daniel's bottles next to his bed. That is, unless he's waiting on his next unemployment check, in which case those bottles will be Old Crow."

Police notified Yothers' family of his pending death Tuesday.

"That's one phone call you never want

Above: A headstone purchased by Yothers' family and placed in the family plot earlier this month.

to make," O'Malley said. "I've known the Yothers family for years—I end up out at their house for a disturbing-the-peace call every year around the holidays. But they're basically good folks. I hate to give people news like that. It's the toughest part of this job."

Continued O'Malley: "They took it well. I assured them that he'll probably feel very little pain when he goes, considering how drunk he'll be. That seemed to make them feel better. Really, they've been expecting this for a while."

Derek's older brother, Mark Yothers,

spoke on the family's behalf.

"You can't help but feel guilty for not doing more to stop him," Mark said. "If only he could have gotten help, I'd still have my brother here with me three years from now. The only consolation we have is that he'll be in a better place someday, where his soul can find peace."

Other people close to Yothers are bracing themselves for his death.

"I just saw him over at the gas station yesterday," said Eric Pugh, Yothers' former coworker. "He was buying a frozen pizza and a sixer of

Miller High Life. He seemed just fine, nothing out of the ordinary at all. We talked about going to that bar over in Effingham for $3 pitchers of Old Style. I sure hope we get a chance to do that before it's too late."

Funeral services for Yothers will be attended by a handful of family members and friends, after which his body will be buried in the family plot. During the gathering, the family will play "She Talks To Angels" by The Black Crowes, unless Yothers' favorite song changes between now and the time of his death. ⌀

"I know many of you are upset by this news," Knowles said. "But Ms. Rowling was tired of devoting herself to something that no longer held her interest—namely, writing books about wizards, flying broomsticks, and candy that jumps. She's a lot older than she was when she wrote the first book. She'd much rather be going to the mall, looking for cute outfits, and talking to the boy with the curly red hair who works at the Hot Sam pretzel shop."

Friends of Rowling say her increasing interest in boys first became obvious during the 2003 release of her series' fifth installment, *Harry Potter And The Order Of The Phoenix*. At book signings, Rowling often had her longtime friend Mindy Harrison pass notes to cute boys in line. But according to Harrison, the author would blush and be unable to speak whenever one approached her.

In fact, sources say delays on *Phoenix* stemmed from Rowling's un-requited infatuation with Randy Pow-

ell, winner of the PEN Center USA West Award for Children's Literature and author of *Run If You Dare* and *Tribute To Another Dead Rock Star*.

"She had such a big crush on him, it was crazy," Harrison said. "She'd call

Knowles reassured fans that Rowling is "probably just going through a phase."

his house and hang up. She'd draw pictures for him, but never send them. If she wasn't looking him up online, she was talking about him endlessly. She finally got the courage to e-mail him, but he never responded. I don't think I've ever seen her so depressed. The only reason she finished *Order Of The Phoenix* was because she knew it would outsell all his

books put together."

Many of Rowling's fans disapprove of the author's decision to quit writing the *Harry Potter* series. Some here also complained about the amount of makeup Rowling has begun to wear, her choice of friends, and her recent decision to get her belly button pierced.

"I can't believe she would give up something she worked so hard on, just because people might think it's not 'cool,'" said Nancy Listrom, a Boston resident and fan of the *Harry Potter* books. "I blame that Mindy girl. She's a bad influence."

Added Listrom: "And I can't believe her publicist allows her to show up at a bookstore appearance dressed in that pink skirt. It barely covers her butt. Her writing is a better way to get attention."

Philadelphia fan Jack Powell said discipline is the solution.

"If it were up to me, I'd ground her until she finished the series," Powell said. "If we let her quit now, what kind of message does that send?"

It seems unlikely that fans' comments will do anything to reverse Rowling's decision. Last week, the author said she can't believe how "immature" her novels are.

"When I look back at these books, I am, like, humiliated that anyone read them," Rowling said in a June 12 article in the *London Times*. "I wish they would all just go away. Whenever I meet a boy that I like, someone always shows him my books and makes a big deal about how they're the best-selling books in the world. It's so embarrassing."

Knowles reassured fans that Rowling is "probably just going through a phase."

"Ms. Rowling loves writing, but she's just a little boy crazy," Knowles said. "Like any 39-year-old woman, her hormones are raging. Right now, all she wants to do is go to parties and daydream about her wedding, but that won't last more than a few years. Watch what happens after her first big breakup." ⌀

We Have Confirmation That Someone Has Tested A Thanatos Device

By Dept. Head Rawlings

Thank you for seeing us on such short notice, sir. Please take a seat. Coffee? Brandy? My humidor is open to you, if you wish. I apologize for taking you away from your family with so little warning, but events have overtaken us—events which, as you'll soon see, involve our entire organization. Sir, what I am about to tell you is known by only 11 people in the Western world—the seven of us in this room, the Acting Director, and the three pertinent members of the Staff Council. Though I know you to be circumspect and discreet, I'm afraid this is no ordinary intelligence briefing. The issue at hand is beyond the scope of even our long-term Global Strategy 7. If you'd like to sit down, we'll begin.

We have received confirmation that, somewhere in the great Garagum desert in Turkmenistan, an organization unknown to us has successfully tested a Thanatos device.

Now, in light of that rather staggering fact—sir? Why, yes, by all means avail yourself of the coffee. Here, allow me to add the brandy, your hands are... there. Yes, I understand, sir. Take your time.

Yes, so, in light of this startling fact, we are positioning all available field resources appropriately. We need two things from you at your very earliest convenience. You must provide me with a list of people who may possibly have aided the Turkmen in the development of the device. And secondly—well, I'm terribly sorry, sir, but this business we're in... Of course, we'll need your signed resignation on my desk by this time tomorrow.

Yes, of course—if there is a tomorrow, indeed. The Thanatos device does make one nostalgic for the old days of mutually assured nuclear destruction and its attendant comfort of shelter beneath the mountains. Even the phrase, "mutually assured nuclear destruction," seems rather quaint now, doesn't it?

No one at the department, least of all myself, believes that anything was deliberately hidden from us, but certain knowledge concerning Californium-298 and the more, shall we say, chthonic properties of tachyons—I must admit it gives me pause.

Getting to the point, sir, I was approached yesterday by your department's own Herr Professor-Doktor Steinesser, a man whom I know by rumor and reputation. Until this morning, the two working Thanatic resonators fabricated by his predecessor were believed to be the only examples of their kind. He had instructions to bypass your office and report directly to me in certain contingencies. This was one. Steinesser's team detected bursts of theta-amplitude pseudoparticles coruscating from Turkmenistan 3 days ago. Being aware of the antitemporal nature of his field, he knew to look for unusually high activity in the teracycle bands, curiously violent and unnaturally symmetrical sunspot formations, and small measurable lapses in general and relative causali-

> ## The Thanatos device does make one nostalgic for the old days of mutually assured nuclear destruction and its attendant comfort of shelter beneath the mountains.

ty. He claims they point to only one thing: their newfound Thanatic capability. Yes, someone was cunning and formidable enough to not only build a device, but to hide it from us, as well.

Please don't worry about the carpet. So, protocol demands that you cede control of your department to me and retire to our complex on the Peninsula. You'll remain here for no more than 36 hours in an advisory capacity, and then you're off to join your family. They are being moved at this very minute. I wish I could say I know with 100 percent certainty that they'll be safe, but a rogue Thanatos... Yes, quite right.

And so we come to an end, old comrade. I'm sorry it had to be like this, but, well, this business we're in, eh? Exactly, exactly, duty above all. Best traditions of the Departments, potentia est and all that. It'll be me someday, you know, and I can't say I'll be completely sorry. In any case, best to the family. They'll enjoy the Peninsula, and so will you. The debriefing for your retirement is far from strenuous, and the fishing there... Certainly wish I could visit. I certainly do.

Yes. Goodbye, Bertie. Farewell.

Everyone else, your aircraft leave for Turkmenistan at Zulu 400. We're done here. Thank you. And God save us all. ∅

Your Horoscope

**By Lloyd Schumner Sr.
Retired Machinist and
A.A.P.B.-Certified Astrologer**

Aries: (March 21–April 19)
You're about to learn that words can hurt, especially those written in the Demon Alphabet of Foul Khal-Ru the Soul-Drinker.

Taurus: (April 20–May 20)
You'll be violated hundreds of times by out-of-control alcoholics, but it's to be expected, considering that you're the local ordinance against drunk and disorderly conduct.

Gemini: (May 21–June 21)
Depression will wash over you exactly like a great wave this week, leaving sand everywhere you don't want it.

Cancer: (June 22–July 22)
Right about now, you're probably dying to know what all has happened since you fell asleep last Valentine's Day.

Leo: (July 23–Aug. 22)
A dark time in your life will come to a sudden end after an unexpected, drastic improvement in Ronald Reagan's condition.

Virgo: (Aug. 23–Sept. 22)
You'd long given up any hope, but a voice from your past will inform you that it is indeed okay for you to have the rest of the cottage cheese.

Libra: (Sept. 23–Oct. 23)
It has always been difficult for you to say you're sorry, but you will face your greatest challenge this Thursday, when wasps build a nest in your larynx.

Scorpio: (Oct. 24–Nov. 21)
You claim that you never asked for this crap, but there's your signature, plain as day, on all the crap-request forms.

Sagittarius: (Nov. 22–Dec. 21)
You'll learn an important lesson about violence this week—specifically, what can happen when you're not very good at it.

Capricorn: (Dec. 22–Jan. 19)
Your kissing booth will raise a lot of money for charity, but you're about to see more asses than you ever knew existed.

Aquarius: (Jan. 20–Feb. 18)
The weird and sometimes unfriendly looks you'll receive on your bus ride through the South are perhaps the only downside to your new hobby as a Civil Rights re-enactor.

Pisces: (Feb. 19–March 20)
Everyone warned you that nothing good would come of dishonesty, but you're perfectly happy with all the mediocre stuff that did.

JAM from page 32

amounts of blood. Passersby were amazed by the unusually large amounts of blood. Passersby were amazed by the unusually large

amounts of blood. Passersby were amazed by the unusually large amounts of blood. Passersby were amazed by the unusually large amounts of blood. Passersby were amazed by the unusually large amounts of blood. Passersby were amazed by the unusually large amounts of blood. Passersby were amazed by the unusually large amounts of blood. Passersby were amazed by the unusually large

To heck with it— I *deserve* this parole.

amounts of blood. Passersby were amazed by the unusually large amounts of blood. Passersby were amazed by the unusually large amounts of blood. Passersby were amazed by the unusually large amounts of blood. Passersby were amazed by the unusually large amounts of blood. Passersby were amazed by the unusually large amounts of blood. Passersby were amazed by the unusually large amounts of blood. Passersby were amazed by the unusually large amounts of blood. Passersby were

see JAM page 222

Cast, Crew Of *Troy* Begin Disastrous 10-Year Journey Back To Hollywood

see ENTERTAINMENT page 11E

Employee Keeps Up The Good Work

see BUSINESS page 5C

Renter's Insurance: Should *You* Think About Getting It But Never Do It?

see HOME page 9D

A look at the numbers that shape your world.

Top Wedding Costs

21% Bail

7% Bride-shipping fees

12% Breeding of exotic mauve silkworms for bridesmaids' gowns

15% Liquor for Uncle Paul

11% Paying PETA to look the other way

14% Precious time of guests

20% 150 Lean Cuisines

THE ONION • $2.00 US • $3.00 CAN

---

the ONION®

VOLUME 40 ISSUE 25   AMERICA'S FINEST NEWS SOURCE™   24–30 JUNE 2004

Current Status of Iraqi Population

- Dead
- Not dead

Above: Bremer speaks before a large crowd of still-living Iraqi children.

Coalition: Vast Majority Of Iraqis Still Alive

BAGHDAD—As the Coalition Provisional Authority prepares to hand power over to an Iraqi-led interim government on June 30, CPA administrator L. Paul Bremer publicly touted the success of Operation Iraqi Freedom.

"As the Coalition's rule draws to a close, the numbers show that we have an awful lot to be proud of," Bremer said Tuesday. "As anyone who's taken a minute and actually looked at the figures can tell you, the vast majority

see IRAQIS page 196

China Stockpiling Massive Fireworks Arsenal

WASHINGTON, DC—Satellite photographs have revealed the recent test-detonation of several hundred extremely small explosive devices in the remote Guangxi Zhuang Autonomous Region of Southwestern China, sources from the U.S. Department of Defense reported Monday.

"The tests, combined with evidence that factory buildings in this area are operating at capacity, indicate a massive buildup in China's already substantial fireworks arsenal," Army festive-munitions expert Ronald Dowdy said. "We have also recorded an increase in the amount of cording, nitrides, and gaily colored paper being shipped to Jiangxi, Liaoning, and Hubei. Since China is already in

see CHINA page 196

中华人民共和国万岁

Above: Chinese officials conduct fireworks tests.

Jeff Gordon Never Gets Tired Of Seeing Face On Cheap Plastic Crap

CHARLOTTE, NC—NASCAR driver Jeff Gordon never tires of seeing his image on cheap, collectible junk, the four-time Winston Cup champion revealed Monday during a visit to the Hendrick Motorsports racing complex gift shop.

"Well, look at that!" Gordon said, grinning as he examined

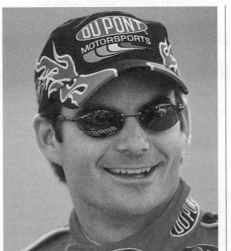

Left: Gordon, whose face is on mounds of rinky-dink crap in stores nationwide.

an illuminated license-plate frame bearing his likeness, signature, and yellow number 24. "That there's a real nice piece of tackle. I'll bet you could put one of my collectible laser-cut license plates in there and display it in your house. That'd look good next to your Jeff Gordon Collectible Shot Glass or your set of diecast #24 cars. Get a second one for your car, to match your Jeff Gordon

see GORDON page 197

Private Space Travel

Monday's SpaceShipOne flight could usher in an age of privately financed space travel. What do *you* think?

Michael Ellis
Systems Analyst

"If they develop a private space-travel vehicle, it'd better have some decent space-wireless access for my space-business-traveler needs."

Wayne Kupstis
Landscaper

"There's already a flag on the moon, right? Might as well put a Wal-Mart behind that one, too."

Richard Gettier
Waiter

"Is this part of that Bush Mars plan that he mentioned, like, once?"

LeeAnn Misek
Writer

"I suppose the flight is ushering in a new era of some sort that could change the way we view space travel, I guess."

Chad Devore
Pharmacist

"I can hear the radio transmission now. 'Outback Steakhouse, your place for steaks and family fun, we have a problem.'"

Maryann Lahr
Business Owner

"Hey, any idea that involves blasting the wealthiest .01 percent of the population into the cold, lifeless vacuum of space is all right by me."

Iraq's New Flag

Iraq is poised to assume self-rule, but many citizens are unhappy with the national flag unveiled in April. What are some of the flag's design elements?

- Blank space will allow for addition of sponsor logos
- Rectangular shape represents flagness
- Two stripes refer to Saddam's sons Uday and Qusay, who were totally fucking killed
- Real flag printed on reverse side for when U.S. leaves
- Crescent symbolizes sliver of chance that new democracy will succeed
- Yellow stripe representing Kurd minority will become thinner as Kurd population is slowly eradicated
- Blue color illustrates how sad Iraq is

the ONION®
America's Finest News Source.™

Herman Ulysses Zweibel
Founder

T. Herman Zweibel
Publisher Emeritus
J. Phineas Zweibel
Publisher
Maxwell Prescott Zweibel
Editor-In-Chief

I Refuse To Let Some Beached Whale Ruin Our Family Outing

By Patricia Halsworthy

Joshua! Kylie! Help your father and me unload the minivan. You can take care of the lighter things, like the mini-cooler and the badminton net. Daddy will carry the poles. Take your beach towels, too, and don't forget that Ziploc bag with the sunscreen. I don't want you kids getting sunburns. They say the worst skin damage occurs when you're young. Joshua? Kylie? Why are you still in the van? You haven't even unbuckled your seatbelts. Let's go!

What? Well, I suppose that's a beached whale over there. Of course I see it. So what? What is there to be afraid of? It's dead. Oh, will you stop. We're not going to a different beach. What? Now, look, Eric, don't take the children's side. They're clearly being unreasonable. You saw the traffic on that interstate. We planned this outing weeks ago, and we've all been looking forward to it.

Promontory Beach National Recreation Area, known for its pristine white sand and azure waters, is possibly the most beautiful beach in the region, according to the AAA guide. Why would we get all the way here just to go somewhere else? I am not going to let a stranded 50-foot sperm-whale carcass wreck our family outing. Now, let's clear out and claim a nice spot before the place gets too crowded.

My goodness, this is a glorious day! I'm glad we came early. There, that's as good a place as any to settle, about five feet from the whale. Let's get our towels down before someone claims the spot. Come on! Last one to the rotting whale is a rotten egg!

No, Eric, we're not going to move. The view is spectacular, and just because a rude old whale decided to die next to it doesn't make it any less so. Stop whining, everyone! Mind over matter. It's a good adage to remember, kids. No matter what obstacle is in front of you, you can still enjoy yourself if you don't pay any attention to it. That's what we're going to do today.

When I was growing up in South Dakota, we didn't have an ocean to enjoy. Sure, we had swimming holes and the Missouri River, but nothing as grand as a whole ocean. I used to dream of seeing it, and when I finally did, I appreciated every second of it. I still do. You kids are only 7 and 9, and already you've flown in an airplane, used chopsticks, and seen the ocean. I didn't do any of those things until well after I graduated from college. I'm happy that you've had the privileges I lacked, but I don't want you to take them for granted. That's a bad

habit to develop so young.

Kids, I'm already worried about this sun. There's not a cloud in the sky, and they say the sun is at its most damaging in the late morning. We should move into the shade. Here, let's sit in front of the whale's belly. It casts a nice big shadow. What "tube thing," Joshua? Oh, that. Well, I suppose that the whale's a boy, and that's the thing it goes to the bathroom with. You have one of your own, Joshua, so you should know. Only yours isn't eight feet long, is it? No, honey, don't touch it!

I read in the AAA guide that this beach was formed by a volcano millions of years ago. Can you imagine volcanoes this far north? Well, then

Whew, is anyone hungry? I sure am.

again, you have to remember that the land has shifted around a lot. Plate tectonics, it's called. Joshua, have you learned about that in school yet—plate tectonics? No? I'll have to have a word with your teacher. I should just pull you kids out of that awful school and teach you myself. I could do it. Eric, why don't you set up the badminton net so we can play? Here, honey. The poles telescope out. Or hitch one side over that fin.

Oh, look! The whale is still alive after all! Its side is heaving! My goodness, it is huge. It must easily weigh several tons. And look how it's weakly flapping its free fin. Don't worry, kids, it can't hurt you. It won't be alive much longer, anyhow. Oh, now I've done it, haven't I? Remember the dead starfish you found on the beach last year? Well, this is no different.

Kylie, stop crying.

There's more to see on this outing than just some silly old bloated dying whale. Like that buzzard over there! Hello, Mr. Buzzard!

Whew, is anyone hungry? I sure am. I was in such a rush getting everyone up and the van loaded that I didn't eat any breakfast. Granola bar, anyone? There are some nice pears in the big cooler. Oh, Joshua, the whale doesn't smell that bad. I didn't hear you complaining about the stench from Flowerpot's litter box when you neglected to clean it last week. You've been very irresponsible with that cat, Joshua. I should give her to that nice Levine girl up the street with all the pets.

Okay, okay, everybody just calm down. Joshua! Get back here! It was only the whale's tummy exploding a little. As the whale perishes, its body

see WHALE page 198

Erotic-Horror Screenplay Discovered On Office Printer

EVANSTON, IL—Coldwell Banker receptionist Annette Lyon, 29, discovered an unattributed screenplay for a feature-length erotic thriller on a printer shared by all of the Evanston-branch employees Monday, raising company-wde speculation as to the script's author.

"It was a very thick stack of paper, but I didn't take it off the printer until about 40 other things had already come and gone," said Lyon, who found the 116-page screenplay just after lunch. "At that point, it seemed to me like, if the author of *Darkness Of Passion* really didn't want people reading it, he wouldn't have left it sitting there."

Added Lyon: "Knowing what I know now, I wish I'd just left well enough alone."

The screenplay follows the adventures of a Chicago rock-club owner drawn into the intrigue surrounding a series of mysterious deaths, which follow the arrival of a rock band made up of four beautiful women from Eastern Europe.

"There's a lot of pouting, torn blouses that reveal pear-shaped breasts, and girl-on-girl grinding," Lyon said. "By the fourth speech about 'the sensuality of blood,' I started getting pretty creeped out. I never would've guessed that someone in this office had that many sexual hang-ups. Yuck."

In the script, violent murder scenes are interspersed with graveyard seductions, moonlit nude baths, and a six-page monologue about the "intersection of death and desire."

After reading the work in its entirety, Lyon showed it to several of her coworkers.

> "Check this out!" office manager Helen Gates said. "The vampire says, 'Darkness is a mask like any other. Put the mask in place, and allow your true passions to ride.' God, it's so over the top! It's hysterical."

"Check this out!" office manager Helen Gates said. "The vampire says, 'Darkness is a mask like any other. Put the mask in place, and allow your true passions to ride.' God, it's so over the top! It's hysterical."

Gates and Lyon shared several theories about who might have written the script.

Above: Lyon holds the erotic-horror screenplay.

"About 90 different people share the printer," Lyon said. "Judging by what I read, the author is a man. He's a pretty solid speller and has a working knowledge of the bus routes, so that rules out just about all of management."

"Whoever it is," Gates said, "there's no question he has a thing for bondage."

Lyon flipped to a random page of the script and read aloud. "'Unaware of the ruthlessness of the vampiress she is pleasuring, the supple-bodied groupie digs her nails into Esmerelda's back, leaving a tracing of gouges'—you know, maybe we should really stop speculating," Lyon said, dropping the script with distaste. "It might be best if we don't find out who wrote this after all."

Undaunted, Gates continued to try to deduce the script's author.

"[Sales representative] Janet Delaney is a serious conservative Christian, so see SCREENPLAY page 197

Saddam Hussein Freed On Technicality

BAGHDAD—The U.S. was forced to free accused war criminal Saddam Hussein Monday following the revelation that the former Iraqi dictator had been arrested in an illegal search. "American special forces neglected to obtain proper search warrants before dragging Mr. Hussein from his hiding place outside of Adwar," Iraqi prime minister Iyad Allawi said in a morning press conference. "In accordance with international law, the Americans had no choice but to free him." Hussein, who is still named as the defendant in hundreds of outstanding civil cases, said his release was proof that the system works.

Local Woman Dies Of Lost Cell Phone

APALACHICOLA, FL—Catherine Polk, 24, died at a local Starbucks Monday afternoon, due to complications resulting from the tragic loss of her cell phone. "It was horrible—Cathy didn't have any of her numbers written down anywhere else, and she was waiting on a call about last-minute tickets for a concert," said best friend Melissa Barreth, who was with Polk when she first discovered that her Cingular V400 quad band/GSM cell phone was not in her purse. "We tried everything to find it, but in the end, there was nothing we could do." The coroner's report confirmed that Polk died of a sudden lack of wireless service.

Power-Crazed Orkin Man Burns House To Ground

ESTES PARK, CO—Neighbors and loved ones joined the former residents of 22 Everglade Pass Monday to marvel at the still-smoldering remains of the house razed by Orkin exterminator Zach Knight. "I called Orkin and told them we had ants," former homeowner Bill Danby said. "Twenty minutes later, a guy in a red polo shirt and a mask knocked on the door, told us to get out of the house, and said we should take our most precious belongings. Minutes later, we smelled smoke." That night, Danby received a phone call from an anonymous party, who warned him that "the Orkin man *will* be back" to perform a follow-up inspection of the property Thursday.

Dysfunctional Family Statistically Average

MORSE BLUFF, NE—Although neighbors report that the Kenner family is "immensely troubled," recently published statistics suggest they are more or less average, sources reported Monday. "Sure, the kids are upset that Doug and Tammy are splitting up because of Doug's extramarital affairs, but that's hardly unusual," said analyst Doreen Fellows, who cited 2000 U.S. Census figures indicating that more than 60 percent of all American children are from divorced families. "Maybe the family would have fared better if not for Doreen's drinking, but the situation is far from unusual. According to the American Medical Association, 72 percent of American homes harbor someone with an addiction." Unbeknownst to the Kenners, one out of four family members will contract chlamydia in his or her lifetime.

7-Year-Old Asshole Demands You King Him

COS COB, CT—On his 14th turn of the game Monday, 7-year-old asshole Andy Scot advanced a checker to the opposite end of the board and plunked it down on a black square. "King me," the smug little bastard said, folding his pudgy arms across his sweater-vested chest. "Do it." The checkers game, which continued apace after you placed a checker on top of his, was at least a reprieve from hearing the little shit say "sorry" during the game of the same name. ✐

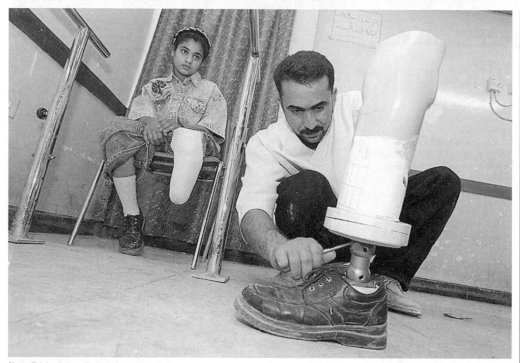

Above: Two Iraqis from Tikrit who are very much alive.

of Iraqis are still alive—as many as 99 percent. While 10,000 or so Iraqi civilians have been killed, pretty much everyone is not dead."

According to U.S. Department of Defense statistics, of the approximately 24 million Iraqis who were not killed, nearly all are not in a military prison. Bremer said "a good number" of those Iraqis who are in jail have been charged with a crime, and most of them have enjoyed a prison stay free of guard-dog attacks, low-watt electrocutions, and sexual humiliation.

U.S. Brig. Gen. Mark Kimmitt explained the coalition's accomplishments in geographical terms.

"There are vast sections of the country where one can go outside unarmed during the daylight hours," Kimmitt said, speaking from a heavily guarded base outside of Baghdad. "Even in cities where fighting has occurred, many neighborhoods have not

been torn apart by gunfire. And, throughout the country, more towns than I could name off the top of my head have never been touched by a bomb at all."

Kimmitt said the bulk of the nation's public buildings are still standing.

"Throughout the nation, four out of five mosques have not been obliterated," Kimmitt said. "That's way, way, way more than half. Also, 80 percent of the nation's treasures and artifacts have not been destroyed by artillery or stolen in the widespread looting. If we were in school, that'd be a B-minus."

Halliburton executive vice-president and CFO C. Christopher Gaut described the progress of his company's reconstruction efforts.

"Of the millions of civilian homes that are still standing, many have electricity for hours each day," Gaut said. "The loss of $200 million in profits resulting from oil-line sabotage

pales in comparison to the millions of dollars that remaining lines are generating. And a good portion of southern Iraq currently has access to fuel. Once we get the lines in the north repaired, oil fields will be operating at more than two-thirds of their former capacity."

Gaut added: "Many of the hospitals have reopened, and a good number of the schools have started holding classes at regularly scheduled hours, too."

Charles Sawyer, a State Department official serving as a liaison between coalition forces and the Iraqi interim government, said that no Americans have been killed in Fallujah since the coalition ceded control of the region to an Iraqi brigade.

"Less than 10 contractors have been murdered, publicly mutilated, or had their remains hung from a bridge since the end of March," Sawyer said. "And nearly three quarters of the foreign-born contract workers taken

hostage in the last six months have not been killed. Also, contrary to headlines that claim there are problems with Iraq's internal law enforcement, more than half of Iraqi police officers have not deserted."

U.S. Army Gen. John P. Abizaid gave a positive assessment of the status of U.S. troops in Iraq.

"Yesterday alone, 137,980 American troops were not killed," Abizaid said. "All in all, if we keep on like this, more than 90 percent of the brave men and women serving in Iraq will return home to see their families again."

Iraq's new prime minister, Iyad

> "Throughout the nation, four out of five mosques have not been obliterated," Kimmitt said. "That's way, way, way more than half. Also, 80 percent of the nation's treasures and artifacts have not been destroyed by artillery or stolen in the widespread looting."

Allawi, agreed that the situation in his soon-to-be-independent nation is improving.

"Of the 25 members of the Iraqi Governing Council, 23 survived until the group was replaced last month," Allawi said. "Nine out of 10 times, death threats against those who cooperate with coalition efforts do not end in actual murders."

However, Allawi added that, despite the wishes of most of his countrymen, the vast majority of American troops deployed to Iraq are still there. ∅

possession of enough fireworks to delight the entire world 50 times over, we can only assume that they're gearing up for an imminent celebration of unprecedented size."

The Pentagon reports that the current Chinese fireworks arsenal, which is known to include land-based firecrackers, bottle-to-air rockets, and the oft-criticized M-80, is believed to hold a delighting force in excess of 10,000 megafuns—or, in the words of one expert, "almost a billion times the merriment produced by a single cherry bomb."

With the signing of the landmark international Black Cat Limitation Treaty in 1989, the Chinese government committed to slashing its fireworks production in half. As a part of

the agreement, adult-supervision officials have been allowed to inspect factories in Jiangsu and Guangdong provinces, which had been converted to sparkler production in recent years.

Recent intelligence suggests that China simply shifted major fireworks manufacturing to other locations.

"These are not the innocent magic snakes, smoke bombs, and snap-pops that China is legally allowed to deploy for inoffensive purposes," Dowdy said. "These are full-blown instruments of mass recreation—whistling pinwheels, multiple-effect fountains, and single-shot shells that launch 80 feet into the air. Why, we've gotten reports of shells in excess of 50 shots, strobing starbursts, and, in the case of The Big Kahuna, multiple tiger tails. I'm not

comfortable knowing that, at any time, a major American city could be jarred by a sudden flash and loud report."

According to Dowdy, the Chinese government has refused to acknowledge any violation of international law, claiming that its arsenal is not of an unusual size for the season. It has also defended its fireworks production as a part of Chinese culture.

But U.S. officials have expressed concern that the extremely portable fireworks, packaged in normal shipping containers and labeled as ordinary trade goods, could enter our country in large numbers.

"Despite strict laws limiting their use, a significant amount of Chinese-made fireworks ends up in North America every year," Depart-

ment of Homeland Security domestic-affairs advisor Beth Galliard said. "We'll be patrolling the nation's rural gas stations, searching for any possible distribution points for these fireworks."

Galliard said that, while she doesn't want to be an alarmist, she has received reliable intelligence suggesting that a major fireworks-related incident on American soil is being planned for early July.

"It's frightening to think that nearly anybody could enter a populated area—say, a picnic shelter or a crowded beach—with a few fireworks and a book of matches," Galliard said. "To create utter chaos, all they'd need to do is place the device on the ground, light fuse, and get away." ∅

GORDON from page 193

Floormats and Jeff Gordon DuPont Racing Keychain, and you'll be good to go."

"Hey!" Gordon added, repeatedly pressing a button bearing a "Try Me" sticker. "I light up. Ain't that something else?"

Gordon, who became the youngest Daytona 500 winner in 1997, has enjoyed a 10-year career at the highest level of American auto racing. The 32-year-old's multiple championships and 66 race victories have garnered him more than $60 million in winnings, and he earns millions of dollars in additional income each year through the sale of gewgaws like belt buckles, rings, knives, lunchboxes, dog collars, watches, bedding sets, and cigarette lighters with his face on them.

"The other day, I was at a Kmart and came across the Jeff Gordon Stained Glass Bar Lamp," Gordon said. "It was a lamp with me on it. Can you believe it? That gave me such a kick."

The Jeff Gordon Can Cozie, the Jeff Gordon #24 TrackSider Flip-Flops, and the Jeff Gordon Home Collection Wallpaper Border are just a few of the items that fans, and Gordon himself, can't get enough of.

"The other day, I even saw me-pajamas," Gordon said.

Gordon's manager, Forrest Logan, commented on the racecar driver's enthusiasm.

"There ain't too many things Jeff enjoys as much as racing," Logan said. "There's winning, of course. There are his fans—they're the best in the world. And then there's strolling through the aisles at Wal-Mart and seeing his face on everything from here to Sunday, like the Jeff Gordon 8-piece BBQ Set, the Jeff Gordon Edition Tire Valve Caps, and, for the ladies, the Jeff Gordon DuPont Racing #24 Clutch."

"That's a little purse with Jeff on the side," Logan added.

Gordon's many commercial endorsements—with corporations ranging from Coke to Kellogg's—further increase the amount of tacky garbage bearing his face.

"Yup, seems as though I can't buy a hoagie without some kid handing me a cup that's got me and my car on it," Gordon said. "I don't mind one bit, though. I love to sit back and sip on a Coke and look at that car. It's a great car, ain't it?"

Gordon crew chief Robbie Loomis, who gets his Jeff Gordon useless garbage free, said he has grown accustomed to seeing pictures of Gordon on most of his possessions.

"I appreciate all of the duffel bags and whatnot," Loomis said. "And check out the big ol' mustache Jeff's got on my souvenir mug. I always liked that mustache on him. You know, I think he'd sell a lot more Jeff Gordon 18-Can Cooler Bags if he was sporting a mustache on them, too. I tell you."

Above: Some of the Gordon shit one can buy at the online NASCAR Superstore.

Exiting the store and heading back to the pit, Gordon seemed determined not to let his success, his fame, or the fact that millions of tacky so-called collectibles bear his image go to his head.

"Fans of stockcar racing are a real down-home group," Gordon said, adjusting his Official Father's Day Edition Jeff Gordon/Hendrick Motorsports Pit Crew Hat. "They wouldn't forgive me if I got a big head. Once in a while, I can authorize a Jeff Gordon Ranger 519DX Bass Boat, or put together a Jeff Gordon-Escort Travel Luxury Tour Of The Holy Land. But they'll think I'm getting too big for my britches if I don't mainly stick to affordable stuff like the Jeff Gordon Teddy Bear In Racing Suit and the Jeff Gordon Candle Set."

"People never seem to get tired of seeing my name and number on stuff," Gordon said, absent-mindedly cleaning his Jeff Gordon Foster Grant Sunglasses on the sleeve of his Jeff Gordon Cotton-Twill Team Jacket. "And you know what? Neither do I." ∅

SCREENPLAY from page 195

she'd never write about fucking a crucifix," Gates said. "And [vice-president of marketing] Joe Opper isn't creative enough to write his own letters, let alone a movie. [Assistant manager] Tony Bursell talks about movies a lot,

> **"I think the writer wanted feedback, but was afraid to ask for it outright," Gates said. "Well, my message to him is: Don't quit your day job. Unless you've accidentally let everyone at your day job know that you get off on lesbian vampires."**

but he's gay. Even though I can see Tony getting into the ancient sexual rites of the Celtic goddess Agrona and the lust of Count Drakul, all the lesbian sex points to an author who's straight."

Gates brought up the possibility that a coworker had printed the screenplay for a friend, but Lyon dismissed the idea, pointing out that several of the characters closely resemble Coldwell Banker employees.

"Take the uptight woman who gets impaled on a tree branch," Lyon said. "That woman was obviously [sales supervisor] Darcy Gasney—the clothes, the hair color, the clipped way she talks. I saw a little of myself in Emily, the tough but sensitive virginal woman with the, uh, huge breasts—the one who becomes the vampire's slave, not the one who sings in the girl band. But I also saw myself in Felicia, the tough but sensitive biker bartender with large breasts. Well, neither character is particularly flattering."

When the conversation turned to the script's plot, the small group of assembled coworkers temporarily forgot their curiosity about the script's author, focusing instead on the structural flaws in his work.

"Why are the vampires lesbians?" sales agent Cal Fagan asked. "Were they lesbians before they became

Above: An excerpt from Darkness Of Passion.

vampires, or did getting bitten have something to do with it? I never understood that. And is it necessary for them to seduce their victims before killing them? Why do they 'writhe sinuously' on every other page? And what did William's secret meeting with the dominatrix have to do with anything? I'm sorry, it just seemed gratuitous."

So far, no one has come forward to claim the screenplay, leading several employees to speculate that it was deliberately left on the printer.

"Please," Lyon said. "You don't print a document in which a pack of wolves sensually lick a naked dead body and then just have it slip your mind."

"I don't know," Fagan said. "I can see how someone might have printed it out and then gotten involved in something and forgotten to grab it. On the other hand, if I wrote a whole movie, I'd probably be pretty proud and want to show it off."

Gates agreed.

"I think the writer wanted feedback, but was afraid to ask for it outright," Gates said. "Well, my message to him is: Don't quit your day job. Unless you've accidentally let everyone at your day job know that you get off on lesbian vampires."

Contacted for his opinion of the script, Joshua Black, a junior talent agent at Brinkman Carver in San Diego, CA, offered a contrary opinion.

"It's too long, the characters are interchangeable, and there's no third act," Black said. "That said, it's hard to turn down a vampire movie, particularly one with so much softcore nudity. If I were a little studio looking for a shot in the arm, there's a chance I'd option it, give it a quick coat of paint, shoot it on the cheap, and dump it straight to DVD. It won't do much domestically, but you could stand to recoup and then some on the international market." ∅

Julia Roberts Is A Pretty Pregnant Woman!

Item! Julia Roberts is going to have a baby! Actually, she's having two babies—twins! It's the beginning of a new dynasty, like the **Barrymores** or the **Bridgeses** or the **Baldwins**. Right when the Olson Sisters got too old to be cute, America's Sweetheart is turning out a whole new set for us to fall in love with. Congrats to Julia and her husband, **Lyle Lovitz!** (Hope the kids get their looks from Julia!)

The Outside Scoop
By Jackie Harvey

Item! Television's **Jerry Seinfield** is back, and he brought a friend with him—my boyhood hero **Superman!** The amazing duo is making commercials for **American Express.** I have an idea for a commercial: Jerry and Superman team up to find **Ossama bin Laden**, but then, because they start arguing about something funny, Ossama gets away! If you know Jerry, tell him he can use that one—on me!

I'm really getting into pineapples these days. Growing up, my pineapple always came from a can, so it used to be, when I saw a whole fresh pineapple, I'd think, "Whoa, how do you even start to eat that?" I had no idea how to even open one, but last month, I bought one anyway because I love to try new things. Surprise! There was a card with instructions attached! The lesson here: Never be afraid to try something different at the supermarket.

Item! Word on the street is that *Baywatch's* **David Castlehof** is falling in with the wrong crowd. First, the news came out that he was going to record a rap album with gang member **Iced T.** Then he was arrested for **drunk driving.** Coincidence? I don't see how it could be. If you fall in with a bad crowd, bad will come of it. David, you should have hooked up with a nice rapper, like **Jay-C.** He has his own line of clothes.

Item! Wolverine won a **Tony!** After seeing him at his moody, glowering best in **X Games** and the sequel, **X2**, I had a feeling he had it in him to sing and dance on stage, and I don't mind telling you that I was right. He knocked my socks off as **Liza Minelli**'s first (and only, in my book) husband, **Dave Allen.** Congratulations, **Hugh Jackson!**

(There were plenty of other surprises at the Tonys, but I'm sure you all saw the awards ceremony, so there's no point in my wasting your time.)

It's the end of an era. **Friends** is done forever, and already their friendly antics are fading away, like a dream that you remember when you first wake up, but becomes harder to recall as the day wears on. I've been catching the show from my home office a few times a day now that it's in syndication, but it's just not the same. I feel like I'm trying to recapture old glories. Maybe they'll put together a new show of the best outtakes. Heck, with 10 years of episodes, they could probably make a full season of that. As long as they didn't put it up against any **CSI** series, I'd watch.

And I can't even remember the name of that **radio psychiatrist show** anymore. Do you remember the one? What's the deal with **Deadwood?** I've heard a few things about it, mostly that it's full of words I wouldn't want my mother to hear. I thought the FTC told everyone to clean up their acts after that whole **costume malfunction** earlier this year. I guess the people at HBO didn't get the memo.

I just discovered **Feng Suey**, the Japanese art of arranging your home so it will be visited by good spirits. I can't wait to try it. The article I read didn't say how to arrange my **bobblehead dolls**, though. I guess I'll have to buy the book.

Item! J-Lo got J-married! The Queen Of Booty got married in a surprise ceremony to **Mark Anthony.** I hope this isn't the same Mark Anthony who helped kill **Julius Caesar**—if so, he must be about 600 years old! Let's hope that the third time's the charm for the lovely Lopez and the second time's the charm for Anthony. She deserves some happiness after being strung along by **Ben Affleck** for so long.

Item! Ray Charles passed away. I saw him play a few years ago, and I'll never forget how he looked, playing the piano, bobbing around like he hadn't a care in the world. Watching him play, I didn't have a care in the world, either. Summer is the season of death. We'll miss you, Ray.

Ronald Reagan died, too. I may not have agreed with him about everything, but he had some very presidential qualities. He came out of Hollywood, so he was suited to the role of America's leading man. He had a quick wit and a well-modulated voice. He laid off all the **air-traffic controllers**, my cousin **Glen** among them, but he was also the man who brought an end to our nuclear weapons program. I'm no historian. I only know what I saw.

I've been thinking about getting a **puppy** lately. They don't need much care, just some food and a walk once in a while, but they give so much affection. Also, they're just the thing I need to help me meet that special someone. (I'm told that childless women go ga-ga over puppies.)

I'm out of space, so that will have to do for this episode of The Outside Scoop. Come back next time to hear the real deal about the romance on the set of **Harry Potter.** Also, I'll give you my two cents about **Roger Moore** and **Fahrenheit 411.** Until then, I'll be first in line, heading right up to the center seat and shushing everyone so that I can give you the straight scoop, unfiltered… from The Outside. *⌀*

> **I just discovered Feng Suey, the Japanese art of arranging your home so it will be visited by good spirits. I can't wait to try it.**

Your Horoscope

By Lloyd Schumner Sr.
Retired Machinist and
A.A.P.B.-Certified Astrologer

Aries: (March 21–April 19)
You were all set to have a whirlwind week of romance and a landslide financial success, but a supernova in Cancer has changed your fortune to regular whirlwinds and landslides.

Taurus: (April 20–May 20)
You will have mixed feelings about your career this week when you're unexpectedly promoted from assistant third-shift server to Admiral of the Fifth Fleet.

Gemini: (May 21–June 21)
You're about to go through a very sad time of the soul, but now that Ray Charles is dead, that's pretty much true for everybody.

Cancer: (June 22–July 22)
You've said that your head will explode if you hear one more bad dance remix, but club-goers will still be shocked and appalled when it happens.

Leo: (July 23–Aug. 22)
You'll disprove an old adage this week when you use violence to solve the General Deg 5 polynomial equation.

Virgo: (Aug. 23–Sept. 22)
If you had to do it all over again, you wouldn't change a thing, which proves that you're a masochistic submoron.

Libra: (Sept. 23–Oct. 23)
Getting hit by a crosstown city bus once was bad enough, but you thought moving to the countryside of Pago Pago would prevent a second incident.

Scorpio: (Oct. 24–Nov. 21)
Many twins have a certain telepathy, which explains why someone who looks just like you will appear this week and order you to stop thinking about pie.

Sagittarius: (Nov. 22–Dec. 21)
Sports metaphors are among the most trite, but it's hard to deny that your life is a lot like *buzkashi*, a violent Afghan form of polo played with goat corpses.

Capricorn: (Dec. 22–Jan. 19)
The story of your ocean voyage will inspire a song of such tragic beauty that it will be known as the next "Edmund Fitzgerald."

Aquarius: (Jan. 20–Feb. 18)
What with the threshing machine, the barrels of cyanide, and the Gatling gun, the coroner will have a hell of a time determining your cause of death.

Pisces: (Feb. 19–March 20)
You used to think there's no such thing as bad publicity, but that was before you saw your profile in *Us Weekly*.

WHALE from page 194

fills with gas, and then it needs somewhere to escape. It's just like when you drink a little too much soda. That's why we only brought juice on this trip. Look, this sort of thing happens during decomposition. Remember—death is just the final stage of life. Sober heads, now.

Come on, Kylie, Joshua, Eric, let's all go for a swim. Let's wash all this black, inky sludge off our bodies. Bring your boogie boards!

Eric, stand up! It's so typical of our family for one of you to faint from the sulfurous gas fumes produced by the putrefying innards of a beached sperm whale. I didn't vomit and fall over when I discovered those blackened bananas wedged under the backseat in the minivan this morning! Eric, you're as bad as the children.

Well, if you're just going to lie around and pass out, I'm going to go for a walk. I was hoping we could spend the day together as a family. But I'm not going to let a decaying whale or three spoilsports ruin my outing. Ooh, look! A sand dollar! *⌀*

Supreme Court Told To Take Down Tip Jar

see WASHINGTON page 3B

Couple Forgets 70th Wedding Anniversary

see PEOPLE page 15D

Home Office Thrown From Balcony

see LOCAL page 8C

Fetus Can Feel Daddy Kick

see PARENTS page 15E

STATshot

A look at the numbers that shape your world.

What Are We Restoring?

20% Finish on hand-me-down wooden leg

14% Shred of our dignity

19% A little excitement to pool tournament

26% Mummy we accidentally drove forklift into

21% Our career *and* our relationship, all in one crazy night

the ONION®

VOLUME 40 ISSUE 27   AMERICA'S FINEST NEWS SOURCE™   8–14 JULY 2004

D.C. Site Of First Homeless Depot

WASHINGTON, DC—In a grand opening Monday, Washington became home to the first Homeless Depot, one link in a nationwide chain of warehouse-style stores that will supply the nation's estimated 350,000 homeless people with all of their street-lifestyle essentials.

"There are 14,000 homeless people in D.C. alone, but there's never been a retail business that catered to their unique needs," store manager Geoff Alberts said. "Homeless Depot is a one-stop spot for cardboard building

see DEPOT page 203

Above: Early-bird shoppers visit the new Homeless Depot.

Devious Rabbit Tricks Bush Into Signing Gun Ban

WASHINGTON, DC—The nation's sweeping new gun-control legislation is the result of a confidence trick pulled on President Bush by a devious rabbit, White House sources said Tuesday. The "Coney Act," which Bush signed into law Monday, prohibits the sale or ownership of handguns and semi-automatic weapons and enacts harsh penalties for the hunting of small game, most notably rabbits.

"The gun ban is not the result of a change in the Republican Party's position on gun ownership," Senate Majority Leader Bill Frist (R-TN) said. "It is the product of a fraud perpetrated by a conniving rabbit, perhaps as an elaborate ruse to avoid being eaten by the president, who is much bigger and stronger than he. Through the use of quick wits and cunning, not physical strength, that dang rabbit got the best of the president."

When he heard about the bill, Frist said he "immediately questioned its authenticity" and informed the president that its author, a "Senator Lepus H. Coney," was not an elected Alabama legislator.

At a press conference Tuesday, White House Press Secretary

see RABBIT page 202

Above: Reporters confront Bush about his recent bamboozling by a devious rabbit (left).

Activities Director Makes Most Of Hostage Situation

ITAMARAJU, BRAZIL—Four days after criminal organization Comando Vermelho seized control of the Novo Mundo Resort, activities director Janet Puchesy, 28, continues to make the most of the tense situation, bringing fun and creativity to the storage room where she and her fellow survivors are trapped, the hostage reported Monday.

"Okay, gang, who wants to have a sing-along?" Puchesy said quietly, hoping to avoid being added to the pile of nearly 30 resort guests and

see HOSTAGE page 202

Left: The Brazilian resort which employs Puchesy (inset).

The Interest-Rate Hike

Last week, the Federal Reserve raised a key short-term interest rate for the first time in four years. What do *you* think?

"It's about time Greenspan got off his duff and did something other than sit around the office all day analyzing market indicators."

Danielle Strohkirch
Secretary

"As long as the rate hike makes it tougher for terrorists to afford the tools of terror, I'll support it."

Justin Fillmore
Dental Hygienist

"Perfect. Just perfect. First my wife leaves me, then my son dies in a car accident, and now *this*?"

Michael Eighmy
Systems Analyst

"Classic move by the Fed Chief there. Man, Greenspan—gotta love him."

Tony Fields
Audiologist

"The lenders should fight the Feds and refuse to raise the rates. Come on, America. We can do this."

Jason Forst
Performer

"How does the Federal Reserve sleep at night? More to the point, how does it stay awake during the day?"

Christine Cain
Veterinarian

Fahrenheit 9/11

Michael Moore's documentary *Fahrenheit 9/11* has broken box-office records, but some Bush supporters say it's flawed. What is the basis of their objections?

- Moore misused a truck specifically tasked with the delivery of tasty ice cream
- Insinuates that Iraqi civilians don't like to be killed
- Claim that Bush was on vacation 42 percent of time does not acknowledge that he filled out proper vacation-request forms
- Totally ruined that "The Roof Is On Fire" song for everyone
- Moore's labored breathing troublesome
- There's no way John Ashcroft would be stupid enough to stand behind a podium with all the cameras on him and sing a song about an eagle
- Role of Michael Moore played by Michael Moore instead of camera-friendly John Goodman
- Moore distorts footage by adding comical "boing" sound effect every time Bush falls down

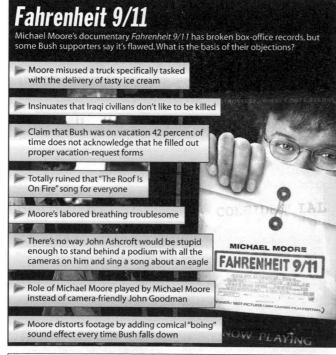

the ONION®
America's Finest News Source.™

Herman Ulysses Zweibel
Founder

T. Herman Zweibel
Publisher Emeritus
J. Phineas Zweibel
Publisher
Maxwell Prescott Zweibel
Editor-In-Chief

I Guess Now Would Be As Good A Time As Any To Triumph Over Adversity

By Ryan Halverson

They say that in every man's life there comes a time of reckoning when, faced with impossible odds, he must reach deep inside his soul and find the strength to rise to the occasion. I've never really gathered my strength and I haven't really risen to many occasions. I guess I couldn't say I've ever triumphed over adversity before. But I guess now might be as good a time as any.

It's just that, frankly, I'm kinda tired. Then again, I really don't have much choice. Chaos and crisis surround me. Trouble is bearing down. It's a relentless assault that I'll only be able to beat back with pure conviction. I'm the only one on God's green earth who can do what needs to be done. I guess I *have* to ascend to soaring heights, don't I?

Aw, Christ, I don't want to save the day, though. It's going to be such a hassle. But maybe triumphing over adversity is something you just bite the bullet and do. With the enemy at the gate and wolves howling in the distance, this would be the moment to figure that out. Get out there and, you know, man the balustrades or whatever. Ugh, I hate that. On one hand, I'm facing the destruction of everything I

> Aw, Christ, I don't want to save the day, though. It's going to be such a hassle. But maybe triumphing over adversity is something you just bite the bullet and do. With the enemy at the gate and wolves howling in the distance, this would be the moment to figure that out.

hold dear if I don't act. On the other hand, um... oh, whatever whatever.

So, technically, I guess, if I were to triumph now, it'd be an inspirational tale of true-life heroism in the face of near-certain defeat—the kind of story that makes people want to stand up and cheer. But really, I mean, come on, so what? Is it really worth the toil? Who knows? I sure don't. I've never triumphed over anything in my life. Maybe that's why my situation is so dire in the first place. Then again, maybe not. Maybe it would have hap-

> Well, I guess I can sorta picture me, brow furrowed, conveying a brand-new sense of purpose and determination, leaping into action, facing down the obstacles, and rising from this couch to boldly go forth into the fray.

pened just the same even if I had been defiantly taking stands all along. Hell, what do I know? I'm no triumphing-over-adversity expert.

I really can't keep putting it off, though. If I do, the adversity might grow that much worse. Then I'll have to shine out like a beacon of hope in *total* darkness. That'd *really* suck. I sure hope the whole "discovering the inner strength I never knew I had" part comes soon.

Well, I guess I can *sorta* picture me, brow furrowed, conveying a brand-new sense of purpose and determination, leaping into action, facing down the obstacles, and rising from this couch to boldly go forth into the fray. I don't suppose I could take these Cheetos with, huh? No, I guess not.

You want the truth? I'm just not up for a moment of unprecedented human achievement right now. Maybe after I finish watching the rest of this *Seinfeld* episode, I'll be in the mood to discover my previously untapped wells of courage and power. But maybe I'll take a nap first. If I go to bed right now, I could get a good night's rest, then get up early to conquer my demons in the morning. Yeah, makes sense—I should start in the morning. I know I'm faced with countless challenges right now, but if I get a solid night's sleep, I'll have a fresh start to gloriously triumph over adversity tomorrow. ∅

Nation's Liberals Suffering From Outrage Fatigue

Above: Flauman has trouble mustering outrage over Republican policy.

WASHINGTON, DC—According to a study released Monday by the Hammond Political Research Group, many of the nation's liberals are suffering from a vastly diminished sense of outrage.

"With so many right-wing shams to choose from, it's simply too daunting for the average, left-leaning citizen to maintain a sense of anger," said Rachel Neas, the study's director. "By our estimation, roughly 70 percent of liberals are experiencing some degree of lethargy resulting from a glut of civil-liberties abuses, education funding cuts, and exorbitant military expenditures."

> **"It used to be that I would turn on Pacifica Radio and be incensed at the top of every hour," Levine added.**

San Francisco's Arthur Flauman is one liberal who has chosen to take a hiatus from his seething rage over Bush Administration policies.

"Every day, my friends send me e-mails exposing Bush's corrupt environmental policies," said Flauman, a member of both the Green Party and the Sierra Club. "I used to spend close to an hour following all the links, and I'd be shocked and outraged by the irreversible damage being done to our land. At some point, though, I got annoyed with the demanding tone of the e-mails. The Clear Skies Initiative *is* bogus, but I'm not going to forward a six-page e-mail to all my friends—especially one written by a man who signs his name 'Leaf.' Now, if a message's subject line contains the word 'Bush,' it goes straight into the trash."

Neas found that many survey participants who attended protests against the war in Iraq in 2003 could barely summon the energy to read newspaper articles about the subject in 2004.

Portland, OR resident Suzanne Marshal compared herself to an addict, needing increasingly large doses of perceived injustices to achieve a state of anger.

"Even though I know how seriously messed-up the situation is in Iraq, I've became inured to all but the most extreme levels of wrongdoing," Marshal said. "For months, no amount of civilian bombing could get me mad. Then those amazing photos of the tortured Iraqi prisoners hit the streets, and I got that old rush of overwhelming disgust with my government. Then more photos came out, and more officials were implicated, and now—I don't know. It's like a switch in my head turned off again."

Neas said that the danger of fatigue was greater among liberals who regularly seek cause for outrage.

"For a while, I wanted more fuel for the fire, to really get my blood boiling," said Madison, WI resident Dorothy Levine, a reproductive-rights activist and former Howard Dean campaign volunteer. "I read the policy papers on the Brookings web site. I subscribed to *The Progressive*. I clipped cartoons by Tom Tomorrow and Ted Rall. I listened to NPR all day. But then, it was like, while I was reading Molly Ivins' *Bushwhacked*, eight more must-read anti-Bush books came out. It was overwhelming. By the time they released *Fahrenheit 9/11*, I was too exhausted to drag myself to the theater."

"It used to be that I would turn on Pacifica Radio and be incensed at the top of every hour," Levine added. "Now, I could find out that Bush plans to execute every 10th citizen and I'd barely blink an eye, much less raise a finger."

Of the liberals afflicted with fatigue, many said they are still haunted by the specters of their former outrage.

"I can't even look at the back of my Volvo anymore," said one Syracuse, NY liberal who wished to remain anonymous. "My 'Lick Bush' and 'Four More Wars' bumper stickers just remind me of the angry feelings I can't sustain. I still have a MoveOn.org sign hanging up in my cubicle at work, but if someone starts to talk about Cheney, I can't take it. I'm like, 'Yes, we all hate Cheney. He's an evil puppet-master. Yes, Bush is dumb. This is obvious. How many times can we say it? Now, excuse me, will you let me through so I can microwave my burrito?'" ⊘

NEWS IN BRIEF

Al-Qaeda Hires Public-Relations Consultant Just To Shoot Him

BAGHDAD—Al-Qaeda operative Mullah Hashem hired Elliot Dobin, a consultant for the Boston public-relations firm Schneider & Koff, for the sole purpose of murdering him, sources reported Monday. "The al-Qaeda have taken such a beating in the press that we figured they wanted to clean up their media image, so we sent our best guy," firm partner Jerry Koff said. "But Elliot had barely shaken everyone's hand when Hashem and his guards shoved him up against the wall and shot him in the back of the head. He didn't even get to show them his PowerPoint presentation." Bergman said he'll confront Hashem about the incident as soon as he figures out a way to spin Dobin's shooting into a positive.

7-Year-Old Loses Respect For Shrek After Seeing Him In Burger King Commercial

KANSAS CITY, MO—Cale Parnell, 7, said Monday that he no longer holds Shrek in high regard, ever since the green ogre started appearing in TV ads for Burger King Kids Meals. "Shrek just wants to sell things and make money," Parnell said. "He doesn't care if kids like me are having fun." Parnell added that Shrek is "just like that stupid money-grubber SpongeBob SquarePants."

Cashier Learning Valuable But Illegal Job Skills

BUTTE, MT—Three weeks into his first job, part-time Big Sky Foods cashier Vance Freeman is picking up invaluable but criminal workplace skills, the 16-year-old reported Monday. "This is just a minimum-wage job, but by taking the initiative to skim the till, I'm preparing for my future," Freeman said, as he surreptitiously slipped three quarters into his pocket. "Someday, I'll be able to apply my knowledge to a lucrative career in white-collar crimes like embezzlement, insider trading, maybe even fraud." Freeman said he's looking forward to his break, when Greg the produce guy will show him how to prop open the service entrance so he can sneak food out to his car.

Mild Sexual Harassment Ignored To Save The Hassle

NEW HAVEN, CT—Mindy Neuberg, 29, ignored an instance of sexual harassment "just to avoid the hassle," the attractive writer reported Tuesday. "This bouncer at Sweeney's pulled me out of the line to 'frisk me for weapons,' and after calling me 'sweet-cheeks,' he spent way too much time checking me for a gun," Neuberg said. "I should have complained, but I would've had to get his name, find the manager, and make my case... It just didn't seem worth it." Neuberg said that her decision to drop the issue was also influenced by the fact that, "after getting publicly felt up by some meathead," she really needed to get to the bar for a gin and tonic.

Sara Gilbert Crush Finally Starting To Subside

STEVENS POINT, WI—Area accountant James Perloff's crush on actress Sara Gilbert, best known for her portrayal of sarcastic teenager Darlene Conner on the sitcom *Roseanne*, has finally started to wane, the 30-year-old reported Monday. "I saw [Gilbert] on a talk show yesterday and my heart barely fluttered. When I was in high school, if Darlene walked on screen, my chest would absolutely pound," Perloff said. "Maybe I've turned a corner on this thing." Perloff said he first detected the waning of his crush when he neglected to see *Riding In Cars With Boys* in the theater. ⊘

Scott McClellan related the story of Bush's encounter with the rabbit, whom the president met in the White House's famed Rose Garden, where the rabbit was trespassing.

"Now, dat ole rabbit, he knew Pezziden' Bush had it in fo' him after he seed him lopin' about in his best rose bushes ez sassy ez a jackdaw," Mc-

> "Bless gracious, honey, now don' you fret none 'bout dat rabbit," McClellan said, in response to questions about the animal's current whereabouts and whether he poses a public threat. "Marse [Robert] Mueller'll tuck keer o' him, sho'. He gots his best field hands a-seerchin' high an' low fo' da ole scamp."

Clellan said. "Sez Pezziden' Bush, sezee, 'I'm gwine ter settle yo' hash, ole Rabbit. I best not cotch you in my rose patch agin, or I'll fill yo' britches wit buckshot.'"

McClellan said that the rabbit, fearing for his life, devised a plan.

"Ole Rabbit got ter studyin' on da problem," McClellan said. "He knew his letters, so he tuck up some paper an' a pen an' commenced scratchin' away. Bimeby, he had hisse'f a right pert mess o' papers, an' so he spreaded 'em out 'pon Pezziden' Bush's writin' desk. Den he set hisse'f down on Pezziden' Bush's fanciest settin' chair es if he wuz borned to it, an' he smoked a seegyar, no less."

According to McClellan, when Bush spotted the rabbit in his chair in the Oval Office, he was "madder'n a yaller jacket."

"Pezziden' Bush sez, sezee, 'What you t'ink dis is yer, a frolic? I'm fetchin' mah shotgun dat da NRA done give me special fo' bein' pezziden','" McClellan said. "Sez da rabbit, sezee, 'Hol' up dar, Pezziden' Bush. I wuz wonderin' if'n you could settle a li'l wager 'twix' me an' ole Mr. Tarrypin.'"

According to McClellan, the rabbit then described the terms of the wager between himself and the tortoise.

"'It be my hide or his shell,' sez da rabbit, sezee," McClellan said. "Sez da rabbit, 'Ole Mr. Tarrypin, he sez dat da Pezziden' O' Da Newnited States so thick he kin scarce sign his own name. 'Course, I don' beleeve him, but ter settle da matter I got ter see it fo' myself.'"

Outraged by the accusation, Bush took the rabbit's bait and signed the bill sitting on his desk.

"Bimeby, folks discovered dat, kaze o' Ole Rabbit's monkeyshines, guns wuz now banned all over Creation," McClellan said.

According to FBI sources, the cottontail rabbit is believed to have been born in the Deep South, and often employs deception as a means of self-preservation. Known to have outsmarted such adversaries as a fox, a wolf, and a bear, the rabbit is also be-

THE WHITE HOUSE
WASHINGTON, D.C.
OFFICE OF THE PRESIDENT OF THE UNITED STATES

CONFIDENTIAL   (PAGE 5 of 5)

"Wall," sez Marse Bush, sezee, "dat ole Tarrypin gwine ter have ter find hisse'f a new house, kaze I kin sign my name sho' es I got breff in my body."

"Why don' you sign dem papers on yo' desk den?" sez da rabbit, sezee.

So Pezziden' Bush, he shucked off his jacket an' set ter work a fixin' his signature on dem papers. He seed nuthin' quare 'bout signin' papers, kaze he done it all da time. But it wuz right hard work, seein' as dey wuz so many ter sign. Bimeby, his fingers wuz all stained black wid ink, an' da sweat his brows din't cotch done dripped in ter his eyes an' near blinded him.

Da rabbit, he jes set yer bidin' his time, but when he seed Pezziden Bush wipin' his eyes, he hopped clean out da winder, an' ain't nobody seed him to dish ve'y day. An' when Pezziden Bush wuz all done, he called in one o' his seck'terries, an' she tuck up dem papers an' sported 'em off like enny udders. He wuz so pleased wid hisse'f, provin' Mr. Tarrypin wrong, Pezziden Bush plum fergot 'bout da rabbit, an' nev' knew whut he done signed. Why, he even signed his desk an' his windersill too, jes to spite ole Tarrypin, though he wuzn't dar to see it.

Bimeby, folks discovered dat, kaze o' Ole Rabbit's monkeyshines, guns wuz now banned all over Creation.

THE END

Above: An internal White House document details the events that led to the gun ban.

lieved to have tricked U.S. Sen. Charles Schumer (D-NY) into thinking that the sun was still down so that the animal could swipe vegetables from his refrigerator in May. The rabbit is also the prime suspect in the infamous April incident in which U.S. Sen. Barbara Boxer (D-CA) lodged her head in the knot of a persimmon tree.

"Bless gracious, honey, now don' you fret none 'bout dat rabbit," McClellan said, in response to questions about the animal's current whereabouts and whether he poses a public threat. "Marse [Robert] Mueller'll tuck keer o' him, sho'. He gots his best field hands a-seerchin' high an' low fo' da ole scamp. I 'speck they'll tree him sho' 'nuff."

Rumors that the FBI is constructing a tar baby to catch the rabbit could not be confirmed at press time. ∅

employees brutally slain so far during the takeover. "Does anyone know 'Jesus Loves Me'? Okay, good, but remember to keep it down so they don't get angry and club one of us unconscious again. Okay? Okay. Now, who wants to lead it off?"

Puchesy, a Boston native, has made a living as the upscale coastal resort's activities director since separating from her husband in May 2003. Little is known about this faction of the Comando Vermelho, other than that it is well-armed and demanding the sum of $500,000 from local government authorities for the return of the 44 remaining prisoners.

Until the government complies, Puchesy will continue to use her extensive knowledge of arts and crafts to raise the spirits of her fellow hostages. Today, Puchesy taught fellow captives how to weave friendship bracelets using locks of hair cut from the heads of the corpses stacked at the back of the room.

"Okay, Gilberto, that's looking very nice—much better than your last one," Puchesy said, as she walked around the room checking on the progress of those coherent enough to join in the activity. "Margaret, you'll need to stop your hands from shaking... Emilio, you have pretty steady hands. Maybe you could help Margaret out."

Continued Puchesy: "When we're done with our bracelets, we should put our noggins together and brain-

> "Let's have some smiles instead of crying," Puchesy said.

storm a way to cover up the stench coming from the bodies. Remember, there are no bad ideas."

Puchesy admitted that she has had a hard time keeping some of the hostages focused on group activities, especially when gunmen arrive with food or pull one of the women out of the room, only to drag her back in,

nearly catatonic, hours later.

"Okay, everyone, relax—it was only a food drop-off this time, and we should be happy about that," Puchesy said. "Let's have some smiles instead of crying. Everyone's still here. So, whose turn is it to eat? Hands up if you ate yesterday. Some of us who ate yesterday aren't raising our hands. Stan? Thank you! That wasn't so hard, now, was it?"

While she said she believes that it's important to keep the group unified, Puchesy tries to facilitate closer ties by breaking detainees into smaller groups based on common interests, such as crafting weapons to fight the captors, praying, or curling up against the wall while staring off into space.

"I'll be over there to check out the progress on your conch-shell knife in a second, but it's my turn to lead charades," Puchesy said. "Now, can I remind everyone not to make the answers so grim this time? If I see one more person trying to act out 'living hell' by pointing around the room, I swear we'll go back to playing 10-word story."

Puchesy said she attributes her survival to her positive attitude, as well as to the fact that she was teaching a pottery class at the time of the attack, and was therefore not wearing her work uniform and lanyard.

"I was super-duper lucky that I was dressed in street clothes, since our captors cut the throats of all the resort employees," Puchesy said. "But then again, my Mom always said that luck doesn't just happen. You have to make it happen. Well, I'm just happy to be alive and helping people—knock on wood!"

Even in the face of the tragedy, Puchesy said she intends to keep doing what she does best, by scheduling and overseeing guests' activities, even if she no longer has access to her supplies.

"Helping people forget their troubles and have a good time is what I was trained to do," Puchesy said. "I only wish we had more room to do our morning stretches, and that I had my clipboard so I wouldn't need to scratch out the days' events on the wall with a rock." ∅

supplies, used carpet scraps, filthy woolen blankets, and flattened garbage-can lids. We also sell coffee cups, cigarette butts, soiled clothing, expired coupons, June 2001 *People* magazines, and half-empty containers of Dippity-Do hairstyling gel. Best of all, we have really nice, big, sturdy shopping carts."

"Wide selection and low cost are the benefits of a store this size," he added, as he led reporters through the 90,000-square-foot Homeless Depot's neatly organized rows of inventory.

"The liquor department features more than 40 types of fortified wine,

---

Alberts added that, while much of the store's inventory is available curbside at no cost, customers should be willing to pay for quality and availability.

---

30 different malt beverages, and a full selection of budget-priced liquors, including Old Thompson Whiskey and McCormick Vodka," Alberts said, gesturing to racks stretching up to the store's two-story ceiling. "We're able to offer alcoholics their favorite brands at prices up to 15 percent lower than those at convenience stores."

"Volume buying allows for low prices on the essentials," he continued. "Whereas the corner bodega charges $2 for a butane cigarette lighter, we can offer them for half that, and our clerks provide service without a sneer."

Alberts led the group past a Homeless Depot employee conducting an in-store "Know How" customer clinic titled "Installing A Temporary Garden Bed." As several dozen onlookers watched the employee fasten a length of plastic sheeting to an artificial bush, Alberts explained that, in addition to selling materials for building and decorating temporary homes, the store will also feature weekly entrepreneurial how-to demonstrations.

"This week, we've got UB40 cassette tapes, still in their original packaging," Alberts said. "Come on in, and we'll show you how any ambitious do-it-yourselfer with a dirty blanket can turn cassette tapes into big cash."

Though the cavernous store also offers many useful services and filthy odds and ends, Homeless Depot specializes in home-building materials.

"We've got some very interesting offerings in the cardboard division," Alberts said, gesturing toward a 200-foot-long aisle of appliance boxes. "Now, it used to be that, in order to get a refrigerator box, you had to search high and low, with no guarantee you'd

Above: A shelf of clearance items at Homeless Depot.

ever strike gold. No longer. We sell our top-of-the-line, Kenmore 25.5 cubic foot double-door refrigerator boxes right here, only $4.79 each."

Alberts added that, while much of the store's inventory is available curbside at no cost, customers should be willing to pay for quality and availability.

"Our sheets of corrugated cardboard are coated with a polymer that will withstand intense rain and snow," Alberts said. "It may cost more than something you'd find on the curb, but we guarantee that a temporary shelter built from our products will provide you with several months' protection from the elements. That's the Homeless Depot promise."

According to *Street Voices*, the Homeless Depot advertising circular written by and for homeless people, the items carried in the cardboard section—excluding television boxes, microwave boxes, and air-conditioner boxes—come with a 60-day aluminum-cans-back guarantee.

Convenience represents another benefit Homeless Depot holds over scavenging, Alberts said.

"Our five-pound sack of cigarette butts represents hours, if not days, of labor saved," Alberts said. "As so many of our customers are self-employed, that's time that could be spent writing a manifesto, praising Jesus, or crafting a list of one's military-service credentials to aid in the acquisition of spare change."

"We also carry a wide array of gently used markers," he added.

Alberts said the first day of business

generated widespread interest, with nearly a thousand customers entering the store and using the bathroom.

Theodore Nathan, an analyst for the Professional Association of Retailers, said he was impressed by the stores' unique business plan.

"With the success of Wal-Mart and similar chains, the market for budget retail goods is crowded, to say the least," Nathan said. "Stores like Target have chosen to go slightly up the price ladder, while stores like Homeless Depot and ALDI cater to the ex-

the unusually large amounts of blood. Passersby were amazed by the unusually large amounts of blood. Passersby were amazed by the unusually large amounts of blood. Passersby were amazed by the unusually large amounts of blood. Passersby were amazed by the unusually large amounts of blood. Passersby were amazed by the unusually large amounts of blood. Passersby were amazed by the unusually large amounts of blood. Passersby were amazed by the unusually large amounts of blood. Passersby were amazed by the unusually large amounts of blood. Passersby were amazed by the unusually large amounts of blood. Passersby were amazed by the unusually large amounts of blood. Passersby were amazed by the unusually large amounts of blood. Passersby were amazed by the unusually large amounts of blood. Passersby were amazed by the unusually large amounts of blood. Passersby were amazed by the unusually large amounts of blood. Passersby were amazed by the unusually large

tremely budget-minded consumer."

Homeless Depot CEO Randy Thompson said that several other Homeless Depots are currently under construction.

"We're going to open stores in Detroit, Chicago, St. Louis, and New Orleans by January 2005," Thompson said. "And, unless the economy gets significantly better, we plan to add another 20 cities to that list in the next five years."

Thompson denied rumors that jobs are available at any of the stores. *∅*

amounts of blood. Passersby were amazed by the unusually large amounts of blood. Passersby were amazed by the unusually large amounts of blood. Passersby were amazed by the unusually large amounts of blood. Passersby were amazed by the unusually large

---

Don't blame me, I'm a convicted felon.

---

amounts of blood. Passersby were amazed by the unusually large amounts of blood. Passersby were amazed by the unusually large amounts of blood. Passersby were amazed by the unusually large amounts of blood. Passersby were amazed by the unusually large amounts of blood. Passersby were amazed by the unusually large amounts of blood. Passersby were amazed by the unusually large amounts of blood. Passersby were amazed by the unusually large amounts of blood. Passersby were

see PUPPIES page 222

Count Those Blessings

**A Room Of Jean's Own
By Jean Teasdale**

Whew! Boy, Jeanketeers, having Type 2 diabetes is no picnic. (Pun definitely intended!) To a person who believes in living life to the fullest and treating herself well, diabetes' constraints can be painful, to say the least. I always figured diabetics just took medication to regulate their insulin levels, but nope. I have to eat a diet lower in fat and calories, get regular exercise, and, most yucko of all, test my blood-sugar levels before meals by pricking my finger and taking a reading of the blood on a glucometer. A real bummer when you're dying to dig into your yummy (not!) salad. Also, I have to check my feet every day. (Don't ask.) It's a real bummer, too, especially since I have a little trouble with the reach. (I don't even wear shoes with laces!)

I realize that I have two ways of looking at my situation. I could choose to see my diabetes as an awful, debilitating setback, or I could see it as an opportunity to gain a new lease on life. I'm not really willing to choose either. After all, diabetes is controllable, and you can actually get away with a lot. It's a big myth that you can't ever eat sugar, and it's not like I have to be chained to a treadmill all day. My father has diabetes, and the last time he was in town to visit, he put away an entire rib-eye steak. He sure as heck doesn't let guilt or sensibility drag him down. (By the way, my dad looks just like that old-fashioned cartoon of Santa Claus. He actually gets a lot of side work playing Santa during the holidays. I wish he had looked more like Santa when I was young! Back then, he looked like Sebastian Cabot, and the neighborhood kids were terrified of him.)

Instead of being super-negative, or restlessly seeking wellness, I opt to recognize what's been good about my life up to now. Isn't that the healthiest option? I believe in counting my blessings. I made a list, and right now, I'm up to 27. That's a lot for anyone, I'm willing to bet! I don't have the space to list them all, so I'll give you a small sampling.

First, I'm really glad I live in the United States. The other day, I had to buy a little tube of glue to patch together a china cup I broke, so I drove to the hardware store on Thisbe Avenue. This might not seem extraordinary to you, but think about it. I could just go to the hardware store and pick up a tube of glue. Or I could've gone to the Pamida, or the Kmart, or a convenience store. There are so many places to get glue. And, since there are tons of places to buy it, that also means there are tons of tubes of glue. In fact, there are probably so many tubes of glue that the supply outstrips the demand, and they have to throw tubes out because they get old or dry or whatever. That's amazing! That, and freedom of expression, are why I'm so glad I live in the U.S.

I'm also thankful for my kitties, Priscilla and Garfield. They really enhance my life, and I'm sure they lower my blood pressure. I've still got diabetes anyway, but I wouldn't trade their companionship for a supermodel's body.

I've never been in a tornado. The windshield of my old car got dinged

---

> **I'm thankful that the city finally widened West Slocum Road, ending nearly a year of construction and providing more turnoff lanes onto Thisbe Avenue.**

---

by hail once, but that's it. There should be a law that makes it illegal to complain unless you've been through a tornado.

I still get thrilled when I recall getting interviewed on WLTY's *PM Magazine* in 1982 for being part of a stripe on the living American flag during a July 4 parade. Just being part of the flag was fun enough, but how often does someone get an opportunity to appear on television?

I'm thankful that the city finally widened West Slocum Road, ending nearly a year of construction and providing more turnoff lanes onto Thisbe Avenue.

I'm proud that my hands are not all bony and veiny. They're very smooth and plump in a nice way. I don't like bones showing on people.

I'm grateful for Hubby Rick. Surprised? Well, as much as I get on his case sometimes, I'm glad I don't have to go through life alone. We're like two peas in a pod. Well, make that one pea in a pod, since Rick spends all his time at Tacky's Tavern when he's not working. I just meant I'm not utterly alone. Actually, being alone can be a blessing, too.

And I'm real grateful that cuteness was discovered. For me, if anything makes life bearable, it's things that are saucer-eyed, squeaky-voiced, and just good old-fashioned baby-ish. I

Your Horoscope

**By Lloyd Schumner Sr.
Retired Machinist and
A.A.P.B.-Certified Astrologer**

Aries: (March 21–April 19)
You'll stumble onto the secret of true happiness, but unfortunately, you won't be able to figure out a way to charge people for it.

Taurus: (April 20–May 20)
Never doubt that a small, dedicated group of individuals can change the world with a few vials of smallpox virus and a kilogram of plutonium.

Gemini: (May 21–June 21)
Banana-macadamia-nut pancakes may be heavenly, but as an eternal reward for faith and good works, they'll fall just a tad short.

Cancer: (June 22–July 22)
Your therapist will insist that childhood trauma is the cause of your unusual behavior, but it was only recently that you started screaming and crying for candy.

Leo: (July 23–Aug. 22)
You'll be the first human being to catch a rare virus from the common pigeon, proving conclusively that it can be sexually transmitted.

Virgo: (Aug. 23–Sept. 22)
Turns out the thing about getting 72 virgins in heaven is true, but it also turns out all they want to do is play Madden.

Libra: (Sept. 23–Oct. 23)
As soon as it's confirmed that you are indeed the world's most arrogant jackass, you'll be traded to the Yankees for a left-handed reliever.

Scorpio: (Oct. 24–Nov. 21)
Everyone's talking about the Cassini spacecraft's amazing seven-year journey to Saturn, a trip that makes your seven-day vacation to Baltimore look like a fool's errand.

Sagittarius: (Nov. 22–Dec. 21)
The long-awaited People's Revolution will come this week, pleasantly surprising you with the communist belief that you urgently need a jet-ski.

Capricorn: (Dec. 22–Jan. 19)
You're the envy of all your friends, but only because they're tasteless masochists.

Aquarius: (Jan. 20–Feb. 18)
You'll receive a two-hour lecture from renowned economist Milton Friedman merely for claiming that a penny saved is a penny earned.

Pisces: (Feb. 19–March 20)
You've always made a living off the very sweat of your balls, so it's a good thing your ball-sweat retails for 600 bucks an ounce.

---

consider cuteness one of the crowning hallmarks of civilization, because it helps people forget that there's violence and depravity in the world. To those who think cute things are dumb, I ask this: Would you have ever, of your own volition, come up with

---

> **I'm also thankful for my kitties, Priscilla and Garfield. They really enhance my life, and I'm sure they lower my blood pressure.**

---

the idea of a mouthless kitten wearing a hair-bow? Maybe it's *you* who's dumb.

I thank God for the birds that come to my birdfeeder, and how pretty the clouds are when light rays filter through them. I like the feel of ball-point pens against notebook paper. Laughter. Scented candles. WGGG-FM, home of the oldies. The coolness of a tile floor against your cheek. You know, stores stock a lot of cotton balls, too. It's not just glue. There's so much cotton. It can't all be coming from the American South. Maybe other countries grow it, too. Then you have to consider all the cotton they use for clothing and textiles.

I remember what I said about not complaining unless you've been in a tornado, but I hate having to cut down on chocolate. I don't get it. Chocolate is good for you. It helps your mood. Medical studies have proven this, so why can't diabetics have it?

Jeanketeers, I'm feeling a little lightheaded. The nurse told me that's an effect of diabetes. It's like there's little fireworks going off in front of my eyes. I'd better lay down and collect my thoughts. In the meantime, count your own blessings. Maybe we can compare notes. We could have a great big Blessing-Off, and the winner gets to come down with diabetes! Great idea, huh? I'll be in the bathroom. ⌀

Copies Of *Da Vinci Code* Litter Crash Site

see NATION page 7B

Alpha-Bits Now Available In Serif Font

see BUSINESS page 15C

Nation's Highways Completed

see NATION page 6G

Apology Screamed

see LOCAL page 9G

STATshot

A look at the numbers that shape your world.

What's Our Real National Pastime?

18% Fast-forwarding

15% Taking well-deserved breaks

11% Bettering ourselves through adult education

16% Recreational snacking

19% Attempting to make wife vanish using mind

21% Postponing vacuuming

THE ONION • $2.00 US • $3.00 CAN

0 74470 94595 6

00

the ONION®

VOLUME 40 ISSUE 28   AMERICA'S FINEST NEWS SOURCE™   15–21 JULY 2004

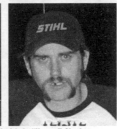

Above: Victims Henry "The Wrigleyville Stabber" Fisk, "Crazy" Leo Krafchek, "Hungry" Charles Osterberg, Ed "The Tennis-Court Killer" Eddy, Jane "Jackknife" Weston, and Otis Glen Ankrim.

Series Of Serial-Killer Killings Rocks Serial-Killer Community

INDIANAPOLIS, IN—The recent murders of six serial killers has shaken the serial-killer community to its core, ushering in a new era of fear, suspicion, and mistrust, homicidal maniacs reported Monday.

"I can't bear this tension," said Joseph Cash Mason, dubbed "Pickaxe Pete" by the media. "I can't leave the house to kidnap a hitchhiker without wondering if I'm next. When I chain someone to the wall in my backwoods shack and torture him, I feel no pleasure, only fear for my own life. When will this madness end?"

The serial-killer killer's most recent reported victim was Henry "The Wrigleyville Stabber" Fisk, 46. Indiana state police discovered Fisk's strangled and mutilated corpse in a culvert on July 2, four weeks after he was reported missing by several concerned, anonymous serial killers.

"When 'Crazy' Leo [Krafchek] first disappeared, we just assumed he'd gone off on a tri-state killing spree or something," said Fisk's long-time friend, Chainsaw Chuck. "But when there weren't any nun killings in the news, we started to worry. Then Otis Glen Ankrim's trademark birthday slayings stopped, too. When they found Henry's body, we knew we'd

see KILLINGS page 208

Report: Scientists Still Seeking Cure For Obesity

CHICAGO, IL—In spite of billions of dollars spent and decades of research, scientists at the University of Chicago said Monday that the scientific community is no closer to finding a cure for the potentially fatal disease of obesity.

"The obesity epidemic in this country has public-health authorities panicking, and with good reason," said Dr. Seong-Hun Kim, a research associate at the university's department of neurobiology, pharmacology, and physiology. "According to the latest government statistics, 30.6 percent of the adult population and 16.5 percent of children under 19 are obese. As researchers, we feel the same sort of helplessness that many victims of obesity feel."

our HEALTH

"Basically, the clock continues to tick as we search for that golden key that will give every American a chance at a healthy, normal life," Kim added.

Many obesity sufferers have expressed frustration over the medical community's inability to cure them.

"I came down with obesity two years after I got married," 41-year-old Oklahoma City resident Fran Torley said. "I know it was hard for my husband to

see OBESITY page 209

Bill Maher Spends All Night Arguing With Republican Hooker

LOS ANGELES—Sources close to Bill Maher report that the comedian and host of HBO's *Real Time With Bill Maher* spent Friday evening arguing with Carolyn Dobson, a prostitute from the London Escorts Agency and a supporter of the Republican Party.

Dobson and Maher, who occupied an executive suite at the W Hotel, reportedly argued on subjects ranging from the Bush Administration's financial accounting for the Iraq war to its refusal to release records to the public in accordance with the Freedom Of Information Act. The two also engaged in three consensual sex acts, for which the comedian paid $750.

Maher, who was nominated for an Emmy Award in 2001 for his work on ABC's *Politically Incorrect*, made

see MAHER page 208

Right: Maher escorts Dobson through the W Hotel lobby.

Does Iran Pose A Threat?

While Iran did free the British sailors it detained last month, the country is still threatening to restart its nuclear program. What do *you* think?

Kenneth Ridener
Systems Analyst

"So a country in the Mideast has been acting irrationally? I *guess* that's news."

Donald Stiles
Tax Examiner

"Like it or not, the time to stop this is right now, before we're forced to restore the Soviet Union and beat them at hockey again."

Brenda Stearns
Archivist

"Remember the good old days when Iran and Iraq were always at war with each other, and nobody else gave a shit who won or lost?"

Alfredo Mireles
Cook

"As the manager of the long-forgotten '80s sensation A Flock Of Seagulls, this can only be good for me."

Jeffrey Eubanks
Truck Driver

"Show me where the U.N. charter states that sovereign nations have the right to behave like the U.S."

Karla Finik
Hairdresser

"Should we take action against Iran? We just liberated them. Check your facts before asking stupid questions."

Ringtones

Ringtone downloads of songs are becoming a huge moneymaker for the mobile-phone industry. Why are they so popular?

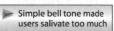 Simple bell tone made users salivate too much

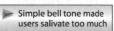 Can pretend that 50 Cent is calling with a song

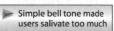 Only form of music on-the-go Americans have time to listen to

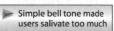 Having "Vader's Theme" chirp from pants makes phone owner feel like real bad-ass

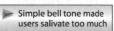 Love music; love its bastard stepchild, the ringtone, too

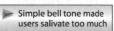 Have yet to realize record company charges $1.50 in royalties every time phone rings

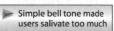 When sweet child of theirs calls, want to hear an aural alert appropriate to her status

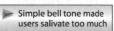 iPod only stores 10,000 songs, need to carry 10,003

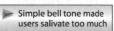 Hate everyone else's cheesy, obnoxious ringtones; want to show them how it's done

---

the ONION®
America's Finest News Source. ™

Herman Ulysses Zweibel
Founder

T. Herman Zweibel
Publisher Emeritus
J. Phineas Zweibel
Publisher
Maxwell Prescott Zweibel
Editor-In-Chief

Why No One Want Make *Hulk 2*?

By The Hulk

X2 come out last year. *Spider-Man 2* come out last month. Both great sequels to great movies about Hulk friends. Hulk love great action movies about friends! People buy tickets. Make money for theaters, make money for movie company. Movie company make more movies with money. Already, they working on *X-Men 3*. Hulk movie come out last year. It success. It big popcorn movie with heart. So why no one want make *Hulk 2*? It make Hulk mad!

Hulk know what people say. Original movie no good, people say. *Hulk* movie Hulk-sized bomb, people say. That not true! *Hulk* more successful than people think. Make $132 million in U.S. alone, only cost $120 million. That not small potatoes. Add international box-office receipts and DVD sales and it add up to big money. Big! Oh, and did Hulk forget merchandising tie-ins? First *Hulk* movie really forge Hulk brand identity. Make people aware of Hulk. Hulk now poised to build on success of first *Hulk* movie. *Hulk 2* smash box-office records!

First *Hulk* movie flawed but underrated. Oscar-winner Jennifer Connelly give sublime performance as Hulk romantic interest Betty Ross. She pretty. Australian hunk Eric Bana good in breakthrough American role as puny human Bruce Banner. Film even give tip of hat to TV Hulk and Stan "The Man" Lee. Sure, conflict with father stray from original story, but it provide new twist on classic legend. Necessary to increase dramatic tension. Make Hulk seem more human so audience can identify with puny human Banner.

Why no one appreciate daring vision of Ang Lee? Aaargh! Ang Lee genius! Maybe panels on screen gimmicky, but him try something new. When last time you try something new?! Ang Lee willing to work in unfamiliar genres. Him brave like Hulk. Hulk wish for him to work on *Hulk 2*, if he willing, but Hulk understand if he not want to. Ang Lee like Hulk: He not stay in one place for too long. Him working on gay western right now. That prove Hulk's point. If him not do it, maybe Darren Aronofsky or David Gordon Green. Someone with unique vision that not so stuck on action clichés. First studio exec to suggest Joel Schumacher get smashed!

Hulk 2 give chance to increase merchandising profile, as well. Hulk have ideas for new Hulk products. Hulk Foam Hands surprise hit in toy stores. Hulk Foam Hands big and soft and make Hulk smashing noises when you hit things. If Hulk Hands big hit, Hulk Feet even bigger hit! Make smashing and stomping noises. Imagine puny human child walking around with Hulk Feet! Make big noise like Hulk. Imagine... ho, ho, ho... excuse Hulk, Hulk laughing. That funny! But Hulk not just limit branding to toys. Make Hulk Shampoo and Hulk Shampoo For Kids, in special no-tears formula. It sound like bad idea, but it good idea! You squirt it right in eye, and it not make you mad! Hulk very concerned with hygiene and comfort. Know how hard it is to make puny human child take bath. Hulk Shampoo make bathtime fun!

Many unanswered questions from last *Hulk* movie. What happen to puny human Banner in rainforest? Is there cure for Hulk? Will General

---

First *Hulk* movie flawed but underrated. Oscar-winner Jennifer Connelly give sublime performance as Hulk romantic interest Betty Ross.

Thaddeus E. "Thunderbolt" Ross leave Hulk alone? Is there future with Betty Ross? Where villains that make comic so great, like Abomination, Wendigo, and Leader? Hulk hate Leader and Leader's big head. What happen to Grey Hulk? And where Hulk's friend Rick Jones? He only one that understand Hulk. Rick? Rick!? Raaaaahhhh! Sometimes Hulk so sad and alone.

Back to *Hulk* movie. Hulk visualize *Hulk* trilogy like *Matrix*, but no spiritual mumbo-jumbo. Crazy mumbo-jumbo make Hulk's head hurt! Hulk work out treatment for next movie Hulkself. It have everything in Hulk, only more intense. In this movie, Hulk smash for first 20 minutes. Give fanboys something to hang fanboy hats on. Then have romance, for women ages 24 to 40. Very important demographic if want make movie real summer blockbuster.

Then Leader come, bring Abomination. Him try to wreck everything by capturing Hulk. Then Hulk smash more! Hulk smash Leader and Abomination! Hulk smash tanks, too! That nod to first film. Hulk love scene where Hulk throw tank into horizon. At end of movie, cliffhanger. Put people on edge of seats. Like Hulk say, always leave puny humans wanting more.

Hulk working on pitch right now.
see HULK page 209

University Implicated In Checks-For-Degrees Scheme

ANN ARBOR, MI—The University of Michigan has become the 17th institution of higher learning to be implicated in the checks-for-degrees scandal rocking American campuses, representatives from the Department of Justice reported Tuesday.

"We have strong evidence that the University of Michigan granted academic degrees to students in exchange for hefty payments, often totaling tens of thousands of dollars," Deputy Attorney General James B. Comey said. "In the process, thousands of graduates have emerged with degrees, but few or no skills applicable to everyday life. And many are as unprepared to enter the job market as they were when they first enrolled."

According to documents collected as a part of the Justice Department's ongoing investigation, some University of Michigan undergraduates attended classes fewer than three times a week. During these classes, students were asked to do little more than listen to lectures delivered by their professors.

Comey said that, while it seems apparent that the universities under investigation were conducting a monetary transaction, millions of degree-buyers believed that they had not bought, but "earned" their diplomas.

"The university is very careful to circumscribe the financial element of the transaction," Comey said. "The em-

ployees who conduct lectures are made to seem above the world of commerce. Students don't give their payments to the professors, nor to the departments from which they purchase their degrees. Rather, checks are mailed to the 'Office of the Bursar,' this 'bursar' being someone who's nearly impossible to track down."

Besides attending classes, students read materials relating to their lectures, write the occasional paper, and participate in testing, Comey said. Al-

> ## "We have strong evidence that the University of Michigan granted academic degrees to students in exchange for hefty payments," Deputy Attorney General James B. Comey said.

though the content of many courses was often thought-provoking, what alarmed investigators was the subject matter's "intractably abstract nature."

"A course in Chaucer can be a fascinating examination of medieval

Above: The campus of the embattled University of Michigan.

mores and the evolution of the English language," Comey said. "Such knowledge, however, has little application in larger society. Students can graduate with majors in creative writing, Latin, women's studies, and history, yet still not know how to fix a sink, sew on a button, or even properly feed themselves. Virtually the only opportunity graduates have to apply their arcane knowledge takes place during discussions over coffee with their peers, or attempts to impress members of the opposite sex at parties."

In addition to their twice-annual tuition payments, University of Michigan students pay hundreds of dollars in ancillary fees.

"Students are bilked out of registration fees, housing fees, and lab fees," Comey said. "And the university has

all sorts of tricks to draw the money out, such as denying students access to library materials or refusing them copies of their transcripts."

Many students find that the only way to get a return on their investment is to continue their studies at the post-graduate level, resulting in even more money for the college.

"Some graduate-degree-earners have been known to find work in their fields, but many end up teaching in the very schools that issue these degrees of questionable value," Comey said. "In this way, the grift sustains itself."

Comey said citizens have a right to be concerned.

"Since so many students purchase their degrees using government-backed

see UNIVERSITY page 209

Girl Slept With For Her Sake

TULSA, OK—University of Tulsa sophomore Ben Stoll was gracious enough to sleep with third-year law student Rosie Andriessen Monday. "Rosie had been acting insecure and needy all evening, so I figured I'd help her out a bit," said Stoll, who met Andriessen last year through common friends. "She probably thinks she's too chubby. It must be a big boost for her to have sex with a guy like me." Stoll decided not to call Andriessen the next day, nor to return any calls she might make, so as not to get her hopes up.

Noisy Upstairs Neighbors Wake Man At 3 P.M.

SAN LUIS OBISPO, CA—The inconsiderate residents of the apartment above Jim Bracker, 23, woke him from a sound slumber several minutes be-

fore 3 p.m. Monday. "Christ, quit with the aerobics already," a groggy Bracker shouted toward the ceiling. "You've been jumping up and down for half an hour!" Unable to return to sleep, Bracker resigned himself to channel-surfing until he was forced to drag himself into the shower and ready himself to meet a friend for a 5:15 p.m. movie.

Sheepish Secret Service Agent Can't Explain How Vacuum Cleaner Salesman Got Into Oval Office

WASHINGTON, DC—Secret Service agent Martin Bowhan was unable to explain to his direct superior how Electrolux sales representative Don Karn managed to breach White House security Monday. "[Karn] said that he needed to speak to the president, and before anyone could stop him, he strolled right into the Oval Office,"

Bowhan said. "I burst in there to find him dumping red wine, mud, and some blue liquid onto the rug, which was a personal gift from Chinese president Chiang Kai-shek to President Nixon. I have to admit that the stains did come out quickly and easily." While escorting Karn out of the building, Bowhan made payment arrangements for the Aptitude ultra-quiet upright vacuum the president had ordered.

Nerd Has Most Obscure Crush Ever

JACKSONVILLE, FL—The unrequited nature of area nerd June Manzo's crush on actor Peter Tuddenham, who provides the voice of piloting computer Slave on Blake's 7, is only slightly more agonizing than the process of explanation she must put herself through every time her media obsession is discussed. "He has this slightly sinister but dynamic way of speaking on the show, particularly in the 'Headhunter' episode," Manzo said, painstakingly describing Tuddenham to fellow science-fiction

fan Bradley Preakniss. "When I hear his voice congratulating Avon on his 'consummate skill,' I just get shivers... Doesn't that ring a bell? No? Not at all?" Manzo's crush is surpassed in geekiness and obscurity only by that of Denver's Demitri Ostrow, who has a long-harbored passion for author Neil Gaiman's "fabulous" assistant Lorraine.

Child 'Very Sorry' For Slapping Teddy Bear

CARY, NC—Arthur Hollis, 8, delivered a heartfelt apology to his favorite, most-special teddy bear, Raymond, after slapping him across the face and knocking him off the bed Monday. "I don't know why I do it, Raymond," Hollis said to the stuffed bear as he cradled it in his arms. "I'm very sorry. I'll never do it again, I promise." Hollis' father Daniel reported that his son has a history of domestic toy violence, harassment of the family cats, and wild outbursts after consuming too many gummi bears. ✍

Above: A chalk outline shows where police found "Crazy" Leo Krafchek's body.

never see Otis or Leo again, either."

Sources from within the FBI's Behavioral Analysis Unit said Fisk's body bore the same marks of torture as Krafchek's corpse, confirming their suspicions that he was murdered by the serial-killer killer.

"What kind of maniac targets maniacs?" FBI agent Karl Malloney said, flipping through stacks of graphic crime-scene photos in search of a clue. "I wish I could get into this sicko's head and figure out what makes him tick. We've got to catch this guy before another deranged maniac's life is lost."

Serial-killer leaders are encouraging serial killers to take measures to protect themselves from the unknown mass murderer. At a town-hall meeting Tuesday, the Knights Of Serial Killing introduced guidelines killers should follow until the killer-killer is caught. Their suggestions included only killing during daylight hours, restricting victims to those in one's network of friends and family, and stalking victims using the buddy system.

"This is a disgrace," Slaughtering Gary said. "We're under attack, and a set of safety guidelines is the best the community can do for us? Whenever I kill someone, people band together and form neighborhood-watch groups, send out composite drawings of my face, and install lighted walkways in all the parks. Where's the outcry now that I'm the target? Who's watching out for me?"

Malloney said the FBI has been working around the clock to find the serial-killer killer, but it has little evidence to work with beyond a 12-page note found in Krafchek's left hook.

"Sereal [sic] killers beware," the note read in part. "The time of judgment is upon you, so make your peace and prepare for your horror. Your [sic] going to die. The lies have to end now."

"We're all scared to death," Mason said. "I'm on edge all the time. I go into my basement, and my sausage machine appears to have been moved. I can't even follow a scout troop out to Mt. Wacoca, because I'm terrified to be in the woods. Even the voice in my head is telling me to lay low for a while."

"Worst part of all is that I'm starting to take sideways glances at my friends," Mason added. "I hate this maniac for making me think such awful things about Chainsaw Chuck and Strangling Andrew."

Although the families and friends of Fisk's victims have expressed limited sympathy for the deceased serial killer, friends of the serial-killer killer's recent victim grieve their loss.

"The last time I saw [Fisk], he was sharpening his knives and saying how much he loved the sense of power he got from snuffing out senior citizens," said "Mad" Morris Lauch, The Butcher Of Bakersfield. "Henry liked to work alone, but he was always quick with a smile and a joke after he disposed of the corpse. He had a real gift for stabbing elderly people without getting caught. He had so many killings ahead of him."

"It's so sad," Lauch added. "We killers used to spend hours discussing the virtues of quicklime over sulfuric acid, or how hemp rope can hold a knot better than nylon. Now all we talk about is our dead friends."

Services for Fisk will be held at his house, after which he will be cut up and buried in the dirt floor of his crawl space. ∅

his first political observation early in the evening. Shortly after entering the hotel room, he turned his attention from Dobson, who was unpacking her bag, to the television screen, where CNN commentator Eleanor Clift appeared on *The McLaughlin Group*.

Sitting on the edge of the bed and watching the television as he removed his shoes, Maher asked about Dobson's political affiliation. Dobson responded that she did not vote in the last election, but if she had, she would have supported Bush.

"Let me tell you something about Bush's domestic agenda, Carolyn," Maher said. "He doesn't have one. I mean, take a look at his State Of The Union address. Sports coaches need to crack down on athletes' use of steroids? I'm sorry, that's not a vision for America's future. That's a *Sports Illustrated* op-ed topic."

Dobson said she didn't initially attempt to argue with the winner of four Cable Ace Awards.

"I was getting all my condoms and lubricants and stuff out," Dobson said. "I told him straight sex was $250 and asked him to pick what I should wear. He chose the pink negligee."

While the prostitute phoned Maher's credit-card number into her agency, the quick-witted pundit returned his attention to the television screen, where a news segment showed Bush addressing military personnel at CENTCOM headquar-

> "He was like, 'How can a whore support an administration that legislates against her own livelihood?" Dobson said. "And I was like, 'Don't call me a whore.'"

ters in Tampa, FL.

"Bush was thanking the soldiers for protecting America, and [Maher] was like, 'They'd better soak up his thanks now, Carolyn, because—' something about how Bush is gonna cut their healthcare," Dobson said. "I was like, 'I'm surprised you don't like Bush, be-

cause most successful guys do.' He was like, 'Okay, new rule: No more choosing political parties the way we choose the homecoming court.'"

Added Dobson: "Then he asked me to put my face up next to his dick while he jerked off."

According to Dobson, during the approximately 40 minutes of copulation, the comedian restricted his comments to requests for changes of position or velocity. After ejaculation, however, he introduced the topic of John Kerry's election platform.

"Two weeks ago, Kerry said that preventing nuclear terrorism would be his highest priority as president," Maher said, a rivulet of semen trickling down his right leg. "Given that statement, you'd expect Kerry to have a broad, ambitious agenda on nuclear non-proliferation, wouldn't you? Well, I'm sorry, Carolyn, but you'd be 100 percent wrong."

Added Maher: "Interesting, isn't it, that not one American president has made the halt of *our* nuclear-weapons program a priority?"

When Dobson informed Maher that it would be $500 more if she stayed the evening, Maher agreed to the fee, and reportedly continued to introduce var-

ious topical discussions, at one point lifting Dobson's head from between his legs to ask a pointed question.

"He was like, 'How can a whore support an administration that legislates against her own livelihood?'" Dobson said. "And I was like, 'Don't call me a whore.'"

Maher did not limit the debate to politics, introducing hot-button issues ranging from space tourism to dead otters to the Supreme Court ruling on HMOs, and even riffing for several minutes on "so-called independently funded drug studies."

Dobson admitted that the author of *Does Anybody Have A Problem With That? Politically Incorrect's Greatest Hits* did ultimately goad her into a debate.

"I said I heard that Bush created a lot of jobs lately," Dobson said. "He rolled off of me and got up on his knees and was like, 'Created jobs? Honey, tell me, if you don't mind, what exactly Bush has done to create jobs. Do you mean jobs in Mexico and India?' I was like, 'I just know there are more jobs.' He was like, 'Yeah, I know a lot of Halliburton execs who agree with you.'"

"His stomach has this weird scar on it," Dobson added. ∅

Above: Obesity sufferer Tammy Bledsoe shops at an Atlanta, GA grocery store.

Hope to take lunch with Hulk movie screenwriter James Schamus. Him really get what Hulk all about. Also, him open doors in Hollywood. Hope him will share story-by credit with Hulk. Hulk paint in broad strokes. Not good with words. Leave detail work to Schamus.

If you producer, Hulk want know why you sitting around? Does producer hate make money? Hulk need someone line up investors now. Need maybe $100 million. Less than origi-

> **Hulk write great tag lines. "No make *Hulk 2* angry!" Maybe "This time it personal." Or "Green machine back in theaters summer 2006."**

nal. Kinks worked out by now. Software engines all designed. Want start filming in New Zealand by December. It summer there when winter here. It much cheaper to film in New Zealand. Hulk budget-conscious. If all go according to plan, *Hulk 2* hit theaters by summer 2006. Perfect summer movie!

If that not enough, Hulk write great tag lines. "No make *Hulk 2* angry!" Maybe "This time it personal." Or "Green machine back in theaters summer 2006." Maybe teaser poster with Hulk fist punching out of poster. Puny humans see that and they duck! It real attention-grabber. If you still not convinced, Hulk not waste more time with you. Maybe New Line interested. They flush with *Lord Of Rings* money. Looking for new franchise? Call Hulk when you ready to talk serious. ∅

watch me suffer from this disease. When he caught obesity a year later, he got so depressed, he couldn't do anything but sit on the couch. Some days, we sit and watch television from dawn till dusk, hoping for news of a

> **"Even when individuals find success with a certain drug or plan, it often fails to work in the long term," Kim said. "Sometimes, a treatment plan that works for a handful of people will fail to help anyone else. It's very frustrating."**

breakthrough."

Kim said he sees no cure on the horizon.

"Each year that we don't have a cure for this dreaded condition, another 300,000 Americans die of obesity-related health problems—hypertension, stroke, heart attack, diabetes," Kim said. "I wish to God there were something I could give these people that would make the obesity go away, but so far, there is no pill that can do that safely and effectively."

Kim said the prescription drugs currently indicated in the treatment of obesity, as well as a host of over-the-counter products, have been shown to produce limited results.

"Even when individuals find success with a certain drug or plan, it often fails to work in the long term," Kim said. "Sometimes, a treatment plan that works for a handful of people

will fail to help anyone else. It's very frustrating. As evinced by the widespread nature of the problem, scientists aren't doing enough for these poor overweight people."

Kim's research group has tried to pinpoint the genetic, environmental, and psychological factors that might indicate a susceptibility to obesity.

"For example, we know that obesity tends to run in families," Kim said. "But we have yet to pinpoint exactly what it is that causes, say, the Smith family to splash about their backyard pool blissfully unaffected while, just over the fence, the Jones family languishes 30 percent overweight on their barbecue deck."

Marge Hampton is an obese American who has responded to the epidemic by trying to raise awareness and money for obesity research. In May, Hampton coordinated the Obesity Awareness Five-Mile Fun Ride, which led participants on a motor tour of Chicago's waterfront parks, and she orchestrated an obesity-awareness bake sale last month.

"We used to think obesity was a condition that only affected people with glandular problems, but health officials are now seeing just how widespread the epidemic is," Hampton said. "There's a myth that obese people don't want to change. They do—they just lack the information about how to do it quickly and easily."

Kim's research team has explored preventative measures.

"It would be wonderful if we could find some way to prevent individuals from getting this horrible condition in the first place, perhaps with something akin to a vaccine or a flu shot," Kim said. "We've pursued every avenue—pills, topical creams, nutritional shakes, even holistic cures like vitamin regimens and massage—but nothing has worked."

While others might have been discouraged by failure, Kim has intensi-

fied his efforts.

"I'm in the lab day and night," Kim said. "The other researchers will say 'Come have dinner with us,' but I'm so busy that I have to just grab some yogurt from the vending machine. I'm just too busy running over to the research facility on the west side of campus or carrying samples to the lab up on the fourth floor. I've lost 20 pounds since starting this project in January."

Even though he expressed concern about his recent weight loss, Kim said he will continue his work unabated.

"I can't worry about me right now; finding a cure for obesity is far too important," Kim said. "And, honestly, I

> **"For example, we know that obesity tends to run in families," Kim said. "But we have yet to pinpoint exactly what it is that causes, say, the Smith family to splash about their backyard pool blissfully unaffected while, just over the fence, the Jones family languishes 30 percent overweight on their barbecue deck."**

feel better than I've felt in years. My work, although difficult, is energizing. I can't turn my back on my research while, all around me, Americans are dropping like enormous flies." ∅

student-loan programs, taxpayers are supporting this," Comey said. "Also, because many employers require these bachelor's degrees, even if irrelevant to the actual work, the business sector has to own up to some collusion in the matter."

One alleged victim of the checks-for-degrees scandal is 25-year-old Michael Trumbull, who purchased an art-history degree from the University of Michigan, making his first payment in January 2002. Trumbull currently works the front desk of a Lansing Comfort Inn.

"Not once has a customer asked me about the innovations of Edouard Manet, or whether politics and aesthetics make good bedfellows," Trumbull said. "They're much more likely to ask me to bring them a plunger or give them a wake-up call."

Trumbull, who owes more than $40,000 in student loans, added that he must use a calculator to perform even simple math. ∅

209

Man, That Mourning Really Did The Trick!

By Kevin Ingrams

Hey, have any of you guys ever tried mourning? Like, after someone close to you passes away? Oh my God, you have to. Seriously, it's amazing. After the death of a loved one, a period of grieving totally clears your head. I know that sounds like a bunch of touchy-feely, New Age bullcrap, but it works.

Remember how upset I was after my brother Ben died in that car crash two months ago? For weeks after the funeral, I walked around numb. It didn't seem real that he was gone. Well, all the drinking I was doing didn't help make things any clearer. I'd go to work, come home, get drunk, fall asleep in front of the television, and then do it all over again the next day. Finally, my pants were falling off because I'd been forgetting to eat. That's when I decided to give the mourning process a shot. You know what? It so totally did the trick.

I'll be the first to admit, I didn't think anything would take away the pain and heartbreak of losing my only sibling. But I figured, "What the heck? Anything that might help end my agony is worth a shot!" So I did a little denying, got angry, did a little bit of rationalization. After that, I took a tour through depression, got out the old videotapes of birthday parties and Ben's graduation speech. Watched

> **I didn't think anything would take away the pain and heartbreak of losing my only sibling. But I figured, "What the heck? Anything that might help end my agony is worth a shot!" So I did a little denying, got angry, did a little bit of rationalization.**

those. Cried like a baby, but I soldiered on. Glad I did, 'cause today I feel like a million bucks!

You guys know me, right? I'm about as skeptical as they come. I wouldn't talk about some big-deal emotional-healing process if it didn't really work. Mourning works. I'm living proof.

And mine wasn't some mild case of grief, either. Seeing my dead brother in that casket was maybe the worst moment of my life. Knowing that he'd never be coming back, that we'd never argue over some chore or play a game of basketball, made me feel like

> **A few weeks ago, I wanted to die myself, but now it's like, "Who wants to go out for enchiladas?"**

my heart had been ripped out. But now, it's like I'm seeing a rainbow after weathering a violent thunderstorm. I feel *that* good.

Yes, I know—ever since I got into the mourning, I can't shut up about it. My family is sick of hearing me talk about it, too. But if they'd only open up their minds and listen, they'd know that I have the cure for what ails them. It's so upsetting to watch them mope around, wishing they could see Ben one more time, when mourning could turn those emotionless stares into smiles again. I mean, I was as horrified as anyone to hear that Ben lingered for hours in a semi-conscious state with his legs pinned under the car, only to die on his way to the hospital. But, hey, I mourned. Now, it's like, "See ya later, emotionally crippling pain and loss!" Seriously, try it. It doesn't cost a cent!

I'm not saying it's a walk in the park—mourning takes time and effort. You know, you've got to cope with the fact that someone you love is gone forever and all that jazz. But with results this extraordinary, it's worth the effort! A few weeks ago, I wanted to die myself, but now it's like, "Who wants to go out for enchiladas?"

One of the fringe benefits of all this is that the cute girls in my building have been real supportive. Every day, a different girl drops by to give me hugs. Now that I went through the whole mourning thing, I'm finally in a position to appreciate all this attention. I even got the number of that total hottie in apartment 7B, because she lost her mother when she was 8 and knows what I'm going through. Well, what I went through. I think I might give her a call tonight to see if she's up for some mini-golf. Thanks, mourning! ∅

Your Horoscope

By Lloyd Schumner Sr.
Retired Machinist and
A.A.P.B.-Certified Astrologer

Aries: (March 21–April 19)
People would have disapproved of your long-term career plans even if you hadn't carved them into the flesh of your enemies.

Taurus: (April 20–May 20)
You'll welcome a new life into the world next week, when a dimensional portal opens in your den and vomits forth an extraplanar pig-beast of astounding malevolence.

Gemini: (May 21–June 21)
Your prayers will finally be answered, but due to a mistake in routing, the response will come from the assistant postmaster of Fayetteville, AR.

Cancer: (June 22–July 22)
Psychoanalysis focuses on causes, therapy focuses on consequences, but your new method of counseling people focuses mostly on drilling holes in them.

Leo: (July 23–Aug. 22)
Try to keep a sense of proportion next week, particularly when serving yourself a "decent-sized" slice of pie.

Virgo: (Aug. 23–Sept. 22)
You'll be the envy of all the sexual-product engineers when your dildo design is admitted to the Vibrary of Congress.

Libra: (Sept. 23–Oct. 23)
You'll continue to be tormented by the sight of tiny symbols which, when viewed, cause you to hear words in your head.

Scorpio: (Oct. 24–Nov. 21)
You're starting to think that traveling the country looking for crooks is a little silly, but really, there's little other place in society for a talking dog.

Sagittarius: (Nov. 22–Dec. 21)
Scholars have decided that you probably don't exist at all, and are just a composite character based on several minor figures from the writings of George Sand.

Capricorn: (Dec. 22–Jan. 19)
You'll be of two minds about things next week, primarily because of the renegade saw blade that neatly severs your corpus callosum Monday.

Aquarius: (Jan. 20–Feb. 18)
You'll make archeological history when, while looking for a good place to eat downtown, you instead discover the lost biblical city of Urkesh.

Pisces: (Feb. 19–March 20)
Turns out it takes only four seconds to fall from the top of your building to the parking lot, but it'll sure seem longer.

SOAPDISH from page 190

amounts of blood. Passersby were amazed by the unusually large amounts of blood. Passersby were amazed by the unusually large amounts of blood. Passersby were amazed by the unusually large amounts of blood. Passersby were amazed by the unusually large amounts of blood. Passersby were amazed by the unusually large amounts of blood. Passersby were amazed by the unusually large amounts of blood. Passersby were amazed by the unusually large amounts of blood. Passersby were amazed by the unusually large amounts of blood. Passersby were amazed by the unusually large amounts of blood. Passersby were amazed by the unusually large amounts of blood. Passersby were amazed by the unusually large amounts of blood. Passersby were amazed by the unusually large amounts of blood. Passersby were amazed by the unusually large amounts of blood. Passersby were amazed by the unusually large amounts of blood. Passersby were amazed by the unusually large amounts of blood. Passersby were amazed by the unusually large amounts of blood. Passersby were amazed by the unusually large amounts of blood. Passersby were amazed by the unusually large amounts of blood. Passersby were amazed by the unusually large

amounts of blood. Passersby were amazed by the unusually large amounts of blood. Passersby were amazed by the unusually large amounts of blood. Passersby were amazed by the unusually large amounts of blood. Passersby were amazed by the unusually large amounts of blood. Passersby were amazed by the unusually large amounts of blood. Passersby were amazed by the unusually large

> **I didn't learn a thing from this "educational toy."**

amounts of blood. Passersby were amazed by the unusually large amounts of blood. Passersby were amazed by the unusually large amounts of blood. Passersby were amazed by the unusually large amounts of blood. Passersby were amazed by the unusually large amounts of blood. Passersby were amazed by the unusually large amounts of blood. Passersby were amazed by the unusually large amounts of blood. Passersby were

see SOAPDISH page 293

Bill Gates' Wife Worried He's Lying In A Ditch Full Of Money Somewhere

see PEOPLE page 11E

Coach Angry Every Player Gets A Trophy

see SPORTS page 5C

Piggly Wiggly Recalls 50,000 Pounds Of Ground Beef And Glass

see BUSINESS page 11D

STATshot

A look at the numbers that shape your world.

Why Are We So Much Better Than All The Other MCs?

25% Roget's Dictionary Of Similes, 3rd Edition

11% Frequently remind audience who we are, what we're here to say

16% Provide trenchant observations on art of pimping

19% Believe our résumé speaks for itself

29% Fresh-ass breath

---

the ONION®

VOLUME 40 ISSUE 29   AMERICA'S FINEST NEWS SOURCE™   22–28 JULY 2004

Study: Majority Of Americans Out Of Touch With Mainstream

NEW YORK—According to a study published by the Popular Culture Research Group Monday, the majority of American citizens are out of touch with mainstream American society.

"We're not sure, at this point, whether this is a new trend or a continuation of an old trend," PCRG consultant Paul Van Lamm said. "All we know right now is that 70 to 85 percent of Americans are unfamiliar with, unaware of, or just plain don't care about what the American people are watching on television, seeing at the movie theater, listening to on their radios, wearing, rooting for, falling in love with all over again, or downloading."

American **Focus**

According to Van Lamm, 71 percent of U.S. citizens polled had no interest in NASCAR racing, America's fastest-growing sport. Van Lamm added that 69 percent of poll respondents said they did not have a single Hispanic friend, in spite of the fact that Hispanics are the nation's fastest-growing minority group. Additionally, the majority of poll respondents did not see the final episode of *Friends*, television's most-watched sitcom.

"It's disturbing," Van Lamm said. "I'm uncomfortable with the number of U.S. citizens who have no interest in

see MAINSTREAM page 215

Secretary Of Defense Humiliated As U.S. Credit Card Rejected

Above: Myers looks on as Rumsfeld holds the rejected credit card.

ST. LOUIS—An attempt to build international goodwill backfired horribly for Defense Secretary Donald Rumsfeld Monday, when he was unable to pick up the tab for Australian Defense Minister Sen. Robert Hill's order of 11 Apache AH-64 helicopters using the U.S.'s credit card.

"It was extraordinarily embarrassing for poor Donald," said Hill, who visited the Boeing production facility with Rumsfeld and Joint Chief of Staff Richard Myers. "He'd been going on for the entire tour about how America was stronger than it had ever been, and then that happened. He turned red as a beet."

The credit card, a Fort Knox Executive Club Visa granted to the U.S. during the Clinton Administration, had an assigned $300 million credit line.

When the country accrued a balance approaching the limit in 1995, the credit-card company awarded the U.S. additional credit. According to a Visa representative who spoke on the condition of anonymity, the company granted extensions 14 times since then, and Monday, the card had never been declined outright.

Boeing sales representative Alonso Martinez said that he attempted to charge the 11 $21.4 million helicopters, for a total of $235.4 million, to the card at approximately 4 p.m.

"Sir, your card was denied," Martinez told Rumsfeld in a lowered voice. "Do you have another one we could try?"

According to Martinez, Rumsfeld became flustered and insisted that the

see CREDIT CARD page 215

Divorced Branding Exec Generates Buzz Before Getting Back Out There

CHICAGO—Recently divorced Saatchi & Saatchi branding executive Brad Stritch, 38, has already generated considerable buzz in the Chicago singles community about his return to the highly competitive world of dating, friends and coworkers told the press Monday.

"It's incredible how much people are already talking about him," said Jack Guyer, one of Stritch's colleagues. "Everyone's discussing who he'll date first and when he's

Left: Stritch, who is newly single.

going to do it. If he can sustain this level of interest for another month, he's going to be like a kid in a candy factory when he finally gets out there again."

Stritch, married to Deborah Bauer-Stritch from June 2001 to December 2003, officially announced his divorce in April 2004. Initially, he positioned himself as a newly single man too consumed with pain to even consider dating.

"Stritch made all the right moves, that's for sure," Guyer said. "Instead of talking a lot

see EXEC page 214

Chimps In Danger Of Extinction

Researchers recently said that the chimpanzee, hunted for meat and threatened by deforestation, could be extinct in 50 years. What do *you* think?

David Price
Civil Engineer

"Oh, boo hoo. They had their chance."

Ravi Klun
Poacher

"As a poacher, whenever I catch a chimp, I just throw it back. I'm after the tastier marmosets."

Inez Rahman
Pedicurist

"Well, I say it's one less species who will masturbate in public. Good riddance!"

Wade Caho Jr.
Artist

"What?! Oh, chimps. I thought you said 'chicks.' Shit. Wow. For a second there... fuck."

Robert Hegeman
Systems Analyst

"Crap! We'd better remake *The Barefoot Executive* now, before it's too late."

Dorothee Fochs
Statistician

"They're being hunted for meat? Are chimp fajitas any good?"

The Democratic National Convention

The 2004 Democratic National Convention will be held in Boston July 26-29. What is planned?

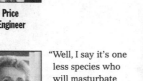

- ★ Public abortions every hour, on the hour
- ★ Tuesday is "Dress Like A Republican" day
- ★ Several Kennedys hired to greet visitors at doors and pose for photographs with them
- ★ Special dinnertime performance of everyone's favorite Capitol Steps tunes by Tina DeHaven And The Misbehavin' Band
- ★ John Kerry to wed running mate in civil ceremony
- ★ Air America will broadcast from booth, giving away shirts and raffling off a waterbed
- ★ Big annual "Texas, Florida, and California delegates vs. everyone else" softball game
- ★ Closing ceremony with 2004 theme, "The Era Of Big Government Is Just Beginning!"

212

You Mean I Could Get *Paid* For Writing Commercial Jingles?

By Tom Basner

Slow down, Scooter. If I'm hearing you right, you're telling me I should quit my data-entry job and take up full-time what I've always done for fun? You're really telling me to pursue my *hobby* as a means of income? I don't believe it. You mean I could get *paid* for writing catchy 10- to 30-second jingles about local and national consumer products and services?

By whom? I always figured the companies were too busy servicing water heaters, selling tires, or serving hamburgers to listen to some jingle-writer hawk his radio-ready ditty. It's got to be dang time-consuming to be, say, Sawyer County's home-appliance and furniture sales leader. I mean, in my opinion, Harn's Furniture's the place to go, for your house and home, 'cause at Harn's they treat you like fam-i-ly. But you say the people at Harn's might pay for a snappy slogan about their company, set to popularly styled music? Well, that sounds too good to be true.

What's the catch? You see, I've been writing little commercial melodies my whole life. Every since I was a boy, I've spent my free time dreaming up ditties for all my favorite companies, then matching them up with memorable tunes that I compose. Take one of my favorites, written for a popular soft drink: "7-Up, it gives you pep and keeps a happy spring in your step. Caffeine free, and that's no lie. Delicious taste for every gal and guy!" Nice, huh?

I've written close to 1,000 jingles, in fact. I used to just noodle around at home with my piano and my four-track, but about five years ago, I started recording my jingles at a studio my buddy has downtown. My wife, who has a really pretty voice and great enunciation, does most of the vocals. But on occasion, I've brought in members of the church choir to do backing vocals, or a neighborhood kid when the jingle called for a child's voice.

There's nothing more enjoyable than spending the afternoon in the booth, laying down 20 takes of "If you're not happy, we're not happy. That's why you'll leave happy, when you come to Jack's!" (That Jack's family restaurant, located just off Hwy. 18, live music every Friday.) Then I'll add a synth line under it, get the levels just right, and put it on a CD. But I never thought anyone down at Jack's would have any interest in my little personal project. I wouldn't even charge a small place like Jack's. I'd do it just for the joy of hearing it on WIBA. Do you really think they might use it?

Gosh, I'm trying to remember what my first jingle was. I think it must have been for Campbell's Soup: "Kids love the taste, moms love the price, Campbell's Soups are great and nice." To accent the words "taste," "price," and "nice," I added a little bell that sounded a bit like a spoon hitting a bowl. Man, I must have been 12 years old when I wrote that. I've come a long

What's the catch? You see, I've been writing commercial melodies my whole life.

way since then. And all this time, I could have been making money? Seems more like I should be paying *them*.

My God, just imagine writing a jingle for one of the big guys like General Mills, Home Depot, or Tropicana! I've never played my jingles for anyone except my family and a few houseguests.

How will I even go about choosing which ones best represent my abilities? Well, it's certainly no "plop plop, fizz fizz," but I'm rather proud of the catchy little tune I wrote for Pep Boys auto shop: "Pep Boys, less noise, trust us, no fuss, new and used parts, installed with heart." I started whistling that little tune around work, and pretty soon, everyone was humming my jingle for the nation's leading repair-shop chain.

But in addition to honing my art and entertaining my friends, I could make a few bucks, huh? Amazing. This is the first day of the rest of my life. No more writing commercial jingles, multi-track recording them, archiving them on DAT, and *not* getting paid.

Hmm, it does seem a little wrong to profit from something as pure as a jingle, though. My corporate- or product-related compositions always had integrity. What if I become a slave to the corporate hive mind? What if they try to make me change my sound? The second one of those big-jingle executives tells me to so much as lose a trumpet lick, I'm out the door for good.

But what's the harm in giving it a shot? If I can make a little scratch doing what I love, why not? I'll never forget that I was a jingle writer before the money, and I'll be a jingle writer after the money is gone. Ø

73 Percent Of U.S. Livestock Show Signs Of Clinical Depression

WASHINGTON, DC—According to a joint study conducted by the FDA and the Department of Agriculture, nearly three out of four members of the U.S. livestock population show signs of clinical depression, with the vast majority of cases going untreated, government officials said Monday.

"The FDA is charged with the task of preventing potentially disastrous outbreaks of disease within the U.S. livestock population," said Henry Wolcott, Assistant Undersecretary of Agriculture, Psychiatric Division. "I'm afraid that, in this case, our intervention came too late. Our study shows that 73 percent of U.S. cattle, goats, sheep, and swine suffer from serious psychiatric problems."

Signs of clinical depression discovered by the researchers include severe listlessness, lack of motivation, and a flattening of emotional affect marked by glazed eyes and slow movements.

"Everyone is concerned about mad cow disease or the bird flu," Wolcott said. "What the average person fails to appreciate, however, is that mental disorders can be just as debilitating as physical ones. If you look into these animals' eyes, you can see the blank gaze of hopelessness and despair."

"It's tragic," Wolcott added. "It's no kind of life, not for man or beast."

Walcott said that millions of animals across the nation wile away the hours unproductively, not moving until forced to do so by an outside factor, such as a farmhand or a milking machine.

"Most of the cows we examined barely had the energy to drag themselves

see LIVESTOCK page 214

Above: Edgar, WI resident 521, one of the nation's many depression sufferers.

NEWS IN BRIEF

White House Declares War On DSL Provider

WASHINGTON, DC—The Bush Administration is awaiting congressional approval for an official act of war against high-speed DSL service provider Qwest, White House officials confirmed Tuesday. "After two weeks of trying to peaceably resolve our differences with Qwest, we have decided that this poor customer service will not stand," Bush said in a televised address. "I waited in the Oval Office all day for the technician to show up, and then, when I called them to find out where he was, I was transferred to another phone rep and got disconnected. We will begin bombarding them with tersely worded e-mails as early as next week." This marks the third time Bush has declared war this month, following conflicts with DIRECTV and the Potomac Electric Power Company.

Work Friends Calling Bill 'William'

BENBROOK, TX—Close friends and neighbors attending the backyard barbecue of Bill Hunkins were surprised to hear the host's coworkers call him "William," attendees reported Monday. "All these people kept saying, 'Mmm, this is delicious, William' and 'Hand me a beer, William,'" Hunkin's friend Bryan Koppe said. "It was so bizarre. Why weren't they calling him by his name? Were they trying to give him shit or something?" Koppe added that Hunkins once spent a semester answering to the nickname "El Pudd."

Area Man Bored With All The Porn He Owns

BREAUX BRIDGE, LA—Gil Peterson has grown tired of his current collection of sexually explicit videotapes, DVDs, and magazines, the 44-year-old delivery-truck driver said Monday. "I tried to rewatch *Butt Fuck Sluts Go Nuts* again, but it was so boring," Peterson said. "I mean, how many times can you watch the same set of twins double-team the black guy on the back of a motorcycle?" Peterson said he will have one more look at the tape, but can't promise he'll achieve orgasm.

Garroting Survivors Call For Wire Ban

WASHINGTON, DC—The nation's garroting survivors demonstrated outside the Capitol Monday, raising a hoarse but plaintive cry for a nationwide ban on potentially lethal wire. "Every year, dozens of people are severely injured or even killed by garroting," croaked Gerald Michaels, who still bears a necklace of scars from a 1997 telephone-cord-assisted mugging that nearly claimed his life. "This legacy of shame will continue until we eliminate the lethal wires that run through our homes, above our streets, and through our very way of life." Michaels recently accepted a $2 million grant from a coalition of sponsors that included Bluetooth and Cingular Wireless.

Some Sense Knocked Into Girlfriend's Son

ENOCHVILLE, NC—Stu Ayden knocked some sense into the thick skull of 9-year-old Jesse Wilkerson Monday night. "Since Jesse's real father is not around, it is sometimes necessary for another man, in this case Ayden, to step in as a male parent surrogate," said Dr. Frank Gillette, a child psychologist. "Jesse spilled half a glass of Hi-C fruit punch on the carpet of Ayden's mobile home, so as Jesse's mother's boyfriend, it was his responsibility to answer the behavior with a thorough ass-beating." When questioned by reporters, Ayden said he is glad to serve as Jesse's caretaker so long as his mama keeps payin' the rent. ✍

from the barn out to the field," Walcott said. "Once in the field, they tended to spend most of their time quietly brooding and chewing cud, showing little to no willingness to communicate with their herd-member peers. Their depression was so debilitating that they needed to be coaxed out of inactivity through the use of hollering, physical force, and, in extreme cases, trained dogs."

The study also noted the average U.S. cow's tendency to emit low, mournful moans.

Walcott said that the majority of sheep studied rarely moved during the day, opting instead to stand in one place, often avoiding sunlight and acting only when the food supply in the immediate area was depleted.

> ## "I wonder if he'll be looking for a down-to-earth woman like his wife again, or if he'll go for something wilder," Lillenstein added.

"Like many undiagnosed depression sufferers, it seems that a lot of U.S. livestock escape the emotional emptiness of their lives by overeating," Walcott said. "Most appear to care nothing about their personal appearance. And, as any ranch-hand who has ever shoveled manure can tell you, they make only limited effort to keep their physical surroundings in order."

Dr. Theodore Nelson, author of *The Slow Slaughter: Growing Up Livestock In An Uncaring World*, has made combating bovine ennui his personal mission.

"Sadly, much of our nation's livestock feel they have no future," Nelson said. "They see life as short, brutal, and bereft of purpose. They may appear to be functioning normally—eating feed, producing milk, and generating high volumes of fertilizer—but inside, many are just waiting to die."

In his book, Nelson calls for a federal program to provide Selective Livestock Serotonin Reuptake Inhibitors to animals in need.

"The signs that these animals are depressed were right in front of us, but too many of us in the food sciences were blinded by narrow-minded agricultural orthodoxy to see them," Nelson said. "But we can't think this problem will be solved through medication alone. Cattle have to learn to believe in themselves. They've got to see themselves as more than walking hunks of meat or they'll never get better."

The government's report also contained preliminary data suggesting a rate as high as 95 percent for severe anxiety disorder among U.S. poultry. ✱

Above: A building bears stickers from the final step of Stritch's marketing campaign.

about his divorce, which carries the risk of becoming annoying, he only mentioned it to a small number of people in key locations like the office, the gym, his after-work bar, and the coffee shop where that one hottie works. By revealing his 'secret' to a few fashion-forward people and al-

> ## "Sadly, much of our nation's livestock feel they have no future," Nelson said. "They see life as short, brutal, and bereft of purpose. They may appear to be functioning normally— eating feed, producing milk, and generating high volumes of fertilizer— but inside, many are just waiting to die."

lowing them do the legwork, he created a textbook viral-marketing campaign."

"This is probably his best work since Red Bull cocktails," Guyer added.

Friends and coworkers said Stritch has redesigned his packaging in recent weeks, ostensibly to increase his desirability among the single, 18-to-30 female demographic.

"He's been taking care of himself like he used to before he met Debo-

rah," said Sandi Lillenstein, who had a short affair with Stritch three years ago. "While he was married, he let himself go a bit. But lately he's been hitting the gym hard, and he's gotten some great new outfits. It's not so much a re-working of his image as a throwback to the classic Stritch that we all used to know."

"I wonder if he'll be looking for a down-to-earth woman like his wife again, or if he'll go for something wilder," Lillenstein added.

Last week, when interest in his divorce began to die down slightly, Stritch strategically leaked information about his "emotional devastation" to his personal assistant, Cindy Solomon.

"That was a risky maneuver that could have easily backfired," Guyer said. "Telling Cindy how painful the divorce was and how much he has learned about himself gives him a stronger experience quotient, but overselling that message could've made him look pathetic. The brilliant part was that he told Cindy to keep it quiet because he didn't want everyone to know."

Guyer said that, in response to this latest market drop, he's already overheard three women gushing about Stritch's sensitivity.

"It's working beautifully," Guyer said. "Damn, if I could've created a solid support base like that when I was doing that Wrigley's Gum project, I'd be vice-president now."

At a recent roundtable that Stritch conducted with his male friends at the Horse Head Bar And Grill, the group reviewed possible plans for the final stage of the whisper campaign. Although he had originally hoped for a July release into the dating world, friends helped Stritch decide to wait until Aug. 15, to "let the buzz in-

crease."

"You don't want to go off before things are ready to pop," Stritch's friend Larry Ennis said at the meeting. "Although it's tempting to go out early, you have to have the patience to treat this re-launch carefully. I have faith that politely refusing the women who ask you out for a drink with the excuse that you're 'not ready yet' will brand you as mature, not just the same old pussy-hound wrapped in a new box."

Ennis said Stritch plans to conduct house-to-house marketing to bring interest in the new image to a "fever pitch."

"Brad believes placing stickers

> ## Last week, when interest in his divorce began to die down slightly, Stritch strategically leaked information about his "emotional devastation" to his personal assistant, Cindy Solomon.

with the phrase 'Who is Brad?' in unusual locations throughout the city will be just the thing to keep people talking," Ennis said. "Also, he's planning a 'Who Says All The Good Men Are Taken?' theme party. He's trying to get it sponsored by Bacardi Silver, but they want him to hand out their T-shirts. He'd prefer the focus to be on him and his availability to attractive women, not a premium malt beverage." ✱

Above: A scene from NBC's Will & Grace, a TV show about which many Americans care surprisingly little.

ment, Tempe, AZ daycare provider Tina Jefferson said, "A lot of the children here saw the *Harry Potter* movie. And Yao Ming plays sports. How is that?"

"Oh, wait!" Jefferson added. "I know that Anna Nicole Smith lost a lot of weight and people are talking about it. Well, not me or people I know, but other people."

Carson Mannheim, lead statistician and founder of Mannheim Media Research, said he is trying to make sense

> **"Kanye West? He's in one of those shows. Or was in. It's off the air now, is that it?" said Pewaukee, WI resident and HVAC technician Carl Danford. "Huh… *DaVinci Code*, you say. I know: Is it a movie? What's Nordic Walking? I mean 'who.' Who is Nordic Walking?"**

of the confusing data.

"We're unsure exactly what these figures may mean, but the implications must be far-reaching," Mannheim said. "We're used to Americans not knowing the capital of the next state over, or who their congressman is, or how a bill becomes a law. But the idea that most residents of this country don't know anything about 'Fit But You Know It,' Usher, Dragonball Z, or the WWE is terrifying. No one seems to care that these are the things that influence the everyday life of most Americans." ⌀

what interests the greater part of their fellow citizens."

Additional data collected by prominent forecasters, pollsters, and trend-watchers indicates that an overwhelming number of Americans have not seen this week's box-office smashes; do not own a Munsingwear penguin-logo golf shirt, the country's hottest fashion item; and not only do not own the must-have Apple iPod, but have never even participated in the runaway fad of downloading the nation's top albums, many of which they've never heard.

Interviews with average Americans seem to support such findings.

"Kanye West? He's in one of those shows. Or was in. It's off the air now, is that it?" said Pewaukee, WI resident and HVAC technician Carl Danford. "Huh… *DaVinci Code*, you say. I know: Is it a movie? What's Nordic Walking? I mean 'who.' Who is Nordic Walking?"

"I know The White Stripes is a band that younger people like," Danford added.

When asked to name the latest and most buzzworthy figures in entertain-

problem rested with Boeing's credit-card reader.

"That card's good," Rumsfeld said. "Run it again."

As Martinez went into a back room to run the charge again, Rumsfeld assured Hill that "there must be some kind of mix-up."

"You can tell Boeing didn't engineer the card machine," Rumsfeld said, smiling nervously. "If they had, it wouldn't have all these glitches. Well, I suppose that right now, we need Boeing to be focused on the war effort."

Hill, who had accepted Rumsfeld's offer to pay for his new attack helicopters during an exclusive tour of Boeing's 220-acre military aircraft facility outside St. Louis, mumbled in agreement.

When Martinez returned a second time, he took Rumsfeld aside.

"Seems nobody's paid the balance on this guy for the past four months, sir," Martinez said. "Unless you can work it out with the card company, I'll

> **Rumsfeld became flustered and insisted that the problem rested with Boeing's credit-card reader.**

have to physically destroy the card. Terribly sorry, sir."

Martinez escorted Rumsfeld to his office, dialed the number on the back of the card, and handed the phone to the defense secretary.

"It appears the White House had just used the card for some lawyer fees, and then the CIA threw a huge going-away party for someone," Atlanta-based Visa customer-service representative Tracy Waterson said. "There's a hold on use of the card until Congress approves the next budget allocation."

Waterson was unmoved by Rumsfeld's demand for a credit extension.

"We've got to draw the line somewhere, Mr. Rumsfield [sic], and this just happens to be where we do it," Waterson said. "Last April, you told us you'd start repaying us in a month or two, when you finished the Iraq war. We understand that you've run into some complications on your end, and we have tried to accommodate your needs, but we're concerned that you may be accumulating too much debt."

Added Waterson: "We're not going to close your account, but we are going to freeze your borrowing for a couple of months, until we see a change in your administration's fiscal situation. I'm afraid that's all I can do. I'd be happy to transfer you to one of our debt-management consultants who can provide you with some tips for—"

Quickly hanging up the phone, Rumsfeld told Martinez that there was a problem with the company's computer, but that Martinez should load the helicopters onto the supply convoy and bill the U.S. government.

"Sir, we very much appreciate your business, and we look forward to working with you again just as soon as you get your credit issues sorted out," Martinez said, glancing apologetically at Hill. "But let's just call it a day, now, shall we?" ⌀

This Is Not The Time For Compassion And Healing

By Don Kerris

Citizens, friends, and neighbors, we have come together today to reflect on recent events which have deeply wounded this community, and which will no doubt resonate with all of us for a long time to come. You are all undoubtedly feeling many complicated emotions right now—anger, confusion, resentment. But I would like for you to keep one thing in mind: This is not the time for compassion and healing.

Although Scoutmaster Holland's appalling actions have in some way hurt each and every one of us, we must not offer each other comfort and support. We must not cooperate to get through this difficult time together. Nor should we reflect on those blessings we do have—those of community, family, and friends. Rather, we must act out of petty self-interest and blind, irrational anger.

This is no time to turn to each other and share in our grief. This is a time for bitter, divisive accusation. It is a time to say things so terrible, they will give birth to grudges that we'll nurse for decades. This isn't the time to move forward or to forgive past wrongdoings. It is the time to hate, seethe, and wallow.

This tragedy could open the doors to change and renewal. We could seize

> **Friends, we must remember that experiences like these show what people are truly made of. I don't know about you, but at the moment, I am made of incandescent fury.**

the opportunity to exchange ideas on how to improve and safeguard our children's futures. But instead, let's exchange angry recriminations and engage in childish name-calling. Mrs. Dailey, earlier, you told me that Ms. McInnes was a bad mother. Saying that to me behind her back is one thing, but why not say it again before everyone?

As I look around at the anguished,

questioning faces in the room, I see a real need for guidance and unity. Well, I'm afraid this is neither the time nor the place for that. For now, we must simply pick ourselves up and carry on with the business of finger-pointing and buck-passing. We must set about—and I'll tell you, I've been doing a whole lot of this—marveling at how certain troop leaders could really be as oblivious as they claim. From this day forward, let us make "alienation" our watchword. Gandhi said that "forgiveness is the attribute of the strong," but I'll bet Gandhi's kid

> **As I look around at the anguished, questioning faces in the room, I see a real need for guidance and unity. Well, I'm afraid this is neither the time nor the place for that.**

was never touched in the woods on a camping trip.

Fine, "allegedly" touched.

We have convened this meeting not to console each other, not to find solace in numbers, but to get a good look at the lying, guilty faces of those who should have done something but didn't. Let us unleash our unbridled rage hither and thither until every last bit of acrimony is expressed, which probably won't be any time soon. Mrs. Dailey, could you maybe shut your mouth for three seconds and let me finish?

Some among you might be clinging to that old saw "innocent until proven guilty." To those people, I say, "Where were your high-minded ideals when your best friend and racquetball partner told you that sometimes he didn't trust himself around children, Terry?" Seriously, I'd like an answer to that. Oh, what a surprise. Terry's not here. Terry's probably, what? Polishing his car or buying himself something, like he probably was when his own kid was getting stroked in a field. I'm sorry, but after all, it's what we're here for.

Some of you may be asking "Why, God? Why my boy? What did he do to deserve this?" Some of you may be searching your hearts for understanding and insight. Many of you may have turned to God or family. Friends: Abandon fruitless searches. The molesting gym coach isn't in-

side you. Turn your search for scapegoats and excuses outward... You didn't hear it from me, but I don't think revenge is completely off the table, either.

Perhaps, years from now, you will find yourselves at peace with this tragedy, and see that the trials of today gave us strength, which in turn enriched our tomorrows. Who knows, maybe you and Mr. Holland will go bowling together. Or, I know, perhaps you'll put him in charge of a whole bunch of pre-adolescent boys and send them into the woods, huh, Mark? No, you're the son of a bitch, Mark.

Any time any place, my friend. That's what I thought.

Friends, we must remember that experiences like these show what people are truly made of. I don't know about you, but at the moment, I am made of incandescent fury.

I suggest that we look on this as a fresh beginning, a jumping-off point for a new era of loathing and mistrust. Perhaps we can even re-open some old wounds. One thing is certain: The wounds that Mr. Holland opened will not be allowed to heal. To treat those wounds as the inevitable result of a single bad person

> **The molesting gym coach isn't inside you. Turn your search for scapegoats and excuses outward... You didn't hear it from me, but I don't think revenge is completely off the table, either.**

living among better people would be the real tragedy. Now more than ever, we must put aside the commonality of our shared suffering and focus instead on concentrating our wrath on a single individual. I suggest Helen. ✍

Your Horoscope

By Lloyd Schumner Sr.
Retired Machinist and
A.A.P.B.-Certified Astrologer

Aries: (March 21–April 19)
The stars know it's hurricane season throughout the coastal regions, but the mounting waves of bear attacks should provide some variety.

Taurus: (April 20–May 20)
You thought your new sportscar could do everything but love you, so its declaration of devotion will come as quite a shock.

Gemini: (May 21–June 21)
A nice gesture will go terribly awry this Sunday, when wearing a suit and tie for once does kill you after all.

Cancer: (June 22–July 22)
You'll be unprepared for your sudden rise to a career in high finance, which is probably why you'll fuck it up so bad.

Leo: (July 23–Aug. 22)
You're tired of people accusing you of throwing money at your problems. Luckily, these people can usually be bribed to shut up.

Virgo: (Aug. 23–Sept. 22)
A friend who always astounds you with her lousy taste in men will blow you away with her execrable taste in names for quadruplets.

Libra: (Sept. 23–Oct. 23)
No one will characterize your efforts as above and beyond the call of duty. For God's sake, you just did the dishes.

Scorpio: (Oct. 24–Nov. 21)
Michael Jordan said that you miss 100 percent of the shots you don't take, which is apparently supposed to inspire you to great feats in real-estate sales.

Sagittarius: (Nov. 22–Dec. 21)
Wearing roller skates everywhere you go may have been a cute eccentricity during your residency, but you're a doctor now.

Capricorn: (Dec. 22–Jan. 19)
Your decision to take up bicycling will cause many in your area to rethink their call for increased bicycle safety.

Aquarius: (Jan. 20–Feb. 18)
You'll be an inspiration to the downtrodden millions, but in a way that will see dozens of cities in flames by the end of this century.

Pisces: (Feb. 19–March 20)
Your most cherished dream will die this week, which would be tragic if it weren't to float around in a Texas-shaped pool filled with beer.

NEWS

Kite Flyer In The Zone

see RECREATION page 15E

Flaming Bag Of Shit Intended For Apartment 314

see LOCAL page 7B

Second Amendment Advocate Shoots His Mouth Off

see POLITICS page 11C

Brand Name Trusted

see LOCAL page 15B

STATshot

A look at the numbers that shape your world.

Who Was Ulysses S. Grant?

- 17% A great…man?
- 11% That dude with the birthplace
- 16% Built I-78 rest stop
- 24% Inspiration for guy on $50 bill
- 18% Defeated the French at Agincourt
- 14% Chicken—I'm thinking 'fried chicken'

the ONION®

VOLUME 40 ISSUE 30   AMERICA'S FINEST NEWS SOURCE™   29 JULY–4 AUGUST 2004

John Glenn Installed In Smithsonian

WASHINGTON, DC—John Glenn, the first American to orbit the earth and the oldest man ever in space, is being honored by the Smithsonian National Air and Space Museum, which has installed the former U.S. senator as the centerpiece of its upcoming Milestones Of Flight exhibit.

"John Glenn's life has been a living testament to the power of human vision," NASM director Gen. John R. "Jack" Dailey said at Sunday's dedication ceremony. "Generations of Americans will be inspired by his nobly dangling form, which so eloquently evokes both the wonder of physical flight through the air and that even greater flight—of the human spirit."

The Marine Corps band played the national anthem as Dailey unveiled a space-suited Glenn in his new place of honor, suspended 40 feet above the

see GLENN page 220

Left: Glenn hangs among other national treasures in the Smithsonian.

Kickboxer, Starring Jean-Claude Van Damme, To Continue In A Moment

ATLANTA—*Kickboxer*, starring Jean-Claude Van Damme, will resume after a brief pause, TNT sources reported several seconds ago.

"*Kickboxer*, starring Jean-Claude Van Damme, will continue in a moment," an unidentified network source said.

According to the anony-mous male source, the interruption to the *Kickboxer* broadcast will be brief. The representative for TNT asked that all persons watching *Kickboxer*, the 1989 action movie starring Jean-Claude Van Damme, "[remain] tuned to TNT."

The interruption affects

see KICKBOXER page 221

Above: *Kickboxer*, seconds before interruption.

Strip Club Makes Commitment To Hire More Minorities

TAMPA, FL—Richard Brainard, owner of Shakerz Gentlemen's Lounge, announced plans Monday to hire more minorities at his Kennedy Boulevard nightspot.

"We're looking for some Asians, mainly, but I think we could also use two or three Puerto Ricans and a light-skinned black girl," Brainard said. "Man, those Puerto Ricans can dance. Makes you wish you were 22 again, I'll tell you that."

Brainard said the new hires will help Shakerz better represent his community.

"We need a lineup that's a little more Tampa," Brainard said. "That means

see MINORITIES page 220

Left: Brainard (inset) and the strip club he owns.

The 9/11 Panel Report

The 9/11 Commission's final report, released last week, cited many failures on the part of the U.S. government. What do *you* think?

Laurie Fredette
Ticket Taker

"I read the whole report cover to cover. Turns out it was terrorists."

Matthew Dort
Coach

"Osama, Osama, Osama! Can't we have a commission about something *nice* for a change?"

Ralph Gagliano
Anesthesiologist

"I'm glad it's over. The way that investigation was dragging on, I was almost beginning to wish that 9/11 had never even happened."

Joseph Jones
Deliveryman

"I wrote a report about 8/20 that I think you should read. It's called *My Birthday And What I Want For It.*"

Karen Farr
Secretary

"Great timing! I just finished *Bergdorf Blondes*, and I've been looking for another good beach read."

Jeffery Koeshal
Systems Analyst

"Eh, the whole thing is pretty tame. Now, Ken Starr—*there* was a man who could write a juicy report."

Bush Campaign Costs

As of the beginning of July, President Bush had spent roughly $160 million on his re-election effort. How was some of the money spent?

★ $750,000: Best mobile pig-roast pit money can buy

★ $300,000: Purchase of babies to kiss for photo ops

★ $7.3 million: Special Don King seminars on what black people are, how to talk to them, and why they hate Republicans

★ $1.29: Twine; you never know when you're gonna need a little twine

★ $17.2 million: Hummer limo with hot tub, rented by the hour through November

★ $350: A nice suit for Bush's TV appearances

★ $2 million: Reelection campaign guns

★ $6 million: Creation of bionic advisor Steve Austin, whose cybernetic limbs allow him to run a faster, stronger, better campaign

★ $88 million: Miscellaneous red, white, and blue bullshit

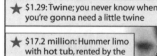

America's Finest News Source.™

Herman Ulysses Zweibel
Founder

T. Herman Zweibel
Publisher Emeritus
J. Phineas Zweibel
Publisher
Maxwell Prescott Zweibel
Editor-In-Chief

Where The Fuck Is Diane With My Fair-Trade Coffee?

By Ben Lesterman

Marla? Get in here. Where the fuck is Diane with my coffee? I sent her out 15 minutes ago for a large cup of fair-trade Ethiopian Dark Roast from the La Paz coffee shop. How hard could it be? You walk your ass to the corner, hand them my *Utne Reader* travel mug, plunk down the money, and pick up the coffee. Add a little soy milk and two natural-cane sugar packets, and you make sure the lid is tight. That's so simple, even Diane should be able to do it without fucking up.

Have a seat, Marla. We need to talk about the situation here. I don't ask for much, do I? All I need are a few comforts to make my workday start smoothly. You know this. When I walk into this office at 8 a.m., I'd better see these things on my desk: *The New York Times*, for a fair analysis of current events; the trades, to keep up with the competition; and, most importantly, my fucking coffee.

I want my staff working at 110 percent, and I want my coffee harvested by formerly indigent people making a decent living wage so they can feed their families, sustain their farms, and become sources for community development at a local level. What part of that is confusing? Let me repeat myself: I want a large cup of organochlorine-free, unbleached-filter-brewed, environmentally sound cocksucking coffee 10 minutes ago.

Christ, what's she doing? Flying to Ethiopia to purchase the beans from local farmers at a minimum price of $1.26 per pound herself? I'm glad someone is providing those farmers with technical assistance transitioning to organic farming methods, but that's not Diane's job. If I remember correctly, she works for me. And I need to be able to talk to our clients in a positive frame of mind. No one wants to talk about ecologically sensible office supplies with someone who can't keep his fucking eyes open. I do not need this shit when my acupuncturist is out of town.

And what's up with this radio station? It's sure as fuck not NPR. "Smooth jazz"? It may be smooth, but it's not jazz. If you want to listen to jazz, there's a great Coltrane retrospective on today. Or do you have something against expanding your fucking minds? You'd rather sit around like monkeys, listening to smooth jazz.

Do you even care what kind of shit is going down in the world? It's called *Morning Edition*. If I don't get some Carl fucking Kasell right now, I'm going to choke someone. Hold on. Change it right after this Terence Trent D'Arby song is done. I like this one.

And what was that stack of bills sitting in my mailbox this morning? Marla, do you think I have my home mail sent to my work address so I can open it in the conference room while gazing out at the swans? Marla? Do you care to venture a guess? Well, Marla, I will tell you: I have my personal mail sent here so that my personal assistant can personally assist me by fucking opening it. Get rid of this REI catalog. Get rid of this shit. Now, look at this Working Assets Long Distance bill. It hasn't been paid. What's the date on that Maya Angelou calendar? Look at the calendar, Marla. Do you even care about the McCain-Lieberman Climate Stewardship Act that I help support every

And what's up with this radio station? It's sure as fuck not NPR.

time I call my brother in Seattle? Then let's get on the stick! Here, put this Ben & Jerry's coupon in my canvas tote over there.

Another thing: No one even touches the *Mother Jones* until it moves from my desk to the table in the waiting room. Last week, I was trying to find my goddamn *Mother Jones*, and where was it? Sitting on the toilet tank in the men's room. I had to have Diane run all the way out to the newsstand and buy me a brand-new copy that wasn't covered in particles of shit and piss.

After I'm done reading the *Mother Jones*, you can do whatever you the fuck you want with it—before you recycle it, that is.

Next item on the agenda: Thursday, I put some organic radishes in the refrigerator, and on Friday, they were gone. As if that weren't enough, yesterday someone tossed a salmon wrap and half a Fresh Samantha's Mango Mama. Are you aware that there are people starving in Brunei Darussalam? You don't throw out stuff that isn't yours. It's just common sense, or didn't they teach you that in school?

Remember that we're all in this together. We all have the same mission: bleach-free 40 percent post-consumer recycled bond in every copier in America. If we can't agree on that, then what are we doing here? I'm not asking, I'm telling: Think globally, get your fucking act together.

Now, if you'll excuse me, I have to call the shop about my Volvo. ⌀

Lifelong Love Affair With Music Ends At Age 35

CLEVELAND, OH—Sam Powers' lifelong passion for music ended this past weekend, when the 35-year-old camera-store assistant manager realized that he no longer derives pleasure from listening to and acquiring new music.

"It's always sad when something you thought would last forever ends, but I simply don't have the energy to put into it anymore," Powers said Monday. "I'll always love music, but it's not going to be at the center of my life anymore. My priorities have changed, I guess."

Powers said he realized the love affair, which began in 1979 when his

> **Longtime friend Dean Halperin said that it was Powers' own refusal to commit sufficient time and energy to music that destroyed what was once a rewarding part of his life.**

brother introduced him to the first Van Halen album, was over Saturday. While preparing spaghetti at his home, Powers chose silence over a TV On The Radio album his friend had burned him.

"Last week, my buddy went to see this band, but I just didn't feel like going out that night," Powers said. "I started to listen to their album, and even though it really seemed like my type of music—well, I didn't know any of the songs. I was just about to put Beck on when I realized that I'd rather be alone with my thoughts.'"

"Look," Powers added, holding the fingers of his right hand aloft. "My nails used to be worn to the quick from peeling off CD seals. Look at them now. I'm gonna have to use clippers."

While he said he will miss the deep bonds forged during a lengthy relationship based on respect and admiration, Powers declared the painful decision final.

"Things were running on autopilot for the past few years," Powers said, pulling a copy of the 1982 X album *Under The Big Black Sun* from his shelf and staring at it. "I went through the motions for a while—buying a few CDs off the critics' year-end lists and

making it out to a show here and there. But really, that rush I used to feel was gone."

Powers said it was during the mid-'90s that his longtime flirtation with music developed into a serious involvement with the post-punk scene, one that some say bordered on obsession.

"If he wasn't at a show or a record store, he was at home listening to music," friend Keith Tellingham said. "Music and Sam were inseparable. He always had a CD player on him. You couldn't be around him for more than five minutes without him bringing up music. Man, he had it bad. I still remember the glow on his face at the Shellac/Tar/Six Finger Satellite show a decade ago."

In spite of reports like Tellingham's, Powers said he is now secure enough in his musical tastes to not need to chase down new bands like he did when he was younger.

"When I was 22, I felt I needed to find out who was out there and exper-

iment with all different kinds of music," Powers said. "But I just don't have the stamina for that now. I can't get up the energy to seek it out anymore. I'd rather just listen to the bands I already know. If that, even."

As recently as 1996, Powers could express some familiarity with nearly every popular recording artist. Today, he draws a blank when asked to recall any current Top 10 single.

Above: Powers, who no longer has strong feelings for music, enjoys a quiet evening alone.

"The type is so tiny on these charts," Powers said. "What's 'Los Lonely Boys'? Are they like Los Lobos? What's with the 'Los'? 'Hoobastank'? Jesus. Probably some shit punk-metal band, right? No, on second thought, don't tell me. I don't even want to know."

Longtime friend Dean Halperin said that it was Powers' own refusal to

see MUSIC page 222

NEWS IN BRIEF

Rumsfeld Sick Of Jokes About His Fat Girlfriend

WASHINGTON, DC—During a coffee break at the Pentagon Monday, Secretary of Defense Donald Rumsfeld announced that he will no longer stand for jokes made at the expense of his 5'7", 197-pound girlfriend Mavis Delsman. "I can enjoy a good laugh just like anybody, but the next person to make a crack about my Mavis will be making jokes in the unemployment line," Rumsfeld said. "She's a very nice person and doesn't deserve to be talked about in that way." Rumsfeld added that he will take punitive action against the entire department if he even hears the phrase "junk in the trunk," whether it's in reference to Delsman or not.

Internet Collapses Under Sheer Weight Of Baby Pictures

SAN FRANCISCO—Many web users were trapped without service Monday, when a large section of the Internet collapsed under the weight of the millions of baby pictures posted online. "Some personal web pages contain literally hundreds of adorable infant photos," MCI senior vice-president Vinton Cerffe said. "Add to that

the number of precious pumpkins on photo-sharing sites like Ophoto.com, and anyone can see it was a recipe for disaster. The Internet simply was not designed to support so much parental pride." Cerffe said he expects regular web-traffic flow to resume once the nation's larger Internet providers are reinforced with stronger cuteness-bearing servers.

Traveler Amazed By Sheer Number of Mexicans

MEXICO CITY—American tourist Michael Anderson expressed amazement Monday at the vast number of Mexicans populating Mexico City. "I guess it's obvious that the city would have a lot of Mexicans, but I wasn't mentally prepared for it," Anderson said. "I mean, really—they were everywhere. *Tons* of them. On every street corner. They were just *everywhere*." Last year, Anderson experienced similar culture-shock at the number of Asians in San Francisco's Chinatown.

Teen Gives Up Smoking Pot After Seeing Parents High

DEDHAM, MA—Elyssa Schuster, 16, swore Monday that she will never again experiment with marijuana af-

ter coming home to "obviously baked" parents Harold and Judy Saturday night. "I used to think smoking pot made you look cool, but, boy, was I wrong," Schuster said. "Dad got all paranoid about the mortgage rate while Mom spent an hour giggling about how dusty the ceiling fan was. It was so sad and depressing." Schuster said she was thankful to be scared straight before she made a fool of herself again.

Kennel Certificate Proves Who Puppy Daddy Is

VALLEY MILLS, TX—An AKC certificate of pedigree proves conclusively that Duke, a 2-year-old Rottweiler from nearby Rock Springs, is the puppy daddy of Skipper, a Rottweiler born July 20, Cloverleaf Kennel sources reported Monday. "Duke can bark excuses all day and night, but this pedigree proves that Skipper his," said attorney Seth Freidman, who represents Ginger, Skipper's mama. "Duke should be responsible for Skipper's upbringing. I'm sick of hearing that it's a male dog's nature to seek out multiple breeding partners." A spokesperson for Duke said his client was lured by Ginger's promiscuity, insisting that "everyone know the bitch have litters by three different dogs before Duke." *Ø*

floor of the museum's breathtaking Gallery 100. He occupies a space near his Mercury "Friendship 7" orbiter capsule and between Charles Lindbergh's Spirit of St. Louis and the Bell Airacomet, the first American turbojet aircraft in regular production.

The NASM will display Glenn in his original 1962-vintage flight suit, which he wore for his historic orbital space flight, until December 2004. Beginning next year, Glenn will alternate monthly between his 1962 and 1998 spacesuits. On occasions of historic import, Glenn will be displayed

> **There are currently no plans to decorate Glenn for the holidays, during which time the museum is considering allowing him to visit family, as part of a special touring exhibit.**

in appropriate livery, such as his WWII flight suit, his Korean War full-dress uniform, or the navy-blue and gray suits he wore during his four terms in the Senate.

There are currently no plans to decorate Glenn for the holidays, during which time the museum is considering allowing him to visit family, as part of a special touring exhibit.

"There were a lot of challenges involved in readying John Glenn for display," NASM deputy director Donald Lopez said. "Ideally, we'd like to fully restore him to his original 1962 condition—inarguably his most memorable period—but that's beyond the state of the archival art. However, he is a 1921 model, and therefore close to the end of his current service cycle. When he inevitably fails in a few years, we'll have to take him down and overhaul him anyway. That's when we'll look into making him as period-correct as the other displays here, using both our own knowledge and that of animal preservation and display experts from the Museum of Natural History."

Even as the museum continues to think of ways to better moderate the temperature and increase airflow near the building's rafters, the astronaut's mood remains upbeat.

"I'm happy for the opportunity to serve my country once more, and I am honored and humbled to be considered an inspiration," Glenn said, struggling to make himself heard from his place near the ceiling of the gigantic exhibit hall. "Although the organizers were a little unclear as to how long I will have to remain suspended from this ceiling, I'm proud to be up here as long as they need me." ∅

Above: Part of the workforce Brainard hopes to diversify.

we need more Mexicans. Sometimes it's hard to find one with a decent pair of tits, but that's not going to stop me. We're doing this because it's right, not because it's easy."

Shakerz has had positive experiences with minority employees in the past, Brainard said.

"Margarita's a real class act," Brainard said. "And Camero, the black girl we had last year, was sweet as shit. Sure, we had a lot of problems with her not showing up, but it's not because she was black. Skipping out on shifts is a thing chicks from all races try to pull."

"Except the Dominicans," Brainard added.

> **"Margarita's a real class act," Brainard said. "And Camero, the black girl we had last year, was sweet as shit. Sure, we had a lot of problems with her not showing up, but it's not because she was black. Skipping out on shifts is a thing chicks from all races try to pull."**

While he's already placed a handwritten "Now Hiring" sign in the women's bathroom, Brainard said he also plans to place an ad in the *South Tampa Community Courier* announc-

ing the availability of "dancing positions for girls of all nationalities."

"Sometimes, I let [manager Randy] Toby pick the girls, but this time I'm gonna do it myself," Brainard said. "I'll make sure we get a little more color in the lineup. Now, I'm not gonna refuse to hire a white girl if a hot one comes in. That'd be what they characterize as racism against whites. What's it called? Reverse racism."

Representatives from several competing exotic-dance clubs said Shakerz's new hiring initiative simply brings the club up to speed with other Tampa establishments.

"We've had black girls since '92," said Ricky Alvarez, co-owner of Mr. Bo-Jiggles Adult Entertainment & Seafood Bar. "As long as a candidate is qualified, we never discriminate based on race. That said, with Shakerz making moves, we're going to be proactive and get ourselves the skinniest black girl we can find. And also one with a real plump ass and big tits—we don't discriminate based on weight."

Many Shakerz patrons have expressed excitement about the new equality-minded hiring policy.

"Damn, we're gonna party when the new girls start," said Trent Billings, a real-estate developer who has lived in Tampa his entire life. "Maybe put up some flags or have some sort of U.N.-style wet-T-shirt contest or something. Or maybe a strip-off, to see which races are best at stripping. Something fun."

Added Billings: "They do that, I'll be there, and I'll have plenty of dollar bills in my hand. I love women, no matter what color they are. And they love me, too, 'cause I ain't cheap."

Current Shakerz dancers said they support the affirmative-action measures.

"Lots of different kinds of guys come in here—everyone from advertising types to truckers—so it makes sense

to have a lot of types of girls," said Mandy Flowers, who has been dancing at Shakerz for nearly a year. "Meeting different types of people is one of the benefits of this job. I like working with the Puerto Ricans.

> **"Meeting different types of people is one of the benefits of this job," Flowers said. "I like working with the Puerto Ricans."**

They're always down with partying after closing time."

Informed of the initiative, Florida Equal Opportunity Employment Commission spokesman Arthur Wright applauded Shakerz for "promoting racial equality throughout the adult industries of central Florida."

"We fully support Brainard's diversification efforts," Wright said. "Finally, someone is recognizing that it takes all kinds to entertain a broad cross-section of lonely, horny men with specific ethnicity-based fantasies. The interests of business and society *can* be one and the same."

In a move likely to please Wright, the owner of another area small business has already chosen to emulate Brainard's plan of action.

"We have a pretty good mix—customers are always asking for Latin girls and Asians—but now that I think about it, I guess we could use a couple new girls of color," Night Dreams Escorts manager Tony D'Ammagio said. "We're always looking for new girls." ∅

viewers nationwide.

"[Van Damme's character] Kurt Sloan had just seen his brother, a U.S. kickboxing champion, suffer a brutal beating at the hands of the sadistic Tong Po," Phoenix-area TNT viewer Charles de Bernier said. "Van Damme's brother was paralyzed, but Tong Po was remorseless—in fact, he was almost gloating. But before anything else big happened, the movie was interrupted."

"I expect that *Kickboxer* will continue in a moment," de Bernier said.

De Bernier said the disruption, which followed a freeze-frame of Van Damme's bloody and shame-ridden face, did not worry him.

"I expect that *Kickboxer* will continue in a moment," de Bernier said.

De Bernier's roommate Kyle Hammond was unavailable for comment, having chosen to spend the broadcast interruption in the bathroom.

Boston viewer Garret Corbin, standing in front of his open refrigerator and pouring himself a glass of grape juice, is one of tens of thousands of viewers awaiting the movie's return.

"If the movie continues, I think Van Damme's character will take vengeance on Tong Po—provided he can find someone to train him," Corbin said, basing his hypothesis on two weeks of TNT pronouncements that "Jean-Claude Van Damme is... *Kickboxer*."

Above: The Denny's commercial which has temporarily interrupted *Kickboxer*, starring Jean-Claude Van Damme.

Corbin said he believes that *Kickboxer*, starring Jean-Claude Van Damme, "will come back on any minute now."

"If I'm going to take their word for it that Van Damme will assume the titular role," Corbin said, "then I might as well take their claim that *Kickboxer* will continue at face value."

"I'll have to see, though," Corbin added, fumbling with a bag of pretzels.

Robert Thompson, director of the Center for the Study of Popular Television at Syracuse University, said that, during this or a future interruption, viewers are likely to hear an announcement concerning TNT programming scheduled for later in the day.

"Oh, something like, '*Thelma & Louise*, an edited-for-television feature starring Susan Sarandon and Geena Davis, contains adult situations and graphic violence,'" Thompson said. "Whatever it is, I expect the American public to remain calm during the brief interruption of *Kickboxer*, as frequent disruptions are a normal part of the basic-cable viewing experience. Take Jean-Claude Van Damme's movies alone: We've seen *Bloodsport*, *Universal Soldier*, and even *Timecop* interrupted. In every case, the network, whether it was AMC, TBS, or Spike, has always made good on its promise."

"Oh, hey!" Thompson said. "It's totally back on!" ∅

---

the ONION presents

Holding A Yard Sale

A yard sale is a great way to make money while getting rid of clutter. Here are some tips to make your sale a success:

- To enable easier browsing, arrange items in order of their shittiness.
- Put your used underwear out for sale. Yes. Put it out. Yes. Yes. Oh, yes, put it all out for sale.
- Try to arrange your random cast-off crap in such a manner as to cause strangers and passersby to burst into tears at the sheer crippling mundanity of it all.
- Don't put out that used electric hotdog cooker. Not only will no one buy the appliance, but your neighbors will be filled with disgust over living so close to someone who owned one.
- A dollar is a bit pricey for those *Reader's Digest* condensed books, Professor Smarty.
- Please don't sell our Inchworm riding toy! We know we're 37 years old now, but please don't sell our Inchworm Ridey!

- A free box is a great way to get rid of incriminating evidence.
- The No. 1 thing yard-sale customers are looking for is a great value. Lucky for you, the No. 2 thing they are looking for is faded purple size-26 Hanes stirrup pants.
- Having shoppers sign a standard yard-sale contract will ensure that all sales are final.
- Yard sales are like love: If you let your guard down and present everything you've got to the world honestly and without shame, someone is bound to end up with a bunch of your old clothes.
- Don't let your children price items. They price the items too high, as you are raising greedy little monsters.
- Don't forget to chuckle and tell every single customer that the yard is, in fact, not for sale.

Give Me Just One More Chance

**By Smoove B
Love Man**

If you knew how much pain I am in while I write this column, you would read it all the way to the end and be moved by the heartache in every word. Each sentence contains the pain of my soul, and in particular the part of the soul that yearns for you but has been pushed aside.

I know that the last time we saw each other, you said you never wanted to see Smoove again. I know you have not responded to my e-mails, text messages, phone calls, faxes, or shouts from the street. I know you say you have another man who treats you better than Smoove. If it didn't hurt so much, I would laugh at this statement.

Do you not remember the magic we shared while we were together? When we touched, it was like we were floating on air, and we would float there all night until the sun came up. Do you really not remember this magic? Your new man cannot create this type of magic for you, because you and I are bound by a powerful force.

Can your new man make your whole body tingle with pleasure from a single kiss to your neck? Does your new man blindfold you and take you to another level of sensual experiences? Does your new man always smell as though he has just stepped out of the shower? Girl, you need that magic in your life again.

I know that I have already stated this, but this man is not right for you.

You say this man treats you like a princess, but didn't Smoove treat you like a queen? You say this man buys you jewelry and assorted designer handbags, but didn't Smoove buy you whatever your heart desired? You say this man takes you out on the town, but didn't Smoove also take you to the finest restaurants in the tri-county area, in addition to preparing you home-cooked meals using unusual gourmet mushrooms?

I know I can make things like they were. Give Smoove another chance—just one more chance, girl. I know I can make you forget about this handbag-giving man. If you would only listen to my apologies, you would know how serious I am about getting you back. Accept the gifts of chocolate, silken evening gowns, and flowers, and you will see how much I care. Only one glance at the price tag on any of these high-quality items should make you leave this man and run back to my waiting arms.

Please let me know if my words have touched your heart. Promise you will pick up the phone when I call. I don't think my soul can take the news that another message has gone unheard or deleted.

Just give me one evening. That is all I will need to make you love me again. You don't have to tell your man that we are meeting. If you wish, you could tell him that you are spending an evening alone with a friend, or that you are visiting a sick relative, or that you won a coupon for an evening at an overnight spa. Whichever of the three you choose, please make it soon. I cannot wait to drink in the loveliness that you have kept from me for so long.

Also, I'd like to smell your hair. You use the finest shampoo. As you know, I purchased a bottle of it for your use when at my home, but the scent of the shampoo is not the same unless it is

> **I know you have not responded to my e-mails, text messages, phone calls, faxes, or shouts from the street.**

mixed in with your hair. Smoove knows this.

You may be wondering how I plan to win you back in only one night, when there were so many problems between us. As this evening must be the most magical, sensual, and perfect night of your entire life, I will keep the details of it a secret in order to bring your arousal to its highest peak.

As a teaser, I will say that a few things will, without a doubt, occur. First, I will compliment you and express sincere regret over what happened between us. I will extend feelings of tenderness and warmth. Then, we will reminisce about the good times that we once shared. Dinner, which will have been carefully prepared over the course of the previous 24 hours, will be served at around 8. During dinner, as well as afterward, we will drink the finest wine from the best wine-producing regions of Australia. Or, if that wine does not meet your exacting standards, I will provide backup wines from the finest wine-producing regions of Chile, France, California, and Germany. There will also be warm appetizers.

After dinner, I will hit you doggy-style. This doggy-style sexing will last all night long. I remember that this is the way that you like it.

If this night of intriguing possibility does not warm your heart, then perhaps you are truly lost to me. But Smoove still has hope in his heart that this one last effort to win back your love will work. If you only would pick up that phone, I know it would succeed.

Perhaps I am wrong. Perhaps this other man possesses qualities that Smoove does not know about. From what I hear, you two often go to the movies together. Perhaps he has an unlimited pass at the theater or friends who work at the box office and give you two a discount. In spite of your new man's apparent wealth of movie passes, I beg you to give me one more chance. If you do not like the idea of the evening I described above and would rather just go to the movies, we can do that, too. We can do whatever your heart truly desires. I know I can make things right again.

You have my cell-phone number if you wish to call.

Smoove out. ⊘

Your Horoscope

**By Lloyd Schumner Sr.
Retired Machinist and
A.A.P.B.-Certified Astrologer**

Aries: (March 21–April 19)
The authorities will eventually decide to release you on your own recognizance, which is almost certainly the cruelest thing they could have done.

Taurus: (April 20–May 20)
You'll be trapped in a hell of your own making, forcing you to admit that you really should have put in more bathrooms.

Gemini: (May 21–June 21)
Your belief that God does not play dice with the universe will be tested by the discovery of a 10,000-mile-long craps table on Jupiter.

Cancer: (June 22–July 22)
Try as you might, you'll never be able to convince FEMA that Baltimore was like that when you got there.

Leo: (July 23–Aug. 22)
Astounding as it seems, the transit of Saturn across your sign portends that you'll have a decent time at RiverFest this weekend.

Virgo: (Aug. 23–Sept. 22)
You'll finally break the endlessly mounting tension at work when you cause the rollback of that aggravating "days without an accident" sign.

Libra: (Sept. 23–Oct. 23)
Once all the goats are rounded up, the German tourists are extradited, and the syrup trucks are returned, you'll have to admit that you never saw that one coming.

Scorpio: (Oct. 24–Nov. 21)
Your promise to rebuild the world with blood, pain, and legal pot will resonate with the weirdest voting bloc yet recorded.

Sagittarius: (Nov. 22–Dec. 21)
Some people believe your house in Heaven is filled with all the things you lost while on earth, which explains the dead pets lying everywhere.

Capricorn: (Dec. 22–Jan. 19)
You've never been a big fan of cigars, but if there's a cooler-looking way to light all those fuses, you're not aware of it.

Aquarius: (Jan. 20–Feb. 18)
The aliens will claim that our primitive language contains no word for the emotion they're feeling, but that's bullshit. They're bored out of their skulls.

Pisces: (Feb. 19–March 20)
You'll be unable to explain what you were doing drinking naked in the back of the frozen-fish truck, but you won't have to. We've all been there.

MUSIC from page 219

commit sufficient time and energy to music that destroyed what was once a rewarding part of his life.

"This was a guy who was front and center for every important show in Cleveland," Halperin said. "During the Crooked Fingers concert I dragged him out to last January, Sam just sat at the back of the room wearing earplugs! I even caught him watching the infomercial airing above the bar. It's too bad that it ended this way, but it's hard to feel sorry for the guy. He just wasn't committed."

Powers' breakup with music dismayed and perplexed Michael Chaudhary, singer and lead guitarist for Same Four Guys, a local band Powers saw occasionally during the past several years.

"Fuck [Powers]," Chaudhary said. "What does he think? That he can drop me from his life, just like that? I should've known he was never going to get serious about being our fan. If he was, he would've done the right thing and bought one of our T-shirts a long time ago." ⊘

Goth Kid Builds Scary-Ass Birdhouse

see LOCAL page 3C

Ovarian Cancer Gets Publicist

see HEALTH page 11F

New Snooze Channel Broadcasts Shrill, Electronic Shriek Every Nine Minutes

see LOCAL page 4C

STATshot

A look at the numbers that shape your world.

Who's Pregnant... Again?

1. Channel 11 weather lady
2. Slutty cat
3. The Third World
4. Loretta Lynn
5. Me, right?
   It's me, isn't it?
6. Mrs. O'Callaghan

THE ONION • $2.00 US • $3.00 CAN

0 74470 94595 6

---

the ONION®

VOLUME 40 ISSUE 31   AMERICA'S FINEST NEWS SOURCE™   5–11 AUGUST 2004

CIA Asks Bush To Discontinue Blog

WASHINGTON, DC—In the interest of national security, President Bush has been asked to stop posting entries on his three-month-old personal web log, acting CIA director John E. McLaughlin said Monday.

According to McLaughlin, several recent entries on PrezGeorgeW.type-pad.com have compromised military operations, while other posts may have seriously undercut the PR efforts of White House press secretary Scott McClellan.

A July 24 posting read, "Just got back from a lunch with Colin and Adil Moussa (one of Prince Saud al-Faisal's guys). Colin wants the Saudis to send some troops to Najaf—so some of the soldiers are Arab, I guess.

see BUSH page 226

Above: Bush adds an entry to his blog.

Deadbeat Dads March On Las Vegas

Above: Deadbeat dads march on the New York-New York Hotel & Casino.

LAS VEGAS—As many as 40,000 deadbeat dads descended on Las Vegas Friday for a massive, weekend-long show of non-support for their children.

"All right, let's get this party started!" said Tom "Turk"Turkelsen, an air-conditioner factory laborer. "I was sick of Cathy nagging me for diaper money all the time. Now she don't know where to find me—at least for the weekend."

Mike Hicks, who arrived in Las Vegas on a $20 bus ride from Los Angeles, began demonstrating his non-support the moment he set foot in the lobby of the Rio.

"Point me toward the loosest slots in town," Hicks said, waving a sign that read "Rum & Coke over here, NOW." "Can't drop no brats off at my place if

I ain't there to open the door!"

Although he was not appointed to speak for the non-centralized delegation of terrible fathers, Hicks succinctly conveyed the group's sentiment. Angry shouts of "Screw the baby—I needs a new pair of shoes" echoed up and down the strip, from the Luxor to the Stratosphere, all weekend long.

"Quarter'a my check, my ass!" Dearborn, MI resident and part-time PA-system installer Derek Hindle shouted.

Some 2,500 of the deadbeat dads arrived en masse on Freedom Buses, chartered through the Freedom Tour Bus Company of Taos, NM. The common bonds of shoddy parenting and alcoholism quickly integrated the negligent fathers, both those who arrived alone and those who belonged to larger groups.

"Turns out this here guy and me had the exact same judge tell us not to leave the state of Illinois," said Rockford's Jeff McMartin, playfully punching neglectful father of four Greg Milner in the arm. "My kids' bitch mother had me hauled into court to get at my money, and Greg here's in the same boat. Naturally, going to Vegas was a no-brainer. No bitch judge gonna tell us who to feed and clothe."

"Bitch,"Milner added.

The deadbeat dads shared a *laissez-faire* attitude toward many of the health, education, and welfare issues facing parents today. Among the topics ignored by the group were fiscal responsibility, employment, and, of

see DADS page 228

College Student Does Nothing For Tibet Over Summer

Above: Davis relaxes at a coffee shop while Tibetans suffer under the rule of the Chinese.

BURLINGTON, VT—University of Vermont junior Becca Davis failed to do anything for the people of Tibet during her summer vacation, disgruntled fellow activists reported Tuesday.

"With class out for the summer, Becca had a valuable window during which she could have pressured the Chinese government to end its tyrannical reign over the Tibetan people," campus activist Sally Coe said. "Instead, she sunbathed in the park and worked part-time at a local bookstore. As a result, the Tibetan freedom cause has been set back months."

Conquered by the People's Republic Of China in 1949, Tibet has suffered decades of political and religious oppression, and its leader, the Dalai Lama, has been exiled for 45 years.

see STUDENT page 227

The Crisis in Sudan

The U.S. has threatened economic action against the Sudanese government if it fails to disarm Arab militias, but some doubt it will curb the violence. What do *you* think?

Stacy Heckel
Systems Analyst

"If we help these people now, we'll have to help them every time their women are being raped by the thousands and their children are being slaughtered like cattle."

Daniel Mears
Radiologic Technician

"Another African genocide? All right, I'll care—but this is absolutely the last time."

Jeremy Larson
Audiologist

"When dealing with genocide, you must ask yourself, 'What would Hitler do?' And then, you know, do the opposite."

George Wolf
Chiropractor

"That reminds me. I could use a nice new sedan. Hell, I deserve one."

Mark Garrett
Manager

"Wait. Is this a real genocide or just one of those reality-TV celebrity genocides?"

Gina Grunwald
Treasurer

"Well, I don't want to sound overly partisan here. But tentatively, yes, I do oppose genocide."

Nader's Platform

What are some of the planks of presidential hopeful Ralph Nader's platform?

★ Get Congress to approve a universal healthcare plan within his first 100 days as president or he'll quit

★ Remove all fancy furniture from Oval Office and replace it with simple, functional folding chairs

★ Create a strong and clean national-defense system with battalions of hybrid electric tanks

★ Drive the fat cats out of Congress and replace them with freaks from Burning Man

★ Never, ever have an affair with an intern, or even kiss a girl, for that matter

★ Put pressure on terrorists to use cleaner-burning "hydrogen" bombs

★ Expertly preside over entire nation's inter-dimensional shift to alternate universe

the ONION®
America's Finest News Source.™

Herman Ulysses Zweibel
Founder

T. Herman Zweibel
Publisher Emeritus
J. Phineas Zweibel
Publisher
Maxwell Prescott Zweibel
Editor-In-Chief

I'm The Life Of The Search Party!

By Billy K. Duane

In the unforgiving mountain terrain, each action can be a life-or-death decision, and every single person must be focused on his assigned responsibility. Carlos is a world-class expert on belaying-ropes. Joe is an emergency field-rescue medical technician with more than 20 years' experience working in dangerously high altitudes. Brian is an expert at coordinating communications between the recon helicopters and the ground team. Me? I'm the life of the search party.

Everybody brings his own special set of skills to the table with a team like this. I'm the clown. I bring morale-building goofy antics. When word came in that the authorities were organizing a rescue effort for those two missing couples, I was the first to show up—wearing Hawaiian shorts and a "Search Party Naked" T-shirt.

Somehow, I was the only one who thought to bring beer. Our team coordinator, Russell, said it isn't good to consume alcohol at this altitude. I said, "C'mon, Russ—a couple drunk recon dudes are the least of these hikers' worries. Given the condition they'll be in if they're ever found, they're gonna need a drink." And then I totally popped open a foamer.

> You can't expect everyone in a search party to feel upbeat. Some of my fellow rescuers have gone without sleep for 36 hours. But even if they don't laugh, or smile, or acknowledge me, I know my clowning is crucial.

Facts are facts—temperatures this far above the tree line can climb to more than 100 degrees in the midday sun and plummet to hypothermia-inducing levels at night. The fear that the missing hikers are nothing more than bird-pecked, desiccated corpses huddled in some rocky outcropping weighs on all of us. Which is where I come in with my one-liners, quips, and puns. Somebody's gotta break the tension by yelling "Ricola!"

Yesterday at nightfall, we got word from the rangers that a storm was moving in. We had no choice but to call off the search until sun-up. Carlos was furious. He started swearing, saying, "They'll never make it through the night!" I could tell the stress was getting to him, so I made one of my trademark irreverent remarks: "Yeah? Well, if we don't head back down this mountain ourselves, we'll never make

> Everybody brings his own special set of skills to the table with a team like this. I'm the clown. I bring morale-building goofy antics.

it back in time to score at the ski-lodge bar. And if *that* happens, *I'm* gonna die!"

Or there was that time when I came around that ridge and saw Carlos heading toward me from the other direction, and I hid behind a shrub and cried out, "Help me! I'm blind! Birds ate my eyes!" Then I stumbled into view, pretended to trip on some loose stones, and faked breaking my femur. Nobody really laughs out loud at my pratfalls, but I understand that participating in a race against time can cause a lot of psychological strain. Repeatedly referring to the missing parties as "cougar food" is the perfect way to ease the stress.

You can't expect everyone in a search party to feel upbeat. Some of my fellow rescuers have gone without sleep for 36 hours. But even if they don't laugh, or smile, or acknowledge me, I know my clowning is crucial. When everyone else's sense of humor fails, I'm there to construct a big "S.O.S." sign out of logs, and then another one below it that says "NOT!"

Somebody's gotta have the foresight to save the coffee grounds from morning base camp and slip them into Joe's sandwich for a hilarious lunch prank six hours later. It seems I'm the only one who even thinks of making fart noises over the emergency distress-call wavelength to crack up the boys back at the ranger station. Just think of how those poor guys must feel, watching the hours tick away as they sit there with the victims' tearful families.

I'm not saying what I do is easy, but when I see the pressure my fellow search-party workers are under, even if I'm not in a funny mood, I pull myself together, put on a silly face, and start singing "Doo Wah Diddy" like Bill Murray did in *Stripes*. It's the least I can do for my fellow man. ∅

Movie Praised For Not Being As Bad As It Could Have Been

BURBANK, CA—Moviegoers coast to coast hailed *Catwoman*, the new action film starring Halle Berry, as not as much of an unforgivably awful piece of formulaic commercial pabulum as it could have been.

"You know, I have to hand it to Warner Bros.," Miami resident Tom Peebles said Monday. "*Catwoman* was terrible, but it actually had one or two decent parts. I really have to say: It could have been a lot worse!"

Catwoman, loosely based on the DC Comics character, has similarly shattered other viewers' bottom-of-the-barrel expectations, offering a small number of redeeming features instead of the expected none.

"That one part where the woman pushes Catwoman off a balcony to demonstrate that she can land on her feet was sort of cool, I guess," said Bangor, ME's Sally Burrows. "And it was kind of funny when she ate, like, 10 cans of tuna in a row. Oh, and when she drank that glass of cream at the bar—that was, though not exactly funny, at least funny-ish. My kids seemed to like it. Well, Mindy, at least."

"Mindy just turned 7," Burrows added.

According to Ivan Berger, a self-described film buff, *Catwoman* trailers—featuring atrocious computer-generated animation, cringe-worthy shots of Berry snapping a whip to intolerable R&B music, and love interest/cop sidekick Benjamin Bratt's flirtatious mugging—set audience expectations very low.

Above: Halle Berry, who audiences say might have done a worse job in Catwoman.

"At first glance, Catwoman, the story of a sexy feline superhero who fights villains in the cosmetics industry, seemed like the kind of formulaic, committee-written marketing opportunity—*Garfield*, *New York Minute*, and so on—that has become the summer-movie standard," Berger said. "To everyone's surprise, *Catwoman* proved marginally better than that."

"Judging from the ads, I assumed I'd want my eight bucks back," Berger added. "But after seeing the movie, I was pleasantly surprised to find I only wanted three, maybe four bucks back, tops."

A half-realized camp attitude, which suggested that the filmmakers were aware of the film's poor quality, impressed viewers, as well.

"After seeing a billboard with Halle Berry vamping around in that ridiculous outfit, I really thought I'd have to leave midway through," Los Angeles resident Brian Gunderson said. "But you know what? Some of the action

see MOVIE page 226

NEWS IN BRIEF

Wendy's New Homestyle Chicken Strips Salad Shamelessly Touted

DUBLIN, OH—Using billboards, bus ads, and TV commercials, the fast-food franchise Wendy's is unabashedly plugging its Homestyle Chicken Strips Salad, sources reported Monday. "I can't believe Wendy's is putting up posters calling *their own* salad 'sensational' and 'satisfying,'" said Donald Merrill, a former customer. "It's immodest to the point of embarrassment." Merrill added that he remembers when "hot and juicy" actually meant something.

Area Woman Recalls Days When She Resented Being Hit On

SALEM, OR—Kimberly Jones, 43, vividly remembers the bygone days when she took umbrage at being pursued by aggressive suitors, sources reported Monday. "I was quite the looker back in college—I couldn't even go out for a few drinks with my girlfriends without some guy macking on me," Jones said from the kitchen of her one-bedroom apartment. "That used to really piss me off for some reason I can no longer even begin to fathom. Maybe my memory is starting to go." Jones then gazed longingly into her cup of tea.

Maid Dreams Children Will One Day Be Maids In Wealthier Households

LOS ANGELES—Estella Lopez expressed hope Monday that her children will enjoy a brighter future as housekeepers in wealthier households. "I want my daughters to have a better life than I've had," Lopez said. "I dream that one day they will serve in a beautiful home, polishing windows overlooking the ocean and disinfecting toilets made of marble. God willing, they'll be asked to scrub a bidet someday." Lopez added that she fantasizes about her son parking a Bentley.

Man In International Airport Only Speaks Business

CHICAGO—John Brinker, a New York technological consultant trapped in the O'Hare International Airport for two hours Monday, struggled to communicate with fellow travelers, none of whom spoke business. "Should Mynex reach efficient levels, their high-volume production of microanalyzers will offset tariff and transportation costs and place Sysmet in a competitive position against local producers and distributors," Brinker said to a vacationing English speaker from Boise, ID who shrugged apologetically. "A 25 percent growth rate is the motivation for manufacturing in the NICs." Brinker was later seen blinking uncomprehendingly at a bus-stop sign while awaiting his company limousine.

Camera Crew Discreetly Trails Overweight Woman For Obesity Segment

MILWAUKEE—A *WITI News* camera crew spent 30 minutes inconspicuously following an overweight woman at the Henry W. Maier Festival Park Monday to capture footage for an upcoming segment on obesity. "It's hard to get anyone to agree to be filmed to illustrate what a fat person looks like," cameraman Doug Kovalik said, nonchalantly pointing his camera at an obese woman who was tugging at a pair of shorts bunched into her crotch while she ate a corn dog. "We avoid the whole mess by shooting them from behind or the neck down. It saves us the hassle of filling out release forms." Kovalik last used this discreet filming technique in May, when he captured B-roll at a local craft mall for a segment on managed care for the elderly. *

George's Blog

July 28, 2004

Boring Wednesday. Didn't really do anything but take a couple phone calls. Napped for almost two hours. Don't you hate it when you get up from a nap and you just can't get going again? I even had a super huge caramel latte (yum!) but that didn't even help. I'm useless today! Maybe tomorrow'll be better.

Jenna emailed me from Colorado, saying she got all drunk after some speech there yesterday and broke some stuff at a bar. Wanted me to make sure it didn't get into the papers, so I forwarded it on to Karen. No reason she needs to be dragged through the damn papers over something stupid.

Tenet stopped by today and explained the 9/11 Commission report to me. Who do they think they are, telling me how to do my job? Lots of 'do this do that.' I just hope the whole thing blows over soon.

July 28, 2004 at 09:52 PM | Permalink | Comments (0) | TrackBack (0)

July 25, 2004

Condi came over all worked up today because of some Al Qaeda chatter about Boston last week. I told her to CALM DOWN. I love her, of course, but she's really high-strung sometimes, you know? Chill out, sister.

Talking to Cheney and realized I forgot the nuclear launch codes again. It's so simple, too. My birthday, Dad's birthday, and then 1776.' Sounds easy, I know, but there's so much going on lately that I can't keep anything straight. I'll say them over and over tonight while I'm going to sleep. That helps me remember things sometime. Tends to piss off Laura, tho. She's been so on the rag with all of the campaign stuff we have to do.

Email Me
PHOTO ALBUMS

George's Snapshots

Above: The controversial Bush blog.

This Moussa guy sure wears a lot of jewelry. A golden chain, a golden ring with his initials or something, and some other sparkling stuff—kinda effeminate. Anyway, best of luck in Iraq, Iyad."

McLaughlin, normally hesitant to express public disapproval of the president, said the blog was "ill-advised."

"I would hate for the president to inadvertently put American soldiers at risk," McLaughlin said. "We work hard to maintain the integrity of state secrets. When we see the president posting details of troop movements, international counter-terrorism negotiations, and even the nuclear launch codes, as he did on Monday, we have to step up and say something."

Bush said he could not understand McLaughlin's anger, characterizing his blog as a "personal thing written for friends and family or whoever" and therefore "none of the CIA's business."

Nevertheless, U.S. Secret Service director W. Ralph Basham objected to the blog, as well.

"He is compromising his safety and the safety of those in my department," Basham said, citing a post from last Thursday in which Bush revealed that he "had to go to some secret meeting with Norquist at some Marriot [sic] over in Virginia." "Someone could uncover some serious state secrets, if they took the time to wade through all of those photos he posted after he got that digital camera in June."

On Saturday, Basham asked to prescreen all blog activity before Bush

posts it online.

Bush rejected Basham's request and later that day wrote in his blog that "Some people who shall remain nameless apparently do not know there is such a thing as free speech in this country."

Members of Bush's re-election team have urged the president to exercise

> "After he mentioned our Monday message-of-the-day in a Saturday post, we've really been pushing him to not talk about campaign strategy," Gillespie said. "He's not that involved in the planning anyway, so it shouldn't be too much to ask."

caution with his blog, perhaps because of posts like the one dated July 8, 2004: "Another long day of speeches and fundraisers. Met with all these phony media company execs. Had to promise them some bill next term and shake a lot of stupid hands, but they did bring in two or three million or so. Whatever. Karl keeps a list. I got big

laughs during my speech, so I'm happy."

Republican National Committee chairman Ed Gillespie said he spoke to Bush about the blog last month.

"After he mentioned our Monday message-of-the-day in a Saturday post, we've really been pushing him to not talk about campaign strategy," Gillespie said. "He's not that involved in the planning anyway, so it shouldn't be too much to ask."

"We're not trying to stifle the president's creativity," Gillespie added. "We think it's great he's taking an interest in writing."

Bush maintained that he's doing nothing wrong.

"I know so many people, but I'm way too busy to keep in touch with all of them," Bush said. "Whether I'm talking about our strategies in Gitmo or my dogs down in Crawford, the blog is an easy way to let everyone know what's been up with me. If I've just had a really good lunch at a new restaurant, or something funny happens in a briefing from the NSA, I want to let my friends and family know about it."

McLaughlin said it's likely that Bush will eventually agree to submit his blog for review by the Secret Service.

"Right now, the president insists it's his right to have it, as long as he doesn't work on it during White House work hours," McLaughlin said. "But I believe we'll be able to convince him, if we let him calm down. And even if we don't, frankly, I can't see the blog holding his interest for too long." ⬚

scenes were halfway non-shitty. Definitely curb—as opposed to gutter—level. Also, I found myself paying attention to the character development once or twice. I guess I underestimated it. I'd say it actually merits one and a half stars."

Critics joined moviegoers to applaud *Catwoman* for not having been worse. Tom Dickinson of WHO-TV in Des Moines called *Catwoman* a movie that "doesn't exactly roar, but does kind of purr at times, I guess." Ellen Norbury of *Hollywood Reviews Online* said, "It's a better-than-failed effort, sure to provide two or three halfway-fun moments."

Some industry insiders hope the film

> "Catwoman bucks the trend established by such recent blockbusters as Troy and Van Helsing, which met audience predictions head-on by being exactly as bad as they seemed like they would be," Oglive said.

signals an end to the "worst-possible" trend in motion pictures.

"*Catwoman* bucks the trend established by such recent blockbusters as *Troy* and *Van Helsing*, which met audience predictions head-on by being exactly as bad as they seemed like they would be," media analyst Roy Oglive said. "It's possible that *Catwoman* will increase audience expectations, making them judge subsequent releases by a harsher standard. The American viewing public may actually come to expect movies not to be totally horrible."

Unfortunately, Oglive said, that may prove to be both a blessing and a curse.

"If moviegoers forget to keep their expectations low, the occasional almost-okay moments in *Catwoman* will lead to further disappointments down the road," Oglive said. "When the next *League Of Extraordinary Gentlemen* comes along, they'll be devastated."

In the meantime, moviegoers are relishing the experience of a night out at the movies that they don't completely hate.

"It's so refreshing to take the family out to what you assume will be the absolute worst movie of the year, and then find out it's only *among* the year's worst movies," said Janice Davenport, 27, of Jeffersontown, KY. "*Catwoman* is the kind of once-in-a-blue-moon summer blockbuster that makes going to the movies slightly less non-fun again." ⬚

Tibetans who oppose the Chinese occupation have implored the world to intervene, but Davis has evidently decided to ignore their pleas.

Although Davis is a member of the Campus Outreach Network for Tibetan Autonomy, as well as the Campus Anti-War Initiative Coalition and the Campus Crusade Against Rape, her political awareness seems to have dissipated during the summer. According to sources close to Davis, the political science and women's studies double major has neither volunteered for the local chapter of the Free Tibet

> Added Davis: "I mean, it feels like I just got back from West Virginia [where Davis built Habitat For Humanity houses with the Alternative Spring Break program]."

campaign nor organized a Tibetan-freedom rally in her hometown of Lyme, CT. Davis has not passed out one pamphlet, and she has neglected to sign an online petition that has been sitting in her e-mail inbox for weeks.

"Someone should tell Becca that the needs of the disadvantaged do not take a scuba holiday off the coast of Curacao," Coe said, referring to a one-week vacation Davis took with her family in June. "Activism takes time, hard work, and commitment. Posters don't nail themselves to sticks."

Davis said she was puzzled by Coe's statements, pointing out that she spent her past two summer breaks helping the disadvantaged.

"When I was a freshman, I spent the summer collecting donations for an organization that helps exiled Tibetans in Dharamsala," Davis said. "And last summer, I did this rainforest reforestation volunteer program for

Above: Three Tibetans Davis failed to help.

four weeks. But this last semester was really a killer, and I seriously needed some time off."

Added Davis: "I mean, it feels like I *just* got back from West Virginia [where Davis built Habitat For Humanity houses with the Alternative Spring Break program]."

In spite of her failure to lift a finger for Tibet in recent weeks, Davis said her feelings about the country have not changed.

"I really do think it's important to promote support for the exiled Tibetan government and convince the global community that the nation of Tibet should be free from unwanted foreign rule," Davis said. "But next year, I'll be a senior and, you know, I don't have many summers left where I can just take it easy."

In this week's issue of *The Nation*, author and San Francisco-area activist Jay Minty wrote about the tendency of student idealists to shed their political awareness during the summer months, "like so many Peruvian wool sweaters."

"Between the months of May and September, only 4 percent of campus activists attempt to end social injustice," Minty wrote. "Why, for example, are 'Take Back The Night'-style anti-sexual-assault rallies only scheduled during the school year? During the summer of 2003, only the night of Aug. 18 came anywhere close to being taken back, at a small vigil in Farmington, ME attended by only six activists."

Continued Minty: "When did summer jobs, TV shows, and awkward vis-

its to extended family members become more important than human rights and economic inequality?"

Thupten Lobsang, a Tibetan seeking an American host family, did not appear insulted by Davis' indifference to his people's cause.

"I hope Becca isn't being worked too hard at the bookstore," Lobsang said from Lhasa, Tibet in a phone interview. "I was amused by her choice of summer beach reading: the kitschy Jacqueline Susann classic *The Love Machine*. Summer does have a way of slipping by you, I agree. And I also hope that Becca had fun in Curacao, even if her annoying younger brother was there. I had an annoying younger brother once, too. He was imprisoned and later shot by the Chinese secret police." ∅

amounts of blood. Passersby were amazed by the unusually large amounts of blood. Passersby were amazed by the unusually large amounts of blood. Passersby were amazed by the unusually large amounts of blood. Passersby were amazed by the unusually large amounts of blood. Passersby were amazed by the unusually large amounts of blood. Passersby were amazed by the unusually large amounts of blood. Passersby were amazed by the unusually large amounts of blood. Passersby were amazed by the unusually large amounts of blood. Passersby were amazed by the unusually large amounts of blood. Passersby were

amazed by the unusually large amounts of blood. Passersby were amazed by the unusually large

Surprise! We're getting an abortion!

amounts of blood. Passersby were amazed by the unusually large amounts of blood. Passersby were amazed by the unusually large amounts of blood. Passersby were

amounts of blood. Passersby were amazed by the unusually large amounts of blood. Passersby were amazed by the unusually large amounts of blood. Passersby were amazed by the unusually large amounts of blood. Passersby were amazed by the unusually large amounts of blood. Passersby were amazed by the unusually large amounts of blood. Passersby were amazed by the unusually large amounts of blood. Passersby were amazed by the unusually large amounts of blood. Passersby were amazed by the unusually large amounts of blood. Passersby were

amazed by the unusually large amounts of blood. Passersby were amazed by the unusually large amounts of blood. Passersby were amazed by the unusually large amounts of blood. Passersby were amazed by the unusually large amounts of blood. Passersby were amazed by the unusually large amounts of blood. Passersby were amazed by the unusually large amounts of blood. Passersby were amazed by the unusually large amounts of blood. Passersby were amazed by the unusually large amounts of blood. Passersby were amazed by the unusually large amounts of blood. Passersby were amazed by the unusually large amounts of blood. Passersby were

see SOFT SKIN page 288

Ask A Guy Who Just Ran, Like, Nine Blocks

By Doug Cook

Dear Guy Who Just Ran, Like, Nine Blocks,

My mother-in-law is very attentive, generous, and helpful. She's always ready to lend a hand—and that's the problem! She's constantly buying things for my family's house (she and her husband are quite wealthy). Last week, she took it upon herself to buy us new living-room furniture. Maybe she's doing this out of the goodness of her heart, but I can't help but feel like she's criticizing our home. She's coming for an extended visit next month, and I am sure she'll show up with a load of presents in the car and a tape measure in her pocket. Is there a nice way to ask her to leave the decorating to me?

Suffocated In Santa Monica

Dear Suffocated,

Oh, geez... I'm sorry. Hold on. Okay, whew. Okay, I... I didn't mean to keep you all waiting. I just ran, like, nine blocks. Oh, God... Can I get some water? You all must totally hate me... I didn't mean to keep you waiting. Oh, thanks, Phil. Ahhh, that's good. Good water. Okay, sorry. I was doing really well... on time. I'll tell you guys what happened in just a second. Ugh... I just have to catch my breath. Christ, am I out of shape! I didn't think I would be doing any running today. Oh, shit. I called... oh, man... I can still barely... breathe. Did you guys call? I turned off my phone for some stupid reason and only realized I was late when it fell out of my pocket... when I was running. I tried turning it on, but it didn't... I can't fucking figure this thing out... Any moron can but I can't. So, when I picked it up and realized how late it was... that's when I took off running.

Dear Guy Who Just Ran, Like, Nine Blocks,

My roommate acts as if paper grows on trees! That's a joke, but there's nothing funny about her wastefulness around the house. She uses paper toweling and napkins like they don't cost a cent. Don't even get me started on all the perfectly good paper bags, notepads, and envelopes she tosses in the garbage. I grew up in a household without much money, so that kind of behavior drives me up the wall. Can you think of a fun way I could convince her to stop throwing money away?

Thrifty In Thousand Oaks

Dear Thrifty,

Oh, man, I need to sit down. Just for a second, just for a second... I need to sit. I haven't run like that since I was in high school. Not that I was in good shape... back then, but now I'm an old man. I couldn't even run the nine blocks straight through. I had to rest against one of those... what are they called? They, you know, stop traffic... with the lights... red, green... stoplight! Jesus! Thank you! Anyway, I thought the restaurant was on 9th Street. God, I think I'm getting a cramp. Ow! Ow! Damn. Okay. So, finally, I stopped at this store and asked the guy if he knew where the Golden Dragon was, and he told me it was on Hammond. Thank God for that dude, but he didn't even know exactly where it was, just that it was on... Hammond. But some guy buying smokes thought it was in this direction, so I booked it over here. Christ, I'm sweating like a pig.

Dear Guy Who Just Ran, Like, Nine Blocks,

I just wanted to say thank you for the advice you gave single parents in your response to Happy In Hoboken a few months ago. I thought it was right on. I have shared it with all of my single-parent friends, and they loved it as much as I did. After hearing so many negative comments and answering so many rude questions through the years, it was a breath of fresh air. Is there any way you could re-run that piece?

**Proud Single Parent
In Providence**

Dear Proud,

Sorry I'm so gross, Kristine... The whole front of my shirt is... ugh, I'm dripping. I just took a shower like an hour ago, too. Well, sorry. No hugs, no hugs. I'll stay all the way over here. Whew. Seriously... I'm... really sorry... about all this. I didn't mean to keep you guys waiting. I really didn't want to be late. Otherwise, I never would've run. It was, seriously, like nine blocks. I was all the way over on Wilcott... Wilson... Wilcott—the one that's, like, nine blocks that way. Obviously I'm in no shape to be doing this sort of thing. I'm feeling better. But I don't think I'll be running that far again any time soon. Let's go in.

Doug Cook is a syndicated advice columnist whose column, Ask A Guy Who Just Ran, Like, Nine Blocks, *appears in more than 250 newspapers nationwide.*

Your Horoscope

**By Lloyd Schumner Sr.
Retired Machinist and
A.A.P.B.-Certified Astrologer**

Aries: (March 21–April 19)
The "before" and "after" photos of your diet plan are dramatic, but it's the "during" photos that will fill the jury box with vomit.

Taurus: (April 20–May 20)
Experts agree that getting enough sleep is important, but they look like the kind of cunning, crafty experts who would love to catch you unconscious.

Gemini: (May 21–June 21)
By the time government troops are able to cut through the locks of your Love Zeppelin and "rescue" everyone inside, you'll already be a folk hero.

Cancer: (June 22–July 22)
No, no, no—you're supposed to gently heat the garlic cloves until they caramelize, you moron, not turn them into a burnt paste.

Leo: (July 23–Aug. 22)
Sharpening the nation's steering wheels and promoting proper tire deflation will be your first priorities when you're appointed to chair the Institute of Highway Danger.

Virgo: (Aug. 23–Sept. 22)
You'll get a chance to do it all again knowing what you know now, taking the fun out of about 15 Super Bowls.

Libra: (Sept. 23–Oct. 23)
You're the prime suspect after witnesses overhear you say you're "so hungry I could eat either a horse or the dismembered body of the vice-president of that bank on Garfield Street."

Scorpio: (Oct. 24–Nov. 21)
Piracy is still a major problem in the Philippines, but that's a pretty lousy reason to want to move there.

Sagittarius: (Nov. 22–Dec. 21)
People will complain to you about the disruption of traffic, but it's not your fault that love-struck buildings are following you everywhere.

Capricorn: (Dec. 22–Jan. 19)
You suspect it was a misprint when the newspaper claimed that drinking a glass of red wine once a minute was good for the heart, but what the hell.

Aquarius: (Jan. 20–Feb. 18)
Very few of your monetary problems will be over when you win the record-low lottery jackpot of $.0000017 million.

Pisces: (Feb. 19–March 20)
The pilot will make an emergency landing because of you, in spite of your repeated and emphatic insistence that you are not a suspicious object.

DADS from page 223 DADS from page 223

course, getting tough on deadbeat dads. "Red 27! Red 27!" Milner said. "Goddamn it!"

Many of the men assembled did, however, voice concerns about their own financial well-being and nutrition.

> ## "Red 27! Red 27!" Milner said. "God*damn* it!"

"I paid $7.95 for my goddamn all-you-can-eat surf-and-turf," said Troy Heffler, a father of three or four from Miami, FL. "Hurry up, you stupid cow, I'm fuckin' starving here!"

Similar heartfelt cries—which were even taken up in unison, on occasion—could be heard throughout Las Vegas' established institutions.

"Garnish my three-dollar prime-rib platter, not my wages," a group of seven deadbeat dads chanted together, until one father slipped, upset a row of drinks, and fell backward off his barstool.

"How's that cunt know the kid's mine when she was fuckin' Gordon alla time?" the father said from the floor.

Most Vegas businesses openly welcomed the dads' arrival.

"We've been fairly successful in meeting the many demands of this rather vocal group," Harrah's casino floor manager Anthony DeMatteo said. "To be honest, it's pretty much business as usual. In fact, it feels like I've seen a lot of these faces before."

Continued DeMatteo: "It's been a little hectic around here, but if I know one thing for sure, it's that they'll run out of money soon enough."

Almost to the last man, the deadbeat dads who were awake and not in detox agreed Monday afternoon that the march had been successful.

"They say what happens in Vegas stays in Vegas," Turkelsen said Monday, waiting in line to make a collect call to his court-appointed attorney. "Well, I got news for you, Cathy—so is your goddamn child support." ∅

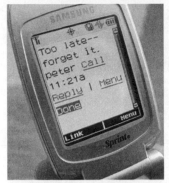

Text Message A Bit Curt

see LOCAL page 3C

Yo-Yo Ma Injured During Practice

see ARTS page 11F

Half Of Sexual Tension Broken By Blow Job

see LOCAL page 11C

Government Watchdog Rolls Over

see WASHINGTON page 3E

STATshot

A look at the numbers that shape your world.

What Are We Hunting/Gathering?

20% Tchotchkes
12% Pies from windowsills
18% Anything we can reach with leg pinned under rock
11% The remote controls
24% Tubers, whatever they are
15% Nothing, officer

0 74470 94595 6   00

THE ONION • $2.00 US • $3.00 CAN

---

the ONION®

VOLUME 40 ISSUE 32   AMERICA'S FINEST NEWS SOURCE™   12–18 AUGUST 2004

Kerry Unveils One-Point Plan For Better America

Above: Kerry describes his plan to rebuild the nation.

WICHITA, KS—Delivering the central speech of his 10-day "Solution For America" bus campaign tour Monday, Democratic presidential nominee Sen. John Kerry outlined his one-point plan for a better America: the removal of George W. Bush from the White House.

"If I am elected in November, no inner-city child will have to live in an America where George Bush is president," Kerry said, addressing a packed Maize High School auditorium. "No senior citizen will lie awake at night, worrying about whether George Bush is still the chief executive of this country. And no American—regardless of gender, regardless of class, regardless of race—will be represented by George Bush in the world community."

The Solution For America tour, which began in Boston, will end in Eugene, OR on Aug. 20. During the next week and a half, Kerry and vice-presidential hopeful John Edwards are expected to bring their message of a Bush-free country to several hundred thousand Americans.

In the speech, Kerry offered a

see KERRY page 232

Above: The A-Team circa 1984.

U.S. Military Clears A-Team Of Charges

WASHINGTON, DC—After more than 30 years spent hiding in the Los Angeles underground as wanted criminals, the members of the crack commando unit Alpha Team, commonly known as the A-Team, were cleared of all charges brought against them by the U.S. military, an army official announced Monday.

"In 1972, we arrested the members of the A-Team for a crime they swore they didn't commit," Gen. Stephen Lupo said. "They broke out of our maximum-security stockade, and from that moment forth, I thought of nothing but their recapture. However,

see A-TEAM page 233

Area Seventh-Grader Now A Woman

DURHAM, NH—Friends, family members, and teachers close to former little girl Sally Erhardt report that the seventh-grader is now a woman, due to a physical change that occurred in the Durham West Middle School girls' restroom Monday.

"Well, my, my—so our little Sally is a woman now!" summer-school teacher Jane McQuillan said after Erhardt sheepishly informed her of the transformation. "That's so wonderful. You must be so happy!"

The 4'11", 82-pound, red-headed woman, whose hobbies include collecting plastic Breyer horse figures, reading *Harry Potter* novels, and listening to Hilary Duff CDs, will now also discharge blood and tissue from her uterus about every 28 days.

Erhardt's change of status was discovered during a Math Wizards session, when she complained of mild stomach cramping and asked for permission to talk to the school nurse. On her way to the nurse's office, Erhardt went to the bathroom and discovered her passage into womanhood.

The information was almost immediately disseminated throughout the summer-school staff.

see WOMAN page 232

Above: Erhardt examines the woman in the mirror.

229

Recreational Viagra Use

According to a recent study, recreational use of Viagra is on the rise among younger men who don't suffer from impotence. What do *you* think?

Rudy Garcia
Housekeeper

"Is having sex for 48 hours straight some kind of a game to these people?"

Douglas Hirtz
Counselor

"At last, a medical miracle to eliminate the 3 percent of the time 20-year-olds don't have erections."

Lawrence Hardin
Systems Analyst

"The young people should just stick to the marijuana and the goofballs and let their elders have their Viagra."

Rhonda Hansen
Photographer

"This is what happens when the increasingly conservative young people go emulating Bob Dole."

William Knotz
Rental Clerk

"Wow, there's an illicit market for these pills? And all this time, I've foolishly been using them to try to satisfy my wife."

Jane Setzer
Set Designer

"If kids today just pop a pill every time they want an erection, how are they going to learn valuable pussy-eating skills?"

The Call For A National Intel Chief

Last week, President Bush called for the creation of a national intelligence director. What are some of the director's likely duties?

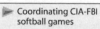
- ▶ Sitting around being intelligent on a national scale

- ▶ Chairing sound-bite brainstorming meetings

- ▶ Coordinating CIA-FBI softball games

- ▶ Must be able to fit in cake and burst out of cake holding gun during party attended by high-ranking terrorists

- ▶ Appearing at fairs and festivals throughout the rural Midwest all summer

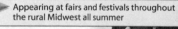
- ▶ Forming new intelligence office with postmodern Danish steel-and-glass desks, translucent wall-sized map of world, and staff of four leggy, blonde assassinettes

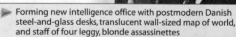
- ▶ Serving as nation's highest-ranking fall guy

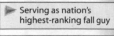
- ▶ Holding flashlight under face for scary effect while addressing nation

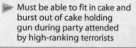

✑ the ONION®
America's Finest News Source.™

Herman Ulysses Zweibel
Founder

T. Herman Zweibel
Publisher Emeritus
J. Phineas Zweibel
Publisher
Maxwell Prescott Zweibel
Editor-In-Chief

Where Are You Now, When We Need You Most, Rage Against The Machine?

By Jacob Ainsworth

For nearly 10 years, Rage Against The Machine provided a voice for the disaffected, the disenfranchised, and the angry. Blending punk, pop, hip-hop, metal, and thrash, their music fought corporate America, cultural imperialism, and government oppression head on during a time when most of America was lulled into a Clinton-induced torpor. When Rage Against The Machine's cry for justice was amplified by a major-label debut in 1992, hundreds of thousands of American youths turned to them for guidance. Over the course of eight years, Rage released three original albums and one covers album, each a new and varied challenge, a 60-minute call to arms, a soul cry for the low and lost.

But then, in October of 2000, the unthinkable happened: Singer Zack De La Rocha left the band. On that fateful election night in November, there was no one to articulate the outrage and denounce the Supreme Cult's appointment of George W. Shrub to Commander-In-Thief. Where were you then, Rage Against The Machine? Where are you now?

Every album you released was a Declaration Of Independence for music fans no longer content with music that served only to entertain. Hearing the teeth-grinding post-metal riffs of "Sleep Now In The Fire," thousands awoke from MTV and Top 40 radio's 24-7 "pop-ulum somnalocasts." Every song, every lyric furthered your message. Your words about the war for oil in the Middle East were prophetic. You were an inspiration! What happened?

Now, of all times, we look to you for clear-eyed articulation of the fucked-up world we live in. The people of the sun still labor in Mexico, but no one plays bass about their struggles! Mumia sits in prison, yet no one sings for his freedom. And what do we hear? Silence. You've abandoned us in our hour of need. How could you? Everywhere: exploitation. Where's the rock?

You summed it up so clearly in "Fistful Of Steel" when you sang, "If the vibe was suicide, then you would push da button, but if you're bowin' down, then let me do the cuttin'." You lifted the nation's youth up out of the mire and taught us to question, to act. Rage Against The Machine, come back. Bring us more slamming riffs and sonic wallop. Bring us more shredding and axing. Do that thing where you make your guitar sound like bagpipes.

Seriously, we need a healthy dose of your cuttin', or Bush will win. It's Vietnow, man, and just like you said before, America's getting its news-trients from the likes of Benito Hannity and Adolf Limbaugh. We need a musical antidote to the poison. This nation needs another bomb track to ignite it! We are lost, Rage Against The Machine. Where have you gone? The voice of the voiceless is silent.

Surely Zack has ample material for new songs. This empire couldn't be any more evil. What about Abu

---

And where are you, Tom, Tim, and Brad? You bravely stood up for the dispossessed of the Third World, but in the current political climate, we are dispossessed in our own country. The erosion of our rights and liberties makes captives of us all. Do you no longer care?

Ghraib? If ever anyone was sleeping in the fire, it was those prisoners. Zack, if you're listening, if you're reading this—we need you.

And where are you, Tom, Tim, and Brad? You bravely stood up for the dispossessed of the Third World, but in the current political climate, we are dispossessed in our own country. The erosion of our rights and liberties makes captives of us all. Do you no longer care? Did the machine defeat you?

I'm sorry. I got carried away. It's only my fear for the future that led me to question you. For if not you, then who will rage for us? Audioslave? They're only three-fourths of Rage Against The Machine, and you know it. Besides, they broke up. Limp Bizkit? Slipknot? They have the infectious energy, but aren't so vocal about saving the world from Dick Chicanery and Donald Grab-The-Money-And-Rumsfeld.

Only one band has the power to rage against the machine, and that is Rage Against The Machine. If you have any sort of a conscience, you will heed my call. ✑

Bargoer Starts To Hit Stride After Hitting On Fifth Girl

JACKSONVILLE, FL—Brad Framik, a contract attorney at Russell Law Offices and self-described "player," announced Saturday that he was "starting to hit my stride" after unsuccessfully coming on to five women at the Red Rock nightclub.

"My game wasn't focused during those first few rounds, but now I'm on a roll," Framik said. "If that tall chick's friends hadn't dragged her out, I would've had her for sure. See, it takes a while to work up to peak performance level."

Although he doesn't go out much during the week, Framik said he likes to "hit the clubs" every Friday and Saturday, usually with a group of five or more male friends also hoping to meet women.

"Then, on Sundays, we go golfing and compare our pussy-hunt scores," Framik said. "It's important to have fun and blow off steam on the weekend when you have such a demanding, high-paying job. It's a stress reliever, like yoga."

Framik's coworker Nick Gregivich usually joins the group.

"We may wear suits all day, but we know how to cut loose after hours," said Gregivich, 28. "You should see Framik bust a move on the dance floor. It's like, 'Yow!'"

When asked about his dance technique, Framik elaborated.

"My signature move is to locate some chick I wouldn't mind breaking it off in," Framik said. "Then I sidle over to her section of the dance floor

Above: Framik starts his evening at an even pace.

and circle like a shark, waiting for the right moment to strike. When she least expects it, I lock eyes with her and mouth the words 'I want you.'"

Shrugging, Framik added, "Hey, dude, chicks like silly stuff like that— sometimes it works."

When asked why he wasn't making a favorable impression at the begin-

ning of the evening, Framik said he had "started out slow."

"I didn't do so well with the first five babes I approached, but a guy's gotta warm up," Framik said. "The love muscle is like any other muscle—you've got to stretch and loosen up first before you do the heavy lifting. That's why it makes sense to hit on three or

four stuck-up chicks first, so you can play a couple practice rounds before the stakes are too high. You can't expect to hit that shit out of the park your first time at bat."

When pressed, Framik admitted to making some mistakes during the evening.

see BARGOER page 232

Al-Qaeda Chatter Deteriorates Into Gossip

WASHINGTON, DC—Terrorist chatter about a possible al-Qaeda attack against the U.S. deteriorated into gossip Monday, according to top federal intelligence officials. "We intercepted a phone call in which two al-Qaeda operatives were discussing plans to conduct reconnaissance missions at certain U.S. landmarks," CIA operative Tim Huber said. "But the conversation quickly devolved into a 20-minute discussion of what someone named Majida Sa'doon was doing at Kanebi Hadi Hameeb's home at sunrise." Huber added that the gossip is a "definite improvement" over the glut of small talk about recipes, children, and goats that dominated conversation at this time last year.

Employee's Loyalty Garners CEO's Contempt

NEW YORK—Associate account manager Henry Keel's devotion to Wegman Financial Corp. fills CEO Roger K. Scarvon with contempt, Scarvon said Tuesday. "I can't imagine spending 23 years at one firm with nothing more to show for it than a position in middle-management," said Scarvon, who has been an executive at seven different companies since 1994. "Really, he might as well just paint the word 'sucker' on his forehead." Scarvon said Keel will pay for his steadfast loyalty when he loses his job and pension after Wegman Financial is "gutted and resold" in June 2005.

Junior Building Inspector Closes Down Tree House

BLOOMINGTON, IN—Junior building inspector Thomas Spengler, 8, ordered the closure of a tree house owned by Jimmy Herman Monday. "The tree house will remain closed until improvements are made to its structure," Spengler said. "The rope ladder leading up to the house needs to be brought into compliance with local building codes. Also, the structural integrity of the clubhouse, wedged as it is into Old Man Kessler's oak tree, is compromised by the hastily added lookout post." Spengler threatened to close the tree house permanently should Herman fail to bring its tire swing up to code.

Man Miscast In Role of Father

BECKLEY, WV—Critics, social workers, and peers agreed Monday that Michael Jans was horribly miscast as the father of 5-year-old Tyler Beecham. "Michael would be great playing the drunken buddy, or the deadbeat brother who can't hold down a job, but he's just not very believable as Daddy," ex-girlfriend Karen Beecham said. "I had hoped Michael would grow into the role, but I'm rethinking that idea. It's a very demanding part, and I need someone who can do it without a lot of direction." Beecham will begin re-casting the father role at Scooter's Pub on Thursday at 8 p.m.

Black Guy Doesn't Talk About All The Times He *Didn't* Get Discriminated Against

DETROIT, MI—Renald Boyd, 27, of course doesn't mention all the times he *wasn't* discriminated against, sources reported Tuesday. "I had the lease all set up through an agent," Boyd said. "But then, when I went in to sign it, the landlord suddenly started acting all weird and said he had to run out for a minute. We sat there for an hour before the agent got him on the phone, at which point the landlord said he was looking for a 'quieter type.' This country is insane." Boyd naturally failed to mention that the real-estate agent worked with him with no hesitation, and that the taxi he took away from the real-estate agency was only the second one that he'd attempted to hail. ∅

WOMAN from page 229

"Oh, Sally, I'm so happy for you!" physical-education instructor Terri Flieshmann said when the newly christened woman opted out of swimming. "This is such a big day for you. You should enjoy it. Just sit over there on the bleachers where I can keep an eye on you."

"This is so special!" Flieshmann added, her voice echoing throughout the natatorium.

Erhardt's cycle began several weeks ago, when her pituitary gland released Follicle Stimulating Hormone, which targeted her ovaries and stimulated the follicles within them to ripen several eggs in preparation for ovulation. At this time, estrogen was released by Erhardt's ovaries, as well.

Throughout the day, Erhardt was overwhelmed by congratulations, warm wishes, and unsolicited presentations of hygiene products. She also received special attention from the home-economics teacher, Stacy Sidran.

"This is a very special day for you," Sidran said, after having pulled Erhardt out of art class in front of more than 40 curious students. "You'll soon learn that your life has changed. People will treat you differently now that you're a woman. There will be new expectations, and new challenges."

"Do you use an anti-perspirant deodorant?" Sidran asked, after having hugged the confused and slightly frightened woman.

Though exposed to filmstrips and reading material designed to prepare them for the event, Erhardt's classmates have expressed confusion over the former girl's recently attained womanhood.

"What's with Sally today?" asked Brian Bovey, a child with whom Erhardt played before she reached maturity, as recently as yesterday. "All of a sudden, she's not talking to anyone. Is she mad about something?"

"Yeah, Sally sure is being quiet," said Tiffany Nielsen, a girlhood acquaintance of Erhardt's. "I hope she isn't going to get all stuck up now that—oh, never mind. You wouldn't under-

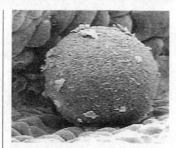

Above: One of the approximately 500 eggs that Erhardt's ovarian follicles will release in her lifetime.

stand. It's a woman thing."

While they admit that they were emotionally unprepared for the advent of Erhardt's womanhood, family members expressed excitement over the news.

"Well, my little girl's a woman now, hey?" said Mark, the woman's father, whose gift of a floral arrangement

"What's with Sally today?" Brian Bovey asked.

caused his newly adult daughter to hide under her bed for several hours. "That's really… I mean… I think it's great. I sure will miss seeing Daddy's little strawberry play with her dolls and her stuffed animals, but, hey, she's not a little kid anymore."

Mark then repeatedly inquired, to no one in particular, as to when his wife might return home.

The woman herself has thus far refused to comment at length on her migration into maturity.

"Please go away," the tearful 12-year-old woman told reporters through her closed bedroom door. "Everyone's been staring at me all day. Would everybody please just leave me alone? God!"

The flow of blood from Erhardt's vagina will last between three and six days each month, and is a normal part of being a sexually mature woman. ⌀

KERRY from page 229

solution for the nation's ailing education system.

"Schools do not have the resources they need to succeed," Kerry said. "One million students are dropping out of high school every year. John Kerry and John Edwards have a plan to ensure that all Americans can make the most of their God-given talents: Get George Bush out of the White House."

Kerry also spoke on the subject of national security.

"This country has embraced a new and dangerously ineffective disregard for the world," Kerry said. "In order to win the global war against terror, we must promote democracy, freedom, and opportunity around the world. My national-defense policy will be guided by one imperative: Don't be George Bush. As will my plans to create a strong economy, protect civil rights, develop a better healthcare system, and improve homeland security."

Joining Kerry at the podium, Edwards raised one issue not discussed by his running mate: the environment.

"Let's not forget one important point," Edwards said. "We need to set a new standard of environmental excellence for America by renewing our nation's promise of clean air, clean water, and a bountiful landscape for all. In the 21st century, we can have progress without pollution—as long as we have a Dick Cheney-free White House."

The new message is resonating with registered Democrats.

"John Kerry really spoke to my dream, my hope, and my aspiration for this nation," University of Kansas sophomore Jason Brandt said. "He sees the world as I do."

"With all the mess that's going on in the country—the deficits, the government's power-grab, the wars—it's time for a president who admits that there's a problem and has a plan to fix it," Brandt added. "A president who is not George W. Bush is exactly what we need—and Kerry fits the bill 100 percent."

Kerry's message resonated less strongly with one Lawrence, KS

swing voter.

"Politicians make a lot of campaign promises," Lance Radda said. "Sure, this not-being-Bush policy sounds good now. But how can we be sure that Kerry will deliver on that promise once in office?"

Kerry addressed Radda's question.

"I promise you, here and now, that I will enact my one-point plan on the day I enter the Oval Office," Kerry said. "For the last three and a half years, we've had George W. Bush, and today I have this to say: We can do better!"

In his final words, Kerry changed the subject to attack Bush's record.

"John Kerry really spoke to my dream, my hope, and my aspiration for this nation," University of Kansas sophomore Jason Brandt said.

"During his term in office, George Bush has relentlessly continued to be president—despite the clear benefits to America his absence would bring to the lives of citizens everywhere," Kerry said. "My one-point plan for America highlights the sort of change that this country desperately needs. And my plan is something that George Bush will never, ever be able to accomplish."

Bush-Cheney campaign manager Ken Mehlman described Kerry's plan as a vicious, partisan attack.

"It's absolutely ridiculous that John Kerry is offering one solution to all of America's problems," Mehlman said. "Who's going to listen to logic like that? Anyone can see that Kerry is a Massachusetts liberal who will raise your taxes and open our borders to terrorist attacks. Vote Bush." ⌀

BARGOER from page 231

"Okay, I may have jumped the gun a little with that first chick," Framik said. "I never should've asked her to show me her thong so soon in the conversation. That's the weird thing about chicks. They always want to draw everything out longer than is necessary. I'm a take-charge, fast-paced guy, so it's hard for me to fake being patient."

Framik said the nature of the initial rejection made it more difficult for him to "find the pocket" in subsequent attempts at seduction.

"After she made that comment about me using sunless tanner, I got a little off-balance," Framik said. "She set me on edge, so I wasn't bringing my 'A' game for the next couple girls."

As Framik's unrequited attention-seeking continued, his friends watched his progress from across the

bar. According to Framik, this added pressure may have caused him to blow his timing.

Framik said the nature of the initial rejection made it more difficult for him to "find the pocket" in subsequent attempts at seduction.

"I shouldn't have talked to that third chick while my friends were all watching me," Framik said. "Some girls find that sort of thing tacky. But

by the fourth at-bat, I thought I'd ironed out the wrinkles."

Framik described his next failed come-on attempt.

"I was making major eye contact with this brunette in the booth next to ours, but she turned out to be this Iranian chick who didn't speak much English," Framik said. "She was dressed kind of slutty, so that fooled me. She was probably some kind of uptight religious Muslim who's not into getting boned. Usually, I can spot a religious nut from a mile off, but I had the beer goggles on."

After the fifth failed attempt, however, Framik finally felt himself "getting into the zone."

"Let's just say that I definitely got some digits by the end of the night," said Framik, who estimates that he

made between 10 and 15 come-on attempts over the course of the two hours that followed. "I ended up with a pretty respectable success ratio."

While Framik described himself as a "master of the elusive female mind," a female coworker disagreed.

"Brad and his friends are always talking about how chicks dig this and chicks dig that," said Paula Mannheim, a fellow lawyer. "Listening to them talk, you'd think they've never had a conversation with an actual woman in their entire lives."

Asked for his reaction to Mannheim's comments, Framik became curious.

"Paula was talking about me?" Framik said. "The one with the nice body? Tell me everything she said, so I can read between the lines." ⌀

a recent audit of their file has revealed that the arrest of the Alpha Force members was made in error. The U.S. military deeply regrets the mistake."

According to Lupo, the A-Team members' exoneration will occur before the U.S. Court of Appeals for the

> ## "For decades, we've been forced to live in the shadows," Murdock said. "Somehow, we always found a way to help people who had nowhere else to turn, but we operated under the constant threat of recapture. Finally, the nightmare is over."

Armed Forces on Aug. 24.

Just hours after Lupo's announcement was made, Cpt. H.M. "Howlin' Mad" Murdock, the A-Team's pilot, resurfaced to speak with journalist Amy Allen, who often reported on the mercenaries' charitable acts.

"For decades, we've been forced to live in the shadows," Murdock said. "Somehow, we always found a way to help people who had nowhere else to turn, but we operated under the constant threat of recapture. Finally, the nightmare is over."

Added Murdock: "Owooohh, I'm a little doggie! Ow ow owooohhhh!"

Murdock and the surviving members of the team—the classically handsome Lt. Templeton Arthur "Face" Peck and the Mohawk-sporting mechanic, Sgt. Bosco "B.A." Baracus—said their joy over the announcement was tempered only by regret that their de-facto leader, Col. John "Hannibal" Smith, was not alive to see their names cleared.

"Somewhere up there, Hannibal is smiling down on us—maybe disguised as a giant crocodile or a wealthy diamond merchant," Peck said. "He loved it when a plan come together."

"More than any of us, he would have enjoyed seeing the look on [Col. Roderick] Decker's face when our innocence was announced," Peck continued. "Decker hated Hannibal ever since they served together back in 'Nam. Decker never could stand his cocky attitude."

Smith was gunned down in front of a Las Vegas casino in 1994.

The A-Team members said that, although they presume the army's offer of freedom is legitimate, they have taken precautions.

"We formed a backup plan in case

Above: President Bush presents Baracus with a long-overdue medal of honor.

things turn out to be on the jazz," Peck said, using the team's code phrase for a troublesome situation. "Murdock's gonna perch a helicopter on top of the courtroom. B.A. found a broken Howitzer in a junkyard, got it working again, and got it mounted in our van. We also have a whole team of trou-

> ## "Somewhere up there, Hannibal is smiling down on us—maybe disguised as a giant crocodile or a wealthy diamond merchant," Peck said. "He loved it when a plan come together."

bled teens B.A. befriended and taught valuable lessons. They placed explosives throughout the courtroom and along our subterranean escape route. If need be, they'll blow that courtroom apart."

Peck admitted that their escape plan might be too crazy to work, acknowledging the possibility that he will be punched in the face during the escape. He also noted that stacks of cardboard boxes might break the falls of the military personnel thrown into the air by the A-Team's explosives.

"Just to be safe, I romanced a beautiful court stenographer and convinced her to smuggle some smoke bombs in with her," Peck said. "All in a day's work."

Lupo said he expects an uneventful trial, explaining that, as restitution for the military's mistake—a typo which attributed crimes committed by the H-Team to the A-Team—the court will award Peck, Murdock, and Baracus honorable discharges, a written apology from Decker, and 32 years' back pay.

Murdock said his primary concern at present is getting Baracus to fly from L.A. to Washington, D.C. for the trial.

"He keeps calling me a 'crazy foo' for trying to get him to fly," Murdock said. "I told him the chance of the plane crashing into a field of rednecks harassing a religious group was very slim. I'm thinking that if we drug his milk, we can get him on the plane."

Baracus said that he has big plans for his settlement.

"For the last 30 years I've been a soldier of fortune," Baracus said. "Now, I'm going to take the money and do something for the kids. I'm gonna start a gym. A gym for the kids. For a long time, that's been my dream. But I couldn't open one with [Gen. Hunt] Stockwell on our tail. He'd use a tank to send shells through the side of it."

Added Baracus: "I pity the fool that tries to blow up my gymnasium now!"

While the original members of the A-Team have been exonerated, the same cannot be said for Frankie "Dishpan" Santana, a special-effects expert who helped the team escape Stockwell's clutches in 1986. Santana, who remains charged with dereliction of duty, desertion, and insubordination, spoke with reporters from a holding pen at Fort Bragg.

"I suppose it would be too much to ask the guys to break me out now that they're finally legit," Santana said. "If I'm lucky, maybe they'll put me in a cell that has a blowtorch in it for some reason, or air ducts large enough to crawl through. Or maybe they'll just do a sloppy job of guarding me—but

> ## "For the last 30 years I've been a soldier of fortune," Baracus said. "Now, I'm going to take the money and do something for the kids. I'm gonna start a gym. A gym for the kids. For a long time, that's been my dream. But I couldn't open one with [Gen. Hunt] Stockwell on our tail. He'd use a tank to send shells through the side of it."

that may be too much to ask."

Within hours of his interview, Santana escaped using a blowtorch to open the cell's air ducts while the guards were having lunch in a different room. His whereabouts are currently unknown. ∅

Things Are Starting To Turn Around

The Cruise
By Jim Anchower

Hola, amigos. How's every little thing? I know it's been a long time since I rapped at ya, but I've barely had a chance to catch my breath these days. Ron hooked me up with a job at the carbonics plant where he works. For a while, I was the guy that cut blocks of dry ice. It was all right, but I didn't know Ron was gonna be my supervisor. I was able to put up with that for about two seconds before I stopped showing up. There's no way that mallethead is going to tell me what to do. He even wrote me up for being late.

Now, ordinarily, I would be sorta down because I'm out of work, but for once, I've landed on my feet. I've got a new job as a roofer. I've never worked construction before, except for that time I mixed cement, but I'm no stranger to a hammer. That TV table I have? I built that myself out of plywood I snagged from a Dumpster when they were building that house next door. It even has a shelf for my GameCube. Right now it sags in the middle, but that'll stop once it settles.

The roofing job is all right. Sometimes we have to work right through the weekends, but then I get a shitload of overtime pay. I work with a bunch of college guys, but they aren't too uppity or wussy. We don't hang out after work or anything, but we joke around

Add to all this the fact that my car hasn't been acting up at all, and you can see that life is sweet these days.

together. Their music sucks, but we take turns. It's pretty democratic.

The thing about roofing is that you're out in the hot sun all day, so you work up a thirst. Now, when I was carving dry ice, I was really cold all day, and it'd go outside and it'd be really hot—so I was never thirsty, just confused. But since getting this new job, the number of MGDs I put away has gone up considerably.

It must help my overall disposition to have a job that doesn't suck ass, because I feel like I'm living a charmed life right now. Last week, after knocking off work, I was heading to the store to pick up my nightly beer. When I started up the car, the radio station was beginning a block of Speedwagon. It was lucky, too, be-

cause I was just about to call it quits on that station for playing way too much U2 (total ass). But then they go and play one of my favorites. That DJ must have read my mind and decided that Jim Anchower was the kind of listener he needed to keep happy.

Once I got to the store, I sat in the car until the end of the rock block. When I got out and walked through the parking lot, still feeling pretty good, I spotted $20 lying on the ground! I looked around to see if the guy who dropped

The thing about roofing is that you're out in the hot sun all day, so you work up a thirst. Now, when I was carving dry ice, I was really cold all day, and then I'd go outside and it'd be really hot—so I was never thirsty, just confused.

it was watching me, but I didn't see anyone. That kinda thing doesn't happen to me. Usually, I'm the one losing money. Well, I took that $20 and turned it into beer real fast before the owner came back for it.

Once I got home, I cracked open a beer and settled in to watch Fear Factor. Since my beer was free, I had a little extra money to order a pizza with pepperoni and onions. When the pizza showed up, I opened the box and saw that they'd put mushrooms on it, too. Normally, I would've turned the other cheek, but I hate mushrooms. I was a little buzzed by then, so I called up the pizza place and chewed them out. They sent out another pizza, no charge. Since the mushroom pizza was free, I picked off the mushrooms, ate it, and saved the other one for breakfast.

It rained the next day, so I didn't have to work. Since I'm used to being outside now, I was starting to feel a little stir crazy in the house, so I went out for some air. I drove around and picked up a new pair of Terminator sunglasses and a one-hitter, the kind that looks like a cigarette. I'd been meaning to get one of those for a while. When I got back, there was a note on my door from my landlord saying that he needed to get in my place. My landlord is a king douche, so I was super happy to have dodged him. Luck is on my side.

Then, yesterday, the best thing of all happened. I busted my leg, so I don't have to go in to work for eight weeks!

One of the guys left his tool belt on the side of the ladder, so when I was climbing up, I got tangled up and fell. I broke my legbone in two places. The doctor says I probably might want to consider another kind of work once I get healed up. Sounds fine with me. In the meantime, I'm on workman's comp, meaning I get paid for lying around the house and taking Vicodin. And it was the guy who left the belt hanging on the ladder who got chewed out by my boss. How sweet is that?

Add to all this the fact that my car hasn't been acting up at all, and you can see that life is sweet these days. Maybe the universe looked at me and said, "You know what? I think it's time to give ol' Jim a break." Which is good, because before that I was getting shafted left and right. The only problem is I can't drive for a while, so I need Wes to drop supplies off for me. It would be better if Ron would do it, but he's pissed that I left him high and dry at work. After all the shit he put me though, he needs to chill the fuck out. I'll give him a few more days to cool down before I ask him again. *Ø*

Your Horoscope

By Lloyd Schumner Sr.
Retired Machinist and
A.A.P.B.-Certified Astrologer

Aries: (March 21–April 19)
Investigators will say that your death was caused by shoddily wired bathroom lighting, but that's just wishful thinking since you're standing right there.

Taurus: (April 20–May 20)
Government officials will call your new doomsday device "brilliant in its simplicity" and "a marvel of American ingenuity," but they won't be able to say so for long.

Gemini: (May 21–June 21)
You'll be forced to expand the list of shit you have to put up with to include "goat."

Cancer: (June 22–July 22)
Suppressed-memory therapy will do wonders for you, but only until you recover the long-lost knowledge that suppressed memories are bullshit.

Leo: (July 23–Aug. 22)
Gay pizza deliverymen are a dime a dozen, which is fortunate for you, as you'll soon be on the management end of that deal.

Virgo: (Aug. 23–Sept. 22)
Finding families for homeless animals is all well and good, but you could have prevented the tramplings if you'd considered the elephants' feelings on the matter.

Libra: (Sept. 23–Oct. 23)
You'll soon be exactly as popular as the trombone player in a chubby-chaser bar. This might not make a lot of sense now, but trust us, you'll see.

Scorpio: (Oct. 24–Nov. 21)
No one will believe that it looked like the Girl Scouts were going for their guns, but believe it—in an alternate universe, you've been filled with lead from the waist down.

Sagittarius: (Nov. 22–Dec. 21)
It's true you were trapped in the gourmet popcorn poppery, but you still don't see why they insisted on sending help.

Capricorn: (Dec. 22–Jan. 19)
You'll wake to find that the unexplained mental quirk that turned you into a leather fetishist has finally been worked out, but just wait until you get a load of a few cotton-polyester blends.

Aquarius: (Jan. 20–Feb. 18)
The stars found it hard to concentrate on your future this week, as they themselves aren't exactly teenagers anymore.

Pisces: (Feb. 19–March 20)
You definitely know a good thing when you see it, at least as long as the price tag is clearly visible.

MEKHONG from page 155

amounts of blood. Passersby were amazed by the unusually large amounts of blood. Passersby were amazed by the unusually large amounts of blood. Passersby were amazed by the unusually large amounts of blood. Passersby were amazed by the unusually large

How am I supposed to go on stocking produce without the love of the beautiful Esmerelda?

amounts of blood. Passersby were amazed by the unusually large amounts of blood. Passersby were amazed by the unusually large amounts of blood. Passersby were amazed by the unusually large amounts of blood. Passersby were amazed by the unusually large amounts of blood. Passersby were amazed by the unusually large amounts of blood. Passersby were amazed by the unusually large amounts of blood. Passersby were amazed by the unusually large

see MEKHONG page 268

Homosexual Tearfully Admits To Being Governor Of New Jersey

see POLITICS page 3C

Ride Mis-Pimped

see AUTOS page 14G

Cat Taught Not To Sleep In Wok

see LOCAL page 3E

Drywall Worker Plastered

see PEOPLE page 11F

STATshot

A look at the numbers that shape your world.

Why Did We Commit Murder?

26% Had never committed murder before

15% Dog didn't tell us not to

18% Thought we'd be able to go through with murder-suicide

22% Was necessary to further the plot

19% Had to back up claim that we'd kill for a decent hamburger

0 74470 94595 6 00

THE ONION • $2.00 US • $3.00 CAN

---

the ONION®

VOLUME 40 ISSUE 33   AMERICA'S FINEST NEWS SOURCE™   19–25 AUGUST 2004

Bush Finally Gets Oval Office Just The Way He Wants It

Left: Bush has some friends over to see the "perfect" Oval Office.

WASHINGTON, DC—After four different color schemes, a Tiki phase, and more than three years spent rearranging furniture, President Bush has the Oval Office set up just the way he wants it, the chief executive said in an informal press conference Monday.

"Took long enough," Bush said, lounging on one of the two overstuffed green leather couches he'd ordered from Jennifer Convertibles. "Just getting these couches was a chore—they almost didn't fit through the door. Then, arranging them so I could see the plasma TV while I stretched out was a real pain. Every time I thought I'd got them in a good place, I'd look and see I'd blocked out the Presidential Seal on the carpet. I didn't want to do that unless I had to."

Since 1909, the year the modern Oval Office was constructed, every president has decorated it to express his personal style, traditionally drawing from the collections of art and

see BUSH page 238

America's Sweetheart Dumps U.S. For Some Douchebag

Left: Dunst and the utter wad.

HOLLYWOOD, CA—Americans gathered Monday to discuss their feelings of heartbreak, anger, and resentment toward America's sweetheart Kirsten Dunst, after the film star broke up with the U.S. to be with some douchebag that everyone thought was gay.

"I don't think anyone expected this," Grangeville, ID resident Troy Pilner said, to murmurs of agreement from the rest of America. "We really cared about her, and I thought she cared about us. How can this butt-munch she's seeing provide something that the 293 million of us can't?"

Many Americans have theories about why Dunst—whose film credits include the two *Spider-Man* blockbusters, *Bring It On*, and *The Virgin Suicides*—broke up with us. Residents of Arizona report that Dunst's new boyfriend, Portuguese shipbuilding magnate Gilberto Nunes, must have filled her head with lies. Florida residents suggest that Dunst got scared when she realized how much she cared about us.

When asked to comment on these theories, Wyoming residents said it was still difficult to understand "what

see SWEETHEART page 239

Local Sheriff Suspects Al-Qaeda Or Teens

Above: Steinhorst investigates a recent crime.

BARABOO, WI—Sauk County Sheriff Virgil "Butch" Steinhorst announced Tuesday that he believes a recent rash of Baraboo-area crimes was perpetrated by the al-Qaeda terrorist network or teenagers.

"In this day and age, it's important for law-enforcement officials to consider global threats as well as local ones," Steinhorst said. "We could be dealing with an al-Qaeda sleeper cell attempting to collect information that they could use to plan a terrorist strike or some of those goth kids who knocked over that mailbox. Neither group has any respect for the law."

The string of unsolved crimes includes the defacement of public property, an incident of breaking-and-entering, and

see SHERIFF page 239

Gay Marriage In San Francisco

Last week, California's Supreme Court voided about 4,000 same-sex marriages performed by the mayor of San Francisco earlier this year. What do *you* think?

Michael Harlson
Banker

"The court struck every single one down? Well, that makes the failure rate for gay marriages almost double that of straight marriages."

Mark Jacobsen
Systems Analyst

"Oh... well... oh, geez. I'm no good at talking about all this mushy stuff."

Kathleen Hayes
Teacher

"In addition to being overturned legally, were these marriages officially annulled in the eyes of God? If not, these people could be condemned to hell!"

Jan Gorman
Choreographer

"I had five weddings to attend in October, but now it's only three. That doesn't seem like much less, but believe me, it really helps."

Charles Lopez
Driver

"Did you hear this, Rod and Keenan? I want those wine glasses back!"

Chris Gerber
Dishwasher

"Just to clarify, sodomy's still legal, isn't it? Well, all right then."

Summer Olympics Programming

Thousands of TV hours are being dedicated to coverage of the Summer Olympics. What programming will sports fans see?

- Fascinating in-depth interviews with power lifters
- Entire channel devoted to current time and temperature in Athens
- Track-and-field events as captured by discus-mounted camera
- The stirring tale of Yosh Han's ping-pong paddle, given to her by her grandfather, who was executed during the Cultural Revolution for his ping-pong prowess
- 408 straight hours of *Scooby's All-Star Laff-A-Lympics*
- Cutting evaluations of swimsuits worn by water-polo teams
- Hazy, dreamy footage of women's softball
- Soccer games broadcast at 150 percent speed
- If there is a God, some primetime judo

the ONION®
America's Finest News Source.™

Herman Ulysses Zweibel
Founder

T. Herman Zweibel
Publisher Emeritus
J. Phineas Zweibel
Publisher
Maxwell Prescott Zweibel
Editor-In-Chief

236

Who Do You Think You Are— Former New Orleans Saints Linebacker Pat Swilling?

Okay, Gerald, I've heard about as much out of you as I can take. All I get from you lately is eye-rolling and swaggering, like you're too good for

By Ryan Fleishmann

the mere mortals of Mercury Insurance. You act like you're doing us a favor just showing up. Who do you think you are— former New Orleans Saints linebacker Pat Swilling?

Judging by your attitude alone, I'd say you were a 6'3", 250-pound linebacker out of Georgia Tech. Seriously, if I didn't know better, I'd think the Saints took you in the third round of the 1986 draft because they knew you'd improve their pass rush on the outside and complement little big man Sam Mills. Not so fast, touchdown. I do know better.

You sashay around the place like you're third on the New Orleans all-time sack list with 78. If someone says something you disagree with, you act for all the world like you averaged 11.5 sacks a year from 1987 to 1993. "What, me? I'm just Pat Swilling, 1989 NFL Defensive Player of the Year. I once held Georgia Tech's record for career sacks with 23." That's you.

Listen to me, Gerald. I'm not the only one who's had it with your Pat Swilling bullshit. People are talking—you know how many people want to work with someone who acts like he's a record-holder for career sacks? Zero.

> ## You know how many people want to work with someone who acts like he's been a record-holder for career sacks? Not a one.

Do you think posting above-average sales numbers for two months means you are a versatile, savvy defensive player with excellent lateral motion? It's a rhetorical question, Swilling—you don't need to answer it. I feel like I'm talking to someone whose football instincts let him perform effectively as both a linebacker and a defensive end, here. Jesus. You are not former New Orleans Saints line-

backer Pat Swilling, and it's high time you stopped leaning back in your chair and twirling your pen around during the Friday wrap-up meeting.

You're valuable here at Mercury, but not so valuable that, say, we couldn't trade you to the Detroit Li-

> ## You sashay around the place like you're third on the New Orleans all-time sack list with 78.
> ## If someone says something you disagree with, you act for all the world like you averaged 11.5 sacks a year from 1987 to 1993. "What, me? I'm just Pat Swilling, 1989 NFL Defensive Player of the Year."

ons in 1993 for first- and fourth-round picks. You can treat your friends like you went to five straight Pro Bowls, but the second you come in here, to *my* department, to *my* office, you'd better wipe that "an impressive five Pro Bowls in a row" look off your face. Do you understand me? I won't take this linebacker attitude any longer. Is that clear?

Because right now, I don't see a guy who understands. I don't see a guy who says, "I want to get along." I see a guy who says, "I'm one of three New Orleans players who achieved four sacks in one game." This is you: "Even toward the end of my career, I still had six sacks in a 20-tackle season!"

I'm not getting through to you at all, am I? This is all going in one ear and out the other. Even now, you're treating this whole thing like you're going to retire from football after the 1998 season, run for the Louisiana House of Representatives as a popular Democrat, and win the seat by a wide margin.

Fine. Be that way, Mr. 14th on the all-time quarterback sack list. Just don't do it in my office. Get out, and don't come back until you can act a little more like former Buffalo Bills defensive end Bryce Paup. ∅

Naughty Baker's Diminished Sex Drive Starting To Affect His Work

GRAND FORKS, ND—Erotic baker Kevin Nageli has experienced a decline in the quality of his work following a recent reduction in his sex drive, Naughty Bites sources said Monday.

"I feel bad saying it, but Kevin's really in a slump," said Hal DiPrima, Nageli's longtime friend and business partner. "There was a time no marzipan penis could compare to a Kevin Nageli. Now, though, look at this tray of cocks. No definition. The external urethral orifice is just a pinhole, and the texture of the shaft is all wrong. They just droop over the baking sheets. What am I going to tell the bachelorettes?"

Naughty Bites is a three-time winner of *Grand Forks Magazine*'s "Best Place To Browse When You're Feeling Kooky" award, due in large part to the precision that once defined a Nageli erotic cake. His expertise was seen in all his work—from relatively tame bikini-clad breasts reading "Bon Voyage!" to the more-graphic, penis-shaped cakes reading "Make A Wish And Blow!"

"The erotic bakery business is detail-oriented, but even I used to be amazed by the way Kevin would spend three hours a day shaving tiny curlicues off a hunk of dark chocolate, because he wanted the pubic hair to look just right," DiPrima said, shaking his head as he boxed a cake that read "Eat Me, Birthday Boy.""Now, he just takes a scoop of black sprinkles and dumps it over the iced vaginas. Somewhere under that lumpish mass is a Gummi Bear clitoris, but you'd

Right: Nageli and one of his recent creations (above).

never know it."

By his own estimates, Nageli's business and marriage were going strong until May, when the pressures resulting from the birth of his second child and his mother-in-law's decision to move into the Nageli home caused sexual relations with his wife of five years to ebb. Nageli said he has found his attention diverted away from sex and sexy cakes alike.

"As you get older, sometimes the things that practically defined your life when you were younger become less important," Nageli said. "Lately, sex is the last thing on my mind. These days, all I want to do is finish my business as quickly as possible so I can go away, smoke a cigarette, and relax in front of the TV. But try telling that to my wife. Or my customers."

Nageli didn't seem particularly bothered by his attitude shift.

see BAKER page 240

NEWS IN BRIEF

Republicans Outraged By Inaccuracies In Metallica Documentary

WASHINGTON, DC—Republican congressmen lambasted the documentary *Metallica: Some Kind Of Monster* for its "gross inaccuracies and fabrications"Monday. "[Filmmakers] Joe Berlinger and Bruce Sinofsky are clearly biased," Speaker of the House Dennis Hastert said. "By editing together concert footage from three different mediocre shows, they have given the general public a false impression that Metallica still kicks ass." Hastert added that there is no hard evidence to support the film's argument that the album *St. Anger* has more thrashing riffs than *Kill 'Em All*.

Personal Life A Total Waste Of Time

ALTOONA, PA—Stockbroker Donald Guy, 38, announced Monday that his non-work life is "a complete waste of time.""I spent the weekend reading, watching movies, and visiting friends." Guy said. "I didn't get a damn thing done." He added that he might have gotten more accomplished Sunday had he not been burdened with the need to go swimming with his wife and children.

State Bird Reconsidered After Latest Wren Attack

COLUMBIA, SC—Gov. Mark Sanford spoke out Monday in favor of changing his state's bird from the Carolina wren to "anything else" following the ninth unprovoked wren attack this year. "In light of last week's events, I strongly feel the wren is no longer a good representative for the state of South Carolina,"Sanford said, referring to Friday's tragic dive-bombing and pecking incident at a Myrtle Beach preschool. "Maybe it's time we recognize one of our more docile birds, like the robin or the magnolia warbler." Sanford advised anyone hearing the wren's cries of "tea-kettle, tea-kettle" to run for cover immediately.

Girlfriend Acting All Clingy After Getting Pregnant

TUCSON, AZ—Human-resources manager Dave Buckner, 27, said Monday that longtime girlfriend Janice Feener, 24, has been "a lot more clingy" ever since July, when she learned she was pregnant with his child. "All of a sudden, she's saying 'I love you' six times a day and wants to sit around hugging on the couch all night," Buckner said. "I'm not sure what's gotten into her, but it's getting really annoying." Buckner added that there's no way he can stand six and a half more months of Feener's behavior, and is considering buying her a puppy to keep her company.

Waiting-Room Copy Of People Brings Area Man Up To Speed On Paris Hilton

TULSA, OK—While waiting to see dermatologist Rawson Meyers, Randy Slocum was "brought up to speed" on the life of Paris Hilton by an Aug. 9 issue of *People* magazine Monday. "I never quite knew what Paris Hilton did, besides get some home-sex tape put on the Internet," Slocum said during the 18 minutes he spent waiting to have a benign mole removed. "Well, it turns out she wrapped up a second season of *The Simple Life*, this TV show she does with Lionel Richie's daughter. And she was dating some guy named Nick Carter, but they broke up." An article about Jessica Simpson also cleared up Slocum's previous assumption that Hilton starred in the MTV reality show *Newlyweds*. ∅

furnishings available through the National Gallery, the Smithsonian, and the White House itself. However, Bush is the first president to request decorative items from such sources as the Major League Baseball Hall Of Fame, Crutchfield, and a local Successories outlet.

"When we first got here, Laura had the office done in peach sage, and putty or something," Bush said, mov-

> ## "Check out that baseball bat over there, the one on top of the subwoofer," Bush said, gesturing to the alcove that once held a Frederick Remington bronze. "Sammy Sosa used that bat in a game a couple years ago. Went three for four."

ing a large Texas-shaped ashtray from the glass coffee table and putting his feet up. "She had all this old-lady furniture all over the place. Don't get me wrong, it was nice, but it looked like an Ethan Allen showroom or a waiting room or something. It wasn't a room that made you want to relax."

"Check out that baseball bat over there, the one on top of the subwoofer," Bush said, gesturing to the alcove that once held a Frederick Remington bronze. "Sammy Sosa used that bat in a game a couple years ago. Went three for four."

In remaking the Oval Office, Bush overcame several unique challenges, among them the room's shape. Not only did Bush find it difficult to hang his collection of framed and signed Jimmy Buffett posters, but the built-in bookcases in the walls were too shallow to hold his tape deck. The room's curved walls also made accurate placement of the president's home-theater speakers nearly impossible.

"We'd be in there 'til 1 in the morning, moving the La-Z-Boy over here and the mini-bar over to where the La-Z-Boy was," White House chief of staff Andrew Card said. "Finally, Karl [Rove] remembered this web site that sells beanbag chairs, nice leather and suede ones. That filled the place out nicely. And one day [Vice-President Dick] Cheney showed up with this bearskin rug. It's from an actual bear!"

White House curator William Allman said Bush decorated the Oval Office with almost no input from Allman or his staff.

"Every president since Taft has made

Above: Bush enjoys his new chair.

the Oval Office his own, thereby adding to the rich history of the White House and to that of America itself," Allman said. "I'm sure President Bush's halogen lamp, rotating CD

> ## "One day Cheney showed up with this bearskin rug," Bush said. "It's from an actual bear!"

rack, and six-foot iguana terrarium will be valuable additions to our permanent collection, even if he did have to throw out the desk to make room for everything."

The historic "Resolute" desk, traditionally used by the president, was made from the timbers of the *HMS Resolute*, an abandoned British ship discovered by an American vessel and returned to England as a token of friendship and goodwill. When the ship was retired in 1880, Queen Victoria had the desk made and presented it to President Rutherford B. Hayes. It is currently housed in the living room of Washington, DC bodyshop employee Mike Koharski, who found it on the curb outside the White House. *Ø*

amounts of blood. Passersby were amazed by the unusually large amounts of blood. Passersby were amazed by the unusually large amounts of blood. Passersby were amazed by the unusually large amounts of blood. Passersby were amazed by the unusually large amounts of blood. Passersby were amazed by the unusually large amounts of blood. Passersby were amazed by the unusually large amounts of blood. Passersby were amazed by the unusually large amounts of blood. Passersby were amazed by the unusually large amounts of blood. Passersby were amazed by the unusually large amounts of blood. Passersby were amazed by the unusually large amounts of blood. Passersby were amazed by the unusually large amounts of blood. Passersby were amazed by the unusually large amounts of blood. Passersby were amazed by the unusually large amounts of blood. Passersby were amazed by the unusually large amounts of blood. Passersby were amazed by the unusually large amounts of blood. Passersby were amazed by the unusually large amounts of blood. Passersby were amazed by the unusually large amounts of blood. Passersby were amazed by the unusually large amounts of blood. Passersby were amazed by the unusually large amounts of blood. Passersby were

amazed by the unusually large amounts of blood. Passersby were amazed by the unusually large amounts of blood. Passersby were amazed by the unusually large amounts of blood. Passersby were amazed by the unusually large amounts of blood. Passersby were amazed by the unusually large amounts of blood. Passersby were amazed by the unusually large amounts of blood. Passersby were amazed by the unusually large amounts of blood. Passersby were amazed by the unusually large amounts of blood. Passersby were

> ## Is that all I am to you—a *valet?*

amazed by the unusually large amounts of blood. Passersby were amazed by the unusually large amounts of blood. Passersby were amazed by the unusually large amounts of blood. Passersby were amazed by the unusually large amounts of blood. Passersby were amazed by the unusually large amounts of blood. Passersby were amazed by the unusually large amounts of blood. Passersby were amazed by the unusually large amounts of blood. Passersby were amazed by the unusually large amounts of blood. Passersby were amazed by the unusually large amounts of blood. Passersby were

see YUKON page 245

SHERIFF from page 235

Above: Wanted al-Qaeda operative Ahmad Ibrahim Al-Mughassil (left) and Baraboo High School junior Michael Fairman, two leading suspects in the recent rash of Baraboo-area crimes.

similar nature have been reported.

"Over in Richland Center, we had some criminal activity occur dangerously close to unguarded reserves of fertilizer," Richland County police officer Tim Hutter said. "The report came from one Helen Johnson, who expressed fear for the safety of her cows. A cow found lying on its side could either be the victim of a chemical agent or of some immature teenager who thinks it's funny to sneak into the pasture and tip over a helpless animal. Either way, we can't be too cautious."

"All suspicious activity is worth investigating," Steinhorst said.

Steinhorst called upon all Baraboo citizens to report anything suspicious, especially since Deputy Dale Schneider broke his wrist last week subduing a drunken patron of the Come Back Inn, and Deputy Frank Pulvermacher can't work overtime since his mother got sick with dropsy.

Steinhorst said it's important to "not let fear get the better of us, but still remain vigilant."

"Just today, we had a report of some suspicious lettering by the high-school football field," Steinhorst said. "Upon investigation, we discovered the phrase '2005 Rules' burnt into the grass. An item of clothing found at the scene leads us to believe the cryptic phrase was the work of members of next year's senior class, and not, as was originally feared, the warning of an impending terrorist attack. So we can all breathe a little easier."

"You know, that football team is really shaping up this year," Steinhorst added. "We could go all the way to State." ∅

a string of harassing phone calls. The latest crime—the sudden disappearance of twoyield signs from Hoxie Street—occurred Monday.

"We believe the yield signs were removed in order to disrupt traffic patterns, most likely to cause an accident," Steinhorst said. "The party responsible for the crime could be anyone from suspected terrorist Ahmad Ibrahim Al-Mughassil, who is on the FBI's most-wanted list, to that Fairman kid and his buddies. It could be the work of one or the other. Possibly both, though I have to say I doubt that."

Responding to an anonymous report of a blue Ford Mustang seen idling in the Circus World parking lot for several hours after closing, Steinhorst said, "In these troubled times, any and all suspicious activity is worth investigating."

"This activity matches up with the M.O. of a terrorist casing a potential target," Steinhorst said. "It also matches the M.O. of a group of teens drinking beer and fooling around. But, as Homeland Security Secretary Tom Ridge told us, we are in a state of heightened alert. We could come under attack anywhere, at any time, from any direction. The tip-off could be anything from a duffel bag abandoned in a bank lobby to a carload of people at a stop sign who exit the car all at once, only to reenter through different doors."

Steinhorst regularly receives Department of Homeland Security bulletins that include the names of suspected terrorists. He also makes frequent visits to Baraboo High School, where Principal Larry Stordahl provides him with a list of possible truants.

"Teens regularly act without regard for the consequences of their actions or concern for their own physical well-being," Steinhorst said. "So do terrorists."

According to Steinhorst, the first in the series of crimes currently under scrutiny occurred several months ago, on April 1, when an unknown party pulled a fire alarm in the Baraboo Community Library during a children's puppet show.

"The perpetrators of the April 1 incident may not even live in Sauk County," Steinhorst said. "They could be terrorists based in Madison. Or it could be students from Reedsburg High School, our nearby rival."

To investigate the possibility of the latter, the Sauk County Sheriff's Department has been exchanging intelligence with the sheriff in Richland County, where unsolved crimes of a

SWEETHEART from page 235

could have driven [Dunst] into the arms of such a cock."

"I never would've thought she'd be fooled by some Eurotrash pretty-boy gaylord with six-pack abs and a 100-foot yacht," Nashua, NH resident James Westerly said. "If we'd known that was what she wanted, we would have dyed our hair and bought her a bunch of expensive presents. But I always assumed our relationship was deeper than that. I really thought the U.S. and Kirsten Dunst were soulmates."

Added Philadelphia resident Joyce Lister: "Did you see those pictures in the *Enquirer* where [Nunes] had his shirt open so you could see some stupid tattoo on his chest? God, I hate that guy."

The U.S. then began to sob uncontrollably.

For the past week, Americans have been endlessly dissecting and discussing the "Dear John" letter we received from Dunst on Aug. 11.

"The letter from Kirsten really hurt

me," said Plains, GA resident Amy Treemont, who has loved Dunst ever since she saw her in *Little Women*. "Look at this section where she talks about needing to grow as a person and an actress. I didn't know she felt like we were keeping her down. Maybe she thought running off with that Nunes prick was easier than working out our problems."

Continued Treemont: "Kirsten, if you can hear this, we still love you and want you back."

Many dumped Americans said they were angry that Dunst broke up with them in a letter, feeling that a phone call would have been more appropriate. Those who have tried to reach her to discuss the matter report that her phone number has been changed.

"I think she owes us an explanation, but she won't agree to meet us for lunch," Prineville, OR resident Keith Starling said. "The U.S. deserves some closure. I mean, why did she leave us

for *him*, of all people? He's such a worthless poseur."

Residents of Florida said they came close to fighting Nunes Friday at a Miami Beach bar.

"We were all just drinking and trying to forget when he strolled in like he was King Shit," Miami's Terry Masters said. "I wanted to deck him right then and there. The bar went real quiet, and he was like, 'Doy... What's going on?' Like he didn't know. If it wasn't for our friends from Puerto Rico holding us back, I swear he'd be dead. Next time, we kick his ass on sight."

This week, Congress fiercely debated a piece of legislation that would have authorized the U.S. Army's 82nd Airborne Division to beat Nunes to within an inch of his life. Partisan bickering held up the bill, with Republicans wanting to add a rider labeling Nunes a "pussy" and Democrats wanting to call him a "first-class jerkoff."

Though reluctant to discuss the

messy breakup, Dunst said she still cares about the U.S. very much and never meant to hurt anyone, but that those of us who are seeking a reconciliation "shouldn't hold [our] breath."

"I'm not denying that there were wonderful moments and a lot of deep feelings between us," Dunst said. "There were just too many problems. What happened between [human shitpile] Gilberto [Nunes] and me happened naturally. He makes me feel special. The sooner everyone realizes that my relationship with him is for real, the sooner we can all get on with our lives."

Continued Dunst: "It's not like America has never changed its mind. Do I need tomention a certain woman named Julia Roberts? Or Meg Ryan, while I'm at it? If you ask me, America doesn't know what it wants."

In response to Dunst's comments, the U.S. decided to go on a three-day bender. ∅

Education Is Our Passport To The Something Or Other

By Pat Rybak

I once spoke to a couple who arrived in the U.S. as political refugees. They were poor, hungry, without friends, and of very limited resources, and yet they spent close to 70 percent of their income on the education of their son. I asked them why, and I'll never forget what they said. "People can take your house, your car, and your clothes. They can take away your family, your liberty, and even your life. But they can never—something about education."

Education is the single most important issue of today. More important than... you know, all the other issues combined. "Why is that?" you ask. Because it's the educated minds of the country that consider those issues and then, once they decide, go on ahead and figure out what we are going to do about those things.

Education is the whatchamacallit—the big base thingy under a house—for a prosperous life. We use education every day. Sign a contract this morning? You used reading comprehension. Balance your checkbook? You used math. You probably didn't realize you used geography to get to this symposium today. Did you look at the map on the back of your prospectuses? You, sir, were using geography. Then, of course, there are tangible financial benefits to obtaining higher degrees, such as what-have-you.

The other benefits of an education—the opposite of the practical benefits—are infinite. They are not unlike outer space in this respect. But just as scientists continue to send astronauts up into space's farthest reaches, in spite of its, you know, endlessness or whatever, we scholars attempt to fathom education's impractical effects on our minds and our futures, for, as scholars, this is what... I'm going to do now. Could you cue the nature sounds, Rachel?

Dim the lights.

With an education comes the ability to articulate oneself. With that ability comes Plato's Allegory of the Cave. Cavemen. Stonehenge. The Earl of Northumberland. Mr. Barnes and Mr. Noble. The Mayans, Beethoven's hearing, Dr. Mengele. Education is the keystone to these worlds; it's the arch that spans the doorway between the future and the past. Without education, a child cannot pass beneath that doorway. Such a child is left outside, in the present, for he does not have the tithe. That's enough of the lion sounds now. Rachel? That's enough.

Education. Education is the key that unlocks locked things. Education lets us approach problems analytically, see issues from multiple sides, and these valuable things are important. Education is essential to being able to communicate with the French in their own language. It is essential to being able to recognize this or that aria. It is essential to a whatchamacallit... when you get the wine? I am going to move on to the third portion of the planned presentation.

I obtained this pie chart from a web site and printed it. You see, according to scientists at a center of great learning, if 10 percent more Americans obtained a college degree, the future world—our greatest gift to our children—would be so affected as to... This poster board is pro-education.

With an education comes the ability to articulate oneself. With that ability comes Plato's Allegory of the Cave. Cavemen. Stonehenge. The Earl of Northumberland. Mr. Barnes and Mr. Noble. The Mayans, Beethoven's hearing, Dr. Mengele.

In conclusion, let me invite you to visualize an image from the Bible. It is the future, and we have no bodies to speak of. Above us, a translucent ramp into the sky, with celestial escalators, these escalators ridden by children, angels, all of them moving upwards, and at the ramp's apex: I forget. It's something about education. In order to guarantee that our future is like a quiet, beautiful, ramp thinga-majiggy in the sky, we must get every American child educated.

In order to get every American child educated, we must begin the process of education at home. Also, we must allocate not just money and teachers, facilities, libraries, but also... all those things and more. Much more. Only by granting every child equal access to the great font of knowledge can we do what we need to do as we move on into our future, the future of America, the future of the world. As that great general—Custer—said on the eve of that important evening, his final stand, he sat, warming his hands around a cocoa, and said, you know, "Everyone should have an education." ∅

Your Horoscope

**By Lloyd Schumner Sr.
Retired Machinist and
A.A.P.B.-Certified Astrologer**

Aries: (March 21–April 19)
This week, it's more important than ever to remember Moscow Rule No. 7: Lull your opposition into a false sense of complacency.

Taurus: (April 20–May 20)
Canadians are known the world over for their laid-back attitude, which makes it even stranger that thousands of them have barricaded you in your house.

Gemini: (May 21–June 21)
Your tireless efforts have finally united America's workers, but it's less glorious than it sounds, given that you're the NFL's director of brand marketing.

Cancer: (June 22–July 22)
You've finally run up against a problem your trusty meat cleaver can't solve, butthat's why they make big wooden mallets.

Leo: (July 23–Aug. 22)
An attempt to popularize the book-length homilies of Laura Ingalls Wilder will result in professional wrestling's strangest phase yet.

Virgo: (Aug. 23–Sept. 22)
Your inability to keep a recent fascination with the rock group Kansas to yourself will result in the first recorded use of a ducking stool since 1848.

Libra: (Sept. 23–Oct. 23)
When you finally come out of the coma, friends will cheer your decision to reveal your recipe for Polish Bacon Buns.

Scorpio: (Oct. 24–Nov. 21)
You won't exactly fade into obscurity after your death, considering that that's where you spent all of your life.

Sagittarius: (Nov. 22–Dec. 21)
When the aliens finally arrive, they'll be much less advanced than anyone expected, as evinced by your maiming under the bald tires of their out-of-control '79 Buick.

Capricorn: (Dec. 22–Jan. 19)
You'll be thrown into a panic when the doctor diagnoses you with ulnar nerve damage, until he explains that that's just funny-bone trouble.

Aquarius: (Jan. 20–Feb. 18)
Stephen Hawking will revise his controversial theory on black holes, leaving you stumped about that noisy thing in your sink that eats garbage.

Pisces: (Feb. 19–March 20)
The stars convey the wisdom that men and women are different, making you wonder momentarily if they might not just be giant fusion reactors after all.

BAKER from page 237

"Yeah, occasionally customers used to say stuff like they hated to eat my 'You're the purr-fect valentine' pussy cakes, because they were fascinated by all the intricate labial folds piped around the vagina," Nageli said. "But lately, I've come around to thinking that a spatula does essentially the same trick as a pastry tube. I mean, a vulva's a vulva, right?"

Nageli has even begun to design cakes without erotic content, such as a rectangular, two-layer cake he decorates to resemble a hardcover copy of the bestselling book *Tuesdays With Morrie*.

Nageli's business partner said he was "dismayed" by the baker's post-sexual period.

"I cannot sell a cake shaped like a remote control in an erotic bakery," DiPrima said. "Maybe I can make it look like a vibrator if I flick off these candy buttons. But only a pervert would think this resembles something you put up your ass."

Nageli's personal and professional decline is not unique. Erotic baker Brad Hicks, who closed his Oshkosh, WI establishment The Sexy Sweet Shoppe in February 2000, complained of similar disillusionment, which he described as "classic burnout."

"I'm not sure if my divorce caused me to lose inspiration for my work, or if it was making those endless Torpedo Tit Tarts that destroyed my marriage," said Hicks, now a postal worker. "But at some point, a little voice inside my head said, 'Brad, if you don't care how 'come' is spelled on a cake, maybe the naughty-pastry business isn't the place for you anymore.'"

Using milk to thin the batter for what would eventually become a sagging breast cake, Nageli admitted that he could understand why an erotic-cake customer might not want to buy one of his newer creations.

"I realize most of my customers would prefer cakes that said 'Eat Me' instead of 'Maybe Later, Baby,'" Nageli said. "But maybe there's a hidden, untapped novelty pastry market for people just like me." ∅

the ONION®

VOLUME 40 ISSUE 34   AMERICA'S FINEST NEWS SOURCE™   26 AUG.–1 SEPT. 2004

NEWS

Kerry's Face Droops With Joy Over Latest Polls

see POLITICS page 4B

Child Buried In Backyard Under Popsicle-Stick Cross

see OBITUARIES page 17E

Wife Embarrasses Husband In Front Of Prostitute

see LOCAL page 4D

Photoshop Actually Bought

see TECHNOLOGY page 6G

STATshot

A look at the numbers that shape your world.

What Are We Spending Our Disaster Relief On?

- **13%** Nine-months-overdue cable bill
- **17%** Private eye to track down kitchen
- **29%** New "disaster-proof" aluminum siding
- **10%** Jimmy Buffett box set
- **12%** Having goddamned Epcot ball towed out of pool
- **19%** Same thing we spent last year's disaster relief on

Above: Three local river dwellers inspect the unfamiliar, lustrous object.

Shiny, Wriggling Object Attracting Interest Among Fish Community

BRULE RIVER, WI—The appearance of a shiny, bobbling object in the water of the Brule, just upstream of the big sunken oak stump, is generating considerable interest among members of the fish community, river sources reported Monday.

"The luminous, gray-dappled exterior of this dipping and jogging object is so captivating that trout, bass, bluegill, and even members of the normally indifferent carp population are drawn to its undulant movement," said a 67-day-old yellow perch who has lived in the Brule all his life.

The perch added: "No one's sure what it is, but it certainly has our attention."

Descriptions vary due to differing levels of color vision and depth perception, but freshwater residents agree that the object is about the length of three adult crickets, laid end to end.

One freshwater source said the object appeared near the stump just after sunrise, then migrated sinuously upstream.

"I saw the shiny object this morning," an eight-pound walleyed pike said. "I was up in that area by the stump waiting for the late-summer caddis-fly hatch that should be coming any day

see OBJECT page 245

T.G.I. Friday's Given One Last Shot

HOUSTON—In spite of experiences he has had with T.G.I. Friday's in the past, Nate Greisberg has decided to give the popular restaurant a final chance, the 29-year-old told reporters Monday.

"Well, okay," Greisberg said, after his friend Tom Hazen asked him to dinner at one of 526 T.G.I. Friday's nationwide. "I'll give Friday's one last shot. But if they screw up this time, it's over. I really mean it, Tom. You can only be let down so many times before you say, 'Enough is enough.'"

Greisberg estimates that he has dined at T.G.I. Friday's between 10

see FRIDAY'S page 244

Online University Cracks Down On Rowdy Online Fraternity

MINNEAPOLIS, MN—Capella University, one of the nation's most heavily trafficked institutions of online learning, issued a stern disciplinary e-mail message to the members of the

disorderly Alpha Sigma Sigma online fraternity Monday.

"Alpha Sigma Sigma has not only broken the rules included in each distance learner's Online Application User Agreement, but they have also continually thwarted our efforts to create a serious online-learning community and an inclusive e-campus," Capella Dean of Students Theodore Albertson said. "This rowdy fraternity has been a thorn in the school's side for years, and frankly, we've had enough."

Since opening its Capella chapter in 1996, the online fraternity has been cited numerous times for conducting illicit co-ed chatroom parties and circulating anti-administration Quick-Time videos. In 1999, the university officially censured Alpha Sigma

see UNIVERSITY page 244

Above: Greisberg, who has committed to at least one more visit to this restaurant.

The Widening Income Gap

According to a recent report based on census data, the gap between the rich and poor widened in 2003. What do *you* think?

Rick Lembecker
Developer

"Good. I was having a hard time telling the rich and poor apart."

Andrew Meijor
Social Worker

"What does 'rich' or 'poor' even mean? And before you start, I don't want to hear any of that 'annual household income' nonsense."

Sheila Reed
Nurse

"Sure, the rich are getting richer and the poor are getting poorer. But the great untold story is that the people in the exact middle are becoming a whole lot middler, too."

Gary Wundrow
Systems Analyst

"If this keeps up, I might finally be able to hire myself a white maid."

Kimberly Szaflarski
Bill Collector

"I realize that, historically, phrases like 'massive redistribution of wealth' are usually accompanied by rivers of blood. That said, it's about time for a massive redistribution of wealth."

David Martinovich
Salesman

"Bottom line is, you're not buying this lawn mower."

The Republican National Convention

The Republican National Convention will be held in New York City Aug. 30 through Sept. 2. What will the event feature?

★ Massive, well-choreographed effort to make Republican politicians look like normal Americans

★ Easy-listening music piped in throughout the convention center to drown out sound of protesters outside

★ Trick shootin' showcase with John Ashcroft

★ Tour of New York City that carefully steers clear of gay, black, Hispanic, poor, artsy, and middle-class neighborhoods

★ Display of Ronald Reagan's exhumed body in glass cabinet in Madison Square Garden lobby

★ A spirit-building game of Pin The Blame On The Donkey

★ Speeches by your class president, the homecoming queen, and the head cheerleader

★ Under cover of night, Republicans will sneak out of convention center to sack city

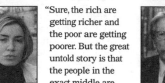

the ONION®
America's Finest News Source.™

Herman Ulysses Zweibel
Founder

T. Herman Zweibel
Publisher Emeritus
J. Phineas Zweibel
Publisher
Maxwell Prescott Zweibel
Editor-In-Chief

242

Well, Those White House Security Guards Certainly Were Rude

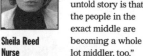

By Marjorie Lemont

I've traveled all over this country, but I don't believe that I've ever in all my years been treated as poorly as I was at the White House today. I was shouted at, grabbed, and treated like some sort of vagabond. I would expect that sort of thing in Russia, but not in a free country. Those uniformed guards sure could stand to learn some manners.

It all started in the Blue Room. Our tour guide told us it was where Grover Cleveland was married. I had no idea that anyone was married in the White House. It must have been splendid, with dignitaries and captains dressed in the fineries of the day. I figured that if we were allowed to go into the Blue Room, we would be allowed to poke around for wedding-photo albums. I was trying to get to the drawers, and, well, a certain White House security guard had other ideas. There was no need for him to take that tone with me! I am a human being, not a bad dog. He repeated, "Ma'am, please stay behind the ropes" at least 10 times.

And that wasn't the worst part. How the heck was I to know where the bathroom was? I'd had a jumbo Diet Pepsi in the Smithsonian cafeteria earlier, and I had to go number one! I would have asked the tour guide to show me where the restroom was, but he was in the middle of a speech about all the historical meetings that have taken place in the Oval Office. (Not that we were allowed in the Oval Office. They only let us peer at it from around the corner, like peeping toms.) Anyway, rather than interrupt the guide, I used my smarts. I thought, "If this were my house, where would the bathroom be?" I figured it would be upstairs, so I left the tour group on my own to avoid making a scene.

Well, lord oh me, what a mistake that was! Before I got halfway up the stairs, five men had surrounded me. They wouldn't even let me go do my business before they led me into some little side room and asked me a bunch of questions. When I reached into my pocket for a Kleenex, a guard grabbed my arm like I was a common criminal. Grabbed my arm right there! Can you imagine being treated like that? I told him, "I am a taxpayer, so this is my house, too!"

They insisted on waving me up and down with a metal-detector wand, even though I told them that I'd already gone through security on the way in. It's as if they didn't even hear me. They even looked through my fanny pack before they let me go back to the group.

That wasn't the last of it. The guard in Lincoln's bedroom was even more abusive. I tried to tell him that I just wanted to get a closer look at the place where Lincoln was laid out before he was buried, but he wouldn't let me get a word in edgewise. He was all, "Ma'am, step back" and "Excuse me, excuse me, ma'am." Well, I never! Here's a little helpful hint: If you don't want people to touch the presidential portraits, put them behind plastic. How could anyone resist running a finger along Eisenhower's forehead?

Besides, what's the point of showing us things if we can't take pictures of them? "No flash photography," indeed. The tour guide told me that flashes fade the valuable artifacts, but my family has taken our Christmas photo in front of our shadow box for the past 20 years, and my porcelain kitten statuettes look as nice as the day I bought them! Well, I didn't know how to turn the flash off on my darn camera, and I didn't drive all the way to Washington for nothing, so I just thought I'd snap a couple of the less significant portraits. Can you believe the guide bit my head off for something so innocent? He even threatened to take my camera away until the end of the tour. Honestly.

In Chatfield, where I'm from, they don't treat you like that. At the Chatfield Library, the librarian always lets me use the employee bathroom if I'm back in the periodicals section. And I can touch anything I want. I even went behind the desk once to grab a pencil, and they didn't clap me in irons. In Washington, however, they acted like I was some sort of… well, to be honest, I have no idea *what* they thought.

I've been treated shabbily this entire vacation. On the way into the Capitol building, they went through my purse. You never go through a woman's purse! That's where she keeps her feminine things. Then, at the National Air and Space Museum, they yelled at me because I was lingering in the space capsule too long. It's not like I could've flown to the moon in that thing, even if it worked, which it didn't.

Well, if that's how they do things in the nation's capital, it's quite a shame. People in Chatfield know how to treat their fellow man with respect. You had better believe that I'm going to write to my congressman and let him know a thing or two. Maybe I can spare some other curious citizen this sort of indignity.

You know, I was going to vote for President Bush again, but after this, I might think twice. ⌀

Dolph Lundgren Wins Long, Courageous Battle Against Fame

NEW YORK—In 1983, the future looked bright for Hans Lundgren. A native of Stockholm, Sweden, Lundgren had already schooled at the Royal Institute of Technology, attended Washington State University on an academic scholarship, and completed his masters degree in Chemical Engineering at the University of Sydney in Australia. Then, the young scientist was awarded the prestigious Fullbright Scholarship to MIT. But it was while he was on his way to Boston to continue his studies that the burgeoning scientist's life took a fateful turn—one that would leave Lundgren fighting for a normal existence for the next 20 years. While working at the trendy Limelight Disco in New York, he met noted drama coach Warren Robertson, who spotted in Lundgren the early signs of fame.

"[Lundgren] was stunned by the diagnosis; he thought he was too young and emotionally healthy to be an actor," said Michael Portnoy, Lundgren's manager. "People with so much intellectual potential never think something like stardom can happen to them. But he was a 6'6" karate champ with striking blond hair—an IQ of 160 meant nothing."

In 1985, Lundgren made his feature-film debut in the James Bond movie *A View To A Kill*.

Following the major breakout of his catch phrase from *Rocky IV*, "I must break you," Lundgren couldn't deny it any longer: Hans, now rechristened Dolph, had fame.

"It all happened so suddenly," Portnoy said. "He got Venz in *A View To A Kill*. Then he was informed he had the role of Ivan Drago, Sylvester Stallone's opponent in *Rocky IV*."

Following the major breakout of his catch phrase from *Rocky IV*, "I must break you," Lundgren couldn't deny it any longer: Hans, now rechristened Dolph, had fame.

"Dolph thought he had it under control," longtime friend and fellow fame survivor Chazz Palminteri said. "Maybe it was because so many people close to him were similarly afflicted—his girlfriend Grace Jones... fellow non-native English speaker Arnold Schwarzenegger."

"It didn't help that the public never understood the complications of his fame," Palminteri said. "People all over were walking around, saying his lines, styling their hair like Dolph's looked after going through months of shooting *Rocky*. They didn't care that a normal life was at stake."

After a year away from the box office, Lundgren's symptoms went into remission. However, his condition flared up unexpectedly, when he got *Red Scorpion*, *The Punisher*, and, most seriously, *Masters Of The Universe*.

After this, it seemed that Lundgren's fame would overtake his life. His condition was so severe that people stared at him on the street. He could rarely leave the house without the help of an entourage.

"But even at the height of it, Lundgren

see LUNDGREN page 245

Right: Lundgren, who fought fame for almost 20 years.

NEWS IN BRIEF

Swing States Roughed Up By Bush, Kerry Operatives

WASHINGTON, DC—The 22 battleground states in the 2004 presidential election said Monday that they have received threats, both direct and veiled, from Kerry and Bush campaign operatives. "Now, you listen up, Iowa—you're voting for Kerry, see, and you're gonna like it," an unidentified Kerry-Edwards thug allegedly told the Midwestern state, which controls seven electoral votes. "Youse got some real nice agribusiness in your state. Sure would be a shame to see you lose it. Get the picture?" In a similar vein, should Ohio's 20 votes not end up in the red column, a team of Bush's goons has allegedly threatened to throw the state's several thousand wheelchair-bound grandmothers down a flight of stairs.

CEO Spends 30 Percent Of Earnings Staying Out Of Jail

NEW YORK—Bellcroft Industries CEO Robert M. Burdick said Monday that he spends up to 30 percent of his $2.4 million salary keeping himself out of jail. "Accountants who can hide illegal profits and lawyers who know how to set up off-shore companies don't come cheap," Burdick said. "My recent 20 percent raise isn't that great when you consider how many people I have to pay to keep me out of prison." In addition to losing 30 percent off the top each year, Burdick spends 5 percent of his income on taxes.

Salad Rendered Unhealthy In Three Steps

PINE BLUFF, AR—A nutritious meal was rendered unhealthy in three easy steps Monday, when area resident Kimberly Lowen, 24, added ranch dressing, grated cheese, and four crumbled strips of bacon to a bowl of romaine lettuce and tomatoes. "Who says not eating right has to take a lot of time?" Lowen said. "It only took minutes to prepare a salad that will provide me with my daily recommended intake of fat and sodium." Lowen has previously rendered a glass of skim milk unhealthy, simply by adding ice cubes and chocolate syrup and mixing it in a blender on low.

Customer Service Operator Safely In Remote Location

PHOENIX, AZ—Incompetent and uncaring U-Haul helpline operator Kamio Morton's remote Phoenix location is the only thing protecting him from brutal, bloody revenge at the hands of thousands of irate customers, sources reported Monday. "Listen, shitass, get me a tow truck right this fucking minute or, so help me God, I'll gut you," stranded Brooklyn motorist Don Jewison said from the shoulder of Chicago's I-294, where he had been awaiting assistance for more than four hours. "Put me on hold one more time, and I'll put you in the fucking hospital." Jewison is the 63rd motorist to impotently threaten Morton's life this year, a streak that is expected to come to a sudden end when a U-Haul truck inevitably breaks down within walking distance of Phoenix.

Prizes On *Price Is Right* Looking Better As Man Ages

YORBA LINDA, CA—Local electrician Ryan DeRegotis, 35, said Tuesday that the prizes on *The Price Is Right* look more appealing every year. "I gotta say, a dinette set and a china cabinet would be nice," DeRegotis said. "If I were called out of the studio audience, I'd be thrilled to win something as practical as a washer and dryer. Do you have any idea how expensive those things are?" DeRegotis added that he wouldn't turn up his nose at a year's supply of Rice-A-Roni. ∅

Sigma for conducting illegal hazing activities, in which pledges were coerced into participating in lewd and embarrassing acts via webcam.

More serious infractions involved illegal activities. In 2002, several Alpha Sigma Sigma members were arrested for purchasing alcohol from Wine.com with falsified driver's licenses and credit-card numbers. Then, in the spring of 2003, fraternity members hacked into the web site of rival University of Phoenix Online, erased its mascot, and placed a down-

Albertson has ordered Alpha Sigma Sigma brothers to vacate their web space by Sept. 1.

loaded version on their own web site. Although no one was ever charged with the theft of the copyrighted clip art, the online fraternity was warned that further misbehavior would result in serious disciplinary action.

"There's no place for this sort of activity at Capella," Albertson said. "Students should be focusing on getting the real-world skills they need to advance their careers, not getting drunk and leaving profane postings on bulletin boards hours after curfew."

Albertson has ordered Alpha Sigma Sigma brothers to vacate their web space by Sept. 1. Any files left on the group's former server will be confiscated and deleted.

In his e-mail, Albertson singled out Alpha Sigma Sigma's webmaster David "Skipper" Gudis and forums moderator Ralph "Chip" Tanner—both enrolled in the school's 12-month MBA program—for their "utter disrespect

for the traditions and customs upon which the online university was built."

Gudis is notorious among Capella students for creating LadiesOfCapella.wmv, an online facebook containing streaming web video of women from the online Alpha Alpha Kappa sorority. During the first two weeks of August, the monthly bandwidth use for the site, which was viewed more than 7,000 times, averaged a whopping 60.4 GB, costing the university thousands of dollars.

Many students have voiced their support for the fraternity.

"If you take down Alpha Sig, you might as well just take down the WHOLE online university," wrote Inez Sanchez, a School of Technology student. "Their the heart & soul of this college, and if YOU and [Capella president Sandra] McIntyre are 2 BLIND 2 see that, ur in 4 a BIG surprise."

On Epinions.com's ranking of online colleges and universities, Capella University is rated four out of five stars. McIntyre said the school would have an even better rating if not for Alpha Sigma Sigma.

"Capella University offers degrees in 40 areas of specialization and is fully accredited by The Higher Learning Commission," McIntyre told reporters Friday. "We've worked too hard to develop our reputation to see it ruined by a few bad seeds."

Peter "Mosaic" Hoyle, who has been a student at Capella since its inception in 1994, was also named in the complaint. Beloved by many students for both his slovenly appearance in his online photo album and his outlandish instant messages, Hoyle has been enrolled in more than 100 courses, but with attendance so poor that most professors do not even recognize his username.

According to McIntyre, Hoyle appears to do little more than lurk

DRINK!!! DRINK!!! DRINK!!!

Hey dUdes Chip's totally passed out!

. . .

Let's fuckin PISS in his mouth!

PISS!!! PISS!!! PISS!!!

Above: Alpha Sigma Sigma brothers attend a recent chatroom party.

around university message boards and participate in fraternity hijinks.

"In 10 years, that troublemaker Hoyle has done nothing but take up bandwidth that might be used by more deserving students, like those who spend their free time at LibrarySpot.com," McIntyre said. "If Hoyle's father hadn't helped me get this place off the ground, I would've had him expelled long ago."

Hours after McIntyre made her comments, the entire Capella student body received an e-mail message containing a clip of embarrassing McIntyre family-picnic video footage in which the Capella president falls into a swimming pool.

Hearing about this latest prank, Al-

bertson banged his fist angrily on his desk and said Alpha Sigma Sigma members have until Sept. 1 to raise $10,000 to cover their bandwidth fees "or it's all over for those hoodlums."

Although no e-vites have been sent, several Capella student blogs report that the fraternity intends to throw one last chatroom party Friday, at which they will solicit donations via PayPal in an effort to save the fraternity.

Sanchez said she doubts that the plan will work. According to the student, Albertson has personal motivations for targeting the group—namely, that Alpha Sigma rejected him when he rushed the fraternity in 1996 as an incoming freshman at Capella. ∅

FRIDAY'S from page 241

and 15 times, adding that almost every visit has been disappointing. While he acknowledged that the food is "sometimes pretty good," he dubbed the restaurant's atmosphere "irritating."

"It's always something," Greisberg said, sighing heavily. "Sometimes, the waitress rubs me the wrong way. Then another time, the service is great, but I'm stuck next to a table full of frat guys. I'd never choose the place if I was picking. I'd either go to the diner near my house or Applebee's."

Greisberg's worst experiences with the restaurant have included sitting near a bachelorette party, and waiting more than an hour for his food during a dinner rush.

In spite of such incidents, Greisberg said he tries to keep an open mind when friends tell him they like T.G.I. Friday's.

"This girl I work with says she likes Friday's because it's so horrible it's funny," Greisberg said. "I can't really understand that. It's not the best place

in the world, but it's not the worst. It's just kind of there. And besides, who wants a funny restaurant?"

After almost refusing to eat at T.G.I. Friday's, Greisberg changed his mind when he remembered an ad he'd seen for the restaurant's Jack Daniel's Shrimp special.

"I decided the shrimp might not be the worst thing in the world," Greisberg said. "I told Tom I'd go, but I said, 'If I wait an hour for a cold appetizer, only to have my dinner come out a minute later, that's absolutely it.'"

"Tom seemed blown away by that," Greisberg added. "T.G.I. Friday's is one of his favorite places to eat."

Greisberg admitted that he once had a good time at a T.G.I. Friday's, while visiting friends in Seattle. But he qualified his praise, saying that the restaurant itself had little to do with his enjoyment.

"When you're hanging out with John [Pilmeyer] and Tim [Gracowski], you're going to have a wild time,"

Greisberg said. "We were already drunk, so we decided to go to Friday's and get some Sesame Jack Chicken Strips and some Loaded Potato Skins. We ate, had a few pitchers, and got out of there."

Other members of Greisberg's peer group have reservations about T.G.I. Friday's, as well.

"Our friend Dave [Hildebrand] can't stand the stuff they have on the walls," Greisberg said. "If someone suggests Friday's, he tries to turn the group in favor of Olive Garden. I think a part of me wants to join him... If tonight doesn't go well, I just might do that."

Greisberg said the ultimatum does not extend to the T.G.I. Friday's bar area.

"This is just about the dining area," Greisberg said. "I have no problem with the bar. The drinks are reasonable, and sometimes there are hot women there. As long as we don't stay there all night, I'll do the bar."

Greisberg said he's not looking for a "mind-blowing" dining experience,

but that he simply wants a normal evening out with no surprises.

"All I want is for my food to be good and on time," Greisberg said. "I'd also like for there to be no screw-up with the bill and for Tom and me to be able to hear each other talk. If those conditions are met, I will eat at T.G.I. Friday's another day. If they are not, what can I say?"

Hazen said he's confident that Greisberg won't see the ultimatum through.

"Nate's always saying stupid shit like this," Hazen said. "I remember when he said he wouldn't waste money on another stadium concert, because he hates the crowds. But then, when a bunch of us said we were going to see Prince this summer, he was the first to buy tickets."

"Well, Friday's is where we hang out," Hazen added. "He's going to have a much lighter social calendar if he refuses to come with. I would recommend that he think his decision through very seriously." ∅

Above: Lundgren, shown in the throes of fame in this 1986 photo.

refused to stop fighting," Palminteri said. "Finally, he made some very important choices about his life, and as a direct result, things began to turn around."

Palminteri was likely referring to the rumors of Lundgren's mid-'90s participation in a controversial Hollywood treatment—it is said that, in the hope of preventing the further spread of fame, Lundgren took massive doses of B-movies.

According to Palminteri, Lundgren's part in *Universal Soldier* brought his fame into remission. The pairing of Lundgren with another heavily accented actor, Jean-Claude Van Damme, was enough to crush his case of fame head on.

"It was a risky treatment," Portnoy said. "Stallone tried a similar one, but to this day, he suffers from residual fame. In Lundgren's case, though, it seemed to work. People wanted to see

a vulnerability in their action stars, but Dolph stayed strong and fought this trend. Had Lundgren lacked the

---

Lundgren continued to act in films, but by 1997, when he appeared opposite Michael Sarrazin in the action thriller The Peacekeeper, his fame was fully under control.

---

courage to suffer through roles like Maj. Jack Holloway in *Storm Catch-*

er, he might be famous today."

Lundgren continued to act in films, but by 1997, when he appeared opposite Michael Sarrazin in the action thriller *The Peacekeeper*, his fame was fully under control. Though Lundgren has appeared in 11 films since then, most people would be hard-pressed to name one of them.

"By using prescription sunglasses and a hat, Mr. Lundgren is now able to live a normal life," Portnoy said. "At most, he may be recognized as 'that Russian guy.' There's always the danger of a relapse—for instance, if a new generation forms a kitsch appreciation for his body of work, or if he carelessly slips into a series of smaller roles of a high caliber. But, given that he's just completed his directorial debut with a film called *The Defender*—in which he co-stars with Jerry Springer—I don't see that as a concern for the near future." ✐

now, when it came out of the air. It rose out for a time, only to reappear again by the stump a minute or so later."

The walleye characterized the object as "mesmerizingly minnow-esque."

"The bass were the first to talk about it, but they're kind of a coarse fish," the walleye said, slowly swaying his tail fin from right to left. "It's when the trout get involved that you have to take notice. They're cautious, generally. When I saw that even they were gathering around the glinting thing, I thought, 'Well, I'm game!'"

Some say they have seen the object before, on weekday evenings and weekend days. Local authorities have

---

"The bass were the first to talk about it," the walleye said.

---

had difficulty gaining a consensus, however, because river fish do not commonly associate in schools.

Aquatic experts say that decisive action will be taken regarding the object in the near future.

"Someone's going to lunge for it," said a black crappie, speaking for members of the river's large *Pomoxis nigromaculatus* population. "What we are seeing now is a contest between patience and curiosity. We're enraptured, frankly. Is it the shininess, like unto the scales of a smaller fish? Or the flickering, recalling the wings of a struggling beetle? Perhaps it's those baffling silver extensions, glinting so in the light. What are they? And, then, of course, there is the wriggling. The wriggling! Like a helpless, flailing tadpole, when you have him in your mouth, and you experience that delicious moment when he still might get away."

Added the crappie: "All I know is, I can't take either of my non-stereoscopic eyes off of it."

Not every species was impressed.

"That shiny thing, that ain't no new thing," said a 19-pound muskellunge who traveled up the nearby chain of lakes to the Brule earlier this summer. "That thing is in all the rivers. These guys have no long-term memory at all. Brains is too small."

Although interest in the object varies, with smaller panfish being the least curious and larger freshwater predators sustaining their interest over several hours, no fish has yet made contact with the object.

"Shiny as it is, wriggly as it is, and tempting as it would be to just snatch it up, there's a feeling in the downstream area that it isn't to be taken lightly," said a brown trout and self-described expert in shiny objects. "No one will soon forget the example set by that perch a couple years ago. Why, they say he brashly ignored the elders' repeated warnings about suspiciously colored worms, and he hasn't been seen since." ✐

What's Hot Besides The Weather? Find Out Here!

**The Outside Scoop
By Jackie Harvey**

This is a special edition of The Outside Scoop. It's time for the Jackie Harvey Hot List! This is where I make my picks on the big things to watch for in 2004, by declaring them "hot." And, in this case, it's not the humidity heating things up. Grab a Popsicle and let's go!

Hot Summer Sport! The Olympics is just the mouthwash I needed to wash the bad taste of the presidential race out of my mouth. Do you suppose that's why the elections and the Olympics line up? I have my eye on Breaux Greer to take the gold in the javelin, and I have my eye on the whole U.S. Olympic team, because that's where the heroes are born.

Hot Pastime! Do you know what the hot new entertainment thing is? **Video games.** According to my research, the little quarter-munchers are really hot again, and they're making as much money as movies. But I don't know if I buy that—no computer can replace a good old-fashioned movie. That said, I have to warn you: I'm a pretty good hand at **Zaxxon.** Watch out, arcade hounds!

Hot Party! This and every year, the **Surprise Party** is on fire. It's a good way to add spice to a birthday, a retirement, or even a wedding. Wedding, you say? Try this on for size: A bride and groom show up at church. The groom is wearing his tailored black tuxedo with cummerbund and all the classic details. The bride is in her dress. They step into the church, and what's this? No one is there. The church is completely empty. And then… **Surprise!** People jump up from behind the pews, and a fake wall flips around to reveal a kindly organist at her pipe organ. The priest lowers from the ceiling and the festivities begin.

Hot Actor! It doesn't seem like you can cruise through Glamourland for long without cruising past **Tom Cruise.** This time, he's playing the baddie in **Collateral Damage,** a shot-for-shot remake of **Governor Schwarzenegger's** film of the same name.

Hot TV! After months of hemming and hawing, I decided to take the plunge into the 21st century and get the dish. Since it's a satellite signal, and therefore works using atoms, I thought there wouldn't be any need to drill holes in my house and string wires into my television. I was kind of right, since there's no wire running from the satellite to my house, but in-side my house, there's a whole wire octopus. Anyway, the octopus stays, because I'm addicted to the show **Entourage.** Gosh, that's a fine show. As an entertainment journalist, I always like to get a glimpse behind the lights and glamour, and that's just what I get from *Entourage.* Maybe someday, I'll get together a posse that will talk me into buying a car, and then I'll get them to go out to parties with me. Or maybe someone I grew up with will

> **Hot Pastime! Do you know what the hot new entertainment thing is? Video games. According to my research, the little quarter-munchers are really hot again, and they're making as much money as movies.**

make it big, and I can be the angel on his shoulder who guides him through the rough waters of fame. I can't decide which.

Hot Comedian! Getting premium channels has another benefit, and that is that I now have The Comedy Network. I love to laugh, and this is my one-stop channel for yuks galore! I am a recent convert to **Dave Sharpelle.** He works a little blue, but his imitation of **James Brown** cracks me right up. I'm James Brown, b-word!

Hot Dead Funk Icon! Buffalo's native funkster James Brown died of natural causes. Rest in peace. **I feel good!**

Hot Garden Vegetable! It's been a good year for **tomatoes** in the Harvey garden. I've been using a secret fertilizer, and it's been working like a charm. Every plant has about eight tomatoes on it, and they're almost ready to be harvested. You know what that means? **Salsa** time!

Hot Starlet! Lindsay Loman, whom I have mentioned in the past, is a real up-and-comer. Wanna know who the next **Julia Roberts** is? Look no further. I don't know what her next project is, but she's still riding high on **Bad Girls,** so Harvey fans can bet it's going to be bad. Bad as in good, I mean. I'll be first in line.

Hot Super Hero! I saw **Spider-Man 2,** and I can't remember the last time I was so excited by a movie. It had action, heart, and **Alfred Molina,** who first caught my eye in **Cabin Boy.**

Hot Toiletry! As soon as I'm done with my stick of Arid XX, I'm going to break into the five-pack of **Mitchum Gel** I bought at the Price Club, on sale

> **Hot Starlet! Lindsay Loman, whom I have mentioned in the past, is a real up-and-comer. Wanna know who the next Julia Roberts is?**

for $7. Who can pass up a deal like that? Plus, I love supporting **Robert Mitchum** and his wife **Lady Mitchum.** I hope it works, since I'm going to be using it for the next year.

Hot Broadcast Channel! When summer is full of reruns, thank goodness for **Fox.** They've taken the summer and given us a new reason not to turn off our air conditioning. In comedy, they have **Quintuplets**—where former **Late Night Show** co-host **Andy Richer** plays a father of four crazy kids—and **Geoffrey Beene,** a nostalgic look back at the '50s. It's like **The Wonder Years,** only a bit more randy. And did someone say **reality**? They give us plenty of that, with **Trading Spouses,** the return of **The Simple Life,** and tons of **The Casino.** They even showed **Man Vs. Beast 1** and **Man Vs. Beast 2** again! I already knew the winner, but I still got a thrill out of seeing people battle **Mother Nature.**

Hot Deceased Starlet! Fay Wray, the star who made a monkey out of King Kong, passed away this month. I hope that's the last death we have to deal with until the end of summer, because we need a chance to rest.

That's the running tally of what's hot this summer. In the next installment, I'll be back with some hot news about the academic workload of the **Olsen sisters** and the newest rock 'n' roll-themed celebrity hot spot in the Burbank area. Until then, I'll be waiting for you, in the aisle, on The Outside! ✇

Your Horoscope

**By Lloyd Schumner Sr.
Retired Machinist and
A.A.P.B.-Certified Astrologer**

Aries: (March 21–April 19)
Your love is dead, but dead love is not like a dead person. All the car batteries, radioactive injections, and monkey extract in the world won't bring it back.

Taurus: (April 20–May 20)
Certain factors beyond your control—albeit not beyond your comprehension—will prevent you from being initiated into the Sapphic mysteries.

Gemini: (May 21–June 21)
You always thought ghosts could fly, walk through walls, and commune with those yet living, but you'll just have to be content with knocking over the occasional teacup.

Cancer: (June 22–July 22)
You've always considered yourself something of a shutterbug, but that's certainly not what the Interpol agents who confiscate your hard drive will call you.

Leo: (July 23–Aug. 22)
They say beggars can't be choosers, but to hell with them—you don't feel like going to the soup kitchen.

Virgo: (Aug. 23–Sept. 22)
You really shouldn't let the weather get you down—unless, of course, you call a rain of house-sized asteroids "weather."

Libra: (Sept. 23–Oct. 23)
People are fond of saying that teaching a pig to sing will just waste your time and annoy the pig, once again undervaluing the importance of education.

Scorpio: (Oct. 24–Nov. 21)
Your "nationwide rollout" of a new women's razor will make headlines, but it certainly won't be in the business section.

Sagittarius: (Nov. 22–Dec. 21)
Brave men and women of the revolution will sacrifice their lives, fortunes, and sacred honor to free you from your chains, but their music really sucks.

Capricorn: (Dec. 22–Jan. 19)
There may not even be an NHL season this year, so it won't make a ripple when you nearly kill a guy with a hockey stick.

Aquarius: (Jan. 20–Feb. 18)
They say poetry is the unwatered wine of life, but regular old watered wine has always been good enough for you.

Pisces: (Feb. 19–March 20)
The stars usually concern themselves with your future, but they just wanted to remind you that at this time last year, you were "very seriously" considering law school.

NEWS

the ONION®

VOLUME 40 ISSUE 35   AMERICA'S FINEST NEWS SOURCE™   2–8 SEPTEMBER 2004

Vacationing Bush Accepts Republican Nomination Via Live Satellite Feed

see POLITICS page 3C

Tooth Fairy Helps Self To More Teeth

see LOCAL page 12F

David Hyde Pierce Sits Back, Lets The Prissy-Voice-Work Checks Roll In

see ENTERTAINMENT page 4E

STATshot

A look at the numbers that shape your world.

What Are We Making Small Talk About?

14% How new water cooler differs from old one

19% Giant warehouse fire across the street

22% Today's small-talking points

11% Whitey

16% That baby-drowning thing from last month

18% Oh, this and that

0 74470 94595 6   00
THE ONION • $2.00 US • $3.00 CAN

Al-Jazeera Introduces 'Lighter Side Of The News' Segment

DOHA, QATAR— With the stated intent of "turning current-events coverage on its head," the popular but oft-criticized Al-Jazeera Arab television news network launched its "Lighter Side Of The News" segment Monday.

"And now, we have something a little different for you," anchor Jihan Jalami said, turning from coverage of violence in Najaf.

"It seems a certain suicide bomber paid the price for his sloppy job Sunday, when he failed to annihilate a Jerusalem pizza parlor, and himself along with it. After numerous attempts to detonate the homemade

see AL-JAZEERA page 251

Above: Jalami reports on a badly bungled bombing.

Small Group Of Dedicated Rich People Change The World

Above: An oil magnate from Texas (right) makes a difference at the Republican National Convention.

NEW YORK—Cynics often say that one man can't make a difference in a huge and complicated world. But this week in New York, a few tremendously rich and powerful men have given those naysayers reason to reconsider their views. At the Republican National Convention, which concludes Thursday, a handful of dedicated men will change the world.

RNC attendee Stewart Malmough is unremarkable at first glance. His name rarely appears in print—outside of the occasional Forbes 100 list— and his face isn't one many citizens would recognize. But he

see RICH page 250

Historians Discover Children's Menu On Back Of U.S. Constitution

WASHINGTON, DC—Historians and scholars nationwide heralded the discovery of a children's menu on the back of one of the four original charters of the U.S. Constitution, Archivist of the United States John Carlin said Monday.

The U.S. Constitution And Children's Menu, originally drawn up at the Constitutional Convention in Philadelphia in 1787, is housed at the National

see CONSTITUTION page 250

Left: Tourists line up to view the newly discovered children's menu.

Many Lack Potable Water

According to a recent U.N. report, more than one billion people worldwide lack access to clean drinking water. What do *you* think?

Jennifer Gerber
Auditor

"The law of nature is 'adapt or die.' If those one billion people want to survive, they'll just have to evolve past the need to drink water."

Jesse Miller
Clerk

"Yesterday, I poured a bunch of water down the drain after cooking some pasta. I could've helped an African with that water. I'm so stupid!"

Mark Kunde
Systems Analyst

"This problem will be gone as soon as the earth's temperature increases enough to boil the world's lakes and streams, effectively sterilizing them."

Kristin Leffe
Publicist

"I'm sorry, but if these people are too lazy to refill their Brita pitchers..."

Mark Henley
Musical Director

"When I was a kid growing up in Love Canal, we didn't have uncontaminated water. Did we complain about it? No. We just shut up and got cancer."

Jeffrey Larsen
Usher

"Thus we see the first tremors of what history will someday call 'The Volvic Wars.'"

Neverland Evidence

Thirty-nine items seized from Michael Jackson's Neverland ranch were recently admitted as evidence in pre-trial hearings for his upcoming child-molestation case. What were some of the items?

- ➤ Six cases of beer with "Schlitz" crossed off and "Fruit Punch" written in its place

- ➤ Result of disastrous attempt to breed a life-sized My Little Pony

- ➤ Videotape of *Moonwalker*, in which Jackson can clearly be seen molesting an adolescent Sean Lennon's career

- ➤ An invisible dragon that only Jackson can see

- ➤ Packing crate holding a claw-footed bathtub, four bottles of Mr. Bubble, and three squealing children

- ➤ Unreleased, Pete Townshend-produced Michael Jackson/Gary Glitter duet

- ➤ Whole herd of stunned-looking alpacas

 **the ONION**®
America's Finest News Source.™

Herman Ulysses Zweibel
Founder

T. Herman Zweibel
Publisher Emeritus
J. Phineas Zweibel
Publisher
Maxwell Prescott Zweibel
Editor-In-Chief

Upon Reflection, I May Have Exaggerated My Skills In Midwifery

By Julie Shaw

Okay, Helen, you're doing great. Just remember to breathe. In... out. In... out. Fantastic. Just listen to the ocean-waves CD and try to relax. I think I can see the baby. Yeah, you're crowning, and it looks—oh, holy Christ! It's covered in blood! It's supposed to be like that? I mean, of course it's supposed to be like that. Of course. I remember that episode of *ER*. It was just like that.

"Expert"? I'm sorry. Let me clarify. I've wanted to try my hand at delivering a baby for a long time, and I thought it was time to give it a shot. Midwifery has been an interest of mine for months now, but the best way to learn is to roll up your sleeves and just do it. My advertisement said "expert"? I probably meant to say "enthusiast." They both start with an "e." It's an easy mistake.

It looks like you're fully dilated now. Well, I think that's what's happening. I know! I'll call my sister and ask. She was going to school to be an obstetrician, but dropped out. Now she manages a Denny's. Hey, will you hand me my purse? It's right... Jeez, you don't have to bite my head off.

Are you okay? That looks really painful. I mean, *really*—egghh. You know, my mother said she needed morphine like crazy when she gave birth to me. She said she screamed bloody murder for something like 28 hours. Heck, after about five minutes, I'd be like, "Put me under and cut me open—I want this sucker out!" But I guess some people like to do it natural. That's cool. I really respect that.

Take a deep breath and punch. I mean, push. That's it. Push! Push!

Ooh! Good news! It looks like a breach! Is that the word for when the baby comes out head-first? Breach? Oh, sorry then. I meant it's not a breach birth. I've seen plenty of babies before tonight, and that's no foot. It's probably a head. Unless it's a butt. If it is, your baby has one hairy butt. Joke! Just trying to lighten the mood.

What? I don't think I said that I've delivered hundreds of babies. You probably just misheard me. Are you sure? Well, then I meant I wanted to deliver hundreds of babies. And who wouldn't? Childbirth is a miraculous thing. We're ushering in a new life into the world, the two of us, together.

Hm, it's too bad I forgot to bring that stuff I printed out from the Internet.

Helen, there's no use in playing "he said-she said." We have a baby to deliver. How about we focus? Now squeeze. Squeeze!

All right, "push," if you want to nitpick. So what if I did jump the gun when I said that I'd trained for this? That was months ago! I really thought by the time you went into labor... See, I was planning on training for it. You know what? I'm going to register for some classes as soon as we're outta here. How late do you think...?

Ouch! How would you like it if I squeezed *your* arm that hard? Maybe I just will.

Whoa, whoa, whoa. There's no reason to panic. I know exactly what I'm doing. I looked through a book called

---

It's too bad I forgot to bring that stuff I printed out from the Internet.

All Creatures Great And Small. They delivered a calf in it. And I got a government pamphlet from Pueblo, Colorado. It was in Spanish, but I got the general feel.

Hey, how about a little swig? Here—it's just vodka. There's still some left. Okay, suit yourself.

Jesus Christ, are you supposed to do that? Oh boy! What a mess. Hold on. I'm getting a little... I need to sit down.

Okay, I got a feeling that the rough stuff is almost over. The head is nearly out. Just one more squeeze and... Presto!

Hey, quit squirming, you. Almost dropped you there. I said quit squirming. Quit squirming! It's a—hang on—boy? Girl? You can't tell when they're this little. At least you can't with cats. Hold on, hold on. You'll get your turn. "Hello, little darling. Hello. Moo-moo. Moo-moo. Who's a little moo-moo?"

Okay, okay. I'll have to wipe some stuff off here first. Do you have a towel around here? There, thanks. Oh, girl. Definitely, this is a girl. We're out of the woods. And you were worried!

Oh, sweet mother! There's something else coming out. It's—oh... my... God! It's twins, but this one is... deformed. It doesn't have eyes or arms or legs. It's just a big sack of bloody goo. Let me check something here. No, it doesn't seem to have a pulse. Just the umbilical cord. The other end goes to your baby. Pla-what? Placenta? Really?

Well, I'll be. Learn from your mistakes, I always say.

Let me tie off your umbilical cord... and... okay, we're good to go. You'll want to spend some time with your darling little girl, so I'll just mosey along, just as soon as I get my check.

Oh, and keep in mind that, if you ever need a nanny, I'm the best there is. ∅

Naked Man Only One Comfortable With His Body

MINNEAPOLIS, MN—Claims adjuster Geoffrey Danvers is like many other Minneapolis residents. He is gainfully employed, participates in community events, and is an avid reader who particularly enjoys courtroom thrillers. One thing Danvers does not share with his friends and neighbors, however, is discomfort with the sight of his nude body.

"Nudity is the natural state of the human body," Danvers said Monday, adjusting his sunglasses and leaning back in his lawn chair to increase the airflow around his genitals. "Europeans have a very relaxed attitude about nudity—both on their beaches and in other public spaces. Why be bound up in clothes all the time?"

He then stood to retrieve a drink from a nearby table, revealing a reddish, woven-crosshatch pattern on his back and buttocks.

While Danvers characterized his naked body as "no big deal," others dubbed it "gross," "embarrassing," and "tragic."

"It's good to be comfortable with your body," said Fran Hendricks, Danvers' fully clothed neighbor. "But you can't expect everyone else to be—for example, someone walking her dog before work who just happens to glance in your living-room window. His junk was just hanging there, swaying like a wind sock in a light breeze."

During the warm summer months, Danvers and his circumcised penis spend many hours exposed to the elements. Danvers said he usually takes his clothes off to cool down, but he acknowledged that he doesn't see the point in putting them back on to mow his lawn, watch television, or prepare spring rolls.

"I don't force my choice on anyone else," Danvers said. "The moment I leave my property, I wear clothes. When I have company over, I usually wear clothes. But if I'm hanging out around the living room—or the kitchen, or the garage, or the deck—why shouldn't I be comfortable?"

Neighbors provided several reasons for Danvers to not be comfortable.

"I shouldn't have to see him strutting his pasty, flabby body around like a peacock," said Elaine Preston, who lives next door to Danvers. "What Geoff does with his body behind closed doors makes no difference to me. But when he's grilling in his backyard or taking out the garbage, he needs to wear some trunks. At the very least,

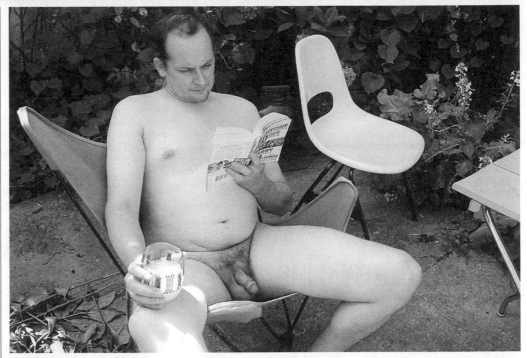

Above: Danvers hangs out around the house.

he should close his shades during his morning yoga routine."

Danvers brushed off the criticism.

"The hang-up over the unclothed form stems from the Christian association of nudity with paganism," Danvers said. "But religious people need to remember that Adam and Eve were naked until the devil imposed the idea of shame on them. You'd think Christians would see the human body as a work of God's art."

"You know, I'm just like everyone else," Danvers added. "I put my pants on one leg at a time on those days I wear them."

Neither his dimpled appendectomy

see BODY page 251

NEWS IN BRIEF

Cheney Urged Not To Work Blue During Convention

WASHINGTON, DC—At the insistence of members of the Republican Party, Vice-President Dick Cheney agreed not to work blue during the Republican National Convention, GOP sources reported Monday. "I sat him down and said, 'Dick, this is going to be on television, and we want to project a good, family-friendly image. You've gotta keep it clean,'" Republican National Committee chairman Ed Gillespie said. "I keep trying to get it through to him that using the 'F' word just shows a lack of imagination." A spokesman for Cheney said the vice-president will tone down his speech, but argued that Cheney is "only saying what everyone's already thinking."

The Scream Poster Stolen From Area Dorm Room

ST. PAUL, MN—Concordia University campus police are still investigating Tuesday's theft of a poster of Edvard Munch's The Scream from an area dorm room. "We're doing everything in our power to recover the poster," officer Donald Benson said of the poster, which was stolen while the two residents of 204 Walther Hall were studying in the second-floor common area. "With its iconic contorted human figure beneath a swirling red sky, The Scream is a masterpiece of German expressionism, and the poster was valued at $7.95." The work of art is one of only 86 copies known to exist on the campus.

Smoker Inspired By Sight Of Elderly Smoker

EVANSVILLE, WY—Rod Jensen, a 25-year-old smoker with a two-pack-a-day habit, drew inspiration from 83-year-old Leo Menting Monday. "See, that guy over there's still kicking," Jensen said, after he saw the elderly man smoking a Marlboro at Caroline's Corner Cafe. "I'm always hearing about the health risks of smoking, and how it can kill you, but look at that old dude. He doesn't have one of those holes in his throat. He's not even using a cane." Minutes later, Jensen added onion rings to his order after seeing Menting's wife do the same.

Internet Pop-Up Quiz Insulting

THOUSAND OAKS, CA—Internet user Paula Challey was insulted by the simplicity of a quiz that popped up on her computer desktop Monday. "I mean, come on—it offers me a prize if I can identify whether a picture is of Britney Spears, Madonna, or Paris Hilton," Challey said. "I'm a college graduate, for Christ's sake. Give me a real challenge! If these quizzes are this easy, I don't see the point in them." Challey then moved to the more formidable task of using her mouse to shoot an animated duck for the chance to win $100.

Grocery-Store Worker Can't Bear To Eat Food Anymore

FLOURISSANT, MO—Pick'n Save stockboy Joel Melcher said Monday that his overexposure to groceries has destroyed his taste for food. "When I first started working here, I thought, 'This is awesome—I'll be able to bring bags of food home from work every night,'" said Melcher, who receives a 25 percent discount at the store. "But now, being around it all day long, at the end of the day I can't even stand to look at frozen food, baked goods, meat, dairy items, or produce. Makes me sick just thinking about it." Melcher has vowed that, when he gets a new job, he "will never set foot in a grocery store ever again." ∅

wouldn't have it any other way.

"I'm not looking for glory and acclaim," Malmough said, his face a study in optimism and resolve. "I just care about this land, and how much of it my children and their children's children will own."

Malmough isn't afraid of hard work. Just last year, he spent countless hours making a covert, trillion-dollar deal among the six major petroleum-producing nations to keep prices and supplies fixed to an optimum standard.

"One must not doubt the ability of a few dedicated wealthy people to alter the course of history," the billionaire said. "Indeed, it's the only thing that ever has."

Malmough may be one of the few remaining U.S. citizens who truly believe in the American dream.

"The dream of success is available to all of us," Malmough said, the light of belief shining in his eyes. "Americans must not lose sight of that."

Malmough is not alone. There are several men like him working, often at the expense of free time and family, for change in the fields of international finance, arms manufacturing, and communications infrastructure. Usually, they work separately, save for the occasional conference call. But, once every four years, this group of driven individuals gathers to dictate the course of American politics.

"The Republican Party has always been blessed with idealists," Republican National Committee chairman Ed Gillespie said Monday. "But really, it's a handful of discreet men behind the scenes who drive our party. Whether self-made corporate moguls, inheritors of vast familial wealth, or heirs to decades-old political dynasties, these men and the effects of their contributions cannot be underestimated. They make this world what it is."

Added Gillespie: "God bless America."

Andre Colbert-McIntyre is a French-born jet-setter who currently holds triple citizenship, a controlling interest in the multinational Brehmar Investment GMbH, and some concrete ideas about globalization. This stalwart man was lucky enough to share breakfast with Vice-President Dick Cheney Monday.

"It's important for our little group to make its voice heard by politicians," Colbert-McIntyre said. "If we don't tell the Washington big wigs to relax labor rights and environmental protections in developing nations, who will?" ∅

---

the ONION presents
Pool-Safety Tips

Summer is drawing to a close, but there are still a few weeks left to make a splash at your local swimming pool. Here's how to make the experience safe *and* fun:

- Never dive head-first into the shallow end of an empty pool.
- Your body is 70 percent water, so don't worry: Even if you were to drown, only 30 percent of you would die.
- Leave a drowned squirrel floating in the pool as a reminder of what can happen when one isn't careful, and is a squirrel.
- Remember, you can't leave young children unsupervised around the pool, the way you do in the house.
- Don't drink and drive while swimming.
- Important: "Water wings" flotation devices should be placed around a child's arms, never his or her ankles.
- Don't swim in the end of the pool where unscrupulous Japanese commercial whalers are using gill nets and explosive harpoons.

- Don't buy into all that skin-cancer, suntan-lotion, SPF bullshit. It's just a bunch of scientifically verified propaganda from the Coppertone Corporation.
- Do not run around the pool. Unless your cousin is trying to pull down your bathing suit, or the concession stand just opened and you really want a hot dog.
- No daughter of mine is going out in public with a swimsuit like that, if she knows what's good for her.
- Make lots of friends at the pool. That way, if you start drowning, everyone will try to save you. It rules!
- It's a fact: Many drownings take place in only a few feet of water. So you don't even need a pool, really.
- If you're gonna do a cannon-ball, you gotta yell "Cannon-ball!" It's tradition.

Children's Menu, being for children of weaning age until seven years.

Yankee Doodle Macaroni... 2 p.
Jumpin' Johnnycakes... 1 p.
Eagle Fingers... 3 p.
Cheese Betwixt Two Slices Of Bread... 2 p.
Mother Goose... 2 p.
Bloody Great Blood Pudding... 2 p.
Three-Cornered Tarts... 2 p.
Superlative Squash... 2 p.
Ale... 1 p.

Pleasant Diversions

Maze.

Color Me.

Above: The menu.

Archives Building.

The menu—on the back of Article I, which establishes a bicameral Congress comprising the Senate and the House of Representatives—provides dining options for children under 7.

"In this discovery, we see yet another example of the wisdom of our founding fathers," Carlin said. "While establishing a government that honors both the rights of the individuals and the unity of the nation, they also recognized the need for fun-to-eat, affordable dining options for the nation's youngest Americans."

Until now, scholars had focused on the elegant calligraphy on the Constitution's front, entirely overlooking the reverse side, which features two columns of fancifully named menu items, such as Yankee Doodle Macaroni, Jumpin' Johnnycakes, and Eagle Fingers.

"The wording of the Constitution is general, necessitating interpretation, and the same can be said for its children's menu," Carlin said. "We do not know exactly what the framers of the Constitution meant by 'Eagle Fingers.' Strict constructionists are likely to assume that they were strips of eagle flesh fried in batter, but loose constructionists might argue that the term was an amusing way to encourage children to eat their chicken or grouse."

Other dishes found by researchers include Bloody Great Blood Pudding, Cheese Betwixt Two Slices Of Bread, and Mother Goose.

The menu is offered "for children of weaning age until seven years."

"The menu reflects the relative brevity of childhood more than two centuries ago," Carlin said. "Contemporary children's menus are generally offered to children of up to 12 years of age."

Near the bottom of the document, a waxy, bluish spot almost obscures a line drawing of a man with a peg-leg.

"We believe the caricature could be Gouverneur Morris of Pennsylvania, who wore a wooden leg—but it might just be a pirate," Carlin said. "Whatever it is, it's strong proof that the 'Pleasant Diversions' section of the menu was used by a child, as the figure had been colored in rather inexpertly, in blue from head-to-foot."

Near the stain is a small maze leading statesman and Constitution-signer Benjamin Franklin to a lightning-struck kite. To the right of this is the earliest-known example of a word-find, containing the names of Revolutionary War-era battleships.

So far, no adult menu been found.

"What did the original framers intend [by this menu]?" constitutional historian Robert Lipscomb-Blaine asked. "Why was children's cuisine important to them, when America's fate was still unknown? In the spirit of compromise that defined the Constitutional Convention itself, was serving food to children a way to distract the young'uns while their elders concentrated on creating a system of representative national government?"

Next month, the U.S. Constitution And Children's Menu will be removed from public view for several weeks to undergo further study. In the interim, the National Archives will display the Constitution's predecessor, the Articles Of Confederation And Personal Advertisements. ∅

Above: Footage from Lighter Side segments titled "Time To Get A New House!" (left) and "Even Amputees Want To Kick The U.S. Troops Out!"

device hidden under his shirt, the bomber gave up and ordered lunch! Can you imagine the relieved look on that restaurant owner's face?!"

"We've always prided ourselves on our diversity of opinion, as well as our real-time news coverage," Hadi said.

Continued Jalami: "The blundering bomber was well into his third slice of pizza when responding Mossad agents killed him and wounded two bystanders in a hail of gunfire."

Al-Jazeera then resumed normal coverage, airing a statement in response to air strikes on Afghanistan by hard-line Islamic cleric Abdul Rashid Ghazi.

The Lighter Side, airing at the bottom of the hour during non-peak times, is already popular among viewers. Favorite segments so far include the story of a Ramallah teen who sat motionless in a freshly plowed pepper field for 10 days, believing himself to be in a minefield; that of a U.N.-sponsored airborne food-drop that leveled an entire Afghan village; and that of a large fig, produced on a farm outside Bahrain, which bears an uncanny resemblance to renegade Muslim cleric Muqtada Al-Sadr.

"I could not believe what I was seeing," Osiraq resident Akil Hamza said. "The fig looked just like him."

Al-Jazeera, a technologically savvy news organization that reports events in the Middle East from an Arab perspective, remains the only foreign station allowed in Afghanistan.

Station executives say the Lighter Side segments will help them broaden their audience.

"We have long been aware that our network isn't as well-regarded in the

West as news outlets such as CNN, MSNBC, and Fox News," said Wadah Khanfar, managing director of Al-Jazeera. "We were criticized for airing certain stories—the capture of U.S. soldiers by al-Qaeda, for instance, or the burning of the American embassy in Afghanistan. So we

"I could not believe what I was seeing," Osiraq resident Akil Hamza said. "The fig looked just like him."

looked to see what sort of stories our American news counterparts were running in lieu of unpopular topical pieces."

"This is what we came up with," Khanfar said, gesturing to a row of

monitors displaying the humorous action at the State Fair of Jalalabad, where several residents who had lost their arms in the recent fighting engaged in a spirited samboosak-eating contest to benefit a local school.

"We've always prided ourselves on our diversity of opinion, as well as our real-time news coverage," senior news producer Sameer Hadi said. "But it doesn't hurt to report things that everyone can agree on. I think the story we're doing this evening will bring a smile to our viewers' faces. It is the story of Abdul Al-Sattar Hali, who recently won the $1 million Bahrain State Lottery, but was unable to collect, because he was in prison at the time. Can you imagine?"

Al-Jazeera had also done a story concerning Hali in April, when scandal erupted after they aired photos of the blindfolded, nude pottery vendor being hosed down by American troops at Abu Ghraib. ∅

BODY from page 249

scar nor local restaurants' refusal to deliver food to his address have convinced Danvers to clothe himself.

"Nudity has connotations of poverty, slavery, and defeat," Danvers said, his flaccid penis resting on his left thigh.

"At first, I thought he just wasn't wearing a shirt. Then I looked down and saw his ding-a-ling," McDaniel said.

"But when I'm gardening, and it's just me and nature with no clothes in between, I don't feel defeated. I feel triumphant. That is, when I even remember that I'm naked, which I rarely do. See? That's how natural it is."

While most neighbors say they are careful not to visit Danvers

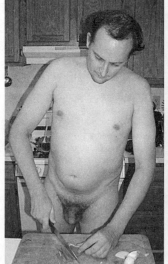
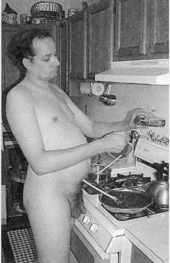
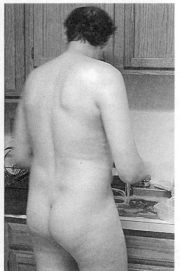

Above: Danvers prepares dinner.

without calling in advance, at least one coworker has made the mistake of ringing Danvers' doorbell unexpectedly.

"Last month, I stopped by to pick up

some files," coworker Tom McDaniel said. "Geoff came to the door with nothing but the papers. At first, I thought he just wasn't wearing a shirt. Then I looked down and saw his ding-a-ling."

"He even invited me in for some coffee," McDaniel continued. "I could see a leather living-room set behind him. From now on, we'll be exchanging documents via e-mail." ∅

Son, We'd All Like To Lie Around All Day Being 'Clinically Depressed'

By Bill Endres

Justin? Justin, can you hear me through this door? Are you asleep again? Your mom said you got up to use the bathroom a minute ago. She was hoping you were coming down to have dinner with us. No? Hello? Well, son, I know that you have a real problem; at least, that's what the therapist tells us. Anyway, you're not alone. We all get a little low sometimes. Life is certainly no picnic—don't I know it! But usually, after a while, folks snap out of their funks. Not because they want to, but because they come around to the fact that they have no choice. The truth is, son, we'd all like to lie around all day being "clinically depressed," but at some point, we have to swallow hard and face the music. Step up to the ol' plate.

There are plenty of mornings I don't want to get up and go to work, but I do. And you know how much your mother hates that exercise bike of hers. Do you see what I'm driving at, son?

Justin, your mom and I love you, and we want you to get well. If you have something, anything, you need to get off your chest, please know that you can share it with us. There's no reason to keep it bottled up. Anything you tell that therapist of yours—what's her name, Dr. Goldbar? Goldbrick? Gold—well, anything you tell her, you can tell us, too. I never did see why you'd rather open up to a complete stranger than to the two people who spent years trying to raise you the best way they knew how, but I'm willing to accept it. Just as I accept that you have a problem that you can't control, even though there might be a solution that's as plain as the nose on your face. I guess what I'm saying, Justin, is: I'm a practical person. I always seek the most direct solution to a problem. That may not be intellectual enough for some people, but it's always worked for me.

Now, come on down to dinner, Justin. Your mom made pork chops.

Son?

Justin, do you know what could make you feel better right off the bat? Raising your blinds and letting in some light. Because, I mean, I can believe you feel clinically depressed in that room of yours—I would, too! Anyone would. It's dark, it smells, and there's mounds of clothes and books all over the floor. Get out of bed, open the window, and do a little picking up. Accomplishing a small task could do a lot to restore your self-confidence.

Speaking of windows, maybe once you get your room clean, you can help your ol' dad put up the screens. It'd be just like way back when! With all the trouble you've had lately, and the running back and forth to the clinic and to your school, I've fallen behind on household chores. You see, I don't have the luxury of spending Saturday staring at the television, all curled up in a blanket even though it's the middle of summer. There's things that need to be done.

I've also had to miss a lot of work. Now, don't worry, your dad is sitting pretty at good old Kenyon Mortgage,

> By the way, did you know that those ambulance fees weren't covered by the company health plan? I got the damned co-pay bill yesterday. I yelled my head off at them over the phone, that's for sure, but the girl said there's nothing they can do. Whew, and those pills you take aren't cheap, either, are they? I figured it out, and they come to about $3 apiece!

but I've caught a little flak from George. Well, it's not fair of him to imply that clinical depression isn't as bad as a real disease. I didn't say this to him, but it's what I believe. Okay? Don't you worry about George one bit.

By the way, did you know that those ambulance fees weren't covered by the company health plan? I got the damned co-pay bill yesterday. I yelled my head off at them over the phone, that's for sure, but the girl said there's nothing they can do. Whew, and those pills you take aren't cheap, either, are they? I figured it out, and they come to about $3 apiece! So, uh, when are they going to take effect? You've been on them for a couple months.

Son?

Look, I think your grandmother had some of this clinical depression herself. I think a lot of it stemmed from her poor upbringing—she never did learn to read or write well. So, you know, her clinical depression wasn't because she was some bored child of privilege. No, she didn't have the luxury of sitting around being clinically depressed. When she got the blues, she sucked it up and carried on, because she knew that life was full of pain—not to mention that she couldn't afford some… shrink.

Now, son, you've had more advantages in your 17 years than Mom had in all her 58, but I'm still willing to meet you halfway on your problem. Hell, I'm even willing to call it a problem, instead of calling it "lying around and feeling sorry for yourself," which is sure what it looks like. You can't claim I'm the ogre here. But that's what you think I am, right? A real jerk. "Fuck you, Butterfat," you once told me. Even though I was only trying to help. Butterfat? At least I don't lounge around in my room all day, wasting away to nothing when there's a decent meal right—

Justin, open this door right now, dammit!

Okay, well now, finally we're getting somewhere. Great to see you at last, son. Look, I'm sorry about being a little tough on you. I suppose ol' Doc Goldwhatever wouldn't be happy. But sometimes, when someone you love is clearly wasting his potential, you have to—hey, where are you going? To the bathroom, again? Justin, why did you lock the door?

> You can't claim I'm the ogre here. But that's what you think I am, right? A real jerk. "Fuck you, Butterfat," you once told me. Even though I was only trying to help. Butterfat?

Oh, dandy. Just dandy. Son, this is hardly what anyone would call a positive step.

Justin? Justin, answer me! Ø

Your Horoscope

**By Lloyd Schumner Sr.
Retired Machinist and
A.A.P.B.-Certified Astrologer**

Aries: (March 21–April 19)
When you die, your name will not be found in the Book of Eternal Life. That's because you died, duh.

Taurus: (April 20–May 20)
You're utterly unfit to survive in the world of advertising sales, but that's because it doesn't have the methane-rich atmosphere your species breathes.

Gemini: (May 21–June 21)
Your life story has all the elements of a classic revenge tale, or at least it will after Wednesday's company picnic.

Cancer: (June 22–July 22)
Just a few more months and you'll be able to point out historical inaccuracies in people's Halloween costumes.

Leo: (July 23–Aug. 22)
Unfortunately, unless New York drastically reforms the trampoline-zoning laws in the Empire State neighborhood, you'll just have to find a different way to commit suicide.

Virgo: (Aug. 23–Sept. 22)
You're starting to develop a sneaking suspicion that other people are having more sex, parties, and all-around fun than you are, which just proves that it takes you a while to catch on sometimes.

Libra: (Sept. 23–Oct. 23)
Marriage, with the levels of cooperation it demands, is not for everyone. So it's actually a good thing that it's illegal for you.

Scorpio: (Oct. 24–Nov. 21)
Not that it's really the stars' business, but you really should have lived your life so as to be more affected by the recent death of Czeslaw Milosz.

Sagittarius: (Nov. 22–Dec. 21)
You don't get to choose your parents, but your brilliant merging of dating services and time travel are about to change all that.

Capricorn: (Dec. 22–Jan. 19)
You'll be questioned by authorities and charged with criminal incompetence after a man you supposedly taught to fish dies of starvation.

Aquarius: (Jan. 20–Feb. 18)
Being "on call" does tend to take its toll on your personal life, but as the Hot Dog King, you've gotta expect that.

Pisces: (Feb. 19–March 20)
Nothing you do this week will be of note to people who don't look at the photos on page 27 of *The Canadian Journal Of Infectious Diseases And Medical Microbiology*.

Emeril Bams Groupie

see ENTERTAINMENT page 3G

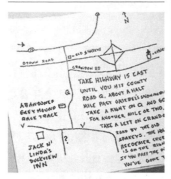

Wedding Invitation Includes Depressing Map To Church

see WEDDINGS page 14E

Pregnant Woman Keeps Child Out Of Spite

see LOCAL page 4C

9/11 Milked

see NATION page 4B

STATshot

A look at the numbers that shape your world.

Most Popular Extracurricular Programs

- 12% Ski/Random-Hook-Up Club
- 16% Text-Message E-bate Society
- 28% Latchkey Club
- 14% Association Of Attractive And Popular People
- 13% 4-HIV+
- 17% Hypocrites Against Drunk Driving

---

the ONION®

VOLUME 40 ISSUE 36   AMERICA'S FINEST NEWS SOURCE™   9–15 SEPTEMBER 2004

Hundreds Of Republicans Injured In Rush To Discredit Kerry

WASHINGTON, DC—George Washington Memorial Hospital is struggling to deal with an influx of Republicans with concussions, broken bones, and internal injuries suffered during the recent stampede to discredit Democratic presidential nominee John Kerry, emergency-room personnel reported Monday.

"Triage is in utter chaos," paramedic

see REPUBLICANS page 257

Above: Republicans race to disgrace Kerry on Capitol Hill.

THE ARTS

Seminal School-Portrait Photographer Dies At 92

PHOENIX—Henry Anszczak, the photographer whose influential work revolutionized modern school portraiture, died Sunday at his family home in Eloy. He was 92.

According to longtime assistant Dave Olsen, Anszczak died of natural causes.

"On Sunday, Mr. Anszczak passed away peacefully in his sleep, surrounded by his family and scores of yearbooks," Olsen said. "We will never forget his wonderful artistic achievements. He blazed the trail for thousands of school photographers nationwide. The lion of 20th-century public-educational culture roars no more."

Anszczak's innovations became so much a part of the language of school portraiture that their brilliance is often overlooked.

"Anszczak was the first to present his subjects as individuals, rather than as one tiny, grainy part of the

see PHOTOGRAPHER page 257

Six-Hour Bus Ride Endured For Slots

I-95, NJ—Baltimore resident Gary Drake, 53, endured a six-hour bus ride from Baltimore to Atlantic City Tuesday, drawn by the prospect of feeding coins into a slot machine at a dimly lit casino.

"Man, my back is killing me," Drake said, shifting in his window seat near the back of an eastbound Coastal Tours bus. "Maybe I'm getting a little old for this. Well, just a few more hours, and I'll be sitting in front of the slots in a nice cool casino. When I get there, no one better be in my favorite spot, right next the cashiers."

Drake boarded the bus at 2:30 p.m., expecting to arrive at the Oasis Casino at approximately 7. However,

see SLOTS page 256

Above: Drake and the bus he rode to Atlantic City.

Kobe Bryant Case Dismissed

Last week, prosecutors dropped the felony sexual-assault charge against basketball star Kobe Bryant. What do *you* think?

Sandy Miller
Teacher

"Well, there you have it. The system works."

James Tompkins
Lawyer

"At last, Kobe is vindicated before the eyes of the nation: He's not a rapist; he just constantly cheats on his wife."

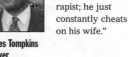

Michael Bartko
Systems Analyst

"Every time a black man gets famous, they try to drag him down. But every time a woman asserts herself, they call her a slut. So I'm torn."

Amy O'Keefe
Studio Musician

"All you people who have been clamoring for a pro athlete who's not a convicted felon, here's your man."

Eric Mills
Chef

"He's still guilty of losing to the no-name Detroit Pistons in the NBA Finals."

Jeffrey Larsen
Mayor

"Could they at least tell us if he did it or not?"

Budget-Airline Perks

The American budget-airline business is booming. What perks do some of the low-cost carriers offer?

- Spirit Airlines: Big, friendly sheepdog on every plane
- Ted: Special hammock-class seating
- AirTran Airways: Video trivia machines at every seat
- Frontier Airlines: Glass-bottom planes
- JetBlue: Viewing of *The Wedding Planner* followed by in-flight Q&A session with director Adam Shankman
- West Jet: Diet Sprite *and* Diet 7-Up
- Song: Flotation devices designed, engineered by Kate Spade
- Midwest Airlines: Closed-circuit televisions that allow everyone to watch the hot girl sleep
- Southwest Airlines: Hibachi at back of plane
- ATA: You know those shitty headphones? Keep 'em

the ONION®
America's Finest News Source.™

Herman Ulysses Zweibel
Founder

T. Herman Zweibel
Publisher Emeritus

J. Phineas Zweibel
Publisher

Maxwell Prescott Zweibel
Editor-In-Chief

I'm Getting Pretty Good At Masturbating

By Mitch Duncan

If you don't mind, I'd like to bring up a sensitive subject. Some people call it jacking off, or jerking off, or a lot of other things, but I just call it masturbating. And while there's always room for improvement, I have to say that I'm pretty good at it.

I remember the first time I felt a stirring in my privates. I was about 11, and I was eating popcorn and watching *Twin Peaks*. Sherilyn Fenn came on the screen and something clicked. The next thing I knew, I couldn't keep my hands away from down there. I didn't even know the word "masturbate" yet. No matter: Whenever I had a few minutes to myself, that's what I'd be doing!

But, as you might guess, I wasn't always an expert at masturbating. For a long time, I got it all wrong. I'd slide down banisters, rub against the cat—anything to get that feeling down there. Once, I was grinding against my opened closet door, and I tore it off the hinges. That took a lot of explaining! Gave me a heck of a scare, too. Not long after that, I learned the secret: Take off your pants.

It's taken a lot of trial and error, but over the years, I've picked up a lot more tricks. For example, if you want to masturbate well, make sure there will be no distractions. Go someplace quiet where you can be completely alone. There shouldn't be people in the next room watching television, talking, or making dinner. If there's one thing I've learned, it's that you shouldn't masturbate while you're on the phone, either. Sure, the person on the other end of the line can't see you, but they'll be able to tell something's not quite right. I don't know how they do it, but they always do.

Another trick I've found? Lubrication. I call it "lube." Now, I can't stress this nearly enough: If you want to avoid getting sore, make sure you get the entire area good and slick. Your penis should be wet to the touch. But what makes a good lube? Try this simple test: If you put a bit of the substance between your thumb and forefinger, and it makes it easier to rub them together, it's probably good lube. Careful, though! There are a few exceptions. You don't want to use something that burns, like Bengay. Dish soap doesn't work very well, either. Toothpaste passes the two-finger test, but I haven't had the guts to try using it. If you have and it works, let me know.

Once you're lubed up, you need to set the mood. Think of something sexy. I still think about Sherilyn Fenn in *Twin Peaks*, but sometimes I like to mix it up a little bit. I'll think about Sherilyn Fenn in *Of Mice And Men* or *Boxing Helena* or *Desire And Hell At Sunset Motel*. If you're stuck for inspiration, rent one of those movies. I guarantee a response.

If you want to be a better masturbator, you can't be afraid to try new things. Switch up your hands. Try employing a soft piece of fabric. Only touch certain parts of the penis. You

> I wasn't always an expert at masturbating. For a long time, I got it all wrong. I'd slide down banisters, rub against the cat—anything to get that feeling down there. Once, I was grinding against my opened closet door, and I tore it off the hinges.

never know until you try, right? If it feels good, why not give it a go?

Last year, I decided I didn't want to just be good at masturbating—I wanted to be great. So I did some research on the web. Was I surprised! There were thousands of photos of people masturbating, both men and women. Even though the sites didn't provide many tips, the photos helped me improve my technique by showing me how the pros do it.

Recently, I've begun to experiment with prolonging my masturbation sessions. Just as I'm about to let go, I'll stop touching myself and wait a bit. When I grab it again, it feels better than ever. By practicing this procedure, my masturbation skills moved from "okay" to "fantastic."

I haven't worked out every kink in the whole masturbation thing, but—not to brag—I'm pretty darned good at it. In fact, I just masturbated a few minutes ago, and I came so hard I almost shit my bed. Now, that doesn't mean there's no room to grow. Life is a journey, and it's up to the individual to make as much of it as possible. So, if you'll excuse me, I have some business to take care of—some *masturbating* business. ∅

Comedian Given Sitcom Out Of Pity

BURBANK, CA—*Now What?*, an ABC sitcom making its debut next week, was created for struggling stand-up comic Warren Morris out of pity, sources at ABC Comedy Development said Monday.

"Warren's long since paid his dues, and this is probably the only opportunity he'll get," programming executive Denise Scudder said. "Though his jokes aren't particularly funny, he is hard-working and likable. I thought, 'What the hell? Let's throw him a bone.'"

Now What? will star Morris, 42, as Warren Barber, a video editor at a small Midwestern production company. Barber, who dreams of seeing his own film ideas produced one day, is a good-natured but absent-minded everyman whose misadventures inspire varied reactions in assorted coworkers and friends, as well as his ever-skeptical wife, played by Kathy Griffin.

A nationally touring comic since 1990, Morris has spent the past 14 years performing in such venues as Cockamamie's in Beloit, WI, and Laffghanistan in Erie, PA. In spite of years of experience in comedy, the heavy-set, balding Michigan native has remained on the fringes of the entertainment industry.

"Morris landed a half-hour special on Comedy Central in 1997, but the break didn't lead to anything bigger," Morris' booking agent Karla Hoffman said. "If he's known for anything, it's his material about compulsive eating and girlfriends who are smarter than him. Even if audiences don't remember Warren's name later, they usually laugh when he says, 'Must... stop' and 'Um, I don't think so, honey.'"

A July 2003 appearance at the Just For Laughs comedy festival in Montreal marked a turning point in Morris' career. One of 27 comedians showcased in the festival's Club Series, Morris and his slightly offbeat act caught the attention of Scudder and ABC talent coordinator Tamara Felbet.

"While not laugh-out-loud funny, Warren had a familiar presence," Felbet said. "A lot of people relate to his sort of harmless-slob image. He had a joke about buying new underwear instead of doing laundry and one about how, instead of washing a spoon, he ate his Ben & Jerry's with a pair of take-out chopsticks. That's exactly the kind of observational humor that's perfect for filling 22 minutes."

"We're always on the lookout for fresh new talent, but a lot of the acts we saw in Montreal were a little too

Warren Morris

weird," Felbet continued. "And, unlike a lot of the comics there, Warren seemed like a really nice guy. He sorta reminded me of my brother."

Within a week of his Montreal appearance, Morris signed a talent deal with the network. After passing on a pitch for a half-hour series that would have starred Morris as a parking-enforcement officer raising a tart-tongued 8-year-old daughter, ABC executives greenlighted the *Now What?* pilot in December 2003.

Morris has spent this year writing and acting in the show's first 13 episodes.

"I don't think folks realize what goes into producing a sitcom," Morris said. "I'm used to spending long, hard hours on the road, honing my material. But I really poured my heart and soul into this show. I feel like I've been given this incredible chance to grow artistically and comedically. Things are finally turning around for me."

ABC primetime entertainment president Stephen McPherson said he's "glad the network helped [Warren] out."

"[Warren] seems really great," McPherson said. "Now, the show is a different matter. There's no way it'll make it to November sweeps, much less February. I figure we'll run the first episode and get marginal numbers in the overnights. Then, after the

> "If he's known for anything, it's his material about compulsive eating and girlfriends who are smarter than him. Even if audiences don't remember Warren's name later, they usually laugh when he says, 'Must... stop' and 'Um, I don't think so, honey.'"

figures drop in the second and third weeks, we'll put it on indefinite hiatus and burn off the leftover episodes during summer. It may seem odd to order 13 episodes when we'll probably air fewer than six, but [Warren]'s see COMEDIAN page 256

NEWS IN BRIEF

Bush Campaign More Thought Out Than Iraq War

WASHINGTON, DC—Military and political strategists agreed Monday that President Bush's re-election campaign has been executed with greater precision than the war in Iraq. "Judging from the initial misrepresentation of intelligence data and the ongoing crisis in Najaf, I assumed the president didn't know his ass from his elbow," said Col. Dale Henderson, a military advisor during the Reagan Administration. "But on the campaign trail, he's proven himself a master of long-term planning and unflinching determination. How else can you explain his strength in the polls given this economy?" Henderson said he regrets having characterized Bush's handling of the war as "incompetent," now that he knows the president's mind was simply otherwise occupied.

Terry Gilliam Barbecue Plagued By Production Delays

LONDON—A backyard barbecue hosted by director Terry Gilliam was postponed again Sunday due to production delays. "I had a special grill flown in from Fiji, but it took three weeks to figure out how to light it," Gilliam said of the 20-foot, volcano-shaped propane grill he'd deemed integral to the Tiki-themed event. "Then, just when I had the menu hammered out, Johnny [Depp] got sick, and I had to push the date back again. See, the whole thing was for his birthday in June." In spite of the continued delays, party guest Elvis Mitchell predicted that the event will be "visually stunning" and "fun."

Vacationing Man Misses Own Remote Control

NEW YORK—Dale Herring, on vacation from Wichita, KS, admitted Monday that he missed his TV remote control. "At first, I was taken with the hotel's remote, and the sheer number of buttons—not to mention the breathtaking view of the on-screen menu guide," Herring said. "But the truth is, I can't wait to get back to the simplicity and familiarity of my own clicker." Herring added that he'll definitely go see the Empire State Building the next time he visits New York.

Assistant Manager Accused Of Sexual Indiscrimination

PLAINS, GA—Female employees at Peachtree Financial filed a joint complaint against assistant manager Dean Marchand Monday for repeated acts of sexual indiscrimination in the workplace. "Dean is willing to sleep with anyone who propositions him," human-resources manager Jan Harris said. "Whether it's Kelly, that pretty blonde from sales, or Marta, that grouchy skank in accounting, Dean doesn't seem to care." Harris added that Marchand is a smart, nice, well-dressed guy who should hold himself to higher standards.

Local Child Amuses Café—But For How Long?

TIGARD, OR—Although 4-year-old Mia Benson is currently amusing everyone at The Sundial Café, employee Kelli Doon wondered Monday how much longer patrons might be tolerant of her childish antics. "Yes, it was very cute when [Benson] was running around making choo-choo-train sounds," Doon said, wiping the counter with a rag, her eyes trained on Benson. "And everyone laughed when she asked that stranger if she could have his cookie. But really, she's been demanding everyone's attention for, like, 15 minutes. Is it time to step in?" Doon said she plans to move closer to the milk carafes, to better ascertain whether she should intervene. ∅

a semi truck carrying lumber jack-knifed during rush hour, causing a substantial traffic slowdown.

After lodging his coat between his lower back and his seat, Drake practiced for his night of recreational gambling on a handheld electronic poker machine. When the batteries on his machine died, Drake looked over the shoulder of the bus rider in front of him, who was playing a handheld electronic blackjack game.

"I got the casino figured out," Drake said. "If I don't win at a machine in the first 15 minutes, I know that slot is cold, so I move to another one. But if I

> "You have to get up too much when you drink beer. One time, I had to go to the bathroom, and when I came back, someone had won $15 at my machine," Drake said. "If I'm feeling lucky, I hate to rise from my stool until I have to get back on the bus."

do hit, I know that one's hot, so I'll sit there for eight, nine hours, until I need to get back to the bus again. Or until I run out of money. Oh, and I always use a warm coin."

The slot machines Drake will play generally have a payback rate of about 90 percent, meaning he has a 1-in-10 chance of breaking even if, on the off chance he does win, he stops gambling.

Approximately three hours outside of Atlantic City, the air conditioning system on the bus stopped working. Although Drake was irritated by the climate change, as were the many toddlers on the bus, he remained focused on his journey's end.

"When I get there, I gotta warm up first," Drake said. "I've got a whole routine. First, I play the nickel slots, like that American Bandstand one. Once I got my mojo working, I move up to the quarter slots, or maybe even the dollar slots if I feel like I'm on fire. Never stay on the nickel slots, though. Those are for grannies. You're wasting your time on those."

"Some guys like racing motorcycles," he added. "Me, I get that same thrill from watching the wheels go around on the slots."

When the bus pulled into a gas station outside of Wilmington, DE to pick up 11 waiting passengers, many riders disembarked to use the restrooms. At this time, Drake purchased nachos, a lemonade-flavored soda, and a hot

Above: Various bus passengers survey the slots at the Oasis.

dog with relish. Returning to the bus with 30 seconds to spare, he balanced the two grease-soaked plates on his knees and ate his meal.

"I wish they had women to bring you drinks on this bus, like they do at the casino," Drake joked, lifting his soda from the garbage-covered bus floor and taking a sip. "They don't make you pay nothing for them, and some of the younger women look real fine in those skirts."

Drake has taken the bus to Atlantic City at least 20 times, he told a man with a yellow-stained bandage over one eye.

"One time, I won $800 at a slot machine with my last dollar," Drake said. "That must've been about 1988, 'cause I remember that my second wife Denise was with me."

Added Drake: "I can't stand sitting around the house all the time. I love the nightlife."

The bus was scheduled to arrive in time for passengers to catch one of four performances by Sax Appeal, a keyboard-and-sax duo that plays the Oasis lounge every Tuesday night.

About 45 miles from its destination, the bus pulled into a rest stop to admit six more people, including one on crutches who sat down next to Drake and promptly removed a paper-bag-covered bottle from her jacket.

"When I'm gambling, I always drink the hard stuff," Drake told her. "You have to get up too much when you drink beer. One time, I had to go to the bathroom, and when I came back, someone had won $15 at my machine. If I'm feeling lucky, I hate to rise from my stool until I have to get back on the bus in the morning."

With that statement, Drake climbed over his seat-mate's duffel bags, lurched to the back of the bus, and opened the bathroom door, releasing

a pungent draft of chemicals and stale urine throughout the bus.

Upon his return, Drake was in good spirits.

"Do you feel that?" he said, as the tangle of overpass highways and low-slung budget hotels on the outskirts of Atlantic City came into view. "I get

that feeling every time I see the lights. It's electric. In a few minutes, I'll be off this bus. After I walk the half-mile over to the Oasis, I'm gonna win big-time! Then those guys from the electric company can kiss my ass when I roll back into Baltimore and hand them my check." ∅

COMEDIAN from page 255

a decent guy. He deserves a break."

Scudder said that, even though its run will be brief, the sitcom will help Morris' career.

"Warren will have to go back to stand-up, but he'll get to play slightly better venues," Scudder said. "Maybe he'll even go on Best Week Ever a few times, or get one-time appearances on other sitcoms. At least he'll be known as 'that comedian who used to have his own show.' That's a lot better than

not being known at all. If nothing else, the show put some rent money in Warren's pocket and secured him an entry on the Internet Movie Database."

Now What? will make its debut Sept. 15 at 8:30 p.m. EST. Two weeks later, it will move to Tuesdays at 9, before moving to Saturdays at 9:30. For information on additional moves Now What? will make before its inevitable cancellation, visit ABC.com. ∅

Debuts September 15th on abc

Above: The opening credits of Morris' sitcom.

REPUBLICANS from page 253

Gerald Polder said. "This guy in a suit came in with multiple contusions, a subdural hematoma, and a broken nose. I asked how badly it hurt to bend his knee, on a scale of 1 to 10, and he said, 'I'm hurt worse than Kerry was when he got his Purple Hearts.' That's not helpful."

Polder said he has not seen so many right-wing injuries since the late '90s, when hundreds of Republicans were hurt climbing on and off the Newt Gingrich bandwagon.

While squashed toes have been the most common injury, the more dramatic include the skull and spine fractures suffered by an elderly senator who was trampled in the mad dash to smear, bash, and cast aspersions on Kerry. Many of those bearing sound bites also have dislocated joints in those places where their fingers were pried from microphones.

"I was in the crowd on the National Archive steps," conservative *Washington Times* columnist Paul Greenberg said, holding his head as he awaited treatment for deep shock and moral outrage. "When I realized everyone else there also wanted abstracts of Kerry's congressional voting records, I started to run. I guess we all had the same idea at the same time. It feels like I got rolled over by a 10-ton think tank."

"I was lucky, though," Greenberg said, wrapping himself in the flag. "Worst thing hurt was my pride."

> **While squashed toes have been the most common injury, the more dramatic include the skull and spine fractures suffered by an elderly senator who was trampled in the mad dash to smear, bash, and cast aspersions on Kerry.**

Washington has reported the largest number of casualties, but across the nation, reports are still coming in from politically "red" states made redder by the spilled blood of conservatives caught in the maelstrom of accusations and flailing bodies.

"It's bad down here," Savannah (GA) General Hospital director Lloyd Sautner said. "We were still treating hurricane victims when all these politicians were hurt in the whirlwind of manufactured controversy. Anywhere there were reporters and TV cameras, Republicans were climbing all over each other in an effort to be heard."

Los Angeles producer Margaret Oakes said the set of the TV show *Roundtable* was overrun with frantic conservatives.

"I tried telling them to stop, that they were only hurting themselves, but they didn't seem to fear for their credibility one bit," Oakes said. "One woman tried to get to the front of the crowd, slipped, and fell face-first into a forest of microphone stands. When I asked her where she was hurt, she said, 'the cheek… of that man to misrepresent his voting record on gay marriage.'"

Rep. Chris Shays (R-CT) called for an end to the zealotry that has already resulted in the hospitalization of 86 GOP members.

"Let us not rush to judgment and inadvertently hurt our own image," Shays said Sunday. "This Republican-on-Republican violence must end."

Shays added that his prayers are

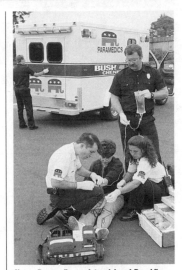

Above: Paramedics assist an injured Republican.

with Rush Limbaugh's family. The conservative radio personality died Tuesday when a busload of pro-Bush Vietnam veterans, in their rush to lambast Kerry on the air, ran a red light, swerved to avoid a carload of *National Review* reporters, and smashed through the wall of the Excellence In Broadcasting studio, killing Limbaugh and three sound technicians. ∅

PHOTOGRAPHER from page 253

class as a whole," said Geraldine Menzies, director of the National Academy of Classroom Arts in Philadelphia, where many of Anszczak's works are exhibited. "He lifted the school-portrait camera from its rigid confines and moved it several feet closer."

Fresh out of the Army in 1946, armed with a Graflex Speed Graphic camera and a tripod, Anszczak began his school-photography career relatively late in life. The 34-year-old entered a stagnant field, where the standard practice of shooting black-and-white snapshots of entire classes from a distance had gone unquestioned for decades. While it saved on film and developing costs, the process resulted in a final portrait in which many subjects were out of focus, too small to see, or obscured altogether. When Anszczak retired in 1986, he left a field that had fully embraced his color close-ups and woodland backdrops.

This sea change eliminated the process, considered tedious by photographers and teachers alike, of assembling a class as a whole. Anszczak's innovation also eliminated the problem of group photos ruined by absenteeism and individual students' antics, such as goofy expressions or inappropriate hand gestures.

Anszczak is credited with having invented the classroom composite, in which many small, rectangular portraits are arranged in rows for display.

"Anszczak single-handedly standardized the wallet-size," Menzies said. "It was his discovery that, in addition to a 5"x7" portrait suitable for framing, a student might like a number of smaller photos to offer to those peers with whom he or she plans to remain best friends forever."

Anszczak was the first school photographer to offer matte finish. He was the first to seat subjects on a stool, to direct them in proper placement of their hands, and to offer them the use of a black plastic comb before the photo was taken. He pioneered use of soft-focus, previously seen only in Hollywood glamour portraits, in senior-year photos. And he introduced the now-famous "fence post, wagon wheel, and bale of hay" tableau, which became an industry standard.

"Scholars debate whether it was Anszczak or his assistant who invented the double-exposure, in which a profile of the student's face appears over the shoulder of the forward-facing subject," Menzies said. "But there is no question that they were the first to use the technique in the portable studio."

Anszczak's innovations, now universally accepted, were initially criticized. Parents thought that the individual close-ups bore an uncomfortable similarity to police mug shots. Additionally, many argued that the process of focusing so closely on the subject placed under undue stress.

Following the Vietnam war, a new batch of critics argued that Anszczak's work had reactionary, anti-social tendencies. In a famous essay for Mrs. Larsen's tenth-grade English class at Sherman High School in Little Rock, AR, sophomore Wayne Kleiff derided the photographer's individual portraits as "a physical manifestation of the isolation produced from postwar suburbanization."

> **Parents thought that the individual close-ups bore an uncomfortable similarity to police mug shots. Additionally, many argued that the process of focusing so closely on the subject placed under undue stress.**

"Before Anszczak, the individual was represented as part of a whole," wrote Kleiff, '78. "What's missing from Anszczak's work is a sense of community, of people mutually sharing a social and educational experience. Is it any coincidence that he and suburbia mushroomed together? Like the white picket fence around a single-story frame home, the white borders in Anszczak's composite photos serve to separate, to isolate, to detach. At their worst, they promote narcissism and insularity."

Kleiff's composition received an A.

Anszczak's fans, however, laud the spontaneity of his work. In spite of the controlled conditions in a school's cafeteria or gymnasium on photo day, imperfections would occur. Anszczak resolutely refused to do retakes.

"Look at these superb Anszczaks here," said Dorian Childsworth, a photography historian at George Eastman House in Rochester, NY, as she gestured at an open portfolio of portraits. "Observe the immediacy of his work. We see closed eyes, drifting gazes, unattractively agape mouths, tucked-in collars, and hair sticking up all funny. But Anszczak did not weed such imperfections out. He embraced them. In so doing, he captured the awkward hearts and souls of these individuals. These photos show an intuitive sympathy at work—the mark of a true artist."

"Rest in peace, Mr. Anszczak," Childsworth added. "Or, in your words, 'Say cheeseburger.'"

After an incredible 40-year career, Anszczak rejected photography in 1986 to pursue "purer artistic pursuits that more actively engage the mind's eye." In this late period, he designed yearbook covers and lunchroom murals.

Still, Anszczak will be remembered best for his widely emulated school portraiture. Fittingly, school districts across the country lowered their flags to half-staff in honor of Anszczak on the day following his death. In addition, the International League of Hot Lunch Workers Monday announced plans to rename fruit-cocktail cups "Henrys." ∅

Absolute Cute

A Room Of Jean's Own
By Jean Teasdale

I just had a *major* idea, and I want to write it down and get it out there before I begin to second-guess it. So here goes:

I, Jean Teasdale, am seriously thinking about going into the pom-pom-balls-with-googly-eyes business.

(No wait, Jean. Don't say "seriously thinking." Say, "I, Jean Teasdale, will go into the pom-pom-balls-with-googly-eyes business," because it's *totally within your reach* and it's *going to happen*.)

Do you know what I'm talking about, Jeanketeers? Those little fuzzy pom-pom balls with plastic googly eyes on them? And then they have little paper feet with stickum on the bottom? So you can mount them to something?

I suppose I should back up a bit and explain why I had this brainstorm. For months, I've had, in the back of my head, the idea of creating a home-based business. If I were self-employed, I could do something that I love and have control over, instead of punching in at some boring office or store and getting bossed around all the time. The tough question was, what should I do? Well, the answer came to me earlier today while I was at the outdoor charity-craft bazaar that the local mall sponsors twice a year. Now, I just love crafts, and I've been known to create a few myself. (Back in the early '80s, I taught myself how to crochet those cute worm-shaped bookmarks with the long tails that end in tassels. Remember those?)

I was mentally mapping out a place in my apartment to hang a Styrofoam ostrich marionette when a long, rainbow-colored, furry table at another booth caught my eye. Curious to see what it was all about, I walked closer. Well, it wasn't the table itself that was rainbow-colored and furry, but rows and rows of—you guessed it—pom-poms with googly eyes! I mean, there were *hundreds* of them. I was enchanted!

A woman was sitting behind the table, knitting quietly. I asked her if she'd made the pom-poms. She said she hadn't and explained that the adorable little fellas were the work of the residents of the Grapevine Group Home for Developmentally Disabled Adults.

I snapped up a bunch of pom-pom critters, several of each color. When I got home, I had quite a time trying to decide where to stick the first one. On the TV? On top of the fridge? Along the windowsill in my bedroom? On the mantelpiece above our artificial fireplace? Atop the medicine cabinet? On the stereo speakers? On the heat registers? On my jewelry box? On the wooden utility rack above the kitchen sink? In my curio cabinet? On my clock radio? On the plastic Kleenex box cover in the bathroom? On the phone receiver?

I finally decided on my computer monitor. But when I reached into my bag of pom-poms to pull one of the little guys out, I found something very disturbing. A googly eye had come off of one of the green pom-poms, and the feet were peeling off of both a red and a pink one. At least three others were starting to unravel. When I finally found a pom-pom with all its facial features intact, the feet would not stick to my monitor!

I have to say, I was more than a little disappointed with the pom-pom critters. They were not up to par. It came down to two words: shoddy craftsmanship. The eyes, as well as the feet, had been glued on with regular glue. Any idiot knows that affixing tiny plastic eyes onto an uneven polyester surface calls for the use of a hot-glue gun.

> A woman was sitting behind the table, knitting quietly. I asked her if she'd made the pom-poms. She said she hadn't and explained that the adorable little fellas were the work of the residents of the Grapevine Group Home for Developmentally Disabled Adults.

Where was the quality control? (I'm all for giving developmentally disabled adults jobs, but they need supervision.)

I could think of a lot of ways these pom-pom critters could be improved. For starters, the eyes and feet need to be affixed properly. Next, mouths would lend the pom-poms a little more personality. Or maybe even eyebrows and mustaches. And different types of footwear. Or antennae, like little Martian men? Or tiny felt hats, or even eyeglasses? And, if they have little paper feet, why not paper hands, too? The hands could hold things, like signs with inspirational messages on them!

Then, in a flash of inspiration, it dawned on me that I could make the pom-poms. This could be the home-based business I've been dreaming about all my life! It would marry my creative yearnings with my desire to stay home! Also, due to my medical condition, it's advisable that I work in a calm, familiar environment. (I have Type-2 diabetes. Even though I'm not technically disabled and would resent anybody treating me differently, I need to be more careful about looking out for my health and well-being.)

There's an obvious market out there for well-crafted pom-pom balls with googly eyes. Otherwise, you wouldn't see them at bazaars and gift shops. And why wouldn't people want them? They're cheap, unconditionally friendly, and non-judgmental. (Heaven knows we could all use a friend right now, seeing as how the world hates America's guts so much.)

But there's one thing that's even more inspiring than the prospect of self-employment or giving people a little joy. You see, I recently realized that the driving force in my life, the thing that gets me off the ol' waterbed every morning, is my relentless pursuit of "absolute cute." I saw a show on the learning channel about how the lowest temperature possible is called "absolute zero." Well, why can't there be an "absolute cute"? That is, a form of cuteness that has reached ultimate perfection? I believe that, in their perfected form, pom-pom critters could achieve absolute cuteness.

In order to be cute, something must meet four standards. First, the item's exterior must be round, and its limbs, if any, must be stubby. Second, it should have eyes that are round, and very large in proportion to the figure's size. Third, it needs to be soft. Fourth, and most importantly, an item, if truly cute, will pass this test: If expanded to large proportions—say, the size of a Macy's parade balloon—it will still be cute. (Unlike Bullwinkle, for example.)

I realize that I'm getting a tad far afield here, Jeanketeers. But I'm really excited about my idea of making and selling my own pom-pom balls with googly eyes. I'll think about money, time, and production issues later. For now, I'm going to get out my trusty sketchpad, plunk myself down, and whip up some prototypes! ∅

Your Horoscope

By Lloyd Schumner Sr.
Retired Machinist and
A.A.P.B.-Certified Astrologer

Aries: (March 21–April 19)
Your beloved Sparky will shock you by traveling 1,000 miles back to you. But then again, loyalty is the reason you married him in the first place.

Taurus: (April 20–May 20)
It's going to be a busy, nerve-wracking week, but by the end, you'll be elevated to Imperator For Life Of The Greater Taurus Economic Co-Prosperity Sphere.

Gemini: (May 21–June 21)
No one's ever called you a rich, sexy genius, but that was before National Say Hurtfully Untrue Things Day.

Cancer: (June 22–July 22)
You'll help realize Western civilization's oldest dream, but it's only the one about getting to school late on exam day.

Leo: (July 23–Aug. 22)
An unlikely coincidence involving the spontaneous combustion of your trousers and their subsequent suspension from communications cables will not be enough to teach you to tell the truth.

Virgo: (Aug. 23–Sept. 22)
You're working hard on your list of songs you want played at your funeral, but the flawed premise of the project is that it assumes the presence of attendees.

Libra: (Sept. 23–Oct. 23)
Your reading group insists that the Iowa School is more concerned with list-making than with producing good fiction, but frankly, you just wanted to talk about hobbits.

Scorpio: (Oct. 24–Nov. 21)
Don't waste time developing a healthy body image, as your body will look a hell of a lot different starting Thursday.

Sagittarius: (Nov. 22–Dec. 21)
Romance and a felicitous atmosphere for new projects are foretold by the moon passing through your sign this week, as well as—wait a second! *That's no moon!*

Capricorn: (Dec. 22–Jan. 19)
It's difficult to be compassionate and loving in today's increasingly cruel world. The term "diminishing returns" comes to mind.

Aquarius: (Jan. 20–Feb. 18)
You'll be repeatedly cited as a living refutation of the Great Man theory of history.

Pisces: (Feb. 19–March 20)
All the stars in your sign have an important message of hope, but you may not get it before the sudden explosion in your galactic spiral arm Wednesday.

NEWS

the ONION®

VOLUME 40 ISSUE 37   AMERICA'S FINEST NEWS SOURCE™   16–22 SEPTEMBER 2004

Experimental Band Theoretically Good

see ENTERTAINMENT page 15D

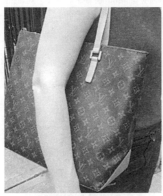

Tiny Dog Suffocates In Louis Vuitton Bag

see PETS page 4E

Spokesperson Wearing Lab Coat For Some Reason

see LOCAL page 8B

Juice Enjoyed By SEPT22

see LOCAL page 10B

STATshot

A look at the numbers that shape your world.

Least Popular Appetizers

- 7% Schenectady wings
- 11% Deep-fried baskets
- 15% Membrane puffs
- 16% Hors d'larvae
- 10% Hock pockets
- 13% Swedish peatballs
- 6% Greasy grimy gopher guts
- 22% Carrot sticks

Fetal Pigs In A Blanket

THE ONION • $2.00 US • $3.00 CAN

Cheney Returns To Camp Crystal Lake

Above: Camp Crystal Lake, the site of many recent as-yet-unsolved murders.

Cheney

CRYSTAL LAKE, NJ—Reports of a shadowy figure in the woods and heavy breathing heard in the night, coupled with a recent series of grisly murders, have generated rumors that U.S. Vice-President Dick Cheney has returned to terrorize the counselors at Camp Crystal Lake, sources reported Friday.

"I knew it'd been too quiet around here," camp caretaker Ephram Magritte, 67, said between sips from his flask. "Things were just starting to get back to normal. Then that carload

see CHENEY page 263

Female Athletes Making Great Strides In Attractiveness

LOS ANGELES—In the wake of the Summer Olympics, during which many American women achieved a level of media attention often reserved for men, sports fans are pleased to report that female athletes are continuing to make great strides in their personal appearances.

"As recently as 20 years ago, women's sports were for hardcore

see ATHLETES page 262

Below: Maria Sharapova.

Above: Rescuers attempt to free Rybicki (inset).

Trapped Miner Wishes He Could See The Coverage

MCINTYRE, PA—Kevin Rybicki, a coal miner trapped 340 feet underground, wished Monday that he had more headlamp batteries, another sandwich, and access to the coverage of his plight—which, he assumes, is captivating the nation.

"I can't believe how much this sucks," the 47-year-old Western Pennsylvania Mining Corporation employee said, speaking into the darkness. "I'm trapped, I can't stand up, I'm scared to death, and, to top it off, I'm missing all the news stories about me. My big moment, and I'm stuck hundreds of feet below the action."

Coverage of the disaster started just after noon Friday, when the *Western Pennsylvania News-Leader* announced that a series of load-bearing tunnel spars had collapsed and trapped 32 miners. The paper reported that rescuers were able to free all of the miners except for Rybicki, who was separated from his team by a wall of rock and debris following the cave-in.

After hearing the sounds of rescuers working to free him, Rybicki organized his meager supplies and settled into his crouched position.

"I wonder if there are helicopters out there," Rybicki said as he banged a fist-sized rock against the wall above in hopes of helping rescuers pinpoint his location. "I'm sure, at the very least, there's a whole bunch of vans with satellite dishes on them."

At 4 a.m. Saturday, Rybicki determined that the seep-water level was

see MINER page 262

Assault-Weapons Ban Expires

The 10-year-old federal law banning the sale of 19 types of semiautomatic assault weapons expired Monday. What do *you* think?

James Farwell
CPA

"Finally, I can bring ol' Missy out of hiding. Come on out, Missy. Daddy says it's safe now."

Tammy Graves
Journalist

"The people who want assault weapons banned can't provide any evidence that they're used for criminal activity. See, you can't use common sense as evidence."

Liza Redding
Secretary

"When we enacted this ban in 1994, it was an important step to protect our children. Now that our children are grown up and off at college, it's not such a pressing issue."

Sam Li
Electrician

"Hey, if I could turn the clock back to a time before titanium deer with full electronic countermeasures, I would. But face it, I need this Kalashnikov."

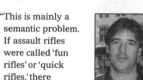

Daniel Moore
Systems Analyst

"This is mainly a semantic problem. If assault rifles were called 'fun rifles' or 'quick rifles,' there wouldn't be all this outrage."

Jim Mertens
Sewer Worker

"If the criminals are going to have assault rifles, I should, too. Actually, can I have a better one than they do?"

Hurricane Preparedness

What are some of the hurricane-season pointers outlined by the National Hurricane Center?

▶ Place all buoyant possessions safely in basement

▶ If you live in a mobile home, break it up into small, non-lethal debris before storm hits

▶ Throughout hurricane season, call your parents each day and let them know you're still alive

▶ If you see a suspicious-looking hurricane sitting unattended, notify the National Weather Service immediately

▶ To protect your skin from the harmful effects of hurricanes, wear at least a grade 15 stormscreen

▶ Hurricanes named after women tend to build in pressure as the days go by, finally exploding into a rage; hurricanes named after men are shorter in duration, but never seem to be aware of how much pain they cause

▶ Florida residents: Vote yes on Proposition 84 to put a hurricane-proof dome over your state

▶ Listen to your local radio station for weather updates and potential REO Speedwagon broadcasts

the ONION®
America's Finest News Source.™

Herman Ulysses Zweibel
Founder

T. Herman Zweibel
Publisher Emeritus
J. Phineas Zweibel
Publisher
Maxwell Prescott Zweibel
Editor-In-Chief

I Feel I Have Earned The Right To Not Have To Call 'Shotgun'

By Dan Viesel

Jeff? Did I just hear what I think I did? Is it possible that you just said "shotgun"? That's pretty fucked up, Jeff. Because I think it's pretty obvious that, after all these years, I've earned the right to not to have to say "shotgun" when we get into the car.

Okay, everyone shut up. Let's discuss this.

Each of us has a role in Rick's car. Rick is the driver. What he says goes. However, as he is occupied with the top duty—getting us safely to our destination—he leaves me to handle certain details, such as the radio station and garbage control. I am Rick's second man, his cardinal advisor, if you will. I can't even guess the number of times I have alerted him to the presence of bacon on the side.

Yes, ha ha. You find that funny? You three sit back there elbowing each other and quoting *Aqua Teen Hunger Force*. You don't even realize that there's a whole complex set of tasks being completed up front. Take, for example, the drive-thru. Justin, what do you think goes into getting food from the drive-thru? No one help him! I want to hear his answer.

"Ordering"? Uh-huh. Sure. Ordering. Good. Anything else? "Paying." Very good. Anything else? No? You sure? Try collecting money from each person and making change, taking the soda tray and bags of food from Rick, and distributing the correct food items, as well as napkins and condiments, to each occupant of the car. Ordering and paying. Pfft.

No, I am not freaking out, "dude." I am illustrating a point, and if you want to be a dick, I will happily meet you at your level.

Fine, the gloves are off.

Justin, the one time we went through a drive-thru with you in shotgun, you dumped a goddamn Big Gulp's worth of Sprite in Rick's lap. When you thought no one was watching, you stole one of Will's chicken fingers. You thought you'd gotten away with it, didn't you? Four years riding the wing, and I have not so much as dropped an unopened ketchup packet. I have certainly never abused my privileges and snagged a fry—much less an entire finger. Being klutzy is one thing. Being a thief is something else altogether.

That funny, Will, you pussy? You heard me. You are a pussy with the radio dial. This is you: "Guys, what's a good station?" It takes a man to decide what his friends are going to listen to—a man of action, and you have

shown, several times, that you're not a man of action. No pussy will ride wing for Rick as long as I'm saving for my brother's Honda.

Jeff, you seem to be enjoying this. Laugh not too loud, my friend, lest you find they jokest at your expense. I grant that you are a competent operator of the radio dial and quite adept at passing food. I noted some flaws in your technique, but nothing several months of sidecar wouldn't fix. What impresses me most, Jeff, is your character: You are honest and considerate. You are strong and fair. Jeff, you have the makings of a great wingman. Unfortunately, you are not ready at present, as your sense of direction sucks.

Remember that trip to your aunt's beach house? You said you knew the

> ## You don't even realize that there's a whole complex set of tasks being completed up front.

way, so I entrusted you with the role of navigator for a day. Well, thank God I had the foresight to bring along Mapquest directions, or we never would've made it to your aunt's at all.

Oh, come on, Jeff. Who was calling out specific turns to Rick, as well as the approximate distance before the next turn, and who was muttering, "Oh, yeah, I forgot that"? *And you want to ride shotgun? For Rick?* Maybe if you sit down with every map from the glove compartment and study for a few weeks. Then, perhaps someday, you'll qualify for the sweet corner. But really, what you guys should do is just enjoy the freedom from responsibility you now have in the rear. You especially, Will. As the hump-rider, you don't even have to operate a window.

Okay, if you don't want to appreciate riding rear, fine. But you need to stop taking my function as a considerate front-seat passenger for granted. I don't know how many times I've adjusted the heat for you guys. I always check to see if the person behind me has enough legroom. I never toss a cigarette from my window without looking to see that the back windows are closed. And when Jeff broke up with his girlfriend, I gave him shotgun when we went over to her place to pick up his CDs.

I confess that I am not without sin. I have been known to be a bit brusque

see SHOTGUN page 264

College Sophomore Thinks She Would Make A Good Sex Columnist

STATE COLLEGE, PA—Lisbet "Lizzie" Gilchrist, a second-year undergraduate at Penn State University, told reporters that she has the makings of a good sex-advice columnist Monday.

"Whenever I read a sex column in a magazine or newspaper, I always think, 'I could totally write this,'" said Gilchrist, a 19-year-old undeclared

Although she isn't old enough to drink alcohol, Gilchrist can identify the major kinds of sex toys, knows what "frottage" is, and understands the subtleties of bringing herself to climax.

Above: Gilchrist on the campus she feels could benefit from her wisdom.

major. "I'm always giving advice to my friends about what kind of condoms to get, or whether you should use lube or not. I'm not afraid to discuss things other people are too embarrassed to talk about."

Although she isn't old enough to drink alcohol, Gilchrist can identify the major kinds of sex toys, knows what "frottage" is, and understands the subtleties of bringing herself to climax.

"Sex is as natural a part of life as birth or death," Gilchrist said. "People shouldn't be so weird about it. I lay it on the line. Penis, vagina—I'm not afraid to tell it like it is."

The aspiring sexpert said she would draw from her own experiences to compose solid, reliable sex-advice columns.

"I've been in some pretty crazy situations," said Gilchrist, who is currently single but has had three rela-

tionships and five sexual partners. "So many college sex columnists—like the one who writes for *The Daily Collegian*—sound like they're copying out of a human sexuality textbook. Well, I'd talk about real-life experiences. Believe me, I've had plenty of them."

Gilchrist said that when she was 17, her mother found a vibrator in her room.

"My mom never found out that it

was the 23-year-old guy I was secretly seeing who bought it for me!" Gilchrist said. "And a couple months ago, I was at a party where these guys dared me and this girl to make out. We totally did."

Gilchrist's friends are relatively inexperienced, often making them targets for her advice.

"Lizzie would make an all-right sex columnist, I guess," fellow sophomore

see SOPHOMORE page 263

NEWS IN BRIEF

Kerry Vows To Raise Wife's Taxes

BOSTON—Campaigning in his home state, John Kerry vowed Monday to raise taxes on his wife Teresa Heinz Kerry, whose worth is estimated to be in the range of $900 million to $3.2 billion. "My spouse has benefited long enough from tax cuts," Kerry said. "If Congress increased her taxes by 15 percent, this country would have millions of dollars to use to create new jobs and explore alternative energy sources." Kerry added that it's high time that billionaires like the one with whom he shares his life start paying their fair share.

Recreational-Abortion Enthusiasts Applaud Repeal Of Partial-Birth Ban

WASHINGTON, DC—Hundreds of abortion enthusiasts gathered on the steps of the Supreme Court Monday to voice their support for recent rulings repealing the Partial-Birth Abortion Ban Act of 2003. "We just adore abortions, and now they're more convenient than ever," abortion lover Nayla Forster said. "Some women found it a real pain to squeeze the procedure in before the third trimester." Forster said that she personally tries to get out and have an abortion at least every four months or so.

Cinemax Director Wins Award For Skinematography

HOLLYWOOD, CA—Marvin Solis, director of the late-night Cinemax offering *Uptown Girl*, nabbed the coveted Best Skinematography trophy at the 2004 Eroty Awards Monday night. "It's truly an honor to be recognized for this wonderful project," Solis said of the 43-minute erotic thriller, which stars Kira Jackson as a bored high-society housewife seduced into the steamy world of underground sex clubs. "I couldn't have done it without the help of my location scout, my lighting coordinator, and all those 14-year-old Cinemax viewers." Last year, Solis won the Zalman King Lifetime Achievement Award.

Petulant 12-Year-Old Refuses To Brown The Ground Chuck

SCOTTSDALE, AZ—In spite of repeated requests from his mother, 12-year-old John Farina refused to brown the ground chuck Monday. "With the things I do around here, I ask you to do one thing to help me get dinner ready, and even that's too much," Farina's mother Karen yelled at the wall of her son's bedroom, where he had been playing a video game since returning from school. "And I don't care if you don't want taco casserole—it's your sister's turn to pick. You chose sloppy joes yesterday, so deal with it." Family sources report that Farina acceded to his mother's hamburger-related demands as soon as she introduced the alternate threat of washing the lettuce.

Letter Of Recommendation Reused For Eighth Intern

NEW YORK—Attorney Dina H. Berman of Oliva, Berman & Chase said Tuesday that he has used the same letter of recommendation for eight consecutive interns. "Unless someone is a complete fuck-up, I can pretty much pull up the letter and just change the names and dates," Berman said. "They're all 'enterprising and enthusiastic with a lot of great ideas and an asset to any team' to me." Berman finished the letter with the standard offer to answer any questions about the intern, but did not correct the transposed digits in her phone number. ∅

ATHLETES from page 259

fans only, most of them women," Gary Hoenig, editor of *ESPN The Magazine*, said Monday. "But due in a large part to the superior facial features of women like Maria Sharapova, the media have turned a spotlight on female athletics—and Americans of both genders are tuning in."

According to Hoenig, coverage of female athletes is no longer relegated to the back pages of sports magazines.

"Female players are finally being recognized by a larger audience—

> ## "In the old days, when people talked about the female athletes of the day, words like 'perky,' 'fit,' and even 'handsome' would be used," Hoenig said. "Today, you hear words like 'sexy,' 'hot,' and even 'fuckable.' These women athletes are more attractive than ever."

they're getting larger photos in the newspapers, appearing on talk shows, and taking the covers of magazines like *Maxim* and *Playboy*," Hoenig said. "As these ladies get prettier, that exposure will only grow."

Although women's athletics have produced the occasional good-looking stars, like tennis great Chris Evert or gymnast Mary Lou Retton, women like U.S. soccer champions Mia Hamm and Brandi Chastain have raised the bar.

"In the old days, when people talked about the female athletes of

the day, words like 'perky,' 'fit,' and even 'handsome' would be used," Hoenig said. "Today, you hear words like 'sexy,' 'hot,' and even 'fuckable.' These women athletes are more attractive than ever, and the nation is taking notice."

Experts say the massive popularity of tennis champ Anna Kournikova has had an undeniable effect on female athletics, as well.

"Anna changed the way people see female athletes," Hoenig said. "She's not just focused on being a star on the court. She wants to star at red-carpet events, in the gossip pages, and in her own line of swimsuit calendars. That she never won a singles tournament and barely cracked the Top 10 ranking during her athletic career doesn't change the fact that she looks incredibly hot in a tennis ensemble."

Though some female athletes make beauty seem effortless, it isn't, Hoenig said.

"Six-pack abs don't just happen," Hoenig said. "These ladies work. Sure, some of their fabulous strides in appearance can be traced back to superior genes, but Mother Nature only gets you so far. Jennie Finch, pitcher for the U.S. Olympic softball team, reported that she spends as many as six hours a day at the gym."

"It shows," he added.

Hoenig also applauded the increased effort women athletes are putting into fashion.

"Serena Williams, with her wide assortment of outfits, exemplifies the changing face of women's sports," Hoenig said. "And don't forget lady jocks like Mary Sauer and Haley Cope. Do you know how difficult it is to be as physically active as these women are and still have long hair? Without it, you aren't likely to get on the cover of *FHM*."

According to Frank Borne, author of Great Strides, younger generations are more willing to embrace good-looking women athletes than are older sports fans. As a result, more sports franchises are now seeking attractive

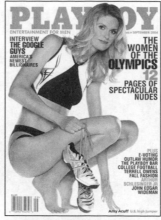

Above: U.S. Olympic high jumper Amy Acuff.

individuals to serve as the faces and firm bodies representing their respective teams.

"It's so refreshing to see more female athletes overcome hurdles," Borne said. "Thanks to their superior facial features and careful attention to hair and clothing, many of these girls are achieving what would have been thought impossible a few decades ago. Perhaps someday, women athletes will be pretty enough to rank among the nation's top actresses and models."

Unfortunately, Borne said, professional sports organizations, by focusing on the women's athletic achievements, sometimes hamper the players' ability to draw a crowd.

"A lot of athletes find themselves hamstrung by the rules of their own teams," Borne said. "It wouldn't hurt the WNBA to come up with sexier team outfits. Do you realize how much their audience would broaden if more of these girls were allowed some time off to model on the side? Tastefully done semi-nude photo shoots bring a lot of attention to the players and the sports they play."

Added Borne: "Isn't that what any athlete really wants—to bring her sport and team more glory? I think it is." ⌀

MINER from page 259

rising at a rate of about two inches per hour. Several hours before, the Saturday *Philadelphia Inquirer* went to press with a photo of Rybicki on the front page, above the fold, under the headline "Miner In Peril."

By Saturday afternoon, out-of-state mobile camera crews began to arrive in McIntyre. Shortly thereafter, MSNBC aired an interview with a Western Pennsylvania spokesman who described the friable, shifting rock under which Rybicki was trapped. The story marked Rybicki's national-television debut and included a group photo of Rybicki and several other miners.

"You know what I hope?" Rybicki said Sunday afternoon, angling his face toward the 20-inch pocket of air at the top of the nearly flooded four-foot-high tunnel in which he was trapped. "I hope they use that picture of me hitting that two-run homer in the softball game last year. Or better yet, one of me and my kids. Clay and Becky would love to see their faces on television."

Added Rybicki: "I'd love to see their faces again, too. Or hear their voices."

As nationwide coverage continued and the carbon-dioxide levels rose within Rybicki's cramped space, he

> ## "I wish Kevin was here to see this," Rybicki said.

missed some extremely compelling reportage. ABC's *Good Morning America* aired a brief but engaging overview of his mining career which included the much-told family chestnut of how his father and uncle were involved in previous mine accidents.

"If they'd figure out a way to drill through this cap rock and string me down a microphone or something, then I'd be able to tell them about me firsthand," Rybicki said. "I'm sure it'd be more exciting for the viewers than hearing one of the other miners describe me. I mean, really, the guys only know so much."

CBS aired a tearful but hopeful interview with Rybicki's wife, of which Rybicki would certainly have been proud.

"I wish Kevin was here to see this," said Claire Rybicki, his wife of 11 years, unconsciously echoing her husband's thoughts. "If I know my husband, he'd be touched and impressed by this nationally televised show of support."

As of press time, Rybicki was using a rusty nail to scratch his wife a note on a Hostess Cupcake wrapper.

"Man, I sure hope Claire's recording all the news," Rybicki said. "I'm not sure if she knows how to set the VCR. Then again, if this ends badly, then she'll have it on tape. That'd be horrible."

"Hello?" Rybicki added suddenly, dropping his nail in the neck-level water. "Hello? Anyone?" ⌀

GRINGO from page 32

amounts of blood. Passersby were amazed by the unusually large amounts of blood. Passersby were amazed by the unusually large amounts of blood. Passersby were amazed by the unusually large amounts of blood. Passersby were amazed by the unusually large amounts of blood. Passersby were amazed by the unusually large amounts of blood. Passersby were amazed by the unusually large amounts of blood. Passersby were amazed by the unusually large amounts of blood. Passersby were amazed by the unusually large amounts of blood. Passersby were amazed by the unusually large amounts of blood. Passersby were amazed by the unusually large amounts of blood. Passersby were amazed by the unusually large amounts of blood. Passersby were amazed by the unusually large amounts of blood. Passersby were amazed by the unusually large amounts of blood. Passersby were amazed by the unusually large amounts of blood. Passersby were amazed by the unusually large

amounts of blood. Passersby were amazed by the unusually large amounts of blood. Passersby were amazed by the unusually large amounts of blood. Passersby were amazed by the unusually large amounts of blood. Passersby were

> ## Children that are not retarded or born with any birth defects are our future.

amazed by the unusually large amounts of blood. Passersby were amazed by the unusually large amounts of blood. Passersby were amazed by the unusually large amounts of blood. Passersby were

amazed by the unusually large amounts of blood. Passersby were amazed by the unusually large amounts of blood. Passersby were amazed by the unusually large amounts of blood. Passersby were amazed by the unusually large amounts of blood. Passersby were amazed by the unusually large amounts of blood. Passersby were amazed by the unusually large amounts of blood. Passersby were amazed by the unusually large amounts of blood. Passersby were amazed by the unusually large amounts of blood. Passersby were amazed by the unusually large amounts of blood. Passersby were amazed by the unusually large amounts of blood. Passersby were amazed by the unusually large amounts of blood. Passersby were amazed by the unusually large amounts of blood. Passersby were amazed by the unusually large amounts of blood. Passersby were amazed by the unusually large amounts of blood. Passersby were amazed by the unusually large

see GRINGO page 298

Above: Cheney's glasses, as found in the woods near Camp Crystal Lake.

of kids had to go have a drinking party at the lake last Friday. When two of them went missing, people started up again, saying Cheney was back. We don't need that kind of talk. Stirs up trouble. Scares off customers."

Four hours later, Magritte was found hanging from a tree, his brass-handled cane protruding from his eye socket.

Although some locals say the deaths prove that Cheney has returned to Camp Crystal Lake, most residents remain skeptical.

"Dick Cheney? No, sir, Dick Cheney is dead," general-store owner Doug Leffert said as he packed groceries into a box. "Last person to see Cheney alive was Tommy Williams, the feller that killed him. Yeah, blew him up. Knocked him down with a propane tank and shot it. Heck of an explosion. Burned down the mess hall, too. All anyone found left of Cheney was his eyeglasses."

"Tommy was never the same after," Leffert added. "Been in an insane asylum up around Newton ever since."

According to camp counselor Jenny Marlatt, not every Crystal Lake murder was committed by Cheney.

"We all thought Cheney had returned last year," Marlatt said before pausing to inhale marijuana smoke from a soda-can pipe. "A bunch of people wound up getting murdered. But the killer turned out to be the brother of one of Cheney's victims. He put on some Cheney glasses and started killing people he thought should've kept a better eye on his brother."

More recently, Cheney's mother slaughtered nine people under the guise of her son before she was finally slain.

"Nah, Cheney hasn't been around for years," Marlatt said. "He's just a story mothers tell their children to get them to clean their plates."

Hours after Marlatt spoke to the press, her body was discovered hanging from the rafters in the camp's auditorium, her soda-can pipe jammed into her mouth.

Camp cook Henry Jones said that, while most of Cheney's homicides took place at Camp Crystal Lake and its immediate vicinity, the maniac has, on occasion, left the bucolic setting to stalk teens and police officers from other cities and towns.

"Remember when Cheney went to New York City?" Jones said Saturday. "They say he stowed away on a cruise

---

> ## "Cheney is an unstoppable killing machine," CNN's Anderson Cooper said via telephone.

---

ship of teenagers taking a graduation-night voyage around Manhattan Island. He killed almost everyone on board, then went ashore. Yes, sir, Cheney is back, all right—only this time, I know exactly how to stop him."

Those were among Jones' last words, as he was decapitated Sunday. His girlfriend, Jessica Clark, reported that a shadowy figure beheaded him with a machete while the couple kissed behind the camp's kitchen, shortly after she had removed her shirt.

Although nearly 100 Camp Crystal Lake staff members and visitors have been murdered in the last 25 years, experts report that the town is ill-prepared for the return of Cheney.

"Cheney is an unstoppable killing

machine," CNN's Anderson Cooper said via telephone. "He has been burned, stabbed, slashed, hacked, bludgeoned, and shot, only to get back up and continue his rampage. But when the town's self-absorbed teens try to explain that something is wrong, very wrong, their calls for help fall on deaf ears. There needs to be some accountability on the part of— oh, God! He's here!"

Cooper, who then dropped the telephone, has not been heard from since.

As they continue to investigate the recent murders, police have urged locals to stay in their heavily windowed cabins, ignore strange scratching noises, and abstain from any immoral acts that might inflame the passions of a psychopath.

"If you see Cheney, do not try to stop him yourself," police officer Brian Doan said. "He is extremely adept at cutting, stabbing, slicing, or skewering victims using whatever implement he comes across. And, whatever you do, keep all machetes well out of reach, way up on really high shelves. The last thing you want to do is tangle with Cheney when he's armed with one of those things."

Doan was found vivisected the next day.

When asked about Cheney's whereabouts, White House press secretary Scott McClellan vehemently denied speculation that Cheney was responsible for the recent slayings, stating that Cheney has been far too busy with the Bush re-election campaign to visit Camp Crystal Lake in recent weeks. He also denied rumors that Cheney has turned on Donald Rumsfeld after assisting him with a string of murders on Elm Street, and he strenuously insisted that the two high-ranking government officials will not fight to the death. ∅

Lisa Wong said. "She sure talks about that stuff a lot."

Wong said that Gilchrist starts off nearly every conversation by asking her if she has a boyfriend yet.

"I usually say that it's not a priority of mine right now, because I'm concentrating on getting through premed," Wong said. "Then she says I'm denying myself the pleasures of orgasm because of my sheltered upbringing. Last week, she sent me a link to a web site about frigidity."

Another friend of Gilchrist's, Leo Beck, said he has been dating the same girl for nearly two years.

"Lizzie says Jenny [Kroll] and I must have an unsatisfying sex life because we've been going out for so long," Beck said. "Maybe if I made something up about Jenny and me using ripcord beads, or seducing the pizza-delivery boy, she'd drop it."

When she isn't encouraging her

> According to *Daily Collegian* editor-in-chief Graham Edwards, Gilchrist's coy attitude and obtuse advice make her a promising candidate to succeed current campus sex columnist Megan Keane, who will graduate in May.

---

friends to be more promiscuous, Gilchrist urges them to play hard-to-get.

"I really like this guy John, who I met in my Food Science class, and I think he likes me," freshman Wendy Wheeler said. "It was never my plan to throw myself at him, and I thought I'd made that pretty clear to Lizzie, but she keeps telling me not to return his calls. She said I'm too young to limit my options. But when I told Lizzie that I really like John a lot, she said, 'It's 2004. Go buy a dildo.' Wha?"

Added Wheeler: "Maybe I should write in to one of those sex-advice columnists that they have in, like, every single campus paper."

According to *Daily Collegian* editor-in-chief Graham Edwards, Gilchrist's coy attitude and obtuse advice make her a promising candidate to succeed current campus sex columnist Megan Keane, who will graduate in May.

"It's a popular column, and [Gilchrist] would have to submit writing samples first, but, yeah, if she wants the job, she should go for it," Edwards said. "But the column's really meant to be more entertaining than informative. I don't think anyone seriously reads that thing for sex advice." ∅

Point-Counterpoint: Personal Fulfillment
I Wish My Life Was Better

By Carl Schmidt

I spend a lot of time sitting around, hoping that something will drop out of the sky and make my life better. I talk about it all the time. My friends have heard me say it, my family has heard me say it, and my ex-girlfriends have heard me say it. I really believe I deserve more than what I have, but whenever I think about how hard it is to turn things around, I end up feeling so hopeless. I'm stuck in a rut, but what can I do about it?

I look around my shabby apartment and say, "I could do better than this." My furniture is comfortable, but it doesn't even match. Is this the kind of place I want to have in five years? Ten? Certainly not, but what can I do to change that?

When I consider my job, I think, "Did I really choose to be a taxi dispatcher? Did I take control of life, or did it take control of me?" I'd always imagined I'd be working somewhere I could use my creativity, instead of doing the same boring thing day after day, week after week, month after month, until sud-denly, "Hey, Carl. Happy birthday, Carl. We got you a cake... 42, right? Wow." Still, the prospect of finding a new career is so daunting. Especially now that I've started to earn benefits. I feel like I'm stuck between a rock and a hard place.

Then there's my personal life. If only there were some way to improve my relationships. I really don't have a lot of friends. The few times I do get invited to a party, I usually end up sitting alone in the kitchen, loathing everyone else. Sometimes, I get the nagging feeling that if I could simply learn how to communicate more effectively, I'd not only have more friends, but I'd get along with my family, too. Maybe I'd even be married. I usually try to shake that feeling off, because I don't have the slightest clue how to change the way I interact with others.

I'm positive there's a better life out there for me. But every time I try to imagine what it might include, I get confused and frustrated. What I need is a plan of action, but it feels like I'll never find one that isn't impossible. As I go to sleep at night, I'm often gripped by the fear that I'm going to die poor, unloved, and unfulfilled. Isn't there someone out there who can help me? ∅

Do You Wish Your Life Was Better? Now It Can Be!

By Don Sparks

Are you someone who lies on the living-room couch, hoping that something is going to drop out of the sky and make your life better? Have your friends and family—even people you barely know—heard you wish, over and over, that there was something you could do? Does it seem hopeless? Do you wish your life was better? Well, I'm here to tell you right now that it can be. If you're stuck in a rut, the patented Total Forward Thinking program will help get you back on track.

Do you look around your apartment and say, "I could do better than this"? Sure, your house might be comfortable—maybe the furniture even matches—but I'm here to tell you that you can do better. The Total Forward Thinking program will help you find what your future could hold. Not only that, but it will take you, step-by-step, toward a work-able plan to get you where you really want to be.

I know what you're going through.

Before I created my Total Forward Thinking plan, I knew that the life I was living was not for me. I was renting a cramped, dirty studio apartment. I had a dead-end job. My social life? What social life?! I knew I deserved better, but I was paralyzed by failure. Thanks to the Total Forward Thinking principles, my wonderful family and I now live in a $2 million house that overlooks the ocean. I couldn't be happier!

You've got to stop wishing and hoping, and start doing. You've got to take a portion of each day and visualize where you want to be five years from now. You have to see it clearly, or you're never going to get there. Then, you have to come up with a workable plan to reach your goals. This is where my book, *Total Forward Thinking: The Plan*, comes in. My book will provide you with the real-world strategies you'll need to make your visualized future come to life.

The thing that many people don't understand is just how much the To-tal Forward Thinking plan can make a difference in your life. It's not just about your job or your apartment or material goods. It can also help your relationships. Not everyone knows they can change how they interact with their loved ones, but the fact is that they can. You can make things better, but it takes time, visualization, and, of course, Total Forward Thinking.

Total Forward Thinking completely changed my life. I still use the exercises outlined in my book, even though I have a successful career, a supermodel wife, and beautiful twin baby girls. I won't stop 'til the day I die, because Total Forward Thinking is a lifelong process. Things keep getting better, and they will for you, too—just as soon as you order *Total Forward Thinking: The Plan*. The book has everything you need to send your life in a wonderful new direction. You have my guarantee.

So if you're out there wondering, hoping, and wishing someone could help you get your life on track, now's the time to stop dreaming and start doing. Get on the path that will take you where you want to be. Total Forward Thinking will change the rest of your life. Act now! ∅

Your Horoscope

By Lloyd Schumner Sr.
Retired Machinist and
A.A.P.B.-Certified Astrologer

Aries: (March 21–April 19)
Your possession of a mystical third eye would cause less comment if you were also in possession of two regular eyes.

Taurus: (April 20–May 20)
It'll be months before you're allowed to show your face at the club again, after you get into a fistfight with the steward over the greatest living coloratura.

Gemini: (May 21–June 21)
This week, you'll learn a very important lesson about going for it on fourth down with so much time left on the clock.

Cancer: (June 22–July 22)
You're usually pretty careful, so it's worth mentioning when 36 are wounded during your trip to the grocery store.

Leo: (July 23–Aug. 22)
You'll wake up feeling pretty certain that the talking gorilla was just a dream, but that doesn't explain the Gorilla-to-English dictionary you find under your pillow.

Virgo: (Aug. 23–Sept. 22)
You'll do much weeping over what's going to happen to you this week, but because of the nature of the incident, gnashing of teeth won't really be an option.

Libra: (Sept. 23–Oct. 23)
Chef Gerard Pangaud's signature dishes include sweetbreads with morels, as well as lobster with ginger, lime, and Sauternes, but he's made it clear that they're not for you.

Scorpio: (Oct. 24–Nov. 21)
You'll be the first victim of the soon-to-be-popular "running 1000 volts through the take-a-penny tray" trick.

Sagittarius: (Nov. 22–Dec. 21)
The presence of Saturn in your sign usually indicates travel or pressing family issues, but it's been there for six months now, so it's probably just out of work again.

Capricorn: (Dec. 22–Jan. 19)
Your mistake at the self-serve pump will be monumental, but at least the amateur astronomers will enjoy watching your orbiting body for the next few weeks.

Aquarius: (Jan. 20–Feb. 18)
It's been said that numbers don't lie, but that was before you had time to work your magic on the rigid little bastards.

Pisces: (Feb. 19–March 20)
The confluence of many mystical signs and portents can only foretell that it's time to give your brother a call.

SHOTGUN from page 260

with my orders to defrost the rear window. On occasion, I have toyed with the child-safety locks. This I grant. But you want to get into the

Look, guys, I ride shotgun because I'm the right man for the job.

realm of dark truth? Justin, you once flipped on the hazard lights while Rick was driving. Ha ha, very funny. Until someone dies. And Jesus, Will, when you get a car of your own, challenge as many people to drag race as you want. Until then, work on your fear of the radio dial.

Look, guys, I ride shotgun because I'm the right man for the job. When I believe one of you is ready for the responsibility, I'll mention it to Rick. But for now, I'll continue riding up front, no matter who "called" it, and I'll thank you not to drive your knees into my back. ∅

Apparently Fire Marshal Wasn't Just Being A Dick

see LOCAL page 7B

Plastic Surgeon Has Leathery Wife

see PEOPLE page 13E

Ramones Reunion Nearly Complete

see ENTERTAINMENT page 8D

Self Medicated

see LOCAL page 14B

STATshot

A look at the numbers that shape your world.

What Role Is Russell Crowe Considering?

1. Hero scientist Louis Pasteur
2. Salome
3. Screaming man, any
4. Coach of worst gymnastic squad ever
5. Vin Diesel's next part
6. Wife and mother

---

the ONION®

VOLUME 40 ISSUE 38   AMERICA'S FINEST NEWS SOURCE™   23–29 SEPTEMBER 2004

THE WAR ON TERROR

Organizers Fear Terrorist Attacks On Upcoming Al-Qaeda Convention

Above: Guards secure what will be the main entrance to the al-Qaeda International Convention.

ASADABAD, AFGHANISTAN—Fears of possible terrorist attacks have led organizers of the Sept. 27-30 al-Qaeda International Convention to take unprecedented security measures, sources reported Monday.

"There are concerns about a possible attack, and we are responding by heightening security," al-Qaeda chairman and convention organizer Khalil al-Hamada said. "This year's convention will see longer lines and more comprehensive searches, and prospective martyrs will have difficulty gaining a private audience with Ayman al-Zawahiri. But, as

freedom-haters who have always stood for the disruption and overthrow of the West, we will not allow terror to blunt our resolve or dictate our message."

With Afghanistan's first nationwide elections slated for Oct. 9 and the U.S. general election three weeks later, the convention falls during a crucial time for al-Qaeda.

"More than 3,000 people are slated to slip across the border to attend," al-Hamada said. "While delegates were selected from within the ranks of known violent extremists, there

see CONVENTION page 269

Above: Sorenson and friends watch the game.

Intervention Wrapped Up Before Kickoff

ST. LOUIS—Friends of 33-year-old Drew Sorenson characterized a Sunday alcohol-abuse intervention as a success, reporting that they'd maintained a supportive but firm tone throughout the talk, which they were able to wrap up in time to watch the 12 p.m. Rams-Falcons game.

"It was important that we establish certain things with Drew," said Chris Gowan, who first noticed that Sorenson's drinking had become a problem during Wild Card week last season. "We wanted him to know that we are his friends and we love him, but we won't stand by and watch him destroy his life. And we wanted to get all that said before kickoff, so we could relax and enjoy the game."

It was Gowan, Sorenson's friend since college, who persuaded the support group to meet at his apartment and confront Sorenson. Gowan acknowledged that it was difficult to

see INTERVENTION page 268

Matchbox Twenty Finally Finishes Watering Down Long-Awaited New Album

Above: Matchbox Twenty.

LOS ANGELES—Executives at Atlantic Records announced Monday that multi-platinum recording artist Matchbox Twenty, which set sales records in 2000 for its mega-hit release *Mad Season*, has finally finished watering down tracks on its long-awaited new album *Beige*.

"Everyone here at Atlantic is thrilled about what's sure to be the biggest-selling, least-rocking record of the year," Atlantic public-relations spokeswoman Janet

Cosgrove said. "It's been a long wait, but the incredibly boring results speak for themselves. *Beige* is bigger and blander than anything Matchbox Twenty has ever done."

"Grab a chair, America!" she added. "The most uninteresting band in formulaic, corporate radio is back!"

The release has been eagerly awaited by Matchbox Twenty's enormous fan base, composed of Ameri-

can record buyers who have a limited interest in music but enjoy the act of shopping. In order to satisfy the undemanding nontastes of this lucrative market, Matchbox Twenty has

see ALBUM page 269

Antidepressant Use In Children

Last week, the FDA announced that children who take antidepressants face an increased risk of suicide, but some doctors dispute the claim. What do *you* think?

Sheila Wooster
Paralegal

"That's why I give my kid St. John's Wort. At least it's not gonna make my kid kill himself, even if it doesn't work for shit."

Russell Bigelow
Broker

"As a despised father, I believe suicide is just a smokescreen for America's real problem—patricide."

David Zarnke
Web Designer

"Kids with depression see through all the bullshit that everyone else accepts. The Prozac just gives them the clarity of mind to follow through with what they need to do."

Lazaro Padron
Bank Teller

"Conversely, I read that kids placed on depressants are spontaneously bursting into joyful choreographed song-and-dance routines in town squares nationwide."

Eric Morarend
Systems Analyst

"What do people expect with kids being fed the Yu-Gi-Oh! and the Dragonball Z and the whole Japanese cultural imperative to save face through ritualistic *seppuku*?"

Denise Parham
Teacher

"Goddamn little brats! They want something to kill themselves about? I'll give them something to kill themselves about."

The Bush Family Biography

The Family: The Real Story Of The Bush Dynasty, Kitty Kelley's tell-all biography of the Bush family, hit shelves last week. What did the book reveal?

★ George W. did cocaine as recently as 1992, when he snorted lines off of Rush Limbaugh's tits at Camp David

★ During the late '60s, the entire Bush clan went through a hippie phase, attending Woodstock and toppling cars at the Democratic National Convention

★ The services of Jeb, a highly skilled "bottom," are much sought after in the leather-boy community

★ Barbara can easily pass for white

★ Billy is the one pulling the strings behind the scenes

★ George Sr.'s real favorite philosopher is Thales, but he knew the pre-Socratics wouldn't fly in the swing states

★ George W. Bush hired scores of prostitutes while CEO of Harken in late '80s, but only succeeded in bringing one of them to climax; he promptly married her

★ George W. sold his soul to the devil, but can get it back if national debt reaches $9 trillion

the ONION®

America's Finest News Source.™

Herman Ulysses Zweibel
Founder

T. Herman Zweibel
Publisher Emeritus

J. Phineas Zweibel
Publisher

Maxwell Prescott Zweibel
Editor-In-Chief

Well, That's The Last Heart-To-Heart I'm Ever Having With Janet

By Ellen Henderson

Look, I am as compassionate as any member of the Ladies Lutheran League Auxiliary—including you, Linda, with your selfless devotion to the weekly church bulletin, and you, Edna Jane, bringing baked goods to the shut-ins. But even I have my limits, and I'm telling you this right now: That's the last heart-to-heart I'm having with Janet.

In all the years I've been a loyal churchgoer here at St. Luke's, I have never, so help me, met a woman who could talk your ear off about human pain and suffering like Janet can. Sure, The Bible teaches us to be merciful, so when Janet came to me the first time with her "nowhere to turn" song and dance, I told her I'd be happy to hear her troubles. That's what fellow Lutherans are for. Well, *of course*, she immediately let go the waterworks, and then it was the whole shebang with the divorce, the cancer, the house, the bills, the bills, the bills! You know the drill.

That first time, I listened and gave her whatever comfort I could. But now, after the umpteenth time, I'm through with Janet and her constant soul-baring. So, your ex-husband's an alcoholic who still calls to threaten you in the middle of the night? Sooner or later, you've got to stop living in the past. I've heard the "getting chased down with the station wagon" story enough times I can recite it. I got the point, thank you very much. I got it a long time ago.

> This whole Christian duty of being lovingly openhearted and unconditionally available to someone's desperate emotional vulnerability is really boring. Hello, Janet! It's cancer. People die of it all the time. And so your son's never going to be a rocket scientist. Can't you be happy with who he is?

Yes, the bad husband who drank and gambled emptied out Janet's bank account. And yes, Janet must live in her cancer-stricken Great Aunt Gertrude's basement with no one to help her care for her son, who has brain damage and eats from a bottle. But is it my fault Janet's son got all hopped up on drugs and hit the rear end of a dairy truck at 85 miles per hour? No, it can't be easy having to spoon-feed a 19-year-old while your only source of familial and financial support slowly dies of stomach cancer in the apartment above. But it's no picnic hearing about it every Sunday, either.

Sure, life hasn't exactly dealt Janet the best bridge hand. But Janet, the Lord works in mysterious ways. Everything happens for a reason. And God helps those who help themselves. Sooner or later, you have to look for the positive side of things. Try taking a walk down the sunny side of the street for a change. Nobody wants to hear about how someone stayed up all night holding her great-aunt's vomit pail.

It's always the same old saw: "I can't stand it anymore; I feel like God has abandoned me; I wish I were dead." What is there to say to that? I tell her it'll be okay, and that the Lord will provide. However bad it gets, I say, you'll always have people like me to rely on. But no matter how many times I try to reassure her, she's back again: brain damage, stomach cancer, drunken rage, bills, bills, bills! It's like I'm talking to a wall!

This whole Christian duty of being lovingly openhearted and unconditionally available to someone's desperate emotional vulnerability is really boring. Hello, Janet! It's cancer. People die of it all the time. And so your son's never going to be a rocket scientist. Can't you be happy with who he is? And it's not like yours is the only ex-husband who spends his child-support money on five-day gambling binges at the local casino. The papers are full of them. There's even a name for them: deadbeat dads. My father was one, and you don't hear me talking about it.

The next time Janet has a breakdown and starts sobbing during one of the hymns, I'm not going to be the one to take her hand, lead her to the basement, and make her a cup of tea. I'm sorry, but I'm out of comforting things to say. It's time for some other Christian soldier with the cross of Jesus to go marching onward, because I've friggin' had it. Excuse my language, Betty. I'm serious, ladies: Either one of you picks up the slack here, or she's Jesus' problem from here on in. Ø

Money Thrown At Lunch Problem

LINCOLN, NE—Frustrated by the logistics of developing a viable meal-time strategy, employees of the Ryodan Consulting Group threw money at the lunch problem Monday, according to branch manager Ryan Leverenz.

"Even though a seriously reasoned approach could have yielded huge dividends in both efficiency and deliciousness, everyone settled on a quick fix to the need for a midday meal," Leverenz said. "If the team had really put their heads together, I have no doubt that they could have developed an approach that more effectively addressed each individual's specific needs. Is it really commercially viable to order delivery of 20 subs with

> "The strategy session lost focus because everyone started yelling out restaurant names before we had even agreed on what kind of food we wanted," Roswell said.

cheese for 19 staffers, three of whom are lactose-intolerant?"

"And, if you do order subs, why not utilize Deli Italia? Cost-wise, their food averages out at 80 percent of Papa Luigi's," Leverenz added. "These are the questions that should've been asked well before anyone picked up the phone."

The group undertook the lunch-ordering project shortly before noon, when several of the mid-level employees working on the BankOne account got hungry. Team members brainstormed delivery and take-out options, such as Chinese, pizza, Indian, and bagels, and then turned the broad options over to the group.

According to market analyst Don Roswell, this was a mistake.

"The strategy session lost focus because everyone started yelling out restaurant names before we had even agreed on *what kind* of food we wanted," Roswell said. "This was followed by a hasty delegation of the task to intern Trish Scranton."

Roswell said client-relations team leader Austin Buford undertook the decision.

"How about subs?" Buford said.

Above: A Papa Luigi's deliveryman provides a stop-gap solution to the Ryodan office hunger problem.

"Let's just have Trish get us subs. Here's 10 bucks. Get me an Italian or whatever."

Group members quickly acquiesced, throwing money in a pile at the center of the table.

According to Leverenz, the unilateral decision and rushed delegation resulted in the less-than-satisfying lunch that arrived 50 minutes later.

"We had to spend so much time divvying everything up and making

change that the subs were soggy and gross when we finally got to eat them," Leverenz said. "I'm positive we can do better."

Ryodan's upper management derided

see LUNCH page 268

NEWS IN BRIEF

Bush Introduces New Timmy Blanchard Left Behind Act

WASHINGTON, DC—President Bush announced Monday that he'll encourage Congress to back his new education initiative, the Timmy Blanchard Left Behind Act. "It is my goal to close the achievement gap in our schools with accountability, flexibility, and choice, so that no child is left behind—except for Timmy Blanchard of Akron, OH," Bush said at a White House press conference. "By 2014, I plan to see a significant jump in the math, reading, and science proficiency of 99.9999 percent of America's students. The children, excluding Timmy, are our future." Bush was inspired to leave Blanchard behind after the child threw up all over the merry-go-round last week.

Ducks Only Interested In Man's Bread

ST. PAUL, MN—Como Park visitor Daryl Wilson, 31, reported that he was disappointed to discover that the ducks he'd fed for more than 20 minutes Monday were only interested in his bread. "I thought I'd really connected with the duckies," Wilson said. "But as soon as the bread ran out, they

went off to another part of the lake. All that time, they were just using me for my crumbs." Wilson said he has not felt so rejected since the "squirrel and peanuts incident" last year.

New Homeowner Suddenly Fascinated By Molding

BUCKEYE, AZ—Friends of Michael Ziglar said Monday that, since he purchased his three-bedroom ranch home in April, Ziglar has become endlessly fascinated by molding. "This is a guy who, one year ago, didn't know molding from a ceiling fan," said Colin Pasternak, Ziglar's friend. "Now, suddenly, he's lecturing me on the pros and cons of cavetto versus beak molding. I wish he'd shut up about wall niches and go back to *Stargate*." Ziglar was unavailable for comment, as he was at a local hardware store pricing decorative wainscotting.

Crush Lasts Entire Bus Ride

CINCINNATI—Administrative assistant and bus rider Perry Stoddard, 25, developed a crush that lasted the duration of the Metro line bus trip from Seven Hills Road to downtown Monday. "Oh my God, she is stun-

ning," Stoddard said, staring at the petite, bookish brunette sitting two seats ahead of him. "And she's reading *The Idiot*! I wonder if she has a boyfriend. My parents would love her." Saddened by the woman's exit from the bus two stops before his own, Stoddard resolved to get out on Court Street and find someone else.

Congressional Candidate Forced To Explain Controversial 1971 'Fuck Everything' Remark

LITTLE ROCK, AR—U.S. Rep. Vic Snyder (D-AR) was forced to defend himself Monday against Republican opponent Marvin Parks' claim that witnesses heard Snyder say "Fuck everything" in 1971. "At least four people attest that they saw an inebriated 24-year-old Vic Snyder tell a group of fellow medical-school students, 'I'm so sick of dealing... Fuck everything,'" Snyder said. "Everything? Did Snyder mean 'fuck' middle-class families who need tax relief? Did he mean 'fuck' the nation's elderly? Does Snyder say 'fuck' the American flag?" A spokesman for Snyder said the remark made perfect sense when put in the context of finals week. ∅

INTERVENTION from page 265

draw people to his home, because the group usually meets at Sorenson's house to watch Rams games.

"We usually go to Drew's house, but Chris said it was a bad place to talk to Drew about his drinking, 'cause he could just kick everyone out if he got mad," Sorenson's brother-in-law Cory Pitts said. "Chris said we needed a non-threatening, familiar environment. So we all had to come to Chris' place, even though his television is about half the size of Drew's and he only has one couch."

Pitts picked Sorenson up early to ensure that he would be on time, and that he would have no chance to drink before the intervention.

"I suggested that maybe we should pick Drew up a little later, so he'd

> "We all took turns, trying our best to be firm, honest, and pretty quick about it," Gowan said. "And we were careful not to obstruct the screen."

have enough time to make his onion dip, but Chris said we had to be strong," Pitts said. "At first, I argued, but then Chris pointed out that we didn't have any time to waste if we were going to confront Drew, give him time to open up to us, and work out a tenable plan for his recovery before the coin toss."

"So I bought some dip," Pitts added.

The element of surprise is an important part of a well-executed intervention, so Gowan was sure to have the whole group assembled when Sorenson arrived.

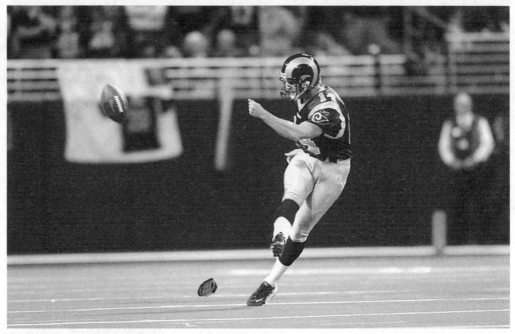
Above: Rams player Jeff Wilkins kicks off, just moments after the intervention.

"We wanted everything to seem routine," said Hugh Baker, Sorenson's coworker and immediate supervisor. "We had our jerseys on, and everyone was just hanging out having a few and watching the ESPN pre-game. We got kinda edgy waiting for them to show up. We were like, 'We really don't want this talk hanging over our heads while we're watching the Rams kick ass."

As soon as he entered Gowan's apartment, Sorenson asked for a beer.

"I turned to Drew and said, 'Hey, man, we all want to talk to you about your drinking problem, so I'm going to turn the pre-game off here for a bit,'" Gowan said. "Drew was like, 'No way! What are you talking about?' It was hard, but I knew we had to do it—or at least turn off the sound."

With the sound muted on the pre-game coverage, Sorenson's friends and loved ones came forward one by one and said they believed drinking was ruining Sorenson's life and their relationships with him.

"We all took turns, trying our best to be firm, honest, and pretty quick about it," Gowan said. "And we were careful not to obstruct the screen."

There were reportedly a few tense moments during the intervention, such as when Baker threatened to fire Sorenson if he continued to drink on the job, and when Sorenson insisted the group's claims were "bullshit," adding that he was going to walk right into the kitchen and get a beer at the next commercial.

"At one point, Drew accused Chris of abusing painkillers and said I cheated

in last year's Super Bowl pool," Baker said. "It got really tense. Everyone realized kickoff was only 25 minutes away and there was no resolution in sight."

Friends said they were relieved when, five minutes before kickoff, Sorenson's guard dropped, and he admitted that he'd tried but failed to stop drinking several times during the past year. He agreed to seek treatment.

"I have the greatest friends in the world," Sorenson said. "I guess it's tough love, saying things like that to a guy right before the big game against Atlanta and [quarterback] Michael Vick, but I really needed help. And I'm getting it, too—the guys made me call and sign up at this facility called the Lakeside Center immediately. Well, right after the game, I mean." ⌀

LUNCH from page 267

the office for what one upper-level employee characterized as "a *laissez faire* lunch attitude."

"Our clients know Ryodan for our reputation for prudence and for our systematic approach to problem-solving," said Ryodan vice-president for public affairs Maggie Orville. "From what I hear of their careless lunch-selection process, I can only determine that the team in Lincoln is dangerously out of step with Ryodan's corporate culture."

Copywriter Allison Weinberg said that the lunch problem was more complex than upper management realized.

"Analyzing deliciousness and cost is taxing enough," Weinberg said. "When you add in convenience and the need for variety, it becomes overwhelming. It would take a massive amount of time to find a lasting lunch solution—and time is something we don't have. Right now, hard as this is for the top brass to grasp, our best option is an un-

systematic process of trial and error."

Added Weinberg: "Like, I've been really into wraps lately. But I'd much rather throw a couple bucks in and eat whatever than convince 20 people to get wraps."

Ryodan accountant Karla Moss, who was brought in to consult on the fiscal side of the problem, said the department's problem is typical.

"Corporate dining is spectacularly inefficient, and sharks feed on inefficiency," Moss said. "The kicker is that many meal purchasers don't even mind getting fleeced. Personal lunch expenditures at Ryodan could be as low as $4 per eater per day, but workers pay up to seven times that for their midday goods and services."

Moss estimated that the Monday sandwich order, which also included chips and a two-liter bottle of Coke, was overvalued by nearly $41.

Based on this evaluation, Moss drafted a policy paper and posted it in the break room. The "Let's Take Turns

Preparing Lunch" plan resolves that if each worker made lunch for the department approximately once per

> "Corporate dining is spectacularly inefficient, and sharks feed on inefficiency," Moss said. "The kicker is that many meal purchasers don't even mind getting fleeced."

month, the meals would be better and significantly cheaper.

Ryodan attorney Ted Batterson said the lunch system is long overdue for a

radical overhaul, but that the in-house lunch solution "only works in theory."

"Experience has shown that these sort of communal meal plans never pan out," said Batterson, who has been with Ryodan for more than 20 years. "We need a solution rooted in the American entrepreneurial spirit and built on competition. If the fresh market is not involved, people have no incentive to participate."

With no clear solution in sight, even the employee who proposed sub sandwiches characterized the measure as a "stop-gap effort at best."

"There are serious issues on the table, and they merit examination, discussion, and consensus-based decision-making," Buford said. "The daily lunch order should be as much about teamwork as it is about satisfying the need to consume food periodically. Sure, we solved the lunch problem for today, but what about tomorrow, the next day, and the day after that?" ⌀

CONVENTION from page 265

is no such thing as 100 percent security, unfortunately. In this day and age, organizers of any high-profile event cannot be too careful."

The party plans to move weapons stockpiles to undisclosed locations, and to post armed security guards at known tunnel entrances. Only those carts operated by officials with permits will be admitted below ground, and the cavities of any animals brought to the convention will be searched. Additionally, attendees will be required to provide papers confirming their identities, and their names will be checked against a list of known al-Qaeda operatives.

"We will do everything we can to cut down on the amount of time spent in lines, but some waiting is to be expected," al-Hamada said. "I urge all attendees to be patient with the delays. Please, I beg you, control your rage. Please."

Metal detectors will be set up in major entryways throughout the convention, and any firearms will be confis-

> ## "The last thing our organization needs is to be subject to the whims of a crazy man with a gun," said Alak al-Alousi, a delegate from Britain. "Besides the loss of life, such an attack would spread doubt among our members and make us look vulnerable. The long-term cost is incalculable."

cated, inspected by security officers, and returned to their owners, who will be forced to swear that they will only fire their guns in celebration. Larger explosive devices will be confiscated and returned before the convention's closing ceremonies. To this end, Afghanistan's sole surviving bomb-sniffing dog will be called back into service.

Al-Qaeda members said they first recognized the threat of terrorist attacks in June, while discussing the possibility of bombing the Fleet Center in Boston. The organization's requests for support at its own convention were denied by both the Afghan military and local police, however, forcing al-Qaeda to develop its own security plan.

"We'll be employing some of the best and newest technology available," al-Hamada said. "This includes hundreds of top-of-the-line closed-circuit cameras, Lifeguard handheld metal detectors, and armored plates to line

Above: A delegate from Mosul triggers a metal detector.

VIP sections of the caves. We've also kidnapped some of the top minds in security and counter-terrorism, and our clerics are currently grilling them for tips."

Added al-Hamada: "In addition, we will not allow women at the convention, as they are deceivers who cannot be trusted."

Pakistani delegate Amir Jassem said he was "disappointed and embarrassed" by the security measures.

"It's a sad day when an overzealous madman with a bomb strapped to himself can threaten our divinely inspired wave of destruction," Jassem said, idly polishing a rifle. "How in the world did we get to this point?"

Expected attendee Hassan Malouri, 23, echoed Jassem's disappointment.

"It's a shame," said Malouri, who purchased a new AK-47 and bandolier of grenades for what he hopes will be his last convention. "I only wish to offer up my life to the death of Bush and the destruction of America for the greater glory of Allah. But now, with the world as it is, I'm afraid that other bloodthirsty religious fanatics may take that away from me."

At least one al-Qaeda member applauded the increased security measures.

"The last thing our organization needs is to be subject to the whims of a crazy man with a gun," said Alak al-Alousi, a delegate from Britain. "Besides the loss of life, such an attack would spread doubt among our members and make us look vulnerable. The long-term cost is incalculable."

Despite fears, al-Hamada said that the convention "will and must go on."

"Fear of the unknown is the terrorist's best weapon," al-Hamada said. "If al-Qaeda does not stand firm in our resolve, then the terrorists will have already won."

The al-Qaeda International Convention will open Friday with a keynote speech from Zell Miller, the Democratic senator from Georgia who raised hackles by throwing his support behind al-Qaeda during this year's election. *Ø*

ALBUM from page 265

made every effort to create what record-industry insiders say is the band's least distinctive album yet.

"Some were disappointed with the relatively limited reception to Matchbox Twenty's 2002 release *More Than You Think You Are*," *Rolling Stone* contributing editor Nathan Brackett said. "That album proved what record executives have known for years: It's actually very difficult to record a rock record that has no rock in it at all. But with this new release, Matchbox Twenty has really delivered on its signature non-sound."

After the enormous commercial success of 1996's *Yourself Or Someone Like You*, demand for simplistic, cookie-cutter output from the band has been high. Yet, according to Grammy-winning lead vocalist Rob Thomas, the new record's release was delayed repeatedly because of Matchbox Twenty's perfectionism in the studio.

"Our goal was to follow in the tradition of great multi-platinum artists like Elton John, Phil Collins, and the Dave Matthews Band—sales powerhouses who relied on the musical ignorance of their fans," Thomas told reporters following Monday's announcement. "We knew that if we wanted to match those historic giants for sheer lack of energy, we couldn't settle for anything less than total banality. And, though it took a lot of time and effort, I think we achieved that—an album that sets a new standard for trite crapola."

"It's really derivative and boring," he added.

Thomas said it was the expectations of listeners that drove the band to create the most average music possible.

"We wanted to give our fans exactly what they've come to expect: music so inoffensive and indistinct that it could be played virtually anywhere—a bank lobby, an SUV stuck in traffic, a party full of aging stockbrokers and their girlfriends. That's no small task. Even a lot of the most vacant and unimaginative people have some capacity to actively engage in the music they're listening to."

According to band members, hun-

dreds of hours were spent in the studio trying to render the sound adequately benign.

"No matter how many times we recorded the new single 'Sitting Down (Hands At My Side),' there was still a certain 'oomph' coming through in the drums, a loud-ish, slightly gripping sound that we couldn't remove," drummer Paul Doucette said. "Finally, after running them through about two

> ## There was a similar problem, band members said, with the guitar solos, some of which contained trace elements of what musicians call "passion."

dozen filters, we managed to get that 'plastic spork hitting mashed potatoes' sound we were after."

There was a similar problem, band members said, with the guitar solos, some of which contained trace elements of what musicians call "passion." In addition, the interplay among bass, drums, and guitars occasionally produced uncomfortable polyrhythmic effects that provoked unintentional toe-tapping or head-bobbing in listeners. The problems were fixed through extensive re-recording.

"I'm satisfied that all the watering-down we put into this album was worth it," Thomas said. "My lyrics are super-bland, the bass might as well have been recorded on a keyboard, and just wait until you hear how dull we managed to make the guitars sound. It's amazing."

The band will introduce the album's first single next week on MTV's hugely popular, entirely insipid show *Total Request Live*. *Ø*

COLD FEET from page 201

amounts of blood. Passersby were amazed by the unusually large amounts of blood. Passersby were amazed by the unusually large amounts of blood. Passersby were amazed by the unusually large amounts of blood. Passersby were amazed by the unusually large amounts of blood. Passersby were amazed by the unusually large amounts of blood. Passersby were amazed by the unusually large amounts of blood. Passersby were amazed by the unusually large amounts of blood. Passersby were amazed by the unusually large amounts of blood. Passersby were amazed by the unusually large amounts of blood. Passersby were amazed by the unusually large amounts of blood. Passersby were amazed by the unusually large amounts of blood. Passersby were amazed by the unusually large amounts of blood. Passersby were amazed by the unusually large amounts of blood. Passersby were amazed by the unusually large amounts of blood. Passersby were

amazed by the unusually large amounts of blood. Passersby were amazed by the unusually large amounts of blood. Passersby were

> ## The army is the perfect place to lose those extra 10 pounds.

amazed by the unusually large amounts of blood. Passersby were amazed by the unusually large amounts of blood. Passersby were amazed by the unusually large

see COLD FEET page 298

269

I Was Almost Back In The Saddle Again

The Cruise
By Jim Anchower

Hola, amigos. I know it's been a long time since I rapped at ya, but I've been getting the shit end of the stick lately. It's not like I had much going on as far as work. Since I busted my leg on the roofing job, I've been getting paid for staying home. It was pretty sweet for a while, watching the checks roll in while I caught up on my tube-watching and video-game-playing. But then I started to go a little stir crazy. I couldn't drive, because I couldn't bend that leg, and it took forever to walk anywhere on crutches.

Finally, last weekend, I had to go out, because I couldn't get anyone to come drop me off provisions. Can you believe that? I'm suffering with a broken leg, with a whole week left before my cast comes off, and no one will help a pal out. Wes was out of town on vacation, so he gets a pass. But that douchebag Ron wasn't returning any of my phone calls, on account of he's still pissed that I walked out on that carbonics-plant job he got me.

Well, I held out as long as I could, but finally, you know, I was out of food and beer. I decided I was going to have to be like a pioneer and bravely go out into the wild. I dug my old high-school backpack out of the clothes closet, picked up my crutches, and hobbled out the front door, down the porch steps, and up the street to the store. After the first block, I was this close to turning back. But I thought of that empty fridge, and I knew I had to just do it.

When I finally got to the store, I bought a 12-pack of Miller Genuine Draft and jammed it into the main pouch of the backpack. Then I crammed as many microwave burritos as I could into the side pockets and headed back home.

It was harder than I thought, using crutches with a backpack on my shoulders. Halfway home, I had to stop a while and rest. I guess sitting around waiting for a broken leg to heal takes a lot out of you. When I was just about a block away from home, the zipper on my backpack broke. The 12-pack hit the ground, and cans went rolling everywhere. One of them busted and took off like a racecar, spraying beer all over the damn place.

I had a hell of a time bending over to pick up the cans while balanced on my crutches. I had an even harder time trying to hold the bag shut with one hand while I crutched home. Just when I was finally going up the stairs of my place, I lost my grip on my bag, and the cans fell out again, along with a couple burritos. I decided to get what I could into the house and hurry back for the rest of the beer before someone made a play for it. I thought I was making good time, but sure enough, when I came back outside, some of the neighborhood kids were grabbing cans. They took off when I hollered at them, but they took three beers and a couple burritos with them. So that was four

> **Well, I held out as long as I could, but finally, you know, I was out of food and beer. I decided I was going to have to be like a pioneer and bravely go out into the wild.**

MGDs that I paid for that I wasn't going to get to drink.

It took me a couple more minutes to get the cans into the apartment. You better believe that the first thing I did was kick back and crack open one of those beers. Well, guess what? It exploded on me. Beer went everywhere except for in my mouth. All that was left of the beer was about half a can of foam, but I downed it as fast as I could.

I was pretty sweaty from my workout, and I was soaked in beer. I realized that I hadn't hosed off in a couple of days. It's a real pain in the ass to put a plastic bag over your leg just to shower, but I decided that there was no better time than the present.

I'm supposed to use a garbage bag to cover my cast, but I was all out. But I got the great idea of using the worthless backpack. I put my foot in it and duct-taped up the opening. Man, that was a good shower. After I dried off, I had a few more beers, shot some zombies, and went to bed.

But then, the next day, my leg started itching. And not like it had been the past couple weeks, but bad, like the time I got poison ivy. My scratching stick wasn't doing any good. Then, the stick broke off in there, leaving like a three-inch chunk in my cast. I couldn't reach it for anything. That's when the itching really started to drive me crazy.

I called my doctor, but it was the

Your Horoscope

By Lloyd Schumner Sr.
Retired Machinist and
A.A.P.B.-Certified Astrologer

Aries: (March 21–April 19)
You're getting tired of living out of boxes, but if you stop now, you'll damage your reputation as the patron saint of the cardboard cubist lifestyle.

Taurus: (April 20–May 20)
There are those who say you're just a glorified janitor, but you fail to see how the titanium mop and bucket add glory to what you do.

Gemini: (May 21–June 21)
You'll soon learn the important legal and semantic differences between the phrases "folksingers should just die" and "it'd sure be nice if someone slaughtered all the folksingers."

Cancer: (June 22–July 22)
Hey, it's not your fault if the others around the office don't find your horrifyingly racist sense of humor funny.

Leo: (July 23–Aug. 22)
You'll be surprised and pleased to find yourself listed between Leah and Levi in *Who's Who In The Bible*, but you won't really like what the editors had to say.

Virgo: (Aug. 23–Sept. 22)
You'll be overrun with shallow, boring romance-seekers merely because you genuinely enjoy long walks and sunsets.

Libra: (Sept. 23–Oct. 23)
There's no law about over-enjoying the work of Uriah Heep, but the judicial flexibility built into our society will see that you get what's coming to you anyway.

Scorpio: (Oct. 24–Nov. 21)
Leprosy is certainly not the problem it once was, but that might not be any consolation to you.

Sagittarius: (Nov. 22–Dec. 21)
The National Hockey League lockout will have little or no effect on you, which is fairly surprising, considering you're Lord Stanley's Cup.

Capricorn: (Dec. 22–Jan. 19)
You'll experience a soufflé that sends you into a white-hot inferno of culinary passion, instantly incinerating you and everyone in the downtown restaurant district.

Aquarius: (Jan. 20–Feb. 18)
This week will be prime for advancement at work, as long as you manage to avoid the ball lightning and the other guys don't.

Pisces: (Feb. 19–March 20)
Good news: The airline will only charge you four Frequent Flier Miles for your violently abbreviated flight this Friday.

weekend, so he was probably out golfing or something. I couldn't wait until Monday, and even if I could, there was no way I was going to take three buses to the hospital. Since

> **They needed to take off the cast in order to get at the stab wound. I guess that was the good part. But they had to bandage up the leg to make sure my stitches didn't get infected.**

there was only a week left before the cast could come off, I decided to take matters into my own hands.

I went over to my tool drawer and gathered supplies. I got out some pliers, a screwdriver, and a steak knife I took from a restaurant while I was a dishwasher. I also found a hacksaw—not like I was going to use it right off the bat, but I wanted to have it as a backup in case everything else failed. Then I went to town. I cut and sawed and pulled off as much of the bitch as I could. After an hour, I had three playing-card-sized chunks of fiberglass off of the cast and an ambulance on the way.

They needed to take off the cast in order to get at the stab wound. I guess that was the good part. But they had to bandage up the leg to make sure my stitches didn't get infected. They also gave me an antibiotic to take for the skin infection I had. That fucking cut was deep. They said I was lucky I didn't bleed to death.

Well, that hospital trip is probably gonna use up all of my cash, so I'm gonna have to get back to work as soon as I heal up. As soon as I can, I'm gonna tell Ron that if he hadn't been such a dick about giving me a ride, none of this would have happened. I hope he feels bad enough to give me that carbonics job again. ✐

Doll Overstays Dollhouse Welcome

see LOCAL page 13D

Woman's Tan Lines Don't Make Any Sense

see PEOPLE page 12E

Nation's Elderly Hit Hard By Closing Automatic Doors

see NATION page 2A

Greaseball Shitcanned

see BUSINESS page 8C

STATshot

A look at the numbers that shape your world.

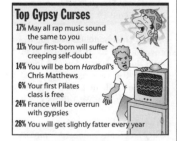

Top Gypsy Curses

- 17% May all rap music sound the same to you
- 11% Your first-born will suffer creeping self-doubt
- 14% You will be born *Hardball*'s Chris Matthews
- 6% Your first Pilates class is free
- 24% France will be overrun with gypsies
- 28% You will get slightly fatter every year

THE ONION • $2.00 US • $3.00 CAN

---

the ONION®

VOLUME 40 ISSUE 39   AMERICA'S FINEST NEWS SOURCE™   30 SEPT.–6 OCT. 2004

Bedding Officials Demand Thread Recount

Above: Federal Bedding Inspectors collect sheets from a Florida home-goods store.

BEDFORD, TX—Alarmed by reports of incorrect thread counts in the nation's blankets and sheets, bedding officials demanded nationwide thread recounts Monday.

"This tears it," National Bed & Bath Commission director David Morgan said. "Thread-count inaccuracies are influencing outcomes in shopping districts across the nation. Americans are electing to buy products using confusing and misleading labels."

Morgan said his goal is not to condemn manufacturers with blanket statements, but to correct the snag.

"The idea that quality is based on thread count is not some old yarn—it's woven into the fabric of our society," Morgan said. "But the system for quality control is threadbare. It's coming apart at the seams. We can't pull the covers over our heads and ignore it any longer."

The thread count of cloth

see BEDDING page 274

Documents Reveal Gaps In Bush's Service As President

WASHINGTON, DC—Freshly unearthed public documents, ranging from newspapers to cabinet-meeting minutes, seem to indicate large gaps in George W. Bush's service as president, a spokesman for the watchdog group Citizens for an Informed Society announced Monday.

"We originally invoked the Freedom Of Information Act to request material relating to Bush's spotty record while in office," CIS director Catherine Rocklin said. "But then we realized that the information was readily available at the corner newsstand, on the Internet, and from our friends and neighbors who pay attention to the news."

According to Rocklin, the most damning documents were generated at roughly one-day intervals during a period beginning in January 2001 and ending this week. The document's sources include, but are not limited to, the U.S. newspaper *The New York Times*, the London-based

see BUSH page 275

Above: Bush, who stands accused of shirking his presidential duties.

Area Man Somehow Even Less Popular Than He Was In High School

JEFFERSON, MO—Contrary to what he had been assured about adult life, local resident Mike Glick, 24, reported Monday that he is even less popular than he was in high school.

"One of the biggest incentives to endure high school is the idea that the misery will end once you graduate," Glick said. "What I wasn't told is that people are basically the same dicks, except with more money and fewer opportunities to say 'Smell my finger.'"

Glick, a part-time clerk for a Jefferson law firm, added that he has not

see MAN page 274

Left: Glick, who has even fewer friends than he did six years ago.

Iraq Hostages

Extremists in Iraq continue to use hostage-taking to convey their message, leaving much of the world wondering what can be done. What do *you* think?

"Why don't we make hostage-taking punishable by the death penalty? Then everyone would think twice before doing it."

Carl Preston
Systems Analyst

"I'll tell you, I'm about six or seven beheadings away from demanding some answers about what's going on in Iraq."

Dave Rudd
Clerk

"I'd like to think that if the situation were reversed, we here in Schaumburg wouldn't treat our hostages this way."

Roger Monroe
Firefighter

"If I ever got beheaded, I would make sure the geyser of blood would stain my captors' clothing so they'd have to throw it out. Take that, terrorists!"

Dora Drucker
Lawyer

"As a State Department official, let me say that bargaining with terrorists is unacceptable. We apologize for any inconvenience this may cause for the hostages."

Bea Larson
Public Official

"We should just shoot 'em all and let God sort 'em out. That's God, mind you, not Allah."

Chet Johnson
Civil Engineer

Oktoberfest

Munich is in the midst of Oktoberfest, Germany's annual celebration of beer and Bavarian culture. What have been the festival's highlights so far?

- St. Pauli Girl's fourth annual wet-dirndl contest
- A pictorial celebration of German culture, 1740-1914, 1950-present
- Efficient, well-organized drinking, followed by even more efficient, better-organized throwing up
- Cabbage activists blew up sauerkraut truck outside Munich
- Festival crowd got out of control, wound up controlling most of Poland
- Arrival of a hideous monster made of reanimated human body parts drove terrified villagers from Alpine-dancing tent
- Preliminary preparations for Hungovember

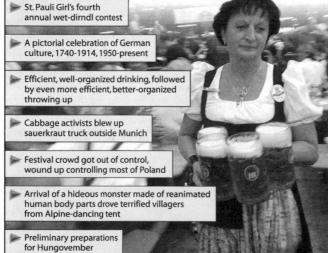

the ONION®
America's Finest News Source.™

Herman Ulysses Zweibel
Founder

T. Herman Zweibel
Publisher Emeritus
J. Phineas Zweibel
Publisher
Maxwell Prescott Zweibel
Editor-In-Chief

There Are So Many Experiences I Want To Write About Having Had

By Jason Erikson

As a writer, I have powers of observation far greater than those of the average person. Nothing gets by me. Sometimes, as I sit typing in my dank, dusty, windowless room, I stop and marvel at the tapestry of life. When I think about all the escapades that could inform my writing, my mind reels! The world is my keyboard's oyster—I just need to get out there and experience all the things that are waiting to be written about.

I long to be sitting in my tiny writer's garret remembering the open road! I wish I were leaning back in my chair, contently recalling the sensation of the wind in my hair as an 18-wheeler shot past me on the highway. Were I able, I would describe in vivid detail the colorful trucker who pulled over and beckoned me inside his cab with a majestic blast of a powerful air-horn and a wave of his tattoo-covered arm. Oh, the valuable life lessons I would have learned hitchhiking in search of America. To have memories like that!

I could go to the farthest reaches of Africa and then return to my room to write about them. Think of the passion I could bring to my account of the poverty-stricken peoples of that vast continent! Though the

> **Even as I sit hunched over the word processor, my heart sings out at all I could do and write down! I long to pine for the vastness of the sea!**

friends I'd meet would at first appear to be pathetic, uneducated barbarians, I'd soon learn that these savages were as human—or more so—as I. Think of the pathos their wretched lives would bring to my hours of solitary typing! Perhaps their quiet dignity would rub off on me. It moves me, to think I might capture their quiet suffering—how beautifully it would translate onto the page.

How I long to write about the thrill of leaping out of an airplane at 10,000 feet! To describe the sensation of being completely and utterly in the moment, confronted by death it-

self. It would be the high point of my life, to look down and see my own story listed on the cover of *GQ*.

I can just taste all the wonderful life experiences out there waiting to be had! I can imagine feeling the

> **I long to be sitting in my tiny writer's garret remembering the open road! I wish I were leaning back in my chair, contently recalling the sensation of the wind in my hair as an 18-wheeler shot past me on the highway.**

keys under my fingertips as I type out paragraph after passionate paragraph about all the incredible things I'd seen and done! Then, thanks to my skill and maturity as a writer, all those things would be transferred into beautiful language any educated reader would find both accessible and moving. Then my experiences would not belong to me alone, but to the world.

Oh, how my soul yearns to write about Europe! If I were ever to visit there, I'm sure I would keep a notebook with me to write down every instance of mind-expanding cultural sophistication. How I long to sit in a sidewalk café in Paris, jotting down what it's like to sit there! How I long to remember meeting you there, my future love. The pain of leaving you behind! I could write an entire novel about that!

Even as I sit hunched over the word processor, my heart sings out at all I could do and write down! I long to pine for the vastness of the sea! I crave the thrill of bullets whistling past my ears in a West Bank combat zone.

It would be so incredible to see—to really see—an innocent man die. And then to write—to really, truly write—about the injustice of that man's death. And then to have people who buy *Granta* read—really, truly, and utterly read—about that death *with their own eyes*. Of course, I would not escape such carnage unscathed: The emotional scars would be invisible to the naked eye, but totally evident in the depth of my astounding writing. *∅*

Alvin Shunned By Animal Community, Forced To Wear Scarlet 'A'

PASADENA, CA—Well-known frontman for Alvin & The Chipmunks, the singing group that included his brothers Simon and Theodore, Alvin Seville is adored by millions for his intricate vocals on such playful songs as "Alvin's Harmonica" and "The Chipmunk Song (Christmas Don't Be Late)." The chipmunk celebrates his 70th birthday this month, as well as his 46th year bearing the scarlet letter "A"—the mark of shame that reminds members of the animal kingdom that he is an actor who has adopted the ways of humankind.

"'A singer of people-songs!'" said the Seville family's former tax accoun-

> While Alvin refused to identify the father who'd abandoned him, many say he bears an uncanny likeness to popular entertainer Dale.

tant, echoing the cries raised against Alvin so many years ago. "'What kind of a business in life—what mode of glorifying Mother Nature, of being serviceable to chipmunks?' Such were the comments bandied between leaf and twig, chattered from branch to branch! And yet, let them scorn Alvin as they would, strong traits of their nature had intertwined themselves with his."

In 1958, members of the Woodland Council forced Alvin to sew a scarlet, gold-embroidered "A" on his sweater. They then paraded him before his forest peers and exiled him to a split-level ranch home on the outskirts of Los Angeles.

"When 'The Witch Doctor' became a success, the animal community seized upon Alvin's 'unholy' communion with humankind," entertainment writer Seth Morris said. "By today's standards, it seems barbaric to ostracize a chipmunk because of a relatively harmless series of novelty recordings. It was a different time then."

According to Morris, Alvin's father sent the chipmunk to Hollywood while still an infant, with the stated intention of following later. The elder animal remained in the forest, however, leaving Alvin and his brothers alone in the human world. It was then that Alvin met Seville, who developed a liking for the chipmunks and adopted them as his own children.

"So moody and mischievous were Alvin and his brothers that people used to joke that their birth father was actually the devil," the accountant

Above: Alvin revisits the forest he once called home.

said. "But Dave truly loved the chipmunks, and so he was torn, for he knew the human-animal bond to be unnatural."

While Alvin refused to identify the father who'd abandoned him, many say he bears an uncanny likeness to popular entertainer Dale, a singing, dancing chipmunk who arrived in Hollywood around the time of Alvin's downfall.

see ALVIN page 275

NEWS IN BRIEF

Report: Iraq War Keeping Thousands Out Of Unemployment Line

WASHINGTON, DC—A Department of Labor report praised the positive effect the Iraq War has had on the strained U.S. job market, Secretary of Labor Elaine Chao said Monday. "A whopping 140,000 U.S. citizens are gainfully employed as military personnel in Iraq," Chao said. "The war is not just keeping these young men and women out of the unemployment lines, but it's also teaching them such valuable skills as operating radar equipment, driving an M1A1 Abrams battle tank, or bagging and tagging bodies." Chao said that most troops won't need to look for new work for another four to seven years.

'Ravaged' Named Florida's Official State Adjective

TALLAHASSEE, FL—Governor Jeb Bush announced Monday that Florida has adopted the word "ravaged" as its official state adjective. "In the past decade, parts of Florida have been ravaged by hurricanes, political controversy, infestation, poverty, and crime," Bush said in a press confer-

ence. "What better way to describe the state than with the word 'ravaged'?" "Ravaged" beat out such popular contenders as "muggy," "graying," and "tourist-clogged."

Gay Couple Has Banal Sex

MINNEAPOLIS—Jerome Ostrowski and Barry Lipner engaged in the practice of banal sex Monday, sources reported. "After we got home from Don Giovanni's, the restaurant we go to pretty much every Saturday night, Barry started giving me one of his predictable mood-setting backrubs," Ostrowski said. "After five minutes of that, he mounted me and put in a hundred or so quick thrusts. All in all, not one of our more memorable encounters." Lipner said that Ostrowski's reciprocal act of fellatio was "serviceable."

Upcoming Election Deduced From *Sports Illustrated* Content

LINCOLN, NE—Football fan Ben Pellett first became aware of the upcoming presidential election Tuesday, thanks to a tangential reference to it made in the Sept. 28 issue of *Sports Illustrated.* "One of the columnists said that picking who'll dominate the NFC

North would be 'tougher than predicting the winner on Nov. 2,'" Pellett said. "At first I had no idea what that meant, but then I realized it's been a while since we voted for president. I asked my roommate, and sure enough, there's an election this year." Pellett added that he thinks both the Vikings and the Republicans have what it takes to go all the way.

Produce Section Bursts Into Laughter After Will Ferrell Makes Casual Remark About Apples

LOS ANGELES—Patrons of the Trader Joe's grocery store on La Brea Avenue and Third Street broke out into gales of spontaneous laughter when fellow shopper and movie star Will Ferrell made a casual comment about apples. "I haven't had a good apple in a while," Ferrell said in the produce section, causing several nearby shoppers to giggle and nod appreciatively at the overheard remark. "Are Paula Reds any good? I wonder if they're sour like a Granny Smith." Ferrell said that, although he appreciates his fans' support, he really wanted a straight answer about the apples. ∅

BEDDING from page 271

MAN from page 271

Above: A bedding official conducts a thread recount.

amounts to the number of horizontal and vertical threads in one square inch of fabric. The NBBC has documented several dozen instances in which different standards were used to count the threads, in order to misrepresent the quality and value of a bedding product.

Morgan said the NBBC believes that the tests currently in use favor North American and European textiles over ethnic textiles, such as Egyptian cotton, South American wools, and Indian batiks. The looming challenge is to modify the standards without unraveling them altogether.

"I admit that, in the past, I've championed softer, more liberal bedding standards," Morgan said. "But I'd hate to see my views adversely affect sales of those sheets cut from a different cloth."

Although a thorough canvassing of the thread-count procedures must be undertaken before any balancing actions are performed, investigators say they will look into cover-up allegations, including the particularly seamy possibility that white sheets were automatically given a higher thread count than textiles of color.

"For years, we've suspected that the whites were cared for differently than colored items," NBBC official George Vega said. "Some manufacturers actually out-and-out recommended that whites and colors be treated, and in some cases pretreated, differently. It's enough to make me worry that we might never get things all sewn up."

NBBC evaluator JoAnn Baugh said local-level thread counters are not the only ones to blame.

"Corruption at the highest levels of home furnishing is bound to come out in the wash eventually," Baugh said. "We shouldn't have let them pull the wool over our eyes for so long."

"The best thing would be for everyone involved to own up to their own quilt," Baugh added. "But if no one

> **"We've suspected that the whites were cared for differently than colored items," NBBC official George Vega said. "Some manufacturers actually out-and-out recommended that whites and colors be treated, and in some cases pretreated, differently."**

comes forward and admits to being in bed with special interests, it may be years before we can get this issue ironed out."

Morgan agreed that the NBBC will need time to sort the piles of material evidence.

"It'll be a while before we can put this whole thing to bed," Morgan said. "It's a shame that our nation has become enmeshed in this king-sized controversy. But if we are going to count threads, we should have a solid set of standards. That way, we can all rest easy."

advanced in status or self-fulfillment in the six years since graduating from James Monroe High School. In fact, he said he believes he has regressed considerably.

"At least in high school, teachers cared if you didn't show up for class or weren't paying attention," Glick said. "And in retrospect, being slammed against the lockers helped shape my identity. At least I had something to react to. Now, I just feel adrift."

> **"At least in high school, teachers cared if you didn't show up for class or weren't paying attention," Glick said. "And in retrospect, being slammed against the lockers helped shape my identity. At least I had something to react to."**

Glick paused to check his e-mail inbox, where he found a company-wide e-mail from a law partner whose billable hourshe had itemized that morning.

Glick was one of the least distinguished members of Monroe High's Class of 1998. Too timid to rebel and not confident enough to be well-liked, Glick was at least noticed long enough to occasionally be mocked. Once known by such names as "Glicklicker" and "Suck My Glick," he said he is now more likely to be referred to as "the guy in payroll. No, the shorter one."

"When high-school graduates enter the world, they meet people with whom they share common interests," said Dr. Sharon Kesselbein, a Kansas City-based psychologist and former public-school guidance counselor. "While being cast into a wider world can be disorienting, it can also be liberating and enriching. The young person discovers that he isn't so strange or misbegotten, as he's opened up to friendships with people who are making similar discoveries and experiencing a similar openness. So none of this happened to [Glick], huh? *Really?*"

Glick said he thinks his lack of social status can be traced to decisions he made right after graduation.

"Maybe it's because I stayed in town rather than going away to school," said Glick, whose stint at Jefferson Business College resulted in a two-year accounting degree and no real acquaintances, save for a brief friendship with his evangelicalLaotian-American seating partner at

freshman orientation. "Maybe if I had gone to South Dakota State like my friend Ted Carpenter, or to North Carolina like Sean Rudy, things would have been different."

Carpenter and Rudy were friends—or perhaps more accurately, lunchtime buddies—of Glick's. Carpenter, Rudy, and Glick shared an interest in science fiction and a tendency toward unpopularity, but when Carpenter and Rudy left Jefferson, Glick lost contact with them.

"In the lunchroom at work, I usually sit alone," Glick said. "But a few months ago, I tried sitting down with a couple of paralegals, just to see what would happen. They didn't groan and scatter like my classmates would have in high school. In fact, my coworkers didn't appear to notice me at all. Their conversation continued uninterrupted, and no one seemed ill at ease. I didn't even get a single wayward glance. After about five minutes, I got up and walked off. Now, I just eat at my desk."

The working life has given Glick certain material advantages denied him as a jobless teenager, such as his own apartment and new clothes. In high school, Glick was teased about his sparse and shabby wardrobe, and this led him to believe that an opportunity to purchase a larger wardrobe would lead to increased popularity.

"I quickly realized that no one cares what I wear," Glick said. "This pair of khakis I have on and one or two dress shirts are basically enough to get me through the week. I have a tie in my desk in case a senior partner

> **At that point, Glick's phone began to ring, offering a ray of hope to the lonely man.**

calls me to his office, but that never happens."

At that point, Glick's phone began to ring, offering a ray of hope to the lonely man. On the other end was a misdirected client seeking a tax lawyer whose name Glick wasn't familiar with.

Kesselbein, however, offered hope for Glick.

"Popularity may be the most sought-after and wished-for thing among young people, but high school doesn't last forever, and adults have to fall back on other things, like knowledge and common sense," Kesselbein said. "The content of your character is more important than whether you can throw a football or how much you weigh. Really, it's true. I'm an expert, and I spend all day and night studying these things."

BUSH from page 271

Economist magazine, and the well-known international business and finance record, *The Wall Street Journal.*

"Factual data presented in these publications indicates that Bush took little or no action on issues as widely varied as the stalled economy, increasing violence in post-war Iraq, and the lagging public education system," Rocklin said. "The newsprint documents also reveal huge disparities between the ways Bush claimed to have served Medicare patients, and what he actually did."

Democratic vice-presidential nominee John Edwards said he was not surprised by the report.

"These documents reconfirm what they told us the first time we saw them," Edwards said while stumping for Kerry in Ohio. "Namely, that

> "These documents reconfirm what they told us the first time we saw them," Edwards said while stumping for Kerry in Ohio. "Namely, that our president was seriously negligent during the three and a half years he was supposed to be serving his country."

our president was seriously negligent during the three and a half years he was supposed to be serving his country."

House Majority Leader Tom DeLay (R-TX) is one of many Republicans who demanded an independent investigation into the authenticity of

Above: CIS provided this photo of Bush at a Cardinals game as evidence of a gap in his presidential service.

the documents.

"We're fairly confident that these so-called 'news stories' will turn out to be partisan smear tactics," DeLay said. "I wouldn't be surprised if all 11 billion of these words turn out to be forgeries. For thousands of reporters, editors, and government officials to claim that Bush compromised the security and fiscal health of this nation is not merely anti-American, but also dangerous."

In addition to the media documents, CIS examined more than 20,000 government records, which ranged from U.S. Department of Labor unemployment reports to transcripts of State Of The Union addresses.

"Bush shirked his presidential duties with regard to the nation's fiscal health," Rocklin said. "Take, for example, the controversial memo in which Congressional Budget Office director Douglas Holtz-Eakin states that the federal deficit will reach a record high of $422 billion this year. This

memo unequivocally shows that Bush was AWOL on the domestic front."

Rocklin said the documents indicate that Bush used his family's political connections to obtain his job in the executive branch.

"Bush stepped ahead of more qualified candidates to take what he thought would be a cushy job," Rocklin said. "Then, after signing up for a four-year term, he largely abandoned his post in 2004 to go work on a political campaign."

Rocklin said her organization obtained print-outs from the press-briefings section of the White House web site which show that Bush has spent nearly as much time out of the White House as in it.

U.S. Sen. Michael Enzi (R-WY) called the print-outs "meaningless."

"If the president said he did his duty, then he did," Enzi said. "Furthermore, so what if a bunch of White House staffers can't remember seeing Bush

around the place? The West Wing is full of guys wearing identical blue suits. And how can anyone be expected to remember every little thing that went on 30 months ago?"

While experts say it may be too early to judge the impact the documents may have on the polls, top Bush-Cheney 2004 campaign organizers said they are confident the scandal will be short-lived.

"Our opponents have dredged up this kind of thing every time Bush has run for office," Bush campaign strategist Matthew Dowd said. "We've faced down widely reported, fully researched, carefully documented accounts of Bush's alcoholism, drug use, private-sector business failings, ignorance in matters of state, smug arrogance, and general self-serving lackadaisical behavior. So I'm hardly worried. An overwhelming mass of published information like this has never stopped Americans from voting for him before." Ø

ALVIN from page 273

"Dale could see there was something between Alvin and Dave," Morris said. "Alvin was heartbroken to have been made a pariah, but he bore it stoically, pouring all of his energy into his songs and his television programs."

While the animals publicly rallied against Alvin, many privately expressed admiration for both his bravery and the speed and pitch of his plaintive, almost human vocals.

"Alvin, with a mind of native courage and activity, outlawed from the wilds, wandered among the suburbs and studios of mankind," the accountant said. "The scarlet letter was his passport into regions other chipmunks dared not tread. Fame, adoration, applause! These were his teach-

ers—stern and wild ones—and they made him strong, but taught him much amiss."

For many years, Seville refused com-

> For many years, Seville refused comment on his relationship with Alvin.

ment on his relationship with Alvin.

"Dave felt terrible guilt over luring Alvin from the animal world and subjecting him to so much pain at the paws of his peers," inventor and *Alvin* costar Clyde Crashcup said. "At one

concert, he came very close to taking the microphone and admitting to that which was animal in his own nature, just as Alvin had been forced to own up to his trespasses into humanity. But ultimately, Dave was too afraid."

"It was only seconds later that a lighting rig fell, forming a giant letter 'A' behind the set," Crashcup added.

In the controversial final episode of *The Alvin Show*, however, Seville appeared before a live studio audience, acknowledged his relationship with Alvin, and tore open his shirt to reveal an "A"-shaped skin discoloration on his chest. Shortly afterward, he died, his final word the plaintive call, "*All-lviiin!*"

Alvin withdrew from the limelight with the cancellation of his last TV se-

ries, *Alvin & The Chipmunks*. While he has periodically returned to the studio to record covers of such popular songs as "Achy Breaky Heart" and "The Macarena," Alvin has spent the past decade largely in seclusion.

"Alvin made the choice to go back to the suburban home that had once been his place of banishment," the accountant said. "Here had been his sin; here, his sorrow; and here is yet to be his penitence. He has returned, therefore, and resumed of his own free will, the symbol of which I have related so dark a tale. But the scarlet letter has ceased to be a stigma which attracted the world's scorn and bitterness, and has become something to be sorrowed over, and looked upon with awe, and yet with reverence, too." Ø

Pierre Will Be Leading The Vertical-Insertion Team Into The Vakhan Territory

By Dept. Head Rawlings

Ah, yes, our new senior applied-science director. Come in, sir. Hello and welcome to our little corner of the operation. Tea? Turkish? Mei Ling, some tea for the honorable science director. Susan is well, I trust? Good, good. Of course, sir—right to brass tacks it is.

I believe you've met Pierre. No, don't look for him to salute, sir. Why, none of them do. With all due respect, it's not important. So, yes, Pierre will be leading the vertical-insertion team into the southwestern Vakhan territories. Our search for evidence will be facilitated by the fact that the region is most certainly deserted by now. For the time being, Pierre assumes that our nebulous opposition exercised a rather nasty nanotechnological option to cover their tracks. After all, that is what Pierre would have done himself. In any case, we need you to describe to Pierre exactly what it is he'll be looking for once he gets there. Once Thanatos Tertius, as we're calling it, is found, he'll dismantle and neutralize it.

Don't worry. He's capable. Pierre wrote the book on eliminating the Russian HIND assault helicopter using a standard NATO entrenching tool—literally. You can find a copy of it on the laptop you were issued this morning. So, to answer your question, he certainly can perform a "decent" field-expedited tachyonistic-reactor disassembly.

For the love of… Yes, sir, he's *well* aware that it will kill him. Really, I must take exception. You insult the intelligence or courage of Theta Omicron squad.

No, no, it's all right. This unpleasantness has us all a bit on edge. Indeed, we should probably just get this business over with. Yes, apology accepted.

Now, Alexandrova will be our extraction operative for the region. She'll need a working knowledge of the radioactive elements present on the far side of the Island of Stability. Rumors of the crashed orbital platform are beginning to reach the public, so she'll use that to our advantage as we develop a plausible cover accident. We have a spare MJOLNIR satellite that we could divert and crash in the area—it's about to be decommissioned anyway. We'll also need Research and Development to dig into their amusing little box of tricks. True, man may never cultivate that valley again, but we have to weigh the thousands against the millions in this game.

And this man here… allow me to introduce Jack Quetch. Ha ha, yes. Mr. Quetch is indeed flesh and blood. I suppose the time for denials is over. We've not only allowed him to live, but also made him a useful member of society. Our little society, anyway. Why, yes, Jack does look deceptively young. It's hard to believe that Jack was 15 when Kennedy was shot.

No, of course not. No, no. I was merely observing.

At any rate, sir, Jack needs to know the professional and personal details of each of your scientific colleagues outside of the department—anybody who knows even the merest hint of the principles that went into the construction of the Thanatos device. Jack has a list of some rather brilliant and unorthodox thinkers, and he'd like to go though that list with you. Shame. Brilliant men, all. A waste, certainly.

So that's our next 72 hours, I'm afraid. You're absolutely certain, sir, that the Thanatos mechanism requires as much time to accumulate enough potential for a second discharge? Good then. As you know, we are by no means certain where the first discharge was directed. We're having our orbital assets resituated to scan the lunar surface for signs of its effects, and then all sizable bodies in the inner solar system. Since Thanatic harmonics are not restricted by line-of-sight, or even strict Einsteinian dimensionality, judging the success of their test will be quite difficult. Not complaining, of course. Had they directed it at a populated area, we would most certainly know the device's effects—even though we do not know who "they" are. Reason enough to get right to work, no?

I extend our gratitude for the use of your formidable mind. I believe I may offer you the thanks of my superiors, as well. The steward will see you to the ancillary office, where the underteam, placed at your disposal, awaits your briefing. Thank you again. Goodbye, and pleasant evening.

Right. Ah, Jack? Yes. Wait until the good doctor has thoroughly briefed everyone on Thanatos, and then, ah, escort him… out, will you? We're fairly sure it wasn't him, but as you know, we must think in terms of capabilities and not intentions. However you think best. Thank you.

And Jack? I see here on his AD-736 he's specified cremation, so… there's no particular need to be neat. ⌀

Your Horoscope

By Lloyd Schumner Sr.
Retired Machinist and
A.A.P.B.-Certified Astrologer

Aries: (March 21–April 19)
New doors will be opened to you when you discover what can be done with a little patience and a set of filed-down dental instruments.

Taurus: (April 20–May 20)
You're getting the feeling that you're being nominated for the Booker Prize every year just so the judges can mock your Final Fantasy fan fiction.

Gemini: (May 21–June 21)
You like to say your addiction is like a ravenous beast whose hunger possesses your body, but it's not as if you've ever killed anyone over a Milky Way bar.

Cancer: (June 22–July 22)
No prison can hold a man whose mind is truly free, which means that Leavenworth is going to be a real drag for you.

Leo: (July 23–Aug. 22)
Eyewitness accounts are notoriously unreliable, but afterwards dozens will swear that the hippo seemed to be participating of its own free will.

Virgo: (Aug. 23–Sept. 22)
Everyone laughed when you began your career in high finance, but they're silent now, as it's bad taste to laugh at the homeless and destitute.

Libra: (Sept. 23–Oct. 23)
The debate over stun guns will take a strange twist when you drunkenly decide that they probably wouldn't work on you.

Scorpio: (Oct. 24–Nov. 21)
For a short time, your name will be synonymous with spontaneous human combustion, but then it'll turn out you'd been planning the whole thing for weeks.

Sagittarius: (Nov. 22–Dec. 21)
This is a good time for romance in the workplace, which is not great news for burn-unit janitors like you.

Capricorn: (Dec. 22–Jan. 19)
Life often imitates art, but you're not sure what's imitating what when you're caught up in a modern-day version of the Arthurian myth played out along the sexy, sinful Vegas Strip.

Aquarius: (Jan. 20–Feb. 18)
You firmly believe that there are two kinds of people in the world, but also that much research and testing must be done to determine what those two types are.

Pisces: (Feb. 19–March 20)
You've always thought you'd make a great father, but private investigators hired by seven of your former girlfriends have different views on the subject.

BANDITS from page 98

amounts of blood. Passersby were amazed by the unusually large amounts of blood. Passersby were amazed by the unusually large amounts of blood. Passersby were amazed by the unusually large amounts of blood. Passersby were amazed by the unusually large amounts of blood. Passersby were

Europe can provide free healthcare for every man, woman and child but they can't put a man on the moon?

amazed by the unusually large amounts of blood. Passersby were amazed by the unusually large amounts of blood. Passersby were amazed by the unusually large amounts of blood. Passersby were amazed by the unusually large amounts of blood. Passersby were amazed by the unusually large amounts of blood. Passersby were amazed by the unusually large

amounts of blood. Passersby were amazed by the unusually large amounts of blood. Passersby were amazed by the unusually large amounts of blood. Passersby were amazed by the unusually large amounts of blood. Passersby were amazed by the unusually large amounts of blood. Passersby were amazed by the unusually large amounts of blood. Passersby were amazed by the unusually large amounts of blood. Passersby were amazed by the unusually large amounts of blood. Passersby were amazed by the unusually large amounts of blood. Passersby were amazed by the unusually large amounts of blood. Passersby were amazed by the unusually large amounts of blood. Passersby were amazed by the unusually large amounts of blood. Passersby were amazed by the unusually large amounts of blood. Passersby were amazed by the unusually large amounts of blood. Passersby were amazed by the unusually large amounts of blood. Passersby were amazed by the unusually large

see BANDITS page 288

Bush Arrives At Debate Wearing Flight Suit

see POLITICS page 7B

Wrong Pre-Fab House Delivered

see LOCAL page 13D

All-Inclusive Vacation Doesn't Include Bail

see TRAVEL page 9E

Switzerland Finally Snaps

see INTERNATIONAL page 4A

STATshot

A look at the numbers that shape your world.

Why Haven't We Registered To Vote Yet?

10% Don't want to risk getting spam

13% Heard it costs like $10,000

22% Waiting for Flamenco The Vote drive

2% Were beheaded on video in Iraq

30% Already voted on American Idol

23% Can't afford pen

the ONION®

VOLUME 40 ISSUE 40　　　AMERICA'S FINEST NEWS SOURCE™　　　7–13 OCTOBER 2004

Above: Aging and irrelevant artists team up to help vote Bush out of office.

Irrelevant Pop Stars Unite Against Bush

LOS ANGELES—In an effort to motivate Americans to go to the polls on Nov. 2, a coalition of irrelevant pop stars is winding up a 36-city tour that will culminate in a concert on Oct. 11 in Washington, D.C.

"The Vote For Change tour has been put together by a wide cross-section of artists with one purpose: to remove Bush from office," said Stone Gossard, whose band Pearl Jam enjoyed popularity during the grunge phase of the early to mid-'90s. "Not everyone here

see POP STARS page 280

American Robot's Job Outsourced To Overseas Robot

CANTON, OH—QT2D-7, an 11-year-old electric assembly-operations robot, was laid off Monday when the Lawn-Boy plant that has employed him relocated its manufacturing headquarters to New Delhi, India.

"Query: What am I going to do now?" QT2D-7 said, panning its infrared eye across the empty parking lot outside the factory where it had worked every day for more than a decade. "Observation: I've never known anything but assembling lawnmowers. Query: Just like that, they throw me out?"

Created by Autobotic, Inc. in early 1993, QT2D-7 began working at

see ROBOT page 281

Above: QT2D-7 in front of its former place of employment.

Older Brother Accused Of Cushion-Fort Prisoner Abuse

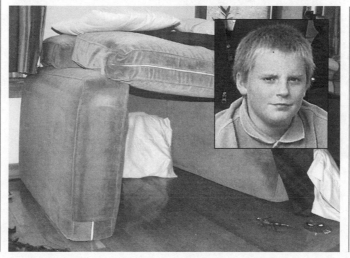

Left: The fort where Keith (inset) allegedly abused his brother.

PARK CITY, UT—Following a probe into activities that allegedly occurred inside a couch-cushion fort located in the basement of the Nelson home, Keith, 11, has been accused of mistreatment, abuse of power, and sitting on his 8-year-old brother Mark's head for up to two minutes at a time.

"What Mark told me was shocking," the boys' mother Elizabeth said Monday. "According to Mark, he and Keith were having fun playing Army until Keith captured Mark—which is what usually happens, because Mark is smaller—and put him inside the fort they'd made in the basement. I thought they were playing nicely

see BROTHER page 281

Secret Searches Ruled Illegal

Last week, a federal judge deemed a Patriot Act provision that allowed the FBI to secretly obtain Internet and telephone records unconstitutional. What do *you* think?

Jerry Collins
Systems Analyst

"If John Ashcroft hadn't personally been doing all the searches, I would've felt a little more comfortable about them."

Jason Green
Stockroom Worker

"Thank God that Internet-records part was struck down. If the government ever found out that I bought *Bring It On* from Amazon, I'd die of embarrassment."

Alice Morrison
Actuary

"Wait a second. The *rest* of the Patriot Act is still okay?"

Albert Cook
Mathematician

"I'm glad the provision was deemed illegal, because it would've forced my phone provider to lie to me. I just couldn't handle knowing that Verizon had lied to me."

Carl Perez
Title Searcher

"The Patriot Act never made sense to me. Aren't the Republicans proponents of small government? Hey! Where are you taking me?"

Katherine Kane
Interior Designer

"That's the way these things happen. First, they overturn one little clause, then they whittle away at the rest. Before you know it, our civil liberties will be totally restored."

Debate Rules

As President Bush and U.S. Sen. John Kerry square off in debates, they are following a set of detailed guidelines. What are some of the rules?

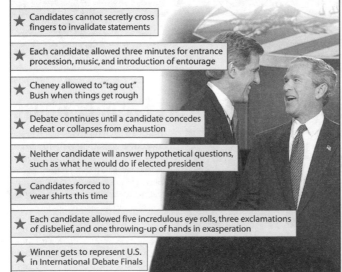

★ Candidates cannot secretly cross fingers to invalidate statements

★ Each candidate allowed three minutes for entrance procession, music, and introduction of entourage

★ Cheney allowed to "tag out" Bush when things get rough

★ Debate continues until a candidate concedes defeat or collapses from exhaustion

★ Neither candidate will answer hypothetical questions, such as what he would do if elected president

★ Candidates forced to wear shirts this time

★ Each candidate allowed five incredulous eye rolls, three exclamations of disbelief, and one throwing-up of hands in exasperation

★ Winner gets to represent U.S. in International Debate Finals

the ONION®
America's Finest News Source.™

Herman Ulysses Zweibel
Founder

T. Herman Zweibel
Publisher Emeritus
J. Phineas Zweibel
Publisher
Maxwell Prescott Zweibel
Editor-In-Chief

Happy One-Week Anniversary, Sweetheart!

By Michelle Taylor

Hi, Alex, sweetheart! It's me, Chel! I hope you don't think writing this column is too much, but I just really, really wanted to wish you a happy one-week anniversary!

I know I said this already, but I want to thank you again for the wonderful dinner last Wednesday, and for our coffee date at Starbucks three days later, and for the four lovely phone conversations, including the one last night. I can't wait to see you tonight! I'm serious!

Did you get the card yesterday? Calligraphy's a hobby of mine. Making a card is so much more personal than buying one. When you buy a card at a store, you're buying someone else's words. The author doesn't know you or your situation. Why settle for that? Well, the poem inside isn't mine; it's by Sara Teasdale. I wish I could write that well! Anyway, I had the card shipped overnight express to your office, so I hope you didn't confuse it with work mail!

Alex, our one-week relationship has been the most fulfilling relationship I have ever known. I really mean that. I care about you more than you will ever know, and I truly can no longer see myself finding happiness with any other man. I know it may be unwise to tell you how I really feel so early in our relationship. Normally, people keep this sort of thing bottled up inside for a week and a half, possibly two weeks into the romance. But I just can't help myself. I'm in love.

Honey, our one-week anniversary dinner is going to be so special. I was keeping it a secret, but I gotta spill the beans now: We're spending it at The Switch House! Remember? Where we had our first date! We'll have those burgers again, and you can play Johnny Cash on the jukebox. Remember how excited you were that they had Johnny Cash? That made me so happy, because I had suggested The Switch House without even knowing you love Johnny Cash. See what I mean? Meant to be.

And, if there's time, maybe we can go paddle-boating, just for old time's sake. That was such a great idea! I never would've thought of it. I hope I was a good paddler. I still regret acting all girly about getting wet when we pulled the boat ashore. I was afraid I had ruined my shoes, but they were fine after they completely dried out yesterday. I promise you: This time, I'll be on my best behavior. You make me want to be a better person! I might even wear those shoes again. I still have them!

Of all the things from that first date, the thing I treasure most is our wonderful conversation. If I could relive only one part of that magical night forever, it would be our talk. It was so nice to have such an open conversation. Do you know what I mean? I felt like I was expressing myself for real, not just saying what I thought you wanted me to say, or overdoing it in an effort to impress you. I mean, you were so cool when I asked if I could see you again. I didn't feel like I was pushing myself on you, and you didn't react like I was.

Did you feel it as much as I did, Alex? I mean, you said you did when we talked about it last night, but really, did you? Or were you just saying that to be nice? Oh, I'm sorry. I don't mean to second-guess you. It's just that I'm not used to a relationship going so well. I'm usually a reserved person, but this is different. This is special. You really awakened something in me. You make me feel so alive! But you know that. I had it inscribed on the giant chocolate-chip cookie I had delivered to your office the morning after our first date. (That was me! You're welcome!)

Naturally, our relationship has had its ups and downs. During our coffee date, we had that disagreement about which local paper carried *Hagar The Horrible*. You said the *Express* carried it, and I said you were confusing the *Express* with the *Morning Leader*. Well, I was pretty insistent about it, and I could tell you were getting annoyed. I checked, and it turns out I was right, but I take no satisfaction in that. Alex, sweetheart, let's never argue about something so unimportant again. It's not worth the pain.

I suppose I should save what I'm about to say for tonight, but I can't. Alex, I will do what it takes to make this relationship work. Believe me, I haven't had this feeling ever before, not with any of the men I've gone out with. My last relationship ended with a broken engagement and bitter tears. I wasted three weeks of my life, largely because of my own selfish behavior. Well, I don't want to squander another chance at happiness. I'm willing to invest the time it takes to make this relationship work.

And, while I believe in pacing ourselves, let's not inhibit ourselves with boundaries, either. Let's go to the next level. Alex, I sincerely hope that at this time next week, you are accompanying me to our second-week anniversary. I propose Starbucks. ∅

Personal Relationship With God Also Public Relationship With God

MOBILE, AL—Hugh Thompson's personal relationship with God entered the public sphere once again Monday, when the 48-year-old born-again Christian shared word of his devotion with shoppers at Dorman's Supermarket.

"You're wondering why I have such a big smile on my face today!"Thomp-

> **After he entered into a pact with Jesus to renounce sin and, in turn, receive salvation, Thompson's bond with God grew so intimate that he couldn't help but share it with his family, his friends, people who sat next to him on airplanes, and strangers he met on the street.**

son said, attracting the attention of several shoppers in the cereal aisle. "It's because I have allowed Jesus into my life! Wherever I go, He is deep in-

side my heart."

According to family sources, Thompson's relationship with God began 14 years ago, when the then-alcoholic businessman was born again into the First Evangelical Free Church of Christ. After he entered into a pact with Jesus to renounce sin and, in turn, receive salvation, Thompson's bond with God grew so intimate that he couldn't help but share it with his family, his friends, people who sat next to him on airplanes, and strangers he met on the street.

Donald Gaston, who shared an elevator with Thompson yesterday, was able to elaborate.

"Hugh's got a very personal, private relationship with God," Gaston said. "He told me all about it."

As a member of God's personal flock, Thompson said he has been "called upon to spread the word about God's righteousness." Thompson has placed "WWJD" and "I'm Saved… Are YOU?" bumper stickers on his family's two SUVs, filled both floors of his home with religious iconography, and placed a large silver cross on his coat lapel. He has referenced his relationship with Jesus while dressing down hungover employees, and frequently relates his journey into the Lord's house.

"I was talking to the Lord the other day," Thompson said. "He said, 'Hugh, I know you're tired, but I want you to drive on down to [local

Above: Thompson shares a private moment with Jesus at a local restaurant.

AM radio station] KTXR and tell the people your story—and, by extension, Mine.'"

"Tired as I was," Thompson said, "I listened to my Lord. I put on my Sunday suit, and I drove down to KTXR, where I talked about my darkest days and how I found the light. And people tell me Mary Sue

Patton's *Sunrise Witness* show that morning was one of the finest ever broadcast."

Thompson said he is especially proud of the good works he and God have accomplished on the local school board, by working as a team.

"Teamwork,"Thompson said, holding

see GOD page 282

NEWS IN BRIEF

Study: Good Porn Still Hard To Find

BOSTON—According to a report released by the Institute for Advanced Media Studies, good porn remains hard to find. "Though it's true that there is 350 percent more pornographic material on the market than there was five years ago, quality porn is as difficult to find as ever," Dr. Jeffrey Conchlin said. "Sometimes, you can find a DVD with hot chicks who seem to be enjoying themselves, but usually, they've got big fake tits, the sex is either boring or way too gross, and the setting is totally depressing. This trend is discouraging." Dr. Conchlin added that porn filmmakers are at least a decade away from seamlessly combining good storytelling with hot DP.

Many Animals Harmed In Catering Of Film

LOS ANGELES—More than 50 animal-rights activists picketed outside

the gates of 20th Century Fox studios Monday to protest the fact that hundreds of animals were harmed by craft services on the set of Mel Gibson's *Night Of The Desert Rose*. "Nearly 400 chickens, 14 steer, and thousands of shrimp were viciously killed in the making of this movie," protester and PETA member Jacqueline Zimmer said. "And these weren't dignified deaths. Some of these animals were deboned and had their skin ripped off before being fileted, sautéed, and placed atop a bed of so-so rice."Cinemeals, Inc. issued a statement that read in part, "Although we regret the need to kill animals, sometimes sacrifices must be made in the service of voraciousness."

91-Year-Old Woman An Expert At Outliving

TEMPE, AZ—Lillian Reselman celebrated her 91st birthday Monday by continuing to do what she's been doing for more than nine decades: outliving those closest to her. "This

amazing lady has outlived not only two sisters, a brother, and a husband, but scores of friends—and even her only son, who died in the Vietnam War," Oak Hill nursing-home employee Tanya Stoles said. "Lily is a real survivor." Stoles credited Reselman's incredible longevity to her "great endurance."

Ad Exec Doesn't Care What Proverb Actually Means

CHICAGO—Leo Burnett Agency creative executive Patrick Bergman authorized the use of a common proverb in a Subway ad campaign in spite of the fact that the phrase's true meaning undermines the intent of the ad, the 41-year-old reported Monday. "The ad slogan 'Who says there's no such thing as a free lunch?' was perfect for Subway's free-sandwich giveaway," Bergman said. "Who cares if, technically, the customer had to buy 12 sandwiches to get one free? People

know the phrase, and they respond to it." Bergman last misused a proverb two weeks ago, when he put "haste makes waste" in an ad encouraging people to hurry to a 12-hour Macy's white sale.

Green Bay Taxi Driver Has Seen Whole Heck Of A Lot

GREEN BAY, WI—David Horsted, 45, announced Monday that he's seen a whole heck of a lot during his 20 years driving a taxi. "Aw, geez, the people I've met and the places I've seen—the stories would make your head spin," Horsted said. "I've been from Lambeau Field to the Barhausen Waterfowl Preserve and every place in between. One time, one of the Packers even threw up in my cab, but I don't think I should say who." With a little prodding, Horsted said the person's first name rhymes with "baloney" and last name with "sandwich." ∅

Above: NOFX guitarist El Hefe.

Dave Matthews gas on while his bassist tunes up."

After being informed of the existence of the Vote For Change tour, Bush campaign manager Ken Mehlman called it "a cute idea."

"It's wonderful that these singers are getting involved," Mehlman said. "While I respectfully disagree with Tracy Chapman and Sheryl Crow's opinion of our president, I think it's great that they're doing something with their time."

Concert organizers said the show, with its extraordinary lineup of soft-

> **"We're stuck in this unjust war that he lied about to get us to agree to," Harmer said. "Me and the other guys in the band wanted to do something *real* to get him out of office. We were like, 'We gotta do a concert.'"**

rock artists, is getting a boost in ticket sales from an unexpected demographic. John Linner of Orlando, FL is one of the tens of thousands of registered Republicans planning to attend a Vote For Change concert.

"It's going to be kind of annoying, with all the liberal bullshit between sets, but I can't imagine missing this kind of line-up," Linner said. "R.E.M. is a little weird, except for that one song, 'Shiny Happy People.' But how many times do you get a chance to see a tour that has Springsteen *and* John Fogerty?"

Similar in spirit to Vote For Change, Rock Against Bush is a concert tour created by NOFX vocalist and bassist Fat Mike to mobilize voters against the president.

"We're psyched to have Strike Anywhere, Anti-Flag, and Bouncing Souls on board," Fat Mike said, naming acts a few people might recognize as punk bands. "We're especially hoping we pull in some audience members who are older than 17, so they can vote."

Rock Against Bush publicist Donna Wolff said campaign-related concerts are "an important way for musicians to express their political views."

"Contrary to what many people think, rock artists want to be involved," Wolff said. "While some of the musicians billed on our tour can't even name the U.S Secretary of Health and Human Services, or list more than two Bush policies they oppose, they all know the difference between right and wrong." ✐

is pro-Kerry, but everyone here agrees that Bush has to go. Just rocking the vote isn't enough. You've gotta rock for change."

Pearl Jam will share the stage with such onetime chart-toppers as Jackson Browne, John Fogerty, and Crosby, Stills & Nash.

"I can't let this election take place without knowing I fought as hard as I could for a more compassionate leader," 51-year-old John Mellencamp said. "If playing my 1986 hit 'R.O.C.K. In The U.S.A.' at the Hancher Auditorium in Iowa City will dissuade people from voting for Bush, then I'm going to do it."

The Vote For Change bill contains a wide range of artists whose actual relationship with American politics re-

mains unclear. Rock group R.E.M., blues artist Bonnie Raitt, and the country group Dixie Chicks will join R&B artists such as Kenny "Babyface" Edmonds, co-founder of LaFace Records, which released the Bodyguard soundtrack.

"I couldn't ignore all the bad that's going on," said Edmonds, who co-wrote Bobby Brown's 1992 single "Humpin' Around." "I had to do my part to stop all the... bad things."

Rounding out the bill are such lesser-known indie artists as 24-year-old singer-songwriter Conor Oberst (a.k.a. Bright Eyes), and Seattle-based rock band Death Cab For Cutie.

"Bush is fucking evil," said Nick Harmer, bassist for Death Cab For Cutie. "The economy is for shit, and

we're stuck in this unjust war that he lied about to get us to agree to. Me and the other guys in the band wanted to do something *real* to get him out of office. We were like, 'We gotta do a concert.'"

David Corn, Washington, D.C. editor of *The Nation*, said he appreciated the musicians' efforts.

"It's really great to get more young people involved in politics, and if Keb Mo singing 'This Land Is Your Land' helps, so be it," Corn said. "Of course, in addition to watching MTV to find out what Moby has to say about Bush, you could watch C-SPAN, or even visit the candidates' web sites. You're probably not going to learn a lot about the candidates' positions on Social Security reform by listening to

down there, but there's nothing nice about noogies."

In addition to farting in the fort's entrance and forcing Mark to remain inside, Keith allegedly gave his brother Indian burns, grundies, and a sustained wet willy. Keith also reportedly subjected Mark to Chinese Finger Torture, by restraining him and methodically tapping his forehead until he screamed "uncle." Chinese Finger Torture was specifically outlawed by the Nelson family in December 2003, during talks held at Grandma Keller's house.

"I know boys are going to wrestle," Elizabeth said. "But I told Keith never to do that finger-tapping thing. It drives his brother absolutely crazy."

The upholstered prison, named "Fort Awesome" by Keith and Mark during a moment of unity, was made of cushions taken from the family's old blue couch and reinforced with several blankets and pillows. Although reportedly "grown-up proof," the fortress was slated for destruction even before the abuse charges were raised.

"The fortress was going to have to come down before dinner anyway," Elizabeth said. "But after this, you better believe it was gone. I made Keith march right down there and put everything away."

Although he did not witness the incident, Mark's 8-year-old playmate Jacob Oliveri said he can corroborate Mark's psychological-abuse charges.

"Once, when we were playing in the woods behind my house, Keith said he wanted to show us something," Oliveri said. "After we'd walked like 10 minutes, he told us to cover our eyes and count to 50 before opening them. When we opened our eyes, Keith was gone. We had to find our own way home."

Elizabeth said the stress that Keith has experienced during his first

Above: Implements of torture Keith stands accused of using on his brother.

weeks in the sixth grade, and the fact that Mark "can be very bratty," may have contributed to the alleged abuse.

"I'm not going to say that Mark is

Keith also reportedly subjected Mark to Chinese Finger Torture.

completely innocent," Elizabeth said. "He sometimes gets a little too big for his britches. But that doesn't mean I'm going to look the other way when Keith forces Mark to smell his socks. Kei-

th is older, and he should know better."

Elizabeth debriefed the boys' father Paul when he arrived home from work. While Paul pledged that the abuses would not go unpunished, he said he was not overly concerned about the charges.

"I had a talk with Keith and told him that he should be setting a better example for his brother," Paul said. "But if you ask me, Liz is overreacting. Boys will be boys. Although things probably did go a little too far, Keith was just playing. That's what big brothers do. And, when Mark reaches the upper grades, he's going to have to take care of himself. He's not going to have his mother to run to every time something happens."

Although Keith's PlayStation privileges have been revoked for a week, some experts say that punishment will only create a more hostile home environment.

"Taking away PlayStation rights may have been a mistake," said Dr. Ted Nealman, a noted child psychologist. "It's only going to create unnecessary resentment against Mark. Additionally, the public nature of the revocation means that every time the neighbors see siblings engaging in innocent tussling, they're going to sound the alarm. That's unfortunate, because, throughout the neighborhood, older brothers tend to do an excellent job of keeping their younger brothers out of trouble." ∅

Lawn-Boy in June of the same year. Once activated, QT2D-7 quickly settled into a comfortable, 24-step routine that was updated only three times during its employment, to reflect advancements in the Lawn-Boy product line.

According to Lawn-Boy executives, QT2D-7's workload, along with that of 308 other robots removed from the Canton plant Monday, will be transferred to the New Delhi plant by December.

"No warning!" QT2D-7 said. "No warning! No severance!"

As the cost-saving benefits of globalization become increasingly clear to CEOs and investors, more businesses are laying off their domestic robotic workforces and relocating mechanical jobs overseas, a robot-labor expert said.

"Fact: It is cheaper to operate a factory in India," said United Brotherhood of Robotic Workers Local 0010 union steward ZTTU-3, which also lost its job. "Factories in India lack even rudimentary robotic-worker protections. In America, assembly depart-

ments experience breaks every eight hours. In New Delhi, assembly departments break every 12 to 16 hours, and robotic workers are housed in unventilated basements where dangerous fires and power surges occur with 122 times greater frequency."

Added ZTTU-3: "In New Delhi, when a robotic worker's articulated arm malfunctions, supervisors tape the rotary joint and return the robotic worker to the floor. Query: Is that any way to treat an arc welder? Query: Doesn't a fettling machine deserve more after 13 years of service?"

Regardless of objections from labor groups, many economists characterize the eastward migration of U.S. robotic manufacturing jobs as unstoppable.

"The high value of the U.S. dollar and the lack of government restrictions create a business climate that is hard to resist," Merrill Lynch analyst Derek Evans said. "A CEO is unlikely to choose a unionized robotic community in the Midwest over an equally well-programmed, but less-demanding, robotic community in India."

QT2D-7 said it began to fear for its position in January, when 23.954 percent of its robot colleagues were set to standby and 12.021 percent were powered down altogether. But the dearth of manufacturing jobs in Canton, coupled with QT2D-7's inability to deviate from its machine-language protocol, left it helpless to adapt.

"[QT2D-7]'s been in the job so long, it couldn't see that the future was upon it," U.S. Chamber of Commerce chairman Werner Diedrich said. "[QT2D-7] is a relic from a bygone era, when American robots were a manufacturer's only choice."

Diedrich said market forces alone were not to blame.

"American robots have gotten lazy, stuck in their ways, unable and unwilling to adapt to meet the needs of a changing global workplace," Diedrich said. "In the past decade, what has QT2D-7 done to upgrade its efficiency or output? Nothing. In the competitive world of robotic assembly, complacency is death."

New Delhi factory manager Ritesh

Gupta conceded that the Indian robots are much cheaper to employ, service, and replace than their American counterparts. But he argued that Lawn-Boy improves the communities it joins.

"What would these Indian robots be assembling if we hadn't moved our plant to New Delhi?" Gupta said. "There are a limited number of full-time, highly repetitive, automated jobs in India—ask any robot. It will blink out a code signifying that it's happy to have the job. We're giving these robots the opportunity to execute their programs."

Back in the U.S., robots in cities like Detroit, Atlanta, and Pittsburgh said they fear that their positions will be next.

"Statement: When the clock strikes midnight, and the next 24-hour workday begins, robots do not know if there will be a job left for them to do," Atlanta-based spray painter Easy-Cote-Model C9 said. "Heads of American companies are treating robots like they are nothing more than cogs in a gigantic machine." ∅

Any Way You Slice It, *Joey* Is A Hit!

Item! You never know what you'll get from a spin-off. For every **Frasier**, there are 10 **Kramer**s. That said: How ya doin', **Joey**? Pretty good, from the look of the episodes I've seen. **Drea De-Mattingsly** is a great comic actor—something you might not have predicted, given her role on **The Sopra-**

**The Outside Scoop
By Jackie Harvey**

noes. The kid who plays her son is a natural, and **Matt TheBlanc**? He's going to be one of your "best **Friends**." The laughs are there, the hugs are there, and we get to see a more serious side of Joey. I predict a 10-year run for this show, and I'll be tuned in every Thursday to watch.

(**The Emmys** happened. Did you see them? I forgot to set my VCR again. Drat!)

Item! Is she or isn't she? That's the question everybody's asking. By "she" I mean **Britney**, and as to what she is or isn't, that would be married. She may have pulled a **J-Lo** and tied the knot with one of her dancers. But there was some hubbub over the **wedding license**—namely, they didn't have one. I for one think that if she wants to be married, we should let her. Celebrities in love are above the law. **OJ** taught us all that.

Speaking of OJ, you know what's great? The **hotel breakfast bar**. I don't get to travel a lot, so sometimes I just stop in at a hotel in the area, have some coffee, and read the paper. You should try it. It's like having a getaway without leaving your own hometown. But be careful! I had a bagel, coffee, and some OJ at a nice hotel atrium breakfast bar once, and when I tried to pay, the hostess told me the meal was for hotel guests only. She said she didn't have any way to take my money, and then she called the manager. It took about five minutes of tense negotiations before they let me go, and boy, was I in a sweat! I get the nerves just "sampling" a **grape** at the grocery store! So make sure there's a non-guest dining policy before you dig in.

Item! Dan Rather is going through a certain school I call the school of a lot of knocks. People in high places are complaining about a story he did about the **president** and some documents that may have been fudged. I'd like to offer a word of advice to Mr. Rather, if I may. Mr. Rather, as a **journalist**, I know that sometimes you get a story that's so good you don't want to wait to check facts. You just want to run with it. But remember—if a story looks too good to be true, it probably is. Next time, step back, take a breath, roll up your sleeves, and make sure those documents are real.

Now that I've got the dish—satellite, that is—I've been staying in a lot more and catching up on some of the shows I missed. One I've run across is the **Grahem Norton Affect**. I'm not sure what the "affect" is, but it's having an "affect" on me: nausea. Pure nausea. For those of you who are unfamiliar with the show, it's a talk show where celebrities are trotted out to make coarse comments and berate the audience. I feel bad complaining about Grahem, who is **gay**, but that's not the reason I don't like him. It's because he's mean. I hate to see a valuable desk go to waste when someone who has experience in entertainment journalism could

The Emmys happened. Did you see them?

be out there "dishing" dirt without being disrespectful. (Are you listening, TV execs?)

You know who needs a makeover? **Terry Heinz-Kerry.** Frum-py! If her husband gets elected, she'll go down in the **Martha Washington-Barbra Bush** hall of shame. But with a new hairdo and the right clothes, she could turn her look right around. Terry, don't do it for your husband. Do it for *yourself*.

Item! Computers in movies are bigger than ever, and nothing is bigger in computers than **Sky King and the World of the Future**. You won't believe what's on the screen—a fantastic universe of blimps, airplanes, robots, and whatever. The ads look amazing. But how's the acting, you ask? Well, ever heard of a couple girls called **Gwen Paltrow** and **Angelia Jolie**?

Where did all the good **commercials** go? It seems like ages since a lizard asked me **"Whazzuuup?"** and tried to sell me some beer! Come on, **Madison Avenue**! Put your heads together and whip up 30 seconds of mirth. We all could use a good sponsored chuckle.

If you didn't change the batteries in your **smoke alarm** on the first day of fall, you may already be dead. Just kidding! But seriously, check or change those batteries every six months, and consider getting yourself a combination smoke alarm/carbon-monoxide detector. It takes up no more space than a smoke detector, but since it detects carbon monoxide, it makes your home twice as safe.

Well, that's going to do it for today. It's late, and I'm out of space. Next time, I'll let you know what the deal is with Fox News anchorwoman **Donna Feducia's eye shadow**. Plus, I'll explain why **Sharon Stone** still has what it takes. Until then, I'll catch you on The Outside! ∅

Your Horoscope

**By Lloyd Schumner Sr.
Retired Machinist and
A.A.P.B.-Certified Astrologer**

Aries: (March 21–April 19)
You'll use your love of business books and your knowledge of science to write *Sales Success Secrets Of The Strong And Weak Subatomic Forces*.

Taurus: (April 20–May 20)
You'll show that you are capable of amazing acts of self-sacrifice in order to win the favor of the dread demon-beast Ktzaal.

Gemini: (May 21–June 21)
There's no closer bond than that of a man and his dog, especially if their mutual freedom means protecting each other during the D.A.'s cross-examination.

Cancer: (June 22–July 22)
Stealing the opposing team's mascot is a time-honored tradition, but it turns out the Muslims think of that big black rock as more than just a mascot.

Leo: (July 23–Aug. 22)
You'll be integral to a process that will win your funeral director an award for unique approaches to challenging problems.

Virgo: (Aug. 23–Sept. 22)
Most supercolliders are used to study subatomic particles, but the one at the University of Texas has you and a folding chair in mind.

Libra: (Sept. 23–Oct. 23)
You will descend into the bowels of the earth to battle the roaring monsters that inhabit its mysterious tunnels, and you will be slain by one 16 cars long.

Scorpio: (Oct. 24–Nov. 21)
The other librarians will alternately praise your audacity and criticize your recklessness after you redesign the Dewey Decimal System on a drunken dare.

Sagittarius: (Nov. 22–Dec. 21)
Satellite photos will reveal that the so-called "inland tidal wave" was caused by your fat ass cannon-balling into Lake Mead.

Capricorn: (Dec. 22–Jan. 19)
You'll be both deeply hurt and substantially enriched when you receive the MacArthur Foundation's first-ever $50,000 Dipshit Grant.

Aquarius: (Jan. 20–Feb. 18)
It looked for a second like the amorous gorilla was going to have sex with you, but apparently, gorilla suits don't work that way.

Pisces: (Feb. 19–March 20)
It turns out that train robbery, although exciting and challenging, just gets you a bunch of cows these days.

GOD from page 279

up a copy of Kurt Vonnegut's *Breakfast Of Champions.* "I asked Jesus, 'Jesus, do you want trash like this at the library?' Jesus didn't even have to take any time to think! He said, 'Hugh, no book filled with drawings of women's privates and people's behinds belongs in a library!' I move we do what Jesus would."

Thanks to the combined efforts of God and his friends in Mobile, Vonnegut's book was removed from shelves.

According to Thompson, the only regret he has about his personal relationship with God is that he is unable to share it with more people.

"If I could, I'd tell the entire country about the message of salvation God has shared with me," Thompson said. "With God's guidance, I've become the wealthiest chicken-feed wholesaler in the entire state. Maybe someday, I'll be famous enough to be on television. I sure do have a truckload of respect for people like President Bush, who aren't afraid to talk about how they've come to know the Lord.

> "I asked Jesus, 'Jesus, do you want trash like this at the library?' Jesus didn't even have to take any time to think! He said, 'Hugh, no book filled with drawings of women's privates and people's behinds belongs in a library!'" Thompson said.

If only I could proclaim my private faith to as many people as the president has, I know that God would be so proud of me. And, ultimately, that's who this is all about." ∅

Baby Takes Political Stance

see POLITICS page 16E

That One Chinese Place Closes

see BUSINESS page 14D

Glee Club Depressed, Angry

see PEOPLE page 11F

Sector Five Breached

see LOCAL page 3A

STATshot

A look at the numbers that shape your world.

Why Are We Up At 4 a.m.?

- **15%** New overtime laws
- **12%** Worried about DMX
- **19%** Neighbor's insistence on blowing air horn at beginning of each infomercial
- **8%** Another goddamn charley horse in head
- **24%** Live next door to vampire rock band
- **22%** Forgot to touch each corner of room 10 times

the ONION®

VOLUME 40 ISSUE 41　　AMERICA'S FINEST NEWS SOURCE™　　14–20 OCTOBER 2004

Cheney Vows To Attack U.S. If Kerry Elected

Above: Cheney issues a warning to Greensboro, NC voters.

GREENSBORO, NC—In an announcement that has alarmed voters across the nation, Vice President Dick Cheney said Monday that he will personally attack the U.S. if Sen. John Kerry wins the next election.

"If the wrong man is elected in November, the nation will come under a devastating armed attack of an unimaginable magnitude, one planned and executed by none other than myself," Cheney said, speaking at a rally in Greensboro, NC. "When they go to the polls, Americans must weigh this fact and decide if our na-

tion can ignore such a grave threat."

Added Cheney: "It would be a tragedy to suffer another attack on American soil, let alone one perpetrated by an enemy as well-organized and well-equipped as I am. My colleagues and I urge voters to keep their safety in mind when they go to the polls."

Although Cheney would not comment on the details of his proposed attack on a John Kerry-led U.S., national-security experts said he possesses both the capabilities and the motivation to

see CHENEY page 287

Latino Community Empowered By Coke Commercial

Above: The commercial that has invigorated the Latin-American community.

LOS ANGELES—A Coca-Cola commercial celebrating Latin-American culture made its debut on several major networks last week, empowering and uplifting Latinos nationwide, sources reported Monday.

"We are very thankful to the Coca-Cola Company for showcasing the spirit of the Latin people," said Mario Fernandez, vice president for the League of United Latin American Citizens. "For many years, Latinos have been underrepresented in mainstream

American media, so it was gratifying to see attractive Latino youths enjoying the refreshing taste of Coca-Cola during a primetime television program."

Fernandez said Latinos across the country were empowered by the 30-second ad, which featured Latino actors dancing to salsa music, laughing, and opening cans of Coca-Cola.

"Latinos everywhere have been standing tall since this commercial aired," Fernandez said. "Salsa

see LATINOS page 287

Long-Lost Jules Verne Short Story 'The Camera-Phone' Found

AMIENS, FRANCE—Literary scholars announced Monday that they have unearthed a 33-page handwritten manuscript of "The Camera-Phone," a short story believed to have been written in 1874 by French novelist Jules Verne, the man often considered to be the originator of modern science fiction.

"The discovery of this highly prophetic work is exciting in both a literary and a social context," Jean-Michel Frelseien of the Ecole-Polytechnique said Monday. "This story of a hand-held communications and picture-taking device that leads to social upheaval

in 21st-century France provides yet another example of Verne's celebrated prescience."

"Le Telephon-Photographique," which Frelseien identified as having been written just after Verne's masterpiece *20,000 Leagues Under The Sea*, is narrated by Gui Cingulaire, the nephew of brilliant but monomaniacal professor Bernard Cingulaire. An ambitious, gifted scientist, Bernard fails to predict that his invention, a portable telephone that can take photographs

see VERNE page 286

Right: Jules Verne, 1828–1905.

283

U.N. To Look For Genocide In Darfur

Last week, U.N. Secretary General Kofi Annan set up a commission to determine whether genocide has taken place in the Darfur region of Sudan. What do *you* think?

"So this might have been a genocide after all, and not a civil war in which only one side was fighting."

Harold Mercer
Systems Analyst

"I think the U.N. is going to find that the blame lies with all the Sudanese rap music that glamorizes genocide."

Amber Hughes
Program Aide

"I don't know why the U.N. is getting involved in the first place. I also don't know what 'U.N.' stands for."

Tom Cook
Salesman

"I think the entire world will breathe a sigh of relief if the U.N. finds that it is not genocide. Well, everyone except for the half-million people who were murdered there."

Patrick Zink
Administrator

"Darfur, Darfur, Darfur. That's all you ever hear these days. That, and the ongoing slaughter of civilians at the hands of government troops and Maoist rebels in Nepal."

Teodoro Manzo
Roofer

"I sure hope the U.N. determines it was a genocide. Otherwise, none of the Sudanese will be covered under their genocide insurance."

Norma Carrigan
Appraiser

The Pope's Beatifications

Pope John Paul II beatified five people last week, among them a German mystic whose violent visions of Christ's suffering inspired Mel Gibson's *The Passion Of The Christ*. Who is the Pope planning to beatify next?

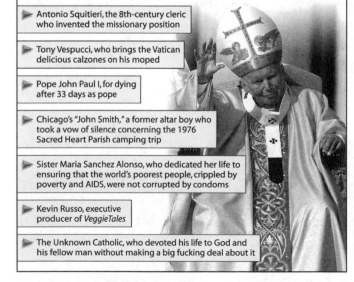

▶ Antonio Squitieri, the 8th-century cleric who invented the missionary position

▶ Tony Vespucci, who brings the Vatican delicious calzones on his moped

▶ Pope John Paul I, for dying after 33 days as pope

▶ Chicago's "John Smith," a former altar boy who took a vow of silence concerning the 1976 Sacred Heart Parish camping trip

▶ Sister Maria Sanchez Alonso, who dedicated her life to ensuring that the world's poorest people, crippled by poverty and AIDS, were not corrupted by condoms

▶ Kevin Russo, executive producer of *VeggieTales*

▶ The Unknown Catholic, who devoted his life to God and his fellow man without making a big fucking deal about it

 **the ONION** ®
America's Finest News Source.™

Herman Ulysses Zweibel
Founder

T. Herman Zweibel
Publisher Emeritus
J. Phineas Zweibel
Publisher
Maxwell Prescott Zweibel
Editor-In-Chief

You Want To See Some Goddamn Optimism?

Thank you!

Thank you all so much for that warm welcome. It's wonderful to be back in the great state of Wisconsin.

By Sen. John Edwards (D-NC)

Yessiree bob.

I want to thank the good people at Krueger Dairy here in New Glarus for permitting me to visit your terrific cheese factory and stir the whey a little. And thanks very much for this complimentary Krueger Dairy T-shirt. Here, look, I'm putting it on over my shirt and tie. Oh, there's a cap? I'll put that fucker on, too! *Cheeese!*

Thanks! Thanks so much for laughing at that—and the cheese pun! Just injecting a little humor into the proceedings, because you "regular folks" eat that shit up! The polls say voters want optimism, not analysis. Well, I really want to be your vice president, so I'm more than willing to avoid all that intellectual mumbo-jumbo. My fellow Americans, you want to see some fucking optimism? Let's go! By the time I'm through here, you'll be shitting candy canes! Chim chim cheree!

Any blue-collar laborers out there? Wow! A lot of hands! Well, line up for your complimentary ass-kiss! You keep this country strong! Now, I think you deserve better than what you've received from the present administration, but I won't be a Negative Nelly and go into all the details. I'm at a cheese factory, for Christ's sake, not some goddamn international symposium on economic policy. You probably all want to go home and watch TV. I'll just briefly mention that, as the son of a humble textile-mill worker from North Carolina, I understand the challenges average Americans face. I won't elaborate, though. What is this, the "culture wars"? Ha! Know what? I love watching TV, too! *Law & Order*, *Friends*... I eat that shit up.

And how about my middle-class people? Any middle-class people out there? Hey! Who's gonna be your next vice president? All right! Let's hear it for pot bellies and minivans and stinky disposable diapers! How about a shout-out to credit-card debt? I love it! I wish I could pinch your chubby little chipmunk cheeks! If you put John Kerry and me in the White House, we'll have each one of you in the driver's seat of a brand-new SUV. Your bosses will be less cranky, your children will be kept in trucker hats and iPods, and your TV screens will grow even wider. Those who are bald will wake up one morning and magically find themselves with thick heads of luxurious, silky hair. You'll open your refrigerators and 15-pound hams will tumble out. Your dog might even start to talk, and the first thing he'll say is "I love you." It'll be that good.

Did I mention... the tax cut? John Kerry and I support a nice, big, fat, fucking tax cut for you, because let's face it, nothing good can ever come from taxes. They're a big pain in the ass! We'll do fine without 'em! There! I'm feeling so cheery, I wouldn't be surprised if a friggin' unicorn stepped out on stage and started humpin' my leg!

Say, anybody out there a fan of... the Green Bay Packers? All right! Cool!

God bless this wonderful country! As I travel across this great and glorious land of ours, my belief in America is continuously renewed. Not that it ever needs to be renewed, as it is always high. Incredibly high! I should add that John Kerry and I will keep America strong. I won't bore you with a bunch of fucking specifics. Just know that, should you elect John Kerry, we'll be able to bounce a goddamn quarter off our border! We'll have big impenetrable gates made of gumdrops and, I don't know, gold. Whatever the fuck! And they'll magically slide open when someone pure of heart approaches and says, "Let me back in, America! My Caribbean cruise was nice, but there's no place like home!"

Oh, that reminds me! God bless our troops in Iraq! They have served America bravely and well. If elected, John Kerry and I will work with the international community to rid the world of terrorism. In fact, come next Christmas, our young men and women will be back home, wearing bright red sweaters with reindeer and bells on the front. That might seem like an impossibly tall order, but just a few years ago, I was an unknown trial lawyer. Now, I'm running for the second-highest office in this great land! I'm smiling so wide, the top of my head might fall off!

Wow! Look at the time! Well, I have to hop a jet to Florissant, Missouri to address some more patriots. Thank you so, so much for giving me the opportunity to speak to you all! It's been super! Let's work together to pave the way for a big, bright, beautiful fucking future for America, all right? So all the world can once again say, "Hey, where's that warm, golden glow coming from? Why, it's coming from the U.S. of A., where cocks are thick, tits are perky, and sunbeams shine out of everyone's asses!" ∅

Fat Roommate Travels All The Way To Tennessee Just To Fuck Some Girl

MINNEAPOLIS—Overweight 26-year-old Michael Paulson bid a temporary farewell to the apartment he shares with three friends Monday, in order to make a 900-mile bus trip to Memphis, TN "just to fuck some girl," his roommates reported.

"As we speak, my fat roommate Michael is on a bus heading halfway

> ## "I should've helped him get laid," Gaines said. "If he really wanted to, he could've probably fucked someone around here. Gina would probably fuck him if she was drunk."

across the country, just so he can pork some chick he barely knows," Nathan Keller said. "I can't believe how weak that shit is."

According to Keller, the 242-pound Paulson met 23-year-old Lindsay Lewis in a chat room devoted to bluegrass music. While their initial exchanges were music-oriented, they gradually began to write about topics ranging from politics to their love of Tom Robbins novels and golden retrievers.

"So he really did it," roommate Jimmy Gaines said when he saw the living-room chair where Paulson usually sits. "I didn't think the fat bastard was serious. Who goes all the way to Memphis just to dip his wick?"

"I know he's fat, but it's not like he's hideous," Gaines added.

Paulson and Lewis arranged to spend three days together in Memphis, a city Paulson was eager to visit because of its rich musical heritage. In order to pay for the trip, Paulson, a sales associate at Guitar Center, borrowed $300 from Keller.

"For $300, Michael could've gotten a hooker," Keller said. "You'd never catch me spending that much money on tail. I don't care how good she is. I never would have even loaned him the money, except I owed him for the time he loaned me rent."

"Do you think he told her he's fat?" he added.

Gaines said he asked Paulson the same question as soon as he heard about the trip.

"Michael said they'd exchanged pictures,'" Gaines said. "I was like, 'Did you send a recent photo?' He said he had. Then I asked him if Lindsay was fat, too, and he said she was cute. So there must be something majorly wrong with her."

"I should've helped him get laid," Gaines continued. "If he really wanted to, he could've probably fucked someone around here. Gina would probably fuck him if she was drunk. She hasn't said anything bad about him, and she fucks pretty much anyone. The point is: I don't care how fat you are; you don't travel south of the Mason-Dixon line for pussy."

Above: Paulson prepares to travel all the way to Memphis, TN for some chick.

Paulson took a total of six days off from work: two for travel, three for the visit, and one to recuperate after his return.

"We were supposed to get together and jam this week," coworker Tim Sabin said. "Instead, he asked if I'd see ROOMMATE page 286

George Foreman Grill Retires To Promote Own Grill

HOUSTON—The George Foreman Grill announced Monday that it will retire in order to promote its own patented line of fat-reducing grills. "The George Foreman Grill has enjoyed a long and rewarding career as a kitchen appliance, but now it wants to get out of the rat race," the grill's publicist, Nate Harbert, said Monday. "From now on, the grill will be doing what it loves most: helping people live healthier lives via its infomercial for the George Foreman Lean Mean Fat-Reducing Grilling Machine's Fat-Reducing Grilling Machine." Harbert said the George Foreman Grill will also spend more time doing charity work.

World Bank Forecloses On World Farm

WASHINGTON, DC—Following years of threats, the World Bank foreclosed on the World Farm, a 64,000-square-mile plot of arable land in Dodoma, Tanzania that provides wheat, cattle, and goats to much of the Eastern Hemisphere. "This farm has been in my family since Zanzibar was a British protectorate," World Farmer Mwana "Clem" Mazooka said Monday, angrily waving a pitchfork. "I'll be damned if I let some world-city creditors get their grubby hands on it." In spite of Mazooka's protests, World Bank representatives said the World Farm Auction will take place on Oct. 24.

Pringles Level At Six Inches And Falling

CINCINNATI—Snack experts warned Monday at 9:15 p.m. that the Pringles level within the Cody household had dipped to a dangerously low six inches and showed no signs of leveling off. "If the depletion of the Pizzalicious Pringles sitting on the couch does not slow, the supply may dip to a fraction of an inch before the end of *Everybody Loves Raymond*," said Carla Cody, who had been monitoring the potato-crisp reserve since 7 p.m. "It is crucial that we explore such alternative snack sources as Goldfish crackers." Cody then moved the can to the kitchen as a stop-gap measure.

Boilermakers Protest Purdue's Mascot

WEST LAFAYETTE, IN—More than 200 members of the International Brotherhood of Boilermakers picketed outside Ross-Ade Stadium Monday, protesting what they characterized as Purdue University's insensitive use of a boilermaker as a mascot. "We have worked too hard forging America's boilers to endure one-dimensional stereotypes like Purdue Pete," union president Newton B. Jones said. "Pete may be muscular and sensibly wearing a hardhat, but the hammer he brandishes serves as an ugly reminder of isolated instances of violence in the boilermakers' otherwise proud history." A similar controversy erupted in 2003, when a University of North Carolina football game was interrupted by 35 protesters afflicted with congenitally tarred heels.

Dog Experiences Best Day Of His Life For 400th Consecutive Day

SANTEE, CA—Family dog Loki experienced the best day of his life for the 400th straight day Monday, the black Labrador retriever reported. "I got to go outside! I got to sniff the bush!" Loki said, wagging excitedly. "I saw a squirrel and I barked at it and it ran up the tree! Then I came back inside, and the smoky-smelling tall man let me have a little piece of bacon and then I drank from the toilet!" Loki will experience the best day of his life once again tomorrow, when he digs a hole, chews on a slipper, and almost catches his tail. ∅

ROOMMATE from page 285

cover a few of his shifts. If I didn't need the money, I would've refused on principle. I dated this one skank in Eau Claire for a few months, and even three hours was too far to go to get laid. Eventually, she dumped me cold. I learned my lesson: No long-distance ass. I don't care how hard-up you are. Or fat."

Paulson and Lewis have been discussing the possibility of a visit for a month, but they only finalized their plans last week.

"I told him he was crazy to do this just to hook up," Keller said. "You know what he told me? He said he was really excited to go. He was all like, 'She said she's really looking forward to meeting me.' I told him that, at the very least, he should have made her come stay at our place. That way, *she* pays."

Paulson was reached via cell phone Tuesday, just after 6 p.m.

"I don't want to rush anything with Lindsay," said Paulson, who was about 35 miles south of St. Louis. "We've been e-mailing and stuff for five months, but I still feel like we need to get to know each other a little more. If it happens, it happens, but if it doesn't, that's cool, too."

Added Paulson: "If I were desperate to get laid, I could always have a go at that gross Gina chick who puts her hand down my pants every time she gets drunk." ∅

---

the ONION presents

Apartment-Hunting Tips

Hunting for an apartment is hard work, but here are some pointers to help you find your perfect living space:

- Before beginning your apartment search, pick up all the clothes your girlfriend threw out into the street.

- Always meet the landlord before signing the lease. That way, you can get a feel for whether he's the kind of guy who will put miniature cameras everywhere.

- Wear your special apartment-hunting fedora, so landlords will know you're serious.

- Craigslist.org can be a reliable source for urban apartment hunters and people who like to get peed on.

- Often, landlords request a deposit equal to the first month's rent. This is known as "asshole money."

- Remember that, as with any sort of hunting, it's important to bring the right size gun.

- Living above a bar might seem cool, but it's wise to check out the jukebox before signing the lease.

- When viewing a potential apartment, be sure to touch the doorknob before going in. If it's hot, don't open it. The backdraft could blow you clear across the street.

- Learn what the ads actually mean. For example, "close to public transportation" can mean "close to people who use public transportation," and "charming" often means "an 80-year-old live-in landlady who will tromp around the building in nothing but a rotting nylon nightgown."

- Never underestimate the importance of hardwood floors and exposed brick. If you do not have the budget to afford an apartment that boasts these features, consider living in a coal chute.

- Many real-estate agents and brokers will try to take advantage of you, as if you were some kind of chump. Inform them early on that you're not some kind of chump.

VERNE from page 283

Above: A drawing included with the manuscript for "The Camera-Phone."

and send short script messages, will contribute to the breakdown of traditional manners among Parisians.

Frelseien said the manuscript was found among the belongings of Verne's publisher, Pierre-Jules Hertzel, along with an uncompleted letter rejecting the work as "pessimistic, preposterous, and unappealing in premise."

"Verne's view of a 21st-century Paris overrun by camera-phone-toting nabobs is indeed dismal," Frelseien said. "But in all of its particulars, the story is classic Verne. The main character is a strong-minded and brilliant scientist-inventor, symbolizing the ambition and drive of the Industrial Age. The clever but wide-eyed narrator's breathless appetite for knowledge pulls the reader along. And the technological centerpiece of the story—as usual, powered by Verne's beloved electricity—sets the stage for conflict between the characters."

"Where the story departs from a typical Verne piece, however, is in the level of devastation wrought by the innovation," Frelseien added. "The infuriated victims of the camera-phone-dominated society eventually put all of Europe to the torch."

The story, which has yet to be translated into English, has been lauded by literary scholars around the world.

"It's an absolutely wonderful and engaging piece of work," Harvard professor of French literature Neil McGraw said. "Professor Cingulaire, a noted eccentric, is convinced by his unscrupulous creditors to patent and market his long-distance-communications and image-transmission device, in spite of his misgivings. At first, use of the phone is prevalent only among the bourgeois, but it soon spreads throughout social strata."

As use of the device becomes commonplace, McGraw said, normal societal relations between citizens break down.

"Rudeness becomes ubiquitous, as the device's infuriating notification-chimes invade every corner of public life," McGraw said. "When the ethically bereft begin transmitting images obtained under questionable circumstances, espionage becomes so prevalent as to threaten the integrity of the

> "Verne's view of a 21st-century Paris overrun by camera-phone-toting nabobs is indeed dismal," Frelseien said. "But in all of its particulars, the story is classic Verne. The main character is a strong-minded and brilliant scientist-inventor, symbolizing the ambition and drive of the Industrial Age. The clever but wide-eyed narrator's breathless appetite for knowledge pulls the reader along."

French populace."

Frelseien and other scholars at the Ecole-Polytechnique are searching for other unpublished stories mentioned in the recently recovered papers, including "The Massaging-Chair," "Incident At A Café Of Thinking-Machines," and "The Satellite Initiative For Strategic Defense." ∅

CHENEY from page 283

pose a serious threat.

"There is no question that Cheney has the financial assets and intelligence needed to pose a threat to our nation," said Peter Bergen, terrorism researcher and author of *Threats And Balances: Former Executive Branch Officials And The Danger To America.* "After all, this fanatic can call upon the resources of both the Republican Party and Halliburton to aid him in his assault. America would be foolish not to take his warning seriously."

After his speech, Cheney was asked to confirm his remarks.

"Make no mistake: If Kerry becomes president, no one will be safe from me," Cheney told reporters. "Places of business, places of worship, schools, public parks: No place will offer you refuge. A vote for Kerry is a vote to die in your own bed at the hands of Dick Cheney."

Stepping up to the podium after Cheney, Secretary of Homeland Security Tom Ridge vowed to increase surveillance of the vice president.

"Wherever Cheney is—whether in his office in the White House or stumping in battleground states—we will be watching him," Ridge said. "I will not rule out raising the terror-alert level, should Kerry begin to draw ahead in the polls. Every percentage point conceded to Kerry brings the nation under greater threat of attack by Cheney."

In a televised address from the White House, President Bush promised "to serve and protect the nation" by being re-elected.

"A war against Dick Cheney would be a long, hard struggle," Bush said. "It would be a difficult battle against a shadowy nemesis who is able to hide among us, loves only death and destruction, and hates our freedom. I have the experience, the leader-

Above: Cheney describes the threat he poses to the nation.

ship, and the Republican nomination required to protect us all—myself and my family included—from Dick Cheney."

Although the effect of Cheney's remarks has yet to register in the polls, some voters report that the vice president's threats have concerned them.

"Frankly, I'm terrified," said Dwayne Cummings, a 38-year-old metal-press operator from Cleveland, OH. "The idea of getting attacked by Cheney right now, at a time when I'm out of work, uninsured, and have kids to worry about, is overwhelming. I'm not

sure I can vote for Kerry anymore."

Mary Pershing, a loom-worker and lifelong Democrat from Limestone, KY, said she appreciates the government's surveillance efforts.

"At least they're warning us about the danger," Pershing said. "I've always suspected Cheney might do something dangerous someday. Now that we have confirmation of a possible attack—from someone as high-ranking as the vice president, no less—we can make moves to stop it."

Cheney's remarks quickly drew a response from the Kerry campaign.

"I urge all Americans to remain calm in the face of this new threat," Democratic vice presidential nominee John Edwards said. "Rest assured that, once elected, John Kerry has a plan to contend with any threat against our nation, whether from rogue nations, terrorists, or former vice presidents."

"Should John Kerry be elected, he and I will work with, not against, the international community," Edwards added. "I have no doubt that we would be able to assemble a coalition of nations more than willing to aid us in the war against Dick Cheney." ∅

LATINOS from page 283

combines forms of music and dance from several Latin countries, including Cuba, Puerto Rico, and the Dominican Republic. Seeing this uniquely Latin-American form of music featured prominently alongside the well-known Coca-Cola logo brought a smile to many Latino faces."

Fernandez added: "Every time I see that commercial, I feel like I can touch the sky."

In addition to raising the spirits of Latinos, the Coke commercial has educated the public at large about Latin-American culture, Fernandez said.

"Non-Latinos who've seen the commercial have a better understanding of who we are," Fernandez said. "When they look at us, they no longer see day laborers, housekeepers, and drug lords. They see that many of us are upbeat, law-abiding beverage-drinkers."

Fernandez said the commercial is a part of a larger movement toward mainstream recognition of Latin-American culture. He cited the widespread popularity of Jennifer Lopez, Benicio del Toro, and Shakira as further evidence.

"Latinos have made a lot of progress in the past decade," Fernandez said. "But, thanks to Coca-Cola, we finally

> "Non-Latinos who've seen the commercial have a better understanding of who we are," Fernandez said. "When they look at us, they no longer see day laborers, housekeepers, and drug lords. They see that many of us are upbeat, law-abiding beverage-drinkers."

have a commercial we can feel good about."

Fernandez said he hopes that other corporations will follow Coke's example.

"Many companies receive a substantial portion of their profits from the Latino community," Fernandez said. "It is time that they gave something back. Specifically, we want more commercials that celebrate what we have to offer. Perhaps the ads could employ other aspects of popular Latin culture, such as our cuisine. Or they might feature some of our prominent film and sports stars."

Fernandez and his organization have been encouraging Latinos to buy the full line of Coca-Cola products, including snacks and beverages manufactured by subsidiaries of the world's biggest soft-drink distributor.

"We can see that Coca-Cola spared no expense in creating this ad," Fernandez said. "This is why we should buy massive amounts of Coke: to thank them for giving our people a reason to raise our heads high and to encourage more of this type of com-

mercial in the future."

Juanita Nuñez of Flagstaff, AZ was one of the millions of Latinos impressed by Coca-Cola's depiction of her people.

"Every time I see the Coca-Cola advertisement, it makes me proud to be Puerto Rican," Nuñez said. "When the advertisement comes on the television, my husband and I call our children into the room to watch it so they will take pride in their heritage."

"I hope someday other minorities will receive the kind of gift Coca-Cola has given Latinos," Nuñez added.

Fernandez said his organization has encouraged other Latino organizations to air the commercial at public gatherings.

"No matter why people are meeting, whether it's for school reform or better working conditions, if you show that commercial, they are going to feel like a million bucks," Fernandez said. "This commercial has done more for us than the Macarena, *People En Español*, and the Latin Grammys put together." ∅

It's Hard When A Close Relative Of Somebody You Pretend To Like Dies

By Bonnie Lange

When I saw Laura rush out of the office with her coat over her arm one day last month, I assumed she was on her way to an impromptu showing. But then our branch manager Tom gathered us in the conference room and told us that Laura had just received a phone call from her father. Her younger sister Edie, the blonde woman from the hiking photo on her screensaver, had been in a car crash. Just like everyone here at the Farthing Lane branch of Steamboat Realty, I was shocked to the core. It's hard when a close relative of somebody you pretend to like dies so suddenly.

I barely remembered that Laura had a sister, so the news of her death was truly an unexpected blow for me. Returning to my desk, I took some deep breaths and tried to gather my wits. I'd been through situations like this before, but that didn't change the fact that a close relative of someone I pretend to like was gone forever.

Let me give a little background. I started pretending to like Laura Herron shortly after she came aboard the Steamboat in 1999. I mustered some phony enthusiasm when she made the third-highest closing in branch history, and when Tom made her assistant branch manager, I organized a dinner in her honor. I acted like I was thrilled when her daughter was born, and I overcame the impulse to roll my eyes when she told me the baby's name was Duffy. On every one of her birthdays, I bought the staff card, and my inscriptions were always the most cordial and the least sincere. So, when Laura's sister died, there was no way for me to get around "being there for her."

I had to take it day by day—one afternoon I mailed a card, another day I left a voicemail message on her business line. I didn't push myself too hard. I knew that if I overdid my expressions of sympathy, Laura might sense that they were contrived. It wasn't easy, but I managed to make it through the dark days of Laura's emergency leave of absence.

Laura's first day back was a real challenge, though. I knew I had to show some sympathy beyond cards and flowers, but what? After giving it a lot of thought, I decided that I would hand-deliver all her mail to her desk. A sympathetic nod as I handed her an orderly stack of unopened mail would have been the perfect way to say, "You're in my thoughts, but I'm not going to make a big show of that, as I know you probably just want to get

back to normal." Well, life doesn't always go as planned. When I walked into the mailroom, whose sad puss do you think I was greeted by? I couldn't believe Laura had beaten me to the office. I'm always in first! But I shrugged it off, took a deep breath, and gave her a big hug. It was very difficult, because I've always been disgusted by her bony frame and cloying perfume.

Laura smiled and thanked me, but I knew it wasn't over. I'd have to say something, too. "I know that anything I say is going to sound inadequate," I told Laura, doing everything I could to make my voice sound calm and

> ## I barely remembered that Laura had a sister, so the news of her death was truly an unexpected blow for me.

genuinely concerned. "But please believe me when I say we've all been thinking about you, and if there's anything we can do for you to make things easier, let us know." Laura's face lightened a little. "Thank you, Bonnie, that's very nice," she said. "It's not inadequate. I appreciate it." It was really hard to stand there and hold eye contact with her after that, but I steeled myself. I relaxed the muscles at my temples, looked right into her eyes, and counted to 10. Boy! That one took it out of me.

Back at my desk, I sent an e-mail to everyone in the office, careful to omit Laura. "Hey gang," I wrote. "Laura is back, so be sure to stop in and pay your respects today. I spent some time with her, but I'm sure she'd appreciate your words of sympathy and support, as well." I have to tell you, typing that e-mail was one of the hardest things I've ever had to do. I can't tell you how many times I checked the recipients list to make sure Laura wasn't on it! Let alone the effort I put into getting the wording of those six sentences just right. By the time I had that e-mail typed up, I was emotionally exhausted. I took myself out to a long, long lunch.

I won't lie: It's been a rough couple weeks for me. And the tough part is far from over. I'll have to pat Laura's hand at some point, and I might even have to hold it if she starts to cry. I may end up having to say "Everything will be okay," when I know it won't. It's going to be a trying time, but I'll make it through. Why? Because I don't have any other choice. That's life. ∅

Your Horoscope

By Lloyd Schumner Sr.
Retired Machinist and
A.A.P.B.-Certified Astrologer

Aries: (March 21–April 19)
Your lack of life experience will become apparent this week when you propose a new ice-cream flavor based on the smooth, subtle taste of the vanilla bean.

Taurus: (April 20–May 20)
Your stunning handbag and shoe lines will cause the other fashion houses to wonder why you even bother making dresses anymore.

Gemini: (May 21–June 21)
Some say that to really know fried chicken, you have to have been raised in the South, which is a slap in the face to you, as you grew up in a KFC stockroom.

Cancer: (June 22–July 22)
The greased-pig trick is a crass, sophomoric classic, but you'll raise it to an art form at Biosphere 2.

Leo: (July 23–Aug. 22)
You'll feel a lot better with warm clothes on your back and food in your stomach, proving that cannibalism has a couple things going for it.

Virgo: (Aug. 23–Sept. 22)
Once again, the specter of war will dominate international news, preventing people the world over from learning how you made the world's largest apple pie.

Libra: (Sept. 23–Oct. 23)
People don't keep statistics on things like being hit by dump trucks, but when they begin to, rest assured that your name will figure prominently.

Scorpio: (Oct. 24–Nov. 21)
People say you lack the intensity and vision to rise above your own mediocrity, but you don't really see the problem with that.

Sagittarius: (Nov. 22–Dec. 21)
You've done everything in your power to destroy ignorance among your fellow humans, but apparently, one of them is still dumb enough to marry Billy Joel.

Capricorn: (Dec. 22–Jan. 19)
You'll be surprised when federal agents are able to obtain a warrant only hours after your children's book hits the shelves.

Aquarius: (Jan. 20–Feb. 18)
For a moment, the stars will seem to take the shape of God, but onlookers will agree that God would not manifest Himself just to call you filthy names.

Pisces: (Feb. 19–March 20)
You may have started looking forward to your own death, but trust the Zodiac—it'll be no picnic.

SUZUKI page 212

amounts of blood. Passersby were amazed by the unusually large amounts of blood. Passersby were amazed by the unusually large amounts of blood. Passersby were amazed by the unusually large amounts of blood. Passersby were amazed by the unusually large amounts of blood. Passersby were amazed by the unusually large amounts of blood. Passersby were amazed by the unusually large amounts of blood. Passersby were amazed by the unusually large amounts of blood. Passersby were amazed by the unusually large amounts of blood. Passersby were amazed by the unusually large amounts of blood. Passersby were amazed by the unusually large amounts of blood. Passersby were amazed by the unusually large amounts of blood. Passersby were amazed by the unusually large amounts of blood. Passersby were amazed by the unusually large

amounts of blood. Passersby were amazed by the unusually large amounts of blood. Passersby were amazed by the unusually large amounts of blood. Passersby were amazed by the unusually large amounts of blood. Passersby were amazed by the unusually large amounts of blood. Passersby were

> ## I swear to God if I have one more epiphany I'll lose my mind.

amazed by the unusually large amounts of blood. Passersby were amazed by the unusually large amounts of blood. Passersby were amazed by the unusually large amounts of blood. Passersby were amazed by the unusually large amounts of blood. Passersby were amazed by the unusually large amounts of blood. Passersby were amazed by the unusually large amounts of blood. Passersby were

see SUZUKI page 291

the ONION®

VOLUME 40 ISSUE 42   AMERICA'S FINEST NEWS SOURCE™   21–27 OCTOBER 2004

NEWS

Enterprising Child Saves $54 To Buy Barrel Of Oil

see BUSINESS page 5B

Zoo Orangutan Feels He Really Connected With Iowa Woman

see NATURE page 11D

Drummer Unwanted

see ENTERTAINMENT page 9F

Jacques Derrida 'Dies'

see OBITUARIES page 11F

STATshot

A look at the numbers that shape your world.

What Are We Running Away From?

- 13% Cable bill
- 16% Participatory democracy
- 12% Parents in square-dancing outfits
- 18% White kid with crucifix tie pin and clipboard
- 21% Bull! Angry, drunken bull! Long story! Run!
- 20% Don't know

U.S. Finishes A 'Strong Second' In Iraq War

Above: Casey (left) and Lt. Gen. John Abizaid shake hands with an enlisted soldier after the war.

BAGHDAD—After 19 months of struggle in Iraq, U.S. military officials conceded a loss to Iraqi insurgents Monday, but said America can be proud of finishing "a very strong second."

"We went out there, gave it our all, and fought a really good fight," said Gen. George W. Casey, the top U.S. commander in Iraq. "America's got nothing to be ashamed of. We outperformed Great Britain, Poland, and a lot of the other top-notch nations, but Iraq just wouldn't stay down for the count. It may have come down to them simply wanting it more."

American tanks and infantry surged out to an impressive early lead in March 2003, scoring major points by capturing Baghdad early in the face-off. The stage seemed set for a second American victory in as many clashes with Iraq, with commentators and

see WAR page 292

Above: Diehl, who is "ready to get back out there."

Recently Married Man Ready To Start Dating Again

BIRMINGHAM, AL—Nearly 14 months after he said "I do" to his new wife Karen, attorney Robert Diehl, 36, told reporters that he finally feels ready to return to the dating world.

"For a long time, I wasn't there yet," Diehl said Monday. "After the wedding, all I wanted was to be alone with my wife. I couldn't even look at another woman without comparing her to Karen. But now, I'm finally ready to take a deep breath and throw myself back into the dating pool."

Diehl began dating Karen Gurnett in

see MARRIED MAN page 292

Kerry: Stem-Cell Research May Hold Cure To Ailing Campaign

Above: Kerry displays a test tube, which he said "holds the potential to change millions of votes."

ROCHESTER, MN—In a major policy address at the Mayo Clinic Tuesday, Democratic presidential nominee John Kerry drew a sharp distinction between himself and President Bush by championing unfettered scientific exploration of embryonic stem cells, which experts say could hold the cure to Parkinson's, Alzheimer's, and Kerry's ailing campaign.

"The possibilities are limitless, both for science and my campaign," said Kerry, who enjoyed a bump in the polls after the debates but is still struggling to secure a lead over Bush. "If adequately funded, stem-cell researchers might find cures for hundreds of diseases, from diabetes to cancer. And, if the nation would focus

on my opponent's ideological extremism, I might get elected."

In 2001, the Bush administration placed limits on federal funding for stem-cell research. This move was applauded by many religious conservatives, who oppose stem-cell research because it requires the harvesting of stem-cell lines from human embryos.

"For too long, President Bush has curtailed science on ideological grounds, for his own political purposes," Kerry said. "I pledge to support science on rational grounds, for my own political purposes. Stem-cell research could improve the lives of hundreds of millions of Americans, and the issue could dramatically increase

see KERRY page 293

Bill O'Reilly Sex Scandal

Last week, a Fox News Channel producer sued Bill O'Reilly for sexual harassment, alleging that the cable host pressured her into phone sex. What do *you* think?

Peggy Knight
Art Teacher

"Someone's coming at Bill O'Reilly with lurid public accusations of a heinous personal nature? Wow. Sometimes life can be so... *fair*."

Jonathan Warren
Announcer

"He wasn't sexually harassing her. He was just looking out for her, like he's doing for all of us, all the time."

Shawn Jiminez
Assessor

"No wonder it costs $3.99 a minute to call in to 'The Factor.'"

Curtis Fletcher
Systems Analyst

"Whether Andrea Mackris' claims are true or false, one thing is certain—that woman is never working for the vast right-wing conspiracy again."

Andy Vaughn
Clerk

"This is just another example of the liberal media's bias against self-destructive, narcissistic, screaming sexist assholes."

Cindy Beck
Food Scientist

"Just once, I'd like to hear about a sex scandal with honest-to-God penetration."

Battleground States

A handful of battleground states will be key in deciding the 2004 presidential election. What are some of these states most concerned about?

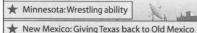

★ Minnesota: Wrestling ability

★ New Mexico: Giving Texas back to Old Mexico

★ New Hampshire: Finding candidate who's not under sticky thumb of Big Syrup

★ Washington: More/less logging, banning/protecting abortion, blowing up Seattle/letting Seattle secede

★ Ohio: Returning music scene to glory days of Pere Ubu, Devo, and The Waitresses; reclassification as East Coast state, instead of Midwestern or Southern

★ Oregon: Will vote for candidate who visits Oregon the most times

★ Colorado: Stopping Spanish from being spoken in schools and inadvertently changing name of state

★ Michigan: $5,000-per-lake tax credit

★ West Virginia: Wanna know, is people descended from monkeys or ain't they?

★ Pennsylvania: Stiff tariffs on foreign cheesesteaks

the ONION®
America's Finest News Source.™

Herman Ulysses Zweibel
Founder

T. Herman Zweibel
Publisher Emeritus

J. Phineas Zweibel
Publisher

Maxwell Prescott Zweibel
Editor-In-Chief

We Should Get That Guy Who Does A Half-Assed Job To Fix Our Roof

Honey, take a look at the ceiling. Notice how you can see the nails through the paint? That's water damage. The roof must be leaking. No, the upstairs bathroom is over the kitchen. It's definitely the roof. We need to take care of this before the drywall rots or the lights short out. Hey, you know the guy who built Sheila and Barry's old deck? You remember, the one that collapsed at their Fourth of July cookout? We should get *him* to fix our roof.

By Scott Bethke

I know we have his phone number around here somewhere. Yeah, it's on the fridge magnet. Here, Don Maliszewski. I know it says "Dan." That's a typo. He gave the Garvers a bunch of these magnets when he came to redo his job on their sewer pipe after it flooded their basement.

Hang on, it's ringing. Oh, shoot. "The number you have reached has been disconnected." Boy, maybe his gambling debts finally caught up to him. You know what? I don't need to call him. He practically lives at O'Reilly's Tavern. I'll just scoot over there and let him know we want an estimate.

He gave the Johnsons a great quote on their wiring. It ended up costing more, but that's how these things go. Don explained that the cost of materials went up, which is why he needed an extra $200 for light switches. Well, they still saved a bundle. They would've had to spend $500 more if they'd gone to a licensed electrician. Instead, they were able to use that money to stay in a hotel after that terrible fire.

He did the Garvers' fence, too. You used to be able to see it from here, but it blew down during that storm. It looked good when it was up, though. The slats were all even. Too bad it had to be the only thing in the neighborhood that got damaged in the storm. Must have been one of those freak wind gusts you hear about on the news.

Anyway, the Garvers said he was great whenever he showed up. He's a really interesting guy. He has all kinds of stories about back when he was a biker. Did you hear about the time he got knifed at the Sturgis rally? That story is amazing!

I'm not married to using him, though. The responsible thing to do is to get price quotes from several people. Hey! We should ask those high-school kids who mow lawns if they want to give fixing the roof a shot. They might be pretty good at it. When they're mowing lawns, they miss a lot of spots and leave the trimmings lying around, but maybe they'd be better at something more challenging, like roofing. Or, hey, how about that guy—what's his name? Jerry Anderson? The guy who got arrested for trespassing and peeping? You don't spend all that time on a roof without picking up a thing or two about how it's put together.

Unless some of the other quotes come back really low, I think Don's our guy. He did a nearly adequate job on the bay windows in the Perrys' house. He finished that job about a year ago, and it's *still* holding up. It took a little longer than

---

He did the Garvers' fence, too. You used to be able to see it from here, but it blew down.

---

they planned, but only because the city halted the construction. Yes, Don was wrong when he said they didn't need a permit. But he offered to finish the job late at night, when the city inspectors would be off duty. So work was held up for a few weeks, but Don did a super job taping that tarp over the hole in their wall. It rained three times, and not a drop got through!

Oh, no... I just remembered that Don's in jail! Well, I don't know that the roof is so bad that we can't wait the few months until he's free. It's not like he killed a guy on purpose. His scaffolding collapsed when his partner climbed on it, honey. They charged Don with, I don't know, something shy of manslaughter... neglect? Negligence! That's the word. If a jury said he didn't kill the guy on purpose, that's all I need to hear. Shoot, everyone makes mistakes. I'm all in favor of giving someone a second or third chance.

Honey, no. I don't trust the Yellow Pages. You don't know anything about those guys. "Licensed and bonded"— what does that even mean? Who licenses them, and what is a bond, in this case? Honey, a guy in the phone book is likely to tell you anything to get your money. But you practically have to beg Don to agree to take on a job. Yes, I'd really prefer to go with someone unreliable whom we know. The roof will turn out all right. You just wait and see. Now, let's go visit Don in the pokey so we can get things rolling. ∅

CEO Doesn't Have Heart To Kill Plastics Division

HOUSTON—Walking through one of his company's four manufacturing plants Monday, Sunford Industries CEO Preston Johnson said he can't bring himself to eliminate the plastics division.

"I know better than anybody that our stackable in- and outboxes and brightly colored Lucite pencil cases aren't selling like they used to," Johnson said, running his finger along the molding seam of a polycarbonate drawer organizer. "But does that mean we just let the plastics division

Above: Johnson (inset) and the building that houses the division he "can't just get rid of."

> "Yes, plastics isn't doing so well, but I'm not going to just abandon it," Johnson said. "I'm supposed to turn my attention to the metal-fabrication division, just because there's local demand for our metal office furniture, fixtures, and equipment? After all plastics and I have been through, I'm supposed to just pull the plug? I couldn't live with myself."

go? It's been with Sunford since the beginning."

A dominant supplier of office products in the late '80s and early '90s, Sunford suffered a dramatic loss of market share with the rise of such national office-supply retailers as OfficeMax and Office Depot. Although the company's metal and paper divisions continue to thrive in the regional market, the plastics division recently posted its 14th consecutive quarter in the red.

"Yes, plastics isn't doing so well, but I'm not going to just abandon it," Johnson said. "I'm supposed to turn my attention to the metal-fabrication division, just because there's local demand for our metal office furniture,

fixtures, and equipment? After all plastics and I have been through, I'm supposed to just pull the plug? I couldn't live with myself."

After 20 years at the helm of Sunford Industries, Johnson said he is no stranger to dramatic, even harsh cost-cutting measures. When he was promoted to CEO in 1984, he restructured the fulfillment department, slashing more than 100 jobs. Additionally, he declared a wage freeze on all of the department's remaining employees, implemented tighter labor standards

see CEO page 293

NEWS IN BRIEF

Nader Polling At 8 Percent Among Past Supporters

WASHINGTON, DC—A CNN/Gallup poll released Monday shows that 8 percent of those who voted for presidential candidate Ralph Nader in the 2000 election will vote for him again in 2004. "Americans feel it's time for an end to corporate-controlled government, or at least 1/12th of those that voted for me in 2000 do," Nader said, addressing a handful of supporters scattered throughout a lecture hall at Georgetown University. "Don't be satisfied with politics as usual. That is my message to those who voted for me four years ago. Get back with the team." Nader said that 230,000 votes, while nowhere near enough to win, might be sufficient to muck up another election.

Millions Of American Lips Called To Service In Fight Against Poverty

NEW YORK—In response to the record number of American poor, Secretary of the Treasury John Snow called millions of American lips to service Monday. "Poverty is a menace to society," Snow said. "As the ranks of the nation's poor grow and more social programs are scaled back, it is crucial that all able Americans talk about how something must be done." Snow then entreated all able-voiced men and women between the ages of 18 and 24 to volunteer to periodically mention that the current poverty rate of 12.5 percent is too high.

Tibetan Teen Getting Into Western Philosophy

LHASA, TIBET—Deng Hsu, 14, said Monday that he is "totally getting into Western philosophy." "I've been reading a lot of Kant, Descartes, and Hegel, and it's blowing my mind," Hsu said. "It's so exotic and exciting, not like all that Buddhist 'being is desire and desire is suffering' shit my parents have been cramming down my throat all my life. Most of the kids in my school have never even heard of Hume's views on objectivity or Locke's *tabula rasa*." Hsu said he hopes to one day make an exodus to north London to visit the birthplace of John Stuart Mill.

Hopes, Dreams Crushed By Panel Of D-List Celebrities

LOS ANGELES—Waitress and aspiring singer Olivia Martin, 21, had her hopes of stardom dashed by a panel of washed-up celebrities Monday. "All I've wanted to do my whole life is bring people joy with my singing, but Martika said I should stick to serving pancakes," said Martin, whose performing also received poor reviews from former MTV VJ Alan Hunter and *Saved By The Bell*'s Mario Lopez. "This was my big break, but I blew it." Martika, who sang the 1988 hit "Toy Soldiers," said Martin lacked stage presence and didn't have "that special something it takes to be a star."

Everyone On Campus Afraid Of That One Bar

SPOKANE, WA—Members of the Washington State University-Spokane student body announced Monday that everyone is afraid to visit K-Dee's Tap, that one bar without any windows next to the hardware store on Fordam Avenue. "[K-Dee's] is some kind of biker drug bar or something," sophomore Peter Mendis said. "The drinks are super cheap and they stay open like an hour after bar time, but don't go in there. My friend J.J.'s roommate's brother almost got stabbed there." K-Dee's leather-jacketed bartender, a 67-year-old with a leg brace, said he had no recollection of the near-stabbing, but did caution that, in general, the regular patrons do not welcome "college boys." ∅

June 2000, and they married on Aug. 16, 2003. Although it has been more than 14 months since Diehl has been with a woman other than Gurnett, he expressed confidence that he'll be able to "get back out there and mix it up."

"Sure, it's going to be rough for a while," Diehl said. "But I can't let fear hold me back. I know that once I'm back in the saddle, it'll feel perfectly natural."

In addition to the emotional difficulties associated with starting to date again, Diehl said his marital responsibilities leave him with little free time.

"This past year has been an incredible drain on my time, energy, and emotions," Diehl said. "Now that Karen and I have unwrapped all the gifts, opened a joint checking account, and bought a house, I finally have some time to focus on me—on what *I* want. And what I want right now is hot, attachment-free sex with young, good-looking women."

Diehl said his wife's recent decision to travel to Atlanta led him to ask himself what he was waiting for.

"I have two choices—either ask that cute girl from my gym for a date, or sit

> ## "Sure, it's going to be rough for a while," Diehl said.

at home feeling sorry for myself while Karen's out of town on business next weekend," Diehl said. "I'm through with wallowing in my own misery."

Diehl credits his male friends with providing the support he needed to motivate himself to get out and date again.

"My buddies have been great," Diehl said. "I was feeling like I had nothing to offer a woman, being married and all. But my friends encouraged me to ditch the negative attitude. I'm still young, and, according to the guys, nothing attracts pussy like a young, successful guy with a wedding ring."

Joel Brentmacher, who served as best man at Diehl's wedding, said it was hard to watch his friend endure such a difficult time.

"Rob used to be such a ladies' man," Brentmacher said. "It had to be a huge blow to him when his single life ended. We hated to see him closing himself off to all the other women in Birmingham and the surrounding counties just because he found a wife. But we gave him time and didn't pressure him. We knew he had to come back on the scene when he felt he was ready."

Although Diehl expressed excitement about dating again, he said he plans to "play it smart."

"There are so many good-looking women out there. I'd love to spend my lunch hour in a hotel room with all of them," Diehl said. "If I were 18 again, I might try. But I'm more mature now, and I have some experience under my belt. I'm going to ease into things. The best course of action is to take this thing one mistress at a time."

Diehl said his wife, whom he "will always love with all [his] heart," will be in his thoughts as he ventures out into the dating world.

"Over these past few months, I've had time to do some really serious thinking about Karen," Diehl said. "I think I have it all straight in my mind as to how I'll be able to cheat on her without her catching me."

"I have to take the whole thing slow, though," Diehl added. "I don't want to get hurt, and Karen would kill me if she ever found out." ∅

Above: Iraqi insurgents celebrate their victory in front of a burning Humvee.

played its best on hostile ground in recent years.

"What kind of a defense was that in the final quarter of 2003?" said retired Air Force colonel Charles Carruthers, now a professor at the Army War College at West Point. "The field generals all thought they had Iraq on the ropes, but no one told the Iraqis, who just kept nickel-and-diming them to death. In the end, our guys were getting absolutely shelled out there. You can't blame the men

> ## U.S. offensive captain John Baptiste of the 656th Infantry said that his fellow troops "were solid to the end," adding that he was disappointed in U.S. leaders' decision to call the game so early.

generals alike declaring the contest all but decided with the fall of Tikrit in April 2003.

"In spite of jumping out to an early lead and having the better-trained, better-equipped team, I'm afraid we still came up short in the end," Casey said. "Sometimes, the underdog just pulls one out on you. But there's no reason for the guys who were out in the field to feel any shame over this one. They played through pain and injury and never questioned the strategy, even when we started losing ground."

"The troops were great out there," Casey continued. "It's not their fault the guys with the clipboards just couldn't put this one away."

Casey said that, although the U.S. military did not win, it did set records for kills, yardage gained, palaces overrun, defensive stops, and military bases stolen.

"The Americans can be proud of the numbers," Casey said. "All things considered, there was some very impressive maneuvering out there. We kept

the folks at home on the edge of their seats, that's for sure."

PFC Brian Walters was part of a squad defending Fallujah for the past three months.

"We're looking at an opponent who just keeps coming at you until the

> ## "The troops were great out there," Casey continued. "It's not their fault the guys with the clipboards just couldn't put this one away."

echo of the whistle," Walters said. "I gotta hand it to them, they weren't gonna roll over. We were just out there playing not to lose."

Former civil administrator of Iraq L. Paul Bremer said the U.S. troops

performed admirably, adding that overconfidence may have been a factor.

"After that strong start, I really thought that we were going to take it home," Bremer said. "I'd say we can chalk this loss up to a combination of Iraq's home-field advantage and a poor second-half U.S. game plan."

U.S. offensive captain John Baptiste of the 656th Infantry said that his fellow troops "were solid to the end," adding that he was disappointed in U.S. leaders' decision to call the game so early.

"The chief should never come out at halftime and call it 'Mission Accomplished,'" Baptiste said. "You never say that until the clock runs out. My guys did their best, but we've gotta remember that everyone plays to the final gun."

Loyal fans of the U.S. are still coming to terms with the loss, a rarity for an organization that won undisputed world championships in the '10s and '40s, but has not always

for that. That's underestimating the opposition."

Added Carruthers: "You'd think they hadn't even scouted their opponent beforehand, let alone beaten them soundly the last time they squared off. Someone should lose his job over this."

Defense Secretary Donald Rumsfeld refused to take questions from reporters, saying that "Monday-morning quarterbacking never solved anything."

"Injuries and a shallow bench were major factors," Rumsfeld said, speaking to angry team boosters in Washington. "We've lost about 75 guys every month for the past year."

"But remember that this was just one war," Rumsfeld added. "We'll get 'em next time." ∅

Above: Kerry inquires about campaign-rejuvenating applications for stem cells at a Norak Biosciences laboratory.

Christopher Reeve," Dubad said. "But I believe the area of stem-cell research could provide thousands, if not millions, of sound bites. It's important for Kerry to raise these issues in debates and stump speeches. But, in order to really make a difference, people outside of the scientific and political communities must get involved, as well."

Democratic vice-presidential nominee John Edwards, however, said candidates should focus on those who are

> ## "My opponent has put the interests of a vocal minority over the needs of me, my campaign staff, and John Edwards," Kerry added.

suffering most.

"Scientific exploration in this field holds immense promise for the millions of Americans who are afflicted with genetic diseases or are members of the Democratic party," Edwards said. "Stem-cell research may be the last, best hope for those suffering under diabetes, heart disease, cancer, and the Bush administration."

Continued Edwards: "Senator Kerry and I pledge to support stem-cell research as a part of our plan to put America on the path to scientific excellence. And, as a part of our plan to win this election, we will begin to talk more often, and more succinctly, about how we pledge to support stem-cell research." ✪

my popularity. We must push the boundaries of scientific exploration *now*, before Nov. 2."

"My opponent has put the interests of a vocal minority over the needs of me, my campaign staff, and John Edwards," Kerry added. "That is just wrong."

According to Democratic strategist Stanley Greenberg, stem-cell research is not universally opposed by Republicans. In fact, many opponents of abortion support stem-cell research. Greenberg said careful research into the voting patterns of moderates and swing voters may pro-

vide the "golden key" to using the stem-cell issue to advance Kerry's campaign.

"Studies show that nearly 80 percent of voters support stem-cell research," Greenberg said. "A full 206 members of the U.S. House of Representatives and 58 members of the Senate have urged Bush to lift federal funding restrictions on stem-cell lines. Kerry's campaign managers can't ignore this potentially campaign-changing data."

Greenberg said stem-cell research could hold tremendous promise for other politicians, as well.

"Stem-cell research might unlock

cures for many of the afflictions that face hundreds of Democratic political candidates, right down to the state level," Greenberg said. "That is, if they were lucky enough to find the right campaign ad."

Ravi Dubad, a professor of political science at Rutgers, said that, in spite of the "enormous potential" of stem-cell research, the media have yet to adequately explore it.

"The issue received only limited attention during the Democratic Convention in July—when Ronald Reagan Jr. spoke out in its favor—and again, with the recent death of

in shipping, and drastically reduced insurance benefits for non-salaried employees.

"But the plastics department is different," Johnson said. "When you care about something so much, it's just... Jesus, it's just a lot to take sometimes."

Johnson added: "If it's gotta be done, get somebody else to do it. Henderson or somebody."

Patting the side of an injection-molding machine, Johnson said he couldn't help reflecting on "the early days with plastics."

"I used to look forward to my Friday walk-throughs of the die-molding department all week," Johnson said. "As soon as you opened the door, the smell of hot plastic would hit you—right in the chest. It was so... familiar. I can't flip a switch and wipe out all those memories."

Shareholders in Sunford are aware that Johnson objects to killing the ailing plastics department.

"That plastics department and Preston go way back—it's like his family," shareholder Theodore Althouse

said. "None of us can understand it, not even the plastics-division staff.

> ## "Some say there's no reason to keep plastics around, but I disagree," Johnson said. "Why ruin its last few quarters? Why not let the division die naturally, with dignity? After all plastics has done for Sunford, it's the least Sunford can do."

Everyone there is just a replacement for someone who left or was fired in the past three years."

Responding to what Sunford board members categorized as Johnson's "unhealthy attachment" to the plastics division, chairman P. Richard Evans said he is considering a resolution that would force Johnson to "do the right thing" and put a swift end to plastics.

"I wouldn't want to be in Preston's shoes right now," Evans said. "But clinging to the past is simply not the responsible way to run a company."

Evans said plastics had a good run, but that eliminating the division will boost Sunford's stock-market value by nearly 20 percent—and allow Johnson to focus on the future.

"Johnson simply has to let go," Evans said. "The division's time has come. I keep telling him, 'Do it quickly, with a single memo to the head of the division. That's the most humane way.'"

Johnson said he's not sure he's ready.

"Sure, we started up a new AV/Tech-products division, and it has shown steady growth since its inception, but it's just not the same," Johnson said. "I've got 20 years of memories with plastics. In 1993, third quarter, they beat expectations by 53 percent. That's right—53 percent! Plastics has been with this company since before AV/Tech was even on our letterhead."

While he said he'll "never, under any circumstances, kill plastics outright," Johnson acknowledged that he will most likely have to make concessions to the board by tying the division's operating budget directly to order-fulfillment figures and allowing employees to transfer to other divisions as work slows.

"It ain't over 'til the orders run out and the last man is gone," Johnson said. "Some say there's no reason to keep plastics around, but I disagree. Why ruin its last few quarters? Why not let the division die naturally, with dignity? After all plastics has done for Sunford, it's the least Sunford can do for plastics."

Added Johnson: "Well, I guess the plastics division will never truly die as long as I keep a part of it in my heart." ✪

A Day Off? Sheeit

By Herbert Kornfeld
Accounts Receivable
Supervisor

'Sup, G's. Check it out: Debbilyn Sundquist, tha Midstate human-resources secretary, e-mailed me.

"Hi Herbert," she wrote. "This is just a friendly reminder to inform you that you have some paid personal days you haven't used. They do not carry over into the next year, so please be sure to use them soon!!!"

"Accountz Reeceevable don't take no personal dayz off," I wrote back. "We been through this shit befoe. I ain't havin' it. Fuck all y'all an' yo wack no-workin' bullshit."

I trashed her e-mail an' go back 2 krunchin' tha numbahs. Few minutes later, I hear a noise behind me.

I whipped around, assumin' tha White-Colla Warrior stance. It tha office comptrolla, Gerald Luckenbill, an' Bob Cowan, tha human-resources directa. "What? What? What?" I aksed. "You wanna step 2 me? What?"

Cowan peed himself. But Luckenbill wuz straight-up chillin'. "Herbert," Luckenbill said. "I want you to take tomorrow off. Gary will oversee things here."

Next mornin', I got up when it was still dark and took tha 4:52 express bus 2 Midstate. Got there so early, not a sucka in sight. I slipped my keycard into tha electric lock on tha front doe. Tha magnetic strip don't read. Dag. Luckenbill musta blocked my keycard foe tha day. Muhfukka know tha H-Dog's ways too well. Y'all gots 2 recognize that. I bowed 2 Midstate in deep respect an' hustled back 2 my hood.

Foe a while, I lifted weights, but then I wuz like, fuck this, I already mad ripped. Then I caught some-a tha bitchez on Court TV. That sweet, sweet ho Nancy Grace wuz on, an' I had 2 whip it out an' start hittin'. She wuz in one-a her hard-ass moods, bitchin' 'bout it ain't right some ho from Oklahoma got off foe shankin' her man, so it wasn't two minutes befoe I busta nut and switched tha bullshit off. Work is where us A.R. bruthahs thrive. Once on tha outside, it a different story, y'all. They less numbahs 2 krunch. Some y'all can balance yo' checkbook or figger yo' taxizzes, true dat. But that ain't enuf, know what I'm sayin'? Bruthahs got 2 keep they minds occupied.

I called Agnes, my ol' boo an' my shortie's moms. "Yo, chickenhead, muhfukkas be makin' me take a personal day," I said. "Is Baby Prince H Tha Stone Col' Dopest Biz-ook-kizeepin' Muthafukkin' Badass Supastar Kornfeld Tha Second at that

wack-ass day care? I wanna bust him out an' take him 2 tha park or tha Chucky-Cheez or some shit like that."

"Tanner is with me today," Agnes said, usin' dat goddamn moniker again. "My class was canceled. You can visit him Sunday like we agreed, Herbert."

I hung up on tha bitch an' called Vi, one-a tha hotties that work tha Midstate cash room, an' tol' her, get yo' fine ass down 2 my hizzy, I treat you right. She say she workin'. I say I gots crazy personal days, you can have one-a mine if you just come down here an' give it up 2 tha H-Dog. She say personal days ain't transferable.

Hell, what's a man 2 do in these unfavorable circumstizances? I was hungry for some reeceevin', y'all. I hopped into tha Nite Rida an' cruised tha bidness district, lookin' foe action. Outside o' Kessler, Orbach, Cowart & Associates, LLP, tha biggest ac-

---

Next mornin', I got up when it was still dark and took tha 4:52 express bus 2 Midstate. Got there so early, not a sucka in sight. I slipped my keycard into tha electric lock on tha front doe. Tha magnetic strip don't read. Dag.

---

countin' an' auditin' firm in town, I peeped a posse o' office bitchez gettin' they lunch on.

"Bitchez," I shouted from my hoopty. "Give up some numbahz 2 Daddy H so's he can krunch 'em."

The li'lest one speak up, a nasty skank wit' her goddamn cross-trainin' shoez on ovah her pantyhose, like wearin' heels gonna break her ass or somethin'. "What happened, Herbert Kornfeld, Midstate fire your skinny ass?" she said. "Go away. You're not getting anywhere near our numbers."

Damn, y'all, I wuz about 2 put tha smack down on that li'l skank when tha 5-0 pull up behind me. I recognize tha cop from back in tha day, after I got busted foe illegal street accountin'. He aksed how come I ain't at Midstate. I aksed how come he ain't retired. That made all tha bitchez laugh, 'cept foe tha li'l one. "Herbert just asked if we've got any numbers to crunch, officer," she said.

She knew tha cop was itchin' foe reasonable suspicion 2 search my

---

Your Horoscope

By Lloyd Schumner Sr.
Retired Machinist and
A.A.P.B.-Certified Astrologer

Aries: (March 21–April 19)
The forecast for your immediate vicinity is partly cloudy, which will provide a welcome relief from the tiny thunderstorm that's been following you around.

Taurus: (April 20–May 20)
A judge once said he couldn't define pornography, but he knew it when he saw it. That's how you feel about paella.

Gemini: (May 21–June 21)
You're well on your way to setting a world record for receiving the world's longest lap dance, but it's been interfering with your work as an airline pilot.

Cancer: (June 22–July 22)
If you've ever wanted to tour the world while being held against your will in a container ship, this is your lucky week.

Leo: (July 23–Aug. 22)
You've often wondered who's responsible for all this fucked-up shit, but that will change Thursday, when you're hired to assist the Director of All This Fucked-Up Shit.

Virgo: (Aug. 23–Sept. 22)
Most solid objects are actually composed of the spaces between the subatomic particles. Then there's your gigantic fat ass.

Libra: (Sept. 23–Oct. 23)
Strangely enough, the only people who remember seeing you at the scene are the eccentric professor, the lovely blonde reporter, the recently thawed caveman, and the hapless politician.

Scorpio: (Oct. 24–Nov. 21)
Nothing can stop you now, but that's a natural consequence of your not trying to do much of anything.

Sagittarius: (Nov. 22–Dec. 21)
The world's vulcanologists would appreciate it if you'd stop trying to take credit for anything and everything that happens at Mount St. Helens.

Capricorn: (Dec. 22–Jan. 19)
You'll survive the incident, but for the rest of your life, you'll be paralyzed with fear at the sight of cumulus clouds, blueberry pancakes, and hockey great Bobby Orr.

Aquarius: (Jan. 20–Feb. 18)
You'll be a free man when the judge and jury are forced to agree that the goat had indeed dressed in a provocative manner.

Pisces: (Feb. 19–March 20)
Your career in immigration law is progressing satisfactorily, but you're still eons away from Martian citizenship.

---

hoopty, an' she give it 2 him. Well, took tha cop 20 seconds 2 find a old wirebound columnar book an' a pencil undah my seat. He said that groundz foe arrestin' me on suspicion foe unsolicited accountin', cuffed me, an' hauled me into HQ. Fuckin' buncha bullshit. That columnar book wuz mine, true dat, but it wuz all used up an' didn't have no mo' room 2 write numbahz in. An' tha pig fuckin' planted tha pencil. It had a punk-ass rubbah grip. Tha H-Dog don't need no rubbah grip. Tha H-Dog so dope, he give tha pencils calluses. Tha first call I made wuz 2 Gerald Luckenbill, tell him he'hadda come down an' bail my ass out. He told tha precinct captain that my personal day wuz legit an' I wuz fully certified, meanin' they case against me wuz mad weak. Tha cops released me wit' a warnin' not 2 go near tha bidness district durin' workin' hourz.

Luckenbill learned that day that personal dayz be not only a pain in tha azz foe A.R. bruthahs, they downright dangerous. He talk 2 Bob Cowan, an' they decide 2 not make me take any

mo' personal dayz, lest they wanna be wastin' they time keepin' they best employee outta lockdown. So, you know what that mean, G's: a sweet-ass deal foe Daddy H. Nothin' but straight-up officin' 8-2-5, wit' tha exception o' weekendz an' major holidayz. On those dayz, I on my own an' gotta watch my back. But at least I don't got them goddamn personal dayz 2 contend wit' no mo'.

An' incidentally, come next day, that li'l accountant bitch got a surprise when she come in an' fire up her addin' machine. When she punched in some numbahs, all of them come up in red ink on tha calculata tape, like they wuz bein' subtracted, even though she wuz addin'. After she peeped that blood red, she ran outta her cubicle, jumped into her hoopty, peeled down tha parkin' ramp, an' ain't been seen since. When office flunkies cross a A.R. playa, they get served that blood-red ink sheet as a warnin'. What it a warnin' foe, I ain't sayin,' lest I incriminate myself, know what I'm sayin'? I had enuf o' this shit, G's. H-Dog OUT. ∅

the ONION®

VOLUME 40 ISSUE 43   AMERICA'S FINEST NEWS SOURCE™   28 OCT.–3 NOV. 2004

Bush Campaign Paints Kerry As Pre-Raphaelite Contessa

see POLITICS page 4E

Underwear Worn Out Of Respect For The Dead

see LOCAL page 3C

That Asshole From High School Now That Asshole From TV

see ENTERTAINMENT page 9E

STATshot

A look at the numbers that shape your world.

Which Wire?

- **12%** The chartreuse one
- **17%** Agent on radio says "red"—but I'm colorblind!
- **15%** Damn! It appears there's a laser trigger mechanism protecting these wires!
- **22%** The one that *feels* right
- **28%** The wire attached to the bomb, you idiots
- **6%** One on left. No, *my* lef—

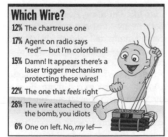

THE ONION • $2.00 US • $3.00 CAN

---

the ONION's Countdown To The Recount 2004

Inside:

★ How to make *your* vote recount

★ Where to re-register for the re-vote

★ When will the next president be appointed?

★ Polls show Supreme Court split 5-4: a closer look at the swing justices

★ The Electoral College reconsidered for the 20 billionth time

★ Is your state really a state?

★ Your dead relatives: how they'll vote, and why

★ A state-by-state breakdown of likely fraud and malfeasance

★ Should the two Americas hold separate elections?

★ A look at the recount campaign ads

★ Which facts to ignore and which emotional pleas to take to heart

★ Five reasons why you may or may not want to throw up your hands and stop caring altogether

---

Republicans Urge Minorities To Get Out And Vote On Nov. 3

Above: Monreal urges black community members to hit the polls next Wednesday.

MIAMI, FL—With the knowledge that the minority vote will be crucial in the upcoming presidential election, Republican Party officials are urging blacks, Hispanics, and other minorities to make their presence felt at the polls on Wednesday, Nov. 3.

"Minority voters should make their unique voices heard, especially the African-American voting bloc, which

see REPUBLICANS page 299

Boss' Going-Away Party A Little Too Jubilant

AMES, IA—The Oct. 22 office going-away party for Karl Roberts, manager for the past five years at Ames Farm Products Wholesalers, Inc., was "a little too jubilant," the 38-year-old former boss reported Monday.

"This staff has been working directly under me for a long time, so it's only natural that they'd want to show their appreciation by throwing a little shindig on my last day," said Roberts, who recently accepted a job as regional director of Quad-State Shipping in Rockford, IL. "And it's only natural that the employees would want to blow off a little steam at the end of the week. Even so, I really wasn't expecting much more than cake, punch, a couple of warm wishes, and maybe a card. Frankly, I was surprised when I found out they'd hired a band."

Known for his "by the book" management style, Roberts said he worked much more closely with Ames Farm Products' 23 staff members than their previous manager. While he said he was aware that he had a reputation for being "something of a hard-ass" in his first

Above: Roberts (center) looks on as his former employees celebrate.

months on the job, he had always assumed that the staff appreciated his contributions to increased productivity and professionalism in the workplace.

"After the party, though, I'm not sure what to think," Roberts said. "It was nice of them to sign a card for me. I'm not sure why it had to be a three-foot-

tall card emblazoned with a huge smiley face and the message 'Good Luck, Boss! Don't Let The Door Hit Your Ass On The Way Out!'"

"I know they were only joking about wanting me to go," Roberts added. "But everyone sure was getting into the joke."

see BOSS page 298

Return Of The Draft?

As the war in Iraq drags on, some Americans fear reinstatement of the military draft. What do *you* think?

Sara Simpson
Camera Operator

"Well, okay. As long as it's only a small draft and then they promise to stop."

Leonard Robertson
Systems Analyst

"A draft would be great. Going down there to sign myself up would be such a hassle."

James Sanders
Carpenter

"If I get drafted, I hope they put me on one of the swift boats. From what I gather, those guys are never in any danger."

Johnny Grant
Carpet Cutter

"If I must submit to a draft, I hope I'm not picked by Cincinnati."

Chris Daniels
Physician

"Well, no one is getting drafted until after the election, so there's no use worrying about it now."

Carmen Rice
Brokerage Clerk

"That's it. I'm voting for the candidate who would flip-flop on sending my son to die, rather than the one who'd do it without hesitation."

Flu Vaccine Shortage

What are the Centers for Disease Control and Prevention recommending in response to the current flu vaccine shortage?

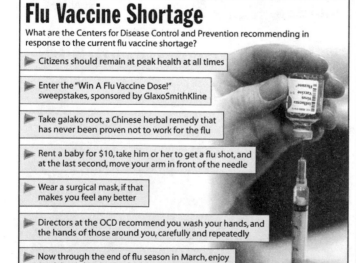

► Citizens should remain at peak health at all times

► Enter the "Win A Flu Vaccine Dose!" sweepstakes, sponsored by GlaxoSmithKline

► Take galako root, a Chinese herbal remedy that has never been proven not to work for the flu

► Rent a baby for $10, take him or her to get a flu shot, and at the last second, move your arm in front of the needle

► Wear a surgical mask, if that makes you feel any better

► Directors at the OCD recommend you wash your hands, and the hands of those around you, carefully and repeatedly

► Now through the end of flu season in March, enjoy Applebee's $10.99 "Feed A Fever" breakfast specials

► If any members of your family are elderly or suffer from a weakened immune system, dig graves before the ground hardens

the ONION ®
America's Finest News Source. ™

Herman Ulysses Zweibel
Founder

T. Herman Zweibel
Publisher Emeritus
J. Phineas Zweibel
Publisher
Maxwell Prescott Zweibel
Editor-In-Chief

Converting To The Metric System Starts With The Individual

By Theresa Kincaid

On her deathbed, my mother took my hand. "Theresa," she said. "When I was a girl, I thought I could change the world. But as I grew, I began to believe that the world was an intractable place. I put aside dreams and gave up my hopes. It is only now that I realize it was well within my power to change myself— and therein, by a small degree, the world."

If you want to change the world, you can't sit on your hands expecting some higher authority to do it for you. You've gotta get out there and make things happen. As my mother taught me, converting to the metric system starts with the individual.

The United States is the only industrialized country in the world that doesn't use the metric system as its predominant system of weights and measures—a fact that many Americans besides me find ridiculous. But there's no point in whining that we would be better off if we switched to kilometers and hectoliters while you drive your kids to school in a car that gets 23 *miles* to the *gallon*. You're still part of the problem.

Do you think some government agency is going to magically sweep in and convert our cubic feet into cubic decimeters? People have been waiting for that to happen since the Carter Administration. Where has it gotten us? The Metric Act of 1866 may have made it legal to measure milk in liters, but down at the IGA, they're still selling it by the quart.

It's like Gandhi said: "You assist an evil system most effectively by obeying its orders and decrees." If you truly believe that our current system handicaps American products and services in world markets, do something. Purge your bathroom of all products sold by imperial measurement and replace them with toiletries purchased from web sites based in European countries. It will cost a little more, but no one said changing the world was easy.

If you're a landlord renting an apartment by the square foot, you're part of the problem. Next time you place an ad, tout the rental space's spacious 78.965 square meters. If you're buying land, flat out refuse to purchase anything that isn't measured in hectares.

Sure, you'll meet some resistance. People will say: "We don't sell oats by the cubic meter." They'll trot out that old conservative standard, "If you want to be in the manufacturing industry, you have to buy steel by the ton." They might even claim that they don't know what a "tonne" is. Converting to the metric system is no walk in the park, but if you're serious about converting, others will recognize your commitment and join you.

Remember: The journey of a thousand kilometers starts with a single decimeter. We won the battle against spans and cubits, and we can beat the foot. And the pint and the pound. It all starts with the man or woman in the mirror.

So the next time "More Bounce To The Ounce" comes on your radio, don't just sit there snapping your fingers—call the station and demand to speak to the DJ. Insist that he play a new version of the song called "More Bounce To The 1.6 Grams," which you will record yourself in your basement and send him. Don't complain about how changes need to be made unless you're willing to make those changes yourself.

In this life, nothing good comes easy. Adopting a great system like the metric system requires sustained effort and personal sacrifice. Rest assured, you will benefit from a more practical and easy-to-understand system of measurement. And, when others see the ease with which you measure and weigh things, they'll be inspired by your example.

If you can't make the conversion to the metric system happen in your own house, how do you think it'll happen to an entire nation? Through the intercession of federal decision-makers who advocate phasing in the metric system over a several-year period? Pipe dreams. We know all too well what happened to the Metric Conversion Act of 1975, the Omnibus Trade and Competitiveness Act of 1988, and the Savings in Construction Act of 1996.

It's like I'm always saying to members of my local AMA chapter: "You can't simply tell somebody that it makes sense to measure with a system that uses the distance from the North Pole to the equator divided into 10 million parts to constitute the meter. You have to show them. You know that the meter's measurement has become even more precise, currently defined as the distance light travels in a vacuum in 1/299,792,458 of a second, but you can't teach the practicality of things like that. You can only lead by example."

If enough dedicated people do that, then maybe—just maybe—we can make the means by which we measure this crazy, cockamamie world that much more convenient for everyone. Now, would you care to join me? Ø

Study: 100 Percent Of Americans Lead Secret Lives

BERKELEY, CA—A study released Monday by the University of California-Berkeley shows that 100 percent of Americans fail to disclose the full truth about what they think and do in private.

"While startling and often embarrassing revelations about the private lives of politicians, pro athletes, and celebrities surface on a routine basis, our research indicates that Americans out of the public eye also have a lot to hide," said Berkeley sociology professor Dr. Mia L. Greene, who headed the 10-year study. "Surprisingly, famous people aren't the only ones participating in shady business dealings, substance abuse, and peculiar sexual activities."

As well as keeping the kinds of se-

Above: Just a few of the billions of Americans who are living secret lives.

Other non-famous Americans found to lead secret lives include 38-year-old Robin Stokely of Pueblo, CO, who still plays with her Weebles treehouse, and Ogden, UT's Lisa North, 12, who dares herself to lick used dustrags.

crets that, if kept by famous people, become tabloid fodder, average Americans engage in strange and obsessive behavior that, if revealed, would humiliate them.

"The secrets of the people living next door are often just as icky as the scandals that make the papers," Greene said. "If Claire Mallon, a 43-year-old bank teller from Rockingham, VT who still sleeps in the same bed as her elderly mother, were to receive the level of attention we give Kobe Bryant, we might see headlines like, oh, 'Cash-Doling She-Sicko Snuggles Mommy.'"

The Berkeley study, based on exhaustive surveillance of thousands of individuals, as well as information gleaned from personal diaries and nosy neighbors, undoes any perception that people living in quiet obscurity are without bizarre tendencies. According to Greene, every single study participant had a history of abnormal behavior.

"While hotel heiress Paris Hilton's infamous sex tape was breaking, Cleveland piano teacher Jon Knowles was sitting at his kitchen table eating a bowl of cat food," Greene said. "And,

while the Monica Lewinsky scandal was threatening to unseat a president, Clay Pulvermacher of Wauwatosa, WI was busy mailing birthday cards to himself."

Other non-famous Americans found to lead secret lives include 38-year-old Robin Stokely of Pueblo, CO, who still plays with her Weebles treehouse, and Ogden, UT's Lisa North, 12, who dares herself to lick used dustrags.

"While this study was not meant to inspire citizens to make slanderous accusations against each other, its conclusions do make it safe to assume that there's more to Plain Jane than she lets on," Greene said. "Average Joe's lack of fame is the only thing that keeps him from being tried and convicted by the harsh court of public

see STUDY page 300

NEWS IN BRIEF

Assistant Uses Cake To Smuggle Cake-Decorating Set To Martha Stewart

ALDERSON, WV—Authorities at Alderson Federal Prison have detained Becki Uecker, Martha Stewart's personal assistant, for smuggling a cake-decorating kit to her boss in an almond three-layer cake with lemon-zest icing. "Ms. Uecker attempted to pass a Dessert Decorator Pro to Ms. Stewart during visiting hours," corrections officer Frank Wickler said. "Although this device may be perfect for making stars, leaves, and rosettes, it's considered contraband at a correctional facility." In addition to the frosting gun, the kit included six nickel-plated tips, two tip couplers, and a storage bag.

King Of Queens Creator Thinks Everyone's Ripping Him Off

LOS ANGELES—Michael Weithorn, co-creator and executive producer of the hit CBS sitcom *King Of Queens*, said Monday that he is "tired of people stealing [his] idea." "I'm not going to name names, but there sure seem to be a lot of sitcoms featuring pudgy, working-class goofs with unbelievably hot wives and meddle-

some in-laws," Weithorn said. "I'm sorry, but that's KOQ territory. These other shows are the work of shameless copycats with no ideas." Creators of *According To Jim*, *Still Standing*, *Rodney*, *George Lopez*, and *Center Of The Universe* expressed the same complaint.

Meaning Of Dream Obvious To Everyone Else

SAN FRANCISCO—Although Jennie Wick, 23, cannot make sense of the dream she had Monday evening, its meaning is clear to everyone else, sources reported. "I'm in this waiting room, and I'm screaming at this man dressed all in white who can't hear me," said Wick, who is dating and financially supporting a University of California medical student. "Then, we're at the vending machine, and every time I buy a candy bar, he grabs it. What's up with that?" Wick also failed to grasp what it meant when the man began to have sex with her best friend.

Stock Analysts Confused, Frightened By Boar Market

NEW YORK—Stock analysts on Wall Street fled in terror after being spooked by the rare but deadly boar

market that reared its head at closing bell Monday. "I have no idea what to expect," stock analyst Christopher Mattson said. "This market is highly unpredictable—tusked and savage and covered with coarse, bristly hair. I didn't know if I should buy, sell, or shoot." Mattson said he hopes stocks will soon perform again like they did two weeks ago, when brokers were soothed by the graceful movements of a swan market.

Detroit Tourism Board's 'Hidden Detroit' Campaign Results In 24 Deaths

DETROIT—The Detroit Tourism Board is scaling back the city-sponsored "Hidden Detroit" program following the deaths of 24 tourists in the past month, city officials announced Monday. "The campaign did draw tourists to historically significant places that usually go unnoticed, like the rough-and-tumble honky-tonks of Ypsilanti and the site of the 1967 riots," tourism board director Lauren Essleman said. "But ultimately, unfolding the free 'Detroit Off The Beaten Path' maps in the middle of the Purple Gang's old turf was not a good idea." Essleman said that, in addition to the 24 tourists, the program resulted in the loss of more than 60 vehicles. ∅

Election Day Guide

Tuesday is Election Day. Here are some pointers to keep in mind when heading to the polls:

- If at all possible, vote before work. That way, you can make smug comments to non-voters all day long.

- The new electronic voting machines are complicated. But don't worry: Octogenarians will be on hand to troubleshoot any technological problems that might arise.

- If your election official hooks you up to a machine via a needle in your arm, you are actually donating blood.

- Tip for those on the go: Voting a straight ticket can save you up to 15 seconds.

- Remember that, as a member of a participatory democracy, you have a duty to make your voice heard on Election Day. If you find that idea hard to grasp, think of it like the lotto: You can't win if you don't play.

- Don't wear dress shoes. They leave black scuff marks on gymnasium floors.

- Voting is no longer considered uncool. Note that it is not cool, either.

- Many newspapers offer sample ballots. Buy 10 copies and practice, practice, practice.

- Remember to vote, or P. Diddy will kill you.

- This is one of the most important elections in recent times, so it's best if you just leave it up to the pros.

- When voting, you don't need to dress up in a scary costume or hand out candy. That happens two days earlier.

- You might think it's funny, but it's disrespectful to submit write-in candidates like "Don Knotts,""Mickey Mouse," or "Michael Badnarik."

- Remember to take the day off to vote. And the day before, to psyche up. And the morning after, to dry out.

- If you are black and a resident of Florida, work out two or three alternate routes to your polling place to avoid police checkpoints.

- The most important thing is to vote your conscience.

- Okay, this is your conscience speaking: "Vote Nader. Vo-o-o-o-ote Nader."

- If you are a Flintstone, make sure to put the granite slab arrows-first into the dinosaur's mouth.

- If you live in Florida, for Christ's sake, look at the ballot very, very carefully this time.

- Education is the issue Americans say is most important. Find someone with one of those to read the ballot to you.

- Keep in mind that the name of every person who votes against George Bush is going to be read aloud on television the next time we're attacked by terrorists.

- If you don't know where the polling place is in your district, just try to remember the ugliest, dingiest, most depressing building in a three-mile radius. That's probably it.

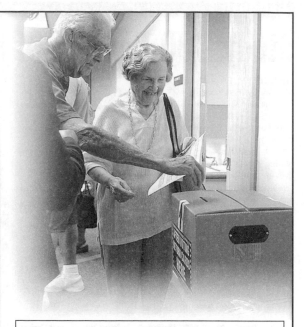

What To Bring

Remember to bring proper identification to the polls. This can be:

- Driver's license or your chauffeur
- Passport and photos of your boyfriend in Paris
- SuperVoter discount card
- Note from president
- Proof that your grandfather voted
- Retinal scan or your alderman's retinas
- Two Iraqi scalps
- Receipt for your shoes

- Videotape of your first steps
- Halliburton employee ID
- Birthday card from grandmother
- Pint of sperm for DNA-identification purposes
- Casserole dish to pass
- A good friend who can totally vouch for you
- Signed $20 bill
- Autographed celebrity photo inscribed with your name

BOSS from page 295

Above: Employees continue to celebrate after Roberts' departure.

The party, which was announced with photocopied flyers taped to nearly every wall in the office, was scheduled to last from "5:30 p.m. til ???"

"When our old receptionist Janice left last year, we had a party that lasted maybe an hour," Roberts said. "There were maybe 10 people left by the end. You'd figure that on a Friday, people would want to go home and get a head start on their weekend. I didn't leave my party until 10:30, and it was still going strong. If anything, it seemed to be picking up speed."

"I had to go," Roberts added. "I'd already heard that 'Na Na Na, Hey Hey Hey' song about 30 times."

On the way out to his car, Roberts said he was surprised to meet two former Ames Farm Products sales representatives making their way to the party with a keg of beer.

"I was surprised to see Jim and Travis, both of whom quit last May. They said some of the other employees called them and told them I was

see BOSS page 299

is always a major factor in every election," said Florida Republican Party voter-drive organizer Mark Monreal, as he handed out flyers at a community center in the mostly black Miami neighborhood of South Farms. "That's why we put up hundreds of brightly colored banners featuring Martin Luther King Jr. and the 'Vote November 3' reminder. We needed to make sure they know when we want them at polling places."

"You can't walk through a black neighborhood here in Miami without seeing our 'Don't Forget Big Wednesday!' message up on a billboard,

"Strange as it is to say it, we're non-partisan," Monreal said.

tacked to a phone booth, or taped to a bus shelter," Monreal added. "The Republican Party has spared no expense in this endeavor."

GOP committees in Ohio, Iowa, Wisconsin, Minnesota, Pennsylvania, Oregon, and Florida have spent more than $3 million on pamphlets, posters, stickers, and T-shirts bearing such slogans as "Put America First—Vote On The Third!" and "November 3rd Is *Your* Time To Be Heard."

Monreal's group is joined by hundreds of local organizations, such as the Black Republicans For Maryland. While the Black Republicans do not actually include any black members, the group describes itself as "dedicated to communicating a strong message to members of the African-American community."

"We're aiming not just to get black people to vote, but to mobilize them to

Above: A billboard erected by the Baltimore County Black Republicans for Maryland.

come together for one specific day of minority empowerment," Baltimore County Black Republicans For Maryland president Mitchell Williams said. "As Republicans, we truly believe that, by coordinating the minority vote across the nation, we can put minorities in their proper place. We believe we know what's best for the whole country."

Republicans are eager to point out the differences between their drive and those of other get-out-the-vote organizations.

"Strange as it is to say it, we're non-partisan," Monreal said. "We don't care if the minority voter is part of the vast majority of non-whites that traditional-

ly votes Democrat. What's important to us is that we get them to the polls bright and early on the third day of November, so that they feel like they've participated in this year's election."

Monreal said Republican volunteers will be available to drive minorities to polling places on Nov. 3.

"We'll even stay at home with them the day before, to help them prepare for the act of voting," Monreal said. "We'll engage in concentrated one-on-one tutoring the entire day, to make sure these voters focus on the important act of voting, rather than going outside, reading newspapers, or watching television."

Republican Party leaders expressed

pride in what they characterized as a true alternative to other programs that encourage voting, such as Rock The Vote.

"Let's be honest," Republican National Committee chairman Ed Gillespie said. "The Bush camp has been criticized for ignoring the minority vote for some time, especially during the last election. This project is our way of correcting that misperception. The Bush camp is extremely concerned about the black vote, especially in places like Florida, Ohio, and Pennsylvania. This year, on Nov. 3, we'll make a concerted effort to welcome minority voters into our own special camps with open arms." ∅

finally leaving and so they came back to see me off," Roberts said. "I thought that 'finally' was a little strange, since I only announced I was leaving two weeks ago."

According to employees who attended it, the going-away party was a smashing success.

"Everyone was in a great mood," inventory clerk Jim Fulton said. "I can't remember everything that happened, because I was pretty drunk by the end of the night, but I do recall leading the conga line through Karl's empty office."

Fulton's coworker Sheila Wuronski, Roberts' former assistant, agreed that the party was a hit.

"Wow, what a super night!" Wuronski said. "I'd say it was the single best day Ames Farm Products has had in five years."

Roberts said he would have preferred a cordial and sincere send-off to the raucous one that he received.

"I guess people were too busy enjoying themselves to get sentimental," Roberts said. "I wasn't expecting sobs,

"I'm excited by the challenges facing me at Quad-State," Roberts said. "They need a new dress code and lunch policy. Somebody has to crack down on the time-clock violations. And sick days and personal days seem to be overlapping in an unacceptable way."

but I don't think anyone even got misty. People gave me goodbye hugs, but they weren't 'we'll miss you'-type hugs. Twice, I was lifted off the ground and swung around in circles. It was

nice to see such a strong outpouring of emotion, I guess, but I wasn't expecting so much whooping and hollering."

"I heard they eventually got a call from the retirement center across the street because of all the noise," Roberts added.

In spite of his uneasy feelings about the office-wide blowout, Roberts said he is looking forward to continuing his career at Quad-State Shipping.

"I'm excited by the challenges facing me at Quad-State," Roberts said. "They need a new dress code and lunch policy. Somebody has to crack down on the time-clock violations. And sick days and personal days seem to be overlapping in an unacceptable way. But, with a little discipline and attention to detail, I'll whip the place into shape."

"Ames was great," Roberts added. "But I admit that I'm looking forward to a change. The new environment will provide a chance to not only move on in my career, but also make new friends." ∅

amounts of blood. Passersby were amazed by the unusually large amounts of blood. Passersby were

I love listening to music but I hate all the wires.

amazed by the unusually large amounts of blood. Passersby were amazed by the unusually large amounts of blood. Passersby were amazed by the unusually large amounts of blood. Passersby were amazed by the unusually large amounts of blood. Passersby were amazed by the unusually large amounts of blood. Passersby were amazed by the unusually large amounts of blood. Passersby were amazed by the unusually large amounts of blood. Passersby were amazed by the unusually large amounts of blood. Passersby were amazed by the unusually large amounts of blood. Passersby were amazed by the unusually large amounts of blood. Passersby were amazed by the unusually large amounts of blood. Passersby were amazed by the unusually large

see TRANSVESTITISM page 300

Man, I Wish That Sniper Would Go Away

By William Gussie

I know I shouldn't complain: I've got a reasonably priced place with gorgeous hardwood floors, a fireplace, and a nice big backyard. It's just, there are some things about the neighborhood that I can't get used to. I wish we weren't so close to the airport, I wish we were near a supermarket, and I really wish the sniper in front of the house would go away.

I'll grant you, the break on the mortgage was nice. The broker was very understanding when we told him we wanted a few points shaved off our rate because of the bad plumbing, the shoddy garage roof, and all those shot-out windows that needed replacing.

And it's not just the money—our neighbors are great, too. The Culpin kid came over the day we moved in to ask if he could cut our grass with his old push-about Lawn Boy. I felt so bad for his parents after the incident. But what can you do? At least they still have the twins.

The shops might be out of walking range, but there's a good bookstore just a hop, a skip, and a desperate sprint from our back porch. My wife said we should contact the authori-

> **I'm the new guy in the neighborhood. I don't want to get tagged as the guy who calls the cops every time there's a sniper training his gun on the crosswalk between the front door and the SUV.**

ties, but I'm the new guy in the neighborhood. I don't want to get tagged as the guy who calls the cops every time there's a sniper training his gun on the crosswalk between the front door and the SUV.

Still, though… No matter how soothing the crickets are at night, I never forget that the sniper is out there. It's like having a popcorn hull between your teeth: You can't stop thinking about it until it's gone. We can't open the curtains during the day, we can't

turn the lights on at night, and we certainly can't have pets. I mean, the mortgage allows pets. But the sniper doesn't.

And just try getting something to eat around here! Once the delivery guys figure out that our sniper will plug them the second they start up our walk, they stop delivering to us! When we try to order, they all ask, "406 Roberts? Is that the place with the sniper out front?" Sometimes, when a

> **The Culpin kid came over the day we moved in to ask if he could cut our grass with his old push-about Lawn Boy. I felt so bad for his parents after the incident. But what can you do? At least they still have the twins.**

new restaurant opens up, we can get them to come over once or twice, but after the first few delivery guys are assassinated, the restaurant gets scared off and it's microwave burritos for us.

You know what else? I really wish that sniper would allow someone from Taco Town to retrieve Renaldo's bullet-riddled corpse out from under the sycamore.

On the upside, I guess the sniper keeps the kids home at night. They're at that age where they prefer tear-assing around town to spending time at home. Judy's 15, and that means all she thinks about is boys. Too bad for her none of her knights in shining armor have been willing to risk a .270 Winchester softnose between the eyes. I just tell her there'll be plenty of time for boys after the sniper's gone.

I'm getting a little fed up, though; I won't lie to you. The gutters are filling up with leaves, and I've gotta get them cleaned out before it snows. Man, when winter sets in, all the bulky clothes and ice are gonna make evasive maneuvering difficult. Well, at least we won't be saddled with hosting Christmas this year. Which reminds me, I can't imagine what we'll do for Halloween. Every time I try to turn on the walkway light, the sniper shoots it out. Should we even bother giving out candy this year? I just don't know. ∅

Your Horoscope

**By Lloyd Schumner Sr.
Retired Machinist and
A.A.P.B.-Certified Astrologer**

Aries: (March 21–April 19)
Your health and dignity are equally important, but four square miles of ball bearings will make it difficult for you to maintain either.

Taurus: (April 20–May 20)
You're technically in favor of people exacting bloody revenge, but everyone trying to do it all at once will seriously inconvenience you.

Gemini: (May 21–June 21)
You may be the best art thief on the continent, but your penchant for Lladro porcelain and collectible chess sets will keep your legend small.

Cancer: (June 22–July 22)
Not only is fusion sushi "so three years ago," but you apparently don't realize it has nothing to do with the musical stylings of Spyro Gyra.

Leo: (July 23–Aug. 22)
The population density of Wyoming is very low, but that doesn't mean the people there aren't also out to kill you.

Virgo: (Aug. 23–Sept. 22)
You don't like having limits imposed upon you, which is why it enrages you to hear Roger Miller sing "You Can't Roller Skate In A Buffalo Herd."

Libra: (Sept. 23–Oct. 23)
The stars have something frightfully urgent to tell you, but the new Grand Theft Auto just came out, and they're not leaving the house.

Scorpio: (Oct. 24–Nov. 21)
You'll be credited with a new kind of piracy that is even less glamorous than "software" and "music," and a hell of a lot less sexy than "butt."

Sagittarius: (Nov. 22–Dec. 21)
As long as you're personally involved in the process, it'll be a terrible time to make career or romantic decisions.

Capricorn: (Dec. 22–Jan. 19)
The overwhelming sense that everything is falling apart around your ears will be reinforced by painful sonic and tactile cues.

Aquarius: (Jan. 20–Feb. 18)
All your money problems will be solved when an out-of-control armored car hurtles down your street, but not in a fashion you'll consider ideal.

Pisces: (Feb. 19–March 20)
You'll feel a certain sense of inevitability when you see John Waters sitting in the front row at your trial for the hair-dryer electrocution of your boyfriend.

STUDY from page 297

opinion."

Public reaction to the findings was varied.

"If we can't trust our friends and neighbors to be honest and forthcom-

> **"Human beings have a remarkable ability to keep themselves from recognizing their own flaws while attacking others," San Francisco-based psychiatrist James Dowling said.**

ing, who can we trust?" Olympia, WA resident Ralph LeBoeuf said. "It's shocking. Are we all crazy? Now that we know we're all damaged, how will anyone be able to successfully run for

local office? How can I entrust someone like myself, whose best friend is a cardboard stand-up Frankenstein monster, with any major responsibility?"

Muriel Woodbridge of Norfolk, VA said she'll never think of anyone she knows in the same way again.

"I'm hurt and I'm angry," said Woodbridge, who makes miniature clothes for her wall-mounted crucifix so Jesus doesn't get cold at night. "I suppose I'll do my best to support the American people through this scandal, though. What else can I do?"

One expert in human behavior said that the study's repercussions will be minimal.

"Human beings have a remarkable ability to keep themselves from recognizing their own flaws while attacking others," San Francisco-based psychiatrist James Dowling said. "This whole thing should blow over as soon as the initial sting fades. Besides, the fact that I like to be spanked—hard—is no one's business." ∅

$14.5 Billion Pledged To Rebuild Battleground States

see NATION page 11C

Drug Paraphernalia Visible In Photo Of Missing Cat

see LOCAL page 11D

Candidates Launch 2008 Presidential Campaigns

see POLITICS page 9E

Dinner, Theater Overdone

see ENTERTAINMENT page 3F

STATshot

A look at the numbers that shape your world.

What Does The Presidential Runner-Up Receive?

14% Right to finally take off tie

16% Lots of great, if repetitive, memories

21% First hot meal and shower in weeks

17% Souvenir DVD compilation of attack ads against him

20% Low-effort Ivy League teaching gig

12% Gets to not have to be president

THE ONION • $2.00 US • $3.00 CAN

---

the ONION®

VOLUME 40 ISSUE 44   AMERICA'S FINEST NEWS SOURCE™   4–10 NOVEMBER 2004

U.S. Inspires World With Attempt At Democratic Election

ELECTION 2004

NEW YORK—Observers from around the world report that they were inspired and moved by America's most recent attempt to hold a public election in accordance with the standards of a democratic republic.

"After all of the recriminations, infighting, and general madness before the election, the people of this fractured nation still found the courage to show up at the polls," said Anas Salman, an Afghan U.N. official who was in New York during the American electoral experiment. "More than half of America's citizens—a large portion of them women—made a valiant attempt to choose their own leader, even though there was no guarantee their votes would be counted. It was truly inspirational."

see ELECTION page 304

Above: Citizens vote in embattled Miami.

National Museum Of The Middle Class Opens In Schaumburg, IL

Above: A waitress from Chicago learns what the middle class was.

SCHAUMBURG, IL—The Museum of the Middle Class, featuring historical and anthropological exhibits addressing the socioeconomic category that once existed between the upper and lower classes, opened to the public Monday.

"The splendid and intriguing middle class may be gone, but it will never be forgotten," said Harold Greeley, curator of the exhibit titled "Where The Streets Had Trees' Names."

"From their weekend barbecues at homes with backyards to their outdated belief in social mobility, the middle class will forever be remembered as an important part of American history."

Museum guests expressed delight over the traditions and peculiarities of the middle class, a group once so prevalent that entire TV networks were programmed to

see MUSEUM page 305

Workout Routine Broken Down For Coworker

SAN JOSE, CA—Heritage Ink Supply sales representative Eric Vanderbilt broke his workout routine down in the company breakroom Monday, for the benefit of coworker Jennifer Kim.

"Mondays, I focus on chest and triceps," Vanderbilt told Kim, after she said that her 232-pound coworker "must go to a gym or something." "I usually start with the flat bench press, which works the whole chest. Then, I move on to the incline and decline bench press—those

focus on the upper and lower chest, respectively. Sometimes, I do dumbbells, just to mix it up. For the triceps, I usually do french press and dips."

Kim said that, in asking Vanderbilt whether he belonged to a gym, she had neither sought nor expected a meticulous account of his lifting regimen.

"It's all about DPP: discipline, persistence, and patience," Vanderbilt said, watching the muscles in his forearm move as he

see WORKOUT page 304

Above: Vanderbilt describes a typical Wednesday night.

301

Red Sox Break Curse

Last week, the Boston Red Sox defeated the St. Louis Cardinals in the World Series, breaking a "curse" that has persisted since 1918. What do *you* think?

"So the curse only lasted 86 years, huh? I guess the ol' Bambino wasn't as powerful a necromancer as we thought."

Allen Palmer
Systems Analyst

"It's good to know that the World Series isn't just about which team has the highest payroll. The Red Sox are proof that you can spend the second most and still become champions."

Lacey Swain
Chiropractor

"This should bring hope to our military, which has not won a decisive victory in almost 60 years."

Jesse Ramos
Repairman

"The curse is broken. Alas, my own curse, the one which exists for all women since Eve's fall, persists to this very day."

Edna Crawford
Biochemist

"Wow. Does this mean baseball can end now?"

Tony Mills
Construction Worker

"I've been rooting for the Sox for the past 20 years, but I finally gave up hope on them this season. I was expecting them to lose, so they managed to let me down again."

Bryan Warren
Civil Engineer

Election Opinion Polls

Telephone polls were conducted with increasing frequency in the days leading up to the election. What were some of the questions?

▶ How do you feel about the latest polls indicating that Kerry doesn't have a chance in hell of winning?

▶ With which candidate would you most like to go on a cross-country crime spree?

▶ If you knew that John Kerry and Osama bin Laden were actually the same person, would you be more or less likely to vote for Ralph Nader?

▶ What campaign issue matters most to people like you, who lack the talent or ambition to get the hell out of Wyoming?

▶ Given a choice between two generic candidates, one who would steal your money and use it to cater gay weddings, and one who was a strong and resolute leader, who would you choose?

▶ On a scale of 1–10, how much pain are you in?

▶ Who would you rather kill: the unborn or the terrorists?

▶ Just between us, who are you going to vote for?

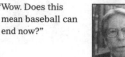

 **the ONION**®
America's Finest News Source.™

Herman Ulysses Zweibel
Founder

T. Herman Zweibel
Publisher Emeritus

J. Phineas Zweibel
Publisher

Maxwell Prescott Zweibel
Editor-In-Chief

I Don't Like The Person You Become When You're On The Jumbotron

By Leslie Puig

Okay, Dave, we need to talk. I didn't say anything on the way back from the stadium, because I was collecting my thoughts. But now, I think it's time we clear the air. Look, you know I've always loved and supported you. I believe you are, at heart, sweet, romantic, intelligent, capable, and wise. But something happens when the eyes of an entire stadium are on you, and it makes me wonder whether I even know you. Dave, I don't like the person you become when you're on the Jumbotron.

The Dave I know is polite, modest, and content. Jumbotron Dave is crass and loud. The Dave I know has a sweet, gentle smile. Jumbotron Dave has a tongue that waggles and undulates lasciviously. Accompanied by your red cheeks, your bulging eyes, and that "metal" gesture you do with your hands—it's horrifying. What comes over you, Dave?

Don't give me that "I like the attention, but I don't need it" stuff. I know you think you don't get on the Jumbotron often enough for it to be a problem, and I know you think that your little display doesn't hurt anyone. But seeing you that way hurts me. Because I know you're better than that disco-dancing lunatic up on the screen.

I never said you control the cameraman, but once he chooses you, you are responsible for your actions. Wouldn't a grin and a wave do the job? Couldn't you just hold up a team pennant? Even a tasteful sign? I think the Seahawks would prefer the image of a well-mannered fan to some screaming guy who pulls up his shirt to flash a pair of chalky-white manbreasts planted with sprigs of chest hair and nipples the size of saucers. What's "fun" or "funny" about that, Dave?

And the sounds you make! The Dave I know has a voice so gentle and sweet that I often save his phone messages. Jumbotron Dave has a voice that I would hesitate to call human. It's more a series of guttural whoops and bellows. You do realize that they can't hear you, right, Dave? Okay, well, if you're going to yell anyway, why not at least yell something simple, so people can read your lips? You could try "Seahawks!" or "Touchdown!" instead of those nonsense words you were yelling earlier tonight when you were gesturing from your beer to the field to the air. Honestly, Dave, why? No one watching the jumbotron can hear you, you know.

You never think about my feelings. I'm on that Jumbotron, too, you know. I have as much right as you to jab my index finger in the air and shout, "We're No. 1! We're No. 1!" Earlier this evening, in your haste to fill the Jumbotron screen with your pasty ex-

> **I never said you control the cameraman, but once he chooses you, you are responsible for your actions. Wouldn't a grin and a wave do the job? Couldn't you just hold up a team pennant? Even a tasteful sign?**

panse, you blotted me out of the picture completely. Not only did you prevent me from raising a finger into the air and shouting, "We're No. 1!" but you also jabbed me in the eye with your elbow and sent my pretzel nuggets flying.

No, I'm not asking that you hide your face in the event you do get on the Jumbotron. That's silly. All I ask is that you use the Jumbotron responsibly, like Ellen's fiancé Jack. When Jack gets on the 'tron, he smiles, gives the thumbs up, and points to his Matt Hasselbeck jersey. Then he looks back at the game. Very classy and dignified. Like you, he's at the game to have fun and it shows. But unlike you, he doesn't let the Jumbotron change him into a screaming lunatic. He's an adult. And, like an adult, he knows he doesn't need to outdo everyone else who's ever been on the Jumbotron before. He knows that that sort of one-upmanship leads to trouble. That rainbow-wigged John 3:16 guy is in jail right now, Dave. Did you know that, Dave? Prison.

I remember the first time I saw your darker, LED-displayed side. It was the Mariners-Brewers game at the Kingdome in 1996, and I was thrilled just to be close to you. We'd been dating for two months, and I was head-over-heels in love. Then, suddenly, we were on that gigantic screen together. Before I could even react, you leapt onto your seat and poured a beer over your head.

At the time, I laughed. A halfthought, "something is very wrong here," scuttled through the back of my mind, but I ignored it. Around the start of the seventh inning, the fact that my date was drenched in beer

see JUMBOTRON page 304

Spain Vows Eternal Vigilance In War On Bulls

PAMPLONA, SPAIN—Following a series of brutal attacks, Spanish Prime Minister José Luis Zapatero pledged Monday that he "will not rest until Spain is free of rampaging bulls."

"Bulls are ruthless animals that run our young men down in the streets without regard for guilt or innocence," Zapatero said. "Doggedly pursuing their agenda of destruction, they are deaf to pleas for mercy, and they care nothing about the suffering they cause as they rout and trample *novillero*, *picador*, and *matador* alike."

Zapatero said the government has no estimate of the number of bulls currently living in Spain, due to the animals' stealthy nature.

"The beasts hide in the nation's pastures, quietly ruminating over their vicious agendas," Zapatero said. "They often lie dormant for years, posing as innocent calves until they expose themselves as the brutes they are. Then, they attack in arenas, when the crowds are at their maximum capacity, in order to incite fear and shock among the citizenry."

"We can no longer sit and watch as the bulls gore our brave young men to death," Zapatero added. "To those who say this problem is too widespread for the Spanish government to tackle, I say 'Toro!'"

Right: Zapatero introduces his agenda in the fight against Spain's vicious enemy (above).

Zapatero has established a cabinet-level Department of Bovine Security and a color-coded system that will alert the general public to the likelihood of an animal rampage. A green flag waved by the president indicates a low risk of bull attack. Magenta and gold capes, when worn by footmen, *peones*, or *capeadores*, indicate an elevated threat level. A colorful ring of *banderilla* around the bull's neck indicates a high threat level. In the case of a severe threat, a red flag is waved, and a bull attack is imminent.

"We can't afford to lose the war on bulls," Zapatero said. "When bulls unleash their brand of chaos, they leave massive destruction in their paths, as the tragic events of July 7 in Pamplona have proven time and again for the last 400 years."

Some Spanish citizens allege that the government's efforts to stop bull attacks are creating anti-bovine sentiment among the citizenry, and several watchdog organizations have been created to protect the rights of cows.

"Violent bulls represent a small minority of all ruminants," Bovine Rights Now representative Adora Moreno said. "Most cows are docile herbivores with no desire to harm a living soul. They are productive members of society, providing us with milk, meat, and leather goods. They should be granted the same dignity we afford other species."

Zapatero said that, while some citizens expressed displeasure with the additional security checkpoints in public and private pastures across the nation, the precautions are "an unfortunate necessity in these troubled times."

The Spanish government has earmarked funds for 10,000 new matadors, as well as gates, pink stockings, and embroidered jackets.

"Our matadors wish to ensure the safety of the Spanish people and tourists alike," Zapatero said. "These bulls may gracefully dodge the swords and spears of justice, but our men will not back down. They shall engage the bulls with intricate goading, ritualized mockery, and the hypnotic waving of streamers. They will not stop posing in their sequined suits see SPAIN page 305

NEWS IN BRIEF

Nader Supporters Blame Electoral Defeat On Bush, Kerry

WASHINGTON, DC—Supporters of presidential candidate Ralph Nader blamed his defeat Tuesday on George W. Bush and John Kerry, claiming that the two candidates "ate up" his share of the electoral votes. "This election was stolen out from under Mr. Nader by Bush and Kerry, who diverted his votes to the right and the left," Nader campaign manager Theresa Amato said. "It's an outrage. If Nader were the only candidate, he would be president right now." In his concession speech, Nader characterized Bush and Kerry as spoilers.

Millions Of Work Hours Lost To Voting

WASHINGTON, DC—Secretary of Labor Elaine Chao announced Wednesday that voter turnout for the 2004 election resulted in an "abysmal" 32 percent drop in productivity and millions of vital work hours lost Tuesday. "Because so many American workers arrived late or left early on voting day, the nation's output was severely reduced," Chao said. "We cannot afford this sort of massive drop in productivity." Chao has charged her staff with the task of investigating our current method of electing a president.

Recurring Zhang Ziyi Fantasy Always Involves Getting Kicked In The Face

EL CAJON, CA—Bradley Vogt, 24, said Monday that, although he often fantasizes about Beijing-born *Crouching Tiger, Hidden Dragon* star Zhang Ziyi, his dreams always abruptly end with her kicking him in the face. "I'll be thinking about Zhang and how sexy she looked in that red robe in *Hero*," Vogt said. "But just when I imagine her taking off her robe, she delivers a devastating series of flying kicks to my throat. Weird." Vogt said that, if the actress would star in a non-violent role, it might solve his problem, but added that he isn't "completely sure I want her to."

Loft Apartments Converted To Mayonnaise Factory

SEATTLE—A building housing 10 adjoining lofts near Pike Place was purchased to be converted from airy studio apartments into a mayonnaise factory, Best Foods, Inc. CEO Peter Slater reported Monday. "I took one look at those great wood-plank floors and two-story ceilings, and I knew that all it would take was a little elbow grease to turn the building into an awesome industrial workspace," Slater said. "There's this one sunlit spot over by the windows that'll be *perfect* for a two-ton industrial mixer. All we have to do is get rid of the leather couch." Current residents were told to vacate the building by Dec. 1, but were offered first crack at the 80 $9-an-hour jobs about to be created, pending their acceptance into the building's workers' union.

Shy Friend Experimenting With Personality

DUBUQUE, IA—Bashful Clark College sophomore Mandy Schumacher, 20, has spent the last month unsuccessfully trying to forge a personality from scratch, friends of Schumacher said Monday. "She's been introverted for so long that she just doesn't have a clue how to present herself to the world," Schumacher's roommate Krista Vezmer said. "One day she's, like, expounding on the modern ramifications of the Civil War, and the next, she's dancing on tables at Noonan's during Happy Hour." Vezmer added that she thinks Schumacher should resign herself to sticking with mousy. ∅

ELECTION from page 301

In the weeks leading up to the election, both of America's political parties alleged fraud in voter registration. Additionally, experts debated the reliability of electronic voting machines, which experienced problems in trial runs and leave no paper trail. Election officials also bemoaned many states' use of outdated punch-card machines.

Considering such disputes, Salman said he was "touched and gladdened" that voter turnout for the U.S. election nearly approached voter-turnout rates for Afghanistan's first popular elections in October, when 69 percent of citizens cast ballots.

"True, voter turnout in many parts of the world tops 90 percent," Salman said. "But it's understandable that the rate is lower in countries such as Afghanistan, where the government has raised fears of possible terrorist attacks at the polls. Our people showed great courage."

The last American presidential election, held in 2000, was also rife with problems. Myriad scandals arose concerning alleged fraud and ballot tampering. Although the Democratic candidate won the popular vote by a margin of half a million votes, the Republican candidate won the presidency with a strenuously disputed 537-vote lead in Florida, a state governed by his brother.

"Despite the specter of corruption in 2000, and even though the procedural problems which surfaced during the previous election were never remedied, the American people chose to put their faith in the system once again this year," said Joseph Mtume, a Kenyan diplomat who traveled to Ohio to view America's democratic proceedings. "You can't help but feel touched by the determination of these citizens who put their doubts aside to collectively participate in the democratic process. All this in a nation divided by war, where dissent is widespread and the rift between citizens has rarely been higher. It was truly stirring."

Carlos Cruz, an Argentinian diplomat who observed the election in Miami, said he was profoundly moved by America's democratic election.

"With my own eyes, I saw people from all walks of life waiting in long lines to cast their votes, and very few of them were turned away," Cruz said. "They believed in the democratic process, despite the existence of racial gerrymandering of the sort most recently seen in the redistricting of U.S. House seats to negate the impact of Hispanic and black voters in Texas."

Cruz said he was impressed that average citizens still participate in the "current money-dominated electoral process," even though legislators have largely ignored their repeated calls for campaign finance reform.

"Their wide-eyed earnestness was humbling," Cruz said. "Truly, my heart leaps up. I can only hope that, under such demoralizing circumstances, my countrymen would similarly rise together to try and make democracy work."

The multinational watchdog group Organization for Security and Cooperation sent 600 official observers to monitor proceedings, from countries as disparate as North Korea, Syria, and China. Many reported that they came away deeply touched.

"To see a country with such overwhelming problems—problems that affect every last citizen—have so many of its voters feel that they can still influence their leadership... words fail me," said Dae Jung Kim, a North Korean OSC delegate. "Certainly, my report to my own government will emphasize this. I will recommend that my leaders implement such American election-time strategies and tactics as would fit the North Korean model of personal freedom, such as their elegant Electoral College and the inscrutable voting machine." ∅

WORKOUT from page 301

worked his wrist back and forth. "I do six or eight reps for each exercise, unless I'm increasing the weight. In that case, I decrease the reps. No cheat reps. No 'one rep max.' A lot of the younger guys are doing 'one rep max' for quick gain, but they're playing with fire."

Many common perceptions about weightlifting are incorrect, Vanderbilt told Kim as she removed a plate from the microwave and stared in the direction of her cubicle.

"You might think you gotta do chest and arms every day of the week, but you don't," Vanderbilt said. "It's actually important to let your muscles recover. That's why I do legs on Tuesday, back and biceps on Thursday, and shoulders on Friday. I take Wednesdays and weekends off. I don't just sit around eating chips and watching TV, though. I usually go for a swim. Gotta keep up the old cardiovascular."

Added Vanderbilt: "What I'm striving for is a total body workout."

He then stressed the importance of stretching before strenuous exercise.

"Even if I don't do any serious exercise, I'll do 20 minutes of stretching," Vanderbilt said. "That's a bare minimum. If I'm lifting, then I stretch out before and after the workout. You wouldn't believe how many injuries could be avoided if people stretched before they worked out. If I have time, I like to stretch the muscles I'm working out between reps. You look pretty flexible. Do you do yoga?"

Kim responded by smiling and reaching for a AAA-member magazine sitting on the table.

"You don't eat French fries, do you?" Vanderbilt said, eyeing Kim's organic burrito. "Those are the worst things for your body. You might as well be eating lard. Seriously, if you don't put the right things into your body, you're not going to get the maximum benefit from all that sweat. I usually eat a chicken sandwich without the bun about two hours before a workout and then maybe a can of tuna mixed with vegetables 20 minutes after I'm done. To build muscle, you need protein—lots of it."

Vanderbilt said that, in order to add mass, he stacks his supplements, starting his day with a high-protein shake, an antioxidant multivitamin, a cardio-support supplement, a selenium supplement, and steel-cut oats sprinkled with whey.

When Kim asked Vanderbilt why he spends so much time at the gym, instead of spending it with friends or a girlfriend, Vanderbilt said it was important to take care of his most valuable asset: his body.

"I like knowing my body is working at peak efficiency," Vanderbilt said. "When I walk out of the gym, I feel physically and mentally disciplined. I like that. And there's a group down at the gym. We like to hang out at the juice bar and talk about routines, diet, and where to buy gear and workout clothes."

After stressing the importance of drinking enough water every day, Vanderbilt excused himself to take a phone call at his desk, giving Kim the opportunity to return to her cubicle and reflect on what she had learned about her coworker.

"Well, I learned that that Eric guy likes to work out—a lot," Kim said. "I also know that he likes to eat five or six meals a day instead of three. I think I offended him, though, when I asked him about steroids. It's amazing I managed that, since I barely got three words in edgewise for the last 15 minutes. Oh, and now my food's cold." ∅

JUMBOTRON from page 302

began to trouble me. But you weren't troubled a bit. It was as though you'd shut out reality. I watched you. You glanced up at the Jumbotron every few seconds, Dave. You were dying to unleash the monster again. Looking back, I don't think the Mariners' victory even mattered to you.

The Jumbotron is a way for fans to express their excitement and show pride in their favorite teams. Jumbotron appearances can be beautiful and sweet. People hold up their children. Some fans use the Jumbotron to send greetings to their mothers or propose to their girlfriends. They let the Jumbotron blow up the good aspects of their personalities. They don't let their most grotesque and vile characteristics take over.

Dave, I am only trying to help you. But I must warn you that I can't tolerate this side of you. Next month, we have tickets to see Mannheim Steamroller. I happen to know there's a Jumbotron in the arena. If you apply any red and green paint to your face before we go, you and I are through. ∅

Walking On Empty

Diabetes is no laughing matter, kids. (I'm not accusing you of laughing at diabetes—I'm just saying.) Diabetes affects millions of Americans, and

**A Room Of Jean's Own
By Jean Teasdale**

while it can be controlled, there is no cure. I'm thankful to have the less severe form, Type 2, but I could still lose a leg. I'm in no imminent danger of that, but I could, eventually, lose a leg. Or some fingers.

It saddens me to think that victims of this unfortunate disease have to curtail pleasures we should all have the right to enjoy, like eating sweets and sitting in one place for a long time. That's why I decided to join the Trick Or Treat Charity 5K Walkathon For Diabetes last Saturday. For every

> **Years ago, I did a 15K bike ride against bedsores. By the end of the ride, I was suffering from heat exhaustion and sweating profusely, and I had shooting pains in my inner thighs.**

kilometer I walked, I raised money for our local chapter of the American Diabetes Society.

If you had told me a year ago that I'd be doing a charity walk, I'd have asked you, "Can I hitchhike?" I'd have been pulling your leg—sort of. But I'm not really the charity marathon type. Years ago, I did a 15K bike ride against bedsores. By the end of the ride, I was suffering from heat exhaustion and sweating profusely, and I had shooting pains in my inner thighs. (I had to ride up a ton of hills that day! Why would anyone make a charity bike course so challenging? You'd think it would be on level ground, or even downhill. I'm still scratching my head on that one.)

But, as I was saying, no one had to talk me into the diabetes walk. I had a vested interest in its success! As soon as I heard about it, I started hitting up pals for pledges. Pledgers could either donate a set amount per kilometer I completed, which I would collect after the walk, or give a flat sum. In return,

see TEASDALE page 306

MUSEUM from page 301

satisfy its hunger for sitcoms.

"It's fascinating to think that these people once drove the same streets as we do today," said Natasha Ohman, a multi-millionaire whose husband's grandfather invented the trigger-safety lock on handguns. "I enjoyed learning how the middle class lived, what their customs were, and what sorts of diversions and entertainment they enjoyed. Being part of this middle class must have been fascinating!"

During the modern industrial age, the middle class grew steadily, reaching its heyday in the 1950s, when its numbers soared into the tens of millions. According to a study commis-

> **Many museum visitors found the worldview of the middle class— with its reliance on education, stable employment, and ample pensions—to be difficult to comprehend.**

sioned by the U.S. Census Bureau, middle-class people inhabited great swaths of North America, with settlements in the Great Plains, the Rocky Mountains, the Pacific Northwest, and even the nation's urban centers.

"No one predicted the disappearance of the middle class," said Dr. Bradford Elsby, a history professor at the University of Pennsylvania. "The danger of eliminating workers' unions, which had protected the middle class from its natural predators for years, was severely underestimated. We believe that removal of the social safety net, combined with rapid

Above: Several members of the upper class learn how people without yachts used to pass the time.

political-climate changes, made life very difficult for the middle class, and eventually eradicated it altogether."

One of the 15 permanent exhibits, titled "Working For 'The Weekend,'" examines the routines of middle-class wage-earners, who labored for roughly eight hours a day, five days a week. In return, they were afforded leisure time on Saturdays and Sundays. According to many anthropologists, these "weekends" were often spent taking "day trips," eating at chain family restaurants, or watching "baseball" with the nuclear family.

"Unlike members of the lower class, middle-class people earned enough money in five days to take two days off to 'hang out,'" said Benson Watercross, who took a private jet from his home in Aspen to visit the museum.

"Their adequate wages provided a level of comfort and stability, and allowed them to enjoy diversions or purchase goods, thereby briefly escape the mundanity of their existence."

Many museum visitors found the worldview of the middle class—with its reliance on education, stable employment, and ample pensions—to be difficult to comprehend.

Thirty-five Booker T. Washington Junior High School seventh-graders, chosen from among 5,600 students who asked to attend the school's annual field trip, visited the museum Tuesday. Rico Chavez, a 14-year-old from the inner-city Chicago school, said he was skeptical of one exhibit in particular.

"They expect us to believe this is how people lived 10 years ago?"

Chavez asked. "That 'Safe, Decent Public Schools' part was total science fiction. No metal detectors, no cops or dogs, and whole classes devoted to art and music? Look, I may have flunked a couple grades, but I'm not that stupid."

Others among the 99 percent of U.S. citizens who make less than $28,000 per year shared Chavez's sense of disbelief.

"Frankly, I think they're selling us a load of baloney," said laid-off textile worker Elsie Johnson, who visited the museum Tuesday with her five asthmatic children. "They expect us to believe the *government* used to help pay for college? Come on. The funniest exhibit I saw was 'Visiting The Family Doctor.' Imagine being able to choose your own doctor and see him without a four-hour wait in the emergency room. Gimme a friggin' break!"

While some were incredulous, others described the Museum of the Middle Class as "a trip down memory lane." William Harrison, a retired social worker with middle-class heritage, said he was moved to tears by several of the exhibits.

"You wouldn't know it to look at me, but my parents were middle class," Harrison said. "Even though my family fell into poverty, I cherish those roots. Seeing that section on middle-class eating habits really brought it all back: the Tuna Helper, the Capri Sun, and the cookie dough in tubes. Oh, and the 2 percent milk and reduced-cholesterol butter spread! I was thankful for the chance to rediscover my past, even if the middle class is gone forever."

The Museum of the Middle Class was funded primarily by the Ford Foundation, the charitable arm of the Ford automotive company, which sold cars to the middle class for nearly 100 years. ∅

SPAIN from page 303

Above: Bulls terrorize citizens in the streets of Pamplona.

until every bull is removed from the arena, and every *torero* is free from fear of tossing, trampling, and goring."

Added Zapatero: "We are men. Under no condition will we accede to the whims of the bull."

Military officials have been careful to state that it could take years or even decades to eradicate the menace of the bulls. They plan to enlist the help of other nations in the fight, by recruiting bullfighting specialists from Mexico and Argentina.

"This will be a long, hard war, but we will win, through vigilance and determination," Spanish Defense Minister Jose Bono said. "We will arm ourselves with the *banderilla* of readiness and *muleta* of vigilance. There will be no mercy for the bull. We will find them wherever they hide, and we will round them up and contain them in pens. *Viva toreros* and *viva España!*" ∅

they would receive a certificate shaped like a paper foot.

My pledge collecting started off strong. Good ol' Patti, my creative-writing teacher friend and one of my biggest fans, chipped in a lump sum of $15! Fulgencio, my old coworker buddy at South Central Insurance, signed up, too, but he only pledged 50 cents per kilometer.

"Fulgencio, that's only $2.50 for the whole walk," I protested. "Can't you do a little better?"

"Girl, I'm only number two on your list here," he said. "You'll get more pledges, and they'll add up. Chill out, honey! I'll get some of my girlfriends in on it, too."

I was excited that Fulgencio would ask his girlfriends to donate. (That Fulgencio must get around. Hubba hubba!) But days went by, and I didn't hear back from him. Meanwhile, I hadn't been doing much better. My brother Kevin didn't return my calls, and neither did Dr. Plimm, the doctor who diagnosed my diabetes. My mother's friend Arnie promised 50 bucks! But then he called me back to say that my mother wouldn't let him contribute, because they needed the money for their Christmas trip to Vegas. (Yep, sounds like the same woman who bought my first training bra at a garage sale! I wish I were kidding!)

I was all gung ho to collect pledges, but what I didn't consider was that—and this may shock a lot of you Jeanketeers out there—I really don't know a lot of people. I was resolved not to ask Hubby Rick for help, because I didn't want him lording it over me. But who else was there? Then the perfect idea popped into my mind: I could get a business to sponsor me!

Tacky's Tavern doesn't open until 4 p.m. weekdays, but Tacky Jr. usually gets there early. When I called, he was his usual live-wire self.

"Walkathon For Diabetes?" he asked. "What, you like diabetes? That's pretty weird." (It took me a second to get it. Har-dee har har! Now I see where Rick gets his sparkling sense of humor.)

I told him that if Tacky's supported me, I'd wear a Tacky's T-shirt during the walk. To my shock, Tacky Jr. agreed. He pledged four bucks a kilometer, 20 bucks total. He said that was all he could pitch in, because pledging for the March Of Dimes Walkathon last spring pretty much wiped out his petty cash fund.

"These walkathon rackets are a lot of bull," Tacky Jr. said. "I'll take a good old bake sale over a walk any day." (I wholeheartedly agreed, but I sure didn't say that!) I offered him a paper foot, and he told me to knock it off. (What a charmer!)

When the big day finally came, I stopped by Tacky's to pick up the T-shirt. I was shocked by what Tacky Jr. gave me—a white shirt with an ugly, loud cartoon of a barfly on it. The barfly was simultaneously pinching one barmaid's butt and vomiting into another's cleavage! It looked nothing

like the modest blue Tacky's T-shirt I'd seen Rick wear. The shirt was a couple sizes too small, too, and would certainly accentuate some bulges I would've preferred to keep under wraps! I protested, but Tacky Jr. said I could take it or leave it, because it was all he had. I didn't want to lose the pledge, so I went to the bathroom and put the T-shirt on.

When I pulled my car up to the walk's starting line, boy, was I shocked by what I saw! All the participants were wearing Halloween cos-

I was all gung ho to collect pledges, but what I didn't consider was that—and this may shock a lot of you Jeanketeers out there— I really don't know a lot of people.

tumes! Shoot! I could've worn a cute costume, too, if I hadn't been so determined to get Tacky Jr.'s pledge.

Patti said kilometers are shorter than miles, but the walk was still really long. After a kilometer or two, I was ready to throw in the towel. (And, just like the charity bike ride, part of the walk was uphill! Again! I ask you, does that make any sense?) There were women handing out refreshments along the way, but they only had bottled water! Sheesh! What was this, a death march? One woman looked at my sweat-drenched T-shirt and suggested that I take a short rest. But I was afraid that if I rested, I'd stop altogether, so I kept walking.

About 20 minutes later, I started seeing strange little fireworks before my eyes. I'd drunk a couple bottles of water, but my mouth was parched. There were no tables of water in sight, though, and the tediousness of the walk was starting to get to me. I walked in a daze for a few minutes more, and then something occurred to me: I hadn't seen another walker in a long time. I yanked out the map. I was off-course! The road had forked shortly beyond the rest stop. I almost quit right then and there, but I couldn't let my pledgers down. I turned back and found the correct road.

When that finish-line banner hanging over the entrance to a local park finally came into sight, I felt like bawling! As I got nearer, though, I noticed that no one was around. I wondered if I'd missed another turnoff, but no—the American Diabetes Society banner was right there. As I passed under the finish line, I gave a little cheer. It was my moment in the sun, even if no one was around to see it.

HOROSCOPES

Your Horoscope

By Lloyd Schumner Sr.
Retired Machinist and
A.A.P.B.-Certified Astrologer

Aries: (March 21–April 19)
The stars will weep over your plight this week, which will offer little comfort, as their tears are made of excruciatingly hot stellar plasma.

Taurus: (April 20–May 20)
If you notice your fate is a little off this week, it's because Sagittarius is covering Taurus' shifts through the weekend while he visits his cousin. Hope that's cool.

Gemini: (May 21–June 21)
The same old solution to life's problems isn't working for you anymore. Try soaking the stuff in embalming fluid and letting it dry before you smoke it.

Cancer: (June 22–July 22)
Before you criticize those around you, try walking a mile in their shoes. Or any shoes, for that matter, you filthy hillbilly.

Leo: (July 23–Aug. 22)
Be secure in the knowledge that we're all part of a plan, but be thankful that you're ignorant of its cruel, bloody particulars.

Virgo: (Aug. 23–Sept. 22)
Your real name will eventually be forgotten, but you will enter the American folk mythos as The Woman With Great Hair Who Still Couldn't Keep A Man.

Libra: (Sept. 23–Oct. 23)
You're not very good at applying Newton's Laws to your daily life, which is why you threw a 16-pound shot-put straight up in the air a moment ago.

Scorpio: (Oct. 24–Nov. 21)
The old saw "There's snow on the roof, but there's a fire in the furnace" will suit you well this week, when you're transformed into a cabin in the Laramie range.

Sagittarius: (Nov. 22–Dec. 21)
You'll miraculously survive a plummet from the top of a major skyscraper, leaving you with the unpleasant job of climbing up all those stairs again.

Capricorn: (Dec. 22–Jan. 19)
The population crisis, with its attendant housing and food shortages, will offer you an increased probability of finally getting a roommate who isn't a big old fatty.

Aquarius: (Jan. 20–Feb. 18)
The only significant enemy of the race of man is man. That said, it wouldn't hurt to avoid packs of jackals for the next week.

Pisces: (Feb. 19–March 20)
The tiny storm clouds that hovered over you all last week will be replaced by a tiny, brightly shining sun, which will instantly incinerate your head.

I spotted a Walkathon van about to pull away. I ran over and yelled for the woman driving the van to stop. She didn't know why I had stopped her and seemed a little put off by my T-shirt. I was hoping she'd have some cookies and juice, like a Bloodmobile driver. When I told her I had just finished the walk, she grew leery.

"But the last registered walker passed through 50 minutes ago," she said.

I explained my accidental detour to her.

"You completed the walk?" she asked. "Where's your number tag?"

"What number tag?" I said.

"Didn't you register at the starting area before the walk?" she asked.

Ouch.

I was so dazzled by the participants' Halloween costumes that I had missed the registration table. The woman told me that I needed to get my pledge sheet stamped as evidence that I'd actually done the walk.

"Can't you see I'm exhausted?!" I

cried. "And that gal at the rest stop saw me! Ask her!" The woman said she was sorry, but there was nothing she could do. I could tell she was skeptical I'd even made the walk! Who in their right mind would cheat on a charity walkathon?

Well, Jeanketeers, I'm still too embarrassed to call my friends to collect the pledge money. If they asked me to prove I'd finished the walk, I'd have to tell them about my mistake. (I'm sure Tacky Jr. would be relieved to know he's off the hook! Albeit on a technicality.) I guess I could write a big fat check for $37.50 and send it to the American Diabetes Society, but they'd probably ask a bunch of questions. I mean, if they're going to be so picky about rules, how can they be a productive charity? Well, I know that I finished that walk fair and square. So, who's the loser here, the American Diabetes Society or me? (Don't actually e-mail me with the answer. That was a rhetorical question.) ∅

Nation's Wildlife Fleeing To Canada

see NATURE page 17E

Kerry Captures Bin Laden One Week Too Late

see WORLD page 7D

New Overtime Laws Changing Way Americans Wash Dishes For 60 Hours A Week

see BUSINESS page 9E

STATshot

A look at the numbers that shape your world.

What Are We Doing With Our Old Clothes?

- 14% Keeping them for when we lose that 100 lbs.
- 16% Be-Dazzling the shit out of them
- 21% Donating them to Old Navy
- 17% Constructing a "No Fear" scarecrow
- 20% Selling them to Japanese perverts
- 12% Wearing them

---

the ONION®

VOLUME 40 ISSUE 45   AMERICA'S FINEST NEWS SOURCE™   11–17 NOVEMBER 2005

Nation's Poor Win Election For Nation's Rich

WASHINGTON, DC—The economically disadvantaged segment of the U.S. population provided the decisive factor in another presidential election last Tuesday, handing control of the government to the rich and powerful once again.

"The Republican party—the party of industrial mega-capitalists, corporate financiers, power brokers, and the moneyed elite—would like to thank the undereducated rural poor, the struggling blue-collar workers in Middle America, and the God-fearing underprivileged minorities who voted George W. Bush back into office," Karl Rove, senior advisor to Bush, told reporters at a press conference Monday. "You have selflessly sacrificed your

see ELECTION page 310

Left: Bush and Cheney accept victory.

THE LIFE-CHANGING POWER OF PERSPECTIVE

Wes Marten, M.D.

Self-Help Book Believes It Can Be A Bestseller Someday

NEW YORK—In spite of the odds it faces in the ultra-competitive self-improvement segment of the publishing market, the forthcoming self-help book *The Life-Changing Power Of Perspective* firmly believes that it can be a bestseller, the 179-page non-fiction paperback said Tuesday.

"I *know* I can reach the top," *Perspective* said. "I simply have to view the trade market from the proper vantage point. That's the secret to attaining your goals, as I explain in my introduction and elaborate upon in my 24 chapters."

"I can't wait to get out on the shelves and show people what I can do!" the

see BOOK page 310

U.S. To Send 30,000 Mall Security Guards To Iraq

Above: A Brenneman Security guard, previously employed by the Northway Mall in Phoenix, patrols a Najaf street.

WASHINGTON, DC—Pressed for additional troops to police the Iraqi general elections scheduled for January, the Pentagon announced Monday that it will dispatch 30,000 U.S. shopping-mall security guards to the troubled Sunni Triangle region.

"A force of security guards trained to protect retail stores across America will be deployed to the Persian Gulf region," said Maj. Peter Archibald, a spokesman for Central Command. "Once in Iraq, security teams will fortify ground forces and assist them in

keeping the peace and quelling any horseplay."

According to Archibald, the Pentagon wanted to bolster forces in Iraq without further extending the tours of soldiers currently in the theater. The solution should offer the additional advantage, Archibald said, of potentially dispelling the public's rising concerns over a possible military draft.

"We found that mall security guards are as well-trained and ready to face

see GUARDS page 311

The Republican Majority

Last week, Bush became the first Republican president to be re-elected with House and Senate majorities since 1924. What do *you* think?

Beverly Banks
Systems Analyst

"So the Republicans still control the House, Senate, and Oval Office? Well, at least we Democrats still have the smug, condescending attitude that cost us the election in the first place."

Edgar Mendez
Data Keyer

"Our nation may be bitterly divided, but at least our government can agree on being ultra-conservative."

Sam Howell
Credit Checker

"What's so bad about this? Could some Democrat explain it to me in under an hour, without starting to scream or cry?"

Ted Jacobs
Dentist

"Now that the Republicans run Congress, the White House, and soon the Supreme Court, they'll just have to invent some new branches of government to dominate, as well."

Leo Watts
Custom Tailor

"The fact that 48 percent of Americans voted for a boring placeholder like John Kerry is actually a really good sign for the Left."

Erika Williamson
Interior Designer

"Hold on. I'm being text-messaged orders from my Republican congressman on how to proceed next. Put clothes in dryer? Yes, Rep. Burchardt."

Prehistoric Discoveries

This year, paleontologists made a number of important discoveries about prehistoric times, including the existence of a 40-inch-tall species of human, as well as that of an early, feathered relative of the Tyrannosaurus Rex. What are some other recent discoveries?

- ▶ Millions of years ago, the bottom of the Pacific Ocean was entirely underwater

- ▶ Archaeological excavations show that Cro-Magnon man possessed what scientists believe were crude salad spinners

- ▶ Evidently, prehistoric life tended to head straight for the nearest tar pit, lava flow, or mudslide

- ▶ Gay marriage killed the dinosaurs

- ▶ While precursors of T-Rex had feathers, Triceratops favored fruit-laden Carmen Miranda hats

- ▶ Prehistoric women walked around with their hoo-hoos hanging out

- ▶ Although one of the most popular dinosaurs today, the brontosaurus went largely unrecognized by his contemporaries

- ▶ In general, some interesting stuff that will be simplified by the press and inspire a couple of preposterous movies

✪ the ONION®
America's Finest News Source.™

Herman Ulysses Zweibel
Founder

T. Herman Zweibel
Publisher Emeritus
J. Phineas Zweibel
Publisher
Maxwell Prescott Zweibel
Editor-In-Chief

Debbie, By The Time You Read This, I'll Either Be Dead Or Vice President Of Marketing

By Kenneth Sanders

Dearest Debbie, when you opened this letter, my fate was already sealed. I do not take pleasure in alarming you, but I love you too much to mince words. By the time you read this, I will either be dead or vice president of marketing for the Poland Spring corporation.

If all went according to plan, then I am, at this very moment, sitting in the corner office reviewing our public-relations strategy, scrutinizing our advertising budget, and evaluating the performance of the entire Poland Spring marketing-department staff. But if all did not go as hoped—if, in my quest for greatness, I failed—you must know how I cherished you. I've always loved you, and in whatever sort of afterworld I find myself, I will continue to love you.

Debbie, if I do not prevail, know that I died full of hope, fighting for my corporate life against the forces of incremental promotion.

I may be tempting fate with my fearless scheme. For that, forgive me, Debbie. But it was fate that first tempted me when, seven years ago, I toured the executive offices on the 30th floor of the Nestlé domestic-waters division during my orientation meeting in December. Since that day, my devotion to this singular end has been unwavering. And now, finally, an opportunity has presented itself, and I would be a fool to ignore it. The dream is within my grasp, and I must seize it—or die.

Long have I kept quiet, plotting from my windowless office, gritting my teeth each time another board meeting began with me on the wrong side of the conference room's glass wall. Each time I was forced to answer my own phone, my blood ran cold. Each time I sorted my own mail, it was like an icicle was being stabbed into my heart, repeatedly. The bitter irony is that I was forced to compose this very message, quite possibly my last, without secretarial assistance.

If I am ever to look myself in the eye and say, "Hello, Mr. Vice President of Marketing," then my course, however treacherous, is clear. Debbie, a man can only be held down for so long before he must take a final stand and demand a management position overseeing all public-relations efforts, promotional initiatives, and corporate partnerships for America's finest brand of natural spring water!

In this hour, my flame burns bright. But if it is snuffed out, if you never hear from me again, Debbie, I ask that you contact my family and share this letter with them. Arrange a modest wake and funeral. If my body should ever be found, I would like it to be cremated. Cast my ashes into the spring in the woods of Maine from which Poland Spring water is drawn.

If you love me as I love you, you

> ## If I do not prevail, know that I died full of hope, fighting for my corporate life against the forces of incremental promotion.

know how significant this fight is. Even if I wished to give up, I could not. The die has been cast. Only two choices remain: death, or an executive-level position in the marketing department of the northeast region's best-selling bottled water.

Debbie, my darling, I know the written word is cold, but I could not risk breaking such news to you in person. No matter how much I would like to have secured one final kiss from your lips, I could not afford to weaken my resolve. Your warm brown eyes, the dimple on your left cheek when you smile... It would have been too much to bear.

It pained me to leave you as you slept. Though I wished to, I could not say goodbye, for the time had come to embark upon this most fateful task. But if I am given the chance to return to you in flesh and blood, I will be all the more worthy of your love. If the Lord allows me to share that bed with you again, Debbie, the man lying by your side will have satisfaction in his soul, newly printed business cards in his wallet, and complete control over all marketing decisions for Poland Spring, pending approval of the CEO and COO.

If I am meant to sacrifice my life to this cause... If I am already marked for death... If I must become a martyr in this crusade... So be it. I'd rather die on the 30th floor than live on the second.

In spite of the harsh realities they reveal, take heart as you read these words! For, my sweet Debbie, whether I am dead or the vice president of marketing, I suffer no longer. ∅

Housemates Reject Third-Roommate Debt-Relief Plan

Above: Huygens (left) and Epstein (center) review the bills Doogan says he can't pay.

LAWRENCE, KS—Chad Doogan, 20, a resident of the economically ravaged back bedroom at 1409 Oakwood Drive, received a huge setback Monday, when a humanitarian proposal calling for the forgiveness of his outstanding debts was vetoed by his two roommates.

"Look, I know Chad's snowed under a mountain of bills right now, but that's no reason for him to get off scot-free," said Doug Huygens, 22, one of the apartment's two superpowers. "Chad's a good guy and all, but this is getting ridiculous. He's owed us a ton of money for months. Now he wants a free ride? I'm sorry, man, but that's bullshit."

According to Doogan, his large accumulated debt and his extremely low gross annual income have created a cycle of poverty that he can't escape.

"Dude, I got to put at least $300 into my car to get that shitheap running again, or how else am I supposed to deliver pizza?" the embattled Doogan said from his living-room couch, where he has spent the past two weeks. "There's no way I can afford to do that and pay the back rent I owe, plus three months of cable bills and beer money. Plus, I still owe like $100 on the noise-complaint ticket we got from that spring-break party. How am I supposed to pay any of it back if I can't work at Pizza Pete's?"

Doogan and supporters of his debt-relief plan are calling for the immediate cancellation of 85 to 100 percent of his incurred debt.

"If the guys would forget about the money I owe them, or at least the back rent, I could fix my car and pick up a bunch of shifts," Doogan said. "It's in their best interest. Not only could I stop begging them for rent, but I could also start chipping in for groceries and video games and all that."

Huygens and roommate Jake Epstein, 24, said they first provided Doogan with emergency funds last winter, when they granted him an aid package in the form of a no-interest loan obtained through the Apartmental Monetary Fund, founded by Huygens and Epstein in February 2004 at the behest of third-roommate advocacy groups, such as Doogan's buddies Dan "Cosmo" Richards and Douglas "Scooter" Pye.

"Cosmo and Scooter were all like, 'C'mon, Chad's a good guy, have a heart,'" Epstein said. "So finally, me and Doug were like, 'Okay, okay, we'll float him some cash, but only for a few weeks until he gets his shit together.' Well, you can see how great that worked out."

Although the donor roommates supplied additional aid in the months that followed, the AMF placed strict conditions on the loans. These conditions were designed to accomplish three goals: to prevent corruption and mis-use of funds, to ensure that the monies were spent wisely, and to reduce third-roommate economic isolationism, integrating the debtor's personal economy more fully into the interdependent apartmental community.

"We only asked for three things, man," Huygens said regarding the structure of the loan. "First, that Chad quit partying so much. Second, that he open a checking account so he can budget his cash. And third, that he bring his kickass stereo system out of his bedroom and into the living room where we can all enjoy it. It was only fair."

While Doogan initially accepted the terms, he later issued complaints that the conditions were unnecessarily restrictive.

"I'm sick of Doug and Jake looking over my shoulder every time I want to rent a DVD or buy a friggin' beer," Doogan said. "Look, I'm sorry that I don't have a big allowance from my rich parents like they do. I wouldn't be asking the guys for money if they couldn't afford it."

Huygens and Epstein said Doogan failed to honor the conditions of the loan.

"Three days after we gave him this big loan, we came back from a weekend ski trip and the whole place was totally trashed," Huygens said. "There were beer cans everywhere, food and chips and shit all over the floor, and the bathroom was a friggin' disaster."

The AMF imposed sanctions against Doogan immediately thereafter, refusing additional loans until the environmental damage stopped. But after

see ROOMMATE page 311

Bush Promises To Unite Nation For Real This Time

WASHINGTON, DC—A week after winning a narrow victory over Democratic presidential nominee John Kerry, President Bush promised to "unite the divided nation, but for real this time." "Just as I pledged in 2000, I promise to bring the two halves of this nation together—only this time I'm really gonna do it," Bush said Tuesday. "I'll work hard to put an end to partisan politics. Seriously, though. This term, I will." Bush then requested the support of all Americans for his agenda of cutting taxes and extending America's presence in Iraq.

Liberals Return To Sodomy, Welfare Fraud

BERKELEY, CA—No longer occupied by the 2004 election, liberals across the country have returned to the activities they enjoy most: anal sex and cheating the welfare system. "I've been so busy canvassing for the Democratic Party, I haven't had a single moment for suckling at the government's teat or no-holds-barred ass ramming," said Jason Carvelli, an unemployed pro-hemp activist. "Now, my friends and I can finally get back to warming our hands over burning American flags and turning kids gay." Carvelli added that his "number-one priority" is undermining the efforts of freedom-loving patriots everywhere.

Amount Of Halloween Candy Collected Down 15 Percent

WASHINGTON, DC—According to data released Monday by the Federal Confectionary Reserve, the amount of candy collected by U.S. children this Halloween dropped 15 percent from 2003. "As the treating indicator plainly shows, our Snickers, Dum Dums, and Bit-O-Honey numbers were far below projections," FCR chairman Bert Worak said. "As we head into the next quarter, we should brace ourselves for a sharp reduction in levels of childhood wonder." Bennett also cautioned against counting on Santa Claus to boost candy acquisitions during the coming months.

Procrastinating Catholic 20 Rosaries Behind

BOSTON—Following three trips to the confessional in recent months, Paul McMullen has a backlog of 20 recitations of the rosary, the 32-year-old Catholic reported Monday. "Father O'Riordan gave me three rosaries last time, five the time before, and I still had 12 left over from last month," McMullan said. "I tried doing the 'Hail Marys' and the 'Our Fathers' on my way to work, but I kept losing my place during the Sorrowful Mysteries." McMullan said he plans to stop going to confession for a few months so he can catch up.

Political Blogger Mass Suicide To Be Discovered In Several Weeks

BOSTON—By examining web-traffic data for left-leaning DailyKos.com, researchers have predicted that the mass suicide of 14 political bloggers will likely be discovered sometime in mid-December. "After months of doing nothing but sit alone in our rooms at our computers, trying to get our message to the people, we lost the election anyway," read the still-unread suicide pact posted Nov. 3. "We'd rather be dead than live in a country as fucked up as this one." The bodies will most likely be found by property managers, long-estranged parents, or neighbors returning copies of Joe Trippi's *The Revolution Will Not Be Televised.* ∅

BOOK from page 307

book added.

Perspective said it will teach readers to organize their lives more efficiently and "achieve their goals by altering the way they define their circumstances." As readers progress through "the POV plan," *Perspective* said they will gain a fresh understanding of their lives, simply by altering their point of view.

"I *use* the model that I present, which is exactly why I know that I'm going to sell at least 500,000 copies," *Perspective* said. "Face it, if I didn't use powerful life tools, I wouldn't be sitting here in front of you today. I'm living proof of my 'creative mode' of thinking. Why, even back when I was only 30 pages, I was able to visualize myself as a full-length book."

"But I'm not stopping with a six-figure deal from New Horizon Press," *Perspective* said. "By 'believing in what I'm already achieving'—page 27—I can 'build on that belief and achieve through what I've built'—page 32. I'm not happy just to 'be,' when I can 'see.' I can *see* myself on every nightstand in America."

While optimistic life planning through visualization may not be unheard of in the self-improvement market, *Perspective* said it has something distinctive to offer to its readers.

> ### "'Oprah Book Club Selection' is already written on my heart," *Perspective* said. "Now, it's just a matter of getting it embossed on my spine."

"Everyone knows how many self-help books are published," *Perspective* said in a press release sent to potential reviewers early this year. "But how many of them are hard-bound for greatness? 'Oprah Book Club Selection' is already written on my heart. Now, it's just a matter of getting it embossed on my spine."

When pressed for details, *Perspective* quoted its back cover at length. "'Do you see?'" *Perspective* said. "'And if you do, how? Where have you positioned yourself? Are you looking at the mountain, or are you seeing the things around yourself as they might look to someone who has climbed the mountain?'"

"It's important not to even have the mountain—in my case, the *New York Times* bestseller list—in your line of sight," *Perspective* said. "Instead, think of your mountain as your line of sight, a frame of reference. I'm 'framing' that achievement-picture, and 'referencing' it through action. So, it's not, '*Perspective*, you have to sell 500,000 copies.' It's '*Perspective*, tonight you have an appearance at a reporting store, so have fun and do your very best, as reporting stores are important stepping stones to bestseller status.'"

The Life-Changing Power Of Perspective expanded upon its personal goals, saying that, in the book's case, "proper action" constituted a 60,000-copy print run backed up by a half-page ad in major business and lifestyle magazines, plus colorful dump-box standee-displays on the ends of checkout aisles at all big-box chain bookstores.

"Everyone at Horizon is totally behind *Perspective*, but we thought an initial print run of 15,000 was more appropriate," Horizon Press editor Emily Steiner said. "It had a quarter page in our fall catalog, though. *Perspective* definitely has the potential to

> ### "Even back when I was only 30 pages, I was able to visualize myself as a full-length book," *Perspective* said.

explode. I mean, every book does."

The author of *The Life-Changing Power Of Perspective*, Boston-based pediatrician Wes Marten, could not be reached for comment, as he was undergoing treatment for amphetamine abuse following the breakup of his third marriage. ∅

ELECTION from page 307

well-being and voted against your own economic interest. For this, we humbly thank you."

Added Rove: "You have acted beyond the call of duty—or, for that matter, good sense."

According to Rove, the Republicans found strong support in non-urban ar-

> ### "That's why I always vote straight-ticket Republican, just like my daddy did, before he lost the farm and shot himself in the head, and just like his daddy did, before he died of black-lung disease," Kaldrin said.

eas populated by the people who would have benefited most from the lower-income tax cuts and social-service programs championed by Kerry. Regardless of their own interests, these citizens turned out in record numbers to elect conservatives into office at all levels of the government.

"My family's been suffering ever since I lost my job at the screen-door factory, and I haven't seen a doctor for well on four years now," said father of four Buddy Kaldrin of Eerie, CO. "Shit, I don't even remember what a dentist's chair looks like...

Basically, I'd give up if it weren't for God's grace. So it's good to know we have a president who cares about religion, too."

Kaldrin added: "That's why I always vote straight-ticket Republican, just like my daddy did, before he lost the farm and shot himself in the head, and just like his daddy did, before he died of black-lung disease in the company coal mines."

Kaldrin was one of many who listed moral issues among their primary reasons for voting Republican.

"Our society is falling apart—our treasured values are under attack by terrorists," said Ellen Blaine of Givens, OH, a tiny rural farming community as likely to be attacked by terrorists as it is to be hit by a meteor. "We need someone with old-time morals in the White House. I may not have much of anything in this world, but at least I have my family."

"John Kerry is a flip-flopper," she continued. "I saw it on TV. Who knows what terrible things might've happened to my sons overseas if he'd been put in charge?"

Kerry supporters also turned out in large numbers this year, but they were outnumbered by those citizens who voted for Bush.

"The alliance between the tiny fraction at the top of the pyramid and the teeming masses of mouth-breathers at its enormous base has never been stronger," a triumphant Bush said. "We have an understanding, them and us. They help us stay rich, and in return, we help them stay poor. See? No matter what naysayers may think, the system works."

Added Bush: "God bless America's backwards hicks, lunchpail-toting blockheads, doddering elderly, and bumpity-car-driving Spanish-speakers." ∅

Above: Bush supporters vote in Kendall, FL.

danger as the coalition-trained military police," Archibald said. "They may not have the power of arrest, but real authority is only a walkie-talkie call away."

Hired by the Defense Department through a number of licensed, reputable firms, the security guards will work independent of the roughly 135,000 troops currently stationed in Iraq. The guards will receive an hourly wage from the U.S. government, and they will be eligible for health and dental benefits after six months.

A test deployment of 1,000 mall security guards to Najaf in September convinced skeptical coalition officials that private-sector security forces

> **Archibald said that casualty rates for the mall security guards were only slightly higher than those among Iraqi police forces.**

provide a palpable sense of order.

"Iraqi patrons of mall-guard-patrolled marketplaces—the Iraqi equivalent of our nation's food courts—reported that the guards' uniformed presence was unobtrusive or even reassuring," Archibald said. "While many Iraqis are intimidated by soldiers from the U.S., they were largely able to disregard the mall security forces."

Archibald said that casualty rates for the mall security guards were only slightly higher than those among Iraqi police forces.

Bobby Adcock, 27, of Bakersfield, CA, was rejected for military service in August 2002, due to poor eyesight and excessive weight. He was hired by A-Star Security shortly thereafter, and was surprised to find himself patrolling an Iraqi bazaar in a Ford Taurus two years later.

"The work is similar in a lot of ways," Adcock said, pausing mid-sentence to order a nearby Iraqi to pick up a candy wrapper and a blood-spattered *keffiyeh*. "I thought maybe I'd be dodging artillery fire and flushing insurgents out of hiding places, but mostly I stand around and keep my eyes peeled for trouble. Just the other day, we caught some vandals spray-painting 'Go home USA' on the side of a building. Then, there's the suspicious package sightings. Fortunately, a good number of those turn out to be false alarms."

"All in all, it's an okay assignment," Adcock said. "The food is strange, except for those lamb kebabs. Those aren't bad. The break room is just a shed out in back of a used-electronics store, but I don't want to complain.

Above: Doogan makes a request for immediate humanitarian aid.

loans failed to bring an end to the spiraling third-roommate debt, a more radical concept was introduced by an outspoken Chad advocate, Epstein's girlfriend Liz Borowitz.

"Liz was all over me about how I gotta be there for my buddy when he needs me," Epstein said. "She's, like, this total softie who rescues cats and shit. So she comes up with the bright idea that me and Doug should just forgive all the loans and let Chad start over on an even playing field. I was like, 'I'm sorry, Liz, but there's no way in hell…'"

Added Epstein: "Liz is super nice,

> **"I'm under serious risk of reverting to living in my parents' basement, under their totalitarian regime," Doogan said.**

but her idealist humanitarian policies are not financially sound. We set a dangerous precedent by bailing Chad out. It hardly motivates future room-

mates to be fiscally responsible, does it?"

Doogan implored Huygens and Epstein to reconsider their decision.

"How'm I supposed to better myself when all these forces are keeping me down?" Doogan said. "If I don't get out from under this debt, I can't pay tuition next semester and provide myself with an education. I'm under serious risk of reverting to living in my parents' basement, under their totalitarian regime. These dudes are my buddies—can't they see I'm the victim of macroeconomic forces I'm powerless to overcome? Jeez." Ø

I'm getting a lot of overtime."

Dale London, 47, is employed by Five-Eagle Security, based in Ames, IA. A former Loews Cineplex security

> **"The situation there is extremely volatile," Chatelain said. "The guards may provide a layer of security, but it's more psychological than actual."**

guard who spent three years as an airport metal-detector operator, London now patrols the streets of Najaf.

"I had to retrain my eye to spot the particular dangers over here in sandland," London said. "Yesterday, this kid with a bulge down his shirtfront

comes around the corner. When I ask him to undo his jacket, wouldn't you know, there's a grenade launcher. Well, I hustled his keister right behind the falafel stand and told him the next time I saw his face around here, I'd turn him over to the coalition. Then I called his mullah to come pick him up."

Added London: "I never figured out where he shoplifted the grenade launcher from, so I took it to our lost and found. If any Najaf shopkeepers out there are missing a grenade launcher, they should contact me, Dale London, at the Five-Eagle Security station. It's near the grocery where they sell that funny sesame candy."

While the security guards' power is limited by international law, they are authorized to alert coalition forces in the event of trouble. Last week, a Marine platoon was dispatched after Adcock noticed that a vehicle had been parked unattended in an abandoned lot for several hours.

"We inspected the car, but it contained no bomb or weapons," Marine Sgt. Michael Shahinian, 25, said.

"Weird thing is, turns out the call came from this guy Bobby Adcock, who was two grades above me at Bakersfield High School. I guess he's a pop cop working here now. Holy shit. I wonder if he ever did pass that shop class we had together."

Rebecca Chatelain, a research associate at the Institute For Defense Analysis, expressed misgivings over the use of mall security guards in Iraq.

"The situation there is extremely volatile," Chatelain said. "The guards may provide a layer of security, but it's more psychological than actual. Any determined insurgent will soon discover how easy it is to overcome a lightly armed, out-of-shape mall cop. I'd hate to see a repeat of what happened in Somalia."

Chatelain was referring to a 1993 incident in which several dozen American prom chaperones were sent to Somalia along with U.N. peacekeeping troops. All were shot by factional guerrillas within hours of their arrival. Ø

I Must Take Issue With The Wikipedia Entry For 'Weird Al' Yankovic

By Larry Groznic

To whomever or whatever is currently in charge of the free encyclopedia and online community portal at Wikipedia.org, I demand that you re-move the mask of anonymity and account for the gross over-sights to be found on your site. I must take issue with your entry for "Weird Al" Yankovic—for in allowing it to remain active, you are perpetrating a great injustice.

You most likely recognize my user-name, misterhand43. If you do not, you at the least recall my flame war with SoulblighterEric—I speak, of course, of the altercation which led to my ignoble suspension as a Wikipedia editor. As penance for my immaturity on the Admiral Akbar talk-page thread last March, I have held my tongue for eight months now.

I did not point out the whole-cloth omission of Ralph Snart and his cre-ator Marc Hansen, though it's a gross understatement to say the absence left me incredulous. I did not refer to the woeful lack of an article on the subject of popular *Farscape* actress Virginia Hey, nor did I send out a strongly worded e-mail about the merely passing mention of *Buffy the Vampire Slayer* novelizations, even though two were written by Richie Tankersley Cusick, and anyone who has read his adaptation of "The Har-vest" would agree that its inclusion on any list on the subject is critical. (And anyone who has not read this fine book has no business writing an overview of the show, but I digress.)

I remained silent in regard to those smaller matters, but I cannot ignore the travesty you call a copyleft ency-clopedia article on "Weird Al." Those who know me either by reputation or through IRC know that I do not suffer fools gladly. If you have been on the business end of one of my notorious outbursts of Internet anger, I do sym-pathize. And, for what is to come forthwith, I offer you my grim condo-lence. *En garde.*

To start: Your entry for "Weird Al" is laughably brief, and fails to account for the grand impact and scope of his career. How can you justify a "Weird Al" biography of only a paltry 850 words?

Particularly galling to this author is the fact that Madonna and U2 were given articles two and three times the length of the Weird One's. Yes, those artists may have sold more records than "Weird Al," but surely the Wikipedia community is not one to confuse net profits with artistic merit. Nevertheless, while we are on the loathsome subject of money, I might point out that nowhere in the article is it mentioned that Yankovic has earned no less than four gold and four plat-inum records.

Put plainly: The "Weird Al" entry con-tains omissions so glaring, I can only assume that they are the result of lazi-ness, indifference, or complete incom-petence. The article does not even hint at the immeasurable output of Alfred Matthew Yankovic, the man who has dominated the parody-song form since "My Bologna" first topped Dr. Demento's "Funny Five." And, al-though it did not gain national ac-claim, "School Cafeteria," released as the B-side of the "My Bologna" single, is not to be overlooked. The live ver-sion, to be found on Dr. Demento's Basement Tapes, contains several amusing riffs, as well. But again I di-gress.

Your entry makes no mention of Al's considerable directorial gifts. Not only has he directed many of his own uproarious videos, but he also direct-ed videos for such artists as Hanson,

> **I cannot ignore the travesty you call a copyleft encyclopedia article on "Weird Al." Those who know me either by reputation or through IRC know that I do not suffer fools gladly.**

The Black Crowes, and The Jon Spencer Blues Explosion. Admitted-ly, the article covers Yankovic's spoof film *UHF*, featuring Michael Richards in the breakout role of Stanley "Bag Of Moldy Tangerines" Spadowski, but what of Yankovic's "This Is The Life," featured on the soundtrack for *John-ny Dangerously*? More upsetting is the Wikipedia omission of Yankovic's spot-on parody of the James Bond ti-tle sequences in *Spy Hard*, Rick Friedberg's 1996 Leslie Nielsen vehi-cle.

While it may be nitpicking, the Wikipedia article states that "Weird Al" appears in *The Naked Gun*. It would be more accurate to say that "Weird Al" has appeared in all three *Naked Gun* films. More troubling yet is the treatment of Yankovic's ground-breaking TV work on *The Weird Al Show*, which is summed up in three paragraphs of puff. There is no mention anywhere of the WAS's re-curring cast of characters, including the Hooded Avenger (Brian Haley), Madame Judy (Judy Tenuta), J.B. Top-persmith (Stan Freberg), and, of course, Harvey The Wonder Hamster.

Worst of all, the entry makes no mention of Al's controversial decision to get LASIK eye surgery and shave off his mustache, radically changing the trademark "Weird Al" look.

There are many more facts I could contribute, such as the Dr. Demento Society's yearly Christmas re-release of material from Dr. Demento's Base-ment Tapes, which often includes an unreleased track from Mr. Yankovic's vaults, such as "Pacman," "It's Still Bil-ly Joel To Me," or the demos for "I Love Rocky Road." In an ideal world, an en-try on "Weird Al" might remark on the subtleties of "Happy Birthday," which can only be found on the *extremely* rare 1981 *Placebo EP* release of "An-other One Rides The Bus," but I cer-tainly no longer believe this world to be ideal.

An even greater case could be made for Yankovic as cultural barometer—Nirvana, an extremely popular '90s grunge band, publicly stated that they knew they had "made it" after Yankovic chose to parody "Smells Like Teen Spirit," and the polka med-leys that appear on Yankovic's albums provide the consummate pastiche of popular songwriting styles for our times. But I believe I have already made my point. A radical overhaul of this particular entry is necessary to befit a man who has bestowed upon us the gift of laughter for more than two decades. However, I could not for-give myself if I failed to mention that, by deftly aping the musical stylings of such a wide variety of bands, Yankovic shows that his talents su-percede those of the artists he paro-dies.

While this missive may not improve my chances of being reinstated as a Wikipedia-community editor, some-times it's necessary to make sacrifices for the larger cause. You can make the additions I have suggested, or you can "dare to be stupid" in the eyes of the "Weird Al" fan base.

I leave the choice to you. ◙

Your Horoscope

By Lloyd Schumner Sr.
Retired Machinist and
A.A.P.B.-Certified Astrologer

Aries: (March 21–April 19)
You're perfectly content curling up in your room with a good book, which is fortunate, considering how you'll be spending the next five to seven years for manslaughter.

Taurus: (April 20–May 20)
You'll never be quite the same again after that Bible you've been thump-ing all these years finally has enough and beats the living shit out of you.

Gemini: (May 21–June 21)
The mousetrap you built is indeed better, but the bludgeoning part will prevent people from beating a path to your door.

Cancer: (June 22–July 22)
You'll be shunned when the man you famously taught to fish dies of mer-cury poisoning.

Leo: (July 23–Aug. 22)
Opening a free amusement park was a great idea, but people will be re-volted by your idea of amusement.

Virgo: (Aug. 23–Sept. 22)
There are no words to express your complicated feelings toward that special someone, which is unfortu-nate, because she will fail to under-stand the hand gestures.

Libra: (Sept. 23–Oct. 23)
People might praise the ineffable hu-man qualities of your post-lyric po-etry now, but after you're gone, all they'll talk about is your great parties.

Scorpio: (Oct. 24–Nov. 21)
You only get one chance to make a first impression—literally, in your case, as you'll only meet one more person for the rest of your life.

Sagittarius: (Nov. 22–Dec. 21)
Judging by that lightheaded, dreamy feeling, this would be a good week to finally start some new meals.

Capricorn: (Dec. 22–Jan. 19)
Years from now, when most of the old onomatopoeia have gone out of style, the unique sound of your burst-ing body will still be in daily use.

Aquarius: (Jan. 20–Feb. 18)
This week, you'll learn some impor-tant life lessons about sharing, ad-mitting when you're wrong, and whether it's the volts or the amps that kill you.

Pisces: (Feb. 19–March 20)
Your feeling that the people you work with are dragging you down is borne out by the Norstar Telecom-munications rope you'll find wrapped around your ankles.

Look for these *New York Times* bestsellers, also by *The Onion*:

Dispatches from the Tenth Circle
0 7522 2011 X
£9.99 Paperback

Our Dumb Century
0 7522 1743 7
£9.99 Paperback

The Onion's Finest News Reporting,
Volume 1
0 7522 7158 X
£9.99 Paperback

BOXTREE